DATE DUE

NO 2 04		
DE 17 04		
JE 9 05		

DEMCO 38-296

Labor Conflict

IN THE UNITED STATES

Garland Reference Library of the Social Sciences 697

Labor Conflict

IN THE UNITED STATES

An Encyclopedia

edited by
RONALD L. FILIPPELLI

editorial assistant
CAROL REILLY

GarlandPublishing,Inc.
New York & London 1990

To Sandra

○ ○

Library of Congress Cataloging-in-Publication Data

Labor conflict in the United States: an encyclopedia/edited by
Ronald L. Filippelli.
p. cm.—(Garland reference library of the social sciences; 697)
ISBN 0-8240-7968-X
1. Strikes and lockouts—United States—Encyclopedias.
I. Filippelli, Ronald L. II. Series: Garland reference library of social science; v. 697.
HD5324.L32   1990
331.89'2973—dc20   90-3534

Design by
Renata Gomes

MANUFACTURED IN THE UNITED STATES OF AMERICA

Table of Contents

Preface

○ ○

Few serious students of history would argue with the assertion that conflict, often violent, has been a major theme in the history of the United States. It is an aspect of our history that most consensus histories underplay, preferring instead to stress those factors that brought us together as a people. But one need only recall the four wars fought on American territory, the bitter suppression of the native American peoples, the long, sad history of racial violence, and the frequent explosions of discontent from the American underclass to get some sense of the constancy of conflict in American history.

Struggles between capital and labor were part of this tremendous upheaval as the United States underwent its industrial revolution. But in several ways they were different from the other conflicts. They took place over the entire span of American history, and they continue to this day. Although the amount of conflict fluctuated from year to year and decade to decade, depending upon a variety of external factors, there has been no period of the nation's history from which the struggle between capital and labor has been absent. Therefore, the conflicts chronicled in this book can be seen as individual battles in a long war. There have been truces, but in general they have not lasted long. Any alert citizen will acknowledge that although the terms and weapons of battle may have been altered over the years, the war goes on.

For the purposes of this book, labor conflict has been defined in several ways.

First and foremost, it means the struggles that took place between workers and their employers over the terms and conditions of employment. Thus, most of the entries in this book deal with attempts by workers, either spontaneously or in an organized fashion, to resist pay cuts, improve their wages, shorten their workday, enhance their safety, or fashion a collective voice through the creation of a union. The intensity and durability of employer resistance to these attempts in America has been, and is, I believe, unmatched in the rest of the industrial world. All industrial nations have histories of labor–management violence, but I believe it accurate to say that in no industrial country has the history of industrial relations been marked by such rancor as in the United States. As any cursory reading of the entries in this book will reveal, American employers have been quick to employ force to crush attempts by their workers to establish some measure of control over their work lives. Frequently these efforts have evoked like responses from the workers. This is most interesting because, although the American strike rate has been very high compared with that of other countries, its labor movement has been among the least radical in political terms. The weakness of socialism in the American labor movement has been the subject of much historical inquiry, and while revolutionary unionism is a part of the American story, it is a subordinate theme at best. Yet the seeming paradox remains; ours is a violent industrial relations history. Of course, a caveat is in order. Most relations between workers and employers did not lead to conflict. The vast majority of negotiations between unions and management ended without a strike or a lockout. At no time in American history did a majority of workers belong to unions. By concentrating on strikes, as we do in this volume, we risk distorting the reality of the employment relationship in historical perspective. However, this is justified, I believe, because it was in the bitter struggles between capital and labor that the terms, conditions, legal setting, and political and social relationships among workers, employers, and the state were largely determined. In focusing on labor conflict we might be studying the actions of a minority, but it was a conscious minority, and it is almost always the conscious minority which moves the historical process.

The *Encyclopedia* also includes examples of labor conflict other than strikes and lockouts, though not in nearly so exhaustive a fashion. There are, for example, entries which deal with conflict between various racial and ethnic groups. These were included when the basis of the conflict had to do with competition for jobs, involvement in a strike, or when a union was involved. Examples of race riots are included when they had competition between whites and blacks for jobs as a focus or when they involved organized labor. For the same reasons the book includes several accounts of violence by white workers against Chinese workers.

There is also, of course, a good deal of political conflict included. Left-wing political movements in American history naturally focused on the working class in general and the trade union movement in particular. This intersection of radical politics and working-class economic action frequently led to conflict. Often this was manifested in traditional conflicts between employers and employees, but under other

circumstances it involved, at least in part, challenges to the authority of the state. When this was the case, such as in the Haymarket Riots of 1886, it is interpreted as labor conflict and included. Slave revolts and uprisings of indentured servants would also fall into this category. Conflicts that led to landmark court decisions are also included, although they might not have been otherwise noteworthy.

Nevertheless, the vast majority of the entries in the encyclopedia chronicle what could be considered traditional labor–management conflict. In these conflicts the weapons of workers ranged from strikes, picketing, and boycotts, to sabotage, violence, and mass protest such as rallies, marches, and sit-ins. Employers had a much greater arsenal. In addition to lockouts, strikebreakers, private armies, blacklists, and espionage, they also frequently called upon the considerable power of the state—police, military, and legal—to crush labor.

Of course, this work is meant to be comprehensive, not exhaustive. The 254 entries represent only a tiny portion of the many thousands of strikes and other labor conflicts that have taken place throughout American history. Any knowledgeable reader will be able to quarrel with a selection or note omissions. The entries were chosen in several ways. First, it is hoped that all of the conflicts that labor historians have agreed are pivotal in American history are included. These are the strikes that appear in all standard labor histories. No reference work on labor history could omit treatment of Homestead, Pullman, the Steel Strike of 1919, and many more. In addition, an attempt was made to include conflicts from a broad range of trades, industries, and geographical areas. For example, in terms of their economic impact beyond the direct participants, the Actors' Strike of 1919 and the New York City Newsboys' Strike of 1899 were not significant. But they and many others are included because they illuminate how conflict has been diffused through every aspect of the employment relationship. Of course, many of the entries deal with conflict at the heart of the American industrial economy, in the coal mines, the steel mills, the textile mills, the auto factories, and on the railroads. This is simply because strikes in those key industries have tended to have much broader impacts. While any strike is important to those involved in it, or to the community in which it takes place, strikes at the heart of the economy have an impact far beyond the workplace where the dispute takes place. Also, because of the pattern of industrial development in American history, labor conflict has been more prevalent in the Northeast and Midwest. Therefore, while these areas receive the most attention, an effort was made to include a number of entries from sections of the country, such as the South, which have traditionally been given less attention in the study of labor history. The same can be said of racial and gender considerations. In terms of numbers, the history of labor conflict in the United States has been dominated by white males, but women and minorities have always been important participants. For a variety of reasons, traditional labor histories have neglected them. This volume contains a number of entries which are representative of the role played by these groups.

Labor Conflict in the United States draws upon the scholarship of untold numbers of historians who have examined the history of labor in America over the years. Most of the conflicts included have been written about elsewhere in more detail, but including abbreviated accounts of them in one volume provides a sweeping, comprehensive treatment of the history of labor relations *in extremis* in America. In the process, however, a good deal more is available to the reader. One will find here an enormous amount of material on working-class culture and community, on women, on blacks and other minorities, and on the development of labor law. The role of the state as the guarantor of the rights, privileges, and power of capital emerges as one of the major themes of labor history, indeed of American history. No one can read over and over again of the use of police, military force, legislation, and the courts against workers and their organizations without acknowledging that reality. Because the working class and working-class organizations were fundamental to the rise and fall of the American left, these accounts include a great deal of material on the history of American radicalism. Of course, there is also much here on the institutional history of the American labor movement. The struggle for the hearts and minds of American workers between pure-and-simple economic unionists, Socialists, anarcho-syndicalists, and Communists is told in a variety of settings, as is the conflict in the labor movement between craft and industrial unionists. Finally, and perhaps most important of all, herein lies the story of thousands of ordinary workers, most of them forgotten, who through these struggles rose above the mundane to make their mark on history, some in truly heroic fashion.

The entries were written with students and interested laymen in mind but should also be useful to scholars. The accounts are drawn from the best available scholarship and are written in a straightforward narrative style. The entries are not meant to be definitive but rather to give the reader a grasp of the issues, events, personalities, and outcomes associated with each conflict. There has been no attempt to impose either stylistic or ideological conditions on the authors, and the reader will encounter a variety of perspectives. No scholarly apparatus is included and no attempt has been made to include an exhaustive bibliography for each entry. The "Further Reading" section at the end of each entry includes books and articles from which the information in the entry was largely drawn and often includes additional sources for a more in-depth study of the subject. Cross references are not used. When a strike covered elsewhere in the book is mentioned in an entry, it is printed in bold type.

Three other aids for the reader are included. One is a chronology of labor his-tory with the labor conflicts included. This will enable the reader to place individual conflicts in a broader context. A second is a brief glossary of frequently used industrial relations terms. The brevity of the entries often precludes sufficient explanation of some terms. It is hoped that the glossary will compensate for that. Finally, in addition to the bibliography at the end of each entry, a selected general bibliography is included.

Acknowledgments

○ ○

The idea for this project originated with Gary Kuris of Garland Publishing. At Garland excellent editorial support, good counsel, and understanding came from Kennie Lyman who encouraged but never pushed. Of course, the contributing historians who wrote the entries made the book. They saw the value of the project to laymen, students, and teachers, and they delivered what they promised. They are listed in "The Contributors" section and at the end of each entry. David Brody of the University of California at Davis, Cletus Daniel of Cornell, and Leon Fink at the University of North Carolina supervised the writing of entries by their graduate students. My sincere thanks go to all of these scholars who took time from their teaching and research to assist in the creation of this volume. I am indebted to the administrative support provided by the Department of Labor Studies and Industrial Relations and the College of the Liberal Arts at the Pennsylvania State University. Arlene Smith, Mitzi Daily, and Sara Waltz handled countless administrative matters while I stole time from my other duties to work on the *Encyclopedia*. Very special gratitude is due Carol Reilly, my editorial assistant and resident computer wizard. Her hard work and skill were critical to the successful completion of this project. For countless reasons, this book is dedicated to Sandra.

The Contributors

○ ○

Ronald L. Filippelli, Editor
Pennsylvania State University

Carol Reilly, Editorial Assistant
Pennsylvania State University

Harold Aurand
Pennsylvania State University

David Bensman
Rutgers University

Mary Blewett
University of Lowell

Marie Bolton
University of California/Davis

Kate Bronfenbrenner
Cornell University

Mari Jo Buhle
Brown University

Paul Clark
Pennsylvania State University

Dorothy Sue Cobble
Rutgers University

Harriet Davis-Kram
Queens College/City University
of New York

Alan Derickson
Pennsylvania State University

Thomas Dublin
State University of New York/
Binghamton

Melvyn Dubofsky
State University of New York/
Binghamton

Gerald Eggert
Pennsylvania State University

Paul Faler
University of Massachusetts/Boston

Gary Fink
Georgia State University

Kenneth Fones-Wolfe
University of Massachusetts/Amherst

Gilbert Gall
Pennsylvania State University

Russell Gibbons
Community College of Allegheny County

Peter Gottlieb
Pennsylvania State University

Cyril Griffith
Pennsylvania State University

Howard Harris
Pennsylvania State University

Shelley G. Herochick
International Ladies' Garment Workers'
Union

Richard Hindle
Pennsylvania State University

Raymond Hogler
Colorado State University

Leslie Hough
Georgia State University

Robert Ingalls
University of South Florida

Philip Jenkins
Pennsylvania State University

Donald Kennedy
International Association of Machinists

Joyce Kornbluh
University of Michigan

Robert Korstad
University of North Carolina

Mario Maffi
University of Milan

Mark McColloch
University of Pittsburgh/Greensburg

A. Ray McCoy
Pennsylvania State University

Carl Meyerhuber
Pennsylvania State University

Stephen Norwood
University of Oklahoma

Louis Pappalardo
Community College of Allegheny County

Joyce Shaw Peterson
Florida International University

James Quigel
Pennsylvania State University

James Rose
University of California/Davis

Frieda Rozen
Pennsylvania State University

John Russo
Youngstown State University

Dorothea Schneider
Occidental College

Bryant Simon
University of North Carolina

James Stewart
Pennsylvania State University

Carole Turbin
Empire State College/State University of New York

Daniel Walkowitz
New York University

James Wolfe
Iron Molders' International Union (Retired)

Chronology

○ ○

1636   Maine Indentured Servants' and Fishermen's Mutiny.

1648   Boston Coopers and Shoemakers form guilds.

1661   Virginia Indentured Servants' Plot.

1663   Maryland Indentured Servants' Strike.

1675   Boston Ship Carpenters' Protest.

1676   Bacon's Rebellion in Virginia.

1677   New York City Carters' Strike.

1684   New York City Carters' Strike.

1741   New York City Bakers' Strike.

1768   Florida Indentured Servants' Revolt.

       New York City Tailors' Strike.

1770   Boston Massacre.

1774   Hibernia, New Jersey, Ironworks Strike.

1776   American Revolution begins.

1778   Journeymen printers in New York combine to increase their wages.

1786   Shay's Rebellion in western Massachusetts.

1791   Philadelphia carpenters carry out the first strike in the building trades.

1792   Philadelphia shoemakers form the first local union organized for collective bargaining.

       Philadelphia River Pilots' Strike.

1794   Federal Society of Journeymen Cordwainers formed in Philadelphia.

       Whiskey Rebellion in western Pennsylvania.

1800   Gabriel Prosser leads a slave revolt in Virginia.

1805   A journeymen cordwainers' union in New York City includes a closed-shop clause in its constitution.

1806   Philadelphia shoemakers found guilty of criminal conspiracy after striking for higher wages.

1812   War with England begins.

1819   Depression begins.

1822   Denmark Vesey leads a slave rebellion in South Carolina.

1824   Pawtucket, Rhode Island, Textile Strike.

1825   The United Tailoresses of New York, a trade union organization for women, organized in New York City.

       Boston House Carpenters' Strike.

1827   The Mechanics Union of Trade Associations, made up of skilled craftsmen in different trades, formed in Philadelphia—first city central federation.

       Philadelphia Carpenters' Strike.

1828   Depression begins.

       The Workingmen's Party formed in Philadelphia.

       Paterson, New Jersey, Textile Strike.

1829   The Workingmen's Party of New York formed.

1831   New England Association of Farmers, Mechanics and other Workingmen formed.

Nat Turner leads a slave rebellion in Virginia.

Lynn, Massachusetts, Shoebinders' Protest.

1832   Boston Ship Carpenters' Ten-Hour Strike.

1833   Lynn, Massachusetts, Shoebinders' Protest begins.

Manayunk, Pennsylvania, Textile Strike.

New York City Carpenters' Strike.

1834   National Trades Union, first attempt at a national labor federation, formed in New York.

Lowell, Massachusetts, Mill Women's Strike.

Manayunk, Pennsylvania, Textile Strike.

1835   Ten-Hour Movement among skilled workers.

Paterson, New Jersey, Textile Strike.

1836   National Cooperative Association of Cordwainers, the first national union of a specific craft, formed in New York City.

Lowell, Massachusetts, Mill Women's Strike.

New York City Tailors' Strike.

Philadelphia Bookbinders' Strike.

1837   Depression begins.

1840   President Martin Van Buren establishes the ten-hour day for employees on federal public works projects.

1842   Massachusetts Supreme Court, in *Commonwealth* v. *Hunt*, rules that labor unions, as such, are not illegal conspiracies.

Anthracite Coal Strike.

1844   Lowell Female Labor Reform Association formed.

1846   Mexican War begins.

1847   New Hampshire passes first state law fixing ten hours as the legal workday.

1848   Pennsylvania's child labor law makes twelve the minimum age for workers in commercial occupations.

1850   New York City Tailors' Strike.

1852   Typographical Union founded—first national union of workers to endure to present day.

1859   Iron Molders' International Union founded.

1860   President Abraham Lincoln elected.

New England Shoemakers' Strike.

1861   Civil War begins.

1862   Congress passes the Homestead Act.

1863   Emancipation Proclamation frees the slaves.

Brotherhood of Locomotive Engineers founded.

1864   Cigar Makers' Union founded.

1866   National Labor Union founded—an attempt at creating a national federation of unions.

Molders' Lockout.

1867   Knights of St. Crispin founded—a union of factory workers in the shoe industry.

1868   First federal eight-hour law passed—applied only to laborers, workmen, and mechanics employed by the government.

Anthracite Coal Strike.

1869   Colored National Labor Union founded.

Noble Order of the Knights of Labor founded.

Troy, New York, Collar Laundresses' Strike.

1870   First written contract between coal operators and coal miners signed.

1872   National Labor Reform Party formed.

Lynn, Massachusetts, Shoe Workers' Strike.

1873   Depression begins.

1874   Tompkins Square Riot in New York City.

1875   Conviction of Molly Maguires for anthracite coalfield murders—twenty are eventually hanged.

Anthracite Coal Strike.

1876   Amalgamated Association of Iron, Steel, and Tin Workers founded.

Workingmen's Party founded—first Marxist party in the United States. Later becomes Socialist Labor Party.

Greenback Party formed.

1877   Federal and state troops are called out to crush a nationwide railroad strike.

Cigarmakers' Strike.

San Francisco Anti-Chinese Riots.

1878   Socialist Labor Party founded.

Greenback Labor Party organized.

International Labor Union founded.

1881   Federation of Organized Trades and Labor Unions of the United States and Canada founded—

predecessor of the American Federation of Labor.

Brotherhood of Carpenters and Joiners founded.

Revolutionary Socialist Labor Party formed.

1882   First Labor Day celebration held in New York City.

Congress passes Chinese Exclusion Act.

Cohoes, New York, Cotton Mill Strike.

1883   International Working People's Association (anarchist) formed.

Cowboy Strike.

Lynchburg, Virginia, Tobacco Workers' Strike.

Molders' Lockout begins.

1884   Federal Bureau of Labor established in the Department of the Interior.

Fall River, Massachusetts, Textile Strike.

Union Pacific Railroad Strike.

1885   Congress passes Foran Act to forbid immigration of laborers on contract.

Anti-Chinese Riots in the West.

Cloakmakers' General Strike.

McCormick Harvesting Machine Company Strike.

Southwest Railroad Strike.

Yonkers, New York, Carpet Weavers' Strike.

1886   Eight-hour-day movement fails.

Anarchist rally in Chicago leads to "Haymarket Massacre."

American Federation of Labor founded with Samuel Gompers as first president.

Anti-Chinese Riots.

Augusta, Georgia, Textile Strike.

Cowboy Strike.

Eight-Hour Strikes.

McCormick Harvesting Machine Company Strike.

Southwest Railroad Strike.

Troy, New York, Collar Laundresses' Strike.

1887 Seven anarchists sentenced to death for the Haymarket bombing (five eventually executed).

Port of New York Longshoremen's Strike.

1888 First federal labor relations law enacted—applied only to railroads.

International Association of Machinists founded.

Burlington Railroad Strike.

Cincinnati Shoemakers' Lockout.

1889 Baseball Players' Revolt begins.

Fall River, Massachusetts, Textile Strike.

1890 United Mine Workers of America founded.

Carpenters' Strike for the Eight-Hour Day.

1891 People's (Populist) Party formed.

Savannah, Georgia, Black Laborers' Strike.

Tennessee Miners' Strike.

1892 International Longshoremen's Association founded.

Seamen's Union founded.

President Grover Cleveland elected.

Strike in Homestead, Pennsylvania, by iron and steel workers gains national attention.

Coeur d'Alene Miners' Strike.

New Orleans General Strike.

1893 Depression begins.

American Railway Union founded.

Western Federation of Miners founded.

Federal court in Louisiana applies the Sherman Antitrust Act to unions for the first time in finding a sympathy strike to be in restraint of trade.

National Civic Federation formed.

1894 Nationwide Rail Strike led by the American Railway Union paralyzes nation's transportation.

Coxey's Army marches on Washington, DC.

Cripple Creek, Colorado, Miners' Strike.

Great Northern Railroad Strike.

1895 U.S. Supreme Court, in *In re Debs*, upholds an injunction restraining the Pullman strikers based on the power of the government to regulate interstate commerce.

Socialist Trade and Labor Alliance founded.

Haverhill, Massachusetts, Shoe Strike.

1896 President William McKinley elected.

Leadville, Colorado, Miners' Strike begins.

1897 Lattimer, Pennsylvania, Massacre.

1898 Spanish-American War begins.

Congress passes the Erdman Act providing for mediation and arbitration of railroad labor disputes.

American Labor Union founded.

Marlboro, Massachusetts, Shoe Workers' Strike begins.

1899 Brotherhood of Teamsters founded.

Buffalo, New York, Grain Shovellers' Strike.

Cleveland, Ohio, Street Railway Workers' Strike.

Coeur d'Alene, Idaho, Miners' Strike.

New York City Newsboys' Strike.

1900 International Ladies' Garment Workers' Union founded.

Anthracite Coal Strike.

Machinists' Strike.

1901 President William McKinley assassinated.

Theodore Roosevelt becomes president.

Socialist Party of America founded.

United Textile Workers founded.

Machinists' Strike.

National Cash Register Strike.

San Francisco Restaurant Workers' Strike.

Steel Strike.

1902 Anthracite Coal Strike.

Chicago Teamsters' Strike.

1903 Department of Commerce and Labor created by Congress.

Women's Trade Union League founded.

Cripple Creek, Colorado, Miners' Strike begins.

Oxnard, California, Sugar Beet Strike.

Telluride, Colorado, Miners' Strike begins.

Utah Coal Strike begins.

1904 Theodore Roosevelt reelected.

New York City Interborough Rapid Transit Strike.

Packinghouse Workers' Strike.

Santa Fe Railroad Shopmen's Strike begins.

1905 Industrial Workers of the World founded in Chicago.

New York Supreme Court, in *Lochner* v. *New York*, declares maximum hours law for bakers unconstitutional.

1906 Eight-hour day widely installed in the printing trades.

1907 Goldfield, Nevada, Miners' Strike begins.

1908 President William Howard Taft elected.

Federal court, in *U.S.* v. *Adair*, finds section of the Erdman Act banning yellow-dog contracts unconstitutional.

U.S. Supreme Court, in *Danbury Hatters* Case, holds a boycott by the United Hatters Union against a manufacturer to be a conspiracy in restraint of trade under the Sherman Antitrust Act.

U.S. Supreme Court, in *Muller* v. *Oregon*, declares an Oregon law limiting working hours for women unconstitutional.

IWW Free-Speech Fight in Missoula, Montana.

1909 National Association for the Advancement of Colored People founded.

Georgia Railroad Strike.

IWW Free-Speech Fight in Spokane, Washington.

McKees Rocks, Pennsylvania, Steel Strike.

"Uprising of the 20,000" Garment Strike in New York.

Watertown, Connecticut, Arsenal Strike.

1910   Bethlehem Steel Strike.

Cloakmakers' Strike.

Chicago Clothing Workers' Strike.

Los Angeles strike wave.

Philadelphia General Strike.

1911   U.S. Supreme Court, in *Gompers v. Bucks Stove and Range Company*, upholds an injunction ordering the AFL to remove the company from its unfair list and cease a boycott.

Fire kills 146 workers at the Triangle Shirtwaist Company in New York City.

Illinois Central and Harriman Lines Rail Strike begins.

Southern Lumber Operators' Lockout begins.

1912   President Woodrow Wilson elected.

Massachusetts adopts the first minimum wage act for women and minors.

Chicago Newspaper Strike.

Fur Workers' Strike.

IWW Free-Speech Fight in San Diego, California.

Lawrence, Massachusetts, Textile Strike.

Louisiana Timber Workers' Strike begins.

New York City Hotel Strike.

Paint Creek and Cabin Creek, West Virginia, Mine Strikes.

1913   U.S. Department of Labor established.

Ludlow, Colorado, Massacre.

Machinists Strike and Boycott.

Michigan Copper Strike.

Paterson, New Jersey, Textile Strike.

Rubber Workers' Strike.

Studebaker Motors Auto Workers' Strike.

Wheatland, California, Hop Riot.

1914   Congress passes the Clayton Antitrust Act. Ostensibly limits the use of injunctions in labor disputes.

Amalgamated Clothing Workers founded.

Fulton Bag and Cotton Mill Strike begins.

1915   Congress passes the LaFollette Seamen's Act—regulates working conditions for seamen.

Standard Oil Strike.

Youngstown, Ohio, Steel Strike begins.

1916   Congress passes Federal Child Labor Law—later declared unconstitutional.

Congress passes the Adamson Act establishing the eight-hour day for railroad workers.

Six killed and forty wounded in bombing of San Francisco preparedness parade—labor leaders arrested.

American Federation of Teachers founded.

Arizona Copper Strike.

Everett, Washington, Massacre.

Minnesota Iron Range Strike.

New York City Transit Strike.

New York Cloakmakers' Strike.

San Francisco Open Shop Campaign.

Standard Oil Strike.

1917   United States enters World War I.

Supreme Court, in *Hitchman Coal and Coke* v. *Mitchell*, upholds the legality of yellow-dog contracts.

Green Corn Rebellion in Oklahoma.

Tom Mooney sentenced to death for role in San Francisco preparedness parade bombing in 1916.

Bisbee, Arizona, Miners' Strike.

Butte, Montana, Miners' Strike.

East St. Louis Race Riot.

Pacific Northwest Lumber Strike.

1918 War Labor Board is created.

World War I ends.

1919 Huge postwar strike wave sweeps across the nation.

Communist Party of America founded.

Farmer–Labor Party founded.

Red Scare begins.

Actors' Strike.

Boston Police Strike.

Centralia, Washington, Massacre.

Chicago Race Riot.

New England Telephone Strike.

Seattle General Strike.

Steel Strike.

1920 President Warren Harding elected.

Trade Union Educational League founded.

Alabama Miners' Strike.

Clothing Workers' Lockout.

West Virginia Coal Wars begin.

1921 Depression begins.

Supreme Court, in *Duplex Printing Press* v. *Deering*, rules that the Clayton Act notwithstanding, federal courts could enjoin unions for actions in restraint of trade.

Congress restricts immigration to the United States and establishes the national origin quota system.

Seamen's Strike.

West Virginia Coal Wars.

1922 Conference for Progressive Political Action founded.

Anthracite Coal Strike.

Bituminous Coal Strike.

Herrin, Illinois, Massacre.

Railroad Shopmen's Strike.

1924 President Calvin Coolidge elected.

Samuel Gompers dies. William Green becomes president of the American Federation of Labor.

1925 Brotherhood of Sleeping Car Porters founded.

Anthracite Coal Strike.

1926 Congress passes the Railway Labor Act, which requires that employers bargain with unions and forbids discrimination against union members.

Passaic, New Jersey, Textile Strike.

1927 Nicolo Sacco and Bartolomeo Vanzetti are executed.

Bituminous Coal Strike.

1928 President Herbert Hoover elected.

New Bedford, Massachusetts, Textile Strike.

1929 Stock market crash and the beginning of the Great Depression.

Trade Union Unity League founded.

Conference for Progressive Labor Action founded.

Gastonia, North Carolina, Textile Strike.

1930   National Unemployed Council formed.

Imperial Valley, California, Farmworkers' Strike.

1931   Congress passes Davis-Bacon Act providing for payment of prevailing wages to workers employed on public works projects.

"Scottsboro Boys" arrested in Alabama.

Harlan County, Kentucky, Miners' Strike.

Tampa, Florida, Cigar Workers' Strike.

1932   President Franklin Delano Roosevelt elected.

Congress passes the Norris-LaGuardia Act, which prohibits federal injunctions in labor disputes and outlaws yellow-dog contracts.

Bonus March of World War I veterans on Washington, DC.

American Federation of Government Employees founded.

California Pea Pickers' Strike.

Century Airlines Pilots' Strike.

Davidson-Wilder, Tennessee, Coal Strike begins.

Ford Hunger March in Detroit, Michigan.

Vacaville, California, Tree Pruners' Strike.

1933   Congress passes the National Industrial Recovery Act, Section 7(a) of which guarantees rights of employees to organize and bargain collectively.

Frances Perkins becomes secretary of labor and the first woman named to a presidential cabinet.

Newspaper Guild founded.

Briggs Manufacturing Strike.

California Farmworkers' Strikes.

Detroit, Michigan, Tool and Die Strike.

Hormel, Iowa, Meat-Packing Strike.

New Mexico Miners' Strike.

1934   Southern Tenant Farmers' Union founded.

Harlem, New York City, Jobs-for-Negroes Boycott.

Imperial Valley, California, Farmworkers' Strike.

Minneapolis Teamsters' Strike.

Newark Star-Ledger Newspaper Strike begins.

Rubber Workers' Strike.

San Francisco Longshoremen & General Strike.

Textile Workers' Strike.

Toledo, Ohio, Auto-Lite Strike.

1935   U.S. Supreme Court declares the National Industrial Recovery Act unconstitutional.

Congress passes the National Labor Relations Act (NLRA), which protects the rights of workers to organize and bargain collectively.

Committee for Industrial Organization (CIO) formed inside the American Federation of Labor.

Negro Labor Committee founded.

United Auto Workers founded.

Oklahoma, Kansas, and Missouri Metal Workers' Strike.

Pacific Northwest Lumber Strike.

Southern Sharecroppers' and Farm Laborers' Strike.

1936   President Franklin Roosevelt reelected.

Steel Workers' Organizing Committee formed.

Atlanta, Georgia, Auto Workers' Sit-Down Strike.

Berkshire Knitting Mills Strike.

General Motors Sit-Down Strike.

RCA Strike.

Rubber Workers' Strike.

Seamen's Strike.

Seattle Post-Intelligencer Newspaper Strike.

1937   U.S. Supreme Court declares the NLRA constitutional.

American Federation of Labor expels the CIO unions.

American Federation of State, County and Municipal Employees union founded.

General Motors Sit-Down Strike.

Hershey, Pennsylvania, Chocolate Workers' Strike.

Little Steel Strike and Memorial Day Massacre. -

1938   Congress passes the Fair Labor Standards Act, which establishes the forty-hour workweek, the minimum wage, and bans child labor in interstate commerce.

Congress of Industrial Organizations (CIO) is founded with John L. Lewis as president.

Chicago Newspaper Strike begins.

Hilo, Hawaii, Massacre.

Maytag Strike.

1939   Chrysler Auto Strike.

General Motors Tool and Diemakers' Strike.

1940   President Franklin Roosevelt reelected.

Philip Murray replaces John L. Lewis as CIO president.

Ford Motor Strike.

1941   United States enters World War II.

AFL and CIO give no-strike pledges for the duration of the war.

Allis-Chalmers Strike.

Captive Coal Mines Strike.

Detroit, Michigan, Hate Strike against black workers.

International Harvester Strike.

New York City Bus Strike.

North American Aviation Strike.

1942   National War Labor Board is established—establishes the "Little Steel Formula" for wartime wage adjustments.

United Steel Workers of America founded.

1943   Fair Employment Practices Committee is established.

Congress passes the Smith-Connally Act to restrict strikes and union political activity during the war.

Bituminous Coal Strike.

Detroit, Michigan, Hate Strikes against black workers.

Detroit, Michigan, Race Riot.

1944   President Franklin Roosevelt reelected.

Philadelphia Transit Strike.

1945   President Franklin Roosevelt dies.

Vice-President Harry S. Truman becomes President.

World War II ends.

Kelsey-Hayes Strike.

New York City Longshoremen's Strike.

Montgomery Ward Strike.

Oil Workers' Strike.

1946   Huge postwar strike wave sweeps across the nation.

United Mine Workers win a health and welfare fund in bargaining with the coal operators.

Bituminous Coal Strike.

Electrical Manufacturing Strikes.

General Motors Strike.

Pittsburgh Power Strike.

Railroad Strike.

Steel Strike.

1947   Congress passes the Taft-Hartley Act (Labor Management Relations Act) restricting union practices and permitting the states to ban union security agreements.

R. J. Reynolds Tobacco Company Strike.

Telephone Strike.

1948   President Harry S. Truman is reelected.

Progressive Party formed.

1949   CIO expels two unions for alleged Communist domination.

Hawaii Dock Strike.

1950   United States enters Korean War.

CIO expels nine unions for alleged Communist domination.

United Auto Workers and General Motors sign a contract that provides for pensions, automatic cost-of-living wage adjustments, and guaranteed increases over the life of the contract.

"Salt of the Earth" Strike of New Mexico Miners begins.

1952   President Truman seizes the steel industry when the steel companies reject the Wage Stabilization Board recommendations. Supreme Court rules the action unconstitutional.

George Meany becomes president of the AFL.

Walter Reuther becomes president of the CIO.

President Dwight D. Eisenhower is elected.

Steel Strike.

1953   AFL and CIO agree to a "no raiding" pact. AFL expels the International Longshoremen's Association for corruption.

Louisiana Sugar Cane Workers' Strike.

1954   Kohler Strike begins.

1955   United Auto Workers win supplementary unemployment benefits in bargaining with Ford.

AFL and CIO merge with George Meany as first president.

Southern Telephone Strike.

1956   President Dwight D. Eisenhower is reelected.

East Coast Longshoremen's Strike.

Steel Strike.

1957   AFL-CIO expels Teamsters, Bakery Workers, and Laundry Workers for corruption.

1959   Congress passes the Labor–Management Reporting and Disclosure Act

(Landrum-Griffin), which regulates the internal affairs of unions.

Steel Strike.

1960 President John F. Kennedy is elected.

Negro American Labor Council founded.

General Electric Strike.

Seamen's Strike.

1962 Presidential executive order gives federal employees' unions the right to bargain with government agencies.

New York City Newspaper Strike begins.

East Coast Longshoremen's Strike.

1963 President John F. Kennedy is assassinated.

Vice-President Lyndon B. Johnson becomes President.

Congress passes Equal Pay Act prohibiting wage differentials based on sex for workers covered by the Fair Labor Standards Act.

1964 President Lyndon B. Johnson is reelected.

Title VII of the Civil Rights Act bars discrimination in employment on the basis of race, color, religion, sex, or national origin.

1965 United Farm Workers Organizing Committee formed.

California Grape Workers' Strike.

1966 New York City Transportation Strike.

1967 Copper Strike begins.

1968 President Richard M. Nixon is elected.

Civil Rights leader Martin Luther King, Jr., is assassinated while supporting a strike by Memphis, Tennessee, sanitation workers.

New York City Teachers' Strikes.

1969 Charleston, South Carolina, Hospital Workers' Strike.

1970 Postal strike is first nationwide strike of public employees.

Hawaii becomes the first state to allow local and state government employees the right to strike.

Congress passes the Occupational Safety and Health Act.

General Motors Strike.

Postal Workers' Strike.

1971 New York City Police Strike.

1972 President Richard M. Nixon is reelected.

Farah Clothing Workers' Strike and Boycott.

Lordstown, Ohio, Auto Workers' Strike.

Philadelphia Teachers' Strike begins.

1974 Coalition of Labor Union Women is founded.

Congress passes the Employment Retirement Income Security Act regulating all private pension plans.

Baltimore Police Strike.

1975 First legal statewide public employees' strike in nation's history occurs in Pennsylvania.

Congress defeats a union-sponsored attempt to reform the nation's basic labor law.

Washington Post Pressmen's Strike begins.

1976 President Jimmy Carter is elected.

Congress defeats a union-sponsored attempt to have a law enacted that would improve the ability of construction unions to organize and carry out effective strikes.

1977 Bituminous Coal Strike begins.

Coors Beer Strike and Boycott begins.

J. P. Stevens Boycott begins.

Willmar, Minnesota, Bank Workers' Strike.

1978   Wilkes-Barre, Pennsylvania, Newspaper Strike begins.

1979   Lane Kirkland becomes president of the AFL-CIO.

Independent Truckers' Strike.

1980   President Ronald Reagan is elected.

Joyce Miller of the International Ladies' Garment Workers' Union becomes the first woman to sit on the AFL-CIO executive board.

1981   President Ronald Reagan fires most of the nation's air traffic controllers for striking illegally and orders their union, the Professional Air Traffic Controllers Association, decertified.

The largest labor rally in American history takes place in Washington in protest against the policies of the Reagan administration.

Baseball Players' Strike.

1983   Phelps-Dodge Copper Strike begins.

1984   President Ronald Reagan is reelected.

Yale University Clerical Workers' Strike.

1985   Hormel Meatpackers' Strike begins.

Los Angeles County Sanitation District Strike.

Yale University Clerical Workers' Strike.

1986   Trans World Airlines Flight Attendants' Strike.

USX (United States Steel) Lockout.

1987   Paperworkers' Strike and Lockout begins.

Professional Football Players' Strike.

1988   President George Bush is elected.

1989   Eastern Airlines Workers' Strike.

Mine Workers' Strike against Pittston Coal Company.

Glossary

Adamson Act: An act passed by Congress in 1916 that established the eight-hour workday in the railroad industry.

AFL: Abbreviation of the **American Federation of Labor.**

Agreement: A contract between an employer and a union, or between an association or group of employers and one or more unions.

American Federation of Labor: A national federation of labor unions formed in 1886. Its predecessor organization was the Federation of Organized Trades and Labor Unions which had been founded in 1881. The AFL succeeded the **Knights of Labor** as the most important trade union federation in the United States. Its membership was primarily made up of unions organized along craft lines.

American Plan: The name given to an anti-union campaign carried on by employers and their organizations from the early 1900s through the 1920s. Also called the **open shop** campaign.

Anarchism: A sociopolitical theory which has many schools. As it applies to labor organizations, it attempts to combine individualism with socialism. Individualistic anarchism distrusts the state and places its faith in individual initiative. Socialist anarchism places the blame for society's ills on the institution of private property and, therefore, on capitalism. It argues for the replacement of private property with property owned by voluntary social groups and emphasizes the welfare of the group and the community rather than that of the individual. Revolutionary anarchists believe in the use of violence to achieve an anarchist society, while philosophical anarchists place their faith in education.

Arbitration: The settling of disputes between labor and management through the use of a neutral third party, or arbitrator, who renders a decision on the merits and facts of the case.

Back-to-work movement: A movement generally organized by an employer to reduce the effectiveness of a strike by convincing some strikers to return to work against the wishes of the union and before a satisfactory settlement has been reached.

Bargaining agent: The union or association which represents a group of workers in collective bargaining and other functions with an employer.

Blackleg: *See* **scab.**

Blacklist: A list of workers' names circulated among employers for the purpose of jointly refusing employment to union members in general or to union activists in particular.

Bolsheviks: In the American industrial relations context, the name given to American Communists and other supporters of the Russian Revolution of 1917, or the term used by employers, the press, and government agencies to associate all labor radicals and/or militants with communism, revolution, and violence for the purposes of defeating unions.

Boycott: In industrial relations, the term signifies an action by a union to refuse to deal with or buy the products of a business, or to convince others to refuse to deal with or buy the products of a business as a means of exerting pressure during a labor dispute. A secondary boycott is the refusal to deal with or buy goods from a business that is a customer or supplier of a business with which the union has a dispute.

Building trades: Occupations in the construction or building industry. The building trades are generally unionized along craft lines.

Business agent: The paid representative of a local trade union or other labor body who administers and looks after the affairs of the union, particularly in terms of its relations with the employer. Business agents, sometimes called walking delegates, are usually associated with **craft unions.**

Business union: A type of union which accepts the capitalist system and places the emphasis on negotiating **agreements** with employers concerning wages, hours, and conditions of employment.

Captive mines: Coal mines whose output is consumed by the companies that own them. They were often owned by steel and other metals manufacturing companies.

Central labor union: A body consisting of various AFL locals in a particular city, county, or other geographic area.

Checkoff: The practice whereby the employer deducts union dues from pay-

checks and delivers these deductions to the union.

CIO: Abbreviation of the **Congress of Industrial Organizations,** formerly the **Committee for Industrial Organization.**

City central: Same as **central labor union.**

Clayton Act: Passed by Congress in 1914 during the administration of President Woodrow Wilson. The act specified that labor unions were specifically excluded from the operation of the antitrust laws. This was ostensibly meant to remove unions from the threat of **injunctions** issued under the nation's antitrust laws. However, because of its interpretation by the courts, the Clayton Act was used successfully by employers to bring suits against labor unions.

Closed shop: A shop where only members of a union in good standing are hired or retained as employees.

Collective bargaining: The process of determining wages, hours, and working conditions through negotiation between representatives of one or more unions on the one hand, and of an employer or group of employers on the other. Results in a labor **agreement.**

Committee for Industrial Organization: Organized in 1935 by the officers of seven national unions in the AFL who favored **industrial unionization** of the mass-production industries as opposed to the AFL's craft union approach.

Committee of Fair Employment Practice: A federal agency created on June 25, 1941, at the request of President Franklin D. Roosevelt. It was charged with investigating and redressing grievances arising from employment discrimination, in particular against blacks, in defense industries.

Company store: A store owned and operated by an employer for the use of its employees. Common in the coal towns. Workers were often forced to buy at company stores, often at prices higher than normal.

Company town: A town entirely owned by an employer. Common in the mining and textile industries but also appeared in many other industries. Workers were often required to rent housing from the company and make purchases at the **company store.** During strikes, workers were often evicted from company-owned housing and denied credit at the company store.

Company union: A labor organization whose membership is confined to the workers of one company, and which is organized and dominated by the company. Company unions were often formed to forestall the organization of independent unions.

Congress of Industrial Organizations: A confederation of a number of national and international unions and organizing committees formed in November 1938. Successor of the **Committee for Industrial Organization.** Stressed industrial rather than craft organization.

Conspiracy doctrine: A common-law interpretation by the courts that was used in the nineteenth century to prevent unionization on the grounds that as combinations to raise wages and reduce hours unions were illegal conspiracies in restraint of trade.

Coxey's Army: Led by Jacob Coxey, a group of unemployed workers who went to Washington, DC, in 1894 to protest unemployment and to demonstrate in favor of legislation that would provide funds for communities to pay the unemployed for work on public improvements.

Craftsman: *See* **skilled worker.**

Craft union: A union made up of workers engaged on a single industrial process or a specific type of work, usually involving a specific skill.

Davis-Bacon Act: A law passed by Congress in 1935 which establishes prevailing wage laws on construction projects financed with federal government funds. The act provides that all workers on federal projects shall be paid at rates equal to prevailing scales for such labor in the localities in which the work is undertaken. In areas where unions are strong, the prevailing wage has come to be the union wage.

Defense Mediation Board: *See* **National Defense Mediation Board.**

Discrimination: Unfair and unequal treatment of workers by employers or unions because of race, nationality, religion, or gender. Also used to describe unfair and unequal treatment of union members by employers.

Double time: A rate of pay for overtime work double that which the worker receives for work during regular hours.

Dual unions: Two labor unions that compete to organize workers in the same industry or trade. A practice usually attacked as divisive in the labor movement.

Emergency strike: A labor dispute in which a strike would imperil the national health and safety. Under the **Taft-Hartley Act** the President of the United States is empowered to seek an injunction to end such strikes for eighty days.

Employee representation plan: *See* company union.

Employers' association: A voluntary non-profit organization of business competitors established to look after the common interests of all member firms or employers in an industry or particular branch of an industry in a specific area. Frequently, they were used to coordinate employer or industry response to unions by coordinating the hiring of **strikebreakers**, organizing sympathy lockouts, and through other means.

Erdman Act: A law passed by Congress in 1898 that mandated that railroad labor disputes should be settled by means of arbitration and mediation, that **yellow-dog contracts** were illegal on the railroads, and that railway employers were prohibited from discriminating against union members in the discharge of employees.

Escalator clause: A clause contained in some collective **agreements** whereby wage rates are adjusted according to increases in the cost of living.

Fact finding: A process by which a neutral third party investigates an impasse between labor and management and makes recommendations for a settlement. Recommendations are not binding on either party.

Featherbedding: Requirement in some collective **agreements** that requires the employer to hire some employees whose services are not required.

Federal local union: A local union directly affiliated with and chartered by the **American Federation of Labor** rather than by one of its affiliated national or international unions.

Federal Mediation and Conciliation Service: A United States Government agency established by the **Taft-Hartley Act**. It is charged with helping to settle disputes between labor and management through conciliation and mediation.

Federated Trades and Labor Council: Same as **central labor union**.

First International: An organization of labor and Socialist bodies formed in London in 1864 under the leadership of Karl Marx and bearing the official name of the International Workingmen's Association.

Fringe benefits: Term used to describe items, other than direct wages, such as vacations, holidays, insurance, pensions, and other benefits that are given to an employee under his employment or union contract.

General strike: A strike extending over a whole community, province, state, or country and including workers from a variety of occupations and industries. Often used as a form of sympathetic strike to help workers in a dispute with an employer. In the theory of **syndicalism**, the general strike is a revolutionary weapon used to paralyze the present economic and political systems.

Goon: A term applied to a person hired by the employer or the union to terrorize the other, usually during a strike or union-organizing campaign.

Grievance: An allegation by a worker, the union, or an employer that the collective **agreement** has been violated.

Hiring hall: Hall managed by unions, or by unions and employers, where employers come to hire workers in industries, such as shipping, longshoring, and construction, in which employment is often casual.

Illegal strike: *See* **wildcat strike.**

Indentured servant: A person who is bound to serve an employer for a certain number of years in order to pay off a debt. Many immigrants indentured themselves in order to pay the cost of passage to America.

Industrial relations: The relations between employers and employees in an industry. Often taken in the narrower sense of relations between unions and employers.

Industrial union: A union in which membership is open to all workers in the industry, irrespective of occupation, skill, or craft.

Industrial Workers of the World: Formed in Chicago in 1905. A revolutionary workers' organization whose unions were organized as **industrial unions**. Its goal was to organize all workers into "one big union" and replace capitalism with socialism through direct, nonpolitical action.

Industrywide agreement: A collective **agreement** covering all employees and employers in an industry.

Industrywide bargaining: Collective **bargaining** covers an entire industry and results in an **industrywide agreement.**

Injunction: An order issued by a court to restrain one or more persons from carrying out an act that they have threatened to commit, from continuing an action already underway, or from repeating an action carried out in the past on the grounds that the complaining party will suffer irreparable damage if the act in question is permitted. Was frequently used by employers to prevent or break strikes, picketing, or boycotts.

International union: A union containing members in more than one country. In the United States the name most often means that unions also have members in Canada.

Iron-clad agreement: Same as **yellow-dog contract.**

Jurisdictional dispute: A dispute between two or more unions over the right to organize workers in certain categories of work or in certain industries.

Labor Department: A cabinet-level department of the United States Government established in 1913 and charged with overseeing the nation's labor laws, policies, and conditions.

Labor espionage: The use by employers of secret agents to infiltrate the ranks of organized labor in order to weaken or destroy the union.

Labor–Management Relations Act of 1947: *See* **Taft-Hartley Act.**

Labor's Nonpartisan League: Formed in 1936 to bring the resources of organized labor together for political action.

Labor spy: *See* **labor espionage.**

Leftist: A person who holds radical views on political, social, and economic issues, usually taken to mean a Socialist, Communist, or anarchist. Usually a perjorative term in American labor history. *See* **Bolshevik; Red.**

Left winger: Same as **leftist.**

Little Steel: Refers to steel companies other than the United States Steel Corporation.

Local union: Basic unit of most national or **international unions.** Usually organized around a group of employees in one plant or one small locality.

Lockout: The closing by an employer of a workplace to bring pressure on workers to agree to the employer's terms. Also used by employers to prevent a union from striking one employer, while allowing another to operate, in order to bring pressure on the struck employer to settle. This practice is called whipsawing.

Lodge: Name used for local units of certain national and **international unions.** *See* **local union.**

Marxism: A socioeconomic school of thought founded by Karl Marx and Friedrich Engels. Also called scientific socialism to distinguish it from utopian socialism. Marxist theory outlines how capitalism will inevitably decay to be replaced with a Socialist economy based on the social ownership of the means of production and the control of society by the working class.

Master agreement: An **agreement** signed by the most important employer or employers in an industry that sets the pattern for agreements throughout the industry. *See* **industrywide agreement.**

Mediation: The process whereby a neutral third party is asked to help to solve a dispute between labor and management.

Multi-employer bargaining: **Collective bargaining** in which more than one employer participates.

National Defense Mediation Board: A federal board established before the outbreak of World War II to prevent labor disputes and strikes in defense plants. After the outbreak of the war, it was replaced by the **National War Labor Board** in early 1942.

National Industrial Recovery Act (NIRA): Passed by Congress in 1933. A measure meant to revive industry during the Great Depression by establishing codes of fair competition in each industry. Among other things, these codes fixed minimum wages and maximum hours, and abolished **sweatshop** working conditions and child labor in several industries. The NIRA also included Section 7(a) which protected workers' right to join a union of their own choosing. The NIRA was declared unconstitutional by the Supreme Court on May 27, 1935.

National Labor Board: Established in 1933 to deal with disputes between labor and management. Its role was basically **mediation,** although it did have quasi-judicial functions under Section 7(a) of the **National Industrial Recovery Act.** It was dissolved in 1934 and was later replaced by the **National Labor Relations Board.**

National Labor Relations Act: Passed by Congress in 1935. It guarantees workers the "right to self-organization, to form, join, or assist labor organizations, to bargain through representation of their own choosing, and to engage in concerted activities for the purpose of collective bargaining or other mutual aid of protection." It is commonly called the Wagner Act.

National Labor Relations Board (NLRB): Federal government agency established to enforce the provisions of the **National Labor Relations Act.**

National Labor Union: Formed in 1866. An early attempt at the formation of a national labor organization. It included local unions, trade assemblies, eight-hour leagues, and national craft unions. Disappeared in 1872.

National Mediation Board: Independent federal agency established in 1934 to help carry out the provisions of the **Railway Labor Act.**

National Railroad Adjustment Board: Federal agency established in 1934 under the **Railway Labor Act** to help settle disputes in the railroad industry arising out of grievances or contract application.

National Recovery Administration (NRA): Agency established to administer the **National Industrial Recovery Act.**

National War Labor Board: (1) Federal agency established in April 1918 to deal with labor–management disputes in defense industries during World War I. (2) Federal agency established to effect the peaceful settlement of labor–management disputes during World War II. Also had jurisdiction over wage and salary rates during the war. The successor to the **National Defense Mediation Board.**

New Deal: A popular term for the reform presidential administration of Franklin Delano Roosevelt during the Great Depression.

Norris-LaGuardia Act: Passed by Congress in 1932 for the purpose of limiting the issuance of labor **injunctions** by federal courts. Also declared **yellow-dog contracts** to be illegal.

Open shop: A shop in which an employer exercises the right to hire workers whether or not they belong to a union. In American history it was generally used as a weapon against unions and meant in practice that employers hired only non-union labor. The opposite of **closed shop.**

Operative: *See* **semiskilled worker.**

Picketing: (1) Publicizing, by marching outside of a struck workplace, the existence of a labor dispute and the union's version of the dispute. (2) The stationing of workers outside of a struck workplace in order to convince or intimidate other employees, **scabs,** or customers from entering the workplace.

Piece rate: Payment of workers based on the number of units produced rather than on the basis of time.

Piecework: Work performed under a **piece-rate** system of payment.

Pinkertons: Employees of the Pinkerton Detective Agency formed by Allan Pinkerton. They were frequently hired by employers to break strikes through **labor espionage,** violence, or the protection of **scabs.** *See* **strikebreaker.**

Preferential shop: A system established in a labor **agreement** whereby union members, when available, are given preference in hiring over non-union workers, or which requires that a certain number of employees be union members.

Railway brotherhoods: Trade unions of railway employees: Brotherhood of Locomotive Firemen and Enginemen, Order of Railway Conductors, Brotherhood of Railway Trainmen, Order of Railroad Telegraphers, Brotherhood of Maintenance-of-Way Employees, Brotherhood of Railroad Signalmen, Brotherhood of Railway Carmen, and Brotherhood of Railway and Steamship Clerks, Freight Handlers, Express and Station Employees.

Railway Labor Act: Passed by Congress in 1926. Gives railway (and now airline employees) the right to organize into unions of their own choosing for purposes of collective bargaining. Amended in 1934 to establish the **National Mediation Board** and the **National Railroad Adjustment Board** to help settle labor–management conflicts arising during collective bargaining and the administration of the contract.

Rank and file: Members of a union other than officers.

Red: Perjorative term used against radicals, usually Communists, Socialists, or anarchists. *See* **Bolshevik; leftist.**

Revolutionary unionism: Unionism that advocates the overthrow of the present economic, social, and political systems. *See* **Industrial Workers of the World; syndicalism; Trade Union Unity League.**

Runaway shops: Businesses which move from one location to another to escape unionization or protective labor legislation.

Sabotage: Advocated in **revolutionary unionism** to paralyze industry and create the circumstances for the transition from a capitalist to a worker-controlled society. Tactics range from the destruction of machinery, the making of defective products, to the work slowdown.

Scab: An expression describing, (1) a union member who continues to work during a strike, (2) a non-union worker who accepts work during a strike, (3) a non-union man who accepts union work for which he is not qualified or at a lower wage than the prevailing or union rate.

Scientific management: School of management associated with the work of Frederick Taylor and other exponents of the efficiency movement. Includes management control of work through industrial engineering, time and motion studies, job analysis, **piece-rate** wages, and heavy supervision.

Scrip: Pay for work, not in regular money, but in the form of certificates issued by the company that could only be used in the **company store.** Most common in the mining industry.

Secondary boycott: *See* **boycott.**

Semiskilled worker: Worker whose job requires little training and skill. Associated with the increased use of machinery.

Seniority: The standing of an employee with relation to all other employees in terms of length of service. Seniority is often used to determine employment rights and privileges, such as promotion, transfer, layoff, and recall.

Sherman Antitrust Act: Passed by Congress in 1890. It was designed to control monopoly practices by business. However, it was applied as well to the activities of unions. Under the act, **injunctions** were frequently issued by judges on the grounds that unions and/or strikes were illegal combinations in restraint of trade.

Shop steward: Representative of a union on the shop floor. Stewards represent workers in grievances against the company and act as a link between the rank and file and the local union.

Sit-down strike: A strike in which, rather than leaving the workplace, strikers remain at their posts and refuse to work. When used, this often resulted in the occupation of factories by the strikers. This form of strike, used extensively in the auto and rubber industries, made it impossible for the employer to use **scab** labor.

Skilled worker: One who possesses special expertise, usually acquired through an apprenticeship with another skilled worker, in a particular occupation involved in handcraft or industrial production, construction, transportation, and communication.

Slowdown: The planned reduction in the pace of work by a group of employees for the purpose of restricting the output of the employer. Used either to make work for more people, or bring pressure on an employer to agree to the demands of the workers.

Smith-Connally Act: Passed by Congress in 1943. A wartime measure authorizing the government to take over any plant or enterprise affected by a strike or other labor dispute if the enterprise was considered essential to the war effort.

Socialism: A socioeconomic theory in which the means of production are owned by the community, rather than by private owners, and are managed for the collective good rather than for private profit—production for use rather than production for profit. There are many schools of socialism. *See* **Marxism; anarchism; syndicalism.**

Socialist Labor Party: A political party espousing Marxist doctrines, organized in the United States in 1876 under the name of the Workingmen's Party. Became the SLP in 1877.

Socialist Party: Founded in 1900. Espoused moderate Socialist views.

Soldiering: A term used to describe loafing, loitering, or pretending to be working while on the job. *See* **slowdown.**

Speedup: Increasing the rate of production of the worker without increasing wages. Usually used with reference to assembly-line or mass-production operation.

Stretchout: Requiring the worker to operate more machines and/or perform more tasks without increasing time or wages.

Strike: A voluntary stoppage of work on the part of a group of workers, by common agreement, or by order of their union usually for the purpose of obtaining or resisting a change in the conditions of employment.

Strikebreaker: Someone hired by the employer to break a strike either through taking work in a struck workplace, **labor espionage,** violence, or the hiring of workers to cross the picket lines. *See* **Pinkertons; scab.**

Sweatshop: A factory or shop where workers were required to work under unhealthy conditions, for long hours, usually for low **piece-rate** wages. Prevalent in the garment and textile industries.

Sympathy strike: A strike called by workers without a direct grievance with their employer in order to support a strike by other workers, either against the same employer, or another employer.

Syndicalism: A sociopolitical theory of French origin. Combines the economic principles of **socialism** with the direct action at the point of production of trade unions and the political theory of **anarchism** which rejects political action. *See* **Industrial Workers of the World.**

Taft-Hartley Act: Passed by Congress in 1947. It amends the **National Labor Relations Act** and the **Norris-LaGuardia Act.** Created the **Federal Media-**

tion and Conciliation Service. To the unfair labor practices for employers proscribed by the National Labor Relations Act, it added a list of unfair labor practices by labor organizations. Its passage was considered a triumph by business interests over organized labor.

Taylorism: *See* scientific management.

Trade Union Educational League: A Communist organization formed in 1920 to train Communist workers in leadership skills, ideology, and tactics so that they could work within AFL unions to capture control of them and convert other workers to communism. In 1925, in response to a change in political direction from the Communist International in Moscow, the name of the TUEL was changed to the Trade Union Unity League. Its purpose was to organize its own union affiliates in various industries as a competitor of the American Federation of Labor.

Trade Union Unity League: *See* Trade Union Educational League.

Union label: A notice attached to a product that informs the consumer that the product has been manufactured by union workers.

Union shop: A contract provision in which the employer promises to keep only union members on the payroll and in which non-union workers can be hired but must join the union within a stipulated time.

Voluntarism: One of the controlling principles of the American Federation of Labor whereby the affiliated unions possessed considerable autonomy to work out their own problems of organization and workers were seen as having the freedom to determine the form of labor organization they wanted.

Wagner Act: *See* National Labor Relations Act.

War Labor Board: *See* National War Labor Board.

War Manpower Commission: A federal agency established in 1942 to manage the mobilization and utilization of manpower for the war effort.

Wildcat strike: A strike that is not authorized by union officials. Usually in violation of a no-strike clause in a collective agreement.

Wobbly: A slang term for members of the Industrial Workers of the World.

Women's Trade Union League: Organized in 1903 to promote the unionization of women workers. Also active in the field of workers' education.

Yellow-dog contract: A contract in which a worker agrees not to become a member of a union while in the employ of the firm. Outlawed by the Norris-LaGuardia Act.

Selected Bibliography

●●●●●●●●●●●●●●●●●●●●●●●●●●●●●●●●●●

The sources cited in the "Further Reading" section following each entry constitute an excellent bibliography of American labor history. The following bibliography is provided for those who want to pursue a more in-depth study of labor relations. It is meant to be comprehensive but not exhaustive.

BIBLIOGRAPHIES AND REFERENCE WORKS

Fink, Gary M., ed. *Biographical Dictionary of American Labor Leaders*. Westport, CT: Greenwood Press, 1974.

———. *Labor Unions*. Westport, CT: Greenwood Press, 1977.

Labor History. "Annual Bibliography of Periodical Articles on American Labor History." *Labor History*, Annually from 1967.

McBrearty, James. *American Labor History and Comparative Labor Movements: A Selected Bibliography*. Tucson, AZ: University of Arizona Press, 1973.

Neufeld, Maurice, et al. *American Working Class History: A Representative Bibliography*. New York: Bowker, 1983.

Who's Who in Labor. New York: Arno Press, 1976.

SURVEYS AND PERIODS OF DEVELOPMENT

Bernstein, Irving. *The Lean Years: A History of the American Worker, 1920–1933*. Boston, MA: Houghton Mifflin, 1960.

———. *The Turbulent Years: A History of the American Worker, 1933–1941*. Boston, MA: Houghton Mifflin, 1960.

Brody, David. *Workers in Industrial America, Essays on the 20th Century Struggle*. New York: Oxford University Press, 1980.

Commons, John R., et al. *History of Labor in the United States*, 4 vols. New York: Macmillan, 1918–1935.

Dubofsky, Melvyn. *Industrialism and the American Worker, 1865–1920*. Arlington Heights, IL: Harlan Davidson, 1985.

Filippelli, Ronald L. *Labor in the USA: A History*. New York: Knopf, 1984.

Foner, Philip. *History of the Labor Movement in the United States*, 6 vols. New York: International, 1947–1983.

Galenson, Walter. *The CIO Challenge to the AFL: A History of the American Labor Movement, 1935–1941*. Cambridge, MA: Harvard University Press, 1960.

Green, James R. *The World of the Worker*. New York: Hill and Wang, 1980.

Grob, Gerald N. *Workers and Utopia: A Study of Ideological Conflict in the American Labor Movement, 1865–1900*. Evanston, IL: Northwestern University Press, 1961.

Lens, Sidney. *The Labor Wars: From the Molly Maguires to the Sitdowns*. Garden City, NY: Doubleday, 1973.

Montgomery, David. *Beyond Equality: Labor and the Radical Republicans, 1862–1872*. New York: Knopf, 1967.

———. *The Fall of the House of Labor: The Workplace, the State, and American Labor Activism, 1865–1925*. New York: Cambridge University Press, 1987.

Ware, Norman. *The Labor Movement in the United States, 1860–1895*. New York: Appleton, 1929.

INDIVIDUAL UNIONS, TRADES, AND INDUSTRIES

Aurand, Harold. *From the Molly Maguires to the United Mineworkers: The Social Ecology of an Industrial Union, 1869–1897*. Philadelphia, PA: Temple University Press, 1971.

Brody, David. *Steelworkers in America: The Non-union Era*. Cambridge, MA: Harvard University Press, 1960.

———. *The Butcher Workmen: Study of Unionization*. Cambridge, MA: Harvard University Press, 1964.

Christie, Robert A. *Empire in Wood: A History of the United Brotherhood of Carpenters and Joiners of America*. Ithaca, NY: Cornell University Press, 1956.

Clark, Paul. *The Miners' Fight for Democracy: Arnold Miller and the Reform of the United Mine Workers*. Ithaca, NY: Cornell ILR Press, 1981.

Corbin, David. *Life, Work, and Rebellion in the Coal Fields: the Southern West Virginia Coal Miners, 1880–1922*. Urbana, IL: University of Illinois Press, 1981.

Daniel, Cletus. *Bitter Harvest: History of California Farmworkers, 1870–1941*. Ithaca, NY: Cornell University Press, 1981.

Derickson, Alan. *Workers' Health, Workers' Democracy: The Western Miners' Struggle, 1891–1925*. Ithaca, NY: Cornell University Press, 1988.

Eggert, Gerald. *Railroad Labor Disputes, The Beginnings of Federal Strike Policy*. Ann Arbor, MI: University of Michigan Press, 1967.

Fink, Leon. *Workingmen's Democracy: The Knights of Labor and American Politics*. Urbana, IL: University of Illinois Press, 1983.

Licht, Walter. *Working for the Railroad: The Organization of Work in the Nineteenth Century*. Princeton, NJ: Princeton University Press, 1983.

Ligenfelter, Richard. *The Hardrock Miners: A History of the Mining Labor Movement in the American West, 1863–1893*. Berkeley, CA: University of California Press, 1979.

Ozanne, Robert. *A Century of Labor–Management Relations at McCormick and International Harvester*. Madison, WI: University of Wisconsin Press, 1967.

Perlman, Mark. *The Machinists: A New Study in American Trade Unionism*. Cambridge, MA: Harvard University Press, 1964.

Peterson, Joyce Shaw. *American Automobile Workers, 1900–1933*. Albany, NY: SUNY Press, 1987.

Schact, John N. *The Making of Telephone Unionism, 1920–1947*. New Brunswick, NJ: Rutgers University Press, 1985.

LABOR RADICALISM

Buhle, Paul. *Marxism in the United States: Remapping the History of the American Left*. London: Verso, 1987.

Cantor, Milton. *The Divided Left: American Radicalism, 1900–1975*. New York: Hill and Wang, 1978.

Cochrane, Bert. *Labor and Communism: The Conflict That Shaped American Unions*. Princeton, NJ: Princeton University Press, 1977.

Conlin, Joseph. *Bread and Roses Too: Studies of the Wobblies*. Westport, CT: Greenwood Press, 1969.

David, Henry. *The History of the Haymarket Affair*. New York: Collier, 1963.

Draper, Theodore. *The Roots of American Communism*. New York: Viking, 1957.

Dubofsky, Melvyn. *We Shall Be All: A History of the IWW*. Chicago, IL: Quadrangle, 1969.

Green, James. *Grass Roots Socialism: Radical Movements in the Southwest, 1895–1943*. Baton Rouge, LA: University of Louisiana Press, 1978.

Herreshoff, David. *American Disciples of Marx*. Detroit, MI: Wayne State University Press, 1967.

Kornbluh, Joyce L., ed. *Rebel Voices, an I.W.W. Anthology*. Ann Arbor, MI: University of Michigan Press, 1964.

Laslett, John H. M. *Labor and the Left: A Study of Socialist and Radical Influence in the American Labor Movement,*

1881–1924. New York: Basic Books, 1970.

Levenstein, Nelson. *Communism, Anti-Communism and the CIO*. Westport, CT: Greenwood Press, 1981.

Shannon, David. *The Socialist Party of America*. New York: Macmillan, 1955.

AUTOBIOGRAPHY AND BIOGRAPHY

Anderson, Jervis. *A. Philip Randolph: A Biographical Portrait*. New York: Harcourt Brace Jovanovich, 1973.

Brophy, John. *A Miner's Life: An Autobiography*. Madison, WI: University of Wisconsin Press, 1964.

Clark, Paul, et al. *Forging a Union of Steel: Philip Murray, SWOC, & the United Steelworkers*. Ithaca, NY: Cornell ILR Press, 1987.

Cormier, Frank, and William J. Eaton. *Reuther*. Englewood Cliffs, NJ: Prentice Hall, 1970.

De Caux, Len. *Labor Radical: From the Wobblies to CIO, A Personal History*. Boston, MA: Beacon, 1970.

Dreier, Mary. *Margaret Dreier Robins: Her Life, Letters and Work*. New York: Island Press Cooperative, 1950.

Dubinsky, David, and A. H. Raskin. *David Dubinsky: A Life With Labor*. New York: Simon and Schuster, 1977.

Dubofsky, Melvyn, and Warren Van Tine. *John L. Lewis*. New York: Quadrangle, 1977.

Flynn, Elizabeth Gurley. *The Rebel Girl: An Autobiography. My First Life, 1906–1926*. New York: International, 1973.

Foster, William Z. *Pages from a Worker's Life*. New York: International, 1939.

Goldman, Emma. *Living My Life*. New York: Knopf, 1931.

Gompers, Samuel. *Seventy Years of Life and Labor*, 2 vols. New York: Dutton, 1925.

Goulden, Joseph. *Meany*. New York: Atheneum, 1972.

Grossman, Jonathan. *William Sylvis: Pioneer of American Labor*. New York: Columbia University Press, 1945.

Haywood, William D. *Bill Haywood's Book*. New York: International, 1929.

Jones, Mary. *Autobiography of Mother Jones*. Chicago, IL: Kerr, 1925.

Josephson, Matthew. *Sidney Hillman: Statesman of American Labor*. Garden City, NY: Doubleday, 1952.

Larrowe, Charles P. *Harry Bridges: The Rise and Fall of Radical Labor in the United States*. New York: L. Hill, 1972.

Levy, Jacque. *Cesar Chavez: Autobiography of La Causa*. New York: Norton, 1975.

Mandel, Bernard. *Samuel Gompers: A Biography*. Yellow Springs, OH: Antioch University Press, 1963.

O'Connor, Richard. *Heywood Broun: A Biography*. New York: Putnam, 1975.

Pesotta, Rose. *Bread Upon the Waters*. New York: Dodd, Mead, 1945.

Powderly, Terrence. *The Path I Trod*. New York: Columbia University Press, 1940.

Salvatore, Nick. *Eugene V. Debs: Citizen and Socialist*. Urbana, IL: University of Illinois Press, 1982.

Schneiderman, Rose, and Lucy Goldthwaite. *All for One*. New York: Paul Eriksson, 1967.

Seretan, Glen L. *Daniel DeLeon: The Odyssey of an American Marxist*. Cambridge, MA: Harvard University Press, 1979.

Van Tine, Warren. *The Making of the Labor Bureaucrat: Union Leadership in the United States, 1870–1920*. Amherst, MA: University of Massachusetts Press, 1973.

Whittemore, L. H. *The Man Who Ran the Subways: The Story of Mike Quill*. New York: Holt, Rinehart & Winston, 1968.

Ziegler, Robert H. *John L. Lewis, Labor Leader*. Boston, MA: Twayne, 1988.

COMMUNITY STUDIES, IMMIGRATION, AND SOCIAL HISTORY

Barton, Josef. *Peasants and Strangers: Italians, Rumanians, and Slovaks in an American City*. Cambridge, MA: Harvard University Press, 1975.

Bodnar, John. *Immigration and Industrialization: Ethnicity in an American Mill Town, 1870–1914*. Pittsburgh, PA: University of Pittsburgh Press, 1977.

———, et al. *Lives of Their Own: Blacks, Italians, and Poles in Pittsburgh, 1900–1960*. Pittsburgh, PA: University of Pittsburgh Press, 1982.

Cantor, Milton. *American Workingclass Culture: Explorations in American Labor and Social History*. Westport, CT: Greenwood Press, 1979.

Cumbler, John. *Working-Class Community in Industrial America: Work, Leisure, and Struggle in Two Industrial Cities, 1880–1930.* Westport, CT: Greenwood Press, 1979.

Dawley, Alan. *Class and Community: The Industrial Revolution in Lynn.* Cambridge, MA: Harvard University Press, 1976.

Dubofsky, Melvyn. *When Workers Organize: New York City in the Progressive Era.* Amherst, MA: University of Massachusetts Press, 1968.

Faler, Paul. *Mechanics and Manufacturers in the Early Industrial Revolution, Lynn, Massachusetts, 1780–1860.* Albany, NY: SUNY Press, 1981.

Frisch, Michael, and Daniel J. Walkowitz, eds. *Working Class America: Essays on Labor, Community, and American Society.* Urbana, IL: University of Illinois Press, 1983.

Gutman, Herbert. *Work, Culture and Society in Industrializing America.* New York: Knopf, 1976.

Hareven, Tamara K. *Family Time and Industrial Time: The Relationship Between the Family and Work in a New England Industrial Community.* New York: Cambridge University Press, 1982.

Harvey, Katherine. *The Best Dressed Miners: Life and Labor in the Maryland Coal Regions, 1835–1910.* Ithaca, NY: Cornell University Press, 1969.

Ingalls, Robert P. *Urban Vigilantes in the New South: Tampa, 1932–1936.* Knoxville, TN: University of Tennessee Press, 1988.

Kessner, Thomas. *The Golden Door: Italian and Jewish Immigrant Mobility in New York City, 1880–1915.* New York: Oxford University Press, 1977.

Kleinberg, S. J. *The Shadow of the Mills: Working-Class Families in Pittsburgh, 1870–1907.* Pittsburgh, PA: University of Pittsburgh Press, 1989.

Meyerhuber, Carl I. *Less Than Forever: The Rise and Decline of Union Solidarity in Western Pennsylvania, 1914–1948.* Selinsgrove, PA: Susquehanna University Press, 1987.

Oestreicher, Richard. *Solidarity and Fragmentation: Working People and Class Consciousness in Detroit, 1875–1900.* Urbana, IL: University of Illinois Press, 1986.

Rischin, Moses. *The Promised City: New York's Jews, 1870–1914.* Cambridge, MA: Harvard University Press, 1962.

Rosenzweig, Roy A. *Eight Hours for What We Will, Workers and Leisure in an Industrial City, 1870–1920.* New York: Cambridge University Press, 1983.

Saxton, Alexander. *The Indispensable Enemy: Labor and the Anti-Chinese Movement in California.* Berkeley, CA: University of California Press, 1971.

Shergold, Peter. *Working-Class Life: The "American Standard" in Comparative Perspective, 1899–1913.* Pittsburgh, PA: University of Pittsburgh Press, 1982.

Thernstrom, Stephan. *Poverty and Progress: Social Mobility in a Nineteenth Century City.* Cambridge, MA: Harvard University Press, 1964.

Walkowitz, Daniel. *Workers City, Company Town: Iron and Cotton Worker Protest in Troy and Cohoes, New York, 1855–1884.* Urbana, IL: University of Illinois Press, 1978.

Wilentz, Sean. *Chants Democratic: New York City and the Rise of the American Working Class, 1788–1850.* New York: Oxford University Press, 1984.

Yearly, Clifton K. *Britons in American Labor: A History of the Influence of the United Kingdom Immigrants on American Labor, 1820–1914.* Baltimore, MD: Johns Hopkins University Press, 1957.

WOMEN AND MINORITIES

Blewett, Mary H. *Men, Women, and Work: Class, Gender, and Protest in the New England Shoe Industry, 1780–1910.* Urbana, IL: University of Illinois Press, 1988.

Brownlee, W. Elliot, and Mary M. Brownlee. *Women in the American Economy: A Documentary History, 1675–1929.* New Haven, CT: Yale University Press, 1976.

Buhle, Mari Jo. *Women and American Socialism, 1870–1920.* Urbana, IL: University of Illinois Press, 1981.

Cantor, Milton, ed. *Black Labor in America.* Westport, CT: Negro Universities Press, 1969.

Cantor, Milton, and Bruce Laurie, eds. *Class, Sex, and the Woman Worker.* Westport, CT: Greenwood Press, 1977.

Dublin, Thomas. *Women at Work: The Transformation of Work and Community in Lowell, Massachusetts, 1826–1860.* New York: Columbia University Press, 1979.

Dye, Nancy Schrom. *As Equals and as Sisters: Feminism, Unionism, and the Women's Trade Union League of New York.* Columbia, MO: University of Missouri Press, 1980.

Foner, Philip. *Organized Labor and the Black Worker, 1619–1973.* New York: Praeger, 1974.

———. *Women and the American Labor Movement,* 2 vols. New York: Free Press, 1979–1980.

Genovese, Eugene. *From Rebellion to Revolution: Afro American Slave Revolts in the Making of the Modern World.* Baton Rouge, LA: Louisiana State University Press, 1979.

Gottlieb, Peter. *Making Their Own Way: Southern Blacks' Migration to Pittsburgh, 1916–1930.* Urbana, IL: University of Illinois Press, 1987.

Gould, William B. *Black Workers in White Unions: Job Discrimination in the United States.* Ithaca, NY: Cornell University Press, 1977.

Greenwald, Maureen. *Women, War, and Work: The Impact of World War I on Women Workers in the United States.* Westport, CT: Greenwood Press, 1980.

Gronman, Carol, and Mary Beth Norton, eds. *'To Toil the Livelong Day': America's Women at Work, 1780–1980.* Ithaca, NY: Cornell University Press, 1987.

Harris, William H. *The Harder We Run: Black Workers Since the Civil War.* New York: Oxford University Press, 1982.

Henry, Alice. *The Trade Union Woman.* New York: Appleton, 1915.

Jacobson, Julius, ed. *The Negro and the American Labor Movement.* Garden City, NY: Doubleday, 1968.

Kessler-Harris, Alice. *Out to Work. A History of Wage-Earning Women in the United States*. New York: Oxford University Press, 1982.

Marshall, F. Ray. *The Negro and Organized Labor*. New York: John Wiley, 1965.

Meier, August, and Elliot Rudwick. *Black Detroit and the Rise of the UAW*. New York: Oxford University Press, 1979.

Norwood, Stephen H. *Labor's Flaming Youth: Telephone Operators and Worker Militancy, 1878–1923*. Urbana, IL: University of Illinois Press, 1990.

Spero, Sterling, and Abram L. Harris. *The Black Worker*. New York: Columbia University Press, 1931.

Tentler, Leslie Woodcock. *Wage Earning Women: Industrial Work and Family Life in the United States, 1900–1930*. New York: Oxford University Press, 1979.

Wertheimer, Barbara. *We Were There: The Story of Working Women in America*. New York: Pantheon, 1977.

LABOR, POLITICS, AND INTERNATIONAL AFFAIRS

Calkins, Fay. *The CIO and the Democratic Party*. Chicago, IL: University of Chicago Press, 1952.

Carew, Anthony. *Labour Under the Marshall Plan: The Politics of Productivity and the Marketing of Management Science*. Detroit, MI: Wayne State University Press, 1967.

Filippelli, Ronald L. *American Labor and Postwar Italy, 1943–1953: A Study in Cold War Politics*. Stanford, CA: Stanford University Press.

Foster, James. *The Union Politic: The CIO Political Action Committee*. Columbia, MO: University of Missouri Press, 1975.

Gall, Gilbert. *The Politics of Right to Work: The Labor Federations as Special Interests, 1943–1979*. Westport, CT: Greenwood Press, 1988.

Godson, Roy. *American Labor and European Politics*. New York: Crane, Russak and Company, 1976.

Greenstone, J. David. *Labor in American Politics*. Chicago, IL: University of Chicago Press, 1977.

Karson, Marc. *American Labor Unions and Politics, 1900–1918*. Carbondale, IL: Southern Illinois University Press, 1958.

Larson, Simeon. *Labor and Foreign Policy: Gompers, the AFL, and the First World War, 1914–1918*. Rutherford, NJ: Fairleigh Dickinson University Press, 1975.

Milton, David. *The Politics of U.S. Labor: From the Great Depression to the New Deal*. New York: Monthly Review Press, 1982.

Radosh, Ronald. *American Labor and United States Foreign Policy*. New York: Random House, 1969.

Rehmus, Charles M., and Doris McLaughlin. *Labor and American Politics: A Book of Readings*. Ann Arbor, MI: University of Michigan Press, 1967.

Stedman, Murray S., and Susan W. Stedman. *Discontent at the Polls: A Study of Farmer and Labor Parties, 1827–1948*. New York: Columbia University Press, 1950.

Taft, Philip. *Defending Freedom: American Labor and Foreign Affairs.* Los Angeles, CA: Taft, 1973.

Wilson, Graham K. *Unions in American National Politics.* New York: St. Martin's Press, 1979.

Zieger, Robert. *Republicans and Labor, 1919–1929.* Lexington, KY: University of Kentucky Press, 1969.

WORK ORGANIZATION AND CONTROL

Edwards, Richard. *Contested Terrain: The Transformation of the Workplace in the Twentieth Century.* New York: Basic Books, 1979.

Gilbert, James B. *Work Without Salvation: America's Intellectuals and Industrial Alienation, 1880–1910.* Baltimore, MD: Johns Hopkins University Press, 1977.

Gordon, David M., et al. *Segmented Work, Divided Workers: The Historical Transformation of Labor in the United States.* New York: Cambridge University Press, 1982.

Jacoby, Sanford. *Employing Bureaucracy: Managers, Unions, and the Transformation of Work in American Industry,* 1900–1945. New York: Columbia University Press, 1985.

Juravich, Thomas. *Chaos on the Shop Floor: A Worker's View of Quality, Productivity, and Management.* Philadelphia, PA: Temple University Press, 1985.

Montgomery, David. *Workers' Control in America.* New York: Cambridge University Press, 1979.

Nelson, Daniel. *Managers and Workers: The Origins of the New Factory System in the United States, 1880–1920.* Madison, WI: University of Wisconsin Press, 1975.

———. *Frederick W. Taylor and Scientific Management.* Madison, WI: University of Wisconsin Press, 1980.

Rodgers, Daniel T. *The Work Ethic in Industrial America, 1850–1920.* Chicago, IL: University of Chicago Press, 1974.

Tomlins, Christopher L. *The State and the Unions: Labor Relations, Law and the Organized Labor Movement in America.* New York: Cambridge University Press, 1985.

Yellowitz, Irwin. *Industrialization and the American Labor Movement, 1850–1900.* Port Washington, NY: Kennikat Press, 1977.

The Encyclopedia

ACTORS' STRIKE OF 1919. On May 26, 1913, one hundred twelve actors met in the Pabst Grand Circle Hotel on Fifty-ninth Street in New York City and formed the Actors' Equity Association. At first the organization did not consider itself a trade union, but rather defined its role as a professional association charged with raising employment standards for actors in the legitimate theater. By 1919, Actors' Equity had enrolled some 3,000 members, or roughly one-half of the eligible actors across the country. Relations with the producers, however, had deteriorated to the point that Actors' Equity applied for a charter in the American Federation of Labor as part of the Federation's Associated Actors and Artistes of America.

At the time, the chief adversary of Actors' Equity was the Producing Manager's Association (PMA), which enrolled most of the major producers in New York and in other centers of legitimate theater. This included the huge chains, such as the Shubert Organization and Klaw and Erlanger, as well as smaller, but not unimportant, producers such as George M. Cohan, and Florenz Ziegfeld. Relations between Actors' Equity and the producers had been rocky from the beginning. Although negotiations with the PMA's predecessor had resulted in an agreement on a standard actor's contract in 1917, many of the producers failed to put it into effect. By 1919, those that had were interested in rolling back some of the concessions they had made in 1917, particularly regarding limitations on unpaid rehearsal time and the eight-performance week. For its part, Actors' Equity wanted full enforcement of the standard contract, including the eight-performance week, arbitration of differences between Equity and the PMA, and the closed shop. While the managers were inclined to consider the workweek issue, they were adamant about the closed shop. There would be no recognition of Actors' Equity as the exclusive representative of the performers. Nor, as a corollary, would there be arbitration with Equity interposed between the actors and their employers. This attitude grew even harsher when the actors accepted the AFL charter.

The first skirmish took place at the Century Theater in New York where Actors' Equity called out the cast of "Chu Chin Chow." The move failed when a majority of the cast refused to heed the union's call. Three who did walk out and subsequently lost their jobs—Lucy Beaumont, Ida Mulle, and Clara Verdera—became the first of Equity's Gold Star members because of their courage.

The events at the Century Theater impressed the need for organization and solidarity on Equity's leadership. They knew that they needed unified direction. To that end they elected Frank Gillmore to lead the struggle. They also realized that they might need the support of the other theatrical unions, particularly the International Association of Theatrical Stage Employees, and the Musicians Union. At a meeting attended by 1,500 actors on August 1, 1919, Equity members gave their leaders the power to make alliances with the other unions if necessary.

For their part, the producers set out to crush Actors' Equity and to reestablish the employment relationship in the industry based on individual contracts between actors and employers. The PMA put its members under $10,000 bond not to issue Equity contracts. They also brought all branches of the industry into their united front against Equity. PMA formed an alliance with the Vaudeville Managers' Protective Association, the National Association of the Motion Picture Industry, and the Columbia Amusement and Burlesque Interests of America. All were national in scope and their inclusion was aimed at cutting off the possibility of employment for Equity members in all branches of the theater across the nation. Twice during the strike, the producers also tried to form a company union to draw support away from Equity, but in both cases the attempt failed.

The strike began on the evening of August 7, 1919. The players in "Lightnin'" at the Gaiety Theater were the first to walk out, leaving a full house of disgruntled playgoers. Similar scenes were acted out at twelve other theaters with shows produced by members of the PMA. By the end of the strike, eighteen New York productions were closed and five productions in rehearsal were canceled. The show moved outside of the theaters from then on as fascinated New Yorkers watched actors such as Ed Wynn, Eddie Cantor, Marie Dressler, and Ethel, Lionel, and John Barrymore walk the picket line. The display of solidarity and the publicity surrounding the strike led to a rush of new members for Actors' Equity whose rolls grew to nearly 4,000 during the strike. In addition, the dispute also led to the formation of a union of chorus men and women as a branch of Actors' Equity. Marie Dressler and Ethel Barrymore were instrumental in encouraging the militancy of the chorus.

In response the PMA members pledged a strike fund of $1 million and brought suit for breach of contract against Equity and its members to the tune of $500,000. In order to keep his "Follies" open, Florenz Ziegfeld obtained an injunction from a New York Supreme Court judge restraining Eddie Cantor and the rest of the cast from joining the strike. Although Cantor and the "Follies" cast eventually walked out anyway, the tactic did keep Ziegfeld's review from going dark during the first days of the strike. The Shubert Organization filed its own $500,000 suit against Equity for losses suffered. And the producers scored one of their biggest publicity victories when George M. Cohan, the famous writer of popular and patriotic songs and a bitterly anti-union producer, pledged every dollar he possessed for the fight against Equity. So determined was Cohan that he assumed the presidency of one of the ill-starred company unions, the Actors Fidelity League, and pledged to retire completely from the theater if Actors' Equity won.

As the strike wore on, Equity called out all of its members currently in rehearsal for plays or musicals to counter the producers' resort to the courts. Equity also extended the strike to the road in order to deprive the producers of income from out-of-town productions. In Boston, in spite of an injunction, six theaters went dark. Philadelphia reported the closing of two theaters, and similar successes were noted in Chicago, St. Louis, Washington, Providence, and Atlantic City.

The fame of the strikers and their innovative tactics gained broad support among the general public. Newspapers in New York and other theater centers were generally favorable to the actors. Frequent parades and motorcades of famous strikers also generated publicity and kept the dispute in the public eye. Perhaps Equity's most inspired tactic was the production of its own shows. The first took place at New York's Lexington Avenue Opera House where for a top price of two dollars, most of which went into the Equity strike fund, patrons could watch a galaxy of stars such as W. C. Fields, the Barrymores, Cantor, and Dressler in dramatic and musical productions laced with a generous dose of pro-union propaganda. The productions earned thousands of dollars for the support of the strikers. Equity productions were also mounted in Brooklyn, Philadelphia, and Chicago.

After several weeks, events began to conspire to bring about a settlement. One, oddly, was the visit of American Federation of Labor president Samuel Gompers to New York on his return from participating in the Versailles Peace Conference. Gompers spoke out in support of Actors' Equity and advised the producers, many of whom, including George M. Cohan, were his friends, to negotiate with the union. Gompers' position undercut the producers' argument that they were not anti-union, having dealt with other theatrical unions for years, but that they believed unionization for actors would ruin the theater. At about the same time, the International Alliance of Theatrical Stage Employees and the Musicians Union threatened to strike, and the Teamsters refused to haul trunks and scenery to and from the struck theaters.

The pressures brought the producers to the bargaining table. The so-called undercover negotiations that commenced were an open secret on Broadway. The first crack in the united front of the producers came when the New York Hippodrome broke ranks and signed with Actors' Equity on August 30, recognizing the union for both the actors and the chorus. Suspicion also grew in the Shubert Organization that its main rival, Klaw and Erlanger, was about to follow the lead of the Hippodrome. Having lost both the economic and the public relations battles, the producers sued for peace, offering recognition of Equity and the eight-performance week. The strike ended on the evening of September 6 when the lights went on once

again on Broadway. Unionization had come to stay for American actors.

So ended the formative struggle for the unionization of actors in the American theater. It had lasted for thirty days, had spread to eight cities, had closed thirty-seven plays, had prevented the opening of sixteen others, and had cost the actors and the industry nearly $3 million. By the end of the strike, Actors' Equity had gone from a small, shaky organization, to a confident, battle-tested union with over 14,000 members. Relations between actors and producers, however, would remain bitter for years to come. [Ronald L. Filippelli]

FURTHER READING

Falukender, Robert E. *Historical Development and Basic Policies of the Actors Equity.* Ph.D. dissertation, University of Pittsburgh, 1954.

Harding, Alfred. *The Revolt of the Actors.* New York: William Morrow & Company, 1929.

Ritterbush, Alice M. *Variety's Involvement in Broadway Labor–Management Disputes.* Ph.D. dissertation, Tulane University, 1968.

o o o

AIR TRAFFIC CONTROLLERS' STRIKE OF 1981. In the private sector of our economy, workers are afforded a right to strike under the National Labor Relations Act (NLRA), which was enacted in 1935. Congress excluded public employees from the coverage of the NLRA by providing that federal, state, and local governments were not "employers" within the definition of NLRA. As a consequence, governmental bodies remained free to enact laws concerning collective bargaining. A majority of states have now adopted legislation providing for collective bargaining by their employees.

Beginning with an executive order issued by President John F. Kennedy in 1962, the federal government has recognized the right of its workers to engage in union activities and collective negotiations.

Those rights were codified in the Civil Service Reform Act of 1978, a comprehensive statute enacted during the presidency of Jimmy Carter. Under the Act, most executive branch employees may "form, join, or assist any labor organization" or refrain from such activities "without fear of penalty or reprisal." The Act further states that it shall be an unfair labor practice for any labor organization "to call, or participate in, a strike, work stoppage, or slowdown, or picketing of an agency in a labor–management dispute if such picketing interferes with an agency's operation." The Federal Labor Relations Authority, which administers the Act, has the power to revoke the exclusive recognition status of any labor organization that willfully engages in a strike, or to take "any other disciplinary action" against a striking union. A related federal statute makes it a felony for any federal workers to participate in a strike against the government.

The Professional Air Traffic Controllers Organization (PATCO) was at one time the designated bargaining agent for federal air traffic controllers employed by the Federal Aviation Administration (FAA). Between its organization in 1968 and the mass strike in 1981, PATCO had engaged in a number of slowdowns, "sickouts," and other forms of work actions against the FAA. Those tactics, as well as PATCO's expertise in the political arena, helped the union to gain substantial concessions from the government. Even though compensation is not a subject for negotiation under the federal statute, air traffic controllers were earning an average of $33,000 annually in 1981, with a generous fringe benefit package.

In June 1980, Robert Poli was elected president of the union. Poli's strategy for the forthcoming contract negotiations was to undertake a nationwide strike which, Poli believed, would prompt congressional approval of greater economic gains for the membership. Poli began by demanding

such exorbitant items as a $10,000 per year salary increase and a thirty-two-hour work-week. The union also accumulated a large fund which was to be used to compensate any workers who were discharged as a result of the strike. Poli and other union leaders made no secret of their strike preparations and openly discussed the strike plan with members throughout the country. On the political front, the union endorsed Ronald Reagan's successful presidential bid in October 1980 and received Reagan's grateful acknowledgement of its support.

In June 1981, the FAA made a substantial contract offer to PATCO. The Reagan administration agreed to request congressional approval for an immediate pay increase, overtime pay after thirty-six hours, an increase in severance pay, and other items for the controllers. The final offer represented more than an 11 percent increase in compensation, or more than twice the increase given to other federal employees. Poli tentatively accepted the FAA's offer and agreed to submit it for approval to the membership. According to the PATCO strategy already in place, however, the union executive committee rejected the offer and persuaded the rank and file membership to do likewise, which it did by a vote of 95.3 percent in favor of rejection. Poli then issued new demands to the FAA and imposed a strike deadline of August 3, 1981. The FAA rejected PATCO's demands.

The strike began on the scheduled day. By using controllers who refused to strike, military personnel, supervisors, and retirees, the government was able to continue operating the air transportation system. Within ten days, the system was functioning near normal levels. Other unions within the industry, such as the pilots, attendants, and machinists, refused to join the strike, and it was soon apparent that the strike had failed to paralyze airline traffic as PATCO had planned.

Shortly after the strike began, President Reagan took vigorous action. Within hours after the strike commenced, he issued the following warning to all striking controllers: "This morning at 7:00 A.M. the union representing those who man America's air traffic facilities called a strike—I must tell those who failed to report for duty this morning they are in violation of the law and if they do not report for work within forty-eight hours, they have forfeited their jobs and will be terminated." The FAA also sent a telegram to all strikers informing them that "any unauthorized absence from the facility when scheduled or directed to report for duty indicates that such persons are participating in the strike." Some 1,200 controllers returned to work, but approximately 11,500 remained on strike and were subsequently discharged.

The union mounted a legal challenge against the discipline imposed on strikers, but the courts uniformly upheld the FAA's actions. One lead case held that a prima facie case for discipline would be proved where an employee "withheld his services in concert with others." The existence of general knowledge of a strike together with an unjustified absence made out a case for discipline, unless the employee had a legitimate excuse for absence from work. As to the proof of an intent to strike, the court said: "Neither participation in strike planning nor express agreement with others to perpetrate the strike is a necessary ingredient that a particular employee participated in a strike." Consequently, an employee's unexplained absence during the work stoppage sufficed as proof of an "intent" to engage in the strike.

Some controllers argued that they had been coerced or intimidated by the picket lines and were therefore justified in refusing to work. The court agreed that intimidation might be a defense to the charge of participating in the strike, but pointed out that the employee needed a high standard of proof. The employee, the court said, had

to show "that his failure to report for work was the result of a threat or other intimidating conduct, directed toward him, sufficient to instill in him a reasonable fear of physical danger to himself or others, which a person of ordinary firmness would not be expected to resist." The vast majority of controllers were unable to make such a showing.

A further legal argument made by the fired employees was that discharge was too severe a penalty since some strikers were initially permitted to return to work. The court also rejected that contention. It said that leniency shown to strikers in the past did not preclude the government action in this case. "That other government workers have struck and been allowed to return to work, or that a court may have viewed it permissible under some circumstances to continue government strikers in employment, cannot be viewed as forever binding the government against the removal of any strikers under any circumstances." The FAA, then, had discretion to penalize some controllers more severely than others.

The union was also punished for instigating the strike. At various times, the PATCO officers were subject to injunctions, the union was fined, and charges of unfair labor practice were filed against it. As a result of those charges, the union was eventually decertified by the Federal Labor Relations Authority, and the Authority's action was upheld by a federal appellate court.

The PATCO strike was an extremely significant event for American labor. Many observers viewed it as signalling the decline of labor as an important force in American politics; despite PATCO's political sophistication, the union seriously underestimated the opposition of President Reagan, Congress, and the American public to its illegal strike. Other commentators argue that President Reagan's drastic action encouraged employers generally to deal harshly with unions and to engage in open anti-union strategies. By any standard, the PATCO strike was a resounding defeat for labor. Nevertheless, the hostility and adversarialism engendered by the conflict lasted less than a decade.

By mid-1987, air traffic controllers had chosen a new union, the National Air Traffic Controllers Association (NATCA) to represent them. NATCA and the FAA negotiated a three-year contract effective January 12, 1989. The agreement covered working conditions, but not pay or economic benefits. According to a *New York Times* report, the parties' relationship was characterized by a spirit of cooperation and congeniality. The negotiators celebrated their agreement with a banquet, which a union executive vice president described as follows: "It was a big group of friends. You couldn't distinguish one side from the other." Thus, the bitter struggle of 1981 had become only a matter of historical interest. [Raymond L. Hogler]

FURTHER READING

Meltzer, Bernard, and Cass Sustein. "Public Employee Strikes, Executive Discretion, and the Air Traffic Controllers." *University of Chicago Law Review*, Vol. 50 (1983), pp. 731–799.

Northrup, Herbert. "The Rise and Demise of PATCO." *Industrial & Labor Relations Review*, Vol. 37 (1984), pp. 167–184.

Shostak, Arthur. *Air Controllers' Controversy: Lessons from the PATCO Strike.* New York: Human Sciences Press, 1986.

o   o   o

ALABAMA MINERS' STRIKE OF 1920. Organized labor had reached its peak of power in Alabama during World War I. Most Alabama employers had historically been extremely hostile to any idea of unionization, but they reluctantly accepted unions during the war because of labor shortages and federal government pressure to maintain uninterrupted production. By 1919, labor had a presence in the crafts, on the railroads, in the iron and steel industry, and in the mines. The mines had been unorganized since the complete defeat of the United Mine Workers in 1908, but most became union again under wartime conditions.

On November 1, 1919, after the failure of the negotiations on union demands for a wage increase, which had been drawn up at the 1919 United Mine Workers convention, America's bituminous miners, including those in Alabama, walked out. On November 8, an Alabama court issued an injunction ordering the Alabama miners back to work. Negotiations continued and the UMW accepted a compromise proposal from President Woodrow Wilson that had been advanced by U.S. Attorney General A. Mitchell Palmer. Palmer promised UMW District 20 officers in Alabama that operators would rehire the strikers and accept the settlement.

Unfortunately, active unionists were not rehired in Alabama, and many were blacklisted. When Palmer inquired as to why the operators had disregarded his instructions, J. L. Davidson, secretary of the Coal Operators Association, claimed that those denied employment were general malcontents and troublemakers who had intimidated other employees. In effect, the operators had decided not to recognize the union any longer. They refused to appear before the coal commission appointed by President Wilson to decide wage increases for the bituminous miners. When the coal commission adopted a rate, the Alabama operators refused to put it into effect.

After failing to get Wilson and Palmer to pressure the Alabama operators to implement the commission's recommendations and to recognize the union, UMW District 20 adopted a "blue book" agreement to present to the operators which called for a compromise form of union recognition. Miners were instructed to strike those who refused to sign. By the summer, approximately fifty-one smaller operators had signed the blue book agreement and recognized the union, but most had not and some 2,000 miners were on strike. In an effort to avert a wider strike, Governor Thomas E. Kilby of Alabama appointed a commission to investigate the situation. The operators agreed to testify but adamantly refused to consider union recognition.

The mine labor force of Alabama had been integrated for a long time. Blacks and whites worked together, although blacks generally held the lower level jobs. But black workers did support the union. Attempting to discredit the union, the operators charged that the UMW was promoting racial equality. Although the union denied it, there is no question that black and white miners showed solidarity during the strike. In one instance, a white miner shot and killed a deputy sheriff and a black strikebreaker while they were attempting to arrest a black striker.

The use of black strikebreakers led to violence: the homes of three black strikebreakers were dynamited, a train carrying strikebreakers was fired upon, and the companies claimed that strikers had fired into a boarding house where black strikebreakers lived. For their part, the miners blamed the violence on company policies. Their ire was directed mainly at the private mine guards who had been deputized by the sheriff, and particularly toward those employed by the Corona Coal Company. Corona company guards were charged with illegally and brutally evicting miners and their families from company houses. On one occasion, with the miner absent, and only his family in the house, company guards fired 147 bullets into the dwelling, wounding two women.

Corona's general manager, Leon Adler, violently opposed the strike, claiming that strikers had no right to hold meetings. He vowed that he and his deputies "would disperse their meetings as fast as they assembled" and that they would paint the union hall red "even if it had to be done in blood." Not surprisingly, this tense climate produced violence. A few days after Adler's statement, he and a deputy were killed during a confrontation between strikers and Corona's guards. When the guards, with Adler at their head, marched into town and opened fire on the union hall, the miners responded in kind. Twenty-eight union members were arrested for the killings, but no one was convicted.

The shoot-out forced the governor to send troops to the mining districts. But the presence of troops did not end the violence. Strikebreakers on the way to the Majestic Mines were fired upon, with one killed and two wounded. With the troops in place, the operators showed no inclination to settle the strike. Strikers had been replaced by strikebreakers at many of the mines, and the demand for coal was low because of a national economic slowdown. As the strike wore on, the suffering of the strikers increased. Van Bittner, director of District 20, requested money from UMW president John L. Lewis to purchase 1,000 tents for the use of evicted strikers. Although the strikers received small amounts of strike benefits, little help could be expected from a national union that faced battles across the nation's coalfields and whose finances were in bad shape.

As the strike dragged on incidents of violence on both sides continued. One of the most serious occurred when a National Guardsman killed a striker at Nauvo on December 23, 1920. The dead striker's son-in-law then sought out the guardsman and killed him in turn. A few weeks later, a group of masked men broke into the Walker County jail and removed the accused murderer of the guardsman. Police found his body the next day. Nine national guardsmen were indicted for the murder, but although the state held several trials, the case was ultimately dismissed.

With no apparent end of the bloody strike in sight, Governor Kilby intervened and appointed a three-man board to make recommendations. Both sides agreed to abide by the decision. The governor's board rejected the union's request for recognition because it would raise the price of coal to the consumer. Nor did the board grant the union relief from contract work. The board recognized "the right of the coal operator to operate his mine property as he sees fit," and believed that the state should, "at any cost, protect such operator in the peaceful possession and operation of his property."

The recommendations were a severe blow to the union. They did not even include a requirement that the strikers be hired back, although the governor did make that a personal recommendation. With his troops exhausted, and the entire weight of public opinion behind the governor's recommendations, Van Bittner called off the strike on February 21, 1921. The arrogance of the operators was demonstrated shortly after when they began to cut wages. Appeals from the union to the governor, who had also been assured that no wage cutting would occur, fell on deaf ears.

The defeat in the Alabama miner's strike demonstrated how ephemeral the union gains of the war years had been in the face of determined opposition from anti-union employers. The defeat in Alabama also increased the amount of non-union coal on the market, thus putting more pressure on the organized mines in the central competitive field. The defeat had been expensive in dollars and cents as well. The UMW contributed nearly $2 million for organizing expenses and relief of the strikers. Finally, the defeat of the miners gave heart to the anti-union offensive in Alabama. Employers in the state eagerly signed up for the "American Plan" anti-union crusade. Soon after the defeat in the mines unionization on the railroads suffered a devastating blow. In a few years unionism in Alabama had reverted to its prewar level. [Ronald L. Filippelli]

FURTHER READING

Straw, Richard A. "The United Mine Workers of America and the 1920 Coal Strike in Alabama." *Alabama Review*, Vol. 28 (1980), pp. 104–128.

Taft, Philip. *Organizing Dixie: Alabama Workers in the Industrial Era.* Westport, CT: Greenwood Press, 1981.

o o o

ALLIS-CHALMERS STRIKE OF 1941. Well before America entered into World War II after the Japanese bombing of Pearl Harbor on December 7, 1941, the Roosevelt administration had begun to send much-needed material to the allies and to mobilize American industry for the defense effort. Critical to Roosevelt's plan was labor peace. To this end the government created the National Defense Mobilization Board (NDMB), to which all industrial disputes were to be referred, and called on the labor movement, and in particular the Congress of Industrial Organizations (CIO), to curb its militancy in the service of national preparedness.

The administration had good reason for concern. During 1941, the CIO's aggressive organizing had produced an enormous strike wave. In that year 2.4 million men and women engaged in some 4,228 strikes. Many of these strikes affected the heavy-industry sector so vital to defense production. Almost 70 percent of those who struck were under the leadership of CIO unions. In the surge of militancy, nonunion giants like Bethlehem Steel and Ford were organized. The United Mine Workers, in a month-long strike, finally eliminated the wage differential between the northern and southern Appalachian coalfields.

Although the strikes were largely successful—not only bringing union representation to millions of new workers but also increasing real wages—they also provided an issue for enemies in Congress to seize upon to discredit both the labor movement and the New Deal. Under the guise of national defense, conservatives sought legislation that curbed the right to strike and picket and mandated compulsory arbitration in some disputes. As the leader of an administration with so much labor support, Roosevelt found these changes unacceptable. Instead, the President tried informal means through appeals to the patriotism of labor leaders. To facilitate this policy, Roosevelt elevated Sidney Hillman, president of the Amalgamated Clothing Workers, a CIO union, to associate director of the Office of Production Management (OPM). But even though Hillman claimed credit for avoiding a number of serious strikes during 1940 and 1941, the informal influence he applied with his peers in the labor movement could not end strikes entirely. Too many were the product of local issues and were under the de facto control of local union officials.

The seventy-six day Allis-Chalmers strike that began in January of 1941 illustrated the limitations of the government's policy. The Milwaukee company was one of the major defense contractors, holding some $40 million in Navy orders. United Auto Workers Local 248 represented most of the workers. The history of unionization attempts had been bitter. The company resisted organization and continued to try to undermine the union after the UAW had won representation rights—in particular by infiltrating anti-union workers into the factory to disrupt the union. For its part, Local 248 was under the leadership of Harold Christoffel, a militant closely associated with the Communists in the UAW.

The incident that touched off the strike occurred when Allis-Chalmers fired six union members, all of them militants. The workers had been particularly aggressive in collecting back dues and fines from anti-UAW workers. Christoffel immediately called for a strike vote and received over-

whelming support. On January 21, 1941, the local called its members out and shut down the plant. Response to the strike was overwhelming. In a plant of 7,500 workers, as many as 5,000 joined the picket lines. The union demanded a union security agreement, even though the existing contract had three months to run. The Department of Labor's conciliation service tried but failed to end the conflict. Hillman and William S. Knudsen, co-directors of the OPM, called union and company representatives to Washington. There government representatives proposed arbitration with agreement by the company to carry out the union's demand if the union's charge of company anti-union activity held up. The union agreed, but the company rejected the offer. Hillman then exercised his powers of persuasion. He suggested that the union security issue be solved by implementing a "maintenance of membership" formula. This meant that all workers already paying dues to the local would have to remain members until the contract expired. Hillman's intervention failed largely because the company saw maintenance of membership as a first step toward the closed shop.

With the strike more than one month old, the Department of the Navy wired management and the union that the plant must reopen at once. The newspapers of March 21, 1941, reported that the War and Navy department's were seriously considering taking over the struck plant. Christoffel stood firm, refusing the Navy's order. But his action brought the wrath of public opinion down upon the strikers. The press generally applauded the government's determination to end the strike by force. The chairman of the House Judiciary Committee announced that he would not hesitate to pass a law to send strikers "to the electric chair." The company informed the union of its intention to reopen on March 28 in accordance with the Navy department order. City and county police agencies announced their intentions to protect any workers entering the plant.

Local 248 responded with a huge mass meeting, a show of strength that made clear the risk the government would run by trying to force the reopening of the plant. By this time UAW officials at a higher level, fearful up to now of the negative publicity from the strike, felt compelled to back the strikers. So too did CIO president Philip Murray who demanded to be told upon what authority the ultimatum to the strikers had been issued. Murray also inquired as to why the government did not demand compliance from the company with the original proposal of the OPM.

Faced with opposition from both CIO and UAW officials, the government retreated. But the state and local authorities did not. On March 31, Milwaukee police, using an armored car and firing tear gas, made a violent assault on the picket line. Although they suffered injuries, the strikers held firm. State militia sent to the scene had the same disappointing results. After three days of futile attempts to force the picket line at bayonet point, the militia was recalled, and the governor of Wisconsin ordered the plant closed.

With the departure of the militia, the company's last hope of averting a settlement with the union disappeared. On April 7, seventy-five days into the strike, the company agreed to accept the maintenance-of-membership security clause. The union accepted, and the first great attempt at government strikebreaking in the name of national defense failed. [Ronald L. Filippelli]

FURTHER READING

Lichtenstein, Nelson. *Labor's War at Home: The CIO in World War II.* New York: Oxford University Press, 1982.

Preis, Art. *Labor's Giant Step: Twenty Years of the CIO.* New York: Pathfinder Press, 1972.

o   o   o

ANTHRACITE COAL STRIKE OF 1842. By 1830 the use of anthracite coal for home heating and industrial purposes was commonplace, and the future of the fuel seemed assured in the expanding markets of the young country. Shortly thereafter, the labor disturbances, which were to become commonplace for more than a century in the anthracite fields of northeastern Pennsylvania, began. The first significant industrial conflict occurred in Schuylkill County in 1842.

With the opening up of the Schuylkill coalfields to speculation in 1829, the area experienced an economic boom unlike any the country had seen. The speculative frenzy for coal lands brought a surplus of undercapitalized coal operators and resulted in a surplus of mine labor as well. When the bubble burst at the end of 1830, the region descended into a depression broken only by two brief upturns—the first due to a coal shortage in the severe winter of 1831–1832, and the second during the brief economic upturn that preceded the national economic collapse of 1837.

Economic conditions had reached their nadir by 1842. Working miners saw their conditions worsen as the price of coal continued its steady decline. Unemployment had reached 20 percent of the workforce, and new miners, lured by shipping company advertisements, continued to arrive from Wales. The discontent of the workers broke out on the night of May 14, 1842, when arsonists burned the barn of a coal operator, supposedly because of the callousness of the operator's wife toward the misery of the miners and their families. When told that the miners could not afford a decent diet, she is reported to have advised that they eat "dry bread and potatoes."

The miners also objected to the pay system whereby they received not cash wages but "store orders" for goods at local stores. The system resulted from the fact that the Schuylkill coalfields were in the hands of numerous undercapitalized small operators, most of whom were chronically short of cash. Because of this, the store owner was forced to extend credit to the coal operators and take the risk that they would redeem the store orders later. In these circumstances, the merchant felt justified in charging higher prices in order to protect himself. The victims of the system were the miners who received fewer goods for their work than they would have had they been able to shop where they pleased with cash wages. In effect, this was the first step toward the establishment of the company store, owned by the operator, which became a common point of conflict in later coal strikes almost everywhere in the United States.

The system broke down on July 7, 1842, when a number of workers struck for a cash wage payment system. The strike was the spark that ignited the accumulated discontent across the region. On July 9, strikers paraded through Pottsville and stopped the loading of coal onto barges on the Schuylkill Canal. At nearby Minersville, there were reports that the strikers had threatened to burn down the town. By Monday, July 11, the industry was completely paralyzed.

At this point, what had been largely a spontaneous movement by both unemployed and employed miners, began to fall apart for lack of organization and leadership. The authorities, taken by surprise by the militancy of the workers, regained control of the situation. Miners who wanted to return to work were guaranteed protection by the militia and the sheriff. Many coal operators, for their part, had decided to keep their mines closed. By the end of July the movement had largely dissipated. There were some incidents of violence and a small number of strikers were jailed for their part in the strike. Apparently, the operators did respond to the demand for cash wages for a time, but this so strapped

them that it led to a greater decline in the number of working miners.

Although little detailed evidence remains of the miners' strike of 1842, it was apparently the first major uprising of coal miners in the history of the United States—the first battle in a century-long war between coal miners, the so-called "shock troops" of labor, and the coal companies. [Ronald L. Filippelli]

FURTHER READING

Berthoff, Rowland. "The Social Order of the Anthracite Region." *Pennsylvania Magazine of History and Biography*, Vol. 89 (1965), pp. 261–291.

Itter, William A. "Early Labor Troubles in the Schuylkill Anthracite District." *Pennsylvania History*, Vol. 1 (January, 1934), pp. 28–37.

o   o   o

ANTHRACITE COAL STRIKE OF 1868. This strike led to the formation of the first industrywide union in hard coal mining. All usable deposits of anthracite in the United States are located in a 1,400 square mile area of northeastern Pennsylvania. Although geographically concentrated, the industry seemed immune to serious labor organization. Erosion divided the area into four coalfields or basins separated from each other by mountains. Transportation lines combined the four fields into three trade regions: the Schuylkill, the Lehigh, and the Wyoming-Lackawanna. Mine workers identified their welfare with that of their region and were not prone to cooperate with the other regions.

Ethnocentrism fractured the labor force in each region. Five nationalities—German, Irish, Welsh, English, and Scottish—worked in the hard coal fields. Each group preserved its identity by establishing its own churches and social organizations. The social structure reinforced the ethnic divisions. The English, Welsh, and Scottish workers received the highest paying jobs. The Irish were regarded as an undesirable criminal class. Language isolated the Germans.

Working conditions provided the diverse workforce with a common set of experiences and grievances. The anthracite mines were among the most dangerous in the world. Wages were low. Moreover, mine operators depressed their employees' real income by forcing them to shop in company stores which charged excessive prices. Rent for company housing also tended to be exorbitant. Deductions for the company doctor, taxes, and, in some cases, the church, left the miner little or no cash on payday.

Danger and economic abuses caused the mine workers to combine. Between 1842 and 1860 they conducted a number of localized strikes which were easily crushed. During the Civil War they formed local unions in an effort to keep up with the war-induced inflation. Labor shortages and a high demand for coal brought them success. But the mine owners launched a counter-offensive at the end of the war. The Wyoming-Lackawanna accepted a pay cut after a series of disastrous strikes in 1865. By 1867, wages had fallen below the 1857 level and labor seemed to be in complete disarray.

Pennsylvania's legislature provided the stimulus for reorganization in 1868 by legalizing the eight-hour day. Miners in the Mahanoy Valley demanded the shorter day without a comparable reduction in wages. When the operators refused the demand, the miners walked off their jobs. Armed strikers carrying signs reading "Eight Hours" marched through the Schuylkill and Lehigh regions shutting down the mines. Elated by their success, they decided to extend the strike by marching into the Wyoming-Lackawanna region. Remembering that Lehigh and Schuylkill had remained working while they were defeated in the 1865 strikes, the Wyoming-Lackawanna men ignored the marchers. Unable

to shut down the industry, the strikers surrendered the eight-hour day. They did, however, gain a 10 percent wage increase.

Partial success encouraged the mine workers to establish an inclusive organization. During September, the local unions merged into countywide associations. Meeting in Providence, Pennsylvania, on November 7, 1868, delegates from the new county unions agreed to form an industry-wide organization. It took time to resolve the petty jealousies inherent in such a merger, but on March 17, 1869, a convention of county delegates established the General Council of the Workingmen's Associations of the Anthracite Coal Fields of Pennsylvania.

The Workingmen's Benevolent Association (WBA), as the new union was known, reflected the philosophy and background of its leader, John Siney. An Irishman who worked in England before migrating to America in 1863, Siney expounded three basic principles: collective bargaining, compulsory maintenance of a standard wage, and refusal to work alongside non-union members. He believed that the key to labor's economic problems lay in the industry's unstable market. The WBA, therefore, tied wages to coal prices, which it tried to maintain by restricting production.

The union's policy failed to address the structural realities of the anthracite industry. Three large corporations dominated the Wyoming-Lackawanna region and were quite capable of maintaining coal prices in their primary market without labor's help. Neither they nor their employees could support the notion that the purpose of a strike was to control production. As a result, membership in the Wyoming region rapidly declined after 1871. Restricted to the Lehigh and Schuylkill regions, the WBA continued to negotiate contracts until it was destroyed in the **Anthracite Coal Strike of 1875**. [Harold W. Aurand]

FURTHER READING

Pinkowski, Edward. *John Siney: The Miners' Martyr.* Philadelphia, PA: Sunshine Press, 1963.

Yearley, Clifton K. *Enterprise and Anthracite: Economics and Democracy in Schuylkill County, 1820–1875.* Baltimore, MD: Johns Hopkins University Press, 1961.

○   ○   ○

ANTHRACITE COAL STRIKE OF 1875. This was a six-month lockout/strike that destroyed the Workingmen's Benevolent Association (WBA) in the anthracite fields of Pennsylvania. The leadership of the WBA regarded the instability of the coal market as the fundamental cause of labor's problems. Accordingly, they sought to maintain coal prices through the timely suspension of production. As the constitution of one of its local branches proclaimed: "the object of this society is to make such arrangements as will enable the operator and the miner to rule the coal market."

The proposed alliance, at first, was warmly received in the Schuylkill region. The small entrepreneurs who dominated the industry in that area had long argued that overproduction was ruining coal mining. Moreover, they realized that they could not police themselves.

By 1873, however, conditions that made the proposed alliance plausible changed dramatically. Franklin B. Gowen, president of the Philadelphia and Reading Railroad, had moved to protect his company freight by controlling the mines along its right-of-way. By 1873, the railroad had acquired a 60,000 acre coal estate and entered a pool arrangement with the carrier producers of the northern fields. Gowen was thus in a position to "rule the coal market" without labor's aid.

In January 1874, the union struck against a proposed reduction in wages. Caught without a large reserve of coal, Gowen restored the pay cut. But the WBA's ability to disrupt his plans convinced Gowen that he must destroy the union.

Throughout 1874 the Reading stockpiled coal in anticipation of a prolonged conflict. In November, Gowen announced that his company had enough coal to last until spring and ordered its collieries closed. Thirty-one independent operators in the area, dependent upon Gowen's railroad for transportation of their coal to market, also suspended work. In January, the operators announced a non-negotiable 10 percent reduction in wages for 1875. The WBA called a strike, but the call made little difference. Most of the miners had effectively been locked out since late November.

Gowen attempted to overawe the strikers with a show of force. He increased the Reading's Coal and Iron Police until it approached the size of an army. The police force was, in Gowen's words, "armed to the teeth."

Not intimidated, the strikers turned to violence. They sidetracked Reading locomotives, upset or set on fire cars loaded with coal, burned breakers and other buildings, and stoned strikebreakers. The violence, however, helped Gowen develop his claim that the union was the pawn of a secret Irish terrorist society, which came to be identified as the **Molly Maguires**. He instructed his agents to record all instances of violence or threats of violence, which he then published.

By June, both the union and its members had exhausted their resources to continue the fight. Conceding defeat, union leaders called for a token concession to preserve the principle of arbitration. But the operators ignored the appeal. Reduced to near-starvation, the mine workers resumed work on June 14 at a 20 percent reduction in wages. An unknown minstrel summarized the strike by singing: "Well, we've been beaten, beaten all to smash."

In many ways, however, the WBA destroyed itself. It was unable to resolve the tension between German, English, and Irish workers. Nor was it able to overcome the regional animosities that divided the industry. Perhaps most importantly, it never examined its premise that capital would willingly share the benefits of a regulated market with labor. Nevertheless, the Worker's Benevolent Association left a legacy of cooperative action that encouraged other attempts to organize the hard coal fields. [Harold W. Aurand]

FURTHER READING

Aurand, Harold. *From the Molly Maguires to the United Mine Workers: The Social Ecology of an Industrial Union, 1869–1897.* Philadelphia, PA: Temple University Press, 1971.

Schegel, Marvin W. *Ruler of the Reading: The Life of Franklin B. Gowen.* Harrisburg, PA: Archives Publishing Company, 1947.

Yearly, Clifton K. *Enterprise and Anthracite: Economics and Democracy in Schuylkill County, 1820–1875.* Baltimore, MD: Johns Hopkins University Press, 1961.

o   o   o

ANTHRACITE COAL STRIKE OF 1900. This dispute firmly established the United Mine Workers in the hard coal fields. The UMW began to organize the region in 1894. Progress, however, was erratic until the spontaneous strike of 1897 convinced many workers to join the union.

Feeling that a demonstration of the union's ability to improve working conditions would aid their recruiting efforts, local officials requested permission to strike in early 1900. John Mitchell, president of the United Mine Workers, urged a delay. He was hesitant to challenge the interlocking cartel of railroad-mining companies which controlled the industry with less than 10 percent of the work force enrolled in the union.

In July, however, Mitchell called a convention of anthracite delegates to dis-

cuss problems. Meeting in Hazleton, Pennsylvania, on August 13, 1900, the convention compiled a list of twelve grievances and invited the coal companies to discuss the issues. Management ignored the request.

Rebuffed, the convention asked permission to initiate a strike. Still concerned that the union lacked sufficient resources to conduct a successful strike, the National Executive Board postponed action on the request and instructed President Mitchell to open direct negotiations with the presidents of the coal companies. Mitchell was unable to establish meaningful contact with management. On September 12, the union offered to arbitrate the issues in an effort to avoid a conflict. Management did not respond to the proposal, and the UMW called a strike for Monday, September 17, 1900.

The response to the strike call surprised everyone. Approximately 80,000 workers walked off their jobs on September 17 and within ten days 97 percent of the industry's labor force (146,000 men and boys) were idle.

Two serious incidents of bloodshed marred the strike. On September 21 a battle between strikers and a sheriff's posse near Shenandoah left one dead and seven wounded. A mine guard was killed and thirteen people wounded in a confrontation at Oneida two weeks later. The Shenandoah "riot" prompted Pennsylvania governor William A. Stone to send 2,500 members of the National Guard into the area.

The strike carried important political implications in this year of a presidential campaign. A prolonged conflict threatened the East Coast with a coal famine and the party in power, the Republicans, would receive blame for the public's discomfort. Moreover, the spectacle of 146,000 strikers mocked the GOP's slogan of "a full dinner-pail." Senator Mark A. Hanna, chairman of the Republican Party's National

Committee, pressured management to grant concessions to the men. The coal companies responded by posting notices of a 10 percent wage increase and several smaller concessions on their properties during October. On October 24, the union called off the strike.

In one sense labor lost the strike. The miners failed to secure most of their demands and management successfully ignored the UMW throughout the dispute. From a broader perspective, however, the strike was an outstanding victory for labor. The United Mine Workers achieved an unprecedented unity among the anthracite miners, and it demonstrated that it could wring concessions from the anthracite combine, as the interlocking cartel was known. [Harold W. Aurand]

FURTHER READING

Cornell, Robert J. *The Anthracite Strike of 1902.* New York: Russell and Russell, 1957.

Green, Victor R. *The Slavic Community on Strike: Immigrant Labor in Pennsylvania Anthracite.* Notre Dame, IN: Notre Dame University Press, 1968.

Gluck, Elsie. *John Mitchell.* New York: John Day and Company, 1929.

o   o   o

ANTHRACITE COAL STRIKE OF 1902. This dispute altered the public's perception of organized labor and government–labor relations. The anthracite mine owners resented the political pressure which caused them to conclude the **Anthracite Coal Strike of 1900** with a few concessions. As soon as work resumed they began preparing for another conflict with the United Mine Workers of America (UMW). They attempted to weaken the union by assigning its prominent members to the least desirable workplaces in the mines. Storage facilities were expanded and coal stockpiled. They built stockades around their collieries.

John Mitchell, president of the UMW,

wished to avoid an open conflict. Several times he requested a conference with the presidents of the railroad mining companies that dominated the industry. Only one, Eben Thomas of the Erie Railroad, agreed to meet with him. During the March 1901 interview, Thomas indicated that the "coal interests" might consider negotiating with the UMW in 1902. But in 1902, Thomas told Mitchell that events during the year demonstrated that the union could not be trusted.

Thomas alluded to the large number of unofficial strikes which plagued the region as the mine workers grew impatient with Mitchell's conciliatory posture. Meeting in Shamokin, Pennsylvania, in March 1902, a convention of anthracite miners' delegates displayed their indignation by formulating a set of final demands: recognition of the UMW, an eight-hour workday, a 20 percent increase in the piece rate, a minimum wage scale, and a 2,240-pound ton—the "miner's ton" in effect in the region weighed as much as 3,360 pounds!

Mitchell urged the convention to postpone issuing the ultimatum and ask the National Civic Federation, a labor–management body whose goal was a reduction of strikes and lockouts through strict adherence to collective bargaining agreements, to mediate. The delegates agreed on the condition that he would authorize a strike if the Federation's intervention failed. The National Civic Federation, of which Mitchell was a member, arranged a conference between the two parties. But after several sterile meetings with the operators, the miners' committees forced Mitchell to call a suspension of work to begin on May 12. Despite management's warning that the strike "would be a fight to the finish," more than 100,000 mine workers obeyed the call.

Some of those who remained on the job did so with the union's permission. Traditionally, firemen, engineers, and pumpmen were allowed to work during strikes for they kept the mines free of water. But on May 21, Mitchell ordered these men to join the suspension on June 2 if they did not receive an eight-hour workday (they worked twelve-hour shifts) without a reduction of pay. Management refused to grant the shorter workday.

The operators moved quickly to replace the striking pumpmen. Employment agencies in Philadelphia and other major cities recruited men for work in the hard coal fields. The coal companies increased their private police forces to protect the strikebreakers; within one month the governor of Pennsylvania commissioned 1,170 new coal and iron policemen. Under such heavy protection the operators kept their mines dry during the strike.

The coal regions remained calm during the first two months of the strike. In separate incidents company guards killed two people when they came close to colliery stockades. Neither the shootings nor the use of strikebreakers provoked the mine workers to violence. But on July 30, strikers in Shenandoah attacked Deputy Sheriff Thomas Beddall as he escorted two non-union men to the railroad station. The confrontation ended with one dead, more than twenty seriously injured, and fifty hurt. Local officials asked Pennsylvania governor William A. Stone for aid in restoring order. Stone then ordered 1,500 members of the National Guard into the area.

The level of violence increased as the strike continued into October. Homes of "scabs" were set on fire; men returning to work were beaten; and in one incident outraged strikers attempted to prevent the funeral of a "blackleg," as strikebreakers were often called in the anthracite region. On October 6, Governor Stone ordered the entire Pennsylvania division of the National Guard—8,500 men—into the hard coal regions.

The strike dragged on because the mine owners could not replace their pro-

duction people with imported labor. Since 1889, Pennsylvania law required state certification of anthracite miners. To be certified, a candidate had to demonstrate he had worked at least two years in the hard coal mines and also pass an examination administered by a board of nine miners. The certification law insured that not one ton of anthracite would be raised to the surface as long as the miners remained loyal to the union. Unable to resume production, but assured that the mines would not be flooded, the coal companies decided to wait until hunger made the strikers regret "their foolish and inconsiderate" action and compelled them to return to work.

But the public, fearing a coal famine, refused to wait until the miners were starved into submission. Noting that anthracite was "a prime necessity of life," editors of major newspapers exclaimed "we must have coal!" The editors placed the onus for the impending fuel shortage upon the mine operators who instigated the strike and then refused to end it. Arguing that the strike was a public question, not a private dispute, the editors called for intervention by the federal government.

President Theodore Roosevelt was well aware of the political implications of a prolonged energy crisis. As early as June he directed the Commissioner of Labor, Carroll D. Wright, to report on the causes and conditions of the strike. He also asked Attorney General Philander Chase Knox if the federal government could intervene in the conflict. Knox replied that in his opinion the president had no power to take action in the matter.

Unable to use the power of the government, Roosevelt tried persuasion. He invited the mine owners and union representatives to meet with him on October 3. The President asked both parties to put the public's welfare before their own. Referring to the union as a "set of outlaws," the mine operators reminded Roosevelt of his constitutional duties and asked him to employ the military to "squelch the anarchistic conditions" in anthracite. Roosevelt kept his composure, but that evening wrote to Mark Hanna, "Well, I have tried and failed."

After reviewing the proceedings of the failed meeting, Secretary of War Elihu Root thought he saw a way of ending the impasse. Acting on his own, but with the President's knowledge, Root met with J. P. Morgan and composed a letter from the operators suggesting that the issue be "submitted to an arbitration commission appointed by Roosevelt. The operators, however, did not hesitate to instruct the President on what types of people should be appointed to the commission: an engineer from the military; a mining engineer; a person engaged in the mining and selling of anthracite; "a man of prominence, eminent as a sociologist"; and a judge from the Eastern District of Pennsylvania.

Subsequent negotiations led to the addition of a Catholic prelate to the commission and the operators' acceptance of a labor leader serving under the rubric "eminent sociologist." On October 16, Roosevelt announced the members of the commission: Brigadier General John M. Wilson; E. M. Parker, mining engineer; Judge George Gray; E. E. Clark, Grand Chief of the Order of Railway Conductors; Thomas H. Watkins, anthracite businessman; and Bishop John L. Spalding of Peoria. He also appointed Carroll D. Wright recorder of the commission. Mitchell called a meeting of anthracite union delegates for October 20 and at the gathering ordered the men to return to work on October 23.

Receiving their instructions from President Roosevelt on October 24, the Anthracite Coal Strike Commission decided to hold formal public hearings. Before the hearings began they toured the anthracite regions to acquaint themselves with conditions in the area. The hearings lasted three months; during that time the commission heard the testimony of 558 witnesses. Finally, on March 22, 1903, the commission announced its decision. It granted a 10 percent increase in the piece rate and gave some classifications of workers an eight-hour workday and others a nine-hour workday with no reduction in wages. The commission declined to fix a standard ton and to compel the operators to recognize the UMW as the bargaining agent for their employees. Indeed, it recommended a separate union of hard coal miners. The commission provided a formal grievance procedure by instituting the Anthracite Board of Conciliation. Composed of three representatives of labor and three operators, the Board was to settle any grievance that arose. An umpire, selected by a judge of the circuit court of the United States was to make the final decision when the Board could not agree.

In terms of the Shamokin demands, the hard coal miners gained very little by striking for 165 days. But they won public respect for organized labor. And, for the first time, government intervened in a strike not to break it, but to bring it to a peaceful resolution. [Harold W. Aurand]

FURTHER READING

Cornell, Robert J. *The Anthracite Coal Strike of 1902.* New York: Russell and Russell, 1957.

Greene, Victor R. *The Slavic Community on Strike: Immigrant Labor in Pennsylvania Anthracite.* Notre Dame, IN: University of Notre Dame Press, 1968.

Mitchell, John. *Organized Labor.* Philadelphia, PA: American Book and Bible House, 1903.

U.S. Anthracite Coal Strike Commission. *Report to the President on the Anthracite Coal Strike of May–October, 1902.* Washington, DC: Government Printing Office, 1903.

o o o

ANTHRACITE COAL STRIKE OF 1922. The strike of the anthracite miners in 1922 has been overshadowed in labor history by the bituminous strike and the railroad shopmen's strike of the same year. But the anthracite shutdown was an epic confrontation between capital and labor. It lasted 163 days and caused a serious fuel shortage in the northeastern United States. Indeed, the impact of the strike was so great that many users of anthracite turned to other fuels, thus signalling the decline of the industry.

The anthracite industry had serious problems even before the great strike. The retail price of the fuel had doubled between 1913 and 1922 because the oligopoly that controlled the industry, with a virtual monopoly over the home heating fuel market in the northeast, had decided to charge all the market would bear. Unlike the bituminous fields, which were much larger, anthracite coal was located almost entirely in five counties of northeastern Pennsylvania. It was controlled by seven railroad companies tied together through interlocking directorates and bound to large banking interests through joint stock ownership.

This business combination also held the miners in conditions of near servitude. The average miner earned from $1,400 to $1,600 annually, well below the level necessary to maintain a family above the poverty level. Nevertheless, the operators were not above blaming the miners for the high cost of coal. Bulletins published by the coal companies portrayed the miners as prosperous but made no mention of the soaring profits in the industry.

Negotiations between the operators and the mine workers began on March 15, 1922, and quickly reached impasse. The operators called for a 2.5 percent wage reduction. There was no justification offered for this demand. In addition, the operators refused to accept the dues checkoff, whereby union dues would be deducted automatically from the miner's salary by the company. The attack on the checkoff was foolhardy. Since it cost the companies nothing, it signalled a decision on the part of the operators to rid themselves of the union. Indeed, the companies

wanted to replace collective bargaining with annual wage arbitration, a proposal they knew the United Mine Workers (UMW) would refuse. This hard-line attitude practically guaranteed labor unrest, which in its turn, provided the opportunity for competing fuels such as gas, oil, and electricity to capture part of the home fuel market.

For its part, the UMW demanded a 20 percent wage increase. The miners believed the demand to be moderate, enabling them to earn a living wage, what UMW vice-president Philip Murray called the "industrial birth right of every American. . . ." The miners based their demands on the argument that labor costs represented only a small part of the retail price of coal. The real culprits, according to the union, were high profits, excessive freight rates, and middleman costs. If profiteering were stopped, the UMW argued, wages could be advanced by 20 percent and prices reduced at the same time. The union was determined not to sacrifice the interests of their members to the anthracite oligopoly.

The two sides were so far apart on their wage demands that it was clear from the beginning that no compromise could be reached. On April 1, 1922, production in the anthracite mines ceased. On the same day the bituminous miners also struck. The resulting stoppage by 600,000 miners constituted the largest strike by miners in the history of the nation. "The men who go down in the earth to dig the coal that fires the furnaces of the nation and warms its homes," wrote AFL president Samuel Gompers, "shall not be crucified on an altar of greed!"

In spite of the diametrically opposed positions of the two parties, the anthracite strike was largely peaceful mainly because management made no attempt to use strikebreakers. Pennsylvania law restricted anthracite mining to state certified miners with two years of experience. This made the recruitment of replacement miners almost impossible. The shutdown of the anthracite fields was complete. Indeed, the only real disturbance took place in the town of Luzerne, near Wilkes-Barre, where striking miners stoned firemen whom they mistakenly suspected of operating part of a mine.

As coal stocks diminished and fall approached, public pressure on the federal government to intervene increased. The *Washington Post* suggested temporary government control of the mines if the dispute lasted until winter, and the idea of nationalizing the mines was raised more frequently as the strike wore on. Most of the pressure came from the northeast— New York City, and New England in particular—for which an anthracite shortage in winter posed a problem of near catastrophic proportions.

Along with talk of nationalizing the coal mines came increased interest in the use of substitute fuels. None of this made an impression on the coal operators or the union. On May 18, the operators reiterated their demands. For its part, the UMW refused to compromise the principle of a living wage for anthracite miners. The impasse in the anthracite strike was matched by a similar lack of movement toward settlement in the bituminous strike. The prospect of a winter without both fuels finally brought President Warren Harding into the disputes. He arranged a White House meeting between UMW president John L. Lewis and coal operators from both the anthracite and bituminous fields. Still, Harding was content to bring the sides together. He did not exercise any presidential pressure for a settlement and none came. The meetings held on July 1, 1922, ended where they had begun—in deadlock.

Recognizing the failure of his hands-off efforts, Harding then proposed a return to work of the miners at the old rates with the dispute to be settled by arbitration. In the meantime, a newly appointed Federal Coal Commission would study the coal industry in detail. Harding's proposal made no impact on the miners. It was little more than what the coal operators had been asking, the replacement of collective bargaining with arbitration. Nor was the idea of a Federal Coal Commission new, it had been circulating in Washington for some time.

The UMW's refusal to submit the dispute to arbitration, and the operators' acceptance of the plan, brought the onus of public opinion down on the miners. Nevertheless, newspapermen could not mine coal, and as the strike continued into the middle of August, a winter fuel shortage in the northeast became inevitable. The settlement of the strike came on September 2, after Pennsylvania senators David Reed and George Pepper offered a plan that called for the dropping of the arbitration issue by the operators in exchange for a return to work by the miners and the extension of the old contract until August 31, 1923. In the meantime, there was to be an investigation of the industry by a government agency. The proposal merely postponed the settlement of the issues for another year. It did nothing to rationalize the chronic problems in the industry. Both sides, by now exhausted, accepted the proposal—the operators because they feared that the government might nationalize the mines, and the union because Lewis believed that inflation was inevitable and would provide the miners with an increase in wages.

In the aftermath of the settlement President Harding asked Congress to create a commission to investigate the coal industry. He also asked for the creation of a federal fuel distribution authority to control the distribution of existing stocks of coal. The Cummins-Winslow Act became law on September 22. It created the Federal Fuel Administration, with a life span of only one year, to apportion the limited stocks of coal available for the winter. In addition, the Borah-Winslow Act created a United States Coal Commission to investigate both the anthracite and bituminous industries.

Although the union was happy to emerge from the strike having turned back the operators' demand for a wage cut and the arbitration of future contracts, there were no winners in the strike of 1922. The long summer strike opened the door to alternative fuels. Because of the shortage of anthracite coal, the winter of 1922–1923 was a difficult one for the northeastern United States. Yet after the settlement, Congress lost interest in the coal emergency and turned to other matters, ultimately ignoring the massive study of the coal industry done by the United States Coal Commission. The Commission had recommended limited government regulation of the industry. Nothing was done. The conditions and issues which had caused the strike of 1922 remained to contribute to walkouts which paralyzed the industry in 1923 and especially in the bitter **Anthracite Coal Strike of 1925–1926**. Each time, anthracite lost a share of its market to competing fuels, and the industry took another step toward disaster. [Ronald L. Filippelli]

FURTHER READING

Kanarek, Harold K. "The Pennsylvania Anthracite Strike of 1922." *Pennsylvania Magazine of History and Biography*, Vol. 99 (1975), pp. 207–225.

o   o   o

ANTHRACITE COAL STRIKE OF 1925–1926. The emergence of competing fuels for home heating after World War I seriously threatened the dominance of Pennsylvania anthracite coal in the markets of the eastern United States. Yet even in the face of the threat from oil, gas, and bituminous coal, the traditionally rancorous relations between miners and mine operators in the anthracite fields of northeastern Pennsylvania did not improve. The industry suffered strikes in 1920 and 1923,

and a massive 163-day strike in 1922. At each suspension of production, markets disappeared to competing fuels.

The year 1925 was to be no exception. The issues that had torn the industry apart for so long remained unresolved. The union demanded a 10 percent wage increase and the operators asked for wage reductions. The union wanted the dues checkoff, and the industry flatly refused to assist the union. For their part, the operators wanted annual arbitration of the wage scale, while the union rejected it as an attack on collective bargaining.

Early negotiations produced bitterness and recrimination on both sides and went nowhere. Facing yet another fuel shortage, the governors of the New England states met and agreed to sponsor a massive publicity campaign to educate citizens to the benefits of using substitutes for anthracite. The *Boston Globe* editorialized approvingly that the action of the governors would help to "strike off the shackles of bondage" in which New England was held by the hard coal industry.

Appeals to President Calvin Coolidge to intervene, however, fell on deaf ears. The laissez faire president had decided on a hands-off policy toward the negotiations. The governor of Pennsylvania, Gifford Pinchot, also approached the dispute with caution. Past interventions had gotten him little but political criticism, particularly from the operators. Pinchot begged off by claiming that because of the number of states affected, the anthracite dispute was a national matter and should be dealt with at that level.

With the political leadership on the sidelines, observers watched the deadlocked negotiations with a fatalistic resignation. As the strike deadline approached, it was clear to everyone that the fourth strike of the decade was inevitable. This time, however, it would be a fight to the finish. The strike began on September 1, 1925, and it soon became evident that it would not be settled soon. After several weeks, panicky public officials began pressuring Coolidge to intervene. The plea of the Brooklyn congressional delegation illustrated the tenor of the appeals. "The poor in Brooklyn and elsewhere," they claimed, were "begging piteously for coal withheld because of extortionate prices." Still, however, Coolidge refused to change his stance, even when the call for presidential action came from United Mine Workers president John L. Lewis himself.

As winter approached the economic effect on the anthracite region was no less severe. The mayors of sixty coalfield communities wrote to the companies asking them to grant the dues checkoff. But the companies stood firm. With no movement anywhere, Governor Gifford Pinchot changed his position and invited the negotiators to Harrisburg to hear his proposal. The operators, who considered Pinchot pro-labor, found excuses not to attend. Nevertheless, Pinchot went ahead with the meeting with only the union present.

Pinchot suggested a modified checkoff and arbitration provisions. The plan offered something for both sides, and did not include a wage hike. It was particularly tailored toward the consumers in that it asked the operators for a pledge of no price increases for five years. In exchange, no wage increases could be granted that would require a price increase. That would be determined by a board appointed by the governor. The proposal required the operators to open the books to the board.

Pinchot's plan had the support of much of the coal region business community and the union. John L. Lewis immediately signalled the UMW's acceptance of the proposal, but the operators were in no mood for a compromise. The request that they open their books to the governor's board particularly rankled them. They rejected the proposal to fix prices for five years. They argued that only supply and demand, not arbitrary agreement, set prices. Pinchot slammed the operators as "hard-boiled monopolists" without regard for the public. The angry governor signalled his intention to call a special session of the Pennsylvania General Assembly for the purpose of regulating the anthracite industry.

At this juncture, President Calvin Coolidge cautiously entered the fray. He asked Congress for powers to act in coal emergencies and for legislation to regulate the industry. But the proposal was met with an almost total lack of enthusiasm. Even in the face of an impending disaster, few could stomach any tampering with market forces. Even the United Mine Workers and the AFL rejected legislation, believing that it would restrict the right to strike and collective bargaining.

By the end of December, four months into the strike, John L. Lewis realized that his men could not go on for long. Fraternal assistance from other unions, UMW strike funds, and help from local charities only marginally alleviated the suffering of the strikers. As the new year approached, future prospects were unusually bleak, especially since a Republican governor and a Republican President had failed to move the coal operators, themselves overwhelmingly Republican, to compromise. But conditions for the operators were less than ideal as well. Coal stockpiled before the strike was running low. These pressures, not outside intervention, brought the adversaries back to the bargaining table on December 29, four months after the previous session.

By the end of January the negotiators had rejected several hundred proposals. The stickling point proved to be the operator's desire for wage arbitration. Realizing that the market conditions for anthracite were worsening and that market factors would inevitably drive wages down, the operators reasoned that they could only benefit from periodic wage arbitration. The union rejected this outright for the same reason.

While the negotiators met, Pinchot submitted two bills to a special session of the Pennsylvania legislature. One gave the governor the authority to enter into compacts with other anthracite-consuming states to fix prices. A second would create the Anthracite Coal Supply Commission to regulate the industry in Pennsylvania. The commission would have the right, after a strike of three months, to seize the mines and impose a settlement that could be appealed by both the union and the operators to the Pennsylvania courts. The operator's lobbied hard against Pinchot's bills, managing to kill them in the House Mining Committee which they effectively controlled. Once again Pinchot assailed the operators as betrayers of the public interest. There was in America, according to the Pennsylvania governor, "no other monopoly . . . so defiant of public opinion, so scornful of the public interest. . . ."

While the drama in Harrisburg played out, the miners and the operators, both reaching exhaustion, continued to negotiate. The full dimensions of what they had lost were beginning to dawn on both sides. Anthracite markets that had existed before the strike had disappeared forever to competing fuels. The northeast had weathered the winter without anthracite and would never again be dependent upon the fuel. On February 12, 1926, the two sides agreed to a compromise: a five-year contract at the old wage scale and arbitration of wages during the contract only if both sides agreed. The checkoff appeared nowhere in the document.

The strike had been an enormous failure for everyone. Market losses suffered in the strikes of the 1920s, particularly the 1925–1926 strike, could never be recovered. Anthracite production declined from approximately 90 million tons before the strike to 68 million in 1930. The workforce of 150,000 fell below 100,000 by 1935. No doubt oil, gas, and electricity would have ultimately conquered anthracite coal as home heating fuels without the strike, but the fratricidal strike of 1925–1926 hastened the decline of hard coal and the anthracite region immeasurably. [Ronald L. Filippelli]

FURTHER READING

Anthracite Bureau of Information. *The Anthracite Strike of 1925–26: A Chronological Statement.* Philadelphia, PA: Anthracite Bureau of Information, 1926.

Greene, Victor. *The Slavic Community on Strike: Immigrant Labor in Pennsylvania Anthracite.* Notre Dame, IN: University of Notre Dame Press, 1968.

Kanarek, Harold. "Disaster for Hard Coal: The Anthracite Strike of 1925–1926." *Labor History,* Vol. 15, No. 1 (Winter 1974), pp. 44–77.

o   o   o

ANTI-CHINESE RIOTS OF 1885 AND 1886. On September 2, 1885, a group of white coal miners armed with guns attacked the Chinese quarter of Rock Springs, Wyoming killing twenty-eight Chinese and wounding fifteen others. The men responsible were members of the Knights of Labor lodge in Rock Springs. They were not a small minority of the lodge's members. Rather, the massacre could aptly be described as a mass action by the Knights' members. The victims too were mainly miners, employees of the Union Pacific Railroad. After the slaughter and the burning of their homes, the Chinese fled. They were later returned to Rock Springs by the Union Pacific, but only under military escort of federal troops sent by President Grover Cleveland to protect them.

The virulent anti-Chinese feeling in the Wyoming Territory was demonstrated later when territorial courts tried to apply justice in the incident. Only sixteen white miners were arrested and all of those went free when law enforcement officers were unable to find anyone to testify against them. Congress did later appropriate $150,000 to cover losses of property, but no indemnity was paid for the lives lost. Only the Union Pacific Railroad took action, firing approximately one-third of its white miners and replacing them with Chinese workers.

The events at Rock Springs pointed up the growing hostility of white workers to Chinese immigrants. Resentment of the Chinese, while fueled by racism, also had its roots in white workers' fears that Chinese workers lowered standards, took work from white workers, and were used to keep the wages of white workers low. The animosity in Rock Springs went back to the depression year of 1875 when white miners struck against a demand by the company to increase production. Union Pacific broke the strike by importing Chinese labor. By 1880, Chinese miners outnumbered white miners by two to one, although it is likely that whites worked the high yield coal seams, thus earning more with less effort. So long as this pattern held, there was peace between the two groups.

This changed in 1885 when the Knights of Labor demanded, among other things, the discharge of the Chinese miners. The grievances of the Knights focused on the Chinese as cheap labor competition. This was exacerbated by a company decision to reduce the differential in earnings of white and Chinese miners by distributing access to the richer seams more evenly between the two groups. There were probably several reasons for this, including the increased availability of white labor because of a growing depression in the East, and the increased difficulty of recruiting Chinese miners because of the Chinese Exclusion Act passed by Congress in 1882.

The outbreak at Rock Springs set off a chain reaction across the West. In Seattle and Tacoma, Washington, angry mobs of white workers and their supporters called for the expulsion of the Chinese. In Tacoma, several hundred were driven from the city. Seattle witnessed an even worse confrontation. Some 200 Chinese workers and their families were placed aboard the steamboat Queen of the Pacific and sent to San Francisco. Those unlucky enough not to get aboard had to be protected from an angry crowd by the militia. The confrontation between the troops and the mob resulted in the killing of two rioters and the wounding of several others. The Washington example was followed in a series of towns in California and Oregon. In Truckee, California, Chinese workers were expelled and labor contractors were forced to agree not to hire any more. In all, some thrity-five cities and towns in California and Oregon expelled or tried to expel their Chinese communities between January and April of 1886.

The anti-Chinese expulsion movement soon grew into a budding political movement—The California Anti-Chinese Non-Partisan Association—built around Chinese exclusion. A number of California labor leaders supported the bipartisan effort. Indeed, although the movement represented a cross-section of California's political, business, and professional elite, organized labor did play a prominent role. During the expulsions, Knights of Labor lodges often took the lead, and seem to have been involved in a major way in almost every incident.

Nevertheless, to place the blame for the events largely at the door of labor would be inaccurate. The real leaders of the anti-Chinese hysteria seem to have been local merchants who gained no benefit from the importation of "coolie labor," but who, instead, were placed at a disadvantage by the large businessmen, railroads, and mining companies who employed the Chinese. On the other hand, the small town merchants depended for their livelihood on the white workers and their families who shopped at their stores and patronized their banks. When an economic downturn threatened the perilous economic position of the white workers, it is no surprise that an alliance against the Chinese developed between them and the small businessmen. [Ronald L. Filippelli]

FURTHER READING

Crane, Paul, and Alfred Larson. "The Chinese Massacre." *Annals of Wyoming*, Vol. 12 (January 1940), pp. 47–55; (April 1940), pp. 153–160.

Cross, Ira. *History of the Labor Movement in California*. Berkeley, CA: University of California Press, 1935.

Saxton, Alexander. *The Indispensable Enemy: Labor and the Anti-Chinese Movement in California*. Berkeley, CA: University of California Press, 1971.

o o o

ARIZONA COPPER STRIKE OF 1916. In 1916, in eastern Arizona, Mexican and Mexican-American miners struck against three copper giants—the Arizona Copper Company, the Shannon Copper Company, and the Detroit Copper Company, a property owned by the giant Phelps-Dodge Company. The grievances of the Mexican workers, who made up some 75 percent of the copper workers, centered around the "Mexican wage" system under which Mexican workers received half of the pay of Anglo workers for the same work. In addition, they received only half of their compensation in currency, with the other half coming in the form of credit at the company store. The system guaranteed the copper companies a direct return on a considerable portion of their wage bill.

Discrimination by the copper companies was matched by discrimination by the Western Federation of Miners (WFM), the largest union in the hard-rock mining areas. The WFM shortsightedly viewed the Mexicans primarily as cheap labor competition for Anglo workers and showed little interest in organizing them. By 1915, the WFM's disdain for the Mexicans had become a self-fulfilling prophecy. Mine operators used them as replacements for

Anglo workers and as strikebreakers. Thus, in 1915, the Federation, under the direction of organizer George Powell, set out to organize the Mexican workers of eastern Arizona.

After Powell succeeded in organizing local unions in the mining towns of Clifton, Morenci, and Metcalf, the union demanded that representatives of three companies meet with them to discuss grievances. The request was met with firm refusal, and 5,000 miners struck on September 11, 1915. The companies had counted on the loyalty of the Anglo workers, but they were disappointed. The Anglos went out with the Mexicans. With the strike in progress, the WFM demanded a sliding scale of wages equal to other parts of the state, written leases for company houses, the end to the selling of jobs by foremen, and recognition of the union.

Predictably, the companies blamed the strike on "outside agitators." In truth, the companies, all of which were controlled by absentee owners, feared that the troubles would spread to other of their properties in the West. They immediately began to try to reopen the mines with strikebreakers. After setting up a camp for replacement workers in Duncan, a short way from the struck mines, the managers of the three companies "fled" with much publicity to Texas and called on the governor of Arizona to send in the militia to protect their private property. No doubt the companies expected a repeat of what had happened in Ludlow, Colorado, only a few years earlier when the governor sent in troops. That action resulted in the infamous **"Ludlow Massacre"** in which miners, women, and children were killed.

Apparently, however, Governor George Wiley P. Hunt of Arizona had learned another lesson from the strike. He vowed to have no repetition of the Ludlow events in Arizona. Instead of troops, Hunt sent a representative to investigate the strike. After noting the general peaceful character of the strike, the governor sent troops with instructions to cooperate with the strikers to protect property. He also issued orders to prevent any strikebreakers from entering the strike district. He did so because he believed that history had shown that the importation of strikebreakers in an industrial dispute almost inevitably led to violence and "other disastrous consequences."

The actions of the governor, and the decision of the sheriff to appoint strikers as deputy sheriffs charged with protecting company property, enraged the companies. They blasted Hunt for using troops paid for by the taxpayers to drill strikers so that they could function efficiently as deputy sheriffs. From their strike headquarters in El Paso, Texas, the companies unleashed a four-month-long torrent of criticism, blasting the governor as a sympathizer of the radical Industrial Workers of the World. But no denunciations of "lawlessness" by the operators could obscure the fact that, as the magazine *The Outlook* wrote, "for more than nineteen weeks a strike of copper miners has taken place . . . virtually without violence."

Thwarted by their inability to use strikebreakers, and suffering from an increasingly poor public image, the companies agreed to talk. The militancy and solidarity of the workers had exceeded anything the companies expected. The strike had been carried on with only lukewarm support from the WFM and without strike benefits, and strikers and their families suffered extreme hardship. Outside contributions by unions and other sympathizers kept the struck communities from starvation. Under orders from the governor the state militia distributed the relief supplies in an orderly manner.

The combination of militancy on the part of the Mexican workers and the evenhandedness of the governor forced the companies to surrender. Two federal mediators helped to fashion a settlement that included elimination of most distinctions between Anglo and Mexican workers, withdrawal of company objections to union recognition, a system of monthly negotiations between workers' representatives and the companies on problems, and the reemployment of strikers.

Surprisingly, the miners did not attribute their success to the WFM. They resented the fact that the union had done little or nothing to help them in their struggle. On January 12, 1916, they withdrew from the WFM and affiliated with the Arizona State Federation of Labor. For their part, the companies never forgot the role that Governor Hunt had played in the affair. They did their best to defeat him in the next election, but the governor, whom Mother Jones called the greatest governor that the country had ever produced, won in a disputed election. [Ronald L. Filippelli]

FURTHER READING

Byrkit, James W. *Forging the Copper Collar: Arizona's Labor–Management War, 1901–1921.* Tucson, AZ: University of Arizona Press, 1982.

Foner, Philip S. *History of the Labor Movement in the United States*, Vol. 6. New York: International Publishers, 1982.

Kluger, James R. *The Clifton-Morenci Strike: Labor Difficulty in Arizona, 1915–1916.* Tucson, AZ: University of Arizona Press, 1970.

o   o   o

ATLANTA UAW SIT-DOWN STRIKE OF 1936. The sit-down strike at the Chevrolet-Atlanta Division and Fisher Body Division Atlanta Plant, of the General Motors (GM) Corporation began on November 18, 1936. A small number of union activists had attempted to organize the plant in the Lakewood section of Atlanta since the late 1920s with limited success. In August of 1929 there had been a brief job action, under the auspices of the American Federation of Labor (AFL) Auto Workers union, over the issue of mandatory overtime. A number of the leaders of the strike were fired and the strike was lost.

General Motors established a company union after that, but it failed to gain the confidence of the workers. At the same time, the AFL Auto Workers union, which later became the United Auto Workers (UAW), affiliated with the Congress of Industrial Organizations (CIO), were also unable to recruit many union members. Workers in the plant, however, did form a local union, UAW Local No. 34. In 1935, Lakewood workers participated for a month in a successful strike in sympathy with their counterparts at a GM transmission plant in Toledo, Ohio. But even after that, most of the workers in the plant, like most GM employees nationwide, were not UAW members. The national leadership of the UAW planned a campaign to organize GM beginning early in 1937. Wyndham Mortimer, first vice-president of the UAW, with allies like Roy Reuther, planned a New Year's assault on General Motors. The effort was to focus on the Flint, Michigan and Cleveland, Ohio Fisher Body plants, which produced most of the body stampings that were essential to GM production.

The Atlanta sit-down strike appears not to have been a part of this national strategy, but rather a reaction to local conditions. The local union had the definite impression that the UAW elsewhere was better prepared for a strike than they were, which wasn't necessarily the case. Dissatisfaction with management at Lakewood had increased in 1936, with short workweeks, arbitrary treatment of workers, and harassment of union activists. In fact it was such an incident of harassment that precipitated the strike in November, 1936. Several union members were wearing CIO lapel buttons in the plant. When management insisted that the buttons be removed, workers, led by Local No. 34 president Charles Gillman, shut down the assembly line and sat down in the plant.

Women workers left the plant and went to the union hall to prepare sandwiches and coffee, which were delivered to the workers still inside the Lakewood factory. Management balked at allowing food to be brought into the plant, but when UAW regional director Fred Pieper said they would clean up afterward, management relented. On the morning of November 19, negotiations between Local No. 34 leaders and GM reached a compromise. If the workers would leave the plant, management would not try to restart the plant, or move the machinery to another location. So the workers of the Lakewood plant, many of them not yet UAW members, left and set up picket lines around the plant for three long months.

The sit-down strike at the Lakewood plant in Atlanta was symbolically important in demonstrating that GM workers, North and South, were prepared to take on the corporation on behalf of the UAW, even when many of them had not yet formally joined the union. It was also pivotal in opening the final drive by the UAW to organize General Motors, using the sit-down strike as the key weapon. The winter of 1936–1937 was bitterly cold, even in the South, but Local No. 34 members were faithful on the picket line, while their union brothers and sisters sat down for weeks in Flint and elsewhere. The strike was on. The United Auto Workers had organized the largest automobile company in the world, and the historic sit-down in Atlanta had begun it all. [Leslie S. Hough]

FURTHER READING

Herring, Neill, and Sue Thrasher. "UAW Sit-down Strike: Atlanta, 1936." In *Working Lives: The Southern Exposure History of Labor in the South.* New York: Pantheon Books, 1980.

Lens, Sidney. *The Labor Wars: From the Molly Maguires to the Sit-downs.* Garden City, NY: Anchor Books, 1974.

o   o   o

AUGUSTA, GEORGIA, TEXTILE STRIKE OF 1886. A number of changes in structure, technology, and transportation transformed the textile industry during the 1880s. One of the results of this change was the development of the South as a major center of textile production. The growth was centered in the states of Georgia, South Carolina, and North Carolina, which shared the benefits of the Piedmont region—location, cheap power sources, the availability of raw materials, and cheap labor. Augusta, Georgia became the capital of the industry in the South. By 1886, the city had eighteen cotton mills employing nearly 3,000 workers.

One of the great attractions of Augusta, and the region as a whole, was the abundance of cheap labor. As an added bonus for the employers, the workers were not immigrants from Europe, carrying with them ideas about unionization and socialism. Rather, they came from the farms and small towns of the region and were, for the most part, of Anglo-Saxon stock. In addition, they were extremely poor and hungry for jobs. In many cases, the southern manufacturers used the family system of employment whereby parents often took their children into the mills with them to supplement the meager family income.

Southerners worked in the mills for less than their northern counterparts. In Augusta, workers averaged 80¢ per day. Children, who made up a quarter of the work force, worked for as little as $1.50 per week. Augusta workers not only were paid less than northerners, but they worked longer hours for the smaller rewards. The workday averaged eleven hours.

The depression of 1883 ended the early period of soaring growth for the industry. In the fall of 1884, the companies cut wages. For the first time the formerly docile workers struck back. After a 10 percent wage cut, spinners at the Augusta Factory closed down the mill on November 15. The men were fired, and the mill reopened the following day. When the spinners struck, they did so spontaneously without organization. Up to the 1880s, the textile industry in the South was completely non-union. But as the industry grew, so too did the interest of the Knights of Labor, the leading labor organization of the period. By 1886, the Knights had more than 4,500 members in Georgia and had organized Local Assembly 5030 in Augusta under the leadership of the Reverend J. S. Meynardie, a Baptist preacher.

The issues that most concerned the workers were low wages and the pass system, a practice in Augusta whereby workers could not move freely from a lower paying factory to a higher paying one. This permitted the industry to maintain wage differentials for the same work in the city. After the employers refused to discuss these issues with Local 5030, Meynardie publicized the plight of the Augusta workers at the 1886 Knights of Labor Convention in Cleveland. The *New York World* picked up the story and ran accounts of thirteen-hour workdays, abused children, exploited women, and other horrors.

The publicity enraged the Augusta mill owners and southern business leaders in general. They were sensitive to attacks from the North, especially unfavorable comparisons between southern and northern working conditions. The mill owners retaliated with a barrage of articles and public statements denying the charges, painting a picture instead of satisfied workers who would be no trouble if not stirred up by outside agitators.

The employers' characterization of their workers was at odds with the facts by 1886. On June 11, fifty workers at the Algernon Mill walked out in a dispute over the recording of piecework rates by a foreman. The employers threatened a citywide lockout unless they returned. The response brought criticism of the employers in the local press, thus forcing them to back down. But the bad feelings engendered by the incident festered. On June 18, two spinners were discharged at the Riverside Mill. The action brought a slowdown in the mill. Several weeks later, fearful of a general increase of labor militancy, the large King Mill granted its workers a wage increase. The unilateral action of the King Mill both angered the other mill owners, who announced that there would be no general wage increase in Augusta, and whetted the appetites of the workers in the other mills for more money.

By July 12, the worst fears of the employers were confirmed. Two mills were shut down over a wage dispute, and demands for increases arose in every other mill in the city. Up to this point, Local 5030 had not been involved in the ferment. The Knights of Labor preferred arbitration to strikes, and, in an attempt to resolve the dispute, they sent W. H. Mullen, editor of the *Labor Herald*, to Augusta. Mullen met with a representative of the mill owners and extracted a promise to end the pass system, but nothing more. Mullen told the Augusta workers to stand firm.

By the end of July, 1,300 workers were on strike. The mill owners had come together as well. The King Mill, which had set off the round of demands by granting its workers an increase, took the lead and locked out its 650 workers. The owners then announced a lockout in all the mills unless the strikers returned to work by August 10. When the workers overwhelmingly rejected the ultimatum, the "Great Lockout" began.

Aid for the strikers came from other Knights of Labor lodges in the South, and the Knights' Grand Master Workman Terrence Powderly sent prominent Knights Frederick Turner and W. H. Mullen to confer with both the strikers and mill owners. In the meantime, the city, in the midst of a situation the likes of which it had never seen, and with its economy suffering enormously from the strike, had set up a local arbitration committee to confer with both sides. Turner proposed that the mills be opened and that the issues of the strike be handled by impartial compulsory arbitration. The proposal died when the employers refused to include the wages of officers and managers in the arbitration with the wages of workers. Instead, they placed blame for the failure of the compromise on the Knights for "usurping" the legitimate role of management.

The failure of the arbitration proposal meant a battle of attrition. The Knights geared up for a long strike. The general executive board donated thousands of dollars in strike relief. Even the Augusta City Council appropriated money for the relief of needy workers but only to those who were not members of the Knights. Unfortunately, the public outcry and pressure from the mill owners forced the council to rescind the action. Unfortunately, the Knight's relief committee, through incompetence or greed or both, misappropriated several thousand dollars in relief funds. Although the national Knights settled all of the debts, the incident further damaged the union's reputation in the city and with the workers.

By mid-September the employers began to import strikebreakers. At the same time strikers were ordered to vacate company houses. Soon the Augusta Factory began operating with a small crew of non-union workers and strikebreakers. Slowly the other mills began to reopen as well. Nevertheless, the strikers held out for nearly two more months. In early November an agreement was reached. The employers agreed to end the pass system and not to retaliate against the strikers. For its part the Knights promised not to conduct boycotts if members were dismissed for just cause. The wage issue, which had precipitated the strike in the first place, was ignored. So too was the matter of shorter hours.

The defeat of the union in the labor relations climate of the South of 1886 is not surprising. Indeed, the Augusta workers did remarkably well considering the disadvantages they faced. One of the reasons for this was undoubtedly the fact that the city officials and merchants of Augusta, while they opposed the strike as a tactic, were not anti-worker or, in any serious way, anti-union. They focused their efforts on ending the strike in order to return prosperity to the city. Nor did the Augusta mill owners, for whatever reason, use dictatorial tactics in responding to the strike. To be sure the lockout was economically draconian, but there was no violence in the strike and no use of police or militia. Indeed, mill owners proved willing to discuss the strike with the Knights on several occasions. Finally, while Local 5030 of the Knights proved to be erratic, the national officers of the order consistently tried to mediate the dispute and end it in compromise.

In sum, in spite of the outcome, the strike could certainly be seen as a success for its time. When one looks at the bloody and dismal history of the attempts to organize the southern textile industry in the twentieth century, the relative calm of Augusta in 1886 was remarkable indeed. [Ronald L. Filippelli]

Further Reading

McLaurin, Melton A. *Paternalism and Protest: Southern Cotton Mill Workers and Organized Labor: 1875–1905.* Westport, CT: Greenwood Press, 1971.

Reed, Merl E. "The Augusta Textile Mills and the Strike of 1886." *Labor History*, Vol. 14, No. 2 (Spring, 1973), pp. 228–246.

Van Osdell, John G. *Cotton Mills, Labor and the Southern Mind: 1880–1930.* New Orleans, LA: Tulane University Press, 1966.

○ ○ ○

BALTIMORE POLICE STRIKE OF
1974. In July 1974, the city of Baltimore
experienced a police strike that was commonly described at the time as the most
thorough and effective action of its kind
since the legendary **Boston Police Strike
of 1919**. This was a real withdrawal of
labor, as opposed to a mere slowdown or
partial walkout, and the full-fledged strike
lasted for five days, from July 11 to July
15. This was followed by major reprisals
that left long and bitter memories. Most
police industrial actions of the 1970s resulted in at least partial success; by contrast, the outcome of the Baltimore strike
was extremely damaging to the cause of
police unionism.

The Baltimore action was also unusual among police disputes in that it was
intimately bound up with strikes by civilian employees of the city. In previous years,
police job actions had more commonly
been the result of grievances affecting only
officers, while police union political activism had tended to be deeply conservative
and even racially divisive—for example, in
the New York City campaigns against the
creation of a civilian complaints review
board. In Baltimore, a more traditional
union solidarity was evident, which may
explain the extremely hard line taken by
authorities against the police. Oddly, the
Baltimore event is less well known in the
contemporary literature on police unions
than are other strikes such as those in
Detroit (1967), **New York City (1971)**,
San Francisco (1975), and New Orleans
(1979).

In 1973, Baltimore had 3,500 police
officers, including a much higher proportion of minority officers than other major
cities. Unionization was well advanced.
Local 1195 of the American Federation of
State, County, and Municipal Employees
(AFSCME) was open to patrolmen, sergeants, and detectives, and by the eve of
the 1974 strike, membership had swelled
to over 2,000. Nine hundred seventy-seven
more officers made up Lodge 3 of the
Fraternal Order of Police (FOP), which was
open to all ranks. The AFSCME local was
especially noteworthy because while some
400,000 police officers nationwide belong
to a national or regional union federation,
AFSCME was one of the smallest of these
groups, accounting for only 9,000 or so
officers. In 1974, Baltimore was by far the
biggest police local in AFSCME.

For many years the Baltimore police
unions had confined their actions to lobbying the mayor or city council. By 1974,
however, AFSCME had gained exclusive
bargaining rights from the city, although
Baltimore was also unusual among large
cities in that neither state legislation nor
local ordinances provided for recognition
of bargaining.

The police strike grew out of a wider
confrontation between the city of Baltimore
and other AFSCME workers. There were
thus a series of more or less simultaneous
stoppages which contributed to a general
crisis atmosphere. At the beginning of July,
sanitation workers belonging to Local 44
were on strike despite repeated orders and
fines by Circuit Court Judge James W.
Murphy. The issues in this case involved a

pay increase, but the employees were also seeking the elimination of a controversial points system under which workers could be dismissed for unauthorized absences. There followed a series of sympathy strikes by workers from the Department of Recreation and Parks, and the Department of Education. A strike by city jail guards provided the opportunity for a minor inmate uprising. In all, some 3,000 workers were affected.

Police officers also had their own wage demands, but sympathy with other city workers was undoubtedly a factor in their decision to launch their own protest. On July 7, police began a limited job action involving precise enforcement of all laws, as well as slowdowns in other job areas. On the evening of July 10, a six-member strategy committee of Local 1195 met and decided to begin a partial police strike. Clearly, the decision was a popular one, as reflected by growing union membership.

The effectiveness of the strike was the subject of much contention. Police Commissioner Donald D. Pomerleau suggested that only 500 or so officers were striking, but other estimates put the total number of strikers at 1,500 or more. Police supervisors were unable to maintain public order, and street violence became widespread over the next few days. Nonstriking officers found themselves working a seven-day week on twelve-hour shifts.

Throughout the crisis, the city and state authorities maintained a solid front against compromise and absolutely refused to consider any settlement that involved amnesty. On July 12, Maryland governor Marvin Mandel ordered the use of 115 state troopers (and the state's much-prized armored car) in the streets of Baltimore. The courts also played a decisive role in efforts to crush the strike. On July 13, Judge Murphy threatened to jail the leaders of the various groups of municipal

employees, including Thomas Rappanotti of the Metropolitan Police Council. A fine of $10,000 a day was levied against police local president George Hoyt until the strike ended, and the local union was fined $25,000 a day. (Later, Rappanotti would also become the target of a contempt fine.) There was the added threat that any officer jailed for non-payment would lose his job. On July 14, Pomerleau threatened the dismissal of all officers who failed to return to work immediately. In addition, eighty-two probationary officers were fired for striking.

By July 15, most of the striking city workers were returning to work, and a new offer gave the police a 21 percent pay increase over two years. However, several hundred officers held out, refusing to settle without unconditional amnesty. In the political circumstances, this demand was entirely unsuccessful. Only 230 officers voted to ratify the pay offer on July 16, but thereafter, officers trickled back to work, and reprisals began. Within a week, over a hundred striking officers were dismissed or demoted with further suspensions occurring in August. AFSCME lost its sole right to bargain on behalf of the Baltimore police; and Pomerleau cancelled the automatic dues checkoff to the union. A particular source of grievance was the role of Governor Mandel. The union erroneously believed that he would intervene with the commissioner to prevent retaliation against the strikers.

The combination of dismissals, suspensions, fines, and limitations on union activity effectively crippled the police local and raised vital questions about the effectiveness of the strike weapon as opposed to slowdowns and walkouts. The *New York Times* (July 28, 1974) remarked that the Baltimore strike had been closely monitored by other cities and police departments as an object lesson for future struggles. [J. Philip Jenkins]

FURTHER READING

Bopp, William J. *Crises in Police Administration.* Springfield, IL: Charles Thomas, 1984.

Juris, Harvey, and Peter Feuille. *Police Unionism.* Lexington, MA: Lexington Books, 1973.

Walker, Samuel. *The Police in America.* New York: McGraw Hill, 1983.

o   o   o

BASEBALL PLAYERS' REVOLT OF 1889–1890. Since the early 1980s, labor–management strife in professional sports has become commonplace. [*See* **Baseball Strike of 1981**, and **Football Strike of 1987**.] Yet labor–management conflict in professional sports has a long history in the United States. During the 1880s, a series of disputes in professional baseball resulted in a struggle between players and owners for control of the sport.

In December of 1875, William Hulbert, owner of the Chicago White Stockings in the ill-fated National Association of Professional Baseball Players (NAPBP), took the lead in the formation of the National League of Professional Baseball Clubs. The NAPBP, like several earlier attempts at the formation of a viable league, had been a players' league. Not only did players predate administrators, but the earliest commercial major league was a players' league. The clubs were little more than barnstorming aggregations with constantly changing rosters. But the new league was completely in the hands of the owners; men such as Hulbert and Charles Fowle of the St. Louis club. The League looked after the interests of its owners by mandating that there could be no more than one team in any city, thus making expansion and competition much less likely.

Under Hulbert's aggressive leadership, the National League made short work of the NAPBP. He quickly lured the old league's top stars away with lucrative salaries. Soon the cash-starved NAPBP surrendered to the inevitable, and four of its teams joined the National League.

Hulbert first attacked the poor image of the game, and the players, as dishonest and plagued with excesses of gambling and alcoholism. He expelled franchises in several cities for playing Sunday games and selling liquor. In 1877, four players were blacklisted for gambling and fixing games. In all, thirty-four players fell victim to the blacklist in the early 1880s, some because of their resistance to the owners' new domination of the game. In order to stop the common practice of "revolving"— whereby players offered their services to the highest bidders, breaking contracts and changing teams several times during a season—the owners installed a reserve clause that prohibited a team from offering a contract to any other team's top fourteen players, thus binding them to one team unless the team decided to sell their contracts.

Hulbert's efforts to clean up the sport and reinforce management control did not guarantee profits, nor did they succeed in retaining a monopoly for the National League. On November 1, 1881, a group of rival promoters met in Cincinnati and formed another competing league, the American Association of Baseball Clubs. The two leagues competed bitterly in the same cities, with the Association gaining the upper hand in several major markets. The presence of the Association led to a bidding war for player talent, thus rendering the National League's reserve clause ineffective. After one season of competition the National League compromised and recognized the new circuit. Credit for the strategy went to A. G. Mills, Hulbert's successor as National League president. Mills proposed peace with the Association with the reserve clause as the cornerstone. He argued that the competition between the leagues benefitted only the players and convinced the new league's owners to agree that they would respect each other's reserve lists by refusing to sign any players on another team's list. This effectively put the owners back in complete control of the game. It also gave the National League owners the time they needed to undermine and destroy the Association and yet another short-lived challenger, the Union Association of Baseball Leagues.

The monopoly power in the hands of the owners led them to overstep the bounds in their relations with the players. In 1885, they imposed a salary ceiling of $2,000. The autocratic management and the hated reserve clause led to seething resentment on the part of the players. Revolts broke out on the St. Louis and Louisville teams in the Association. The resentment that this sparked led to the creation of the Brotherhood of Professional Baseball Players in 1885, the first union of professional athletes. Brotherhood membership grew rapidly and soon drew the ire of the owners. Relations between the two sides deteriorated as management attacked the players in the press and the union took the owners to court to end the reserve clause. By 1888, the two sides were at an impasse that could not be resolved by either negotiations or arbitration.

Instead of a strike, the player's union chose to break away and form its own league, the Players' National League of Baseball Clubs. The leader of the effort, John Montgomery Ward, who had also organized the Brotherhood, was a leading player for Providence and the New York Giants. He had graduated from the Pennsylvania State College and attended Columbia Law School. His education, rare for professional athletes of the day, thrust him into a leadership position. Although highly paid, Ward was dedicated to the cause of the players. He was a skillful propagandizer for the players and was able to gain numerous supporters for the Brotherhood and the Players' League among the nation's sporting press.

The new league quickly won the support of the vast majority of the players. Financiers, guaranteed good players by the

Brotherhood and eager to capitalize on baseball's growing popularity, accepted the opportunity to challenge the National League's monopoly in the major cities and start clubs in the new league. In a short time, franchises were operating in Boston, New York, Brooklyn, Philadelphia, Cleveland, Chicago, and Buffalo.

The Brotherhood organized the league and divided up the players. Each team was ordered to contribute $25,000 to a central war fund. Each player was to receive a salary equal to his 1888 pay, and individual club profits above $20,000 were to be pooled and shared equally by all. The first $10,000 of a club's profits belonged to the owners and the second $10,000 was to be divided equally among the players. Each club was directed by a committee of eight, half of whom were players. The league's democratic structure was topped by a senate with sixteen members, two from each club, eight of whom were players. Profits from gate receipts were split by the home and visiting teams. After operating expenses, profits were divided into an insurance fund for salaries and a prize fund for the pennant winner. Only after these requirements were satisfied did the owner's profits materialize.

In place of the reserve clause, players received guaranteed three-year contracts. At the end of the contract period, players could offer their services to other teams. This compromise promoted both league stability and economic freedom for the players. Finally, although the hated blacklist was abandoned, severe penalties were set for gambling and drunkenness.

National League owners denounced the new league's organizers as "hot-headed anarchists." The upstanding Ward was maligned as the "chief conspirator" who was using "terrorism peculiar to revolutionary movements." It was pointed out in the owner's organ, *Spalding's Official Base Ball Guide*, that the Central Labor Union of New York had supported the players. Such tarring of the Players' League with radicalism was one reason that Ward refrained from aligning the Brotherhood with the American Federation of Labor.

The battle among the three leagues took place on three fronts—the recruitment of players, the support of the public, and the courts. Numerous attempts by the National League and the Association teams to sue defecting players for breach of contract failed. It was clear that the reserve clause would not hold up in court. From the outset, the Players' League received the support of the athletes, who, according to one source, "held together like rocks." Most of the talented players, men such as Connie Mack of Philadelphia and Charles Comiskey of Chicago, went to the Brotherhood. This solidarity prevailed in the face of the National League's offer of three-year contracts and $10,000 signing bonuses.

The battle for public support was even more intense because the leagues were in head-on competition in the seven largest cities. As the 1890 season opened, a pattern of economic warfare emerged, with the National League putting pressure on the players' financial backers. The league's strategy was to drive a wedge between the Brotherhood and their backers. The National League made certain to schedule its games in direct conflict with those of the Players' League. Extensive promotions, including free tickets and frequent ladies' days, forced the Players' League to follow suit.

The battle was costly to both sides. One estimate put the National League's losses at the end of the season at $300,000. Undoubtedly the Brotherhood suffered more. Although the Players' League slightly outdrew its competitors at the gate, it was in serious financial trouble by the end of the 1890 season. At this point the National League's leadership announced its willingness to meet with the rival league's backers as equals but not with the "renegade" players. Ward called for a boycott of the

meeting, but the players' financial backers were anxious to make peace and recoup their losses. They split with the Brotherhood at the league meetings in November. Ward tried to raise money from the players to buy out the owners, but to no avail. When several teams sold out to the rival National League, the Players' League disintegrated.

Although the National League took the members of the Brotherhood back with no reprisals, the salary ceilings and the reserve clause were reinstated. The players reverted to the status of powerless workers. Even though the courts had ruled time and again against the legality of the reserve clause, the power of the owners allowed them to reimpose it. The collapse of the Player's League did not signal the end of attempts at the unionization of baseball players. In 1900, the League Protective Players' Association was formed, but it disappeared when the new American League organized in that same year to successfully challenge the monopoly control of the major baseball markets by the National League. A subsequent agreement between the National and American leagues to honor each other's rights to players quickly ended the brief opportunity that the players had enjoyed to offer their services to the highest bidder.

Ten years later, in 1910, the players formed the Baseball Players' Fraternity after Detroit players were heavily fined for striking for two days to protest the suspension of their teammate Ty Cobb for fighting with a newspaper reporter. The Fraternity lasted just six years, and its one accomplishment was the adoption by the leagues of the "waiver rule" which allowed other teams to sign a player before he was sent to the minor leagues by his club.

With the demise of the Fraternity, unionization did not return to professional baseball until 1946 when players formed the American Baseball Guild. The goals of the new union were similar to those that had motivated their predecessors to form an independent players' league, including the end to the reserve clause, which bound a player to one team. The Major League Baseball Players Association replaced the Guild in 1954 and remains the union of professional baseball players at the time of this writing. [Ronald L. Filippelli]

FURTHER READING

Dworkin, James B. *Owners Versus Players—Baseball and Collective Bargaining*. Boston, MA: Auburn House, 1981.

Frommer, Harvey. *Primitive Baseball*. New York: Macmillan, 1988.

Seymour, Harold. *Baseball: The Early Years*. New York: Oxford University Press, 1960.

Voigt, David Quentin. *American Baseball*, Vol. 1. Norman, OK: University of Oklahoma Press, 1966.

o   o   o

BASEBALL PLAYERS' STRIKE OF 1981. Major league baseball is the oldest professional sport in the United States and is the first sport whose players unionized and embraced collective bargaining. Over several sets of negotiations the players built a strong union bargaining position which established a model for labor relations in other professional sports.

Before the players unionized, baseball owners maintained monopolistic control of their labor force through, among other devices, the reserve clause, which bound a player to one team unless he was traded or released or decided to retire. Exempted from the nation's antitrust laws, major league baseball was a self-regulating monopoly which engaged in noncompetitive labor practices.

The economics of the industry made the owners vulnerable to collective action on the part of the players. Although baseball teams play many more games than other professional sports teams, most contests are not sold out. In addition, notwith-

standing national television contracts, most revenue comes from local sources—local ticket sales, local media broadcasting, stadium concessions, and parking. With only nine players on the field at one time, owners have a strong economic incentive to sign quality players, improve the team's record, and thereby become more profitable.

The Major League Baseball Players Association (MLBPA) was formed in 1952 and was dominated by team owners until 1966 when Marvin Miller was selected as executive director. Miller, a former assistant to the president of the United Steel Workers of America, brought a traditional trade union perspective to the MLBPA and was an exceptionally skilled labor relations practitioner. In his second agreement, which he negotiated in 1970, Miller inserted a clause providing for grievance arbitration of disputes arising during the life of the labor contract. This approach replaced a system where the commissioner of Major League Baseball, who was selected by the owners, ruled on all disputes.

Two years later, after a ten-day work stoppage, a clause that called for the determination of players' salaries by neutral arbitrators in certain situations when an impasse occurred was inserted in the new agreement. Once a player became eligible for salary arbitration, after three years of service, an impasse could be submitted to binding arbitration if he could not agree with management on a new contract.

Before the mid-1970s, players who signed contracts became, through the reserve clause, the property of one team. This effectively gave management a monopoly in the labor market. However, in 1975, arbitrator Peter Seitz decided that pitchers Andy Messersmith and Dave McNally, who had performed without a contract the previous season, were free agents and therefore free to sign with any team in baseball. This decision, establishing "free agency," was a frontal assault on the reserve clause.

In 1976, the owners shut down the spring training camps for seventeen days and locked the players out when an impasse developed over the issue of free agency. The impasse was resolved with the insertion into the contract of a clause requiring the players to have six years of service before being eligible for free agency. Free agency continued to be an issue in the 1980 bargaining as the owners attempted to regain control over player mobility by restricting free agency.

The heart of the dispute was compensation for free agents who signed with another team. The owners wanted to institute a system whereby any team that signed a free agent would have to compensate the team that lost the player with another quality performer. This would have effectively ended the system, but the players refused to consider it. A strike appeared imminent until the two parties agreed to separate the issue of free agency from the other issues. A joint labor–management committee was set up to study the issue. When this committee could not agree on the issue, the owners announced that they would put into effect a compensation plan of their own, and the union announced its intention to strike.

The MLBPA filed an unfair labor practice charge with the National Labor Relations Board (NLRB) alleging that management had pleaded inability to pay at the bargaining table and then had refused to open its books which constituted bad-faith bargaining. As part of its involvement, the NLRB tried to get a U.S. District Court injunction to postpone the strike but failed. The strike began on June 12, 1981. The owners purchased $50 million in strike insurance from Lloyds of London and created a $15 million strike fund to cover strike-related expenses. The MLBPA relied on rank and file solidarity which held throughout the stoppage. In all, 713 games were canceled when, after fifty days, a settlement was reached.

Both sides compromised to reach an agreement. Free agency compensation rules were tightened and the players retained the right to move to other clubs without much market restraint. Under the new rules, free agents were ranked as either A or B players depending on their performance. Players in the top 20 percent were rated A; those in the 21 to 30 percent category were rated B. If a player had twelve years of experience or had gone through the reentry draft before, he was exempt from the ratings. If a team signed an A-rated free agent, it had to compensate the team that lost the player with a player of its own choosing from a pool of unprotected players. In addition, the team that lost a free agent was given an extra choice in the free agent draft. When a team lost a B-rated free agent, it received two extra selections in the amateur draft.

These free agency rules proved to be complex and did not restrict player movements or slow the rapid increase in salaries. Therefore, in 1985, the rules for free agency were changed at the bargaining table so that compensation for teams that lost free agents was eliminated. The reentry draft, which had been set up in 1976, was abolished. The rules lifted virtually all barriers to players becoming free agents once they had completed six years of service. From that point on, players were bound only by the length of their existing contracts.

The damage inflicted by the baseball strike of 1981 was limited to that season. Games were canceled, income was lost, and attendance figures were down. However, in subsequent years attendance levels reached new records, and baseball popularity achieved a new high. The 1981 strike was an attempt by the owners to turn the clock back and regain control over free agency, which they had bargained away in previous contracts. The strike demonstrated that free agency was a permanent part of the landscape of major league baseball. In the wake of the strike, the bidding for free agents continued to increase salaries, but, because of the growing popularity of professional baseball, team profits soared. As the decade closed, a new round of bidding for high-priced free agents occurred. The 1981 strike was the only stoppage of the decade and anchored in place the system of free agency and salary arbitration that has dramatically changed the face of labor relations in America's national pastime. [Donald Kennedy]

FURTHER READING

Dworkin, James B. *Owners Versus Players: Baseball and Collective Bargaining.* Boston, MA: Auburn House, 1981.

Staudohar, Paul. *The Sports Industry and Collective Bargaining.* Ithaca, NY: Cornell ILR Press, 1986.

o   o   o

BERKSHIRE KNITTING MILLS STRIKE OF 1936–1937. Throughout much of the Depression decade of the 1930s, the American Federation of Hosiery Workers (AFHW) attempted to organize the Berkshire Knitting Mills—the largest full-fashioned hosiery mill in the world. This effort resulted in a thirteen-month strike in 1936–1937, which, labeled the "Berky" strike, became the best known labor–management conflict in the history of the city of Reading, Pennsylvania.

Full-fashioned stockings were made largely from silk. They were called full-fashioned because the stocking was knitted to fit the leg snugly by adding stitches at the broad part of the leg and dropping them at the narrower parts. The full-fashioned industry offered employment to skilled knitters, who enjoyed good wages, and to other relatively unskilled workers who filled mass-production jobs.

Skilled knitters in several cities turned to unionism in the first decade of the twentieth century. In 1909, Local 706 of the American Federation of Hosiery Workers

was formed in Philadelphia, Pennsylvania, the center of the American hosiery industry at that time. In 1913, Local 706 and four other locals from across the United States founded the American Federation of Full-Fashioned Hosiery Workers (AFFHW). In the early years, the AFFHW was dominated by a craft philosophy and organized skilled male workers. Eventually the union changed its name to the American Federation of Hosiery Workers and became more industrial in structure. Women hosiery workers, who were the vast majority of the industry's labor force, achieved representation in the AFFHW for the first time at the 1918 convention, and by the mid-1930s they outnumbered unionized male workers by two to one.

Berkshire Knitting Mills was one of three divisions of Wyomissing Industries which was located in a suburb of Reading, Pennsylvania. The other two divisions were the Textile Machine Works, which manufactured knitting machines, and Narrow Fabric, which produced lace and ribbon. Berkshire was built in order to test the machines which Wyomissing Industries produced.

Wyomissing built a huge complex that included, in addition to the factory buildings, offices, garages, a dispensary, recreation hall, power plant, cafeteria, foundry, and a thirty-six-acre recreational tract. The company offered employees life insurance, medical coverage, and a profit-sharing plan. Over the years, the corporation donated money to the local hospital, art museum, library, historical society, and other community activities.

Because of Berkshire's dominant position in the industry, the American Federation of Hosiery Workers had launched several campaigns to unionize the company. The AFHW launched an unsuccessful general strike in 1930 and one year later conducted a two-week organizing drive that also failed. In the summer of 1933 a successful strike closed down the Reading hosiery industry, including the mighty Berkshire. The Reading Hosiery Strike was the first case presented to the National Labor Board (NLB) after it was established by the National Industrial Recovery Act (NIRA) in 1934. The NLB mediated the strike and devised the "Reading Formula" which had four parts: the union agreed to end the strike, management would rehire all striking employees without discrimination, a secret ballot election would be held to determine if the employees wanted to join the AFHW, and any unresolved issues would be submitted to the NLB.

Election day was August 15, 1933, and over 14,000 workers went to the industrial polls. The pro-union forces carried thirty-seven mills and over 13,000 votes. The vote at Berkshire was 2,662 votes for the union representatives of Branch 10, AFHW, and 976 for the company representatives. In the wake of this resounding union victory, Berkshire implemented a multi-faceted plan to avoid collective bargaining. After firing 3,000 employees who struck the firm, Berkshire set up a company union, delayed bargaining a contract with the AFHW, and when a brief document was finally agreed to, Berkshire signed a similar pact with the company union.

In April 1934, because of the lack of progress in negotiations, the AFHW announced the termination of the earlier agreement and attempted to bargain a new agreement throughout 1935 and into 1936. When these attempts proved fruitless, the AFHW called a strike for October 1, 1936.

The union's main goal in the strike was to stabilize the hosiery industry. The AFHW wanted to maintain the hosiery code enacted by the NIRA and to achieve meaningful recognition as the bargaining agent for Berkshire's employees. Throughout 1936, the union maintained daily mass-picketing at Berkshire's gates because the company announced that it was open for business. Many manufacturers in the area supported the AFHW's effort because they feared the price-cutting which would follow the collapse of the NIRA standards.

The union competed for the loyalty of Berkshire's workers, most of whom lived in the city of Reading, by visiting them at their homes. The union also looked for support from Reading's Socialist mayor; announced a nationwide boycott of Berkshire's products; lobbied to remove borough, county, and state police from the area around the plant; and used the media to tell its story to the community.

In mid-February 1937, Branch 10 called a general strike of some 12,000 employees in twenty mills in the Reading area. The stoppage began on March 1, 1937. Sit-down strikes occurred at four mills while workers at the rest of the hosiery factories walked out. The strike achieved agreements at all of the mills except Berkshire. The "Berky" strike dragged on for over a year and finally ended when union strike funds were exhausted.

In the summer of 1937, the union filed an unfair labor practice charge with the National Labor Relations Board (NLRB) alleging that Berkshire had interfered with its employees' right to organize, had dominated a company union, and had discharged workers for union activity. The NLRB upheld the union's charges and ordered the disestablishment of the company union, the reinstatement of the terminated, and a back-pay award for several hundred employees. Berkshire appealed, and the case eventually went to the Supreme Court which upheld the NLRB's order. In August 1946, Berkshire paid over $500,000 in back-pay awards. Despite its court victory, however, the union lost the strike.

The Berkshire Knitting Mills Strike was the most significant labor-management conflict in the history of the full-fashioned hosiery industry. It pitted the world's largest full-fashioned hosiery mill against the union that was attempting to stabilize an industry that had been ravaged by the Great Depression. Even though the vast majority of Berkshire employees voted for collective bargaining, the corporation was able to thwart their will through a multi-faceted anti-union policy. This posture plus the developing labor policy of the federal government and the corporation's integrated hosiery operation enabled it to prevent a union victory. Throughout the strike, Wyomissing Industries continued to operate unimpeded in its other two divisions—Narrow Fabric and Textile Machine Works. This guaranteed a steady source of revenue even though its knitting mill was affected by the strike. This factor, perhaps more than any other, explains why the AFHW lost the most important strike in its history. [Donald Kennedy]

FURTHER READING

Kennedy, Donald. "Corporate Structure, Technology, and the Full-Fashioned Hosiery Industry: The Berkshire Knitting Mills Strike of 1936–37." *Labor Studies Journal*, Vol. 3 (Winter, 1979), pp. 257–280.

Rogin, Lawrence. *Making History in Hosiery: The Story of the American Federation of Hosiery Workers.* Philadelphia, PA: The Federation, 1938.

o   o   o

BETHLEHEM STEEL STRIKE OF 1910. One of the most important strikes in the pre-union history of the steel industry took place at Bethlehem Steel in 1910. The conflict resulted from the refusal of the company to discuss grievances with representatives of 700 skilled workers at the company's main Bethlehem, Pennsylvania plant. Instead, the three men carrying the demands were fired.

The grievances of the skilled workers, mostly machinists, grew out of discontent with low wages and long hours, and particularly with the company's refusal to pay time and a half for overtime. The company had voluntarily paid the premium before 1907, but it then arbitrarily discontinued the practice in the midst of a business slump. In addition, the workers wanted an end to Sunday work.

The firing of the workers' representatives touched off a work stoppage in the two largest machine shops. The decisiveness of the workers' action alarmed Bethlehem management. Company president Charles M. Schwab calmed the situation by promising the workers that he would accede to their demands, including the rehiring of the fired workers, but only if they would return to work first. No negotiations would take place under strike conditions.

On February 5, 1910, two days after the strike had begun, the workers met to consider Schwab's offer. Circumstances had changed significantly since the skilled machinists had walked out. Unskilled workers and apprentices had joined the strike in the hopes of improving their conditions as well. In addition, sentiment for the organization of a lodge of the International Association of Machinists began to surface. Schwab tried to head off any move to continue the strike by painting a rosy picture of Bethlehem Steel's economic future. The remarks had the opposite effect. Workers calculated that with the volume of orders held by Bethlehem the company would not risk a long strike. So convinced, the men voted to continue the strike.

The machinists and the company knew that the strike could only be successful if the entire plant were shut down. A walkout by the machinists alone, although damaging, could be handled by the importation of skilled men from other cities. The support of the unskilled workers would be essential. Schwab tried to divide the two groups by offering the machinists a token raise, but that failed, and the skilled and unskilled workers agreed to remain out until both groups' wages were increased.

Both the International Association of Machinists (IAM) and the American Federation of Labor (AFL) assisted the strikers. The resolve of the strikers was also enhanced by a company decision to accept only individual applications for a return to work. The strikers would not be allowed to return as a group. The policy was an indication that Schwab had no intention of capitulating. By the end of the first month of the strike, hundreds of workers had left Bethlehem for other jobs.

During the first three months the strike remained violence free. The community, though generally favorable to the company, had more or less stayed out of the dispute. But as the strike wore on, and the strikers' financial resources diminished, tempers grew short. The goal of shutting down the plant entirely had not been realized, and the nearby Saucon Valley plant had barely been touched by the strike. The strikers directed most of their hostility at the still-large number of nonstriking workers. Tensions on the picket line led Eugene Grace, operating head of the company, to ask the city of Bethlehem and the Commonwealth of Pennsylvania to increase police protection for the plant.

City and state officials responded with alacrity to the company's request. Governor Edwin S. Stuart dispatched twenty-five state policemen to the scene. The appearance of men from the Pennsylvania constabulary added to the tension rather than decreasing it. Called "cossacks" by the workers, particularly by the eastern European immigrants, the state police had become infamous in labor circles for their brutal treatment of workers in labor disputes especially in the coal and steel towns of western Pennsylvania. As it turned out, Bethlehem was to be no exception. Police reacted harshly to taunts from the strikers and their supporters. Violence inevitably followed. In one unfortunate incident, an innocent bystander in a barroom was killed by a stray bullet from a constable's gun.

Under the protection of the police reinforcements, Schwab announced that the plant would resume full operations on February 28. But the strikers responded overwhelmingly to the appeal of their leader, David Williams, not to return to work while the "cossacks" were in town. Frustrated, Schwab threatened to sublet $2 million in armaments contracts to Carnegie Steel Corporation, thus lowering the number of jobs in Bethlehem. To counter this threat, the strikers took the innovative action of going to Washington to urge the nearly two dozen countries doing business with Bethlehem Steel to cancel their contracts.

Williams turned up the pressure at home as well. He hinted at the possibility of a general strike by the AFL in Pennsylvania and noted with satisfaction that Bethlehem was having precious little success in recruiting skilled workers. Not to be caught unawares, Schwab called together the business leadership of Bethlehem and chastised them for their relatively neutral stance during the dispute. Unless they came to the defense of the company, he threatened that the plant might close for good. Schwab railed against city officials for allowing the strikers to use the municipal hall as a venue to attack the company. His threats had their intended results. The businessmen passed a resolution to advise Congress and foreign governments that the local business community totally supported the company. They also sent a delegation to meet with President William Howard Taft to make certain that the government would not cancel its contracts with Bethlehem.

The strikers also appealed to President Taft, asking for a federal investigation of the causes of the strike. Taft and Congress complied with the union request, and Bethlehem Steel announced its full cooperation. At this point, both sides, certain of success, waited for vindication from the Department of Commerce and Labor investigation. The report issued on May 4 was a disappointment. In its documentation of

Bethlehem's wage rate, it did provide evidence to support the strikers' claims of low wages and poor working conditions; however, it did not take sides or draw conclusions. It angered Schwab because it did not state that Bethlehem's conditions met the industry standard, no better and no worse. Schwab forced Dr. Charles P. Neill, the Commissioner of Labor in Washington, to issue a public statement that while Bethlehem's "conditions of labor . . . may well be called shocking, . . . they are not confined to the Bethlehem Steel works."

The entire episode ended up as a public relations nightmare for the company. Schwab was eager to settle the strike. So too were the workers. They had not succeeded in stopping production at the Bethlehem works, and unless they could convince more unskilled workers to join them then, they had very little hope of ever doing so. Many of the skilled workers had been forced to leave the city to find work elsewhere, and those remaining were fast approaching the end of their financial resources. Under pressure from Schwab, many of Bethlehem's businessmen had cut off credit to strikers. On the strikers' side, support from the labor movement was more moral than real. During the entire strike fraternal aid amounted to only $6,700, or less than $1.00 a month per worker.

On May 18 the strike ended. The only gain made by the workers after 108 days of struggle and sacrifice was the right to refuse overtime. There were no wage increases, and only those workers who had not damaged company property or attacked its reputation could return to work. This eliminated most of the strike leaders. Union recognition was not part of the settlement.

Although the terms of the settlement were a victory for Bethlehem Steel, the cost of the strike was high to the company and to the industry. The Department of Commerce and Labor investigation turned up material about their labor policies that embarrassed the steel companies. After the strike, the government widened its scrutiny of the industry when the Senate passed a resolution for a full-scale inquiry. The study yielded a four-volume report which was an indictment of the wretched working conditions of the steelworkers. [Ronald L. Filippelli]

FURTHER READING

Brody, David. *Steelworkers in America: The Nonunion Era.* Cambridge, MA: Harvard University Press, 1960.

Cotter, Arundel. *The Story of Bethlehem Steel.* New York: Moody Magazine and Book Company, 1916.

Hessen, Robert. "The Bethlehem Steel Strike of 1910." *Labor History,* Vol. 15, No. 1 (Winter, 1974), pp. 3–18.

o   o   o

BISBEE, ARIZONA, MINERS' STRIKE OF 1917. Beginning in the fall of 1916, the Industrial Workers of the World (IWW) initiated a vigorous campaign to organize Arizona's four metal-producing districts that supplied 29 percent of the nation's copper. By 1917, their organizing efforts won support from some members of the International Union of Mine, Mill, and Smelter Workers (formerly the Western Federation of Miners) and members of several American Federation of Labor (AFL) unions who joined them in a general walkout from the metal mines in June and July of 1917. They were protesting the failure of the companies to arbitrate grievances, adjust wages to meet the wartime increase in the price of copper, and the metal industry's discrimination against union activities and union workers.

Denouncing the strike as "pro-German," the copper corporations refused to bargain with the union, stockpiled arms and ammunition, hired additional gunmen and guards, and publicly declared their intention of removing labor agitators from the area. The Bisbee sheriff wired the Arizona governor that most of the strikers were foreigners, that the strike appeared to be an anti-U.S. plot, and that bloodshed was imminent.

On July 6, 1917, a loyalty league was organized in the region, pressuring citizens to join and turn in the names of IWW citizens and sympathizers. Within the week, sixty-seven IWW members were rounded up in Jerome, forced into cattle cars and shipped to the California border. Two days later, vigilantes in Bisbee rounded up 1,200 persons and loaded them on a twenty-seven car train that ended in the desert near Hermanas, New Mexico. There, the Bisbee refugees were kept in a stockade under army guard until mid-September when the camp was disbanded because the federal government refused to continue supplying food.

Most of the deportees returned to Bisbee. Some were arrested; others were allowed to stay unmolested. A year later, a federal grand jury indicted twenty-one leaders of the Bisbee Loyalty League. No one was convicted.

The President's Mediation Commission, sent in to settle the strike, found that of the 1,200 deportees, 360 belonged to no labor organization. It also found that 662 were either native born or naturalized citizens. Many had been soldiers or sailors, were registered under the Selective Service Act, owned Liberty Bonds, and supported the Red Cross.

The copper strikes in Arizona were ended by the deportations and by the President's Mediation Commission, which reported that the strike was neither pro-German nor seditious but "appeared to be nothing more than the normal results of the increased cost of living, and the speeding up processes to which the mine management had been tempted by the abnormally high market price of copper." The strike settlement, however, specifically excluded any miner who spoke disloyally against the government or who was a member of an organization that refused to recognize time contracts.

The copper companies were protected by the umbrella of the Sabotage Act of 1918, which classified the mines as "war premises" and their output as "war materials." Army troops that had been sent in during the 1917 Arizona strike were given the authority to "disperse or arrest persons unlawfully assembled at or near any 'war premise' for the purpose of intimidating, alarming, disturbing, or injuring persons lawfully employed thereon, or molesting or destroying property threat."

Federal troops stayed in Arizona until 1920 in an effort to curb the "Wobbly menace." They protected strikebreakers, dispersed street crowds, and patrolled "troublesome" sections of the communities. They were billeted in quarters built for them by the mine owners and were informed about industrial relations and workers' activities by reports from private company detectives.

Although in 1918, the U.S. Justice Department proceeded to prosecute the vigilantes who had been armed and financed by the Phelps-Dodge Company, the department refused to indict Walter Douglas, president of Phelps Dodge, who was most responsible for the deportations. The case, which went on appeal to the U.S. Supreme Court, ended when the highest court ruled that the vigilantes were not subject to federal prosecution.

Unionism in Arizona's copper camps failed after the 1917 Bisbee strike and the deportation that followed in response to AFL and IWW organizing efforts. [Joyce L. Kornbluh]

FURTHER READING

Jensen, Vernon H. *Heritage of Conflict.* Ithaca, NY: Cornell University Press, 1950.

Perlman, Selig, and Philip Taft. *History of Labor in the United States, 1896–1932*, Vol. 4, *Labor Movements.* New York: Macmillan, 1935.

Report on the Bisbee Deportations Made by the
  President's Mediation Commission to the President of
  the U.S., November 6, 1917. Washington, DC:
  Government Printing Office, 1918.

o   o   o

BITUMINOUS COAL STRIKE OF 1897. Few strikes have had as much impact on the development of collective bargaining in the United States as the important struggle between the fledgling United Mine Workers of America (UMW) and the coal operators of Pennsylvania, Ohio, Indiana, and Illinois—the so-called Central Competitive Field. The strike not only gave stability to the UMW but also brought a semblance of stability to one of the most unstable and competitive industries in America.

At the end of the nineteenth century, coal was the basic source of power for American industry. The ease with which coal could be found and the relatively small amount of capital required to enter the industry attracted large numbers of entrepreneurs to the coalfields. The result was overbuilding and overproduction in an industry highly sensitive to the fluctuations in the economy. In times of depression, such as in the desperate years from 1893 to 1897, overproduction reached epic proportions.

Labor costs accounted for from 60 to 80 percent of the costs of mining. Thus, when competition and business downturns pressured the coal operators, their first response was to cut wages to gain competitive advantage. Not surprisingly, wage cuts were almost always at the heart of the epic struggles between capital and labor that characterized industrial relations in the coal industry. So long as the miners were unorganized, there was little they could do to stem the snowballing effects of wage-cutting wars in the highly decentralized industry. Only a union of all of the miners could take wages out of competition by negotiating a uniform rate across the fields, and only by doing this, it appeared, could stability be brought to the industry.

The formation of the United Mine Workers of America in 1890 was the first step toward this goal. Although the union remained small in its first few years, its potential as a magnet for the discontent of the miners was demonstrated in 1894, in the depths of the depression, when some 180,000 miners answered the union's call for a general strike in order to cut production and raise the price of coal and wages. In an extraordinary display of militancy and endurance, the miners stayed out for eight weeks, returning only when it became clear that the presence of non-union West Virginia coal on the market was undercutting the effectiveness of the strike.

By 1897 conditions in the coalfields were worse than ever. Coal prices, and wages, had continued their dramatic decline. Instead of shutting down altogether, many operators continued to produce, cutting wages or reducing the work available to miners. This greatly increased the excess miners working the pits and impoverished the miners and their families. Accounts of near starvation in the coal towns were commonplace. Under these circumstances even the operators knew that some kind of revolt was likely to come. Indeed, many of the operators welcomed it. The industry journal noted that a general strike would have the salubrious effect of cleaning out excess coal, "and might have the effect of establishing a sensible and practical differential in the four principle mining states . . . , thus enabling all miners to make fair living wages."

On July 4th, Independence Day, the industry journal got its wish. The small United Mine Workers union, some 10,000 strong, called for a general strike. As in 1894, the response was overwhelming. Some 100,000 miners, the vast majority of whom were not union members, answered the call from union president Michael

46
o

Blatchford in the first four days. The Central Competitive Field was completely paralyzed, and mining operations were suspended as far afield as Kentucky and Tennessee. Faced with this show of solidarity, the operators soon surrendered. The strike was a remarkably peaceful affair as coal mining strikes went. In large measure this resulted from the fact that both the union and the operators realized that the eventual settlement of the strike was likely to lead to a more stable industry.

The fruits of the union victory came in January of 1898 when representatives of the miners and the operators met in Chicago and signed the "Inter-State Joint Agreement." The accord established wage rates based on differentials for the various districts that factored in all of the variables effecting the mining and marketing of coal. It also established the eight-hour workday, and provided for an immediate wage increase of ten cents per ton. The goal of the agreement was to equalize costs of production among all operators and thereby establish equality of competition. The UMW's success led to a 1,000 percent increase in membership during 1897 and 1898.

In addition, the parties to the agreement established a permanent parliament of operators' and miners' delegates who would meet each year to work out a new agreement. The union's role was to "afford all possible protection to the trade and to the other parties hereto against any unfair competition resulting from a failure to maintain scale rates." In other words, it was the union's job to police the agreement by insuring that the operators complied with the wage scales set down in Chicago. That the employers assigned this crucial task to a trade union was a recognition of how critical uniform wage scales were to stability in the industry. This support by the northern operators for the union's role also extended to the largely non-union southern fields. There, the UMW was assured in the operator's journal, it would receive the hearty support of the operators for an organizing drive.

Although the operators did not forcefully resist the strike, this fact should not detract from the impressive show of strength that the UMW had demonstrated. For its time, the strike was a masterful display of organizational skill, ranging as it did across four states at hundreds of work places. The strike was also seen as critical to the fledgling labor movement at the turn of the century. Eugene Debs toured Indiana to address the strikers, and the organizers of the Industrial Workers of the World later pointed to the 1897 coal strike as a milestone in the organization of the American working class. Indeed, the victory in bituminous coal made the United Mine Workers of America the premier labor organization in the country. It also proved to be one of the first indications of an increase in labor militancy that marked the country in the years from 1897 to 1904. [Ronald L. Filippelli]

FURTHER READING

Evans, Chris. *A History of the United Mine Workers of America, 1860–1900.* Indianapolis, IN: The United Mine Workers of America, 1900.

Ramirez, Bruno. *When Workers Fight: The Politics of Industrial Relations in the Progressive Era, 1898–1916.* Westport, CT: Greenwood Press, 1978.

Roy, Andrew. *A History of Coal Miners in the United States.* Columbus, OH: J. L. Trauger, 1907.

o o o

BITUMINOUS COAL STRIKE OF 1922. This was the second of the three major strikes called by the United Mine Workers of America (UMW) during the decade that followed World War I. The strike affected many union and non-union mines throughout the Central Competitive Field, which stretched from western Pennsylvania to Illinois. The stated goals of the strike were the maintenance of union contracts, increased wages and benefits, and the unionization of non-union operations. The strike reflected both the unsettled conditions within the UMW hierarchy, as well as the declining market position of coal produced in the Central Competitive Field.

The miners of the Central Competitive Field were influenced by two new forces during the 1920s. The first was John L. Lewis, a man of insight, intelligence, and ruthless ambition. In 1922, Lewis' possession of the UMW national presidency was due to fortuitous circumstance and adroit maneuver rather than election by a supportive rank and file. Determined to make himself absolute master of the UMW, Lewis was as "ruthless in the suppression of minorities as any king." Lewis began to build a union machine, utterly loyal to his person. Union rivals accepted sinecures or were purged. Critics charged the "Lewis gang" employed not only election fraud, but a "Fascist terror," which included beatings, abductions, and even murder. Local district autonomy was systematically eliminated, and both district and national UMW conventions were gatherings orchestrated by Lewis. Lewis loyalists such as Pat Fagan and Philip Murray made their way to the upper echelons of the UMW hierarchy. The rank and file eventually acquiesced, sacrificing union democracy for order, stability, and victories won at the bargaining table.

The 1920s also brought depression to the miners of the Central Competitive Field. While Lewis wielded the carrot and the stick within the UMW, depression became the established reality in the northern bituminous fields. There were too many miners and mines and too much coal. Comparative advantage was being lost to non-union operations in West Virginia, Kentucky, and Tennessee. Southern operators enjoyed lower freight rates and a non-union wage scale. Oil and natural gas also invaded traditional energy markets. In 1924, the share of the nation's bituminous

mined in union fields fell to 24.6 percent, compared to 29 percent in 1920. Between 1920 and 1927, the market share of Pennsylvania and Ohio coal fell from 60 percent to 39 percent. Coal miners averaged 220 workdays a year in 1920, 149 in 1921, 174 in 1924, and 191 in 1927. Approximately 663,000 miners worked 8,078 mines in 1921, a number that shrank to 522,000 working 6,450 mines in 1928. These trends did not bode well for the bituminous industry, and the situation was particularly bleak for northern union operations which were losing markets in an interregional competition with southern Appalachia.

Western Pennsylvania bituminous reflected the general state of the industry in the North. Although Westmoreland County led Pennsylvania in coal production, and Allegheny County ranked fifth, bituminous miners worked fewer than 150 days in 1921. There was plenty of coal to be mined. The Commonwealth of Pennsylvania estimated 1.4 million recoverable tons of coal in Allegheny County, 3.2 million in Westmoreland County, and 2.4 million in Armstrong County. Both markets had dried up. It was no surprise when the Freeport Thick Vein Coal Operators Association refused to accept a continuance of the union wage scale in 1922. Henry Kinloch, superintendent and part owner of the Valley Camp Coal Company, emerged as the Association's chief advocate for an adjusted union scale. Valley Camp operated two large mines near New Kensington. Kinloch had operated on a union scale since 1917 and enjoyed a particular rapport with the union miners in his employ. Valley Camp made no attempt to force the issue and shut down its mines. Most of the district's operators chose to emulate Valley Camp's policy of watchful waiting, and also ceased operations in April 1922.

Non-union operators in such diverse places as the Kiskiminetas Valley, Somerset County, and the coke fields near Connellsville, resisted the UMW. Lewis Hicks operated a dozen mines in the Kiskiminetas Valley and was determined to stamp out the union in his mines. Hicks imported trainloads of black strikebreakers. The vicious brawls which erupted between white union miners and black miners in remote patches at Edri and Foster were little more than race riots. They set the stage for even more pervasive racial conflict in the **Bituminous Coal Strike of 1927**. Ten miles downriver, opposite Apollo, three Slavic strikebreakers from Natrona were murdered as they slept when dynamite was thrown into their bunkhouse at the Patterson mine. Seventy-five miles to the south, deputy sheriffs and the Coal and Iron police fought union pickets in the coke district. In nearby Somerset County, John Brophy directed a strike which became a stalemate that lasted for almost two years.

Judged by the harsh standard of the coalfields, the 1922 strike was a relatively mild affair. The **Herrin Massacre**, in which union miners murdered more than a dozen men, brought much opprobrium to the UMW, but such was not typical of the conflict. Since many coal operators closed down, confrontation was reduced significantly, and the strike's outcome was not determined on the picket line. In western Pennsylvania, 45,000 union miners left the pits on April 1, 1927. They were joined by 15,000 miners aspiring to be union men. These men demanded union recognition, preservation of the union wage scale, and the dues checkoff. The strike failed, and some were inclined to attribute the defeat to John L. Lewis. Lewis, however, had not favored a strike which flew in the face of depression and shrinking union resources.

In 1922, Lewis continued his efforts to wrest control of the UMW from rivals, and a strike beset by financial problems endangered the consolidation of his authority. But his hand was forced from below. At a special convention in February, rank and file militants pushed a broad program including nationalization of the mines, establishment of an independent labor party, a six-hour workday, expansion of the union, and wage increases. Lewis knew that he did not have enough money to finance union expansion, particularly in such anti-labor strongholds as the coke fields. Lewis correctly identified the calls for nationalization and the creation of a labor party with left-wing sentiment in the UMW. He was content to call for federal regulation of coal production and pricing. By the time the union had walked out in April, UMW demands had been reduced to a maintenance of the status quo in wages, the checkoff, and organization of the non-union fields.

By mid-July, the solidarity of the coal operators began to dissolve, something that would not happen until four years later. President Warren G. Harding lent his offices to both parties suggesting that standard wages be $7.50 per day for daymen, 94¢ a ton for machine-cut coal, and 88¢ a ton for pick miners. The Pittsburgh Coal Producers countered with the 1917 scale including $5.00 per day for daymen, 70¢ a ton for machine-cut coal, and 88¢ a ton for pick miners. Some operators, including Henry Kinloch of the Freeport Thick Vein Association, were evidently displeased with the proceedings and decided upon independent negotiations. Lewis extended the olive branch to the independents and offered to negotiate in Cleveland. They accepted and signed a UMW contract *status quo ante*.

The fading resolve of the operators proved to be small consolation for Lewis. He abandoned hope for a uniform, nationwide contract, and ordered some men back to work while others remained on the picket line. That move defied the UMW tradition that demanded that all union miners stay out until a uniform contract was reached for the entire union membership. Lewis virtually abandoned his fledgling membership in the coke district, Somerset, and the Kiskiminetas, because operators there did not sign a union contract of any kind. Lewis's decision was not an act of faithlessness or cowardice, but an attempt to make the best of a deteriorating situation. The UMW was destitute, and striking miners could not replenish a treasury already weakened by an industrywide depression.

Many locals refused to heed Lewis' order to return to work. Unimpressed with their president's change of course, they attempted to adhere to the tradition of one union, indivisible. "Conscientious objectors" at established locals were aided by roving pickets from the coke district. Local meetings and rallies were disrupted, and beatings selectively administered. The men under contract eventually went back to work but not without shame. For the UMW, the 1922 coal strike had opened a deep internal schism. The disaffected levelled charges of betrayal against the national union, and especially against Lewis. He was perceived not only as a grasping despot but also as a traitor to the rank and file.

On June 2, 1923, the Progressive Miners International Committee met at the Labor Lyceum in Pittsburgh. Participants included UMW insurgent Alex Howat, Communist miner Thomas Myerscough, Communist Party leader William Z. Foster, and a number of other radicals. Five coal mining states and two Canadian provinces were represented. The organization denounced "dual unionism," and advocated "boring from within" to capture the UMW. Its agenda included the ouster of Lewis, as well as labor party politics and nationalization of the mines. The Progressives elected a slate of officers and organized districts which coincided with those in the UMW, adding one to represent abandoned miners in the coke district. Lewis condemned the proceedings as the work of "UMWA traitors, Communists, IWWs, and dualists." The Progressives were never able to defeat Lewis, nor was he ever able to stamp them out. However, their stubborn resistance to the Lewis regime would do much to deny the UMW the internal unity that it would so desperately need in 1927. [Carl I. Meyerhuber, Jr.]

FURTHER READING

Blankenhorn, Heber. *The Strike For Union.* New York: H. W. Wilson, 1924.

Brophy, John. *A Miner's Life: An Autobiography.* Madison, WI: University of Wisconsin Press, 1964.

Dubofsky, Melvyn, and Warren Van Tine. *John L. Lewis: A Biography.* New York: Quadrangle, 1977.

Meyerhuber, Carl I., Jr. *Less Than Forever: The Rise and Decline of Union Solidarity in Western Pennsylvania, 1914–1948.* Selinsgrove, PA: Susquehanna University Press, 1987.

o   o   o

BITUMINOUS COAL STRIKE OF 1927. This was the third and last industrywide strike called by the United Mine Workers of America (UMW) during the decade following World War I. It was the most comprehensive work stoppage ever directed by a union in the Central Competitive Field, made up of the bituminous coal regions of Pennsylvania, Ohio, Indiana, and southern Illinois. In 1927, the UMW was led by the most articulate, assertive, and decisive man ever to hold the union's presidency—John L. Lewis. A year earlier, Lewis defeated John Brophy ending more than a decade of uncertainty that had engulfed the upper echelon of the union's hierarchy. Under Lewis, democracy gave way to autocracy, and dissent was buried by the friends of order. A measure of internal unity was particularly important to the UMW in 1927. For the first time the union faced unified, intransigent, corporate opposition in the bituminous industry.

As in the **Bituminous Coal Strike of 1922**, the union miner and coal operator fought to control the economics of a bituminous industry mired in depression. In 1927, coal production would fall 60 million tons below 1920 levels. Demand, which had peaked during the war, declined throughout the 1920s. Between 1924 and 1926, more than 2,000 bituminous mines closed and 116,000 miners lost their jobs. The price of coal fell 24 percent during that period. In 1929, only 35 percent of all bituminous producers reported profits, compared to 90 percent in 1920. Operators in the Central Competitive Field bore the brunt of the depression in bituminous, for on the eve of the strike their share of the market had fallen below 40 percent. The chief culprit so far as the northern operators were concerned was interregional competition. The advantages enjoyed by southern operators were both relative and absolute. The new southern coal seams were close to the surface, and therefore less expensive to mine. They produced high quality industrial steam coal. Southern freight rates were lower, and so were the wages paid to miners. In 1926, West Virginia surpassed Pennsylvania in bituminous production. During that year, West Virginia miners, paid on a tonnage basis, earned $5.85, those in Alabama earned $4.57, compared to $6.18 paid in Pennsylvania's union pits.

It was the disparity between union and non-union wages that brought the bituminous operators and the UMW into conflict. In 1924, John L. Lewis met with the operators in Jacksonville, Florida, and negotiated a wage agreement that became known as the Jacksonville scale. Under that agreement, the $7.50 per day wage for daymen established by the union in 1922 was retained, and wages for tonnage men remained the same.

Widespread operator dissatisfaction with the Jacksonville scale appeared less than a year after the contract was signed. In September 1924, some central Pennsylvania operators complained that they could not pay the "impossible wage scale" and

therefore shut down. Charles O'Neill, spokesman for the Central Pennsylvania Coal Producer's Association, requested a meeting with the UMW for the purpose of reducing wages. Operator associations in western Pennsylvania made similar requests in March 1925. The UMW refused the operators, and "No Backward Step" became the battle cry of the union miners.

In 1925, the operators of the Central Competitive Field had not reached an agreement on specific solutions to their wage problem. Some wanted to return to 1917 wage scales, others preferred less extreme measures, calling for a "continuously competitive" scale in which wages would be adjusted according to the price of coal. Virtually all agreed that the Jacksonville scale had to be terminated, but many were prepared to continue with the union. The eventual direction of the operators was charted by Pittsburgh Coal Company. In 1925, control of Pittsburgh Coal was acquired by the Mellon family of Pittsburgh. Following the UMW rejection of wage adjustments, Pittsburgh Coal closed all its mines. It established its own police force that occupied its properties. In August 1925, Pittsburgh Coal reopened on a non-union basis. The UMW had been there for thirty-five years. Most of the company's 17,000 miners were union men. That did not matter. The miners were ordered to accept the new regime or find new employment.

Pittsburgh Coal had simply abrogated the Jacksonville scale. Competitors soon followed. Bethlehem Mines; Buffalo, Rochester, and Pittsburgh coal companies; and others repudiated the UMW in 1925. The Jacksonville scale did not expire until April 1, 1927. Pittsburgh Terminal Coal, Valley Camp, and Clearfield Bituminous were among those companies which fulfilled its provisions until expiration. All three, however, announced that renewal would not be forthcoming. Industrywide overdevelopment, overproduction, and a dog-eat-dog competitive environment forced these companies to imitate Pittsburgh Coal. William Warden of Pittsburgh Coal openly subscribed to the doctrine of "survival of the fittest" and argued that the well-being of his firm depended upon how well its management used its "brains and physical strength." Warden's colleague J. D. A. Morrow concurred, adding that there "was no strike and there were no problems" at Pittsburgh Coal. His company was "done with the union." It would not sign a contract with the UMW "no matter what wage reductions they might be prepared to accept."

Pittsburgh Coal matched its intransigent anti-union rhetoric with deeds. Union miners were a hard lot, and the company fully expected them to resist the imposition of an open shop. Pittsburgh Coal borrowed the superintendent of Pennsylvania Railroad's security so that he could organize its Coal and Iron Police. Provisions were made for the importation of strikebreakers to work the company pits. Eviction proceedings were begun, and recalcitrant union miners were systematically removed from company housing. Eventually, Pittsburgh Coal obtained court orders to finish what it could not achieve through the use of raw force and violence. Bethlehem Mines imitated Pittsburgh Coal step by step, but companies such as Valley Camp and Clearfield Bituminous were clearly squeamish about using such blatant union-busting tactics. Eventually even they resorted to deputy sheriffs, evictions, court orders and strikebreakers. In short, the strategy and tactics adopted by Pittsburgh Coal set the tone for the proceedings in 1927.

The union responded with picket lines, surety bonds to block evictions, and violence, particularly against strikebreakers. Those strikebreakers were drawn from every ethnic community, race, and geographic region of the nation, but opprobrium fell chiefly upon the black strike-breaker. The UMW had apparently learned little from the widespread use of black strikebreakers in 1922 and had done little to deal with racism in the union or in the mines. When the operators introduced black strikebreakers in large numbers, the union responded first with violence, and then with public race-baiting. UMW vice-president Philip Murray complained to the Pittsburgh Council of Churches that the presence of blacks constituted a public menace because they engaged in widespread dope peddling and bootlegging. Murray also pandered to social fears by accusing black miners of "mingling" with white women. Robert Vann, editor of the Pittsburgh *Courier* and a civil rights activist, fired back that the UMW was making black miners scapegoats in order to mask its own failures. Vann urged the neophytes from the south to avoid the non-union deathtraps and to join the UMW. He urged the union to desist in its distortions about blacks and to employ black organizers to recruit the newcomers. "No real man wants to be called a scab," Vann warned. An open shop victory for the operators meant the reestablishment of "industrial feudalism" for all miners, black and white. Unfortunately, no one at UMW headquarters heeded Vann's advice, and strike violence degenerated into little more than a sporadic series of race riots which endured for more than a year.

Guards, evictions, strikebreakers, and racial violence were not new to the soft coal fields in 1927. What makes the 1927 Coal Strike noteworthy was the degree of repression to which the northern bituminous miner and his family were subjected. Had this strike taken place in southern Appalachia, it might simply be viewed in the tradition of **Harlan County**, Matewan, and the Mingo County Wars. It is, perhaps, ironic that a strike perceived by the UMW as essentially defensive, generated such a ferocious repudiation by the operators.

In 1927, the UMW sought no expansion into non-union fields, and demanded little beyond the maintenance of the Jacksonville scale. The western Pennsylvania operators, some of whom had worked with the union for decades, adamantly rejected the status quo and eventually sought the utter destruction of the UMW. To that end, civil liberties ceased to function in the soft coal fields. Guarded day and night, the coal camps were accessible only to those who carried an authorized company pass. Heat, light, running water, and medical care were dispensed by company fiat. Debt peonage, the threat of eviction, company police, and the courts enforced the will of the operators.

In November 1927, J. N. Langham, presiding judge of the Indiana County Court of Common Pleas, issued an injunction against UMW miners on strike at the Clearfield Bituminous Coal Company mine located at Rossiter. The order was so sweeping and punitive that it can only be construed as an invitation to the union to disband. Langham ordered the union not to picket, march, dispense relief, or to gather for meetings or rallies. Vile language and physical intimidation were forbidden. However, his order also forbade the union men "from saying or doing anything to cause [those working] to quit or cause men seeking work to refrain [from doing so]." Communication by billboards, signs, or newspaper advertisements was forbidden. All of this denied the union access to tactics common to an industrial strike and quite rightly raised questions about the violation of First Amendment rights. But that was not unusual. What raised a furor was the judge's prohibition against the singing of hymns and the holding of church services on two lots owned by the Magyar Presbyterian Church near the mine.

The prohibitions against hymn singing account for the notoriety of the "Rossiter injunction," and during the strike, Rossiter became synonymous with repression in the soft coal fields. Ironically, Clearfield Bituminous Coal Company did not qualify as the industry's most vicious strikebreaker. Rossiter, situated in northern Indiana County about seventy miles northeast of Pittsburgh, was founded by the New York Central Railroad and named for the treasurer of that company. During the first quarter of the twentieth century, Clearfield Bituminous, a New York Central subsidiary, its miners, and their town prospered. The company abided by the Jacksonville scale until it expired on April 1, 1927. Like other operators, Clearfield Bituminous hoped for a readjustment of wage scales. When wage adjustments did not materialize, the company opened on a non-union basis. Deputy sheriffs took control of the streets and the mines. Management imported strikebreakers and, in doing so, professed a curious paternalism. Superintendent F. D. Welsh assured observers that his company never hired "colored men," "Spaniards," "Mexicans," or "people of the class." His company believed that there were many efficient black miners, but they were not welcome in his mining camps. Welsh explained that employment of blacks would decrease the "standing of the community, particularly its schools."

Rossiter was a company town and virtually everything in it belonged to Clearfield Bituminous. The only properties to which the striking miners had access were the two lots owned by the Magyar Presbyterian Church. The titles to those lots had been donated by Clearfield Bituminous to the original congregation years before the strike. When the original congregation faded away, the property was ceded to a lay preacher and his flock. The preacher happened to be the vice-president of the Rossiter UMW local. The strategic value of the church lots was apparent, because the strikebreakers had to pass it on their way to work. "Church services" coincided with shift changes at the mine, and passing scabs probably had things sung and said to them that were not found in hymnals or prayer-books. Judge Langham was probably correct when he perceived that "We'll Get You Bye and Bye" was sung in a way designed to intimidate strikebreakers. However, his heavy-handed insensitivity and excessive judicial zeal characterized a court system clearly unsympathetic to the cause of the union miner.

Faced with a number of Rossiters, the UMW was bankrupt by spring 1928. Lewis called off the strike in July. The collapse of the strike was not caused by pusillanimous leadership, corruption, or mismanagement. The anti-union faction in the UMW blamed John L. Lewis for the failure, but the rank and file stood with their president even in defeat. "No Backward Step" was, in fact, the goal of the union miner. Unlike 1922, Lewis left no one to die on the vine; the UMW men understood that they had simply been beaten by a stronger party. The union miners were dispersed, and their union reduced to a shell, but the UMW was not destroyed. The union would remain dormant for six years, and then rise again when better times arrived in 1933. [Carl I. Meyerhuber, Jr.]

FURTHER READING

Dubofsky, Melvyn, and Warren Van Tine. *John L. Lewis: A Biography.* New York: Quadrangle, 1977.

Filippelli, Ronald. "Diary of a Strike: George Medrick and the Coal Strike of 1927 in Western Pennsylvania." *Pennsylvania History*, Vol. 43 (July 1976), pp. 253–266.

Meyerhuber, Carl I., Jr. *Less Than Forever: The Rise and Decline of Union Solidarity in Western Pennsylvania, 1914–1948.* Selinsgrove, PA: Susquehanna University Press, 1987.

o   o   o

BITUMINOUS COAL STRIKE OF 1943. In 1943, most bituminous coal miners were covered by a variation of the labor agreement between the United Mine Workers (UMW) and two industry groups representing the northern and the southern coal operators. When the parties assembled in March of that year to negotiate a new contract, the American people, engulfed in World War II, watched with trepidation. Despite having initially taken a cooperative stance in terms of the war effort, the union came to the bargaining table with an ambitious list of proposals. John L. Lewis, the combative president of the miners' union, soon made it clear that he intended to aggressively pursue the UMW's demands.

Lewis, who had staked his standing in the labor movement on the defeat of Franklin D. Roosevelt in 1939, had chafed under the President's wartime domestic policies. The UMW leader felt that labor had been asked to make inordinate sacrifices relative to business and industry. Most disturbing to Lewis was the government's intrusion into labor–management relations, particularly the creation of the National War Labor Board (NWLB) and its imposition of the "Little Steel Formula." The formula, designed to control the wage demands of American workers, limited pay increases to 15 percent beginning January 1, 1941. This limit, presumably, would last until the war's conclusion.

The demands the UMW presented to the coal operators on March 10, 1943, clearly exceeded the NWLB formula. At the top of the miners' list was a two-dollar-a-day wage increase. In addition, the union proposed double time pay for Sunday work, paid vacation benefits, and an end to the practice of charging miners for equipment, tools, and materials used in their work. Completing the list of demands was a proposal to pay miners for the time they spent traveling to and from their work underground. The portal-to-portal pay request would become a crucial issue in the negotiations.

With the March 31, 1943, contract expiration date fast approaching, and with the UMW's policy of no contract–no work in mind, the union and the operators agreed to a thirty-day extension. Little progress was made during the month of April as the mine operators looked increasingly to the NWLB for support in their resistance to the union's demands. On April 22, with only days left before the extension expired, Secretary of Labor Frances Perkins certified the dispute to the NWLB.

Lewis and his membership viewed the NWLB, and its wage policies, with great resentment. For his part, Lewis refused to cooperate with the NWLB, even threatening to end the thirty-day contract extension if the industry did not continue negotiations. The miners followed suit by engaging in spontaneous, scattered walkouts to protest the involvement of the NWLB. As the number of miners off the job grew to 60,000, the NWLB suspended its proceedings. The dispute was again at a standstill. It would take the direct involvement of the President to get the mines back into production.

Roosevelt moved quickly. In an April 29 telegram to Lewis, the President called on all miners to return to work on behalf of the war effort. He went on to state that "if work at the mines is not resumed by ten o'clock Saturday morning [May 1], I shall use all the power vested in me as President and as Commander-in-Chief of the Army and Navy to protect the national interest and to prevent further interference with the successful prosecution of the war." When the miners failed to appear at the mines on the first of May, Roosevelt was forced to follow through on his pledge.

The President's primary objective was to resume the production of coal. Ideally he wanted to do this without appearing to surrender to Lewis. Few viable alternatives, however, were available to him. Eventually he chose to seize and operate the mines on behalf of the United States Government. On May 4, with the encouragement of John L. Lewis, the miners went to work under the American flag. At the same time the

government announced that even though it now operated the mines, it would not negotiate with the union. The UMW would be required to continue bargaining with the industry under NWLB supervision.

When Lewis sent the miners back to work, he set another strike date for June 1. While some progress toward a settlement was made, movement was slow and on June 1, approximately 500,000 miners again walked off the job. This time, however, they were on strike against the government. Because the NWLB would not allow the union and the industry to continue negotiations as long as a strike was ongoing, Lewis decided to engage in a strategic retreat. On June 7, UMW miners returned to work, with June 20 set as the next bargaining deadline.

When NWLB efforts to settle the dispute failed in the ensuing weeks, the stage was set for the third walkout in two months. Like the previous strike against the government, the June 20 walkout was a short one; Lewis ordered his members to return to work on June 22. Hemmed in by the NWLB, and with few options available to him, Lewis made the decision to bide his time while the government operated the mines. Couching his decision in the most patriotic of terms, Lewis this time agreed to a longer extension of the contract. The next strike deadline was set for October 31.

Lewis' game of cat-and-mouse with the coal industry and the United States Government was not without cost. While Lewis and the UMW had previously earned the resentment of the American public, their actions in the midst of the war swelled the crescendo of fear and loathing to new levels. Lewis was vilified on the nation's editorial pages; his reputation was further sullied by widely published letters from servicemen condemning the mine workers' walkout. One such serviceman expressed his disgust in a letter that ended, "speaking for the American soldier, John Lewis, damn your coal-black soul." The ongoing dispute also had ramifications in the legislative arena. On June 25, the U.S. Senate voted to override President Roosevelt's veto of the Smith-Connally War Labor Disputes Act. This legislation gave statutory powers to the NWLB, granting it increased authority to settle disputes such as the miners' strikes. Viewed by many as a blatantly anti-labor proposal, the atmosphere created by the strike of 1943 paved the way for its passage.

Clearly on the defensive, Lewis and the miners' union embarked on a gambit that they thought might break the deadlock. Once, in July and again in September the union negotiated agreements with the Illinois Coal Operators' Association and presented them to the NWLB for approval. The UMW hoped that these agreements would serve as a pattern for an industry-wide settlement. Both contracts included provisions previously recommended by the NWLB, as well as portal-to-portal pay and other gains. In both cases, the NWLB rejected the contracts as being in violation of the government's anti-inflation program. The second agreement was rejected on October 26. On October 31, with the expiration of the four-month contract extension, 500,000 miners once again laid down their tools.

The shutdown of the coal industry again spurred the direct involvement of the President in the dispute. While the extension had been in effect, the government had gradually returned control of the mines to the operators. On November 1, the President ordered the mines placed under government supervision for a second time. In this instance, the President went a step further, ordering the secretary of the interior, Harold Ickes, to negotiate directly with the UMW. Bargaining quickly ensued, and on November 3 a Memorandum of Agreement was signed between the union and the government. The miners promptly returned to work.

The Lewis–Ickes agreement incorporated those provisions of the second Illinois contract approved by the NWLB. The provisions of the pact not approved were reworked in an effort to comply with NWLB guidelines. The contract that was negotiated between the government and the UMW served as the basis for settlements with the northern and southern operators. Eventually both agreements were approved by the NWLB, although it would be months before all the mines were returned to their owners. With the reversion of the northern mines to private ownership on May 31, 1944, this turbulent chapter in the history of the coal industry closed. Lewis had won at least some of the gains he had fought so hard for, including portal-to-portal pay; the price, however, had been high. [Paul F. Clark]

FURTHER READING

Dubofsky, Melvyn, and Warren Van Tine. *John L. Lewis: A Biography.* New York: Quadrangle, 1977.

Lichtenstein, Nelson. *Labor's War at Home: The CIO in World War II.* Cambridge, U. K.: Cambridge University Press, 1982.

o   o   o

BITUMINOUS COAL STRIKE OF 1946. At the conclusion of World War II, the United States faced the challenge of reconverting to a peacetime economy without creating widespread unemployment or allowing rapid wage and price increases that would result in spiraling inflation. Labor, for its part, was determined that the gains it had made and held during the war would not be lost in the face of an employer counterattack, as had been the case following World War I. Hopes for an orderly and peaceful reconversion were soon dashed as a flood of strikes swept over the country in late 1945 and early 1946. From steel to auto, meat-packing to electrical, industries nationwide were shut down as unions tried to insure that their members would share in the prosperity of the postwar era. The turmoil of the period would soon extend to the coal industry.

On March 2, 1946, UMW president John L. Lewis communicated to the bituminous coal industry his intention to reopen negotiations. When the United Mine Workers (UMW) and the coal operators opened talks on March 12, Lewis proposed not only significant wage increases and improvements in working conditions but also the establishment of an employer-financed welfare fund that would provide health care and retirement benefits to miners and their families. Talks proceeded slowly and on April 1st, with the expiration of the old contract, some 400,000 miners walked off the job. On April 11, Lewis broke off negotiations with a flourish, telling the operators that "To cavil further is futile. We trust that time, as it shrinks your purse, may modify your niggardly and anti-social propensities."

Over the next several weeks, both the strike and negotiations continued intermittently. By mid-May, with both parties rejecting a presidential request for arbitration, the dispute was clearly at an impasse. On May 21, with the nation's coal supplies dwindling and no settlement imminent, President Truman ordered his secretary of the interior, Julius Krug, to take over the mines on behalf of the United States Government. He also directed Krug to negotiate an agreement with the UMW. Eight days later, on May 29, Krug and Lewis signed a contract ending the coal strike, at least temporarily. The contract between the miners' union and the government contained a number of significant advances for UMW members, including a substantial wage increase, better vacation pay, and improved safety protection. Most importantly, the new agreement established a health and welfare fund financed by a five-cent royalty on each ton of coal mined.

While operating the mines under the contract it had signed with Lewis, the government spent the next several months attempting to bring the union and the industry together in order to return the mines to private ownership. At the same time that slow progress was being made in this direction, the UMW engaged in a running dispute with the government over the interpretation and administration of their agreement. Before a new contract could be reached with the operators, Lewis surprised the Truman administration, and the nation by demanding on October 21 that the government negotiate a new agreement with the UMW. At the same time he set a strike deadline of November 20.

Secretary Krug rejected Lewis' charge that the government had breeched its agreement with the miners, as well as the UMW's position that the contract could be reopened unilaterally. In support of his position, Krug produced a formal opinion from the U.S. Attorney General suggesting that the union did not have legal grounds to terminate the contract. In a last-ditch effort to avert a confrontation between Lewis and the government, Krug engaged in a futile attempt to bring the union and the industry together. Lewis refused to cooperate or to rescind his strike call, complaining in his characteristically grandiloquent style, "You [the government] now, at the last hour, of the last day, yield to the blandishments and soothing siren voice of the operators and seek to place the United Mine Workers of America and its members between Scylla and Charybdis."

The Truman administration moved quickly to head off a walkout, applying for a federal injunction to restrain the miners' union from striking the government-run coal industry. Judge T. Alan Goldsborough approved the government's request on November 18. Since Lewis had originally announced that the union's contract with the government would terminate on November 20, which in the context of the UMW tradition of no contract–no work meant that a strike would then ensue, the court was in essence placing responsibility for the pending walkout on Lewis' shoulders. Lewis, however, did not rescind the termination date. On November 20, without a formal strike notice, bituminous miners across the nation refused to report for work.

On November 25, with public opinion squarely behind the government, the Truman administration asked Judge Goldsborough to hold Lewis and the UMW in contempt of court for violating the November 18 injunction. Following several days of hearings in federal district court, Lewis and the UMW were found guilty of civil contempt on December 3. Judge Goldsborough subsequently fined Lewis $10,000 and the UMW $3.5 million. The UMW immediately initiated an appeal to the Supreme Court. On December 7, Lewis, citing a pending coal shortage, directed his members to return to work.

Three months later, the Supreme Court sustained the ruling of the federal district court on the grounds that the government was within its power to obtain an injunction when the nation's welfare was threatened by a strike. The Supreme Court did, however, find the $3.5 million judgment against the UMW excessive and reduced it to $7 million, while maintaining the $10,000 fine against Lewis. The reduction of the fine was predicated on Lewis' compliance with the court's order to officially withdraw its contract termination notice. On March 19, 1947, Lewis complied and withdrew the notice.

Throughout these proceedings, the bituminous coal mines remained under government supervision. In the spring of 1947, prior to the expiration of the government's authority to run the mines on June 30, the Truman administration brought the union and the operators together to negotiate a new agreement. By

mid-July, the industry and the union had signed a contract. The agreement that was eventually reached with the operators included most of the provisions originally demanded by the union more than a year earlier, including the establishment of an employer-financed fund to provide health and retirement benefits to miners and their families. It is ironic that this episode, which included one of John L. Lewis' most humbling defeats, culminated in the attainment of one of his most lasting achievements—the UMW health and welfare fund. [Paul F. Clark]

FURTHER READING

Alinsky, Saul. *John L. Lewis: An Unauthorized Biography*. New York: Vintage Books, 1970.

Dubofsky, Melvin, and Warren Van Tine. *John L. Lewis: A Biography*. New York: Quadrangle, 1977.

o   o   o

BITUMINOUS COAL STRIKE OF 1977–1978. The coal strike of 1977–1978 was the longest nationwide strike in the history of an industry accustomed to periodic disruptions. The dispute between the United Mine Workers of America (UMW) and the Bituminous Coal Operators' Association (BCOA) largely centered on two issues—the right of miners to strike over grievances during the course of the contract and the future of the jointly administered fund that provided health benefits to UMW members. It would take 110 days, a rapidly increasing power shortage as the coal reserves of public utilities ran out, and the intervention of the President of the United States to finally bring the walkout to an end. Among the key factors contributing to the long impasse were the disarray and disorganization of the union's leadership and industry leaders who viewed the negotiations as a unique opportunity to win long-sought gains at the bargaining table. Given the enormous costs of the strike, in the end, neither side could claim victory.

The work stoppage was set in the context of a union in turmoil. Beginning with the election challenge, and subsequent murder, of union reformer Jock Yablonski in 1969, and continuing with the election of the Miners For Democracy (MFD) reform administration in 1972, the years leading up to 1977–1978 had been tumultuous for the UMW. The months just prior to the strike witnessed a wave of wildcat strikes that had sent shock waves through the industry. In addition, the union had just suffered through a bitter and divisive national election that saw the incumbent president, Arnold Miller, barely win reelection in a three-way race. These events, combined with the uninspired leadership style of the Miller administration, had left the union unprepared and unorganized as national contract talks opened on October 6, 1977.

The events of the preceding months also had an impact on the substance of the negotiations. The wildcat strikes of the 1970s were caused, at least in part, by a perception on the part of rank-and-file miners that the designated method of settling disputes with management, the grievance and arbitration procedure, was being abused by the coal companies. Many miners believed that the industry used arbitration as a tactical weapon, inevitably pushing problems to the costly and time-consuming last step of the grievance process. Based on perceived popular support among the membership, the Miller administration conceived a right-to-strike scheme as the solution to this problem. The UMW proposed that during the course of a contract, if a local dispute arose that could not be settled in the grievance procedure, the local union would have the option to arbitrate the dispute or to strike. In the heat of the election campaign, Arnold Miller had made a strong political commitment to this plan. The right-to-strike option, therefore, became a central issue in contract talks.

Skeptical of the union's claim that the implementation of the right-to-strike option would, ultimately, reduce wildcat activity and improve labor–management relations in the industry, the BCOA, the bargaining representative of most of the major coal companies, rejected the proposal out of hand. On the heels of a period that had seen man-days lost to wildcat strikes rise from 419,200 in 1973 to a record 1,940,300 in 1976, the industry made it clear that the return of labor stability was one of its highest priorities for this round of negotiations. Not only did coal management reject the union's right-to-strike proposal as anathema to the goal of labor peace, it proposed a far-reaching plan of its own to deal with the wildcat issue. This proposal involved a systematic set of disciplinary measures, including fines, suspensions, and discharge, that would be levied against striking miners. The chasm separating the union and the industry on this issue alone suggested that the 1978 talks would be difficult ones.

The list of contentious issues, however, did not end with the right-to-strike question. Just four months prior to the opening of negotiations, the jointly administered UMW Welfare and Retirement Funds had notified miners of a cut in medical benefits effective July 1. For the first time in the thirty-year history of the Funds, miners would be forced to share the cost of medical care. The rationale for the cut was that the Funds' income, which was based on royalties from each ton of coal produced, had been severely reduced by lost production due to wildcat strikes. Whatever its cause, the erosion of their blanket medical coverage was a tremendous blow to the UMW membership. Sensing the importance of this issue, Miller took the position early in the talks that the union would not move forward in negotiations until the industry agreed to cancel the cuts completely and restore health benefits.

Industry negotiators, however, were reluctant to discuss the issue as a precondition to other issues. From their point of view, the Funds-health benefits issue was closely tied to the industry's number one bargaining concern—labor stability. With the parties at loggerheads on these two key issues, the scene was set for a long impasse.

By the December 6 strike deadline, after two months of bargaining, very little progress had been made. Only the two major issues, labor stability and health benefits, had been seriously discussed, and there had been very little movement on either issue by either side. Despite some suggestions by Arnold Miller that the contract deadline be extended, coal miners at mines all across America walked off the job at 12:01 A.M., December 6, 1977.

From the first day of negotiations, the UMW leadership experienced problems, separate from the substantive bargaining issues, that had considerable effect on the bargaining process. Perhaps the major problem in this regard was the state of readiness of the union for nationwide bargaining with the coal industry.

The Miller-led UMW negotiating team came to the table unprepared to engage in the complex process of industrywide negotiations. The union's disarray was rooted in the fact that of all the international officers and staff who had successfully negotiated the adminis-tration's first contract in 1984, Arnold Miller was virtually the only significant figure who remained. Staff defections and Miller's falling out with his vice-president and secretary-treasurer were responsible for this situation. In addition, Miller had devoted all of his time and energy in the last year to his June reelection bid. As appeals and challenges to that election dragged on through October, little attention was given to preparations for the upcoming talks. So disorganized was the UMW when it entered negotiations that the Federal Mediation and Conciliation Service (FMCS), a government

dispute resolution agency, took the highly unusual step of lining up staff and consultants for the union in an effort to aid the negotiations process.

Even when Miller finally turned his attention to the business at hand, he was a man whose energy had been sapped by infighting and poor health. His behavior had reportedly become unpredictable and his attendance at bargaining sessions become sporadic. Miller's uneven performance only served to exacerbate the union's troubles at the bargaining table.

Although talks continued after the December 6 shutdown, progress was slow as the union continued to refuse to tie the health benefits issue to the question of labor stability. Late in January, however, the pace of negotiations picked up, and on February 6, negotiators reached a tentative settlement. In addition to a substantial wage increase, the proposed agreement provided for a fundamental change in the provision of health benefits. In addition to reducing these benefits, the proposed agreement would have replaced the jointly-administered, industry-financed health fund with company-by-company insurance plans that included deductible fees. Also included was a labor stability clause that allowed coal companies to fine and fire miners for unauthorized work stoppages.

Opposition to the proposal within the union was swift and sharp. This dissatisfaction was reflected in the pact's rejection by the union's bargaining council, a group composed of district level officials that constituted the first step in the contract ratification process. On February 15, at President Jimmy Carter's personal request, contract talks resumed. The result of these negotiations was a slightly revised version of the original proposal, which, like the first pact, was overwhelmingly rejected by the bargaining council.

Under increasing pressure from the White House, negotiations continued. In late February, the UMW and the coal industry reached yet another tentative agreement. This proposed settlement was based largely on an agreement the UMW had recently signed with the non-BCOA Pittsburg and Midway Coal Company. The contract was similar to the February 6 pact in terms of wages and the implementation of a new health benefits system; the labor stability language, however, was drastically different. Industry proposals to discipline miners who participated in wildcat strikes were dropped, with the exception that coal companies still retained the right to discharge anyone who instigated such job actions. As in the previous proposals, the UMW's right-to-strike option was not included. Since this tentative settlement was based on one previously approved by the bargaining council, the union's leadership moved quickly to win membership ratification. Dissatisfaction with the pact was evident in the coalfields however, and on March 5, UMW members rejected the proposal by a two-to-one margin.

The rejection of a possible settlement elicited strong reaction from the public and President Carter. As coal supplies fell to critical levels forcing schools to close or drastically reduce their energy use, and as violence against non-union miners, coal truckers, and company property increased, so did opposition to the strike among the American public. At the same time, President Carter intensified his involvement in the dispute by calling for a Taft-Hartley injunction. This action met with strong opposition from UMW miners. When a temporary back-to-work order was issued by a U.S. District Court on March 10, the order was largely ignored. The only apparent effect of the government's intervention was to escalate tensions and increase the chance of a violent confrontation.

This confrontation, however, never materialized. The UMW and the BCOA resumed negotiations, and on March 14 they once again reached a tentative agreement. The following day the bargaining council approved the pact by a twenty-two to seventeen vote. Relieved of the pressure of the Taft-Hartley injunction when a Washington judge denied the government's request for a continuance of the original back-to-work order, UMW miners accepted the proposed contract by a 57 to 43 percent margin on March 24. During the week of March 27, UMW miners returned to the mines, marking an end to the 110-day strike.

In the weeks and months following the strike, miners, the press, and the public speculated about what the strike had accomplished. Had the mine workers won? Had the gains justified the losses and sacrifices of a record strike? Or had the miners simply been beaten; worn down by the hard line of the coal operators and the weakness and ineptitude of their own leadership?' Without question, the final pact negotiated by union and industry bargainers did include significant concessions from the BCOA, many of which were not included in the previous pacts rejected by the bargaining council and the membership.

From the union's point of view, perhaps the biggest achievement was preventing the industry from winning language addressing the "labor stability" issue. The resolution of this issue, however, was not really a victory for the union, as a broad arbitration precedent allowing operators to discharge wildcat strike leaders remained intact. In addition, the UMW's high priority demand for the right-to-strike had also been dropped.

Beyond the labor stability question, the union did convince the BCOA to moderate its proposals on revamping the health benefits plan. While the union bargainers could not keep the free medical care miners had enjoyed under the UMW funds for thirty years, and were forced to agree to the funds' replacement with company-by-company private insurance plans, the union did win a reduction of the maximum deductibles UMW members would have to pay for medical care in the future.

The wage offer in the approved agreement was similar to those made in the rejected agreements. Miners' wages would increase $2.40 an hour, or more than 37 percent, over three years. As in the other key areas, the UMW's accomplishments here were watered down by concessions to the industry. Specifically, the operators gained the right to establish production incentive programs at mines where miners voted their approval.

While the UMW won other concessions, very few of the demands spelled out at the 1976 UMW convention were included in the new agreement. The union's role in the 1977–1978 negotiations, and throughout the 110-day strike, had been largely defensive. Whether the successful ratification vote reflected support for the contract or desperation brought on by the long strike was not clear. What was clear was that the 1977–1978 negotiations and strike had further fractionalized an already divided union. [Paul F. Clark]

FURTHER READING

Clark, Paul F. *The Miners Fight for Democracy: Arnold Miller and the Reform of the United Mine Workers.* Ithaca, NY: ILR Press, 1981.

Seltzer, Curtis. *Fire in the Hole: Miners and Managers in the American Coal Industry.* Lexington, KY: The University Press of Kentucky, 1985.

o   o   o

BOSTON HOUSE CARPENTERS' STRIKE OF 1825. The first great strike that centered on the issue of the ten-hour workday began in Boston when the master builders refused the demand for shorter workdays from their journeymen carpenters, nearly 600 of whom took part in the strike.

The journeymen chose the timing of their strike carefully. They called it in the spring when the building season was in full swing. In addition, a recent fire and a push for public improvements increased the demand for the skills of building trades workers of all kinds. The journeymen called for "ten hours of faithful labour" to constitute a day's work. They also called for an increase in wages they termed "derogatory to the principles not only of justice but humanity." They argued that journeymen, housewrights, and carpenters could not maintain their families on existing wages. But from the beginning it appears that the issue of wages was secondary to that of shorter hours. Both the carpenters and the master builders concentrated on that key issue.

The master builders received the demand for shorter hours with "surprise and regret" and labeled a combination of workers to reduce hours "fraught with numerous and pernicious evils." The argument of the master builders is interesting in that it reflects the assumption of upward mobility in the trade by stressing that when the journeymen became master builders themselves, they would have to live with the new shorter hours in the trade when hiring their own journeymen. This was hardly likely, since by 1825 the construction industry was largely dependent upon merchant capitalists for financing, and most journeymen could be classified as propertyless wage earners.

Also significant was the argument that shorter hours would lead both apprentices and journeymen to "temptations and improvident practices" from which they were protected by working from sunrise to sunset. The master builders feared the consequences of the measure on the morals and well-being of society. Back of this condemnation of the shorter-hours movement on moral and traditional grounds lay the economic argument. No matter how justified the change to ten-hour workdays, contracts for the season had already been signed, and they were predicated on the existing wage and hour structure. In the face of this dilemma, the master builders resolutely refused to consider any changes and also refused to hire any journeyman associated with the movement.

But the resolution of the conflict, which resulted in defeat for the journeymen, depended more on the power of the merchant capitalists than on the determination of the master builders or the house carpenters. While the journeymen were employed directly by the house carpenters, the master builders, as the master carpenters were called, were in turn employed by the prospective owners who financed the projects. It was these "gentlemen engaged in building the present season" who resolved that the actions of the journeymen were a departure from practices that had prevailed in New England "from time immemorial." Any concession to the house carpenters, they argued, would open the door to idleness and vice among the entire working class and eventually to a "spirit of discontent and insubordination to which our native mechanics have hitherto been strangers." In summary, the gentlemen engaged in building called on the public at large to resist combinations of workers which, because they created an unnatural monopoly of labor, were unjust and injurious to all other classes. In the face of such consequences, the merchant capitalists resolved to support the master builders at "whatever sacrifice and inconvenience." What they meant was that they were willing to extend their contracts and, if necessary, to suspend building completely.

In the face of this united front between capitalists and contractors, the strike collapsed and the sunrise to sundown system remained the hallmark of building trade work in Boston for several more years. [Ronald L. Filippelli]

FURTHER READING

Commons, John R., et al. *History of Labour in the United States*, Vol 1. New York: Macmillan, 1936.

o   o   o

BOSTON MASSACRE OF 1770. Although it is widely accepted that colonial workers played an active role in the revolutionary movement, one of the best examples of working-class unity for political ends and the solidarity of urban workers occurred as the result of a dispute over a job at a Boston ropewalk. Part of the hostility of Boston workers toward British soldiers stemmed from the fact that when off duty, the redcoats often competed for jobs with colonial workers at much lower wages.

On March 2, 1770, three British privates in the 29th regiment sought work at the ropewalk belonging to John Gray. When a journeyman, William Green, insulted them, the soldiers challenged him to a fight. After a brief scuffle, the soldiers left and returned with several companions, who were also driven off. Once again the soldiers sought aid and were joined by thirty or forty redcoats armed with clubs and sabres. As a response to this show of force, workers from neighboring ropewalks came to Green's assistance and turned the intruders away. In order to reduce the tension, the employer, John Gray, discharged several journeymen whom the British commander accused of instigating the trouble.

On the evening of March 5, some British soldiers, smarting from their humiliation in the clashes with the workers, beat up a number of Bostonians. The incident resulted directly from the taunting of the soldiers by a barber's apprentice. When a soldier struck the apprentice, a melee resulted. The soldiers fired, killing a number of persons, including Sam Gray, one of the ropewalk workers who had been involved in the original dispute. News of the events of March 5 spread rapidly throughout the colonies, and resentment over the incident, popularly known as the Boston Massacre, fueled the revolutionary spirit growing among the colonists. [Ronald L. Filippelli]

FURTHER READING

Morris, Richard B. *Government and Labor in Early America*. New York: Harper and Row, 1946.

o   o   o

BOSTON POLICE STRIKE OF 1919. During World War I, workers generally supported America's war effort and attempted to maintain levels of productivity without resort to strikes or other disruptive activities. Under the authority of the War Labor Board, many employers entered into collective bargaining arrangements which provided labor peace and stability in the industrial relations system. That tenuous labor–management accord disintegrated following the armistice, however, and there was a tremendous resurgence of worker militancy. A wave of strikes spread throughout American industry in 1919, including the massive work stoppage in the steel industry and the general strike in the city of Seattle. Like their private sector counterparts, the Boston police force attempted to improve their wages and working conditions through industrial action.

In 1919, rank-and-file police officers in Boston worked from seventy-two to ninety-eight hours per week, depending upon shifts and duties. They were paid between $900 and $1,400 annually, out of which they paid $207 for uniforms and equipment. The inflationary pressures resulting from the war and the escalation of wages and prices in other sectors of the economy particularly exacerbated the problem. Unskilled factory workers in the Boston area, for example, often earned from $75 to $100 per week, while many police officers earned less than $23 weekly.

Between 1906 and 1918, the department was headed by Police Commissioner Stephen O'Meara, a man of integrity and compassion who commanded the respect of most officers. Following O'Meara's death in December 1918, Edwin Curtis was appointed commissioner, and he demonstrated little sympathy for the grievances of the police officers or their attempts to negotiate over working conditions. According to one study, Curtis was generally viewed as "an uncompromising martinet with no previous experience in police administration and no great affection for the Boston Irish."

The immediate cause of the Boston strike was the connection between the police department and organized labor. Traditionally, the American Federation of Labor (AFL) had declined to issue charters to local organizations of police officers. But at its convention in June 1919, the AFL reversed that policy, and a number of police unions, including the Boston local, applied for a charter; the Boston group became affiliated with the AFL in August. In response, Commissioner Curtis promptly amended the rules of the department. Rule 35, Section 19, made clear that the AFL affiliation jeopardized the police officers' jobs. The rule stated, "No member of the force shall belong to any organization, club, or body composed of present and past members of the force which is affiliated with or part of any organization, club, or body outside of the department. . . ." To implement the new policy, Curtis prepared a form letter which notified the recipient that he had been discharged from the service. One thousand copies of the letters were printed.

Undaunted, the police officers continued to meet as a union and elected a slate of officers to be their official representatives. Curtis refused to yield on the principle of affiliation; he filed charges against a total of nineteen officers, commencing with the union leaders, for violation of the rule and instituted disciplinary proceedings against them. Fearing the likelihood of a strike, Boston mayor Andrew

Peters appointed a committee of citizens headed by James Storrow to mediate the dispute between Curtis and the rank-and-file officers.

During late August and early September, the Storrow Committee studied conditions within the force and developed a compromise plan which was supported by major Boston newspapers. Among other concessions, the union executive committee agreed to give up its AFL charter and to cooperate with a separate committee in investigating its grievances. The proposals were made known to the public on September 7, but on that same day, Commissioner Curtis issued his decision upholding the suspension of the officers who had violated the nonaffiliation order. Police officers held a mass meeting on September 8 to determine their course of action, and of the 1,136 officers voting, 1,134 voted to strike. Shortly thereafter, Storrow and Mayor Peters met with Calvin Coolidge, who had been elected governor of Massachusetts in 1918, but Coolidge declined to become involved in the situation.

The strike began on the evening of September 9. That night there were numerous incidents of looting and violence in various parts of the city. On the following morning, Mayor Peters declared that a state of riot existed, and, under statutory authority, he ordered the state militia to impose order in the city. By the evening of September 10, troops were present throughout Boston. In a disturbance in South Boston, the militia shot and killed three people and injured several others; that event effectively quelled further riots in the area.

On Thursday, September 11, Governor Coolidge assumed an active role in the affair. He sent an additional contingent of militia into the city and placed Commissioner Curtis rather than Mayor Andrews in charge of the troops. Coolidge also contacted Franklin D. Roosevelt, then secretary of the Navy, to request federal support if necessary. In anticipation of a possible expansion of the strike, Coolidge mustered a reserve force of 40,000 guardsmen and militia.

Sympathetic unions in Boston and throughout the country supported the police strike. There was a call for a general strike of all workers in Boston, and the Massachusetts Federation of Labor authorized a strike vote by all Boston locals. Although the general strike did not materialize, many labor groups continued to contribute financial and moral aid to the strikers. Samuel Gompers, president of the AFL, telegraphed Coolidge on September 13 in an effort to resolve the dispute. Gompers proposed that all strikers be permitted to return to work, as if there had been no previous disciplinary action. Coolidge replied that he had no authority to interfere with the maintenance of discipline in the department. More aggressively, Gompers then asked Coolidge to remove cCommissioner Curtis and to satisfactorily adjust the legitimate grievances of the police officers.

Coolidge's response earned him a national-political reputation. First, Coolidge adamantly refused to remove Curtis as commissioner, stating that Curtis acted on authority vested in him by the people. Second, Coolidge pointed out, the strikers had abandoned their duty. That fact, Coolidge continued, was the primary consideration determining the outcome of the strike. Coolidge stated:

Here, the Policemen's Union left their duty, an action which President Wilson described as a crime against civilization. Your asserting that the Commissioner was wrong cannot justify the wrong of leaving the city unguarded. That furnished the opportunity; the criminal element furnished the action. There is no right to strike against the public safety by anybody, anywhere, any time. You ask that the public safety again be placed in the hands of these same policemen while they continue in disobedience to the laws of Massachusetts and in their refusal to obey the orders of the Police Department. Nineteen men have been tried and removed. Others having abandoned their duty, there places have, under the law, been declared vacant in the opinion of the Attorney General.

Consequently, Coolidge concluded, there was no opportunity for compromise and he declined to take any action toward reinstatement.

Public sentiment was overwhelmingly in favor of Coolidge's strong stand against the strikers. In the increasingly conservative political climate, Coolidge became a champion of the forces of law and order and a challenger of radical labor factions. Citizens throughout the country wrote congratulatory letters; to handle the volume of mail, the post office increased its deliveries to sixteen a day. Some weeks later, Coolidge issued a second statement concerning reinstatement of the strikers; he was even more vitriolic toward the police than on the first occasion. "The authority of the Commonwealth cannot be intimidated," Coolidge said. "To place the maintenance of the public security in the hands of a body of men who have attempted to destroy it would be to flout the sovereignty of the laws the people have made. . . . There is no middle ground." Again, Coolidge's political stature increased. He was reelected governor by a large margin, and in 1920, the Republicans chose him as the vice-presidential candidate on the Harding ticket. Following Harding's death in 1923, Coolidge became President of the United States.

The city of Boston gradually hired new police officers to replace the strikers. Because there were initially few applicants for the jobs, the city was forced to relax its hiring standards, to increase the starting pay for officers, and to provide additional fringe benefits such as a uniform allowance. With such improved economic benefits—many of which were requested by the strikers—the commissioner had attained a full police complement by the end of 1919.

The consequences of the 1919 Boston police strike were momentous. Nearly 1,100 striking police officers lost their jobs, and the city incurred the financial and social burden of the militia's occupation of the city and the deaths of and injuries to members of the public. The intense public outcry against the strike permeated police labor relations for many years. The ramifications remain evident in public sector labor relations to the present day.

Because the National Labor Relations Act does not cover labor relations in the public sector, states and local governments are free to establish their own systems of collective bargaining. As of 1985, twenty-eight states and the District of Columbia had laws affording police the right to organize and bargain collectively. No state authorizes strikes by police, although a growing number of states do permit strikes by other groups of public employees. Despite that, police strikes do occur. Between 1970 and 1980, a total of 245 unlawful police strikes took place. These strikes were not generally destructive of the civil order of the municipality; in some instances, city authorities were able to provide a stronger police presence during the strike than on a routine patrol day. Accordingly, although police strikes hardly amount to civil anarchy, it is unlikely that they will ever be legalized and accepted by the public. That, in large measure, is the legacy of the Boston Police Strike. [Raymond L. Hogler]

Further Reading

Delaney, John Thomas, and Peter Feuille. "Police." In *Collective Bargaining in American Industry: Contemporary Perspectives and Future Directions.* David Lipsky and Clifford Donn, eds. Lexington, MA: Lexington Books, 1987, pp. 265–306.

Lyons, Richard L. "The Boston Police Strike of 1919." *New England Quarterly*, Vol. 20 (1947), pp. 147–168.

Russell, Francis. *A City in Terror: 1919—The Boston Police Strike.* New York: Viking Press, 1975.

Zibel, Howard J. "The Role of Calvin Coolidge in the Boston Police Strike of 1919." *Industrial and Labor Relations Forum*, Vol. 6 (1969), pp. 299–318.

o   o   o

BOSTON SHIP CARPENTERS' PRO-TEST OF 1675. In 1675, a group of ship carpenters rode one of their number out of Boston on a rail because he had worked in the yard without having served his full seven-year apprenticeship. The carpenters were fined five shillings apiece payable to the colonial government and a like amount payable to the victim. John Roberts and the eight other defendants admitted the charge of having forcibly carried John Langworthy "upon a pole and by violence" from the north end of Boston to the town dock. According to the Boston town records, the defendants justified their conduct on the ground that "he was an interloper and had never served his time to the trade of a ship carpenter and now came to work in theire yard and they understood such things were usuall in England." [Ronald L. Filippelli]

FURTHER READING

Morris, Richard B. *Government and Labor in Early America.* New York: Harper and Row, 1946.

o   o   o

BOSTON SHIP CARPENTERS' TEN-HOUR STRIKE OF 1832. After textiles, shipbuilding reigned as New England's greatest industry in the first half of the nineteenth century. But unlike textiles, which was well on its way to the factory system by 1832, shipbuilding was still carried on by skilled artisans who worked directly for master carpenters, who in turn were employed by merchant capitalists who supplied the raw materials and contracted with the master carpenters for labor. The relationships among merchants, masters, and journeymen could clearly be seen in the struggle of the journeymen ship carpenters for the ten-hour workday.

The ship carpenters, along with several other trades in Boston, were members of the New England Association of Farm-ers, Mechanics, and Other Workingmen which had been founded in 1831. It grew out of the ten-hour workday movement, but when achieving the shorter work day through economic action against employers seemed impossible, the Association turned more toward reform political action.

In the early spring of 1832, the Boston branch of the New England Association passed a resolution in favor of the ten-hour workday. Not only ship carpenters, but caulkers, house carpenters, masons, painters, slaters, and sailmakers apparently responded by trying to persuade their employers. Much of what happened is lost to history, but the fate of the ship carpenters is representative of the difficulties that workers faced when confronted by the power of merchant capitalists in the early years of the nineteenth century.

In response to the demands of the workers, the merchants and shipowners took the lead. They adopted a set of resolutions declaring that the ten-hour workday would seriously damage the industry in Boston by driving work to other cities. Consequently, after May 22 no carpenter or caulker taking part in the demand for ten hours would be employed, nor would work be given to any master carpenter hiring members of the "combination." To put muscle into their stance, the employers contributed $20,000 to an anti-strike fund. The response of the strikers was to repeat their pledge not to work more than ten hours in any day unless they were paid for every extra hour.

Faced with the solidarity of the strikers and pressured by their employers, the master carpenters and caulkers signed an agreement pledging to support the resolutions of the merchant capitalists in regard to the employment of journeymen who were participating in the action for the shorter workday. At the same time they advertised for ship carpenters "not pledged to any combination respecting hours." Carpenters from other cities willing to work during the lockout were offered travel expenses and a guarantee of three months work. The action of the master carpenters and caulkers clearly indicated that the economic ties that bound them to the merchants were stronger than the ties of the trade that bound them to the journeymen.

By July 20 the employers' offensive had apparently succeeded. Having defeated the collective action of their workers, they now permitted the masters to give their workers two hours rest at noon during the hot months of July and August, so long as they understood that they must "commence the day's work at sunrise, and terminate it at sunset." According to one observer, the triumph of the employers had been so great that it had ushered in the "Republicanism of the Dark Ages." [Ronald L. Filippelli]

Further Reading

Commons, John R., et al. *History of Labour in the United States*, Vol. 1. New York: Macmillan, 1936.

o   o   o

BRIGGS MANUFACTURING STRIKE OF 1933. Auto workers of the 1920s often seemed the very model of New Era workers: well paid, semi-skilled, quickly trained, content, and non-unionized. By the time of the **General Motors Sit-Down Strike of 1936–1937** auto workers seemed the model new industrial worker: militant, rights conscious, self-confident, and bent on industrial unionism won by their own strength and solidarity. The most important intermediate event between these two stages of auto workers' history was the Briggs Strike of 1933. The Briggs Manufacturing Company was the largest independent manufacturer of automobile bodies in the entire auto industry. Throughout the 1920s and early 1930s, in its four Detroit plants, Briggs maintained a well-deserved reputation for exceptionally poor working conditions and notably low wages.

Detroit auto workers bitterly commented on Briggs' striking disregard for workers' safety when they advised, "If poison doesn't work, try Briggs." In addition, from 1930 on, Briggs workers complained of an ever accelerating speedup whereby workers were advised to work faster if they wanted to avoid being fired and sent to join depression bread lines. As one Briggs worker described the situation, " . . . the greater the number of unemployed, the greater the effort on the part of those working. As the depression deepened, the men tended to work close to the limit of their capacities."

By the late 1920s, body work, once one of the most highly skilled of all auto jobs, became more routine as skills were subdivided and some of the process of body building became adapted to assembly line construction. Once well regarded and well paid, body workers found both their prestige and their wages lowered while they still remembered better times. They had a reputation for militance and they figured prominently in the informal auto industry walkouts of the 1920s.

The Briggs Strike of 1933 began as workers responded to an increasingly familiar experience—a company announcement of a wage cut. Early January walkouts at the Briggs Waterloo plant (and also at the Motor Products Company) went unreported in the Detroit press but succeeded in persuading the company to revoke the announced wage cuts. Striking resumed on January 22 when metal finishers at the Briggs Highland Park plant announced at an Auto Workers Union (AWU) meeting at Finnish Hall that they had walked off the job. AWU head Phil Raymond advised these workers to go back to work and bring out the entire plant. On January 23 the entire Highland Park plant went on strike, followed on the next day by the other three Briggs plants. The example of the Briggs workers was so powerful that by the end of January workers at

Murray Body were also on strike and Hudson managers had decided to close down in order to avoid a strike. At the strike's peak, close to 12,000 Detroit auto workers had walked off their jobs and approximately 100,000 other workers were affected as other companies, the Ford Motor Company in particular, found it necessary to close down due to lack of bodies.

Briggs strikers quickly began to articulate a list of grievances that went far beyond their initial protest against wage cuts, which reflected years of pent-up frustration with their work. The centerpiece of the strikers' demands was a call for a guaranteed hourly wage that would end the practice of "dead time"—time when workers waited around for production to start up again after company mandated shutdowns of production due to lack of supplies, line problems, or peculiar production schedules. During these times workers were required to be physically at the work site, but they were not paid for their time since they weren't working. Additional demands included a nine-hour workday, a five-day week, time and a half for overtime, the end of compulsory health and accident insurance, gloves and tools to be furnished by the company, and most significantly, recognition of worker-elected shop committees.

The origins of the Briggs strike were spontaneous and rooted in intolerably worsening conditions. The strikers' demands were pragmatic and specific to their situation. When the strikers looked for help in organizing and running their strike, they turned to the only organization in the industry with any experience in strike management or theory—the Auto Workers Union. The AWU was, in 1933, a Communist union, a member of the Trade Union Unity League, and interested in adding members to the Communist Party as well as in organizing an industrial union of auto workers. AWU participation in

the strike led company spokesmen to charge that the strike was Communist led and dominated. Although the Briggs strikers valued AWU president Phil Raymond's pragmatic advice, company charges of Communist domination as well as overdrawn claims by Earl Browder, Communist Party leader, eventually led the strikers to sever their ties to Raymond. However, they remained friendly to the example of union organization represented by the AWU and to the AWU members in their midst. The strikers responded to charges that they were being led astray by Communist organizers with the simple assertion that their strike was "against abominable conditions of labor which goaded practically the whole plant to rise in protest. It is a strike for decent American wages and for decent American conditions of labor."

The Briggs strike resulted neither in the granting of the strikers demands nor the establishment and recognition of a permanent union. After the first week of the strike the company established a guaranteed minimum wage of twenty-five cents an hour. No further concessions were forthcoming. Nonetheless, the Briggs strike stands as a turning point of auto workers' history. In it the strikers proved their militance and solidarity. They mounted a strike that in size, duration, and level of organizational complexity exceeded anything previously seen in the auto industry. In the process they gained a new level of confidence and a sense that the future had to be different. The depression had wiped away many of the more desirable features of auto industry life. Wages were down, company benefits eliminated, and unemployment a constant threat. The 1920s' forms of worker resistance—turnover, restriction of output, sporadic and isolated walkouts—were ineffective in bringing lasting changes to the industry. The Briggs strike helped to convince auto workers that the solution to their situation lie in unionization, the belief that they could mount successful plant-wide strikes, and that in the future such strikes could bring a union into being. [Joyce Shaw Peterson]

FURTHER READING

Detroit Mayor's Non-Partisan Committee. "Report of the Mayor's Non-Partisan Committee on Industrial Disputes (The Fact Finding Committee) in the Matter of the Strike of the Workers at the Briggs Manufacturing Company, Detroit, Michigan." February 21, 1933.

Keeran, Roger. *The Communist Party and the Auto Workers Unions.* Bloomington, IN: University of Indiana Press, 1980.

Peterson, Joyce Shaw. *American Automobile Workers, 1900–1933.* Albany, NY: State University of New York Press, 1987.

o   o   o

BUFFALO, NEW YORK, GRAIN SHOVELLERS' STRIKE OF 1899. Grain shovellers on the Buffalo waterfront struck against the Great Lakes shipping companies, the elevator owners, and the railroads in 1899. The strike paralyzed the nation's largest grain port and had ramifications far beyond its economic impact on the city. The economic and political forces arrayed against the strikers were as unequal in terms of power as they were in most of the great industrial struggles of the last decade of the nineteenth century. Although the grain shovellers were largely Irish, the work force consisted of a polyglot mixture of Irish, Polish, Italian, Swedish, Bohemian; and black workers. Yet the grain shovellers overcame the odds and won their strike. Although largely forgotten by labor historians today, the struggling labor movement of the turn of the century heralded it as one of the great labor victories of the time.

The work of the grain shovellers on the Great Lakes operated under an unusual set of circumstances. Longshoremen did not work for one stevedoring company, as they usually did on the east and west coast ports. Ship captains, elevator managers, and railroad agents all hired longshoremen. In winter, ice closed the ports, which meant that work was heavily seasonal, concentrated in the spring and fall. Saloon owners on the Buffalo waterfront came to act as labor bosses, supplying labor to the employers for a percentage of the men's wages. Many of the saloon owners also ran boarding houses where the immigrant, transient labor force lodged during the warm-weather months.

Thus the saloon became not only the social and domestic center for many workers but also the labor exchange. Not surprisingly, arrangements such as these also made the saloon owners formidable political figures, often controlling the vote of the longshoremen. The system had serious drawbacks for both the workers, who lost much of their wage to the saloon owners, and the companies, who could not predict the cost of loading and unloading ships because of the decentralized nature of the labor contracting in the port. By the time of the strike, however, the system had changed considerably, with a few powerful labor contractors emerging to contract directly and formally with the shipping companies on a long-term basis. These men became, then, the true employers of labor, middlemen between the shippers and the saloon bosses, and consequently, formidable political figures in Buffalo.

Great Lakes Longshoremen first organized in 1884 and 1891 and affiliated with the AFL as the International Longshoremen's Association (ILA). The weak ILA never amounted to much, but it did spur the employers to organize in response. By the beginning of the 1890s the Lake Carriers Association and the Western Elevator Association represented employer interests on the Buffalo waterfront. Also extremely important were the railroads, which controlled most of the elevators and the major shipping companies.

In 1896, a group of freight handlers unionized and demanded recognition from the major labor contractor, William J. Connors. Connors countered with the creation of a rival union for his freight handlers. The split weakened the effort and it collapsed. In the same year the grain shovellers who worked for another large contractor, James Kennedy, also formed a union which was chartered by the ILA as Local 51. Kennedy followed Connors' example and had some of his scoopers form a rival independent union. The grain shovellers struck for an end to the saloon system and a pay increase. But in spite of considerable community support, especially from the churches which wanted to remove the hold of the saloon bosses on the men, the strike collapsed in the midst of the economic downturn of 1896.

By 1899, the economy had revived and so too had the militancy of the workers. By then Connors and Kennedy had merged and tried to force a new wage system on the workers—one that amounted to a severe cut in pay. Local 51 of the ILA had agreed to the changes. The majority of workers, however, rejected the arrangement and formed a new union which they claimed was the legitimate Local 51. The new union refused to work. They wanted the saloon bosses and the contract system eliminated and the old wage system reestablished.

The stand against the saloon system brought the union strong allies among Buffalo's Catholic and Protestant churches and the city's temperance advocates. When the churchmen investigated the way the employment system on the docks worked, they came to understand that the contract pay system and the saloon system were interdependent; so too were the saloon system and the political control of the waterfront wards. These realizations reinforced the support of the clergy for the strikers and gave the union powerful allies in the city's establishment.

This widespread support no doubt accounts for the fact that the strike re-

mained relatively peaceful. When Connors imported strikebreakers, including large numbers of Italian immigrants and blacks, the police assigned extra men to the docks to prevent conflict between the strikers and the strikebreakers. Some violence did occur. Connors loyalists fired on strikers who tried to stop the unloading of a ship. The following day someone shot James Kennedy's nephew to death as he walked on the waterfront. In early May, a third incident attracted the attention of the city. A striker who had returned to work died after a severe beating. Although witnesses testified that he had been assaulted, the police insisted that he had fallen.

Serious as they were, these incidents palled when compared to the violence typical of other labor–management disputes of the era. There were several reasons for this. One was the discipline of the strikers. Especially critical was the union's success in eliciting cooperation from the various, and usually antagonistic, ethnic groups. Another factor was the restraint of the police. Both sides criticized them for favoritism, but it seems clear that their patience and fairness kept the strike from escalating into violence on a number of occasions.

By the beginning of May, the effect of the strike began to be felt across the Great Lakes. The grain trade backed up as ships were stalled as far west as Duluth, Minnesota. The Erie Canal suffered significant drops in tonnage, and empty ships rode in New York harbor waiting to load. The spreading economic impact of the strike brought outside intervention into the dispute between Buffalo grain shovellers and Buffalo labor contractors.

A serious impediment to a settlement was the fact that the union refused to negotiate with Connors and Kennedy. Because they wanted to do away with the saloon system, they demanded direct talks with the Lake Carriers Association. Although the LCA was willing, its contracts with Connors left them open to a suit if they signed independently with the union. Connors, realizing the danger to his empire, recruited strikebreakers throughout the East and Middle West, but the press and city officials opposed the importation of strikebreakers, and the strikers refused to allow the provocation to upset the peaceful conduct of the strike. Indeed, the favorable attitude of the community towards the strikers was a major factor in their ultimate victory.

In May, the LCA asked Buffalo's Catholic bishop to intervene in an attempt to settle the strike. The issue which divided the LCA and the union was the future of the contract system. The union wanted it out completely with the carriers contracting directly with the union for labor. The carriers, willing to return to the old wage scale and to end the saloon system, were not prepared to give up their arrangements with Connors. On May 13, a tentative agreement was reached giving the strikers most of their demands, but continuing the contract system. The question of who would appoint the "boss scooper" of each gang was left to a subcommittee to decide. Pending the compilation of a list of bosses acceptable to the union, current boss scoopers were suspended.

When the men reported to work on May 15, Connors reneged on his promise to honor the agreement. Only those carrying cards in Connors' union could work and many objectionable boss scoopers remained. Meanwhile, the strike had widened as the freight handlers, elevator workers, coal handlers, and marine firemen, inspired by the action of the grain shovellers, also walked out. By the middle of May, the port was effectively closed down, and pressure from the operators to end the contract system and settle the strike increased.

But the long strike had begun to divide the strikers between factions willing to settle for the LCA's last offer and continue the contract system and those who refused to give in on this demand. The split led to a breakdown in the discipline of the strike, and random incidents of violence broke out. Local 51 was clearly losing control of the strike. At this juncture, pressure on the carriers to discard the contract with Connors began to have an effect. The Chicago Board of Trade voted to demand the end of the contract system and railroad and other business interests called for a similar solution. The national officers of the ILA also entered the fray and urged that the workers accept the contract system if they received control over the appointment of boss scoopers.

Pressure from the outside interests finally brought a solution. The strike ended on May 23 with the defeat of Connors. The contract system remained, but Connors gave in on every other issue. The company union was disbanded and a closed-shop agreement for the hiring of grain shovellers went into effect. Connors also lost control over the appointment of boss scoopers. The result was the stabilization of the industry for both the carriers and the workers. The strike also enabled the International Longshoremen's Association to become a powerful force on the Great Lakes. [Ronald L. Filippelli]

FURTHER READING

Thirteenth Annual Report of the Board of Mediation and Arbitration of the State of New York. Albany, NY: State of New York, 1900.

Shelton, Brenda K. "The Grain Shoveller's Strike of 1899," *Labor History,* Vol. 9, No. 2 (Spring, 1968), pp. 210–238.

o   o   o

BURLINGTON RAILROAD STRIKE OF 1888. This strike, often called the Great Burlington Strike, involved a contest between the Chicago, Burlington & Quincy Railroad Company, operating westward from Chicago to Denver and Cheyenne, and two railroad unions, the Brotherhood of Locomotive Engineers (BLE) and the Brotherhood of Locomotive Firemen (BLF). Beginning on February 27, 1888, the strike lasted over ten months until officially called off by the defeated brotherhoods on January 8, 1889. The strike was notable in three ways: (1) it was the first militant action taken by the engineers in over ten years, and the first ever undertaken by the firemen, (2) the Burlington, though weakly supported by other railroad companies, secured impressive judicial weapons for defeating both this and later strikes, and (3) some executive officers of the federal government attempted to move the government to a more neutral stance between strikers and railroad companies during railway labor disputes.

The strike grew out of two devices by which the Burlington kept down the wages of its enginemen (engineers and firemen). Instead of hiring new engineers as needed, the company promoted firemen from the ranks. During the first year, they were classified as third class engineers and received two-thirds regular pay. As second class engineers during their second year, they earned five-sixths full pay. Only in their third and subsequent years did engineers receive full pay. Firemen were similarly classified and paid. The men charged that frequently when they reached first class status they were discharged and replaced by lower ranked, less expensive men. Among other things, the system also provided the company with a large supply of trained engineers in the event of strikes. The second grievance concerned set payments per trip for various runs, depending on the number of cars hauled, length of the trip, and whether it was over the main or a branch line. Since main and branch line work required essentially similar skills and responsibilities, the enginemen demanded a uniform per-mile rate. For several years the unions pressed for both an end to classification and adoption of a uniform mileage rate.

In late January 1888, the two brotherhoods established a joint committee to negotiate these matters with company officials. They wanted engineers to receive three and a half cents per mile for passenger trains and four cents for freight trains. Firemen would receive 60 percent of the amount paid to engineers. The Burlington argued that the enginemen in effect were calling for raises when the times demanded pay cuts. If it met these demands, the Burlington would be paying more than its rivals and weakening its competitive position. During the next month, although it offered to make small adjustments, the company would not yield on either principle. The brotherhoods voted to strike.

Loyalty of the enginemen to their unions completely thwarted efforts of the Burlington to pressure them back to work by threatening them with permanent loss of their jobs. On the other hand, the BLE's long history of not assisting Knights of Labor or other brotherhoods when they went on strike, now bore bitter results. Assisted by the Pinkerton Detective Agency, the Burlington had no difficulty in securing enough engineers from these unions to maintain their usual schedules.

Sensing failure, P. M. Arthur, longtime head of the BLE, and F. P. Sargent, chief of the BLF, turned next to a boycott. On March 5, the BLE called upon all members of the order, regardless of which railroad they worked for, to refuse to move any car to or from the Burlington, and if discharged for refusing, to strike that line. This tactic held promise as the other railroads operating in the area blamed the Burlington for repeatedly slashing rates and touching off rate wars. Accordingly, when requested, they went along with the boycott, refusing to interchange freight with the Burlington lest their own engineers go on strike.

In response to these tactics, the Burlington promptly turned to judicial proceedings. They called upon the judges of federal court districts in the various states served by the Burlington to enjoin connecting railroads, as common carriers of interstate commerce, from refusing to interchange traffic with the Burlington in support of the strikers. Three different judges cooperated by forbidding railroads in their districts from engaging in secondary boycotts. The obedience of the various roads to the judges' orders effectively eliminated that weapon of the strikers. These same rulings would serve as important precedents for the railroads in battling strikers in future battles.

Actions by two federal officials, the postmaster general of the United States and the chairman of the Interstate Commerce Commission, briefly offered hope to the brotherhoods. Hoping to avoid trouble with federal authorities over tie-ups of the mail, the strikers offered not to interfere with mail trains so long as they consisted solely of mail cars and carried no other business of the railroad. The Burlington flatly refused, arguing that it could not afford to run trains carrying nothing but mail. Arthur accordingly pressed the matter with Postmaster General Don M. Dickinson. Already concerned for the mails in the event of the strike expanding into a more general tieup of the railroads, Dickinson ruled that the railroads were under contract to move the mail even if it meant doing so on special trains carrying no other traffic. Since 1888 was a presidential election year, Dickinson, whose efforts had helped put Michigan in the Cleveland column in 1884, may have been as concerned with the political consequences of an anti-labor stand as with moving the mail.

In any event, upset at the ruling, a group of railway executives called on President Grover Cleveland, hoping to persuade him to reverse the policy. Instead, Cleveland sent for Dickinson and, after listening to both sides, threw his support behind the postmaster general. Though spelled out, the policy was not put to a test. The Burling-

ton itself had no trouble running trains and the strike did not spread to other lines.

Early in the strike, the recently created Interstate Commerce Commission (ICC) was meeting in Chicago on other matters. Railroad officials approached Thomas M. Cooley, chairman of the ICC, wanting a statement from the agency supportive of the railroad position. Cooley, long experienced in railroad matters, concluded that the ICC might better investigate the conditions behind the strike and privately suggested that the Burlington's rogue position on freight rates lay at the root of the difficulties. His more timid colleagues on the commission were divided on the issue of holding a public hearing in Chicago that Cooley had scheduled for a few days later. Cooley planned a showdown, but he fell ill with pneumonia the night before the meeting, nearly died, and recovered long after such a hearing would have served any purpose.

As the strike dragged on and victory eluded them, some strikers turned to sabotage. Scabs encountered shouts, stonings, and occasional assault. Engines were disabled, switches thrown, cars set afire, tracks obstructed, trains cut, and pins holding cars to trains pulled. Arthur deplored such actions, but some lesser officials condoned and encouraged them. By the third month of the strike, dynamiting incidents began, but fortunately no one was hurt. The Pinkerton Detective Agency managed to hire a minor union officer to supply evidence against some of those engaged in the incidents. The resulting trial and press coverage considerably damaged the BLE's reputation with the public.

Beginning in December 1888, the defeated brotherhoods approached Burlington officials to learn under what conditions, if any, strikers might be rehired. The company granted only the most limited of concessions. It would not use blacklists to attempt to block employment of strikers on other lines, but would give prospective employers letters of introduction of former employees only if they had not engaged in violence or other "improper conduct." Should it become necessary for the Burlington itself to go outside its current labor force for new employees, it would select the best candidates available, including those who left the company's service so long as they too had not been guilty of violence or other improper conduct against the company. With little else that they could do, the brotherhood representatives "approved" the conditions and called off the strike.

Relatively few of the strikers were ever reemployed by the Burlington, though apparently most secured jobs on other railroads. The Burlington, as might be expected, found permanent places for the strikebreakers and continued to secure engineers by promoting firemen. For several years the Burlington would not allow the brotherhoods to organize on its line. The BLE returned to its previous non-strike policy, and once more refused to cooperate with other unions during strikes, or to federate with the other brotherhoods to strengthen railroad labor in dealing with their employers. [Gerald G. Eggert]

FURTHER READING

Eggert, Gerald G. *Railroad Labor Disputes, The Beginnings of Federal Strike Policy*. Ann Arbor, MI: University of Michigan Press, 1967.

Hall, John A. *The Great Strike on the "Q"*. Chicago, IL: Elliot and Beezley, 1889.

McMurry, Donald L. *The Great Burlington Strike of 1888*. Cambridge, MA: Harvard University Press, 1956.

Salmons, C. H., et al. *The Burlington Strike*. Aurora, IL: Bunnell and Ward, 1889.

o o o

BUTTE, MONTANA, MINERS' STRIKE OF 1917. This was a struggle to restore unionism to the copper mines of Butte, Montana. The combined opposition of the federal government and powerful corporate interests, together with divisions among the mine employees themselves, doomed the effort to reorganize. Because the conflict occurred in a strategic industry during a war, mine operators enjoyed a free hand in crushing the strike. The lynching of union organizer Frank Little represented the nadir of this unrestrained disregard for civil rights.

For decades up to 1914, Butte had been a citadel of hardrock miners' unionism. In 1893, the Butte Miners' Union led the movement to found the Western Federation of Miners and became Local 1 of the federation. But numerous agents of the giant Anaconda Copper Mining Company gradually infiltrated the miners' leadership. By 1912, management operatives had so thoroughly corrupted the local that it acquiesced in the wholesale discharge of radical workers and the institution of a rustling card system of employment screening. Hatred of this corrupt regime exploded in June 1914. A large group of rank-and-file miners dynamited the union hall and formed a new independent body to represent their interests. This secession movement failed, and by 1915 this so-called Gibraltar of unionism had become an open-shop town.

On June 8, 1917, a carbide lamp accidentally ignited the insulation surrounding a cable in the speculator mine of the North Butte Mining Company. Smoke and gases soon filled the shaft that was the primary exit from the mine and rapidly spread throughout the underground workings. Fleeing workers found escape routes blocked by cement bulkheads; although Montana law required that bulkheads be constructed with doors that could be opened, the barriers in the speculator mine had no such doors. Asphyxiated bodies piled up against the bulkheads. This, the worst fire in the history of the western metal-mining industry, claimed 163 lives.

Miners channeled their rage over this needless loss of lives into a movement to reorganize. On June 10, rank-and-file copper workers distributed a leaflet emblazoned with this emphatic proposal: "Miners, Attention! Let's Have a Union." This call for organization enumerated six demands: strict compliance with state safety regulations, dismissal of the state mine inspector, abolition of the rustling card system, control of the hiring process by a union committee, protection of miners' rights of free speech and free assembly, and a wage increase commensurate with the high wartime cost of living. The following day, employees at one Butte copper operation spontaneously walked off the job in an unorganized protest about working conditions.

Foreshadowing their strategy in the months to come, mine operators dismissed this action as the irresponsible work of unpatriotic agitators from the radical Industrial Workers of the World (IWW). Even while new widows were still trying to identify their husbands' bodies, Anaconda and other firms asserted that their employees had no cause for stopping work to protest unsafe conditions. On the front page of the *Butte Daily Post* of June 12, near an article entitled "Ghastly Sight at Morgue," the operators declared that working conditions in Butte "compared favorably with those of any other camp." Needless to say, adding insult to injury in this manner only fueled the resurgence of pro-union sentiment.

A mass meeting on June 13 resulted in the formation of the Metal Mine Workers' Union (MMWU) with approximately 1,000 charter members. The new organization was an autonomous local body, affiliated with neither the International Union of Mine, Mill, and Smelter Workers (IUMMSW) (successor to the Western Federation of Miners) of the American Federation of Labor (AFL) nor the Metal Mine Workers' Industrial Union No. 800 of the IWW. Yet some of its leaders, like long-time radical Joe Shannon, were well

known as Wobblies. Seizing on the involvement of these militants, the operators simplistically denounced the whole resurgence of labor organization as nothing more than a treasonous anarchist conspiracy by the IWW to cripple the war effort.

The Metal Mine Workers at once took up the proposals enumerated in the circular of June 10. The union also added demands for recognition as the miners' bargaining agent and for safety training of new employees. After management refused to meet with the union to discuss these issues, the MMWU on June 15 declared a strike against all the mining firms in the district. Shortly thereafter, the Butte local of the International Brotherhood of Electrical Workers led a strike of the various metal trades—blacksmiths, machinists, and other crafts—against the mine operators for improved pay and working conditions. By the end of the month, about 15,000 men were out of work; virtually all mining in the locality had ceased.

The Metal Mine Workers called on U.S. Secretary of Labor William B. Wilson to investigate their grievances. Federal mediator W. H. Rogers arrived on June 22. But Rogers concentrated on settling not the miners' strike but rather that of the metal-working crafts. Accordingly, employers granted the AFL locals a wage increase, seniority in layoffs and rehiring, and the closed shop. Dropping their demand that the mine operators recognize the MMWU, the craft unionists all returned to work by the end of July leaving the miners to fend for themselves.

IWW leader Frank Little came to Butte in July to support the strikers. Unfortunately, Little felt a need not only to endorse the copper workers' demands but also to condemn vociferously U.S. involvement in World War I as well. In a speech on July 19, for example, the IWW executive board member denounced soldiers serving in the U.S. Army as "uniformed scabs." Other inflammatory public attacks on the war as an imperialist adventure followed. These declarations did nothing to aid the cause of the MMWU.

Little paid dearly for his temerity. In the early hours of August 1, a gang of six masked men broke into Little's room and abducted him at gunpoint. He was dragged behind an automobile to the outskirts of town. There he was hanged by the neck from a railroad trestle. When his body was found the next day, it bore a card with the message: "Others Take Notice! First and Last Warning!" Local, county, and state police made no real effort to bring Little's murderers to justice. Instead, the incident helped justify the introduction of federal troops, who arrived on August 10 to "maintain order" during what had been an orderly strike.

In late July, the operators, while steadfastly refusing to negotiate with the MMWU, had offered individual mine employees a wage increase and a minor change in the rustling system. As the Army patrolled the city, some miners accepted these concessions and went back to work. The majority stayed out. On August 14, the MMWU received a further setback when the IUMMSW smelter workers voted not to join the strike. Undeterred, miners' union pickets shut down the Anaconda smelter in nearby Anaconda, Montana, on August 25. The firm responded by closing its smelter in Great Falls and its mines in Butte as well. The company correctly assumed that the various AFL locals at these operations would have only limited sympathy with the independent MMWU. On September 12, the AFL affiliates voted to return to work. Six days later, Anaconda reopened its facilities. Thereafter, the Metal Mine Workers' Union and its work stoppage disintegrated. Acknowledging defeat, the union finally called off the strike on December 28.

Conducted at a time of growing patriotic fervor, this episode of labor–management conflict led to harsh restrictions on civil liberties. In February 1918, a special session of the Montana legislature passed the Criminal Syndicalism Act, which, in attempting to annihilate the IWW, significantly limited freedom of association for workers and other state residents. In addition, the legislature passed the repressive Sedition Act. Among its sweeping provisions, the law made it illegal to "utter, print, write, or publish any disloyal, profane, violent, scurrilous, contemptuous, slurring or abusive language about the form of government of the United States, or the constitution of the United States, or the soldiers or sailors of United States, or the flag of the United States. . . ." This state statute served as the model for a federal law enacted in May 1918. [Alan Derickson]

FURTHER READING

Dubofsky, Melvyn. *We Shall Be All: A History of the Industrial Workers of the World.* New York: Quadrangle, 1969.

Gutfeld, Arnon. "The Speculator Disaster in 1917: Labor Resurgence at Butte, Montana." *Arizona and the West,* Vol. 11 (Spring, 1969), pp. 27–38.

Jensen, Vernon H. *Heritage of Conflict: Labor Relations in the Nonferrous Metals Industry up to 1930.* Ithaca, NY: Cornell University Press, 1950.

C

○ ○ ○ ○ ○ ○ ○ ○ ○ ○ ○

○   ○   ○

CALIFORNIA FARMWORKERS'
STRIKES OF 1933. The spring of 1933
ushered in a wave of labor unrest unparal-
leled in the history of California agriculture. Starting in April with the Santa Clara
pea harvest, strikes erupted throughout the
summer and fall as each crop ripened for
harvest. The strike wave culminated with
the San Joaquin Valley strike, the largest
and most important strike in the history of
American agriculture.

All told, more than 47,500 farmworkers participated in the 1933 strikes.
Twenty-four of these strikes, involving approximately 37,500 workers, were under
the leadership of the Communist-led Cannery and Agricultural Workers Industrial
Union (CAWIU). In a dramatic reversal of
its previous record of repeated debilitating
losses, twenty of the CAWIU-led strikes
resulted in partial wage increases while only
four strikes ended in total defeat for the
union. The remaining strikes, including
three spontaneous walkouts, two American
Federation of Labor (AFL) led strikes and
two led by independent unions, resulted
in partial gains in four out of the seven
conflicts.

Like their industrial counterparts,
California farmworkers entered 1933
embittered by three years of steadily declining wages and living conditions. Although these workers had endured intolerable conditions for decades, their burgeoning frustration and bitterness was for
the first time being channeled into a combination of ethnic consciousness and labor

militancy. Aroused by outbreaks of urban
industrial action around the nation and
inspired by the appearance, albeit illusory,
of a sympathetic administration in Washington, farmworkers looked to the CAWIU
for the leadership and guidance needed to
transform this seemingly inchoate activism
into an effective labor movement.

Although the CAWIU had been involved in a series of major farmworker
strikes since its inception in 1930, by 1933
it had little to show for its efforts. Despite
a strong showing of workers' support at the
onset of each conflict, in strike after strike
workers had been forced by the brutal
strike-busting tactics of the growers and
local authorities to go back to work or flee
the area without any of their demands
being met.

The union had learned important
organizational lessons from each of these
failures and began 1933 with a corps of
well-trained and committed organizers who
had earned recognition and respect from
farmworkers across the state. By the time
the first of the 1933 strikes broke out in
April, detailed strike plans had been developed based on careful research of wages,
working conditions, and harvest schedules
for each crop. A standard list of demands
had been developed that included substantial wage increases, union recognition, an
eight-hour workday, time and a half for
overtime, a closed shop with a union-con-
trolled hiring hall, abolition of labor contracting, no union or ethnic discrimination,
and free transportation of workers to and
from the fields. A network of farm com-

mittees, representing the multi-ethnic character of the work force, had been elected by workers at mass meetings in each local growing area. And perhaps most important of all, CAWIU organizers had learned by experience to focus their organizing appeals on improving farmworker wages, working and living conditions, rather than on loftier aims couched in revolutionary rhetoric.

Despite these preparations, the CAWIU's 1933 strike campaign got off to an inauspicious start on April 14, when a strike by 2,000 Mexican, Filipino, and white pea pickers collapsed in just two weeks in response to a familiar pattern of violence and intimidation by growers and local authorities.

The next CAWIU venture, the El Monte berrypickers' strike, was to be an even more humiliating debacle. Under CAWIU leadership the strike was called by the approximately 600 Mexican berry pickers employed by Japanese growers in the San Gabriel Valley. Holding firm for their demand of sixty-five cents per crate, strike committee members not only rejected the growers offer of first forty cents and then forty-five cents per crate but also openly challenged the CAWIU leadership of the strike. With the aid of the Mexican consul, the non-Communist leadership was able to undercut the CAWIU's influence through appeals to ethnic pride and by portraying the Communists as outside agitators. They were aided in this effort by local authorities who systematically jailed most of the CAWIU organizers in the area. Leadership of the strike then passed to the Confederacion de Uniones de Campesinos y Obreros Mexicanos (CUCOM), which settled with the growers in mid-July for increases of twenty-five cents for men and twenty cents for women. But because most of the crop had already been picked by scab labor, the majority of the workers were unable to benefit from the settlement.

For the CAWIU, their humiliation at El Monte was tempered by their simultaneous strike victory among 1,000 cherry pickers on twenty of the largest ranches in Santa Clara County. Although the larger ranchers organized an all out assault against the union, this time the violence served to mobilize the strikers rather than to break the strike. Unable to break the strike, and faced with the loss of their crops, growers reluctantly agreed to bring the pickers' wages up to the thrity cents an hour demanded by the union. Although still unable to win recognition, the union ended the strike on June 14, overjoyed with its first solid wage victory in three years of organizing.

Buoyed by their Santa Clara triumph, twenty-nine CAWIU delegates assembled at the union's first district convention on August 5 to engage in a serious round of self-criticism and to plan for the critical late-summer fruit harvests. A detailed organizing strategy was developed including a commitment to build a strong integrated union apparatus throughout the state's important agricultural centers; more aggressive organizing of women and children; "boring from within" established unions to form contacts with dissident elements and win the organizations over to the CAWIU; and building alliances with unemployed agricultural workers.

CAWIU organizers left the convention to immediately embark upon a rapid succession of ambitious and mostly successful strikes. The late-summer harvest campaign began on August 7 and 8 with strikes involving 1,000 Mexican and Filipino sugar beet workers in Ventura County and 400 tomato pickers near San Diego. By August 14, pear pickers around San Jose and peach pickers near Tulare had joined the fray, with still other strikes soon spreading throughout the fruit growing districts of six San Joaquin Valley counties. With the exception of the **Oxnard Sugar Beet**

Strike, almost all of these strikes resulted in significant wage victories for the union. Early in August the average farmworker wage in California had been approximately sixteen and a half cents an hour. By the end of the month the general agricultural wage was firmly established at twenty-five cents an hour. Supervised by CAWIU organizer Pat Chambers, the strikes were meticulously organized with leadership diffused throughout the work force so that it was more difficult for local authorities to break the strike by arresting the main leaders. The CAWIU also succeeded in conducting the strikes in the most law-abiding and nonviolent manner possible, making it more difficult for the authorities to justify using violence to break up the strikes.

The only exception to this general lack of violence was the **Oxnard Sugar Beet Strike**, where the mayor of Oxnard, a sugar beet grower himself, used his authority to brutally break the strike. But with Oxnard the only loss, CAWIU leaders were increasingly confident of the inevitable triumph of militant unionism in California agriculture. This exuberance was quickly chastened when in early September they lost two major grape strikes in the San Joaquin Valley.

First in Fresno and then in Lodi, growers and local authorities broke the strikes by wholesale arrests of strike leaders and by violent attacks on picket lines. Although in Fresno part of the loss could be blamed on the lack of CAWIU discipline, the 4,000 grape pickers in Lodi were a well-organized group. But still they were no match for the growers, who were willing to go to any length to keep the union out of their vineyards. Hundreds of well-armed deputized growers, businessmen, and legionnaires under the command of Colonel Walter E. Garrison, a grower and retired military officer, viciously assaulted 100 unarmed strikers while the police stood idly by. Any strikers who did attempt to defend themselves were arrested by the police for "rioting." The attack continued throughout the day, with strikers and their families being run out of their camps with fire hoses and tear gas. When union appeals to state authorities went unheeded, the strike quickly collapsed and Lodi growers succeeded in keeping their vineyards non-union.

The CAWIU had little chance to mull over their losses in Fresno and Lodi for they had set their sights on the most important harvest of all—the October cotton harvest.

More than 15,000 workers picked cotton in the San Joaquin Valley. Three-quarters of this work force were Mexican, the remainder included southern blacks, Filipinos, and white migrants from the Southwest. Three years of depression had forced their wages down more than 75 percent. With the growers unwilling to pass on any of the 150 percent increase in the price of cotton from the previous year, the pickers were ripe for organization.

As tensions rose each side prepared for the ensuing conflict. Organizers spread through the valley building up locals and developing leadership. Alliances were made with liberal groups to help win public support for the struggle ahead. Demands were formulated including union recognition, a picking wage of $1.00 per hundred pounds, abolition of labor contracting, a union-controlled hiring hall, and no union discrimination. A general strike throughout the region was called for October 4.

Growers held firm to their offer of a twenty-cent increase or sixty cents per hundred pounds and began to mobilize anti-union forces to break the strike. They organized themselves into agricultural protective associations with the somewhat ingenuous motto of "strikers work peacefully or leave the state of California." As soon as the strike began, the protective associations moved quickly to evict strikers from the camps.

But breaking up the picket lines proved more difficult. With a strike area more than a hundred miles long and thirty to forty miles wide, the union sent out roving truckloads of pickets instructed to stop and picket only where they found workers in the field. The growers could then only break up picket lines when and where they found them.

The first major altercation occurred in Woodvile, where, by violently attacking picketers, the growers served only to unite the heretofore ethnically divided work force under the leadership of rank-and-file leader "Big Bill" Hammett and his multi-racial general staff.

By the second week of the strike, violence had greatly escalated as roving bands of armed growers moved through the region attacking all strikers who refused to return to work or leave the area. Law enforcement officials cooperated by arresting all those they thought to be strike leaders. Growers also applied pressure to local merchants, threatening to boycott all stores that did business with striking workers. State labor commissioner Frank C. McDonald joined in the public outcry, denouncing the boycott threat as a thinly disguised effort to "starve out" the strikers and appealing to both sides to allow state mediation of the conflict. Although the union quickly agreed to state intervention, the growers refused and the violence continued.

Despite the growers' efforts, the strike grew to encompass 12,000 workers across Tulare, King, and Kern counties, with most of the cotton crop remaining unpicked in the fields. The violence reached its peak on October 10, when, in the small town of Pixley, a caravan of forty armed growers fired on a large group of unarmed strikers and their families who were gathered in the center of town to protest the arrests of strike leaders. The growers killed two and wounded at least eight more strikers while a group of highway patrolmen watched from a safe distance, refusing to intervene.

Soon after the Pixley attack, growers in Kern County fired on a group of unarmed pickets killing one and wounding several more. After the shootings, the local authorities arrested some of the strikers for rioting and allegedly murdering one of their own people.

Because of the public outcry after the shootings, Tulare County officials were pressured to arrest eight of the growers involved in the Pixley incident. But to placate local growers, they also arrested strike leader Pat Chambers on criminal syndicalism charges.

In response to public pressure, the federal relief office directed the governor to distribute relief to all of the striking farmworkers marking it the first time in American labor history that the federal government offered relief to striking workers.

Federal involvement did not stop there. New Deal administrator George Creel intervened in the conflict, arguing that although agricultural workers were excluded from Section 7(a) of the National Industrial Recovery Act (NIRA), industrial disputes in agriculture were under the jurisdiction of the National Labor Board, which he represented.

Creel came prepared to impose a "fair settlement" on both parties by threatening revocation of federal relief if the union did not agree to fact finding and by assuring growers that without relief strikers would immediately return to work at sixty cents per hundred pounds pending the outcome of the fact finding.

Seriously disturbed by the specter of militant communist unionism which he found antithetical to the New Deal's paternalistic labor relations ideology, Creel's intent was to eliminate the CAWIU's influence in agriculture by undermining its hold over the strikers. But in doing so he seriously underestimated the commitment of the cotton pickers to their strike and to their union. Government threats to condition relief on a return to work failed to sway the majority of the strikers, and the fact-finding hearings began on October 19 with the cotton strike still in full swing. After two days of testimony from growers and a succession of workers, the federal fact finders proposed a seventy-five-cent increase to settle the strike. To induce the growers' cooperation Creel promised that if they granted the seventy-five-cent increase, all federal relief would be immediately cut off and workers returning to the fields would be given full protection from the strikers.

The strikers remained adamant, holding out for eighty cents and union recognition. But on October 27, the CAWIU Central Strike Committee, arguing that the strike had already dragged on long enough, convinced the strikers to go back to work at the seventy-five cents per hundred pounds, without union recognition.

The most dramatic and significant strike in the history of American agriculture ended with no clear victor but with all sides—the growers, the union, and the federal government—claiming victory. Twelve thousand farmworkers under the leadership of some of the CAWIU's most dedicated and experienced organizers had brought the most powerful and determined growers in California to a standstill. What the strike had ultimately made clear, in the words of labor historian Cletus Daniel, was "the irreconcilable conflict between the CAWIU's militant unionism and the federal government's new rational and paternalistic labor policies. . . . "

The union had proven itself in the 1933 strikes, but it had never won recognition. And when the dust settled, little of the pre-strike union organization remained intact. The CAWIU would continue to organize, but it would be unable to overcome the combined forces of the Roose-

velt administration and intense grower opposition. [Kate Bronfenbrenner]

FURTHER READING

Daniel, Cletus E. *Bitter Harvest: A History of California Farmworkers, 1870–1941.* Berkeley, CA: University of California Press, 1981.

Jamieson, Stuart. *Labor Unionism in American Agriculture.* U.S. Bureau of Labor Statistics Bulletin No. 836. Washington, DC: Government Printing Office, 1945.

McWilliams, Carey. *Factories in the Field: The Story of Migratory Farm Labor in California.* Boston, MA: Little, Brown, 1939.

o   o   o

CALIFORNIA GRAPE AND LETTUCE BOYCOTTS. Early in the twentieth century it became clear that California agriculture would be dominated by one-crop commercial farms and marked by an ever-increasing degree of concentration of ownership. In this kind of near-monopoly agribusiness, the demand for low-cost, unskilled labor was to become insatiable.

The labor was supplied largely by Mexican workers with a significant minority of Filipino workers also employed in the fields. Working and living conditions for the large number of migrants that harvested the great California farms were deplorable. Workers did try to reform the system through unionization on occasion, and the California farmworkers were not immune to the surge of militancy that coursed through the American working class in the 1930s. There were thirty-one strikes in 1933 alone, involving 48,000 workers. Most of the strikes were Communist led, and most were broken. Employers used deportation, arrests, the importation of strikebreakers, and violence. None of the attempts led to permanent organization.

During World War II, the government, facing a labor shortage in the fields, instituted the bracero program. The program brought in Mexican workers under a series of presidential agreements with the Mexican government. By the end of the war it was clear that growers had become dependent upon the low-wage, controlled, and regulated labor force provided by the bracero program. The program was also virtually union proof. The United States Government, not the growers, contracted with the Mexican government. Wages and working conditions were arranged and agreed to in advance. The effect was to hold wages virtually even between 1950 and 1960, a period in which factory workers' annual earnings increased by 60 percent.

Public Law 78, which regulated the bracero program, expired in December 1964, over the strong objections of the growers. Less than a year later grape pickers in Delano struck. They were mostly Filipinos and belonged to the Agricultural Workers Organizing Committee (AWOC), a unit of the AFL-CIO. They were soon joined by members of the National Farm Workers Association (NFWA).

After a hard struggle with the growers, the first victories came against Schenley Industries and the giant DiGiorgio Corporation. Both companies agreed to elections to determine representation. The victories were announced at the capitol in Sacramento after a twenty-four-day, three-hundred-mile march of farmworkers from Delano. Schenley signed the first contract recognizing the union on June 21. It included a thrity-five-cents-per-hour wage increase. DiGiorgio settled soon after. In the course of the campaigns, the two labor organizations, one predominantly Filipino and the other Mexican, came together as the United Farm Workers Organizing Committee (UFWOC).

Despite the victories at Schenley and DiGiorgio, the other growers in Delano refused to recognize the union. To counter the resistance, the UFWOC recruited supporters across the nation and enlisted them in a nationwide boycott of table grapes that took on the trappings of a quasi-religious movement. Led by Cesar Chavez, the union appealed to college students and liberals who manned boycott offices, worked for near starvation wages, and finally won the sympathy of the American people for the plight of the stoop labor of the California fields. Chavez hailed the victory as the beginning of a new day.

Victory in the grape fields was followed by war in the lettuce fields of Salinas and Santa Maria. Here the adversary was not only the growers, who were formidable enough, but also the Teamsters union. In order to forestall organization by what they perceived as the more militant alternative, the growers began signing contracts with the Teamsters. Workers who looked with hope to the United Farm Workers felt betrayed and began spontaneously to leave the fields. Tensions between the two unions were relieved temporarily by an agreement that gave jurisdiction in the fields to the UFWOC and the sheds and trucks to the Teamsters. But growers who had already signed with the Teamsters, without consulting their workers, kept their Teamster agreements. Chavez responded by calling the workers out. The growers, claiming to be the innocent victims of a union jurisdictional dispute, asked the courts for relief. When the courts issued the requested injunctions, the UFWOC turned once again to its tested weapon, the boycott.

But the lettuce growers had learned from the grape boycott. This time they sponsored a statewide ballot proposition severely limiting the rights of farmworkers to organize, strike, and conduct boycotts. The UFWOC, with the charismatic Chavez in the lead, persuaded California voters to defeat the initiative soundly. The growers received a second blow shortly after when the California Supreme Court overturned the injunctions that had halted the 1970 lettuce strike. But the court still refused to overturn the existing Teamster agreements.

Indeed, the war between the two unions had intensified. When the UFWOC grape agreements began expiring, the Teamsters moved in and signed what the UFWOC attacked as "sweetheart agreements" with the grape growers. AFL-CIO president George Meany blasted the Teamsters but had little leverage since the huge union had been expelled from the federation years before on corruption charges. Confrontations between UFWOC members and Teamsters began to mar the California labor scene. Teamster "guards" and organizers killed two workers and injured hundreds when they brutally attacked UFWOC picket lines. The battle moved back to Delano where thousands of UFWOC strikers ignored a court order to end the strike and went to jail. Through it all the growers continued to sign Teamster contracts.

In the midst of this turmoil, the California legislature, with the support of Governor Edmund G. Brown, Jr., passed a farm labor relations law. Until this point, no labor law, federal or state, regulated labor–management relations in agriculture in California. The law gave farmworkers the right to organize and bargain collectively. It was a right that farmworkers, exempt from protection of the National Labor Relations Act, had in no other part of the United States. The law also established an Agricultural Labor Relations Board (ALRB) to administer the law.

From practically its first day, the board was controversial. Growers objected vehemently when the ALRB ruled that labor organizers should have access to a grower's property to solicit support. The growers also carried on a constant war against the board in the state legislature and succeeded in hamstringing its operations by interfering with its funding. Finally, the Teamsters and the UFWOC signed an agreement ending their war in March 1977. It reaffirmed the old jurisdictional division of the industry, with the field workers going to the UFWOC and the packing shed and truck workers to the Teamsters. More importantly, the Teamsters pledged not to renew contracts it held in the UFWOC's jurisdiction. The agreement only ratified what the workers had been expressing through their ballots in ALRB elections. In the first year, Chavez's union won 229 elections to 116 for the Teamsters.

The resolution of the jurisdictional battle did not guarantee smooth sailing for the UFWOC. The struggle went on. When the UFWOC tried to renew contracts for 7,000 workers in 1979, the growers once again proved obstinate. During the 1960s and 1970s the struggles of California farmworkers in the grape and lettuce fields of the richest agricultural kingdom in the world captured the imagination of a significant portion of the American people. Cesar Chavez and his humble legions seemed to many to symbolize the rebirth of a democratic and militant labor movement in the service of the poor and weak. The struggle of the farmworkers, La Causa as it was popularly called, merged in those years with other social reform movements, such as the Black Civil Rights movement, the women's movement, and especially La Raza, the rising of consciousness among America's Mexican-American minority. If the results of the conflict eventually proved inconclusive in terms of collective bargaining, there is no doubt that the movement was a success in terms of the struggle for a more just society. [Ronald L. Filippelli]

FURTHER READING

Matthiesson, Peter. *Sal Si Puedes*. New York: Random House, 1969.

Selvin, David. *A Place in the Sun: A History of California Labor*. San Francisco, CA: Boyd and Fraser Publishing Company, 1981.

Taylor, Ronald B. *Chavez and the Farm Workers*. Boston, MA: Beacon Press, 1975.

o o o

CALIFORNIA PEA PICKERS' STRIKE OF 1932. Just before the start of the May 1932 harvest season, growers in the Half Moon Bay area of San Mateo, California, provoked a spontaneous strike among pea pickers when they reduced piece rates from seventy-five to fifty cents a pack. Although the workers were unorganized, the large pay cut represented the breaking point for families just coming out of the slow winter season. The previous year's rate of seventy-five cents a pack had not been enough to tide them over through the winter, especially given the four dollars a month rent they were required to pay the growers for camping out on their land. Unable to feed their families, many of the workers were forced to look to the San Mateo County relief office for charity, only to be told that because they were not permanent residents of the county, they were only eligible to receive two cents per family member per day. A twenty-five-cent pay cut meant that the next winter would be even worse.

Fifteen hundred Mexican, Filipino, Puerto Rican, and Italian pea pickers from sixty farms covering a territory of fifteen square miles walked off their jobs to gather in the town of Half Moon Bay to discuss strike plans. Without effective leadership, the mass meeting dissolved after the sheriff and the powerful labor contractors, backed up by armed San Mateo police, threatened them with eviction from the camps and immediate replacement by imported farm laborers. However, the walkout continued as workers went back to their tents rather than returning to the fields.

Within hours the strikers were joined by organizers from the Cannery and Agricultural Workers Industrial Union (CAWIU). The CAWIU had been established the year before by the American Communist Party's Trade Union Unity League (TUUL) as a successor to the Agricultural Workers' Industrial Union (AWIU)

when the union became involved in an unsuccessful strike among Santa Clara County cannery workers. Sixteen of the TUUL's more experienced farmworker organizers were still imprisoned under California's criminal syndicalism laws for organizing activity during the 1930 Imperial Valley Cantaloupe Workers' Strike. Thus the CAWIU, and its forerunner the AWIU, stuck to a relatively passive strategy of sending a small group of organizers into the field whenever they heard reports of spontaneous strikes. Typically, Communist organizers would assume leadership of the strike and quickly formulate demands including raises, overtime pay, union recognition and protection for union activity, and improvements in living conditions. Again and again, the growers and local authorities would respond with aggressive assaults on the strikers and the union leadership. Mass meetings and picket lines were violently dispersed by police, strikers were arrested and threatened with deportation, and relief supplies were cut off. In a short time, the organizers had no choice but to call off the strike and send those workers who had not yet been deported back into the fields without any of the union's demands having been met.

The Half Moon Bay Pea Pickers' Strike of 1932 was no exception. The strikers willingly handed over leadership of the strike to the CAWIU organizers because they had no leadership of their own. Demands for restoration of the seventy-five-cent piece rate, elimination of the four-dollar monthly rental fee, and improvements in camp living conditions, including shower baths and free medical care, were presented to the growers and publicized throughout the county.

The growers lost no time in mounting a counterattack. A call went out to all local law enforcement officials, farmers, merchants, and businessmen to arm themselves and join the battle to crush the strike by force. Hundreds of "concerned citizens," primarily farmers, were deputized. Well-armed deputies once again threatened the strikers with eviction from the employer-owned camps and replacement by imported scab labor. It quickly became clear to the organizers and the workers that the growers were willing to use extensive force to ensure that their pea crop would be picked—by scabs if necessary.

Confronted with the well-armed deputies and fully cognizant of the strike's inadequate organization and preparation, the CAWIU called off the strike only twenty-four hours after it had begun. For the second time in its brief history, the CAWIU had failed miserably in its efforts to convert a spontaneous strike into a lasting organization of agricultural workers. Once again the union was an organization in name only, with neither members nor strike victories to claim for its own.

Yet the Half Moon Bay strike served as an important turning point for the CAWIU. In response to harsh criticism voiced by national Communist Party leaders regarding the haphazard organizing strategies that they had used among agricultural workers, local organizers themselves began to re-evaluate their strategy. But perhaps most important of all, Sam Darcy, one of the Communist's most astute and committed organizers, was sent out to take control of all organizing in District 13, which included California, Nevada, and Arizona. Under Darcy's leadership, delegates to the District 13 annual Communist Party convention in July 1932, used the Half Moon Bay debacle to engage in a serious bout of self-criticism. Discarding their failed policy of attempting to exploit spontaneous strikes, organizers concurred that the only way they were going to build a lasting organization among agricultural workers was through careful selection of organizing targets; the development of a leadership representative of the agricultural work force in terms of race, nationality, sex, and age with a focus on

concrete demands including wages, working conditions, and union recognition; and, most important of all, the painstaking and diligent building of a mass organizational movement before any economic action was to be taken.

The fortunes of the CAWIU did not take a dramatic turn for the better following the 1932 convention. But the metamorphosis in union strategy and tactics that followed the collapse of the Pea Pickers' Strike set the stage for the dramatic farm-worker struggles of 1933 and 1934. [Kate Bronfenbrenner]

FURTHER READING

Daniel, Cletus E. *Bitter Harvest: A History of California Farmworkers, 1870–1941*. Berkeley, CA: University of California Press, 1981.

Jamieson, Stuart. *Labor Unionism in American Agriculture*. U.S. Bureau of Labor Statistics Bulletin No. 836. Washington, DC: Government Printing Office, 1945.

McWilliam, Carey. *Factories in the Fields: The Story of Migratory Farm Labor in California*. Boston, MA: Little, Brown, 1939.

o   o   o

CAPTIVE MINE STRIKE OF 1941. In 1941, the United Mine Workers (UMW), led by the nation's most controversial labor leader, John L. Lewis, was one of the largest and most influential unions in the American labor movement. In addition, as its founder and chief benefactor, the UMW occupied a position of unrivaled power in the Congress of Industrial Organizations (CIO). When the miners' union went to the bargaining table, these factors and the critical position coal occupied in the industrial picture caused the nation to watch with great interest. The fact that the 1941 talks occurred as the nation mobilized for war heightened the attention focused on the negotiations.

Bargaining between the UMW and the industry, through the Appalachian Joint

Wage Conference, opened in New York City in March. The bargaining structure that had evolved pitted the union against the major industry groups, the northern and the southern operators. Whatever terms were agreed to by the Appalachian Conference were usually then accepted by the smaller operator groups.

After four months of difficult negotiations that included a month-long strike, presidential intervention, and a split between the two industry groups, both the northern and the southern operators accepted almost identical contracts with the miners' union. The 1941 agreement was heralded as a "significant victory" for Lewis and the UMW. Not only was the union successful in virtually eliminating wage differentials between northern and southern mines but also it won a healthy pay increase, paid vacations, a memorial period clause, and an extension of the union shop—a provision that forced all new miners to join the UMW following a short probationary period.

In 1941, the northern and southern operators' groups represented approximately 70 percent of the nation's bituminous coal production. After the union had settled with these groups it promptly moved to have the contract adopted by the remaining coal producers. Virtually all of these operators quickly accepted the previously negotiated agreement. The one exception was the so-called "captive mines," a group of mining subsidiaries owned and operated by steel companies.

The captive mines were willing to accept most aspects of the 1941 agreement with little discussion. They were not, however, willing to accept the union shop provision, first incorporated into the Appalachian agreement in 1939. Despite the fact that 95 percent of workers in the captive mines had voluntarily joined the union, both the UMW and the steel companies were adamant on the issue of union security. Although this issue affected only

5 percent of the work force, it's importance transcended the actual workers involved. The steel companies resistance was rooted in the fear that if they granted the union shop in the mines, they would inevitably have to grant it in the steel mills and the shipyards. The union, on the other hand, feared that failing to win this arrangement in the captive mines would threaten the union shop in the rest of the coal industry. Having drawn the line on the issue of union security, both sides settled in for a protracted struggle.

On September 15, 1941, Lewis ordered the 53,000 miners working at captive mines out on strike. In the context of the burgeoning American war buildup, this walkout caused great consternation among government officials and the general public alike. However, within a matter of days, the UMW president proposed a thirty-day truce during which time the miners would go back to work under the new Appalachian agreement but without the union shop, and the National Defense Mediation Board (NDMB) would consider the dispute. The operator's quickly accepted Lewis' proposal; the strike had lasted just one week.

By mid-October Lewis grew impatient with the lack of progress and set October 25 as the date on which the strike would resume. In the days before the resumption of the walkout, the NDMB scrambled to find a way to resolve the deadlock. With the deadline fast-approaching, the board proposed two alternatives for ending the impasse. First, the dispute could be submitted to the full NDMB for resolution with both sides agreeing to accept the decision or, second, the parties could agree to submit the issue to a tripartite, ad hoc arbitration panel. President Roosevelt, taking a greater interest in the dispute, endorsed the second approach and recommended that the parties name John L. Lewis and Myron Taylor of U.S. Steel to represent the union and the industry, respectively, on the panel.

The steel companies, however, preferred the first alternative proposed by the NDMB. The resultant bickering over how to proceed proved unproductive and, as Lewis had promised, the strike resumed on October 25 despite appeals from President Roosevelt for a continued truce.

Lewis' indifference to the President's appeals earned him the enmity of the American public. Both the conservative and the liberal press castigated him for impairing the defense effort and threatening the nation's security. Roosevelt's efforts to paint the dispute as an unpatriotic act were largely successful and Lewis became a lightning rod for the rising tide of public indignation. This sentiment would not dissipate quickly even though the walkout was short-lived.

On October 29, Lewis, Myron Taylor, and William Davis, chairman of the NDMB, worked out a plan in which the dispute would be formally submitted to the full board for a recommended settlement during which time the miners would return to work. The board's decision, however, would not be binding on either party. Lewis, reportedly, was amenable to this approach because he fully expected the NDMB to grant him the union shop. In fact, all the parties held great hopes that the dispute would shortly be resolved. The next day, October 30, Lewis ordered his members in the captive mines back to work.

Following hearings, the board announced its decision on November 10. By a nine to two vote, the NDMB, composed of labor, employer, and public representatives, unexpectedly rejected the UMW's demand for the union shop. Even the labor representatives on the board split on the decision with the only two favorable votes coming from the block of four labor members. These two labor representatives, Philip Murray of the CIO and Thomas Kennedy of the UMW, immediately resigned from the NDMB effectively ending the board's usefulness as a mediating body in this and subsequent disputes.

On November 17, at Lewis' behest, the captive miners struck once again. This time they were joined by some 150,000 other miners who walked off the job in sympathy with their brothers at the captive mines. With the strike growing, and sporadic violence breaking out in the coalfields, Roosevelt again appealed for an end to the strike. The President proposed that the parties reconsider the use of binding arbitration, an approach suggested earlier by the NDMB. This time, however, Roosevelt suggested John R. Steelman, director of the United States Conciliation Service, as the neutral member of the tripartite panel. The UMW would again be represented by Lewis and the operators by Benjamin F. Fairless, president of U.S. Steel. The union readily agreed to this proposal as it was well known that Steelman supported the UMW's position on the union shop.

On November 22, UMW miners across the country went back to work. Two weeks later, the arbitration panel voted two to one to grant the union shop. As expected, Steelman joined Lewis in the majority, with Fairless dissenting. The operators' subsequently suggested that they had agreed to arbitration without the knowledge that Steelman would be the third party. While this may have been the case, the imposition of the union shop by a third party allowed the captive mine owners to hold fast to their principle of opposing the union shop while resolving the dispute in the face of Lewis' intransigence.

The settlement was a great personal triumph for Lewis. The victory brought him widespread public attention, although he still was reviled by much of the press and the populace. Lewis was, however, forced to yield the spotlight on this occasion. The decision of the panel was issued on December 7, 1941, Pearl Harbor Day. [Paul F. Clark]

FURTHER READING

Bernstein, Irving. *Turbulent Years: A History of the American Worker, 1933–1941.* Boston, MA: Houghton Mifflin, 1971.

Dubofsky, Melvyn, and Warren Van Tine. *John L. Lewis: A Biography.* New York: Quadrangle, 1977.

o   o   o

CARPENTERS' STRIKE FOR THE EIGHT-HOUR DAY OF 1890. After the end of the **Eight-Hour and Haymarket Strikes of 1886**, the American Federation of Labor (AFL) took no significant action on the issue of shortening the workday for two years. Despite the fact that the eight-hour workday had been labor's cardinal demand for a generation, the repressive atmosphere following the Haymarket Massacre injected a note of caution into trade unions' actions. Few of the nearly 200,000 workers reported to have gained shorter workdays in 1886 had been able to preserve their hard-won gains, and the internecine warfare between the AFL and the Knights of Labor occupied much of the labor movement's energy.

By the end of 1888, AFL president Samuel Gompers needed a way to revitalize a moribund labor movement; labor's ranks in cities like Detroit and Philadelphia had been decimated. The widespread popularity that the eight-hour workday enjoyed among rank-and-file workers made it the ideal issue for Gompers. The AFL president launched a new national drive around the "eight-hour question" at the December 1888 AFL convention in St. Louis asserting that it was "perhaps the only one upon which [the workers] can be rallied and aroused from their present lethargy."

The AFL adopted a plan to inaugurate a universal eight-hour workday on May 1, 1890. The federation would arrange for "simultaneous mass meetings" throughout the country to coincide with widely observed holidays on February 22, July 4, and Labor Day, 1889, and on February 22, 1890. These meetings would both educate the public and connect the demand for a shorter workday to the American political rituals accompanying George Washington's Birthday and Independence Day. The AFL also commissioned pamphlets written by George McNeill and George Gunton, names long associated with the eight-hour movement, to outline the three principal short-hour theories prevalent at the time. The AFL distributed more than 50,000 copies of the pamphlets and over half a million circulars to publicize the movement. Finally, the AFL executive council wrote 1,200 personal letters to public opinion leaders throughout the country "to create sympathetic understanding for the . . . movement and to forestall any association of the movement with anarchistic influences."

From the outset, however, some union leaders expressed misgivings about a general confrontation with employers that was to occur in less than eighteen months. Eight AFL convention delegates voted against setting a specific date, fearing that many unions might not be prepared to make the demand. Shortly after, even such strong unions as the International Typographical Union, the Iron Molders Union, and the Furniture Workers Union deemed the action either hasty or inadvisable at the moment. Other organizations agreed to assist eight-hour workday strikers, but made clear their intention not to strike for shorter hours on May 1, 1890.

The most forceful proponent for timely action was Peter J. McGuire, secretary-treasurer of the United Brotherhood of Carpenters and Joiners of America (BCJA). McGuire made two arguments in favor of setting a definite date to demand the shorter workday. First, he believed that even so mild and reasonable a demand as the eight-hour day infused organized labor with a revolutionary spirit. "Courage will come, and the federation [will be made] stronger by the agitation," he declared, pointing to the growth of the BCJA during the 1886 strike. (BCJA Locals in Chicago grew from 600 members to 5,000; in Boston they grew from 106 to 2,400 members.) Secondly, he felt that some workers would win the demand or a compromise as in 1886. If but "10,000 men adopt the nine hour day . . . it will require 1,100 more men to complete the work now done," McGuire argued, employing the theory widely held in labor circles that the shorter workday was principally important as a cure for unemployment. McGuire thus committed the BCJA to action and challenged others to follow.

Gompers exhibited greater caution. The reservations expressed by presidents of affiliated unions caused the AFL president to declare that the 1888 resolution did not *require* all unions to strike for the eight-hour workday on May 1, 1890. At the same time, the enthusiasm generated by the eight-hour movement prevented Gompers from pulling back completely from his support for the issue. On Washington's Birthday 1889, some 240 city labor federations held mass meetings for the eight-hour campaign. On July 4th, the number of rallies grew to 311 and by Labor Day to more than 420. To the founding meeting of the Second International in Paris on July 14, Gompers sent a message informing that body of its impending strike for the eight-hour workday, and the Paris congress resolved to "organize a great international demonstration" on behalf of "the legal reduction of the working day to eight hours."

Caught between the enthusiasm of rank-and-file workers for the issue and the caution of experienced union leadership, Gompers went to the December 1889 AFL convention prepared to compromise. His report proposed that the convention select one or two trades to press the eight-hour demand and assess other affiliates for assistance and educational agitation. When the first effort was successful, Gompers suggested, others would be chosen to proceed in the same manner. The convention accepted the proposal and, for the first time, gave the AFL the right to assess affiliates for a strike fund. Three months later, the AFL executive council selected the BCJA as "the best disciplined, prepared, and [most] determined to lead the movement." On May 1, the BCJA prepared to strike for the eight-hour workday with a strike fund of more than $12,000.

Building contractors generally opposed the voluntary granting of a shorter workday; thus the BCJA's notification that it intended to make the eight-hour workday universal precipitated strikes in April and May. By the middle of May, 208 BCJA locals and 57,420 carpenters had struck for a shorter workday. The discipline and preparations paid handsome dividends; strikes were successful in 137 cities, benefiting more than 46,000 workers. At the same time, the inspirational lead of the BCJA encouraged other local unions to demand reduced hours. May 1, 1890, was a day of general demonstrations in behalf of the eight-hour workday. Printers, bakers, granite cutters, and several building trades unions besides the BCJA won a shorter workday.

The zeal of the eight-hour effort of 1890, however, failed to ensure the continuity and expansion of the movement. The AFL executive committee decided that the United Mine Workers (UMW) would make the next effort to secure the eight-hour workday on May 1, 1891. But mine owners, in an effort to preempt the UMW's effort, confronted the union with a proposal for a nine-hour workday at reduced wages in March, two months before the UMW was ready. The UMW was determined to take its stand on the eight-hour issue then, but it did so without full AFL support. With an inadequate treasury, the UMW incurred financial difficulties as early as April 8, and by May 1, enthusiasm for the strike had waned. Although some miners successfully fought for the eight-hour workday, most strikes were lost. In its wake, the confusion surrounding the UMW's effort killed the remaining backing for an AFL-directed shorter-hours movement. [Ken Fones-Wolf]

FURTHER READING

Christie, Robert A. *Empire in Wood: A History of the Carpenters' Union.* Ithaca, NY: Cornell University Press, 1956.

Fine, Sidney. "The Eight-Hour Day Movement in the United States, 1888–1891." *Mississippi Valley Historical Review*, Vol. 40 (December 1953), pp. 441–462.

Foner, Philip S. *History of the Labor Movement in the United States*, Vol. 2. New York: International Publishers, 1955.

Kaufman, Stuart B., et al. *The Samuel Gompers Papers: Volume 2, The Early Years of the American Federation of Labor, 1887–1890.* Urbana, IL: University of Illinois Press, 1987.

o o o

CENTRALIA, WASHINGTON, MAS-SACRE OF 1919. The anti-radical hysteria that had gained momentum during World War I in the Northwest climaxed in November 1919 in Centralia, Washington, a lumber town with a long history of Industrial Workers of the World (IWW) and anti-IWW activities. The small IWW hall had been wrecked during a Red Cross parade on Memorial Day, 1918, its American flag torn from the wall, its Victrola auctioned in the street, and the desk confiscated by a Centralia banker. The newsstand of a blind IWW sympathizer was demolished in June 1918 because it sold the IWW *Industrial Worker*. The newsdealer was kidnapped, driven out of town, dumped into a ditch, and warned not to return at the risk of his life.

When the IWW opened a new hall in Centralia, the Centralia Protection Association, a local businessmen's group, issued regular bulletins warning of the IWW menace. A secret committee was appointed to work out details of driving the IWW from the town. Word leaked out that there was a conspiracy to raid the IWW hall during an Armistice Day parade in November. Elmer Smith, the IWW lawyer in Centralia, went to the governor to try to get protection for the organization. The owner of the building that the Wobblies rented appealed to the police for help. Wobblies circulated leaflets door-to-door asking townspeople for aid in meeting the threats against them.

On November 11, Centralians jammed the streets to celebrate Armistice Day and watch a parade of returned veterans. The postmaster and former mayor carried coils of rope. When the marching legionnaires reached the IWW hall, they were halted by the commanding officer. Statements conflict as to what happened next. Knowing what was coming and acting on legal advice, Wobblies had prepared to defend their hall against a second attack waiting inside the hall as well as on nearby rooftops. As legionnaires rushed the hall, shots were fired in a brief, bloody gunfight that killed three attackers, including the legion commander.

As paraders broke into the hall, Wesley Everest, an IWW member and a war veteran, ran out the back door being chased by legionnaires. Surrounded by a mob, he offered to give himself up to any police officer in the crowd, but as the men rushed to get him, he shot and killed one of his attackers. Knocked unconscious, Everest was dragged back to the jail by a strap around his neck.

That night, street lights were turned off while a crowd entered the jail, seized Everest and drove him to the edge of town where he was castrated and lynched. His body was hung on a railroad trestle above the Chehalis River and, as word spread through town, automobile parties drove out to see the hanging corpse. His body was taken to the jail the next day, laid in a corridor to be viewed by the eleven other IWW prisoners, and then buried by four Wobblies under guard in an unknown grave so that no pictures could be taken of the body.

Throughout the next weeks, the American Legion organized posses to hunt for IWW members; over 1,000 were arrested. The local bar association threatened its members with disbarment if they defended an IWW member. Newspaper editorials fanned the hysteria declaring, "Even to sympathize with the perpetrators of the tragedy is proof evident that the sympathizer is a traitor to his country." Washington's governor authorized the suppression of all seditious literature and encouraged police chiefs and sheriffs to arrest all radicals in their towns. Local officers of the U.S. Department of Justice closed the offices of the American Federation of Labor's Seattle *Union Record* and arrested its editorial board for urging readers to hear both sides of the story before judging the case.

Seven of the IWW prisoners were declared guilty of second-degree murder and sentenced to maximum jail terms of twenty-five to forty years. One died in prison, five others were paroled in 1933, and the other, who insisted on a full pardon, was finally released in 1940. The American Legion built a monument to the memory of the legion captain killed in front of the IWW hall on Armistice Day. The grave of Wesley Everest was found in 1988; his story was preserved in prose and poetry by Wobbly writers and sympathizers.

The Centralia tragedy climaxed the career of the IWW lumber workers' organization in the Northwest. IWW lumberjacks continued to fight the "gyppo" of the piecework system and kept agitating for better living conditions in lumber camps. Numerically, the union never recovered from the post–World War I anti-radical campaign. [Joyce L. Kornbluh]

FURTHER READING

Chaplin, Ralph, and Ben Hur Lampman. *The Centralia Case: Three Views on the Armistice Day Tragedy at Centralia, Washington, November 11, 1919.* New York: Da Capo Press, 1971.

Federal Council of Churches of Christ in America. *The Centralia Case.* New York: Federal Council of Churches of Christ in America, 1930.

Jensen, Vernon H. *Lumber and Labor.* New York: Farrar and Rinehart, 1945.

Report of the President's Mediation Commission to the United States—Unrest in the Lumber Industry. Washington, DC: Government Printing Office, 1918.

Tyler, Robert L. *Rebels of the Woods: The I.W.W. in the Pacific Northwest.* Eugene, OR: University of Oregon Press, 1967.

o   o   o

CENTURY AIRLINES PILOTS' STRIKE OF 1932. The Air Line Pilots Association strike against Century Airlines was the pilot union's first strike. It was more important to the history of the airline passenger industry than is suggested by either the relatively insignificant size of the contenders or the short duration and narrow geographical scope of the conflict.

The airline passenger industry was in its infancy in 1931, the year that both Century Airlines and the Air Line Pilots Association were formed. Congress had given the industry an initial boost with the Air Mail Act of 1925, permitting private contractors to carry airmail for the Post Office Department. The earliest scheduled passenger flights were in 1928. Congress encouraged further industry growth by passing the 1930 Watres Act, which enabled the Post Office Department to pay airlines according to space available for mail rather than for actual mail carried: subsidies were offered, in effect, for owning larger, safer planes suitable for passenger service.

In this period of government support preceding actual government regulation in the later 1930s, new entrepreneurs were free to enter the industry, but they never won airmail contracts away from the original successful 1925 bidders, who were larger, better established airlines and not necessarily low bidders. New, unsubsidized airlines operated at a relative disadvantage and hoped to influence Congress to change the bidding process in their favor.

In 1931, a free-wheeling entrepreneur from the automobile industry, Errett Lobban Cord, who had owned the Auburn Motor Company, the Duesenberg car, the Cord (the first front wheel drive), and eventually an airplane manufacturing company, decided to enter the passenger airline industry. He formed Century Airlines, which flew routes between Chicago, St. Louis, Detroit, and Cleveland, and Century Pacific Lines in the West. He paid pilots a base wage of $350 a month, compared to an average of over $600 a month on other airlines. Although he was operating without the subsidy of an airmail contract, his fares were half those of the competition and lower than railroad fares. He wanted an airmail contract and submitted a bid offering to carry the mail at half of what other airlines charged. Airmail contractors were alarmed by this threat to their safe positions.

Also in 1931, a small group of pilots formed the Air Line Pilots Association (ALPA) following a nationwide depression-induced paycut for pilots and copilots. Within months, the ALPA had an AFL charter, a Washington lobbyist, and had signed up about 65 percent of all transport pilots. However, it was reluctant to operate in the fashion of other unions and did not try to negotiate its first contract until 1939. (Pilots had tried to form a union in the 1920s, and even earlier, in 1919, they had struck to win the right to refuse to fly in dangerous weather.)

Although he paid pilots far less than the rest of the industry did, Cord announced a further reduction for Century Airlines pilots, starting February 1, 1932, to $150 a month (his pilots earned an additional $3 per hour for daytime flights and $5 per hour for night flights). He hired private armed guards for the airport. They intimidated Century pilots, offering them resignation forms, and a new job at the lower rate. The Century pilots turned to Dave Behncke, president of ALPA, for help. His intervention led to a statement of support from the national AFL and from the Illinois Federation of Labor and nothing else. A strike—or lockout, according to ALPA—followed.

Like employers in airline industry strikes of the 1980s (a pilot strike at Continental, a flight attendant strike at TWA, and a machinist strike at Eastern), Cord tried to operate with employees who would cross the picket line and with new hires. ALPA tried to proselytize these pilots so they would refuse to fly, and Cord retaliated with measures to prevent any contact between ALPA members and his pilots.

Although ALPA pilots on Capital converted few scabs into strikers, ALPA at the national level succeeded in winning influential vocal support. The Chicago City Council, sympathetic to labor, undertook an investigation of Cord's use of private guards at the Chicago airport, and was angered when Cord refused to meet with it.

The most effective support came from Congress, which had shown a continuing interest in the development of the airline passenger industry. Congress recognized that safety was the critical issue if the public was to embrace air travel, and congressmen, who were among the earliest converts to air travel, had obvious reasons for caring about safety. Congressman Fiorello LaGuardia was especially angered by Cord's categorization of pilots with truck or taxi drivers, and he and others succeeded in labeling Cord as an exploiter of labor who did not care about air safety.

LaGuardia threatened to block Cord's application for a mail contract. By the time ALPA's sympathizers were through, Cord realized he would fail in his bid for a contract, as he did, at March hearings. The writer of the most detailed history of the pilots union notes, "As if to underscore the contention that Cord's operations with inexperienced pilots were unsafe, midway through the hearings a Century aircraft crashed in St. Louis while conducting training operations, killing two of the six pilot trainees aboard."

Passenger traffic fell off as a result of the strike, the bad publicity, and the crash, and Cord decided to sell his aircraft and give up Century. He traded his aircraft and related holdings for stock in Aviation Corporation, American Airline's parent company, and for a short time, he was influential in that company, but he soon left the airline passenger industry.

When the whole system of airmail contract bidding came under investigation in 1934, several airlines that did not have airmail contracts charged that ALPA and Cord, their former ally, had colluded to blacken the eye of the unsubsidized airlines via the ALPA-Century strike. Most researchers in the field do not agree.

As a result of the strike and the practical defeat of Cord, ALPA gained a more positive and prominent image than other unions. The remaining airlines seemed to accept pilot unionization without serious opposition.

After the Century strike, Behncke, unlike other union leaders at that time, decided that he could accomplish many of his goals through legislative contacts, and ALPA did not attempt actual collective bargaining for several more years. The ground had been laid for congressional sympathy for the unionization of pilots and for collective bargaining in the airline industry. These views made it possible for ALPA to win protection through fact-finding boards of the National Labor Board of the National Industrial Recovery Act, special protection for compensation formulas under the Airmail Act of 1934, and, finally,

inclusion under the Railway Labor Act a few years later. [Frieda S. Rozen]

FURTHER READING

Baitsell, John M. *Airline Industrial Relations, Pilots and Flight Engineers.* Boston, MA: Division of Research, Graduate School of Business Administration, Harvard University, 1966.

Hopkins, George E. *The Airline Pilots—A Study in Elite Unionism,* Cambridge, MA: Harvard University Press, 1971.

Serling, Robert J. *Eagle—The Story of American Airlines.* New York: St. Martin's/ Marek, 1985.

Smith, Henry Ladd. *Airways, The History of Commercial Aviation in the United States.* New York: Alfred A. Knopf, 1942.

o o o

CHARLESTON, SOUTH CAROLINA, HOSPITAL WORKERS' STRIKE OF 1969. The struggle of Charleston, South Carolina, hospital workers is one of the major examples of the cooperation that developed in the 1960s between the Civil Rights movement and the emerging labor movement among black workers in the nation's service industries. The Charleston strikers took much of their inspiration from the dramatic events during the successful Memphis Sanitation Workers' Strike of 1968, including the assassination of civil rights leader Dr. Martin Luther King, Jr., on April 4. The Memphis strike acted as a spark which set off a series of struggles by black workers throughout the South.

In 1968, five black, licensed practical nurses from the Medical College of South Carolina complained to the Department of Health, Education, and Welfare after being discharged because of a dispute with a white supervisor over hospital procedures. The subsequent investigation turned up a pattern of discriminatory behavior by the hospital including the denial of hospital privileges to black physicians and below minimum wage pay for many black service workers. Although the five nurses were eventually reinstated, the incident caused a stir among the black community that resulted in a series of meetings among black hospital workers. When the concerns voiced at these meetings, including racial discrimination, low wages, and the lack of a grievance procedure, were rejected out of hand by the hospital's administration, the workers turned to Local 1199 of the Drug and Hospital Employees Union (1199) for guidance.

Local 1199 was accustomed to organizing under difficult conditions. Its membership of 34,000 in the spring of 1969 attested to its successes, mostly in hospitals in New York and other large eastern cities. Composed mainly of blacks, women, and Hispanics, it appeared to be the ideal union to take on the formidable task of organizing black workers in the hostile anti-union climate of Charleston. The union's involvement with black workers had given it a prominent place in the Civil Rights movement. With the support of the Southern Christian Leadership Council (SCLC), the organization which Dr. Martin Luther King, Jr., had brought to the fore in the Civil Rights movement, Local 1199 had formed the National Organizing Committee of Hospital and Nursing Home Employees. Dr. King's widow, Coretta Scott King, served as honorary chairperson with SCLC chairman Reverend Ralph Abernathy as a committee member.

Charleston offered the new labor–civil rights coalition the opportunity to test its effectiveness. Local 1199B was created for the Charleston workers. Although nearly all of the strikers were women, strike planning was carried on primarily by four men: Henry Nicholas from the national union, Andrew Young representing SCLC, William Saunders representing Charleston's black community, and Isaiah Bennet who stood for the workers. On March 17, 1969, after repeatedly refusing to meet with union delegates, the hospital administration fired seven union activists, ostensibly for leaving critically ill patients unattended in order to attend a grievance meeting. The workers, including local union president Mary Moultrie, argued that they were dismissed for their union activities.

The strike began on March 20 when 400 black nurses, nurses aides, kitchen helpers, laundry workers, and orderlies walked off their jobs. The next week, workers at the Charleston County Hospital struck in sympathy. The medical hospital administration recruited replacement workers and, claiming that they could not bargain with the union because state law forbade unionization at public agencies, refused to consider the union demands for reinstatement of fired workers, a grievance procedure, union recognition, and a pay raise to at least the federal minimum wage of $1.60 an hour. In response, the strikers turned to the Charleston black community for support.

In late April, the SCLC began to stage mass demonstrations and marches to promote national awareness of the hospital workers' plight. The tactic brought support from around the country. The May 26 issue of the *Nation* compared the fervor surrounding the strike to the Civil Rights movement with its protests, mass marches, willing arrests, and crowds swaying arm in arm singing "We Shall Overcome." In Charleston, the black community threw its support behind the strike. Students boycotted their schools, local ministers raised money from the pulpit, and many militants, such as SCLC head Ralph Abernathy, were arrested for acts of civil disobedience.

In the face of this mounting pressure, hospital chief Dr. William McCord and South Carolina governor Robert McNair held fast to the argument that there was no legal way for negotiations between a union and a public agency to take place in South Carolina. McNair made it known that the state would never recognize a public employees union. But neither McNair's stubbornness, his declaration of martial law, nor the South Carolina National Guard which he sent to Charleston could dissuade the strikers from continuing to march, protest, and go to jail for civil disobedience.

Coretta Scott King emerged as a major figure in the strike. She compared women strike leaders such as Mary Moultrie, Emma Hardin, and Rosetta Simmons to civil rights heroines such as Sojourner Truth, Rosa Parks, and Fannie Lou Hamer. King's presence was important because as a result of her national stature she was able to appeal to liberals across the country for financial contributions to the strikers. It soon became clear to strike organizers that it was necessary to bring outside pressure to bear on the city and state. Much of this support came from the labor movement. Walter Reuther, president of the United Auto Workers, gave $25,000 as did George Meany, president of the American Federation of Labor. But there was a great deal of political pressure as well. Twenty members of the U.S. House of Representatives asked President Richard Nixon to intercede on behalf of the hospital workers, and seventeen senators urged him to send federal mediators.

Rather than moving South Carolina officials, the growing outside pressure seemed to harden their stance. Boycotts of stores and schools by blacks were beginning to take a serious toll on Charleston. The daily marches, the curfew, and the presence of national guardsmen in the streets kept tourists away from the city and white Charlestonians away from the downtown area. Faced with economic disaster, the Charleston business community made a plea for a settlement. But neither the local nor the outside pressure moved South Carolina officials.

A break in the impasse came on June 5, 1969, when the Department of Health, Education, and Welfare (HEW) informed the hospital that it was in violation of the antidiscriminatory provisions for federal contracts and would either have to develop a program to comply with these provisions or face losing $12 million in federal aid. The federal agency suggested that the fired workers be rehired and the minimum wage be raised to $1.60 per hour in compliance with federal standards. Faced with this economic threat, the hospital agreed; but when told by South Carolina senator Strom Thurmond that he had been assured by the Robert Finch, President Nixon's secretary of HEW, that federal assistance would not be cut off, the governor and Dr. McCord reneged on their word.

The labor–civil rights coalition then intensified the pressure on a wider scale. Pickets appeared at the New York headquarters of textile companies with plants in South Carolina, and the Longshoremen's Union threatened to close down the port of Charleston if a settlement was not reached quickly. Under this pressure, HEW reversed itself, and Finch agreed that HEW would fulfill its legal responsibility in the area of equal employment at the Medical College of South Carolina. Secretary of Labor George Schultz sent a federal mediator to Charleston and urged Dr. McCord to settle the strike.

On June 27, a victory rally took place at Zion Olivet Church to celebrate the settlement of the strike. The struggle had gone on for 100 days. The strikers won most of their demands but did not achieve union recognition. Nevertheless, in the words of SCLC activist Andrew Young, the strike had been won "because of a wonderful marriage—the marriage of the Southern Christian Leadership Conference and Local 1199." The first of many beautiful children of that marriage, according to the Reverend Young, was Local 1199B of black hospital workers in Charleston.

Unfortunately, the lack of union recognition proved to be a tragic loss in the long run. The workers tried to maintain the union without recognition. An attempt to arrange for a form of the dues checkoff through the credit union failed. After a few months, Local 1199 pulled its staff representative out of Charleston. Soon the union disappeared. According to Mary Moultrie, president of the Charleston local, the workers were back where they started from soon after the strike. There had been improvements in working conditions and pay, but the lack of a union meant that the workers remained powerless. [Ronald L. Filippelli]

FURTHER READING

"Agony of Charleston." *America* (May 17, 1969), p. 573.

"Back to the Roots." *Newsweek* (May 5, 1969), p. 72.

Bass, J. "Hospital Strike." *New Republic* (June 7, 1969), p. 8.

Foner, Phillip. *Organized Labor and the Black Worker*. New York: Praeger, 1974.

Hoffius, Steve. "Charleston Hospital Workers' Strike, 1969." In *Working Lives: The Southern Exposure History of Labor in the South*, Marc Miller, ed. New York: Pantheon Books, 1980.

Nolan, D. "South Carolina: the Movement Finally Arrives." *Nation* (May 26, 1969), p. 655-66.

"Intransigence in Charleston." *Time* (June 20, 1969), p. 24.

"Settlement in Charleston." *Time* (July 1969), p. 15.

"Strike Gains Clout; AFL-CIO and UAW Help Charleston's Negro Hospital Workers." *Business Week* (May 17, 1969), p. 39.

"Unions Team Up With Black Power: Alliance of Civil Rights and Labor Organizations Behind Charleston Walkout." *Business Week* (April 5, 1969), pp. 22–24.

"Winning Combination: Settlement in One Charleston, S.C. Hospital." *Newsweek* (July 7, 1969), pp. 19–20.

o   o   o

CHICAGO CLOTHING WORKERS' STRIKE OF 1910. Precipitated by a walkout of sixteen young women at shop No. 5 of Hart, Schaffner & Marx, the strike of men's clothing workers spread to other factories until the city's garment industry was brought to a near standstill for almost five months. This mass strike was a harbinger of a series of uprisings in the men's garment trade which culminated in 1914 in the creation of a major industrial union, the Amalgamated Clothing Workers of America (ACWA). The strike also inaugurated the modern era of collective bargaining. Selig Perlman and Phillip Taft's *History of Labor in the United States, 1896–1932*, (1935) called the settlement "the beginning of the most highly elaborated industrial government in America based on equal participation of employer and union." The Chicago strike also prefigured the **Lawrence Textile Strike of 1912** by rallying and involving the community-at-large, which in turn celebrated the militance and solidarity of foreign-born workers of many nationalities.

The clothing workers' strike of 1910 represented a volatile response to the cutthroat competition which characterized Chicago's garment industry in the early twentieth century. The Chicago Wholesale Clothiers' Association (CWCA) had formed in 1890 to represent the interests of large manufacturers against a growing number of smaller concerns as well as the city's largest, Hart, Schaffner & Marx. Refusing to join the association and determined to increase its competitive edge, Hart, Schaffner & Marx withdrew all contract work from independent tailors and small shops and opened a factory employing over 8,000 workers. Other manufacturers reacted by cutting labor costs, and Hart, Schaffner & Marx responded in kind by announcing a lowered piece rate on September 22, 1910.

Although unsanitary working conditions, low wages, and long hours were common throughout the highly competitive clothing industry, garment workers found this new wage—and rate—regimen unacceptable. Annie Shapiro, a daughter of Russian immigrants, faced a quarter of a penny loss for each pocket that she seamed; averaging only seven dollars per week, she foresaw a 12.5 percent overall reduction in wages. She complained first to her supervisor and then turned to the district council of the United Garment Workers (UGW), a craft union mainly representing male cutters. Impatient as the local union leadership stalled, Shapiro talked with other workers, and at week's end a small group of women struck, blew their whistles, and invited others to join their picket line. Three weeks later, on October 27, as approximately 18,000 workers turned out, Thomas Rickert, national president of the UGW, finally sanctioned a general strike.

As the strike spread to other shops and eventually involved over 41,000 strikers, about 10 percent of Chicago's work force, the outdated craft union proved unable to deal with an event of such magnitude. By October 29, the Chicago Federation of Labor (CFL), the Women's Trade Union League (WTUL), and the Socialist party stepped in to organize support committees. While the UGW provided at best only nominal leadership, settlement workers, Socialists, university professors, and WTUL allies did the major work in publicizing the strikers' demands, initiating negotiations with the manufacturers, and managing an extensive relief program. By early November, a Joint Strike Conference Board, chaired by CFL president John Fitzpatrick and comprising representatives from the WTUL and UGW, met with thirty-nine strikers to plan strategy and to oversee negotiations.

Every step was fraught with difficulty. The city's garment workers were mainly recent immigrants or their children. Unfamiliar with local customs they nevertheless "pour out of the shops and factories," according to a WTUL report, "throw down their needles, and in nine different languages demand a better condition of affairs in the industry of garment-making in Chicago." To coordinate their separate protests, the WTUL strike committee called an informal meeting to hear directly from twelve representatives of the trade. League president Mary Dreier Robins then compiled their grievances and demands and produced an informational leaflet for public distribution. The *Chicago Daily Socialist* played an equally important role in spreading news of the strike. Special editions, with runs of up to 50,000, detailed conditions in the shops and daily events on the picket lines. The WTUL and local Socialists also sent dozens of speakers into the neighborhoods and arranged for appearances before various clubs and civic societies.

By far the biggest job was organizing relief for strikers and their families. By the end of November, several settlement houses reported cases of destitution. With the harsh Chicago winter still ahead, a WTUL report noted, "something more than refreshment stations became necessary." Under Robin's direction, the Joint Strike Conference Board opened several neighborhood commissary stations. Sympathetic merchants donated or offered supplies at cost, and local commissaries distributed bread, sugar, coffee, flour, and other goods to families on a rationed basis. Each site could handle as many as 500 applicants per day, including the many Jewish strikers who requested a special line of kosher items. For the 1,250 babies born during the strike, the settlement houses supplied layettes and milk. A special strike committee handled problems related to housing, such as eviction threats or fuel emergencies. A health committee recruited physicians to provide medical care to strikers and their families.

Strike committees also took on the courageous work of protecting picketers from police harassment. As manufacturers recruited strikebreakers and hired private guards to escort non-striking workers, violence escalated. Mounted police were used to disperse the crowds. Nearly 400 strikers were arrested, and eventually two were killed. The death of the first victim on December 3, brought a massive funeral parade of nearly 30,000 marchers. The police banned red flags, and protesters carried instead red and white flags with incendiary slogans. Led by a band playing the "Marseillaise," the funeral cortege made a dramatic public statement.

All of these programs depended upon the voluntary contributions in time and energy of hundreds of men and women outside the garment industry, and the Joint Strike Conference Board's success in rallying such support indicated the extent of sympathy for the strikers within the city at large. A citizens' committee, chaired by Rabbi Emil Hirsch and involving women from Hull House, including Jane Addams and Ellen Gates Star, played an important role. To strengthen its ranks, the WTUL appealed directly to wealthy women and escorted young strikers like Annie Shapiro to their elegant homes. Moved by personalized stories of conditions in the shops, some of these women formed lines of "Aristocratic Pickets," as they were called. The WTUL strike committee alone took in nearly $70,000 in contributions.

Although the Joint Strike Conference Board excelled in mobilizing the community, setting a nationwide standard for strike support in the next decade, its well-intentioned members were less successful in representing the workers' interests in negotiations with the manufacturers: they too readily conceded a central demand, the closed shop.

For the past decade the Chicago Wholesale Clothiers' Association had campaigned against unions, broken contracts, and declared the open shop throughout the industry. Membership in the UGW fell precipitously, and by 1910 represented only about 1,000 highly skilled male cutters. Whereas in 1903 the UGW had enrolled nearly 8,000 women, by the time of the strike there were virtually none. To the majority of unskilled workers, the closed shop represented their only hope for a measure of control over working conditions. In later years, Annie Shapiro ex-

plained simply: "We all went out; we had to be recognized as people."

As early as November 5, the UGW national president Thomas Rickert had signed an agreement with Hart, Schaffner & Marx that allowed for arbitration but not union recognition. The strikers called Rickert a traitor and rejected this proposal and a similar one presented on December 8. On January 14, 1911, however, the workers of Hart, Schaffner & Marx reluctantly agreed to these terms, although 18,000 strikers from other shops stayed out. Without consulting other members of the Joint Strike Conference Board, the UGW declared the strike over on February 3.

Only the strikers from Hart, Schaffner & Marx returned to work with a contract in sight. Drawn up by Clarence Darrow, this contract established wages and hours as well as health and safety measures. Considered a landmark agreement in the men's clothing industry, the agreement included a permanent board of arbitration. The firms affiliated with the Wholesale Clothiers' Association refused to accede to the strikers' demands. Only in 1919, following two more strikes, did the city's employers recognize the right of the union to represent workers in negotiations. By this time, dissident members of the UGW, led by Sidney Hillman, had formed the Amalgamated Clothing Workers of America (ACWA), and the new union acted aggressively to represent the interests of the unskilled. [Mari Jo Buhle]

FURTHER READING

Amalgamated Clothing Workers of America. *The Clothing Workers of Chicago, 1910–1922*. Chicago, IL: A.C.W.A., 1922.

Levine, Louis. *The Women's Garment Workers*. New York: B. W. Heubsch, Inc., 1924.

Payne, Elizabeth Anne. *Reform, Labor, and Feminism: Margaret Dreier Robins and the Women's Trade Union League*. Urbana, IL: University of Illinois Press, 1988.

Weiler, N. Sue. "The Uprising in Chicago: The Men's Garment Workers Strike, 1910-1911," In

A Needle, A Bobbin, A Strike: Women Needlework-ers in America. Joan M. Jensen and Sue Davison, eds. Philadelphia, PA: Temple University Press, 1984, pp. 114–145.

o   o   o

CHICAGO NEWSPAPER STRIKE OF 1912. Between 1905 and 1912, William Randolph Hearst's Chicago newspapers, the *American* and the *Examiner*, found them-selves paying higher wages than their competition because of contracts with their production unions that granted rates higher than the prevailing scale in the Chicago market. The imbalance resulted from the fact that Hearst's contracts with the print-ers, stereotypers, pressmen, engravers, and mailers were signed individually with each union in 1905, while the rest of the news-papers in the city negotiated better rates through the Chicago Chapter of the Ameri-can Newspaper Publishers' Association (ANPA). When Hearst's contract with the Web Pressmen's Local No. 4 expired, he demanded that his newspapers also come under the ANPA contract. An arbitration board, agreed to by the union, supported Hearst and issued an award that reduced the pressmen's wages by 20 to 30 percent and increased their hours.

While the board had ruled decisively against the union on the wage and hour issues, it neglected to discuss manning levels in spite of management's claim that crews sizes at the Hearst's papers were 20 percent above those of the competition. After the old contract expired at midnight on April 30, 1912, Hearst's papers not only put the new wage scale into effect, but they also reduced the number of men who operated the presses by 20 percent, claim-ing that the ANPA contract gave them that right. The pressmen, who had accepted the wage cuts, refused to accept the reduction in manning levels and struck. The Hearst management claimed that the strike was a violation of the ANPA contract with the Pressmen's Union. But union president George Berry argued that while the ANPA contract gave management the right to determine crew size, it was a limited right, subject to union consultation and the in-troduction of labor-saving equipment. Neither had been the case at the *American* and the *Examiner*.

The Hearst strike resulted in an immediate show of solidarity among the Chicago newspaper publishers. All but one of the major dailies cancelled their contracts with the Web Pressmen's Union and an-nounced that they would run their presses on an open shop basis. Management soli-darity resulted in solidarity on the union side as well. On May 3, 1912, Stereotypers' Union No. 4 joined the walkout, and soon they were joined on the picket lines by the Delivery and Mail Drivers' Union and the Newsboys' Union. Instead of solidarity, however, the action of the local Stere-otypers' Union led to a fracture of relations between the Pressmen and the Stereotypers at the national level when James J. Freel, president of the International Stereotypers' and Electrotypers' Union of North Amer-ica, ordered the Chicago local to return to work immediately and honor the contract with the ANPA. In Chicago, however, where relations between the Pressmen and his union had been close, President L. P. Straube of the Stereotypers refused to obey Freel's order. The International then sus-pended the charter of Stereotypers Union No. 4.

Another major problem facing the unions was the lack of support from the printers in Typographical Union No. 16, who remained on the job. The strike had been opposed by the local and national leaders of the International Typographical Union (ITU), including ITU president James M. Lynch, even though a substan-tial minority of local members wanted to support the pressmen. Lynch came to Chicago on May 7 to insure that the ITU local honored the contract with the ANPA.

101

o

His main concern was the campaign by George Berry of the Pressmen to convince the printers to come out in support of the strike. Berry's appeal to the principle of union solidarity was making headway among the printers. In addition, the Chicago Federation of Labor castigated ITU Local No. 16 for staying on the job, denouncing its members as "rotten" and "selfish" and branding them as strikebreakers. Nevertheless, at a mass meeting held on May 19, ITU's members voted to follow Lynch's lead and honor their contracts.

In the meantime, the newspapers had begun to operate with non-union workers and the few union members willing to work. Attempts to deliver the papers resulted in pitched battles between the replacements and the delivery drivers and newsboys who were supporting the strike. Chicago police protected the replacements and arrested large numbers of strikers. Company guards also attacked picket lines. In all, four strikers and supporters were killed by gunfire, and several others were seriously wounded in the disturbances.

With the city officials securely on the side of the publishers, the union story could only be told in the pages of the *Chicago Daily Socialist*, whose circulation expanded rapidly during the strike. This led to retaliation from the major newspapers whose guards attacked *Daily Socialist* newsboys and newsstands.

Toward the end of May, Samuel Gompers, AFL president; John Fitzpatrick, president of the Chicago Federation of Labor; and George Perkins, president of the Cigar Makers Union tried to mediate the dispute. Their efforts were rejected by the publishers who told them that under no circumstances would they resume contractual relations with the pressmen, an organization "that could not guarantee a contract," or "control its own membership."

The publishers were less harsh on the Stereotypers because the international union had refused to sanction the strike and

had ultimately revoked Local No. 4's charter. In its place a new Local 144, was chartered. Leaders of the strike were denied membership, and members of old Local 4 could only join if they repudiated the strike. Local 144 got less than a warm welcome from the Chicago labor movement, however. Its application for membership on the Chicago Allied Printing Trades Council was initially rejected, and was only accepted after John Mitchell, president of the United Mine Workers, who had been appointed by Samuel Gompers to arbitrate the dispute, ruled that Local 144 was the legal representative of the Stereotypers in Chicago. A similar embarrassment occurred when the Chicago Federation of Labor also denied Local 144 membership.

Having failed in his attempt to draw the ITU into the strike, George Berry then tried to widen the strike to other Pressmen's locals employed in the Hearst chain, but he ran into strong opposition from the New York locals who feared the destruction of their union because of the number of non-union printing shops operating in the city. Berry then turned for support to the American Federation of Labor at the organization's 1912 convention. There he ran into the opposition of James Lynch of the Typographers and James Freel of the Stereotypers who blamed Berry, not the newspaper publishers, for the trouble in Chicago. Even Max Hayes, a member of the ITU and a leading Socialist opponent of Gompers, attacked Berry and argued that contracts with employers must be honored.

Shortly thereafter, the united front of the striking Chicago unions began to crumble. In the middle of November, the delivery drivers and the newsboys returned to work. Stereotypers' Local 144 then signed an agreement with the Chicago publishers which officially ended the walkout by the now defunct Stereotypers' Local 4. For all intents and purposes, the strike was effectively over by the beginning of 1913. Nothing had been gained, and the Pressmen's union had been crushed in Chicago. [Ronald L. Filippelli]

FURTHER READING

Taft, Philip. "The Limits of Labor Unity: The Chicago Newspaper Strike of 1912." *Labor History*, Vol. 19 (Winter, 1978), pp. 100–129.

o   o   o

CHICAGO NEWSPAPER STRIKE OF 1938–1941. Although the American Newspaper Guild (ANG) was founded in 1933 in Washington, DC, it took three more years for unionization to take hold in Chicago, one of America's great newspaper cities. When the Chicago Newspaper Guild received its charter in 1936, most of its small membership rested in the city's foreign language papers, such as the German-language *Abendpost*. Very few reporters on the mass-circulation dailies belonged to the union.

When the Guild's organizing drive began to take hold, some of the publishers sought to undercut the appeal of the new union. William Randolph Hearst, owner of the *Chicago American* and the *Herald and Examiner*, and an implacable foe of unionization, offered editorial employees a return to the forty-hour week, minimum salaries, and dismissal compensation. The *Chicago Times* followed suit, although the *Chicago Tribune* and the *Chicago Daily News* did not.

While all of the Chicago papers resisted unionization, the leader of the resistance in Chicago, as elsewhere, was the newspaper tycoon, William Randolph Hearst. The working conditions of news writers had always been bad, marked as they were by no job security, irregular hours, and poor pay. During the Depression these already bad conditions worsened. On the Hearst newspapers mass layoffs occurred, and survivors suffered wage cuts of up to 30 percent. Reporters under-

going these hardships took note that the unionized mechanical employees, such as the printers, engravers, pressmen, and others suffered much less because of their contracts.

In the face of these difficult conditions, and with the example of the upsurge in unionization in the mass-production industries by the CIO, to which the ANG had affiliated, the numbers of Guild members on Chicago's big newspapers began to increase dramatically. Hearst responded by blaming the organizing drive on radicals and fired large numbers of Guild members. When forty Guild members, all branch circulation members, were fired in November 1938, the 600 unionists at the *Examiner* and the *American* struck. A serious union weakness surfaced immediately. The AFL printing trades unions and other AFL and non-union employees crossed the picket lines. The papers, though crippled, were able to continue to publish.

The failure of the AFL unions to honor the picket lines grew out of the bitter jurisdictional disputes between the AFL and the CIO. When faced with an organizing attempt by a more militant CIO union, Hearst, like many other employers, enlisted the support of the AFL against the CIO. In the Chicago walkout, the AFL supported the management position. The Federation blasted the strike as a CIO raid on an AFL jurisdiction. Indeed, a company union, the Chicago Editorial Association, an AFL affiliate, sprang up to contest the Newspaper Guild on the Hearst papers.

Guild strikers skillfully dealt with the hostile publicity coming from the Hearst organization. In a public relations campaign of their own, the strikers urged advertisers and readers to boycott the Hearst newspapers. Merchants who refused the Guild's pleas often found themselves the victims of secondary picketing. Parades were used to generate publicity in a city in which the newspapers were cooperating in a blackout of reporting on the strike.

Ironically, the Guild gained more favorable publicity from an incidence of violence on the picket line than from any other single action. At the direction of *American* publisher Merrill C. Meig, nonstriking circulation truck drivers parked their trucks beside the picket line with their motors racing, thus choking the strikers with carbon monoxide. A fight between strikers and drivers ensued. The following day pictures of Guild members picketing in gas masks appeared in papers across the country.

On January 26, 1939, Hearst signed a contract with the AFL-affiliated Chicago Editorial Association (CEA). The agreement included mandatory arbitration and a no-strike clause. This and other Hearst tactics, such as a $50,000 damage suit against the Guild for losses in advertising and circulation, failed to shake the resolve of the strikers. When Hearst succeeded in having the Guild's sound truck permit revoked, the strikers found a loophole. An injunction forbidding the Guild to carry out normal strike operations was met with an extension of the Guild boycott of Hearst papers with the help of other CIO unions to other cities. Most remarkable of all, after repeated attacks by Hearst agents on pickets, the Guild secured an injunction enjoining the publisher from using violence against the strikers.

After seventeen months of the strike, the National Labor Relations Board (NLRB) found the company guilty of a pattern of violations of Section 7(a) of the National Labor Relations Act, including spying, intimidation, coercion, and helping to create a rival union. The board ordered elections to determine bargaining agents for the workers. The NLRB order effectively brought the strike to a close. It had lasted 508 days, the longest of any of the early Guild strikes. The strike had been costly for both sides. Most of the original 600 Guild strikers never returned to work.

Hearst had been forced to close the *Herald and Examiner* and create a new paper, the *Chicago Herald-American*. There were fewer jobs for newspapermen in the city as a result. Hearst did agree to sign an interim contract with the Guild until the NLRB-ordered representation elections could be held. The agreement called for reinstatement of only 115 of the original 600 strikers, and dismissal pay for fifty-two others.

Five months after the settlement, the NLRB conducted an election at the *Herald-American*. The Guild suffered a stunning defeat. The AFL union triumphed decisively in the editorial rooms and in the commercial departments. Why the Guild lost after holding out so long is difficult to say. Certainly one reason was that more nonstrikers voted than strikers, only a minority of whom returned to the paper. Also, in distributing the dismissal pay to those not rehired, the Guild had made enemies.

Soon after the victory many remaining Guild members were dismissed, and others reluctantly joined the CEA. The Guild demanded another NLRB investigation, claiming continuing coercion and intimidation at the Hearst papers. All that it got was a settlement that gave severance pay for those who were discharged. Meanwhile, the AFL moved to use its Chicago Editorial Association as the building block of a new national union of newspaper editorial and commercial employees, the American Editorial Association.

Ironically, the Chicago Guild strike, while a disaster in the Windy City, inspired the newspaper union across the country. In July 1940, the Hearst chain, after enduring draining strikes not only in Chicago but also in Milwaukee and Seattle, agreed to a modified union shop arrangement with the Guild at most of its papers but not in Chicago, the center of the Hearst empire.
[Ronald L. Filippelli]

FURTHER READING

Carlisle, Rodney. "William Randolph Hearst's Reaction to the American Newspaper Guild: A Challenge to New Deal Labor Legislation." *Labor History*, Vol. 10 (1969), pp. 74–99.

Kritzberg, Barry. "An Unfinished Chapter in White-Collar Unionism: The Formative Years of the Chicago Newspaper Guild, Local 71, American Newspaper Guild, AFL-CIO," *Labor History*, Vol. 14, No. 3 (Summer, 1973), pp. 396–413.

Lens, Sidney. "Reunion: Celebrating the Fortieth Anniversary of Chicago's Hearst Papers Strike." *Progressive*, Vol. 43 (February 1979), p. 66.

o   o   o

CHICAGO RACE RIOT OF 1919. Race riots erupted in cities across the United States during the first two decades of the twentieth century, the bloodiest of which were in northern cities. These riots came during a massive migration of thousands of blacks to the North around World War I, which led to increased contacts and competition between blacks and whites. The steady inflow of blacks increased competition for jobs, housing, and even recreational facilities.

In Chicago, the situation reached the boiling point during July of 1919. The precipitating incident was the death of a black boy, Eugene Williams. Williams and four of his friends had been swimming in Lake Michigan when they noticed a white man throwing rocks at them from a nearby breakwater. They ducked the rocks and continued to swim. Eventually, Williams was hit in the head by a rock and drowned.

The other swimmers tried to enlist the aid of a white policeman, pointing out the white man who had thrown the rocks. But the policeman refused to arrest the man or even to let a black police officer make the arrest. Rumors quickly spread through the city, fanning the flames of racial discontent. Whites heard, for example, that a white youth had been drowned by blacks and blacks heard that a white police officer had killed a black swimmer.

That afternoon, several hundred whites and blacks, along with the police, converged on the spot where Williams drowned. Insults were exchanged and a black man with a revolver shot into the crowd of policeman and hit one officer. Another officer fired back, fatally wounding the black man; then gunfire erupted from both sides. The rioting began that evening and continued unabated for five days. On the first evening, rioting white gangs such as the Ragen Colts and the Dirty Dozen shot, stoned, stabbed, or beat more than thirty blacks. In their homes on the South Side, blacks armed themselves with guns, bricks, and knives and prepared to defend their neighborhoods from invasion. The police officers most often supported the whites. They completely closed off the black community by the end of the second day, yet almost two thirds of the 230 injured were black. On the evening of the second day, white workers and gang members stood on streetcorners near the stockyards carrying clubs, pipes, and hammers. They were waiting to brutally assault black workers as they emerged from the evening shift. One black worker who lost his life that evening was chased by a mob of whites, caught, and stabbed several times in the chest. Black workers were also pulled from streetcars and assaulted.

Carloads of whites raced through black neigborhoods firing randomly into houses and at blacks on the street. Other whites sneaked into the black neighborhoods at night and set homes on fire, although blacks caught and killed several whites. On the fourth night, the mayor called in the militia, which effectively controlled the white mobs.

But by that time, thirty people, sixteen whites and seventeen blacks, had been officially acknowledged as killed in the riots. This included seven black men who had been shot by the police. Officials also noted that 500 people of both races had been injured.

The riot occured in a period of especially nasty competition for jobs and housing in Chicago. Fifty thousand blacks had migrated to Chicago between 1917 and 1919 alone, joining a massive number of European immigrants who were working in the stockyards. The influx of blacks and European immigrants had created a very serious housing shortage. The shortage prompted those blacks who were financially able to seek housing in traditionally white neighborhoods. Whites, fearing their property values would drop, began to bomb the homes of blacks who had moved into white neighborhoods. The offices of realtors were also bombed if they were suspected of selling homes in white neighborhoods to blacks. No arrests were made of the bombers. A series of clashes between whites and blacks over parks, swimming areas, and other recreational facilities soon followed.

The longstanding competition between whites and blacks for jobs was an even more important source of interracial tension. The meatpackers, the city's major employers, had been engaged in a long struggle against unionization. For more than a decade, white stockyard workers had staged a number of strikes to protest poor wages and working conditions, but the meatpackers had used blacks to break the strikes.

Each strike defeated by the use of black replacements increased racial tensions and became part of the foundation for the events which took place in the summer of 1919. The use of black strikebreakers began in July 1894, when the packing and slaughterhouse workers struck in sympathy with Eugene V. Debs' American Railway Union. In response, the packers hired blacks for the first time in the history of the meat-packing industry. The meatpackers brought in black strikebreakers so quickly that they had to be housed in the stockyards. The striking white workers were defeated within a month and viewed the black workers as the cause, especially after employers followed suit and began hiring blacks to replace striking whites.

Many workers died in the struggles between white trade unionists and black strikebreakers. For example, during a strike by stockyard workers in 1904, under the leadership of the Amalgamated Meat Cutters and Butcher Workmen (AMCBW), strikers killed several black workers. One black worker and his ten-year-old son were assaulted by a mob of 500 men. White strikers blinded one black strikebreaker by stabbing him in both eyes. Another 2,000 white strikers hurled bricks and other objects at 200 black strikebreakers and the police who were escorting them into the stockyards. The AMCBW's president, Mike Donnelly, was ignored when he urged the white strikers to avoid violence. The frustrated Donnelly later advocated that black strikebreakers be drowned.

During the Teamsters strike in 1905, employers imported trainloads of black strikebreakers, which solidified white workers' fears that blacks posed a serious threat to their jobs. In the one hundred days that the strike lasted, twenty died and over 400 hundred were injured.

The competition for jobs was particularly fierce during the summer of 1919. Soldiers returning from World War I overwhelmed the labor market at a time when most employers were restructuring for a peacetime economy and laying off workers. Membership in labor unions increased rapidly as workers sought to protect themselves against the cutbacks. But the workers remained sharply divided along the lines of race. Not many blacks belonged to unions. Some were specifically excluded by union constitutions. Other unions that allowed blacks to join practiced segregation and required the establishment of all-black locals. The racial divisions gave the employers a powerful weapon against the white workers as industrial tensions increased. Near the end of July 1919, nearly 250,000 workers in Chicago were on strike, locked out, or threatening to strike.

Just three weeks prior to the riot, 2,000 employees of the Corn Products Refinery struck. The employer brought in 600 blacks as strikebreakers and used several black men as armed security guards to defend the plant. The gulf between white and black workers was particularly wide in the stockyards during July when 90 percent of the white workers were unionized and nearly all of the black workers were not.

The record shows quite clearly that white workers vented their rage against the encroachment of black workers during the Chicago riot of 1919. In more than twenty other cities that summer, racial conflicts among workers fanned the flames of broader racial explosions, but the Chicago riots still stand as among the bloodiest in the nation's history. [A. Ray McCoy]

FURTHER READING

Tuttle, William M., Jr. "Labor Conflict and Racial Violence: The Black Worker in Chicago, 1894–1919." *Labor History*, Vol. 10 (1969), pp. 408–432.

———. *Race Riot: Chicago in the Red Summer of 1919*. New York: Atheneum, 1975.

Waskow, Arthur I. *From Race Riot to Sit-In: 1919 and the 1960s*. Garden City, NY: Anchor Press, 1966.

o   o   o

CHICAGO TEAMSTERS' STRIKE OF 1902. The strike by Teamsters against the major packing houses of Chicago in 1902 combined a traditional labor–management conflict over wages and working conditions with the growing resentment in the nation against the increase in beef prices that followed the corporate consolidation of the meat-packing industry. Opposition to monopoly in the industry, the so-called "beef trust," brought workers, farmers, butchers, and consumers together in support of the Teamster action.

Chicagoans had been agitated about the stranglehold that the meatpackers had on them and their city for some time, and when the federal government initiated antitrust proceedings against the major meatpackers, they wholeheartedly endorsed the action. On May 20, after learning that the "big six" packing firms—Armour, Swift, Hammond, Cudahy, Schwartzschild and Sulzberger, and Nelson Morris—had met on a weekly basis for ten years to fix prices and divide the market, the U.S. Circuit Court in Chicago issued an injunction against the companies.

The strike followed the injunction by five days. At midnight on May 25, Teamsters at the union stockyards refused to work. Their grievances focused on the sixteen- to eighteen-hour workday and wages of sixteen cents to twenty-five cents an hour. They wanted the ten-hour workday, overtime pay, a five- to seven-cents-per-hour raise, and the right to arbitration of future disputes. To enforce their demands, the Teamsters held out the threat that the drivers who carried meat to the retail markets would join the strike if the meatpackers refused to talk. A strike which disrupted the movement of meat from the stockyards to the distribution houses was bad enough, but one that stopped deliveries from the distribution houses to the markets raised fears of famine. The union's boldness resulted, no doubt, from their general awareness of the resentment against the packers and their knowledge that the rest of the unions in the industry would support them.

Their assumptions proved to be correct. Only clerks, salesmen, and management personnel remained to drive the wagons. Union pickets made sure that no company wagons left the stockyards. The beef business in Chicago came to a complete halt. When the packers appealed to the major express companies, their drivers refused to work. When the railroads were asked to help, freight-handlers and switchmen stymied the move. Coal haulers warned the hotels and markets not to take delivery from non-union drivers or their supplies of fuel would be cut off.

The solidarity of the Chicago labor movement brought the city to a near crisis by the end of May. After only five days, 40 percent of the city's meatmarkets had exhausted their supplies and 70 percent of the restaurants had removed meat from the menu. In addition, Teamsters in other meat-packing centers such as St. Louis, St. Joseph, Omaha, and Kansas City held themselves in readiness to widen the strike against the "big six" if the Chicago Teamsters gave the word.

Surprisingly, in the face of this solidarity, the meatpackers refused to talk to the strikers and began to import strikebreakers. The issue of recognition of the Packing House Teamsters' Union, Local 10 particularly raised the ire of the employers. Had they been forced to pay union scale, their wage bill would have almost doubled. About the hardship caused by a lack of beef, a staple in diets of the time, the companies seemed unconcerned.

The obstinancy of the packers raised the labor struggle to a new level. Consumers undertook a boycott of the "big six," urging that people buy instead from the small companies that had signed union-scale contracts. Lists of "good" and "bad" meatpackers were widely publicized by Chicago newspapers, and organized labor in the city instructed its members to boycott the major meat companies. Butchers in the city also brought pressure on the companies either by closing their shops in support of the strike or pledging to buy only from union-contract packers. Kosher butchers in the Jewish quarter agreed not to buy any meat until the strike ended.

In this setting, class consciousness merged with consumer consciousness. Chicago's citizens did not remain passive in support of the boycott but enthusiastically took part in anti-beef trust rallies and demonstrations. Workers complained of trust control over their trades, butchers complained of the price charged them by the packers, and consumers railed against exorbitant prices. This combination of forces against monopoly capitalism also surfaced during the riots that broke out at the beginning of June. Stirred up by union accusations that the meatpackers had stolen the city's water, evaded taxes, and sold rotten and worthless meat during the Spanish-American War, the rioting lasted for several days. The riots were aimed at stopping the movement of non-union meat throughout the city. But many others besides the strikers participated. They were joined by other unionists, shopkeepers, and "young women in summer gowns and well-dressed clerks and businessmen." The inter-class nature of the crowds indicated that the resentment against the "beef trust" was communitywide and surmounted class divisions. The intensity of this community spirit became particularly evident as the crowds blocked police efforts to protect company property.

The strike ended on June 5, 1902. It had climaxed with three days of rioting involving thousands of people. The solution was a compromise denying formal recognition to the union but granting arbitration of future disputes (i.e., de facto recognition of the union), a wage increase, and premium pay for overtime. In the context of the times and considering the power of the "beef trust," the strike had been a success. But most assuredly, the Teamsters owed what success they did have to the support of a wide range of Chicago's citizens—citizens imbued with the anti-trust spirit that had been building for a decade, especially in the Middle West, and outraged by monopolistic control of a necessity of life. [Ronald L. Filippelli]

FURTHER READING

Commons, John R. "Types of American Labor Organization: The Teamsters of Chicago."

Quarterly Journal of Economics, Vol. 19 (1905), pp. 400–402.

Piott, Steven L. "The Chicago Teamsters' Strike of 1902: A Community Confronts the Beef Trust." *Labor History*, Vol. 26 (Spring, 1985), pp. 250–267.

o   o   o

CHRYSLER STRIKE OF 1939. On October 18, 1939, the United Auto Workers (UAW) struck the Chrysler Corporation in a nationwide walkout that continued for the next forty-five days. That conflict—from which the union emerged victorious—marked the beginning of two important developments. In reference to the young autoworker union's relationship to the company, the 1939 battle inaugurated an industrial relations pattern of repeated struggles between the company and rank-and-filers on the shop floor over production standards, a pattern quite unlike the bureaucratic structures that evolved at both General Motors and Ford. And equally as important, the strike also began an alliance between UAW officials and leaders of Detroit's black community, who joined together to defeat Chrysler's attempt to use its black workers as a strikebreaking force.

The Chrysler Corporation's desire to use the major 1939 internal split in the UAW to its advantage formed the immediate background of the strike. The union had essentially divided into two warring factions—the "Progressive" coalition of UAW president Homer Martin, which was considered the more conservative, and the "Unity" caucus of vice-presidents Wyndham Mortimer, Walter P. Reuther, and former Martin ally Richard Frankensteen. Eventually, the Martin forces formed the UAW-AFL as a rival to the UAW-CIO, which the "Unity" caucus came to dominate. The company, which the union had organized in a sit-down strike in 1937, determined that it would try to take ad-vantage of the union's political war to re-assert as much control as possible over production standards. Thus, it refused to extend the former contract beyond a month at a time after March 1939, claiming it did not know which union was the true collective representative. Then, in September, Chrysler announced that it would not extend the contract further. Workers also soon found that management had begun to intensify production through increased line speed.

The speeded-up production quotas weighed heavily on Chrysler's workers. In the company's flagship Dodge Main plant, many of those who could not meet the new standards were either fired or sent home with the company insisting that it had no duty to bargain with the union over grievances since no contract was in effect. After several chief stewards were fired in early October—the union's executive board counted more than 105 firings and 23 incidents of major discipline in Dodge Main—UAW chiefs realized the need to respond. A national strike vote taken on October 15 resulted in authorization by approximately 90 percent, 13,751 for a walkout versus 1,324 against. Besides a general wage increase, the union demanded joint determination of production standards. Company officials, however, were confident that they held the upper hand. "Production schedules are the management's function," declared General Manager Herman Weckler, "You may as well know we do not intend to give your union control of production."

Despite this initial corporate optimism, the Chrysler workers' insistence on staying out until their grievances had been dealt with forced an ill-advised company response. The strike had been effective in shutting down operations completely, and after several weeks, Chrysler executives attempted to sponsor a "back-to-work" movement among its black workers—many of whom did not trust the auto union. In this gambit, the automaker was encouraged by Homer Martin's rival UAW-AFL faction, which also hoped to use the racial issue to its advantage in its competition with the UAW-CIO group.

Chrysler was the second largest employer of black workers in the Detroit area—after Ford—but, as elsewhere, they had been relegated to the most arduous, low-paying jobs. The Dodge Main plant's 1,700 black workers formed a sizable core for a potential back-to-work movement, but in reality that was not the main objective. Chrysler's strategy aimed at provoking interracial violence between white and black Chrysler workers which would then force Michigan's pro-labor governor, Frank Murphy, to call out the National Guard to break the strike.

On November 27, an assemblage of 181 blacks and 6 whites with a police guard of 1,000, tried to walk through the mass picket line of over 6,000 Chrysler strikers at Dodge Main. They did so without violence. The next day the total number of blacks participating was 430, hardly enough to run the huge plant. Nor had the expected race rioting erupted, largely due to the efforts of black ministers Malcolm Dade, Charles Hill, and Horace White, who, while friendly to the UAW-CIO, were far more concerned about potential white–black violence in the racially tense city. Through their intercession, the city's political elites and even its business leaders were calling on the company to abandon its manipulations. Chrysler settled the strike on November 29, 1939. The union won advances in contract recognition of the steward system and restraints on unilateral management control of production standards.

It was an important victory, for it gave Chrysler's workers at the rank-and-file level confidence that their own actions could affect the amount of work which they were required to do. This concern with shop floor control thereafter loomed prominently in other labor struggles between the UAW and Chrysler through the late 1950s. Moreover, the 1939 Chrysler engagement also signified a stride forward in the UAW-CIO's relationship to the black community. As long as the union failed to organize black autoworkers, it would never be secure. The crisis brought the union's officers into closer contact with important allies in the black community, which would become important to the **Ford Motor Strike of 1940**, as well as to the union's continuing efforts to build a cohesive industrial union. [Gilbert J. Gall]

FURTHER READING

Jefferys, Steve. *Management and the Managed: Fifty Years of Crisis at Chrysler.* Cambridge, U.K.: Cambridge University Press, 1986.

Meier, August, and Elliot Rudwick. *Black Detroit and the Rise of the UAW.* New York: Oxford University Press, 1979.

ᵒ   ᵒ   ᵒ

CIGARMAKERS' STRIKE OF 1877. The 1877 strike of cigarmakers in New York City was the largest labor conflict the city had ever seen up to that time. It brought to the public view the plight of Bohemian tenement cigarmakers, a group of immigrant workers largely overlooked until then. The leadership of the strike led to new standards for the organization of labor conflicts and organizations in industrial America. Samuel Gompers and his ally Adolph Strasser, head of the Cigar Makers International Union (CMIU), received their battle training as two of the organizers and leaders of the strike.

At the root of the conflict was a large-scale restructuring of the thirty-year-old North American cigar industry whose center was New York City. Traditionally a craft that employed skilled male workers at relatively good wages, cigarmaking had become a sweated industry by the 1870s through the subdivision of labor and the use of cigarmolds which allowed the employment of semiskilled workers (most of them recent immigrants and many of them women) at very low wages. In addition, New York's cigar manufacturers used the depression of the 1870s to restructure their production toward low-cost brands, employing thousands of recently emigrated Bohemians and Germans. For greater cost savings production was shifted from factories to tenement apartments that were rented to the workers and their families by the manufacturers, and in which the workers lived and made cigars. The tenement workers received the lowest piece wages in the industry. They were not admitted to the CMIU which had waged a bitter fight against tenement production since the early 1870s.

The immediate cause of the great strike, which followed immediately upon the heels of the **Railroad Strikes of 1877**, was the latest in a series of wage reductions in two New York City cigar factories in August of 1877. A month later, the few hundred strikers at these factories were joined by thousands of Bohemian cigarmakers who spontaneously quit work at factories and tenements throughout New York City. Dissatisfied with starvation wages and dismal working conditions, the workers walked away from their benches without clear goals or an organization to lead them.

By mid-October, when 2,500 workers had quit at twenty-five firms, a mass meeting convened on the German Lower East Side; and with the help of members of the CMIU, an organization of strikers was formed called the Cigarmakers Central Organization. The group was independent from the union, although it would benefit from the organizational expertise and nationwide connections of some unionists who were members. It organized and represented all strikers, Germans and Bohemians, tenement and factory workers, men and women.

The Central Organization energetically took on the many tasks that needed to be done: it counted the strikers and kept track of the number of workers and firms affected by the walkout, it formulated unified demands of all strikers, and it organized relief for the striking workers through a nationwide campaign of financial support. The effectively organized strike gave the underpaid workers in the cigar industry an unprecedented amount of favorable publicity in the city's press and among immigrant and labor organizations nationwide. Over $38,000 in financial support was collected in the course of the three-month strike. But it was the organization of relief that attracted most attention among the strike's observers. Rather than making cash payments to the thousands of needy families, the Central Organization opened a number of food banks where strikers could pick up daily and weekly food rations. In order to give the most skilled workers some work at a time when New York's cigar production was at a standstill, the strikers also opened a cooperative cigar factory employing about 150 workers under the supervision of Samuel Gompers as foreman.

At first the cigar manufacturers had not been prepared for this unified response to their wage cuts, and their response to the walkout was confused and ineffective. Efforts to train young women as cigarmakers and employ them as strikebreakers failed because of the resistance of the picketers and the reluctance of non-immigrants to go to work in the tenements. But the strikers' front began to crumble by the middle of November. Economic need forced many workers back to the benches at the old wages, and evictions of cigarmakers from their tenement apartments put severe pressure on the strikers' organization. By mid-December, enough workers had returned to work for a partial resumption of production, and the manufacturers declared the strike to be over. But thousands of workers held out until late January when a vote of the remaining strikers officially ended the walkout.

By all conventional measures the strike was a failure. Only a few of the firms had temporarily given in to the strikers' demand for higher wages. By and large, wages did not rise in the industry until well into 1878–1879. The tenement system continued to flourish for the better part of a decade. But the cause of the tenement workers did not vanish; nor did Bohemian cigarmakers revert back to their former invisibility among the city's laboring people. Although the Central Organization itself did not survive long after the strike and the CMIU was also temporarily weakened by the defeat, the union re-emerged in better shape than before by the late 1880s with an increasing number of Bohemians as members. Because of the continuing popularity of the union among immigrant workers, the CMIU shed some of its craft exclusivity and welcomed women and semiskilled workers, although it continued to exclude tenement cigarmakers. A multiethnic cigarmakers union with a loyal rank-and-file membership and vigorous leaders would eventually become a national example for its successful mix of craft and industrial unionism during the early American Federation of Labor era. [Dorothee Schneider]

FURTHER READING

Gompers, Samuel. *Seventy-Five Years of Life and Labor*, Vol. 1. New York: Dutton, 1924.

Schneider, Dorothee. "The New York Cigarmakers Strike of 1877 in New York." *Labor History*, Vol. 26 (Summer, 1985), pp. 325–352.

o   o   o

CINCINNATI SHOEMAKERS' LOCKOUT OF 1888. The struggle for control of the Knights of Labor between the mixed assemblies and the craft assemblies in the late 1880s, part of the larger struggle between inclusive reform unionism and exclusive craft unionism, can be seen in microcosm in the case of the Cincinnati shoemakers. The precipitous decline of the Knights from their pinnacle of power in 1886 to their near disappearance seven years later was mirrored in the agony of District Assembly 48 in Cincinnati.

On February 1, 1888, some 2,500 workers, almost half of whom were women, were locked out of Cincinnati's shoe factories by the city's Shoe Manufacturers' Association. The lockout resulted from a complicated set of circumstances arising from the provisions of the agreement that the Knights of Labor had signed with the city's shoe manufacturers in December of 1887. The contract provided practically no protection for the workers. Although no prejudice was to be shown against members of the Knights, the manufacturers had complete freedom to organize the work and introduce new technology. Wages, in reality piece rates, were to be determined by discussions between the employers and their employees, with no formal participation by the Knights. In the event of an impasse, a committee consisting of seven manufacturers and seven employees were to "arbitrate" the differences. Only when an agreement had been reached did the Knights have the opportunity to approve the settlement. Until that point, no strikes or lockouts were permitted. Under these very restrictive circumstances, the Knights were permitted to organize the shops.

During the fall of 1887, one manufacturer, Blacker, Gerstle & Co., had introduced a new process for beading shoes. Because there was no piece rate for the process, the employer agreed to pay the old rate, six cents per dozen, with any difference to be made up later if the committee on wages agreed on a higher rate. But a member of the committee on wages told the beaders that the new rate had been set at nine cents per dozen. This the beaders told the bookkeeper who paid eight women at that rate. When the company found out, the women were informed that three cents per dozen would be subtracted from their pay. The women refused to take the cuts, arguing that the wage committee member who gave them the erroneous information should take the cuts. The company then fired the women and hired replacements. The remaining beaders and their co-workers, the lasters, refused to work with the replacements and struck in violation of the contract. At that point the Shoe Manufacturer's Association closed all their factories in Cincinnati until the Knights agreed to discipline their members and honor the contract.

Although the Knights as an organization had not been party to the original dispute, their members were affected by the lockout, and they could not remain outside of the controversy. Indeed, at a mass meeting on February 2, the shoeworkers unanimously declared that the dispute should be placed in the hands of the joint executive board of the Knights of Labor Assemblies, "their authorized representatives, and that any settlement arrived [sic] be placed before the various local Assemblies for their sanction."

The employers, however, refused to meet with the executive committee. In addition, internal divisions among the Knights were eroding the solidarity of the workers. Five of the local assemblies had been trying for some time to remove themselves from the jurisdiction of District Assembly 48, headed by Hugh Cavanaugh. They wanted to affiliate with National District Assembly No. 216, a craft assembly made up exclusively of shoemakers. Cavanaugh, on the other hand, urged the Knights' general executive board to deny the request because District Assembly 48 had entered into contracts with the shoe manufacturers of Cincinnati as the representative of the shoemakers.

The jurisdictional split became entwined with the growing discontent of the locked-out shoeworkers over the progress of the dispute. Many were unhappy about having to make sacrifices in a dispute which involved eight women and a total of $12.68 in wages. They took their anger out on Cavanaugh even though they had not permitted District Council 48 to intervene. Nevertheless, at a mass meeting at Workingmen's Hall on February 8, Cavanaugh did manage to convince the hostile crowd to refer the dispute to the District 48 Executive Board and to the union's general executive board in Philadelphia.

Events in Cincinnati moved swiftly from that point. Cavanaugh and his District Board reached an agreement with the employers calling for an end to the lockout, the rehiring of the eight discharged beaders, and the maintenance of the *status quo ante* until the Knights' general executive board ruled on the legality of the agreement that the Knights and the manufacturers had signed in December of 1887. This was the contract in force at the time of the dispute at Blacker, Gerstle & Co. Unfortunately, the agreement was rejected by the workers at a mass meeting, and the Blacker workers refused to return to work. With their arrangement with the employers collapsing, District Council 48 instructed the master workman of each local assembly to order their members back to work. The plea had little effect. Few workers returned, and the lockout continued.

Cavanaugh received support for his position from the general executive board in Philadelphia. No shoeworker assemblies could affiliate with the national district council of shoeworkers until the present agreement with the Cincinnati manufacturers had expired. Cavanaugh also agreed with the manufacturers to order the Blacker workers back to work, and that if they did not obey, to suspend their local assemblies. At this point National District Council 216, the national shoeworkers assembly, intervened and ordered its Ohio executive board member to assume control of the lockout in the name of N.D.A. 216 and to pay no attention to orders from District Assembly 48. This action coincided with the desires of the rebels in the local assemblies. Their justification was that the Knights' constitution gave jurisdiction in trade matters to the national assembly for the craft and not to the mixed district assemblies. It could be clearly seen in this confrontation the issue of craft autonomy versus the heterogeneous, mixed industrial nature of the Knights founding philosophy.

In the light of this new challenge, Cavanaugh followed through with his threat. On February 14, he suspended the two major rebel local assemblies, the Garfield and the Hannah Powderly. The next day, a group of lasters from the Garfield Assembly met and formed the Lasters' Mutual Association of Cincinnati. They had effectively seceded from the Knights of Labor. When the women of the Hannah Powderly Assembly also ignored Cavanaugh's directive, he declared the Blacker factory open to all members of the Knights, in effect inviting members of the order to scab on the striking Blacker workers.

Once again the tactic failed, and once again Cavanaugh escalated the conflict by suspending the General Custer Assembly for supporting the two other suspended assemblies. At that point Cavanaugh's remaining support among the shoeworkers crumbled. The Andrew Jackson Assembly withdrew from District Assembly 48, declaring that its members henceforth belonged to National Council 216. Finally, Assembly 280, the most important in Cincinnati, rejected Cavanaugh's actions.

By this time, however, the lockout was taking its toll on the majority of workers who had been out of work for nearly three weeks. Recognizing the opportunity that the jurisdictional fight among the Knights offered them, the manufacturers reopened their factories to all Knights who would recognize the authority of District Assembly 48. With every shoemaker local assembly in Cincinnati having been suspended by Cavanaugh, the employers saw the opportunity to rid themselves of the militancy of the craft organizations. In addition, the manufacturers also began to hire non-union workers. They required only that the "scabs" sign a declaration of loyalty to the decisions of District Assembly 48 but not that they join the Knights. In addition, they resolved to blacklist the men who had led the revolt against Cavanaugh and his district assembly and to allow no organizations to function inside the factories.

The issue was further complicated by the arrival in Cincinnati of T. B. Mcguire and A. A. Carlton who had been sent by the Knights' national general executive board to take over the rapidly deteriorating situation. The two men met with all parties and declared their support for Cavanaugh and the contract he had signed with the manufacturers. The workers were ordered to return to the shops, but no mention was made of the locked-out workers' rights to their old jobs. The decision aggravated the internal problems rather than solved them. On March 5, a mass meeting of some 800 women and 1,200 men, after verbally attacking Cavanaugh and the emissaries from Philadelphia, decided to return to work but only if the manufacturers agreed to take everybody back. The manufacturers refused the everyone-or-no-one offer. Thus frustrated, the workers had only one recourse—to request District Assembly 48 to call a general strike if the shoemakers were not re-employed. Cavanaugh and the district assembly board refused.

By this time Frank Skeffington, Master Workman for National District Assembly 216, was deeply involved in the dispute. He had earlier recommended that the workers return to the factories and immediately apply for transfer to Assembly 216. When the employers failed to allow the workers to return on their terms, Skeffington counseled the workers to attempt to take over District Assembly 48. They could then call for the general strike in the industry. The attempt ended in failure in an acrimonious mass meeting on March 11. Time was now decidedly on the side of Cavanaugh and the employers. The factories were slowly filling their rosters with non-union workers. Any call for a general strike was likely to fail. Late in March both the rebels and Cavanaugh's forces agreed to arbitration by a panel made up of an attorney representing the rebels, a priest representing District Assembly 48, and Terrence Powderly, Grand Master Workman of the Knights of Labor. The panel recommended that the shoemakers return to work. The rebellion had failed, but in the process the Knights' position in the shoe industry of Cincinnati had all but disappeared.

For their part, the manufacturers resolved never to sign a contract with a labor organization again and to operate on an open shop basis. The jurisdictional squabbling among the Knights had been costly to the industry in the short run and disastrous to the Knights in particular and to trade unionism in general in the long run. The defeat in the lockout of 1888 marked the beginning of a precipitous decline of the Knights in Cincinnati. When the Panic of 1893 hit the city, what was left of the noble order disappeared. Hugh Cavanaugh stepped down from his position in Cincinnati but went on to become a national officer of the Knights, a position he held until 1893. [Ronald L. Filippelli]

FURTHER READING

Morris, James M. "The Cincinnati Shoemakers' Lockout of 1888: A Case Study in the Demise of the Knights of Labor." *Labor History*, Vol. 13 (Fall, 1972), pp. 505–519.

————. *The Road to Trade Unionism: Organized Labor in Cincinnati to 1893.* Ph.D. dissertation, University of Cincinnati, 1969.

o   o   o

CLEVELAND, OHIO, STREET RAILWAY WORKERS' STRIKE OF 1899. Cleveland, Ohio was growing as rapidly, with as great an ethnic diversity, as any American city during the late nineteenth century. This period was in Cleveland, as in most of industrial America, also a period of considerable turmoil between labor and management. Beginning in the 1870s, an extended series of strikes occurred that dramatically changed the relationship between employers and their workers.

While the extremely destructive riots associated with the **Railroad Strikes of 1877** that occurred in Pittsburgh and elsewhere did not take place in Cleveland, the city's establishment, including such notables as John Hay, earlier Abraham Lincoln's secretary and later secretary of state, and Standard Oil tycoon John D. Rockefeller, felt threatened by repeated incidents of labor unrest, particularly in Cleveland's iron and steel industry. These conflicts continued throughout the late nineteenth century and culminated in 1899 with a street railway strike that symbolized the discontent of Cleveland's workers with the blatant disregard of their interests and demonstrated their willingness to act collectively in support of their fellow workers.

By the 1890s, street railways were necessary for most Clevelanders to get to work or otherwise move about the city. A process of consolidation had reduced the number of street railways to only two. One was the Cleveland Consolidated Street Railway Company, also called the Big Consolidated, owned by Henry A. Everett. Everett had owned one of the earlier street railway companies that had been part of a bitter strike in 1892.

The issue for the workers was not so much money, but the tyrannical practices of management, especially the speedup of street railway operations. Many employees of the Big Consolidated were members of Division 106 of the Amalgamated Association of Street Railway Employees of America (AASREA). The Amalgamated Association called a strike in 1899, primarily over the issue of the speedup. The strike was temporarily settled when Everett agreed to change schedules, ending the speedup. When the new schedules were not implemented, the Amalgamated Association operators resumed the strike. Everett, for his part, brought in strikebreakers, and the union decided that a consumer boycott of the Big Consolidated was the only hope for victory. Violent protest against the company did take place but was carried out, for the most part, by sympathizers of the strikers, not by the striking operators themselves.

The most remarkable aspects of the strike were the completeness of the consumer boycott of the Big Consolidated, and the secondary boycott implemented to force compliance with the boycott of the company's street rail lines. A series of spotters were put into place to note who rode the cars, and these "scab" riders were then refused service by many merchants in Cleveland who were sympathetic to the strikers. According to the major newspapers in the city, this elaborate boycott, enforced by a secondary boycott, was amazingly successful for a period of months. Individuals who rode the struck carrier were not only refused service in their own neighborhoods, but were shunned elsewhere as well. The organization, commitment, and involvement required to carry out such an effort was monumental. The effectiveness of the boycott diminished when foul weather reached Cleveland in the fall of 1899. By the end of 1899, the strike ended with the return of most of the union operators to work at the Big Consolidated with the issue of the speedup unresolved. Nevertheless, the solidarity of the strikers and their sympathizers displayed here is powerful evidence of the close cooperation that working-class folk were able to inspire in late-nineteenth-century Cleveland. [Leslie S. Hough]

FURTHER READING

Hough, Leslie S. "The Turbulent Spirit: Violence and Coaction among Cleveland Workers, 1877–1899." Unpublished Ph.D. dissertation, University of Virginia, 1977.

Whipple, James B. "Cleveland in Conflict: A Study in Urban Adolescence, 1876–1900." Unpublished Ph.D. dissertation, Western Reserve University, 1951.

o　o　o

CLOAKMAKERS' GENERAL STRIKE OF 1885. In August 1885, cloakmakers organized in the Knights of Labor virtually shut down the cloak trade in New York City. Their general strike was one of the labor victories that helped build the momentum for the Knights' meteoric rise in 1885 and 1886. It also demonstrated the order's effectiveness in organizing across lines of gender, religion, and ethnicity. The local organization that emerged from the strike had an even longer-term significance, eventually evolving into a local of the International Ladies' Garment Workers' Union.

Although the Knights of Labor originated among Philadelphia garment workers, the order's strength in the 1870s was in the coal-mining regions. In the early 1880s, however, the Knights penetrated the urban-immigrant enclaves, challenging the craft, gender, and ethnic animosities characterizing much of the labor movement. Workers in the garment trade split into two main groups: inside workers, more likely to be men, who worked in the large stores; and operators, more likely to be female workers, who did stitching at home or in sweatshops as part of a large and widely dispersed subcontracting system.

The first efforts to organize workers in the New York women's garment industry occurred in 1880. In 1882, German, Austrian, and Hungarian immigrant garment workers made a second effort through the auspices of the Knights of Labor. Permanent organization finally came in July 1883, when shop workers went on strike against low wages and long hours. Their demands consisted of a minimum daily wage of $2.50 for a ten-hour day with piece rates set so that operators could average about $15.00 per week. Like earlier efforts, inside workers dominated the 1883 strike which eventually led to the formation of Knights Local Assembly 3038 and the United Cloak and Suit Cutters Union, also affiliated with the Knights.

Over the next two years, the program of the Knights of Labor broadened the base of garment-worker unionism. Influenced by the order's insistence on including all workers, local assemblies in the clothing industry began to recruit operators, especially new immigrants located in tenements and sweatshops. The ritual of the Knights struck the large numbers of Jewish immigrant workers as an oddity. One worker recalled his initiation:

[T]he District Master Workman and his deputies, all Irish, came to perform the ceremony of installing us. We were all new in America and we did not understand a word of what was said. We could only see how one of them took a piece of chalk and drew a large circle on the floor and told us all to stand around the circle. Then another deputy placed a small sword on the table, and a globe was hung on the side of the door of the meeting-hall . . . Many of us on seeing the sword were not sure whether we were all going to be slaughtered or drafted into the army.

Nevertheless, the excitement generated by the Knights of Labor's upsurge in 1885–1886 overcame the hesitancy immigrants had about joining with workers of different ethnic and religious backgrounds. Equally important for the garment industry was the order's attempts to include women. One interesting aspect of the 1883 strike had been the gender segregation— male and female strikers met in different locations. In the summer of 1885, gender segregation did not disappear, but female operators were an important component of the organizations in various branches of the industry.

The events of August 1885 temporarily submerged the differences between male and female cloakmakers and between inside workers and operators. Workers rejected the exploitive conditions of the garment industry and combined in a "revolt for bread and butter." More than 1,500 cloakmakers completely shut down that branch of the trade. While the strikers had three separate meeting places—inside workers met at Golden Rule hall, operators gathered at No. 56 Orchard Street, and a special meeting for women took place at the Florence Building—the garment manufacturers and the public understood that the cloakmakers were "united in action." For the first time, inside workers and operators exerted equal influence and coordinated their demands. Furthermore, they combined the typical requests for shorter workdays and higher wages with an insistence on "polite treatment."

Because of the harsh conditions of the trade, the cloakmaker's strike won widespread public and press support. The *New York World*, for just one example, expressed a good deal of sympathy for the "poor foreigners." Even the contractors tried to make an alliance with the strikers; they hoped that the establishment of standards in the contracting system would bring some stability in the industry. Indeed, the contractors refused to take work from the manufacturers until the strike was settled.

The solidarity of the cloakmakers and public sympathy for their plight combined to make the strike brief. On the morning of August 24, the Manufacturers' Association sent a message to the strikers requesting a meeting. At 4 o'clock that afternoon, a committee from the Cloakmakers met with the strike committee of the Manufacturers to settle the strike. The Manufacturers agreed to advance wages and to negotiate price lists with the shop committees to cover each of the 800 different grades of manufactured goods in the industry. In addition, the Manufacturers' Association accepted the principle of a preferential shop for union members and both sides appointed four members to an arbitration committee designed to avert future strikes. The strikers accepted the negotiated settlement provided that each manufacturer agree to sign his name to it. This 1885 settlement marked the first time that employers and workers in the industry signed an agreement and established an arbitration committee.

Organization in the garment industry nevertheless faltered within the year. After the victory of August 1885, a new line of division appeared in labor's ranks. Although affiliated with the Knights of Labor, garment-worker labor unionism proceeded along craft lines, as demonstrated by the names of the various organizations: Gotham Knife Cutters, Dress and Cloak Makers, Cloak Finishers, Independent Cloak Operators, Cloak Pressers, and United Cloak and Suit Cutters Association. Despite the establishment of an arbitration board, the cloakmakers were again on strike during the great labor uprising of the following spring, demanding the abolition of the contract system. However, this time the incipient craft unions were not united; the cutters and the contractors sided with the manufacturers seeking to maintain the contracting system, leaving the weaker Cloak Operators and Cloak Pressers unions to wage the battle. It was no contest. The manufacturers not only successfully divided labor's ranks but also imported large shipments of ready-made garments from Germany. By the summer of 1886, garment-worker unionism had reverted to a small core of craftsmen but not before demonstrating the sporadic strength immigrant clothing workers would show until more permanently organized in the twentieth century. [Ken Fones-Wolf]

FURTHER READING

Levine, Louis. *The Women's Garment Workers: A History of the International Ladies' Garment Workers' Union.* New York: B. W. Huebsch, Inc., 1924.

O'Neal, James. *A History of the Amalgamated Ladies' Garment Cutters' Union Local 10.* New York: Local 10, 1927.

o   o   o

CLOAKMAKERS' STRIKE OF 1910. In 1909, a great series of strikes by women garment workers, popularly called the **"Uprising of the 20,000,"** shook the shirtwaist industry of New York. The strikes resulted in improved working conditions and wages for the garment workers and a tremendous increase of membership for the International Ladies Garment Workers Union (ILGWU). Only five months after the shirtwaist strike, another even larger strike paralyzed the women's clothing industry. This was the great cloakmakers strike which brought some 60,000 workers, mostly men, in the cloak and women's suit industry to the picket lines. Together the shirtwaist and cloakmakers' strikes created the foundation for strong and stable unionism in the needle trades.

Like their sisters in the shirtwaist factories, the cloakmakers worked in horrible conditions. In addition to a lack of sanitary conditions, workers had to pay for their own sewing machines and repairs. Inside contracting, which was widespread in the industry, created depressed wages. In 1910, the average wage for operators was fifteen to eighteen dollars per week, with pressers receiving fourteen dollars. During the busy season, the workday extended to as many as sixteen hours. For women, who made up about 10 percent of the workers, conditions and wages were even worse.

Union planning for the cloakmakers offensive predated the events of the 1909 waistmakers strike, a largely spontaneous event. But the victory in 1909 acted as a catalyst for the cloakmakers' drive, and by July 1910, the union was strong enough to demand union recognition, the forty-eight-hour workweek, premium pay for overtime, and the abolition of subcontracting. The strike began on July 7. It was evident from the beginning that there would be solidarity between the two major ethnic groups in the industry, the Jews and the Italians. Almost immediately, small employers who could not stand a long strike began to settle with the union. But the larger manufacturers vowed never to cede to the demand for union recognition and the closed shop. To create a fighting organization, they formed the Cloak, Suit, and Shirt Manufacturers' Protective Association and pledged not to bargain with the union.

The Association's assignment was to coordinate anti-strike activities. This included the hiring of private guards and strikebreakers. In addition, the Association obtained an injunction restricting picketing. When the strikers defied the injunction, New York City police scattered the pickets with clubs and horses. The strike attracted the attention of the National Civic Federation (NCF), the national labor–management organization formed to mediate industrial disputes. The NCF asked Supreme Court justice Louis D. Brandeis, the first Jew on the high court, to help to arrange a settlement for the strike. Under Brandeis' prodding, the ILGWU removed the closed shop from its list of demands, replacing it instead with what he called the "preferential shop." This would require an

employer to hire a union member when available but still permit him to hire non-union workers. AFL president Samuel Gompers, a member of the NCF, urged the union to accept. Neither Brandeis nor the union leaders anticipated the hostility toward their proposal from the strikers. With the newspaper of the Lower East Side, the *Jewish Daily Forward*, ridiculing the preferential shop as "the scab shop with honey," the strikers rejected the compromise overwhelmingly.

No matter what the strikers thought, the authorities had expected the preferential shop compromise to end the strike. When it didn't, the New York Supreme Court made the injunction against the strikers permanent, labeling the strike a common-law, civil conspiracy to deprive non-union men and women of the right to work. Police were instructed to disperse all pickets. Even the manufacturers' attorney described the injunction as perhaps the strongest in American history in a labor dispute. Gompers and other labor leaders uniformly blasted it as another example of the tyranny of capital.

Although the earlier attempt at negotiations had collapsed with the failure of the preferential shop solution, negotiators for the union and the Association had continued to make contact. This paid off on September 2 when the manufacturers presented a new proposal with additional concessions. The ILGWU strike committee, with the consent of only several hundred shop chairmen, accepted the employers' offer. No attempt was made to poll the 60,000 on strike. The settlement, called the "Protocol of Peace," included a fifty-hour workweek, bonus pay for overtime, ten legal holidays, wages in cash instead of checks, and a joint labor–management board to improve safety and health conditions in the shops. No strikes were permitted before arbitration, and joint union–management committees were established to handle grievances.

Wages were to be determined by negotiations in each shop.

The Protocol also lacked a time limit, although it could be terminated by either side with notice. Finally, although the settlement compelled employers to acknowledge the value of the union, it did not include the closed shop. Instead, the preferential shop reappeared. Non-union labor could only be hired when no union members were available. The preferential shop was to continue to be a stumbling block as both sides tried to live by the Protocols. Issues concerning the ability of the employer to contract work out would later become points of conflict. In addition to the preferential shop, many members objected to the no-strike-before-compulsory-arbitration clause. While at the time the Protocols of Peace were hailed as an innovative cooperative solution to the problems of industrial conflict, they soon became a point of serious contention between the parties. [Ronald L. Filippelli]

FURTHER READING

Berman, Hyman. *The Era of the Protocol: A Chapter in the History of the International Ladies' Garment Workers' Union.* Ph.D. dissertation, Columbia University, 1956.

Clark, Sue, and Edith Wyatt. *Making Both Ends Meet.* New York: Macmillan, 1911.

Foner, Philip S. *History of the Labor Movement in the United States*, Vol. 5. New York: International Publishers, 1980.

o o o

CLOAKMAKERS' STRIKE OF 1916. The chief significance of the cloakmakers strike of 1916 was that it marked the end of the "Protocol of Peace," the agreement that had governed relations between labor and management in the ladies garment industry since the great cloakmakers' strike of 1910. In addition to raising wages and reducing the workweek, the Protocol had many features that raised controversy in the International Ladies Garment Workers Union (ILGWU). The Protocol was a kind of treaty for the industry. It had no termination date, prohibited strikes, and established a permanent Board of Arbitration to resolve major disputes.

While the inability to strike bothered many ILGWU members, the most controversial feature was the "preferential" rather than the closed shop. Employers had the right to choose whom to employ, but supposedly only between one union member and another. Non-union help was only to be hired when union workers were unavailable. In practice, employers used the preferential shop to rid their workplaces of union militants and continued to contract out work to non-union workers. Indeed, resentment over the workings of the Protocol brought on an internal conflict in the union which led to the defeat of the ILGWU president, John Dyche.

The end of the Protocol came when employers refused to submit the disagreement over the interpretation of the preferential shop to arbitration as called for in the agreement. On April 16, the employers, acting in concert through their association, locked out 25,000 workers. In response, the ILGWU called out all of the other cloakmakers in the New York market. By early May, a general strike involving 60,000 workers paralyzed the women's garment industry in the city.

The strike lasted for fourteen weeks. The other unions of New York rallied to the support of the striking garment workers. The Women's Trade Union League, which had been instrumental in helping to organize the garment workers, contributed $30,000. The ILGWU itself, its treasury fattened by the organizing successes that it had enjoyed during the peaceful period of the Protocol, spent heavily to insure that the gains made in the past five years were not lost.

Faced with this impressive show of union solidarity, and with public opinion swinging to the workers, most of whom were immigrant women, the manufacturers agreed to negotiate. The settlement came on August 4, 1916. It replaced the Protocol with a standard collective bargaining agreement of two years duration. Manufacturers won the right to hire and fire as they pleased, and the union regained the right to strike if attempts to resolve disputes peacefully failed. Of particular importance to the union, the contract provided for recognition of the ILGWU. Protocols which had been established in the cloak industry in Philadelphia and Boston were also subsequently replaced by standard collective agreements. The next year, similar cooperative arrangements were discarded in the dress and waist industry.

It is too much to say that the Protocol of Peace failed. During the five years of its existence the ILGWU grew to be the third largest union in the American Federation of Labor. The agreement had also outlawed homework, established the fifty-hour workweek, and generally raised standards in what had been a terribly substandard industry. During the period of relative peace and prosperity that the Protocols provided, the ILGWU began its innovative policies in education, health care, and housing for its members. Nevertheless, as a substitute for collective bargaining, the experiment had failed. Workers in the garment industry preferred the certainty of negotiated contracts to the open-ended uncertainty of permanent arbitration. [Ronald L. Filippelli]

FURTHER READING

Berman, Hyman. *The Era of the Protocol: A Chapter in the History of the International Ladies' Garment Workers Union.* Ph.D. dissertation, Columbia University, 1956.

Foner, Philip S. *History of the Labor Movement in the United States,* Vol. 6. New York: International Publishers, 1982.

Seidman, Joel. *The Needle Trades.* New York: Farrar & Rinehart, 1942.

o   o   o

CLOTHING WORKERS' LOCKOUT OF 1920 AND 1921. Cooperation with government and industry during World War I plus the business boom that followed the war had given much of American labor leadership a false sense of security about the place of the labor movement in American society. This optimism proved to be premature as the postwar years brought a concerted attempt by industry to destroy the labor movement. The effects of this assault were intensified by the business recession that began in the middle of 1920.

The Amalgamated Clothing Workers of America (ACWA), who represented workers in the men's garment industry, was among the unions which bore the brunt of these attacks. These problems occurred while the industry was in the throes of a recession that had led to the bankruptcy of hundreds of firms. Union contracts that expired were frequently abandoned, and thousands of workers were laid off.

The industry attack was part of the "American Plan," a drive to smash unions and return to the open shop, which was launched in California and swept east. On October 7, 1920, the New York Clothing Manufacturers' Association proposed a seven-point program designed to eliminate the ACWA from the industry. The key demand was for the establishment of a piecework system that would permit the measurement and control of unit labor costs. They also asked for individual production standards and "adequate freedom" in hiring and firing, as well as in the introduction of new machinery. In the absence of union agreement, the manufacturers vowed to send work to non-union "out-of-town" shops.

As a counteroffer, ACWA president Sidney Hillman offered to have the union assume responsibility for output, to reduce labor costs where necessary, and to work out adjustments of wages and prices in cooperation with the manufacturers. The employers rejected Hillman's offer and locked the workers out on December 8, 1920.

The timing could not have been worse for the union. Depressed conditions in the industry had led to massive layoffs and a depletion of the ACWA's treasury. A feature of the lockout was a series of damage suits brought against the union for conspiracy. One suit, taking advantage of the radical preamble of the ACWA constitution, applied for an injunction against the union not only for its actions, but also "for its ideals." While most of the damage suits came to nothing, the union did suffer from a number of injunctions, including one from a New York Supreme Court judge who prohibited all picketing because the court "must stand at all times as the representative of capital, of captains of industry, devoted to the principles of individual initiative, to protect property and persons. . . ."

One of the key victories for the union was Hillman's ability to make concessions to manufacturers' associations in Rochester, Boston, and Chicago to keep those shops from joining in the lockout. This meant that nearly half of the union's membership remained on the job and able to support their locked-out brothers and sisters. It also brought great pressure on the New York manufacturers who feared the loss of markets to their competitors in other cities.

Hillman also directed a massive relief effort for the strikers. In addition to fraternal contributions from other unions, the ACWA rented a warehouse to store food supplies and opened seven cooperative commissary stores to provide food at low prices. The stores effectively served some 50,000 strikers and their families for four months. The union also ran classes in English, literature, history, and economics, as well as in trade unionism, for the strikers. Volunteer teachers, authors, and entertainers staffed the "Amalgamated Labor College."

The key to victory was the solidarity of the workers who were able to hold firm at a time of business depression and high unemployment. On the other hand, the united front of the employers began to crack in April. With one production season lost and the prospect of the loss of another, a number of smaller firms broke ranks and signed with the union, bringing some 20,000 workers back to the shops. In May, the hard-line leadership of the employers' association resigned after several of the big manufacturers withdrew from the Clothing Manufacturers' Association. The new officials began to talk with the union, and in June, the six-month struggle came to an end. The manufacturers agreed to retain the forty-four-hour workweek, the union shop, and the system of joint administration of grievances. In return, the union conceded group production standards and small wage reductions to be determined by a joint labor–management committee.

Considering the anti-labor environment in which it occurred, the great lockout in New York resulted in a victory for the ACWA. But while the union assured its survival in the key New York market, it did not achieve the kind of rational, cooperative, and stable labor relations that Hillman desired. In the next few years, the New York Clothing Manufacturers' Association disbanded and the ACWA was forced to deal with individual firms for several years. Strikes hit the industry in 1922 and 1924. Hillman's goal of integrating the union into the production structure of the industry had to wait for a more propitious time. [Ronald L. Filippelli]

FURTHER READING

Amalgamated Clothing Workers of America, 1914–1952. *ACWA Documentary History*. New York: Amalgamated Clothing Workers, Vol. 6, 1914–1916.

Epstein, Melech. *Jewish Labor in U.S.A: 1914–1952.* New York: Trade Union Sponsoring Committee, 1953.

Josephson, Matthew. *Sidney Hillman: Statesman of American Labor.* Garden City, NY: Doubleday & Co., 1952.

Soule, George. *Sidney Hillman.* New York: The Macmillan Company, 1938.

o   o   o

COEUR D'ALENE, IDAHO, MINERS' STRIKE OF 1892. This was a defensive engagement to resist a wage cut and to preserve unionism in the silver-lead mines of northern Idaho. It was fought out as a no-holds-barred brawl. The strike both precipitated the founding of the Western Federation of Miners (WFM) and helped set a discordant tone for labor–management relations in nonferrous metals for many years to come. The defeat of the miners in this battle thus eradicated not unionism, but rather the last hopes for harmony between labor and capital in western mining.

By 1892, hardrock mine owners in the Coeur d'Alene were ready for a decisive confrontation with organized labor. The burgeoning union movement in the district had become increasingly oppressive to the operators. At the beginning of the previous year, the four local unions in the area had formed the Central Executive Committee of the Miners' Union of the Coeur d'Alene, commonly known as the Coeur d'Alene Miners' Union. The new central organization had quickly enforced a standard daily wage of $3.50 for all underground workers. It had also led a successful campaign that replaced mandatory payroll deductions for a company medical plan with a union-controlled hospital. With silver and lead prices falling in an increasingly crowded market, unionism became vulnerable to counterattack.

The operators prepared systematically. They organized the Mine Owners'

Protective Association in 1891 under the leadership of prominent engineer and entrepreneur John Hays Hammond, an executive of the Bunker Hill and Sullivan Mining and Concentrating Company. The Association retained the Pinkerton Detective Agency to spy on the miners' organization. In December 1891, Pinkerton operative Charles Siringo was elected to the sensitive position of recording secretary in the Gem Miners' Union. Siringo provided the operators with a steady stream of reports on union activities and plans.

On New Year's Day of 1892, the owners announced that all extractive operations in the district would cease in two weeks. The reason given for this action was a dispute with the Northern Pacific and Union Pacific railroads over freight rates for hauling ore. Given the paucity of alternative opportunities for employment, a large share of the 2,000 laid-off workers left the area as soon as the mines shut down on January 15.

In mid-March, the operators won the freight rate changes they had sought from the railways. Accordingly, on March 18, they declared that mining operations would resume on April 1 and that a new scale of wages would prevail throughout the district. Henceforth, skilled miners would receive the customary $3.50 for ten hours' labor, but unskilled carmen and shovelers would receive only $3.00 per ten-hour day. With the introduction of highly productive steam-powered drilling machines in the Coeur d'Alene beginning in the late 1880s, the need for laborers to shovel broken ore and to push cars of ore out of the mines had increased substantially. Conversely, the demand for craftsmen adept at hand drilling had declined. Increasingly, these displaced skilled workers fell into the reservoir of competitors for unskilled work. Thus, at the bottom of the dispute was the concern over the distribution of the fruits of technological advance.

On March 21, the Coeur d'Alene Miners' Union formally rejected the management ultimatum. The union insisted simply that wages be maintained at the *status quo ante* level. By clinging to a common wage for all underground labor, the miners' unions hoped to salve the sting of the degradation of their craft. Within a week, the owners' association published a lengthy attack on the union, arguing that unskilled labor deserved lower pay. The union immediately replied that all mining work required skill and that all underground workers shared the same extraordinary safety and health hazards. With this exchange of broadsides taking the place of any semblance of collective bargaining, both sides mobilized for battle.

On April 1, the districtwide shutdown became a lockout. Four days later, the Owners' Protective Association announced their intention to suspend operations until June 1. Yet by the end of the month, the operators had begun to bring in replacement workers to extract ore. Importation of strikebreakers was necessary because the miners' organization enjoyed strong and widespread community support throughout the Coeur d'Alene, making the recruitment of local labor impossible. Having just built a hospital to serve the general public, the hardrock unions stood as benevolent pillars of the community, in a very different light from the mining corporations directed by absentee owners. In early May, after a federal judge enjoined the union from interfering with labor recruitment, the importation of new workers accelerated. Tensions rose as the strikers engaged in skirmishes with both the men who had taken their jobs and the large contingent of armed guards who protected them.

On July 9, the miners of Gem discovered that their trusted recording secretary was a spy for the operators. In the wake of this disclosure, union leaders could no longer restrain rank-and-file anger. Two days later, gun fights broke out at two sites in Gem. After exchanging rifle fire with guards and strikebreakers at the Frisco mine for two hours, strikers demolished the company's ore-processing mill with dynamite. Down the creek at the Gem mine, gunshots killed five combatants—three unionists, one strikebreaker, and one private detective. That evening in nearby Wardner, 500 armed men seized the Bunker Hill and Sullivan mine and threatened to blow it up if the company's non-union miners were not immediately discharged. Bunker Hill acceded to this demand. About 300 strikebreakers fled the district in a panic.

Before the day was over, Governor Norman Willey had sent six companies of the Idaho National Guard to Shoshone County and asked for additional federal troops. On July 13, Willey proclaimed martial law for the county. The next day, the combined state–federal force of about 1,500 under General James Curtis arrived in the Coeur d'Alene to aid the mine operators. They would occupy the district for four months.

Military force easily broke the strike. General Curtis summarily removed pro-union sheriff Richard Cunningham and replaced him with W. S. Sims, a company doctor. Assisted by Siringo, Dr. Sims personally directed the wholesale arrest of union members and their supporters. Over 300 men were herded into two crude stockades, so-called bullpens, beginning on July 15. Many of these prisoners were kept under overcrowded, unsanitary conditions for several weeks. (Of the nearly 600 arrested during the strike, no one was ultimately found guilty of any infraction of the law except contempt for the sweeping federal injunction.) In addition, Curtis closed down both the union commissary and two mines that had resumed production on the union's terms.

Needless to say, strikebreakers returned to work without interference. With military protection, mass importation of additional workers began at once. The state and federal troops safeguarded mine property as well. Ore production gradually returned to normal. By the fall of 1892, the strike was over. On November 19, Governor Willey finally lifted martial law.

Yet this clear-cut victory proved to be a small one for Coeur d'Alene employers. The district miners' union and its local affiliates survived. Union members not only regained their old jobs within a short time but soon were pressing the former strikebreakers to either join the union or leave camp. Moreover, mine workers became active in the Populist party. In the next session of the Idaho legislature, a Populist–Democratic coalition denied any appropriation for the National Guard, causing its virtual disintegration.

The setback of 1892 also led directly to broader mine labor organization. On May 15, 1893, forty-two representatives of local hardrock unions from across the Rocky Mountain region, including five delegates from the Coeur d'Alene, met in Butte, Montana, to form the Western Federation of Miners. In large part, the activists from widely scattered pockets of unionism agreed to unite in order to prevent a recurrence of the Coeur d'Alene defeat. In 1896, Edward Boyce, a veteran of the warfare in northern Idaho, became the president of the Western Federation. During his six years leading the international union, Boyce shaped an increasingly radical policy. Without question, Boyce's radicalism, as well as his tireless commitment to union organizing, derived in some measure from his personal experience of incarceration during the 1892 strike. [Alan Derickson]

FURTHER READING

Jensen, Vernon H. *Heritage of Conflict: Labor Relations in the Nonferrous Metals Industry up to 1930.* Ithaca, NY: Cornell University Press, 1950.

Lingenfelter, Richard E. *The Hardrock Miners: A History of the Mining Labor Movement in the American West, 1863–1893.* Berkeley, CA: University of California Press, 1974.

Smith, Robert W. *The Coeur d'Alene Mining War of 1892.* Corvallis, OR: Oregon State University Press, 1963.

o o o

COEUR D'ALENE, IDAHO, MINERS' STRIKE OF 1899. Less a strike than an escalation of ongoing guerrilla warfare, this battle was waged as armed struggle, pure and simple. As had become typical in the hardrock mining fields, an outburst of violent collective action by frustrated workers brought on harsh repression by state and federal authorities. Unlike the **Coeur d'Alene Strike of 1892**, this confrontation left the metal miners' movement in northern Idaho in disarray.

The local unions in the silver-lead mines of Shoshone County not only survived a major defeat in 1892 but rapidly rebuilt their strength throughout the district. Organized miners persuaded some former strikebreakers to join their ranks; they intimidated others to leave camp. In August 1894 the unions' central executive committee signed a pattern-setting agreement with a number of mine operators. The contract formally restored a daily wage of $3.50 for all underground employees, barred discrimination against union members in hiring, and called for arbitration of disputes. By 1899, every operator in the Coeur d'Alene except the Bunker Hill and Sullivan Mining and Concentrating Company hired union men and paid the Butte uniform scale of $3.50 per day.

Bunker Hill, by far the largest and most powerful operator in the district, forced job applicants to sign "yellow-dog" contracts promising no union activity in order to gain employment. Moreover, the firm retained informants within the union who reported employees who became union members. These men were fired immediately. Bunker Hill and Sullivan paid skilled miners $3.00 and unskilled mine laborers $2.50. This inferior wage structure galled both hardrock workers and the companies that had to compete against Bunker Hill. As long as the largest firm in the area paid lower wages, the standard of living of all Coeur d'Alene miners was insecure.

The Wardner Miners' Union, Local 18 of the Western Federation of Miners (WFM), adopted a different approach to organizing Bunker Hill. In order to avoid detection by informants, the local relied on two highly trusted members to recruit and initiate new members surreptitiously. By the spring of 1899, this secret campaign had organized approximately 250 men, more than half of the Bunker Hill workers. On April 13, the Wardner local publicly called on the remaining non-union employees to join them.

Ten days later, a union committee demanded that Bunker Hill recognize the union and conform to the wage standard prevailing elsewhere in the district. The company agreed to increase miners' wages to $3.50, but refused to raise laborers' pay beyond $3.00. At the same time, mine superintendent Albert Burch declared that he would see that all union members were terminated. By the evening of April 23, the Wardner Miners' Union had launched a strike against Bunker Hill.

The work stoppage was, however, less than complete. Management had, after all, spent years selecting an anti-union work force. Further, it had already conceded union scale wages for its skilled miners. In addition, the union's history of coercion and violence against nonmembers undoubtedly alienated some of the Bunker Hill workers.

The prospect of failing to bring this corporation to terms was especially infuriating to organized miners throughout the Coeur d'Alene. From its creation in the mid-1880s, the firm had been the nemesis of unionism. Since 1887, it had paid the lowest wages in the district. It had adamantly opposed the establishment of the Miners' Union Hospital in 1891. It had also played a leading role in the formation of the Mine Owners' Protective Association that year and in the wage-cutting and union-busting campaign of the following year. Management invariably claimed that the numerous disabling and fatal accidents that occurred at its properties were the victims' fault. In addition, in 1899, most miners believed (erroneously) that Bunker Hill and Sullivan had been acquired by Standard Oil, the architect of the lead trust, and the very epitome of ascendant plutocracy in the United States.

On the morning of April 29, the Northern Pacific westbound train picked up at least 200 passengers at Burke. The train made an unscheduled stop on Canyon Creek at the Frisco powderhouse where it took on 4,000 pounds of dynamite. Another 200 or so miners boarded the train at Gem and a like number got on near Wallace, having walked down to the rail line from Mullan. By the time it reached Wardner, the train was jammed with men, a large share of whom were armed and masked.

At the Bunker Hill and Sullivan property, the strikers and their supporters confronted a similarly armed group of one hundred or more non-union employees. A gun fight broke out, and one striker and one nonstriker were killed. The strikers managed to plant a heavy charge of dynamite in the ore processing mill and detonate it. The resulting explosion demolished the mill and surrounding structures.

Because the Idaho National Guard was serving in the Philippines, Governor Frank Steunenberg immediately summoned the U.S. Army. By the time General H. C. Merriam and his troops arrived, tranquillity had returned to the district. Nonetheless, Steunenberg declared martial law on

May 3 and dispatched state auditor Bartlett Sinclair to the scene to guide the military authorities. Sinclair supervised the arrests of over 700 union members and union sympathizers. As had been the case in 1892, a primitive stockade was used to confine the mass of prisoners. Many were detained for weeks under unhealthful conditions without charges.

On May 8, the state announced the institution of a new yellow-dog screening system for all mine employees. Sinclair branded the miners' unions as criminal enterprises and declared that "the employment of men belonging to said or other criminal organizations during the continuance of martial law must cease." To implement this proclamation, he required that applicants for employment at any mine in the district obtain a permit from Bunker Hill's physician, Hugh France, now the "duly appointed and authorized agent for the state of Idaho for this purpose." In order to receive a permit, a union member had to "renounce and forever abjure all allegiance" to the miners' organization. Trainloads of strikebreakers were brought in from Joplin, Missouri, and other distant mining centers.

These measures broke the strike and the miners' movement in the Coeur d'Alene. Many unionists left the area after their release from prison. Hundreds had already fled before the troops arrived. Despite the fact that he had not been present at the scene of the shooting, Paul Corcoran, secretary of the Burke Miners' Union, was convicted of the murder of the nonstriker James Cheyne and sentenced to seventeen years in prison.

The decisive role of military force in defeating the union underscored for WFM leaders the need to win control of the state. Specifically, disasters such as this helped to drive the union to adopt a Socialist political stance. Thoroughly disillusioned with both major parties, international president Edward Boyce, a charter member of the Wardner Miners' Union, led the movement toward socialism. In addition, the debacle should have made the futility of violence unmistakably clear to western hardrock unionists. Unfortunately, this lesson was lost on many in the Western Federation. [Alan Derickson]

FURTHER READING

Haywood, William D. *Bill Haywood's Book: The Autobiography of William D. Haywood.* New York: International Publishers, 1929.

Jensen, Vernon H. *Heritage of Conflict: Labor Relations in the Nonferrous Metals Industry up to 1930.* Ithaca, NY: Cornell University Press, 1950.

Phipps, Stanley S. *From Bull Pen to Bargaining Table: The Tumultuous Struggle of Coeur d'Alene's Miners for the Right to Organize, 1887–1942.* Ph.D. dissertation, University of Idaho, 1983.

o   o   o

COHOES, NEW YORK, COTTON MILL STRIKE OF 1882. On April 6, 1882, the Harmony Mills of Cohoes, New York, one of the largest cotton mill complexes in North America, posted notice that it would reduce wages 10 percent. The company claimed that depressed market conditions left them no alternative; the cotton workers' disagreed, however, and immediately gave two weeks' notice that they would quit rather than accept the pay cut. Thus began a bitter four-month strike which attracted national attention as poorly paid Irish and French-Canadian cotton-worker families struggled against one of the nation's new corporate giants.

By the 1880s, the Harmony Mills had come to dominate the political and economic life of Cohoes, a wool and cotton producing city at the confluence of the Hudson and Mohawk rivers near Albany and Troy, New York. The company had bought out all of its competitors two decades earlier, using its local monopoly to establish a company town. The company employed over 5,000 operatives, nearly one-quarter of the city's total population.

Company paternalism extended into most aspects of the mill workers' lives: Harmony Hill, the company housing complex, was a physically self-contained village shut off from the rest of the city by a cliff and the mill buildings themselves; workers shopped at the company store; the children attended the Harmony Mills Sunday School presided over by the mill superintendent. Even the most skilled mule spinners could not earn enough in the cotton mills to support a family. One-quarter of the families were, in fact, headed by widows—poor women seeking multiple jobs for themselves and their children in the textile mills in order to survive. The hours were long, the work tiresome, and the pay poor.

Absentee ownership of the mills complicated the struggles of local workers. The mills' owner, Robert Garner, lived in New York City. Harmony Mills was only one of his investments. His varied holdings helped him weather the strike in Cohoes, and he remained publicly absent from any involvement in its settlement. Workers had to negotiate with D. J. Johnston, the superintendent in charge of day-to-day operations, and his son, Robert Johnston, the general manager. The Johnstons lived in the grand mansion overlooking the 500 company tenements.

A series of strikes in 1880 set the stage for the 1882 event, helping to explain both the virulence of the latter conflict and its tactics. In a nine-day strike during February 1880, led by the women weavers, mill hands won a 10 percent wage increase, ten minutes extra for lunch, and an end to a newly imposed system in which overseers could dock them for every piece of imperfectly woven cloth. When two spinners in the men's Mule Spinners' Union, a group which had actively supported their weaver sisters, were subsequently fired for doing union business while on the job, a second strike ensued. Lasting nearly a month, the focus of this struggle shifted to a dispute over the company's decision to withhold two weeks' back pay from 414 striking workers it alleged had stopped work without giving the stipulated two weeks' notice. After a local magistrate served the company with summonses requiring that it show cause why the money should not be refunded to the men, management settled the dispute out of court. The company had been forced to swallow a bitter pill, one it did not soon forget—it had not recognized the union, but it had effectively agreed that it could not fire whomever it pleased.

When the company posted its notice of a wage reduction on Thursday, April 6, 1882, the spinners also recalled the previous battle, and this time they preceded their stoppage with two weeks' notice. During the ensuing two weeks, worker proposals to meet the problem of overproduction with an alternative to a wage cut fell on deaf ears: Harmony Mills' managers, obviously committed to full production at a lower wage, rejected a proposal from the spinners' committee that the mills shut down or run at three-quarter time for a month or two. With the two sides deadlocked, the workers shut the mills down on April 19. The 1882 Harmony Mills' strike had begun.

In the next six weeks the cotton workers, most of whom were immigrant Irish and French-Canadian women and children, basked in the attention and support which a local, regional, statewide, and national union movement and national press coverage gave to their struggle against such a wealthy foe. Almost immediately, the weavers, most of whom were women, and the spinners and carders, most of whom were men, reorganized the unions they had disbanded as part of the 1880 settlement agreement. Thousands gathered at weekly rallies, addressed in both French and English, to hear state and national labor leaders such as John Swinton, Robert Blissert (head of the New York City Central Labor Council), and Samuel Gompers, as well as local labor chiefs like the Cohoes spinner Joseph Delehanty, and Troy iron-molder organizer Dugald Campbell. All of the speakers attacked the Harmony Mills and urged resistance. Picnics and vaudeville benefits regularly raised funds for the striking families. About $2,300 in donations enabled the newly established workers' supply store to remain well stocked. Local merchants offered striking workers 5 percent reductions or contributed to the strike funds. The largest contributions, however, came from powerful iron-molder locals: the Troy Iron Molders' Union, No. 2 (which included Cohoes molders) gave $500, while Albany local, No. 8, gave $100.

Only after six weeks did the Johnstons take action to open the mills. On June 1, the mills quietly reopened, hoping to attract tired and hungry strikers ready to accept the wage cut. For fear of creating too much excitement among strikers, no bell was rung. Only one adult and two children appeared for work, however, so the mills closed again. The next week the company tried once more, but the work force still comprised only twelve hands, five strikers and seven section bosses. Once again the company closed the mills.

In mid-July, with the strike now entering its third month, the company increased the pressure. After rejecting an effort at mediation by Robert Blissert, it announced that arrangements had been made to bring fifty Swedish families to Cohoes to replace families which had left town for work elsewhere. At the same time, the company issued eviction notices to fourteen strike leaders and 150 women who resided in the company boarding houses. Management heretofore had feared that evictions would arouse public support for the workers as it had in 1880, but now it took the chance that the strike's duration would have taken its toll on the cotton workers' meager resources. Indeed, the local press estimated that nearly one in

three families had gone outside the city for work, many leaving the area permanently. Many of those who stayed, the pro-labor Troy *Press* reported, were discouraged by the insufficient strike funds. Joseph Delehanty, the spinner who had assumed a leadership position in the strike, turned the eviction into a temporary source of worker solidarity. Until this strike, management had always collected rent two weeks after occupancy, but now they insisted on payment two weeks in advance. Delehanty refused, forcing his eviction for non-payment of advance rent. He was to be the only tenant actually evicted, and his action turned the company's threat into a psychological victory for the strikers. Delehanty became a martyr, and his vindication prompted further resistance.

On August 4, fifteen weeks after the first shutdown, the Harmony Mills reopened for the third time, and the struggle intensified. Each day for the next three weeks, management sought to break the cotton-worker community's solidarity, and to entice strikers back to work. The company hired five deputy sheriffs to guard the returning workers against daily crowds of hooting strikers and their children. Simultaneously, it intimidated non-striking maintenance workers at the mills to pressure their relatives into working. Strikers, for their part, kept pressure on vacillating neighbors, and the Spinners Union published a list of sixteen "rat spinners" who had returned to work. Between this hammer and anvil stood the impoverished cotton-worker families. Accounts of near starvation increased in August. Then, on August 16, the company issued general eviction notices to all strikers, ostensibly to make room for the Swedish families. Destitute and demoralized, on August 26, after four months of resistance, the Harmony Mills cotton operatives voted to return to work under the wage reduction.

The operatives lost, but the strike testified to the capacity for organization and resistance within an industry of mostly unskilled immigrant women and children whom the organized labor movement had all but forsaken. More immediately, out of the battle came a permanent association and heightened worker political consciousness. At the same meeting at which the workers voted to return to work, they also agreed to unite in an assembly of the Knights of Labor. Then, scarcely two months later, they demonstrated their newfound political power. Carrying the banner of the Democratic party and the new Cohoes Working Men's party, Joseph Delehanty, their leader, was elected state assemblyman from Albany County. [Daniel Walkowitz]

FURTHER READING

Walkowitz, Daniel J. "Workingclass Women in the Gilded Age: Factory, Community and Family Life Among Cohoes, New York, Cotton Workers." *Journal of Social History*, Vol. 5 (1972), pp. 464–490.

———. *Worker City, Company Town: Iron and Cotton-Worker Protest in Troy and Cohoes, New York, 1855–84.* Urbana, IL: University of Illinois Press, 1978, pp. 219–229.

o   o   o

COLONIAL STRIKES. Although collective action by journeymen workers, as distinguished from combinations by licensed trades, guild groups, or employers' trade associations, was rare, conflict between workers and employers in the form of strikes, slowdowns, and conspiracies goes back to the earliest days of the Colonial period. Overseer John Winter, who was constantly struggling to keep his employer's indentured servants and fishermen at work on Richmond Island, off the coast of Maine, reported in 1636 that they "fell into mutany" against him for withholding the previous year's wages. Apparently, the workers conspired to run away and many did. When Winter tried to blacklist

the runaways on the Maine coast, other workers resisted. The frustrated Winter advised his employer, Robert Trelawney, not to use bound workers in the future unless their indentures contained a penalty for breach of contract. It seems that troubles on Trelawney's estate were endemic. In 1641, his servants refused to work unless they received better food, and Trelawney's carpenters staged what was probably one of the first slowdowns in American labor history. The carpenter's knew that the labor shortage for skilled workers in the colony gave them leverage. When Trelawney criticized their action, they told him that if he didn't like it they would leave, fully aware that there were no other carpenters to be had.

If one of the first slowdowns occurred in Maine, then it is probable that the first lockout took place in the Gloucester, Massachusetts, shipyards when colonial authorities forbade a group of troublesome shipwrights to work without further orders from the governor. Massachusetts was also the site, in 1741, of an agreement among Boston caulkers, a group known for its solidarity and its radicalism, to protect themselves against inflation by not accepting paper money from their employers in payment for their labor.

Strikes among journeymen artisans were rare in the Colonial period, but they did occur. New York tailors struck against a pay cut in 1768. They offered to work on their own for "three shillings and six pence per day" plus meals. They took care in the public offer of their services not to mention that they were on strike, but merely asserted that they could not support their families on the wages of journeymen. Instead, they had decided to compete directly with their former employers, the master tailors.

In 1778, during the American Revolution, the journeymen printers of New York City demanded a substantial increase in wages to offset the effects of wartime inflation. The demands of the printers were directed to the master printers. But the journeymen, like the tailors before them, were hesitant to be labeled as a combination against the master printers. No doubt this reluctance sprang from the fear of how the British forces occupying the city would deal with such a combination of working-men, especially considering the manner in which unions were repressed in England, where they were subject to the common-law conspiracy doctrine.

In the manufacturing industries, only the iron industry suffered strikes. When their wages were not paid at the Hibernia Iron Works in New Jersey in 1774, the carpenters struck. And there is also fragmentary evidence that German immigrants, recruited to work in the iron industry, staged slowdowns to demand higher wages. [Ronald L. Filippelli]

FURTHER READING

Commons, John R., et al. *History of Labour in the United States*, Vol. 1. New York: Macmillan, 1936.

Morris, Richard B. *Government and Labor in Early America* New York: Harper and Row, 1946.

o   o   o

COORS BEER STRIKE AND BOY-COTT OF 1977–1987. One of the longest labor disputes in American history began on April 5, 1977, when Local 366 of the Brewery Workers Union struck the Adolph Coors Brewing Company of Golden, Colorado, the nation's fifth largest brewer. Coors beer had grown dramatically in popularity because of the publicity over the fact that it was the favorite beer of Presidents Dwight Eisenhower and Gerald Ford, as well as popular movie actor Paul Newman. The strike began as a traditional labor–management dispute. The company, which had been a union shop for forty-two years, sought to limit seniority rights and dimin-

ish the authority of Local 336 over its 1,472 members.

The company's demands rankled the union because they were the latest in a list of concessions that the company had won over the years from Local 366. By 1977, Coors workers could be disciplined or discharged for a list of actions that included conduct which violated the common decency of the community, disrespect toward superiors, and disparaging remarks about the employer or the product. In the 1977 negotiations, the company demanded work rule changes that would permit it to assign workers "at its sole discretion" and without regard to seniority. The union interpreted the hard line from Coors as an attempt to force the union to strike. The company denied this, claiming that it was motivated by the need to make its operations more efficient and flexible.

There was considerable evidence that the union was correct in assuming that Coors wanted to rid itself of the union. According to William Coors, company president, the company had lived with the union shop for forty-two years but had always been philosophically opposed to it. In addition, William's brother, Joseph, was a well-known backer of the ultra-right-wing John Birch Society and an implacable opponent of the liberal causes that the trade union movement supported, including the Equal Rights Amendment for women.

Within two weeks of the strike—after they had received a series of letters from the company that threatened them with permanent loss of their jobs—more than half of the strikers crossed the picket lines and returned to work. The company replaced the others with new workers and promptly added a demand for the open shop to its contract proposal. Soon after, the union received another blow when the Transportation Drivers and Mechanics, a sub-unit of Local 336, accepted the open shop contract and voted to leave the union to set up its own "association." Finally, in December of 1978, after the remaining strikers had rejected the company's final offer, those working voted to decertify the Brewery Workers and Coors became officially non-union.

On the defensive, the union expanded the dispute to include Coors' use of lie-detector tests to probe into the lives of job applicants. In a series of affidavits collected by the union, striking employees charged that company-administered polygraph tests required them to answer questions about their sexual preference and their political beliefs. The union also charged that Coors had discriminated in hiring against women, homosexuals, blacks, and Hispanics. The facts seemed to support the charge. Before the strike Coors had hired only ninety-two Chicanos, fifty-nine blacks, and forty-five women among the 1,472 workers in jobs covered by the union contract. Indeed, for nine years Hispanic organizations had been boycotting Coors for its hiring policies.

The confluence of these issues brought the strikers many sympathizers. Homosexual rights, feminist, Hispanic, and labor groups promoted a nationwide boycott of Coors beer. The boycott had an immediate impact, particularly in the all important California market, where sales were down by 15 percent. The boycott also hindered the company's ability to expand. At the beginning of the strike, Coors beer was sold mainly in fourteen western states, with California alone accounting for some 45 percent of its volume. Attempts to market the product in heavily unionized states such as Michigan, Pennsylvania, and New York were negatively affected by the boycott. In New York City, where labor, homosexual rights, and feminist groups had significant influence, the sale of Coors beer met with powerful opposition.

On August 19, 1987, ten years after the beginning of the strike, Coors and the American Federation of Labor-Congress of Industrial Organizations (AFL-CIO) re-solved the dispute. The AFL-CIO agreed to call off the boycott in exchange for a promise from Coors that the company would not interfere with a union organizing drive. In addition, Coors pledged to sign a union-approved contract for any future plant construction. Coors also tried to mend fences with the other groups that had shunned its beer by opening up its hiring practices and by aiming its advertising at minority audiences.

The settlement did not reflect a change of heart on the part of Coors' management concerning unions. Rather, it was a realistic response to the company's need to expand into midwestern and eastern markets to compete with aggressive rival beer manufacturers. In order to do this successfully, it had to shed the anti-union and anti-minority image that the boycotters had succeeded in assigning to the company. [Ronald L. Filippelli]

FURTHER READING

Atchison, Sandra. "Will Labor's Joe Sixpack Come Back to Coors?" *Business Week* (September 7, 1987), p. 29.

"Bitter Beercott: Dispute Over Polygraph Exams at Adolph Coors Company." *Time* (December 26, 1977), p. 15.

"Coors Beer, The Union Buster." *The Nation* (April 15, 1978), pp. 434–436.

Rozek, Edward. "The Brewer of Golden." *National Review* (October 26, 1979), p. 1363.

Tasini, Joseph. "The Beer and the Boycott [Truce with the AFL-CIO]." *New York Times* (January 31, 1988), pp. 18–21+.

o   o   o

COPPER STRIKE OF 1967–1968. For more than eight months, beginning in the intense heat of a desert summer and continuing through the bitter cold that engulfed the upper plains states and the East, most of the nation's copper mines, refineries, and fabricating plants as well as lead, zinc, and brass facilities were shut down by a coalition of twenty-six unions from July 1967 to March 1968.

It came close to being the longest industrywide strike in U.S. history. It affected virtually all of the 400 largest industrial corporations, initiated coordinated bargaining in the three separate nonferrous industry groups, and became the impetus for establishing a multi-million-dollar strike and defense fund within the coalition's lead union, the United Steel Workers of America (USWA).

As with all large and difficult strikes, the results were mixed and the conclusions of the participants and observers were mixed. For the USWA and the coalition of twenty-five industrial and craft unions, it was a classic encounter in which "labor's united ranks held firm until the biggest package in copper history was won." Company perspectives saw "many miners bankrupted, businesses collapsed, and (mining towns) . . . left a financial shambles."

The "Great Copper Strike," as *Fortune* magazine termed it, came at a time when the Industrial Union Department of the AFL-CIO sought to establish coalitions of industrial unions within multi-union bargaining structures with common expiration dates in order to gain maximum strength at the negotiating table. At the height of the strike, AFL-CIO president George Meany warned that it "was a strike that labor cannot afford to lose." A war chest of support from the AFL-CIO's 100-plus affiliates backed up the concern.

To understand the strike, the tumultuous and often violent history of the North American mining industry and its workers is a prerequisite. Hardrock mining in the western states involved those hardy stock of settlers who followed the massive post–Civil War migration. They included gold miners in Colorado and the Dakotas, silver miners in Nevada and Idaho, and copper miners in New Mexico, Michigan, Utah, Montana, and Arizona.

By the last decade of the nineteenth century, railroad interests and development companies had sought to consolidate many of the wealthy mining properties. Miners who sought to organize as had their brothers in the coal states in the East soon learned that the Western gunslinging tradition was to be extended to pioneer "labor relations."

The first union of hardrock miners, the Western Federation of Miners (WFM), was actually conceived in the notorious "bullpens" of the Coeur d'Alene section of Idaho. "We are not ashamed of having been born in jail," declared William D. Haywood, the burly secretary-treasurer of the WFM.

Rejecting a $1.00-a-day wage reduction, the Idaho gold, silver, and lead miners faced an array of anti-labor forces, including strikebreakers, injunctions, and the state militia. As a result of this conflict, troops hastily erected bullpens and thrust several hundred miners in them on July 11, 1892. Almost a century later, historians of the USWA would recall that on that same day state militia were called in to crush the strikers at Carnegie's steel works in Homestead, Pennsylvania.

In Butte, Montana, the miners had already won a wage scale which was to make that town the "Gibraltar of Unionism." It was here, in 1893, that the Federation was formed by forty-two delegates representing gold, silver, and copper miners from a dozen states. Just three years later, the new federation was the driving force behind the adoption of the eight-hour workday law in Utah, the first in the United States.

The WFM became allied with the Industrial Workers of the World (IWW), which issued a call for industrial unionism in opposition to the craft organization concept of the American Federation of Labor. Joe Hill, the movement's martyr, gave the call before his execution by a Utah firing squad: "Don't mourn—organize."

The same year, 1915, the WFM reconstituted itself as the International Union of Mine, Mill, and Smelter Workers.

Before the year was over, a bitter strike in the western mining towns was to begin, and strife continued for two decades. It reached its apex in 1916 with the infamous "Bisbee deportation," when some 1,186 IWW-led miners in Bisbee, Arizona, were rounded up by twice as many hired vigilantes of the Phelps-Dodge Corporation. At gunpoint, they were herded into railroad cars used to transport cattle and shipped across Arizona in midsummer, without adequate food or water, to the New Mexico desert.

Mine Mill was to be one of the eight original unions of the AFL to form themselves into the Committee of Industrial Organization (CIO) under John L. Lewis in 1935. It was to remain a militant member of the CIO until the post–World War II period. Refusing to comply with the Taft-Hartley Act and backing Henry Wallace rather than Harry Truman for President, Mine Mill was expelled from the CIO and labor's mainstream in 1949 for alleged communist domination.

For the next two decades Mine Mill was to be consigned to the labor oblivion as a "left" union, retaining fraternal relationships only with the United Electrical Workers (UE), the West Coast Longshoremen of Harry Bridges, and other independent, non–AFL-CIO affiliates. As such, it was fair game for raiding expeditions by the larger affiliated unions, and the USWA looked upon Mine Mill as its logical target. A bitter union against union conflict ensued, in which the industry took satisfaction, which limited gains in copper negotiations in the years following the end of World War II.

By 1966, merger talks were under way between Mine Mill and the USWA, which the year earlier had gained new leadership under I. W. Abel in the first turnover of Steelworkers leadership in its his-

tory. "We used to call them red," quipped the USWA's vice-president, Joseph P. Molony, "and now we call them red-blooded." By 1967, the two unions had agreed to a merger, which amounted to an absorption of some 40,000 Mine Mill members into the USWA.

Mine Mill's last president, Albert Skinner, hailed the merger as "the development of a new force to obtain decent wages and working conditions in an industry notorious for its anti-union posture." The merger took place in Tucson, Arizona, in January 1967, and was approved by the USWA in June. Six weeks later the new unity was to be tested in the copper fields as 37,000 USWA members in the nonferrous industry went out on strike.

Within a month they were joined by another 13,000 members of the Auto Workers, the Machinists, Electrical Workers, the Teamsters, and construction trades with contracts among the various nonferrous metals fabrication employers. The scope of the strike in both numbers and geography was extensive.

It was concentrated in the copper fields of the West in Arizona, New Mexico, and Montana and of the Midwest in Michigan. It included smelters and refineries in Texas, Michigan, Washington, Maryland, and other states, and metals manufacturing and copper and brass plants in Wisconsin, New York, Connecticut, New Jersey, Maryland, and Ohio. Also affected were lead and zinc facilities in Missouri and Pennsylvania.

The traditional fragmented bargaining dominated by the companies took advantage of the patchwork-quilt pattern of unions in the industry. The companies not only rejected industrywide bargaining, but refused even to meet with the unions in the same city.

In time, the strike would cost the industry some $200 million in after-tax earnings, although *Fortune* noted that while all the "big four"—Anaconda, American

Smelting & Refining, Phelps-Dodge, and Kennecott—"reported severe declines in profits and sales for the year (1967), none went into the red."

World demand for copper was down, to the advantage of the domestic U.S. industry. However, hard-hit Kennecott, with sales down 37 percent and profits falling by 27 percent, willingly shed its Chilean subsidiary by selling 51 percent to the government.

Phelps-Dodge profits plunged by 39 percent, but it, among the "big four," maintained the industry's hard line against the coalition of unions. "The economic and human carnage of the bitter confrontation had become brutal . . . in what one expert observer had aptly called an 'economic holy war,'" wrote *Business Week* as the strike moved into February 1968.

The copper industry rejected the call for companywide bargaining, seeking to retain narrower bargaining units. The National Nonferrous Industry Union Committee was just as adamant. It was led by the USWA's eloquent Molony, a firebrand unionist who had come from the ore docks in Buffalo to the second highest elective office in the million-member Steelworkers. To many, he was the closest to John L. Lewis that the movement had produced in three decades.

As the strike continued to devastate the economies of copper states like Arizona and Utah, the political calls began to build for federal intervention. Finally in January 1968, President Lyndon Johnson named a special investigative commission headed by George Taylor, a widely respected economist and mediator from the Wharton School of Finance at the University of Pennsylvania. The other commission members were George Reedy, one-time White House press secretary and Monsignor George Higgins, veteran labor activist and head of the Social Action Department of the national Catholic Welfare Conference.

The Taylor Commission released its findings on February 20, and they were not to the liking of the union coalition. "The panel completely ignored the union arguments for company-wide talks, uniform terminations, and wage scales," said the National Nonferrous Industry Conference, the bargaining group of the twenty-six unions. The commission recommended three different groupings for bargaining, each with different expiration dates for contracts. One group included copper mining, smelting, and refining, another for other nonferrous metals such as lead and zinc, and a third for metals manufacturing.

President Johnson summoned the negotiators to Washington on March 1. By March 12 the union's Industry Conference approved a compromise settlement, but it was rejected by most of the major producers. The first company to break ranks was Magma Copper, which signed on March 13, followed by Phelps-Dodge on March 16. Asarco, Kennecott, and Anaconda had approved the pact by March 27, and the picket signs came down by the end of the month.

An added impetus was the declaration by the head of the East Coast International Longshoremen's Association, Teddy Gleason, that his members would refuse to unload imported copper as long as the industry resisted a settlement. The West Coast Longshoremen of Harry Bridges had earlier supported the strikers with a similar pledge. With the prospect of the industry's customers being totally cut off from copper sources, the settlement process had come together.

Under the terms of the new contracts, which the union said was a $1.13 package, most workers in the industry won wage gains averaging fifty-six cents an hour, distributed in wage rate restructuring programs, in across-the-board wage hikes, and in increment increases. Major pension improvements were also won.

Coordinated bargaining was preserved for the individual segments and the process would continue in primary copper bargaining. However, as always in the past, it was the extraction segment—the miners and smeltermen—who had to lead first in negotiations and fight the battles on the picket lines.

A by-product of the Great Copper Strike might have set the stage for eventual survival of the USWA in the coming depression of the American steel industry, an event which few would have predicted in the late 1960s. Recognizing the hardship that striking copper workers sustained, with union aid averaging only fifteen or twenty dollars a week, Molony urged Abel to seek constitutional authorization to allocate some dues monies toward strike assistance.

At a special convention in March 1968, a $25 million Strike and Defense Fund was authorized. Abel told the union that they could no longer ignore the "increasingly powerful corporate combinations capable of withstanding even more strike pressure." The Fund was to become the front line of union strategy in the Phelps-Dodge strike of 1983–1986 and the 1986–1987 lockout with USX, the Old United States Steel Corporation, in the steel industry. The war in the copper fields in the late 1960s was prologue to the renewal of industrial conflict in the 1980s. [Russell W. Gibbons]

FURTHER READING

"Copper: A Bitter Aftermath." *Newsweek* (April 15, 1968) p. 80.

"Copper's Holy War." *Newsweek* (January 22, 1968) pp. 75–76.

Steel Labor. Western Edition. (June 1967–March 1968).

"The Great Copper Strike." *Fortune* (June 15, 1968) pp. 310–312.

"Tough Stands Stymie a Copper Settlement." *Business Week* (July 8, 1967) pp. 111–112.

United Steelworkers of America. *Then and Now: The Road Between.* Pittsburgh, PA: United Steelworkers of America, 1973.

o o o

CORDWAINERS' CONSPIRACY CASE OF 1806. In 1806, a group of shoemakers or "cordwainers," in Philadelphia were convicted of the crime of conspiring to demand higher wages from their employer. As a consequence of the case, the common law was used for the first time in America to prevent workers from acting together to improve their wages and working conditions. The *Cordwainers* case had important legal and social implications for American workers. For more than a century, the conspiracy doctrine provided the basic legal framework for the regulation of employment relationships.

The shoemakers' strike was precipitated by a reduction in prices paid by masters to the journeymen shoemakers. Under the system of production at that time, the master shoemakers contracted with journeymen to produce a specific amount of work for a fixed price per item. Workers attempted to maintain standard levels of prices throughout the major eastern cities. In Philadelphia in 1804, the masters cut the amount paid to journeymen for boots, and the Philadelphia workers struck the following year in an effort to attain the prices paid in New York and Baltimore. Criminal charges subsequently were brought against eight journeymen.

According to the indictment, the defendant shoemakers had conspired "to increase and augment the prices and rates usually paid to them and other artificers, workmen, and journeymen, in the same art, and occupation, and unjustly to exact and procure great sums of money for their work and labor. . . ." They also allegedly threatened and menaced other journeymen to prevent them from working. Furthermore, the workers conspired among themselves that none of them would work for a master who employed a shoemaker who was not a member of their society, or who infringed any of the society's rules. The question before the court was whether those activities were unlawful.

The prosecution was represented by Jared Ingersoll and Joseph Hopkinson, both prominent members of the Federalist party. They advanced two lines of argument concerning the unlawful nature of the conspiracy. First, according to Hopkinson, "The mere combination to raise wages is considered an offence at common law." He contended that English common law should be adopted by American courts and that it would prohibit actions by groups, although the same actions might be lawful if done by individuals.

The second line of argument was based on notions of public policy. From that perspective, the prosecution asserted that combination of workers was injurious to the community as a whole; acting in concert, workers would "undertake to regulate the trade of the City." The interests of the citizens were aligned with the interests of the masters, who promoted commerce and resisted the higher costs associated with the workers' wage demands. According to the indictment, the conspiracy of the workers inured "to the great damage and prejudice of the masters employing them in the said art and occupation of a cordwainer, and of the citizens of the commonwealth generally, . . . [and] to the evil example of others, and against the peace and dignity of the commonwealth of Pennsylvania."

A leading Jeffersonian Democrat, Caesar Rodney, acted as chief counsel for the shoemakers. Rodney argued that on strictly legal grounds, the indictments against the defendants were not sufficiently specific to support the criminal charges, because they did not state the precise nature of the crime. In his view, the English common law did not absolutely prohibit combinations of workers to raise wages but rather only those combinations which sought to avoid a statute fixing wages, and there was no such statute in Pennsylvania.

In any event, he added, the entire body of English common law had not been adopted by American courts.

Regarding public policy, Rodney said that the community would not benefit from the prohibition of workers' combinations. To the contrary, he pointed out, masters under those conditions would further exploit labor for their own increased profit, and skilled workers would leave Philadelphia to seek less oppressive working conditions. The source of value to society, in Rodney's view, was productive labor, for only labor constituted the "real wealth of a country." Without the natural combination of workers as a class, masters would become rich and powerful.

Moses Levy, the judicial functionary presiding over the trial, instructed the jury in a manner favorable to the prosecution. He rejected the defendants' argument that the common law was inconsistent with individual rights and liberties and stated to the jury:

An attempt has been made to show that the spirit of the revolution and the principle of the common law, are opposite in this case. That the common law, if applied in this case, would operate [as] an attack upon the rights of man. The enquiry on that point, was unnecessary and improper. Nothing more was required than to ascertain what the law is. The law is the permanent rule, it is the will of the whole community.

According to Levy, then, the rule of law embodied the best interests of society as a whole, and legal principles were the expression of ordered civil life.

A conspiracy of workers, Levy continued, was antagonistic to the welfare of the community. The combination was an "unnatural, artificial means of raising the price of work beyond its standard, and taking an undue advantage of the public." Levy explained to the jury that combinations of workers threatened the foundations of our economic system; if not restrained by law, the shoemakers would raise the price of boots to exorbitant levels. Levy summarized his charge by informing the jury that "in every point of view, this [conspiracy] is pregnant with public mischief and private injury . . . tends to demoralize the workmen . . . destroy the trade of the city, and leaves the pockets of the whole community to the discretion of the concerned." Following Levy's instruction, the jury returned a verdict finding the defendants guilty of "a combination to raise their wages."

The impact of the *Cordwainers* case on workers' efforts to act in their collective interest was of great significance. Between 1805 and 1842, workers were prosecuted under the conspiracy doctrine on some nineteen occasions and were acquitted in only three of those cases. Several of the trials attained particular notoriety; in New York City, for example, workers hanged two judges in effigy to protest their rulings.

In 1842, Chief Justice Shaw of the Massachusetts Supreme Court issued his opinion in the well-known case of *Commonwealth* v. *Hunt*. A group of journeymen shoemakers had been convicted in the lower court of a conspiracy to raise their wages. Shaw reversed that decision on the narrow legal ground that the indictment failed to specify that the conspiracy had an unlawful purpose or was accomplished by unlawful means. Consequently, the defendants could not be convicted of any crime.

The *Hunt* decision is viewed by some scholars as an important judicial contribution to the growth of trade unionism. Other scholars, however, argue that the opinion was neither a radical departure from earlier doctrine nor did it offer substantial protection to workers. One study, for example, concludes that there were more prosecutions under the conspiracy doctrine after *Hunt* than there were prior to the case. More recent scholarship suggests that *Hunt* was largely ideological in import, and the

opinion served to legitimate the common law by giving the appearance of the judiciary's fairness and impartiality toward labor.

Generally, the conspiracy doctrine provided the legal means for controlling the collective activities of workers throughout the nineteenth century. It was oriented toward the interests of employers rather than workers, and it was applied by judges who exhibited a demonstrable class bias. Those judges also articulated the policy supporting the conspiracy doctrine so as to enhance the public's image of capital and to diminish the public's perception of labor. Thus, the doctrine not only imposed punishment on workers but also helped to shape social values as well. [Raymond L. Hogler]

FURTHER READING

Commons, John, and Eugene Gilmore, eds. *Documentary History of American Labor*, Vols. 1–. Cleveland, OH: A. H. Clark, 1910.

Hogler, Raymond. "Law, Ideology, and Industrial Discipline: The Conspiracy Doctrine and the Rise of the Factory System." *Dickinson Law Review*, Vol. 91 (1987), pp. 697–745.

Nelles, Walter. "The First American Labor Case." *Yale Law Journal*, Vol. 41 (1931), pp. 165–193.

Turner, Marjorie. *The Early American Labor Cases: Their Place in Labor Law—A Reinterpretation.* San Diego, CA: San Diego State College Press, 1967.

o   o   o

COWBOY STRIKES OF 1883 AND 1886. The upsurge of labor militancy that marked the second half of the 1880s also had its faint echoes among cowboys on the western ranches. Although for a variety of reasons, they never formed lasting unions and carried out sustained struggles like railroad workers and miners in the West, there is scattered evidence of two significant strikes by cowboys.

At the root of the cowboys strikes lay the same resentment against "Eastern Capital" that marked the great industrial wars in the western mining camps. By the 1880s many of the great western ranches were owned by absentee owners. This infusion of eastern and European capital led to a rationalization of work that resulted in regimentation and a division of labor that brought an end to much of the relative independence that the cowboys had enjoyed. On the large western ranches, cowboys worked in gangs organized to perform one task. Herding, fence patrolling, trail drives, and haying (the putting up of feed) all required different size crews. In addition, cowboys worked in relative isolation from their comrades on other ranches. Because of this and the difficulty of coordination over large spaces, cowboys rarely came together in large numbers to share their discontent.

The constant surplus of cowboys, and the normal winter layoff, also mitigated against collective action. The competition for jobs was exacerbated by the friction between Mexican, black, and white American cowboys. Black and Mexican cowboys usually worked for less than the prevailing wage, causing the Anglo cowboys to call for their exclusion from the range. Jobs were hard to find, and the alternative to a steady position on a ranch, no matter how bad the conditions, was a fall into abject poverty and perhaps crime. Year-round jobs were especially hard to find, and those who had them understood the importance of loyalty to the ranch owners. In most cases, the relationship between rancher and cowboy was one of lord and serf.

Yet even with these difficulties, cowboys did carry out several strikes. The two most important took place in the Texas Panhandle and Wyoming, the two places where corporate ranching was most fully developed. In the Panhandle, in the spring of 1883, a group of large ranchers, organized as the Panhandle Stock Association, had established the twenty-five or thirty dollars standard monthly wage. This was lower than the rate prevailing in Colorado

and Wyoming, and about the same as that paid to black and Mexican cowboys in southern Texas. In addition, the Panhandle season was short and the winters long and hard, creating the need for more money to endure the annual period of seasonal unemployment. Although little is known of the strike, it seems that it was carefully planned and that its leader was a cowboy named Tom Harris. Carried out just before the spring roundup when the ranchers were most vulnerable, the walkout included the majority of the cowboys on all of the large ranches of the region. In general, the old Anglo cowboys, blacks, and Mexicans—those who needed their jobs the most—predominated among the workers who did not strike.

Although a number of different demands were involved at the various ranches, a common demand was for a uniform minimum wage of fifty dollars a month for all cowboys regardless of skill. In addition there were demands for better food and for the right of the cowboys to run small herds of their own on the public domain range land. This last issue struck at the heart of the control that the big ranchers had over the range which was, in law but not in practice, the public domain and open to anyone. The response of the cattlemen was similar to that of American employers elsewhere. They agreed to have nothing to do with the demands. The strikers were evicted from ranch housing and forced to camp on the range.

The ranchers also hired replacements from the plentiful supply of cowboys and managed to carry out the roundup without the strikers. Instead of seeing the strike as a cause for hope for some kind of collective voice, cowboys from New Mexico, Kansas, and southern Texas flocked to the Panhandle to benefit from the job opportunities presented by the strike. There was little the strikers could do to stop this. Picket lines were impractical on the open range, and a troop of Texas Rangers stood by to deal with any violence. The meager resources of the strikers were soon exhausted and they were forced to leave the area. In all, the dispute probably lasted about a month, although the ranchers only had to delay the roundup for two weeks.

The second significant strike took place in Wyoming where the Wyoming Stock Growers' Association, under pressure from outside investors to produce a higher return on investments, began to cut labor costs. They eliminated the "grub line," whereby cowboys unemployed in the winter would ride from ranch to ranch picking up odd jobs in exchange for a few nights room and board. Having removed this traditional means for cowboys to survive the winter months, the owners then cut their permanent crews to the minimum, thus laying off a much higher percentage of their cowboys during the winter of 1885–1886. This led to considerable discontent, and there was talk of a cowboys' assembly of the Knights of Labor being formed in Cheyenne. When the cowboys returned for the spring roundup, they were faced with a cut in wages from forty to thirty-five dollars, and in some cases thirty dollars per month.

Under the leadership of Jack Flagg, the strike that followed resulted in limited success. The ranchers in the three districts affected were forced to restore the wage cuts, but in the fall, when most of the cowboys were laid off, the strikers were told not to return to Wyoming and were blacklisted. Nevertheless, given the obstacles, it is extraordinary that the action had any success at all. There are several reasons that might explain this. First of all, the Wyoming strikers, unlike the Panhandle cowboys, did not leave work until after the roundup had begun. Second, there were fewer replacement cowboys available in Wyoming. Third, and perhaps most significant, on the Wyoming range ranches intermingled their herds. This meant that the cowboys from different ranches worked

together in large groups. This facilitated communication and gave them immediate control of the workplace. By contrast, the Panhandle roundups were carried out independently on each ranch. The Panhandle system separated the workers, while the Wyoming system brought them together.

Neither of the two strikes led to anything resembling permanent organization. The obstacles inherent in the structure of the industry made that almost impossible. Blacklists proved to be effective and most of the strikers moved on to other occupations or areas. Some became small ranchers, and others became rustlers, and a few no doubt became both. [Ronald L. Filippelli]

Further Reading

Allen, Ruth. *Chapters in the History of Organized Labor in Texas*. Austin, TX: University of Texas Press, 1941.

Lopez, David. "Cowboy Strikes and Unions." *Labor History*, Vol. 18 (Summer, 1977), pp. 325–340.

Porter, Kenneth. "Negro Labor in the Western Cattle Industry." *Labor History*, Vol. 10 (1969), pp. 346–374.

o   o   o

CRIPPLE CREEK, COLORADO, STRIKE OF 1894. This dispute involved a most extraordinary development in American labor history. The state government intervened on behalf of the strikers. As a result, the newly founded Western Federation of Miners (WFM) won its first major strike.

The discovery of spectacularly rich gold deposits in the Rocky Mountains west of Colorado Springs in 1890 instantly created a string of roaring boom camps. As silver prices collapsed in the early 1890s, hordes of unemployed miners made their way to the widely publicized gold bonanza. Soon the area had a large labor surplus. That a group of more than 300 men left Cripple Creek to join Coxey's Army in May

1893 gives one indication of the oversupply of workers in the district. Taking advantage of this soft labor market, operators throughout Colorado pressed their employees for wage concessions. In February of that year, silver miners and mine owners in Aspen reached a compromise settlement that set an unfortunate precedent for later developments in Cripple Creek. In order to preserve wage standards, the Aspen union agreed to longer hours.

Six months later, the Isabella mine announced plans to lengthen the workday from eight to ten hours. When the hardrock workers reacted by voting to strike, Isabella management rescinded this proposal. This skirmish led directly to a whirlwind organizing campaign. In the fall of 1893, miners organized local unions in the leading camps of the district—Altman, Cripple Creek, Victor, and Anaconda. These groups soon affiliated with the Western Federation of Miners.

On January 8, 1894, the unions demanded that eight hours constitute a day's work at all mines in the Cripple Creek goldfield. Although a standard wage of three dollars per day prevailed across the district at this time, shifts varied from eight to ten hours. The miners argued that the combination of high elevation, underground air pollutants, and a host of other hazards made working more than eight hours highly unhealthful. Nine days later, management responded by offering their employees a choice. As of February 1, mine workers could work either eight hours for two dollars and fifty cents or ten hours for three dollars. The unions rejected these alternatives and walked out when the deadline arrived. As of February 7, all mines that insisted on a workday longer than eight hours had been shut down. About forty small enterprises that ran on the eight-hour system continued to function.

Within about a month, a number of the struck firms had recruited enough substitute workers to reopen. After union miners roughed up some of the strikebreakers, mine owners on March 14 obtained a federal injunction barring any interference with the operation of the mines. Two days later, the management of the Victor mine sought police protection from a menacing crowd of strikers near mine property. But when El Paso County sheriff's deputies reached Altman, they were arrested by local police sympathetic to the union cause. Sheriff M. F. Bowers asked Governor Davis H. Waite to dispatch the militia to restore order. Waite immediately sent in three companies of the National Guard under General E. J. Brooks. But upon determining that no disorder existed, the Populist governor denounced Bowers' "lying representation" and withdrew the troops.

Denied the easy access to military force that many western mining entrepreneurs enjoyed during this period, the Cripple Creek operators set out to recruit their own army. By mid-May Sheriff Bowers had deputized approximately 1,200 men, who were armed and paid by the operators. As Bowers assembled his deputies at Victor on May 24, the strikers sent them a blunt warning. Union miners seized the Strong mine and blew up the shaft house and machinery with dynamite. Afraid to confront the militant strikers, the deputies retreated from Victor. Nonetheless, early the following morning a band of unionists attacked the deputies' camp. A half hour of gunfire left one dead on each side.

On May 26, Governor Waite issued a proclamation ordering the strikers to lay down their arms and to abide by the law. The proclamation also declared the massing of deputies illegal and called for its immediate dispersal. Waite thus hoped to defuse a crisis that was rapidly becoming a statewide class war. As news spread of the presence of an operator-controlled army in Cripple Creek, groups of hardrock miners throughout Colorado spontaneously mobilized to aid their fellow workers. One heavily armed squad of about 100 commandeered a train at Rico and traveled over 100 miles toward the combat zone before being stopped by a telegram from the governor.

On May 28, Waite came to Cripple Creek to convince the strikers that the power of the state would protect them from the sheriff's deputies. The union authorized the governor to serve as sole arbitrator of the strike. At this point, the WFM locals still demanded the eight-hour workday for three dollars' pay. In addition, they sought preference for union men in employment. In the subsequent negotiations, Waite represented the miners as an advocate, not as a mediator or arbitrator. On June 4, Waite and the mine owners came to terms. The settlement, which the union readily accepted, called for eight hours' work for three dollars. As a concession to the operators, employees now had to eat lunch on their own time. There was to be neither discrimination against union members nor preference for them in employment.

The battle was over, but the army of deputies refused to disband. Accordingly, the governor sent the entire Colorado National Guard to the district to ensure that the agreement would be implemented. When the Guard arrived on June 7, the deputies had already skirmished with WFM miners and split into several marauding groups. Because the state had not imposed martial law, Sheriff Bowers initially refused to submit to the authority of General Brooks of the National Guard. The sheriff ordered his deputies to return to their camp only after Brooks threatened to shoot them if they did not. Meanwhile, the union forces had surrendered to the militia without incident. After further negotiations with state officials, the county deputies finally disbanded.

Peace returned to the district. Two men were convicted of the destruction of the Strong mine building and sentenced to seven years in prison. Both labor and management abided by the terms of the collective bargaining agreement. The tremendous wealth of the gold lode in the Cripple Creek area enabled both mine workers and their employers to prosper, even with the eight-hour day. Similarly, the WFM locals that had arisen in this crisis became deeply entrenched in the years after 1894.

This conflict made even more clear to hardrock unionists the value of having a friend in the state house. In sharp contrast to the behavior of Idaho's governor during the disastrous **Coeur d'Alene Strike of 1892**, Davis Waite had committed both the considerable resources of the state and his own personal skills to the miners' cause. Indeed, Waite became a hero to underground workers throughout the West and helped to inspire other Populist political initiatives in mining centers. The Cripple Creek altercation of 1894 thus had a formative influence on the political orientation of the fledgling Western Federation of Miners. [Alan Derickson]

FURTHER READING

Jensen, Vernon H. *Heritage of Conflict: Labor Relations in the Nonferrous Metals Industry up to 1930.* Ithaca, NY: Cornell University Press, 1950.

Rastall, Benjamin M. *The Labor History of the Cripple Creek District: A Study in Industrial Evolution.* Madison, WI: University of Wisconsin Economics and Political Science Series, 1908.

Wyman, Mark. *Hard Rock Epic: Western Miners and the Industrial Revolution, 1860–1910.* Berkeley, CA: University of California Press, 1979.

o   o   o

CRIPPLE CREEK, COLORADO, STRIKE OF 1903–1904. Almost a decade of relative tranquillity had followed the qualified victory of the Cripple Creek locals of the Western Federation of Miners (WFM) in the **Cripple Creek Strike of 1894**. The resumption of hostilities in 1903 resulted in the virtual fusion of state and employer forces in a united attack on the WFM. As in the concurrent **Telluride Strike** in another part of the state, the combination of vigilantism and military force demolished the local hardrock labor movement.

This was a sympathy strike. On July 3, 1903, employees of the United States Reduction and Refining Company ore mill in Colorado City stopped work to gain an increase in wages. The struck facility processed the gold-bearing ore from the Cripple Creek district. To bring pressure on mill management, the district organization of miners' locals decided to cut off the ore supply being handled by nonstrikers. On August 10, 1903, more than 3,500 miners at fifty-five Cripple Creek mines walked out in support of their nine fellow WFM members striking in Colorado City.

Aware that a large share of the district's hardrock workers were less than enthusiastic about this militant display of solidarity, the Cripple Creek Mine Owners' Association took a hard line. On the third day of the stoppage, the association condemned this disruption of community harmony as "an outrage against both the employers and the employed." The owners announced plans to replace the strikers and operate their mines as soon as possible. On August 18, the El Paso mine reopened with a work force of seventy-five, including twelve union members.

By early September, Cripple Creek had polarized. Merchants throughout the area cut off credit to the strikers. The Western Federation responded by setting up cooperative stores in Victor, Altman, Cripple Creek, and Goldfield. On August 27, businessmen and others formed the Cripple Creek District Citizens' Alliance to marshal public support for the defeat of the union. When the Sunset Eclipse shafthouse burned down on the night of August 29, many assumed that union arsonists were responsible. Three days later, carpenters building a fence around the

Golden Cycle mine were threatened and attacked by strikers.

Within the district itself, the operators had a political problem. The miners had helped elect numerous local and county officials sympathetic to their movement. Dissatisfied with Sheriff H. M. Robertson's less than zealous pursuit of their interests, the mine owners urged Governor James Peabody to send in the state militia. They also offered to finance the costs of military intervention. On September 3, the governor sent a commission to study the situation. After spending only eight hours in the district and meeting with no union representatives, the investigators recommended that the state act to preserve order. Peabody immediately dispatched the Colorado National Guard under General Sherman Bell. According to Big Bill Haywood, secretary-treasurer of the WFM, the militia force of roughly 1,000 was "made up of clerks, businessmen, and lawyers."

General Bell left no doubt as to his mission. "I came to do up this damned anarchistic federation," stated the mine owners' military commander. Similarly, Lieutenant T. M. McClelland believed that the National Guard would not be restricted by Peabody's failure to impose martial law. "To hell with the constitution," raved McClelland, "we aren't going by the constitution." With the militia standing guard, a number of mining properties reopened. On September 8, the Mine Owners' Association openly declared that its aim was to eradicate the Western Federation of Miners from Cripple Creek: "This fight will not be over until the pernicious influence of this organization is swept from the district." The first of many groups of imported strikebreakers arrived on September 17. The Mine Owners' Association estimated that 1,700 were working in struck mines in mid-October.

Meanwhile, the National Guard began a campaign of arresting and jailing union activists, often without charge. A. A. Frye, assistant manager of the WFM store in Victor, was detained for "talking too much" in favor of the strike. The union initiated habeas corpus proceedings to force the release of four men. The military responded with an ostentatious display of power, surrounding the courthouse where the cases were being heard with infantry and cavalry, placing sharpshooters on rooftops, and bringing in a Gatling gun. The attorney for the militia informed the court that a "qualified state of martial law" existed which justified the suspension of habeas corpus. Judge W. P. Seeds was not impressed by this invention, and on September 24 he ordered the unionists released. General John Chase initially defied Seeds but discharged the prisoners after Governor Peabody ordered him to do so.

In late November, union member H. H. McKinney was arrested for attempting to derail passenger trains entering the district. In his confession, McKinney implicated three union leaders—Sherman Parker, W. F. Davis, and Thomas Foster—in the crimes. But he quickly recanted this statement, claiming that he had made it in exchange for immunity from prosecution, a $1,000 payment, and transportation away from the area. Yet the vacillating McKinney was the state's primary witness in the trial of the three unionists in February 1904. On cross-examination, he admitted that detectives employed by the mine operators and the railway itself had hired him to derail a train. Charges against Davis were dropped during the trial; Parker and Foster were acquitted.

On November 21, 1903, two managers at the Vindicator mine died in an underground explosion. Although there was no evidence that the union had caused this unfortunate accident, Peabody on December 4 declared Teller County to be in "a state of insurrection and rebellion." Once again, the governor had not declared martial law, but General Bell acted as if he had. He announced that day that "the military is the whole works at Cripple Creek now, and it is for us to say who is under arrest." As expected, Bell increased his harassment of union supporters. This included censoring the pro-union Victor *Daily Record*, banning public assemblies, deporting unionists from the district, and arresting children who teased his men.

By January 1904, protracted military intervention was proving to be financially burdensome to the operators. Having determined that the troops had done enough to destroy labor organization, the Mine Owners' Association believed that they themselves could finish off the Western Federation. Accordingly, the National Guard contingent dwindled during the winter months, with the last soldiers withdrawn on April 11. Peabody answered one request by the operators for a decrease in the armed force with the assurance that he would "be glad to reduce all along the line in keeping with your wishes, whose interests, . . . are what I am attempting to protect." The gold mine owners undoubtedly realized that vigilantism cost less than keeping an army.

On March 19, the operators' association established a central employment bureau for the district. The bureau screened all applicants for mining jobs and issued cards to those who denied that they were WFM members. Given that no firm would hire anyone who lacked a card, this arrangement served as an effective blacklist. Thus, in Cripple Creek the practical meaning of the open shop movement was the yellow-dog contract. Yet despite the institution of the blacklist and the resumption of production, the Western Federation refused to concede defeat.

On June 6, a massive explosion at the Independence railway station killed thirteen replacement workers and injured six others. Many in the district blamed the miners' organization although no incriminating evidence had been uncovered and the union had disavowed violence throughout this dispute. Capitalizing on this moment of public outrage, the Mine Owners' Association and the Citizens' Alliance met that day to seize political power in the district. Sheriff Robertson was summoned to the meeting and given a choice between resignation and lynching. Robertson resigned. When the purge was over a few days later, more than thirty local and county officials deemed pro-WFM had been driven out of office. Those appointed to fill the vacancies were staunchly anti-union.

The removal of public guardians of the safety of the union ensured that vigilantes could act with impunity. A large crowd, led by the Citizens' Alliance, attacked the Victor Miners' Union hall on June 6 and wounded four men who were defending the building. After a gun battle lasting an hour, the unionists finally surrendered. The mob then destroyed the contents of the hall, including its sizable library. Similar actions wrecked all the other WFM halls and stores in the district that day.

The next day, the Citizens' Alliance and the Mine Owners' Association began systematically to expel union members from the district. General Bell and the National Guard returned to Cripple Creek to help to carry out the deportations. A total of 238 individuals who refused to quit the miners' union were forcibly put on trains to Denver or to the state line. Bell also shut a number of mines that were believed to employ union members. These firms were permitted to resume operations only when they agreed to adhere to the blacklisting system. By the end of the summer of 1904, the Mine Owners' Association, the Citizens' Alliance, and the Colorado National Guard had effectively removed the Western Federation of Miners from its stronghold in the Cripple Creek goldfield. [Alan Derickson]

FURTHER READING

Haywood, William D. *Bill Haywood's Book: The Autobiography of William D. Haywood.* New York: International Publishers, 1929.

Jensen, Vernon. *Heritage of Conflict: Labor Relations in the Nonferrous Metals Industry up to 1930.* Ithaca, NY: Cornell University Press, 1950.

Suggs, George G., Jr. *Colorado's War on Militant Unionism: James H. Peabody and the Western Federation of Miners.* Detroit, MI: Wayne State University Press, 1972.

D

o o o o o o o o o o

o　o　o

DANBURY HATTERS CASE. In 1890, Congress enacted the Sherman Act to regulate monopolies and to encourage competition in industry. The Act stated that "[e]very contract, combination in the form of trust or otherwise, or conspiracy, in restraint of trade or commerce among the several States . . . is hereby declared illegal." Its provisions were enforceable by criminal fines and imprisonment, and federal attorneys were authorized to seek injunctions against violators. In addition, Section 7 of the Act provided that "any person who shall be injured in his business or property by any other person or corporation, by reason of anything forbidden or declared to be unlawful by this Act, may sue therefore in any Circuit Court of the United States . . . and shall recover threefold the damages by him sustained, and the costs of the suit, including a reasonable attorney's fee."

An important question that was not clearly resolved by the legislative history of the Act was whether or not it should be applied against labor unions who engaged in collective activities to impose economic pressures against an employer. That question was answered in the affirmative by the U.S. Supreme Court in *Loewe* v. *Lawlor*, popularly known as the *Danbury Hatters* case. The Court also subsequently upheld the application of the treble damages provision against individual union members.

By the early 1900s, the United Hatters of North America represented most workers in the hatmaking industry. According to evidence presented in the litigation, the union had more than 9,000 members in the United States and Canada and had negotiated collective bargaining agreements with seventy hat manufacturers out of a total of eighty-two in the nation. Non-union manufacturers presented an acute problem for both the United Hatters and the unionized companies, because the non-union operations typically paid wages significantly below the union standard. For that reason, the United Hatters devoted substantial resources to insuring that their contracts were in force throughout the industry.

Loewe & Company was a non-union firm located in Danbury, Connecticut. It employed 230 workers and did an annual gross business of more than $400,000. Martin Lawlor, a union official, approached Loewe in 1901 and requested union recognition and bargaining in exchange for which the company would be entitled to display the union label in its products. Loewe refused. In response, the Hatters called a strike at Loewe, but the strike had little support from Loewe workers and quickly collapsed.

The union's next strategy was to institute a nationwide boycott. Through a nationwide publicity campaign undertaken with the approval and assistance of the American Federation of Labor (AFL), the union urged retail stores not to sell Loewe's products and requested the public neither to buy them nor to patronize stores that sold them. In San Francisco, for example, union agents asked the firm of Triest &

Company to cease handling Loewe's hats. When Triest refused to comply, the San Francisco Labor Council distributed a circular declaring that Triest had been placed on an "unfair" list for so long as they sold Loewe's product. The circular continued, "Union men do not usually patronize retail stores who buy from unfair jobbing houses or manufacturers. Under these circumstances, all friends of organized labor, and those desiring the patronage of organized workers, will not buy goods from Triest & Company."

As a result of the boycott, a number of retailers ceased doing business with Loewe, and his company lost more than $85,000 in one year. In 1903, Loewe sued the union under the Sherman Act claiming that the boycott was a combination in restraint of trade and that he had been injured by the union's illegal activity. The lower federal courts held that there had been no violation of the Act. On appeal, the U.S. Supreme Court reversed.

In an opinion by Chief Justice Fuller, the Court broadly held that the United Hatters union was a combination "which essentially obstructs the free flow of commerce between the States, or restricts in that regard, the liberty of a trader to engage in business." Regarding the issue of whether or not labor organizations fell within the proscription of the Act, Fuller observed:

The act made no distinction between classes. It provided that "every contract, combination, or conspiracy in restraint of trade" was illegal. The records of Congress show that several efforts were made to exempt, by legislation, organizations of farmers and laborers from the operation of the act, and that all these efforts failed, so that the act remained as we have it before us.

Concluding that the Sherman Act had been violated, the Court remanded the matter for a determination of damages.

Some seven years later, the case once again reached the Supreme Court. On this occasion, the Court affirmed an award of $252,000 against the Hatters union and against the individual members of the union. Justice Holmes wrote that "if these members paid their dues and continued to delegate authority to their officers unlawfully to interfere with [Loewe's] interstate commerce in such circumstances that they knew or ought to have known, and such officers were warranted in the belief that they were acting in the matters within their delegated authority, then such members were jointly liable, and no others." Consequently, individual workers became responsible for satisfying Loewe's judgment against the United Hatters.

The *Danbury Hatters* case was a serious blow to the American labor movement, and Samuel Gompers, president of the AFL, commenced a political campaign to overturn the effects of the Supreme Court's reading of the antitrust law. In 1912, Woodrow Wilson was elected President, and the Democratic party gained control of both houses of Congress. To reward labor for its support in the election, Congress in 1914 enacted the Clayton Act, which Gompers and other labor leaders regarded as the "Magna Charta" of the American working class. Section 6 of the statute provided:

That the labor of a human being is not a commodity or article of commerce. Nothing contained in the anti-trust laws shall be construed to forbid the existence and operation of labor, agricultural, or horticultural organizations, instituted for the purposes of mutual help . . . or to forbid or restrain individual members of such organizations from lawfully carrying out the legitimate objects thereof; be held or construed to be illegal combinations or conspiracies in restraint of trade, under the anti-trust laws.

Despite the apparently clear language of the Clayton Act, it did not survive an ensuing interpretation by the Supreme Court.

In *Duplex Printing Press Co.* v. *Deering*, the Court construed Section 6 in such a way that labor remained subject to the antitrust prohibitions. The case involved a machinists union which attempted to organize a manufacturer of printing presses. To accomplish that objective, it engaged in a nationwide boycott of Duplex's products. The union instructed its members not to install or repair the presses and urged prospective customers not to purchase them. When the employer sought an injunction against the union, the lower federal courts held that the Clayton Act protected the union's boycott. The Supreme Court reversed this decision.

Citing the *Danbury Hatters* case, the Court reiterated that a labor boycott was a combination in restraint of interstate commerce. With regard to Section 6 of the Clayton Act, the Court offered the following explanation of its language and intent:

The section assumes the normal objects of a labor organization to be legitimate, and declares that nothing in the anti-trust laws shall be construed to forbid the existence and operation of such organizations or to forbid their members from *lawfully* carrying our their *legitimate* objects; and that such an organization shall not be held in itself—merely because of its existence and operation—to be an illegal combination or conspiracy in restraint of trade. But there is nothing in the section to exempt such an organization or its members from accountability where it or they depart from its normal and legitimate objects and engage in an actual combination or conspiracy in restraint of trade.

Accordingly, the Court reasoned, Congress did not authorize labor organizations to engage in such illegal activities as a secondary boycott where a union tried to influence the employees of a secondary employer in order to coerce the employer with which it had an actual dispute.

After the *Duplex Printing* case, organized labor remained in no better a position than it had been prior to the Clayton Act.

The rule of the *Danbury Hatters* case continued to pose a threat of antitrust suits, and the political efforts of 1912 proved futile in removing labor from the coverage of the law. Not until the Norris-La Guardia Act of 1932 was there any significant modification of the law of antitrust as applied to the collective activities of workers. [Raymond L. Hogler]

FURTHER READING

Berman, Edward. *Labor and the Sherman Act.* New York: Harper, 1930

Lawlor v. *Loewe*, 235 U.S. 522 (1915).

Loewe v. *Lawlor*, 208 U.S. 274 (1908).

Taylor, Benjamin, and Fred Witney. *Labor Relations Law*, 5th ed. Englewood Cliffs, NJ: Prentice Hall, 1987.

o o o

DAVIDSON-WILDER, TENNESSEE, COAL STRIKE OF 1932–1933. These mining communities on the Cumberland Plateau in eastern Tennessee were the setting for a long and bitter strike in the early 1930s. At that time, the mining camps of Davidson, Wilder, and Twin employed the only union miners recognized by management south of the Ohio River. Twin was the location for the New York owned Brier Hill Collieries, while Davidson was the site of the mine owned by the Patterson brothers, E. W. and Hubert. The largest of the three mines, part of the Nashville-based Fentress Coal and Coke Company, at Wilder, was run by general manager W. D. Boyer and superintendent L. L. Shivers.

The miners in these communities had only recently arrived from the farms or sawmills of the southern mountains. Their union, the United Mine Workers of America (UMW), was also relatively new to eastern Tennessee. These and other mines in the area were organized during World War I under the protection of the War Labor Board, which considered them vital to the war effort. With the close of the war, depression hit the coalfields, the companies in eastern Tennessee broke the UMW, and the miners worked non-union from 1924 until 1930. Two pay cuts were put into place during that time. When the company tried a third cut in addition to a reduced work week, the miners at Davidson, Wilder, and Twin reorganized under the UMW and, unlike any of the non-union miners in Tennessee and eastern Kentucky, fought off the wage reduction in their new contract.

In July 1932, when the contract at the three mines expired, the mine owners insisted on a 20 percent wage cut. The workers refused and the mines shut down. In the fall, the Wilder mine opened non-union. The Davidson mine followed suit, only to have its mine tipple destroyed by fire. After the Fentress Coal Company in Wilder carried the first load of scab coal out by train, one of the railroad bridges was destroyed in an explosion. Tennessee governor Henry Horton called out the National Guard, and the battle for Davidson-Wilder commenced.

The tactics of the companies were typical of the era, including an injunction preventing the union men from any action involving the non-union employees at the mine, including "jeering or sneering" at the scabs, and the use of company agents as deputized officers to protect mine property and the non-union workers. The UMW fought successfully against eviction from company houses, and helped to stave off hunger by running an aid truck for the strikers, but the UMW, both nationally and regionally, was weak at the time. UMW District No. 19 president William Turnblazer did visit the strikers at Davidson-Wilder but could offer little tangible help. More support may have actually been received from local supporters, including Myles Horton and the Highlander Folk School.

The Wilder local was headed by a strong leader, Barney Graham, who was shot and killed by company agents. Graham's funeral attracted nearly 1,000, but the workers were without resources, and the union began to shift its attention to finding jobs for those miners still holding out. Despite a valiant struggle of nearly one year, the strike at Davidson-Wilder was lost. [Leslie S. Hough]

FURTHER READING

Bell, Brenda, and Fran Ansley. "Strike at Davidson-Wilder, 1932–1933," In *Working Lives: The "Southern Exposure" History of Labor in the South.* Marc S. Miller, ed. New York: Pantheon Books, 1980.

Perry, Vernon. "The Labor Struggle at Wilder." Unpublished Masters Thesis, Vanderbilt University, 1934.

o   o   o

DETROIT HATE STRIKES OF 1941–1943. The struggle of Detroit's blacks against job discrimination in the automobile factories occurred in the midst of the dislocations in the industry that resulted from production demands in World War II. By 1942, a serious labor shortage prevailed in the industry—an industry in which blacks had historically been excluded from all but the lowest paying and most arduous jobs. The labor shortage of World War II brought hope to Detroit's black community, which had been swollen by large numbers of southern immigrants in search of better paying jobs.

Black organizations in Detroit, such as the National Association for the Advancement of Colored People (NAACP) and the National Negro Congress, formulated their strategies based on their leverage during this period of labor scarcity. They also knew that no progress was possible without federal intervention. Black optimism rested on the apparent determination of the Roosevelt administration to end employment discrimination. They looked for assistance to agencies such as the

Committee on Fair Employment Practices (FEPC), created by Roosevelt's Executive Order in June of 1941, the Negro Employment and Training Branch in the Office of Production Management (OPM), and the Negro Manpower Service of the War Manpower Commission (WMC). In general, this optimism was misplaced. Both the War Production Board (WPB) and the WMC had the mobilization of scarce labor resources for war production as priorities and not the promotion of equal economic opportunity for blacks. The FEPC was crippled by a lack of enforcement authority and meager funding.

In battling discrimination in the Motor City, black advancement organizations worked closely with black union leaders. United Auto Workers leaders at the international level, such as President R. J. Thomas, generally operated on an ad hoc basis, intervening to deal with crises on the shop floor between white and black workers. Like the black organizations, the UAW looked to federal agencies for help. In the union's case, however, the reason was that the resistance of many white workers to the hiring and promotion of blacks had the potential to create serious internal political problems.

Early in the war, the industry underwent a transformation from peacetime to wartime production. The new military orders required far less foundry work, where most blacks were employed, and large numbers of workers were laid off. When blacks were not rehired or transferred to defense work in line with their seniority, they took action. During the summer of 1941, black workers staged wildcat strikes at Chrysler Corporation's Dodge division. The union's response, although sympathetic, was feeble. The international officers were loath to challenge the locals on these delicate issues.

Black UAW members and black advancement organizations took the fight to the union, challenging them to put into operation the non-discrimination principles of the UAW-CIO constitution. The strategy did pay off with union officials and staff, who worked quietly with staff leaders to achieve substantial gains at companies such as Briggs, Kelsey Hayes, Murray Body, and even at General Motors, which had the worst record of employing blacks of any of the major auto companies.

Under these circumstances, progress on economic equality in the auto industry came slowly, but come it did. One of the results of this effort was a growing cooperation between the United Auto Workers and black organizations in Detroit, a cooperation that had not existed earlier when many blacks identified the auto companies as their allies rather than the union. These changes were not always accepted peacefully by white workers. In late 1941, the discontent over the hiring and promotion of blacks led to a series of wildcat "hate strikes" by white workers. They erupted in a number of companies including Chrysler-Dodge, Hudson Naval Ordnance, and Timken Axle. Nowhere were they as virulent, however, as at Packard Motor Company.

While Polish-Americans constituted the largest single group of Packard workers, the company also had a reputation for hiring large numbers of southern whites. Both groups were known for their anti-black sentiments. The attitudes of many of the rank and file contrasted with those of the Local 190's leadership, many of whom were left wing and sympathetic to black aspirations. When the local leadership, under pressure from black activists, persuaded Packard management to transfer two black metal polishers from automobile to defense work, white workers staged a brief sit-down strike. Only the union's willingness to return the two blacks to their previous job averted a crisis. At first the union supported the blacks, but they buckled under to the threat of another strike. So began a six-month controversy over what *Fortune* called "a wrestling match" between the union, the government, and the company "over two American citizen's rights to contribute their skill to the production of tanks." Only a firm commitment from the union that it would discipline any union members trying to prevent the transfers broke the logjam, and the two black metal polishers returned to their new jobs six months after the initial transfer.

At Dodge Truck the transfer of twenty-six blacks caused a walkout of 350 whites. The action on June 2, 1942, closed the 3,000-worker plant. Once again the local union proved unable to take decisive action and only firmness on the part of UAW president R. J. Thomas and government and company officials ended the walkout. With UAW support, two whites who had led the strike were fired.

At Hudson the management was more supportive of offering expanded job opportunities to blacks. Up to that point the few blacks in the company were concentrated in the janitor category. Nevertheless, when two blacks were transferred to machine jobs in January 1942, 200 whites promptly walked off the job. The company gave in and returned the two men to their janitorial jobs. The combination of increased black activism in the local union and the shortage of machine operators in Detroit led the company and the union to cooperate on a campaign to prepare whites for the coming transfers and promotions of blacks. Nevertheless, on June 18, when a few blacks arrived at their new posts, nearly 10,000 whites struck. The UAW informed the local that because of the "display of vicious race prejudice," unless they returned to work immediately, they faced expulsion from the union. In tandem with the union, the secretary of the Navy threatened wholesale firings. The strike was crushed by cooperation between the company, the union, and the government. Soon after, a hate strike at Timken Axle was smashed by the same alliance.

The size and virulence of the Hudson strike gave further impetus to the growing cooperation between black advancement groups and the UAW in Detroit. Yet the union's willingness to try to enforce the anti-discrimination clause of its constitution and its forceful support of black aspirations at Ford Motor Company against fierce management hostility to hiring blacks did not end the hostility many white workers felt for blacks. Indeed, the militancy of the black campaign for equal rights only sharpened the hostility of many whites and led to a revival of the hate strikes.

In all, there were a dozen hate strikes during 1943 in Detroit, the most serious of which occurred at Packard. The company had been slow to change its discriminatory hiring patterns after its first hate strike in 1941. Packard management was known for exploiting the racial prejudices of their workers in order to weaken the union. The UAW went so far as to accuse Packard of deliberately fomenting the strikes. When small numbers of black men and women were added to the work force in February and March, a few work stoppages erupted. In the ensuing months, other small additions of blacks met with wildcat strikes. On several occasions, black workers, angered by the union's inability to do anything, walked off the job. The conflict had torn the Packard local apart. The climax came on June 2 when an agreement between the company, the War Labor Board, the FEPC, and the union led to the return of the black workers to their production jobs. Twenty-five thousand white workers promptly struck.

UAW officials, led by President R. J. Thomas, condemned the walkout and ordered the leaders of Local 190 to get the union members back to work. The halfhearted attempt failed. Thousands of workers milled outside of the plant gates, listening to racist speakers and shouting down UAW leaders. Officials of the badly split local union admitted that they had lost control. At this critical juncture, R. J. Thomas flew to Washington to ask for help from the War Labor Board (WLB) and the War Department. He told them that because of its support for the rights of black workers, the UAW international office was "out on a limb" with the rank and file and needed decisive government action.

Thomas received the help he asked for. Both the WLB and the War Department ordered Packard workers back to work. Thomas, in turn, threatened expulsion from the union for anyone who disobeyed the government order. Under these ultimatums, the strikers reluctantly returned to work. Thomas's firm stand for black rights earned him the respect of Detroit's black leadership and gained a great deal of credibility for the UAW in the black community.

The victory did not immediately lead to significant gains for black workers at Packard. Only the tenacity of the reorganized FEPC achieved this goal after several months of difficult negotiations with the company and Local 190. Nevertheless, the transfer and promotion of blacks was accelerated, and by the summer of 1943, blacks held 300 semi-skilled jobs outside of the Packard foundry. While far from having solved the problem, the concerted effort of Detroit's black leadership, the international officers of the UAW, the FEPC, and the WLB had prevailed against the raging hostility of much of the auto industry's work force both on the factory floor and in the executive suite. [Ronald L. Filippelli]

FURTHER READING

Meier, August, and Elliot Rudwick. *Black Detroit and the Rise of the UAW.* New York: Oxford University Press, 1979.

Lichtenstien, Nelson. *Labor's War at Home: The CIO in World War II.* Cambridge, U.K.: Cambridge University Press, 1982.

o   o   o

DETROIT RACE RIOT OF 1943. Thousands of defense workers flooded into Detroit during World War II. A significant influx of white and black southerners added to the already tense racial situation in Detroit, the home of the auto industry, where large white ethnic and black communities lived largely segregated from one another. The influx of new workers also created a severe housing shortage in the city, causing the federal government to construct several housing projects. Access to these projects for blacks became an explosive issue in the Motor City.

Evidence of racial tensions and outbreaks of racial violence marred most of the war years in Detroit. From 1941 through 1943, a series of "hate strikes," [see **Detroit Hate Strikes of 1941–1943**] wildcat walkouts by white workers protesting the hiring and transfer of black workers occurred at a number of factories. Only determined action by black organizations with cooperation from the top leadership of the United Auto Workers and federal agencies such as the War Labor Board and the Committee on Fair Employment Practices succeeded in breaking through the auto industry's racist employment traditions.

Indeed, the violence that erupted in Detroit over black access to government housing projects can only be understood if viewed against the backdrop of the racial tensions at the workplace. In both struggles blacks received valuable assistance from the United Auto Workers (UAW).

The first housing controversy occurred over access to the federally constructed Sojourner Truth Housing Project. The project, named after the great black abolitionist, was constructed for black workers but was located in a racially mixed, but predominantly white ethnic, working-class area of Detroit. The reaction of whites was predictable. They argued that the project should be white and that if it stayed black mortgage lending in the neighborhood would dry up and housing values would plummet. Although it wavered, the federal government, under pressure from Detroit's black leadership organized in the Sojourner Truth Citizens Committee, officially authorized the Detroit Housing Commission to assign the project to blacks. The Sojourner Truth Committee included supporters from the Congress of Industrial Organizations (CIO), the American-Federation of Labor (AFL), the UAW, and Detroit's religious community.

When the first black tenants moved in on February 28, the Ku Klux Klan with the support of the white "improvement association" attempted to block them. The night before the move, a crowd of whites burned a cross in front of the project. The next day, a violent confrontation resulted when an angry white mob attacked the small group of black tenants. As news of the conflict spread, hundreds of black youths came to the aid of the black tenants. By the early hours of the next day, some 200 blacks and only a few whites had been arrested. It was clear that the police, rather than protecting the black tenants from the angry mob, had sided with the whites.

After the trouble at Sojourner Truth, the support of the UAW became even stronger. Local 600 at the Ford Rouge plant—a local with a large black membership—took the lead in demanding that the authorities investigate the involvement of the Klan and the actions of the police. R. J. Thomas, UAW president, refused to be intimidated by attacks on him from white members in the city. He publicly declared that justice required that the project be occupied immediately, under police protection, by black workers in need of housing. With the support of the united front among the UAW, black leadership, and the federal government, blacks began moving into the project at the end of April.

The ability of the Sojourner Truth Citizens Committee to win the Sojourner Truth battle hinged on the fact that the project was segregated. The importance of that fact became clear when the same coalition attempted to integrate another new government housing project near Ford's new Willow Run Plant. The Willow Run Project, according to the Federal Public Housing Authority's Jim Crow policy, was to be all white. Black workers at the plant would be accommodated in separate developments. Attempts by Detroit's black leadership and the UAW to change the government's decision failed.

The struggles over Sojourner Truth, the attempts to integrate public housing in the city, and the chronic hate strikes were all part of the climate of racial tension in Detroit that the Detroit Association of Catholic Trade Unionists called a "subterranean race war" that could only lead to an explosion of violence. The spark that caused the predicted explosion occurred at Belle Island, an amusement park frequented by black and white workers and their families. On Sunday evening, June 20, shortly after the settling of the worst of the hate strikes at Packard Motor Company, rioting between the races broke out at Belle Island and spread throughout the city. Both whites and blacks were assaulted and a number of white-owned businesses were destroyed, but most of the violence was committed against blacks. Police used persuasion with white rioters, while they employed night sticks, revolvers, and rifles against blacks. Twenty-five of the thirty-four persons killed were blacks, and seventeen had been killed by the police.

Federal troops entered the city on Monday, June 21, and by Tuesday morning peace had largely been restored to the city. During and after the riot, the UAW and particularly President R. J. Thomas proved to be black Detroit's major ally. With Detroit's business leadership silent, Thomas became, according to the Detroit

Free Press "the only Detroiter who has come forward with a set of formal recommendations looking toward a restoration of interracial accord for our riot-ravaged city." Thomas called for the creation of a biracial commission to deal with racial tensions, the construction of housing and recreational facilities, and an enforceable program against job discrimination in the war plants. Finally, the UAW president demanded a grand jury investigation to uncover the riot's causes and to scrutinize the behavior of the law enforcement officials. The Detroit Interracial Fellowship, made up of religious, labor, and social welfare groups, endorsed Thomas's program.

The alliance between the UAW and Detroit's black leadership during the troubles of the war years, and particularly in terms of the race riot of 1943, impressed upon the black leadership the importance of organized labor as an ally. The next autumn a coalition of labor and the black community worked together politically to defeat the incumbent mayor who had pandered to white Detroit during the riots. Although the attempt failed, the cooperation marked the beginning of an alliance between the UAW and black Detroit that came to dominate the city's politics. [Ronald L. Filippelli]

FURTHER READING

Boskin, Joseph. *Urban Racial Violence in the Twentieth Century.* Beverly Hills, CA: Glencoe Press, 1969.

Lichtenstien, Nelson. *Labor's War at Home: The CIO in World War II.* Cambridge, U.K.: Cambridge University Press, 1982.

Meier, August and Elliot Rudwick. *Black Detroit and the Rise of the UAW.* New York: Oxford University Press, 1979.

o   o   o

DETROIT TOOL AND DIE STRIKE OF 1933. During the years following the passage of the National Industrial Recovery Act (NIRA) in 1933 several groups, including affiliates of the American Federation of Labor, the Industrial Workers of the World, and several independent organizations competed to organize the auto workers. The most important of the independents was the Mechanics Educational Society of America (MESA), an organization of skilled tool and die makers who worked in the auto factories and in the contract job shops that served the industry.

MESA had been formed in 1933 as an educational and social society. With the passage of the NIRA, which granted workers the right to organize and bargain collectively, the organization began to move toward becoming a trade union. In August, less than two months after President Roosevelt signed the NIRA into law, MESA had 5,000 members in Detroit, Flint, and Pontiac, Michigan.

At a time when the fervor for industrial unionism was running high, MESA appealed to the highly skilled workers who made or repaired tools, dies, jibs, fixtures, and machinery. It was this concentration on the close-knit tool and die makers community that gave MESA the ability to take on the auto makers in a protracted strike at a time when its competitors were barely able to keep their organizations alive.

In September, the Flint local of MESA presented demands for a 75 percent wage increase, a thirty-seven-hour workweek, and union recognition to the managements of Buick, Chevrolet, and A.C. Sparkplug. When the companies balked because of the possible impact of such wage increases throughout the industry, MESA struck on September 21. It soon became clear that in order to forestall the transfer of work to other plants, the workers in Detroit and Pontiac would also have to be called out. In an amazing demonstration of coordination and persuasion, the inexperienced leaders of MESA managed to narrowly win strike votes in Detroit and Pontiac and expand the strike. So rapid was the action that the Detroit walkout on September 26 predated the presentation of demands to the companies. Considering its almost impromptu organization, the strike was remarkably solid with both the job shops and the main plants in the Detroit area crippled but not shut down. Fortunately for the strikers, the walkout came during the period of model changeover, when the skills of the tool and die makers were most in need.

After the strike began in Detroit, the union began the process of formulating demands. Not surprisingly, the results were considerably scaled down from those put forward in Flint at the beginning. MESA called for a 25 percent wage increase, a minimum wage in the trade, and a forty-hour workweek. The proposals were mailed to the employers, but so inexperienced were the strikers that they failed to request a meeting. Observers were treated to the spectacle of a great strike in which the employers, generally confused by the swiftness of events, had no one with whom to negotiate.

Four days after the strike began in Flint, MESA appealed to Senator Robert Wagner, chairman of the National Labor Board (NLB), the agency created by President Franklin Roosevelt to encourage labor peace under the NIRA. According to MESA, the situation was "out of control." Wagner dispatched John Carmody, an NLB staff member, to Detroit. When Carmody arrived three days later, he found the union determined to negotiate a single settlement covering both the auto plants and the job shops. The auto companies, led by General Motors, wanted company by company settlements. Carmody recognized that the key to a settlement lay with the auto companies, not the smaller job shops. "The Detroit automobile manufacturers," he said, were "slow in realizing that under the industrial set-up by the NRA they are face-to-face with a wholly new relationship between them and their employees." The

companies, in Carmody's eyes, were violating the NIRA's requirement that they bargain with representatives of their employees.

MESA's recourse to the NLB indicated the union's recognition that it was not likely to win a confrontation with the auto industry without outside assistance. When the walkout failed to halt auto production, enthusiasm for the strike began to wane. The strike leaders thus welcomed the NLB's decision to invite representatives of the manufacturers, job-shop owners, and MESA to Washington to try to work out an agreement. MESA's enthusiasm was not shared by the manufacturers, who refused to go. When MESA's representatives did get to Washington, they did not find the support they were looking for. The NLB criticized the union for striking before submitting demands and for not requesting a meeting with the employers. In addition, the NLB had no authority to order the companies to do anything, let alone to negotiate jointly with the union. MESA's leaders returned to Detroit with instructions to request meetings with each of the employers to discuss the demands.

Unhappy with the results of the Washington initiative, MESA's leaders realized, nevertheless, that they had little choice but to follow the NLB's instructions. But at a mass meeting on October 22, the strikers agreed to follow the letter of the instructions but not the spirit. Individual bargaining would take place with each company, but all settlements would have to be identical, and there would be no return to work until agreements had been reached with all of the employers.

The militancy of the strikers produced more frustration than results. When neither the NLB nor the employers endorsed the MESA strategy, violence flared. On October 30, strikers attacked eight job shops, smashed hundreds of windows, and burned blueprints and tool diagrams. MESA condemned the action, but its militant leader, Matthew Smith, admitted later that the condemnation was only pro forma. Smith did not repudiate a certain amount of violence as a method of bringing the seriousness of the situation to the attention of the employers and the government.

In fact, the events of October 30 had a sobering effect on all of the parties. Within the next ten days the union reached agreement with most of the companies involved. On the face of it, the union won little. Wages stayed more or less the same, with minor increases in the smaller job shops. The hours issue was moot because the industry code under the NRA had decided the question. And although the companies agreed not to discriminate against the strikers in rehiring, they did not agree to recognize the union by signing formal contracts. The NLB got around this thorny issue by sending letters to the parties which included the terms of the settlement, thus making the NLB a witness to the agreements.

The results of the tool and die strike are difficult to measure. It is clear that MESA did not succeed in achieving any of its original demands. This failure no doubt resulted from the union's lack of organization and its inexperience. No less important was MESA's inability to close down the industry. Here the lack of support from the production workers was critical. MESA believed at the beginning that because of their critical skills the tool and die makers could go it alone. When this proved false and the union tried to reach out to the production workers, they got little response. In addition, MESA's rivals, particu-

larly the AFL's United Auto Workers, considered MESA a dual union and did not support the strike. Nor was MESA able to hold all of the tool and die makers out. The strike was strongest in the job shops, but success in the auto plants was the key to victory. There, many of the skilled workers reported to work. The companies were also able to farm work out to plants outside of the Detroit area, while union attempts to extend the strike much beyond the city were largely unsuccessful.

Nevertheless, unlike its rivals for the loyalty of the auto workers, MESA, with all of its organizational problems, had been able to maintain a strike against some of America's most powerful companies for a month and a half and come out of it bloodied but undefeated. Membership in the organization doubled during the strike, and the leaders used those new resources to solidify the administrative structure of the organization. The Mechanics Educational Society of America had established itself as a long-term participant on the industrial relations scene in the automobile industry. [Ronald L. Filippelli]

FURTHER READING

Dahlheimer, Harry. *A History of the Mechanics Educational Society of America in Detroit from its Inception in 1933 through 1937.* Detroit, MI: Wayne University Press, 1951.

Fine, Sidney. *The Automobile Under the Blue Eagle: Labor, Management, and the Automobile Manufacturing Code.* Ann Arbor, MI: University of Michigan Press, 1963.

———. "The Tool and Die Makers Strike." *Michigan History,* Vol. 42 (September 1958), pp. 297–323.

E

○ ○ ○ ○ ○ ○ ○ ○ ○ ○ ○

○   ○   ○

EAST COAST LONGSHOREMEN'S STRIKE OF 1956. Negotiations between the International Longshoremen's Association (ILA) and the New York Shippers Association (NYSA) were clouded by the fact that the ILA had been expelled from the AFL in 1953 after the New York State Crime Commission had found the union rife with corruption. In addition, during the 1956 negotiations, the ILA was also involved in successfully fighting off the challenge of the International Brotherhood of Longshoremen, the new union chartered by the AFL in the ILA's jurisdiction.

In the midst of the ILA's troubles, the NYSA, for the first time, developed a coherent program to be followed in bargaining based on the strategy employed by the General Electric Company. The core of the strategy involved the development of the company's "best offer," the preparation of which involved taking into consideration the issues to which workers themselves gave priority. This proposal was then presented both to the union and the union members as the company's "fair" and final offer. The companies were fully prepared to take a strike if the union rejected the take-it-or-leave-it bargaining approach.

For its part, the ILA made coastwide bargaining in the Atlantic ports on the main economic and job security issues its chief demand, insisting that it had to be conceded before any talk about other demands. The NYSA rejected the demand out of hand, claiming that it had no authority to bargain for the other ports, even though

the NYSA members controlled 80 percent of the shipping in the nation. The prime motivation for the demand for coastwide bargaining was the ILA's fear of assaults by the International Brotherhood of Longshoremen in the other ports of the east and gulf coasts. The ILA refused to present the shippers with a proposal until the coastwide issue was settled. Both sides, then, had adopted a take-it-or-leave-it attitude and negotiations deadlocked.

The NYSA filed an unfair labor practice charge with the NLRB charging the ILA with refusal to bargain because they insisted that the talks could not go forward without agreement on the coastwide bargaining issue. Mediators were able to persuade the two sides to present detailed proposals but were not able to move the parties beyond perfunctory bargaining. The NYSA proposal, entitled *Three Years of Industrial Peace*, was released to the ILA and simultaneously sent to the press and to the homes of the longshoremen.

The union, angered by the NYSA's attempts to interpose itself between the union and its members, characterized the carefully orchestrated proposal as only a step in the right direction. In particular, the ILA objected to the omission of coastwide bargaining and the lack of a guarantee of eight hours pay. The employers countered by pointing out that the coastwide issue would be settled as a result of its unfair labor practice charge with the NLRB.

With the negotiations deadlocked, a strike shut down the East Coast ports on

November 16. On November 21, the NLRB acted and the U.S. District Court issued a temporary restraining order preventing the ILA from pressing its demand for coastwide bargaining. On November 22, President Dwight Eisenhower invoked the emergency procedure of the Taft-Hartley Act and appointed a Board of Inquiry. The mandatory eighty-day cooling-off period temporarily brought the strike to an end. Bargaining was hardly feasible, however, because the ILA had appealed to the courts to set aside the injunction against coastwide bargaining; this tied up the parties in legal actions. The hardening of positions was indicated by the fact that both the ILA and the NYSA reiterated that they would stand on their original proposals.

Although Taft-Hartley required that in the absence of an agreement an employer's "final offer" had to be presented for a vote before the expiration of the cooling-off period, no progress was made in bargaining. Predictably, upon recommendation of their leaders, the ILA membership overwhelmingly rejected the "last offer."

With the strike on again, the parties moved gradually toward a settlement and reached a "Memorandum of Agreement" on February 16. The NYSA called it the most generous agreement in the history of the industry. It provided for a three-year agreement with a wage increase of eighteen cents the first year and seven cents more at the beginning of the second and third years. The agreement also included two paid holidays in the first year plus an additional one in each of the next two years. This was the beginning of paid holidays in the industry, and a three week vacation for each man who had worked 700 hours in each of five of the six preceding years. Seniority was accepted "in principle" with an agreement to continue negotiations on the subject. Although the union did not achieve its major goal, there was an informal beginning on coastwide bargaining. Long-

shoremen ratified the contract on February 22 by a comfortable margin. [Ronald L. Filippelli]

FURTHER READING

Jensen, Vernon. *Strife on the Waterfront: The Port of New York Since 1945.* Ithaca, NY: Cornell University Press, 1974.

o   o   o

EAST COAST LONGSHOREMEN'S STRIKE OF 1962. The International Longshoremen's Association (ILA) presented its demands to the New York Shippers Association (NYSA) on June 13, 1962. ILA chief negotiator Thomas Gleason, the union's newly elected vice-president, pointed out to the NYSA that every local union in every port in the North Atlantic had representatives at the meeting. The declaration was made to emphasize the ILA's interest in finally achieving coastwide bargaining and a master contract for all of the North Atlantic ports.

The NYSA took the position that until local negotiations were settled, no money offers could be made on the master contract. The union argued the opposite: no local negotiations could take place until money for the master contract was in place.

Shippers had mixed views about pushing for changes in working practices, but the majority believed that they needed some relief. The union would not address these issues without first knowing what the money settlement was likely to be. In order to get negotiations off dead center, the NYSA made a money offer worth $22 million. In return they wanted rights of cancellation of orders of employment whenever a ship failed to reach its berth or when weather was adverse, clarification of a night-shift differential, obligation of the ILA to provide labor for overtime work, assurances of a full and more efficient work force, extensive revisions of the seniority clause, and an end to featherbedding on the work gangs. The ILA rejected the demands as too high a price to pay for a lucrative money offer.

Working against the strike deadline, federal mediators prepared their own proposal. Arguing that the negotiations had become so blocked that many of the real issues that plagued the industry, such as containerization, were not even being discussed, the mediators recommended a one-year contract with only those changes that were absolutely essential to both sides. Study by both sides could then go on as to how to deal with the implementation of new technology on the docks, while at the same time protecting the employment and earnings of the longshoremen. The employers accepted the proposal provided that any issues left unresolved would be submitted to binding arbitration. But the ILA did not want a study and would not agree to arbitration. In fact, a study was superfluous, since both parties already knew the facts and what the implications were for the industry.

The strike followed, as did the inevitable governmental intervention. On October 1, 1962, President John F. Kennedy invoked the emergency provisions of the Taft-Hartley Act, ordering the workers back to work for an eighty-day cooling-off period. The President's Board of Inquiry quickly decided that the only possibility of breaking the impasse was to separate out the issues of manpower utilization and security and postpone them for future study and negotiations. It made recommendations to that effect, suggesting that a three-year contract be negotiated on less controversial issues and that a five-man special committee, composed of two from each side and a mutually agreed upon neutral, conduct a study and make recommendations on the manning and security issues. Both sides promptly rejected the recommendation. Soon after, the NYSA

made its required last offer which was soundly rejected by the ILA members.

In one last attempt to forestall a resumption of the strike, Secretary of Labor Willard Wirtz and President Kennedy called the parties together and proposed a compromise settlement calling for the postponement of most of the divisive issues for later study and the appointment by the President of a board of prominent mediators to help the parties reach agreement. While the board studied the issues, both parties were asked to continue to work for a period of ninety days. The employers agreed but the union rejected the proposal.

Additional attempts at federal mediation also failed, and President Kennedy established a special presidential board comprised of Senator Wayne Morse, James J. Healey from Harvard, and Theodore Kheel, a well-known arbitrator, and charged them with studying the situation and recommending action to him within five days. Kennedy made it clear that he was prepared to ask Congress for special powers if no settlement were reached. After a quick study, the board presented the ILA and the NYSA with a proposal that extended key existing agreements on difficult issues for two years, a wage increase, pension improvements, better health benefits, and an additional holiday. Manpower utilization and job security were postponed for further study by the secretary of labor.

The recommendation allowed the union a graceful way out of the impasse, and the ILA bargaining committee accepted it. The employers, however, considered it a sellout, nothing more than an opportunity to buy themselves out of a strike. Nevertheless, under strong pressure from the government, the NYSA accepted the recommendations by, in the words of its chief negotiator, "paying a substantial price in advance for whatever later benefits might come out of the unresolved issues." [Ronald L. Filippelli]

FURTHER READING

Jensen, Vernon. *Strife on the Waterfront: The Port of New York Since 1945.* Ithaca, NY: Cornell University Press, 1974.

o   o   o

EAST ST. LOUIS RACE RIOT OF 1917.

The July 2, 1917, East St. Louis, Illinois, riot left nine whites and thirty-nine blacks dead, making it the bloodiest race riot of the period. It claimed more lives than any of the nearly twenty race riots that occurred in American cities between 1915 and 1919. Like other race riots of this period, the East St. Louis riot resulted from white working-class fears spawned by the black migration of World War I. In the seven years preceding the riot, a record number of blacks were moving to cities, where they competed with working-class whites for jobs, housing, and political power. City officials were not prepared to manage the increased competition. They had not even considered the reaction of whites nor had they prepared their police forces to impartially dispense law enforcement. However, conservative political leaders were better prepared. They capitalized on white working-class insecurity by overestimating the size of the black migration to East St. Louis. They stridently accused political opponents of attempting to import blacks to win elections. Local newspapers added to the growing white fear and hysteria by reporting accounts of "threatening" or "gun-toting negroes" gathering on corners and insulting whites. And the business community profited most of all, using the black migration to threaten white workers' job security.

The race riot of 1917 can be traced directly to conflicts between black and white workers that were fueled by employers who wanted to keep whites from joining unions. Labor leaders, unable to find common ground with black workers or contain the racism of their followers, were not equipped to provide a solution.

The riot erupted after the Aluminum Ore Company replaced white strikers and their sympathizers with black workers. Afterward, labor leaders launched a campaign against black migration, placing an ad in the local newspapers containing statements such as "Negro and cheap foreign labor is being imported by the Aluminum Ore Company to tear down the standard of living of our citizens." The goal of the campaign was to pressure the city council to end black migration.

On May 28, 1917, sixty representatives of the Central Trades and Labor Union demanded a meeting with the mayor and city council. Hundreds of white trade unionists showed up for the meeting, where Mayor Mollman told them the city council was preparing a plan to end black migration. The crowd wanted more immediate action. Shouts that East St. Louis would remain a "white man's town" came from some in the crowd. And many responded with cheers and applause when a man yelled "there is no law against mob violence." Following the meeting, the crowd heard that a black man had shot a white man. As news of the incident spread, shouts of "lynch him" and "take the guns from the negroes" rose from the crowd outside of City Hall. Mobs of whites raced through the streets assaulting blacks and destroying businesses which blacks frequented. Authorities made few attempts to stop the rampaging whites. The police arrested a few blacks for carrying concealed weapons and helped others out of the gutters where they had been left to die. Union leaders made no attempt to stop the violence. The brutality continued into the morning of May 29 and ended only after the rioters became exhausted. As the mob dispersed, several men were overheard saying that they intended to rest, return with their guns, and "run the negroes out of town."

Tensions erupted into violence once again during the first two weeks of June, when white strikers of the Aluminum Ore Company began attacking black workers as they changed shifts. The attacks ceased only after national guardsmen were brought in to protect black workers. But by that time, the strife at the worksite had incited random attacks on blacks throughout the city. Even after the strike was called off altogether, the broader racial conflict continued. And throughout the city, police ignored the attacking whites, choosing instead to arrest their black victims. Neither the city officials nor the labor leaders took action against the mob violence. Finally, the conflict reached a turning point on Sunday night, July 1, after shots were fired from a Ford car into blacks' homes. Blacks believed that the drive-by shooting was the act of marauding whites. The same car returned and this time blacks returned fire. The police made no attempt to stop the drive-by shootings. However, they responded immediately after receiving word that armed blacks were about to attack whites. Two plainclothes detectives died when blacks opened fire on the unmarked Ford squad car as it approached the area of the earlier drive-by shootings. News reports described the deaths as premeditated murder, and a protest meeting was scheduled to be held at the Labor Temple on the morning of July 2. Speakers urged whites to arm themselves and return for action. When the protesters reassembled, they marched to a major intersection in downtown and shot the first black person they saw. They continued to march through the streets assaulting blacks and shouting that blacks should leave East St. Louis. By noon they had killed several blacks. Three blacks, though offering no resistance, were beaten with gun butts and kicked by young girls. Later, the homes of blacks were burned to the ground and many were shot as they fled their burning homes. By the evening, black corpses, including many women and children, littered the street. Some deaths were prevented after National Guardsmen were ordered to evacuate blacks who lived in areas bordering the downtown area where the rioting took place. But the Guardsmen were generally ineffective. For the most part, the violence continued, often while Guardsmen looked on.

About a month later, Congress held hearings on the cause of the riot. The congressional committee found that employer hostility to organized labor was an important factor in understanding why the riot occurred but concluded that blame could not be placed on union leaders. Historians today tend to agree that Congress was wrong and that the union leaders' campaign to stop black migration incited whites to riot. During the congressional hearings, for example, union leaders finally admitted that blacks did not take jobs from whites but that there was a shortage of white labor in 1917. Union officials recognized that there was an oversupply of black labor which could be used by employers to crush strikes and avoid collective bargaining. So for whites, the problem was not a shortage of jobs but a lack of job security. Thus, it is clear that the labor leaders' appeal to whites for support was deliberately calculated to increase racial tension and drive blacks from East St. Louis. In doing so, the unions would have removed a major obstacle to their struggle to win recognition and collective bargaining. However, the union appeal laid the foundation for the bloodiest race riot of the century. [Arthur R. McCoy]

Further Reading

Rudwick, Elliott M. *Race Riot at East St. Louis.* Carbondale, IL: Southern Illinois University Press, 1964.

Swan, Alex. "When Whites Riot—The East St. Louis Massacre." *International Socialist Review*, Vol. 34 (October 1973), pp. 12–24.

o o o

EIGHT-HOUR AND HAYMARKET STRIKES OF 1886. The nationwide strike for an eight-hour workday on May 1, 1886, marked the culmination of a tremendous labor uprising. For a quarter of a century, three distinct labor movement subcultures—craft unionists, Knights of Labor, and radicals—explored varying degrees of solidarity. Bound by a common attraction to the millenarian characteristics attached to the eight-hour movement, and sensing that 1886 was a propitious moment for workers to struggle for some control over their own labor, the three labor-movement factions united for a dramatic assault on capital's determination of the length of the workday. The strike and its aftermath in early May illuminated both the power and the weaknesses of the labor movement's coalition.

Three different theories made the eight-hour workday something of a panacea for late-nineteenth-century wage earners. For workers fearing unemployment through technological improvements, a shorter workday was a means to share job opportunities—reducing the hours of labor from ten to eight created 20 percent more jobs. A second theory argued that workers needed more leisure time to enable them to meet their responsibilities as citizens of the republic. Long hours of labor prevented wage earners from attaining the culture and education they needed to be intelligent participants in the political and social life of the nation.

The third theory, formulated by Ira Steward, a self-educated machinist, overlapped with the other two but also, in its way, foreshadowed Keynesian economics. Steward, beginning in the 1860s, developed a theory that fewer hours of work would not lead to a reduction in pay. Wages, he argued, were socially determined; a shorter workday would create a more cultivated and insistent working class demanding wages more in keeping with the full product of its labor. Increased wages for workers, moreover, would stimulate both higher levels of employment and more rapid economic growth by enlarging the market for goods. Thus a shorter workday promised an improved standard of living for labor and a greater propensity to consume, which Steward felt, was the basis of an expanding economy.

Steward's theory gained wide circulation in the years after the Civil War, influencing such labor spokespersons as Samuel Gompers, Peter J. McGuire, George E. McNeill, Terence Powderly, and Albert Parsons. These individuals, in turn, exerted a good deal of authority within the diverse factions of the emerging labor movement. Powderly and McNeill, for instance, contributed mightily to the emergence of the Knights of Labor in the 1870s; McGuire and Gompers were central figures in the craft union movement and later in the American Federation of Labor (AFL); and McGuire and Parsons provided a critical link to immigrant Socialists and anarchists. Steward had connections with each. He was, like Powderly, a member of the Machinists and Blacksmiths Union; he worked closely with Gompers and McGuire in the International Labor Union, a forerunner of the AFL; and he and his disciple McNeill ventured to Chicago in the late 1870s, at Parson's request, to address Socialist rallies. Furthermore, these individuals provided entry into the dominant immigrant groups—the English, German, and Irish communities that contributed so much to the labor movement. In this way, the eight-hour issue bridged political and ethnic divisions within the working class.

For all labor groups, the eight-hour workday had the virtue of being at once a simple demand, yet one infused with revolutionary implications. Its simplicity and reasonableness attracted support from people outside labor's ranks. Indeed, Steward attached the idea of labor's control over the workday to the basic individual rights insisted upon by the abolitionists. Such important abolitionists as Wendell Phillips and James Redpath applauded working-class activism in the eight-hour movement. In the years immediately after the Civil War, enough advocates existed that six states and the federal government enacted eight-hour laws. However, the laws were riddled with loopholes and lacked enforcement power.

Labor groups sought their own means of enforcement. Immigrant and native-born workers, many of whom had fought for the Union in the Civil War, engaged in widespread strikes in 1867 and again in 1872, attempting to force through union measures what the laws had refused to guarantee. Many unionists consciously linked their actions to the recent war against slavery. As Steward put it: "the anti-slavery idea was that every man had the right to go and come at will. The Labor movement asks how much this abstract right is actually worth, without the power to exercise it." Although the strikes failed to win the shorter workday, they did much to publicize the issue and to cement bonds between immigrant and native-born workers.

As the labor movement regrouped after the long depression of the mid-1870s, the eight-hour movement resurfaced. In 1878 and 1879, the International Labor Union publicized the issue in the industrial Northeast. The founding of the Federation of Organized Trades and Labor Unions of the United States and Canada (FOTLU), the immediate predecessor of the AFL, in 1881, gave an added impetus to the drive for the shorter workday. But in the early 1880s, the FOTLU was a minor partner in the labor movement, overshadowed by both the Knights of Labor and the vibrant immigrant-dominated Socialist and anarchist movements. Although activists like Gompers, McGuire, McNeill, and Parsons often were involved in more than one of these factions (in some cases all three), each group gave a different empha-

sis to the shorter workday. The Knights worked principally for an alternative to the wage system and thus downplayed the eight-hour workday, and the Socialist Labor Party's preferred sphere of action was politics, where it felt the shorter workday could be achieved through legislation.

It was the relatively moribund FOTLU, however, that set in motion the events that led to the dramatic eight-hour strike of 1886. In the fall of 1884, the Brotherhood of Carpenters and Joiners of America (BCJA) instructed its delegate to the upcoming FOTLU convention to submit a resolution fixing May 1, 1886, as the date when labor would make eight hours the legal day's work for all wage earners. BCJA leader Peter McGuire, who was also a Socialist, discounted legislative action for shorter hours, particularly in the wake of court rulings against the constitutionality of existing laws. McGuire told his followers: "If you want an Eight-Hour law, make it yourself." To a mass meeting of carpenters he said: "The way to get it is by organization" and self-enforcement. Consequently, the BCJA delegate to the 1884 FOTLU convention, Gabriel Edmonston, lit a fire under the spiritless trade unions by introducing the notion of a universal strike for the eight-hour workday.

The body's resolution to demand eight hours on May 1, 1886, started a remarkable period of growth for the labor movement. Still, the eight-hour movement might have fizzled if the Knights of Labor had not won several startling victories in the summer of 1885. Most notable was a successful strike against Jay Gould's powerful southwestern railroad system [see **Southwest Railroad Strikes of 1885 and 1886**] that gave the Knights a national reputation. There were regional examples as well: in Michigan, the Knights shut down the state's most important lumber mills; female workers in the **Yonkers, New York, Carpet Weavers' Strike** surprised manufacturers with their militance; in Philadelphia, male and female shoeworkers forced employers to recognize the union shop and an arbitration board. In the year following these strikes, the order's membership jumped from just over 100,000 to more than 700,000 but even this growth underestimates the numbers of people who passed through the Knights or sympathized with their aims. The most recent guess at the order's influence suggests that perhaps 1 million workers were or had been members in 1886.

The growth of the Knights expanded labor's ranks to include many who formerly had no home in the labor movement. The FOTLU and its affiliated unions recruited principally from the ranks of skilled workers. Craft-union ranks, then, were comprised of white males, typically of native-born parentage or second-generation German- or Irish-Americans. The Socialist and anarchist movements, based almost exclusively in cities, reflected more heavily the influence of German-speaking immigrants. While including many German-American craftsmen and thus overlapping with craft unions, radical groups also attracted unskilled Germans along with less-skilled Scandinavian, Czech, and other new immigrant workers. The Knights also overlapped with the FOTLU and radical organizations, but the order made a place for women, blacks, and thousands of unskilled workers. While many of the leaders were native born, the Knights exerted a great deal of appeal for German, Polish, and especially Irish Catholics. Many of these Catholic workers were too unskilled for the FOTLU but too religious for the avowedly secular Socialist and anarchist organizations.

In 1885 and early 1886, these diverse constituencies all figured prominently in labor's great uprising. Indeed, the excitement of the eight-hour campaign combined with the Knights of Labor's victories to bring thousand of workers into the labor movement. As trade unions and the order

expanded, radical organizations recruited newly politicized workers aroused by the opportunity to exert labor's power. Radical parties, trade unions, and the Knights grew symbiotically and exhibited a surprising tolerance of each other in the heady atmosphere of the months leading up to the May 1 strike.

As the time for action neared, however, the chasms separating labor's factions widened. Terence Powderly, Grand Master Workman of the Knights, fretted over the number of new members who came into the order thinking its purpose was to lead strikes for the eight-hour workday. Powderly, in fact, opposed strikes on principle because they did nothing to alter the wage system. In late March, he issued a secret circular counseling against the order's involvement in the proposed May 1 strike. Socialists and anarchists, whose strength was perhaps greatest in Chicago, were latecomers to the eight-hour movement. But once committed, they felt betrayed by Powderly. Chicago's German radical press attributed his cowardice to the Grand Master Workman's Catholicism which they denounced, driving further the wedge between Irish and German workers. Craft unionists, on the other hand, were distraught both by Powderly's lack of support for the eight-hour movement and by the attempt of Socialist and anarchist groups to join an alliance for the May 1 strike. In such cities as Philadelphia, Chicago, and Detroit, craft unionists wanted no part of "the red flag of Socialism." It was in this context that the eight-hour movement began.

Despite the reservations of labor leaders, rank-and-file workers responded vigorously to the eight-hour movement. In April, *John Swinton's Paper*, a labor journal, reported: "There is an eight-hour agitation everywhere." On the Sunday preceding May 1, Chicago radicals addressed a crowd of 25,000 persons; press estimates of the numbers of workers involved in the movement topped 250,000. Wage earners smoked "Eight-Hour Tobacco," purchased "Eight-Hour Shoes," and sang the famous refrain from the "Eight-Hour Song" coined by Ira Steward's wife:

Eight hours for work,

Eight hours for rest,

Eight hours for what we will.

In the weeks before the strike, many employers either granted a wage increase or shortened the workday to nine hours in the hope of defusing strike sentiment. Because May 1 came on a Saturday, it was not immediately apparent how many workers would actually strike. But on Monday, May 3, the public learned of the importance wage earners attached to the shorter workday. According to *Bradstreet's*, a business source, in the vicinity of 350,000 workers went on strike. The number of strikers in Chicago alone approached 40,000. In Boston, building trades workers completely shut down construction sites; Philadelphia's textile industry came to a halt. One Detroit employer, the huge Michigan Car Works, displayed an unusual testiness by laying off 125 workers on May 1 where most manufacturers merely put up a facade of conciliation. When that measure failed to trigger a showdown, the company fired P. J. Clair, a Knights of Labor organizer. Word spread like wildfire. By late afternoon, Clair had succeeded in bringing out nearly 3,000 car workers from the four car plants surrounding the Michigan Car Works. The strike there provided the catalyst for reluctant workers at other factories in the city. Eventually, about 5,000 Detroit workers shortened their workday, and labor's ranks in the city swelled from 5,000 to 13,000.

Chicago was both the storm center of the eight-hour strike and the city where labor made the most revolutionary claims for its actions. Not even the fragmented nature of the city's labor movement could stem the groundswell. The strike involved lumber shovers, metal workers, freight handlers, carpenters, tailors, bakers, and even sales clerks. Virtually all ethnic groups participated; Irish, Czechs, Poles, Germans, Jews, and more flocked to the eight-hour banner.

Conspicuously, however, anarchists centered in the International Working People's Association (IWPA) and the Central Labor Union appeared to provide the leadership in Chicago. Albert Parsons and August Spies, both prominent in the IWPA, led a May Day march of 80,000 people up Michigan Avenue. Spies, a German immigrant, inspired the eight-hour strikers with ringing denunciations of capitalism in the *Arbeiter-Zeitung*. The call to class conflict was clear in Spies' editorial: "Capitalism conceals its tiger claws behind the ramparts of order. Workmen, let your watchword be: No compromise! Cowards to the rear! Men to the front!" Still, May 1 passed peacefully despite the march through a route where police, deputized citizens, and hated Pinkerton Detective Agency employees, armed with Winchester rifles, crouched on rooftops.

On Monday the feared violence began. Trouble erupted at the McCormick Reaper Works where workers had battled the anti-union company almost solidly for a year [see **McCormick Harvesting Machine Company Strikes of 1885 and 1886**] and intermittently for nearly a decade. In February 1886, McCormick had locked out union members and imported scabs under police protection. Confrontations between police and picketers occurred periodically for the next several months. On May 3, another clash took place only blocks from where Spies was addressing striking lumber shovers. Spies hastened to the battle and witnessed police shooting into a crowd of workers, who returned a shower of stones. Two workers were killed, and in a fiery leaflet, Spies commanded:

"Workingmen to Arms." Retaliation inspired the rhetoric of the German anarchists.

The "revenge circular," as the Spies leaflet came to be known, called for a mass meeting the next day, May 4, at Haymarket Square to protest police brutality. About 3,000 workers gathered at 7:30 P.M. to hear speeches by Spies, Parsons, and Samuel Fielden. With Mayor Carter Harrison in attendance, the meeting maintained order until about 10:00 P.M. when threatening clouds sent home about two-thirds of the crowd, including the mayor and Parsons. As Fielden began to conclude his speech, about 180 armed police, under the command of Inspector John Bonfield, marched into the square and began dispersing the dwindling crowd. Fielden told the police that it was a peaceable meeting but decided not to protest the command to disperse. As Fielden stepped down, a bomb was thrown into the columns of police. It exploded, killing one policeman instantly and wounding many others. In a blind rage, the police opened fire on the crowd, leaving bodies strewn throughout the area. In a matter of minutes, the Haymarket riot was over. Seven policemen died of wounds and sixty more were injured, although most were casualties of bullets (probably the off-target shots of fellow policemen), not the bomb. At least four and as many as eight civilians died in the riot, with another thirty to forty wounded.

In the days following the bomb, Chicago police arrested hundreds of workers. Rumors of anarchist arsenals and plots gripped the public; a broad cross-section of people demanded the quashing of the radical menace. Newspapers across the country whipped up a popular indignation against the labor movement in general but in particular against immigrant radicals. In Chicago, the center of the agitation, police freely rounded up all known radicals, the vast majority of whom were foreigners. Police detained and interrogated hundreds of immigrant workers, searched their homes without warrants, threatened and abused them, and promised them bribes to give false testimony. For nearly eight weeks, police ran roughshod over the city.

In the end, thirty-one persons were indicted, but only eight were selected for trial: Albert Parsons, August Spies, Samuel J. Fielden, Eugene Schwab, Adolph Fischer, George Engel, Louis Lingg, and Oscar Neebe. Parsons, originally indicted as a fugitive, surrendered to stand trial with his comrades. The charge against the eight was incitement to murder. In a trial famous for the bias of the judge and jury against the defendants, all eight were pronounced guilty (seven to be hanged), although no evidence linked any of them to the bomb or to a conspiracy. Three of the eight had not even appeared at Haymarket Square on May 4, and all eight had airtight alibis at the time the bomb was thrown. Judge Joseph Gary nevertheless instructed the jury to convict the defendants if it determined that the anarchists had ever "by print or speech advised, or encouraged the commission of murder" in their efforts to overthrow the law. Appeals postponed the execution for more than a year. During that time, Lingg committed suicide in his jail cell by exploding a dynamite cartridge in his mouth. On November 11, 1887, four more of the eight—Parsons, Spies, Engel, and Fischer—were hanged. The three survivors—Neebe, Fielden, and Schwab (the latter two had their original sentences changed)—began life sentences in Joliet prison, eventually to be pardoned by Governor John Altgeld on June 26, 1893.

The episode at Haymarket Square had implications for the entire labor movement. It opened the fissures between radicals, craft unionists, and the Knights of Labor that the eight-hour movement had never been able to truly eliminate. Knights leader Terence Powderly, for instance, was vehement in his call for punishment for the anarchists. Gompers, as president of the newly formed American Federation of Labor (AFL), sought clemency for the eight, but craft unionists in many cities denounced independent politics and looked suspiciously at German-dominated unions. As the Knights tried to build a labor party in the fall of 1886, unity faltered along lines of ethnicity and political orientation. Finally, the Knights and the AFL engaged in internecine warfare affecting many trades.

In short, the public disfavor that Haymarket brought upon the labor movement put additional strain on already tense relationships. Furthermore, the great upheaval elicited a strong employer counterattack aimed at recapturing the initiative from organized labor. Workers continued to agitate for improved conditions in the spring and summer of 1886, but aggressive employers, a wary public, and an increasingly fragmented and cautious labor movement combined to lead to the loss of much of what wage earners had achieved. Still, at the turn of the century, AFL president Gompers judged the eight-hour movement of 1886 a success. The crusade had created a permanent labor movement and had resulted eventually, according to Gompers, "in a reduction of fully one hour's labor [per day] of the working people of the United States." [Ken Fones-Wolf]

FURTHER READING

Avrich, Paul. *The Haymarket Tragedy*. Princeton, NJ: Princeton University Press, 1984.

Foner, Philip S. *History of the Labor Movement in the United States*, Vol. 2. New York: International Publishers, 1955.

Oestreicher, Richard. *Solidarity and Fragmentation: Working People and Class Consciousness in Detroit, 1875–1900*. Urbana, IL: University of Illinois Press, 1986.

Roediger, David. "Ira Steward and the Anti-Slavery Origins of American Eight-Hour Theory." *Labor History*, Vol. 27 (Summer, 1986), pp. 410–426.

"The Haymarket" issue. *International Labor and Working-Class History*, No. 29 (Spring, 1986).

o   o   o

ELECTRICAL MANUFACTURING STRIKES OF 1946. The 1946 strikes at the General Electric (GE), General Motors (GM), and Westinghouse plants represented by the United Electrical, Radio, and Machine Workers of America (UE), were the largest and most important in the history of the union. The strikes resulted in qualified victories for UE.

The UE had organized some of the workers at all three firms during the 1930s. By the end of 1941, it had national contracts at GE, Westinghouse, and the electrical divisions of GM. Conditions and contracts were improved during World War II and considerable organization of additional plants took place at GE and Westinghouse. High profits, cost-plus contracts, and substantial overtime all boosted the standard of living of workers in the industry and temporarily lessened corporate militancy at the bargaining table.

The end of the war threatened to reverse this situation and pointed toward a showdown. After several high-level meetings with other Congress of Industrial Organizations (CIO) leaders, the UE held a national wage policy conference for its members in mid-1945. The conference proposed a contract demand of a two-dollar-a-day wage hike for all workers in the industry. The demand was virtually identical to that being put forward by the United Steel Workers of America (USWA) and differed only slightly from the 25 percent raise goal of the United Automobile Workers (UAW).

The arguments that the UE made for the wage increase varied slightly from firm to firm but contained many common elements. The union noted that overtime had been eliminated in most plants, causing a very substantial drop in take-home pay and revealing the fact that hourly wages had not kept pace with inflation during the war years. As war contracts dried up, workers were being shifted to lower rated jobs. New plants were being opened, especially by GE, in low-wage, rural, and southern areas, and the cut-back in second and third shift operations meant the elimination of shift differential payments. The UE also cited the ability of the corporations to pay higher wages, noting that wartime profits had been three to five times higher than in the comparable period before the war, and that productivity per worker had risen substantially during the conflict.

The company response was typified by that of GE at the bargaining table. The firm began by stating "we do not consider prices . . . a proper subject for negotiation or even discussion with your organization." They argued that wage increases would cause inflation, that wages had already risen by 30 percent since 1940, and that the company's financial position did not permit large pay increases.

Negotiations were conducted with all three firms over the last quarter of 1945. On December 13, 1945, since little progress was being made, strike authorization votes, which were required by the wartime Smith-Connolly Act, were held at the three chains. About 79 percent of the Westinghouse workers favored the strike authorization, and the figures were slightly higher at GE and GM.

Two days later the War Labor Board (WLB) issued a final ruling on the UE's request for an end to discriminatory female wage rates. The WLB called for the addition of four cents an hour to all wages in the lamp plants of GE and Westinghouse and the establishment of a two-cents-an-hour fund per worker to be used to minimize the gender wage gap throughout the chains. GE and Westinghouse refused to implement this order, noting that the war was over and that the WLB would soon be eliminated. The subject of the WLB order was now added to the disputes to be settled.

Throughout 1945 the UE continued to bargain, hoping to avoid major strikes.

In the opening week of 1946, United States Steel raised its offer to the USWA to fifteen cents an hour, and the UE asked its three major firms to respond. They refused and on January 15, 1946, strikes began at the UE-represented locations of GM, GE, and Westinghouse.

At GM, the UE represented 30,000 workers in the electrical division, with locals at Dayton's Frigidaire and Delco plants; Warren, Ohio's Packard and Sunlight plants; and the Delco plant in Rochester, New York. Of course, most of the GM plants outside the electrical division were organized by the UAW. The UE unsuccessfully sought joint negotiations with the UAW in October 1945, and January 1946, and the ultimate contract demands were somewhat different. UAW General Motors director Walter Reuther called for a 25 percent pay increase and demanded that GM not raise its auto prices as a result. The UAW began its strike on November 21, 1945, before the other CIO unions. The UE did not join the strike until over a month later.

GM's last pre-strike offer to either union was 10¢ or 10 percent per hour. A special government panel appointed by President Harry Truman called for an increase of 19.5¢ per hour in the auto industry. In the steel industry a similar panel recommended a raise of 18.5¢ per hour which USWA and CIO president Philip Murray indicated he was willing to accept. Following these developments, UE director of organization James Matles privately told his staff that 18.5¢ was now the ceiling and that the UE "would have to fight to reach that."

More settlements began to emerge along these lines. On January 26, the UAW concluded deals with Ford and Chrysler at 18¢ and 18.5¢, respectively. The next day, the UE signed a contract for 18¢ an hour with RCA, where there had been no strike. On February 12, 1946, the UE announced that it was signing a contract with GM at

18¢ an hour and returning to work. (For the period from November 7, 1945, to January 15, 1946, the retroactive pay raise would be 13.5¢.)

UAW president R. J. Thomas expressed public shock at the UE settlement, and Reuther condemned it as a betrayal. Privately, Thomas had a more ambivalent attitude. Reuther would continue the UAW strike until March 13, before agreeing to a virtually identical 18.5¢ contract. Regardless of which party, if any, was at fault, the issue helped embitter relations between Reuther, soon to become the UAW president, and the UE.

The biggest of the 1946 UE strikes was the one at GE. It was the first national strike in the history of the firm and caught GE somewhat by surprise. The company's final pre-strike offer had been a pay raise of ten cents an hour, and the company had clearly expected to make a settlement near this figure. When the strike began, the picket lines were solid and well over 90 percent of GE's production workers honored them. So powerful was the strike that the firm could not seriously contemplate a back to work effort. It concentrated its attention on obtaining injunctions allowing non-union managerial and white collar workers across the picket lines and was successful in about half of its locations. In general, however, public manifestations of support for the strike were plentiful. Mayors and other politicians, students, farmers, and small merchants passed resolutions, signed petitions, donated aid and marched on the picket lines. The UE was particularly successful in mobilizing veterans in support of the strike.

On January 22, 1946, Secretary of Labor Lewis Schwellenbach appointed former WLB chairman William H. Davis and Arthur S. Meier of the New York State Board of Mediation as conciliators in the strike. More serious negotiations began. On March 5, after clashes at several locations, especially Philadelphia, a partial armistice

was reached: employees not in the UE bargaining units could enter the plants in return for a pledge not to carry out production work or discriminate against non-unionists who honored the picket lines.

This truce was the predecessor to the conclusion of a contract on March 13 at the pattern figure of 18.5¢. This raise also applied to women workers, whom GE had tried to exclude from earlier offers. One close observer of the 1946 strikes called this a "shocking defeat" for GE and noted that they "won nothing." The results of the strike strengthened the position of the UE at GE. They also encouraged the stunned firm to adopt a more aggressive, well-prepared, and sustained anti-union approach in labor relations in the future.

The longest and most bitter of the UE's 1946 strikes was at Westinghouse, where 65,000 workers struck. The company made no wage increase offer at all before the strike but instead proposed a standard forty-four-hour workweek as the solution to workers' wage needs. Westinghouse, with 60 percent of its production workers on incentive, versus 20 percent at GE, proposed a major downscaling of piecework rates, as well as a strong productivity clause, seniority concessions, and other givebacks by the union. Wage rates were slightly higher at Westinghouse than at GE, and the firm was determined to reduce this gap, even if it meant a long strike.

Westinghouse refused to agree to a GE-style "open gate" arrangement with the UE. Instead, it sought to break the picket lines by injunctions, which it obtained at about a dozen locations. Union hopes for a settlement rose in mid-March, at the time of the GE contract, but Westinghouse continued to refuse a similar deal. At this point, the federal mediators withdrew from the case, condemning Westinghouse for blocking an agreement, especially by demanding the exclusion of lamp workers from its 15.1¢ an hour wage offer, a package that the UE valued at only 9.7¢ after the incentive concessions and other Westinghouse proposals were included.

With its other strikes settled, the UE was now able to focus most of its attention on the successful conclusion of the Westinghouse strike and the union held out for another six weeks until agreement was reached on May 12, 1946. The general wage increase was eighteen cents an hour, including the lamp workers. Women workers received an average pay increase of an additional four cents to lessen wage differentials. Incentive issues were compromised, but were closer to the UE's proposals than to those of Westinghouse. Maintenance of membership was retained, as was the right to strike over unresolved grievances and a restricted management rights clause. Some concessions were made to the firm. The union now had to pay half the cost of lost time for stewards on grievances, and one observer opined that the long strike had "laid the contractual basis for tightening up a demoralized incentive system."

The UE waged several other important strikes in the electrical manufacturing industry in 1946. Settlements on the eighteen cents pattern were made after bitter battles at the three UE-represented Allis Chalmers plants and an eight-month strike at Phelps-Dodge in Elizabeth, New Jersey, where company guards killed striker Mario Russo.

Taken together, the 1946 UE strikes represented a major victory for the union. It had maintained successful strikes, usually for the first time, at its biggest employers and had won contracts that carried forward most of the wartime gains in standard-of-living and union rights. [Mark McColloch]

FURTHER READING

Harris, Howell. *The Right to Manage*. Madison, WI: University of Wisconsin Press, 1982.

Matles, James J., and James Higgins. *Them and Us*. New York: Prentice-Hall, 1974.

Schatz, Ronald W. *The Electrical Workers*. Urbana, IL: University of Illinois Press, 1983.

o   o   o

EVERETT, WASHINGTON, MASSACRE OF 1916. A decade of free speech fights came to a dramatic climax in the tragedy of November 5, 1916, in Everett, Washington, where the Industrial Workers of the World (IWW) had been agitating along with striking sawmill workers of the American Federation of Labor (AFL) shingle weavers' union. On May Day, 1916, the shingle weavers struck to protest employers' failure to increase wages, and met with armed resistance from hired strikebreakers and other violence from mill owners supported by that state's employers' and lumbermen's associations.

When the IWW organizers opened a hall in Everett, a port city on Puget Sound, the city's sheriff and local police responded with savage opposition. In the summer of 1916, Wobbly organizer James Rowan and other agitators from Seattle were arrested when they attempted to carry on a free speech fight. Everett mill owners adopted anti-IWW tactics that had been successfully used in 1913 in San Diego: the use of vigilante groups of local citizens to harass union activists, break up street meetings, beat organizers, and deport them from town, many with broken limbs and internal injuries.

On October 30, forty-one Wobblies, mostly young loggers and lumberjacks, arrived by boat from Seattle IWW headquarters, intending to lend support for the free speech crusade. The Everett sheriff and his deputies rounded them up at the Everett docks, drove them to a park on the outskirts of town, and forced them to run the gauntlet between rows of hundreds of armed deputies who beat them with spiked bats. Everett citizens were shocked at the amount of dried blood found on the grass the following morning. IWW organizer Jim Thompson addressed a public protest rally of 2,000 sympathetic townspeople who felt that their sheriff had gone too far.

On November 5, 1916, a delegation of 250 singing Wobblies left Seattle for Everett on a passenger boat, the *Verona*, and an additional group of IWW members, plus other passengers, boarded a second boat, the *Calista*, which regularly sailed between the two cities. As the *Verona* approached the Everett docks with the Wobbly passengers singing "Hold the Fort," a British union song, shooting broke out from Pier Two where the sheriff and some 200 armed vigilantes had been tipped off to the boat's arrival by Pinkerton detectives in Seattle. Shooting continued for about ten minutes. At least five IWW members were killed and thirty-one wounded. It was said that additional bodies were later found washed up on a nearby beach. The toll for the Everett vigilantes: nineteen wounded and two dead.

The *Verona*, sailing back to Seattle, warned the *Calista* to return. At the Seattle docks, nearly all the Wobblies on both boats were arrested. Seventy-four were charged with murder of the Everett vigilantes and were secretly removed at night from Seattle to the Everett county jail.

The two-month trial that began in March 1917 focused on the inflammatory propaganda of the IWW as well as on Tom Tracy, the first of the defendants, who was charged with firing the first shot from the *Verona*. The IWW defense lawyer demanded a reenactment on the Everett docks of the November 5 tragedy, demonstrating that it was impossible to identify any passenger from the shore and, more-

over, that the Everett vigilantes, milling around the piers, were likely to have been in each other's line of fire. The court acquitted Tracy and released the seventy-three other defendants.

Despite threats of recall, the Seattle mayor had courageously denounced the Everett vigilantes as murderers. AFL officials in Seattle and throughout the state urged their members to support the IWW. The IWW defense campaign brought national leaders to the area who effectively waged massive publicity efforts on behalf of the union. A new local union of lumber workers was organized in these months: thousands of new members joined the union, and intensive organizing and strike plans were initiated that led to the major **Northwest Lumber Strike of 1917.**

The trial was won in the courts but lost in the press. IWW propaganda, submitted as evidence by the prosecution, produced community shivers, newspaper headlines, and caricatures of IWW members as bomb-throwing anarchists. Coverage of the trial swept the fear of internal violence onto the doorsteps of many American communities and presented an image of a domestic enemy attacking American values of industrial peace and property.

A decade of vigorous, uncompromising IWW free speech activity ended as America entered the war to battle Kaiserism in Europe and radicalism in its own backyard. [Joyce L. Kornbluh]

FURTHER READING

Clark, Norman H. *Mill Town.* Seattle, WA: University of Washington Press, 1970.

Smith, Walker C. *The Everett Massacre.* Chicago, IL: I.W.W. Publishing Bureau, 1917.

Tyler, Robert. *Rebels of the Woods: The I.W.W in the Pacific Northwest.* Eugene, OR: University of Oregon Press, 1967.

F

○ ○ ○ ○ ○ ○ ○ ○ ○ ○ ○

○　　○　　○

FALL RIVER TEXTILE STRIKES OF
1884 AND 1889. Fall River, Massachusetts,
was the leading textile manufacturing city
in the country in the late nineteenth century. Like other great industrial cities of the
era, such as Paterson, New Jersey; Lynn,
Massachusetts; and Pittsburgh, Pennsylvania, Fall River had an ethnically diverse
work force living in distinct urban neighborhoods. In the 1880s and 1890s, the
city's working-class neighborhoods, largely
English, Irish, and French-Canadian, surrounded the great textile mills that hugged
the Quequechan River. As the Fall River
corporations grew in size and power, workers steadily overcame the ethnic, religious,
and language barriers which divided them
and began to organize into unions.

Labor conflict had broken out as early
as 1850 when mule spinners struck the
Metacomet Mill in a dispute over shorter
hours and higher pay. Another failed strike
occurred in 1866 over similar issues. In
1867, the workers succeeded in striking for
the ten-hour workday. But three years later
an attempt by spinners and operatives to
turn back a wage reduction failed in the
face of hunger, threatened evictions from
company housing, and the presence of two
companies of the Massachusetts militia
protecting strikebreakers.

Confident after their victory in 1870,
the employers of Fall River expanded the
industry dramatically, only to see their
efforts dashed by the great depression of
1873. To cope with the catastrophe, the
mills ran on short time and cut wages.

Unable to live on their reduced wages,
workers flocked to join a resurgent labor
movement. In the forefront of the effort
were the women weavers who agitated for
a strike and whose militancy carried the
largely male Weavers' Union along in their
wake. The strike began on January 30,
1875, and was marked by a dramatic solidarity among all branches of the trade. But
perhaps as important was the support given
to the strikers by the working-class communities of Fall River. This working-class
unity led to victory on March 18 when the
mills agreed to rescind the wage reduction
and the workers returned to work.

Like many similar actions of the period, the victory of the textile workers in
1875 was shortlived. Indeed, the owners
had learned a lesson from their defeat. They
too realized that solidarity was necessary
for victory and formed the Board of Trade
to coordinate a wage reduction and a citywide lockout which began in September
of 1875. After four weeks the mills reopened to non-union workers who signed
"yellow dog" contracts agreeing not to join
a union as a condition of employment. In
the disaster of 1875, the weavers, carders,
and loomfixers unions were destroyed.
Only the spinners survived.

The harsh terms of the employers'
victory left a deep residue of resentment
among the textile workers of Fall River, and
by 1879 the flames of unionism had been
rekindled. The spinners, the aristocrats of
the textile workers, took the lead in agitating for higher wages. The employers met
this pressure by threatening to install tech-

nology in the mills which would create a surplus of spinners and weaken their union. In response, the spinners called for a general strike to begin on June 15. The employers, with the Board of Trade acting as the coordinating agency, imported French-Canadian workers as strikebreakers, and by October 26 the strike had been broken. Well over 100 spinners had been arrested for trying to stop the Canadians from entering the mills. The lesson that the spinners learned was that craft unionism alone could not succeed against the combined power of the employers and the implementation of new machines.

As before, the defeat did not put an end to agitation by Fall River's workers. Between 1884 and 1894, there were three strikes in the city. In the course of these struggles, the French-Canadian community, which had arrived in Fall River as strikebreakers during the 1879 strike, became part of the community-union front against the textile companies. Most of the strikes took place, as before, in response to wage cuts ordered by the companies. Also as in the past, the skilled spinners were the backbone of the strike, but unlike 1879, the spinners were able to convince all other branches of the trade to support the strike. Soon a series of spontaneous walkouts closed down most of Fall River's textile mills. Workers of the various trades, such as weavers, card room operatives, and loomfixers reorganized their unions. Indicative of the enthusiasm of the workers for the strike was the formation of the Young Ladies Union of Spoolers, Warper-tenders, and Drawing-in Girls. Once again the employers met the challenge with evictions, strikebreakers, and the use of town police to harass and intimidate strikers.

The strength of the strike lay in the support of Fall River's working-class communities which surrounded the mills near the river. Here the strikers drew support for mass rallies, marches, picket lines, and fund-raising events. Community solidarity also involved the ostracism of strikebreakers. Six weeks into the strike violence erupted. During March, several strikebreakers were attacked and one was killed. The violence was the act of desperate men. In spite of the solidarity of the workers and the support of the community, the united front of the employers did not give way. On May 12, the Weaver's Union voted to return to work. Others soon followed, and by early June the eighteen-week strike, marred by violence, arson, and enormous suffering on the part of the strikers, was over. Yet even this decisive defeat did not quench the Fall River workers' thirst for unionization. Rebuilding of the shattered labor movement began immediately, and by 1889 the unions were ready for yet another test of strength with their powerful adversaries.

By 1889, resentment against the mounting speedup and stretchout in the mills had led to increased agitation for workers' action. This time, however, the pressure did not come primarily from the spinners, whose power had been reduced by the introduction of new machinery in many mills that now required only unskilled female labor for spinning. Instead, the weavers, who were the main victims of the employers' drive for increased productivity, took the lead. Weaving was a labor intensive trade, and productivity could only be increased by sweating the workers. Anger over the speedup and stretchout brought most of the city's weavers into the Weavers' Protective Union where they turned their resentment into action in a struggle for higher wages. On March 7, the weavers voted to strike. On March 11, the usual hum of Fall River's mills was absent. All but a few of the mills were shut down. The momentum of the strike continued to build until by March 22, most of the industry in Fall River and surrounding communities was quiet. Pressure was maintained on the employers by marches, rallies, and intense community ostracism of workers who crossed the picket lines. This anger spilled over into violence on March 22 when a crowd of strikers stoned and severely beat replacement workers as they left the Seaconnet Mill.

Nevertheless, the employers remained adamant. They would "positively not recognize the Weavers Union if the mills remained closed until the belts rot on the shafts," said one. In spite of the remarkable solidarity among the various crafts and the support of an ethnically diverse community, the strikers gave way and voted to return to work on March 27. Once again the textile workers of Fall River had gone to war with their powerful employers; once again they had achieved a solidarity among the trades that was the envy of most unions of the day; once again they had overcome gender and ethnic differences to forge a militant united front with the working-class community; once again they had lost. They would try one more time, in 1894, with the same results.

Although the struggles of the textile workers in late-nineteenth-century Fall River were not successful in terms of wresting some measure of control from the employers, they were a remarkable testimony to the determination and militancy of a working-class community in the face a massive assault on their independence and dignity by a group of industrial America's most powerful employers. [Ronald L. Filippelli]

FURTHER READING

Cumbler, John T. *Working-Class Community in Industrial America: Work, Leisure, and Struggle in Two Industrial Cities, 1880–1930.* Westport, CT: Greenwood Press, 1979.

Lahne, Herbert J. *The Cotton Mill Worker.* New York: Farrar and Rinehart, 1944.

o o o

FARAH CLOTHING WORKERS' STRIKE AND BOYCOTT OF 1972–1974. El Paso, Texas, seemed like an unlikely spot for an epic struggle between clothing workers and an employer. Historically, the industry had been centered in New York and the other urban centers of the Northeast and Midwest, such as Chicago. But by the early 1970s, the garment industry had established a significant beachhead in Texas because of the availability of cheap labor, most of it Mexican-American. The Farah Manufacturing Company, whose main product was men's slacks, was one of the most important of the Southwestern producers. The Amalgamated Clothing Workers of America, the dominant union in the men's clothing industry, was eager to organize Farah as an opening wedge to crack the dozens of clothing manufacturers which had set up shop in the low-wage Southwest.

The attempt to unionize the Farah Manufacturing Company began in 1969 and reached a climax on October 14, 1970, when cutting-room employees at the Farah Gateway plant voted for representation by the Amalgamated Clothing Workers of America (ACWA). Farah had fought the union organizing campaign bitterly. The company's president, William F. Farah, a grandson of the founder, vowed to sell the business before recognizing the union. Farah officials pointed to the fact that the company's workers were better paid than most union shops, and that the benefits, including medical clinics, free eye care, life insurance, holiday pay, and sick leave, were evidence of the company's concern for its workers. Not surprisingly, the company challenged the results of the certification election and kept the matter tied up in the appeals process for nearly two years until the NLRB certified the ACWA on September 15, 1972.

The battle, however, was joined a few months earlier, in May of 1972, when

Farah fired six workers, allegedly for union activities. On May 9, about 500 employees boycotted three plants in El Paso and San Antonio. The next day another 100 to 125 workers walked out in support. Farah notified the strikers that they would lose their jobs if they did not return to work. The company also quickly obtained an injunction that forbade picketing within fifty feet of plant property and an order that restrained strikers from interfering with plant operations and employees who wanted to work. On May 13, the strikers held the first of a series of rallies and demonstrations. Four days later, on a complaint filed by Farah, an El Paso justice of the peace issued 189 arrest warrants for violations of a Texas statute forbidding mass picketing. Nearly 1,000 strikers and picketers were arrested before the ACWA's challenge overturned the law.

Throughout the strike the ACWA filed a long list of unfair labor practice complaints against Farah. Some, like the company's use of dogs against the strikers, brought public opinion behind the strike. NLRB decisions during the long battle consistently favored the strikers. When the NLRB ruled in early February 1974, that Farah must let union organizers enter its plants, it became clear that the company's resistance was nearly over.

The strike lasted ninety-three weeks, but it did not bring Farah to recognize the union. That result came as the effect of a nationwide boycott of Farah slacks sponsored by the ACWA and supported by the AFL-CIO. Stores were boycotted across the country. The boycott was supported across the nation by a galaxy of politicians, such as Senators Edward Kennedy of Massachusetts and Gaylord Nelson of Wisconsin. Even Nelson Rockefeller, then the Republican governor of New York, lent his support. More important than the politicians, however, was the backing given the strike by the Roman Catholic Bishop of El Paso, the Most Reverend Sidney M. Metzger.

Metzger's support brought general condemnation of Farah from Catholic circles across the country. Also critical in the success of the boycott was the fact that the Farah struggle, like the **California Grape and Lettuce Boycotts** led by Cesar Chavez and the United Farm Workers Union in California, became identified with the Chicano movement for an end to oppression of Hispanic-Americans. The boycott succeeded in turning Farah's 1971 profit of $6 million into losses of $8.3 million in 1972. Farah stock, soaring at fifty-six dollars per share the day the strike was called, closed at eight dollars just before the settlement. The union did not come through the contest unscathed; the strike and boycott cost the ACWA treasury some $5 million. [Ronald L. Filippelli]

FURTHER READING

"Bishop and the Boycott: Support for Striking Garment Workers by Bishop Metzger." *America* (March 3, 1972), pp. 178–179.

"Boycott to Aid Garment Workers: AFL-CIO Helping Farah Workers to Organize." *Business Week* (August 26, 1972), pp. 53–54.

Malley, D. D. "How the Union Beat Willie Farah." *Fortune* (August 1974), pp. 164–167.

Ortega, P. D. "Farah Slacks and Pants: Chicanos Extend the Boycott." *Nation* (November 20, 1972), pp. 497–498.

Trillin, Calvin. "U.S. Journal: El Paso, Texas: Strike Against Farah Manufacturing Company." *New Yorker* (February 17, 1973), pp. 83–88.

o   o   o

FLORIDA SERVANTS' REVOLT OF 1768. Only six years before the American Revolution, the most serious rebellion of white workers in America up to that time occurred in eastern Florida. Dr. Andrew Turnbull, a wealthy Scotsman, had established a colony at New Smyrna. He imported as workers some 1,400 indentured servants, most of whom were Greeks but with a sizable number of Italians and Minorcans as well. Shortly after landing at

New Smyrna, the workers found their circumstances so intolerable that a revolt, led by the Greeks and the Italians, broke out.

On August 19, 1768, Carlo Forni, one of the Italian overseers, and twenty supporters rallied the workers of New Smyrna in the town square. He declared himself commander in chief and promised to lead the workers to freedom under Spanish protection in Havana. The excited crowd first liberated the town's store of rum, and when an English overseer tried to stop them, he was seriously wounded. Fired with this success, about 300 servants, nearly all of the Italians and Greeks in the colony, seized firearms and ammunition, plundered the houses of the Minorcans who had refused to participate in the rebellion, and captured a ship loaded with provisions at anchor in the river.

When he received the news at midnight that same night, Andrew Turnbull sent a rider at top speed to request assistance from the governor. Troops captured the rebels' ship soon after and arrested most of the insurgents. However, some, including the leaders, escaped in an open boat and managed to elude the authorities in the Florida Keys for four months. Three of the leaders were convicted of piracy: two, including Forni, were executed, and a third was pardoned on the condition that he act as executioner of his two comrades. The others received amnesty. [Ronald L. Filippelli]

FURTHER READING

Morris, Richard B. *Government and Labor in Early America.* New York: Harper and Row, 1946.

Smith, Abbot E. *Colonists in Bondage: White Servitude and Convict Labor in America, 1607–1776.* Chapel Hill, NC: University of North Carolina Press, 1947.

o o o

FOOTBALL PLAYERS' STRIKE OF 1987. The 1987 twenty-four-day strike by the National Football League Players Association (NFLPA) against the National Football League owners was the culmination of changes in labor relations in the sports side of the entertainment industry that accelerated in the 1970s. In fact, the course of the 1987 strike was consistent with the pattern of disputes which characterized football bargaining since the players unionized over twenty years earlier.

With the formation of the NFLPA in 1965, the players considered striking the last preseason game between the Washington Redskins and the Baltimore Colts. However, when Washington's owner, George Preston Marshall, announced that he would play the game without the strikers, the players abandoned their plans to cease working and played the game. This pattern of the NFLPA calling for work stoppages and then being unable to translate the cessation of work into gains at the bargaining table, also occurred in 1968, 1970, 1974, 1975, and 1987.

Throughout these collective efforts salaries and some benefits have increased, but the union's goal of free agency or progress on the "freedom issues" has not been achieved. Although the strikes generally demonstrated good rank-and-file solidarity, the owners have used their monopoly status and revenue-sharing strategy to prevent players from moving from one team to another and thereby to avoid changing labor relations in the business of football.

In 1974, the players struck training camps for forty-two days in a bitter dispute. They presented a full slate of proposals which focused on the so-called "freedom issues," including the Rozelle Rule, which allowed the commissioner to award compensation for the signing of free agents. This walkout was especially difficult for the NFLPA because rank-and-file solidarity broke down, and when the strike ended, most of the issues remained unre-solved, and the owners had won a clear victory and were ready for another round of bargaining in 1982.

After a fifty-seven-day work stoppage in 1982, which featured excellent solidar-ity among the NFLPA's rank and file, competition between owners in the United States Football League and the National Football League, and a new lucrative tele-vision agreement, players salaries rose from an average of $90,000 in 1982 to $230,000 in 1987. The NFLPA, however, did not achieve its bargaining goal of capturing 55 percent of gross revenues to be placed in a separate fund for player compensation and benefits. The union negotiated a minimum salary schedule based on seniority which was funded out of the increased television revenues. However, management won the 1982 strike by refusing to agree to the union's main proposals, although the play-ers did receive a $1.6 billion package over five years. These developments set the stage for another football season which would be interrupted when the contract expired five years later.

In 1987, the NFLPA represented approximately 1,500 players, which was by far the most of any major professional sport. Fifty percent of its members were minorities. The average career span of 3.2 years for football players was the shortest of any players in professional sports. One-half of America's professional football play-ers retired with a permanent disability caused by injuries suffered while earning a living. Players had a life expectancy of fifty-five years, well short of the average for American males. Consequently, players attempt to maximize their income in a short period of time but in a situation where their bargaining power has often been lacking.

In 1987, the players were represented at the bargaining table by a nine-member executive committee, elected from the twenty-eight player representatives, and the union's executive director, Gene Upshaw.

Management was represented by a six-member executive committee which was selected from the NFL's management coun-cil which was composed of one manage-ment representative from each team. Jack Donlan chaired management's executive committee. These bargaining teams did not determine individual salaries but looked at issues such as minimum salaries, severance pay, free agency, and health issues such as the impact of artificial turf. The agreement negotiated in 1982 expired on August 31, 1987.

Several negotiating sessions were held in the summer, and in order to avoid heavy media coverage, they were rotated from one location to another. However, little prog-ress was made, and by mid-September talk of a work stoppage dominated news cov-erage of the fall season. The strike began officially on September 22, 1987.

Management immediately imple-mented a three-pronged strategy to force the players to come back to work without achieving their bargaining goals. First the owners stonewalled in negotiations to avoid agreeing to a new contract; they launched a media campaign to get the public on their side; and they hired strikebreakers who along with scabs would present replace-ment games for the media and the public. During the course of the summer camps two-thirds of the NFL owners lined up players from those who did not make the teams' active rosters but who agreed for $1,000 to cross a picket line and play in replacement games. This approach was similar to the early history of labor–management relations in the United States and indicative of the aggressive anti-union tactics which many employers pur-sued throughout the 1980s.

The NFLPA focused on the issue of free agency and called on the owners to negotiate a system in which players could move from one team to another. The NFLPA was not able to accumulate a strike fund and did not secure a line of credit on which the players could draw for loans during the stoppage. On the other hand, the NFLPA, after becoming the first professional sports organization to affiliate with the AFL-CIO in 1979, received excellent support during the strike from unions in cities around the United States. In the course of the strike 84 percent of the NFLPA's 1,585 members honored the picket lines.

During the strike the players lost an average of $15,000 per game and a total of $80 million altogether. Although television ratings declined as the replacement games continued, the average owner's profit rose from $800,000 per game before the strike to $921,000 during the stoppage. This profit was wiped out, however, by the $60 million that the owners had to refund to the television networks for one missed weekend of play.

On the twentieth day of the strike the NFLPA's executive director, Gene Upshaw, offered a three-part compromise to end the strike during a half-time appearance on the nationwide Monday night telecast of a replacement game. Upshaw proposed that all strikers be reinstated without reprisals; that the 1982 agreement continue in effect; and that if after six weeks of mediation some issues remained unresolved, they would be submitted to binding arbitration. The NFL owners, who were dealing from a position of strength, rejected the call for binding arbitration of unresolved issues.

In the midst of rumors that many veteran players would soon cross the picket line and report to work, the NFLPA decided to end the strike on October 15, 1987. Once the union ended the strike, the NFL owners refused to allow the players to participate in games on October 18 and 19. They based their refusal on the grounds that they had set October 14 as the last possible day on which the players could report in order to be ready to play the following weekend.

The day the strike ended the NFLPA filed an antitrust suit challenging the college draft, restraints on player free agency, and other practices that it alleged interfered with competition in the labor market. The union also filed a suit asking the federal court to declare the 280 players, who were without contracts, free agents and therefore eligible to sign with any of the twenty-eight teams. In mid-July 1988, a federal judge in Minneapolis rejected the union's request for free agency for these players reasoning that such a decision would disrupt the competitive balance between the league's teams. The antitrust suit may not be finally resolved for several years.

With the conclusion of the 1988 football season, labor relations between the NFLPA and the NFL had not changed from October 15, 1987, when the strike ended. Several meetings were held, but no progress was reported on a new contract and, in fact, no meaningful bargaining had occurred since 1982. For all intents and purposes the collective bargaining relationship had broken down completely and the battle shifted to the courts, the National Labor Relations Board, and perhaps the United States Congress.

The Football Players' Strike of 1987 continued the pattern that had been set when the players first unionized. The NFLPA still has yet to win a battle at the bargaining table or on the picket line. The football players have been unsuccessful because of the economics of their branch of the entertainment industry. With the explosion of public interest in pro football in the 1960s, and ever more lucrative television contracts, the NFL owners decided to pool their television revenues and distribute them among the twenty-eight teams throughout the league. With nearly sold-out stadiums week after week and revenue sharing, which guaranteed a profit regardless of the team's win–loss record, there was no economic incentive for teams to bid for players from another city in order to improve their team's competitive status. Because of the owners' monopoly status and revenue sharing, the football players have not been able to overcome the economics of the industry to achieve a balance of power at the bargaining table and thereby negotiate better agreements from one contract round to the next. [Donald Kennedy]

FURTHER READING

Staudohar, Paul D. "The Football Strike of 1987: The Question of Free Agency." *Monthly Labor Review* (August 1988), pp. 26–31.

——. *The Sports Industry and Collective Bargaining.* Ithaca, NY: Cornell ILR Press, 1986.

o   o   o

FORD HUNGER MARCH OF 1932. The Great Depression hit Detroit's automotive industry with ferocious impact, and by December of 1930, 39,000 families were on the relief rolls in the Motor City. The city also faced a budget crisis as a result of the staggering local relief costs. The problem was aggravated by the fact that the Ford Motor Company, many of whose unemployed workers lived in Detroit, had built its factories outside of Detroit, and thus did not pay taxes to the city. Indeed, Ford not only did not pay Detroit taxes, but it also refused to contribute to local charities. The city's attempts to meet the crisis, including cutting teachers' salaries and shortening the school year, proved to be futile. By March 1932, the city announced that its resources could not cope with more than 20,000 families on the relief rolls.

As the crisis deepened, the Communist Party began to emerge as the organization prepared to try to turn the accumulated discontent of Detroit's unemployed into a social and political movement. Events affecting the city's unemployed workers were part of a larger movement that was developing in major cities across the country. In July 1930, the Communist Party gave this movement some structure when it created the Unemployed Councils at a meeting in Chicago.

The Communist Party's leadership of the movement was exercised through the local chapter of the Trade Union Unity League (TUUL), a Communist Party labor organization that had a small but militant following in Detroit, and the city's Unemployed Council. The target chosen for the first demonstration, the Ford Rouge plant in Dearborn, served the purposes of both groups. It focused attention on Ford's seeming lack of willingness to share responsibility for the plight of the unemployed, many of whom were its own workers. Indeed, Ford had laid off some 91,000 workers since 1929. A demonstration at the huge Rouge plant also highlighted the company's consistent anti-unionism.

On March 6, the day before the scheduled march, William Z. Foster, secretary of the TUUL and a leading Communist Party official, addressed a large, enthusiastic crowd. He asked the assembled to build a strong auto workers union. In addition, the organizers of the march had also drafted a list of fourteen demands for Ford that included jobs for all laid-off workers, the seven-hour workday, no foreclosures on homes of laid-off Ford workers, free medical aid in the Ford Hospital, the right to organize, and more.

The marchers assembled in bitter cold on March 7 in Detroit, just across the city line from Dearborn. The city, under Mayor Frank Murphy, a liberal Democrat, had a liberal policy on public assemblies. After having been cautioned by their leaders to avoid violence, the 3,000 marchers stepped off in good humor, with banners proclaiming their demands for economic relief. The mood of the affair changed abruptly at the city line where the Dearborn police chief and some thirty to forty of his officers armed with tear gas guns blocked the way.

When the marchers swept past them, the police fired tear gas cannisters into the crowd. The angry marchers then attacked the police and drove them toward the Ford plant. Emboldened by their victory, the marchers arrived at the Ford employment office at Gate 3 where they were met by the regrouped Dearborn police, the fire department, and Ford's private police. Once again violence broke out. The marchers showered the plant's defenders with stones, while they themselves were drenched in streams of freezing water by the firemen.

In the midst of the melee, two marchers fell wounded by gunshot. They were carried to the rear by fellow protesters and were followed by much of the crowd as the freezing water and renewed use of tear gas began to turn the tide. The affair seemed to have reached a climax when, unexpectedly, a car carrying Harry Bennett, chief of Ford's private police, tried to force its way through the crowd. Bennett was hated by the workers, and he was attacked and injured. When the police saw the blood flowing from Bennett's head, they assumed that he had been shot. After rescuing Bennett, they turned their guns on the now disorganized crowd and began to fire indiscriminately. When the smoke cleared, the "Ford Hunger Massacre" had resulted in four dead and two dozen wounded, all members of the protest.

One of the oddities of the events in Detroit was the presence of a number of Russian workers inside the Rouge plant during the violence. They had come as the result of an agreement between Ford and a Soviet trading corporation to provide technical training for Russian auto workers. Instead of supporting the marchers, led by the American Communist Party, Soviet officials disavowed any connection to the events of March 7. For Joseph Stalin, the acquisition of technical know-how for his forced industrialization of Russia was apparently more important than the defeat of unemployed American workers at the gates of one of the great capitalist enterprises of the United States.

Police and other governmental agencies began rounding up radicals after announcing that there was evidence that the affair at Dearborn had been the work of criminal syndicalists. A nationwide search was inaugurated for William Z. Foster and two local leaders of the TUUL, William Reynolds and Albert Goetz. The Communist Party and its International Labor Defense, as well as the American Civil Liberties Union, took up the defense of the imprisoned radicals.

The Communist Party used the publicity surrounding the Ford massacre as a propaganda tool across the country. The four dead marchers, two of whom had been active Communists, were lionized in the party press and elevated to the status of martyrs. The Party also organized a "Workers' Jury" to investigate the Ford massacre. Its purpose was "to brand as Murderers" those responsible for the massacre and demand their prosecution. Not surprisingly, it found Ford and political officials of Dearborn and Detroit guilty of a conspiracy to murder the unemployed marchers.

The real grand jury, established by the state of Michigan, returned no indictments, calling the riot the "result of an instigation by a few agitators who go about the nation taking advantage of times of industrial depression and other misfortune for the purpose of influencing those who are unable to find employment to take care of themselves and family." The grand jury also cleared Ford of any guilt in the deaths and injuries of March 7. [Ronald L. Filippelli]

FURTHER READING

Baskin, Alex. "The Ford Hunger March—1932." *Labor History*, Vol. 13 (Summer, 1972), pp. 331–360.

Rosenzweig, Roy. "Organizing the Unemployed: The Early Years of the Great Depression,

1929–1933." *Radical America*, Vol. 10 (July–August 1976), pp. 37–60.

Sugar, Maurice. *The Ford Hunger March.* Berkeley, CA: Meiklejohn Civil Liberties Institute, 1980.

o o o

FORD MOTOR STRIKE OF 1940. After the success of the sit-down strikes against General Motors in 1937, the United Auto Workers turned its attention to Ford, the second largest of the big three auto companies and without doubt the most anti-union. For its part, Ford had not been sitting idly by. Watching events at General Motors carefully, the company prepared for war with the UAW.

Because the struggle with General Motors had exhausted the union, the UAW realized that the Ford drive would have nowhere near the same energy and creativity that marked that effort. This meant the running of a conventional campaign based on leafletting and persuasion. In addition, Ford had the advantage of learning from GM's mistakes. Finally, Ford had the aid of Harry Bennet's notorious Service Department, a company police force with the sole purpose of defeating the union. Ford demonstrated its willingness to use these resources during the famous "Battle of the Overpass." When the UAW, in a bid for national publicity, had several of its top officials, including Walter Reuther, distribute leaflets at the gates of Ford's huge Rouge plant, Bennet's men beat them savagely. For the first time, black workers had been recruited into the Service Department, and they participated in the assault.

Although the union gained some favorable publicity as a result of the assault by Ford's Service Department personnel, it was not enough to breathe life into the organizing drive. By the spring of 1938 the company clearly had the upper hand. Both the organizing drive and the UAW's at-

tempt to recruit blacks were faltering. In addition, the union's already precarious financial position suffered even more as a result of a downturn in the economy in that year. Union staff had to be laid off and the drive, for all intents and purposes, was ended.

The UAW did not return in earnest to Ford until 1940. The intervening years had not only been marked by the defeat at Ford, but also by debilitating internal struggles between AFL and CIO factions in the UAW. Although the dispute had been settled in the CIO's favor, internal rivalries still lingered, weakening the staff. On the positive side, Ford workers had won some favorable decisions before the National Labor Relations Board and the courts, and the union had successfully organized Chrysler in 1939. Still, the disarray on the UAW staff made it necessary for the CIO to send in the veteran United Mine Workers organizer, Michael Wildman, to head the Ford drive.

Both the UAW and Ford recognized the importance of black workers to their success. Blacks in Detroit had been suspicious of the labor movement because of the long years of neglect and discrimination they had faced with most of the American Federation of Labor unions. And although the National Association for the Advancement of Colored People (NAACP) had endorsed the CIO on the national level, it had pointedly not endorsed the UAW in its organizing drives in Michigan. During the General Motors and Chrysler strikes and during the first Ford organizing drive, most black workers remained cool to the union, as did most of the leadership of black Detroit. Ford's reputation among the black community had contributed a great deal to the defeat of the union in 1938.

A Dearborn, Michigan judge gave the 1940 drive some impetus by ruling that a local ordinance prohibiting distribution of leaflets at congested areas, including the gates of Ford Motor Company, was unconstitutional. The UAW immediately took advantage of the ruling. Thousands of copies of a tract called *Ford Facts* were distributed at the gates. Black and white organizers also went door to door in Detroit to locate Ford employees. In a few months, the UAW had signed up several thousand workers and petitioned for an NLRB election. Suddenly, on April 1, 1941, Harry Bennet announced the firing of the members of the Rouge Grievance Committees, with whom he had been voluntarily meeting and discussing.

Word of Bennet's action led to a spontaneous, rolling strike at the huge Rouge plant. Union leaders scrambled to gain control of the movement and organize the work stoppage by setting up picket lines and blocking access to the plant. Although most black workers joined the strike, many stayed inside. The next morning hundreds more avoided the barricades and entered the plant. In all, some 300 whites and between 1,500 and 2,500 blacks remained inside.

The UAW and its black supporters believed that the company's strategy was to provoke a race riot and force the governor to break the strike. Twice on the morning of April 2, black strikebreakers were sent out to break the picket lines. According to the Communist *Daily Worker*, "Iron bolts and nuts flew through the air in a wholesale barrage from the factory roof, while several hundred Negroes with steel bars and knives charged out of the main gate . . . and began pelting the strikers. . . ." More than a score of pickets received treatment at the union's field hospital. The following day, 400 strikebreakers, mostly black, once again charged the picket lines and left several pickets injured. Several hours later a group of pickets severely beat a group of blacks who had driven by taunting the strikers.

The events of April 2 and 3 had a sobering effect on union officials. They feared the effect of the escalating racial animosity on the strike. In order to forestall it, the UAW lined up an impressive cross section of black Detroit leadership, including, most importantly, the NAACP, which took its first stand with labor during the Ford strike. In exchange for UAW assurances that black workers would be treated as equals with whites under a union contract, the group blasted Ford for fomenting race hatred and issued a statement condemning Ford's use of strikebreakers and endorsing the UAW. It was an unprecedented show of support for organized labor from Detroit's black community. The UAW could not have hoped for more. Yet although several hundred black workers heeded the call and left the plant, many did not. It took the strong support of Walter White, national secretary of the NAACP, to finally persuade blacks to reject the back to work movement.

On April 10 the strike ended as a result of the intervention of the Democratic governor of Michigan, Murray D. Van Wagoner. Both sides agreed to return to the *status quo ante* for discharged workers and grievance procedures and promised to facilitate an NLRB representation election. The union won an overwhelming victory, garnering 70 percent of the vote at the Rouge plant, and similar margins at other Ford works.

Along with a contract that gave Ford workers more than the union had achieved at any other auto company, the union also gained 10,000 black members, by far the largest group up to that time. After the settlement, the Rouge Local 600, the largest in the union, became a bastion of black influence in the UAW. [Ronald L. Filippelli]

FURTHER READING

Bernstein, Irving. *The Turbulent Years: A History of the American Worker, 1933–1941.* Boston, MA: Houghton Mifflin, 1970.

Meier, August, and Elliot Rudwick. *Black Detroit and the Rise of the UAW.* New York: Oxford University Press, 1979.

o o o

FREE-SPEECH FIGHTS OF THE INDUSTRIAL WORKERS OF THE WORLD.

From 1908 to 1917, Industrial Workers of the World (IWW) members, or "Wobblies" as they were popularly called, campaigned for the right to organize and agitate at street-corner meetings in more than thirty free-speech fights held primarily throughout the West. Capturing national attention because of their drama, impact, and importance in upholding U.S. constitutional rights, the free-speech fights were an important organizing strategy to gather new recruits among itinerant workers, to distribute Wobbly literature with its message of industrial unionism, and to counteract suppression of information or distortions about unions in the commercial press.

In scores of cities, IWW soapboxers, fighting to protect their right to speak on the streets, were yanked off impromptu platforms by police after starting to say, "Fellow workers and friends" and were marched off to jail. By passing ordinances attempting to suppress the IWW's free-speech rights, city officials, pressured by employers' associations, aimed to crush organizing drives and destroy the union. Although street speeches had been used by other radical organizations before 1909, the IWW dramatized and publicized this technique most effectively, calling on its scattered members to converge on a town or city that prohibited street meetings, invite arrest by speaking at open-air meetings, and allow themselves to be marched off to jail, confident that, in the words of one Wobbly song, "As fast as they can pinch us, we can always get some more."

Overcrowded jails created burdens for cities that reacted to the Wobbly free-speech campaigns, as well as higher costs to taxpayers for necessary services. IWW members demanded separate trials by jury to clog the judicial process and municipal machinery.

In the overcrowded jails, or bullpens—abandoned buildings that were used to house the IWW prisoners—Wobblies sang "rebel songs" from the IWW *Little Red Songbook* and organized themselves into defense and strategy committees to publicize their struggle and rally support. Wobblies attempted their own defense, "wasting" no money on legal fees and using any available funds to support the influx of new groups of IWW members into the community to continue the agitation.

The organization aimed through these tactics to win support from liberal sympathizers who would be allies in their campaign to win the right to speak. Support from political leaders like Senator Robert M. LaFollette, American Federation of Labor (AFL) local unions and labor councils, and other liberal organizations was deemed crucial in these campaigns.

Although across the country the boldness and intransigence of the rebels exasperated town officials, aroused wrath and frequent violence from town burghers, and frequently turned the free-speech campaigns into bitter, bloody fights, to the Wobblies the campaigns were unique direct action techniques, a means of educating workers to the class struggle, and a practical necessity in countering community opposition to organizing the One Big Union.

Within the IWW, however, the free-speech campaigns met some resistance as some activists felt that they led to "fighting the bull instead of the boss." Free-speech fights should be conducted on the job rather than on the street, some held, since they were draining the human resources of the movement through jailings, beatings, and bread-and-water diets. The Wobbly insistence on passive resistance used in the free-speech fights also prompted intense discussions since it put members at a great disadvantage. However, the strategy of passive resistance remained, with no acts of violence committed by the free-speech fighters.

The free-speech movement started in Missoula, Montana, in 1908, developed in Spokane, Washington, and Fresno, California, reached a peak in 1912 with the eighteen-month campaign in San Diego, and continued throughout the Pacific Northwest.

The success of the 1908 Missoula fight was a prelude to the IWW major campaign in Spokane the following year, a good case study of a successful free-speech campaign. Spokane was in the center of the "Inland Empire" of eastern Washington and western Idaho, a region rich in agriculture, lumber, and mining. The most pressing grievance of the thousands of migrant workers who shipped out of Spokane was the way they were cheated by employment companies, which the Wobblies termed "sharks."

Beginning in 1908, IWW organizers mounted soapboxes directly in front of Spokane employment agencies and urged workers, "Don't buy jobs." They crusaded for a boycott of agencies, and demanded that employers hire directly through the union hall.

In turn, the employment firms organized themselves into the Associated Agencies of Spokane, which pressured the city council to ban all street meetings. For a time, the IWW obeyed the ordinance that was applied to other organizations as well. When the ruling was amended to exempt religious groups such as the Salvation Army, the Wobblies decided to fight back.

On October 28, after IWW organizer Jim Thompson was arrested for soapboxing, the *Industrial Worker* sent out a call: "Wanted—Men to Fill the Jails of Spokane." A five-month campaign defying the street ban began in November when thousands of Wobblies from around the West converged on that city to court mass arrest.

Speaker after speaker mounted soapboxes to say "Fellow Workers" before being pulled down by police, arrested, charged with disorderly conduct, and sentenced to thirty days in jail. IWW organizer Frank Little was sentenced to thirty days at the rock pile for reading the Declaration of Independence from a platform. Not all the IWW members were able speakers. A story is told about the Wobbly who stood on the soapbox, started "Fellow Workers," and then in a panic yelled, "Where are the cops!"

By the end of November, 600 were crowded into cells and were fed only bread and water. When they protested, the police closed all the ventilation in the jail and turned on the steam heat. IWW leader Bill Haywood later told a 1914 United States Senate investigation committee that several died from first being in the "hot box" and then "third-degreed" in ice-cold cells.

Police brutality and treatment of the prisoners aroused protest from the community and throughout the state. All goods coming from Spokane were boycotted by the Coeur d'Alene district of the Western Federation of Miners. The AFL Spokane Central Labor Council unanimously voted to demand a repeal of the street ban ordinance.

One after another, eight editors of the Spokane *Industrial Worker* put out an issue and were arrested. Police confiscated all copies of the December 10 issue in which IWW organizer Elizabeth Gurley Flynn, who had tried to delay her arrest by chaining herself to a lamp post, reported that the sheriff used the women's section of the jail as a brothel, with police procuring customers and the sheriff pocketing the profits.

Early in March 1910, the struggle concluded when the mayor and law-enforcement officials, tired of using tax money to maintain extra police and prisoners, agreed to negotiate with an IWW committee and recognized their rights to rent a hall, publish a newspaper, and organize through street meetings. Free-speech prisoners were released. The licenses of nineteen of the most notorious employment agencies were subsequently revoked and later investigations into the practices of employment firms led to regulatory legislation.

Dramatic free-speech fights in Fresno and San Diego, California, in Everett, Washington, and in other cities over the next seven years publicized the grievances of unskilled and semi-skilled workers, added new members to the organization, demonstrated the powerful relationships of business interests to municipal and judicial officials, and helped cement some cooperative efforts between AFL members, Socialists, and Wobblies in a number of communities.

Writing in 1912, one commentator praised the IWW for taking the lead in fighting for free speech: "Whether they agree or disagree with its methods and aims, all lovers of liberty everywhere owe a debt to this organization for its defense of free speech. Absolutely irreconcilable, absolutely fearless, and unsuppressibly persistent, it has kept alight the fires of freedom. . . . That the defense of traditional rights to which this government is supposed to be dedicated should devolve upon an organization so often denounced as "unpatriotic" and "un-American" is but the usual, the unfailing irony of history." [Joyce L. Kornbluh]

FURTHER READING

Brissenden, Paul F. *The I.W.W.: A Study of American Syndicalism.* New York: Columbia University Press, 1920.

Clark, Norman H. *Milltown.* Seattle, WA: University of Washington Press, 1970.

Foner, Philip S., ed. *Fellow Workers and Friends: I.W.W. Free-speech Fights as Told by the Participants.* Westport, CT: Greenwood Press, 1981.

Kornbluh, Joyce, ed. *Rebel Voices: An I.W.W. Anthology.* Ann Arbor, MI: University of Michigan Press, 1964; revised edition, Chicago: Charles H. Kerr Publishing Company, 1988.

Thompson, Fred. *The I.W.W.: Its First Fifty Years.* Chicago, IL: I.W.W. Publishing Bureau, 1976.

o o o

FULTON BAG AND COTTON MILLS COMPANY STRIKE OF 1914–1915. Resolute, tension-lined faces characterized the more than 200 men, women, and children who, on the morning of May 20, 1914, walked out of Fulton Bag and Cotton Mills Company plants in Atlanta, Georgia. The exodus from the plants continued throughout the day, and by evening several hundred additional workers had joined the walkout. The immediate cause of the strike, which climaxed a long, troubled period of labor–management relations, was the company's discharge of several employees who had joined Local 886 of the International Union of Textile Workers of America (UTW). The workers vowed to remain on strike until mill management recognized the union and agreed to adjust several grievances. It quickly became apparent that it was the latter rather than the former that had generated much of the heat fueling the strike. Grievances identified by striking workers included the necessity of signing an extremely arbitrary employment contract, an offensive fining system, child labor abuses, and the excessive brutality practiced by mill supervisors and foremen.

For officials of the American Federation of Labor (AFL) and the UTW, the strike could not have come at a more propitious moment. For some time they had been looking for an opportunity to launch a major organizing drive in southern textiles as the opening thrust in a campaign to unionize the largely unorganized southern work force. The Fulton Bag strike seemed a golden opportunity; indeed, it would have been difficult to create a more promising situation than that presented in the Fulton Bag mills. The location of the mills themselves represented an important factor favoring the unionization of mill workers. Rather than being situated in one of the tightly-controlled, rural communities so typical of the industry, the Fulton Bag and Cotton Mills Company was located near the center of Atlanta, the rapidly emerging key city of the "New South." Although company management had installed a welfare system and practiced the type of industrial paternalism common in the textile industry, it was never able to achieve the same level of control so familiar in the more rural areas of the region.

Furthermore, unlike the small single plant firm typical of southern textiles, Fulton Bag was a large interstate business with additional plants located in St. Louis, New Orleans, Dallas, and New York. It had capital stock of $600,000 and property valued in excess of $10 million. Utilizing twenty boilers, 2,500 looms, and 100,000 ring spindle dyes, the Fulton Bag complex consisted for four electrically powered mills which employed up to 2,100 workers when operating at full capacity.

Chances for waging a successful strike were further enhanced by the existence of a relatively strong local labor movement effectively organized through the Atlanta Federation of Trades (AFT). The AFT leadership staunchly supported the organizing efforts among textile workers and successfully sponsored a membership assessment to help finance the Fulton strike. Meanwhile, the AFT utilized its political influence to assure that government would not intervene against the strikers. At the time of the strike, Atlanta's mayor was a member of the typographical union, and union men held a number of other key positions in local government. Reflecting organized labor's political influence, the city's police force as well as its chief of police clearly sympathized with labor.

A number of other circumstances favored the union cause. At the time of the strike, a group of social gospel reformers was waging a highly publicized campaign against child labor. Composed primarily of Protestant church leaders, progressive businessmen, and professionals, these reformers organized the Men and Religion Forward Movement to lobby for change. Since Fulton Bag employed a sizable number of children, leaders of the movement quickly recognized in the Fulton Bag strike an opportunity to publicize their cause before the 1915 session of the Georgia General Assembly convened. Broadsides paid for by the movement appeared regularly in Atlanta's daily newspapers. While emphasizing child labor abuses, these social reformers also recognized the legitimacy of other worker complaints in the Fulton mills, and they soon became strong supporters of the union cause.

Partially as a result of the agitation led by the Men and Religion Forward Movement, both the U.S. Federal Mediation and Conciliation Service and the U.S. Commission on Industrial Relations sent agents to Atlanta to investigate working conditions at the Fulton Bag and Cotton Mills Company. After the completion of their investigations, these agents wrote reports highly sympathetic to the workers' cause.

Although there is little evidence that organized labor sought to take advantage of the situation, the anti-Semitic wave that swept through Atlanta in the wake of the Leo Frank affair undoubtedly worked to the advantage of the Fulton Bag strikers. Leo Frank had been tried, convicted, and sentenced to death for murdering a young girl who worked in the pencil factory he managed. Responding to the obvious unfairness with which the trial had been conducted, Governor John M. Slayton commuted Frank's sentence to life imprisonment. Shortly thereafter, a mob of vigilantes kidnapped Frank from prison and lynched him in Marietta, Georgia. Like Frank, the owners of Fulton Bag were Jewish industrialists who employed large numbers of women and children, and they were convinced that community sentiment favoring striking workers in their mills was simply another example of religious bigotry.

The strike, which lasted for nearly a year, was a classic labor–management confrontation. Shortly after the outbreak of the strike, mill management began recruiting strikebreakers, evicting workers from company housing, and developing a public relations campaign to turn community opinion against striking workers and their union. Organized labor responded by establishing a union commissary to provide necessary food and clothing and by leasing a large apartment house—dubbed the Textile Hotel—to shelter evicted workers.

By the fall of 1914 it had become clear that the strike would not end quickly. In an effort to conserve its resources, the union established a tent colony on a large vacant lot close to the Fulton Mills. Begun in September 1914, the tent colony was maintained until April of the following year. At times as many as 1,200 workers were fed in the union commissary or housed in the tent camp. The AFL, UTW, local labor organizations, and a host of union sympathizers funnelled thousands of dollars into the strike, but in the end, as so often happened in southern textiles, the union was crushed.

Management's effort to break the strike was made easier by the employment instability of the mills, reflected in annual turnover rates exceeding 500 percent. This created obvious problems for union organizers. Moreover, the existence of a large transient textile labor pool made labor recruitment exceptionally easy. As a result, the union was never able to close down the Fulton mills. During the first few weeks of the strike a shortage of weavers resulted in a substantial reduction in production, but with the assistance of other manufacturers, new weavers were found and normal production resumed.

The lost strike dramatically illustrates the difficulties union organizers confronted when attempting to organize southern textiles, even when, as seldom happened, most circumstances favored the workers' cause. Like most other southern textile manufacturers, Fulton Bag's management never wavered in its determination to resist union recognition and collective bargaining. Operating in a highly competitive industry with exceptionally low profit margins, southern textile manufacturers viewed union organization as a vital threat to their existence in the industry. Instead of negotiating with the union, Fulton Bag recruited new workers, dismissed workers suspected of having union sympathies, and harassed union organizers.

From the beginning, Fulton Bag's owners stated they would close down the mills before changing the labor policies. They assumed they had an absolute property right in their business and believed that union recognition and collective bargaining would compromise that right. Thus, rather than alter any of their management practices, Fulton Bag's owners invested thousand of dollars on anti-labor undercover operatives who infiltrated the union and the work force. These agents gathered intelligence about union-organizing activities, provoked discord among striking workers, and generally created a climate of suspicion and fear that further complicated the union's task. In effect, management, willing to risk everything, declared total war against union organizations. Given Fulton Bag's resolute, unyielding position, labor had little to gain even if they had won. [Gary Fink]

FURTHER READING

Fink, Gary. "Labor Espionage: The Fulton Bag and Cotton Mills Strike of 1914–1915." *Labor's Heritage*, Vol. 1 (April 1989), pp. 10–35.

McMath, Robert C. "History by a Graveyard: The Fulton Bag and Cotton Mill Records." *Labor's Heritage*, Vol. 1 (April 1989), pp. 4–9.

∘ ∘ ∘

FUR WORKERS' STRIKE OF 1912. The ferment that marked labor relations in the clothing industry between 1909 and 1913 also reached New York's fur manufacturing shops. There some 10,000 men and women worked, most of them Jewish immigrants, with a liberal sprinkling of Greeks, Italians, French-Canadians, and others. Attempts to unionize these workers had been tried before, most notably in 1904, but in every case the organizing drive failed. Nevertheless, by 1912, a campaign by the United Hebrew Trades to unionize fur workers had succeeded in signing up a third of the workers in Manhattan's fur district. When the union went to the manufacturers to convert this new-found strength into union recognition and gains for the workers, they met with bitter resistance.

There was no question that improvements were necessary. As in the women's and men's garment industries in general, working conditions in the fur industry were abysmal. The aristocrats of the trade, the cutters, earned only twelve dollars a week for fifty-six to sixty hours of work. Those at the bottom, mostly women, received five dollars. In addition, the shops were filthy and dangerous. A 1911 New York State Commission reported that eight out of ten fur workers suffered from one or another occupational disease, with two out of ten having tuberculosis.

The union's demands generally followed those that their sisters and brothers in the shirtwaist and cloak industries had won in 1909 and 1910. These included union recognition, the closed shop, the nine-hour workday, paid holidays, the abolition of home work and subcontracting, and better wages. The employers' associations rejected the demands. The issues on which the manufacturers refused to yield were union recognition and the closed shop. On June 20, the union distributed the strike call, known as the *Red Special*,

throughout the fur district. By the next day, 8,500 workers had laid down their tools and closed some 500 shops.

No matter the effectiveness of the strike, the employers had no ideas of quick surrender. Instead, they determined to close all of the shops for three weeks and then reopen them on July 8 under the old conditions. Hunger, they believed, would drive the workers back into the shops. They were wrong. July 8 came, but the strike held. Practically none of the nearly 9,000 strikers crossed the picket lines. Nor did they return in subsequent weeks when the manufacturers repeated the tactic.

Anti-strike tactics were not restricted to passive resistance. The employers engaged private guards, "goons" and gangsters according to the strikers, and unleashed them on the picket lines. When provocations led to disturbances, city police stepped in to protect company property and strikebreakers. In the course of the strike more than 800 strikers were arrested, and many suffered injuries from the wild clubbing that usually accompanied attempts to break up the picketing. Nevertheless, the strikers managed, through mass picketing and patrols, to keep the fur district out of business.

Their ability to resist was aided by fraternal contributions from various quarters. The Cloakmakers Union contributed $20,000, and other unions sent lesser amounts. New York's two major socialist papers, the *Jewish Daily Forward* and the New York *Call* raised funds for the strikers, as did other efforts such as door-to-door collections taken up mainly by the women strikers.

After two months it became clear to the operators that the solidarity of the strikers, based largely on the leading role of the Jewish workers, would not crumble. Negotiations finally began and produced a tentative agreement on August 22. It granted everything the union had demanded except a reduction to a half day of work on Saturday and the closed shop. Socialist leader Meyer London, who had been advising the strikers, advised them to reject the offer. He understood that they had effectively won the strike, and that the financial losses suffered by the employers had now begun to seriously threaten their existence. Samuel Gompers, president of the AFL, also urged them not to surrender their advantage.

The strikers did reject the first proposal and held out for the half-day's work on Saturday. Two weeks later, the employers gave in. The strike ended on September 8, after thirteen weeks. The furriers won union recognition, the forty-nine hour workweek, premium pay for overtime, ten paid holidays, the banning of homework, and wage payments in cash. The settlement revolutionized the fur industry. From a bastion of employer power and horrible working conditions, the strike transformed it into an almost completely unionized industry. Part of the settlement followed the pattern set in the so-called "Protocols of Peace" that had ended the **Cloakmakers' Strike of 1910**. A permanent board of arbitration was established, as was a joint board of sanitary control. Workers also had equal representation on a standing conference committee to handle grievances. In sum, the contract was the best that any workers in the needle trades had won since their uprising began in 1909. The fact that it was won without the existence of a national union in the fur industry also speaks well of the determination of the New York furriers. [Ronald L. Filippelli]

FURTHER READING

Foner, Philip S. *History of the Labor Movement in the United States*, Vol. 5. New York: International Publishers, 1980.

———. *The Fur and Leather Workers Union*. Newark, NJ: Nordan Press, 1950.

Gold, Ben. *Memoirs*. New York: William Howard Publishers, n.d.

G

° ° ° ° ° ° ° ° ° ° °

° ° °

GALLUP, NEW MEXICO, MINERS'
STRIKE OF 1933. As in much of the rest
of the United States, the Great Depression
of the 1930s brought both high unemployment and a surge of union sentiment to
the miners who toiled in the coal country
surrounding Gallup. The drastic decline in
production that had begun in the 1920s
had continued, until, by the summer of
1933, half of Gallup's 2,000 miners were
unemployed. In that same year, Congress
passed the National Industrial Recovery Act
(NIRA), which gave workers the right to
organize into unions of their own choosing and to bargain collectively with their
employers. The confluence of the two factors—the dissatisfaction with high unemployment, and the passage of the NIRA—
led to union talk throughout the district.

Mine owners too recognized the
implications of the NIRA. The manager of
the largest company, Gallup American Coal
Company, set out to form a company union in order to circumvent Section 7(a) of
the NIRA. But mine officials lost control of
the attempt, and instead, miners decided
to form an independent union. For assistance, they called on two New Mexico labor
activists, Robert F. Roberts and his wife
Martha, both of whom were Communists
and affiliated with the National Miners
Union (NMU).

The NMU had grown out of a Communist-led attempt to wrest control of the
United Mine Workers of America (UMW)
from its president, John L. Lewis. Lewis
ruthlessly defeated his left-wing opponents,

and when the international Communist line
from Moscow changed in 1928, Stalin
ordered foreign Communists to cease trying
to capture unions through infiltration, the
so-called "boring from within" policy. Instead, The Red International of Trade Unions (Profintern), ordered them to form
independent organizations. Lewis' enemies
in the UMW followed orders and created
the NMU, an affiliate of the Communist-
controlled Trade Union Unity League.

All of the complexities of international labor politics were no doubt lost on
the chiefly Mexican miners of the Gallup
Coal Fields. Under the influence of the
Roberts, they chose the NMU over the
UMW. The issues at Gallup were familiar
throughout America's coalfields. Miners
suspected the companies of shortweighing
their production. Company stores profited
at the expense of the miners, and Mexicans were discriminated against in hiring
and promotion. The two key grievances in
Gallup, however, centered on two successive wage cuts and on a company practice
of forcing miners to do "deadwork," or
maintenance, for little or no pay.

The mine companies, with the Gallup American Coal Company in the lead,
rejected any dealings with the NMU. In
response, the miners walked out on August 29 and closed five major mines. Any
illusions the miners might have had after
their brief success were dispelled the next
day when Governor Arthur Seligman ordered the National Guard to Gallup. The
request for the guard had come not only
from the companies but also from the

UMW. Lewis was determined not to allow his rivals to organize in New Mexico. Enforced by the National Guard, a kind of martial law was put into effect. Mass meetings were forbidden, and guardsmen harassed strikers and their families who tried to meet across the Arizona border.

Governor Seligman's action led to a gradual reopening of the mines with strikebreakers hired from nearby Indian reservations and beyond. John L. Lewis then entered the conflict by urging the operators to make an arrangement with the UMW, "a union . . . committed to the upholding of American institutions." The UMW also offered membership to the strikebreakers, and many accepted, thus avoiding the approbation of being "scabs." This intervention by Lewis raised the stakes for the NMU. The union sent national executive board member Pat Toohey in to lead the strike and began a national drive to raise money for the strikers. With skilled leadership and solidarity among its members, the NMU withstood the assaults of both the UMW and the authorities. Although their leaders were frequently arrested for violating martial law, the rank and file held firm.

As the strike moved into its third month, pressure began to build on both sides for a settlement. Several of the smaller mines had already made an accommodation with the union, although no one granted union recognition. This brought pressure on the larger producers who wanted to begin production for the winter. The state of New Mexico tired of the financial burden of keeping the National Guard in Gallup. And perhaps most important of all, the NMU was nearly out of money. By November 22, the parties had reached an agreement. Many of the grievances had already been allowed for in the NIRA code for the bituminous industry. All that was necessary was for the operators to adopt the code. The employers agreed to rehire one-fifth of the strikers immediately,

and the rest through a preferential hiring list. Jailed NMU leaders were promised freedom if they agreed to leave New Mexico for one year.

Although Gallup was no sweeping victory for the union, it was a triumph for the NMU whose fortunes had been rapidly declining elsewhere in the country. Communist Party publications hailed it as a harbinger of things to come as the depression deepened. Yet on the key issue of union recognition, the companies had not yielded. Although wages improved, working conditions did not. Many of the standards of the coal industry code were ignored by the companies. The NMU could do little about this because nearly one-half of the miners, and most of those who had worked during the strike, belonged to the UMW. Contrary to the companies' promises, many of the NMU strikers were never rehired.

Nevertheless, the NMU stayed in Gallup, assisting its members and successfully representing the interests of unemployed workers through the organization of the Gallup Unemployed Council. This gave the union credibility among workers and those on relief. In addition, the poor working conditions in the mines affected both NMU and UMW members. This increased the pressure for consolidation of the two unions. But external, rather than internal events, eventually brought the two groups together. Because of Adolph Hitler's rise to power in Germany, the international Communist policy had changed again. Communists were now instructed from Moscow to discard the dual unionism of the TUUL and the NMU and to form united fronts against fascism with other Progressive groups. The NMU disbanded in the spring of 1934.

The effect in Gallup was the movement of the NMU local toward membership in the UMW. However, on the eve of the merger, a shooting resulted in the death of the sheriff and two others. The sheriff's death gave opponents of the NMU the opening they needed to destroy the organization. The incident grew out of a dispute between a landowner who had essentially purchased a mostly Mexican company town from Gallup American Coal Company. When the new owner ordered the residents to either buy their houses at exorbitant prices or leave, the NMU organized the resistance. When a group of residents moved the belongings of an evicted family back into their house, they were arrested. Tensions surrounding these incidents resulted in the shooting of the sheriff.

In the aftermath of the shootings, some 100 members of the Veterans of Foreign Wars and the American Legion were sworn in as special deputy sheriffs. Their goal was to arrest radicals. The leaders of the NMU came in for the most attention. In all, more than 100 people were arrested the first night. After the police sorted them out, forty-eight were eventually accused of the murder of the sheriff. In addition, some 100 immigrants were deported for seeking to overthrow the government. Ten of the accused were eventually held for murder, and four for aiding the escape of one of the accused. All were members of either the NMU or other Communist organizations. The Communist Party's legal arm, the International Labor Defense League (ILD), carried on the defense. The events at Gallup had been attracting national attention since the shooting of the sheriff. The entry of the ILD into the case. led to a national campaign in support of the "Gallup Fourteen" to publicize the case and to raise money for the defense. The case gained even more notoriety when Robert Minor and Murray Levinson, two Communist Party officials sent to Gallup to help coordinate the campaign, were beaten and kidnapped on the streets of the city and dropped off in the desert.

Eventually, seven of the defendants were found not guilty, and three were convicted of second degree murder with recommendation for clemency. The judge, who lashed out at "bolshevism" and communism at the close of the trial, interpreted clemency to mean imprisonment for not less than forty-five years. Most of the acquitted were deported to Mexico. By 1939, the sentence of one of the convicted men had been overturned on appeal, and the two others were given conditional pardons after they agreed to leave the state.

Through it all, the UMW offered little support, although it did enter into the effort to secure pardons for the convicted men. This did it little good however. The anti-union sentiment that followed the shooting of the sheriff also engulfed the UMW. By 1937, the union had no membership in the Gallup coalfield. Nevertheless, the UMW stayed in Gallup and through painstaking organizing managed to bring the entire Gallup coalfield under union contract by 1940. [Ronald L. Filippelli]

FURTHER READING

Rubenstein, Harry R. "Political Repression in New Mexico: The Destruction of the National Miner's Union in Gallup." In *Labor in New Mexico: Unions, Strikes, and Social History since 1881*, Robert Kern, ed. Albuquerque, NM: University of New Mexico Press, 1983, pp. 91–142.

———. "The Great Gallup Coal Strike of 1933." *New Mexico Historical Review*. Vol. 52 (1977), pp. 173–192.

o o o

GASTONIA, NORTH CAROLINA, STRIKE OF 1929. In the spring of 1929, Gastonia, North Carolina, textile workers raised their voices in anger over the conditions of mill life to join in a rebellion that reverberated across the Piedmont. Before the year's end labor unrest also rocked Elizabethton, Tennessee, and Marion, North Carolina. Strikes in the latter two areas gained national attention: Elizabethton for the suddenness of the uprising and the viciousness of its absentee owners; and Marion for the lawlessness of its deputies, who shot into a crowd wounding twenty-five and killing six. But the Gastonia strike grabbed the most headlines. Reporters wrote of the city's squalid mill villages and dangerous factories, of a sheriff and a balladeer's murder, yet mostly they marveled at the strike's Communist leadership.

To many, Gastonia seemed an unlikely breeding ground for insurgency. Clinging along the Southern Railway twenty miles below Charlotte, Gastonia had a population of 33,000, most of whom toiled in one of the area's fifty-two textile mills. While not the pool of docile labor that boosters advertised it to be, the locale still lacked trade union or radical traditions. Yet in April 1929, workers at Gastonia's largest firm—the Loray Mill—overcame the hurdles which blocked collective action elsewhere, and, did what few southern laborers ever did, walked off their jobs and fell in line behind Communist Party leadership.

The Great Depression hit the South more than five years before the crash on Wall Street. By the mid-1920s, the textile industry's bloated wartime profits began to shrink. Analysts diagnosed the industry as sick. Overproduction, cutthroat competition, and the industry's unrationalized structure plagued textile manufacturers. As these maladies put a squeeze on profits, managers began to examine cost sheets as never before, and in particular, they scrutinized the columns under the heading of labor expenses.

As the industry's illness crept into Gastonia, local manufacturers searched for remedies to heal the wounds and shore up profits. In 1927, after a careful review of their books, the New England–based management of the Loray Mill, which produced yarn and automobile tire fabric, sent G. A. Johnstone to Gastonia with instructions to cut costs and boost returns. The new su-

perintendent handled a balance sheet like a butcher's knife, and appeared to Loray employees to enjoy doing it. By the opening of 1928, he chopped the work force in half, demoted many skilled workers, introduced faster and more efficient machines, raised workloads, and slashed wage rates. Millhands dubbed this assault the stretchout.

When workers complained, Johnstone imported hands from South Carolina who labored for less. On March 5, 1928, Loray weavers staged a brief walkout against the stretchout. Shortly afterward, millhands paraded a coffin through downtown Gastonia. During the procession, an effigy of the loathed superintendent periodically raised his head and called out: "How many men are carrying this thing?" The group retorted—eight. "Lay off two— six can do the work," the effigy snapped back. After witnessing this black comedy, a local Methodist elder wrote the parent company about the acrimony that festered at Loray and threatened Gastonia's peace. Later that month, Johnstone was transferred to a northern mill and replaced by the less contentious J. A. Baugh. When this news reached the mill village, workers poured out of their homes and danced through the night in celebration, but the tensions which sliced through the community ran too deep to be eradicated by one night of revelry.

Meanwhile, far from conflict-ridden Gastonia, leaders of the Communist Party ordered a shift in the party line. Prior to 1928, the self-proclaimed vanguard of working-class revolution advocated a policy of "boring from within" existing American Federation of Labor (AFL) and independent unions. Afterward, the party mandated the establishment of dual unions. Organized in September 1928, around a nucleus of radicals and Socialists from Passaic, New Jersey and New Beford, Massachusetts, the National Textile Workers Union (NTWU) became one of the party's first rival unions. At the NTWU's opening convention, delegates vowed to broaden their narrow regional base and allocated funds to underwrite sending several organizers into the southern textile fields.

On New Years Day 1929, Fred Beal—a veteran of numerous labor battles in New England's textile centers and a recent recruit to the Communist Party—arrived in Charlotte. After several months of wandering through the mill villages surrounding the Queen City with only marginal gains for the NTWU, Beal got a tip. A well-traveled millhand told him that the Loray mill was a tinder box of grievances and hot for organization. Another informant said to Beal: "If you succeed in organizing Loray, you'll organize the South."

Beal rushed to Gastonia. Once there, he had little trouble assembling a core of union supporters. By early March, they had built a clandestine union structure, but secrets were hard to keep in southern mill villages. A company spy, later promoted to firm employment manager, tipped off mill officials about the budding union movement in their midst. Wasting little time, Baugh sacked five activists.

Unionists demanded an immediate strike. Beal, realizing that he lacked the organizational strength and resources needed to take on management, at first tried to hold back the rank and file. But it was no use. Pushed into the open, on March 30, Beal staged a public demonstration of the union's power at a rally attended by more than 1,000 millhands. Strike sentiment pulsed through the crowd, and the operatives voted unanimously, enthusiastically, and confidently to walk off the job the next day. Thus, on April 1, 1929, began one of the most dramatic and tragic industrial showdowns in southern labor history.

Two days later, the NTWU delivered a list of strike demands to the company. Little of the revolutionary rhetoric so often associated with the Communist Party could be found in the union's initial strike planks. Instead it called for the elimination of piecework, a minimum wage of twenty dollars for a forty-hour workweek, the abolition of the stretchout, equal pay for equal work, a 50 percent cut in rent and light charges, and union recognition. While these demands focused on industrial questions, they remained startling for an industry mired in depression, bereft of a trade union legacy, confronted with a labor surplus, and accustomed to paying a weekly wage of nine dollars for sixty hours of labor. Unimpressed by the NTWU's moderation, Superintendent Baugh scanned the demands and less than three minutes later rejected them.

At this early stage of the battle, the NTWU benefitted from deep support among Loray workers and even had some backers within the larger Gastonia community. The picket lines that formed daily and wrapped around the huge mill reminded the firm of the union's numbers and resolve. Through the first week, the pickets kept strikebreakers away. Because of the textile industry's wage structure and the union's inability to pay strike benefits, the conflict mobilized the entire mill community. Women, both as workers and family members, were often the most outspoken and determined of the strikers; they frequently moved to the front of picket lines and parades, and on several occasions they clubbed militiamen and deputies.

Despite the union's initial demonstrations of solidarity, after the first week, the strike's leadership passed from Beal's able stewardship into the shaky hands of Communist Party leaders. During the transition, revolutionary posturing stole the public spotlight away from worker's industrial demands. National figures, including party chief William Z. Foster and Albert Weisbord of the NTWU, flocked to Gastonia to turn it into "a citadel of class struggle." Weisbord told Beal: "We must prepare the workers for the coming revolution." Comparing the strike to the Civil War, one functionary predicted an uprising as disruptive and profound as that great conflict. Party leaders, moreover, insisted that racial equality should become a paramount issue in the strike despite the fact that Loray had less than a dozen African-American employees, most of whom had left town once the conflict exploded.

Local sympathy, and even tolerance, for the strike quickly evaporated. Following a picket-line scuffle on April 3, the *Gastonia Daily Gazette*—the only local paper—headlined, "Call Out the Militia." When the troops arrived the next day, the newspaper led the applause. Thereafter, the *Gazette*'s editors launched repeated vitriolic attacks against the union. They portrayed the unrest at Loray not as a battle to roll back the stretchout but as something much graver—an assault by alien radicals upon the very fabric of the community—and warned against the party's advocacy of atheism, interracial marriage, and free love. A front-page cartoon depicted the American flag attacked by a coiled snake, captioned, "Communism in the South." "The citizens of Gaston County," in a full-page advertisement, averred that the strike was undertaken "for the purpose of overthrowing this Government and destroying property and to kill, kill, kill." Finally, the union's progressive stance on racial equality unleashed a stream of handbills asking: "Would you belong to a union which opposes White Supremacy?"

Faced with this barrage, many millhands wavered in their commitment to the union. On April 10, for the first time since the strike started, observers spotted cracks in the picket lines. Moreover, the once stocked shelves of the union relief store were now barren, leaving many hungry. Five days later, when efforts to block strikebreakers from entering the mill collapsed, according to one scholar, "the strike, as a strike, was over." But the drama still had several acts left.

Near midnight on April 18, a squadron of masked men set fire to the union's headquarters. While the marauders frolicked about the burning building, National Guardsmen, garrisoned only 500 feet away, slept without hearing a sound. They woke up just after the arsonists escaped, and with smoke still thick in the air, they arrested several union leaders, charging them with destroying their own property. Two days later, the Loray Mill ran at near full strength and the guardsmen left town. They were replaced by the Committee of 100, an assemblage of newly deputized workers loyal to management. At this juncture, the strikers' ranks had dwindled to less than two hundred. But the repression continued unchecked. An anti-parading ordinance outlawed picketing, and on May 7, the company evicted sixty-two families, who promptly erected a tent colony on the outskirts of the mill village.

On June 7, the beleaguered remnants of the NTWU marched from the tent colony to the mill gate in order to persuade those on the job to walkout and join them in their struggle. The unionists were turned away by the police, who then trailed them back to their makeshift homes. A fight broke out. Shots were fired. One union member and four police officers lay wounded. Sheriff D. A. Aderholt was killed. Within hours an angry mob, led by a local attorney, attacked the tent colony and levelled it.

After a judge ordered a change of venue from Gastonia to Charlotte, on August 26, 1929, Beal and fifteen others stood trial for conspiracy leading to the murder of Aderholt. The proceedings became a spectacle, at times resembling a vaudeville show more than courtroom deliberations. Communist Party lawyers used the witness stand as a soapbox for repeated denunciations of bourgeois justice. On the other side of the aisle, while delivering his closing statement, Solicitor John G. Carpenter had the bailiff wheel a stretcher into the courtroom on which an object lay covered by a white sheet. Carpenter paused for a moment and then slowly walked over to the stretcher and snatched off the shroud. Silence fell over the courtroom as there lay a life-sized, blood-stained wax figure of the slain police chief. One juror was struck with such horror at this sight that he went insane, and, as a result, on September 9 the judge declared a mistrial.

For the remainder of September, a "reign of terror" gripped Gastonia. News of the mistrial enraged some local citizens and that night a caravan of cars, headed by a phalanx of police motorcycles, sped through Gaston County and the surrounding areas, terrorizing union supporters and destroying their property. Part of the mob grabbed Ben Wells, a British Communist; they ripped off his clothes and lashed him with a tree branch. Wells later identified his floggers, but they escaped conviction because the court dismissed the foreign radical's testimony on the grounds that he did not believe in God. The NTWU answered the attack with a call for a mass meeting on September 19. A truck headed for the rally was stopped by a group of vigilantes. They fired into the packed vehicle. Ella Mae Wiggins, a twenty-nine-year-old mother of five, strike activist, and balladeer was killed. Although Wiggins had been gunned down at midday with scores of witnesses looking on, the five Loray workers indicted in her murder escaped conviction.

By the time of Beal and the others' second trial, on September 30, the union had called off the strike. Tempers in Gastonia had cooled off as well. Just as the proceedings began, the state's attorney announced that charges against seven of the defendants had been dropped altogether and charges for the other seven were reduced from first to second degree murder. Beal and his co-defendants eschewed propaganda and fastened their testimony to the facts, but at the trial's midway point, a woman from the Young Communist League heralded revolution and railed against God from the witness stand. Sensing an opening, Carpenter charged that the defendants had come to Gastonia "to bring bloodshed and death, creeping like the hellish serpent into the Garden of Eden." During his summation, he asked the jury: "Do you believe in God? Do you believe in North Carolina? Do you believe in good roads?" They must have answered yes, and decided that Beal and the others did not share these bedrock values. After deliberating for less than an hour, the jury reached its verdict—guilty. The defendants received sentences ranging from five to twenty years in jail.

Released pending appeal, Beal jumped bail and fled to the Soviet Union, where be became a celebrated martyr to capitalist injustice. In 1933, a disillusioned Beal slipped back into this country and wrote his autobiography—*Proletarian Journey*—a piercing indictment of the USSR. In 1938, Beal was captured, and served in a North Carolina prison until his pardon in 1942.

The strike that Beal led in 1929 was but part of what turned out to be the opening salvo; in conclusion, the 1929 strike wave, which hit the hardest in Gastonia, was just the opening salvo in a protracted struggle between southern mill workers and owners. In 1930, 1932, 1933, and again in 1934, the region's textile towns would erupt with labor upheaval. During these turbulent years, by exhibiting a greater willingness to question the edicts of management and engage in collective action than in the past, millhands shattered the prevailing paternalistic image of southern industrial relations. [Bryant Simon]

FURTHER READING

Beal, Fred. *Proletarian Journey: New York, Gastonia, Moscow.* New York: Hillman-Curl, 1937.

Bernstein, Irving. *The Lean Years: A History of the American Worker.* Boston, MA: Houghton Mifflin, 1960.

Hood, Robin. "The Loray Mill Strike." M.A. Thesis, University of North Carolina at Chapel Hill, 1932.

Pope, Liston. *Millhands and Preachers: A Study of Gastonia*. New Haven, CT: Yale University Press, 1944.

Tindall, George. *The Emergence of the New South, 1913–1945, A History of the South*. Vol. 10. Baton Rouge, LA: Louisiana State University Press, 1967.

Tippett, Tom. *When Southern Labor Stirs*. New York: Jonathan Cape and Harrison Smith, 1931.

Vorse, Mary Heaton. "Gastonia." *Harpers*. Vol. 159 (November 1929), pp. 700–710.

o   o   o

GENERAL ELECTRIC STRIKE OF 1960. This confrontation resulted in what the labor editor of the *New York Times* called "the worst setback any union has received . . . since World War II."

In 1949–1950 the United Electrical, Radio, and Machine Workers of America (UE) was split into two rival unions, the UE and the International Union of Electrical Workers (IUE). Bitter inter-union rivalry, joined in by other AFL and CIO affiliates, persisted throughout the 1950s and left the GE workers badly divided by 1960. In contrast to 1946, when the UE had organized about 80 percent of GE's workers, the unions had lost ground. In 1960, the IUE represented only about 70,000 of GE's 251,000 domestic employees. The UE had about 10,000, the International Association of Machinists (IAM) had 9,000, and various other unions about 17,000.

The badly weakened unions were confronted in the 1950s by an aggressive GE labor relations stance. The GE approach was known as "Boulwarism" after its originator, GE vice-president Lemuel R. Boulware. He characterized the firm's labor relations policy as "doing right voluntarily." In practice, this meant that the corporation, after reviewing union demands, would present a detailed unilateral offer to all of its unions. The package would be widely publicized, the corporation would attempt to "sell" the offer directly to the work force bypassing the union, and would refuse to change the total value of its package unless it were confronted by "new information." GE would implement the offer among its non-union employees and try to encourage the rival unions to accept it, while attempting to deny retroactivity to any union that resisted.

Boulwarism was quite successful in the annual negotiations from 1950 to 1954. In 1955, eager to carry out a costly expansion program, desirous of a lengthy period of labor peace and affected by the announcement of a lucrative General Motors contract, GE made an upward modification in its original offer. Wage hikes of at least 3 percent a year were granted, plus a substantial cost-of-living-allowance (COLA), and a 1958 job security reopener. IUE president James R. Carey called this "a splendid settlement." In 1957, Boulware was no longer with GE, but the company stated that it would continue the same collective bargaining approach.

By the time of the 1958 reopener, however, the situation had worsened for the IUE. The recession of 1957–1958 meant that about 30,000 IUE members at GE had been laid off. Having completed or scaled back its expansion program, GE took a very hard line at the bargaining table. The company's only offer was to substitute a company controlled savings plan for the scheduled wage hikes of 1958 and 1959. Carey attempted to mobilize his union for a strike but could not obtain the necessary two-thirds vote of the union's GE Conference Board. The reopener expired with no agreement. As one pro-union observer noted, "The IUE emerged from the 1958 negotiations badly defeated and with signs of a deep division within its own ranks."

Carey was stung by this setback and prepared for the 1960 negotiations. At the 1958 IUE convention he had the union constitution changed to allow a simple majority of the GE Conference Board to authorize a strike. The IUE produced a half-hour television film focusing on employment security and used a truck caravan to visit major GE plant sites to build support for its 1960 contract goals. In early 1960, the various AFL-CIO unions voted to support common demands at the bargaining table. The IUE conducted an elaborate survey of its members' contract wishes. Among the minority who returned the survey, a guaranteed annual wage was the top priority.

Carey was especially eager to show his members that he could outdo the rival UE at the bargaining table. The UE had regained the Elmira GE plant in 1959 and narrowly lost a representation election at the huge Lynn complex in 1960. Because of the rivalry, Carey refused the UE request for a common negotiating front in 1960.

IUE negotiations began on July 1, 1960. In late August, GE presented its offer: a three year contract with wage increases of 3 percent in 1960 and 4 percent eighteen months later. The company also demanded the elimination of the COLA. GE's management was increasingly confident of Carey and the IUE's weakness. The company refused to increase its offer at all, although it made several minor adjustments in packaging. The always volatile Carey became increasingly frustrated and erratic during the negotiations. A sympathetic National Labor Relations Board (NLRB) Trial Examiner reported that Carey showed "an explosive temper, several times to the point of threatening physical violence . . . and a few times wholly unrestrained in his opinion of some of the Company's negotiators."

When the IUE conducted strike votes at its GE locations on September 27, the results were ominous. Although a narrow majority rejected GE's offer and authorized a strike, many of the IUE's biggest locals did not. These included the largest, Sche-

nectady, New York, as well as Syracuse, New York; Pittsfield and Worcester, Massachusetts; and Burlington, Vermont. GE refused to extend the old contract terms during negotiations and on October 3, the expiration date, the strike began. Schenectady did not join the battle at first, but after Carey and IUE Local 301 president Leo Jandreau forced through a strike authorization by means of a petition, the local joined the picket lines on October 6. However, all was not well for the IUE. Two-thirds of the workers at Bridgeport crossed the picket lines and so did almost all the workers at Burlington. One thousand broke through to the plant at Syracuse, where there were numerous scuffles and several dozen arrests of strikers. Bucyrus, Ohio was another weak spot for the strike. Decertification petitions were filed there and at Burlington.

GE imposed the new contract at its non-union locations. Despite the strong pledges, AFL-CIO unity did not materialize. The IAM and UAW accepted the GE offer at plants where they represented the workers, as did most of the smaller unions. The UE, excluded from the joint negotiations, worked under the old contract while continuing to bargain. Only the three locals of the American Federation of Technical Engineers joined the IUE on strike.

By October 11, it was clear that the strike was weak and getting weaker. Local 301 leaders came to New York to tell Carey to accept the GE offer of a "truce." Its terms were acceptance of GE's wage and COLA removal offer and negotiation of all remaining items after a return to work. When Carey refused, the key Schenectady Local 301 abandoned the strike. By October 19, 15,000 IUE members were crossing the picket lines. Carey retreated. He was now willing to abandon the COLA and his guaranteed annual wage proposal if GE would slightly improve its wage offer. The company, sensing total victory, refused. On October 20, Carey agreed to a memorandum of agreement on the terms of GE's pre-strike offer. The strike officially ended on October 24.

In the wake of this debacle Carey's position in the IUE deteriorated further. He denounced Jandreau and tried to oust him from his local's leadership. In the Local 301 officer election in December 1960, the Jandreau slate trounced the Carey candidate by a three to one margin. Jandreau argued that Carey "did not have the issues or the organizational strength or the other economic factors that are necessary to lead a successful strike." It was Carey who would face increasing challenges within the IUE, culminating in his ouster in 1965 after the Labor Department invalidated his fraudulent reelection in 1964.

The IUE filed unfair labor practices charges with the NLRB during the strike. After lengthy hearings, the trial examiner issued a report finding that GE had violated the National Labor Relations Act by coming to the bargaining table with a fixed position and by carrying out bargaining directly with the members by bypassing the IUE. Despite this ruling, Boulwarism continued to dominate labor relations at GE. It would not be until new unity and militancy was present in the 1969–1970 strike that GE would be forced to modify the approach it had used so well for twenty years, particularly in 1960. [Mark McColloch]

FURTHER READING

Bella, Salvatore. *Boulwarism and Collective Bargaining at General Electric*. Ph.D. thesis, Cornell University, 1962.

Matles, James J., and James Higgins. *Them and Us*. New York: Prentice-Hall, 1974.

Northrup, Herbert. *Boulwarism*. Ann Arbor, MI: University of Michigan Press, 1964.

o   o   o

GENERAL MOTORS SIT-DOWN STRIKE OF 1936–1937. The automobile industry occupied a central position in the industrial structure of twentieth-century United States. In the minds of many Americans it stood for all that was modern and progressive in economic life. The product itself had early on caught the public's fancy. From suburban living, roadside motels, family auto vacations, and backseat necking, to over-the-road trucking of much of America's manufactured and agricultural goods, and spinoff industries in tires, glass, and petroleum products, automobiles had changed American social and economic life. As auto production became increasingly concentrated into a monopoly of the "Big Three"—Ford, General Motors, and Chrysler—its structure seemed typical of modern consumer-oriented industry, as did its practices of frequent model change, a full model line from reasonable to expensive, and competition over design. Auto workers themselves contributed to the public sense that the industry led the way into the future by their favoring of auto jobs over others; leaving farms, mines, and more heavily onerous jobs in industries like steel, they flocked to the high wages and semi-skilled machine-tending jobs of the auto factories.

All was not well in the auto factories, but few outside the ranks of the auto workers themselves recognized the signs of their unease. Labor relations had been relatively peaceful. Unions were limited to the small, industrially organized Auto Workers Union and to a few craft unions, impotent within the industrial structure of auto. High turnover rates, restriction of output, and sporadic brief walkouts throughout the 1920s attested to workers' grievances, but the Depression had put fear into auto workers' hearts. The **Briggs Strike of 1933** had shown auto workers their potential, but it had not resulted in a union that could bring collective bargaining to the industry. By 1936 something dramatic and spectacular would be required to persuade the public and the auto manufacturers that auto workers were not the robots of assembly line fiction. The grievances of auto work were those of the modern factory. The work was tedious, mind numbing, and fatiguing. Seniority counted for little, a situation that Depression layoffs and rehiring had highlighted. While wages were comparatively good, they were coupled with insecurity. The speedup was ever present, either as reality or as threat. And without union representation, workers had no say in the rules governing their working life.

The United Auto Workers (UAW) originated as a federal labor union. In auto, the federal union structure collected workers into a single auto union for each plant, with each federal union having a direct relationship to the AFL. While the structure of the federal unions was industrial within each plant, there was only loose coordination among all the auto federal unions. Therefore, the danger of fragmentation existed should various AFL craft unions insist upon their jurisdictional rights and claim the members of their craft in the federal locals as their own. Auto workers quickly tired of the federal union idea, finding AFL support unenthusiastic and unreliable. In August of 1936, the UAW affiliated with the recently formed Committee for Industrial Organization (CIO), expressing the belief that auto workers could operate successfully only within an organization wholeheartedly committed to an industrial union structure. Armed with the commitment to collective bargaining implied in the National Labor Relations Act of 1935, encouraged by the Senate's investigation of General Motors' violation of workers' civil liberties, and by announced National Labor Relations Board (NLRB) hearings on General Motors' unfair labor practices, and cheered on by Franklin Roosevelt's overwhelming election victory in November of 1936, the UAW and the CIO stepped up organizing efforts in the auto industry.

In June 1936, Wyndham Mortimer, a veteran auto worker and union activist

from Cleveland's White Motors, arrived in Flint, Michigan, to begin the arduous task of interesting General Motors workers in the UAW. Mortimer and the few Flint UAW leaders he joined faced formidable adversaries in the city of Flint and the corporation of General Motors. The history of Flint was so entwined with the history of General Motors that Flint could truly be referred to as a company town. Two-thirds of those employed in Flint worked for General Motors, and 80 percent of the town's families were dependent on income from General Motors. Mortimer soon discovered that Flint could be hostile; a telephone call warned him to "get the hell back where you came from if you don't want to be carried out in a wooden box!" Four months of steady talking, organizing among non-members, and reorganizing of the local union structure yielded scant results. Mortimer was succeeded by Bob Travis, a more dynamic organizer, who won the confidence and support of a small, loyal, and fiercely committed group among Flint's GM workers.

Those who aimed to challenge General Motors' power in the stronghold of Flint had serious problems to contend with. By late December, diligent organizing efforts had resulted in a Flint UAW membership of 10 percent of the General Motors Flint work force of 47,000. They could anticipate that only a minority of GM workers would join them when the moment to strike arrived. In addition, GM in Flint consisted of numerous separate plants, and the UAW members were unevenly distributed among them. The Flint police and public officials could be counted on to side with General Motors. The bright spot in the local political picture was the November election of Frank Murphy as governor of Michigan. Murphy had long been considered a friend of labor, and auto union leaders hoped they could rely upon his friendship to protect them. With Murphy as governor, Roosevelt in the

White House, the Wagner Act in place, and the support of the CIO, the conditions had never been more favorable for organizing the auto industry. But in the end, the success or failure of the drive would depend on the ability of the organizers and militants to mobilize auto workers and their families and friends in support of the union cause. Auto workers could expect no cooperation from General Motors. A December 22 meeting between UAW president Homer Martin and GM executive vice-president William S. Knudsen had resulted in GM's firm reiteration of its refusal to bargain, justified by the traditional claim that job security, wages, seniority, and union recognition were local issues and not appropriate areas for corporate level decisions.

One of the most dramatic strikes in American labor history began modestly enough with the sitting down of workers in the Cleveland, Ohio, Fisher Body plant on December 28, 1936. In response, and in preparation for any additional strike activity, General Motors acted on plans to keep production flowing by starting to move the dies that stamped out car body panels from Flint, the center of GM body production and the center of the union's efforts, to safer territory outside of the city. Aware of the importance of timing and of seizing opportunity when it arose, aware too of the unlikelihood of ever having a better set of external political circumstances, UAW leaders in Flint moved decisively. On December 30, 1936, in Fisher Body Number One, auto workers made history by refusing to start work after the dinner break. Shortly afterward the smaller Fisher Two was also on strike from within. From the beginning it was clear to the auto worker militants that a conventional outside strike would have little chance of success against General Motors in Flint. Their numbers were too small, there were too many GM plants in Flint with too many gates, and too many auto workers were

unpersuaded of the value of striking and would want to continue to work. Success of the strike action depended upon staying inside and using the sit-down tactic. From within, workers could guard their position, refuse to allow strikebreakers entrance, and dominate the situation with the threat, even if unstated, of sabotage against valuable equipment. Thus the sit-down tactic had many advantages, but it was especially dependent upon outside support. Strikers had to be fed and supplied and informed. There needed to be strong links between those inside and those outside or the strike would fail.

Inside the struck plants, workers organized themselves and devised disciplined routine schedules for each day. With crews for clean up, defense, exercise, and entertainment, the strikers settled in optimistically, expecting a quick victory. For many, sitting down was charged with an excitement and comradery unique in their lives. On the outside, other auto workers, and especially family members, organized to provide for the strikers' needs. A strike kitchen solicited donations of food and efficiently organized cooking and distribution teams. Women led the support effort, turning traditional household duties into militant strike actions. As their strike activities brought them out of isolated households, the women developed a strong sense of comradery and usefulness and also worked to persuade other women, who were more reluctant to have their men on strike, of the justice of their cause and the importance of their support. Some of the women formed the Women's Emergency Brigade to provide militant support should the strikers be threatened.

General Motors initially responded with legal and public relations attempts to regain control over the factories. Seeking a court injunction against the sit-down strikers' occupation of the plants, General Motors was embarrassed when it was revealed that the judge who granted the injunction owned a substantial block of GM stock. In the public relations arena, GM benefitted from the Flint Alliance, an organization of anti-strike Flint residents, businessmen, and politicians who promoted the idea that the strike was a Communist conspiracy carried out against the wishes of the majority of General Motors workers and the people of Flint.

Two dramatic moments proved to be turning points in the strike. By January 11, the sit-downers were settled into their routines but were much stronger in Fisher One than in Fisher Two (where there were more married men worried about their families). Aware that Fisher Two was the more vulnerable plant, General Motors turned off the heat to the building. Cold January weather threatened to make life unbearably uncomfortable for the strikers within. Later in the day the company intensified the pressure by refusing to let the UAW deliver food for the strikers' dinner. Company guards controlled the main gate to Fisher Two, making contact with the outside world in the control of the company guards. The company was moving to isolate the strikers by refusing to allow contact. The time for military confrontation was at hand. Strikers inside Fisher Two demanded that company guards give them the key to the plant. The guards, outnumbered and threatened, retreated to the plants' ladies' room. When Flint police arrived on the scene, they found the embattled strikers far from intimidated by the police presence and determined to stand their ground. Armed with the supplies of their trade—nuts, bolts, car-door hinges, and the building's fire hoses—the auto workers fought to maintain their position and to gain total control over the building and the gate. Policemen responded with tear gas, bullets, and buckshot. Casualties and tension on both sides mounted. Victor Reuther, a leader of the strike committee, and Genora Johnson of the Women's Emergency Brigade made effective use of a

sound truck to rally morale and communicate with the sit-down strikers. A heavy barrage of car-door hinges sent police scattering in retreat and gave workers a significant and widely heralded victory, remembered in labor lore as "the Battle of the Running Bulls."

The violence put the governor in a difficult position. Murphy decided that the potential for further violence required the presence of the National Guard—but under what instructions? Would the Guard regain GM property for the company or guard the strikers from further police attack? Murphy explained the Guard's role to be neutral, preventing further violence on either side, but many in the UAW worried about a change of direction for the National Guard. Murphy's prime objective was to lead General Motors and the strikers to the bargaining table. He believed in bargaining and negotiation and rejected the use of violence by either side. While Murphy recognized both the power of General Motors and the reliance that the workers placed in him not to betray them, at the same time he believed that the sit-in was a violation of property rights. However, he wanted to move the terms of the dispute away from the legality or propriety of the sit-down strike toward discussions that could lead to a peaceful settlement of the issues that had precipitated the strike. His refusal to use the National Guard to eject the strikers from the plants was a key component in the auto workers' eventual victory.

Other outside figures also played important roles in the strike drama. Secretary of Labor Frances Perkins spoke with Governor Murphy every night by telephone. Behind her stood Franklin Roosevelt, carefully avoiding much public association with day-to-day decisions about the strike but encouraging her to bring it to a conclusion. As the strike became prolonged and negotiations moved to higher levels, John L. Lewis, head of the CIO, craftily manipulated company representatives, public officials, and public opinion to gain the first nationally-significant CIO victory. On the General Motors side, Alfred Sloan carried the banner for company and managerial rights, and against any collective bargaining whatsoever, while William Knudson acted as a moderating influence inside GM because of his desire to get production rolling again.

In spite of the strikers' dramatic victory in the Battle of the Running Bulls, by late January many in Flint were tired of hardship, conflict, and a strike that seemed to be stalemated. In spite of Frances Perkins' attempts to bring them together, Sloan and Lewis had still not met. General Motors had applied for a second injunction, and some of the strikers themselves were dispirited and losing hope. At this point UAW leaders created plans for the second of the strike's dramatic turning points. There was within Flint a critical target, Chevrolet Number Four, the plant that manufactured engines for all Chevrolets made in the country. As a strategic asset it was perfect, but as a target for takeover it presented formidable difficulties. For one thing it was securely in General Motors hands, guarded round the clock by GM security forces. Any attempt to capture it would have to remain secret, no easy task since there were company spies in the ranks of the strikers. Turning themselves into superb military strategists, Roy Reuther, Robert Travis, and others devised a plan to spread a false rumor that they intended to take Chevrolet Number Nine, a bearings plant. After succeeding in luring company police from Chevrolet Number Four to Chevrolet Nine, auto workers and company security fought it out at Chevrolet Nine while handpicked, trusted workers secretly captured Number Four. The brilliant maneuver reinvigorated the sagging morale of the strikers.

After the successful capture of Chevrolet Number Four, the parties turned to the bargaining table. Foremost was the demand for union recognition and the conditions that would surround that recognition. With Governor Murphy serving as mediator, the UAW, represented by John L. Lewis, Lee Pressman, and Homer Martin, and General Motors, represented by Donaldson Brown, John T. Smith, and Knudsen, began to bargain seriously. Ultimately, the union agreed to evacuate the plants in exchange for union recognition for its members only, and a guarantee of six months to organize before a collective bargaining election. Specific issues of wages and working conditions were set aside to await subsequent negotiations. On February 11, the forty-four-day strike ended. Jubilant strikers poured out of the occupied factories into the streets of Flint, waving newspaper photos attesting to their victory, and joyfully greeting their families.

Although it was one of the most hotly debated issues of the strike, the question of the legality of the sit-down tactic quickly faded. In 1939, the Supreme Court found the tactic to be illegal. Instead, what remained as the significance of the sit-down strike was the demonstration that the CIO could win a major victory for industrially organized workers—that a minority of motivated and militant workers could force a powerful and gigantic corporation to bargain with them. The publicity surrounding the General Motors strike catapulted Lewis to the front ranks of powerful individuals on the national political scene. At the same time, the strike demonstrated that militant leaders could emerge at the rank-and-file level without much encouragement from labor's leaders and could force their vision and their agenda into being. The success of General Motors workers in the sit-down strike signalled the arrival of industrial unionism and ushered in a new era of industrial relations at the heart of America's major industry. [Joyce Shaw Peterson]

FURTHER READING

Dubofsky, Melvyn, and Warren Van Tine. *John L. Lewis, A Biography.* New York: Quadrangle Books, 1977.

Fine, Sidney. *Frank Murphy: The New Deal Years.* Chicago, IL: University of Chicago Press, 1979.

———. *Sit-Down: The General Motors Strike of 1936–1937.* Ann Arbor, MI: The University of Michigan Press, 1969.

Kerran, Roger. *The Communist Party and the Auto Workers Unions.* Bloomington, IN: Indiana University Press, 1980.

o   o   o

GENERAL MOTORS STRIKE OF 1946. Of all of the conflicts making up the great post–World War II strike wave of 1945–1946, perhaps none was more significant than the United Auto Workers' (UAW) work stoppage against General Motors (GM), the world's largest industrial corporation. The strike, which began November 9, 1945, lasted 113 days and ultimately idled some 300,000 workers. It became noted for UAW vice-president Walter P. Reuther's innovative collective bargaining demands, the corporation's determination to resist them, and the way in which much of the struggle was conducted in the public arena. Though Reuther's leadership in the walkout brought him additional national attention as a labor leader to watch, it was the company's determination not to allow further union inroads into management decision-making on which the strike's long-range import rests.

While the UAW had organized GM in 1937, it was during World War II that the auto union grew most phenomenally and consolidated its position. As in many other industries, the decisions of the National War Labor Board (NWLB) mandated wage restraint on the part of labor, arbitration of disputes, and recognition of the union's security needs through maintenance of membership clauses. At the war's end, more American workers had become union members than ever before. And relatedly, much of American management voiced an increasing disdain for what they perceived as an erosion of their power to manage unionized enterprises. General Motors' managers felt this most keenly, and they approached the end of the war with the hopes of regaining the initiative in labor relations.

The company's determination and Walter Reuther's rising ambitions in both the UAW and American labor generally brought the parties into a confrontation of major proportions. Active in the founding of the union and in various wartime labor relations forums, by 1945, the young Reuther, who had become the director of the union's General Motors department, had strong designs on the presidency of the UAW. During the war there had been considerable unrest among auto workers; tight NWLB restrictions on wage raises in the face of inflation frustrated the union's members, and the no-strike pledge given by top labor leaders made it difficult to do anything about it. Reuther believed he could channel this discontent into a contest against GM, push collective bargaining toward new frontiers, and help advance his political fortunes all at the same time.

The essence of his plan revolved around his demand that union-bargained wage gains be tied to a corporation's profits and the public interest. In the context of the 1945–1946 negotiations, he insisted that the auto company could provide an increase of 30 percent in wages without raising the prices of cars. Believing, with some justification, that GM's wartime profits had been exceptionally rich, Reuther hoped to fuse the goals of union members and the consuming public. With higher wages, the economy would grow through the increasing demand fueled by consumer purchases, and this could be brought about by the sharing of bloated profits. "We shall realize and hold on to our gains only by making progress with the community and not at the expense of the community," he said during the strike. Furthermore, the union's additional demands reflected their desire for increased workplace control. Many GM locals had advanced proposals over a range of issues that would have given workers' collective representatives much more control over the setting of production standards and the organization of authority on the shop floor.

Executives of the corporation—including President Charles Wilson and personnel director Harry Coen—were adamant in rejecting all of Reuther's demands in the pre-strike negotiation sessions. In their view, the only appropriate role for union representation was to negotiate on wages and working conditions—not on control of the productive process or appropriate levels of profit for a corporation. "Why don't you get down to your size and talk about the money you'd like for your people," fumed Coen during a negotiation session, "and let labor statesmanship go to hell for a while?" The corporation's strategy, while certainly committed to bursting Reuther's wage bubble, was in fact far more ambitious than that. The company itself put forth its own demands for contractual changes inaugurated during the NWLB era which it believed had usurped management prerogatives. It wanted to remove the maintenance of membership union security provision, limit the authority of union grievance representatives; transform the seniority, transfer, and promotion provisions in its favor; and free up its ability to mete out discipline without constant union challenges. In this it was simply following a policy it had adopted years before: to limit the sphere of collective bargaining to negotiations over wages, hours, and working conditions; to assure itself that it kept all of its management rights to control enterprise decisions; and to severely penalize workers who participated in mid-contract strikes.

Faced with the GM negotiators' immobility, Reuther held a strike authorization vote which carried by 70,853 to 12,438. On November 7, 1945, GM made a 10 percent wage offer. Reuther refused, but the UAW vice-president countered that he would agree to third-party arbitration of the wage demand if the company would open its accounts to an arbitration panel, which would decide GM's ability to pay, and further agree to provide the wage increase decided upon as equitable without elevating car prices. Nothing could have been less attractive to the company's managers. GM vice-president H. W. Anderson termed the proposal not "an offer of arbitration, but a demand for abdication." Another official put it more succinctly:"We don't even let our stockholders look at the books."

Meanwhile, Reuther continued to assault the "arrogance" of General Motors executives in public forums but with only mixed success. The UAW chief's socially oriented collective bargaining strategy found less than a groundswell of support with the public. A public opinion poll in December 1945 indicated that 42 percent of respondents thought the union was at fault in the strike, contrasted to the 19 percent who believed the corporation culpable. In addition, only 35 percent considered the union's wage stance supportable, while 55 percent repudiated it. Even worse than those figures was the labor movement's rejection of Reuther's bargaining position. Traditional unionists such as John L. Lewis and Philip Murray—whose own unions would strike in 1946—had little truck with the idea of tying wage increases to consumers' economic interests. The idea was scarcely more popular in his own union; his rivals, in pursuing their own collective bargaining goals against other auto makers, were careful not to emulate their flamboyant union colleague.

As the strike dragged on into 1946, the union's ability to prevail eroded.

Reuther had miscalculated the economic impact; GM used the time to retool its factories from the production of war materiel to autos, and its competitors could not take advantage of its downtime because of a lack of raw material and parts. When President Harry S. Truman, concerned about how the massive strike would affect his postwar reconversion policies, appointed a fact-finding board, Reuther grasped at the chance. The presidential board met in Washington and, when GM officials refused to participate unless guaranteed the hearings would not involve determination of the corporation's ability to pay, the board held hearings with the union as sole participant. It recommended a raise of 19.5¢ per hour without a price increase. Reuther pushed this recommendation and continued to hold out. Meanwhile, other unions—like the United Electrical, Radio, and Machine Workers (UE) who had bargaining relationships with GM—began to settle their strikes at 18.5¢, setting a pattern which GM then offered, undercutting the UAW vice-president's position. Finally, during a closing negotiating session, GM president Charles Wilson purportedly put a penny on the bargaining table and said to Reuther, "Walter, this whole strike boils down to this one penny. And you ain't gonna get it."

He was right. The union settled at 18.5¢ per hour, losing on most of the economic issues and on virtually all the managerial authority issues. Though GM was not able to get rid of NWLB innovations like arbitration, it succeeded in numerous other areas; for example, the union gave up the maintenance of membership form of union security and conceded to prewar seniority language that the company had sought. Reuther's concept of linking unionism's collective bargaining objectives with broader social goals failed, mostly because of GM's unyielding stance but also because of the lack of broader support even among union leaders.

From the corporation's perspective, it was a victory well worth the 113-day work stoppage—the UAW would not target the giant auto maker for a strike again for two and a half decades. In a way, GM served as the point-bargainer for much of postwar American management, and the 1946 strike set the tone for much of the history of labor relations through the 1970s. The company fought the fight to resist union erosion of a principle that most managers believed to be sacrosanct: the right to manage the enterprise rested with management and was not negotiable. Having established that, the appropriate bounds of collective bargaining encompassed only wages, hours, and working conditions. It was a labor-relations pattern that would dominate until the economic crisis of the 1980s. [Gilbert J. Gall]

FURTHER READING

Bernstein, Barton J. "Walter Reuther and the General Motors Strike of 1945–1946." *Michigan History*, Vol. 49 (1965), pp. 260–267.

Harris, Howell J. *The Right to Manage: The Industrial Relations Policies of American Business in the 1940s.* Madison, WI: University of Wisconsin Press, 1982.

Reuther, Victor. *The Brothers Reuther and the Story of the UAW.* Boston, MA: Houghton Mifflin, 1976.

o   o   o

GENERAL MOTORS STRIKE OF 1970. Beginning in September of 1970, United Auto Workers pickets marched for fifty-eight days at General Motors plants. It was a confrontation between the nation's largest industrial union and the world's largest manufacturer. The strike pulled 344,000 workers off the job in 145 U.S. and Canadian plants. Every day that it lasted, the conflict cost the company $90 million in sales and the workers $12 million in wages.

The importance of the auto industry to the nation's economy quickly became apparent. General Motors used 10 percent of the nation's steel, 5 percent of its aluminum, and large portions of its rubber, glass, textiles, and machinery. In the first month of the strike, nearly a million workers were laid off at companies doing business with General Motors. In Akron, Ohio, for example, Firestone Rubber Company had laid off 10 percent of its work force by October 10.

For the union, the strike was a call to arms after the death of its historic leader, Walter Reuther, who had helped to organize the UAW in the tumultuous 1930s and who had led the union through the postwar years. Reuther's replacement, Leonard Woodcock, believed that the strike was a necessary test for the young workers who enjoyed the benefits won by the UAW, without knowledge of the great organizing battles of the 1930s and the sacrifices that their predecessors had made.

General Motors also saw the strike as a higher cause than simple economic gain. It was mindful of the fact that its settlement with the UAW would set the pattern for later settlements between the union and Chrysler and Ford. According to Chairman James Roche, the company was obligated to restore the balance that had been lost between wages and productivity, for upon that balance rested the nations "ability to cope with inflation, to resolve the crisis of cost." That, in turn, determined America's ability to reach the "lofty national goals we have set for ourselves." The company publicized the strike as a test of whether the auto industry was destined to join the list of others—textile, consumer appliances, shoes—that could no longer compete with low-wage foreign competition. Casting a shadow over the negotiations was the ominous fact that in July of 1970 imported cars had captured an all-time high of 15.6 percent of the U.S. market.

While negotiators haggled at General Motors headquarters in Detroit, things were quiet and orderly on the picket lines. Since World War II, relations between the union and the company had generally been amicable. General Motors made no attempt to operate during the strike. Unionization was accepted in the auto industry as it was in the nation's other great core industries such as steel, rubber, and electrical manufacturing. The days of strikebreakers, militia, and injunctions seemed remote from the negotiations of 1970, in which conflict was restricted to professional negotiators on both sides of the table.

The settlement came suddenly in mid-November. In the end, the two parties conformed to the established pattern of substantial wage and benefit increases—costs that would ultimately be passed on to consumers in the form of higher prices for automobiles. It was the richest single-company labor settlement in history. In wage gains alone the company would pay out $2.4 million over the three years of the contract. In that same period, the average wage of an auto worker would reach $12,000. The union also won improvements in the pension plan, unlimited cost-of-living protection, a twelfth paid holiday, and other improvements. In all, the settlement amounted to a 30 percent increase over three years. To offset reductions in the work force because of automation, General Motors workers with thirty years of service could retire at the age of fifty-six on a $500 a month pension.

Leonard Woodcock downplayed the enormous bargaining success by noting that although he wasn't satisfied with the settlement, there came a time when gains had to be "weighed against the hardships to be inflicted on the troops who are waging the frontline battle." In truth, the UAW also paid dearly for the settlement. In addition to its members' wage losses, the strike nearly bankrupt the UAW's strike fund. Certainly more significant for the workers in the long run was the fact that General Motors failed to achieve its goal of tying wage increases to productivity increases.

That meant that the settlement was likely to do little to help the U.S. auto industry stave off the challenge from foreign auto manufacturers. [Ronald L. Filippelli]

FURTHER READING

"A Costly End to a Costly Strike." *Newsweek* (November 23, 1970), pp. 101–102.

"Auto Workers Hear the Drums Again." *Time* (September 28, 1970), pp. 69–70.

Serrin, William. "Unknown Who Leads the Walter P. Reuther Memorial Strike." *New York Times Magazine* (September 27, 1970), pp. 28–29+.

"UAW, Getting Poorer and Tougher." *Business Week* (October 31, 1970), p. 75.

o   o   o

GENERAL MOTORS TOOL AND DIEMAKERS' STRIKE OF 1939. The strike that assured the permanence of industrial unionism in the auto industry was not, as is commonly believed, the **General Motors Sit-Down Strike of 1936–1937**, but rather a strike of skilled tool and diemakers in the summer of 1939. A study of this strike sheds light not only on the persistence of anti-unionism at General Motors but also on the role of skilled workers in the building of industrial unions.

The skilled trades in the auto industry included the tool and diemakers, the workers who prepared the metal fixtures, such as the jigs, that held and aligned the auto parts during production, and the dies that produced stamped body and chassis parts. Skilled workers from a variety of traditional trades, such as electricians, welders, and machinists were also required to maintain the machinery and equipment.

These skilled tradesmen, under the leadership of the United Auto Workers (UAW), struck for a month in July and August of 1939. What made the strike unique was that only the few thousand skilled tradesmen were called out. The rest of GM's 200,000 workers did not strike. The point of the strategy was to disrupt GM's preparations for production of its 1940 model line, thus assuring a quick settlement.

The UAW entered the strike with a bevy of problems. The "Big Three" auto companies (Ford, General Motors, and Chrysler) continued to resist unionization, with Ford, the most intransigent, still unorganized. Many workers doubted the union's ability to protect them in the long run, and remained wary of joining the UAW. Others were simply anti-union. Finally, UAW political power had declined with the return of a Republican governor to the Michigan statehouse, replacing the pro-union New Dealer Frank Murphy. Nor was it a propitious time to pressure the industry. Car sales were in a steep decline, and half the work force had been on layoff the year before.

To complicate matters even further, the union had serious internal problems. UAW president Homer Martin was under bitter attack from the left-wing in the auto union. The rancor engendered by this bitter battle left the union adrift at a time when it should have been consolidating the gains it had made in 1937. General Motors also took advantage of the internal disarray of the union and, claiming that it did not know which faction to negotiate with, refused to bargain. The company also stalled grievances in plants where dual grievance committees reflected UAW factionalism. In effect, GM, and in some cases the UAW as well, had largely ceased to administer the collective bargaining agreements.

By the spring of 1939, the Union had begun to put its house in order. Martin had been defeated and replaced by R. J. Thomas. Thomas appointed Walter Reuther, a member of the UAW's board since 1936 and president of a powerful amalgamated local on the west side of Detroit, to direct the UAW's General Motors Department. Reuther set about to reform the department and prepare it for the showdown with the corporation.

Reuther and his lieutenants probably settled on the strategy of a skilled-worker strike for several reasons. First, to call a general walkout of production workers was risky and might well fail given the internal problems of the union and the high unemployment rate. A skilled-worker strike would sidestep these problems, at least for awhile, by allowing the production workers to stay on the job at least until the end of the 1939 model run. Then too, if the production workers were eventually laid off, they might qualify for unemployment compensation. In addition, the highly specialized skills of the tool and diemakers made it nearly impossible to replace them with strikebreakers. Finally, as a group, the skilled workers were much more loyal to the union than the unpredictable production workers.

Reuther presented the company with the union's demands on June 8. They included a wage increase, higher overtime pay, a shift differential, more exclusive seniority provisions, and a series of other issues. The company replied that it could not bargain until the question of who represented the workers, the CIO-UAW or the newly chartered AFL auto union headed by Homer Martin, was resolved.

Skilled workers endorsed the demands overwhelmingly. Their wages and job conditions had declined during the 1930s, particularly in relation to the production workers. The strike began on July 5. By that time, GM's tool and die program for its 1940 model line was only two weeks from completion. Reuther employed a shop-by-shop escalation strategy and by July 24, with some twelve shops closed and 7,600 skilled workers out, GM acknowledged that the 1940 model line was completely stalled.

The major complication for the strikers was the existence of many independent tool and die shops in Detroit. If able to work on GM materials, these shops could probably have produced enough tools and dies to allow GM to go into partial production. But the UAW succeeded in convincing the tool and diemakers in the independent shops that any gains made at GM would eventually help them as well. This and the fraternal bonds of the trade led to the refusal of tool and diemakers in the independent shops to handle "hot dies," or work normally done by the strikers.

Company evaluations of the union's strength had obviously been wrong. The factionalism that GM had counted on did not materialize, mainly because the AFL-Martin group had little or no strength in the tool and die shops. Production workers, in no immediate danger of losing their jobs, had rallied to support the strikers. In view of these realities, the company made contacts with the CIO. Philip Murray, CIO vice-president, federal mediator James Dewey, and GM president William Knudsen began meeting to seek a solution on July 12. Thomas and Reuther were soon brought into the often acrimonious talks.

Early August brought additional pressures on the company. The 1939 model run had ended, and without tools and dies for the 1940 models, 150,000 production workers were idled. GM's competition raced to take their market share as the 1940 model sales year approached. Finally, Michigan's Unemployment Compensation Commission ruled that the laid-off production workers were entitled to benefits. This not only cost GM money, but also extinguished any flicker of hope the company might have had that hardship would force the production workers to bring pressure on the union to end the strike.

The parties reached agreement on August 4. The union won modest wage increases and guarantees that the company would address the discrepancies in wages among plants, using the best-paid plant as the standard. The union also won double time pay for Sunday and holiday work and time and a half for Saturday. GM also accepted union labels on its own dies but refused to agree not to use non-union dies from independent shops if the need arose. The union pledged not to strike during the 1940 model run.

Perhaps the most significant result of the strike was GM's agreement to deal only with the UAW-CIO in most of its plants. In addition, the contract, although it covered only the skilled workers, was the first companywide agreement signed by GM in history. In effect, GM's capitulation marked the recognition that unionization in the auto industry was permanent.

The success at GM also marked the beginning of the UAW's resurgence from its nadir in the faction-ridden years of 1938 and 1939. Membership and morale improved dramatically. The strike also launched Walter Reuther on the road to the presidency of the UAW and a position of leadership in the American labor movement. [Ronald L. Filippelli]

FURTHER READING

Barnard, John. "Rebirth of the United Auto Workers: The General Motors Tool and Diemakers' Strike of 1939," *Labor History*, Vol. 27 (Spring 1986), pp. 165-187.

Boyle, Kevin. "Rite of Passage: The 1939 Tool and Diemakers' Strike of 1939," *Labor History*, Vol. 27 (Spring 1986), pp. 188-203.

o   o   o

GENERAL STRIKES OF 1946. In the immediate aftermath of World War II, the greatest strike wave in American history swept the nation. This upsurge of militancy can be attributed to several factors. There was certainly an attempt by employers, large and small, to roll back the gains made by organized labor during the New Deal and World War II. On labor's part, there was the frustration that had been building up during the war as inflation outran earnings, as well as the pressure of the layoffs and reduction in overtime pay that marked the postwar transition to a peacetime economy.

Historians have generally focused on the story of these strikes in the great mass-production industries such as auto, steel, and electrical manufacturing, in the coal mines, and on the railroads. Certainly they had the greatest economic and political impact. But beneath those great strikes, the upheaval of 1946 also reached numerous small manufacturing companies, transportation companies, municipalities, and other employers. Of particular note were several strikes which spread beyond the initial point of conflict. Because of this, each of these strikes occurred on two levels: the first was the economic conflict between one union and one employer, while the second involved a reaction on the part of large segments of the labor movement and the community in support of the strikers.

At the end of the war, the Yale and Towne Manufacturing Company was the main employer in Stamford, Connecticut, with some 3,000 employees. The company had resisted unionization with determination in the 1930s, and had succumbed only because of a union victory in an election ordered by the War Labor Board. The International Association of Machinists represented the workers at Yale and Towne. After the war, the company was determined to give no wage increases and to eliminate the maintenance-of-membership security clause which required that once workers had joined the union, they had to remain members in good standing until the contract expired. Maintenance of membership had been a requirement of the War Labor Board as a quid pro quo for a limitation on pay increases during the war. In addition, Yale and Towne had demonstrated its distaste for the union by refusing to process a mounting backlog of grievances. Worker discontent boiled over on September 21, 1945, when a wildcat strike erupted as the result of the firing of the union's chief steward. At that point the two sides had been negotiating since March under the terms of the old, expired contract. The company used the wildcat strike as the pretext for terminating its contract with the Machinists. The union countered with a strike beginning on November 7, 1945. For the next two months the two sides confronted one another at the plant gates in a bitter struggle. State police closely monitored the picket lines, including an assault and numerous arrests in late December.

The police action and the general hostility against the company roused the community. On the morning of January 3, 1946, workers from all over Stamford reported to a mass pro-union rally rather than to work. Merchants closed their stores to demonstrate sympathy for the strikers. The rally also had the tacit support of City Hall. Mayor Charles Moore, who had refused to send city police against the pickets, criticized the company for refusing to negotiate. Also, the newspapers, dependent on the merchants for advertising and the citizens for subscriptions, would not take sides in the dispute.

Nevertheless, the company refused to yield. Vandalism and intimidation against the company and its officials began to mar the strike. On March 21 and 22, massed pickets skirmished with police and company officials. The conflict sobered both sides to the potential for violence in the strike. Under this pressure, and with the help of federal and state mediators, an agreement was reached. It included wage increases and arbitration on the maintenance of membership issues, which, to no one's surprise, the union later won.

In Lancaster, Pennsylvania, a similar attempt by a company to break a union after the war also led to citywide mobilization. Like Yale and Towne, the Conestoga Transportation Company, which ran Lancaster's busses and trolleys, had been forced by the War Labor Board to recognize the Amalgamated Association of Street Electric Railway and Motor Coach Employees after an election in 1942. Conestoga also saw the maintenance of membership security clause as a form of forced unionization of its employees. The strike began on August 31. Three weeks later, the company resumed operations with a few union members who had crossed the picket lines and management personnel. The union asked the community for support. At a mass meeting the union and its supporters arrived at a compromise settlement package that proposed a resumption of work and the arbitration of all outstanding issues. The AFL Central Labor Union in Lancaster responded by threatening to call a "labor holiday" for all AFL members in Lancaster County if the company refused the compromise offer.

When the company refused, violence broke out at the car barns during union attempts to bar the trolleys from operating. A number of strikers were arrested for rioting and unlawful assembly. After these events, on September 26, the union agreed to return to work under the old contract and to continue to negotiate so long as none of the strikers was punished by the company. When negotiations produced nothing, the bus drivers staged a one day "work holiday" on December 9. The company took advantage of the strike to terminate its contract with the union. In response, after attempts at conciliation failed, the union walked out again on February 6.

Events during the second strike paralleled what had happened before. The company employed strikebreakers, the pickets resisted, and the police arrested the pickets. Once again, the AFL Central Labor Union called a citywide mass meeting to formulate strategy. There were calls for a general strike on the Stamford model. Within a week, almost all of Lancaster's unionized workers struck in support of the bus drivers. On Sunday, February 17, the Central Labor Union voted for a general strike to last until there was a settlement in the Conestoga Transportation dispute. Fourteen thousand workers answered the call on February 19. Picket lines closed movie theaters, markets, and a host of other Lancaster establishments. Two thousand pickets appeared at the car barns. Three days of the general strike produced a settlement favorable to the union.

The general strikes in Stamford and Lancaster both resulted from attempts by hostile employers to break young unions and revert back to the open shop days of before the war. In both cases, these were viewed by the entire labor movement of the cities as part of a challenge to all of organized labor. They were also seen by large segments of the working and small business classes of the cities as threats to the general interest and well-being of the communities. This confluence of interests led to the widespread support for the strikers in Stamford and Lancaster. Similar circumstances led to similar results in Oakland, California, and Rochester, New York.

In Rochester a local of the American Federation of State, County, and Municipal Employees (AFSCME) had formed to counter sweeping work-rule and pay-system changes by the city. The city responded by firing 489 employees. On May 23, some 5,000 union members from throughout the city rallied at City Hall in support of the AFSCME members. The rally resulted in a city offer to the fired workers to return to their jobs but without the union. They refused and joined with 30,000 AFL and CIO members to paralyze the city with a general strike on May 28. So total was its impact that the Republican governor of New York, Thomas Dewey, and industrialists in Rochester intervened with city officials. The settlement, a bitter pill for the city, returned the fired workers to their jobs and recognized the union.

Unlike the other major general strikes of the period which were generally planned and directed by the central labor councils of the cities, the Oakland strike was a spontaneous outpouring of support for striking department store employees, most of whom were women. That such a relatively small strike could act as the flashpoint for a militant general strike was a good indication of the frustrations that had been building in America's industrial working class during the war. Members of the Department Store and Speciality Clerks Union had begun striking two downtown Oakland department stores in November of 1946. Their dispute had gained the crucial support of the Teamsters' union, whose drivers refused to deliver to the stores. Nevertheless, the stores remained open and the strike showed few signs of the drama that it was to precipitate.

When non-union truckers from Los Angeles tried to deliver goods to the Hasting's store early on December 2, strikers blocked the entrances. The Oakland police massed over 250 men to move the trucks through the picket lines. When word spread of the event, protests spread throughout the city. Thousands of workers without direction left work to assemble downtown. With a spontaneous demonstration underway, the Alameda County Central Labor Council tried to gain control of the movement by announcing a general strike for the following day. The spread of the strike outdistanced anything seen thus far. Over 100,000 workers took part. Five thousand workers joined the retail clerks on the picket lines. Workers patrolled the streets, closed stores, and stopped public transportation. In some ways, the demonstration took on the air of a street carnival as a holiday atmosphere prevailed. For all intents and purposes, the city was in the hands of the strikers. This not only struck fear in the hearts of city officials but also into the leadership of the local labor movement as well. The size and character of the demonstration threatened their control of the situation. On Thursday, December 5, after receiving assurances from the city that police would no longer be used to protect strikebreakers, the AFL Central Labor Council called off the strike.

The AFL's action met with determined resistance. The great demonstration of solidarity had accomplished nothing. There had been no resolution of the department store strike. Some local unions refused to abide by the order at first. Nevertheless, without the official support of the AFL and their own unions, most workers returned to work immediately. The explosive potential of the working class of Oakland had proved to be as big a threat to established labor leadership as it had to the city's officials and employers. [Ronald L. Filippelli]

FURTHER READING

Lipsitz, George. *Class and Culture in Coldwar America: Rainbow at Midnight.* South Hadley, MA: J. F. Bergin Publishers, 1982.

Weir, Stan. "American Labor on the Defensive: A 1940s Odyssey." *Radical America*, Vol. 9 (July–August 1975), pp. 163–185.

o   o   o

GEORGIA RAILROAD STRIKE OF 1909. The Georgia Railroad Strike of 1909 was an example of how the overlapping goals of blacks and the labor movement frequently resulted in conflict between black aspirations and trade union interests. The trouble began when officials of the company decided to reduce operating expenses by removing ten white assistant hostlers, station workers who prepared the locomotives for their runs, and replacing them with blacks. The hostlers belonged to the Brotherhood of Locomotive Firemen and Enginemen (BLFE). In response, the Georgia Railroad's sixty white fireman struck, claiming that the company's action was but one part of an overall strategy to replace white railroad workers with blacks throughout the South.

Blacks had served as firemen on most railroads in the South since before the Civil War, but only white firemen could advance to the more prestigious position of engineer. By 1909, 42 percent of the company's firemen were black. Company spokesmen maintained that black firemen did their jobs well and also worked for less pay than whites.

The dispute was simply an open manifestation of a number of problems on the railroad, the most important of which were complaints by the BLFE members about the hiring of black firemen. The race issue had been smoldering ever since the company began to hire blacks. One year earlier, the BLFE's national convention resolved that "the time had arrived when the railroads of the South must be made to discontinue the employment of Negroes as firemen."

Company motives were far from altruistic. In addition to paying the blacks lower wages, it was probable that they were also using the issue to intimidate the union with the lesson that the white firemen could easily be replaced if they did not reduce their demands.

While the company envisioned using the race issue to its advantage, so too did the union, by appealing to public opinion in the racist climate that prevailed in Georgia at the time. The white firemen walked off the job on May 17. The race issue did, in fact, translate into an immediate economic issue for the whites. The presence of the non-union black firemen in such large numbers permitted the railroad to keep the wages of the whites on one of the lowest pay scales in the entire South. Of course, the option of allowing the black workers into the union was never considered. The BLFE's constitution prohibited Negro membership. As the *New York World* pointed out, the white workers had become the victims of their own economic discrimination against the blacks.

The union began a campaign of race-baiting along the tracks of the Georgia Railroad. Mobs of citizens were recruited in several communities to take vigilante action against the railroad and the black firemen. Black firemen were assaulted, protesters stoned trains, and large crowds turned out to jeer the black workers. In Augusta, the home of the Georgia Railroad, a mob tried to lynch a black worker. Throughout the disturbances local authorities failed to intervene.

Faced with near unanimous white support for the strikers, the railroad ground to a halt. White engineers, although unsympathetic with the strike, announced that their members would not work without police protection. In truth, the authorities feared that intervention might lead to even more violence in the explosive climate of the strike. The combination of this fear, the governor's concern lest he be labeled pro-black, and his obvious sympathies for the strikers, kept the police power of the state out of the dispute.

Even so, the railroad did not surrender. When the union threatened to make the "white man's cause" a national one, President Taft intervened and invoked the provisions of the Erdman Act of 1898, which provided for government mediation if both parties agreed. The union, confident of public opinion, accepted mediation provided that the hearings were held in Georgia. The company assented and re-hired the ten white hostlers but refused to remove any more black workers. During the hearings the trains began to move again.

The strike attracted national attention because of the linkage of labor and racial conflict. The *Outlook* editorialized that the combination of the two was "full of menace" for the nation. *Harper's Weekly* was prophetic when it pointed out that the forces set in motion by the strike might result in the elimination of black firemen from every railroad in the South.

The three-man arbitration panel worked under considerable political and public pressure. The BFLE did not argue that blacks should be fired solely because of race but rather because they weren't intelligent enough to serve in such a responsible, complicated position. They claimed that black firemen endangered the lives of passengers and other employees as well as valuable railroad property. The union also attempted to bring representatives of "outraged citizens" to the hearings, but the panel ruled that they were incompetent to testify.

The railroad admitted that black firemen received lower wages than whites, but they assured the panel that blacks performed as effectively as whites, if not better. The company had no intention of firing these loyal employees. But the company also resorted to racial stereotypes in arguing its case. Claiming that blacks were better suited to the tasks of firemen because they had greater endurance and could stand the intense heat better than whites, the company also made it clear that blacks would never be used as engineers because they lacked the necessary intelligence and moral qualifications for the job.

The panel informed the parties of its decision on June 26. By a two to one vote it upheld the company's position that it had a right to hire black firemen. The arbiters found accusations about the incompetence of blacks wholly unfounded. Finally, as a gesture to the union, the panel ordered the company to equalize the pay of blacks and whites. Equal pay for equal work, the whites believed, would gradually lead to the end of the hiring of blacks because of the lack of financial incentives to the company.

The union was wrong. The railroad continued to hire black firemen until 1928, but by that year the four major railway unions had succeeded in virtually ending the hiring of blacks above the level of unskilled workers on American railroads.

According to one source, from 1928 to 1949, not a single black person found employment on a major railroad as a fireman, brakeman, trainman, or yardman. [Ronald L. Filippelli]

FURTHER READING

Foner, Philip. *Organized Labor and the Black Worker: 1619–1973.* New York: Praeger, 1974.

Hammett, Hugh B. "Labor and Race: The Georgia Railroad Strike of 1909." *Labor History*, Vol. 16 (1975), pp. 470–484.

Matthews, John M. "The Georgia 'Race Strike' of 1909." *Journal of Southern History*, Vol. 40 (1974), pp. 613–630.

o   o   o

GOLDFIELD, NEVADA, STRIKE OF 1907–1908. This was the first of several altercations involving both the Western Federation of Miners (WFM) and its rambunctious offspring, the Industrial Workers of the World (IWW). Internecine labor conflict facilitated the destruction of radical unionism by the local mine operators. The crucial factor in the downfall of the miners' movement, however, was not the internal divisions within the workers' ranks, but rather the intervention of the federal government on the side of the employers.

One in a string of mining camps in the southern Nevada desert, Goldfield boomed immediately upon the discovery of rich gold deposits in 1902. Amid the prosperity, high wages and class harmony prevailed. The Goldfield Miners' Union, Local 220 of the Western Federation of Miners, was formed in April 1904 and took on a respectable role in the community. The union immediately built a hospital, open to the public. When the Citizens' Protective Association was organized in May 1904 to promote civic improvements, its secretary and vice-president were WFM officers.

The honeymoon ended abruptly with the arrival of the Industrial Workers of the World. Having played a leading part in sponsoring the IWW in 1905, the WFM became its Mining Department. The WFM also encouraged the development of Wobbly branches in communities in which it had sizable affiliates. In the spring of 1906, IWW Local 77 was chartered to represent the entire non-mining work force of Goldfield. Carrying the logic of mass unionism one step further, Local 77, within a few months, merged with the Goldfield Miners' Union to form IWW Local 220. Soon this amalgamated body had approximately 3,000 members.

The miners' organization began to pursue a more aggressive policy in their dealings with mine owners. On December 19, 1906, Local 220 called for a wage increase for unskilled mining labor from $4.00 to $5.00 for eight hours' work. The miners struck the next day after the operators rejected this proposal. This uneventful dispute ended within three weeks in a compromise settlement. The gold companies conceded the $5.00 day for skilled hardrock miners but gave the unskilled only $4.50. In return, the operators forced the union to accept change rooms, (locker rooms where employees would be required to deposit their work clothes at the end of a shift and change into other clothes before they left company property). By this procedure the operators aimed to curtail the widespread practice of "high-grading," workers' removal of high-grade ore concealed in innershirt pockets, third pants legs, and double hat crowns. Because of its controversial nature, the operators delayed implementation of this system.

On March 1, 1907, the IWW demanded that all businesses in the community grant the eight-hour workday at once. Employers grudgingly acceded to this ultimatum. The Wobblies then turned their attention to the town's carpenters, who remained members of the American Federation of Labor's (AFL) United Brotherhood of Carpenters and Joiners. On March

6, Local 220 ordered the craft unionists to join their organization or leave town. The building tradesmen refused and began carrying guns to work. On March 8, the organized miners told a leading firm in the district, the Consolidated Gold Mines Company, not to employ any non-IWW men as mine carpenters. When the company refused to become entangled in this jurisdictional matter, the miners struck on March 9.

Within a week local employers had formed the Goldfield Business Men's and Mine Operators' Association. The association announced that its members would employ no members of the Industrial Workers of the World. Aware that on the national level the WFM had fallen out with IWW leadership and was withdrawing its support of revolutionary unionism, Goldfield capitalists moved to separate miners from non-miners. All the businesses in town locked out their employees on March 15. Three days later, all but the mines managed to reopen with no Wobblies employed. Within a month, the WFM miners had disaffiliated from the IWW. This paved the way for the negotiation of an agreement ending the lockout on April 22.

Peace was short-lived. On August 18, Consolidated Mines announced plans to set up the change rooms called for in the agreement reached in January. The announcement precipitated a spontaneous walkout at one of its mines; employees at the firm's remaining properties joined the work stoppage three days later. The miners' union did not defend the right to appropriate small amounts of gold. Instead, it protested the humiliating methods proposed to prevent high-grading. The Consolidated plan would compel workers to walk naked across the change room to reach their clean clothes. On September 8, the company and WFM Local 220 agreed that each underground employee would

have two adjacent lockers in which to keep work and nonwork clothing.

Shortly after the resolution of this dispute, the Panic of 1907 hit. Two banks in the district failed, and others tottered. This financial collapse led Goldfield operators on November 18 to declare their intention to pay employees in scrip. When management refused to discuss the issue, the miners' organization began a general strike across the district on November 27. The depressed market for gold gave the mine owners a golden opportunity to break the union.

A delegation of operators went to Governor John Sparks on December 3 to request military intervention. Despite the orderly nature of the strike, Sparks, who had no state militia, agreed to ask for federal assistance. On December 5, the governor convinced President Theodore Roosevelt to send the U.S. Army to southern Nevada. Three infantry companies under Colonel Alfred Reynolds arrived on the scene of the strike the following day. Although they found no insurrection, they remained in Goldfield. The fact that the president of Consolidated Gold Mines, George Nixon, was a U.S. senator may have contributed to this needless commitment of armed forces. With military protection, the operators immediately cut wages, instituted a blacklisting system, and announced plans to resume production. Accordingly, the mines reopened on December 12 with a skeleton work force. Extensive recruiting efforts led to the importation of groups of strikebreakers by the end of the year.

A team of federal investigators arrived in Goldfield on December 15. Like the military authorities, they found no evidence of any disturbances that the local authorities could not control. Further, the investigating commission criticized the blatant union-busting tactics of the operators and Governor Sparks. Nonetheless, this inquiry did not result in the immediate withdrawal of the U.S. Army from Goldfield. It did, however, create pressure for such a course of action. The state hastily forged a substitute force. Sparks convened a special session of the legislature in mid-January 1908. Legislators passed and the governor signed a bill creating the Nevada State Police on January 29. The state police immediately replaced the Army.

On January 30, the mines in the district posted notices that henceforth they would employ no members of either the WFM or the IWW. Meanwhile, the operators continued to import strikebreakers. They ignored repeated invitations from the miners' union to negotiate over the issues in dispute. Extractive operations soon returned to a high level of output. On April 3, long after it had been beaten, the Goldfield Miners' Union voted to end the strike. Thus, by the spring of 1908, the mine owners had annihilated both the IWW and the WFM from what had been only a year earlier a stronghold of radical unionism. [Alan Derickson]

FURTHER READING

Dubofsky, Melvyn. *We Shall Be All: A History of the Industrial Workers of the World.* New York: Quadrangle, 1969.

Elliott, Russell R. "Labor Troubles in the Mining Camp at Goldfield, Nevada, 1906–1908." *Pacific Historical Review*, Vol. 19 (November 1950), pp. 369–384.

Jensen, Vernon H. *Heritage of Conflict: Labor Relations in the Nonferrous Metals Industry up to 1930.* Ithaca, NY: Cornell University Press, 1950.

o   o   o

GREAT NORTHERN RAILROAD STRIKE OF 1894. The Great Northern Strike was a signal triumph for the recently formed American Railway Union (ARU) and its president, Eugene V. Debs. With the onset of the Panic of 1893, the newly built Great Northern Railroad, which op-erated between Minneapolis-St. Paul and Seattle, began cutting costs. Three times between August 1893 and March 1894 the company instituted 10 percent wage cuts. The railroad brotherhoods, to which many Great Northern employees belonged, protested the second cut and proposed arbitration. James J. Hill, builder and president of the railroad, agreed. When the resulting award reduced the cut to 9 percent, the brotherhoods went along. Although unhappy, they did not bother to protest the third wage cut. The ARU, an industrial type railway union anxious to secure a toehold among Great Northern workers, did challenge the cut and so precipitated the strike.

Debs, the president of the ARU, was thirty-eight years old in 1894. For twenty years he had been a member of the Brotherhood of Locomotive Firemen and, since the **Railroad Strikes of 1877**, the secretary-treasurer of the organization and editor of its journal. Distressed at how railroad companies successfully played off one brotherhood or union against the others during strikes, he advocated federation. When those attempts failed, he founded the American Railway Union in June 1893. The new union embraced all railways workers regardless of position or skill. Once fully organized, Debs believed, the union would be so powerful that its just demands would be acceded to without the necessity of strikes.

Although railroad workers, especially those in the yards and shops, rushed into the new union, but by early 1894, it had not reached the strength that Debs had hoped for. Nonetheless, its leaders better understood the sentiment of the workers on the Great Northern than did the brotherhoods. They called upon Hill to restore wages by April 13 to what they had been before the cuts or face a strike. Hill, doubting that the new union represented any significant number of his workers, made no reply. When the ARU members walked out, they were joined by most brotherhood members as well. At that point Hill promised loyal workers that they would be duly rewarded if they remained on the job.

The various brotherhood officials were contemptuous of the ARU yet fearful of what its success might mean for them. Some declared their neutrality in the strike; others threatened to expel members for participating in it. Some went so far as to assist the Great Northern in unsuccessful efforts to secure strikebreakers. Meanwhile, Debs, realizing that any violence would play into company hands, urged his followers to avoid trouble by protecting company property. To forestall problems with the federal government, the ARU agreed to move mail trains so long as only mail—no passengers or freight—was carried on them. Although Hill refused to run mail under these terms, the strike succeeded completely. Not a single freight train moved during the entire tie-up.

Hill called a meeting with Debs and ARU leaders and suggested that the whole matter be submitted to arbitration but insisted that the brotherhoods be included. Debs refused. Hill next turned to the United States Department of Justice for help, focussing on the issue of blockage of the mail. On April 19, he notified Attorney General Richard Olney that a strike "instigated and . . . conducted by men not in Company's employ," prevented movement of the Great Northern's trains and would be met on "strictly legal grounds." Two days later, James E. White, superintendent of the Railway Mail Service and a long-time enemy of railroad strikes, appeared at the Department of Justice seeking an official ruling. Whether he did this on his own or at Hill's prompting is not known, but he wanted the Department of Justice to issue a precise definition of mail trains. Officials there were sympathetic. Attorney General Olney, a distinguished railroad lawyer and director, before, during, and after his term of office, happened to be in Boston at the moment. However,

acting for him was Solicitor General Lawrence Maxwell, a former railroad attorney from Cincinnati. He accommodated Superintendent White by reversing Postmaster General Don M. Dickinson's 1888 ruling in the **Burlington Railroad Strike** that railroads must carry the mail during strikes even if nothing else. According to Maxwell's new definition, a mail train consisted of every car of any train, as made up by the railroad company, that carried mail. Persons preventing passage of such trains, or of any car or cars on them, brought themselves under the laws against conspiracy to interfere with the mail.

The ruling would prove of great importance in suppressing the **Pullman Strike** only a few weeks later. It had little impact on the Great Northern Strike, however. The railroad ran but one passenger-bearing mail train each way each day over its line. Debs and the ARU let them pass inasmuch as it was the hauling of freight, not passengers, that provided the system with its lifeblood.

Hill next arranged for Debs to present the ARU's position to a session of the St. Paul Chamber of Commerce. Apparently, he assumed that hearing the strike leader would unite the business community against the strike. Debs used the opportunity to advantage, carefully spelling out the issues as he saw them. Whether impressed by Debs's arguments or recognizing in him a leader who might well keep the railroad they all depended on closed down indefinitely, they called for arbitration. The brotherhoods were not to be included. Debs accepted this offer as did Hill, who noted that he had always favored arbitration. Interestingly enough, however, Hill at the same time called on President Grover Cleveland to send troops to restore order on the Great Northern. Not only were the strikers plaguing the line, so were bands of the unemployed who were stealing trains to take them to Washington, DC. There they hoped to join Coxey's Army which was then assembling to demand that Congress provide them with jobs. Attorney General Olney objected to troops, suspecting that Hill wanted the Army to break a strike that appeared about to be resolved. Any "unnecessary interposition of the military," he pointed out, "would, of course aggravate matters."

On May 1, less than three weeks after the walkout began, the arbitration committee handed down its award. It called for restoring 75 percent of the three cuts in wage rates since August 1893. All other issues were deferred. When the chairman of the committee proposed a grand banquet to celebrate the end of the strike, Debs recommended that the money instead be used to buy calico for the wives of the strikers.

The ARU and the press hailed the outcome as a great victory for Debs, especially since wages now equalled 97.5 percent of what they had been before the cuts. Those on the other side accepted Hill's interpretation. He was taking great care, he said, not to contradict the popular view that the ARU had won, implying, in effect that they had won little or nothing.

Actually, Debs's management of the strike had been skillful and shrewd. Even Hill congratulated him. As in the Union Pacific Strikes four years before, success stemmed from the surprising unity of the railroaders and the inability of the company to secure strikebreakers in advance of the walkout. A major new factor was the impressive generalship of a compelling labor leader, Eugene V. Debs. In the weeks that followed, the perception that the ARU had won the Great Northern Strike contributed to the union's eagerness to take on, over the objections of Debs, the nation's major railroads in the Pullman Strike. [Gerald G. Eggert]

FURTHER READING

Eggert, Gerald G. *Railroad Labor Disputes, The Beginnings of Federal Strike Policy.* Ann Arbor, MI: University of Michigan Press, 1967.

Ginger, Ray. *The Bending Cross, A Biography of Eugene Victor Debs.* New Brunswick, NJ: Rutgers University Press, 1949.

McMurry, Donald L. "Federation of the Railroad Brotherhoods, 1889–1894." *Industrial and Labor Relations Review*, Vol. 7 (October 1953), pp. 74–92.

Salvatore, Nick. *Eugene V. Debs, Citizen and Socialist.* Urbana, IL: University of Illinois Press, 1982.

○ ○ ○

HARLAN COUNTY, KENTUCKY,
MINERS' STRIKE OF 1931. Harlan
County, Kentucky, was inhospitable to coal
unionism from the opening of its first
mines in 1911 through the 1930s. Only
during World War I, under the supervision of the federal government's National
Fuel Administration, did county coal operators enter an agreement with the United
Mine Workers (UMW) raising wages, limiting hours, and giving local unions the
right to elect their own checkweighmen
(who insured that members were fairly
paid). Shortly after the war, the Harlan
operators broke off relations with the union, refusing to sign even the most pallid
contract the UMW had to offer. From then
until the Great Depression of the 1930s,
the mine owners easily turned back the
brief efforts to organize their employees.
UMW Local Union 5355 survived with a
few members but not a single contract.

Harlan County miners displayed an
interest in joining a union but had scant
opportunity to exercise the right to organize or even to express their opinions about
collective bargaining. The coal operators
ran both the mines and the county, toler-
ating no dissent to their regime. The Harlan County Coal Operators Association had
a clear policy against dealing with unions.
The Association feared losing Harlan coal's
market advantage if unions raised wages
and increased other costs of production. It
subscribed to a conspiracy theory about unionization in which the UMW and union-

ized northern coal operators were in league
to block the southern Appalachian mines'
access to the major coal buyers in order to
sell more coal themselves.

The Association also dominated
local politics by close connections with
political parties, judges, and the county
sheriff. The sheriff, who was often a coal
operator himself, deputized guards that the
companies hired to patrol their property.
Though elected by county voters, the
candidates for sheriff and other public
offices were usually picked by coal mining
interests. If by chance an independent
candidate entered a race, the operators
resorted to vote fraud or intimidation to
insure that their man won the election.
There was little distinction in Harlan
County between the public laws and the
operators' rules.

This was clearest in the mining towns.
All but three communities were unincor-
porated and thus without any kind of town
government. The operators ran these mining villages as they saw fit, and while their
system included some of the trappings of
employer paternalism, it more consistently
scrimped on housing, roads, playgrounds,
and utilities while exploiting the miners
through high rents and inflated prices at
the company's store—often the only place
to shop in the town. Any miner who dared
to challenge the operator or his supervisors could be summarily fired and evicted
from the company house he rented.
Through the Harlan County Coal Operators Association, the same miner could be

blacklisted and virtually forced out of the region.

The 1930s Depression was the first event since World War I to weaken the operators' regime in Harlan County. The deterioration in the miners' living standards provoked them to move toward unionization again. Hourly wages did not fall precipitously, but the average days worked annually fell to 175, cutting annual earnings to $749 by 1931. Miners in the area gathered secretly to discuss unionization. When Harlan operators imposed a 10 percent wage reduction in February 1931, William Turnblazer, the president of United Mine Workers District 19, began circulating leaflets in eastern Kentucky and eastern Tennessee calling on miners to revive the union and demand elected checkweighmen and the abolition of the unpaid work required by the companies. By the end of the month, Local 5355 in Harlan County had about 500 members. The UMW appointed William Hightower as this local's president, but a recent arrival in Harlan County, William B. Jones, served as local secretary and provided the real leadership.

The coal operators did not hesitate to strike back at the organizing drive. Their informers told them about the surreptitious meetings being held, and the pro-union miners fell under close scrutiny. Following a UMW meeting on March 1 for all miners interested in unionization, where hundreds responded to UMW vice-president Philip Murray's invitation to join the union, operators began discharging UMW members. Hundreds of union members and sympathizers were dropped from the mine payrolls from mid-March to April. Company guards and sheriff's deputies carried out the evictions from company housing that inevitably followed, raising tensions sharply. The 1931 Harlan County strike began as a lockout against the union.

The UMW wanted to conduct a peaceful, orderly organizing drive that would convert hundreds of new members into irresistable pressure on the operators to sign a union contract. Public statements by Local 5355 and District 19 UMW officials stressed the union's desire to avoid confrontation and violence. The mine companies' immediate frontal assault on the campaign threw this strategy into confusion. Discharged and homeless miners looked to the union for relief, but the union could not afford to feed and shelter the hundreds of men and their families. UMW appeals for help to the National Red Cross and state and federal governments proved fruitless, and Harlan operators adamantly refused to discuss an agreement with the union.

Receiving no protection from the union against private deputies or hunger, the locked-out miners resorted to their own version of self-help. The incorporated town of Evarts, where the mayor and police chief showed sympathy for union men, swelled with a new population of homeless families who found shelter in vacant houses and barns. Local 5355 secretary William Jones set up union headquarters in his house in Evarts, and regular union meetings were held in the schoolyard, with attendance ranging from 300 to several thousand. Hungry union men began robbing grocery stores and mine company commissaries in April. Though local union and Evarts officials established patrols to guard the stores, the thefts continued, creating more conflicts with the aggressively anti-union county sheriff John Henry Blair and his deputies. Thrown out of company houses by deputies, shadowed and intimidated by heavily armed guards wherever they went, union members increasingly retaliated against the companies' agents and the non-union miners during April. Union sympathizers sniped from the hills at men who took their jobs, and burned and dynamited company buildings.

The confrontations between private deputies and union forces reached a deadly climax on May 5, when approximately seventy-five armed union miners attacked a convoy of cars carrying ten deputies through Evarts. For thirty minutes, miners and deputies exchanged rifle, shotgun, and pistol fire that left three deputies and one union miner dead and several more wounded on each side. Some families moved away from Evarts following this battle, and town officials closed the public school.

The Battle of Evarts, as the clash became known, galvanized both Harlan miners and Kentucky officials. The miners still at work in Harlan and neighboring Bell County went on strike to support the union men's chief demand for the removal of private deputies. Most of the mines in Harlan County were shut down. Kentucky governor Flem Sampson sent 370 National Guardsmen to Harlan County on May 7, with orders to stop the importing of strike-breakers, discharge company guards, house and feed evicted miners, and permit the union's organizing drive to continue, except for night meetings. Not suprisingly, union miners in Harlan County greeted the Guard's arrival with band music and a march of 200 members.

Once in Harlan, however, the National Guard quickly aligned itself with the local rulers and set about breaking the strike. During May, it prohibited union marches, prevented interference by union men with strikebreakers, and ignored instructions to disarm the private deputies. When the UMW tried to hold a rally for its members at the county courthouse, deputies broke up the meeting with tear gas. The National Guard refused to help obtain relief for the desperate union miners. When further efforts to seek supplies from the Red Cross failed, the striking men had little choice but to return to work.

While the National Guard helped reopen Harlan County mines, Sheriff Blair and other officials vigorously pursued individual union activists. Local 5355 secretary William Jones, local president Hightower, forty-three union miners, and several Evarts officials were arrested and charged with the murder of the deputies killed at the Battle of Evarts. (After the strike, the local union officers and six union members were repeatedly tried and found guilty of conspiracy to commit murder.) More than a hundred other union members were eventually charged in connection with that incident or with counts of robbing stores, banding, and confederating. Sheriff's deputies also claimed to have found radical literature when they raided William Jones' home. This discovery conveniently supported accusations by the county sheriff of radicalism among the union supporters, though the National Guard's earlier investigation had turned up no such evidence.

The UMW had given up its organizing drive after the Battle of Evarts, hoping that intervention by representatives of the state government could help salvage something for the union. The National Guard's activities in Harlan dampened these hopes, but the union proposed a settlement to the governor that would have returned labor relations in Harlan County to the situation that existed before the organizing drive, except that operators would hire both union and non-union miners. The Harlan County Coal Operators Association voted to reject any settlement involving the union and underlined this opposition by refusing even to enter the same room with UMW District 19 president Turnblazer during a meeting called by the governor.

By the middle of June 1931, the Harlan County strike was over. Hundreds of union miners were barred by the operators from resuming their former jobs. They settled into a bitter life in makeshift shelters. Disillusioned with the UMW, these blacklisted men turned to the Communist-led National Miners Union later in 1931 and conducted another strike under its auspices in 1932. The coal operators and their allies in Harlan County again squashed the miners' protest with violations of civil rights and gunplay. After the 1931 strike, it took six years and steady pressure from the federal government to bring about collective bargaining between the UMW and Harlan County operators. [Peter Gottlieb]

FURTHER READING

Ardery, Julia S., ed. *Welcome the Traveler Home: Jim Garland's Story of the Kentucky Mountains.* Lexington, KY: University Press of Kentucky, 1983.

Bubka, Tony. "The Harlan County Coal Strike of 1931." *Labor History*, Vol. 11 (1970), pp. 41–57.

Hevener, John W. *Which Side Are You On? The Harlan County Coal Miners, 1931–39.* Urbana, IL: University of Illinois Press, 1978.

o   o   o

HARLEM JOBS-FOR-NEGROES BOYCOTT OF 1934. In the midst of the Great Depression of the 1930s, Harlem African-Americans mounted a boycott against white employers that lasted six weeks. The boycott was the culmination of several years of agitation by black leaders in Harlem in an attempt to break the rigid color bar which barred blacks from all but the most menial jobs in their own community. It also proved to be the catalyst for the organization of a black trade union that became a major force in the self-help movement in New York's largest black community.

The early leader of the movement was the Reverend John H. Johnson of Saint Martin's Protestant Episcopal Church. Johnson was moved to organize the boycott after receiving numerous complaints from his parishioners, most of whom were members of the Harlem middle class, that there were no black salesgirls in the stores on 125th Street, Harlem's main shopping street. When Johnson took their complaints to the proprietors of Blumstein's, Harlem's largest department store, they rejected any suggestion that they should consider blacks for anything but menial positions. Indeed, the Blumsteins pointed with pride to the fact that one black college graduate worked as an elevator operator.

Johnson, along with many of Harlem's civic leaders, then formed "The Citizen's League for Fair Play." Its membership represented the elite of Harlem society. When negotiations between the League and Blumstein's collapsed, the boycott began in June of 1934. Although some sixty-two Harlem organizations, including social, religious, and business groups, supported the effort, the driving force behind the boycott was the *New York Age*, one of Harlem's two major black weeklies. The *Age's* competitor, the *Amsterdam News* took the opposite position, attacking the boycott as foolhardy, and predicting a backlash from white businesses who employed black workers downtown.

The League, though consisting of a generally conservative element, carried out a militant boycott, picketing Blumstein's and intimidating black shoppers who shopped in the store. The united front of the black community brought results. On July 26, 1934, Blumstein's agreed to hire fifteen black clerical and sales workers in August, and another twenty by the end of September.

With the victory over Blumstein's under their belts, the League faltered, failing to carry the boycott to other merchants along 125th Street. The crisis that paralyzed the organization developed when Blumstein's chose all light-skinned black women to fill the jobs. The incident created a split inside the League between those, largely the more conservative and prosperous elements, who saw nothing wrong with Blumstein's choices, and the militants who resented the obvious discrimination against darker-skinned women.

The conflict over color brought to the surface an old division within the African-

American community between light-skinned people, who had generally been accorded higher social status because of their color, and their darker brothers and sisters. Indeed, it is probable that conservative members of the League actually had a hand in selecting the women that Blumstein's hired. No doubt these men, leaders of Harlem society, chose light-skinned women whose appearance met their standard of attractiveness.

In actual fact, the color dispute was about a good deal more than social status in Harlem. The leaders of the militant wing of the League, Arthur Reed and Ira Kemp, were black nationalists who had earlier formed the African Patriotic League, an offshoot of the black-nationalist Marcus Garvey movement. Kemp and Reed believed that the only hope for African-Americans was the development of their own economy. The Jobs-for-Negroes campaign was an ideal beginning for their program. Once the movement became more radical, the demand would increase to include all of the jobs in Harlem. The crusade for darker-skinned workers was seen as a first step toward this goal and was a means to wrest control of the movement in Harlem away from the leadership of the conservative League members.

The militants' first target was the A. S. Beck Shoe Store where they demanded the hiring of African-American sales personnel. The company responded by securing a court injunction against the picketers. The court issued the injunction on the grounds that neither the Citizen's League nor Reed's African Patriotic League were labor unions, and that therefore, since no labor dispute existed, the injunction was a proper remedy for the owners of the shoe store. The judge characterized the issue as solely a racial dispute.

Before the injunction was issued, the picketing committee had become embroiled in a dispute with another 125th Street business, the Orkin Dress Shop. The shop already hired blacks for 50 percent of its sales force, but the militants demanded that the level be raised to 75 percent and that they be allowed to choose who was to be hired, even if this meant the discharge of blacks already on the payroll. This demand led to a hostile reaction against the committee, but Orkin, fearing a boycott, went to the Harlem YWCA to obtain a list of light-skinned girls suitable for hiring. When the militants learned of this, they initiated a boycott of the store. Nevertheless, when the injunction was issued in the Beck's case, it also brought the Orkin boycott effectively to an end. By the fall of 1935, it seemed as if the radicals had been defeated.

The lesson that Reed and Kemp took from the defeat was a different one, however. Using the judge's rather contorted reasoning on the injunction as a starting point, they reasoned that if they formed a union they would be exempt from the threat of injunctions and therefore could picket and boycott. In 1936, Kemp obtained a charter for the Harlem Labor Union (HLU). In addition to the League, the roots of the organization also lay in another Harlem black nationalist organization headed by Sufi Abdul Hamid, the so-called "Black Hitler," a familiar figure in Harlem protests for a number of years.

Arthur Reed became the leader and chief strategist for the HLU. Its members aggressively picketed stores along 125th Street. But although the union had essentially been formed to legitimate the boycott activities, the effort expanded to include the unionization of black workers in pawnshops, grocery stores, meat markets, and shoe stores. The leaders of the movement also expanded their vision of the union's role to include not only jobs for African-Americans but also economic power for blacks in their own community, including the eventual development of black-owned businesses.

The plans were short-lived. The HLU ran into the combined opposition of the white business community, the conservative African-American elite, the American Federation of Labor (AFL), the Congress of Industrial Organizations (CIO), and the Communist Party, all of which feared the development of an independent black nationalist force in Harlem. In the end, the major contribution of the HLU to the growth of trade unionism in Harlem was to demonstrate to blacks that unions could be a vehicle to economic and social change. [Ronald L. Filippelli]

FURTHER READING

Bloch, Herman D. "Discrimination Against the Negro in Employment in New York, 1920–1963." *American Journal of Economics and Society*, Vol. 24 (1965), pp. 361–382.

Hunter, Gary J. *"Don't buy where you can't work": Black Urban Boycott Movements during the Depression, 1929–1941.* Ph. D. dissertation, University of Michigan, 1977.

Muraskin, William. "The Harlem Boycott of 1934: Black Nationalism and the Rise of Labor-Union Consciousness," *Labor History*. Vol. 13 (Summer, 1972), pp. 361–373.

o   o   o

HAVERHILL, MASSACHUSETTS, SHOE STRIKE OF 1895. During the wage cuts and general hard times of the depression of 1893, shoeworkers in Essex County, Massachusetts, supported a strike in Haverhill that prompted the organization of a national federation of shoeworkers, the Boot and Shoe Workers' Union (BSWU). This federation united all the disparate elements of nineteenth-century labor activity in the eastern centers of national shoe production. The BSWU drew together the Lasters' Protective Union, the powerful assemblies of the Knights of Labor in Lynn and Marlborough, and the new American Federation of Labor (AFL) affiliates in Haverhill, Brockton, and other shoe cities in New England.

Activity by women shoeworkers on a regional basis also distinguished the strike in Haverhill. The stitchers of Haverhill and Lynn supported the role of Mary A. Nason, who emerged as one of the first women to represent women workers on the executive board of a national union. Her successors, Emma Steghagen and Mary Anderson, used this position in the union's bureaucracy to work in alliance with middle-class women in the Women's Trade Union League after 1903.

In 1895, Haverhill was a city of 30,000 with over 150 shoe factories. Thirty percent of the work force were women who exercised a virtual monopoly over the stitching of shoe uppers. Two-thirds of the female work force were native-born of Yankee, Irish, and French-Canadian backgrounds. The remaining third were immigrants from Quebec or the English provinces of Canada. Many stitchers boarded with families in Haverhill and developed close ties with local residents that proved useful to organize widespread community support for the strike.

The depression forced wage cuts of one-third on Haverhill's shoeworkers. Skilled, native-born shoeworkers, men and women, faced the reality of being no better off than the immigrant textile workers of Lawrence and Lowell. One of the motives of the strikers was to fight the introduction of "mill wages and mill customs" into the shoe factories of New England. The central issue of the strike was the "iron-clad contract" that specified low wage rates for a period of several years and penalized any strike action. The initial targets of these contracts were immigrant male workers of Armenian, Jewish, French-Canadian, and Italian birth. Native-born workers in the Laster's Protective Union and the local affiliates of the AFL feared they would be next, and they struck against the iron-clad contract in late December 1894.

On January 1, 1895, the Haverhill strikers held a giant parade through the streets of the shoe district. Among the 2,000 marchers, the parade featured 400 women stitchers, immigrant men depicted as the innocent victims of the contract system, and the powerful local union of cutters, the most skilled of all shoeworkers. The native-born and immigrants, men and women, and the skilled and unskilled joined together to demonstrate their rejection of low wages and the contract system. After the parade, the strikers listened to speeches of support, including a first-time endorsement of a strike by Frances Willard of the Women's Christian Temperance Union. Willard's connections with Boston social reformers as well as Mary Nason's friendly relationship with Mary Kenney, an organizer for the AFL, enabled the women stitchers of Haverhill to raise funds for the strike and gain favorable publicity in the Boston press.

The activists of the stitchers decided the strike. Local and regional solidarity among women shoeworkers made it extremely difficult for shoe manufacturers to get uppers stitched. Attempts to take the work to other shoe cities in New England provoked angry rejections by women stitchers in Lynn and Newburyport. During the strike, Haverhill stitchers defended their militancy, changed the name of their Ladies' Stitchers' local to the Women Stitchers' Union, and endorsed equal pay for equal work. The union organized its members into shop crews, distributing three to four dollars weekly in strike benefits and meeting every other day during the strike to exchange information. Married stitchers with children received benefits in accordance with the number of their dependents. Frequent parades of 200 to 400 women strikers marched in long skirts and thin boots through streets that were alternatively icy, snowy, slushy, and muddy.

The community of Haverhill, including Protestant clergymen and Catholic priests, defended striking women shoeworkers from charges of prostitution and immorality. The citizens of Haverhill saw the strike as a defense of community standards by respectable New England women who were welcome as boarders in their homes, as stitchers in their factories, and as shoppers in their retail stores.

By the first week of March, the strike funds had been exhausted. On March 10, at the strike committee's recommendation, the remaining strikers voted 239 to 199 to return to work. The stitchers cast the majority of the votes against the motion. The strike committee argued that the strike had been partially successful. The ironclad contract in Haverhill was dead, wage cuts were halted, and 118 factories had signed the agreement to arbitrate a uniform price list.

The stitchers of New England had a new organization that helped to breathe new life into a national convention of shoeworkers held in Boston on April 10. The result was a federation of the major organizations of shoeworkers in New England that linked up with AFL affiliates in the Midwestern cities of Chicago and St. Louis. At this convention Mary Nason was elected to sit on the national executive board of the BSWU. However, the convention rejected an endorsement of Socialist principles advocated by the leaders of the Haverhill group, opting instead for a simple federation of existing groups. The convention chose as president, John F. Tobin of Rochester, a member of the Socialist Labor Party, but refused to accept his ideology and politics. This uneasy coalition of New England organizations, with deep roots in local autonomy and equal rights ideology, and the unions in Midwestern cities whose leaders accepted a high dues policy and a centralized union bureaucracy meant future trouble. By 1897, Mary Nason had been purged from the union's executive board, and her strong support for stitchers' locals controlled by women had been replaced by

BSWU locals of mixed membership. [Mary H. Blewett]

FURTHER READING

Andrews, John B., and W. D. P. Bliss. *History of Women in Trade Unions*. New York: Arno Press, 1974.

Blewett, Mary H. *Men, Women, and Work: Class, Gender, and Protest in the New England Shoe Industry, 1780–1910*. Urbana, IL: University of Illinois Press, 1988.

———. The Union of Sex and Craft in the Haverhill Shoe Strike of 1895." *Labor History*, Vol. 20 (1979), pp. 352–375.

o o o

HAWAII DOCK STRIKE OF 1949. As the contract between Hawaii's Stevedoring Companies and the International Longshoremen's and Warehousemen's Union (ILWU) approached the expiration date of March 1, 1950, it became clear that the main issue of contention would be the union's desire to narrow the gap between ILWU wages for longshoremen on the mainland and those in Hawaii. California longshoremen earned forty-two cents an hour more than their brothers in Hawaii. In an attempt to narrow the gap, the union asked for thirty-two cents an hour or, alternatively, a wage increase set by voluntary arbitration. The employers countered with an offer of eight cents and rejected arbitration outright, dismissing it as "passing the buck" to a third party who had no responsibility for the success or failure of the industry.

Because of the importance of the contract, the union, under the leadership of Jack Hall, president of the Hawaii ILWU, exercised the reopener clause in the existing agreement and negotiations began a year in advance, on January 26. No progress was made, and the strike began at one minute past midnight on Sunday, May 1. The strike occurred in the midst of the cold war anti-communism that marked the end of the 1940s and the beginning years of the 1950s. The ILWU and its leadership, especially International president Harry Bridges, had been attacked as Communist, and the union was one of the ten expelled from the Congress of Industrial Organizations for alleged Communist domination.

The "red baiting" also spread to Hawaii where the ILWU leadership came under attack. Three days after the beginning of the strike a "dear joe" editorial appeared on the front page of the *Advertiser*, the most influential paper in the Islands. It marked the beginning of an attack on the union that lasted throughout the strike. "Dear joe" was Josef Stalin, and the editorials charged that the Hawaii longshoremen were serving Stalin in a plot to destroy Hawaii's economy. The editorials had an effect on public opinion, turning many in the community against the ILWU.

The union also faced a solid wall of hostility from Hawaii's business and professional class. The Bar Association's executive committee asked for a federal investigation to determine whether the strike was a "communist strategy." Newspapers called on the federal government to ship food and supplies to Hawaii on military ships that could dock at Pearl Harbor to avoid the picket lines. The governor of Hawaii appointed an emergency food committee, and while downplaying the effects of the walkout at home, he cabled the Department of the Interior in Washington claiming that he could not exaggerate the disastrous effects that a long continued strike would have.

On the morning of May 31, a new element of pressure was applied to the union. Three hundred women carrying brooms and signs urging the strikers to return to work marched in front of ILWU headquarters. This "broom brigade" marched every day until mid-August, becoming a symbol of the 1949 strike. The union claimed the whole thing was a setup by the employers and that most of the marchers were white middle-class women, some of whom came to the picket line in limousines. Indeed, the tactic was the brainchild of the wife of a dairy executive. Nevertheless, to many in Hawaii, the "broom brigade" marchers became heroines.

By the end of May, the Islands were tightly in the grip of the strike. Shortages were announced daily. Poultrymen had to kill 15,000 chicks because of a lack of feed. Hospitals noted shortages of a whole range of supplies, including bandages and infant food. Even the supply of embalming fluid ran out. Some companies went on a thirty-six-hour workweek, and employees took wage cuts. Sugar piled up on the docks, and the Hawaii Council of Churches prayed for divine intervention to solve the strike. By now the strike had a national audience as papers across the country chronicled the struggle in the Islands. In a particularly lurid account, the *St. Louis Globe-Democrat* told its readers that the strike had forced adults, children, and infants onto vastly reduced rations. Mothers "foraged" for canned milk for their babies while the dock workers held out for higher wages and "Bridges' CIO musclemen" patrolled to see "that none weakens to the cry of humanity." In addition, the employers ran double-page ads in the *New York Times*, the *Washington Post*, and the *Washington Star* blasting the ILWU.

On June 15, the governor appointed a fact-finding board and gave it seven days to come up with recommendations. The board submitted its report on June 28, 1949, the fifty-ninth day of the strike. It recommended that the longshore wage be raised by 14¢—from $1.40 to $1.54 an hour. The employers agreed, but the union rejected it by an overwhelming vote. Had they accepted, the wage gap with the West Coast would have widened. The whole point of the strike had been to narrow it substantially.

After the rejection of the board's recommendations, the union found itself in an even more difficult public opinion position. Harry Bridges later claimed that the ILWU should never have agreed to fact finding in the first place. The result was to give fourteen cents a kind of magical presence. The union was never able to shake that figure.

With shortages mounting and negotiations going nowhere, it was inevitable that someone would try to unload ships using "scab" labor. On July 12, the Hawaii Stevedores Limited began business with rented equipment and plenty of workers willing to work for the union rate of $1.40 an hour. On July 16 strikers confronted their replacements at Pier 29 and it took the police and ninety-six arrests to break up the melee. Four days later, several hundred ILWU strikers and supporters stormed the new company's headquarters. In a short, vicious fight, twenty-four were injured, four of whom required hospitalization. In a more constructive vein, the union signed a contract with eight companies who agreed to pay $1.72 an hour.

On July 26, 1949, the Hawaii legislature convened in special session and passed the Dock Seizure Bill. The bill allowed the government to take over the stevedoring operations and hire workers at pre-strike wages. The ILWU ordered its members not to work for the territory and sent word to the West Coast not to handle or sail ships to or from Hawaii. Nevertheless, in a few days the Territory of Hawaii had signed up 1,765 stevedores, mostly from among the ranks of Hawaii's unemployed, and began operations on August 15. But the union knew that as long as no Hawaii ships would be unloaded in California, the government's strategy would fail. In the final analysis, that was why the ILWU won the 1949 strike.

By September, the strike had become a disaster for everyone. Sugar worth $61 million had piled up on the docks. The longshoremen were also suffering. Public welfare payments to strikers were stopped. Rental and mortgage payments were in default. The pressure on both sides began to bring results. The first inkling of a breakthrough came when Harry Bridges and Dwight Steele, head of the Hawaii Employers Council, began talking in San Francisco. In a series of meetings punctuated by calls to the union and the employers in Hawaii, the two men arrived at a compromise contract package. The settlement came on October 23, 1949, after 177 days. The union and the employers agreed on the fourteen-cents-an-hour increase immediately, eight cents of which would be retroactive to March 1, 1949. Seven cents more an hour was to be added on February 28, 1950. There was to be a one-year extension on the contract to 1951. By the end of the strike some 25,000 people on Oahu, 17 percent of the workforce, were unemployed. Some companies had been forced to cut pay by as much as half. Food prices had climbed by 6.5 percent, and some small businesses had failed. In one estimate, the cost of the strike to the islands was put at $100 million. [Ronald L. Filippelli]

FURTHER READING

Beechert, Edward D. *Working in Hawaii: A Labor History.* Honolulu, HI: University of Hawaii Press, 1985.

Holmes, Thomas. *The Spectre of Communism in Hawaii.* Ph.D. dissertation, University of Hawaii, 1976.

"Settlement of the Hawaiian Longshoremen's Strike." *Monthly Labor Review,* Vol. 69 (1949), pp. 653–656.

Zalburg, Sanford. *A Spark is Struck: Jack Hall and the ILWU in Hawaii.* Honolulu, HI: University of Hawaii Press, 1979.

o   o   o

HERRIN, ILLINOIS, MASSACRE OF 1922. In 1922, the United Mine Workers (UMW), led by John L. Lewis, and the unionized bituminous coal operators entered into a critical round of national negotiations. These negotiations began in the context of a coal industry suffering from overcapacity, the consequence of expanded wartime production, and a union whose bargaining power was reduced from the resultant unemployment. Taking advantage of the oversupply of labor, the operators responded to the union's request for a 20 percent pay increase with a demand for a 25 to 35 percent wage cut. In addition, the industry refused to consider Lewis' proposal for a single interstate agreement that would unify pay scales across the country. Unable to make progress toward an agreement, the UMW embarked on a nationwide strike on April 1, 1922.

The bituminous miners were joined in their strike by 150,000 miners from the anthracite region [see **Anthracite Coal Strike of 1922**] who had been unable to reach a settlement with their respective owners. In addition, 75,000 unorganized miners also joined the strike, swelling the total number of coal workers off the job to over 600,000. Despite the large number of miners involved, the first few months of the 1922 strike were relatively uneventful. This would all change on June 21 and 22 as a result of events in a small Illinois mining town. What transpired on those dates subsequently came to be known as "the Herrin massacre."

In 1922, District 12 of the UMW, encompassing the state of Illinois, was one of the most militant, aggressive, and highly organized districts in the union. Illinois was, reportedly, 100 percent union territory and no operator had dared work his mine during a strike since the turn of the century. The union was, therefore, acting somewhat out of character when it granted William J. Lester, owner of the Southern Illinois Coal Company, permission to operate a small strip mine on the outskirts of Herrin, a UMW stronghold, during the strike. The union apparently acceded to the company's request only on the grounds that any coal dug would not be shipped until after the dispute was settled.

Despite the union's initial assent, tension quickly heightened as the mine near Herrin went into production. Antagonism arose between the UMW and the company when members of a renegade union, the Steam Shovel Workers' Union of Chicago, were imported to work the mine. Expelled by the American Federation of Labor (AFL), the Steam Shovel Union was widely reviled for its previous strikebreaking activities. In addition, it rapidly became clear to local union miners, given the large number of heavily armed guards hired by the company, that the Southern Illinois Coal Company fully intended to put its coal on the market as soon as possible, strike or no strike.

On the afternoon of June 21, following a number of skirmishes between UMW miners and company guards, a striker was killed by a bullet allegedly fired from the long-range rifle of a company guard. The killing touched off a firestorm of hatred and violence that had been smouldering since the appearance of the strikebreakers. Word went out across southern Illinois and beyond calling union miners and their sympathizers to converge on the Lester mine.

By that evening, an angry and armed crowd of nearly one thousand had gathered outside the mine. World War I veterans organized the growing army of union men, and an airplane, hired at a nearby field, supported the attackers by dropping dynamite on the mine headquarters. After a pitched gun battle that lasted until dawn, the steam shovel workers, their guards, and company officials surrendered to the striking miners. Caught up in the emotion of the moment, the union attackers pillaged the mine; destroyed company equipment, including a huge Bucyris steam shovel; and, finally, turned their vengeance on their unfortunate captives. Disarmed and defenseless, the prisoners were brutally assaulted.

The mine superintendent, a reputed union-buster by the name of C. K. "Old Peg" McDowell, was summarily shot by two of the mob. Some tried to escape into nearby woods and were gunned down as they ran. By day's end, a total of nineteen men had died at the hands of the strikers.

Public reaction was quick; the union and its actions in Herrin were denounced from coast to coast. The strike, which had been unusually low-key and uneventful, jumped to the front page of newspapers across the country. Lewis, the object of much condemnation, denied that neither he nor the union had anything to do with the events at Herrin. He deplored the tragedy and attempted, with little success, to shift the blame to "sinister forces," including company guards and Communist agitators.

In the months that followed, 214 men, most of whom were miners, were indicted for murder. In the pro-union communities of southern Illinois, it ultimately proved impossible to convict a hometown UMW miner of the murder of strikebreakers imported from distant cities. In trials that dragged on from October until the following spring, eleven defendants were acquitted by Williamson County juries. Charges against the others were dropped. A special assessment to pay for damaged company equipment and court costs, levied by the members of UMW District 12 against themselves, suggested that the miners did accept some responsibility for the rampage at Herrin. In the end, however, community sentiment absolved the miners of legal culpability.

In addition to costing the union considerable public support beyond the coalfields, the Herrin massacre forced the Harding administration to adopt a more active role in the ongoing negotiations between the UMW and the industry. Despite the President's efforts to mediate the dispute himself, the nationwide strike continued through July and into August.

On August 15, after a strike of eighteen weeks, the union reached agreement with operators in seven states. The key provision of the pact was that the old wage scale would remain in effect through March 31, 1923. Eventually, the union settled on this basis with unionized operators in the remainder of the states on strike. The agreement, while hailed as a victory by Lewis, was met without enthusiasm by the rank and file. The UMW not only failed to achieve its goal of a wage increase and a unified agreement, but the terms of the settlement also prevented the union from making inroads into the non-union coalfields. In retrospect, the 1922 strike and the events at Herrin were one of the darker periods in the history of a proud union. [Paul F. Clark]

FURTHER READING

Coleman, McAlister. *Men and Coal.* New York: Arno & The New York Times, 1929.

Lens, Sidney. *The Labor Wars: From the Molly Maguires to the Sitdowns.* Garden City, NY: Anchor Press/Doubleday, 1974.

o   o   o

HERSHEY, PENNSYLVANIA, CHOCOLATE WORKERS' STRIKE OF 1937. In the midst of the Great Depression of the 1930s, workers throughout the United States formed unions in record numbers as unionism came for the first time to many different workplaces. One of these workplaces was the Hershey Chocolate Factory in Hershey, Pennsylvania. The origin and development of trade unionism in Hershey is a fascinating story with implications for the development of industrial capitalism and the tradition of company-planned mill towns.

In the 1930s, the community of Hershey embodied the personality and goals of its founder Milton S. Hershey. In 1900, Hershey sold his caramel business which generated the revenue needed to purchase 1,000 acres in a rural location near Harrisburg, Pennsylvania. The chocolate maker developed an elaborate plan to build a paternalistic community centered around a chocolate factory. This plan included, in addition to the factory, a bank, a post office, a general store, a department store, a zoo, theaters, golf courses, a dairy, a country club, a convention hall, a community center, a hospital, a rose garden, a bakery, an experimental candy shop, public schools, and a junior college. During the Great Depression, Hershey paid for the construction of the Hotel Hershey, a swimming pool, a fencing hall, a sports arena, a stadium, an office building, and more.

Hershey also set up a school for fatherless boys which became perhaps his most famous charitable endeavor. The Hershey Industrial School was founded in 1909 and was established with a trust fund which consisted of 500,000 shares of common stock of the Hershey Chocolate Corporation—about two-thirds of the company's stock. The Industrial School emphasized manual training and instruction in the useful arts. The boys who attended the school also worked on Hershey's farms which sent milk to the chocolate factory. The endowment given to the boys school was administered by the Hershey Trust Company whose directors were the directors of the various Hershey enterprises. Because of this arrangement the school was the principal beneficiary of the fruits of the activities of the diverse Hershey holdings.

Although Hershey's construction boom deflected some of the most harmful effects of the Great Depression, his attempt to create an industrial utopia was changed in the 1930s by his employees to include worker representation through collective bargaining. The first meetings to form a union in Hershey were held in the winter months of 1936–1937 when secret discussions were held by pro-union employees. By early March 1937, the Congress of

Industrial Organizations (CIO) forces reported that over 1,500 workers had signed union authorization cards calling for representation by Local 2 of the CIO. Local 2 was a local effort based almost exclusively in Hershey, although the CIO was contacted and provided some legal and organizing support.

In the spring of 1937, the Hershey Corporation raised men's wages twelve cents an hour and women's wages seven cents an hour. On March 17, 1937, an agreement was reached that recognized Local 2 as the bargaining agent for its members only and called for layoffs by seniority and for spreading overtime among all shifts. Soon after this agreement was signed the company announced a major layoff which included many Local 2 activists who were not the least senior employees.

At a union meeting on April 1, the members of Local 2 voted to strike the Hershey Corporation the following day. At 11:00 A.M. on April 2, 1937, one of the local leaders walked to a designated spot in the plant, waved a red handkerchief, and the sit-down strike began. Within a short time, between 1,000 and 2,000 workers had stopped working and were occupying the factory. Soon the sound of strikers singing labor songs filled the factory air, a CIO flag was raised on the company's flagpole, and many workers climbed to the roof of the plant for a better view of the activity surrounding their workplace. When a five-hour meeting between company representatives and union representatives produced no movement, the sit-downers prepared to spend their first night in the plant.

The next day a tentative settlement was reached. The company agreed to bargain in good faith and promised not to make chocolate if the 1,500 workers vacated the plant. The evacuation took place, but twenty union members remained in the factory for patrol duty. While picketing continued outside the plant, the union's leaders called for the state police to come to Hershey to prevent disruptions. The union did this because of rumors that farmers, company officials, and others were unhappy with the turn of events, and trouble could flare up at any time.

After several days of fruitless meetings, between 800 and 1,000 employees reoccupied the plant. As the reoccupation took place, the Hershey Corporation created a "Loyal Workers Club" that, on the evening of April 6, organized a "Loyalty" parade of several hundred marchers; Boy Scouts, the Local Drum and Bugle Corp, management personnel, Hershey employees in divisions other than the factory, and others marched along with vehicles from the Hershey Fire Company.

Throughout the day of April 7, rumors swept through the community that corporation officials, farmers, and others planned to enter the plant and evict the sit-downers. During the morning hours of that day the "Loyal Workers Club" held a rally at the ice arena which was followed by a second well-organized parade led by four members of the Hershey American Legion. They marched to the factory where they were greeted by the president of the Hershey Corporation and then returned to the arena.

Local 2 leaders continued to negotiate in an attempt to avoid a confrontation. The company remained steadfast that no negotiations could take place until the plant was evacuated. In the meantime, the anti-union marchers, who had returned to the arena, gathered up bars, pipes, sticks, banners, and clubs, which were made at the Hershey Planing Mill, and once again headed back to the factory. While these events took place, all but 200 sit-downers made arrangements to leave the plant. As many of them were leaving the plant they saw the armed marchers and rushed back into the factory and locked the doors.

Soon the door was unlocked and the marchers stormed into the plant, rounded up the sit-downers, and formed a gauntlet at the factory entrance. Strikers were sent down the gauntlet and beaten with clubs, pipes, blackjacks, and fists as they left the factory. Several sit-downers suffered severe lacerations, bruises to the head, internal bleeding, and other injuries. The most severely beaten were two prominent leaders of Local 2.

On Thursday, April 8, the chocolate factory reopened. Local 2 continued picketing for several days as more and more employees returned to work. Eventually, a back-to-work agreement was signed which called for a five-day, forty-hour workweek (which was required under federal law) and no strikes or lockouts. The company agreed to rehire all employees who were on the payroll on April 1, 1937, which meant that the CIO supporters who had been laid off would not be recalled. Both sides agreed to conduct an National Labor Relations Board (NLRB) election within two weeks to decide whether or not a union should represent Hershey's employees.

The election was held on April 23, 1937. When the ballots were counted, 542 had voted for no union and 781 had voted for the CIO. Six days later, the Loyal Workers Club was renamed the Independent Chocolate Workers Union (ICWU) with the same officers continuing to serve. Six months later, the company recognized the ICWU as the bargaining agent for the workers in the factory. The first contract called for no change in wages, hours, or working conditions, did not provide for a grievance procedure, and stated that the company had the right to terminate employees without appeal.

In July 1937, the CIO filed an unfair labor practice charge with the National Labor Relations Board alleging that Hershey management had dominated and interfered in the formation of a union. In May 1938, the NLRB ruled that the Hershey Corporation had broken the law. In anticipation of the NLRB's decision, the Hershey Corporation on April 23, 1938, had signed a stipulation that it would dissolve the company union and refrain from any further violations of federal law and would in the future allow its employees to choose freely whether or not they wanted to embrace collective bargaining.

Approximately two years from the date of the sit-down strike another collective bargaining election was held in Hershey. This time, the Bakery and Confectionery Workers Union, affiliated with the American Federation of Labor, was selected overwhelmingly to be the bargaining agent for the chocolate workers. Beginning with this second election, the industrial history of Hershey changed forever. After the original confrontation, labor and management, over the years, created and nurtured a mature industrial relationship in which both employees and managers enjoyed representation at the workplace. [Donald Kennedy]

Further Reading

Bongartz, Roy. "The Chocolate Camelot." *American Heritage*, Vol. 24 (June 1973), pp. 5–11, 91–99.

o   o   o

HILO, HAWAII, MASSACRE OF 1938. As on the mainland, the 1920s was a dark decade for organized labor in Hawaii. Between 1921 and 1927, unionization practically disappeared from the Islands. So grim was the situation, that in 1927 the Central Labor Council surrendered its charter to the American Federation of Labor and went out of existence.

The effects of the Great Depression revived the labor movement. The passage of the National Industrial Recovery Act, which gave workers the right to organize and bargain with employers, spurred unionization. Not surprisingly, the longshoremen, who had a long history of struggle, were in the vanguard of the movement.

Interest in Hawaii followed the reorganization of the International Longshoremen's Association (ILA) in San Francisco in 1933.

Experience on the West Coast inspired the organization in the port city of Hilo. Harry Kamoku, a Hawaiian seaman with a strong interest in trade unionism, had witnessed the dramatic 1934 maritime strike in San Francisco. Kamoku returned to the islands and created a Hilo local of the ILA.

Kamoku's local found itself forced to strike almost immediately after its formation. The beating of a longshoreman by a dock foreman led to a walkout by the Hilo local. Surprisingly, the action resulted in an informal agreement with the Hilo Terminal and Transportation Company. In the next several years, the union proved capable of defending its members from unjust firings on several occasions.

The actions of the longshoremen were but one part of a series of strikes and organizing drives by unions during the period. Fear of militant, what most considered, radical unions led to the formation by Hawaiian businessmen of the Industrial Association of Hawaii (IAH). In an investigation of labor relations in the Islands, the National Labor Relations Board (NLRB) labeled the IAH as one part of the coercion and intimidation of unions it found to be commonplace in Hawaii. The NLRB found that the employers' association maintained close ties with local police and Army intelligence.

The NLRB also found that working conditions on the waterfront were characterized by dependence and paternalism. Workers, many of them Asians, toiled under circumstances not far from indentured servitude. Many of the men were hired on a daily basis through the use of the "shape-up" method, whereby a large crowd of longshoremen assembled each day hoping to be selected by the gang foreman. In such a system, the foreman's decision was often based on the paying of bribes and the giving of other favors by the men. Although the appearance of the NLRB in Hawaii did not in itself result in unionization, it did serve notice to the employers that the National Labor Relations Act applied there as well as on the mainland.

In 1937, a bitter intra-union struggle between the president of the ILA, Joe Ryan, an AFL stalwart, and Harry Bridges, head of the West Coast longshoremen, had resulted in a split and the formation by Bridges, an Australian immigrant and a Communist, of the International Longshoremen and Warehousemen's Union (ILWU). All but one of the ILA's Pacific Coast locals followed Bridges into the ILWU. So too did the Hawaii locals.

Harry Kamoku, a strong supporter of Bridges, announced that the ILWU in Hawaii would lead in the formation of the Hilo Industrial Union Council (CIO) to organize the entire community. The so-called "march inland" of the Industrial Union Council resulted not only in attempts to organize the waterfront but also the warehouse and plantation workers. The Hawaiian unionists told the ILWU on the mainland that with organizers from the West Coast and $3,000 they could organize 65,000 workers in agriculture, canneries, and allied industries in six months.

This new labor movement, with its base in the ILWU locals on the Hilo waterfront, moved optimistically to organize all workers on the Islands. They met determined opposition from the employers. Companies gave raises and increased their paternalism. The union suffered several defeats on the Honolulu waterfront. The AFL, still locked in a bitter feud with the CIO, also assisted the employers by issuing a federal union charter to the Hawaiian Waterfront Workers Association (HWWA), a short-lived attempt to split the workers.

Inter-union rivalries also played a role in the events leading up to the Hilo Massacre. Several AFL unions, including the

Sailors Union of the Pacific and the Marine Firemen, challenged the Inland Boatmen's Union (IBU), a CIO affiliate, in an organizing drive at the Inter-Island Steamship Company. Taking advantage of the conflicting claims, the company refused to recognize the IBU, suggesting an NLRB election instead. The union struck on February 4, 1938, with 180 of the 215 seaman joining the strike. The company quickly came to terms and recognized the union. Subsequently, two other CIO unions, the ILWU and the Metal Trades Council, organized portions of the Inter-Island Company. All three unions presented the company with demands that included the closed shop for hiring and comparable pay with the West Coast.

The wage issue was troublesome but not unresolvable. Hawaii employers admitted the pay differential with the mainland, but they argued that it could not be eliminated at once, only over a number of years. The industry's profits in the Islands caused the workers to discount those claims. The union demand for the closed shop, or preferential hiring hall, was the major obstacle. Control over hiring meant union independence and strength. No issue raised the hackles of the employers like this one. With negotiations at an impasse, the three unions walked out on May 26.

On July 22, the Inter-Island Steamer *Waialele*, manned by strikebreakers, arrived at Hilo. Two hundred fifty union supporters met the ship and jeered the crew. The incident nearly escalated to serious violence when a police lieutenant threw a tear gas canister into the crowd. The same ship later arrived at Kauai, where it was met by another hostile crowd of strikers. The ship returned to Hilo on August 1. The sheriff ordered the longshoremen not to interfere with its unloading, but they refused. Nevertheless, union plans called only for a nonviolent mass demonstration and sit-down on the pier.

The sheriff met the crowd, a mixture of Japanese, Hawaiians, whites, Portugese, and Filipinos, as it approached the pier. Soon the demonstration turned ugly. Police began clubbing and firing buckshot and birdshot into the crowd. The demonstrators panicked as they attempted to flee from the police. Fifty-one strikers and sympathizers were wounded, the majority of them shot in the back. One strike leader, Ben Nakano, suffered crippling injuries. Miraculously, no one was killed. After the event, the sheriff justified the actions of his men as an attempt to prevent bloodshed. The violence shocked all parties to the dispute. Negotiations resumed immediately, and by August 13, both the IBU and the ILWU had voted to accepted the company offer.

Simply judged on the economic and union security issues that were at the heart of the dispute, the strike was a failure for the unions. Wage increases did not bring them to parity with the West Coast longshoremen and seaman. The union hiring hall was not achieved. But the strike served other purposes. The date of the Hilo Massacre, August 1, 1938, became a holy day of sorts for Hawaii's trade union movement. The events at Hilo inspired labor militancy for years afterward. They were also a demonstration of the ability of different racial and ethnic groups to work together. In addition, for the first time public opinion, almost always hostile to unionization in the past, turned to some degree in support of the labor movement. [Ronald L. Filippelli]

FURTHER READING

Beechert, Edward D. *Working in Hawaii: A Labor History*. Honolulu, HI: University of Hawaii Press, 1985.

Center for Labor Research. *Hilo Massacre: Hawaii's Bloody Monday, August 1, 1938*. Honolulu, HI: Center for Labor Education and Research, University of Hawaii, 1988.

Schwartz, Harvey. *The March Inland: Origins of the ILWU Warehouse Division 1934–1938*. Los Angeles, CA: Institute of Industrial Relations, UCLA, 1978.

Zalburg, Sanford. *A Spark is Struck: Jack Hall and the ILWU in Hawaii*. Honolulu, HI: University of Hawaii Press, 1979.

o   o   o

HITCHMAN COAL AND COKE COMPANY INJUNCTION. The Individual employment contract, called a "Yellow-Dog" contract by workers, was a device used by anti-union employers to stop union organizing drives. By signing, workers promised as a condition of employment not to join a labor union. Before 1907, no court had been willing to issue an injunction against unions for interfering with these contractual relationships between individual miners and the companies. In 1907, the Hitchman Coal and Coke Company, facing an organizing drive by the United Mine Workers (UMW), sought injunctive relief by arguing that these were valid contracts. The contract signed by all Hitchman miners was typical of those that had been in use since the 1870s when they were first used by the stone manufacturers when combating the Molders' Union. It reads as follows:

I am employed by and work for the Hitchman Coal & Coke Company with the express understanding that I am not a member of the United Mine Workers of America, and will not become so while an employee of the Hitchman Coal & Coke Company; that the Hitchman Coal & Coke Company is run non-union and agrees with me that it will run non-union while I am in its employ. If at any time I am employed by the Hitchman Coal and Coke Company I want to become connected with the United Mine Workers of America, or any affiliated organization, I agree to withdraw from the employment of said company, and agree that while I am in the employ of that company I will not make any efforts amongst its employees to bring about the unionizing of that mine against the company's wish. I have either read the above or heard the said read.

Federal district court judge Alston G. Dayton agreed with the company and issued an injunction. Ten years later the Supreme Court of the United States upheld the Hitchman injunction issued by Dayton.

The UMW had been trying to organize the West Virginia coalfields since 1901 with limited success. In 1906, a brief strike against Hitchman Coal and Coke, located in the state's northern panhandle, failed; but the union came back almost immediately and began another organizing drive. Because the West Virginia mines were non-union, they threatened the union standards in use in the unionized mines of the Central Competitive Field that included Indiana, Illinois, Ohio, and western Pennsylvania. The UMW was aware of the existence of the yellow-dog contracts in use at Hitchman. Nevertheless, many miners agreed to join the union. The plan of the union was to gain the support of a majority of the miners and then call a strike for recognition. When Judge Dayton issued the temporary restraining order preventing the UMW from organizing Hitchman's mines, the order was so sweeping that it forbade union organizers from almost any contact with miners, on or off of company property, including talking to them in their homes. Dayton's ruling was in the mainstream of case law on labor relations in the United States up to that time. Ever since the **Cordwainers' Conspiracy Case** at the beginning of the nineteenth century, American courts had given preeminence to property rights over the rights of labor to organize. To Dayton, like many of his contemporaries on the federal bench, the United Mine Workers was an illegal organization whose actions in pursuit of its interests violated both common law and the Sherman Anti-Trust Act's prohibition of illegal combinations in restraint of trade. He believed that the UMW was at its base a "conspiracy . . . glaringly designed to injure and destroy" the company.

Dayton's ruling was destined to have major implications for organized labor until the 1930s. By making it illegal to attempt to organize workers who had signed individual employment contracts, the court had put an almost unbreachable obstacle in the path of trade unions. The circuit court of appeals overturned Dayton's ruling in 1914, arguing that the individual employment contracts indeed did not merit injunctive support since workers could leave employment at will or be discharged at will, they were not contracts at all. Nor did Judge Jetter C. Pritchard believe that the UMW was a monopoly in restraint of trade and thus in violation of the Sherman Anti-Trust Act. He rejected Dayton's argument that the purpose of the union was to injure the company, arguing that to destroy the business would "defeat the very object for which this organization was established, to wit, the procurement of steady employment at remunerative wages."

Seven years had passed between the Dayton and Pritchard rulings. During that time "yellow-dog" contracts were legal in West Virginia. Not surprisingly, they were widely adopted by the state's coal companies, and the UMW organizing effort made little headway. The companies immediately appealed Pritchard's decision to the United States Supreme Court. On December 10, 1917, the Court upheld part of Pritchard's ruling, that the UMW was a legal organization, rejecting Dayton's argument that the union was in itself a violation of common law and the Sherman Anti-Trust Act. However, more significantly, the Supreme Court overturned the circuit court of appeals ruling that disallowed Dayton's injunction. The Court held that the equity power of the judiciary could be used to enforce agreements in which workers agreed not to join a union as a condition of employment. The Supreme Court thus sanctioned the use of individual employment contracts on a large scale. Unions could now be enjoined for interfering with the contractual relationship between workers and employers. No other single measure could exceed the effectiveness of a yellow-dog contract when enforced by an injunction in stopping a union organizing drive.

The decision had profound implications for all American unions, but the worst effects of the ruling were postponed by American entry into the war. Government policy aimed at uninterrupted production for the war effort temporarily prevented coal operators from using individual employment contracts. But immediately after the war many coal companies, particularly in West Virginia, Tennessee, and Kentucky, introduced the contracts. In September of 1920, the Red Jacket Coal Company, the target of an organizing drive by the UMW, sued for an injunction to stop the union from trying to persuade its workers to sign with the union and thus, break their contracts with the company. Red Jacket was later joined in the case by 315 other West Virginia coal operators. The United States District Court, citing the Hitchman case but going beyond in its remedy, issued a permanent injunction. The union appealed, but the circuit court of appeals upheld the district court. The union appealed again to the Supreme Court, but the highest court declined to hear the case, thus making the Red Jacket ruling law. Not until the passage of the Norris-LaGuardia Act in 1932 were yellow-dog contracts declared unenforceable in any federal court in the United States. In this manner the architects of Norris-LaGuardia nullified the effect of the Hitchman decision. But in the fifteen years between 1917 and 1932, yellow-dog contracts were an important tactic used by employers to drive the labor movement in the United States to near extinction. In addition to the mines, they were widely used in the shoe, glass, full-fashioned hosiery, clothing, metal trades, and commercial printing industries. [Ronald L. Filippelli]

FURTHER READING

Lunt, Richard. *Law and Order vs. the Miners.* Hamden, CT: Archon Books, 1979.

Taylor, Benjamin, and Fred Witney. *Labor Relations Law.* Englewood Cliffs, NJ: Prentice-Hall, 1971.

o   o   o

HOMESTEAD STRIKE OF 1892. In 1892, the Homestead Steel Mill, located on the Monongahela River near Pittsburgh, Pennsylvania, witnessed one of the most violent and protracted labor conflicts in late-nineteenth-century America. The conflict pitted the Amalgamated Association of Iron, Steel, and Tin Workers, the largest and strongest trade union in the recently organized American Federation of Labor (AFL), against the Carnegie Steel Company, one of the most powerful companies in the United States. The Homestead Strike was among the most sensational in a long series of violent strikes between organized labor and business. Through these strikes, workers responded to American industrial changes in which factories, structured along traditional craft lines requiring many highly skilled workers, began shifting to huge mechanized plants with large numbers of easily replaceable unskilled workers. The Amalgamated's defeat at Homestead illustrated the larger inability of craft unions to respond successfully to the mass production process and set the pattern for the continued loss of power experienced by increasingly dispensable skilled workers.

Intense competition characterized the steel industry in the late nineteenth century, and manufacturers sought to economize in order to survive. Increasingly, companies built larger plants, integrating the stages of steelmaking into a continuous process. Huge machines operating on an immense scale also speeded up production. Most importantly, mechanization lowered production costs and eliminated many highly skilled positions.

However, increased mechanization failed to improve working conditions. Although machines now performed some of the more dangerous jobs, many arduous and risky manual tasks remained. With very high temperatures of volatile materials, and an airspace polluted by poisonous fumes, steel mills continued to be extremely dangerous places. In addition, steelworkers labored at a punishing pace.

Andrew Carnegie acquired the Homestead plant in 1882 and immediately applied the economizing principles that he had pioneered. Carnegie's success in economizing, which had already made him immensely powerful, originated in his ability to maintain growth while simultaneously and unrelentingly lowering costs, particularly labor costs. He measured his success in terms of cost, not profit, and directed much of his economizing drive against trade unions. Even though Carnegie espoused the rights of workingmen, he resented work rules, wage and hour demands, and strikes. At Homestead, the Amalgamated prevented Carnegie from having complete control over labor costs, therefore he determined that the union would have to go.

The company paid steelworkers on a tonnage basis, so that wages rose and fell with the rate of production. Since the Amalgamated agreed that mechanization increased steel output, it acquiesced in rate cuts. However, it insisted on a share of the benefits, arguing that mechanization made for harder work, fewer delays, and faster operations. But as production rose and increased mechanization reduced the workers' necessary level of skill, the company determined to cut wage rates and lengthen work hours. The company argued that labor costs and higher profits were separate issues, and in contrast to the union, contended that mechanization provided for lighter workloads.

In 1889, Carnegie attempted to institute a 25 percent wage cut, negotiate individual contracts, and effectively end collective bargaining. Mass picketing and the threat of sympathy strikes forced the company to back down, continue its recognition of the Amalgamated, and sign a three-year contract. Although the union touted its success, the workers accepted substantial cuts in income in their new contract, signaling their weakening position.

The Amalgamated's membership grew substantially in the years between 1889 and 1892. In 1891, the Amalgamated had over 24,000 members, approximately two-thirds of those skilled workers in the country eligible for union membership. Out of 3,800 Homestead workers, 750 were union members. However, the union's members were precisely those skilled workers most susceptible to job loss due to mechanization. The compromise position taken by the Amalgamated during the 1889 strike indicated to Carnegie that he could eliminate the union.

With this aim, Carnegie Steel deliberately provoked the strike of 1892. The 1889 contract was due to expire on June 30, 1892. On April 4, 1892, Carnegie wrote to the chairman of the steel company, Henry C. Frick, that Homestead must become non-union after the contract expired. Ruthlessly anti-union, Frick eagerly accepted his instructions, while Carnegie extended his European vacation to avoid a potentially unpleasant situation.

Carnegie's position was difficult. Reflecting a concern for the welfare of the American worker, his public posture differed from his relentless pursuit of profits. He had published more than one essay in which he defended workers' right to organize, and sympathized with workers' hostility to strikebreakers. In 1892, however, he quickly seized the opportunity to eliminate the Amalgamated from Homestead. Although Frick handled the actual events, Carnegie fully supported Frick's efforts, and the two men corresponded throughout the strike.

Frick planned to expel the Amalgamated on the pretext that most Homestead workers were non-union, and therefore the majority must rule. He also prepared for an anticipated strike by increasing production and by constructing a heavy, twelve-foot-high wooden stockade with rifle holes. Topped with barbed wire, the fence surrounded the steel works on all sides down to the river's edge. Previously, the plant was integrated into the town of Homestead, open on all sides and easily entered by workers.

In April 1892, Frick presented his demands to the union: a wage cut averaging 22 percent which targeted the most highly skilled and the least skilled workers; a shift from wages based on a sliding scale of steel's market price to wages totally divorced from productivity; and a change in the termination date of the current contract, from June 30 to January 1, 1894. Frick gave the union until June 24 to accept; otherwise, the company would withdraw recognition and only negotiate individual contracts. Expecting further negotiation, the union rejected this offer. However, on June 29, before the contract expired, the company shut down the mill, locking out the steel workers. By July 2, it had laid off the entire work force.

Anticipating a strike, local union leaders had organized an advisory committee to coordinate the workers' response. The committee met with union and non-union workers on June 30. Despite divisions, particularly between the skilled and the largely immigrant unskilled workers, the entire work force united to defend themselves. Even though the Amalgamated did not represent them, the unskilled workers recognized that with no union at Homestead the company would completely control all wages and working conditions.

Foreseeing the possibility of strikebreakers, the advisory committee mobilized the entire work force to provide a twenty-four-hour watch over the plant and town.

The committee organized workers into shifts to picket the plant, meet incoming trains and riverboats, and patrol the roads leading into town as well as the river bordering it. It also set up a communication system to warn the strikers if the company attempted to reoccupy the vacated plant.

Because steelworkers dominated local politics, power during the strike easily transferred from the town council to the advisory committee. Homestead's mayor was a member of the advisory committee, and many other town officials, including the police chief, were union members as well. The committee directed essential town services, issued laws, and generally maintained order. It provided journalists with badges and expelled anyone who reported false information. Eleven Allegheny County sheriff's deputies arrived to occupy the plant, but the strikers escorted them back to Pittsburgh. When the sheriff refused to deputize strikers, the committee decided to accept sheriff's deputies at the plant. But Allegheny County residents strongly supported the union, so that the sheriff failed to raise enough deputies.

Unable to mobilize local authorities, and unwilling to negotiate with the strikers, the company took direct action. On July 6, a steamer towed two barges carrying 300 Pinkerton guards up the Monongahela River toward Homestead. In spite of elaborate security, the strikers learned of the barges' approach and met them with a small flotilla of boats. In addition, a crowd of strikers and townspeople along the riverbank followed the barges upriver. When the crowd saw the Pinkertons prepare to land at the mill, it broke down the fence around the works, and gathered at the dock. Several hundred of the strikers carried firearms.

From the barge, Captain Heinde, the Pinkertons' leader, announced that they had arrived to take over the plant. Armed with rifles, several Pinkertons started to disembark. Following a shot at the first guard down the gangplank, a volley at the men on the barge killed one Pinkerton and wounded five. The guards returned the fire, shooting indiscriminately into the crowd of men, women, and children onshore. At least three people were killed and over thirty wounded. The gunfire lasted several minutes before the Pinkertons retreated below decks. Shortly afterwards, the steamer left, leaving the remaining Pinkertons helplessly trapped on the barges.

The battle continued for the rest of the day. On the riverbank, the crowd grew as supporters from nearby towns joined the strikers. They erected barricades near the water's edge to fire on the barges and to protect themselves. The guards and men onshore exchanged sporadic gunfire, while others attempted to force the Pinkertons from the barges. Small boats filled the river, firing guns and throwing sticks of dynamite onto the heavy barges, which were damaged but did not sink. Some individuals set fire to a flatcar and pushed it down rails toward the water, but the car was unable to reach it. The crowd also directed oil and natural gas lines at the barges and set the lines on fire, but with no effect.

Meanwhile on the barges, the guards threatened mutiny. Most were not regular Pinkertons but unemployed workers and students who thought they were to perform unarmed guard duty. By the late afternoon, crammed below decks in the sweltering July heat, they gratefully accepted the advisory committee's terms of surrender. Once the Pinkertons surrendered, the advisory committee had to control the angry and vengeful riverside crowd. The crowd burned the barges and attacked the disarmed guards as they were marched into town, injuring all of them.

By the end of the day, casualties were heavy: seven Pinkertons dead, twenty wounded, and among the strikers and townspeople, at least forty wounded and nine dead.

The news of violence spread rapidly across the country. Outraged by Carnegie Steel's use of armed Pinkertons against the strikers and townspeople, a group of New York anarchists, including Alexander Berkman and Emma Goldman, formed a plan to assassinate Frick. On July 23, Berkman made his way into Frick's Pittsburgh office and shot and then stabbed him. Berkman's aim was poor and he only succeeded in wounding Frick before he was overwhelmed and arrested. While Berkman's response was extreme, the violence at Homestead greatly alarmed those sympathetic to both sides.

Although Carnegie Steel issued press statements that because of the battle they would never again negotiate with either the Amalgamated or any other labor organization, the advisory committee continued to occupy the steel mill, as well as run the town. Since the situation at Homestead was temporarily peaceful, Pennsylvania governor Pattison resisted pressure from both the sheriff and the company to call out the state militia to control the town. Finally, however, possibly concerned by the strikers' successful experiment in self-government, the governor ordered the Pennsylvania National Guard to take over the town. On July 12, over 8,000 well-armed troops marched into Homestead.

The advisory committee had convinced the strikers to welcome the troops as neutral representatives of the law who would protect them from the company's private armies. However, the troops' commander, General George Snowden, quickly showed his antipathy toward the strikers. The Guard encamped on high ground, as if surrounding enemy territory, and General Snowden prohibited his men from fraternizing with workers or townspeople. Under Guard protection the company reoccupied the plant and brought in groups of strikebreakers to resume production. The company built accommodations within the mill to isolate the strikebreakers from the town. The strikers picketed the plant, but troops prevented them from entering it.

Although Homestead resumed operations, the company had difficulty in recruiting strikebreakers, and production remained greatly reduced. Often recruitment agents told strikebreakers they were being hired to work at another Carnegie plant and then brought them to Homestead against their will. Once there, they were kept under guard and forced to remain in the plant. Frick offered to rehire the Homestead workers, but they unanimously rejected his offer. Nevertheless, Frick believed Carnegie Steel could outlast the strikers. Not only were the company's resources immense, but the non-union Braddock and Duquesne plants maintained full production throughout the strike.

Heartened by a nationwide display of support, the strikers prepared to hold out in order to force the company to recognize their union and negotiate. Amalgamated members at other Carnegie plants struck in sympathy, realizing that should the Homestead workers fail, the company would attempt to eliminate the union from all its plants. The AFL provided limited support by picketing labor recruitment agencies in several cities. The strikers' primary hope was that their value to the company, based on their skills and experience, would cause the company to acquiesce. However, the strikers failed to realize how reduced the value of their labor had become; the company would rehire them only on its own terms.

In an effort to undermine the strikers' solidarity, the company instituted legal action. Seven members of the advisory committee were charged with the murder of a Pinkerton guard, and many other strikers were charged with lesser crimes. As soon as the accused were acquitted, they were re-arrested and through a little used law, charged with treason against the state of Pennsylvania. Although no Homestead striker was found guilty of any charges, the time, energy, and money required to fight the accusations drained the union's strength and weakened the strikers' morale. The union's counter-charges against Carnegie Steel and the Pinkertons further reduced the union's limited funds, while the company had little difficulty in financing bail and legal advice.

As winter approached and the strike wore on, the townspeople began to feel its effects. The company evicted workers and their families from company-owned housing, and stocks of food and supplies were depleted. Throughout the strike, the steelworkers operated independently and received limited backing but no active support from the Amalgamated leadership and the AFL. In October, the advisory committee appealed to the AFL for help in procuring food, clothing, and shoes for the strikers and their families. It also requested a boycott of Carnegie Steel. The AFL refused the boycott proposal but did designate December 13, 1892, as "Homestead Day," asking all their membership on that day to set aside a portion of their pay to provide a contribution to the Homestead workers. Unfortunately this show of AFL support came only after the company began to restore production at Homestead.

On November 18, the unskilled workers met at Homestead and voted to request that the Amalgamated end the strike. The union voted not to give in but released the non-union strikers from any obligation to continue striking. The next day, the mechanics and day laborers lined up at the steel mill asking for their old jobs back. The company hired several, telling the others that their jobs were filled. On November 20, at a poorly attended union meeting, a close vote determined that the workers would call off the strike and return to work. Again, the company chose a number of former workers at greatly reduced wages, but refused to rehire many

others. All the rehired workers signed individual contracts with Carnegie Steel; the union disappeared from Homestead.

After four and a half months, the Homestead strike ended. The Amalgamated Association of Iron, Steel, and Tin Workers, once the most powerful union in the country, was defeated. Following the 1892 strike, not a single Carnegie steel mill was unionized, and by 1903, all the major steel plants in the country eliminated the Amalgamated. Carnegie Steel continued to profit considerably after the Homestead strike. Unopposed in its economizing drive, the company reduced its work force by approximately one-fourth by 1897. In 1893 alone, the company reduced wages in the steel mills by an average of 25 percent. With union work rules no longer in force, the hours of skilled workers rose from eight to twelve per day.

Workers had shown great solidarity during the strike. Both skilled and unskilled had united against a common enemy in order to ensure the survival of the union. The town of Homestead also demonstrated its support for the strikers. Across the country a groundswell of support for the strikers, and a sense of identification with them, served to lay the groundwork for the **Pullman Strike and Boycott of 1894.** However, the decisive defeat left a mood of despair at Homestead.

The Carnegie Steel Company, with its immense resources, and with the aid of state troops, was able to crush a strike even as determined as that of the steelworkers. Although the unskilled workers joined with the skilled workers after being locked out from Homestead, by continuing to exclude the unskilled from membership, trade unions seriously weakened their ability to counter the strength of large modern companies such as Carnegie Steel. This was especially evident at a time of greater mechanization, in which the skilled workers became as expendable as the unskilled.

The 1890s was a decade marked by accelerated industrial growth and violent labor conflict. The erosion of power experienced by skilled steelworkers was paralleled in other industries as mechanization increased. Metal and coal miners struggled for union recognition, and with the steady influx of immigrant labor, urban sweatshops proliferated. Industrial leaders ruthlessly crushed workers' efforts to organize. Most workers were unable to support their families, leading to widespread poverty. The depression beginning in 1893 further increased workers' difficulties, as their wages were cut, and some 3 million were thrown out of work. By the end of the decade, workers found themselves laboring longer hours for less pay with little job security. Nationwide, trade unions had only about 350,000 members, leaving the vast majority of workers without any representation. The Homestead Strike exemplified the labor defeats of the 1890s, and demonstrated the inability of trade unions to counter the increasingly concentrated power of industry. Workers would not make significant gains until labor organizations included the mass of industrial workers, cutting across lines of skills, race, and gender. [Marie Bolton]

Further Reading

Brody, David. *Steelworkers in America: The Nonunion Era.* Boston, MA: Harvard University Press, 1960.

Foner, Philip S. *History of the Labor Movement in the United States: From the Founding of the American Federation of Labor to the Emergence of American Imperialism,* Vol. 2. New York: International Publishers, 1955.

Schneider, Linda. "The Citizen Striker: Workers' Ideology in the Homestead Strike of 1892." *Labor History,* Vol. 23 (Winter, 1982), pp. 47–66.

Wolff, Leon. *Lockout: The Story of the Homestead Strike of 1892: A Study of Violence, Unionism, and the Carnegie Steel Empire.* New York: Harper & Row, 1965.

o   o   o

HORMEL, IOWA, STRIKE OF 1933. In the spring of 1933 a group of workers at the George A. Hormel & Company packinghouse in Austin, Minnesota, began to form a union. The move was an indication of how relations between Hormel workers and management had deteriorated as a result of the effects of the Great Depression, changes in Hormel management, and bad marketing decisions.

Hormel had avoided unionization before 1933 largely because of the company's paternalistic management practices—the legacy of the company's founder, George A. Hormel, who described himself as a "benevolent dictator." Hormel, who had worked himself up from the slaughterhouse floor, had maintained good relations with his workers, and within the bounds of his paternalism, treated them with respect and affection. Hormel's son Jay was not able to maintain these practices in a company grown large and complex that faced severe competition and all of the pressures presented by the Depression.

The loss of the close personal contact between management and labor that had characterized the company and the community of Austin in the old days only accentuated the negative side of paternalism. These included the lack of overtime pay, rampant favoritism in the granting of wage increases, no seniority system, and the dictatorial power of the foremen.

Sentiment for unionization found its leader in Frank Ellis, who was part Cherokee Indian and had worked in packinghouses since the age of eight. Ellis had union experience, having participated in the nationwide packinghouse strike of 1904. His disappointment with the American Federation of Labor led him to the Industrial Workers of the World (IWW), the legendary anarcho-syndicalist "Wobblies." Along with a number of other IWW members, Ellis had been jailed under a Nebraska criminal syndicalist law for opposing American entry into World War I. This along with assorted beatings at the hands of the police and company guards gave him impeccable radical credentials. When the flame of unionism flared at Hormel, Frank Ellis was well qualified to fan it into a blaze.

Ironically, the incident that set off the unionization drive was an attempt by Jay Hormel to institute a work-sharing program to reduce labor turnover at Hormel during the Depression. The scheme called for reducing the work hours of all employees to reduce the need to lay anyone off. Those who were laid off were to be supported by a voluntary tax on those working. These donations would be used to buy coal and groceries for the unemployed. To Hormel's surprise, workers didn't respond favorably to the plan. When coupled with an industrywide reduction in wages, many were angry at the further loss in take-home pay, seeing it as a "share the misery" plan. Others resented the arbitrary way that it was presented by the foremen whose power over the workers made its acceptance anything but voluntary.

On Thursday, July 13, 1933, workers temporarily shut down the killing floor when a supervisor coerced a worker into signing up for the insurance program. The action had been planned in advance by Ellis and other radical unionists. News of the shutdown led to a mass meeting of workers that evening. Ellis took the lead, suggesting that what was needed was a union of all the workers in Austin, not just those at Hormel. Six hundred workers paid one dollar to sign up for the as yet nonexistent union.

Hormel management was aware of these events. Jay Hormel, trying to keep the movement within the confines of the company's paternalistic tradition, offered a union meeting hall on company property. But Ellis refused the offer. Instead, Ellis and his leadership cadre formed a union for all Austin workers, the Independent Union of All Workers (IUAW), patterned on the IWW's syndicalist philosophy of "one big union." The union received an enthusiastic response from workers across the town, with everyone from waitresses to farmers signing up. The initiation fees provided sufficient funds for Ellis to leave his job at Hormel and devote full time to affairs of the IUAW.

By fall, the union had grown strong enough to take on the Hormel Company, the key to the success of unionization in Austin. After a series of hurried negotiations with the company broke down, Hormel locked the workers out on September 24. The event galvanized the negotiators and on that morning, an agreement between the IUAW and Hormel was signed granting recognition to the union. It also included seniority in principle and the arbitration of grievances.

Having won the first round, the IUAW waited only two weeks to follow up on its victory. Demands for a twenty cents an hour pay increase and other matters were sent to the company. The company balked, pointing out that prices were set in the marketplace and that costs of production had to be kept in line with industrywide costs for Hormel to remain competitive. At this point, confusion born of inexperience entered the equation. Ellis took a strike vote to pressure the company to arbitrate the twenty-cent demand. He got an overwhelming majority, but some workers, misinterpreting what had happened, rushed to the plant and called the night shift out, telling them that the strike was on. Soon the plant was shut down and workers were setting up picket lines. Faced with a *fait accompli*, union leaders called a strike. The next day, when rumors spread that non-union men were inside the plant slaughtering sheep, strike leaders lost control again. The strikers smashed the gates, invaded the plant, beat up non-union workers, and roughed up and evicted Jay Hormel and other company executives. At the end of the rampage the strikers were in complete control of access to the plant, although they did not occupy the plant as some historical accounts have claimed.

Hormel, who up to this point had been conciliatory toward the union, now began to make preparations to break the strike. He threatened to close the plant and move from Austin, and at the same time he began to recruit strikebreakers in Minneapolis. In the meantime, the sheriff appealed to the pro-labor, farmer-labor governor, Floyd B. Olson, to send in the state militia. Olson refused to send troops, but he did secretly mobilize three hundred guardsmen and put them on alert. Olson then sent a representative, Frank T. Starkey of the State Industrial Commission, and offered to come to Austin himself if necessary.

In fact, after Starkey failed to arrange a settlement, Olson did come to Austin to assess the situation. His presence was not welcomed by Hormel, who hated the liberal governor and had campaigned hard against his election. When the governor arrived, Hormel told Olson that the strike had been caused by "outside agitators." Nevertheless, Olson's mediation of the dispute did lead to a tentative agreement. The State Industrial Commission was to draw up a code of conduct for regulations and rulings between the company and its employees and both parties were to agree to accept the decision of the commission on controversial issues. For its part, the union demanded that in return for turning the plant back to management, all strikers would be rehired without discrimination. After receiving assurances from Olson that the Industrial Commission would be fair, the union members voted overwhelmingly for the contract.

As a result of the decisions of the Industrial Commission workers at Hormel received increases of from two to four cents per hour and a 10 percent increase in piecework rates. The amounts fell far short of the twenty cents per hour the union had demanded. The commission also instituted a grievance procedure. The union's big victory came in prestige. In succeeding years, through the use of several sit-down strikes, the IUAW achieved the closed shop. In May 1937, the IUAW agreed to affiliate with the CIO and became part of the United Packinghouse Workers of America.

For his part, Jay Hormel accepted the new order with equanimity and became a model employer. His popularity and the popularity of the company increased markedly among the workers. The son of the founder had finally achieved the popularity his father had enjoyed. The company moved into an era of industrial peace that lasted for half a century. [Ronald L. Filippelli]

FURTHER READING

Blum, Fred H. *Toward A Democratic Work Process: The Hormel Packinghouse Workers Experiment.* New York: Harper, 1954.

Brody, David. *The Butcher Workmen: A Study of Unionization* Cambridge, MA: Harvard University Press, 1964.

Engelman, Larry D. "We Were the Poor People: The Hormel Strike of 1933." *Labor History,* Vol. 15, No. 4 (Fall, 1974), pp. 483–510.

o   o   o

HORMEL STRIKE OF 1985–1986. The Hormel Strike of 1985–1986 was one of the most bitter and controversial labor conflicts of the 1980s. The strike began with the refusal of one United Food and Commercial Workers local—P-9 of Austin, Minnesota—to join in concession bargaining in the meat-packing industry. As P-9 reached out to trade unionists across the country for support in its boycott of George A. Hormel Company meat products, the strike became a national symbol of insurgent labor militance. But the United Food and Commercial Workers' Union (UFCW) opposed P-9's stance as ill-conceived and hopeless. Without international backing, the strike was defeated. As the strikers went down to defeat, the resulting name-calling and recriminations proved an embarrassment to the entire labor movement.

P-9's tragedy took place in the context of deteriorating union bargaining power in the meat-packing industry. In the early 1980s, non-union packing companies—led by Iowa Beef—gained substantial market shares. In addition, Wilson Foods declared bankruptcy and scrapped its union contracts, while Swift and Company sold off many of its plants that were shut down, and then opened new plants with non-union shops. The low wages nonunion firms paid their employees put unionized firms at a competitive disadvantage; by 1983, union packers were demanding—and gaining—wage concessions from plants represented by the UFCW. Whereas the industrywide pattern wage was $10.69 in 1982, by 1984, some locals had signed concession contracts for as little as $6.25 per hour.

The UFCW found itself in a difficult position, especially since the union was the product of a recent merger (1979), and most of the International's leadership came from a union tradition—the retail clerks—that had little in common with the meat-packing industry. To counteract the trend toward ever-lower wage rates in meat-packing, the UFCW, led by Lewie Anderson, head of the meat-packing division, decided on a strategy of establishing a new industry wage standard, lower than the previous level, and then working to bring wages up gradually.

Although Hormel was a large and profitable company, number 240 on the Fortune 500 list, it demanded wage concessions in line with those its rivals were receiving. In 1984, the International negotiated an agreement covering six Hormel plants that provided for a wage rate of nine dollars per hour in 1984, with an increase

to ten dollars the following year. Local P-9 refused to join in this negotiation, and though the local executive committee voted to accept the settlement, the membership voted it down.

Local P-9 represented meatcutters at Hormel's flagship plant in Austin, Minnesota. Hormel had long been the town's leading employer, playing a paternalistic role in community affairs, and practicing a similar style of labor relations. But during the Depression, when Hormel's paternalism wore thin, a group of veterans of the Industrial Workers of the World (IWW) organized the plant. For fifty years thereafter, labor peace prevailed in Austin, as the union negotiated a series of contracts that gave Hormel meatcutters the same wages and benefits contained in the industry's pattern settlements.

In 1978, Hormel management threatened to close down its Austin operation and shift all its meatpacking to its other plants, unless P-9 agreed to make concessions. P-9 agreed to an eight-year contract which increased production quotas and established a lower wage scale for new workers in return for Hormel's agreement to build a state-of-the-art pork slaughtering and packing plant in Austin.

When the company came back in 1984, demanding additional concessions at Austin and its other plants, P-9 ignored the International's advice and refused to participate in negotiations. P-9 leaders believed that the clause in its 1978 agreement that tied Hormel wages to the industry standard was only intended to raise wages, not to lower them. When Hormel acted on its threat to cut wages, P-9 presented its case in arbitration, but the arbitrator ruled in favor of the company, ordering P-9 wages to be cut on the ground that the "me-too" clause in the 1978 contract obligated the local to make concessions if Hormel's competitors succeeded in gaining wage cuts in their labor contracts. The arbitrator also ordered P-9 members to return part of their wages to the company as a back-pay award. The stage was set for dramatic conflict.

In December of 1984, Local P-9 decided to wage a corporate campaign against Hormel as a way of forcing the company to rescind the wage cuts it had unilaterally imposed. For help in organizing its campaign, the local turned to Corporate Campaign, Inc., headed by Ray Rogers, who had devised a corporate campaign strategy for the Amalgamated Clothing and Textile Workers in the mid-1970s as part of the campaign to organize J. P. Stevens.

P-9's corporate campaign against Hormel centered on the company's financial link to First Bank System, Inc. of Minnesota, a large bank holding company that owned 16.4 percent of the meatpacker's stock and often directed the firm's borrowing. For eight months, Local P-9 members engaged in a variety of activities to call attention to the bank's ties to Hormel, but the union could not call for a boycott of the bank, because the Taft-Hartley Act of 1947 prohibited secondary boycotts of this sort. Although Rogers had had success with similar corporate campaigns in the past, First Bank showed few signs of feeling pressure from P-9, in part because First Bank had a broad deposit base composed of 152 banks scattered through five states. By the time Hormel's contract with P-9 expired in August 1984, both sides were determined to have a strike.

The UFCW was displeased with P-9's decision to call in Rogers and even less pleased with the local's decision to strike Hormel. By the summer of 1984, national union leaders argued that the company was paying meatpackers at its six other plants just 69¢ less than the $10.69 that P-9 was demanding. In addition, fearing a strike's divisive effect, the International pressured P-9 to accept a mediator's proposed settlement.

For several weeks, union picketers succeeded in keeping strikebreakers out of the plant, though Hormel did succeed in contracting some work out, and shifting production to its other plants. But the Austin plant resumed operations with strikebreakers in January 1986, after Minnesota governor Rudy Perpich sent in the National Guard. Hormel hired 550 replacement workers from distressed Midwestern packing towns; another 550 former employees were soon crossing picket lines, giving the company a full complement of labor.

With Hormel's Austin plant back in operation, Local P-9, led by its president, Jim Guyette, began sending roving pickets to other Hormel plants, asking meatcutters there to join the battle. At Ottumwa, Iowa, 400 workers who refused to cross P-9's picket line were quickly fired.

To reinforce the picket lines, Ray Rogers began working full-time for P-9, intensifying a corporate campaign against Hormel and First Bank and pressing a national boycott of Hormel meat products.

In March, after P-9 members, in a close vote, passed a resolution calling on the local's executive board to soften its bargaining position and mend fences with the International leadership, President William Wynn withdrew strike authorization. Wynn called a halt to all picketing and boycott activities and cut off strike benefits to P-9 members. Furthermore, the UFCW asked trade unionists throughout the country not to give support to the Austin strikers.

Nevertheless, hundreds of Local P-9 members continued to tour packing towns throughout the country, raising the banner of union solidarity against concession bargaining. The Reverend Jesse Jackson, the black political leader, came to Austin in April, bringing national attention to P-9's struggle. Despite the fact the AFL-CIO Executive Board urged trade unionists to stay out of the battle, hundreds of local unions sent over $1 million to support the strikers. Eleven hundred local unions throughout the country "adopted" 600 families of Hormel strikers.

Back in Austin, the situation deteriorated. As meatcutters deserted the union to return to their jobs, lifelong friends became mortal enemies, and even families were torn apart. The town of Austin itself divided into hostile camps. As conditions went from bad to worse, UFCW president William Wynn and Lewie Anderson denounced Jim Guyette and Ray Rogers for precipitating the debacle, and the latter responded with harsh words about "misleaders" and "sell-outs."

Finally, in March 1986, the UFCW's leadership declared the strike a lost cause; when P-9 leaders refused to call off the strike, the local was taken over by the international office of the UFCW and placed under trusteeship, an action upheld by the courts.

The strikers' response to the trusteeship was to organize in July 1986, the National American Meatpackers Union (NAMU), which claimed jurisdiction in the meat-packing industry. NAMU began picketing P-9 meetings in Austin while calling for dissident locals throughout the industry to leave the International.

One month later, the UFCW negotiated a settlement with Hormel for six meatpacking plants, including Austin. The money terms of the agreement followed those approved at Oscar Mayer's Madison, Wisconsin, plant. It provided for a seventy cent hourly wage increase (to $10.70) for the unionists who crossed the picket line in January, giving them one cent more than P-9 had been demanding. The replacement workers, who had been given only $8.00 an hour at the start of the strike, received increases that would raise them to $10.70 by the end of the four-year agreement. Those who had stayed out on strike were given recall rights for two years if and when

openings became available. In return for these contract provisions, UFCW bargainers agreed to delete the guaranteed annual wage provision won by P-9 members during the 1930s; the union also gave back $1.2 million in profit sharing awarded the Austin workers by the NLRB in 1987. The contract was approved in Austin by a vote of 1,060 to 440.

Sixty unionists refused to accept the new P-9 leadership and the contract it negotiated, preferring to remain on strike. After the courts upheld the UFCW's action in placing P-9 under trusteeship, the controversy faded from public view. The 400 Ottumwa workers fired by Hormel for refusing to cross the roving picket lines were ordered reinstated by an arbitrator on August 28, 1987, but since this occurred after the company shut down part of the facility, it was noted that the shutdown precluded rehiring all the workers.

The trusteeship of Local P-9 was lifted on July 16, 1987, one day after local union elections. The 550 unionists who crossed their local's picket lines voted in the election, as did the 650 permanent replacements hired by Hormel; the 600 striker's who stayed out after January 1986 were not eligible to vote despite the fact that they retained recall rights at the Austin plant.

The controversy between P-9 and the UFCW polarized the labor community. Militants who sympathized with the Austin strikers were disheartened not only by the strike's defeat but also by the abuse heaped on Guyette and Rogers by leading labor spokesmen. Defenders of the UFCW argued that P-9's resistance to concessions was motivated by selfishness, and warned that militancy on behalf of selfish goals would destroy the labor movement.

The Hormel disaster did not end labor's sad story in the meat-packing industry. Non-union meat-packers continued to prosper, and the UFCW's efforts to impose a new industrywide wage standard met scant success. Tensions and divisions continued to plague the union. [David Bensman]

Further Reading

Blin, Dick. "Minnesota Calls National Guard as Hormel Brings in Scabs." *Labor Notes* (February 1986), pp. 1, 14.

Gagala, Ken. "A Wobbly-Bred Campaign." *Labor Research Review*, Vol. 7 (Fall, 1985), pp. 81–88.

"Hormel Union Vows to Resist." *Labor Notes* (April 1986), pp. 1, 14.

Moody, Kim. "UFCW Signs Pacts with Hormel." *Labor Notes* (October 1986), pp. 1, 14.

Monthly Labor Review (November 1986), pp. 51–52.

Weekly Labor Reporter (January 7, 1987), p. 20.

Weekly Labor Reporter (April 1, 1987), p. 298.

Weekly Labor Reporter (July 22, 1987), p. 675.

I

○ ○ ○ ○ ○ ○ ○ ○ ○ ○ ○

ILLINOIS CENTRAL AND HARRI-
MAN LINES RAILROAD STRIKE OF
1911–1914. Soon after the turn of the
century, a number of railroads began to
campaign for wage reductions and the introduction of piecework. In response,
shopcraft laborers formed federations on a
number of the railroad systems. Through
this tactic the workers forced management
to bargain with a coalition rather than with
individual unions, thus making it impossible for the railroads to divide the men.
The tactic proved remarkably successful in
1908 as systemwide federations succeeded
in turning back management attempts to
cut wages or impose piecework on the
Southern Railway; the New York, New
Haven, and Hartford; the Union Pacific; the
Santa Fe; the Missouri Pacific; and the Canadian Pacific.

In an attempt to take control of this
burgeoning movement among railroad
workers, the American Federation of Labor (AFL) established a Railway Employees Department (RED) to coordinate the
systems' federations throughout the country.

The first great test for the RED came
on the Illinois Central and the Harriman
lines. The two systems encompassed an
empire of railroads, including the Union
Pacific, Southern Pacific, and the Santa Fe,
that stretched from Chicago and New Orleans to California and the Pacific Northwest. In June 1911, shopcrafts on the two
systems created their own system federation and made a series of demands on
management, including union recognition.

Company officials refused to deal with the
federation, arguing that it had collective
bargaining contracts with seven of the nine
organizations in the new federation, that
these individual contracts called for a
thirty-day notification of request for
changes prior to the expiration dates of the
contracts, and that the action of the federation was in violation of these termination clauses. The railroad stood ready to
negotiate with each individual union but
refused to talk with the new federation.

The AFL polled to find out if their
members wished to walk out over this issue and 97 percent voted yes. The strike
began on September 30, 1911. The railroad conceded that about 63 percent of its
shopmen had struck in the great strike that
paralyzed the transportation system from
the Mississippi Valley to the Pacific. The
railroads flooded the public with propaganda by purchasing space in most of the
major midwestern and western newspapers
to tell their side of the story. The press
responded by attacking the strikers, labeling them a small group of union "mon-
archs" at best, and under Socialist influence at worst.

Once begun, the strike fell into the
familiar pattern of many of the strikes of
the period. Pickets surrounded company
property and the railroads hired detective
agencies to recruit replacements. Violence
followed. Incidents of sabotage and the
beating of scabs occurred across the country. Law enforcement officials and the
companies' private armies responded in
kind. When the Illinois Central brought in
replacements in New Orleans, a riot that

left six dead and one hundred wounded ensued.

In some areas the strike reached insurrectionary proportions. On October 3, in McComb, Mississippi, hundreds of armed strikers and their supporters attacked strikebreakers who were en route to New Orleans. Several rioters were killed and many more injured on both sides. When the train carrying the strikebreakers limped into New Orleans one reporter wrote that it looked as if it had been through the Boer War. National Guardsmen called out by the governor found McComb in a state of near anarchy, with strikers threatening to massacre the strikebreakers unless they were sent out of town. The company reluctantly agreed and the strikebreakers left town under the protection of the guardsmen's rifles. Even this did not calm the situation. Ultimately, the governor had to declare martial law in McComb. The excesses of McComb were repeated with more or less the same results in New Orleans; Central City and Paducah, Kentucky; parts of Tennessee; San Francisco and Oakland, California; Portland, Oregon; and other places.

In the face of this resistance, management resorted to the courts. Sweeping injunctions were issued against the strike in a number of states and localities. Company requests for injunctions were always honored, but although the carriers had success in the courts, where the unions were rarely present for the hearings, they did suffer severe economic damage. After only a few months without maintenance, the rolling stock of the roads began to decline, and the quality of service inevitably followed. Schedules existed only on paper and mail trains ran late or never arrived at all. So star-crossed was the Illinois Central that during the strike its former president was killed in an railroad accident. The strike also took its toll in revenue. In its 1912 annual report the line

showed an operating loss of more than $3 million, and its stock fell steadily.

In the midst of the conflict, governors of several states and the National Civic Federation offered to try to bring the parties together. Management, however, was adamant. There would be no settlement with the federation, only negotiations with the individual unions.

The strike wore on year after year. The RED strike fund chest, which had sustained the strikers at the beginning, was exhausted after four years of struggle. A questionnaire sent to strikers showed that 10 percent had sought charity and that over 90 percent had moved their families to poorer accommodations, and a staggering 68 percent had broken up their homes. In the face of these hardships, the federation began to suffer defections. In December, 1914, RED recognized the inevitable and stopped its contributions to the strikers. A few months later the AFL officially called off the strike.

The shopcraft workers, after incredible militancy and untold hardships, had failed to gain their immediate objectives. Why had the railroads taken such losses to prevail? Undoubtedly because they saw in the system federations of shopcraft workers the germ of a nationwide railroad union organized on an industrial basis. They had defeated just such an attempt in 1894 during the **Pullman Strike and Boycott** when Eugene Debs' American Railway Union was destroyed. According to Julius Kruttschnitt, board chairman of the Southern Pacific, the company had felt that it was its duty to "resist in every legitimate and proper way . . . such a monstrous system."

On the union side, the strike led the AFL to reorganize its Railway Employees' Department. This rejuvenated organization grew until, by 1916, forty-three system federations held RED charters. When the federal government ran the railroads during World War I, it recognized the RED as the sole bargaining agent for all railroad workers outside of the train service brotherhoods. [Ronald L. Filippelli]

FURTHER READING

Adams, Graham. *Age of Industrial Violence: 1910–1915*. New York: Columbia University Press, 1966.

Person, Carl E. *The Lizard's Trail: A Story from the Illinois Central and Harriman Lines Strike of 1911 to 1915 Inclusive*. Chicago, IL: Government Printing Office, 1918.

U.S. Commission on Industrial Relations. "Harriman Railroad System Strike." *Final Report*, Vol. 10, pp. 9,697–10,066. Washington, DC: 1916.

o   o   o

IMPERIAL VALLEY, CALIFORNIA, FARMWORKERS' STRIKE OF 1930. On January 1, 1930, several hundred Mexican and Filipino lettuce workers in Brawley, California, walked off their jobs in a spontaneous protest against declining wages and intolerable working conditions. In less than a week they were joined by 5,000 other field workers, and the impromptu walkout of Imperial Valley lettuce workers turned into a serious strike, ushering in a decade of farmworker militancy that sent tremors throughout California's powerful agricultural establishment.

Early in the strike, the leadership was reluctantly exercised by the Mexican Mutual Aid Society, a conservative and nationalistic workers' association that had replaced the Workers Union of the Imperial Valley following the collapse of the cantaloupe pickers' strike in 1928. With the same weak leadership they had exercised during the cantaloupe workers debacle two years before, the Society, under the guidance of the Mexican consul, Edmundo Aragon, made conciliatory appeals for a peaceful resolution to the strike to the leaders of the Imperial Valley's vegetable and melon growers' organization. Just as they had in 1928, the growers rejected the po-

lite overtures of the Society out of hand and quickly galvanized local, state, and federal authorities to smash the strike before it gained momentum. Despite its conciliatory and conservative nature, the Society represented to the growers an intolerable challenge to the absolute control they had held for decades over a Mexican work force that they long regarded as inherently tractable and submissive.

The employer onslaught, augmented by threats of wholesale deportations from federal immigration officials, and violent attacks on strike meetings and arbitrary arrests of strike participants by local law enforcement officials, threatened to destroy the strike early on. But the tide suddenly changed when the Communist Trade Union Unity League (TUUL), after reading about the strike in the *Los Angeles Times*, sent in three young organizers to take over leadership of the strike.

Although beginning in 1920 the Communist International in Moscow (Comintern) had advised Communist parties around the world that organizing agricultural workers was essential to "guarantee in full the success of the proletarian revolution," U.S. Communists virtually ignored agricultural workers until the 1930s. It was only after the Comintern sanctioned independent organization of unorganized workers into dual unions, and the newly founded Trade Union Unity League committed itself to the organizing of agricultural workers, that the party, under the auspices of the newly established Agricultural Workers Industrial League (AWIL), made any sincere effort to organize California farmworkers.

When TUUL organizers Frank Waldron (who as Eugene Dennis would take over Communist party leadership in the late 1940s), Harry Harvey, and Tsuji Horiuchi arrived in Imperial Valley in January 1930, they had no previous experience organizing agricultural workers. But they knew enough about organizing to remain undercover as much as possible, only coming out in the open after several days of painstaking cultivation of a rank-and-file leadership. Once out in the open, they immediately established an AWIL chapter and moved to integrate Filipino workers into every aspect of strike activity. The organizers blanketed the valley with leaflets summarizing AWIL strike demands, which included a minimum hourly wage of fifty cents for all workers, with higher pay for more difficult or skilled work; a guarantee of at least four hours' pay any time workers were called into the fields; an eight-hour workday with time and a half for overtime and double time for Sundays and holidays; abolition of the labor contracting system; recognition of the AWIL; no work for children under sixteen; no discrimination on the basis of race, sex, or union membership; improved housing provided by employers; and the establishment of a hiring hall under the exclusive control of the AWIL.

By nurturing rank-and-file activism, and focusing on bread and butter issues of primary importance to the strikers, rather than on abstract ideology, the Communists were able to breathe new life into the faltering strike. But by going public, the AWIL organizers also exposed themselves to an effective employer and government counterattack fueled by an anti-radical hysteria that unleashed violent strikebreaking tactics reminiscent of the Red Scare excesses of 1919.

On January 12, AWIL organizers were arrested on vagrancy charges and thrown in separate jails where they were subjected to brutal interrogation. The International Labor Defense Fund and the American Civil Liberties Union sent representatives to the valley to try to win the release of the organizers, only to see them beaten up by the local sheriff. It took four more days for the organizers to be released on bail, but by that time, the strike was on the verge of collapse. The authorities had been able to block shipments of food and other strike relief effectively starving the strikers back to work. In addition, angered by the AWIL takeover of "their" strike, the leaders of the Mexican Mutual Aid Society, mostly local businessmen, cooperated with the growers and local authorities in undermining the strike. Mexican strikers were threatened with arrest and deportation and were given false promises of free land if they "voluntarily" returned to Mexico.

With the majority of the Mexican strikers either deported or back to work, AWIL leaders called off the strike on January 23, just over three weeks after it began, without winning any of the workers' demands. The strike had failed largely because of the employers' unbridled power to smash the strike with the full cooperation of government authorities. But the collapse of the strike was also due to the total lack of initial planning and organization and the ability of the growers and the Mexican Mutual Aid Society to effectively play upon ethnic divisions in the work force.

Yet, despite its ultimate collapse, the 1930 Imperial Valley farmworkers strike inaugurated a decade of rising ethnic pride and class consciousness among Mexican and Filipino farmworkers which, when combined with the aggressive leadership of increasingly effective Communist organizers, ensured that growers could no longer take their control over their work force for granted. [Kate Bronfenbrenner]

FURTHER READING

Daniel, Cletus E. *Bitter Harvest: A History of California Farmworkers, 1870–1941*. Berkeley, CA: University of California Press, 1981.

Jamieson, Stuart. *Labor Unionism in American Agriculture*. U.S. Bureau of Labor Statistics Bulletin No. 836. Washington, DC: Government Printing Office, 1945.

McWilliams, Carey. *Factories in the Field: The Story of Migratory Farm Labor in California*. Boston, MA: Little, Brown, 1939.

o o o

IMPERIAL VALLEY, CALIFORNIA, FARMWORKERS' STRIKE OF 1934. In early November 1933, organizers from the Communist-led Cannery and Agricultural Workers Industrial Union (CAWIU) returned to the Imperial Valley, where just four years before their first strike among California's agricultural workers had ended in a swift and inglorious defeat. Now they returned to the valley, fresh from their strike victories in the fall fruit harvest campaign, confident that the time was now ripe to bring unionization to the Imperial Valley lettuce fields.

Conditions in the valley in November 1933 certainly appeared more conducive to the CAWIU's success. Wages for lettuce workers were as low as ten cents an hour and working and living conditions, always the worst in the state, had continued to deteriorate. Many of the Mexican and Filipino farmworkers gathering for the winter lettuce harvest were veterans of other CAWIU strikes, eager to once again take on their employers.

Yet the young CAWIU organizers, Stanley Hancock and Dorothy Ray, sent in to lead the lettuce strike, arrived in the valley, enthusiastic but inexperienced. Carried away by the workers obvious militancy, they neglected the more tedious work of careful strike planning and union building.

Yet even the most seasoned CAWIU organizers might have failed in the face of the intense opposition from Imperial Valley lettuce growers. These growers were dedicated to using whatever force was necessary to break the strike and keep the union out of the valley. They had started their anti-union campaign before CAWIU organizers had even entered the valley. Hoping to thwart CAWIU efforts by developing a company union of their own, they took steps to revive the *Union de Trabejadores del Valle Imperial*, which had briefly surfaced during the 1928 cantaloupe

harvest. With the assistance of the Mexican consul, they met with "union" leaders on November 1 to propose a seven-and-a-half-cent wage increase and to offer vague promises of further increases later in the harvest season.

To the growers' dismay, within two weeks lettuce workers staged a one-day strike to protest the failure of some growers to live up to the unwritten agreement. Meanwhile, CAWIU organizers had arrived on the scene, inviting lettuce workers to transform their ineffectual company union into a "fighting union" that would militantly struggle for improvements in wages and working conditions. Workers in the Brawley area responded by organizing a large and influential CAWIU opposition group within the Mexican union. Under pressure from opposition forces, the leaders of the Mexican union met with growers on January 2, warning that unless wages were raised to thirty-five cents an hour, CAWIU sympathizers would capture control of the union. When the growers refused to grant any increase, the Mexican leaders stepped aside and allowed the CAWIU to take over representation of all Mexican farmworkers in the valley.

Eager to capitalize on burgeoning lettuce worker militancy, Hancock and Ray focused all of their energy on planning for a strike to begin on January 8, the peak of the lettuce harvest. Demands were formulated including a thirty-five-cents-an-hour wage, a minimum five-hour workday, free clean drinking water on the job, free transportation to and from work, union recognition, and abolition of the labor contracting system.

Ten thousand strike bulletins printed in English and Spanish were quickly distributed to workers throughout the valley. But in the rush to prepare for the strike, basic organization had been neglected and, in many camps outside of the immediate Brawley area, working strike committees still had not been developed when the

257
o

strike began on January 8. Still, 3,000 farm-workers responded on the first day of the strike, and another 2,000 went out the next day, shutting down most field operations for close to a week.

Growers and local authorities responded to the strike with a zeal for violence and intimidation unsurpassed in the history of CAWIU's struggles. Local law enforcement officials, most of them growers themselves, made clear that they would not permit any picketing whatsoever to proceed in their territory.

On January 9, local police, sheriffs, highway patrolmen, and American Legionnaires brutally attacked a caravan of several hundred strikers en route to a strike meeting in El Centro. Three days later a large force of officials fired a barrage of tear gas into Azteca Hall in Brawley, where more than a hundred strikers and their families had gathered for a strike meeting. Barring the doors from the outside, authorities forced men, women, and children to desperately scramble through broken windows to escape the gas. The hall was then stripped and vandalized by the vigilantes, who completely destroyed typewriters, duplicating machines, and the strike kitchen.

With all picketing and strike meetings declared unlawful activity, hundreds of strikers were arrested, with bail in some cases set as high as $1,800. When attorneys from the International Labor Defense came to the area to assist strikers, they too were arrested and harassed by valley authorities.

Broken by the combined effects of vigilante terror and a lack of preliminary organization, the CAWIU called off the strike on January 18, and lettuce workers returned to the fields. Workers had learned that without the constitutional rights of freedom of speech and assembly, their strikes were doomed to fail. In the aftermath of the strike, public outcry against grower violence would bring several New Deal officials to the area. But federal inter-vention brought little benefit to the CAWIU. Although they were disturbed by the growers' flagrant violations of worker's civil liberties, these officials were even more disturbed by the possibility of a militant Communist presence in the valley. Thus, they did everything within their power to undermine the CAWIU's influence among farmworkers.

Coming off a string of victories in the fall strike campaign, the collapse of the Imperial Valley Strike was an especially bitter loss for the CAWIU. Unable to withstand the combined forces of growers, law enforcement officials, and anti-union reformers, the union had reached an irrevocable turning point. If 1933 had been the heyday of militant agricultural unionism, the collapse of the Imperial Valley Strike in January 1934, foreshadowed a year of successive devastating defeats. [Kate Bronfenbrenner]

FURTHER READING

Daniel, Cletus E. *Bitter Harvest: A History of California Farmworkers, 1870–1941.* Berkeley, CA: University of California Press, 1981.

Jamieson, Stuart. *Labor Unionism in American Agriculture.* U.S. Bureau of Labor Statistics Bulletin No. 836. Washington, DC: Government Printing Office, 1945.

McWilliams, Carey. *Factories in the Field: The Story of Migratory Farm Labor in California.* Boston, MA: Little, Brown, 1939.

o   o   o

INDEPENDENT TRUCKERS' STRIKE OF 1979. In mid-June 1979, in the midst of an oil shortage brought on by a drastic price increase instituted by the Organization of Petroleum Exporting Countries, a spontaneous strike of independent truckers swept across the nation. The strike was triggered by shortages of diesel fuel and its rising cost and by weight and speed limits that reduced earnings. Although the strike was not called by any particular organization, once it began, Mike Parkhurst, president of the Independent Truckers Association, acted as a spokesman for the truckers' grievances.

The strike caught the attention of the nation. Using citizen's band radios to communicate with one another, the strikers blocked factories, refineries, and truck stops. Some merely kept their trucks off the road, while others used them as barricades to block access to refineries and fuel terminals. Violence also marred the strike. Truckers who did not honor the stoppage were sometimes the targets of snipers. In Alabama, a trucker died when his truck swerved off the road after he had been shot in the leg. The wife of another driver, a passenger in his truck, was shot in the chest and critically wounded. In Levittown, Pennsylvania, a demonstration of truckers against high fuel prices turned into a riot in which 2,000 motorists and thrill seekers clashed with police for three days. In many states, including Georgia, Kentucky, and Rhode Island, governors kept trucks moving by calling out the police or the National Guard for protection.

The loosely organized strike disrupted shipments of meat, fresh produce, and household goods, resulting in enormous losses to the economy. In California, which provided 50 percent of the nation's fresh summer vegetables and 40 percent of its fruit, farmers were beginning to plow under potatoes and lettuce that had rotted in the fields. Farmers in North Carolina were losing $1 million a day in cucumbers and peppers, and in Texas, which sent 80 percent of its produce to other states, losses reached an estimated $20 million by the end of June.

The independent truckers had been smarting under a series of price increases for diesel fuel for some time. There had been a 37 percent increase since January 1. By the middle of June, the price had reached 86.9¢ a gallon. Fuel normally accounted for 17 percent of the total cost incurred by an owner-operator—a driver who owned his own truck and either leased himself and his truck to a big, regulated trucking company, or secured loads of unregulated commodities, mostly agricultural produce, through freight brokers. The increase in fuel prices wiped out the typical independent trucker's normal net profit of 4 percent to 5 percent on revenue.

Prior to the strike, the Interstate Commerce Commission, which regulated trucking, granted a surcharge to the big regulated carriers to help to cover higher fuel costs. This covered the approximately 60,000 owner-operators under contract to the regulated carriers, but even then it covered less than half of the increase in diesel prices. The 40,000 independent truckers who arranged their own loads, however, did not benefit from the surcharge at all. These drivers negotiated individually with unregulated brokers for rates that depended on market forces. The only way they could compensate for sudden cost increases was to unite to force rates up by withholding their services. Although by the end of June most of the nation's 100,000 independent truckers were striking, the core of the protest came from the owner-operators who worked through the brokers.

The independents were bitter enemies of the Teamsters union members, who drove for the big regulated companies and continued to drive during the strike. Indeed, one of the goals of the Independent Truckers Association once the strike had begun was to weaken the Teamsters. President Parkhurst demanded that the independents be able to carry freight at the same rate as the Teamsters, a clear challenge to the regulated monopoly that had benefitted the nation's biggest union for so long.

The truckers made several demands of the administration of President Jimmy Carter. They wanted an increase in freight rates, an increase in their allocation of diesel fuel, the raising of the speed limits across the country from 55 miles per hour to 65 miles per hour, and a uniform weight limit in the nine largest trucking states of 80,000 pounds.

By June 27, Carter had increased diesel allocations to truckers and had urged the states to raise their truck weight limits. Four of the nine states at issue agreed almost immediately. Carter balked at raising the speed limit because of safety and economy reasons. And although Parkhurst vowed that the strike would continue until all the demands were met, the concessions by the government clearly led some of the strikers to return to the roads. By the end of the first week of July the strike was clearly waning. Probably more important, however, was the financial pressure on the independent owner-operators. Many had monthly payments on their truck loans of $2,000 a month or more. As independents, they had no strike fund and no support from any other quarter. Although in their most militant moments they had vowed to starve the country into submission, in the end it was they who began to feel the financial pinch.

The crisis led the Carter administration to announce a sweeping new plan to deregulate the trucking industry. Carter attacked the regulatory system as detrimental to consumers, shippers, and independent truckers. Rates, freight, and entry requirements would be deregulated. Although the independent truckers did not achieve all of their demands, they did contribute immeasurably to the end of the federal regulation of interstate trucking in the United States and, in so doing, seriously weakened the power of the International Brotherhood of Teamsters. [Ronald L. Filippelli]

FURTHER READING

Chapman, S. "Truck Stop." *New Republic* (July 7, 1929), pp. 6–7.

"One Hellacious Uproar." *Time* (July 2, 1979), pp. 22–24.

"Truckers Deliver More Inflation." *Business Week* (July 9, 1979), pp. 19–20.

"When Truckers Threatened the Nation." *U.S. News and World Report* (June 25, 1979), p. 10.

o   o   o

INTERNATIONAL HARVESTER STRIKE OF 1941. At the beginning of 1941, International Harvester remained non-union, one of the handful of large manufacturing companies that could make that claim. The company had a history of bitter anti-unionism. Harvester's predecessor, the **McCormick Harvesting Machine Company**, had defeated independent unions in the epic struggles of 1885–1886, at the Reaper Works in Chicago. Since that time, with the exception of a successful strike at its Deering Plant in 1903, International Harvester had successfully maintained open-shop status in all but a few of its holdings.

The first cracks in the company's determined rejection of independent unionization came in 1938 when the Steel Workers Organizing Committee (SWOC) of the CIO successfully organized the Chicago Tractor Works and the company's iron ore mines on the Minnesota iron range. These were followed by other scattered victories by the United Auto Workers (UAW) and by the CIO's newly constituted Farm Equipment Workers Organizing Committee (FE). Still, progress at Harvester was painfully slow, partially because of the CIO's difficulty in regaining its momentum after the economic slump of 1937–1938 but primarily because of the company's skillful implementation of a company union program.

By 1937, every Harvester plant had a works council which, under the direction of loyal long-time employees, provided the company with an effective shield against penetration by the CIO. When the Supreme Court outlawed employee representation plans as company dominated in its Jones and Laughlin decision in 1937, Harvester replaced the works councils with ostensibly independent unions that were still under the control of the old leadership. The CIO's major success at Harvester to that point had come when, under the leadership of organizer Joseph Webber, SWOC captured control of the Tractor Works Council from within. In addition, Webber was able to recruit several outstanding organizers, including Gerald Fielde and Grant Oakes, from the company unions.

Beginning in 1938, under the leadership of Webber, Fielde, and Oakes, the FE labored to organize the huge company. Progress was slow, and by January 1941, the union had no more than 200 members out of 6,000 workers in the critical McCormick Works in Chicago. Unable to break through with traditional organizing techniques, FE relied on its request to the National Labor Relations Board (NLRB) to outlaw the "independent" unions as company dominated. The NLRB ordered their dissolution on February 8, 1941, but although the decision aided the FE's case, it did little to improve the union's standing in the plants. In fact, many of the leaders of the company unions began immediately to organize their members into American Federation of Labor (AFL) federal unions. It was clear to the union even before the NLRB decision that it could not win a representation election in any of Harvester's main plants. With this in mind, FE decided to force recognition through a strike as had been done in the **General Motors Sit-Down Strike of 1936–1937.**

To direct the effort, the CIO sent Robert Travis, one of the leaders of the General Motors strike. The first part of the strategy involved calling strikes at plants at which FE had significant support. Even before the NLRB decision, strikes were underway at the Tractor Works in Chicago, and at plants in Rock Falls, Illinois and Richmond, Indiana. But at the key plants,

a bold stroke was required. In spite of FE's weakness at the McCormick Works in Chicago, Travis determined to shut down this giant capstone of the Harvester corporation. He hoped to force the company to recognize the union in return for a reopening of the plant. On February 28, FE members in strategic departments were instructed to cut power in their departments at a prearranged time and announce to the workers that they should leave the plant because the strike was on. Although several foremen did resist for a time, the overall strategy worked brilliantly. The only violence occurred when a group of anti-union foundrymen fought a pitched battle with FE supporters until police expelled both groups from the factory. Although they must have seemed like an army to the company, the coup was carried out by no more than 200 FE loyalists inside the plant, aided by another 150 or so who entered the plant after the action began. So taken by surprise was Harvester that the union was in complete control of the works by that evening.

The fall of the McCormick Works brought the number of Harvester plants on strike to four. The crisis occurred in the midst of the defense buildup preceding World War II, and it brought the intercession of Secretary of Labor Frances Perkins who called union and company officials to Washington on March 3 for a conciliation meeting. FE officials, led by Grant Oakes, demanded recognition of the union, wage increases of twelve and a half cents an hour, and the reinstatement of strikers. The company refused all demands. With the talks at impasse, mediator John Steelman, head of the U.S. Conciliation Service, recessed the meetings indefinitely. The struggle returned to the picket lines where FE's hopes rested on its ability to keep the four Harvester plants shut and some 15,000 workers idle. The union counted on pressure from the government to bring Harvester to the bargaining table.

The flaw in the strategy was the entry of the American Federation of Labor into the conflict. The AFL, which represented some Harvester workers who had belonged to the old company unions, had protested when it was not invited to the Washington meetings. On March 7, 1941, FE's plans were thrown into disarray when the AFL filed a petition for an NLRB election at the McCormick Works. Soon after, petitions were filed for the other closed plants as well. AFL organizers also called for the city of Chicago to provide police protection for the reopening of the plant. AFL president William Green announced that the AFL was chartering federal locals at various International Harvester plants.

Buoyed by the AFL support, Harvester determined to open the McCormick Works on March 23. With support from other CIO unions, such as the SWOC, Oakes countered with a message to President Roosevelt predicting bloodshed if the company followed through with its plans. AFL organizer Irving Brown announced that the AFL's 4,000 members at the McCormick Works were going back to work no matter what. Brown was right. Despite appeals by CIO leaders to President Roosevelt and to Chicago city officials to delay the opening of the plant in the interests of public safety, the McCormick Works reopened on March 23 when 3,000 AFL members returned to work under the protection of a massive show of force by the Chicago police. By the end of the week, nearly 5,000 of the plant's 6,000 workers were back at their jobs.

With FE's fortunes at a low ebb, its strategy apparently a failure, the government intervened. Four days after the plant reopened, Secretary of Labor Perkins certified the dispute to the new National Defense Mediation Board (NDMB) which had been established to settle labor disputes in defense industries. At the hearings the Harvester representatives, led by Fowler McCormick, argued that the dispute was really an organizational strike, and that the matter should be settled by an NLRB election, not by the NDMB. In addition, the company pointed out the left-wing nature of much of FE's leadership. The AFL supported the company position, believing as it did that it would win any NLRB representational election.

The NDMB essentially agreed with the Harvester and AFL position. It based its decision on the belief that the dispute at Harvester was between two unions, and not between the FE and the company. The Board refused to involve itself in the wage question, thus denying FE credit for any improvements and strengthening the hand of the AFL in any election. Indeed, the entire NDMB strategy was based on the belief that the AFL would win the elections—the result that the company obviously preferred.

Given FE's obvious weakness in membership before the strike, this assumption made sense. In a tremendous surprise, however, FE won elections in three of the six Harvester plants at issue and split the vote at the McCormick Works, thus necessitating a runoff election on July 30, 1941. In a hard fought contest, FE prevailed in the runoff, with a margin of less than 300 votes. The campaign was directed by Robert Travis who somehow managed to rally his loyalists and successfully carry the CIO message to the majority of uncommitted Harvester workers. For its part, the AFL won representation rights at two plants. Two other plants were represented by the United Auto Workers. Nevertheless, the heart of the great International Harvester empire was organized by the FE, a Communist-led union that few believed had any chance at victory.

Unionization did not bring agreement at the bargaining table. After five months, the dispute was sent back to the NDMB and then to its successor, the National War Labor Board (NWLB). In addition to its earlier demands, FE was now demanding a union shop security clause. The NWLB recommended a four-and-a-half-cents-an-hour raise, and a maintenance-of-membership clause instead of the union shop. The company acceded to the wage settlement but continued to object to any union security clause. On May 10, 1942, after considerable pressure from the NWLB and in the midst of the war, International Harvester surrendered. Although it had reluctantly agreed to unionization, however, International Harvester's strong anti-union position had not changed significantly. After the war, collective bargaining between Harvester and FE was consistently acrimonious. With the exception of 1949, every contract negotiation between 1946 and 1958 was marked by strikes. [Ronald L. Filippelli]

FURTHER READING

McKersie, Robert. "Structural Factors and Negotiations in the International Harvester Company." In *The Structure of Collective Bargaining.* Arnold Webber. Glencoe, IL: Free Press of Glencoe, 1961.

Ozanne, Robert. *A Century of Labor–Management Relations at McCormick and International Harvester.* Madison, WI: University of Wisconsin Press, 1967.

o   o   o

IRON MOLDERS' LOCKOUT OF 1883–1884. The historian of the Troy, New York, iron industry dispute, Daniel Walkowitz, points out that, "The fortunes of the ironworker community rose and fell with the success or failure of the molders' union, which remained the largest and most influential union in Troy." By 1882, Molders' Local 2 was thriving once again, having survived a crippling economic panic and a disastrous strike in 1877. The *International Molders' Journal* reveals that at the 1882 national convention, Local 2 had the largest delegation, testifying to the fact that it was the International's largest local union.

The year 1883 opened with less favorable expectations. The *Molders' Journal* reported that 78 percent of the foundry centers were suffering from large inventories and that eight stove foundries were shut down temporarily. In these circumstances the employers asked the Molders to agree to a 30 percent wage decrease. The union refused, and the foundries shut down. After several months of deadlock, all but one of the foundries gave in and reopened at the old wage rates. The exception was the Malleable Iron Company which decided to continue the fight. The dispute at Malleable Iron had first centered on the company's demand that molders either give two weeks' notice before quitting or forfeit two weeks' pay. When the molders refused, the company locked them out. The union's refusal to also compromise on the wage issue merely added to the determination of the company to have its way.

The lockout lasted over sixteen months and was marred by considerable violence. After the company reopened with strikebreakers in late February, crowds gathered each day at the gates to taunt the non-union molders. On March 2, the locked-out molders chased the replacements, but although shots were fired, no one was injured. As the number of scabs increased, Local 2 hired an Albany, New York, molder to infiltrate Malleable posing as a strikebreaker. Immediately upon being discovered and discharged on March 28, he swore before a notary that the foundry manager, William Sleicher, had told replacements that he would give them five or ten dollars for each molder they shot.

The company hired Pinkertons to guard the property and protect the strikebreakers. Nevertheless, fights between replacements and locked-out molders continued through mid-June. On May 23, the city's central labor body, the Workingmen's Trades' Assembly, met to prepare its organization for the struggle.

Soon after, what appeared to be a bombing attempt on a strikebreakers' boarding house was discovered. This mounting tension culminated on June 11 when William Hutchinson, a union molder, was killed by two replacement workers. Two other union men were injured in the shooting. In the immediate aftermath of the shooting, an angry crowd of workers threatened to riot as police took the two strikebreakers into custody.

William Sleicher, the company's manager, was charged with aiding and abetting the murder of Hutchinson. The other employers of the city rallied to Sleicher's defense. Even though evidence was presented that the company had been stockpiling revolvers under Sleicher's orders, the court released him. Hutchinson's killers also went free when one determined member of the jury refused to convict.

With these defeats the union changed tactics. Union molders infiltrated the Malleable Iron Works by concealing their union membership. There they converted many of the non-union molders. On December 11, 1883, after the company rejected a demand for higher wages, most of the working molders left to officially join the union. The company reacted quickly, importing German and Italian strikebreakers, thus further angering the largely Irish molders of Troy. Soon violence began again, erupting almost daily between the locked-out workers and the strikebreakers.

The company and its supporters among the Troy business community brought increasing pressure on city officials to disband the molders' "patrol" which the union had organized to direct the street demonstrations outside of the foundry. The foundrymen threatened to move their businesses from Troy to more hospitable cities if the mayor did not take action. After the mayor complied with their request by arresting the patrol members, fourteen molders were tried for their actions as part of the patrol. After a trial that faced off the business and professional classes of Troy against the Irish molders, the accused went free as the result of a hung jury.

The stalemate in the jury chambers mirrored the stalemate between the company and the union. There had been no winners. Malleable Iron remained nonunion, but the molders had withstood the assault of the business, professional, and political interests of Troy and came out with their union intact. Nevertheless, the reign of the proud Irish iron molders of Troy was coming to an end. Manufacturers complaining of union restrictions and high, noncompetitive wages had begun to leave the city several years earlier. To stem this tide, the union was forced to agree to a 20 percent reduction in wages. It proved to be too little too late. Factors other than labor costs also made the Troy foundries noncompetitive. The next fifty years saw the virtual disappearance of the city's iron industry. [James E. Wolfe]

FURTHER READING

International Molders' Journal, 1883–1884.

Walkowitz, Daniel J. *Worker City, Company Town: Iron and Cotton-Worker Protest in Troy and Cohoes, New York, 1855–84.* Urbana, IL: University of Illinois Press, 1978.

o   o   o

IRON MOLDERS' LOCKOUT OF 1866. There is still confusion about the "happenings" in the foundries in Troy and Albany, New York, in the early spring of 1866. While some histories remember the conflict as a strike, William Sylvis and the Iron Molders' Union declared that it was a lockout. Indeed the *International Molders' Journal* often referred to the struggle as "The Great Lock-out." The confrontation between the union and the stove manufacturers lasted less than two months in Albany and Troy and ended in victory for the union. It might well have been the largest labor–management conflict of the period, for before it ended, it involved foundries in Cincinnati, California, Ironton, and Cleveland, Ohio; Covington, Kentucky; Indianapolis, Indiana; Richmond, Virginia; and even London, Ontario. Records reveal that there were in excess of 7,000 journeymen members of the Molders' Union at that time, and about 1,500 were involved in the conflict, or about 20 percent of the membership.

The iron founders of Troy and elsewhere met in Albany on March 14, 1866, to determine how to collectively remove the union from its growing position of power among the workers. The upsurge of unionism among the molders was part of labor ferment in the United States in a year that saw the founding of the National Labor Union, demonstrations for the eight-hour workday, and a mounting interest in producers and consumers cooperatives.

William Sylvis, the president of the Iron Molders' International Union had been deeply involved in all three movements, and was without question the premier labor leader in America at the time. Sylvis' union had pressed a series of demands on the area foundries, including day rather than piecework wages, with pay equalized based on the highest prevailing rate; union control over hiring; and a ratio of one apprentice to every ten molders. Sylvis welcomed the organization of the manufacturers because he believed that it would stabilize relations between the union and the employers and allow for the extension of union standards across the industry. In this spirit, he sent a message to the members of the Stove and Hollow-ware Manufacturers Convention in March which read: "Gentlemen, allow us to congratulate you upon coming together for the purpose of organization, and to say that we have long held that organization on your part was necessary, because we felt that organization on both sides would result in such a mutual understanding as would prevent the unpleasant differences which so frequently

exist between us." Sylvis insisted that after the struggle started he had made every effort to get them to "meet in a spirit of compromise, but to no purpose."

According to the *Journal* of April 1866, Sylvis' message was received with contempt. Instead the employers formed the National Stove Manufacturers' and Iron Founders Association of the United States with Charles Eddy of Troy at its head. Twenty-three of the thirty-three employer members came from Troy and Albany.

The employers rejected the union's demands outright, arguing that piecework raised productivity, that more apprentices were needed to make up for attrition, and that they would never surrender control of the shop floor to union committees. Troy's foundrymen threw down the gauntlet to the union by posting notices in the foundries stating that in the future the owners and not the union would regulate the number of apprentices. They would also "outlaw shop committees" and "control (their) own workshops." If the molders found this unacceptable, they could look for jobs elsewhere. The critical issue, from the employers point of view, was control of the production process. The molders accepted the challenge. When they refused to accept the ultimatum on March 17, 1866, they were locked out. Skilled stove mounters and pattern-makers quickly joined the fray in support of the molders. This meant that one-ninth of the workers of Troy were involved in the struggle.

Molders' resident William Sylvis promptly notified the local unions in other communities to stay on the job and let Troy and Albany handle the fight. An assessment of 5 percent was levied by the union on the members, and funds were solicited to support the strikers and help in the formation of a cooperative foundry. Just one month after the lockout started and as the cooperative foundry was getting off the ground, a settlement was proposed by the employers. They agreed to guarantee employment for the molders and requested the authority to employ apprentices when journeymen were not available. Foundrymen could hire more apprentices under the plan but only with union permission. The official ratio remained one apprentice for every ten molders. With the agreement, the odious notices came down in the foundries. The optimism, however, was premature. The settlement did not include wage equalization at the highest prevailing rate. The strike dragged on for another month over this issue, but by May 12 all of the foundries had agreed to the proposal, and the great lockout was over.

Sylvis' leadership talents were put to the test in the 1866 conflict in Troy and Albany and were not found wanting. He used the victory to launch a campaign of "cooperation," and the cooperative foundry built in Troy during the strike became the first of a number of employee-owned foundries that flourished from 1866–1886 in the eastern part of the United States.

Like many labor conflicts, the Molders' Lockout brought with it an employer attempt to introduce labor-saving technology. The *Molders' Journal* gleefully reported the failure of the "Yankee Molder." The device had been touted as doing "the work of ten men," but the *Troy Herald* reported, after analyzing its shortcomings, that it failed to do the work of one man. The editor of the *Molders' Journal* reported, "It has been sent off to other regions, and will no doubt, be passed around among other employers whenever a difficulty exists, to frighten men into submission. Its character as a bugaboo in Troy, however, has sadly depreciated." [James E. Wolfe]

FURTHER READING

International Molders' Journal. 1866.

Grossman, Jonathan. *William Sylvis: Pioneer of American Labor.* New York: Columbia University Press, 1945.

Walkowitz, Daniel. *Workers City, Company Town: Iron and Cotton-Worker Protest in Troy and Cohoes, New York, 1855–84.* Urbana, IL: University of Illinois Press, 1978

o   o   o

J. P. STEVENS BOYCOTT OF 1977–1980. In the years 1977–1980, the campaign by the Amalgamated Clothing and Textile Workers Union (ACTWU) to organize J. P. Stevens' southern textile mills received national attention. The campaign was viewed as the spearhead of labor efforts to organize the largely non-union South. Company resistance to intense union organizing efforts resulted in prolonged legal proceedings and spurred labor lobbying efforts to change national labor relations law. ACTWU's use of a consumer boycott strategy and an innovative corporate campaign against Stevens and its financial backers brought the struggle great public visibility.

The Textile Workers Union (TWU) began trying to organize J. P. Stevens' plants in North and South Carolina in 1962 as part of a concerted effort by AFL-CIO unions to bring trade unionism to the South. Working conditions and wages in southern mills were below national standards: wages of textile workers were 20 percent below the average for all manufacturing; many Stevens employees worked a six-day week; pensions were small, vacations short; and health problems associated with cotton dust (byssinosis or "brown lung") common. Nonetheless, intense opposition by the company largely thwarted the union effort; between 1963 and 1976, the union lost eleven of twelve organizing elections in Stevens plants. The exception was an election held in August 1974, in Roanoke Rapids, North Carolina, where employees in seven mills voted

1,685 to 1,448 in favor of union representation. For the following two years, Stevens refused to agree to a first contract covering the seven plants in Roanoke Rapids.

In June 1976, the Textile Workers Union merged with the Amalgamated Clothing Workers Union. At the time of the merger, union leaders announced that organizing J. P. Stevens would be a major priority of the new organization and also announced a consumer boycott aimed at Stevens textile products such as apparel fabrics and home furnishings.

The merged organization had far more resources to throw into the fray than the old Textile Workers Union, whose membership had been decimated in the postwar years by the relocation of union textile firms from the North to the non-union South. ACTWU sent organizers, most of them Southerners with experience in the Civil Rights or labor movements, into all towns where Stevens' eighty-five mills and 45,800 employees were located. In addition, ACTWU's legal department began aggressively filing charges against the company for unfair labor practices in its effort to resist organization.

In 1977, a federal appeals court found Stevens guilty of contempt for continuing to violate federal labor law and repeatedly ignoring NLRB rulings. The court threatened Stevens with stiff fines for future violations and required the company to allow union organizers access to non-work areas in each Stevens plant in the Carolinas. In January 1978, a different federal appeals court threatened company representatives with jail unless they complied with court orders. And in the same month, an administrative law judge found Stevens guilty of bad-faith bargaining in Roanoke Rapids and ordered the company to pay all costs incurred by the union and the NLRB—including the cost of the union's organizing campaign. Additional legal decisions in 1979 and 1980 intensified pressure on Stevens to settle with the union.

In response to the large volume of cases concerning Stevens, the NLRB established a separate task force that worked exclusively on the company's cases. By 1980, the Board had found Stevens guilty of twenty-two out of twenty-three separate cases.

At the same time that ACTWU carried out its organizing efforts and legal strategy, it conducted a widely publicized boycott campaign. In asking consumers and a wide variety of organizations to support the boycott, the union presented its campaign not simply as an organizing drive but rather as a movement for social justice—a civil rights movement for textile workers. The union assigned special coordinators to organize support from women's, students' and religious groups. At its peak, in 1978, the boycott staff comprised thirty-five people. In 1979, the release of the film *Norma Rae*, which was based on the story of a Stevens organizing campaign, helped give the boycott additional visibility.

Conducting a consumer boycott against J. P. Stevens was made difficult by the fact that many of the company's products were not sold under its own brand name. In order to overcome this problem, boycott organizers asked groups of community leaders to visit the management of retail outlets to request that the store cease carrying Stevens products. This activity was supplemented by informational leafletting outside many stores. Although many retailers did acquiesce to the boycott, total sales of Stevens products continued to increase.

The fourth component of ACTWU's

effort to organize Stevens was the corporate campaign led by Ray Rogers, a former ACTWU organizer. Rogers' strategy was to isolate J. P. Stevens from the financial companies that provided it credit. Despite the fact the ACTWU lawyers put frequent holds on the corporate campaign strategy, fearing that it would place the union in legal jeopardy for violating Taft-Hartley prohibitions of secondary boycotting, Rogers brought pressure to bear on three major Stevens backers.

The first target was Manufacturers Hanover, a large New York bank that not only was a Stevens creditor but also had two men connected to Stevens on its board of directors. One was James Finley, Stevens' president; the other David Mitchell, chairman of Avon Products, and a member of Stevens' corporate board. In order to pressure the bank into ceasing its support of J. P. Stevens, Rogers began sending information on the bank's ties to the company, to a large group of unions, and to other organizations. Although Rogers did not ask these groups to threaten to withdraw their pension funds from the bank's management, Manufacturers Hanover was soon receiving many inquiries from union leaders asking why a bank that did so much business managing union pension funds was so closely connected to a notorious violator of national labor laws. In response to this pressure, Finley and Mitchell resigned from the bank's board of directors in March 1978.

The corporate campaign's largest impact was on Metropolitan Life Insurance Company, a mutual insurance firm whose head, Richard Shinn, had nominated James Finley for a seat on the board of directors of the Sperry Corporation. Metropolitan Life also held more than 40 percent of Stevens' long-term debt.

In order to sever Metropolitan Life's ties to Stevens, Rogers threatened to run candidates for seats on the insurance firm's board. Since mutual insurance policyholders are considered the company's owners, they have the right to nominate people to the board and to contest elections. Rogers' strategem threatened Metropolitan Life with great expense, for the company would have had to mail election ballots to all policyholders. Metropolitan Life's chairman Richard Shinn responded quickly to the union's pressure. He first met with ACTWU's leaders then with Stevens' executives. Stevens began negotiating non-stop until a settlement was reached on October 19, 1980.

There is disagreement about how important Shinn's intervention was in bringing about a settlement. Some union leaders believed that Stevens had become more inclined to settle since James Finley had resigned from its board in 1979 and that the increasing legal pressures on the company played an important role in bringing about a settlement. Other observers see the corporate campaign's impact on Shinn as decisive.

While the settlement was widely hailed as a breakthrough victory for the labor movement in its campaign to bring unionism to the South, it was only a partial victory for the union. Stevens agreed to sign union contracts at the ten plants where ACTWU had gained bargaining rights through NLRB certification or through court order. Only 10 percent of Stevens workers were thereby covered. Among other settlement provisions, the company also agreed to hold a certification election within ninety days at any non-union plant where the workers petitioned for one. In return, ACTWU agreed to cease conducting many of its activities against the company. The boycott and corporate campaign were dropped; furthermore, ACTWU agreed that it would no longer focus on J. P. Stevens as its primary organizing target.

In the years following, the union and the company developed a stable bargaining relationship at the plants covered by the 1980 agreement and at two additional plants in Wallace, North Carolina, that were organized as a result of a court bargaining order. But union efforts to organize other Stevens plants failed. While the union has won notable victories in Southern mill towns in the 1980s, Southern industry remains largely non-union, and union political strength throughout most of the South remains weak. J. P. Stevens itself was caught up in the merger and acquisition activity of the 1980s and has disappeared as a distinct corporate entity.

The Stevens organizing campaign had historic importance primarily because it enabled the labor movement to project itself as a crusading movement for social justice. This organizing strategy won considerable public sympathy for the union and improved organized labor's general public image. In the early 1980s, conservative attacks on unions for insisting on "high wages" and "inefficient work rules," that allegedly were responsible for making American industry uncompetitive, tarnished labor's image. Labor's aggressive effort to transform the non-union South gave way to a struggle for survival. [David Bensman]

Further Reading

Bensman, David. "J. P. Stevens" What's Behind the Boycott," *Working Papers for a New Society* (Summer, 1977) pp.20–29.

Brill, Steven. "Labor Outlaws," *The American Lawyer* (April 17–24, 1980), pp. 17–24.

Douglas, Sarah U. *Labor's New Voice: Unions and the Mass Media.* Norwood, NJ: Ablex Publishing Company, 1986.

Hauser, Dedra, and Robert Howard. "An Interview with Ray Rogers." *Working Papers for a New Society*, (January–February 1982), pp. 48–57.

Herriman, Tom. "A Union at J. P. Stevens." *American Federationist* (December 1980), pp. 1–7.

Nation's Labor. Vol. 10 (December 1980), pp. 1–16.

Raskin, A. H. "Show 'Em the Clenched Fist." *Forbes* (October 2, 1978), pp. 31–32.

U.S. Senate. *Labor Reform Act of 1977.* Hearings before the Subcommittee on Labor of the Committee on Human Resources. 95th Congress, 1st Session, Part 1, September 20–23, 26, 1977; Part 2, October 31, November 3–4, 1977. Washington, DC: Government Printing Office, 1977.

○ ○ ○

KELSEY-HAYES STRIKE OF 1945. Immediately after World War II, the United States underwent the greatest wave of strikes in its history. The strike wave began in late August and September of 1945 and reached a crescendo in 1946 when much of America's basic industry was shut down at some time during the year. There were a variety of reasons for the strikes. Certainly workers were apprehensive about the impact of the transition from a wartime to a peacetime economy. Overtime work, which had enabled most workers to cope with wartime inflation, ended suddenly after the surrender of Japan. This meant a significant decrease in real income for many. To make matters even worse, nearly a quarter of all workers had been laid off by the early spring of 1946. Finally, many employers used the conditions of the postwar years to attempt to reverse the gains that unions had made in the previous decade.

In the face of these pressures, labor leaders, still operating under the constraints of the War Labor Board's policies and their own wartime no-strike pledge, tried to heed the rumbling from below while at the same time honoring existing contracts. Much of the tension of those years manifested itself in deteriorating relations between management and workers on the shop floor. Unions had made gains in shop floor control during the frenzied production years of the war, and after the end of hostilities, management moved to reclaim maximum authority. At Kelsey-Hayes Wheel Company in Detroit, a wildcat strike by 4,500 members of the United Auto Workers (UAW) broke out on August 23 over the disciplinary firings of thirteen workers who had ejected a foreman from the shop. Management refused to reconsider the firings. Its control of the workplace was obviously at stake.

The officers of Local Union 174 endorsed the strike, but UAW president R. J. Thomas ordered the union to abide by a War Labor Board decision that reinstated nine of the men fired but upheld the dismissal of the others. The local refused. Soon the tie-up at the plant began to deprive the auto industry of key parts, and other plants began to close. In the face of the growing layoffs and the challenge to its authority, the UAW appointed an administrator to take control of the local union and end the strike. The decision brought support for Local 174 from other auto workers who picketed the UAW executive board meetings in protest.

Management saw its opportunity in the illegal strike. Charging that the international union had failed to cope with the situation, Kelsey-Hayes cancelled all agreements with Local 174. The international could see the ramifications of this decision. If rank-and-file militancy spread then other companies might follow the Kelsey-Hayes lead and break off their contractual relationship with the UAW. Richard Frankensteen, a UAW vice-president and a candidate for mayor of Detroit, failed to convince the strikers to return to work. Michigan Governor Harry F. Kelley had no better luck in his attempt at mediation.

The impotence of the international union was becoming embarrassingly clear. The union took drastic action. Seventeen elected officials of Local 174 were removed from office, and the strikers were ordered to return to work on October 3. Only 200 workers followed the international's orders. Diligent work brought most of the others to accept a compromise whereby the UAW would promise to press the case for reinstatement of the four fired workers if the strike were ended. The conflict had lasted forty-six days. Neither company ultimatums nor international union pleadings or sanctions could break the determination of the strikers. The Kelsey-Hayes dispute demonstrated the depth of the conflict between management and labor for control of the shop floor that existed as America moved out of the regulated labor relations environment of World War II. [Ronald L. Filippelli]

FURTHER READING

Lipsitz, George. *Class and Culture in Cold War America: "A Rainbow at Midnight."* South Hadley, MA: J. F. Bergin Publishers, 1982.

U.S. Congress, House of Representatives. Committee on Education and Labor. "Bills to Amend and Repeal the National Labor Relations Act." *Hearings.* 80th Congress, 1st Session. Volume 3. February 20, 1947. Washington, DC: Government Printing Office, 1947.

o　o　o

KOHLER STRIKE OF 1954–1965. The strike of United Auto Workers (UAW) Local 833 against the Kohler Company of Wisconsin became perhaps the most bitter and long-fought labor conflict of the postwar years. Though modest in scope—the strike involved a local work force of approximately 3,000—the emotions displayed were intense since the walkout pitted a highly paternalistic and adamantly anti-union employer against a strong and determined industrial union. By the late 1950s the strike had become a *cause célèbre*

for American conservatives, who used the dispute and its attendant incidents of vandalism and violence to advance their legislative agenda against "big labor."

The strike, which began April 5, 1954, was the second serious conflict at Kohler. The first spanned the years from 1934 to 1941 and involved an American Federation of Labor (AFL) federal local union, which struck for recognition. The company refused to acknowledge the AFL-affiliated body, preferring to deal with the more docile company union, the Kohler Workers Association (KWA). As in the 1950s, the battle was heated; the strike resulted in several worker deaths during rioting and an eventual company victory. In the late 1940s and early 1950s, elements of the KWA grew increasingly restive at the company's refusal to allow Kohler workers a measure of self-determination. Corporation president Herbert V. Kohler's representative, attorney Lyman C. Conger, clearly reflected his superior's paternalistic resentment of any independent union sentiment among Kohler employees as well as his resolution to fight that sentiment for ideological reasons. When the company's workers voted for UAW representation in June 1952—ousting the KWA—Kohler and Conger believed the election to be a result of a group of malcontents within the association and the malevolent involvement of "outsiders"—most notably UAW secretary-treasurer Emil Mazey, who played a large part in the organizing drive.

Kohler resolved to stand firm against its perceived "militant" opponent. Company negotiator Conger reached an agreement with the new local in February 1953, but it was more of a tactical move than a decision to accommodate the changes. Meanwhile, the UAW pressed National Labor Relations Board (NLRB) charges for Kohler's discharge of prominent UAW supporters during the organizing drive. However, the 1954 bargaining did not go as smoothly. After a strike authorization vote passed by a large margin, the company prepared to defend the plant complex with guns, tear gas, and private police. Local 833's membership subsequently rejected the company's "final" offer, and at contract expiration in early April, 2,500 Kohler workers appeared on the picket lines. Soon the company and the union were involved in protracted legal wrangling over the legality of the mass picketing as well as NLRB hearings into whether Kohler was bargaining in good faith. It became clear to UAW leaders though that the corporation intended to continue operating if possible.

Herbert Kohler and his managers contended that they were defending hallowed employer prerogatives and saw themselves as symbolically defending American free enterprise against "labor dictators." Claiming that the principal UAW demand in the strike was the union shop—which the company maintained it would never "impose" on its employees—Kohler criticized numerous union proposals as destructive "union abuses." Insisting that strict seniority would undercut the worth of the individual, that union vetoes over management decisions would sterilize the economy, and that pattern settlements eroded the virtue of industrial diversification, Kohler denounced the UAW as a promoter of coercion, violence, and the class struggle. For its part, the union insisted that the Kohler company's real aim was to see independent unionism cease to exist at their plants. It pointed out that the company had discharged—supposedly irrevocably—the entire leadership of the local union and held hard and fast to its demand that the strikebreaking force which it had recruited would never be replaced in favor of returning strikers. Giving in to such a demand, the union argued, would totally destroy any effective representation on the part of Local 833.

The strike dragged on into the late 1950s. While about 2,500 of the 3,000 Kohler production workers had been UAW members when the strike began, only about 500 of those crossed picket lines over the entire course of the conflict. However, the company had secured enough replacements from nearby rural areas to continue operations. The locus of the contest moved into the hearing rooms of the National Labor Relations Board through the late 1950s. Paralleling the NLRB cases, the conflict attracted national attention. Senators Barry Goldwater (R–AZ) and Karl Mundt (R–SD), and other conservatives on the McClellan Committee investigation into improper activities in the labor–management field brought the strike into the nation's homes in 1958 through five weeks of televised hearings. Finally, in August 1960, the NLRB, after perhaps one of the most complex hearings in its history, held the Kohler Company guilty of unfair labor practices. In order to gain reinstatement rights, the union immediately called off the strike, filed mass applications for reinstatement, and petitioned for a resumption of negotiations.

Still, Kohler would not relent. It offered reinstatement to 1,400 strikers but not to the 400 leaders it believed had fomented the strike or had engaged in violence and vandalism during the course of the contest. Nor would it recognize the legitimacy of Local 833. The international union pursued enforcement of the decision through the appeals process. The company was forced by the courts to resume bargaining in 1962; in 1964, fifty-seven of seventy-seven strike leaders were ordered reinstated; and in 1965 the courts found the company guilty of contempt and ordered 1,000 Kohler employees rehired with back pay. Finally, in December 1965, eleven years after the strike began, the Kohler Company and the UAW reached a settlement on $4.5 million in back pay and pension credits for the long-time strikers and negotiated a new contract.

Thus ended one of the most highly publicized strikes of the middle and late 1950s, a conflict in which wills and ideologies collided and in which the union emerged the tenacious victor. The costs, in both economic and human terms, were enormous; the settlements, though the largest administered by the NLRB up to that time, nonetheless were far exceeded by the strike-related costs to the strikers, the union, and the company. The efforts of conservatives to use the strike as a rallying point for legislative restrictions on union strike activity were generally unsuccessful; indeed, if anything, the UAW's reputation as a union with staying power increased. Nonetheless, the Kohler strike stands as a stark example that 1930s-style labor–management conflict could erupt even in the supposedly placid labor relations environment of the postwar era. [Gilbert J. Gall]

FURTHER READING

Petro, Sylvester. *The Kohler Strike: Union Violence and Administrative Law.* Boston, MA: Western Island Press, 1965.

Uphoff, Walter H. *Kohler on Strike: Thirty Years of Conflict.* Boston, MA: Beacon Press, 1966.

L

●○○○○○○○○○

○ ○ ○

LABOR RIOTS OF 1830–1839. While immigration had been a constant of American life from the beginning of the Colonial period, during the 1830s the pace quickened considerably. During that decade, the number of new arrivals quadrupled compared to the 1820s. Over one-half million arrived. Most came to be laborers, attracted by the demand for labor on the growing list of internal improvements—canals, roads, and harbors, especially—that dotted the new nation. Most came on their own initiative, but many also, especially from Ireland and Germany, the two major sources of immigrants, were signed up by roving labor recruiters retained by American employers.

Large numbers of the immigrants were Catholics, and anti-Catholic sentiment in the country, always strong, intensified with the arrival of the new immigrants, particularly the Irish. Tensions among Irish immigrants and earlier arrivals, mostly of English stock, became a staple of urban life. Anti-Irish riots marred cities such as Boston, New York, and Philadelphia.

The most serious outbreaks, however, grew out of the position of the Irish as wage earners. Many worked in construction gangs on canals and railroads, often separated from their families, and were subjected to authoritarian bosses, low wages, and abysmal working conditions. Others served as day laborers and casual workers in the cities. The seasonal nature of the work left many of them unemployed and destitute for much of the year.

Under these conditions, outbreaks of violence were not uncommon. Many of the "riots" of the period were in fact unorganized strikes by desperate workers. New York stevedores and riggers and Pennsylvania canal workers fought against low pay and oppressive conditions in 1828 and 1829, only to see their efforts crushed by the police. A riot on the Baltimore & Ohio Railroad in 1829 resulted in the killing of one man and severe property damage. Only the intervention of the militia prevented further disorder. In April 1834, workers on the Boston and Providence Railroad struck for higher wages and their action was termed a "riot." A Massachusetts rifle corp restored order. Such riots, wrote the Boston *Courier*, were the result of the actions of "foreigners." In the fall of the same year, 300 Irish laborers were blamed for the murder of several contractors on the Washington Railroad. On the Chesapeake and Ohio Canal, 1,000 laborers laid down their tools in February 1835, refusing to work until forced back by a company of militia.

The cities were not immune to this kind of class warfare, although in the period under question it seems to have been restricted almost entirely to waterfront workers. Philadelphia coal heavers, almost all of whom were Irish, forced a complete stoppage on the Schuylkill docks in 1835. "Three hundred of them," said the Boston *Courier*, "headed by a man armed with a sword, paraded along the canal, threatening death to those who unload or transfer the cargoes to the seventy-five vessels waiting in the river." Violence also marred another coal heavers' strike in Philadelphia in the summer of 1836. In both cases, the arrest of strikers led to the deepening involvement of labor in the city's politics.

New York City faced similar troubles. In 1836, in the midst of a nationwide upsurge of strikes, ship laborers, riggers, and stevedores struck for higher wages. When the strikers attempted to force men still working to honor the strike, a riot ensued. Police attempts to protect the "scabs" resulted in a fight which left several officers wounded. According to the *Pennsylvanian*, police reinforcements, practically the "whole constabulary," were needed to arrest "some half dozen foolish and hot headed foreigners."

The combination of anti-immigrant sentiment and labor unrest among immigrant workers led to the beginnings of the nativist political movement in the United States, blossomed a decade or so later into the xenophobic Native American, or "Know Nothing," Party. [Ronald L. Filippelli]

FURTHER READING

Commons, John R., et al. *History of Labour in the United States*, 2 vols. New York: Macmillan, 1918.

o   o   o

LATTIMER, PENNSYLVANIA, MASSACRE OF 1897. This was the greatest act of labor violence to occur in the anthracite coalfields. It ended the strike of 1897. The strike of 1897 began at the Audenried strippings of the Lehigh-Wilkes-Barre Coal Company. Management, in an economizing move, centralized its stable operation and demanded that drivers stable their mules after stopping work. Slavic mule drivers at Stripping Number 5 complained that this order would require them to work an extra two hours a day. On August 14, the twenty drivers walked off their jobs in protest and established a picket line. The

mine superintendent Gomer Jones appeared carrying an ax handle and threatened to beat the strikers if they did not return to work. In the ensuing melee, Jones hit a worker on the head. News of the event quickly spread; by August 16, 2,000 immigrant workers had joined the strike and demanded that Jones be fired.

Management responded in the usual fashion. Foremen and clerks who sympathized with the strikers were fired. Two squads of Coal and Iron Police armed with rifles patrolled the area. But the strikers were not intimidated. They invited John Fahy, an organizer for the United Mine Workers of America, to help them form a local union.

Confronted with such determination, the company surrendered. It agreed to rescind the centralized stable order. Management also promised to investigate Gomer Jones within ten days after the men returned to work. Had it not been for the company's bad faith and the Campbell Act, the strike of 1897 would have ended without bloodshed.

The Campbell Act was an answer to the "native" miners' demand for protection against Slavic and Italian immigrants. It placed a tax of three cents per day upon coal companies for each alien they employed. At least one coal company refused to pay the tax but most announced that they would deduct the tax from the immigrants' pay.

The Campbell Act went into effect on August 21, and five days later immigrant miners at Coleraine struck for a wage increase that would cover the deduction for the tax. When the ten days passed without the promised investigation of Gomer Jones, the original strikers again walked off their jobs. The strikers marched from mining village to mining village urging all workers to join them to secure a 15 percent wage increase, the right to select and pay their own doctor, the end of the company store, and equal wages with "Americans."

The miners at the village of Harwood joined the strike. Being employees of A. Pardee and Company, the Harwood strikers realized that their success depended upon their ability to close down the same company's operations in Lattimer. On September 10, approximately 250 people lined up behind two American flags and marched toward Lattimer.

At approximately 3:30 P.M., the marchers met Sheriff James Martin of Luzurne County and a well-armed posse on the outskirts of Lattimer. Suddenly, Martin either fell or was pushed to the ground. His posse opened fire; when the smoke had cleared, more than fifty strikers lay dead or wounded.

Local communities were outraged by the news. In Hazleton, mass meetings condemned the shooting of the unarmed strikers. The citizens called for the arrest of Sheriff Martin and his deputies. They also requested Pennsylvania governor Daniel H. Hastings to keep troops out of the area.

Governor Hastings denied their request; on September 11 he ordered the Third Brigade of the National Guard into the region. A warrant for the sheriff and his deputies, however, was also sworn out. But the troops refused to allow the warrants to be served. Finally the National Guard relinquished its protection, and Martin and seventy-three deputies were arrested. But after a five week trial the jury returned a verdict of not guilty.

The verdict destroyed the Slavic community's attempt to redress the injustice of Lattimer. The community had successfully petitioned the Austro-Hungarian government to seek an indemnity from the United States for the victims of the massacre. But the United States held that the verdict demonstrated that Sheriff Martin's actions were free from malicious intent and necessary to uphold law and order. It, therefore, refused to consider the question.

The Lattimer Massacre had a profound impact upon the anthracite region. It disproved the fears that Slavic and Italian immigrants would undermine the economic position of "native" miners and that they could not be organized. The editor of the Hazleton *Standard-Speaker* best summarized the meaning of the massacre: "The day of the slave driver is past, and the once ignorant foreigner will no longer tolerate it." [Harold W. Aurand]

FURTHER READING

Green, Victor R. *The Slavic Community on Strike: Immigrant Labor in Pennsylvania Anthracite*. Notre Dame, IN: Notre Dame University Press, 1968.

Novak, Michael. *The Guns of Lattimer: The True Story of a Massacre and a Trial, August 1897–March 1898*. New York: Basic Books, 1978.

Pinkowski, Edward. *The Lattimer Massacre*. Philadelphia, PA: Sunshine Press, 1950.

o   o   o

LAWRENCE, MASSACHUSETTS, TEXTILE STRIKE OF 1912. This famous industrial conflict, which catapulted the Industrial Workers of the World (IWW) to national prominence, erupted in January 1912. The previous year the state legislature of Massachusetts had enacted legislation reducing the maximum week for factory workers to fifty-four hours. At the time of a previous state-mandated reduction in working hours, employers had not lowered wage rates. The new fifty-four-hour law took effect in 1912 and January 11 would be the first payday after its implementation. On that day a group of Polish immigrant women workers opened their pay envelopes and discovered less money than they had expected. "Short pay!" they exclaimed, leaving their looms and walking out of the mill. That evening the Lawrence *Sun* reported, "Italian Mill Workers Vote to Go Out on Strike Friday— In Noisy Meeting 900 Men Voice Dissatisfaction over Reduced Pay Because of 54 Hour Law." The next day, Friday, January 12, all the city's textile workers realized that employers had elected to reduce pay in proportion to the reduction in the work-week. An angry group of Italian workers left their looms at the mill of the American Woolen Company, demanding that fellow workers join their walkout and disassembling machines. From that mill, the protestors marched to other mills in Lawrence urging textile workers to join the protest against reduced pay. By evening, more than 10,000 men, women, and children had left work, taking to the streets of the city where they shouted slogans, threw snowballs, rocks, and stones, and shattered factory windows. Yet, at first, the explosion of protest and violence seemed to subside as suddenly as it had surged.

The quiet that followed the outburst of January 12, however, was deceptive. The vast majority of Lawrence's textile workers belonged to no trade union and lacked a tradition of collective action; their protest had been spontaneous. A small group of Italian immigrant workers, however, had earlier established a local of the IWW; they were committed to that organization's pursuit of revolution through direct action by workers at the point of production, and they intended to use the discontent among their unorganized fellow workers to spread the gospel of the IWW. At their behest, Joseph Ettor, an Italian-speaking organizer and leader of the IWW, came to Lawrence on January 13. Over the weekend at a series of meetings, Ettor encouraged the textile workers to protest against their poor conditions of work and low pay by striking en masse. On Monday, the start of a new workweek, Lawrence's toilers took Ettor's advice to heart and began the great strike of 1912.

The strike of 1912 was an event without precedent in the history of Lawrence. Founded in 1845, on the pattern of such earlier-model Massachusetts textile towns

as Waltham and Lowell, Lawrence never experienced an era in which its labor force was dominated by young women of old-stock New England heritage. Even in its early years, the city's mills employed large numbers of immigrant workers, mostly Irish, who toiled in family groups because no individual earned enough to support a family. Thereafter, Lawrence's factories continued to attract waves of immigrant workers. By 1912, the labor force in the mills included not only the children and grandchildren of the original Irish immigrants, but also French-Canadian, Polish, Italian, Belgian, Syrian, and Russian Jewish immigrants. Like the Irish before them, the newer immigrants worked as families, their combined wages being necessary to support the family. Even with all adult and adolescent members of the family at work, most workers and their dependents barely maintained an adequate standard of living. Lawrence had some of the worst housing conditions in the state of Massachusetts and the most dreadful morbidity and mortality statistics. "I have rarely seen in any American city," said the social reformer Walter Weyl, "so many shivering men without overcoats as I have seen in the cloth-producing town of Lawrence." Was it any wonder that the immigrant workers of Lawrence rebelled, or that in their rebellion they turned to the IWW?

At its start no one—not the employers, nor the strikers and their leaders, nor the city fathers—realized how long the strike would last or how divisive it would become. Employers had good cause to expect the conflict to end quickly. Most of their more skilled workers were of Irish Catholic origin, evinced little interest in the radicalism of the IWW, and belonged to a church, most of whose local priests sympathized with the manufacturers. Other skilled workers belonged to an affiliate of the American Federation of Labor (AFL) which openly and bitterly fought the IWW. By contrast, the mass of strikers, mostly newer immigrants, did not speak each other's languages, shared no common culture, and worshipped different faiths. If the strike did not collapse of its own accord because of worker disunity, employers could rely on their control of municipal government and their influence with officials of the state to accomplish their goals. For their part, strikers, and especially their leaders, expected that with almost all the city's textile workers out of the mills, employers would prefer to restore wage levels and to bargain with their employees in preference to having their machinery remain idle. However, the textile manufacturers refused concessions to their workers and the strikers remained firmly united. As a consequence, both sides to the conflict settled down for a protracted struggle, one that did not end until March 12.

When the strike began the IWW had a minimal presence in Lawrence. At best, the IWW could lay claim to 300 paid-up members in its Local 20 (by contrast, the AFL affiliate, the United Textile Workers claimed 2,500 members) out of 30,000 to 35,000 local textile employees. Yet the leaders whom the national IWW sent to Lawrence—Ettor, Arturo Giovannitti, and later William D. "Big Bill" Haywood and Elizabeth Gurley Flynn—worked well and closely with local Wobblies representing each of the dominant ethnic groups: Italians, French-Canadians, Jews, Franco-Belgians, and the English-speaking workers. Working together, the local Wobblies and the national leaders spread the message of the IWW among the non-union strikers who rapidly joined Local 20. They encouraged the strikers both to use their ethnic subcultures as a source of resistance and to submerge their differences in language and religion. Ethnic fraternal societies, religious institutions, and neighborhood social clubs provided strength for the strikers. Using their own networks within neighborhoods and as shoppers for the household, women workers and wives

enabled the strikers to survive a protracted struggle. Throughout the conflict, moreover, the men and women of different ethnoreligious groups heeded Bill Haywood's advice that "there is no foreigner here except the capitalist. . . . Do not let them divide you by sex, color, creed, or nationality." The IWW message took hold. "Whether all the members [Local 20] hold the theories of the IWW or not, a more important thing is true," wrote an observer of the strike, "they have all caught its spirit."

Yet the demands that the strikers presented to their employers a week after the conflict erupted resembled those that might have come from any affiliate of the AFL. The textile workers asked for an increase in wages of 15 percent based on a fifty-four-hour week; double pay for overtime; elimination of premium bonus wage payments; and the promise that no striker would suffer discrimination upon re-employment. The demand did not include union recognition or the closed shop nor any radical aspect of the IWW program.

The textile manufacturers, however, refused to bargain with their workers. Instead, they preferred to use power to smash the strike—their power to starve the workers into submission, and their power to influence local police, state militia, and judges. City police and state militia patrolled Lawrence's streets and guarded its mill gates. They also disrupted picketing and parades by strikers and in the process frequently precipitating incidents of violence that were blamed on radical Wobblies. One such incident during a demonstration by strikers resulted in the wounding of a police officer and the death of a young Italian immigrant woman worker. In reaction, the local authorities charged Ettor and Giovannitti with responsibility, arrested them, and indicted them for conspiracy in the death of the woman. It was that incident which led the IWW to send Haywood and Flynn to Lawrence. Scores of rank-and-file strikers experienced justice in Lawrence's courtrooms where one judge said, "The only way we can teach them is to deal out the severest sentences."

Despite repeated attempts by employers and their allies to induce the workers to resort to violence and despite harsh treatment at the hands of the law, the strikers heeded the advice of Haywood and other IWW leaders to remain peaceful. "Can you weave cloth with the bayonets of your militia, or spin with the clubs of your policemen?" Haywood asked. He told the workers to keep their hands in their pockets, spin no more, and let the soldiers go naked. Almost everywhere he went in Lawrence, Weyl observed among the strikers, "this same objective attitude, this same aversion from violence and the threat of violence."

As the strike wore on with no end in sight, the resources available to the workers locally and those provided by the IWW could no longer sustain the struggle. In response, IWW leaders and their sympathizers devised a stratagem to relieve strikers of a financial burden and to win greater publicity. At the end of January, a group of Italian Socialists in New York suggested that the strikers send their children to families elsewhere who would minister to the needs of these temporary orphans of industrial warfare. On February 11, Margaret Sanger and three other female reformers picked up the first group of 119 children for transport to foster families in New York. Soon after, other groups of children left Lawrence for distant cities. The new tactic worked so well that the textile manufacturers and their friends in city government decided to put an end to it. On February 24, the city police stationed themselves at the Lawrence railroad station with orders to stop the transport of the strikers' children. When the children's escorts refused to heed the police order, the officers used force to maintain their authority, clubbing women and children without distinction.

The clash at the railroad station in Lawrence proved to be the strike's turning point. Across the nation, newspapers and magazines publicized the brutality of Lawrence's "ruling class." The governor of Massachusetts ordered an investigation of the incident. A congressional committee prepared to open an investigation of the entire industrial dispute in Lawrence. And Mrs. William Howard Taft, Mrs. Gifford Pinchot, and other socially and politically prominent citizens journeyed to Lawrence to see the plight of the strikers and the callousness of their employers. Beset on all sides, the manufacturers now decided to compromise. Between March 3 and March 12, they bargained with delegates selected by the strikers. On Saturday, March 12, the American Woolen Company, the largest employer in Lawrence, offered the strike committee satisfactory terms: a flat 5 percent wage hike for all pieceworkers, 5 to 25 percent increases for all hourly rated workers, time and a quarter for overtime, reforms in the premium bonus system of payment, and no discrimination against strikers. Two days later, a mass meeting of strikers accepted the terms and voted to end the walkout. Haywood said of the victory, "the strikers of Lawrence have won the most signal victory of any organized body of workers in the world. You have demonstrated . . . the common interest of the working class in bringing all nationalities together."

The great textile workers' victory of 1912, however, proved short-lived. After the workers returned to the mills, their employers still held the larger share of real power. Employers infiltrated private detectives into the IWW local; they discharged union leaders and shop floor militants; they manipulated the local labor market to the union's disadvantage; and they bestowed benefits on workers loyal to them. A general economic contraction that began in 1913 and that was especially severe in the textile industry helped employers complete the destruction of union influence in the mills. By 1914, not a single local leader of the Lawrence strike remained at work in the city's mills, and one IWW member reported that "reaction . . . has been busily at work within the ranks of Local Union No. 20 . . . sowing the seeds of dissension and despair."

At first, however, the IWW believed that its victory in Lawrence was the start of great things. "The revolutionary pot seems to be boiling in all quarters," reported the IWW newspaper, "the day of transformation is now at hand." "The question of 'Will the IWW grow?'" said a leading Wobbly, "is now answered in the affirmative by the masters who add, 'and damn it, *Can it be stopped?*'" Many Americans thought similarly as they read in their newspapers and magazines about the "rising tide of syndicalism." In the aftermath of Lawrence, they also began to ask whether or not revolution was on the American agenda and whether or not the IWW could be stopped. [Melvyn Dubofsky]

FURTHER READING

Conlin, Joseph R. *Bread and Roses Too: Essays on the IWW.* Westport, CT: Greenwood Press, 1970.

Dubofsky, Melvyn. *We Shall Be All: A History of the IWW.* Chicago, IL: Quadrangle Books, 1969.

Foner, Philip S. *History of the Labor Movement in the United States: The Industrial Workers of the World, 1905–1917.* Vol. 4: New York: International Publishers, 1965.

Renshaw, Patrick. *The Wobblies: The Story of Syndicalism in the United States.* New York: Doubleday, 1967.

o   o   o

LEADVILLE, COLORADO, STRIKE OF 1896–1897. Founded in 1893, a year of wholesale economic collapse, the Western Federation of Miners (WFM) spent much of the rest of the decade attempting to restore their members' standard of living to pre-depression levels. As in many other metal-mining centers throughout the Rocky Mountain region, the hardrock miners' union waged an aggressive, indeed overly aggressive, campaign to recover wage standards in the silver-lead mines of central Colorado in the mid-1890s. The defeat of this strike had its most profound effect not on the local distribution of income but rather on the structure of the labor movement in the region.

For a decade prior to 1893, the prevailing wage in the Leadville mining district was $3.00 per day. The sharp decline of silver prices in 1893 forced the suspension of extractive operations. When the mines resumed production in a very depressed market, they paid their underground workers only $2.50. In September 1893, the Knights of Labor local assembly that represented Leadville miners negotiated a variable wage scale with the major operators in the area. As long as the price of silver remained below $.835 per ounce, the mine workers would receive $2.50. When the silver price reached $.835, wages would return to $3.00 per day.

In part because of its acquiescence in this wage-cutting agreement, the Knights of Labor soon lost support among the Leadville hardrock workers. In May 1895, the Cloud City Miners' Union, Local 33 of the Western Federation of Miners, was established to succeed the Knights. (Because of their concessionary wage policy during the early 1890s, the metal miners' assemblies of the Knights had not been invited to participate in the founding of the WFM.) The new organization mounted an aggressive recruiting drive, pressing mine employees to join or leave the area.

By early 1896, most mine workers in Leadville had won back their pre-1893 rate of pay, even though the price of silver had not surpassed the $.835 threshold. Repudiating the Knights agreement, Local 33 demanded that the operators make the $3.00 wage universal across the district. The mine owners refused. On June 19, 1896, a union meeting attended by 1,200 members voted to strike the low-wage operations.

The work stoppage commenced that night. Soon thirteen mines and their approximately 1,000 employees were idle. The operators quietly organized to meet this challenge. In a secret understanding reached on June 22, they pledged to provide each other mutual assistance and not to enter into any individual agreements with the WFM. The only immediate public manifestation of this new unity was the declaration of a lockout at the mines paying $3.00, putting another 1,300 men out of work.

Attempts by state officials to mediate the dispute failed. The union argued that in a remote mining community with a high cost of living, the $3.00 wage was only a matter of subsistence. Management offered to take the matter to arbitration; the union rejected this proposal. Both sides spent the summer preparing for battle. In July, the union committee administering the strike distributed one hundred rifles and a supply of ammunition to the members. Groups of miners openly drilled with arms and paraded in the streets. For its part, management began to bring in some new strikebreakers and made plans for mass importation of replacement workers.

The mine owners issued an ultimatum on August 19. If union members did not return to work within three days, the operators would introduce strikebreakers en masse. Local 33 refused to capitulate. A few mines resumed production, paying $2.50 per day. The union made a strenuous effort to discourage men from working. Squads of strikers patrolled the railway station and the roads leading into Leadville. They persuaded some potential strikebreakers to leave town, forcibly ran

others out of the district, and beat many of those who remained. This violent policy continued in spite of the union's formal denunciation of the use of force as "cowardly and unmanly." Sheriff H. M. Newman, a union supporter, looked the other way.

Just after midnight of September 21, a group of more than one hundred men attacked the reopened Coronado mine. The employees vigorously defended the property. Three members of the Cloud City Miners' Union died in the ensuing half-hour fire fight. The attackers dynamited an oil storage tank, resulting in the destruction of not only the tank but also a number of buildings. By 3:00 A.M., the union forces had moved on to the nearby Emmet mine, another reopened operation. They blasted a hole in the fence surrounding the property and made a determined charge on this breach in the company's defenses. This attack was repelled by what federal investigators called "a terrible fire of buckshot and rifle bullets." A fourth unionist died in this encounter.

Governor Albert McIntire sent the Colorado National Guard to Leadville at once. By the evening of September 22, more than 650 state troops—ten companies of infantry, a troop of cavalry, and an artillery unit—had reached the scene of the strike. In addition, local businessmen assembled a sizable armed force. Twenty-seven members of the WFM, including international president Edward Boyce, who had not been in the district on September 21, were arrested for inciting a riot. (These charges were later dropped in all cases.) Another attempt to resolve the dispute peacefully through collective bargaining failed.

On September 25, the first large group of strikebreakers arrived from Joplin, Missouri, a notorious recruitment center for non-union mine labor. The operators wasted no time in exploiting the vul-

LORDSTOWN, OHIO, STRIKE OF 1972

nerability of the replacement workers. They required that new employees enlist in the Colorado militia and gave them weapons to defend company property. At one mine alone, General Cassius Moses swore in 175 fresh reinforcements. But when state labor leaders protested this practice, Governor McIntire put a halt to it. Nevertheless, ore production resumed and soon approached pre-strike levels. Many union activists left the area. On March 9, 1897, the strike officially ended, an utter failure.

The unwillingness of the trade-union movement to aid the Leadville struggle disgusted the western miners. The WFM had affiliated with the American Federation of Labor (AFL) in 1896. But at its convention in December of that year, the AFL gave rhetorical, not material, assistance to the embattled strikers. A subsequent fund-raising appeal to affiliated unions yielded almost nothing. A letter from Boyce to Samuel Gompers on this matter went unanswered. Instead, the AFL president wrote to inquire about rumors that the hardrock miners were considering withdrawing from his organization. Even while disavowing any current plans to quit the AFL, Boyce did nothing to allay Gompers' fears by declaring that "the laboring men of the West are one hundred years ahead of their brothers in the East." In May 1897, the WFM convention voted to disaffiliate from the AFL.

The WFM set out at once to build an alternative labor movement for all wage earners west of the Mississippi. In May 1898, the miners' organization dominated the conference in Salt Lake City that founded the Western Labor Union (WLU). Boyce looked to this body to end the labor movement's "inattention to the unskilled." In 1902, the WLU expanded its jurisdiction to cover the rest of the United States and, accordingly, changed its name to the American Labor Union. The WFM thus set the stage for the creation of the Industrial Workers of the World. [Alan Derickson]

FURTHER READING

Dubofsky, Melvyn. "The Leadville Strike of 1896–1897: An Appraisal." *Mid-America*, Vol. 48 (April 1966), pp. 99–118.

Jensen, Vernon H. *Heritage of Conflict: Labor Relations in the Nonferrous Metals Industry up to 1930*. Ithaca, NY: Cornell University Press, 1950.

Perlman, Selig, and Philip Taft. *History of Labor in the United States, 1896–1932: Labor Movements*. New York: Macmillan, 1935.

o   o   o

LORDSTOWN, OHIO, STRIKE OF 1972. Perhaps the most significant strike of the 1970s involved the auto workers at United Auto Workers Local 1112 at General Motors' Lordstown, Ohio complex. While the conduct of the strike itself was important, the greater significance of the strike came from its use as a metaphor for a generation's social-political struggles and as an attack on technological determinism.

In 1964, General Motors (GM) began building what would be its largest and most automated facility in Lordstown, Ohio. The Lordstown assembly plant was considered an industrial engineer's dream with a two mile assembly line incorporating the most modern manufacturing equipment and techniques and ergonomically-designed work stations. By the time GM built its first car in March 1966, the Lordstown plant was 88 percent automated and had cost twice its estimated cost. Within the next four years, GM would add new truck/van and fabricating plants (Fisher Body) to the Lordstown complex.

More than 16,000 people from Ohio, West Virginia, and Pennsylvania applied for what were expected to be the 5,700 clean manufacturing jobs with excellent pay and benefits. Most of those hired were young and from rural areas within a fifty mile radius of the plant. On the eve of the strike in late 1971, the average Lordstown worker was twenty-four years old, some eighteen years below the national average.

The hiring pattern suggests that the new work force was chosen because of its lack of trade union experience, isolation from the youth and political movements of the 1960s, and ability to keep pace on what was to become the world's fastest assembly line. The plan failed for several reasons. First, the young workers at Lordstown were not unsophisticated in terms of trade unionism and labor–management relations. They were often the sons and daughters of steelworkers, miners, rubber workers, and electrical workers. In the heavily industrialized tri-state region, these workers and their families had a long and militant trade union tradition. Second, the auto workers at Lordstown also were not isolated from the culture, values, and political turmoil of the 1960s. The work force had the highest level of formal education of all GM assembly plants. The media, especially television, had further educated and exposed these and other workers to the social and cultural attitudes of the 1960s—attitudes characterized by a lack of automatic acceptance of authority. Finally, many of the young men at Lordstown had been profoundly influenced by the Vietnam experience. Workers who had college experience, and there were many at Lordstown, had been exposed to the anti-war movement and were often cynical and distrustful of hierarchy. The attitudes of Vietnam veterans were even more militant. According to one Lordstown worker: "At nineteen, I felt immortal. When I returned to GM after the war, I felt I had done everything. I had a half a million Vietnamese trying to kill me and I survived. What could management do to me?"

The Lordstown complex was under the control of GM's Chevrolet Division from 1966 to 1971. During this period, the plant produced a series of high quality, mid-sized automobiles using a line-speed of sixty cars per hour. The labor relations climate, while not without conflict over workloads, overtime, and absenteeism, was largely characterized by informal shop rules, such as "doubling up," that undermined managerial prerogatives while relieving the auto workers of the monotony of the assembly line.

In 1970, the Lordstown assembly plan was retooled for production of the subcompact Vega. GM hoped to take advantage of Lordstown's high-speed assembly line and automation to maximize production and lower unit labor costs in order to compete in the expanding small car market. But the production of the Vega was doomed from the beginning. According to John DeLorean, general manager of the Chevrolet Division, the car was the end product of chronic corporate infighting involving the Chevrolet Division and GM's marketing, design, and engineering departments. Consequently, the Vega was poorly designed and engineered, and overweight and overpriced compared to its competition. In addition, the car frequently overheated and was known for molting parts.

In October 1971, the car and van assembly operations at Lordstown were merged as part of an ongoing corporate reorganization into the General Motors Assembly Division (GMAD). The reorganization had been predicated on the belief that GMAD's "get tough" approach could boost GM's sagging productivity and profitability and, in the case of Lordstown, effectively compete with the Japanese and German producers in the subcompact market.

In the auto industry, GMAD had the reputation of a no-nonsense organization which used layoffs, speedups, and a paramilitary approach to discipline. In every plant that GMAD entered, labor–management conflict had developed, and the UAW believed that establishing conflict was part of the unit's *modus operandi*. Before GMAD came to Lordstown, Irving Bluestone, UAW vice-president, had tried to warn corporate leaders of the growing antagonism among auto workers toward GMAD's confrontational methods.

Upon arrival at Lordstown, GMAD immediately attempted to establish its absolute authority over production through layoffs, the elimination of shop rules, the reorganization and rationalization of jobs, and increases in assembly line speed and overtime. Discipline was liberally imposed for the slightest deviation from the new rules. Workers felt hounded, harassed, and demoralized from the use of "direct orders" which forced them to do the job and grieve later.

At first, UAW Local 112 leadership responded by telling workers to file grievances and to "do your job but not to strain." Soon "overworked" and disciplinary grievances began to clog the grievance procedure. When GMAD refused to discuss or settle the grievances, the auto workers came to believe that management was deliberately undermining the dispute settlement procedure while continuing to rationalize production. By the time of the strike, over 10,000 grievances were on file.

Out of frustration and anger, Lordstown auto workers retaliated with what was euphemistically called "spontaneous insubordination." Workers caused strategic bottlenecks, worked to the letter of the rules, showed hostility to supervisors, and in extreme cases, sabotaged the product and equipment. It was not uncommon for cars to come down the assembly line missing parts, with keys broken in the door, or with the parts piled neatly in the front seat. Yet, auto workers claimed that the amount of sabotage was minimal and was used to disguise the poor engineering and quality of materials and parts used by GM in the production of the Vega. They pointed to GM's Wilmington, Delaware plant which also produced Vegas having equally high repair levels. Regardless, the Lordstown repair lots were quickly filled to capacity.

GMAD responded by pushing harder. GMAD refused to add a third shift to meet increased production needs and added

overtime. Further, GMAD denied emergency breaks, delayed access to grievance representatives, and increased the use of disciplinary layoffs for frivolous reasons. As the pace and working conditions became intolerable, absenteeism increased or, alternately, some auto workers deliberately sought disciplinary layoffs to escape the pressure. In addition, when the repair lots became full, workers were sent home early.

As Vega's production problems became known, GMAD publicly humiliated auto workers by describing them as disrespectful saboteurs. At Christmas, management sent a letter to its Lordstown employees withholding Christmas greetings because of poor performance. GM estimated that between October 1971, and January 1972, the actions of auto workers had cost workers $3.6 million in lost wages and the corporation 12,000 cars and 5,000 vans in lost production as well as $50 million in sales.

Local 1112 leadership had attempted to negotiate with GMAD to honor local work rules since GMAD's arrival. However, the protracted negotiations proved fruitless, and the local announced that it would take a strike vote. Under the UAW/GM master agreement, either party had the right to strike or lockout over production standards or safety and health issues.

On February 1, 1972, of the 85 percent of Local 1112's members who voted, 97 percent approved a strike. It was the highest pro-strike vote received by any local union in UAW history. In a last ditch effort to prevent the strike, three GM vice-presidents and several UAW officials, including Bluestone, came to Lordstown to try to reach agreement. These efforts failed and the strike began on March 3, 1972.

The strike was largely uneventful. For a time, the union successfully blocked the entry of nonstriking workers and salaried personnel. The dispute idled some 8,000 union workers at Lordstown and another 9,000 workers at plants which supplied

GM with components. Negotiations broke down when GM refused to provide information regarding the number of auto workers on layoff. In turn, Local 1112's leadership asked for a delay and filed an unfair labor practice charge over the company's failure to provide relevant information.

For all of the tensions that produced it, the strike ended rather quickly on March 25, 1972. The agreement returned 700 laid-off workers to their former jobs and gave full back pay and clear records to many workers who had lost their jobs on disciplinary layoffs. In return, the union dropped thousands of grievances and made no challenge to the company's control of production, hoping instead that the higher manning levels would ease the pressures of the work.

Although the strike itself was unremarkable, the media coverage of the dispute was not. Virtually every major newspaper and television network discussed the issues and history of the troubles at Lordstown. While some blamed the workers as industrial representatives of the rebellious generation of the 1960s, more focused on the events at Lordstown as symptomatic of what came to be called the "blue collar blues"—the alienation and discontent that supposedly came when better educated workers experienced boring, repetitive, fragmented, and highly rationalized production processes. Soon alienated, labor in any form was said to be suffering from a malady described as the "Lordstown Syndrome."

The debate over the causes of the Lordstown strike only intensified in the next decade. Clearly, the actions of auto workers at Lordstown had struck a chord in both individuals and in society. One result was a presidential task force which studied the American workplace and issued a widely-read report, *Work in America*. Industrial psychologists, sociologists and anthropologists, organizational behaviorists, labor relations specialists, and political economists all found different meanings in the events at Lordstown. From these analyses sprang various kinds of job redesign and enrichment programs in American industry as well as the development of various quality-of-worklife and participatory management programs. [John Russo]

FURTHER READING

Aronowitz, Stanley. *False Promises: The Shaping of American Working Class Consciousness*. New York: McGraw-Hill, 1973.

Garson, Barbara. *All the Livelong Day: The Meaning and Demeaning of Work*. Garden City, NY: Doubleday, 1975.

Moberg, David. *Rattling the Golden Chains: Conflict and Consciousness in Auto Work*. Ph.D. dissertation, University of Chicago, 1978.

Widick, B. J., ed. *Auto Work and its Discontents*. Baltimore, MD: Johns Hopkins University Press, 1976.

Work in America. Report of the Task Force to the Secretary of Health, Education, and Welfare. Cambridge, MA: MIT Press, 1973.

Wright, J. Patrick. *On a Clear Day You Can See General Motors*. New York: Avon Books, 1979.

o   o   o

LOS ANGELES COUNTY SANITATION DISTRICT STRIKE OF 1985. In 1935, Congress enacted the Nation Labor Relations Act (NLRA) that afforded a majority of American workers the right to organize, to bargain collectively, and to engage in strikes to attain their bargaining demands. The NLRA, however, did not cover workers employed by federal, state, or local governments; those entities were specifically excluded from the statutory definition of "employers." As a result, public employers were free to enact or to refrain from enacting laws providing for collective bargaining by their employees.

A majority of states presently have laws permitting collective bargaining by at least some groups of public employees, and in 1978, the federal government enacted the Civil Service Reform Act, which provides comprehensive rights for executive branch employees. Strikes by public workers, in most instances, are forbidden by express statutory provision. Ten states, however, have chosen to allow strikes by specified groups of public employees, and the legislative trend appears to favor a more permissive approach to strikes. For example, the two most recent states to enact laws, Ohio and Illinois, elected to authorize strikes as a means of resolving bargaining impasses.

In the absence of legislation, the common law rule is that public sector strikes are unlawful and may be enjoined. Until 1985, when the California Supreme Court held to the contrary, the rule was adhered to by every court to consider the question. As the first, and to date the only, appellate decision to so hold, the California case is of particular significance for public sector labor relations.

The Service Employees International Union, Local 600, began a strike in July 1976 against the Los Angeles Sanitation District. The strike continued for eleven days, and during that time, the employer operated the facility with management and nonstriking personnel. The union eventually settled the strike on the employer's terms. The employer then sued the union for damages resulting from the unlawful strike, and the trial court awarded the employer $246,904 in compensation.

Reversing the judgment, the California Supreme Court issued a number of separate opinions. Three justices, writing the plurality opinion, held that public employee strikes were not unlawful under California's common law. Two justices concurred in the plurality's holding on the ground that tort damages against a public union were not appropriate, but those justices did not agree that the common law protected such strikes. Chief Justice Bird wrote a concurring opinion stating that the strike was permitted by common law and was also protected by the California

constitution. Justice Lucas dissented in the case, arguing that any modification of the accepted common law doctrine should be made by the legislature rather than by the court.

In its opinion, the plurality first describes the traditional reasons which have been advanced to justify the common law strike prohibition. First, strikes by public employees have been regarded as inconsistent with the basic concept of governmental sovereignty. Second, courts often conceded to the state legislature the power to unilaterally implement terms and conditions of employment for employees. Third, influential scholars argued that strikes by public employees gave them a disproportionate amount of power in the process of resource allocation, which was disruptive to our democratic system. Fourth, a strike by public employees ostensibly results in the loss of essential services to the public.

The plurality rejected the first argument as a "vague and outdated theory" based on the notion that governmental power is absolute and unchallengeable. As to the second justification, the plurality said that the California legislature had provided for a system of collective bargaining, thereby surrendering its right to unilaterally fix conditions of public employment.

The court linked together the third and fourth arguments in a discussion concerning the nature of political power in our democracy. Initially, the court rejected the idea that striking public sector unions can force public employers to capitulate to "unreasonable demands." Rather, according to the plurality, public opinion may support resistance to union demands, as in the case of the **Air Traffic Controllers' Strike of 1981**. Further, not all government employment is "essential"; many services, they point out, can be contracted to private sector employers, including transportation, health care, and even education. Thus, the "presumption of essentiality of most governmental services is questionable at best."

After refuting the traditional objections to public sector strikes, the plurality offered various reasons in support of the policy permitting strikes. It observes that strikes may strengthen the collective bargaining process by equalizing the relative power of the parties and encouraging realistic negotiations. Further, the ability of workers to engage in a lawful strike to protect their economic interests is a "basic civil liberty." Because the public has become more tolerant of bargaining and strikes by governmental workers, according to the plurality, courts should adapt to the changed circumstances. The court stated that it was appropriate for the judiciary to alter the common law rule rather than to await legislative modification. In the plurality's view, "If the courts have created a bad rule or an outmoded one, the courts can change it."

In her concurring opinion, Chief Justice Bird held that the right to strike was based on constitutional principles which included "basic person liberty," prohibitions against involuntary servitude, and "the fundamental freedoms of association and expression." Bird reasoned that without the right to strike, "working people would be at the total mercy of their employers, unable either to bargain effectively or to extricate themselves from an intolerable situation. Such a condition would make a mockery of the fundamental right to pursue life, liberty, and happiness by engaging in the common occupations of the community." Accordingly, Bird would not permit a complete legislative ban on public sector strikes. Even though the plurality did not wholly adopt Bird's position, three other justices did agree that any prohibition on the right to strike must be based on a "substantial or compelling justification."

In his dissenting opinion, Justice Lucas relied on one basic argument. He contended that even if modern economic conditions justified strikes by public workers, it was the function of the state legislature to authorize them by statute. The legislature, he said, "may formulate a comprehensive regulatory scheme designed to avoid the disruption and chaos which invariably follow a cessation or interruption of governmental services." Without administrative machinery to control and regulate impasse resolution, the common law rule would remain "hopelessly undefined and unstructured." He pointed out that every state which permits public strikes has provided a comprehensive statutory scheme to accommodate the interest of employers and citizens as well as workers.

The California Supreme Court's decision is significant in a number of respects. It marks a radical departure from the previously universal and well-settled legal principle. Further, it suggests that there may be constitutional limitations on a legislature's power to outlaw public sector strikes. Other state supreme courts in the future could use the *County Sanitation District* case reasoning to invalidate existing strike prohibitions or to permit strikes in the absence of legislation. Although public workers in California have not engaged in an increased number of strikes, the decision has implications which will undoubtedly arise in the future. Whether or not the decision is a sound one, it represents a landmark innovation in the common law. [Raymond L. Hogler]

Further Reading

Hogler, Raymond L. "The Common Law of Public Employee Strikes: A New Rule in California." *Labor Law Journal*, Vol. 37 (February 1986), pp. 94–103.

Schneider, B. V. H. "Public-Sector Labor Legislation—An Evolutionary Analysis." In *Public-Sector Bargaining*, 2nd ed. Benjamin Aaron, Joyce Najita, and James Stern, eds. Madison, WI: Industrial Relations Research Association, 1988.

Spivak, Lawrence. Comment, "County Sanitation District: The Need for a Legislative Response to Public Employee Strikes." *Hofstra Labor Law Journal*, Vol. 4 (1986), pp. 181–217.

o   o   o

LOS ANGELES OPEN SHOP STRIKES OF 1910. Organized labor had practically no presence in Los Angeles at the turn of the century. This contrasted with the power of the labor movement in San Francisco, a "union town." In Los Angeles, a combination of bitter open shop employers and a rapidly growing population had kept unions out and wages up to 40 percent lower than in San Francisco.

These conditions began to undermine union standards in San Francisco and elsewhere on the west coast. In 1910, metal trades employers in San Francisco told their workers that the eight-hour workday would have to go unless their non-union Los Angeles competitors, operating on the nine and even ten-hour day, could be brought into line. San Francisco metal trades unions, with the support of the state federation, sent organizers to Los Angeles. When the employers rejected their contract proposals, the metal trades unions in Los Angeles struck twenty-five shops on June 1, 1910. Other labor stoppages plagued the city's breweries, hotels, and restaurants.

The Merchants' and Manufacturers' Association took the offensive. It contributed $350,000 to fight the strike, hired strikebreakers and detectives, and used its political influence to persuade the city council to pass an anti-picketing ordinance. Under the new ordinance, employers secured seventy-five injunctions which resulted in the arrests of 500 pickets in the first week.

But the unions belonging to the General Campaign Strike Committee also poured resources into the fray, including some $80,000 in strike benefits, legal assistance for those arrested, and soup kitchens. Slowly they made progress, and by September the Los Angeles Central Labor Council had expanded from sixty-two unions with 6,000 members to eighty-five unions with 9,500 members. In addition, there were another 2,500 non-affiliated union members in Los Angeles. Then, on October 1, 1910, a bomb destroyed the *Los Angeles Times* building in downtown Los Angeles, killing twenty persons.

Harrison Gray Otis, publisher of the *Times,* accused organized labor of what he termed the "crime of the century." Otis was an ex-printer and union member, but a bitter battle with the printer's union in 1890 and his emergence as a rich and powerful citizen had turned him to an anti-unionism so virulent that, according to one San Francisco reporter, the mere mention of unions "threw him into a passion verging on insanity." Not surprisingly, Otis and his newspaper were pillars of the open shop movement and of the Merchants' and Manufacturers' Association.

In the midst of the general anti-union hysteria of the city's business community, the press, city officials, and the Merchants' and Manufacturer's Association immediately announced rewards for information and launched investigations into the incident. The one that bore fruit was backed by the mayor of the city and was under the direction of the well-known detective, William J. Burns. Burns, like his competitor, the Pinkerton Detective Agency, had been involved in labor disputes as an employee of management for some time. At the time of the bombing he had already been investigating a series of dynamitings growing out of an open shop war between the National Erectors' Association and the International Association of Bridge and Structural Iron Workers. Burns tied the two investigations together when he arrested Ortie McManigal and James B. McNamara, the first a member of the iron workers and the second a brother of the union's secretary. McManigal confessed, and Burns, in a highly questionable fashion, arrested and practically kidnapped John J. McNamara, the union's secretary-treasurer, from the Iron Workers' Indianapolis headquarters.

Unions and union members from across the country rallied to McNamara's support. With Samuel Gompers and the AFL in the lead, supporters eventually raised a defense fund of $236,000. Clarence Darrow defended the McNamara brothers. The certainty of most union supporters that the McNamara's had been railroaded by the open shop partisans was fatally shaken when the McNamara's confessed to the crime. The effect on the labor movement in Los Angeles and elsewhere was devastating. A promising political alliance between the Los Angeles Central Labor Council and the Socialist Party that seemed on the verge of winning the mayoral race fell apart. The confessions and revelations of the McNamara's crippled the organizing campaign. Most of the workers still on strike returned without union recognition or the coveted eight-hour workday. Los Angeles returned to being perhaps the strongest open shop city in the United States. [Ronald L. Filippelli]

FURTHER READING

Adams, Graham, Jr. *Age of Industrial Violence, 1910–1915.* New York: Columbia University Press, 1966.

Cross, Ira Brown. *History of the Labor Movement in California.* Berkeley, CA: University of California Press, 1935.

Selvin, David F. *Sky Full of Storm: A Brief History of California Labor.* Berkeley, CA: University of California Institute of Industrial Relations, 1966.

o   o   o

LOUISIANA SUGAR CANE STRIKE OF 1953. The National Agricultural Workers Union (NAWU) came to Louisiana in 1948 at the request of socially conscious Catholic activists concerned with the plight of the sugar cane workers. The union was the lineal descendent of the Southern Tenant Farmers Workers Union (SFTU) and was still led by the SFTU's founder, H. L. Mitchell. With the Catholic church active in the effort, and under the leadership of Henry Hasiwar, an NAWU organizer from California, the union succeeded in chartering Local 317, a sugar cane workers local, in January of 1953. The local's membership was 80 percent black, some of whom held leadership positions.

Because of its success in organizing in Louisiana, the NAWU decided to make the state the center of its operations. In December 1952, the NAWU took its first step toward negotiation with the big sugar interests. The union claimed that the growers were violating the Sugar Act by paying workers for nine hours and making them put in nine and a half. In July 1953, Local 317 sent registered letters to Louisiana's biggest growers asking them to enter into collective bargaining with the union over wages and working conditions. But in spite of union reference to the Papal Encyclicals, by Leo XIII and Pius XII, on the right of workers to organize and bargain with their employers, the growers refused to bargain. They denied that Local 317 represented their workers, continued to fire workers for joining the union, and threatened others with eviction from company houses for union activity.

In the face of this obstinancy, the union laid its plans for an offensive against the sugar industry. The union enlisted the aid of Joseph Francis Rummel, archbishop of New Orleans, who tried to persuade the growers to deal with the union. The growers, however, refused to discuss the question or to acknowledge a role for the church in the dispute. With the failure of the intercession of the church, the union had little recourse but to strike. In fact, without support from the Roman Catholic church, it is unlikely that the NAWU would have undertaken the effort to organize the sugar cane workers in the first place. In addition, the union was unable to capitalize on the vulnerable economic position of the Louisiana sugar industry and its dependence on government subsidies. The growers' lobbyists and spokesmen were able to resist government-set minimum wage rates as a hindrance on the free enterprise system, while at the same time maintaining the subsidy system of tariffs, quotas, acreage allotments, and benefit payments that supported the growers.

In the fall, the growers had begun recruiting workers of Mexican descent in Texas specifically to break up the sugar local, and the Department of Labor authorized the use of Jamaicans for cane field work. Meanwhile, Local 317 conducted a strike vote and assessed its members two dollars for a strike fund. On September 27, Local 317 announced a vote of 1,808 to 8 in favor of a strike.

The strike began on Monday, October 12, 1953, when workers failed to report for work on the plantations of the four biggest sugar corporations. On the same day, the union informed the growers of its desire to negotiate rather than to strike. According to Henry Hasiwar, the central issue of the dispute was not wages but the right of the sugar cane workers to union representation.

Not surprisingly, Catholic priests in the Archdiocese of New Orleans assisted the union. Archbishop Rummel appealed to the growers to deal with the union, but after the strike had begun, the largely Roman Catholic planters angrily rejected the church's pleading. One grower chided the church and noted that "the morals of these negro laborers are rock bottom and . . . not worthy of being represented by our Church."

Shortly after the strike began, the sugar plantations cut off the utilities of striking workers and issued eviction notices to union leaders. When the union tried to secure an injunction against the evictions, Judge P. Davis Martinez of the 17th Judicial District Court of Louisiana ruled in favor of the planters, and the federal district court upheld his ruling. In addition, the planters waged a successful propaganda campaign in the local press, charging,

among other things, that the strikers were receiving funds from a Communist-front organization, the National Sharecroppers' Fund.

Generally, there was little violence during the strike. The only shooting incident occurred in Houma on October 22 when men lying in ambush fired two shotgun blasts at a truck transporting replacement workers to the Southdown refinery. In order to persuade the black workers to return to work, the planters paid for radio broadcasts by the Reverend J. E. Poindexter, a black Baptist minister of New Orleans.

Support for the strikers came from the Catholic Committee of the South, Holy Name Societies, and the Christian Family Movement, all of which provided food packages or services for the families of the strikers. The *New York Post* ran an article on the strike in November, detailing the hardships of the strikers, and contributions from other unions, such as the United Auto Workers, also helped to sustain the strikers.

Such support, however, was of little use against the combined forces of the planters, the local press, and the courts. A temporary restraining order forbade members of the United Packinghouse Workers from striking one of the planters in sympathy with the cane workers. Picketing was also enjoined at many plants by court order. Indeed, the injunctions determined the outcome of the strike. The union had no funds to fight legal battles. Appeals to the AFL and to the ACLU for help in court were unsuccessful. Because it was enjoined from picketing or otherwise performing its function as a trade union, the NAWU had no choice but to end the strike. Mitchell called it off on November 10.

The 1953 cane field strike was important because it exposed conditions in Louisiana, but the strike itself was a failure and a setback for unionism in agriculture. The sugar workers failed as had the sharecroppers in the 1930s. Given the racial composition of the NAWU, the weakness of the union, the strength of the sugar lobby, and the anti-union sentiment of Louisiana's press and politicians, the strike had always been a gamble. In fact, its fate had been sealed when the Roman Catholic planters turned a deaf ear to the pleadings of the church. [Ronald L. Filippelli]

FURTHER READING

Becnel, Thomas. *Labor, Church, and the Sugar Establishment: Louisiana, 1887–1976.* Baton Rouge, LA: Louisiana State University Press, 1980.

Marshall, F. Ray. *Labor in the South.* Cambridge, MA: Harvard University Press, 1967.

o   o   o

LOUISIANA TIMBER WORKERS' STRIKE OF 1912–1913. The great growth of the timber industry in Louisiana came as a result of the influx of northern capital into the industry after the repeal by Congress of the Homestead Act in 1876. After 1880, southern pine production doubled every decade until the rich stands of yellow pine had been cut to the point that the industry leveled off. Along with the clearing of huge tracts of virgin timber, the arrival of large-scale industrial capitalism in the timber industry also created jobs for thousands of black workers from the cotton and sugar plantations of Mississippi, Louisiana, and eastern Texas. By 1919, there were nearly 41,000 timber workers in Louisiana, some two-thirds of all of the non-farm workers in the state.

In 1902, Louisiana mill workers first attempted to organize. Strikes at several saw mills resulted in small gains for some workers, and at one company, workers even formed a black local of the Socialist Party. In the fall of 1907, a spontaneous general strike broke out in response to an employer threat to lengthen the workday and cut wages by 20 percent. The threat struck hard at workers who worked long

hours for irregular pay and who often received company scrip rather than cash in their pay envelopes. Employers also collected excessive insurance and hospital fees thus turning a profit even on this venture. The 1907 strike brought the AFL and the IWW into the lumber fields, trying to turn the uprising into stable organizational gains. But their efforts did not have lasting effects, and most workers returned to work with a promise of wage increases when the recession of 1907 ended.

Although nothing lasting resulted from the 1907 affair, temporary Socialist and IWW successes in several areas of Louisiana gave them heart, and they continued to organize. In 1908, Pat O'Neill, a seventy-four-year-old ex-Arkansas coal miner and a member of the IWW, launched a weekly paper, *The Toiler*, in Leesville. Two of his disciples, lumberjacks Arthur Lee Emerson and Jay Smith, founded the Brotherhood of Timber Workers (BTW) at Carson in December of 1910. Within a year, the Brotherhood boasted an interracial membership of between 20,000 and 25,000 workers. According to John Kirby, the leading opponent of the union, the Brotherhood was "covering the country like a blanket."

One of the most apparent strengths of the new union was its ability to appeal to rural Louisiana workers regardless of race. This ability troubled the employers who noted that the fact that the Brotherhood especially looked after the black workers and their families, thus creating "a complicated condition," that would be hard to fight. But fight the employers did. In July of 1911, the employers organization, the Southern Lumber Operators Association (SLOA), locked out the BTW members in an attempt to break the union. At the head of the SLOA sat John Kirby, former president of the National Association of Manufacturers and one of the largest lumber operators in Texas. Kirby gave orders that any mill where organizing was going on should be closed and "remain so until the union is killed."

Kirby was anti-union but not unsophisticated about the internecine conflict between the pure-and-simple unionism of the AFL and the revolutionary anarcho-syndicalism of the IWW. Kirby was on friendly terms with Ralph Easely, president of the National Civic Federation, a national organization striving to ensure industrial peace through labor–management cooperation. Easley assured him that "the American Federation of Labor is the organization that will serve our purposes. . . ." Not surprisingly, Kirby praised the AFL which was "based on the right of property and the respect thereof." "The employers," he went on to stress, "would deal with unions that would guarantee the owners a 'fair and just' return . . . for legitimate investments." At Easley's suggestion, Kirby met in Chicago with Samuel Gompers, AFL president and a member of the National Civic Federation. According to Kirby, Gompers recommended a lockout of BTW members. The AFL would then send in organizers to organize the skilled white workers.

Gompers' role in the affair raised a storm of protest from the AFL leaders in New Orleans. But Gompers refused to answer the accusations. On July 19, the SLOA closed eleven mills and employed the Burns Detective Agency to scour the surrounding states for scab workers. Strikebreakers who accepted the company offer worked behind stockades under the protection of armed guards. The BTW put up a brave challenge, demanding a long list of concessions from the companies, but it was all for show. After seven months, the lockout and blacklisting pushed the union to the point of extinction. Its membership dropped to 5,000.

Their defeat by the employers and the role of the AFL in the affair led the leaders of the BTW to choose the path of militant revolutionary unionism. On May 6, 1912,

some one hundred delegates at the BTW's second convention voted overwhelmingly to affiliate with the IWW. When the IWW accepted the application, the BTW became the Southern District of the National Industrial Union of Forest and Lumber Workers but continued to be known in Louisiana as the BTW.

Shortly after the convention, the BTW presented a list of its old demands to several mills. Once again the SLOA responded with a general lockout. In June, the mills began to operate with scab labor. The timber barons also brought in scores of gunmen from the Burns Detective Agency. According to one account, a near civil war reigned over central and western Louisiana and parts of eastern Texas. The worst incident occurred on July 7, at Grabow, Louisiana. There a group of strikers, sympathizers, and their families were speaking at a mill operating with scab labor. Just after A. L. Emerson, a union officer, began speaking, a gunfight broke out between the strikers and company guards. Three strikers and a guard died in the ten minute battle. Nearly forty strikers, family members, and friends were wounded.

The following day police arrested Emerson and fifty-nine other strikers and sympathizers. In all, sixty-four were indicted on the charge of murdering the guard killed at Grabow. Emerson's arrest added to the tension that had been created by the events at Grabow. Mill workers at Bon Ami, who had been non-union, threatened to strike unless Emerson was freed. A rally of 2,500 in New Orleans called for the release of the imprisoned strikers. When the case did come to trial in October, the jury returned a unanimous verdict for acquittal.

While acquittal was a vindication for the arrested workers, it did nothing to slow the employer's campaign to rid themselves of the union. Guards and scabs continued to arrive at the camps. In spite of this show of force and a dwindling treasury, the union held firm. No small part of this resolve was due to the remarkable racial solidarity during the strike. Women and area farmers also gave support to the strikers by donating food and running strike kitchens. Trains importing scabs, many of whom were black workers, were met by the wives and supporters of strikers who tried to inform them about the strike in the hope of turning them back.

With this kind of working-class solidarity, the strikers held out until the middle of February. Having withstood evictions, strikebreakers, and armed guards, exhausted strikers surrendered when the SLOA mobilized the businessmen and community leaders of the strike areas into a "Good Citizens League." The companies' armed guards became members and were made deputy sheriffs. A reign of terror followed. On February 16, "Good Citizens" members began demolishing the strikers' shanties and driving BTW members out of town. The governor refused to intervene. A complete cessation of law and order in the strike areas led to the inevitable defeat of the union. Most of the strikers were blacklisted. Although the BTW existed formally until 1916, the defeat of 1912–1913 effectively put an end to the union and, until its resurrection in the 1930s, to the industrial union movement in Louisiana. [Ronald L. Filippelli]

FURTHER READING

Cook, Bernard A., and James R. Watson. *Louisiana Labor: From Slavery to "Right to Work."* Lanham, MD: University Press of America, 1985.

Green, James. "The Brotherhood of Timber Workers: 1910–1913: A Radical Response to Industrial Capitalism in the Southern USA." *Past and Present* (August 1973), pp. 161–200.

o   o   o

LOWELL, MASSACHUSETTS, MILL WOMEN'S STRIKES OF 1834 AND 1836.

The first half of the nineteenth century saw a dramatic growth of cotton textiles factories in the United States. Concentrated in the New England states and in the Philadelphia region, factory production steadily displaced the home manufacture of woolen and linen cloth which had predominated in the first decades of the nineteenth century.

The emergence of water-powered textile mills in rural villages and in new factory towns across the Northeast brought with it dramatic and controversial changes. The very first mills in Rhode Island employed a mill work force consisting primarily of children. After the opening of the Boston Manufacturing Company in Waltham in 1814, an increasingly female labor force came to dominate in New England textile mills. The novelty of a work force of young, single women recruited to the mills from the surrounding countryside both impressed and disturbed contemporaries.

Politicians, philosophers, and reformers debated the nature and desirability of these changes. Males dominated much of this debate in contemporary newspapers and periodicals, though on occasion, women too expressed their views in print. Although the debate is revealing about fault lines in American culture in the antebellum period, much of the writing is clearly the product of interested observers who knew very little about the actual lives and aspirations of women in the mills.

While contemporaries debated the impact of textile factories, rural women entered the mills by the tens of thousands. By their willingness to tend power-driven machines for seventy-three hours a week and to accept regulations that largely determined the nature of their lives inside and outside the mills, women gave silent testimony to the importance of mill wages in their lives. Their earnings from mill employment gave them a degree of economic and social independence which set them apart from New England women of earlier generations.

Still, if mill women preferred wages earned within the strictly regulated confines of New England factories over a less-driven dependence on their families back on hill-country farms, they did not accept uncritically all that went on in the mills. Periodically, in fact, Yankee women organized strikes in response to wage cuts or other management moves which they found contrary to their interests. The largest of these actions came in Lowell, Massachusetts, in February 1834, and October 1836, and an appreciation of these protests is crucial to an understanding of the place of mill employment in the lives of Yankee women and of the attitudes that motivated them.

More than 800 women millworkers in Lowell "turned out"—went on strike—in February 1834 to protest a proposed wage reduction. Two weeks earlier, mill agents had posted identical broadsides in the mills notifying workers of the impending cuts. The broadsides stirred up "a good deal of excitement" among women operatives according to one agent. Women circulated petitions seeking the signatures of others who would agree "mutually and cheerfully . . . not to enter the Factory on the first of March: unless the wage reductions were rescinded."

In mid-February, women operatives at one mill held a meeting during the noon hour and excluded a male watchman from their proceedings. The mill agent entered the room and attempted to dissuade the women from their course of action. In a letter to the company treasurer in Boston he noted:

It appeared that before I entered the room, they had appointed a dictatress & voted to be governed by her in all cases. This woman . . . retorted upon me with no little vehemence, & declared that there was no cause for any reduction whatever, that the causes assigned for it were without foundation in fact, that she had to pay as much for a yard of cloth as ever & that there was no truth to the assertions of the Agents.

"Perceiving that this woman had great sway over the minds of the other females," the agent dismissed her. As she left the mill, this operative "waved her calash [a scarf] in the air as a signal to the others, who were watching from the windows." Her fellow workers rallied around her, quit work, and the turnout had begun. The women marched from mill to mill securing additional participants. Their number reached 800—about a sixth of the female work force in Lowell at that time—and following a procession, the group rallied on the town common. According to a contemporary newspaper account, "one of the leaders mounted a pump and made a flaming Mary Woolstonecroft [sic] speech on the rights of women and the iniquities of the 'monied aristocracy,' which produced a powerful effect on her auditors. . . ." The women drafted a petition which expressed clearly their sense of themselves and the motivation of their protest:

UNION IS POWER

Our present object is to have union and exertion, and we remain in possession of our unquestionable rights. We circulate this paper wishing to obtain the names of all who imbibe the spirit of our Patriotic Ancestors, who preferred privation to bondage, and parted with all that renders life desirable and even life itself to procure independence for their children. The oppressing hand of avarice would enslave us, and to gain their object, they gravely tell us of the pressure of the times, this we are already sensible of, and deplore it. If any are in want, the Ladies will be compassionate and assist them; but we prefer to have the disposing of our charities in our own hands; and as we are free, we would remain in possession of what kind Providence has bestowed upon us, and remain daughters of freemen still.

Following this expression of the values behind their actions, striking operatives endorsed a common set of resolutions:

Resolved, That we will not go back into the mills to work unless our wages are continued . . . as they have been.

Resolved, That none of us will go back, unless they receive us all as one.

Resolved, That if any have not money enough to carry them home they shall be supplied.

Mill owners, however, were prepared for the turnout. With the posting of the original announcements of the wage cut, agents lined up additional recruits to replace striking workers. Moreover, they demonstrated no inclination to accommodate the striking women. One agent probably reflected the general sentiment when he referred to the turnout as an "amizonian [sic] display." Women turned out on a Saturday, were paid off on Monday, and by the end of the week, the mills were operating normally.

Although unsuccessful, this first strike in Lowell expressed well the strong sense of independence among mill operatives in the 1830s. Women linked their actions expressly to the revolutionary republican tradition of their "Patriotic Ancestors." They viewed the millowners and agents as "Tories in disguise." They saw themselves as daughters of freehold farmers who were not dependent on their mill earnings for subsistence. If the mills would not hold up their end of the agreement that had drawn women into the mills, they would leave Lowell and return to their rural homes. This economic base permitted Yankee women workers a measure of independence not shared by immigrant operatives who succeeded them after 1845.

In October 1836, Yankee women turned out again. On this occasion an increase in the cost of room and board in company boarding houses prompted the protest. The second turnout was larger than the first, engaging 1,500 to 2,000 workers, fully a fourth of the female work force in Lowell. One account indicates that the

women formed a Factory Girls' Association, with "committees from the several corporations to make provisions for those who have not the means to pay their board." The Association may also have provided stage fare for women who preferred to return to their rural homes to wait out the strike. A contemporary in Lowell, the Methodist minister Orange Scott, estimated that 2,000 women left the city during the strike, an effective strategy to cripple production in the mills.

The strike was considerably more successful than its predecessor, and production in the mills was affected for several months. One agent complained in correspondence to his company's treasurer back in Boston that the decline in production was "no doubt the result of calculation and contrivance" on the part of the striking operatives. Apparently, they would "assail a particular room—as for instance, all the warpers, or all the warp spinners, or all the speeder and stretcher girls, and this would close the mill as effectually as if all the girls in the mill had left." Thus, while perhaps a third of the women workers supported the strike, by drawing out all the operatives in a crucial step of the production process, the leaders of the strike were able to shut down production almost completely. As one local storekeeper commented at the time: "[It] was remarkable, that a few, probably less than half a dozen young women, should manage this whole affair with so much dexterity and correct judgement, that no power, or skill, could be successfully employed against them." The strike resulted in a compromise settlement as several firms rescinded the increases in the cost of room and board, while others did so for operatives paid on a daily basis. The mill agents had their hands full with these independent "daughters of freemen," and they apparently had no choice in 1836 but to accommodate to their demands.

The strikes of 1834 and 1836 were not repeated on a similar scale in Lowell in succeeding years before the Civil War, but labor protest did not completely disappear. In the 1840s, Lowell mill women mounted successive petition campaigns in which they called on the Massachusetts state legislature to limit the hours of labor. Women organized the Lowell Female Labor Reform Association which cooperated with similar male organizations across New England. In 1845, more than 1,000 signed the ten-hour workday petitions in Lowell and in 1846 more than 4,000 did so. State legislators, however, showed little sympathy for the organized women workers and refused to enact any limit. Not until 1874 did Massachusetts pass legislation setting ten hours as the length of the working day in corporations in the state.

Declining wages, deteriorating conditions of work, and the refusal of the state to intervene on behalf of workers led Yankee women to leave mill employment in increasing numbers after 1845. Steadily, the influx of Irish immigrants changed the composition of the mill work force in Lowell and across New England. By 1860, a majority of millworkers in Lowell were foreign born. With the entry of immigrant newcomers, labor protest in the mills declined in the 1850s. After the Civil War, however, as the Irish became the dominant group within the mills, and as they had increasing experience by which to judge their treatment in the mills, they too became a force to be reckoned with by mill owners. Although Yankee women workers had largely departed, struggles between capital and labor continued into the immigrant era. [Thomas Dublin]

FURTHER READING

Dublin, Thomas. *Women at Work: The Transformation of Work and Community in Lowell, Massachusetts, 1826–1860.* New York: Columbia University Press, 1979.

Josephson, Hannah. *The Golden Threads: New England's Mill Girls and Magnates.* New York: Duell, Sloan and Pearce, 1949.

o   o   o

LUDLOW, COLORADO, MASSACRE OF 1913. In September 1913, coal miners in southern Colorado commenced a strike against various mine operators in the region. The largest of the mining concerns was the Colorado Fuel and Iron Corporation (CF&I), which was controlled by John D. Rockefeller, Jr. As a result of the conflict, Rockefeller developed and popularized the "employee representation plan," which directly led to the company unions of the 1930s.

The United Mine Workers (UMW) union presented a list of seven demands to the mine operators in August 1913. Their initial demand, and the one to which the operators were most vehemently opposed, was union recognition. Other demands included an increase in wage and tonnage rates, an eight-hour workday, payment for "dead" work such as timbering, election of checkweighmen, the right to purchase goods and medical services where they chose, and enforcement of the state mining laws. The miners imposed a deadline of September 23; if the demands were not met, they threatened a strike. The mine owners conceded nothing.

The strike began as scheduled. Because the miners lived in houses owned by the mining concerns, they were forced to leave the property. Some 10,000 miners and their families vacated the camps and established tent colonies in the area. The largest settlement was at Ludlow.

The conditions which precipitated the dispute were investigated at length by the U.S. Commission on Industrial Relations. Based on evidence presented before the Commission, George P. West compiled a document entitled *Report on the Colorado*

Strike, which was published in 1915. He observed that in the first instance, "[t]he struggle in Colorado was primarily a struggle against arbitrary power, in which the question of wages was secondary, as an immediate issue." According to West, the antagonism of the miners toward the operators was much more than a matter of economics. The operators effectively controlled all aspects of the miners' lives, including social and political activities.

The strikers passionately felt and believed that they were denied, not only a voice in fixing working conditions within the mines, but that political democracy, carrying with it rights and privileges guaranteed by the laws of the land, had likewise been flouted and repudiated by the owners. It was this latter belief that gave to the strikers that intensity of feeling which impelled them to suffer unusual hardships during their stay in the tent colonies and which gave to the strike the character more of a revolt by entire communities than of a protest by wage earners only.

The conflict, then, was deeply rooted in class antagonism.

The strike progressed through the winter with episodes of violence. Mine owners continued to insist that union recognition would infringe on their ability to manage the mines. In order to maintain operations, the owners transported strikebreakers from outside the region and employed the Baldwin-Felts Detective Agency to protect mine property. Legal officials in Las Animas and Huerfano counties deputized individuals who were neither trained law enforcement officers nor local citizens. L. M. Bowers, the vice-president and executive officer of CF&I, wrote to Rockefeller that the mine operators were putting tremendous pressure on the "little cowboy governor" of Colorado to employ the state militia in escorting strikebreakers into the mines. Bowers assured his superior that "the bankers, the chamber of commerce, the real estate exchange, together with a great many of the best businessmen, have been urging the Governor to take steps to drive those vicious agitators [the UMW organizers] out of the State."

The situation, meanwhile, was attracting national attention. President Woodrow Wilson sent his secretary of labor, William Wilson, to Colorado to meet with Governor Ammons and the coal operators. Once again, the operators refused to deal with the union. Secretary Wilson telegraphed Rockefeller on November 21 to request his assistance in ending the strike. Rockefeller replied that the matter was in the hands of the executive officers in Colorado. Moreover, he informed Wilson, the strike was caused by a small number of men who did not represent the interests of the majority of miners. "The actions of [CF&I officers] in refusing to meet the strike leaders," Rockefeller said, "is quite as much in the interest of our employees as of any other element in the company." The following day Bowers wrote Rockefeller and applauded his "splendid support" of CF&I management. Rockefeller's position, Bowers asserted, would be vindicated in the political realm.

Hundreds of men, including many State and some national officials, have become alarmed since the uncalled-for and vicious demand of the union leaders in this State for recognition of the union and suppression of the open shop. It has become a matter of such importance in these last few weeks that it will doubtless be one of the great issues in politics in 1916. I believe there is no man in either Republican or Democratic parties who would dare to come out in opposition to the open shop.

Bowers' prediction, however, was to prove much too optimistic.

The crucial event in the strike occurred on April 20, 1917, when soldiers of the state militia attacked the tent colony at Ludlow. During the battle, five miners and a young boy were killed by gunfire.

The militia overran the settlement, burning the tents in which the miners' families had taken shelter. Eleven children and two women were suffocated or burned to death where they had hidden in a hole underneath one of the tents. Pearl Jolly, a miner's wife, recounted the event for the members of the Industrial Commission.

They got the machine gun set better and at better range, for it was terrible how those bullets came in there; it does not seem possible how they were coming in. They would say if the bullets were coming in like that, why were there not more shot? Simply because the caves were there and the dogs and chickens and everything else that moved were shot. Between five and six o'clock they set fire to our tents. When they set fire to our tents we decided that we would go from cave to cave as fast as we could. They could see us going though, and we had to dodge their bullets.

Jolly then described how one of the leaders of the strike, a Greek miner named Louis Tikas, was captured and murdered by the militia. Lieutenant Karl Linderfelt struck Tikas over the head with a rifle, breaking the stock. Jolly added, "They stepped on his face. We have a photograph. I don't believe we have it here, but it shows plain the prints of the heels in his face. After he fell, he was shot four times in the back."

As a result of the deaths at Ludlow, workers throughout the state of Colorado armed themselves and engaged in open insurrection. Union leaders issued a call to arms and for several days workers attacked mines between Denver and Trinidad, driving away guards and burning mine buildings. Civil government in the state virtually collapsed. As West observes, "The State of Colorado through its military arm was rendered helpless to maintain law and order because that military arm had acted, not as an agent of the commonwealth, but as an agent of one of the parties in interest, as an agent, that is, of the coal opera-

tors, as against the strikers." Order was restored when, at Governor Ammons' request, federal troops were sent into the coalfields.

Public opinion shifted dramatically against the mine owners after Ludlow. Rockefeller was denounced for his role in the conflict, and President Wilson urged that action be taken to end the hostilities. The press reaction and the threat of governmental intervention prompted Rockefeller to act. He developed two strategies to deal with the situation.

First, Rockefeller undertook a "union education" campaign to discredit the UMW. Through a public relations expert named Ivy Lee, Rockefeller disseminated false information about union leaders and conditions in the mine. A series of bulletins were published and distributed to various influential individuals in the state.

Second, Rockefeller hired Mackenzie King, a Canadian expert in labor relations, to devise a plan of employee representation. That plan eventually became the cornerstone of Rockefeller's industrial policy and a justification for his rejection of the plan proposed by President Wilson. In a 1918 speech entitled *Brotherhood of Men and Nations*, Rockefeller extolled the benefits of his plan. He proclaimed, "I am profoundly convinced that nothing will go so far toward establishing Brotherhood in industry and insuring industrial peace . . . as the general and early adoption by industry of this principle of representation, the favorable consideration of which cannot be too strongly urged upon leaders in industry."

In his detailed analysis of the Rockefeller plan and the circumstances surrounding its adoption, West concluded that it was "conceived and executed by men who were determined that no element of real collective bargaining should enter into it." And rather than providing for genuine industrial democracy, the genius of the plan was "its tendency to deceive the public and lull criticism, while permitting the Company to maintain its absolute power." Employee representation, in that view, was not a means to industrial democracy but an instrument of continued managerial domination.

The Ludlow incident is important in several respects. It provided the most influential early example of an "employee participation" plan and was the forerunner of the programs that are now prevalent in today's workplace. Second, the events at Ludlow demonstrated that public opinion could force capitalists to modify their oppressive labor policies. The intense reaction against Rockefeller resulted in his assuming a role as a leader of social reform. [Raymond L. Hogler]

FURTHER READING

Beshoar, Barron. *Out of the Depths: The Story of John R. Lawson, a Labor Leader.* Denver, CO: Colorado Labor Historical Committee, Denver Trades and Labor Assembly, 1942.

Gitelman, Howard M. *Legacy of the Ludlow Massacre: A Chapter in American Industrial Relations.* Philadelphia, PA: University of Pennsylvania Press, 1978.

McGovern, George, and Leonard F. Guttridge. *The Great Coalfield War.* Boston, MA: Houghton-Mifflin, 1972.

U.S. Commission on Industrial Relations. *Final Report and Testimony,* Vols. 7–9. Senate Document No. 415, 64th Congress. Washington, DC: Government Printing Office, 1916.

West, George. *Report on the Colorado Strike.* Washington, DC: Government Printing Office, 1915.

o   o   o

LYNCHBURG, VIRGINIA, TOBACCO WORKERS' STRIKE OF 1883.

Lynchburg, Virginia, was one of the major centers producing chewing tobacco in the United States in the 1870s and 1880s. Large numbers of blacks from the rural areas around Lynchburg migrated into the city during these two decades, and they readily found work in the large tobacco fac-

tories that dominated this small city in the Piedmont region of Virginia. This was a period of political turmoil in the state, with William Mahone and the Readjusters in control of the legislature for a portion of this time, threatening the reestablishment of conservative Democratic rule in Virginia. Lynchburg was also troubled, particularly during the 1880s. The working folk of the city, particularly those who worked in the tobacco manufactories, attempted to assert their control both in the workplace and in politics. While this flirtation with a more radical approach to both politics and labor relations was short-lived, it was an intriguing example of an attempt on the part of Southern workers to assert their rights.

Of particular interest is the strike of tobacco workers in Lynchburg in 1883. In early 1882, an organization called the Lynchburg Colored Workingmen's Association (LCWA) came into existence, and one of its meetings was addressed by a black state senator. About a year later, another labor organization, the Lynchburg Laboring Association (LLA), announced an important meeting. The exact relationship between the two organizations is unclear, but the Laboring Association was destined to lead what was perhaps the most important strike in Lynchburg's history. After respectfully but firmly announcing its demand for a 12.5 percent increase in wages in the newspaper on two occasions, the Laboring Association called a strike when they received no reply from the owners. The solidarity of Lynchburg's tobacco workers, most of them black, and many of those female, was remarkable. Only one of the city's thirty tobacco factories even tried to operate when the strike was called, and it soon closed when the workers in one of the factory's departments turned out. Unfortunately, attempts to enlist other black workers in Lynchburg in a sympathy strike failed, and criticism of the strike surfaced from an organization calling itself the Lynchburg Labor Union

Association (LLUA). The secrecy of the Laboring Association was objected to, but the criticism of the Labor Union Association seemed to have little effect on the tobacco factory strikers, who numbered between 1,200 and 1,300.

Some white strikebreakers were recruited, but only one factory resumed production with such workers. Lynchburg's newspaper editors denounced the strike in the strongest possible terms, referring to the workers as "of the communistic party . . . without an exception." The end of the strike, which appears to have been gradual, as the resources of the strikers disappeared, was not even noted in the press. While the strike ended without a raise or any other gains, it is clear that the desire on the part of Lynchburg's workers to improve their lot did not end in 1883 with the unsuccessful end of the strike. Lynchburg became, in the late 1880s, one of the centers of greatest strength of the Knights of Labor, electing a Knight to Congress in 1886. [Leslie S. Hough]

FURTHER READING

Hough, Leslie S. "Discontent in a Southern Tobacco Town: Lynchburg, Virginia Workers in the 1880s." Charlottesville, VA: Unpublished Master's thesis, 1974.

McLaurin, Melton A. *The Knights of Labor in the South.* Westport, CT: Greenwood Press, 1978.

Tilley, Nannie May. *The Bright Tobacco Industry, 1860–1929.* Chapel Hill, NC: University of North Carolina Press, 1948.

o   o   o

LYNN, MASSACHUSETTS, SHOE-BINDERS' PROTESTS OF 1831, 1833–1834. The development of early industrialization in boot and shoemaking in New England paralleled the rise of the factory system in cotton textiles. But the two systems of production were very different. In Waltham and Lowell, Massachusetts, textile factories used water-powered machinery in a central location where integrated processes yielded a finished bolt of cloth. Shoemaking remained largely decentralized until just before the Civil War. Men and women shoeworkers stitched the leather for shoes by hand in their artisan shops and kitchens unassisted by machines or sources of power other than human effort. Nonetheless, the activities of merchant-capitalists or "shoe bosses," who owned the leather and marketed the shoes, organized a protoindustrial system of work that made New England the national center of shoe production by 1860. The Lynn shoebinders' strikes in 1831, 1833–1834 were responses by shoeworkers who believed that this system was essentially unjust and immoral. Shoebinders declared in 1834: "These things ought not so to be!"

Once an artisan-craft of apprentices, journeymen, and masters at work in little shops, women began to stitch the part of the shoe called the "upper" as production expanded to satisfy domestic markets after 1780. "Shoebinding," the word invented for this women's work, became a commonplace category in early-nineteenth-century New England. A shoebinder used a long flexible wooden shoe clamp instead of straddling a shoemaker's bench. This clamp, usually fashioned from barrel staves, rested on the floor. The shoebinder held it tightly between her knees, thus freeing her hands to use the awl to punch holes in the leather and to stitch the upper with either a needle or hog's bristle. Shoebinders were not taught to make an entire shoe. The sexual division of labor kept women relatively unskilled and therefore distant from the vibrant political and social life of artisans in their shops.

At first the shoebinder, usually the wife or daughter of a shoemaker, did not earn wages or have any direct connection with the shoe boss. Instead, she worked in her kitchen at the direction of the men in the shoe shop. Often as a wife and mother, a shoebinder had to put down her stitching to attend to bread that needed to be baked or children who needed to be fed. These distractions, that were central to women's household work, made it essential to find additional female hands to stitch uppers. In this way, shoebinding began by 1810 to move onto the wage labor market and into the households of farmers, small tradesmen, and other craftsmen.

Shoe bosses hired shoebinders, directed their work, and paid them wages, usually in credits at general stores. Slowly the work of shoebinding became separated from the work of shoemaking; it was conducted by different workers, in different locations, for different shoe bosses. Networks of decentralized workers reached into the small villages and towns of eastern Massachusetts such as Lynn, Saugus, Reading, and Woburn. More women labored in this outwork system in early-nineteenth-century Massachusetts than worked in textile factories.

A shoebinder might work steadily all day to produce ten pairs of sewn uppers at three to five cents a pair, but she also furnished needles, thread, and sometimes lining material which reduced her earnings. The periodic and irregular nature of outwork, often interrupted by farm chores and family needs, encouraged the shoe boss to develop extensive networks of shoebinders using the turnpikes and freight lines to dispatch uppers to women workers. Bosses preferred to develop this widespread system of production rather than to raise prices per pair in spite of the booming domestic market just before the depression of 1837. This situation provoked an outbreak of early labor protest in 1831 among the shoebinders of Reading and surrounding towns in eastern Massachusetts.

Shoebinders began to organize in the early 1830s to protest low wages, an indication that they recognized the separation of men and women's work. They sought and obtained the support of local shoemakers, but their labor protest expressed

women's concerns and generated women leaders. They invoked artisan ideology that asserted equal rights with employers and political liberties for working people. In doing so, they began to argue for new rights for women. This feminist component of early labor protest paralleled the stirrings of interest in women's rights among the Lowell textile workers in the early 1830s. The sense of connection between the leaders of shoebinder protest and female factory workers suggested a new consciousness for working women as industrial capitalism altered the nature of women's work both at home and in the textile mill.

The women shoeworkers of Reading formed the Society of Shoebinders in the summer of 1831 to protest low wages, to demand replacement of store orders with cash payments, and to obtain a uniform wage scale for binding various kinds of shoes. They published a manifesto in a Boston newspaper that had been signed by over 200 women in six towns. These women were aware of the vulnerabilities of working at home in isolation. The objective of the society was to encourage binders to cooperate in resisting individual wage bargains with the shoe bosses so that inexperienced women would not "work for nothing and find [furnish] themselves," that is provide the shoe boss with free labor. Drawing on their identification with the values of artisan life, they expressed expectations of fairness and good treatment by the shoe bosses. But perhaps the most impressive achievement of the society in 1831 was the organization of outworkers living in different towns.

Five shoe bosses from Reading and neighboring towns rejected the arguments of the Society of Shoebinders, insisting that the wages they paid had been customary for ten years. They attempted to undermine the society by pressuring members and isolating them from support. These tactics were successful, and the society disappeared in 1831. But two years later the shoebinders of Lynn and Saugus challenged their employers over low wages.

By 1833, there were about 1,500 shoebinders in Lynn. A wage cut prompted over half of them to organize the "Female Society of Lynn and Vicinity for the Protection and Promotion of Female Industry." They borrowed and recast the values of artisan life to justify their protest as women workers. They claimed new political and economic rights for women, including the right to public assembly and the right to contribute significantly as wage earners to their families. Shoebinders in Saugus also formed a society and adopted similar objectives and justifications. Each society met in a church friendly to the activism of women in religious life—in Lynn, the Friends' Meeting House and in Saugus, the Methodist Church. This linkage of their protest activities and the churches made the moral dimension of their public activities clear.

In the preamble of the Lynn Society's constitution, the binders accused their employers of "a manifest *error*, a want of justice and reasonable compensation to the females; which calls imperiously for redress. While the prices of *Their* labor have been reduced, the business of their *employers* has appeared to be improving, and prosperous, enabling them to increase in wealth. These *things ought not so to be*!" The leaders of the Society, young unmarried women like chairman Mary Russell and secretary Elizabeth K. Keene, used artisan ideology to argue that shoebinders were not earning a just wage for their work. This economic injustice threatened their independence and respectability and violated their dignity as producers.

To redress their grievances, the shoebinders of Lynn demanded an increase in wages and the extension of the equal rights doctrine of artisan life to women. "Equal rights should be extended to all— to the weaker sex as well as the stronger."

The disadvantage that women experienced "by nature and custom" should not be aggravated by "unnecessary and unjust" treatment as workers. The preamble expressed the belief that "women as well as men, have certain inalienable rights, among which is the right at all times of 'peaceably assembling to consult upon the common good.'"

According to the women, the reduction in shoebinders' wages prevented them from earning "a comfortable support," a feminine version of the competency sought by artisan men to provide for their families and allow some savings for old age. Shoebinders used their roles as wives, daughters, and widows rather than their status as workers to determine the wage level that would provide them with this comfortable support. A wage for a wife should cover household expenses for sewing, washing, and nursing. For a daughter, wages should be high enough to cover her expenses for personal upkeep and board. A widow's wages should prevent her from being forced into the poor house or applying for poor relief from the town. The Society particularly condemned the practice of paying widows in store goods rather than in cash.

These activist shoebinders in 1833–1834 recognized the new demands and opportunities of wage-earning for women and sought to integrate wage work into their lives within a context of justice, morality, and artisan values. They linked morality to political action which they saw as appropriate and necessary to female labor protest. In doing so, they added feminism to their expressions of class consciousness. Their leader, Mary Russell, identified the Society's efforts with the first turnouts of the Lowell textile operatives in February 1834, expressing the hope that "they [the shoebinders] might be equally free from oppression." Textile operatives drew on similar sources of New England ideology to justify their labor protest, but unlike shoebinders, they worked and lived together in the new textile towns.

Artisan shoemakers immediately offered their support to the shoebinders' efforts, but the difficulties of organizing outworkers for collective protest were formidable. By the spring of 1834, the Lynn Society was divided and in trouble. It lasted only until December. Unlike the textile workers of Lowell who began their rebellions in 1834, shoebinders worked in their homes and in isolation from each other, submerged in family life and surrounded by household chores. The social relations of family life and the realities of outwork made long-term collective action for shoebinders unlikely. Shoe bosses responded to female labor unrest in the early 1830s by pushing their networks of shoebinders into a more geographically extensive system of outwork that penetrated the villages and rural areas of New England. In this way, they ignored the moral outrage of shoebinders, and the shoebinders' activities ceased. [Mary H. Blewett]

Further Reading

Blewett, Mary H. *Men, Women, and Work: Class, Gender, and Protest in the New England Shoe Industry, 1780–1910.* Urbana, IL: University of Illinois Press, 1988.

Dublin, Thomas. *Women at Work: The Transformation of Work and Community in Lowell, Massachusetts, 1826–1860.* New York: Columbia University Press, 1979.

o　o　o

LYNN, MASSACHUSETTS, STRIKE OF 1872. The 1872 struggle in Lynn, Massachusetts began as a strike, quickly became a lockout, and ended with the ignominious and decisive defeat of the Knights of St. Crispin (KOSC), the largest trade union in the United States. The KOSC was an industrial union of shoeworkers that

had appeared in 1867. With a membership of nearly 50,000, many of them in Massachusetts, the KOSC attempted to establish "arbitration" (collective bargaining) in a fiercely competitive industry.

The 1872 strike pitted the Crispins, KOSC members, against the shoe manufacturers in Lynn, the largest producer of women's shoes in the United States. The KOSC in Lynn united in one union the factory workers who performed the many specialized tasks in the making of shoes. The Crispins were both machine operatives and handworkers, heirs to the traditions and values of the pre-factory mechanics, who left them a rich inheritance of pride, dignity, and self-esteem. The KOSC had several lodges with a total membership of approximately 1,500, accounting for half of the city's shoeworkers.

The key issue in the struggle was the right of the Crispins to establish wage rates for all shoeworkers in Lynn's 180 shops and to end the disastrous competition that drove down living standards. The Lynn Crispins had achieved extraordinary success in 1870 through their board of arbitration. Representatives of the KOSC and shoe manufacturers together established wage rates for all aspects of shoework in the city. In 1871, the two sides renewed the agreement, giving Lynn two years of industrial peace in a period of economic prosperity.

The harmony ended abruptly in the summer of 1872 when the agreement expired. The KOSC conceded the need for revising some rates and acknowledged the need for reductions, especially in light of a new edging machine that simplified work. But the Crispins sought to renegotiate another settlement on a citywide basis. Manufacturers rebuffed the overture of compromise and abrogated some rates, provoking a strike by the KOSC on July 26 that halted production in the city's largest shops. The employers took quick and decisive action. On August 2, a meeting of forty employers announced a new labor policy: they would no longer accept KOSC wage scales. Each employer would freely set his own rates with his own individual workers and would tolerate no interference by any outside organization. After August 10, they would "employ no person subject to, or under the control of, any organization claiming the power to interfere with any contract between employer and employee."

The fifty employers included the largest and claimed to represent 80 percent of the shoe manufacturers. They were confident, aggressive, and determined "to cut the Gordian knot," a euphemism for defeating the union. To those who counseled compromise to preserve peace, they replied that the issue was not the present but the future: "the welfare and prosperity of our city and the interests of the shoe business." Because the stakes were so great, they would "fight it out to the bitter end." Should they fail, they would either go out of business or leave the city and relocate elsewhere. If victorious, they promised the highest wages that the economy would permit, more regular and steady employment, and aid in enlarging the stock of housing for workers.

The KOSC faced humiliation and extinction. On August 13, a mass meeting of Crispins condemned the employers' offer as "tyrannical terms" that would mean "complete sacrifice of self-respect and personal independence." But the resistance of the KOSC was astonishingly brief and feeble. Their strike lasted less than two weeks and ended in nearly complete capitulation. Unlike the great **Shoemakers' Strike of 1860**, there was no strong plea to the public and little evidence of popular support for the shoeworkers, even though one editor said there was "no good reason why it [collective bargaining] should be abandoned at this time." The women workers played no prominent role, despite the existence of their own organization, the Daughters of St. Crispin, nor was their aid sought. And unlike other conflicts in which employers imported strikebreakers to replace strikers, there is no evidence that Lynn shoe manufacturers recruited replacements. The Crispins resumed work on terms some had thought tyrannical.

There are several possible reasons for the collapse of the Lynn KOSC. The strike of 1872 came after a long seasonal layoff. Many workers had probably depleted their savings and had incurred burdensome debts that they were anxious to repay. Business was brisk and wage rates were adequate if not high. Lack of work rather than low wages may have been paramount for many workers. Perhaps workers were fearful that employers would leave Lynn and resume operations elsewhere. In any event, the Crispins had adopted a position that few were willing to fight to defend.

The 1872 strike virtually ended the KOSC's existence in Lynn. Membership dwindled so precipitously that the lodges surrendered their charters. But employers achieved neither complete control of their businesses nor tranquillity in industrial relations. Strikes would recur periodically in Lynn during the next half century. [Paul Faler]

FURTHER READING

Blewett, Mary H. *Men, Women, and Work: Class, Gender, and Protest in the New England Shoe Industry, 1780–1910.* Urbana, IL: University of Illinois Press, 1988.

Dawley, Alan. *Class and Community: The Industrial Revolution in Lynn.* Cambridge, MA: Harvard University Press, 1976.

Lescohier, Don. "The Knights of St. Crispin 1867–1874: A Study on Industrial Causes of Trade Unionism." *Bulletin of the University of Wisconsin*, No. 355. Madison, WI: 1910.

M

o o o o o o o o o o o

o o o

MACHINISTS' STRIKE AND BOY-COTT OF 1913 AGAINST DUPLEX PRINTING COMPANY. In August 1913, fourteen members of the International Association of Machinists (IAM) struck the Duplex Printing Company, one of only three firms in the United States making printing presses. The strike, over union recognition and working conditions, involved less than 10 percent of Duplex's work force and barely slowed production at the plant. For the IAM, however, the strike had a more pressing urgency. The other two major printing press manufacturing firms had agreements with the IAM and promised to offer an eight-hour workday at higher wages if Duplex would agree to the same. Duplex refused to meet those conditions, thus precipitating the walkout. The IAM, with a greater stake in the outcome, quickly called for a boycott and succeeded in convincing some workers not to handle Duplex presses. Especially troubling was a group of union shippers in New York who refused to deliver Duplex products. This secondary boycott set in motion a chain of events that gave this small strike a much wider significance.

One important factor in escalating the conflict was Duplex's location in Battle Creek, Michigan. Battle Creek was a center of anti-union agitation in the first two decades of the twentieth century. Following the dramatic growth of the American Federation of Labor (AFL) in the years between 1898 and 1903, the National Association of Manufacturers (NAM) countered with a vigorous and well-orchestrated attack on organized labor calling for the open shop or, in other words, the non-union shop. Led by local cereal magnate, C. W. Post, Battle Creek manufacturers made the city a haven for the NAM's open shop movement. Post, through his anti-labor magazine, *Square Deal*, convinced his neighboring employers to root out trade unions through a combination of welfare work, legal actions, and police repression.

The NAM's crusade against organized labor received valuable assistance from federal courts which, in particular, had declared war on one of the AFL's most valuable weapons, the boycott. Drawing upon the Sherman Antitrust Act (1890) which banned all unfair restraints on interstate trade, the NAM had convinced the courts that labor boycotts violated the law. In two important cases, *Loewe* v. *Lawlor* (1908) and *Gompers* v. *Buck's Stove and Range Company* (1911), NMA-backed companies won injunctions against boycotts and sued for damages against the Hatters Union and against the AFL itself. AFL leaders Samuel Gompers and John Mitchell even faced jail sentences for their refusal to heed court demands that they remove the Buck's Stove and Range Company from the *American Federationist's* "We Don't Patronize" list.

Court decisions and the open shop movement pushed the AFL to abandon its traditional non-partisan political stance. In 1906, Gompers issued labor's "Bill of Grievances" and began building an alliance with the Democratic Party. By 1912, when Woodrow Wilson won election as President of the United States, relief from prosecution under the Sherman Act topped the AFL's political agenda. The Wilson administration complied with much of that agenda including the passage of the Clayton Act (1914), which supposedly freed organized labor from prosecution for illegal restraint of trade under antitrust laws. Gompers trumpeted the Clayton Act as labor's "Magna Carta."

When the IAM began its boycott of the Duplex Printing Company following the 1913 strike, it did so in the belief that labor's right to engage in boycotts would be protected. However, the Post forces in the NAM were not yet finished. They encouraged their Battle Creek neighbors, the Duplex officials, to pursue action in the courts against the IAM for its illegal restraint of trade. Lower courts, citing the Clayton Act, gave the union favorable opinions as *Duplex Printing Co.* v. *Deering* proceeded through trials and appeals.

Finally, the case reached the Supreme Court in 1921 during an especially virulent period of labor–capital conflict following World War I. Surprisingly, the Court, by a vote of six to three, reversed lower court rulings and ruled for the company. The Clayton Act, according to Justice Mahlon Pitney who wrote the decision, only protected labor's *lawful* methods for achieving its objects. A secondary boycott—that is, a boycott against Duplex products by workers not involved in the original dispute with the company—was not a lawful method according to the Supreme Court majority.

The Court's ruling on secondary boycotts and its questioning of what constituted lawful activities by organized labor spurred a dramatic increase in business's appeal for court injunctions against labor activities in the 1920s. The Clayton Act, according to Gompers, had been "judicially purloined." Its ability to protect labor's rights was decimated. Not until the Norris-LaGuardia Act (1932) was the AFL given some relief from court-or-

dered injunctions, particularly those related to secondary boycotts. However, that right was not to last; in 1947, the Taft-Hartley Act again made secondary boycotts unlawful. [Ken Fones-Wolf]

FURTHER READING

McLaughlin, Doris B. *Michigan Labor: A Brief History from 1818 to the Present*. Ann Arbor, MI: Institute of Labor and Industrial Relations, 1970.

Taylor, Albion G. *Labor and the Supreme Court*. Ann Arbor, MI: Braum-Brumfield, Inc., 1961.

Tomlins, Christopher L. *The State and the Unions: Labor Relations, Law and the Organized Labor Movement in America, 1880–1960*. New York: Cambridge University Press, 1985.

o   o   o

MACHINISTS' STRIKES OF 1900 AND 1901. As the country began to emerge from the depths of the long depression that began in 1893, the International Association of Machinists (IAM), one of the most militant affiliates of the American Federation of Labor, initiated a drive to correct the many problems that confronted the trade. The drive for the shorter workday and the end of the piecework system of payment loomed largest as union goals.

In 1898, after watching as their much more powerful counterpart in England, the Amalgamated Society of Engineers, went down in a crushing defeat at the hands of the metal industries, the IAM pulled back from a confrontation with employers in America's metal-fabricating plants and railroad repair shops. When the drive was revived in 1900, Chicago, perhaps the strongest union town in America at the time, was chosen as the focus of the union's effort.

In January 1900, the IAM's lodges in the city presented 150 machine shops with a demand for the nine-hour workday, a closed shop, layoffs governed by seniority, recognition of union shop committees, and a minimum wage of 20¢ an hour. When the employers, grouped in the Chicago chapter of the National Metal Trades Association (NMTA), refused to consider the demands, 5,000 machinists struck. The action coincided with strikes by 40,000 Chicago building tradesmen, thus severely crippling the city. Following Chicago's lead, machinists in Cleveland, Detroit, Paterson, and Philadelphia called their members out.

The issues that most distressed the employers were not wages and hours. They were willing to make concessions on those so long as their competitors worked under the same conditions. But recognition of the union and the creation of shop committees to handle grievances appeared to be serious threats to management's control of the shop floor. The Chicago employers were particularly fearful of the implications of dealing officially with the militant local machinists. Their solution, in the face of the solidarity of the machinists, was to try to broaden the effects of any settlement to include the entire industry and to remove power as much as possible from the Chicago machinists and transfer it to the national union. As the president of one company explained, "A man fitted to represent a national organization . . . would be an easier man to do business with. . . ." The assumption was that union officials were more reliable than their members— members who were more likely to move the labor–management issues beyond wages and hours to more central issues of workplace control.

The power of the Chicago machinists and the central position of the Chicago metal industry in the nation turned this employer strategy into a major opportunity for the national union. IAM president James O'Connell seized the opportunity and reached an agreement with the NMTA to transfer unsettled grievances, the wage question, and apprenticeship rules to a board of arbitration having equal representation from the IAM and the NMTA. The agreement also called for a fifty-five-hour workweek by 1901. The agreement satisfied the needs of the Chicago employers and gave the national union recognition. What it did not do was give the Chicago locals what they had demanded. In particular, it did not grant the union any role on the shop floor. Nevertheless, the Chicago membership ratified the agreement overwhelmingly.

The center of the action then shifted to New York City's Murray Hill Hotel where a union negotiating team headed by President O'Connell faced off with the NMTA bargaining committee. The sessions resulted in a further reduction in the workweek and a pledge by the NMTA not to discriminate against union members but little else. The arbitration board was to sit permanently to hear grievances, and the union signed a no-strike pledge.

The settlement in the machinists' strike was applauded by the National Civic Federation (NCF), the labor–management organization whose membership included labor leaders such as President Samuel Gompers of the AFL, John Mitchell of the United Mine Workers, and a host of powerful businessmen. The NCF's goal was to promote labor–management peace and cooperation through stable collective bargaining. This depended on providing recognition and thus security for "responsible" national labor leaders who could negotiate, and compel their members to honor, reasonable contracts.

It was difficult, however, to translate this cooperation at the top to support at the local level. In the spring of 1901, IAM lodges from around the country began to demand hourly wage increases to coincide with the reduction of hours to fifty-four. They were determined that the reduction not result in a loss of pay. When O'Connell pushed the NMTA for a national wage settlement, however, the NMTA balked. Wages, the NMTA now argued, should be arbitrated on a local basis. O'Connell, whose union had grown dramatically in the past few years, called a nationwide strike for May 20, 1901.

Employers too felt betrayed. The Murray Hill agreement, they believed, had settled the matter of union influence on the shop floor once and for all. The closed shop had been rejected, as had shop floor committees. What had actually happened at the local level, however, was that as the IAM's numbers grew, workers enforced a de facto closed shop and unilaterally established work rules. With both sides feeling betrayed, the Murray Hill agreement, which only a year before had been hailed by the NCF as a model of responsible labor–management relations, broke down in mutual recrimination.

The NMTA announced a new statement of principles in May of 1901. The employers reaffirmed their right to hire, fire, and direct the work as they saw fit. Local conditions, not a national agreement, would govern wage levels. Piecework, still a sticking point with the IAM, would continue. Armed with this militant program, the NMTA marched into battle with the IAM. The National Civic Federation, appalled at the unraveling of the Murray Hill agreement, could do little but stand aside and observe the bloodletting.

In the end, the employers succeeded in returning conditions in the industry back to before the Murray Hill agreement. Although the 1901 strikes lasted until the fall in some cities, most were defeated. Across the country, metal trades employers pressed an open shop campaign to destroy the IAM. Only in Chicago, the stronghold of the union, did the IAM win. There, as in no other city in the country, the labor movement thrived. Not until the depression of 1903–1904 did Chicago industry regroup and counterattack in a largely successful attempt to recover some of the ground lost since 1901.

The real victim of the 1901 strike was the National Civic Federation's philosophy of stable and responsible labor–management relations. By 1903, most employers had rejected any ideas of accommodation with organized labor. Instead, they flocked into the young National Association of Manufacturers and the Citizens' Industrial Association, the twin prongs of the nationwide open shop crusade. [Ronald L. Filippelli]

FURTHER READING

Montgomery, David. *Workers' Control in America.* New York: Cambridge University Press, 1979.

———. *The Fall of the House of Labor.* New York: Cambridge University Press, 1988.

Perlman, Mark. *The Machinists: A New Study in American Trade Unionism.* Cambridge, MA: Harvard University Press, 1961.

o   o   o

MANAYUNK, PENNSYLVANIA, MILL STRIKES OF 1833 AND 1834. The wage earners of the town of Manayunk, located north of Philadelphia along the Schuylkill River, conducted a series of bitter strikes against the cotton textile manufacturers during 1833 and 1834 that served as a catalyst for the organization of factory workers throughout the region. The walkouts, which continued unabated for nearly nine months, revealed the deep divisions that industrialization had created in the community as shopkeepers, newspaper editors, and clergymen aligned themselves with one side or the other. Unlike other employers faced with similar turnouts during the same period, at least one Manayunk mill owner attempted to replace striking workers and utilized the services of local magistrates to protect his property. Two major reasons for the intensity of the conflicts were the structure of the local textile industry and the nature of the labor force employed in the mills.

The large-scale production of textiles in the Manayunk area began with the opening of the Flat Rock Canal in 1819. In contrast to other manufacturers in the region, who continued to utilize a mix of machine and hand production, the two major cotton mill owners in town, J. J. Borie and Joseph Ripka, decided to invest heavily in power driven machinery in order to boost productivity by lessening their dependence on the services of skilled workers, especially handloom weavers. They recruited their labor force from among the thousands of unemployed or marginally employed English and Irish immigrants who had flocked to Philadelphia to find work in the regional textile industry. Many of these men and women had been involved in some form of labor organization at home. While they eagerly sought employment in the mills, they quickly became disenchanted with long hours, arbitrary discipline, and unsafe machinery.

A general decline in the value of manufactures during the summer of 1833 led Ripka and Borie to announce a 20 percent wage cut in early August. The workers in Ripka's mills responded by walking out and were soon followed by those employed in Borie's manufactory and two smaller mills. Striking workers and their supporters quickly established an organization, "the Working People of Manayunk," to coordinate the activities of the protesting millhands. In addition to cotton spinners from the factories, machinists, storekeepers, skilled artisans, and a few labor leaders from Philadelphia provided the leadership for the committee. A number of these individuals were immigrants who had already confronted similar situations in Europe. "The Working People" issued a memorial to the local newspapers claiming that "We have long suffered the evils of being divided in our sentiments, but the universal oppression that we now all feel, has roused us to a sense of our oppressed conditions and we are now determined to be oppressed no longer!"

Men, women, and children all participated in rallies and street demonstra-

tions. As the strike continued into the early weeks of September, textile workers in surrounding communities moved to establish the Trades Union of Pennsylvania to strengthen their position with their own employers and to provide relief to the Manayunk strikers. The subsequent fate of both the Trades Union and the strike itself is unclear; it appears that the factories resumed operations sometime in November. Four months later Borie announced a new wage cut of nearly 25 percent which precipitated an immediate turnout by his hands. He responded by advertising in Philadelphia papers for replacement workers. The strikers drew up their own handbills explaining the situation in Manayunk and patrolled the streets to discourage anyone from entering the struck mill. They allegedly beat one mule spinner who attempted to go to work. This prompted the manufacturer to call upon magistrates from surrounding communities to protect workers who sought employment in his mill. Borie also received considerable support from local clergymen who utilized their pulpits to urge an end to the walkout, condemning strike leaders as foreign-born radicals and agitators.

As the strike dragged on for a second month, a meeting of factory operatives developed an ingenious proposal for ending the conflict. Rather than have Borie retain the savings from their reduced wages, millhands suggested that they use the funds generated from the proposed cuts to buy new machinery for the manufactory which would increase its competitive edge. They would retain ownership of the new machinery until such time as their employer could afford to purchase the machinery from them. The plan obviously proved unacceptable to Borie.

Available evidence indicates that the strike ended sometime before the end of May and that workers returned to their machines with a 5 percent increase in wages rather than a 25 percent decrease.

Such a settlement was possible because the textile industry as a whole began to pick up from the recession which had precipitated the proposed wage cuts in the first place. The ongoing conflict in the Manayunk mills had deeply divided the community. The divisions engendered by the walkout found their clearest expression in local partisan politics as wage earners helped to turn the Democratic party into a vehicle of social and economic reform. After decisively beating the Democrats in 1835 and 1836, the Whig Party itself split over the issue of its treatment of local wage earners. Grain mill operators and farmers, sympathetic to the cause of the factory workers, lost control of the party to textile manufacturers who made clear their concept of economic and political power. "We consider the mill owners of Manayunk, and every person employing men, to have a better right to discharge any man from their employment for differences of opinion on political questions than either the President of the United States or the Governor of the state."

With the advent of the nationwide depression in 1837, employers wielded that power with even greater enthusiasm, strengthening their control over the work force. Fearful of losing their jobs during hard times, wage earners in Manayunk and elsewhere abandoned trade unionism and other forms of workplace organization. It was to be many years before factory operatives once again took to the streets to demand fair treatment on the job. [Howard S. Harris]

FURTHER READING

Shelton, Cynthia. *The Mills of Manayunk: Industrialization and Social Conflict in the Philadelphia Region, 1787–1837.* Baltimore, MD: The Johns Hopkins University Press, 1986.

Sullivan, William. *The Industrial Worker in Pennsylvania 1800–1840.* Harrisburg, PA: Pennsylvania Historical and Museum Commission, 1955.

o o o

MARLBORO, MASSACHUSETTS, SHOEWORKERS' STRIKE OF 1898–1899.

In the early morning of November 10, 1898, members of the Boot and Shoe Workers' Union (BSWU) arrived at work in Marlboro to find notices affixed to the factory gates. The major shoe companies of the city had determined to terminate their contracts with the BSWU. Henceforward, workers would be dealt with individually or in committee but without union recognition. Four days later the workers answered by striking and closing down the shoe industry in Marlboro.

By 1898, the shoe industry in Marlboro had moved to the front in terms of efficiency and technology. The largest shoe factory in the country was located there, and the factories of the city's nine major employers averaged 266 workers, far above average for the industry. The work force of the city had changed as the industry grew. By 1895, what twenty years earlier had largely been Irish and Yankee, was one quarter foreign born, with French-Canadians constituting the single largest group of newcomers.

Marlboro's shoeworkers had early taken to unionism, and by 1898 more than half of them belonged to the BSWU, making the industry in the city one of the most unionized in New England. But unlike shoeworkers elsewhere, Marlboro's unions were conservative, preferring local autonomy. In part, this reflected the long-term stability of work in the city. This was complemented by higher earnings and better working conditions in comparison with other New England shoe centers. The fact that the manufacturers lived there and played an active and controlling role in the governance of Marlboro no doubt also accounted for the general social and economic stability of the city.

What then, led to the drastic change in the relations between manufacturers, workers, and citizens of Marlboro in 1898?

The main cause seems to have been increased competition from non-union companies. This led employers to resist wage increases. Companies also wanted to replace the day-rate payment system with an hourly and piece-rate system, charging that the day-rate system led to lower productivity. All of these pressures led to an increase in rank-and-file militancy and sporadic disputes with employers.

Manufacturer William Rice led the assault on the unions, blaming them for driving industry out of New England. The declaration of the open shop that resulted stunned the citizens of Marlboro. The complete cooperation of all of the companies made it clear that it would be a long, hard fight.

Response to the strike among the citizens was mixed. The workers were their friends and neighbors and, in the case of small business, their consumers. But all were equally aware of the importance of the shoe industry to the city and were sensitive to threats from the manufacturers that Marlboro was losing out to competing cities where wages were lower. In fact, the general civility that had marked the city before the dispute also prevailed during the early days of the strike. In some cases, manufacturers extended credit and rent reductions to some strikers, particularly the skilled workers whom they wanted to retain after the strike.

Support for the strikers did not extend to the press. The town's major paper, the *Enterprise*, had close ties to the manufacturers. Unions, in the eyes of the *Enterprise*'s editor, should be tolerated only if they allowed for the smooth running of the factories. Nor were the strikers terribly successful in raising money from other unions. Without strike funds, strikers found minimal temporary relief only from the Overseers of the Poor and local charities.

One bright spot for the strikers was the election victory in December of a fusion ticket of workers and the Democrats called the Workingmen's Party. In fact, however, the new city government played practically no positive role in the strike.

By February, the solidarity of the strike had begun to crumble. Numerous workers had left the city to seek work elsewhere. The manufacturers hired strikebreakers from outside of the city and by January had officially reopened the factories. As frustration grew, fights between strikers and strikebreakers became common, as did petty damage to company property. A request for protection from the governor resulted in the sending in of forty state police to keep order. As this transpired, community support for the strike plummeted. The longer the strike continued, the more merchants and community leaders feared that the manufacturers would leave Marlboro. Indeed, one had. William Rice had already taken one of his shops to Worcester. The message was not lost on Marlboro's businessmen who voted overwhelmingly to withhold financial aid and credit from the strikers.

With their meager financial resources disappearing, the strike started to disintegrate in early February when the cutters began to return to work. By mid-April, the back-to-work movement involved just about everyone. On May 5, the joint council of unions told the few hundred still on strike that they could return if they so chose.

The Marlboro defeat was a disaster for the BSWU. Its national membership dropped to 9,000. The decentralized union structure that the various crafts had demanded had failed the test of economic conflict. The leadership concluded that only a strong, centralized union with a high-dues structure could survive against the power of capital in the industrial age. Fresh from their defeat, the BSWU members strongly supported the change. Dues were increased, and strike and sick benefit funds were established. Only strikes authorized by the BSWU's Strike Committee would receive financial assistance from the union. The focus was to be on collective bargaining agreements. With these changes the BSWU rose slowly from the ashes of Marlboro and reconstituted itself as a viable union. But in Marlboro, a different result ensued. There unionization was broken, and wages and working conditions declined. What was once the city with the highest standards in the shoe industry had become the low-wage center. [Ronald L. Filippelli]

FURTHER READING

Dodd, Martin H. "Marlboro, Massachusetts and the Shoeworkers' Strike of 1898–1899." *Labor History*, Vol. 20 (Summer, 1979), pp. 376–397.

Blewett, Mary. *Men, Women, and Work: Class, Gender, and Protest in the New England Shoe Industry, 1780–1910.* Urbana, IL: University of Illinois Press, 1988.

o   o   o

MARYLAND INDENTURED SERVANTS' STRIKE OF 1663. Bound, or indentured, servants often ran away from their masters. Often these flights involved several servants, but the authorities rarely resorted to conspiracy prosecution in these cases. They were content to capture the runaways and enforce the statutory extra service penalty for desertion. An exception occurred in 1657 when Robert Chessick, who had previously run away and then captured, persuaded a group of servants of several different masters to flee. In the process, they seized a boat and a stock of arms and ammunition. All but one were captured and prosecuted and convicted for conspiracy. Chessick was sentenced to receive thirty lashes and enjoined not to depart from his master's plantation without leave. His co-conspirators received similar punishment.

In Maryland, when bound servants chose to withhold their labor instead of fleeing, they were subject to criminal prosecution. In 1663, the servants of Richard Preston refused to work because of the lack of meat in their provisions. When the servants continued in their "obstinate rebellious condition," even though Preston provided them with fish and sugar and offered to lend them a boat to see if they could find meat to purchase, he turned to the court for assistance.

John Smith, Richard Gibbs, Samuel Copley, Samuel Styles, Henry Gorslett, and Thomas Broxam, all bound servants, answered the charges by arguing that without meat they were too weak to work and petitioned the court to see that their needs were answered by their master. The court ruled for the master, ordering all six to suffer thirty lashes each. Impassioned pleas for forgiveness from the defendants led the judge to suspend the sentence and place them on good behavior. [Ronald L. Filippelli]

FURTHER READING

Jernegan, Marcus W. *Laboring and Dependent Classes in Colonial America, 1607–1783.* New York: Ungar, 1960.

Morris, Richard B. *Government and Labor in Early America.* New York: Harper and Row, 1946.

Smith, Abbot E. *Colonists in Bondage: White Servitude and Convict Labor in America, 1607–1776.* Chapel Hill, NC: University of North Carolina Press, 1947.

o   o   o

MAYTAG STRIKE OF 1938. This strike resulted in a significant setback for the United Electrical, Radio and Machine Workers of America (UE).

In early 1937, following up on their success in organizing the electrical plants in St. Louis, UE organizers moved into the manufacturing towns of the surrounding rural states. They found a receptive climate at the home plant of Maytag, located in the town of Newton, Iowa. The plant employed about 2,000 workers, all male, who produced washing machines. Local 1116 of the

UE was chartered on April 30, 1937, and immediately won a National Labor Relations Board (NLRB) representation election. Shortly thereafter, Maytag agreed to a one-year contract.

As the May 9, 1938, expiration date approached, the situation had changed. The nation was now in a renewed recession, and Maytag, while still profitable, had built up a very large inventory of washers. The firm demanded wage cuts of up to 12 percent and refused to extend the old contract during negotiations. The union refused such concessions to a profitable firm, and on May 9, Maytag unilaterally instituted a 10 percent wage cut. Workers in the plant promptly began a sit-down strike. After a few hours, Maytag contacted union headquarters and arranged for the peaceful withdrawal of the strikers.

The union set up mass picket lines outside the plant, which for the first month were honored by over 95 percent of the workers. After some minor clashes between pickets and strikebreakers, the company was able to obtain an injunction, limiting pickets to three at each gate. Most home mortgages in the town were written by Maytag-controlled companies; the firm also controlled the major auto dealership at which workers had financed their cars. The company used this leverage to advantage. A Loyal Workers Committee was set up by the Maytag attorney, and an anti-strike Citizens and Taxpayers Committee was formed. Foremen and supervisors visited homes to encourage workers to support the return to work.

On June 23, about 500 workers filed back into the plant. Most of them, however, were pro-unionists, who had infiltrated the procession that morning. Once inside the plant, the unionists again halted all production. The company then ousted the mayor of Newton and replaced him with a more compliant figure, George Campbell, who unsuccessfully tried to remove the strikers from the plant.

Two sets of legal charges were now filed against the union. One was a group of contempt-of-court charges issued by Judge Homer A. Fuller against 107 union activists for the new sit-down. The other was criminal syndicalism charges against UE District 8 president William Sentner and five other unionists. The six were arrested and held for several days without bail. When bail was finally set, it was $150,000 to be paid in full.

The UE responded by filing unfair labor practices charges with the National Labor Relations Board (NLRB). The regional NLRB began holding hearings and on June 21 submitted a report to the national board urging action.

The governor of Iowa, a New Deal Democrat named Nelson G. Kraschel, was under heavy pressure from both sides. On July 1, acting under martial law powers, he ordered the plant closed and evacuated. The union removed its men on this basis. The governor also appointed an arbitration board to recommend a settlement.

On July 15, Judge Fuller sentenced Sentner and the other unionists, including UE national president James Carey, to six months in jail for contempt of court. The next day, however, the Iowa Supreme Court stayed the sentences, pending a review before that body. On the same day, the arbitration board recommended a return to work at the old wages for sixty days, after which the company could cut wages by up to 10 percent. There would be no closed shop or checkoff. Both sides refused to accept this recommendation, and on July 19 the governor extended martial law to Newton and Jasper County and sent in the Iowa National Guard. As late a August 1, Sentner was optimistic that the governor would take no further action and that an agreement could be reached soon. He was wrong. On August 4, Governor Kraschel directed that the plant be reopened and that the men go back to work on the terms of the arbitration board ruling. In addition, the firing of twelve union stewards for "illegal strike activities" was also ordered.

Overwhelmed, the union was forced to accept this significant setback, in what UE director of organization James Matles called a "very painful decision." Still unified, the 80 percent of the workers loyal to the strike marched back to work as a unit after ninety-eight days off the job. The twelve fired union activists were all eventually acquitted or had the charges against them dropped, but they never regained their jobs. Several became UE organizers, with one of them, Robert Kirkwood, eventually becoming UE director of organization.

In the wake of the return to work, most of the pending contempt and criminal syndicalism charges were dropped. Sentner's case was an exception. In October 1939, he was found guilty and fined $2,500 and court costs. On March 19, 1941, the Iowa Supreme Court overturned the lower court on the grounds that Sentner's Communist Party membership was "wholly irrelevant" and that the sit-down strike was "not a plot to destroy property".

The UE filed additional NLRB charges in November 1939, charging continued discrimination in the rehiring and layoff of seventy-eight strikers. In May 1940, the UE and Maytag reached an agreement with the NLRB to settle all the cases. Maytag would recognize the union as the exclusive bargaining agent and reinstate most of the seventy-eight workers. Still, the union was not able to win an acceptable new contract. Yet, Local 1116 held together. Most workers continued to pay dues and to support the union. In 1941, Maytag signed a memorandum with the union, rescinding the 1938 pay cuts. After the beginning of World War II the deadlock was submitted to the War Labor Board and under its auspice a contract was finally reached in late 1942.

Writing in 1941, one observer summed up the situation: "A dominant company was able to marshall the full force of local opinion, as well as the local and state police power, in a campaign to reduce wages and perhaps ultimately to destroy the union." While the union local did survive, the setback had been a serious one. Coupled with other attacks in 1938–1939, the UE had been weakened, a weakness that was reversed only when the economic and political situation changed with the coming of World War II. [Mark McColloch]

FURTHER READING

Galenson, Walter. *The CIO Challenge to the AFL.* Cambridge, MA: Harvard University Press, 1960.

Matles, James J., and James Higgins. *Them and Us.* New York: Prentice-Hall, 1974.

o   o   o

McCORMICK HARVESTING MACHINE COMPANY STRIKES OF 1885 AND 1886. By 1884, in the midst of the transformation and consolidation of America's basic industry, the McCormick reaper factory in Chicago was one of the most technologically advanced in the country. Fourteen hundred workers labored in the company's huge Chicago works turning out 55,000 machines a year.

From as early as 1862, unions had represented some of the workers at the plant. The most important of these was the Molders' Union which negotiated contracts for its members from the early 1870s, and which led an unsuccessful strike in most of Chicago's foundries, including McCormick, for the eight-hour workday in 1867. Indeed, the molders were able to maintain their union through the deep depression which began in 1873 and to regain its position during the prosperous years between 1879 and 1882.

In 1884, the company's founder, Cyrus McCormick, died. His place was taken by his son, Cyrus, Jr., who had been superintendent of the plant since 1881. One of young McCormick's first acts was to cut wages 15 percent for pieceworkers and 10 percent for dayworkers during the depression of 1884–1885. In spite of the difficult economic conditions, there is no evidence that the wage cut was made out of necessity. Rather, it was simple economizing on the part of management. Indeed, McCormick had earned record profits in the preceding year.

The wage cut led to a strike by the molders. They waited, however, until the height of the spring production season to press their demands for a rescinding of the wage cut. The company, sure of its ability to withstand a strike, greatly underestimated the resolve of the Molders.

McCormick constructed barracks for strikebreakers and sent instructions to its agents to recruit non-union molders. But there were few takers, as the molders were one of the best organized trades in the Midwest. Nevertheless, the company did succeed in enticing twenty-five non-union molders to replace the strikers. When the strikers realized that their picket lines had been breached, they appealed to the non-striking reaper workers to join them and shut down the entire plant. The company too vied for the loyalty of the reaper workers. In the final analysis, the union won this contest because of the bonds between the mostly Irish molders and the Irish element among the reaper workers who generally intimidated the German, Swedish, and Norwegian workers into staying out.

The streets in front of the plant became a battleground as the molders and their allies fought regularly against Pinkerton guards and strikebreakers to keep replacements from entering the works. On Tuesday, April 7, and on subsequent days, busloads of replacements, Pinkertons, and even Chicago detectives were set upon by the crowd and beaten. McCormick's pleas for help to Mayor Carter Harrison received a cool reception because the industrialist had supported the mayor's opponent in the last municipal election.

With the streets effectively under the control of the union, representatives of the Chicago business community became fearful that the disturbances might spread to their own works. Philip D. Armour of the meat-packing firm, and a leader of the Chicago business community, instructed Cyrus McCormick, Jr., that everyone would be better served by a settlement on the union's terms. McCormick complied with Armour's wishes. The union's victory appeared to be complete. The molders returned to work under the old terms, and the scabs were dismissed. Round one had gone to the molders.

The strike had been a painful learning experience for young McCormick. He resolved to study the reasons for the defeat and not to repeat them. His Pinkerton spies blamed the defeat on the role that the Irishmen had played in the battle. The agency linked the leaders of the strike to sympathies for the **Molly Maguires** and the Socialists, warning McCormick that he had a "nest of dangerous, vicious men in his employ." The strength of the Irish lay in the molders trade, and McCormick's main post-strike strategy was to weed them out, largely by replacing them with new pneumatic molding machines.

When the new machines were in place, all ninety-one molders who had led the 1885 strike were removed from the payroll. The union responded under the leadership of Myles McPadden, a veteran of trade union battles in St. Louis and Pittsburgh before his arrival in Chicago. Shorn of his molders, McPadden successfully led an organizing drive that reached into every department of the plant. By February of 1886, the overwhelming majority of the reaper workers, skilled and unskilled, had been enlisted in the Knights of Labor, the United Metalworkers Union, and the Molders' Union. McCormick's strategy had gone awry.

On February 12, 1886, representatives of the three unions demanded wage increases for all categories of workers, no limitation on time the men spent in the water closets, and no retribution against strikers and union men. In addition, when the molding machines failed, as many of them had, only union molders should be hired to replace them. Finally, non-union men were to be dismissed.

Surprisingly, the company agreed to all of the demands save one. They refused to fire five non-union molders who had been hired early in 1886 when it became clear that the molding machines could not do all categories of work. The three unions rejected the McCormick offer and voted to strike on February 16. The company immediately locked out the workers and shut down the works.

As in 1885, the company put on an extensive drive to recruit strikebreakers. In two weeks, it had enough replacements on hand to reopen the plant. This time, however, the relations with the police were different than in 1885. During that strike, the mayor and police gave tacit support to the strikers, enabling the molders to effectively block the use of strikebreakers. In 1886, on the other hand, the police were led by the anti-union Captain Bonfield. When the company reopened the works on March 1, Bonfield's men swept the pickets aside and escorted the replacements into the factory.

Nevertheless, skilled workers were hard to find. This lack severely reduced the company's production in 1886, but it did not force recognition of the union. Gradually, the numbers of replacements increased, and the union cause dimmed. On May 1, the dwindling strike became intertwined with the dramatic events that occurred in Chicago during the nationwide eight-hour-workday movement. So caught up in the eight-hour-day strike were the city's workers that half of McCormick's replacement workers joined the general strike. The company quickly granted the eight-hour day with ten hours' pay. Two days later an eight-hour-day mass meeting was held near the McCormick factory. Although it was unconnected to the strike of the reaper workers, the demonstration turned violent when the eight-hour strikers attacked the McCormick strikebreakers as they left the plant at the end of their shift. Police intervention resulted in the death of two strikers and the wounding of a number of others. It was as a result of this altercation that August Spies, a Chicago anarchist, wrote the famous circular calling for workers to attend a mass meeting the next evening to protest police brutality. It was at the conclusion of that meeting that the famous Haymarket Massacre, [see **Eight-Hour and Haymarket Strikes of 1886**] in which a number of policemen, workers, and onlookers were killed or wounded, took place.

By the time of the Massacre, the strike at the McCormick works was for all intents and purposes over. But the backlash against radicals and unions that swept Chicago after Haymarket effectively led to the complete destruction of unionism at the McCormick Company. [Ronald L. Filippelli]

Further Reading

Ozanne, Robert. *A Century of Labor-Management Relations at McCormick and International Harvester.* Madison, WI: University of Wisconsin Press, 1967.

———. "Union-Management Relations: McCormick Harvesting Machine Company, 1862–1886." *Labor History*, Vol. 4 (Spring, 1963), pp. 132–160.

o   o   o

McKEES ROCKS, PENNSYLVANIA, STRIKE OF 1909. This strike was the first in a series of industrial conflicts which erupted in western Pennsylvania during the first two decades of the twentieth century.

Known regionally as the "hunky strikes," this wave of ethnic industrial unrest appeared first at McKees Rocks in 1909; and then in Turtle Creek in 1914 and 1916, during the "munitions strikes" of 1916, and the great **Steel Strike of 1919**. In all of these strikes, immigrant labor participated from start to finish, strongly suggesting that unskilled, foreign-born workers were no longer to be taken for granted. To one degree or another, radicals, including new industrial unionists, the Industrial Workers of the World, and Socialists were involved. Worker's control issues were also an important element in these strikes.

In 1909, the existence of immigrants living in McKees Rocks was probably not much different than that in hundreds of industrial ghettos that lined the banks of the Ohio River valley. McKees Rocks was dominated by one company, much like North Vandergrift on the Kiskiminetas and Natrona on the Allegheny. The Pressed Steel Car Company of McKees Rocks had never been known for good wages or working conditions, but that was not unusual. The plant, located on the left bank of the Ohio River, six miles below Pittsburgh, had suffered from a reduction in orders for new railroad cars that followed the Panic of 1907. During the recession that followed, Pressed Steel Car president Frank Hoffstot introduced new assembly line production techniques that improved productivity but accelerated the pace of work in his shops. After reducing wages in response to the recession, Hoffstot devised a complex system for pooling wages, whereby a given pool of workers lost wages due to the incompetence of the pool members, management, or breakdowns in machinery. All of this was in keeping with trends in the Pittsburgh district. Alcoa, Westinghouse, and a host of other employers introduced their own special versions of efficiency expert Frederick Taylor's scientific management schemes. Scientific management usually meant workers were driven at a feverish pace. Coupled with Byzantine pooling, premium, and piece-rate wage systems, work was harder and wage-rates uncertain.

On the weekend of July 10, 1909, Pressed Steel Car employees met informally and complained about their small paychecks. On Monday, July 12, amidst periodic work stoppages, the men continued to voice complaints to supervisors and timekeepers. That evening, a group met and decided to present their grievances on the following morning. Management refused to meet with a committee, and several days later, Frank Hoffstot made a formal announcement to the press: "We will receive no committee . . . there will be no arbitration . . . if they're not happy we don't want them . . . we will not change the pooling system, in fact, we intend to increase it."

When the foreigners learned that their committee, which was composed largely of Slavs and a few Italians, had been rebuffed, the men left their jobs, and within a few hours only skilled Americans remained at work. A large crowd of foreigners gathered at the main gate of the plant and shouted threats at all who tried to enter. A major problem for the strikers was a deep division within the company work force. Pressed Steel Car employed about 1,200 skilled American-born workers, and about 3,500 semiskilled and unskilled. Relations between these groups were far from close, and probably not enhanced when the foreigners pulled the Americans off trolleys and subjected them to physical intimidation. The skilled men had no desire to strike, for they were not affected by the pooling system.

By July 15, Pressed Steel Car was completely shut down. The Americans reluctantly, and for reasons that are not clear, joined the strike. An American executive committee soon eclipsed that of the foreign-born, and C. A. Wise, a skilled worker, emerged as strike spokesman. The strikers hired William McNair, a local attorney, as their legal counsel. With Americans in charge, and respectability assured, strike relief poured into McKees Rocks. Indeed, the Americans were able to use that relief to beat back dissent by the foreigners. What Wise and his associates wanted was order, peace, and to return to work. The Americans were not amused by Hoffstot's arrogance, his Coal and Iron Police, or the strikebreakers he procured through the Pearl Bergoff Detective Agency. But the Americans were never committed to the destruction of the pooling system and were inclined to give concessions on that and other issues in the face of company intransigence. The foreigners, suspicious of the conciliatory posture assumed by the American executive committee, known as the "Big Six," formed their own executive council, which they dubbed the "unknown" committee. The foreigners also stepped up their campaign of violence against the scabs.

Hoffstot's stonewalling, and the resort to violence by the foreign-born probably induced the Americans to capitulate. On July 31, the Big Six announced that the strikers had won a great victory. In fact, Hoffstot had given nothing. The defeated were to be subjected to the humiliation of applying individually for employment as new hires. The foreigners brushed aside their moderate allies and met that night at the Indian Mound near the plant to plan strategy. At that point the Industrial Workers of the World (IWW) entered the picture.

The Industrial Workers of the World was not well known or understood in Pennsylvania. IWW resources were spread rather thin in the region, and with the exception of the stogie makers, the radical union never established much of a following in a major industry. IWW operatives turned up in Butler, East Pittsburgh, Turtle Creek, and even in Grove City. More often than not, the Wobblies did not begin

strikes in western Pennsylvania but moved in and assumed a leadership role once a conflict had begun. Such was the case at McKees Rocks. On August 16, William Trautman appeared and delivered an address to the strikers. Violence had been a fact for more than a month, but at McKees Rocks, the IWW would assume its normal role of scapegoat. On August 22, a gun battle between police and strikers, now virtually all foreign-born, resulted in a dozen deaths and fifty injuries. The state constabulary cracked down, arresting scores of strikers and searching their homes for weapons. The Americans were permitted to keep their guns.

A day before the riot, Albert Vamos, a Bergoff strikebreaker, escaped from the plant. He made his way to the Austro-Hungarian vice-consul in Pittsburgh, and complained that he had been abused in the plant and held there against his will. The case was taken first to William McNair and then to a United States commissioner. Peonage affidavits were sworn out against Hoffstot and the Bergoff Agency. The peonage investigations that ensued brought much public opprobrium to Press Steel Car. Sensing that opportunity was at hand, Wise and the Big Six reopened negotiations with the company. Wise, with the help of the United States commissioner of labor, was able to negotiate a settlement. It included a pledge of no Sunday work, half days on Saturdays, and a 10 to 15 percent wage increase within ninety days. Or so it seemed. An official company statement insisted that no specific promise of a wage increase had been given. If good times returned, the men would get their share. The company had not agreed to end wage pooling but condemned "graft" by supervisors.

Was it a victory for the strikers? Trautman did not think so, and urged the strikers to hold out. He was jailed for his troubles, charged with being a "suspicious person." Undaunted, the IWW sent in

Joseph Ettor to direct the strike. It was mid-September, and thousands of hard-core, foreign-born strikers seemed true to their cause. The Americans, many of whom were probably armed, went back to work under the watchful eyes of the constabulary. Ettor tried to hold his men in line, but Wise and the Big Six met with groups of foreigners and undercut strike discipline. On the morning of September 16, the Big Six, carrying an American flag, led thousands of men, some of them foreigners, through the gates of the plant. The strike was over, and the IWW and its foreign-born constituency were utterly defeated. Pressed Steel Car quickly reverted to its old repressive ways, employing selective discharges and a company union organized by Wise.

The McKees Rocks strike proved that the immigrants were not beyond organization, that they could be reliable strikers, and that they possessed a capacity for militance. The IWW, though willing, proved itself too weak to win a strike in a basic industry such as steel. McKees Rocks also established an undefined but nevertheless pernicious public perception that vaguely linked industrial unrest among foreigners with violence and radicalism. In that connection, the IWW became everyone's favorite scapegoat in the Pittsburgh district until the "reds" took their place in 1919. The IWW, which split into feuding factions, the Detroit and Chicago branches, was probably even weaker after McKees Rocks than before. Nevertheless, the Westinghouse Strikes of 1914 and 1916 were linked to the IWW, a charge denied by both Chicago and Detroit. The 1916 Westinghouse Strike, and the ensuing Braddock Riot that cost several lives, were attributed to "drunken foreigners" whose passions had been inflamed by the IWW. In its own way, the McKees Rocks strike prepared public opinion in western Pennsylvania for the Red Scare. On September 29, 1919, following a coroner's inquest regarding the death of Fannie Sellins, the jury foreman announced to the press that the jury deplored and condemned "the foreign agitators who instilled anarchy and Bolshevik doctrines into the minds of un-American and uneducated aliens of the district." [Carl I. Meyerhuber, Jr.]

FURTHER READING

Corvares, Frances G. *The Remaking of Pittsburgh: Class and Culture in an Industrializing City, 1877–1919.* Albany, NY: The State University of New York Press, 1984.

Dubofsky, Melvyn. *We Shall Be All: A History of the IWW.* New York: Quadrangle Books, 1969.

Ingham, John W. "A Strike in the Progressive Era: McKees Rocks, 1909." *Pennsylvania Magazine of History and Biography*, Vol. 90, (July 1966), pp. 353–377.

o   o   o

MEMPHIS, TENNESSEE, SANITATION WORKERS' STRIKE OF 1968. The strike by Memphis Sanitation Workers, begun on Monday, February 12, 1968, has special significance, in part, because it set into motion the events that led to the assassination of the Rev. Dr. Martin Luther King, Jr., in Memphis on April 4. Additionally, the strike provides an interesting case study of labor–management conflict in the public sector, and it illustrates the important connections between organized labor and Civil Rights organizations during the 1960s.

The strike was precipitated by personnel decisions in connection with a rainstorm that occurred on January 31, 1968. Twenty-two black employees of the Sewer and Drainage Division of the Memphis Department of Public Works were sent home. White employees in identical job classifications remained on the job and received a full day's pay. The controversy escalated after two black sanitation workers were accidentally crushed by a garbage compressor on February 1, 1968. Their widows were informed that no insurance benefits would be forthcoming.

Workers' dissatisfaction with management's response to complaints led to a decision by 400 workers at a meeting on Sunday, February 11, to strike unless grievances were addressed. The attendance at the meeting was particularly noteworthy because Local 1733 of the American Federation of State, County and Municipal Employees (AFSCME) had only forty paid members at the time.

The union struck on Monday, February 12 after the failure of last minute attempts to resolve grievances. Mayor Henry Loeb immediately declared the strike illegal under Tennessee law. On Tuesday, February 13, an AFSCME official from the union's Washington office met with the mayor and called for union recognition, the dues checkoff, and negotiations between the union and the city administration. Mayor Loeb threatened to hire replacement workers and issued a back-to-work ultimatum that was to take effect at 7:00 A.M. on Wednesday, February 14. Negotiations broke down on Wednesday and the hiring of replacement workers began.

Throughout the course of the strike, the mayor remained adamant in his refusal to recognize the union and to allow dues checkoff. Although the mayor refused to recognize AFSCME as the sole bargaining agent for Department of Public Works employees, he participated with AFSCME international president Jerry Wurf in a series of meetings over a five day period beginning on Sunday, February 18. These meetings were arranged and moderated by the Ministerial Association, an informal organization of white clergymen. At the conclusion of this series of meetings, no formal negotiations were held until March 23.

The mayor's refusal to negotiate directly with the union represented a continuation of historical efforts to quash organizing efforts. Local 1733 founder, T. O. Jones, had been fired from his job as a sanitation worker in 1963 for attempting to call a strike. A similar unsuccessful strike call had occurred in 1966.

The involvement of the Ministerial Association was one of many indicators that the momentum of the Civil Rights movement had drastically altered the context in which the workers' struggle for union recognition was being waged. The local NAACP chapter officially endorsed the strike on Friday, February 16, after the city council went on record supporting Mayor Loeb. Strike supporters held an all night vigil and picketed City Hall on Monday, February 19. The next day, the union and the National Association for the Advancement of Colored People (NAACP) called for a citywide boycott of downtown merchants.

Faced with an escalating conflict, on February 22, a subcommittee of the city council urged the city administration to recognize the union. On the following day, the council again refused to consider the recognition question. Over the next several days, daily marches in support of the strikers were held, and the boycott was implemented.

Communitywide support for the strike was critical since the city had been able to obtain an injunction on February 24 barring the union from staging demonstrations or picketing. In response, black community leaders and ministers formed C.O.M.E., the Committee on the Move for Equality. The membership of the Interdenominational Ministers Alliance, which included all of the black denominations, used their pulpits on Sunday, February 25 to call on their congregations to support the strike and boycott. In addition to downtown merchants, boycott targets included two local Scripps-Howard newspapers. Downtown sales were reported to have dropped by approximately 35 percent as the boycott took hold.

Mayor Loeb attempted to bypass the local black leadership by sending a letter to each striker on Thursday, February 29. Workers were invited to return to work without union recognition. The communication was also published as an open letter in one of the newspapers. Strikers were offered a wage increase of eight cents per hour, a grievance procedure, and some insurance and overtime benefits. This offer occurred in the wake of an unsuccessful effort by the Memphis Committee on Community Relations to work out a compromise. Mayor Loeb's refusal to accept the compromise provided additional momentum for the daily demonstrations. Twenty-three union members were cited for contempt of court on February 27.

A meeting between the mayor and black ministers on March 1 failed to resolve the impasse. Mayor Loeb also opposed a proposal by a state senator to create a state mediation board to resolve the impasse on March 4. In the wake of this intransigence, local black leaders decided to further escalate the struggle by bringing in national figures. On Tuesday, March 5, the same day that 116 strikers and supporters were arrested for participating in a sit-in demonstration at City Hall, it was announced that the Rev. Dr. Martin Luther King, Jr., had agreed to come to Memphis. Two days later, the city council formally voted against the dues checkoff proposal.

King's first visit occurred on March 18, two days after NAACP executive director Roy Wilkins had spoken to a Memphis crowd of approximately 10,000. King's visit was preceded by several other important events such as a school boycott by black high school students on March 11, and a proposal by the mayor on March 16 that the dues checkoff issue be decided by city-wide referendum in August. The union rejected the mayor's proposal.

The dues checkoff issue was of critical importance to both sides. Because Tennessee is a "right-to-work" state, no other membership maintenance provisions were available to the union. By holding fast on this issue the mayor hoped to dilute potential union strength.

King called for a citywide march on March 22. Two days later, Mayor Loeb reiterated his opposition to the union's demands. A record snowstorm forced cancellation of the planned march, and it was rescheduled for March 28. King's first appearance had alarmed the city council, setting into motion a legislative effort to override Mayor Loeb's refusal to settle with AFSCME. By resolution of the city council, Frank Miles, a local business leader and former mediator with the Federal Mediation and Conciliation Service, was asked to mediate the dispute. Talks between the two parties broke down on March 27, one day before Martin Luther King's scheduled return to Memphis, and on the same day that the Rev. Ralph David Abernathy of the Southern Christian Leadership Conference (SCLC) addressed a rally.

The march plans were complicated by a factional dispute between the Ministerial leadership and the local black power group, the Invaders. About 5,000 strike supporters participated in the march. Violence broke out after store windows were broken, allegedly by the Invaders. A sixteen-year-old youth was killed and 280 people were arrested. A curfew was imposed, and 4,000 National Guardsmen were called out.

The outbreak of violence was a severe blow to Dr. King who was in the midst of planning the Poor People's March on Washington. His credibility as an advocate of nonviolence came under fire in the media and on the floor of both houses of the U.S. Congress. As a consequence, King felt compelled to return to Memphis to lead a peaceful demonstration prior to the Poor People's March.

In the aftermath of the events of March 28, AFL-CIO president George Meany and President Lyndon Johnson offered assistance in resolving the dispute. Their offers were refused by Mayor Loeb, and other attempts to renew mediation of the strike also failed. The curfew was lifted on April 1. On that day, Frank Miles called city and union officials and arranged a meeting for April 5, an agreement made moot by the Reverend King's assassination on April 4.

On April 5, President Johnson instructed Under-Secretary of Labor, James Reynolds to take charge of mediation to settle the strike. Between April 6 and April 10, Reynolds held a series of meetings with each party. Beginning on April 10, Reynolds set up daily joint meetings with city and union officials that continued until April 16, when a final settlement was announced.

The dues checkoff issue was resolved by establishing a dues collection procedure using the independent employees credit union. As part of the settlement, union members received a ten-cents-an-hour pay increase effective May 1 and another five cents effective September 1. A merit promotion plan, a no-strike clause, a no-discrimination clause, and a grievance procedure were also included in the agreement. The final memorandum of understanding was passed by the city council on April 16. The union voted unanimously to accept the agreement.

The strike and the assassination of King were catalysts for institutionalizing structures to redress historical, systemic patterns of racial inequality in Memphis. Following the settlement, black leaders demanded the creation of a Human Relations Commission appointed by the city and county governments. Such a commission was approved on April 30. An NAACP-organized student boycott of the public schools in 1969 led to legislation changing the selection process for school board members from at-large to district elections, enabling the election of blacks to the Memphis Board of Education.

The success of the strike led to significant improvement in the well-being of the members of Local 1733. In 1973, Local 1733 successfully negotiated the first "career ladders" program in the South,

providing upward mobility for lower-grade workers. Local 1733 of AFSCME now represents approximately 6,000 dues-paying members employed in fifteen divisions of city services. [James B. Stewart]

FURTHER READING

AFSCME Local 1733. Brochure commemorating the role of Martin Luther King, Jr. in the Memphis Strike, n.d.

Garrow, David J. *The FBI and Martin Luther King, Jr.: From "Solo" to Memphis.* New York: W. W. Norton & Company, 1981.

Marshall, F. Ray, and Arvil Van Adams. "The Memphis Public Employees Strike." In *Racial Conflict and Negotiations.* W. Ellison Chalmers and Gerld W. Cormick, eds. Ann Arbor, MI: Institute of Labor and Industrial Relations, 1971.

Tucker, Donald M. *Memphis Since Crump: Bossism, Blacks, and Civic Reformers 1948–1968.* Knoxville, TN: The University of Tennessee Press, 1980.

o   o   o

MICHIGAN COPPER STRIKE OF 1913. The first fifteen years of the twentieth century were marked by sustained industrial warfare in America's mining industries. The battles raged across the anthracite fields of Pennsylvania; the coal patches of West Virginia, Illinois, and Ohio; and the coal and hardrock mining regions of Colorado, Montana, Utah, and Wyoming. Part of this upheaval took place in the copper mines of the Kelewnal Peninsula of Michigan, the preserve of the Calumet and Hecla Mining Company (C & H).

With its control of 60 percent of the district's copper output, C & H set the employment standards for the industry in Michigan. In some cases, workers benefited. The company kept rents low for company houses and provided an advanced level of medical benefits for the time. Company schools educated the miners' children, and clergy on the company payroll ministered to their spiritual needs. Little in the life of the miners and their families, from politics to leisure, was not filtered through company control. In the mines, of course, the same power existed; however, unlike above ground, there was no hint of benevolent paternalism. Authoritarian rule prevailed. According to Bill Haywood of the Industrial Workers of the World (IWW), Michigan's copper miners lived under feudal conditions and had adopted the attitude of servility appropriate to that condition. The meager financial rewards illustrated this. Miner's earned low wages from which were deducted rent payments, equipment costs, and credit at the company store. Men usually spent eleven hours underground each shift—a stint for which they earned from fifteen to eighteen dollars for a six-day workweek.

Nevertheless, by 1913, there had been enough interest in unionization among the miners that the Western Federation of Miners (WFM) had organized five locals in the area. The employers took little notice. Their efficiency experts continued to reorganize work in the mines and place more and more burdens on the individual miners. One change that galvanized resentment among the men was the replacement of the two-man drill with the one-man drill. In addition to the unemployment that it created, miners called the new drill the "man killer" or "widow maker" because of its weight and because it forced miners to work alone, without support in an emergency.

Agitation among the miners increased, but the WFM cautioned patience. The union knew that the lightly organized copper miners were not ready to take on the powerful C & H company. However, the anti-company sentiment could not be denied, and in mid-July, the WFM sent a letter to the management of C & H and other companies requesting a meeting to discuss wages and working conditions. No company responded. The message was clear: no negotiations would take place in the copper fields between the companies and representatives of the workers. Secre-

tary of Labor William B. Wilson, himself a miner, blamed the ensuing strike on the absolute refusal of the companies to even acknowledge the workers' request.

The miners struck on July 23, when 16,000 miners walked out, closing all of the mines in the district. It was a remarkable show of force in an area in which the polyglot ethnic work force had been noted for its docility. They demanded the eight-hour day, a minimum daily wage of three dollars for underground workers, abolition of the one-man drill, and recognition of the WFM. The companies' response was typical of the era. Local law enforcement officials swore in deputies loyal to the companies—some 2,000 in all. As soon as a few minor disturbances marred the picket lines, the governor of Michigan sent in the National Guard. The soldiers were clearly there with serious intentions. They were heavily armed, including two automatic machine guns. The companies added to this gathering army by contracting with the Waddell-Mahon Agency of New York to supply company guards. James Waddell, the president of the firm, boasted that the result in Michigan would be a "triumph for law and order" and the mine owners, thus providing excellent advertising for Waddell-Mahon.

The strikebreaking agency's main task was to recruit replacements for the strikers and protect them. Most were drawn from recent immigrants, recruited in New York, who were kept under close guard after they arrived in Michigan. In the face of this tremendous show of force, the strikers relied on solidarity. Parades kept their spirits high. Well-known labor figures appeared from time to time, including Mary "Mother" Jones, the so-called "Miners' Angel," who had been supporting the struggles of miners for more than forty years. Mother Jones' local counterpart was Anna Clemenc, the wife of a Croatian miner. She could frequently be seen at the head of the miners' marches carrying the

American flag. Her activities rallied the strikers and also brought her into danger from National Guard clubs and bayonets. But although beaten and injured several times, she refused to retreat or to surrender the flag. She was arrested numerous times, once for trying to persuade a strikebreaker not to cross the picket line, and another time for assaulting strikebreakers.

Through it all, the company refused to meet with the workers. According to the manager for C & H, the men could find work elsewhere if they didn't want to accept the company's work policies. As for the WFM, it was considered an outside force and a menace to the prosperity of the district. A citizens' alliance of local businessmen shared that view and mobilized to drive the WFM out of the area.

The companies also turned to the courts for relief and secured an injunction forbidding picketing, mass demonstrations, or any interference with the operation of the mines. Those who defied it were arrested. The injunction and the arrests brought even more oppression to the miners. Kate Richards O'Hare, the Socialist journalist, visited the strike area and told her readers that no law existed in the copper country save for the will of the copper barons. The law was dead, according to O'Hare, and the police were "too busy protecting profits to take notice. . . ." After two strikers were killed in their homes by company gunmen, another observer noted that nowhere in the United States had the mine owners gone to greater lengths to defeat the workers. In all, some 600 strikers were arrested during the strike for inciting to riot or other similar charges, while 500 were arrested for violating the injunction.

As the strike dragged on into the cold of December, the hatred on both sides grew. Three Canadian strikebreakers were shot. The citizens' alliance began to hold mass meetings to intimidate the strikers, and merchants threatened to cut off all

credit to the miners. In this bitter atmosphere tragedy struck. A WFM women's auxiliary had collected money and Christmas gifts for strikers' children from other unions across the country. On Christmas Eve, nearly a thousand people crowded into the Italian Hall in Red Jacket for a Christmas party. In the midst of the celebration, someone, no one has ever proved who, screamed "fire." Although there was no fire, in the panic that followed sixty-two children and eleven adults died.

The event shocked the nation. Contributions flowed in to the strikers. When C & H and the citizens' alliance offered combined contributions of nearly $30,000, the miners rejected it as "blood money." The WFM's president, Charles Moyer, after raising the possibility that a citizens' alliance member had raised the alarm, announced that the WFM would bury its own dead and that the American labor movement would take care of the victims. Moyer's stance won the approval of the labor press, which praised the strikers for their dignity, but it enraged the citizens' alliance. Representatives of the alliance demanded that Moyer retract his statements. When he refused, he was seized by a group of armed men, beaten and shot, dragged to the railroad station and placed on a train for Chicago.

The events at the Italian Hall had turned the attention of the nation to the strike. On January 10, 1914, Secretary of Labor William B. Wilson released a report that indicted the company for forcing miners into peonage while reaping enormous profits. Other newspapers publicized results of investigations that showed the oppressive circumstances under which the miners lived in the armed camp that the copper fields had become. The revelations even led to congressional hearings which turned up more damning evidence of the conditions in the industry.

Nevertheless, none of this moved the employers. They were determined not to deal with the union. By this time, however, the WFM knew that the strike was lost. Strike relief payments for the miners had depleted the union's treasury. All they hoped for was an agreement from the company to take the strikers back and allow them to keep their union membership. The company refused, agreeing to take the workers back but not as union members. On April 12, 1914, the strikers voted by a three to one margin to return on the company's terms. In the end, the enormous sacrifice had gained nothing. Unionization disappeared from the Michigan copper country for another quarter of a century. [Ronald L. Filippelli]

FURTHER READING

Foner, Philip S. *History of the Labor Movement in the United States*. New York: International Publishers, 1980.

Mclaughlin, Doris B. *Michigan Labor: A Brief History from 1918 to the Present*. Ann Arbor, MI: University of Michigan Press, 1970.

Sullivan, William A. "The 1913 Revolt of the Michigan Copper Miners." *Michigan History*, Vol. 43 (September 1, 1959), pp. 3–23.

o o o

MINNEAPOLIS, MINNESOTA, TEAMSTERS' STRIKE OF 1934. One of the three seminal labor conflicts of 1934, the Minneapolis Teamsters' Strike began on May 15, 1934. Led by radical union officials of the International Brotherhood of Teamsters, Chauffers, Warehousemen, and Helpers (IBT) Local 574, a general drivers organization, the stoppage brought most truck traffic in the city to a standstill for the better part of a month. Moreover, frequent streetfighting between workers and employers seeking to break the strike resulted in several deaths, numerous injuries, and an eventual declaration of martial law by the state's governor. Along with the **San Francisco Longshoremen's Strike**, the **Toledo Auto-Lite Strike**, and the widespread **Textile Strike**, the virulence of these 1934 contests between workers seeking unionization and employers' seeking to thwart that desire helped reform national labor policy.

Minneapolis, a transportation hub for trucking, had been a notorious "open shop" city prior to 1934. Officers of Local 574, though, had resolved to change its status. Vincent Raymond Dunne—a Teamster and former Industrial Workers of the World member, as well as founder of the Trotskyist Communist League of America—had become the leader of General Drivers Local 574. In collaboration with his brothers and Farrel Dobbs, a truck driver converted to his cause, Dunne planned to organize the coal yard drivers, and from that position, expand into general trucking. After winning in coal, Local 574 quickly signed up 2,000 to 3,000 truckers and served its demands upon the employers.

The trucking employers, stimulated by fervent open shop advocates in the city's citizens' alliance, responded by forming the Minneapolis Employers of Drivers and Helpers, which promptly rejected the demands. The union then suggested arbitration of the wage issue. When efforts to mediate failed, members of Local 574 authorized a strike and stopped working on May 15. The union officials, utilizing Dobbs's heretofore unknown talent for strike leadership, developed an impressive headquarters, a food service operation, a communication network, and organized picket armies. Roads into the city were manned by pickets, who issued passes for essential deliveries. Soon Local 574 had effectively stopped most truck traffic.

In its initial stages, the strikers enjoyed public support because of their reasonable negotiating stance and because of the employers' refusals to mediate the dispute. Then, the fear of food shortages and employer charges of "communism" began to have an influence. The city's mayor and chief of police backed the trucking concerns, in contrast to Minnesota governor Floyd B. Olson, who, as head of the state's Farmer–Labor party, was clearly a union sympathizer.

The employers' first tactical gambit came on May 19. An employer-paid spy in the leadership of Local 574 dispatched trucks with pickets under false pretenses into an alley behind the *Minneapolis Tribune* building. Police sealed off the corridor and beat the trucks' passengers badly. Afterwards, union pickets armed themselves with bats and lead pipes. On May 21, employer forces sealed off the city's central transportation area, called the public market, in preparation to resume shipping. In military formation, six hundred armed union adherents advanced to the area. When the police arrived in force and drew their guns, a union truck drove into them to break the police into small groups. Hand-to-hand streetfighting erupted with the strikers getting the better of it. The next day, with reports that employers were set to move perishable goods, 20,000 people turned out. In short order, a minor altercation set off a major battle between union and employer forces during which two were killed and fifty wounded. The more· numerous unionists routed their opponents and captured the market. In effect, the union now controlled the city's traffic.

Governor Olson then convinced the parties to foreswear further hostilities, under pain of dealing with the National Guard. The union agreed not to picket, and the employers agreed not to try to move trucks for a day. During that time, government officials tried to break the impasse through collective bargaining carried out by proxies, and ultimately a set of conditions was temporarily agreed upon. The strike would end. The employers would rehire all workers who had been on the payrolls previous to the stoppage, agree to be bound by the labor codes of the National Recovery Act, and arbitrate the wage

question if the parties could not reach a decision. Trucks rolled on May 26.

The employers, however, had not really intended to fully live up to the bargain and began propagandizing in the press against the "agreement" and the union, denouncing its Communist leaders with relish. It became clear to Local 574 that it would have to force recognition or be finished in the city as an effective labor organization. Therefore, it made preparations for the second contest that it knew was sure to come. Meanwhile, the companies did not rehire most of the strikers, refused to name their members to the arbitration panel, and turned deaf ears to the entreaties of mediators. Finally, the unionists challenged the employers to recognize the union and negotiate. The offer was rejected, and on July 16, 1934, Local 574 once again went on strike.

Within two days, Father Francis J. Haas, a priest and labor relations academic functioning as the National Labor Relations Board's mediator, and federal conciliator E. H. Dunnigan, put forth settlement terms for the sides to consider. The union promptly accepted what the mediators had suggested, and added conditions of its own. The employers found almost all of the proposals unworkable. In actuality, they had been secretly planning to provoke a riot in the hopes that violence would force Governor Olson to call out the National Guard, restoring order and at the same time breaking the strike.

On July 20, an employer truck under police escort was interrupted by a picket vehicle. The police immediately opened fire, killing two and wounding sixty-seven. Reporter Eric Sevareid, upon inspecting the injured in the city hospital, noted that most had been shot in the back. Unfortunately, Local 574's leadership probably suspected that violence would occur and may have wanted to create "martyrs" for their cause. Now, it had those martyrs, and enraged crowds were threatening to lynch the mayor and chief of police. Following a mass funeral that drew tens of thousands, the governor ordered the National Guard to take control of the city.

Once again, Haas and Dunnigan tried to mediate, adding new proposals to their former recommendations, one of which was an NLB election that would name the local as bargaining representative if the union won. Wages and conditions would be subject to arbitration. The unionists agreed; the employers once again refused to deal with the local and its Communist leadership.

Governor Olson, fearful that control by the National Guard would work to the employers' favor, took pains to try to ensure that martial law would not result in an employer advantage in the conflict. While picketing was forbidden, all truck movement had to take place under a military permit system and, theoretically, those permits would only be granted for essential foodstuffs for the citizenry. Nevertheless, the state militia began issuing permits in large numbers, in apparent contradiction of the governor's orders. Thus, Local 574 faced conditions which would soon break its strike as the city's truck traffic on July 29 was almost two-thirds of normal.

The labor organization protested, implying it would stop the trucks from rolling if the state did not. Olson reluctantly had the union's rebellious leadership arrested, though one Dunne brother and Dobbs escaped imprisonment. Then, after meeting with rank-and-filers from the union, Olson reconsidered. In a spirit of equity, state authorities raided the employers' headquarters, hoping to secure damaging documents that showed that they hoped to inspire a public riot for their own purposes. Then, on August 6, Olson proclaimed that permits would only be issued to shipments of necessities or to those trucking firms who agreed to accept the Haas-Dunnigan settlement package. Some employers broke ranks, but the die-hards

instituted legal proceedings against the governor's use of martial law. Olson personally argued the case and the state's highest court agreed that the chief executive had rightly used his powers. But it was not legal defeat that finally overcame the last resisting employers but Olson's success at involving the Roosevelt administration behind the scenes.

The governor appealed to the President, who was passing through Minnesota, to put pressure on the employers through the Reconstruction Finance Corporation (RFC). The RFC, which was locally controlled by conservative Republicans from the Hoover administration, determined access to credit for firms. It was these RFC local officials, the governor insisted, who forced trucking employers to declare war on labor under pain of losing their access to credit. Roosevelt interceded through Washington RFC chief Jesse Jones, whose involvement finally created a more compromising state of mind among the recalcitrant truckers. On August 21, the settlement was announced. Strikers would receive preferential rehire rights. In ten days, an election would be held to choose representatives for collective bargaining purposes. Certain minimal wage levels were set, with higher rates to be arbitrated. Other conditions would follow NRA labor codes.

Thus concluded the Minneapolis Teamsters' Strike of 1934. Though only modest gains were achieved economically, the workers who had wanted union representation enough to fight for it had made their point. The city would no longer be known as an anti-union bastion. In addition, Local 574 would thereafter organize thousands in Minneapolis and go on to become a power in organizing over-the-road truck drivers nationally. But perhaps most significantly, the conflict became noted by Washington officials struggling desperately to revive the economy. Industrial warfare on this scale and of this intensity would undercut that effort, and thus finding a method to prevent its reoccurrence would become increasingly important, a fact that Congress acknowledged when it passed the National Labor Relations Act in 1935. [Gilbert J. Gall]

FURTHER READING

Bernstein, Irving. *Turbulent Years: A History of the American Worker, 1933–1941.* Boston, MA: Houghton Mifflin, 1970.

Dobbs, Farrel. *Teamster Power.* New York: Monad, 1973.

Walker, Charles. *American City: A Rank and File History.* New York: Farrar and Rinehart, 1937.

o   o   o

MINNESOTA IRON RANGE STRIKE OF 1916. The most important strike on the Mesabi Range, an area with vast deposits of iron ore in northern Minnesota, pitted radical immigrant miners against the corporate power of the Oliver Iron Mining Company, a subsidiary of J. P. Morgan's United States Steel Company, the largest corporate entity in the world. Although the miners eventually lost the strike, they demonstrated that different ethnic groups could cooperate effectively under radical leadership and against great odds. The strike also pointed up the divisions in the American labor movement between the radical anarcho-syndicalist Industrial Workers of the World (IWW) and the conservative American Federation of Labor (AFL).

The radicalism of the iron ore miners grew, in part, from the Socialist heritage of the Finnish workers who constituted the largest ethnic group on the range. This heritage of socialism was reinforced and changed by the bitter opposition of the mine operators to any form of worker organization. The open shop creed of the employers eventually led the iron range miners to turn away from craft unionism and reform socialism toward revolutionary syndicalism and industrial unionism.

Unionism in Minnesota predated the troubles on the iron range. By 1903, some 200 unions existed in the state and the Minnesota Federation of Labor, affiliated with the AFL, was stable enough to have a full-time president, E. G. Hall. But the AFL had little interest in the largely unskilled and semiskilled immigrant miners of the iron range.

By 1910, the Mesabi iron range, by far the largest in the nation, had an insatiable need for labor. It attracted a cosmopolitan population of Scandinavians, Finns, Slavs, and Italians, with the Finns constituting by far the largest group. The first union to try to organize this polyglot group of workers was the Western Federation of Miners (WFM), which after a period of militant industrial unionism, had by 1911 reentered the American Federation of Labor. Workers on the iron range responded to the WFM call because of the exploitation of labor that characterized the industry. Miners paid exorbitant rates to mine bosses for tools and powder. The industry had an astounding accident rate, and workers were often cheated out of their just wages by company manipulation of the contract-labor system.

Abuses of the contract system led to two WFM-led strikes in 1905 and 1907. Both were unsuccessful, although the 1907 strike did close down the entire Mesabi Range. The defeats led the workers, especially some of the Socialist Finns, to lose faith in the WFM which they believed had led them badly during the strikes. The controversy over the proper route to take to combat the power of capital on the range split the Socialist Finnish Federation between those who believed in Socialist political action and those who supported militant syndicalism. The Socialists looked to the AFL to provide a trade union alternative, while the syndicalists turned to the IWW.

Had the AFL been interested, it might have been able, along with help from the

Finnish Socialists, to organize the mines. But there was no such interest. The WFM had been chastised by its loss in 1907, and the state federation feared both the radicalism of the workers and the power of the Oliver Iron Mining Company. Whatever the reason, the failure of the AFL to take up the challenge of organizing the iron range left the field to the IWW and its allies among the Finns.

Up to 1916, the IWW did not have a significant presence on the iron range. But it was prepared to seize the opportunity when it appeared. On June 3, in the midst of an economic boom in the industry, a small group of miners walked out, and within a week several hundred others followed them. The workers had economic grievances and were dissatisfied with the contract-labor system. The labor shortage on the range gave them leverage. Since the AFL showed no interest, the strikers appealed to the IWW for help. Soon IWW veterans like Carlo Tresca and Joseph Schmidt, who were experienced in organizing workers from various ethnic groups, arrived. They established a strike committee made up of all the nationalities present in the mines. By the end of June, the strike had spread to the entire Mesabi Range and involved at least 8,000 workers, 5,000 of whom had joined the IWW's Metal Mine Workers Industrial Union No. 490. Given the shortage of labor, the company had little hope of importing strikebreakers, but it did use armed guards and special deputies. On July 3, a clash between an industry guard and several strikers left one of the guards and an innocent bystander dead. The incident proved to be the only serious violence in the strike, but it was sufficient as a pretext for the authorities to arrest practically the entire IWW organizing group for inciting the killings.

The removal of the professional organizers did not end the strike. The day-to-day guidance of the strike fell to the Finns who provided leaders, strike headquarters, and community support. Although most of the strikers were, in fact, Yugoslavs and Italians, these more recent immigrants looked to the more politically experienced Finns for leadership.

The role of the IWW in the strike turned the AFL from a disinterested party to a hostile one. State federation president, E. G. Hall, denounced the strike and blasted the IWW for leading the miners astray. Editors and local officials, often sympathetic to the workers but hostile to the radical IWW, seized on Hall's words and the hostility of the AFL to persuade the workers to reject the radicals and seek support from the more conservative AFL.

Yet, while the AFL was willing to denounce the IWW, it showed no real inclination to organize the miners and take over direction of the strike as many Minnesota public officials wanted. There were probably sound reasons for this. Even though the AFL announced that it would assist the miners, it knew that the strike committee would not desert the IWW leaders who had given them so much support and who were in jail at the time. Also, the AFL affiliate with jurisdiction was the WFM, which wanted no part of another attempt to organize the iron range. Finally, the conservative AFL, made up primarily of skilled workers, mostly building tradesmen, was probably not enthralled with the prospect of including thousands of unskilled, radical immigrant miners in its ranks.

As the maneuvering to bring the AFL into the strike as an alternative to the IWW went on, the miners held out through the summer. But with no relief help from the AFL, with most of their leaders in jail, and with little prospect of compromise from the company, the strike was called off in September.

Once again, it appeared that organized labor had forsaken the miners, leaving them largely unassisted as they fought a heroic strike against a powerful corporation. Hard on the heels of the defeat in the strike of 1916, during the patriotic hysteria and anti-radical crusade of the war years, the radical, anti-war IWW was crushed in Minnesota as elsewhere. The lesson to the immigrant miners was that trade unionism could not triumph against the combined power of the corporations and the state. For those who rejected that lesson and continued to struggle, the company instituted a highly efficient internal espionage network that succeeded in ferreting out the trouble makers and instilling fear in a divided work force. In these conditions, the open shop thrived on the iron range throughout the 1920s. [Ronald L. Filippelli]

FURTHER READING

Betten, Neil. "Strike on the Mesabi Range—1907." *Minnesota History*, Vol. 40 (1967), pp. 340–347.

Delli Quadri, Carmen, L. *Labor Relations on the Mesabi Range.* Master's thesis, University of Colorado, 1944.

Sofchalk, Donald G. "Organized Labor and the Iron Ore Miners of Northern Minnesota, 1907–1936." *Labor History*, Vol. 12, No. 2 (Spring, 1971), pp. 215–242.

o   o   o

MOLLY MAGUIRES. This was the name given to a reputed Irish-Catholic terrorist society operative in the lower anthracite regions of Pennsylvania during the third quarter of the nineteenth century. Although a violent, anti-landlord society by the same name flourished in Ireland during the 1840s, Benjamin Bannan, Whig (later Republican) editor of the Pottsville *Miners' Journal* established the lexicon of the American episode.

Blaming defeats of local Whig candidates upon the block voting of the Irish, Bannan launched a virulent campaign against them during the 1850s. Week after week, the *Miners' Journal* portrayed the Irish as a drunken and criminal underclass.

Block voting, however, required some direction. Bannan charged that a secret Irish society, which he called "Molly Maguires," controlled the Democratic Party's insidious and criminal purposes.

Events during the Civil War apparently substantiated Bannan's allegations. In June 1862, John Kehoe, an Irishman and anti-war Democrat, spat upon an American flag during a public meeting at Audenried. F. W. Langdon, a mine foreman, denounced Kehoe. Kehoe allegedly responded by threatening to kill Langdon. Later that day, an unidentified person or persons attacked Langdon while he was alone. The badly beaten Langdon died the next day. A second murder, that of George K. Smith, occurred in Audenried in November 1863. Smith, a mine operator, was supposedly killed for providing a draft office with a list of his employees.

The area gained notoriety for resisting the draft. In August 1862, a large group of men stopped a Harrisburg-bound train of conscripts and permitted unwilling draftees to return home. To avoid a confrontation, the federal government accepted bogus affidavits attesting that Cass Township, Schuylkill County, had fulfilled its draft quota with enlistments.

Thereafter, draft resistance, although widespread, tended to be on an individual basis. But the provost marshall, Charlemagne Tower, equated a series of labor strikes in Cass Township with anti-conscription. The fact that 20 percent of Cass Township's population was Irish did not go unnoticed.

A crime wave accompanied these war related "outrages." Fifty-two murders were reported in Schuylkill County between 1863 and 1867. Most of the murders went unsolved. The ease with which suspects secured alibis to free them convinced many that the region was under a reign of terror administered by a secret society.

The level of violence in the region dramatically declined after 1868. A large number of people attributed the restoration of law and order to the Workingmen's Benevolent Association. Indeed, local newspapers praised the new union of anthracite miners for destroying "the reign of terror and outlawry that existed here a few years ago."

Franklin B. Gowen, president of the Philadelphia and Reading Railroad, disagreed. Gowen was district attorney of Schuylkill County during the peak of the Civil War crime wave and had failed to achieve a single conviction. He blamed his failure upon a secret society. Appearing before a legislative committee investigating the strike of 1871, Gowen revived the notion of a secret criminal society and implied that it controlled the union.

Two years later, Gowen hired Allan Pinkerton's national detective agency to investigate violence in the area. At least five agents were sent into the coalfields. Four of the agents—P. M. Cummings, William McCowan, "W.R.H.," and H. B. Hanmore—infiltrated the union. But they were unable to discover a secret society.

The other detective, James McParlan, alias James McKenna, infiltrated the Ancient Order of Hibernians (AOH), a benevolent, fraternal Irish organization. He soon discovered that the dreaded Molly Maguires were a secret inner circle within this secret society. According to McParlan, members brought their grievances before the lodge's Bodymaster who decided and arranged the appropriate retaliation. All of this was done without the knowledge of the general membership. Gaining access to this inner circle, McParlan collected information on several members.

The Molly Maguire trials, however, extended beyond the incidents to which McParlan was privy. During the detective's testimony, the prosecution, headed by coal company lawyers, shifted attention from the individual defendants to the Ancient Order of the Hibernians. They recited the organization's ritual and reported that the

order had only one objective, that of protecting and avenging its members. But McParlan could not provide direct evidence linking the conspiracy he had uncovered with the secret society that terrorized the area during the Civil War.

John Kehoe provided that linkage. A widely known AOH leader and Democratic officeholder, Kehoe also was connected to the murder of F. W. Langdon in 1862. Insufficient evidence, however, had caused authorities to drop the case. Witnesses to the murder suddenly appeared in 1876. Based upon their often conflicting testimony, Kehoe was found guilty and sentenced to hang.

The Molly Maguire investigation and trials ended with the execution of twenty men—ten in one day. The episode vindicated Bannan's notion that the Irish were a drunken underclass easily led into criminal activity. It also tarred organized labor with the label of terrorism, as Franklin B. Gowen successfully equated the Workingmen's Benevolent Association with the Molly Maguires. [Harold W. Aurand]

FURTHER READING

Broehl, Wayne C., Jr. *The Molly Maguires.* Cambridge, MA: Harvard University Press, 1965.

Dewees, F. P. *The Molly Maguires: The Origin, Growth, and Character of the Organization.* New York: Burt Franklin, 1969 (reprint of 1877 edition).

Wallace, Anthony F. C. *St Clair: A Nineteenth-Century Coal Town's Experience with a Disaster Prone Industry.* New York: Alfred A. Knopf, 1987.

o   o   o

MONTGOMERY WARD STRIKE OF 1945. As the end of World War II approached, the nation, exhausted by a decade of depression, the reform energies of the New Deal, and five years of total war, slowly turned to the right. The conservative turn in domestic politics posed a serious threat to the labor movement, which was robust after its growth during the war but still tentative and unsure of its role and security in the nation. The changing climate of opinion was also evident in the resurrection of the traditional American business anti-unionism—a move that spread rapidly. It was particularly strong in industries which had, for the most part, resisted the Congress of Industrial Organizations (CIO) attempts to organize them, often by breaking the law and disregarding National Labor Relations Board (NLRB) and National War Labor Board (NWLB) orders. Among the most visible of the leaders of this movement was Sewell Avery, the bitterly anti-union and anti–New Deal chairman of Montgomery Ward, the retailing giant.

The immediate target of this sector of the business community was the "maintenance of membership" policy adopted by the War Labor Board. The policy required members of a union to remain members for the duration of the existing contract. It provided a form of union security against company attempts to undermine the union through a variety of methods, and also provided the unions with the certainty of dues payments. In industries such as retailing, where unionization was weak, only the maintenance-of-membership policy prevented the de facto operation of the open shop. For many unions in this position, the War Labor Board's policy had been essential to the growth they achieved during the war. This had been true at Montgomery Ward, a company that the small United Retail, Wholesale, and Department Store Employees (URWDSE) had begun to penetrate for the first time during World War II.

Under pressure from the War Labor Board, Avery had signed a union security clause with the URWDSE late in 1942. But the next year, in defiance of WLB orders, he refused to renew the contract. Instead, management cut wages, fired employees, and demanded a new election from the NLRB. Avery also made known his intention to seek a federal court injunction to restrain the War Labor Board from forcing Montgomery Ward to sign a union contract. On January 15, 1944, the War Labor Board ordered a thirty-day extension of the old contract while the union filed for a new NLRB election. The company announced that it would defy the extension order. On March 29, the War Labor Board issued a second order that the company ignored. In the face of this challenge, the Chicago URWDSE local struck in April 1944 to force government seizure of Montgomery Ward and the implementation of the NWLB directive. Five thousand workers walked out in Chicago, ringing three Ward buildings with picket lines. Virtually the entire Chicago labor movement, with the exception of Communist-controlled locals which supported the wartime no-strike pledge at any cost, supported the strikers. So too did the national CIO, including the champion of the no-strike clause, President Philip Murray.

One day after the strike began, the War Labor Board certified the strike to Roosevelt, and on April 26 the president ordered seizure of the strike-bound Chicago Montgomery Ward buildings. In order to appear evenhanded, Roosevelt blasted both strikers and management. The workers hailed the government's decision as a victory, although they went back to work without a contract. What gave the confrontation an aura of victory for the strikers was the dramatic eviction of the intransigent Sewell Avery from his Chicago office. A picture of Avery, unruffled and with arms folded, being carried from the building by two soldiers appeared on the front pages of newspapers across the country.

After the strike, the union did win the NLRB election overwhelmingly. Roosevelt announced that the company had agreed to comply with the results of the election and continue its contractual arrangement with the union. But Avery promptly repudiated the President, announcing that he had never made such an agreement and had no intention of doing so. To Sewell Avery, who had become something of a folk hero to much of the business community, the results of the election were of "no consequence." Ward would not sign any contract that included a union security clause, including the government supported maintenance of membership formula.

Nor was the seizure of the plant a serious blow to the company's fortunes. The union's attorney subsequently complained that it was a farce. There was no change of management personnel. The *CIO News* complained that even under ostensible government control, management practices at the company remained as before. Workers were being shifted from job to job, discrimination was rife, and seniority and grievance procedures were ignored.

Once the government turned official control of the company back to Ward management on May 9, the union had no recourse but to strike again. Avery refused to consider any union security arrangement and would not even discuss seventeen of the union's twenty demands, including seniority and premium pay for overtime. Once again the War Labor Board ordered Avery to extend the old contract. Once again he ignored the order. On December 9, some 2,000 members of the URWDSE struck Montgomery Ward's Detroit stores. Once again most CIO unions came to the aid of the strikers. The strike quickly spread to six other cities.

Roosevelt intervened again. This time ordering all struck Ward operations to be seized on December 28, 1944. The seizure order conceded a seven-cents-per-hour wage increase, but little else, and nothing that Avery had not already agreed to. After a series of court cases, which first found the seizure illegal and then legal, the Army maintained control of the thirteen seized Ward properties until the war's end in August 1945. At that point, the properties were returned to the company. Montgomery Ward and Avery had successfully defied the government. No maintenance-of-membership clause was agreed to by the company. In effect, Avery had been able to defeat the unionization of his company's sixty thousand employees for the duration of the war by defying government orders. Only after the war was the URWDSE able to organize the Montgomery Ward Company. [Ronald L. Filippelli]

FURTHER READING

Lichtenstein, Nelson. *Labor's War at Home: The CIO in World War II*. New York: Oxford University Press, 1982.

Preis, Art. *Labor's Giant Step: Twenty Years of the CIO*. New York: Pathfinder Press, 1972.

N

○○○○○○○○○○

○   ○   ○

NATIONAL CASH REGISTER STRIKE OF 1901. The strike against the National Cash Register Company (NCR) of Dayton, Ohio, reflected the impact on labor of the transformation of American manufacturing and management practices in the last quarter of the nineteenth century. That transformation, involving new technology and the use of electric power, also included the implementation of management systems that rested on bureaucratic control. This meant that the "foreman's empire" on the shop floor was replaced with control by engineers, accountants, and professional personnel managers. At NCR this new system rested on what later came to be called "welfare capitalism." It included profit sharing, insurance, medical assistance, company schools, company housing, company theater, gardening programs, and more. The goal was to tie the worker more closely to the "family" of the firm, to make him more content, and thus more productive.

At the turn of the century, the National Cash Register plant, under the direction of President John H. Patterson, had the reputation of being an advanced example of the industrial welfare policy in action. Patterson was an advocate of an early model of shared decision-making. He had replaced, to some degree, the hierarchical control over production with a series of decision-making committees. Through participation and constant exhortation, Patterson strove to build loyalty to the firm among the employees.

Patterson's innovations notwithstanding, the growth of the firm in the 1890s required an increase in traditional supervision. While many foremen learned to adjust to Patterson's less authoritarian system, one in particular, James McTaggart, continued to use the harsh methods of the "drive system" that he had learned as a brass foundry foreman at the Yale and Towne Company in Stamford, Connecticut. So resentful of McTaggart did the workers become, that the molders at NCR formed a union in 1897 to deal with their dictatorial foreman. McTaggart responded by firing the union activists. This arbitrary action and a speedup in McTaggart's brass foundry created an explosive situation. When the molders organized again in 1899, they joined the Metal Polishers, Buffers, Platers, and Brass Workers Union of North America. Once again, McTaggart responded with intimidation, firing the union leader and threatening to discharge the others. This time, however, the Metal Polishers gave support and negotiated a contract with Patterson calling for the reinstatement of the discharged men and a closed shop for the molders.

While the confrontation in McTaggart's foundry was underway, a number of unions were organizing NCR workers. This task was made much easier by Patterson's decision to favor unionization because he believed that unionization would give workers a sense of participation in the company and would prevent unpredictable work stoppages during a period of company growth. By 1900, the company had contracts with some twenty unions, including the Wood Workers, Machinists, Carpenters, Teamsters, Metal Mechanics, and the Metal Polishers.

The rapid unionization of NCR caused considerable discomfort for the business community of Dayton, a center of the open shop movement. When NCR's unions refused to be as docile as he had hoped, causing frequent disruptions with strikes and jurisdictional fights among themselves, Patterson himself had second thoughts. Patterson lamented that much of management's time had been consumed in sorting out grievances and "getting elaborate agreements . . . in the hope of preventing trouble."

Nevertheless, it was McTaggart, not Patterson, who caused the impasse which led to the strike. He continued his arbitrary and authoritarian ways, disregarding the contract when it pleased him and harassing the union members whenever he had the opportunity. When he fired four union men for insubordination, and Patterson refused to rehire them, the molders struck on April 29. When the stoppage in the foundry began to create shortages throughout the plant, Patterson locked out the remaining 2,300 production workers.

The NCR strike was but one of a series of industrial disputes which struck Dayton in the summer of 1901. By the end of May, city officials estimated that some 3,500 workers were on strike. Patterson, obviously feeling betrayed by the turn of events, refused to deal with the strikers. But he did not resort to terrorism to drive the workers back into the plant. Unlike many other employers of the period, NCR did not employ Pinkertons or strikebreakers to end the strike, nor did it seek an injunction to end the walkout. Instead, Patterson threatened to follow the lead of the other Dayton employers and institute the open shop. This caused dissension in the ranks of the locked-out workers, many

of whom belonged to unions that were not on strike.

The threat of the open shop brought AFL president Samuel Gompers and national officers of the many unions at NCR to speak with Patterson. They found him amenable to compromise but adamant on the issue of not rehiring the four fired molders. This presented Gompers and the non-striking unions with a dilemma. If they persisted in demanding the rehiring of the fired molders as a condition for a settlement, they risked losing all unionization at NCR. Such a turn of events would have been a considerable victory for the open shop Manufacturers Association of Dayton. Given this reality, Gompers counseled moderation and advised the union to yield on the reinstatement issue. Not surprisingly, the strikers refused to accept his recommendation, and the strike and lockout continued.

When the shutdown had lasted for a month, union solidarity began to crumble. The non-striking unions were beginning to lose patience with the molders and metal polishers who refused to return without the reinstatement of the fired molders. Exasperated, the first crack in the united front came on June 19 when the Metal Mechanics, the largest union at NCR, and the non-union workers returned to work. This move induced the molders and metal polishers to concede on the reinstatement issue if Patterson would agree to fire McTaggart. He refused. After the failure of one more attempt at mediation by Samuel Gompers, Patterson proceeded to establish the open shop in the foundry and polishing departments. On July 2, with non-union men filling many of the jobs in the two departments, half of the striking molders returned to work, defeated and without a union.

The strike had taught Patterson a lesson. He did not retreat from his welfare policies. But he did realize that his innovative management techniques had not penetrated to the shop floor, where traditional methods, such as those used by McTaggart, had undermined his attempts at drawing workers into closer identification with the firm. In order to correct this shortcoming, he created the NCR Labor Department, the first modern personnel department in American industry. The department administered the welfare programs, trained foremen in the new techniques, and curtailed the arbitrary authority of men like McTaggart. Its success led Patterson to re-evaluate the value of having unions at all. With the foremen's arbitrary power gone, the workers had less need for protection, Patterson reasoned. With the Labor Department policing the shop floor, there was no need for the unions to perform the function. After 1901, Patterson refused to sign contracts with his remaining unions. In the next decade all trace of unionism disappeared. [Ronald L. Filippelli]

FURTHER READING

Nelson, Daniel. *Managers and Workers: Origins of the New Factory System in the United States, 1880–1920.* Madison, WI: University of Wisconsin Press, 1975.

———. "The New Factory System and the Unions: The National Cash Register Company Dispute of 1901." *Labor History,* Vol. 15 (Spring, 1974), pp. 163–168.

o   o   o

NEW BEDFORD, MASSACHU-SETTS, TEXTILE STRIKE OF 1928. Although most often thought of as a city whose economy depended on commercial fishing, from the middle of the nineteenth century New Bedford was above all a textile manufacturing city. By 1920, twenty-seven textile corporations, all but one of which were locally owned, called the city home.

The family-owned mills of New Bedford suffered from antiquated management practices and a lack of capital investment. The closed system allowed neither for innovation nor for the removal of incompetent management. New Bedford's textile industry matched *Time* magazine's characterization of the nation's textile industry as being run by men who preferred "golf sticks to spindles." In 1928, ten companies in the New Bedford Cotton Manufacturer's Association had not paid dividends for one to two years.

In the face of the problems of poor management, undercapitalization, and competition, the cotton manufacturers turned to labor costs as their salvation. On April 9, 1928, the employers announced that New Bedford would follow a New England–wide reduction in wages of 10 percent. To the surprise of the companies, the heretofore docile unions of the New Bedford Textile Council, none of which had ever been recognized by the manufacturers, made preparations to strike.

The unions represented a minority of New Bedford's millworkers, but they were generally the most skilled, like the Mule Spinners and the weavers, and therefore the most difficult to replace. The unions representing the various trades belonged to the American Federation of Textile Operatives, a national organization not affiliated with the American Federation of Labor. On April 16, the walkout began, and it was 100 percent effective. This was no small feat, because it meant that the unskilled workers, who were predominantly of Portuguese extraction, supported the walkout. These workers, consistently discriminated against by the largely English and Irish skilled workers, were the key to a successful strike.

Unlike in many industrial cities, the citizens of New Bedford threw their support behind the strike from the beginning. The press and the clergy generally championed the "just" cause of the strikers, while city officials remained neutral. This community support was tested when Communist organizers from the Trade Union Unity League, a Communist-organized dual union movement, arrived in New Bedford to try to direct the strike. The Textile Council urged its members and the community to reject the communist efforts.

Communist strategy focused on the unskilled, unorganized portion of the work force, which they attempted to bring into their Mill Committee. The Portuguese, French-Canadian, and other immigrant groups, who had largely been excluded from the Textile Council's skilled craft divisions, found the Communist call for industrial unionism attractive. The entry of the Communists shifted the focus of the strike away from the conflict between the manufacturers and the unions, toward the struggle between the AFL unions and their community supporters against the Communists.

Police raided the Communist headquarters and harassed their supporters in a number of ways. Disturbing-the-peace citations were issued with regularity against pickets representing the Mill Committee. When the Communist leadership tried to defy the police harassment, a fight broke out and nine strikers were arrested. The city aided the Textile Council strikers in other ways as well. Parade permits were made available to the Textile Council, which represented the "recognized labor forces," but not to the Mill Committee. When the unskilled workers demonstrated against the city's refusal to grant them a parade permit, police arrested the leaders for inciting a riot and parading without a permit.

Meanwhile, by the beginning of June the strikers of both movements were beginning to feel the pressure. The strike had been going on for over six weeks and assistance from the Citizen's Relief Group, which was available only to the anti-Communist unions, had been cut by 10 percent because of a shortage of contributions.

The Loom Fixers Union ended strike assistance to its 900 members altogether.

At the beginning of July, sensing victory, the Manufacturer's Association announced that it would reopen the mills on July 9. They had underestimated the strikers resolve. When the opening day arrived, 20,000 pickets and supporters massed at the mill gates. The owners' hoped-for back-to-work movement among the non-union workers failed to materialize. The failure of their tactic did not, however, bring the manufacturers to the bargaining table. Instead, they protested to union and government officials that the mass picket lines had intimidated workers wanting to return to the mills and that the police had failed to protect company property.

The complaints of the manufacturers gained weight with city officials because of a window-breaking rampage engaged in by the pickets three days after the failure of the attempt to reopen the mills. The police, sensitive to charges that they were not enforcing the law evenhandedly, began to limit the number of pickets and to arrest strikers for vandalism. These new tensions between strikers and police led to the worst violence of the strike on July 24. During a hearing for the rioters, the court declared a ban on picketing. Fred Beal, Communist organizer and leader of the Mill Committee, immediately challenged the ban, daring police to break up his mass picket lines. The police responded by arresting hundreds of strikers. Fearful of the escalation of the conflict, the chief of police called in the National Guard to keep the peace.

This show of force ended the mass picketing, largely as a result of a lack of enthusiasm for the tactic among strikers who were increasingly losing hope in the strike. The decline in the usefulness of the tactic, which had been the most successful used by the Communist organizers, also marked the decline of their influence in the strike. Their strength had always been their ability to mobilize the unskilled immigrant workers. As the hardships of the strike intensified, it became increasingly clear that they were unable to convert this short-run strategy into long-term gains for the workers. This was mainly because the Manufacturer's Association refused to have any dealings with representatives of the Mill Committee. Instead, the operators negotiated with the preferred Textile Council unions.

The settlement came on October 6, when the unions accepted a wage cut of 5 percent and indirect recognition of the unions. The Communists tried to disrupt the reopening of the mills, urging supporters to stay on strike. Once again, the police intervened, arresting Mill Committee supporters on a variety of petty charges. After the strike ended, a New Bedford grand jury indicted twenty-five Communist leaders for conspiring to violate the city's anti-parade ordinance.

Community attitudes toward the Communists, more as outsiders than on ideological grounds, shaped the resolution of the strike in New Bedford. Officials and citizens of the city were not anti-union, but they made a clear distinction between the Textile Council unions, made up of respectable skilled workers drawn mostly from "native" stock, and the largely Portuguese unskilled workers being led astray by "outsiders." This fine distinction set the events in New Bedford apart from disputes in other cities at the time. Largely overlooked in the settlement was the willingness of large numbers of the city's underclass of immigrants to follow Communist leadership and strike for six months against overwhelming odds. [Ronald L. Filippelli]

FURTHER READING

Santos, Michael W. "Community and Communism: The 1928 New Bedford Textile Strike." *Labor History*, Vol. 26 (Spring, 1985), pp. 230–249.

Wolfbein, Seymour L. *The Decline of a Cotton Textile City: A Study of New Bedford.* New York: Columbia University Press, 1968.

o   o   o

NEW ENGLAND TELEPHONE OPERATORS' STRIKE OF 1919. In April 1919, the telephone operators of New England completely paralyzed telephone service for six days in the most massive strike to spread across that region since the Shoemakers' Strike of 1860. Never before in New England had a strike so directly affected so large a segment of the population. Involving 8,000 operators, it was one of the largest strikes ever initiated and led by women. It came at the end of the decade that represents the high point of women's labor militancy in the United States—the decade that began with the **"Uprising of the 20,000"** in New York's garment industry in 1909 and that witnessed mass participation by women in the **Chicago Clothing Workers' Strike of 1910**, the **Lawrence Textile Strike of 1912**, and the **Paterson Textile Strike of 1913**. New England's male telephone workers initially refused to walk out with the operators but joined the strike on the third day. The strike was marked by considerable violence, including many assaults on strikebreakers and riots in Boston, reflecting bitter class antagonisms in the larger Massachusetts cities.

The vast majority of New England's telephone workers, both women and men, belonged to the International Brotherhood of Electrical Workers (IBEW), an affiliate of the American Federation of Labor. The operators, not the men, had been the first to organize. The first telephone operators' local in the United States to survive more than a short time was established in Boston by the IBEW in 1912, with major assistance from the Women's Trade Union League. The new Boston operators' local became Local 1A of the IBEW (the operators were placed in separate "Class A" locals). It achieved recognition by the New England Telephone Company after a threatened strike in 1913. Inspired by the operators' success, the male telephone workers in Boston and elsewhere in New England began to organize and affiliate with the IBEW. By 1919, most of the operators and telephone men in the territory served by the New England Telephone Company (all New England states except Connecticut) had joined the IBEW.

The Boston near-strike of 1913 had sparked organizing drives among telephone operators throughout the country, and by the end of 1918 there were about one hundred locals that had affiliated with the IBEW. In 1918, the "Class A" locals were placed in a separate "Telephone Operators' Department," headquartered in Boston. New England was, however, the only region where telephone operators were ever solidly organized.

Since 1913, when the New England Telephone Company had recognized the operators' union, there had existed in New England a formal procedure for collective bargaining. An adjustment board, composed of an equal number of company and union representatives, negotiated an annual agreement covering wages and working conditions. There were separate boards for the operators and the men. Until 1919, New England's telephone workers had never walked out on strike.

Although they had gained some improvements since they had unionized, the operators in particular had long been dissatisfied with their wages and working conditions. They found little satisfaction in their work, which involved the continuous repetition of a few prescribed motions and phrases at a rapid, "nerve-racking" pace under exacting supervision. Wages were too low for the operators, nearly all of whom were young unmarried women and girls, to live outside their families of origin. Having gained the eight-hour workday in 1913, the Telephone Operators' Union hoped to win even shorter hours and wages that would permit the operators to be self-supporting.

The New England Telephone Strike of 1919 occurred during the one-year period when the telephone service was under government control and operation. As a temporary war measure, the federal government in August 1918 assumed control of the telephone system, which was placed under the supervision of Postmaster General Albert Burleson. Burleson not only showed no concern for protecting the wages of telephone workers in a period of soaring, war-induced inflation but also firmly opposed their right to organize and bargain collectively, suspending it where it had been recognized before the war. In 1918, he discharged telephone operators who walked out on strike in Minnesota's twin cities and in Wichita.

The New England strike was precipitated by the failure of the postmaster general to provide any method for adjusting the wage demands of the telephone operators, after having declared invalid the procedure of collective bargaining in force since 1913. The operators were determined to gain wage increases to offset the effects of the wartime inflation. In November 1918, the general manager of the New England Telephone Company informed the Telephone Operators' Union that under government control he could not act on the proposed wage scale for 1919 that it had submitted to him. The union's seven-woman wage scale committee then visited Washington in an effort to determine which government body had the authority to act in the matter. But despite the union's efforts, Burleson failed to establish a procedure for bargaining. He continued to delay even after the existing agreement expired at the end of 1918. In February 1919, the union decided to compel action on its wage demands by taking a vote giving the leadership the authority to call a strike. The vote showed the operators to be overwhelmingly in favor of a strike.

A strike became inevitable when Burleson, in April 1919, elaborated a procedure for handling the wage demands that denied the telephone operators their right to bargain collectively. Burleson insisted that the operators first present their demands to the general manager of New England Telephone, who could, if he chose, submit a secret recommendation to the Operating Board in New York, which was composed only of telephone and telegraph company officials. The Operating Board would then submit its recommendation to the Wire Control Board in Washington, composed of four government officials, after which the matter would go to the postmaster general for final action.

Telephone Operators' Department president Julia O'Connor, also president of Local 1A, responded by calling a mass meeting of the union telephone operators of New England in Boston to discuss a strike. The national IBEW leadership, which believed the time was inopportune for a strike, made every effort to restrain the operators, as did AFL president Samuel Gompers. But at the mass meeting, the operators shouted down the IBEW vice-president who had been sent to dissuade them from striking. The meeting, attended by 2,000 operators from across New England, voted unanimously to strike.

Like the "Uprising of the 20,000" of a decade before, the New England Telephone Strike represented a rejection of male trade union authority by masses of semiskilled women workers, although the telephone operators had the advantage of being solidly organized before the walkout. Nearly every operator in the five states served by the company joined the strike. The operators were not joined at the outset by New England's male telephone workers, who could have considerably strengthened their position. Only on the third day of the strike, with public and newspaper opinion overwhelmingly opposed to Burleson's position and the issue nearly decided, did the telephone men walk out. May Matthews, secretary of Local 1A,

commented, "The fight had been won, but I guess they had been smoked out by other people in the labor movement."

The widespread participation of young "society women" and affluent college students as strikebreakers provoked considerable violence by working-class sympathizers of the telephone operators and led to rioting in Boston. The strikebreakers included large numbers of women from Providence's East Side in Rhode Island; Fall River's "Hill Section," Worcester's West Side, and Brookline in Massachusetts; and other exclusive city neighborhoods and suburbs, as well as college students from Harvard, MIT, Tufts, and Brown. Although physical attacks were reserved for male college students, the society women were subjected to jeers and taunts on their way to and from the telephone exchanges and were in some cases pressured by the crowds to stop work. The most serious of the riots, precipitated by the strikebreaking of college students, occurred in front of Boston's main exchange, when members of a crowd of 3,000 strikers and sympathizers attacked students as they left the exchange, severely injuring several of them.

On the fifth day of the strike, Burleson abandoned his opposition to direct bargaining, and his first assistant postmaster general arrived in Boston with full authority to approve an agreement negotiated by union and company representatives. The settlement reached included a significant wage increase for the telephone operators and recognized their right to bargain collectively with the company's general manager.

The strike settlement represented the first decisive victory for the telephone workers under the Burleson Wire Administration. Every telephone operator resumed the position she had vacated at the strike call and all seniority rights were guaranteed, a significant contrast to the other telephone strikes during the period of government operation. The *Boston Post* reported that the settlement was widely regarded as a "smashing victory for the girl operators and their men allies."

The 1919 New England telephone strike precipitated organizing campaigns across the country that added thousands of new members to the Telephone Operators' Department in the next few months. But the strike also revealed a serious weakness in New England telephone unionism, as the male telephone workers refused to demonstrate solidarity with the operators in the early stages of the strike. Relations between the telephone men and the operators were badly strained from that time on. In 1920, the New England telephone men withdrew from the IBEW to join a company union. During the 1920s, a period highly unfavorable for organized labor, the Telephone Operators' Department lost nearly all of its locals outside of New England. In 1923, the telephone operators walked out in a second New England strike, which the male telephone workers openly opposed. The strike ended in the total defeat of the operators and the complete elimination of their union movement. [Stephen H. Norwood]

FURTHER READING

Greenwald, Maurine W. *Women, War, and Work.* Westport, CT: Greenwood Press, 1980.

Norwood, Stephen H. *Labor's Flaming Youth: Telephone Operators and Worker Militancy, 1878–1923.* Urbana, IL: University of Illinois Press, 1990.

O'Connor, Julia. "The Truth About the New England 'Phone Strike'." *Life and Labor* (June 1919), pp. 131–133.

o   o   o

NEW ORLEANS GENERAL STRIKE OF 1892. Early in 1892, streetcar drivers in New Orleans won a victory that included a shorter workday and the preferential closed shop. The victory spurred thousands of workers to look to the American Federation of Labor for help in dealing with their employers. Thirty new unions were chartered in the city, and a Workingmen's Amalgamated Council was formed which represented more than 20,000 workers. Of more significance, the Teamsters, Scalesmen, and Packers, three racially integrated unions that performed the manual labor essential to commerce in the port, formed the "Triple Alliance."

On October 24, 1892, the Triple Alliance struck over demands for the ten-hour workday, overtime pay, and the preferential closed shop. The Workingmen's Council moved to take over control of the strike by appointing a committee of directors, most from conservative unions, and one of whom was black. New Orleans' employers rose to the challenge. The board of trade, which represented the financial power in the city, appointed its own small committee to centralize decision-making. The four railway systems that entered New Orleans, plus the big commodity exchanges in cotton, sugar, and rice, pledged their support. The business forces contented themselves with raising a defense fund and appealing to the governor to send in the militia. No negotiations took place during the first week.

The unions increased the pressure by calling a general strike to break the stalemate. Under this threat, the united front of the employers cracked. Those not party to the original dispute pressured the board of trade to negotiate. When a tentative agreement fell through because of failures on both sides, the Workingmen's Council again ordered a general strike. After two postponements, 20,000 workers, practically the entire unionized work force of New Orleans, walked out on November 8. The original dispute had spread into a citywide attempt to establish collective bargaining and the closed shop in New Orleans. Each union demanded recognition, a closed shop, and in many cases, wage and hour gains for its members. Recently organized public utility workers joined the strike against the wishes of the governor and the advice of the labor committee. The effectiveness of the strike was reflected in the decline of bank clearings in New Orleans to half of their pre-strike level.

At this critical juncture, the employers decided to reclaim their control over the city. With the assistance of the railroads, strikebreakers were imported from nearby cities such as Memphis and Galveston. When a call by the mayor for special deputies turned up only fifty-nine volunteers, employers began training their own clerks for riot duty and offered to pay all costs if the militia were called up. With the situation worsening and violence clearly possible, the governor effectively created a form of martial law by issuing a proclamation restricting public gatherings and threatening to call out the militia if the strike were not ended.

Fearful of the bloodshed that would likely ensue with the use of the militia, the unions decided to end the strike in three days. The employers did agree to the wage and hour demands of the triple alliance, but refused to grant recognition to the unions. The attempt to make New Orleans a closed-shop city had failed. In the aftermath of the struggle, forty-five strike leaders were indicted in federal court for violating the Sherman Antitrust Act.

The strike, although largely a failure, demonstrated that black and white workers could and would stay together in the South in support of their unions. This example of solidarity among southern workers as early as 1892 gave a hint of the possibilities for militant trade unionism, rarely realized among the southern working class. [Ronald L. Filippelli]

FURTHER READING

Brecher, Jeremy. *Strike*. San Francisco, CA: Straight Arrow Books, 1972.

Shugg, Roger Wallace. "The New Orleans General Strike of 1892." *Louisiana Historical Quarterly*, Vol. 21 (1937), pp. 547–560.

o o o

NEW YORK CITY BAKERS' STRIKE OF 1741. On April 20, 1741, the *New York Weekly Journal* noted that in the previous week there had been a general combination of the bakers of New York City not to bake because the price of wheat was too high. The action apparently brought some general disturbance among the populace, some of whom were unable to find bread.

The strike was referred to in 1809 during one of the **Cordwainers' Conspiracy Cases**, when it was described as a refusal of certain bakers to bake bread unless certain demands were met. During that same case the attorney for the prosecution referred to the bakers' strike as precedent against the cordwainers, arguing that the bakers were tried and convicted for a conspiracy not to bake bread unless their wages were raised. According to the meager information available on the event, no sentence was ever passed.

In the absence of documentation on the strike, one can speculate on its causes by exploring the context of the dispute. At the time, New York was in the grip of mass hysteria springing from a series of fires that destroyed much of the city. Rumors that the fires had been set by black slaves were widely believed. The militia was called out and a number of citizens fled the city for refuge in the Bowery and Harlem. In the midst of this atmosphere, a number of blacks, both free and slave, were convicted of seditious conspiracy on highly dubious evidence and burned at the stake.

To add to the tension, many feared an attack upon the city by the Spanish, with whom England and her colonies were at war. Wartime conditions led to rapid inflation in commodity prices, including wheat. This put the price of bread 50 percent higher than it had been in the previous year. The fear of insurrection, war, and famine no doubt made for a hostile reception from the citizens and the authorities when the bakers decided to withhold their services. Nor is there much mystery that under these circumstances, their action was prosecuted as a criminal conspiracy. [Ronald L. Filippelli]

FURTHER READING

Morris, Richard B. *Government and Labor in Early America*. New York: Harper and Row, 1946.

o   o   o

NEW YORK CITY BUS STRIKE OF 1941. At five o'clock on Monday morning, March 10, 1941, the Transport Workers Union of New York (TWU) struck the New York City Omnibus Corporation and the Fifth Avenue Coach Company. Although ostensibly separate entities, both companies had the same operating officers and most of the same directors. By 6:00 A.M. the strike was completely effective. Not a single bus from either company was on the streets of the city.

Bus drivers had a long list of grievances that set them apart from other workers. Stomach ulcers, so prevalent as to be called "drivers' stomach," resulted from the nervous stress of the daily routine. Drivers complained of the noxious fumes they breathed, the frequency of colds due to the fan blowing on their necks in the summer, and the recurrent drafts in winter when they were not permitted to wear overcoats. High blood pressure and hemorrhoids were occupational hazards, as were various intestinal disorders caused by the constant jolting of the bus. In addition, drivers were often victims of robberies and were expected to make up any loss of money or receipts.

The union's demands included a twenty-five-dollars-per-week minimum salary, the eight-hour workday and the forty-eight-hour workweek. In addition, the TWU asked for a non-contributory pension plan and pay for the eight national holidays. The companies, which had reached agreements with the union after hard bargaining in 1937 and 1938, responded with an elaborate published financial analysis that demonstrated that they were in difficult financial condition and could not meet the union's demands. Indeed, the companies' counter proposal asked for significant concessions from the workers. The last negotiating session took place on March 6 and was marked by bitter arguments. When the companies refused to alter their proposal and the union refused an offer to extend the existing contracts while negotiations continued, negotiations broke down. Mayor Fiorello LaGuardia urged the union to continue to negotiate, but the union president, Michael J. Quill, responded that the responsibility for the strike lay with the companies which, he explained to the mayor, were profitable.

The city's newspapers and radio stations attacked the union unceasingly, blaming it for refusing to accept the mayor's offer to continue negotiating under the old agreement. Editorial writers pointed out the left-wing character of the union's leadership, calling the union a Communist-dominated tool of Moscow. Martin Dies, chairman of the House of Representatives Un-American Activities Committee attacked the TWU leadership as "reds." The *Daily Mirror* blasted Mike Quill as a Communist agitator, a disorderly trouble-maker, and a radical organizer. The companies ran full-page advertisements telling citizens that if they had to walk rather than ride the bus, they should blame the Transport Workers Union.

Finally, with the intercession of John L. Lewis and Philip Murray, president of the CIO, Mayor LaGuardia was able to bring the parties together to resume negotiations on Thursday, March 13, the fourth day of the strike. Arthur S. Meyer, chairman of the New York State Mediation Board, was agreed upon as mediator. But in spite of Meyer's efforts, no progress resulted from the meeting. After another attempt a few days later, Meyer announced that mediation had been a failure.

Soon a press campaign began that claimed that many of the workers wanted to return to work. The companies ran paid advertisements charging that the TWU's leaders would not let the rank and file return. In this atmosphere, 2,000 strikers, dressed in their uniforms and wearing green armbands, gathered to march in the St. Patrick's Day Parade. The workers, mostly Irish, had been invited to participate by the Grand Knight of the New York Chapter of the Knights of Columbus. But overnight something had changed. The head of the parade committee announced that the strikers could not parade as a unit. Most did march anyway, passing out leaflets along the way.

On the ninth day of the strike, it was clear that the union would not be moved. At that point, the union proposed that it would accept arbitration of its demands *upward* but with no consideration of any counter-demands by the companies. In other words, the companies' demands for concessions were not subject to arbitration. On Wednesday, March 19, Philip Murray came to New York to meet with Mayor LaGuardia. Murray explained to the mayor that in inflationary times, no union could accept arbitration that could result in a decline in standards that workers had already struggled to win.

Mayor LaGuardia then appointed a fact-finding board consisting of two ex-transportation industry executives and a Columbia University law professor. In its report, the board accepted the union's argument that the companies' demands for concessions should not be a subject for arbitration. Although the board supported the mayor on several points, the decision on arbitration from a board appointed by the mayor that included no union representatives was a victory for the TWU.

On March 20, LaGuardia supported the compromise, and the companies agreed. The next day, the twelfth day of the strike, all picketing stopped. The busses rolled the following morning. [Ronald L. Filippelli]

FURTHER READING

Huberman, Leo. *The Great Bus Strike.* New York: Modern Age, 1941.

Whittemore, L. H. *The Man Who Ran the Subways: The Story of Mike Quill.* New York: Holt, Rinehart, and Winston, 1968.

o   o   o

NEW YORK CITY CARPENTERS' STRIKE OF 1833. In May of 1833, at the height of the spring building season, the New York journeymen carpenters decided to get an increase in their wages by demanding "a remuneration equal to the services rendered." They demanded an increase from $1.37 to $1.50 a day. The employers refused and the carpenters stopped working.

In making their case to the citizens of New York, the carpenters pledged to stick with their demands until they won and asked for fraternal support from other trades who felt "friendly towards us in the struggle for our right." Eleven journeymen jewelers apparently responded, as did the Typographical Society which had been aroused by an article in the New York *Journal of Commerce* that advised every good citizen to "set his face like a flint against all combinations either to elevate or depress the price." After the typographers called on journeymen mechanics of every trade to support the carpenters, some fifteen trades passed resolutions of sympathy and took collections for the strikers.

With fraternal contributions amounting to some $1,200, the carpenters were able to sustain the strike until the middle of June when they went back with a victory—$1.50 for a ten-hour day from March 10 to November 10, and $1.375 for a nine-hour day for the rest of the year.

The carpenters' success gave significant impetus to the creation of a labor movement in New York. A few days after the strike, the printers issued a call to the journeymen mechanics and artisans of New York to send delegates to meet as "a general union." Some nine societies answered the call and sent delegates to a meeting held on July 15, 1833, where they resolved to create a "General Trades Union." On August 14, 1833, the organization, the General Trades Union of the City of New York, came formally into being. [Ronald L. Filippelli]

FURTHER READING

Commons, John R., et al. *History of Labour in the United States*, Vol. 1. New York: Macmillan, 1936.

Wilentz, Sean. *Chants Democratic: New York City & the Rise of the American Working Class, 1788–1850*. New York: Oxford University Press, 1984.

o   o   o

NEW YORK CITY CARTERS' STRIKE OF 1677. During the Colonial period, certain trades and occupations were considered to be clothed in the public interest. They were licensed and regulated in the manner similar to modern-day treatment of public utilities. One such trade was carting. The fees for the services of porters and carters were regulated by the town authorities, as were their monopolistic privileges.

More than once the carters resorted to a threat to stop work. At the time of the Dutch occupation of New Amsterdam, they complained to the court that outsiders had entered the trade and had sold their carts, horses, and privileges to cart to non-licensed carters. On another occasion, they were the object of complaint for refusing to carry stone, timber, and other materials for the city as a public service. What was probably the first criminal prosecution for a strike in the colonies involved the carters in New York City in 1677. The carters were apparently prosecuted for contempt of court. The Common Council of New York City dismissed twelve carters "for not obeying the Command and Doing their Dutyes as becomes them in their Places." Upon submission to the court, the payment of three shillings each, and agreeing to carry fifteen loads each to the city wharf, the court allowed them to return to their old places at the same rates. [Ronald L. Filippelli]

FURTHER READING

McKee, Samuel, Jr. *Labor in Colonial New York: 1664–1776*. New York: Columbia University Press, 1935.

Morris, Richard B. *Government and Labor in Early America*. New York: Harper and Row, 1946.

o   o   o

NEW YORK CITY CARTERS' STRIKE OF 1684. In 1684, the truckmen employed by the municipal government of New York refused to move dirt from the streets until the price per load was increased. The strikers were "suspended and discharged" "for not obeying the Command and Doing their Dutyes as becomes them in their Places." A week later, the carters asked to be returned to their jobs. They were ordered to conform to certain "Laws and Orders established," and to pay a fine of six shillings each. [Ronald L. Filippelli]

FURTHER READING

Foner, Philip. *History of the Labor Movement in the United States*, Vol. 1. New York: International Publishers, 1947.

McKee, Samuel, Jr. *Labor in Colonial New York: 1664–1776*. New York: Columbia University Press, 1935.

Morris, Richard B. *Government and Labor in Early America*. New York: Harper and Row, 1946.

o   o   o

NEW YORK CITY HOTEL STRIKE OF 1912. At noon on May 7, 1912, lunchtime crowds in midtown Manhattan were treated to a novel sight. Picketing waiters, busboys, cooks, dishwashers, chambermaids, and bellhops filled the sidewalks in front of luxury hotels such as the Belmont, the Waldorf-Astoria, the Plaza, and the Knickerbocker, as well as at famous midtown restaurants, including Delmonico's and Churchill's. A few days later, the number of striking hotel workers reached 18,000, virtually closing down New York's luxury hotel and restaurant trade. It was the first great strike of its kind in New York history.

Long hours, almost military discipline, low pay, and often dangerous working conditions characterized work in the hotel and restaurant trade in New York City. The "kitchen armies" of the city's establishments were largely made up of immigrant workers with little union experience but with deep resentments toward their employers. Although the Hotel and Restaurant Employees and Bartenders Union (HRE), an American Federation of Labor affiliate, had several small locals in the city, the union had never been able to penetrate the major hotels in New York as it had in smaller cities such as San Francisco, Cincinnati, and St. Louis. Because of the size of the industry and the cheap labor provided by the immigrant labor force, many considered the hotel and restaurant trade of New York immune to unionization.

The 1912 uprising disproved that analysis, but it owed little to the efforts of the Hotel and Restaurant Employees Union. Rather it resulted from hard organizing work done by a rival, the Hotel Workers Industrial Union, a creation of the radical, anarcho-syndicalist Industrial Workers of the World (IWW). The strike leaders, Jacob Bloechinger and Joseph Elster, had both become disillusioned with the timid policies of the HRE, which organized according to craft distinctions. Instead, they defected to the IWW vision of one big industrial union enrolling all employees in the industry regardless of skill or job classification.

The IWW presence in the strike also ensured the support of New York's various Socialist factions, some of which were quite strong among the immigrant workers. The IWW's skill at organizing immigrants was also in evidence during the strike. Organizers made special efforts to reach the workers by printing strike leaflets in many languages and by using multilingual organizers such as Joseph Ettor and Arturo Giovannitti.

What the IWW lacked in financial resources and organizational stability, it made up in enthusiasm and tactics. Parades, mass rallies, and wildcat strikes all were used to keep the effort alive. In a few cases, it paid off. The Plaza Hotel and Churchill's restaurant recognized the union. But most employers held fast to their determination not to deal with the Hotel Workers Industrial Union or any union for that matter. Strikebreakers were not hard to find in a city with the available cheap labor pool of New York. Nor did the Hotel and Restaurant Employees Union offer assistance to their rival. After seven weeks, the fear of loss of jobs combined with severe economic hardship drove most of the strikers back to work. Most of the strikers found jobs in the industry, but a number of their leaders were blacklisted. They fanned out from New York to take part in organizing drives in Boston, Cleveland, Pittsburgh, Albany, Chicago, and other cities. [Ronald L. Filippelli]

FURTHER READING

Hopkins, Mary Alden. "The Hotel Workers Strike." Colliers (June 1, 1912).

Josephson, Matthew. Union House, Union Bar: The History of the Hotel and Restaurant Employees and Bartenders International Union, AFL-CIO. New York: Random House, 1956.

Rubin, Jay, and M. J. Obermeier. *Growth of a Union: The Life of Edward Flore.* New York: Historical Union Association, 1943.

o   o   o

NEW YORK CITY INTERBOROUGH RAPID TRANSIT STRIKE OF 1904. In February of 1904, the Cleveland industrialist Mark Hanna died. Among the many positions that Hanna held, one of the most important was his presidency of the National Civic Federation (NCF), an organization working to replace industrial conflict with cooperation between labor and management. The NCF had gained considerable notoriety by intervening in several major strikes, most notably the **Steel Strike of 1901** and the **Anthracite Coal Strike of 1902**. Both settlements were controversial, with historians generally agreeing that the Steel Strike of 1901 was a disaster for the Amalgamated Association of Iron, Steel, and Tin Workers, while the settlement in anthracite was a partial victory for the United Mine Workers.

Hanna's replacement as president of the NCF, August Belmont, was a New York Democrat and aristocrat, and also president of the Interborough Rapid Transit Company (IRT). Viewed by many as a progressive businessmen, Belmont's appointment had been vigorously supported by W. D. McMahon, president of the Amalgamated Association of Street and Electric Railway Employees.

Belmont's relationship with labor began to sour in September of 1904 when his IRT took over the Manhattan Elevated Company, part of New York's new subway system. Belmont announced that henceforth his underground workers would work longer hours and for lower wages than those on the elevated. The policy received a quick rebuke from the unions who represented elevated employees—the Brotherhood of Locomotive Firemen, the Brotherhood of Locomotive Engineers, and the

Amalgamated Association of Street and Electrical Railway Employees. All three unions demanded that their seniority rosters apply to appointments and promotions on the subway and that subway workers be paid equally with those on the elevated. The company agreed to the seniority and preferential hiring demands but rejected equal wages, thus making the seniority question irrelevant. When the three unions voted to strike, the NCF stepped in and arranged a compromise that included a wage increase.

The friction resulting from the incident led to a worsening of labor relations on the IRT. The discontent resulted in an organizing drive on the IRT by the Amalgamated Association that succeeded in enrolling 80 percent of the company's workers. To his credit, Belmont recognized the contradiction in his role as president of the NCF and his relations with the union. He feared that a strike on the IRT would embarrass the NCF, and he agreed to step down. But Warren Stone, Grand Chief of the Brotherhood of Locomotive Engineers and President McMahon of the Amalgamated Association urged him to stay on a promise that there would be no strike.

Unfortunately, the labor leaders were out of touch with the rank and file. The Amalgamated local wanted the nine-hour workday, a 10 percent wage increase, and limitations on the length of the run for each motorman. McMahon urged the local not to strike before bringing the issues to the national union. Another complicating issue was the place of the motormen. They had been included in the union's demands to the company, but they were members of the Brotherhood of Locomotive Engineers (BLE). The BLE had signed a three-year agreement with Belmont, and the cornerstone of NCF policies was the sanctity of the contract.

Nevertheless, when Belmont rejected the demands as a violation of the contract, the workers of both the BLE and the Amalgamated Association struck on March 7, but they indicated that they would be willing to submit the dispute to arbitration. The company refused. It was on firm ground in doing so because McMahon ordered the IRT local to end the unauthorized strike. Other labor members of the NCF backed up McMahon. President Samuel Gompers of the AFL, John Mitchell of the United Mine Workers, and Grand Chief Stone of the BLE, issued public statements condemning the strike as a breach of contract. Subsequently, the Amalgamated Association and the BLE revoked the charters of their IRT locals. Under siege from all sides and forced to watch as strikebreakers took their places, the workers gave in. The surrender was complete. The IRT took only one-third of the workers back, and those lost all seniority, putting them on a par with the strikebreakers. The open shop prevailed on both the elevated and subway lines of the IRT. For his part, August Belmont remained as president of the National Civic Federation.

The lack of support from the labor movement had doomed the strike from the beginning. Labor leaders such as Samuel Gompers, Warren Stone, and John Mitchell were all important members of the NCF. Their legitimacy in dealing with their business counterparts rested on their ability to keep labor relations within the bounds of mutually agreed upon written agreements. In the Interborough Rapid Transit Strike the labor leaders upheld their end of the bargain. For the men for whom honoring agreements between labor and management was most important, blame for the strike rested with the workers who had broken their word. It was, according to Samuel Gompers, a case of union members failing to take the advice "of the men who have made the labor organizations in the United States what they are today." [Ronald L. Filippelli]

FURTHER READING

Foner, Philip S. *History of the Labor Movement in the United States*, Vol. 3. New York: International Publishers, 1964.

McGinley, James J. S. J. *Labor Relations in the New York Rapid Transit Systems, 1904–1944*. New York: King's Crown Press, 1949.

o o o

NEW YORK CITY LONGSHOREMEN'S STRIKE OF 1887. In 1884, the Knights of Labor had organized the eastern ports, setting up District Assembly #49 in New York. With the Knights at the height of their popularity because of victories on the western railroads, longshoremen flocked to join "the Noble Order." In the pre-dawn chill of a January Manhattan morning in the depression year of 1887, the Old Dominion Steamship Line of New York and Newport News, Virginia, locked out its workers and announced that the company would no longer pay the rate of twenty-five cents per hour, but would hire only at a wage of twelve dollars for a sixty-hour week, a 20 percent slash of wages that were already among the lowest in the North Atlantic ports.

The workers repaired to the Knights of Labor Hall where they called for a portwide boycott of all Old Dominion freight. Quickly, all of the longshoremen in the port came to the support of the locked-out workers whose jobs had been taken by scabs. The Knights of Labor had developed such a mystique that even non-union men refused to touch Old Dominion cargo. The workers informed the company of their willingness to negotiate at any time.

As fate would have it, another dispute arose at the same time under the Knights of Labor jurisdiction. Coal handlers in Hoboken, Weehawken, and other points along the New Jersey shore had their wages slashed. As a result, a bitter strike flared on the Jersey docks, and the New York Knights quickly assumed leadership. Soon coal boatmen came to the aid of the handlers, thus effectively bringing the transportation of fuel to a standstill. The longshoremen in New York, already involved in a dispute with Old Dominion, refused to handle "scab" coal and thus became involved in the coal handlers dispute.

Alarmed by the spreading strikes, the companies appealed to the courts. James T. Quinn, "Master Workman" of the New York Knights, was thrown into jail for conspiring "to destroy and injure the property of the Old Dominion Steamship Company." Nevertheless, the boycott was firm, and little or no Old Dominion cargo moved in the port of New York.

Regardless of the solidarity, little was being accomplished, and the Knights were faced with the prospect of either widening the strike or leaving the field in an embarrassing defeat. They chose the former, and on January 26, 1887, the papers announced a call for a general strike on the New York and New Jersey waterfronts. Little time for preparation had left the Knights vulnerable. As the strike spread, their control over it lessened. At first the success of the action was beyond the wildest hopes of the organizers of the general strike. Only mail ships moved in New York harbor during the first ten days of the stoppage. Although small riots broke out at individual piers, the strike was generally peaceful and well ordered during the first days. However, when the employers brought Pinkerton guards to the docks, order could no longer be maintained.

Luckily, there was no strong attempt to use strikebreakers for cargo handling on the Manhattan side of the river. But the story was different in New Jersey where scabs, protected by police and the Pinkertons, began to move cargo across the river to Manhattan. Slowly, the city's industries began to revive. The Knights searched for some way to stop the carrying of coal to the city. Their dilemma grew worse when the small union of stationary engineers, the

men who burned the scab coal that was coming into the city, refused to strike in sympathy. In desperation, the Knights went to Philadelphia where, with the support of the employees of the Reading Railroad, who threatened to strike unless the company made peace with the New Jersey coal handlers, they secured an agreement. Overjoyed, the Knights called off the general strike on the evening of February 11. Unfortunately, they had done nothing to resolve the conflict between the longshoremen and the Old Dominion Company.

When news of the Knights' action reached the longshoremen, there was talk of a sellout and abandonment. As rumors of defeat swept through the waterfront, demoralization turned to panic, and on the morning of February 14, there was a rush for the piers to go back to work. Shipowners, sensing their advantage, immediately slashed pay and withdrew the meager fringe benefits, such as extra money for working during mealtime, that the longshoremen had previously enjoyed.

The disaster of 1887 was nearly a deathblow to unionism on the waterfront. The longshoremen deserted the Knights of Labor in droves, and disenchantment with unionism set in. A year after the strike, there was not one longshore organization left in the port of New York. [Ronald L. Filippelli]

FURTHER READING

Russel, Maud. *Men Along the Shore.* New York: Brussel & Brussel, 1966.

o o o

NEW YORK CITY LONG-SHOREMEN'S STRIKE OF 1945. The great strike wave that occurred in the United States during the transition from war to peace soon after World War II marked an upsurge of rank-and-file militancy that challenged both management control of the workplace and the ability of union leaders to guarantee an orderly industrial relations climate. Such was the case on the New York docks in October of 1945. On the first day of the month, longshoremen refused to unload a ship because the company had been increasing the weight of the load in the slings that the dockers pushed. When the company refused to agree to the workers' weight limit, longshoremen on other piers in the port of New York spontaneously refused to work, charging that the company's position constituted a lockout.

The walkout came during negotiations between the International Longshoremen's Association (ILA) and the shippers. The issue of sling weights, which could go as high as 7,000 pounds, had been absent from previous contracts. This time, however, the strikers demanded that limits be set in the contract. One day after the walkout, however, the ILA's district council ratified a contract negotiated by the ILA's president, Joseph P. Ryan. The contract included pay raises but made no mention of sling weights. The response was immediate. On October 3, two thousand longshoremen refused to work. Most were members of Local 791 of the ILA, located in the Chelsea area of Manahattan, the local that had initiated the wildcat strike two days before. Soon longshoremen on other piers joined Local 791 in defiance of union regulations and contractual obligations. Ryan was in danger of losing control of his union, as nearly 35,000 dockers abstained from work.

The strikers agreed on a set of demands, including a one-ton limit on sling weights, a minimum of four hours pay when called for work, time-and-a-half pay for working over the lunch hour, and a reduction of the number of shape-ups—the meetings during which men were picked to work—from three to two each day. Ryan moved to cut the protest short, but a formal election on the contract Ryan had negotiated, although favorable, drew only 17 percent of the eligible voters and only several hundred voters out of a membership of 1,500 in Local 791. Nevertheless, Ryan interpreted the small vote as a vote of confidence in his policies. The failure of Ryan's attempt became clear the following day when the workers scorned his orders to return to work. The crisis also brought longstanding resentments against Ryan's authoritarian rule to the surface. When he addressed a Local 791 meeting he was roundly booed.

With his hold on the union, which he ruled as "president for life," shaken, Ryan blamed the strike on Communists. He pointed to the support that the National Maritime Union (NMU-CIO) and International Longshoreman's and Warehouseman's Union (ILWU-CIO) had given to the strikers. Both unions were considered to be Communist-led. There is no doubt that the NMU and the ILWU were supportive of the wildcat strike on the New York docks. Both gave material assistance to the strikers, and Harry Bridges, ILWU president, came from California to urge New York's mayor, Fiorello LaGuardia, to meet with the insurgents. The extent of Communist influence among the strikers is difficult to assess. Certainly, Communist's played an important role in the movement, but at the time of the strike, the Communist party was firmly in its united front stage, and it is unlikely that the movement against Ryan had the sanction of the party's leadership.

Nevertheless, the attacks on the insurgents as Communists did help Ryan to reassert his position, especially with the strongly anti-Communist Catholic members of the ILA. Mayor LaGuardia made an appeal to the longshoremen to return to work, promising that negotiations on a new contract would continue and that any changes would be retroactive to October 1. When that appeal failed, LaGuardia understood that the internal dispute in the

ILA was delaying a negotiated settlement. He offered a new plan whereby prominent outsiders would supervise the election of a new negotiating committee for the union. This time, only the insurgents were willing to accept the mayor's plan. Ryan refused, realizing that it was a threat to his leadership. The shippers and the AFL supported Ryan. Ryan also was aware of a back-to-work movement by the strikers. By October 15, two weeks after the initial walkout, the solidarity in the ranks of the strikers began to crack. Large numbers of men drifted back to work as dissension in the largely ad hoc strike committee began to surface. Some wanted to continue the strike while others argued for a National Labor Relations Board (NLRB) election to oust Ryan. Nevertheless, with its base of support eroding rapidly, the strike committee advised its supporters to return to work on October 19.

With the wildcat strike over, attention turned once again to the negotiation of a contract. On October 24, Ryan was humiliated again when the longshoremen overwhelmingly rejected another contract offer from the shippers that did not include sling weight limits. To make matters worse for Ryan, the insurgents had won a court order preventing the signing of any contract until alleged undemocratic procedures in the ILA could be investigated. This turn of events threatened the stability that had been achieved in the Port of New York with Ryan at the head of the longshoremen. In addition, the nation's largest port had now been shut down for nearly a month. At this juncture, Secretary of Labor Louis Schwellenbach offered a binding arbitration proposal satisfactory to the shippers and to Ryan. The insurgents were left completely out of the process. Ryan and his executive board had eliminated the need to return to the rank and file for a ratification vote.

The final settlement did include significant gains for the longshoremen above those negotiated by Ryan, but it did not include limits on sling weights. In that limited sense, the wildcat strike of 1946 was a failure. Nevertheless, the strike did demonstrate the fragility of the labor–management stability that had been achieved since the passage of the Wagner Act in 1935. It also made clear the gulf that existed between the leadership of the ILA and the members. The explosion of rank-and-file militancy had closed the nation's largest port and threatened the control of one of the country's most entrenched labor leaders. But in the end, the strikers could not persist against the combined forces of the employers, their own union leaders, and the United States Government. [Ronald L. Filippelli]

FURTHER READING

Jensen, Vernon. *Strife on the Waterfront: The Port of New York Since 1945.* Ithaca, NY: Cornell University Press, 1974.

Lipsitz, George. *Class and Culture in Cold War America: "A Rainbow at Midnight."* South Hadley, MA: J. F. Bergin Publishers, 1982.

o   o   o

NEW YORK CITY NEWSBOYS' STRIKE OF 1899. For two weeks, in the summer of 1899, newsboys in New York and in other towns (boys of about ten to fifteen years old) brought delivery of the New York *Journal* and the New York *World* to a halt. It was a unique and significant event in a decade of profound and widespread labor unrest—an event that nonetheless remains almost unknown even today.

Various factors underlay the struggle. Some were the result of the decisive changes that had taken place in the sector, others of a rapidly developing social and economic situation. From the Civil War onward, newspapers had gradually established themselves as a leading cultural and economic power. In a country which was still in the throes of social and geographic mobility, they played a fundamental role by providing information and a levelling off in society (P. T. Barnum: "he who is without a paper is cut off from his species"). They took on an even more central role as the great cities grew, laissez faire turned to monopoly, and the country became a world power.

In those decades, the pace in the cities became faster and faster, diversification in production increased, the job market expanded, new printing techniques were introduced, and colossal newspapers such as Joseph Pulitzer's *World* and William R. Hearst's *Journal* emerged. This was bound to lead to significant restructuring in the organization of the newspapers. One of the most important changes was the introduction of afternoon editions, soon to be followed by evening editions as well. Both were aimed at the huge potential readership of white and blue collar workers who stopped work at five and went back to the suburbs or the tenement districts. The need to capture this audience brought about new developments in techniques and printing, including photographs, banner headlines, sensational frontpage news, and short, incisive articles. A new school of journalism was being born as writers such as Frank Norris, Stephen Crane, Lincoln Steffens, and Abraham Cahan became well known, and sensational treatment of politics, crime, and scandal became known as "yellow journalism."

The chief means of capturing the new audience were the newsboys or "newsies," who acted as the newspapers' loudspeakers in the streets. Newsboys were familiar figures in nineteenth-century cities. Contemporary culture recorded them in a rather contradictory way. On the one hand, there were the sentimental and romantic representations of popular writers such as Horatio Alger, while on the other hand, there was increased concern for the welfare of the boys from reformers such as Jacob Riis. The introduction of the new afternoon and evening editions, as well as other social phenomena, had contributed toward making them key figures in the turn-of-the-century urban setting.

The influx of immigrants in the 1880s and 1890s had created a huge reservoir of cheap labor in a labor market that was undergoing a radical change as it adapted to the demands of mass production. Immigrant labor had been immediately inserted into the new production processes, and the large cities on the East Coast had become the domain of sweatshops and tenements. Both in reality and in metaphor, work took up most of the immigrant's daily existence, regardless of age, sex, religious beliefs, and cultural traditions, and involved the entire family. The reality of homework, piecework, and child labor was widespread and added to an already intense exploitation: child labor in particular—flexible and vulnerable as it was—supplied precious energies for the production process.

Children between the ages of ten and fifteen represented an ideal market for a whole host of jobs which took place in the city streets. These children were too independent to stay at home making boxes or paper flowers or to work in the garment industry, and thus were drawn to street life as an alternative to suffocating tenement flats. The new afternoon and evening editions meant that the child labor force could be extended to include the younger boys who were still at school and were only free after three o'clock in the afternoon.

This was also to have considerable effect on the development of urban culture. Newspaper selling turned out to be an offbeat type of acting school for many boys, as can be seen from the number of famous names in show business who actually started out as newsboys. Another effect was that the two hours between the end of the school day and the beginning of their paper selling transformed a mass of youngsters, curious and hungry for entertainment, into the first regular audience for nickelodeons and moviehouses.

However unlimited the supply of labor might have seemed, the demand for labor was high. In New York alone, not only Pulitzer's and Hearst's papers but also the *Times*, the *Daily Tribune*, the *Sun*, the *Herald*, the *Mirror*, the Brooklyn *Daily Eagle*, as well as a number of minor papers and political party publications were on sale in the streets.

The newsboys' strike broke out in response to the decision by the *World* and the *Journal* to increase the wholesale price from five to six cents per ten journals. (The other papers, which had not taken the same decision and therefore were not hit by the strike, followed events very keenly.) The increase had, in fact, been introduced the year before at the peak of the Spanish-American War and because of the bitter competition between the two papers. But by 1899, with the war over and people's interest in the news noticeably waning, the newsboys were beginning to feel the pinch. After a few months of silence, they moved to action. From Long Island City, where the first boys refused to collect the bundles of newspapers, the protest spread to New York, where a meeting was held on July 19, to fix the following day as the date for beginning the strike. The newsboys then formed a real trade union, appointed a "strike committee" and a "committee on discipline," and finally sent out walking delegates to the various city neighborhoods and to other cities. According to historian David Nasaw, "Every day, they met the delivery wagons at the distribution points, pelted them with stones and rotten fruit, captured as many bundles as they could, and then paraded up and down the streets with banners, leaflets, songs, and cheers, proud of their accomplishment but on the constant lookout for any scab papers that might have gotten through." Day after day there were pickets and clashes with scabs,

huge meetings such as the one held at the New Irving Hall on Broome Street and attended by about 5,000 boys, and demonstrations like the march on Manhattan by the Brooklyn newsboys that was stopped by the police on the Brooklyn Bridge.

During the two-week strike, these teenagers showed a remarkable capacity for organization and agitation, a capacity which undoubtedly came from examples they had from other workers (the Brooklyn streetcar operators were on strike at the same time) as well as from shared family experiences (immigrant labor had already given proof of its combative spirit, especially in the garment trades, New York's industrial heart).

At first, the two newspapers did not take the agitation too seriously. But when sales began to plummet and advertisers started to voice their disapproval, they tried to take some measures. In the meantime, the strike had spread like wildfire to other cities in New York State, New Jersey, Connecticut, Massachusetts, and Rhode Island and had merged with other labor struggles involving bootblacks and messenger boys so that there was even talk of a "children's general strike." Above all, the young strikers were able to gain the solidarity and support of the public and also, albeit not disinterested, of rival newspapers. When, for example, Pulitzer and Hearst thought of using the Bowery "bums" and unemployed as scabs and offered them two dollars a day plus commission, their proposal was turned down by the great majority of the men.

After two weeks, the press run had dropped from 360,000 to 125,000, while the returns had increased from 15–16 percent to 35 percent. Don Seitz, the *World*'s managing editor, wrote in a memo to Pulitzer that "the loss in circulation . . . has been colossal." At that point, the papers decided to compromise. They did not cancel the increase, but to offset it they offered to take back unsold copies from the boys at 100 percent refund. Tired after such a long struggle, the newsboys accepted the offer almost without discussion: they called off the strike, disbanded the union, and resumed work in the streets.

Despite at least partial victory, the struggle had no other effect on the young newsboys except the memory of a collective and concerted action. No attempt at a permanent organization was ever made, and thus, when a similar situation arose again in Boston in 1901 and then in New York and other cities between 1918 and 1918, the newspapers had no trouble in using their past experience and their power to quash the strikes.

But, above all, times had changed by then, and the figure of the newsboy was already slowly fading into the background of an ever-changing city. [Mario Maffi]

FURTHER READING

Barth, Gunther. *City People: The Rise of Modern City Culture in Nineteenth-Century America*. New York: Oxford University Press, 1980.

Nasaw, David. *Children of the City: At Work & At Play*. Garden City, NY: Anchor Press/Doubleday, 1985.

New York Times, New York Sun, New York Tribune (July 21–August 3, 1899).

Seitz, Don. "Memos for Mr. Pulitzer, July 21, 22, 24, 1899." New York World Papers, Rare Book and Manuscript Library, Butler Library, Columbia University, New York.

Trachtenberg, Alan. *The Incorporation of America: Culture and Society in the Gilded Age*. New York: Hill and Wang, 1982.

o   o   o

NEW YORK CITY NEWSPAPER STRIKE OF 1962–1963. On December 6, 1962, the 3,500 members of Local 6 of the International Typographical Union (ITU) struck New York City's four major daily newspapers, the *New York Times*, the *New York Herald Tribune*, the *New York Daily News*, and the *New York Post*. At issue were wage increases and the introduction of new technology affecting the typesetting process.

On one side of the argument stood Local 6 of the ITU, led by Bertram Powers. On the other side stood the Publishers Association of New York, a management organization founded in 1897 for the express purpose of presenting a united front in labor negotiations. From experience, most recently the 1958 walkout of the deliverymen that shut down New York's press for nineteen days, the Publishers Association evolved a simple strategy: to close all member papers as soon as one was struck. Thus, when the ITU picketed four papers, the publishers promptly closed down five more: the *Herald Tribune*, the *Mirror*, the *Post*, the *Long Island Press*, and the *Long Island Star-Journal*. The publishers' united front was critical to the evolution of the strike. The union's decision to strike only those four papers that it believed to be in the best financial condition, although publicized as a way to keep the news available to New Yorkers, was in reality an admission that several papers might not be financially strong enough to survive both a long strike and a costly settlement.

The strike lasted 114 days. Union leader Bertram Powers boasted that the union had been preparing for years for this test of strength. Local 6 had amassed a strike fund of $1.2 million, and the ITU's international had made an additional $500,000 available. But the ITU was not the only union affected by the walkout. While only 2,000 printers were involved, the strike also idled another 18,000 newspaper workers, including newspapermen, truck drivers, pressmen, photoengravers, and a variety of others. In all, some ten unions formed the "unity committee" that directed the strike.

The issues in the strike revolved around money and the introduction of new technology. The printer's asked for a compensation package, including wages and fringe benefits, amounting to a 37 percent increase over two years. The publishers offered 8 percent, the amount they had settled for with the Newspaper Guild after an eight-day strike at the *Daily News* only a month before. The publishers might have agreed to the high wage demands if the ITU had granted them concessions toward modern production methods. The ITU enjoyed rigid work-rule and job-classification contract language, and the union was much criticized for featherbedding. The newspapers wanted to introduce automatic typesetters for the stock market returns and sports scores. The national ITU had accepted these changes in a number of contracts already, with the proviso that personnel savings would come only from attrition, not from the laying off of existing employees. But only a year before the New York conflict, Bertram Powers had been elected to the presidency of the Local 6 on a platform of no backward steps.

Powers became the storm center of the strike as it became clear that the city would be without news for a considerable period. Critics charged that the strike was caused not so much by a dispute over pay but over Powers' ambition to become president of the international union. Others charged, with good reason, that Powers' motivation was to restore the ITU's position as the pacesetting union at the city's newspapers, a position it had lost to the American Newspaper Guild which generally negotiated with the publishers first and therefore set the pattern for the other unions. To Powers, this meant that management was settling with the weakest union first, thus setting a pattern that worked to the detriment of the nine other unions. Powers made it clear that he would not accept the 8 percent Newspaper Guild settlement that had been reached in November.

There were also outside attempts to force a settlement. In January, Secretary of Labor Willard Wirtz appointed an ad hoc board made up of three judges, Harold R. Medina, Joseph O'Grady, and David W. Peck, to hear witnesses from both sides and recommend a settlement. The publishers and the other striking unions testified, but Powers and Local 6 boycotted the hearings. After three days of testimony, the judges reported that the strike was "a deliberate design" to "postpone any negotiation until a time when the publishers would be forced to surrender under the economic pressure of threatened extinction."

By the beginning of February, the shutdown had cost the publishers and newsdealers approximately $41 million. The *New York Times* ordered pay cuts of from 20 to 50 percent for management and for editorial employees working in its foreign bureaus. But although the newspapers were feeling the financial pressure, so too were the unions. The Newspaper Guild had mortgaged its headquarters building and borrowed $300,000 from the AFL-CIO to meet the need for strike benefits for its members. Local 6 put a weekly assessment of $3.00 on all of its working members—those employed by commercial print shops and therefore not affected by the strike. New York Printing Pressmen Local 2 brought suit against the *Post*, the *Herald Tribune*, and the *Mirror*, asking $72,000 in lost pay and other benefits. Because these papers had not been struck but rather closed down in solidarity with the struck papers, the Pressmen union claimed that they had been unlawfully locked out.

The financial hardship gradually forced the sides toward agreement. In early February, two months into the strike, an angry meeting of some 1,200 members of the Newspaper Guild took place. The guildsmen hammered out a resolution calling on both sides to negotiate continuously until they reached an agreement. At about the same time, the "unity committee" of striking unions urged continuous negotiation. The united front of the employers suffered its first defection on March 4, when the *Post*, one of the financially weakest of the papers, began to publish.

The deadlock was broken on March 8, the first day of the fourth month of the strike when the parties agreed to a settlement proposed by Mayor Robert Wagner. By March 31, all of the participating unions had accepted it. Although the pact would be costly, some $18.5 million over two years, the publishers had generally prevailed. Compensation increases amounted to $12.50 per week, some $8.00 of which went to wages, exactly the same as had been granted to the Newspaper Guild. The publishers did agree to shorten the workweek from thirty-six and a half to thirty-five hours, but the time came from shortening the daily thirty-minute washup periods already enjoyed by the workers. Perhaps most significant of all, the publishers won the right to use new automatic typsetting equipment for the stock market tables and the sports scores but agreed "in principle" to share the benefits from the increased productivity with the workers. What that share would be was to be settled by an arbitrator. Finally, in what was seen by many as a key victory for the publishers, the ITU's demand for a contract expiration date of October 31, 1964, the eve of the presidential election, was turned back. The ITU did, however, prevail on the issue of concurrent contract termination dates for all newspaper unions, thus removing the Newspaper Guild as the pattern setter in the industry in New York.

Overall, the strike was a victory for the publishers. The walkout had been massively unpopular among New York's citizens from the beginning. The timing of the strike, just before and during the Christmas shopping season, was also seen by many as a calculated slap at the public. Powers lost much of whatever status he had had. Only under pressure from other union leaders did he reluctantly agree to the final settlement. In effect, the printers and

18,000 other workers had lost thirteen weeks' pay to win a wage boost that was little more than they could have gotten in December.

The financial losses in the strike were staggering. Some estimates put the cost at $200 million, including losses to restaurants, department stores, and hotels. The 20,000 workers on strike lost $47 million in wages, and the participating unions spent $7 million in strike benefits. There were other effects as well. The *Mirror* closed after the strike, displacing 1,400 employees. Four years later, a weakened *Herald-Tribune* succumbed after another strike. The 1966 strike also forced the merger of the *World-Telegram*, the *Sun*, the *Herald Tribune*, and the *Journal-American* into one paper. The merged paper lasted for 236 days and closed in May of 1967. Although the reasons for the closing of a number of New York newspapers could not be attributed only to labor costs and the costs of strikes, it is true that the draining 114-day strike in 1962 and 1963 severely weakened several of New York's already precarious newspapers. [Ronald L. Filippelli]

Further Reading

"After a Three Month Shutdown, What Striking Printers Got." *U.S. News and World Report* (March 18, 1963), p. 98.

Kempton, Murray. "Return of the Luddites." *New Republic* (December 22, 1962), pp. 6–7.

Severo, R. "Automation and the News Strike." *Reporter* (March 14, 1963), pp. 29–30.

Time, (December 14, 1962), p. 46; (December 21, 1962), p. 41–42; (January 18, 1963), p. 68; (March 15, 1963), p. 67.

o　o　o

NEW YORK CITY POLICE STRIKE OF 1971. In January 1971, patrol officers in the New York Police Department undertook a series of labor protests. The actions—which lasted from January 14 through January 19—included walkouts, slowdowns, and a refusal to answer non-emergency calls. The protest was widely described at the time as a "wildcat strike," though the police commissioner later described it only as "a semi-walkout. . . which came very close to being a genuine police strike."

The New York City strike was a dramatic illustration of the success of the "third wave" of police unionization (earlier movements had failed in 1917–1919 and 1943–1946). By 1971, the New York Police Department (NYPD) had roughly 32,000 officers, 95 percent of whom were members of a fraternal or benevolent organization appropriate to their rank. By far the largest organization was the Patrolmen's Benevolent Association (PBA), which was central to the strike. Under its president, Ed Kiernan, the PBA spoke for 25,000 of the 27,000 serving patrol officers.

The immediate cause of the job action was a pay dispute arising from the complex arrangements designed to secure parity between various groups of city employees. In 1966, police sergeants and lieutenants had sought raises which would give them parity with their fire department counterparts. However, the parity system also provided for patrolmen to receive increases proportionate to those of sergeants, and the city had apparently agreed to this in January 1969. The PBA thus believed that its members were entitled to an increase of $100 a month, retroactive over the twenty-seven months of the current contract. However, New York's deepening fiscal crisis made it crucial for the city to backtrack on an agreement that could have cost it hundreds of millions of dollars. The crisis occurred with the expiration of the PBA contract on December 31, 1970. The patrolmen had been supported in their claim by a number of state courts; but on January 14, 1971, the state appeals court reversed these lower court decisions. This seemed to foreshadow a lengthy series of court hearings, with the ultimate decision left to a jury. In the meantime, the city would likely renege on its promise to raise salaries.

The patrol officers' response was immediate and apparently spontaneous. By the January 15, a wildcat strike had spread from the Bronx to all five boroughs and had removed an estimated 85 percent of officers scheduled to work. There were also sympathy actions by police employed by the New York Transit Authority and the Housing Authority. As with the NYPD officers, these were wildcat actions, usually in direct defiance of union orders.

The action did not involve a complete withdrawal of services because patrolmen undertook to respond to emergency calls. In addition, the department succeeded in maintaining skeleton service by replacing patrol personnel with superior officers, detectives, and probationary police. Federal officers took over at diplomatic missions, but the National Guard was not called in. There is no evidence that the strike had any major impact on crime or public order in the city—though this was in large part due to appalling weather conditions which kept people off the streets.

The strike effectively ended on January 19, when union delegates voted 229 to 112 for a return to work—though there were militants who denounced Kiernan and the union leadership for a "sellout." Particularly controversial was the use of the Taylor Law, which provided mandatory penalties against striking public employees. Mayor John Lindsay claimed not to have the power to exercise discretion under this law and could not grant an amnesty as demanded by Kiernan. In the following months, however, the PBA won a decisive series of victories in the courts, including the acknowledgment of their pay claim. In March, the city dropped further appeals and agreed to pay each patrolman $3,300 in retroactive salary adjustments. The union had won a victory, but it would be soured by the fiscal crisis of the following years, when high labor costs were used to justify drastic cuts in police manpower. (In 1975 alone, the NYPD lost 5,000 officers, almost a sixth of its strength.)

In retrospect, the most surprising aspect of the conflict was not that it occurred but that such drastic action did not take place until 1971. The strike was the culmination of five years of increasing strife between Lindsay and the police unions, which had acted as almost an official conservative opposition to the liberal mayor. Traditionally, the NYPD had been a heavily politicized arm of the city's machine politics, but beginning in the mid-1950s, the department had enjoyed much greater autonomy. Following his election as mayor in 1965, Lindsay had attempted to bring the department under closer political control. However, the political situation militated against his success. Lindsay was elected first as a Republican, then as a Liberal in 1969, and finally as a Democrat in 1971. He was thus cut off from a firm base in the traditional politics of the city, and hence of the NYPD.

From 1966 on, Lindsay had sought to initiate a series of reforms in the police department, but each seemed to drive the police rank and file—and the PBA—into ever more acrimonious opposition. In 1966, a key proposal to create a civilian-dominated review board to examine complaints against the police was heavily defeated in a referendum sponsored by the PBA. The success of this referendum had a national impact. According to William Bopp,"In the case of the new police militancy, the starting point was New York City in 1966."

From 1966 onward, the PBA leadership had constantly attacked the Lindsay administration on law-and-order themes, denouncing the mayor's policies of "coddling" and alleged political interference. An early climax occurred in 1968, when there were deep fears of a "long hot summer" of racial violence. The police commissioner ordered selective non-enforcement of laws during politically sensitive periods. In response, the PBA under its president, John J. Cassese, urged full enforcement of laws, "regardless of what orders we may get from any superior officers." In the event, the PBA backed down from a perilous political confrontation. In 1970, police morale was further damaged by anti-corruption investigations such as the Knapp Commission.

By 1971, therefore, there was abundant evidence of hostility and mistrust between police officers and the city authorities, and a feeling that politicians and courts failed to support or even sympathize with the police in an increasingly dangerous job. In summary, the militancy of the police in the 1971 strike can only be understood in the context of much deeper grievances. [J. Philip Jenkins]

FURTHER READING

Bopp, William J. *Crises in Police Administration.* Springfield, IL: Charles Thomas, 1984.

———, ed. *The Police Rebellion.* Springfield, IL: Charles Thomas, 1971.

Juris, Hervey, and Peter Feuille. *Police Unionism.* Lexington, MA: Lexington Books, 1973.

Murphy, Patrick, and Thomas Plate. *Commissioner.* New York: Simon and Schuster, 1977.

Ruchelman, Leonard. *Police Politics: A Comparative Study of Three Cities.* Cambridge, MA: Ballinger, 1974.

Walker, Samuel. *The Police in America.* New York: McGraw-Hill, 1983.

o   o   o

NEW YORK CITY TAILORS' STRIKE OF 1836. By 1836, the confrontation between New York's journeymen tradesmen and their employers, both masters and merchant capitalists, had been building for some time. The growing struggle between employers and workers was complicated by the emergence of a strong nativist movement in the city and by the bitter anti-abolition riots of 1834. White workingmen, fearful of losing their jobs and responding to rumors of a black takeover of white neighborhoods, attacked abolitionist meetings and black homes and churches. Social and economic unrest continued throughout 1835, as the pace of strike activity quickened.

During 1836, ten major strikes paralyzed the skilled trades, and both the waterfront and the building industry were seriously disrupted. Employers, in league with their allies in government and the courts, countered with solidarity of their own by forming trade associations to take legal action against the strikers. They were heartened by an 1835 decision of the supreme court of New York in which a Geneva, New York, shoemakers' society was declared an illegal combination to injure trade and commerce.

The most aggressive of the employers' associations was formed by the master tailors who nullified the price book they had negotiated with their journeymen and announced that they would no longer hire union members. The tailors responded by going on strike and asked the General Trades Union of New York City for support. The masters countered by swearing affidavits against twelve strikers, accusing them of riotous and disorderly conduct.

The tailors strike and the unprecedented and coordinated counterattack of the employers galvanized the New York City labor movement. By the end of February, a host of trades were on strike, including the stevedores, laborers, carpenters, and others. The fear of the spreading protests, which appeared to the New York *Herald* to have become "a general movement over the city," led Mayor Cornelius Lawrence to call in the 27th regiment of the National Guard for a show of force.

In the meantime, both sides had become intransigent in the tailor's strike, and it had turned violent, with strikers, strikebreakers, and law officers engaged in running battles in the various shops. By early March, the tailors' union established cooperative shops. In response, the master tailors continued their court action, and in late March a grand jury indicted twenty journeymen tailors for conspiracy. The indictment drove tensions in the city even higher. Thousands of workers, headed by the striking tailors, marched up Broadway in protest. By the time that the trial of the tailors began in May, the *Herald* wondered if the city was on the eve of revolution.

The court used the Geneva shoemakers case as precedent, and the jury, finding the tailors to be an illegal combination, convicted them. The court had effectively denied them their right to unionize. In the words of the labor paper, *The Union*, the court had succeeded in "an unhallowed attempt to convert the working men of this country to slaves." After the verdict, the mood turned uglier on both sides. While employers exulted in the vindication of their rights to manage their businesses unfettered, workers and their allies, nearly 30,000 strong, rallied at City Hall to protest and raise money for the convicted tailors. It was the largest protest gathering in American history up to that point, involving nearly one-fifth of the population of the nation's largest city. The call at the rally was for the formation of a new political party representing the interests of workers. Although the attempt was to fail, the events of 1836 centered around the tailor's strike did indicate that the working class of New York had become, no doubt, the most radical in America. [Ronald L. Filippelli]

FURTHER READING

Commons, John R., et al. *History of Labour in the United States.* Vol. 1, New York: Macmillan, 1936.

Wilentz, Sean. *Chants Democratic: New York City and the Rise of the American Working Class, 1788–1850.* New York: Oxford University Press, 1984.

o   o   o

NEW YORK CITY TAILORS' STRIKE OF 1850. The year 1850 was marked by a surge of industrial conflict in New York

City. The crisis began in the early spring of 1850 with an upsurge in union organization by militant craft journeymen. In March, the carpenters, who had formed a cooperative to sustain their members, went on strike against wage cutting. The carpenters had some success using tactics that ranged from turnouts to colorful parades and rallies that engaged the attention of the city. The victories of the carpenters over a number of master builders gave heart to the other trades that began to demand higher wages and changes in work rules. As in 1836, the movement began to go beyond economic workplace demands to debate over a range of reform political concerns.

In the midst of this unrest, the tailors staged a mass meeting of both their English- and German-speaking sections on July 10. The largest trade in New York, the tailors, worked under what were considered the worst working conditions in the city. At the rally, the tailors proposed a scale of prices, and by July 15 some 900 were on strike. Ethnic unity, so crucial to the success of the strike, was achieved when the Germans announced that they would adopt the proposed pay scale of the English-speaking workers. The employers refused to pay the wages demanded by the strikers, in part because tailors frequently took work out of the shop to complete at home and never returned it. The employers contended that they should set wages at a level that allowed them to recover what the dishonest workers had stolen from them.

One of the issues that developed after the strike began was the demand for the closed shop. The tailors found that their employers were making use of immigrant strikebreakers. The tailors, as well as other skilled workers, had always assumed that they would be able to enroll all skilled workers in the union and thus achieve, de facto, the closed shop in the trade throughout the city. However, they soon realized that they were unable to induce the "scab" tailors to join the union, and they thus pressed the demand for the closed shop upon the employers. In return for recognition of the closed shop, the union offered to guarantee the safe return of all work removed from the shop by its members.

The tailors' strike turned violent on July 22 when a march to present demands to the firm of Longstreet and Company, notorious for anti-unionism and low wages, was marred by rock throwing and fighting between strikers and strikebreakers. Police then entered the fray, arresting and beating the strikers. The reaction to the actions of the police focused most of the labor movement's attention on the tailors. On July 27, thousands of sympathizers rallied at City Hall Park. Those attending heard every variety of radicalism and trade unionism proclaimed. The New York *Herald* labeled the violence of the tailors' march and the fury of the rally a "striking illustration of socialism."

On August 4, while Irish, English, Scotch, and American tailors met to align with the Germans, a fight broke out at the home of Frederick Wartz, a tailor who had supposedly been working at home at rates under union scale. Police quickly arrived at the scene, and in the confusion, either through pillage by the strikers, or ineptness on the part of the police and firemen, Wartz's house was virtually destroyed. Later that day, another crowd of tailors, again mostly German, marched to confront two subcontractors reportedly giving out work below scale. They found their way blocked by the police. In the ensuing melee, police beat the marchers viciously. At least two tailors were killed, with dozens severely wounded. It was probably the first time in American history that workers had been killed by the police in a trade dispute.

After the bloody events of August 4, dubbed the "tailors' riot" by a uniformly hostile press, the tailors, with financial support from other unions in New York and other cities, formed the Cooperative Union Tailoring Establishment. Although the labor movement celebrated the results of the strike as a victory for the New York labor movement, it was a tenuous victory at best. Most unions that had taken part in the upsurge of militancy in the city did not achieve their goals. Even where unions had some success, such as in the construction trades, their gains were soon threatened by aggressive employers. Nor did the working-class solidarity, which had surfaced immediately after the riots, endure. Many unions backed off from their earlier support, fearful of being tarred with the brush of violence that had attached to the tailors. In trade union terms, the events of the tailors' strike produced very little in concrete gains for New York City workers. But they did contribute to an upsurge of working-class political militancy and radicalism in the city. [Ronald L. Filippelli]

FURTHER READING

Commons, John R., et al. *History of Labour in the United States*, Vol. 1. New York: Macmillan, 1936.

Wilentz, Sean. *Chants Democratic: New York City and the Rise of the American Working Class.* New York: Oxford University Press, 1984.

o o o

NEW YORK CITY TEACHERS' STRIKE OF 1968. In the 1960s, New York City's school system served over one million students. Half of them were black and Puerto Rican. These students, often the victims of poverty, found themselves on average some two years behind white students on standardized tests. Their drop-out rate was extraordinarily high. Black militants and some parents blamed this situation on white middle-class control of the New York City Board of Education and the teachers' union, only 10 percent of whose members were minorities. It is understandable then that during the 1960s, with the

upsurge of the Black Civil Rights movement and the black power movement across the country, blacks in New York viewed community control as a step toward rebuilding their schools. In 1966, the Ford Foundation approached the teachers' union, the United Federation of Teachers (UFT), with a plan to use the Ocean Hill-Brownsville district—one of the city's poorest—as a demonstration project for community involvement in the education process.

Ocean Hill-Brownsville seemed the ideal choice because both teachers and the community had already created a common cause to improve the schools through the UFT's project—More Effective Schools (MES), a program in which substantial sums of extra money were invested in elementary schools to reduce class size and provide special services. The teachers' union had also been a strong supporter of civil rights and of a good educational system. The UFT's rank and file was made up predominantly of left-of-center Jewish liberals, strongly empathetic to civil rights issues. The union's president, Albert Shanker, had marched in Selma, Alabama, and the UFT had provided financial support for Dr. Martin Luther King, Jr. Why then did this common cause fail and deteriorate into a bitter confrontation between teachers and the Ocean Hill-Brownsville community? The answer lies in the conflict between the job security and due process rights of teachers and community control of the schools.

The story began in the spring of 1967 when a handful of dissatisfied parents from Ocean Hill-Brownsville joined with allies from the Council Against Poverty (CAP) and the Committee on Racial Equality (CORE), led by the militant worker priest, Father John Powis, who, according to one observer, "was less interested in raising the reading scores of the children and more interested in forcing a confrontation with a sick society." Powis, with the assistance of Herman Ferguson, a strongly anti-teachers' union black separatist soon to be convicted of conspiracy to murder moderate civil rights leaders, proclaimed the birth of the People's School Board with its mandate that "the people would control the schools."

In the summer of 1967, the People's School Board formed a governing board with Rhody McCoy, an eighteen-year veteran of the school system, as unit administrator. This board, in the Ford Foundation–funded demonstration project schools, would exert most of the powers normally employed by the New York City Board of Education. Board membership was apportioned in a manner that favored community groups over teachers and school supervisors. The board insisted on its right to select any principals who met the New York State requirements, without regard to the school system's civil service lists. Of the several hundred names on the list, only four were black. The state commissioner of education balked at the demand, but did agree to create a special category of "Demonstration Elementary School Principal" allowing the governing board to bypass the civil service lists on an ad hoc basis.

At this point, just as the community board was getting underway in September of 1967, tensions between the teachers and the governing board took a decided turn for the worse when a teachers strike occurred. The strike came about as the result of a confrontation between the new mayor, John V. Lindsay, and the UFT on the role the union would play in collective bargaining with the city. But for Ocean Hill-Brownsville, which was in the first year of its community control experiment with its own elected governing board, the strike presented a serious problem. In addition, the UFT's demand that teachers have the right to remove unruly students was translated into the right of white teachers to remove black students and was seen as racist. Instead of keeping the schools closed in support of the teachers, the board sent

letters to the draft boards of striking male teachers informing them that the teachers were not working, and teachers on the picket line were harassed. The strike ended in two weeks but left relations between the UFT and the Ocean Hill-Brownsville Governing Board in a shambles.

By challenging the UFT, the community board had taken on what had become one of the most powerful unions in New York, rivalling even the powerful United Transportation Workers. The teachers had displayed their militancy during strikes in 1960 and 1962. Given their political awareness, their education, and their militancy, the unionized teachers of New York City were a formidable organization. After they learned the lessons of solidarity in the early strikes, neither injunctions nor threats of imprisonment could open the schools during a strike.

After the 1967 strike, the UFT met with the Ocean Hill-Brownsville Governing Board and made an effort to devise a method to prevent mass transfers by teachers out of the community schools. But feelings ran too high. As teachers and assistant principals, perhaps out of fear, actively sought transfers, frustration and anger took hold on the governing board. The board, increasingly under the control of Powis and other militants, asserted its right to remove teachers from their schools.

Tensions boiled over in April 1968 when anti-white demonstrations against teachers erupted after the assassination of civil rights leader Dr. Martin Luther King, Jr. A fire broke out in Intermediate School 55, and the board alleged that ten teachers left the building, thus shirking their responsibility. Also during April, the personnel committee of the Ocean Hill-Brownsville Governing Board, chaired by Powis, directed unit administrator McCoy to fire six supervisors and thirteen teachers, two of whom were union officers. When Mayor Lindsay and his superintendent of schools, Bernard Donovan, told the dismissed teachers to accept their removal, with assurances that they would be transferred elsewhere, the move outraged the UFT leadership. With union support, the teachers refused to heed the superintendent's orders. The union demanded due process for the teachers. When the governing board refused to hold a hearing, the UFT struck the Ocean Hill-Brownsville schools.

The board of education called in well-known arbitrator Theodore Kheel, but the governing board rejected his recommendations stating that "The Governing Board would not negotiate away the community's right to determine who taught their children." On June 18, McCoy intensified the confrontation by sending a letter to all striking teachers informing them that if they did not return to work they would be rated as unsatisfactory and fired.

In this state of confrontation, the New York State courts ruled that the dismissed teachers at Ocean Hill-Brownsville had been fired illegally and ordered them restored. McCoy and the governing board refused and threatened to replace all of the union teachers in the district. Shanker was equally adamant. The UFT delegates voted to strike the entire New York City school system in the fall if the fired teachers were not rehired at Ocean Hill-Brownsville. In this state of crisis the school year ended.

Faced with the awesome possibility of a systemwide strike, the board of education ordered the Ocean Hill-Brownsville school district to reinstate the teachers or be closed down. Although the governing board refused to consent to take the teachers back, after a confusing meeting with the board of education, it did consent to being forced to take them back. This semantic distinction was not enough for the union. The strike was on, and 54,000 out of 57,000 New York City teachers refused to appear for work on September 9 to open the 1968–1969 school year.

The 1968 strike was actually a series of three strikes.' The shortest lasted two days, and the longest lasted for five weeks. The UFT demanded the restoration of dismissed teachers in the community schools, an agency shop provision which required all teachers to pay union dues whether or not they were members, super-seniority protection against transfer for all UFT officers, and binding arbitration. The first strike was settled one day after it began. Critics of Shanker charged that he was using the Ocean Hill-Brownsville confrontation to push a purely trade union agenda, in particular the agency shop provision which no other municipal union had. But the motion that Shanker offered to the membership in ratification of the agreement with the board of education also authorized the UFT Executive Board to close the schools on forty-eight-hours notice "in the event the agreements with respect to Ocean Hill-Brownsville are broken." Those agreements called for the return of the fired teachers to Ocean Hill with an offer of free transfer to schools in other districts if they wanted to leave.

Trouble began as soon as the teachers tried to return to the schools. The teachers were blocked, harassed, and intimidated by black militants who told them to leave and not to return. When the teachers persisted, they found that they were not given teaching assignments. In the face of this chaos, Shanker took his teachers out again. New York State Education Commissioner James Allen suggested the suspension of the governing board until all teachers were returned to their schools. But the compromise, in its earliest form, failed to provide the union with an acceptable guarantee of the safety of these teachers. The horrors suffered by the teachers at the Ocean Hill-Brownsville schools, and the failure of the mayor and the New York City Board of Education to comprehend the gravity of the problem, left the union unwilling to end the strike without firmer guarantees. Ironically, Ocean Hill-Brownsville schools, the storm center of the dispute, operated throughout the strike with replacement teachers recommended by the bureau of personnel. That meant that there was no pressure on them to compromise. The pressure was on the rest of the city where more than a million children were out of school.

On September 26, Schools Superintendent Donovan assigned observers, backed up by police, to Ocean Hill-Brownsville to insure the safe return of the teachers. With this show of force, the UFT agreed once again to end the strike. But once again chaos reigned. No one in authority was able to force McCoy and the governing board to peacefully accept the return of the illegally dismissed teachers. Riots broke out inside and outside the school on October 1. The following two weeks were marked by chaos. The board of education closed the schools twice, but the governing board would not give way, threatening once again to remove all UFT teachers. When it became clear that the city and the board of education could not guarantee the safety of the teachers, the UFT struck again on October 14, this time for five weeks.

By this time, for the teachers, the price of settlement was to bring the Ocean Hill-Brownsville community control project to an end. In spite of an outpouring of support from the city's labor movement—for example, union custodians turned power and heat off in the schools—the pressure on Shanker was growing. Public opinion in the city was turning against the UFT. The number of teachers voting to authorize the third strike had dropped dramatically. Shanker had to secure an acceptable agreement this time because he would not be able to successfully call a fourth strike. In addition, the union increasingly ran the risk of being labeled racist.

Whitney Young, head of the National Urban League and a long-time supporter of the teachers, and other black moderates began to turn against the teachers. Although he told the governing board that they would have to take the fired teachers back, Young supported the firings by claiming that blacks had "a historic sense of who was prejudiced against them and asked did not Jews have the same historic intuitive sense." Shanker agreed but not as a basis for firing teachers.

The decision to bring in the attorney Max Rubin, who had previously been president of the New York City Board of Education, was the key to the settlement of the strike. He had dealt with Shanker before, and it was believed that he would help to remedy the problem of Shanker's mistrust of the mayor, the board of education, and the commissioner of education. With Rubin directing the negotiations, and with the help of Theodore Kheel, a settlement was reached at the end of the fifth week. It included the following: a formula for teachers to make up lost wages, a state trusteeship over Ocean Hill-Brownsville, a state supervisory commission to protect teachers' rights in New York City schools, and a grievance procedure for teachers subject to involuntary transfer. In the end, the UFT had prevailed but at the cost of animosity between teachers and the black community that would last for years. [Louis Pappalardo]

FURTHER READING

Goldbloom, Maurice J. "The New York School Crisis." *Commentary*, Vol. 47 (January 1969), pp. 43–58.

Mayer, Martin. *The Teachers Strike: New York, 1968.* New York: Harper and Row, 1968.

Raskin, A. H. "He Leads His Teachers Up the Down Staircase." *New York Times Magazine* (September 3, 1967), pp. 4–5+

Shanker, Albert. Interview by author, (February 10), Washington, DC: 1989.

———. "The Real Meaning of the New York City Teachers' Strike." *Phi Delta Kappan*, Vol. 50 (April 1969), pp. 434–451.

Woodring, Paul. "New York Teachers Strike." *Saturday Review* (May 19, 1962), pp. 51–57.

o   o   o

NEW YORK CITY TRANSIT STRIKES OF 1916. When historians catalogue the difficulties of work in industrial society, they usually point to mines and factories as examples of the horrors of industrial labor. Yet arguably, workers on America's urban transit systems—buses and subways—suffered from working conditions equally as oppressive and exploitive.

Working conditions for transit workers in New York were among the worst in the industry. The pay scale put New York at the bottom of the nation's major cities. In addition, the carmen worked ten hours a day on the cars, but other duties or breaks in between runs stretched the day to as much as fifteen hours. The men were also subjected to absolute arbitrary authority from the transit companies. Dismissal without cause could come at any moment, and any hint of union activity, usually detected through an elaborate system of company spies, resulted in immediate job loss.

Resentment against these conditions built slowly, but it burst forth in 1916 when the Third Avenue Company, an amalgam of city and suburban lines, tried to break the hold of the Amalgamated Association of Street and Electric Railway Employees, an AFL affiliate, on its operations in suburban Westchester County. The company refused to deal with the union and made offers of wage increases outside of collective bargaining. In response, the Amalgamated Association struck the suburban lines. Soon the strike spread to the Bronx, tying up the cars on the entire Third Avenue system. With the action on one major line complete, union organizers concentrated on the cars of the New York Railways Company, the Second Avenue Railroad, and the Richmond Light, Heat and Power Company, which ran the trans-

portation system on Staten Island. By August 4, public transportation, including the subway and elevated railways, was paralyzed in all of the New York boroughs except Brooklyn.

Cars that did move through the city were manned by strikebreakers and protected by city police. The companies also launched an advertising campaign that pictured them as the defenders of law and order against the "outside agitators" who had lured loyal employees into irresponsible action. Against the propaganda barrage of the companies, the strikers could rely only on the *New York Call*, the city's Socialist newspaper, which supported the New York Central Federated Union's call for a boycott of all of the struck companies.

While the companies dominated the press, they did have public relations problems. During the strike, the Public Service Commission released a report on a 1913 transit strike which placed blame squarely on the companies, in particular on the Third Avenue Company. In addition, the commission pointed to the fact that the failure of the companies to arbitrate the dispute with their employees had brought on the 1916 strike. The commission's report forced the companies to agree to cooperate with Mayor Mitchell of New York and the chairman of the Public Service Commission to work out a settlement. The resulting compromise recognized the workers' right to a union of their own choosing but rejected the closed shop and also recognized management's right not to formally recognize the union. Under the agreement negotiations with employees would not imply recognition of the national union to which they belonged. Both sides claimed victory. In fact, the agreement solved nothing. What had been achieved was a truce, nothing more.

Signs of the companies' strategy appeared even before the agreement had been signed by all of the parties. The Interborough Rapid Transit Company (IRT) began a drive among its employees for the creation of a company union. Soon after, the other companies followed, insisting that "the adjustment of grievances is better left to the employees' own organization without the interposition of any outside body." The union lost faith in Mayor Mitchell when he supported management's right to persuade employees to join a company union.

In this worsening atmosphere, union and management met to negotiate for the IRT subway and elevated lines. Union demands included wage parity with workers in other major cities, the ten-hour workday to be completed within twelve consecutive hours, time and a half for overtime, and super-seniority for union representatives. In response, the IRT offered its workers individual employment contracts which required them not to join any union not recognized by the employer. The company was clearly willing to take a strike.

When the union voted to strike, the IRT had 3,000 strikebreakers ready to go. The Third Avenue Company then joined the IRT in discharging employees not willing to join the company union. Both companies hid behind the fiction that they were not fighting unionism, only protecting their employees in their right to work. By September 10, the strike had spread to the Third Avenue Transit Company and the New York Railways Company. Both lines were under union contract with the Amalgamated Association, and the press blasted the union for breaking its contracts. Up to this time, the press had not been entirely hostile to the strike, but that began to change.

With all public transit in the city paralyzed, the New York Public Service Commission (PSC) intervened and ruled that the IRT was required by the August agreement to arbitrate the matter of individual employment contracts. The union agreed, but the IRT refused, proclaiming responsibility to its loyal employees. As for the Third Avenue line, the PSC ruled that the union was in breach of contract, adding fuel to the anti-union position of most of New York City's press.

Support for the strike came from the city's labor unions and the Socialist Party. On "Sash Day," 5,000 Socialist women wore "don't be a scab" sashes and marched on transit workers picket lines. On September 14, a "silent parade" of thousands of striking workers marched from Eighty-sixth Street to Union Square. There, in a great rally, they and supporters from other unions threatened a general strike of New York's half a million unionized workers. In fact, the Central Federated Union called for a general strike unless the IRT refused to submit the matter of individual contracts to arbitration.

With the situation at an impasse, and the mayor of New York increasingly siding with the companies in the face of the threat of a general strike, the unions of New York took the fateful step of calling out their members in support of the transit workers. The general strike began on September 27, but it soon became clear that it would fail. Only some 12,000 workers remained off the job that first day. When no others followed them on successive days, most returned to work. The refusal of the city's building trades unions, representing 150,000 men, to support the strike was a critical blow.

In the end, New York's unions refused to break their contracts by conducting a sympathy strike. In addition, the American Federation of Labor (AFL), and in particular its president, Samuel Gompers, rejected the general strike as a weapon. The AFL's approach was built on the establishment of stable contractual relations with management.

Shorn of any hope of a massive outpouring of sympathy strikes, the transit workers continued the strike through the fall on their own. But in spite of a visit from labor leader Mother Mary Jones on October 6, each day the companies managed to restore more and more service by using strikebreakers and returning strikers. By Christmas, the strike had effectively been broken, although the Amalgamated Association never actually called it off. The greatest strike in New York City history had been a dismal failure. Company unionism prevailed on the transit lines of New York. Not until 1934 did the next attempt at independent unionism on New York's buses and subways occur. [Ronald L. Filippelli]

FURTHER READING

Dubofsky, Melvyn. *When Workers Organize: New York City in the Progressive Era.* Amherst, MA: University of Massachusetts Press, 1968.

Foner, Philip S. *History of the Labor Movement in the United States.* New York: International Publishers, 1982.

o o o

NEW YORK CITY TRANSPORATION STRIKE OF 1966. At five o'clock in the morning on January 1, 1966, the greatest urban transportation strike in American history paralyzed New York City. At that hour, the city's 135 miles of subway, and its 2,200 buses lay silent, while pickets representing the 35,000 members of the Transport Workers Union (TWU) and the Amalgamated Transportation Union marched in the still, cold New Year's morning.

The strike transcended the boundaries of economic conflict and became a symbolic struggle between "Irish" Mike Quill, the colorful long-time president of the TWU, and John V. Lindsay, the Yale-educated, newly-elected reform Republican mayor who took office on the day the strike began. Throughout the bargaining and the strike, the city's newspapers, particularly the *New York Times*, painted the strike as a contest between the old style of industrial relations, characterized over the years by back-room deals between the city's Democratic mayors and Quill, and a new open and "progressive" politics that would put the welfare of the citizens of New York, a city then in deep financial difficulty, before the selfish interests of any one group. The *Times* characterized the old system as economic bludgeon and political blackmail.

For Quill and the workers, the issues were less cosmic, centering around wages. The average basic wage for transit workers stood at $6,250 per year and was below the federal poverty guidelines for a family of four in New York City. For its part, the Transit Authority (TA), with which the union bargained, was facing an overall deficit of $60 million. The only way out of the dilemma was to raise the fare, get extra money from the city or the state of New York, or hold the line in negotiations with the transit workers. A fare raise was out of the question for John Lindsay, the new mayor. That left the other alternatives.

Negotiations began on November 3, when Quill presented seventy-six union demands to the Transit Authority, including proposals for a four-day workweek and a 30 percent pay increase. The Transit Authority commissioners put the cost of the proposal at more than $250 million over two years. According to TA chairman Joseph E. O'Grady, there wasn't "enough free gold in Fort Knox to pay this bill." The TA later increased its estimate of the union's demands to $680 million.

From the beginning, Quill was antagonistic to Mayor-elect Lindsay. Lindsay's Republicanism and his upper-class background created a natural gulf between him and the crusty, Irish, working-class Quill. But from the beginning, Quill knew that there would be no settlement until the city promised extra money for the package. He repeatedly tried to involve Lindsay in the negotiations, but the newly elected mayor had decided to stay out of the conflict, relying instead on the Transit Authority commissioners and the Transit–Labor Board made up of three well-known mediators.

As negotiations stalled and as Quill waited for a signal from City Hall that Lindsay would offer money to break the impasse, the drama was played out in the newspapers, on radio, and on television. Quill, with his Irish brogue and leprechaun-like demeanor, was a master of manipulating the media. He was also old and ill. No doubt realizing that this was probably his last hurrah, Quill, who had made a series of accommodations with Democratic city administrations over the years to keep the buses and subways running, had obviously decided to go out like a lion. On December 1, Quill walked out of negotiations and threatened to move the strike deadline up from January 1, to December 15, the peak of the Christmas shopping season. At this point, the lame-duck mayor, Democrat Robert Wagner stepped into the fray. To avoid a paralyzing strike in his last two weeks in office, Wagner convinced Lindsay and the Transit Authority to accede to Quill's demand that Theodore Kheel, a well-known New York labor mediator experienced in transit labor matters, and whom Quill trusted, be placed on the Transit Labor Panel.

On December 26, the members of the Transport Workers Union and the Amalgamated Transportation Union overwhelming voted to strike when the contract expired. Lindsay had still refused to enter the negotiations, and Quill no doubt knew that a strike was inevitable. His public statements, always highly critical of Lindsay, became more sarcastic and cutting. Quill had obviously decided to stand alone with his members in the face of almost total hostility from the media and, from all indications, most of the citizens of New York. Then, on the last day of 1965, the day before the expiration of the contract, Lindsay decided to enter the negotiations. He offered a package of $25 million from the city. Union negotiators received news of the offer at 11:45 P.M., fifteen minutes before the strike deadline. They rejected it out-of-hand. The strike was on. The only way to stop it, Quill told the press in a flurry of hyperbole, "was to shoot the workers down."

In anticipation of the strike, the Transit Authority had sought a court-ordered injunction a few days before. The court complied, but on the morning of the strike, in front of the television cameras, Quill tore the court order into small pieces.

Fortunately, the first two days of the strike fell on holidays, the Saturday and Sunday of New Year's weekend. On Monday, however, the strike triggered a near collapse of the city. A bitter, rainy day greeted millions of New Yorkers who tried, contrary to pleas from Mayor Lindsay to stay at home, to reach their workplaces. The impact of the strike spread far beyond the boundaries of New York, affecting businesses across the country and around the world which depended on the city. A torrent of criticism rained down on Quill from the local and national media, most of which was also centered in New York. Without question, the defiant Quill had become the most hated man in New York.

On Tuesday, January 4, after he had refused a court order from the New York Supreme Court to end the strike, Quill and eight other union leaders were arrested. That very day, while awaiting a routine physical examination at the civil jail, Quill collapsed from congestive heart failure.

The jailing of Quill and his subsequent heart attack only served to stiffen the resolve of the strikers. The ability of the city to withstand the economic damage was another matter. Business losses were put at $100 million a day. At this juncture, New York governor Nelson Rockefeller agreed to make state money available. This, along with money contributed by the city, enabled the settlement to come on the morning of January 13, 1966. It included a 15 percent wage increase over two years and a top hourly rate of $4.00 by July 1, 1967. In all, the settlement cost $61 million. In the end, the solution had come, in spite of all of the talk by the new mayor and the *New York Times*, according to the old formula of the city adding substantially to the Transit Authorities resources. In fact, no state money was ever used in the settlement. The money came eventually from the city and a five-cent increase in the fare.

The 1966 strike proved to be Mike Quill's last appearance on the New York labor scene. He died in his sleep two weeks after the settlement, on January 28. In the next two days, 14,000 people, many of them the rank and file of his union, waited in line in bitter weather to view his body and bid him farewell. [Ronald L. Filippelli]

FURTHER READING

Whittemore, L. H. *The Man Who Ran the Subways: The Story of Mike Quill.* New York: Holt, Rinehart, and Winston, 1968.

o   o   o

NEWARK STAR-LEDGER STRIKE OF 1934–1935. The unionization of newspaper journalists was part of the general upsurge of organization that followed the passage of the National Industrial Recovery Act in 1933. In December of that year, representatives of a number of small units of discontented newspaper employees met in Washington, DC, and formed the American Newspaper Guild (ANG). Many of those present wanted the formation of a trade union for editorial workers. Others did not, wanting instead to create a professional organization with some economic influence. This split, between the trade unionists and those who did not see unionization as appropriate for professionals, was to mark the first difficult years of the American Newspaper Guild.

The Guild's first president, Heywood Broun, hoped that the organization would become a strong trade union for writers. Broun belonged to the New York Newspaper Guild, the strongest advocate for the trade union solution. In the summer of 1934, Broun's chapter supported organizational picketing and a few strikes at a number of small newspapers in the New York metropolitan area. But these actions, while they signalled a turn toward unionization, did not test the rift in the fledgling Guild. That occurred on November 17, 1934, when the staff of the *Newark Ledger* began picketing the paper, thus initiating the first strike by newspapermen against a large circulation daily. The *Ledger* strike was the first real test for the Guild. A defeat would have smashed the union, perhaps ending once and for all any real hope of organizing America's big city newspaper writers.

The causes of the strike were largely economic. Writers on the *Ledger* received poor pay for long hours of work. Instead of raises, the paper made available low-interest loans which were repaid in weekly installments deducted from workers' paychecks. In addition, job security at the paper was almost nonexistent. A small cadre of star reporters, well-treated by management, was surrounded by a constantly changing cast of drifters, alcoholics, and part-timers. In charge of all of this, was *Ledger* publisher Lucius T. Russell, who fancied himself a benevolent aristocrat, but whose employees feared his instability and arbitrariness.

Russell had no intention of sharing power with a union. He refused to reply directly to Guild requests for negotiations, and immediately set out to crush the Guild chapter. No matter that section 7(a) of the NIRA gave workers the right to organize and bargain collectively, Russell would "run his shop on a 'rugged Individualism,' with the individualism on his side." For Russell, unionism was nothing more than "outgrowth of socialistic propaganda."

On November 14, Russell announced that he intended to fire 25 percent of the editorial staff within two weeks, with another 25 percent to go in December. The plan was put into effect immediately. The *Ledger* fired eight workers on the first day, most of them Guild members and one of them an officer of the chapter. It became clear to the workers that their choice was either to strike or surrender.

Nevertheless, there remained considerable reluctance to strike among the *Ledger* editorial staff. They feared the repercussions of the action and urged that the leadership attempt to work it out with Russell. Heywood Broun and the other New York leadership, however, favored the strike, fearing that hesitation could undermine the entire Guild movement. The debate proved to be academic. Russell continued to reject any overtures from the *Ledger* Guild chapter for negotiations. Workers were told to continue to deal individually, like "professionals," with the *Ledger*'s management. Seeing no other way out, the workers voted twenty-four to eight to strike.

While only twenty-six workers struck on November 17 out of an editorial staff of forty-seven, ten more walked out during the next three days. Throughout the strike Russell continued to publish the *Ledger*, although in much-reduced form, by using management personnel, a few staff who refused to strike, and several newly hired writers. Having failed to stop publication, the Guild then turned its efforts toward reducing the newspaper's advertising revenue. Sound trucks pleaded with Newark's citizens not to read the *Ledger*. A citizen's committee was formed to persuade advertisers not to patronize the struck paper. The strikers also made their case in a small strike paper, *The Reporter*, which also carried statements of support from prominent Newarkers.

In a series of advertisements in his and other papers, Russell accused the union of being Communist-dominated, power hungry, and irresponsible. The gulf between Russell and the union widened as

the strike wore on. As hopes for a quick victory on both sides vanished, the adversaries prepared for a long strike. The conflict was to last nineteen weeks, with only one striker crossing the line to return to work.

During the strike, Russell lost direct control of the paper to a group of stockholders who, fearful of the effects of Russell's direction of the strike on the value of their stock, successfully petitioned the chancery court to place the company under trusteeship to conserve the *Ledger*'s assets. But the trustees proved no more amenable to a settlement with the union than Russell, who remained as publisher. An attempt to have the printing trades unions at the *Ledger* intervene with the Guild failed when the trustees offered what a Guild spokesman characterized as an "assortment of phonus bolonus."

On March 7, the trustees applied for an anti-strike injunction. The court issued a sweeping temporary order restraining the strikers, the American Newspaper Guild, and the Newark Guild from picketing in front of the *Ledger* offices, "molesting" *Ledger* employees in any way, boycotting, or otherwise hindering distribution and sale of the newspaper, and circulating any written or printed material which incited any of the enjoined acts.

The draconian appearance of the injunction proved to be worse than its actual impact. The Guild found ways to get around it, including using the Citizens Committee to picket advertisers. Indeed, provisions which made it illegal to distribute *The Reporter* rankled many in the newspaper industry, including some who were also anti-union. When ANG president Heywood Broun came to Newark to test the injunction by picketing and distributing the newspaper, the *Ledger*'s management, anxious to avoid bad publicity that Broun's arrest would have engendered, made no effort to have him cited for contempt.

By now, the strike was three-months old, and the newspaper's losses continued to increase. An attempt by Russell to employ "counter pickets" to attack the Guild enraged the judge who had issued the injunction because Russell had employed the very tactics that the *Ledger's* attorneys had asked the judge to enjoin. Suddenly, and in a most surprising manner, the strike ended on March 28. President Roosevelt, without invitation from either side, had sent a federal mediator, P. W. Chappell, to Newark on March 13. In a series of conferences between the trustees and the Guild, Chappell succeeded in working out a compromise agreement. No doubt the way was eased by the fact that Russell had decided to sell his holdings in the paper, and the prospective buyer, S. I. Newhouse, would not close the deal until the strike had ended.

The agreement called for the reinstatement of all strikers except for the eight discharged before the strike. Their cases were to go to an impartial arbitration committee. All strikebreakers but one were to be discharged immediately. All questions of wages, hours, and working conditions not specifically dealt with in the agreement were left to the arbitration committee to decide. Although not entirely satisfied, the strikers, tired of the hardships of the long winter strike, ratified the agreement overwhelmingly.

What the Guild called a "major victory" for the Newark chapter and the American Newspaper Guild chapters everywhere, proved to be much more of a moral than a substantive triumph. The key problem was that the agreement covered only the trustee period. When the sale to Newhouse went through, the settlement was rendered ineffective. Nor was the strikers' faith in impartial arbitration rewarded. In most cases, the arbitration committee ruled against the union. Ironically, the strike's success had resulted in the sale of the paper to S. I. Newhouse, himself anti-

union. Fifteen months after the sale, the guild chapter at the *Ledger* had all but disappeared.

The brief euphoria over what appeared to be a victory, misplaced though it proved to be, obscured the continuing rift over the role of unions among professional editorial employees. For a while, the normally individualistic writers displayed exceptional solidarity. Non-striking members helped on the picket lines, coming from around the New York metropolitan area and beyond to offer their services. Guildsmen across the country contributed to the strike fund for their brothers and sisters in Newark. But the early enthusiasm waned by the end of the first month of the strike. Contributions began to drop off significantly about mid-December. By mid-February 1935, the National Newspaper Guild took over the management of the financing of the strike. Much of the support it received came from other unions. More than 100 unions endorsed the strike and recommended that members not read the *Ledger*. Many also contributed money. But the issue of support from organized labor also became a divisive issue in the strike. Indeed, so cautious was the Guild over too close affiliation with organized labor that in early February 1935, its executive committee rejected a sizable loan from the International Ladies Garment Workers Union. The wisdom of the ANG joining the AFL also became a point of disagreement. Even Emmet Crozier, leader of the strike and president of the Newark Guild, opposed affiliation. The fact that he was defeated for reelection shortly after the strike by an opponent favoring affiliation was an indication that the pro-AFL forces had gained during the strike. Indeed, the most lasting impact of the *Ledger* strike was that it confirmed the movement of the American Newspaper Guild toward the mainstream of organized labor. [Ronald L. Filippelli]

FURTHER READING

Leab, Daniel J. *A Union of Individuals: The Formation of the American Newspaper Guild*. New York: Columbia University Press, 1970.

————. "Toward Unionization: The Newark Ledger Strike of 1934–1935." *Labor History*, Vol. 11, No. 1 (Winter, 1970), pp. 3–22.

o   o   o

NORTH AMERICAN AVIATION STRIKE OF 1941. On June 4, 1941, members of United Auto Workers (UAW) Local 683 went on strike against a North American Aviation Company plant in Inglewood, California. Coming in the midst of President Roosevelt's pre-World War II defense mobilization build-up, this walkout, which did not have the formal authorization of the UAW headquarters in Detroit, halted production of nearly 25 percent of the nation's fighter aircraft, providing the rationale for military intervention to break the strike. More importantly, because the local UAW leaders on the scene were Communists, the controversy left the international UAW's hierarchy open to charges of harboring union activists who were trying to advance Soviet foreign policy through union activities without regard to the security of the United States. Thus, top UAW officials cooperated with the Roosevelt administration's suppression of the strike. Afterwards, Congress of Industrial Organizations (CIO) union officials at the highest levels seemed less willing to risk militancy for fear of alienating the generally pro-labor federal government, and at the same time, seemed more willing to challenge Communist influence within the industrial union movement.

The immediate background to the North American Aviation Strike involved both the UAW's efforts to organize the burgeoning aircraft industry on the West Coast as well as the tangled internal politics of the union. Several important UAW officials in California were Communists: Lew Michener, director of Region 6; Elmer Freitag,

president of UAW Local 683; Henry Kraus, former publicity director for the international union and then employed by the local; and Wyndham Mortimer, former executive board member now working as an international union representative assigned, some said exiled, to California because of his radical political sympathies. UAW organizing at Vultee Aircraft and North American Aviation, led by Mortimer, had finally started to become effective but not without much struggle against both intransigent employers and competing unions. After a National Labor Relations Board (NLRB) election victory at Vultee in 1940, an authorized UAW strike against the company resulted in an outcry by important defense officials in the Roosevelt administration and the subsequent involvement of the highest CIO officials, such as Philip Murrray, in the aircraft industry organizing drive. Concerned about a backlash of anti-strike legislation, the CIO and the UAW put Richard Frankensteen, a union founder and director of the Chrysler department, in charge of CIO-UAW aircraft organizing. The hope was that all disputes would be mediated by the Roosevelt administration's National Defense Mediation Board (NDMB), which had public, business, and labor members.

For the most part, Frankensteen allowed Mortimer and Michener to run the local organizing efforts in California. Their efforts finally produced a hard-fought victory over the International Association of Machinists (IAM) at the North American Aviation Inglewood plant, which employed some 11,000 workers, in April 1941. The union put forth contract demands bettering IAM accomplishments elsewhere in the industry to solidify its rank-and-file support but faced a fairly intransigent, even anti-union, management. Negotiations soon stalled. Faced with these developments, local UAW officials proceeded with a strike vote on May 22, which won overwhelmingly by 5,829 to 210. The NDMB then began hearings on the dispute. Still fearing competition from an existing IAM organization in the plant, local leaders for a time walked a thin line between the possible eruption of wildcat walkouts or the erosion of shop floor support for the UAW. Finally, in early June, night shift workers began a wildcat walkout, which Kraus took control of the next morning by putting into place an effective mass picket line of nearly 4,000 strikers.

Government officials in Washington responded swiftly. Strikes in defense industries would not be tolerated, and the North American Aviation situation would serve as an example. Philip Murray and UAW president R. J. Thomas sent Frankensteen to California with instructions to end the strike by June 9, with the knowledge that a failure to do so would result in the military being sent in. Frankensteen found Mortimer, Kraus, and the local's leaders unwilling to stop the strike, which they believed was a legitimate trade union action designed to establish their organization at North American. Frankensteen then fired Mortimer and took control of the local on the basis that the strike had not been authorized by the international union and had been fomented by Communists. Rank-and-file North American employees, however, refused to heed Frankensteen's call to return to work. On June 9, with the approval of top CIO and UAW leaders, President Roosevelt had the Army seize the plant and prohibit picketing. The war department then ordered draft boards to cancel the draft deferments of those workers who refused to return to the plant, effectively ending the strike.

Though the UAW functionaries on the West Coast were indeed Communists, there is much evidence to support the argument that the North American Aviation Strike was not a political one, but one that aimed at achieving traditional trade union goals of union recognition and the negotiation of a contract. Nevertheless, the strike marked an important turning point for the industrial union movement in terms of settling its relationship with the federal government, as well as for the young labor federation's internal political life. Thereafter, CIO officials more readily accepted many of the policy objectives of the federal government as parameters limiting what they believed their unions could achieve. The strike also foreshadowed how the Communist/anti-Communist split in the CIO would come to dominate not only the contests for leadership in many CIO unions, but would force the eventual expulsion of Communist-led industrial unions from the CIO in 1949 and 1950. [Gilbert J. Gall]

FURTHER READING

Lichtenstein, Nelson L. *Labor's War at Home: The CIO in World War II.* Cambridge, U.K.: Cambridge University Press, 1982.

Prickett, James R. "Communist Conspiracy or Wage Dispute?: The 1941 Strike at North American Aviation." *Pacific Historical Review*, Vol. 50 (1981), pp. 215–233.

o o o

NORTHWEST LUMBER STRIKE OF 1917. Spurred on by the success in organizing harvest workers on the West Coast, the Industrial Workers of the World (IWW) planned in 1917 to renew their efforts in Northwest lumber camps, where attempts to organize lumberjacks had been made since 1912.

Living conditions in lumber camps were notoriously bad. Going from job to job, men carried rolled up blankets on their backs, since the companies provided no bedding. Typical housing for lumberjacks was a crowded bunkhouse with men sleeping two to a bunk on piles of hay. Unsavory food, unsanitary conditions, long days and low wages characterized the lumberjacks' life and led to sporadic strikes in sawmills and lumber camps after 1912.

The IWW lumber strike of 1917 was the most spectacular controversy in the industry up to that time. The demands of the lumberjacks in 1917, organized in the Lumber Workers Industrial Union No. 500 that was formed at the 1917 IWW convention, indicate major grievances. They called for an eight-hour workday, no Sunday or holiday work, higher wages, satisfactory food served in porcelain dishes with no overcrowding at the dinner tables, and sanitary kitchens.

They also pressed for sleeping quarters with a maximum of twelve people in each bunkhouse, single spring beds and shower baths, adequate lighting, free hospital service, and semi-monthly pay by bank check. They called for an end to child labor in the sawmills and an end to discrimination against IWW members in the camps.

In many areas in the Northwest, close to 90 percent of the men became IWW members. By August 1917, the strike that started on July 1 had paralyzed more than 80 percent of the lumber industry in western Washington, threatening the manufacture of airplanes for the war and the supply of lumber for crating shipment.

Newspaper articles in the Northwest charged that the IWW lumber strike was financed with German gold and organized by the Wobblies to oppose the war effort. The governor of Washington proposed a statewide vigilante committee; police frisked men on streets and on trains for union cards or other signs of IWW membership. IWW members were detained in stockades built in many communities, and IWW halls were raided and wrecked throughout the Northwest. Local lawyers refused to defend Wobblies who were imprisoned, and in Congress some of the senators from the region urged the use of military force to drive the IWW members out of the lumber camps.

As the strike progressed, Secretary of War Baker asked the lumber companies to concede an eight-hour day. Employers, however, refused this request as well as mediation efforts by federal or state officials, linking their own position to national defense. Members of the Lumberman's Protective Association raised a $500,000 "fighting fund" to break the strike. Any employer member who gave into demands for the eight-hour day would be fined $500.

Alarmed by dwindling strike funds, arrests of strike leaders, and the use of scab crews in the camps, the IWW urged members to go back to work in the camps but to "hoosier up," that is, act like "greenhorns" who had never been in the woods before, to strike on, rather than off the job. There was evidence that IWW lumberjacks engaged in "conscientious withdrawal of efficiency" that disorganized and confused production throughout the industry, although efforts to document criminal sabotage proved fruitless.

President Wilson sent a mediation commission to investigate and if possible, settle the crisis. The commission reported that the lumber operators took advantage of the wartime hysteria to fight not only the IWW but all unions. The commission condemned the opposition of the lumber owners to the eight-hour day, since lumber was the only major industry on the West Coast in which it did not prevail.

As the unmet need for lumber for the war effort continued, the War Department detailed Colonel Brice P. Disque of the U. S. Army Signal Corps to organize a "Loyal Legion of Loggers and Lumbermen" to establish harmony between employers and workers. The "4 L" became known as Colonel Disque's "weapon to bomb pro-Hunism out of the Northwest woods." The IWW claimed that the 4 L's was a company union that included employers and charged that the police, the press, and cleverly manipulated mob violence had been used as a club to force workers to become members. Colonel Disque advised unionists to suspend union activities and organizing until the end of the war.

In March 1918, Disque announced that the Northwest lumber industry would go on an eight-hour day. The IWW took credit for this. The IWW lumberjacks celebrated May Day 1918, by burning their old bedding rolls so that the companies were forced to provide bedding or have no workers.

After the armistice was signed, the 4 L's lost its government support, although the West Coast Lumberman's Association urged that it continue. Disque was elected president of the 4 L's, promising to stamp out sabotage and anarchy. Although the organization lasted until the 1930s, membership dropped off as both the American Federation of Labor and the IWW recruited lumber workers after the war, and the organization proved ineffective against companywide wage cuts during the next decade. [Joyce L. Kornbluh]

FURTHER READING

Jensen, Vernon H. *Lumber and Labor*. New York: Farrar and Rhinehart, 1945.

Report of the President's Mediation Commission to the President of the United States—Unrest in the Lumber Industry. Washington, DC: Government Printing Office, 1918.

Tyler, Robert. *Rebels of the Woods: The I.W.W. in the Pacific Northwest*. Eugene, OR: University of Oregon Press, 1967.

o   o   o

NORTHWEST LUMBER STRIKE OF 1935. In 1935, the AFL's United Brotherhood of Carpenters and Joiners asked the AFL Executive Council to turn over to it the AFL federal locals in the lumber and sawmill industry in the Pacific Northwest. William Hutcheson, president of the Carpenters, claimed jurisdiction on the basis that the workers in question worked with wood. The AFL Executive Council com-

plied and turned over the locals, which had been organized on an industrial basis, to the Brotherhood.

In inheriting the ninety locals and approximately 17,000 dues-paying members of the federal locals, the Carpenters also inherited a large dose of trouble. The lumber industry had been hit hard by the depression. Only half of the work force was employed and many of those only part time. Wages in the industry were deplorably low, and working conditions were among the worst anywhere. Unionization in the industry, which had flourished briefly during the heyday of the Industrial Workers of the World, had all but disappeared before the passage of the National Industrial Recovery Act (NIRA) in 1933. The Communist National Lumber Workers Union existed on paper only, and even the company unions were hardly functioning.

Section 7(a) of the NIRA changed all that. Local unions were formed in both logging and sawmilling and the AFL granted them federal charters while deciding what to do with them. In July of 1933, the locals came together to form the Northwest Council of Sawmill and Timber Workers.

When the Carpenters assumed control of the locals, the Northwest Council and the Brotherhood formulated demands that included union recognition, a base wage of seventy-five cents a day, the thirty-hour workweek, seniority, paid holidays and vacations. A strike date of May 6 was set. Not surprisingly, most of the operators rejected the demands out of hand and refused to deal with the union. However, two large companies, Weyerhaeuser and Long-Bell, agreed to negotiate. Before the union could secure contracts with these important companies, the unrest that had been seething beneath the surface for years exploded in a series of wildcat strikes. By the official strike date, 10,000 men were out, while a like number stayed on the job at the two big companies where negotiations continued.

A. W. Muir, who had been sent by the Carpenters to lead the negotiations, agreed to contracts with Weyerhaeuser and Long-Bell on May 9. They called for union recognition, a base rate of fifty cents an hour, a forty-hour week, and time and a half for overtime. Caught up in the militant atmosphere of the actions of their fellow workers, the loggers and millworkers at both companies overwhelmingly rejected the contract offer and joined the strike.

Muir moved to regain control of the situation. He branded the insurgents as Communists and removed the recalcitrant officers of the Northwest Council from office. But Muir's brief success in bringing the Northwest Council into line created far greater problems in the long run. Insurgents demanded that Hutcheson replace Muir. The Northwest Joint Strike Committee, formed by the anti-Muir faction, demanded a return to the original bargaining demands. The strike dragged on for two months and became increasingly marked by violence. Operators turned to state authorities, and the intervention of the Oregon State Police and the Washington National Guard led to bloody encounters between strikers and state forces. In the face of the violence, Secretary of Labor Frances Perkins named a mediation board made up of prominent citizens. The board succeeded in formulating agreements on a company by company basis. By August 14, all the men were back at work, having accepted what amounted to the contract originally offered by Weyerhaeuser and Long-Bell.

The 1935 lumber strike established unionism in the volatile industry. But the conflict between Muir and the insurgents also created the circumstances for dual unionism in the lumber camps. When thirteen dissident locals met in Centralia, Washington on October 12 to plan strategy against Muir, he moved to disband the

Northwest Council and replace it instead with ten district councils, organized so as to split his enemies and render them ineffective.

The bitterness over Muir's tactics, and the fact that the Brotherhood treated the lumber workers as second-class members because they paid less per capita tax than construction carpenters, led to the creation in 1936 of the Federation of Woodworkers. The president, Harold Pritchett, was strongly influenced by a militant Communist minority among the lumbermen. Quickly, Pritchett and his supporters from the anti-Muir opposition moved to take the industrially organized Woodworkers into the Congress of Industrial Organizations (CIO). He met with bitter resistance from a minority of the locals and the Carpenters. The Federation of Woodworkers met in Tacoma, Washington in July of 1937 to decide the issue. The CIO prevailed and a new organization, the International Woodworkers of America (IWA), emerged from the meeting.

No jurisdictional battle between the AFL and the CIO during the 1930s was more bitter. In response to the formation of the IWA, the AFL supporters, under the guidance of Hutcheson, formed the Oregon-Washington Council of Lumber and Sawmill Workers. The jurisdictional battle between the two raged across the Northwest. AFL unions, particularly the Teamsters and building trades councils, refused to handle CIO lumber. In addition, there was internal trouble in the IWA over the left-wing character of Pritchett's leadership.

Pritchett, under constant attack from right-wing forces in the IWA, never succeeded in consolidating his power. When the internal fight threatened to hand the victory to the AFL by default, CIO president John L. Lewis sent Adolph Germer in to take over the IWA organizational drive. Germer, who supported the anti-Communist forces, invigorated the organizational campaigns.

The left–right fight continued until 1941 when the right-wing forces formed the CIO Woodworkers Organizing Committee inside the IWA. The new president of the CIO, Philip Murray, who had been stung by the left-wing's rejection of a recommendation of the National Defense Mediation Board on which Murray sat, engineered the victory of the right-wing forces. An anti-Communist slate of officers took control and immediately signed an organizing agreement with the CIO with Germer as director.

The turmoil in the lumber industry resulted in the unionization of some 80 percent of the lumber workers in the Northwest. Of these, the IWA had some 50,000 and the AFL's Carpenters 35,000. [Ronald L. Filippelli]

FURTHER READING

Bernstein, Irving. *The Turbulent Years*. Boston, MA: Houghton Mifflin, 1970.

Galenson, Walter. *The CIO Challenge to the AFL.* Cambridge, MA: Harvard University Press, 1960.

Rose, Gerald A. "The Westwood Lumber Strike." *Labor History*, Vol. 13 (Spring, 1972), pp. 171–199.

O

o o o o o o o o o o o

o   o   o

OIL WORKERS' STRIKE OF 1945. There had been local unions of oil workers in the Pennsylvania oil fields before the turn of the century, and in 1899, the Brotherhood of Oil & Gas Well Workers organized in the newer fields around Findlay and Bowling Green, Ohio. Both attempts failed, however, in the face of the power of the Standard Oil Corporation. Not until the opening up of the great era of Gulf Coast production did trade unionism return to the industry. With the coming of World War I, oil prices soared and a labor shortage developed. Not surprisingly, unions began to grow again. Once again, Standard Oil stood in the way, refusing to deal with the union. The company viciously broke a strike in 1917 on the Gulf Coast, but in California the union did win the eight-hour workday, a wage increase, and indirect recognition of the union in California.

Out of the success in California and the growth of unionization as the war expanded, the International Association of Oil Field, Gas Well and Refinery Workers of America, an American Federation of Labor (AFL) affiliate, was born in 1918. Internal factionalism and an industry offensive made short work of the young union, however. By the time a bitter and hopeless strike in California ended in defeat in September of 1921, the union was all but eliminated as a force in the industry. The next decade was one of drift and continued decline, and by 1933, the union had only 300 members.

Like much of the American labor movement, unionization in the oil industry was reborn during the Great Depression of the 1930s. With the passage of the National Industrial Recovery Act (NIRA), the officers of the tiny union began to receive a deluge of appeals from oil workers for unionization. In March and April of 1934 alone, thirty-three local charters were granted by the national union.

The oil workers, like workers in auto, steel, electrical manufacturing, rubber, and other industries, were also caught up in the battle inside the AFL between the advocates of craft jurisdiction and those, like John L. Lewis, who fought for the industrial form of organization. When the AFL tried to divide the oil refinery workers who had been organized by the Brotherhood of Oil Workers, the union became one of the eight AFL unions involved in creating John L. Lewis' Committee for Industrial Organization. When the industrial unions were expelled from the AFL in 1935, the Oil Workers, now renamed the Oil Workers International Union (OWIU) joined with them to form the Congress of Industrial Organizations (CIO).

The CIO days were not one long litany of victories. Indeed, between 1938 and 1940 the oil interests crushed the union in its stronghold in Oklahoma. Like most of the labor movement, the fortunes of the OWIU flourished during World War II. In 1941, the CIO's new president, Philip Murray, formed the Oil Workers Organizing Committee. By 1943, the union had won fifty-five of sixty elections and gained more members in one year that the total membership in 1940.

When World War II ended, the oil industry turned its attention to rolling back some of the gains made by the union in the favorable circumstances of the war. Workers used to working a forty-eight-hour week during the war did not want to surrender one-fifth of their wages when production returned to more normal pre-war levels. In negotiations with the major producers in 1945, the union demanded a 30 percent increase in straight-time wages and a return to the forty-hour week. The net result would have kept the amount in the pay envelopes even with wartime. The companies, led by Standard Oil, offered 15 percent, an effective 15 percent cut in take-home pay. The union, now 60,000 strong, struck the refineries in mid-September.

The shutdown was total. The rush of returning veterans for the strikers' jobs never materialized. By the end of September, the gasoline pumps began to go dry across the nation. Secretary of Labor Lewis Schwellenbach called for a labor–industry conference, but two attempts failed to produce any movement in the bargaining. On October 5, 1945, President Harry Truman ordered the Navy to seize twenty-six companies. Forced with this ultimatum, the OWIU ordered their members to return to work under the old conditions.

Standard Oil and the other companies now seized the initiative. Using the Navy as a shield, they determined to crush the union local by local. The union had wanted nationwide bargaining, but the companies had refused to discuss it. Now the companies began to use local bargaining, or ultimatums, to weaken the union at each plant, particularly those not seized by the Navy. The OWIU began to charge Truman with breaking the oil workers' strike. CIO president Murray demanded that Truman pressure the companies to settle. Under pressure from many of his supporters, Truman appointed a fact-finding committee, but most companies defied the President and refused to cooperate.

Soon, however, Sinclair Oil broke the industry agreement to follow Standard Oil's lead and signed with OWIU for an 18 percent increase. The 18 percent figure also appeared as the fact-finding board's recommendation. With the united front broken, other companies began to follow Sinclair's lead. The Texas Company and Shell met the pattern. In February 1946, Standard Oil made the capitulation of the companies official by signing for 18 percent. The last major plant to fall into line was Gulf's Toledo refinery. There the union held out until the company agreed to reinstate union members who had been discharged for their union activities.

The great strike of 1945 established the OWIU as a permanent force in the petroleum industry. The successes of the World War II period had been gained largely as a result of the combination of the protection of a benevolent government and the great demand for labor. The union's solidarity in 1945 proved that it could stand up to the major oil producers acting in concert in what amounted to an enormous concentration of power. [Ronald L. Filippelli]

FURTHER READING

O'Connor, Harvey. *History of Oil Workers International Union*. Denver, CO: Oil Workers International Union, 1950.

Rothbaum, Melvin. *The Government of the Oil, Chemical, and Atomic Workers Union*. New York: Wiley, 1962.

o   o   o

OKLAHOMA, KANSAS, AND MISSOURI METAL WORKERS' STRIKE OF 1935. The tri-state district located where southwestern Missouri, northeastern Oklahoma, and southeastern Kansas come together constituted one of the world's greatest centers of lead and zinc mining. Attempts to unionize the miners and mill-men in the district before the 1930s had little success. Yet the district frequently attracted the attention of the Western Federation of Miners and its successor, the International Union of Mine, Mill, and Smelter Workers, who saw in the poor, underpaid, ill-housed, and often occupationally ill miners, the potential for militant industrial unionism.

The organizing upsurge that marked the Great Depression and the New Deal also reached Picherville, Oklahoma, the heart of the tri-state mining district. Tri-state workers had been hard-hit by the Depression, and as the industry slumped, conditions remained precarious for most workers. In addition, many experienced men were considered unemployable by the companies because of age or job-related illnesses or impairments. The policy affected and embittered large numbers of tri-state miners because silicosis and tuberculosis were rampant in the district.

To capitalize on the discontent arising from these conditions, the International Union of Mine, Mill, and Smelter Workers sent Roy A. Brady into the district in 1933 to begin an organizing drive. When Brady was caught absconding with union funds, he was replaced by Thomas H. Brown, president of the union. By May of 1935, the union claimed that slightly more than half of the mine, mill, and smelter workers had joined the union. Nevertheless, attempts to bring the operators to the bargaining table, whether individually or as a group, failed.

Failure to achieve recognition brought Brown to recommend a strike. With unemployment so high, the strike call was an obvious risk, and there were significant numbers of workers who had not voted in the strike vote, thus increasing the unknown factor for the strike's organizers. Warned of the strike, officials of the larger companies began shutting down operations several hours before the midnight strike deadline. When the strike began, roving squads of strikers blocked access to some mines and smelters, refusing entrance to workers who had reported for work unaware of the strike.

During the strike's first three weeks, production reached the lowest levels ever recorded in the district. Only a few of the smallest properties continued to produce. It was the first successful strike in the tri-state district. But the employers knew that the test would be the ability of the union to sustain the strike, and they believed, correctly, that neither the international union nor its locals had the financial resources to sustain the strike. The operators, particularly the large ones, such as the Eagle Pitcher Mining and Smelting Company, waited until financial hardship made a back-to-work movement inevitable.

By May 18, the strategy was beginning to pay off. Large numbers of workers began to agitate for a return to work. Friction between this group and the pro-strike forces created the potential for fratricidal conflict inside the union. In this atmosphere, the operators set about to create a rival workers organization, the Tri-State Metal Mine and Smelter Workers Union, for those who wanted to return to work. The long-range goal was the creation of a company union. Large numbers of workers who had been unemployed before the strike joined the new organization. So too did large numbers of workers who had struck but who now wanted to return to work. Union leaders had been unable to convince them that union recognition and collective bargaining would compensate for the sacrifices they were being asked to make.

The strike began peacefully, but with the appearance of the back-to-work movement, violence became commonplace. Attacks on "scabs" increased and on May 27 only the intercession of Oklahoma state police saved the officers of the back-to-work movement from serious injury at the hands of angry strikers. When the back-to-work supporters retaliated, a bloody riot flared in Picherville. After the riot, authorities decided that they were no longer capable of keeping the peace between the rival unions. They called for the Oklahoma National Guard—a unit that had been specially trained for anti-strike action.

Not surprisingly, although the Guard had come to keep the peace, the result was the reopening of the operations and an alliance between the Guard and the back-to-work movement. Picketing was severely limited and military protection was given to all companies resuming operations in the Oklahoma portion of the district. The actions had the desired results, and by June 10 half of the mines and mills were back in production in Oklahoma and Kansas, where the National Guard had also been called out. Behind the rubric of law and order, the National Guards of Oklahoma and Kansas threw the power of the state behind the back-to-work movement and assisted in the breaking of the strike.

After the effective end of the strike, the operators and the Tri-State Metal Mine and Smelter Workers established a strong relationship with the express purpose of keeping the International Union of Mine, Mill, and Smelter Workers out of the district for good. Those strikers who returned to work were generally forced to join the company union. Those who refused the terms were blacklisted in the district and forced to uproot their families and search for work elsewhere.

Although the strike had effectively been broken by the beginning of June, it remained officially in progress, and in May of 1937 the International Union of Mine, Mill, and Smelter Workers, now part of the Congress of Industrial Organizations (CIO), undertook once again to organize the miners of the tri-state district. But in league with the operators, and using force and violence, the Tri-State Union once again

turned back the attempt at independent unionization.

After the defeat of the CIO attempt, the domination of the operators and the Tri-State Union seemed complete. But soon, in its Jones and Laughlin decision, the Supreme Court upheld the National Labor Relations Act, including its prohibition of company unions. To counter the Court's decision, the Tri-State Union decided to join the AFL, the bitter rival of the CIO, to which the Mine, Mill, and Smelter Workers belonged. The AFL accepted in spite of the fact that the company union had pilloried the AFL in its publications since its inception. The AFL charter gave the Tri-State Union jurisdiction over all mine, mill, and smelter workers in the district. The AFL had made the successor of the old, bitterly anti-union back-to-work movement a respectable affiliate. [Ronald L. Filippelli]

FURTHER READING

Suggs, George H., Jr. *Union Busting in the Tri-State: The Oklahoma, Kansas, and Missouri Metal Workers Strike of 1935.* Norman, OK: University of Olkahoma Press, 1986.

o   o   o

OXNARD, CALIFORNIA, SUGAR BEET STRIKE OF 1903. Ventura County, California, became the center of the American sugar beet refining industry at the end of the nineteenth century as a result of the passage of the 1897 Dingley Tariff Bill. The legislation placed a heavy tariff on imported sugar. New York sugar refiners took advantage of the protection of the law and built a huge sugar beet factory in the new town of Oxnard. By 1903 the plant employed 700 workers.

The arrival of the sugar beet industry brought a new working class to Ventura County, and racial and ethnic separation followed. Most of the new workers were Mexicans and Orientals. The new workers were residentially segregated into ethnic neighborhoods on the east side of Oxnard, while the old stock residents, mostly German and Irish farmers, lived on the west side. The town was divided by class along the same lines, with a small group of large-scale entrepreneurs, such as Henry, James, and Robert Oxnard, who had built and operated the factory.

The racial divisions of the town were mirrored in the occupational structure. The minority population, Mexican, Japanese, and Chinese, worked overwhelmingly in unskilled jobs. Anglo-Americans dominated the upper reaches of the business community, while whites also held the best jobs in the white-collar and skilled categories. The only significant exception to the parallel stratification by race and class were the labor contractors. These were mostly members of minority groups who played a key role in the distribution of agricultural labor in the county. By 1903, the Japanese were particularly significant in this regard.

While the relationship of the labor contractors to their workers was essentially exploitive, the racial bonds that bound contractor and worker also led to the ability of some contractors to force higher wages. In 1902, however, in order to provide local farmers with an alternative to the Japanese labor contractors, a group of local Jewish businessmen, with the support of the American Sugar Beet Company, formed the Western Agricultural Contracting Company (WACC).

The WACC succeeded in gaining control of some 90 percent of the contracting business by February 1903, forcing the minority contractors to work through them or not at all. This meant that the Japanese and Mexican contractors no longer could negotiate wages directly with the farmers. For the workers it meant one more level of control, and one more commission taken out of their pay. In addition, the WACC required workers to accept scrip good only in company stores instead of cash wages.

The new arrangement led the Japanese workers and contractors to organize a protest meeting in February 1903. Their grievances focused on the reduction of wages, up to 50 percent, that had resulted with the domination of contracting by the WACC. The meeting proved to be the first step toward the formation by Japanese and Mexican workers and labor contractors of the Japanese–Mexican Labor Association (JMLA), the first example in California of an agricultural workers union representing different minority groups. Five hundred Japanese workers joined 200 Mexicans as charter members of the new organization.

The goal of the union, largely led by the labor contractors, was to end the WACC's monopoly of the contract labor system. If the WACC could be eliminated, then the JMLA could negotiate wages and working conditions directly with the farmers. When the JMLA members agreed to stop contracting with the WACC, the action effectively put the industry on strike. The withholding of labor threatened the sugar beet crop because its profitability depended on labor-intensive processes, especially beet thinning in which workers carefully spaced beet seedlings and thinned them so that only the strongest survived.

The hostile Oxnard *Courier* framed the issues quite nicely when it wrote that the strike was "simply a question of whether the Japanese–Mexican laboring classes will control labor or whether it will be managed by conservative businessmen." According to the paper, only a union in the hands of "intelligent white men" could provide the "enlightened management" necessary for the mental and moral uplift of the workers.

For its part, the American Beet Sugar Company informed the JMLA that if they persisted in their demands the company would have to take steps to drive them out of the county and import new labor. The harsh response of the company reflected its concern over the success of the JMLA. By the first week in March, membership had grown to 1,200, more than 90 percent of the agricultural workers in the county. WACC also formed the Independent Agricultural Labor Union (IALU) to contest for the support of the minority workers. Its announced goal was to maintain harmonious relations between employers and employees of agricultural labor.

Introduction of the rival company union into the equation led to bloodshed. On March 23, 1903, a fight between supporters of the two unions led to the shooting of four members of JMLA. The press uniformly blamed the incident on the JMLA for resorting to illegal and forceful methods to prevent workers who wanted to work from working.

The incident of March 23 marked an escalation of militancy in the strike. A series of incidents followed in which JMLA members harassed farmers and labor contractors who continued to work with the WACC. The union also had considerable success persuading imported strikebreakers to join the union. Much of this success rested on the ability of the Mexican and Japanese strikers to appeal for ethnic and racial solidarity to the imported workers. This bond was difficult for the WACC to overcome, led as it was by the Anglo elite of the county. If the WACC could not import labor, then it could not win the strike.

The success of the JMLA in sustaining the strike finally brought the parties to the bargaining table. The union pointed out that it had 1,300 members while WACC at the time had only sixty men under contract. On March 30, 1903, the strike ended with a major union victory. The agreement included a pledge by the WACC to cancel all existing contracts with sugar beet farmers. The farmers also agreed to establish a minimum wage scale that nearly doubled the WACC rates and brought the workers back to the scale that had been in effect before the formation of WACC.

The success of the Oxnard workers led to a reevaluation by the California labor movement of the issue of whether or not to organize Mexican and Oriental workers. During the strike, organized labor's support was lukewarm, coming mostly from Socialist elements. The state AFL stayed away from any formal affiliation with the JMLA because of the strong anti-Asian sentiment among its members and because of its general opposition to organizing agricultural workers. It is interesting that when the Los Angeles Labor Council passed a resolution backing the JMLA, it also reiterated its opposition to Asian immigration.

The ambiguity of the Los Angeles resolution reflected the basic hostility of the AFL to the JMLA. When the JMLA petitioned the AFL for a charter after the strike, Samuel Gompers, amazingly, granted the charter with the stipulation that Asians be excluded. The Mexican branch of the JMLA refused, blasting Gompers and declaring their intention to stand by their Japanese comrades. Despite the eloquence of the JMLA appeal, the AFL held firm to its discriminatory policy. Without hope of an AFL charter, the existence of the sugar beet workers union became increasingly problematic. Apparently the union disappeared a few years later. [Ronald L. Filippelli]

FURTHER READING

Almaguer, Tomas. "Racial Domination and Class Conflict in Capitalist Agriculture: The Oxnard Sugar Beet Workers' Strike of 1903." *Labor History*, Vol. 25, No. 3 (Summer, 1984), pp. 325–350.

Murray, John. "A Foretaste of the Orient." *International Socialist Review*, Vol. 4 (August 1903), pp. 72–79.

P

○ ○ ○ ○ ○ ○ ○ ○ ○ ○

○   ○   ○

PACKINGHOUSE WORKERS' STRIKE OF 1904. In the late nineteenth and early twentieth centuries, skill, ethnic, race, and gender differences divided and fragmented the American working class. The efforts of the American labor movement to overcome these divisions were largely unsuccessful, and if successful, usually short-lived. The Packinghouse Strike of 1904, perhaps more than any other labor conflict in this period, demonstrated that divisions along skill and ethnic lines could be overcome, but it equally demonstrated the enormous difficulty of sustaining that unity, in the face of determined employer opposition.

During the last two decades of the nineteenth century, the meat-packing industry underwent vast changes. Spurred by the development of a national market for meat products and facilitated by the invention of the refrigerated box car, the industry quickly rationalized and reorganized its work process and pioneered the (dis)assembly line method of production. Accompanying this rationalization of the work process was the concentration of the meat-packing industry in Chicago under six corporate giants.

The change in the work process was accomplished at the expense of the skilled all-around butcher, who had formerly set the pace of work. By subdividing the killing and butchering process, the all-around butcher was replaced both by a few highly skilled knifemen practicing only one cutting operation and by a large group of common laborers. The wage structure similarly changed, and although wage rates varied widely—from fifteen cents to fifty cents per hour—the majority of workers earned the lower rates. In a 230-man cattle butchering department in 1904, for instance, 6 percent of the workers earned forty-five to fifty cents per hour, and 71 percent earned fifteen to twenty cents per hour. Total usage of animal by-products also increased the ranks of the lowest paid workers, because these processes were susceptible to mechanization. Reorganization also gave the foreman control over the speed of production, which increased dramatically. These changes also affected the workday. Meat-packing had always been seasonal, but now with changes in the work process, work hours and days became increasingly irregular, conforming to the daily shipment of animals.

A final result of reorganization was a change in the ethnic composition of the work force. Native white Americans, Germans, Irish, and, after the 1880s, Bohemians filled the ranks of the early packinghouse workers. The creation of unskilled jobs led to an influx of Poles, Slovaks, and Lithuanians into the lower occupational levels. Blacks, however, remained a numerically small proportion of the work force. Within the canning and by-products departments, women's employment steadily increased, and by 1905, 11 percent of the packinghouse workers were female.

The changes that swept through the packinghouses spurred union activity. Packinghouse workers had organized in the 1880s and early 1890s into the Knights of Labor and the American Federation of Labor (AFL) and conducted two large strikes in 1886 and 1894. Strong and united packer resistance, divisions along craft lines between various unions, and the instability of the work force and work process during this period of expansion and work rationalization, all served to undermine unionization. In 1897, this situation was in part remedied by the creation of the Amalgamated Meat Cutters and Butcher Workmen of North America. Brought together by the national AFL, this union of a handful of weak local unions opened a new round of union organizing in the packinghouses. The union was national in scope and came at a more stable time in the industry's history. Its path was also facilitated by rising meat prices and a tight labor market.

The Amalgamated focused its efforts on Chicago, where one-third of the nation's packinghouse workers were concentrated. Organizing began in earnest in 1900, and by 1904 the union had achieved amazing success. At first the union followed a traditional program of organizing skilled workers into separate craft locals. However, the union soon switched to a departmental strategy that allowed all workers—skilled and unskilled—in a particular department to join the local. The impetus for this change came in part from the urgings of the Amalgamated's president, Michael Donnelly, who combined his own personal ambition of running a large union with a sincere sympathy for the unskilled. The craft workers also clearly recognized that without unionization of the unskilled, their own craft positions in the job hierarchy would remain insecure, and their wages would be pulled downward.

The unskilled workers responded enthusiastically to the union's appeal. The union's success was in no small part aided by the efforts of a largely Irish leadership that actively sought to integrate the unskilled immigrants into the union. For instance, interpreter's were used at local meetings for the benefit of the newer immigrants.

Although not an industrial union, the Amalgamated's departmental structure did allow for the integration of a labor force divided by skill, ethnicity, and race. The various locals then organized a packing trades council in each city to coordinate their work. The only exception to this departmental structure was the formation of one local to encompass all female workers. Although a step back from their departmental structure, the Amalgamated's position marked a vast improvement over the more traditional AFL policy that excluded women altogether.

Donnelly followed a conservative policy of allowing only individual local negotiations. By 1903, two departments had secured industrywide collective bargaining agreements. Elsewhere, departmental workers' committees also successfully negotiated over hours, wages, seniority, and output restrictions, many times after short strikes. At the shop floor level, the Amalgamated was gaining strength.

During 1904, however, new dynamics were at work. The industrywide agreements only encompassed departments that were solidly organized, and even then the agreements only covered the skilled workers. Pressure soon mounted from the ranks of the unskilled for the negotiation of national standards for all workers. In addition, the packers, who had earlier seen unionization as a positive force promoting labor peace, now hardened against the union in the face of frequent departmental strikes and labor unrest. Finally, the depression of 1904 weakened the union's position as unemployment in Chicago rose.

At the Amalgamated's 1904 Cincinnati convention the determination of the rank-and-file packinghouse workers for a national wage scale won out over the union's more conservative national leadership. It is wrong, however, to assume that the demand for a national wage scale was merely the result of pressure from unskilled workers. More than this, it marked a decision by skilled workers to risk a strike over un- skilled wage rates. Much of their reasoning for this decision derived from a defense of their own skilled jobs. Without a floor on the unskilled wage rate, all wages were in danger of being pulled down. In addition, without the unionization of the unskilled, any strike by skilled workers risked defeat through an employer strategy of elevating the unskilled to skilled work. The fact that this demand for an unskilled wage rate was raised in a depression proved disastrous, although it is unclear at best whether the Amalgamated could have held together if it had followed a more conservative course.

The Amalgamated opened the June negotiations with the packers by demand- ing a general wage increase for all workers, the establishment of the Chicago wage rate as the prevailing rate (and hence, a greater wage increase for the outlying cities), and a minimum wage of twenty cents per hour for all unskilled workers. The packers were willing to renew their present agreements without change but objected to a wage in- crease during a depression. More impor- tantly, however, they refused to negotiate over the unskilled rate, arguing that it was solely determined by supply and demand.

The union countered by dropping its demand for an unskilled wage increase but persisted in demanding that the current minimum rate of eighteen cents per hour be written into the contract. The packers finally agreed to negotiate a minimum rate but offered only sixteen cents. A union referen- dum rejected this offer, and the company raised its offer to seventeen cents, but only for a few departments. By the time the packers offered arbitration, President Don- nelly had already set a July 12 strike date, which he believed could not be rescinded.

Approximately 40,000 packinghouse workers in nine cities responded to the strike call. Chicago strikers alone numbered between 20,000 and 28,000. The strike itself was well organized and largely nonvio- lent. Within days, however, the Chicago

packers started their idle packinghouses using foremen, superintendents, and skilled butchers from outlying non-union plants. Also going to work were a number of Chicago's unemployed and a large group of black strikebreakers.

Before serious negotiations resumed, the packinghouse owners knew they could operate the plants without union labor. The union quickly acceded to arbitration on all issues. However, negotiations broke down over the packers' demands for the continued employment of strikebreakers and the re- hire of union members on an individual basis and only as needed. Intervention by the allied trades—carpenters, carworkers, electricians, etc.—who threatened a sympa- thy strike, brought both sides back to the bargaining table. An agreement was reached, based largely on the companies' terms, al- though it did contain a nondiscrimination rehire clause.

When packinghouse workers returned to their jobs on July 22, tempers quickly flared as union leaders were discriminated against in rehiring at Armour, and bosses at other plants harassed returning workers. With the packinghouse workers near revolt, the Amalgamated's leadership was forced to resume the strike the same day. On July 25, the allied trades joined the strike, but as with the packinghouse workers, the packers found replacements. Critical to the success of this sympathy strike of the allied trades was the fact that stationary firemen and engineers, who were necessary for the running of the refrigeration units, remain on the job.

During the second phase of the strike, violence broke out. Strikers attacked black strikebreakers in Chicago, Kansas City, and St. Joseph, Missouri, and rioting broke out in Chicago. In Sioux City the militia had to be called out. The Amalgamated's leader- ship worked hard to maintain discipline and keep the strikers' hope and solidarity alive. Mass meetings were held, union literature was printed in six languages, food relief was distributed, and a giant parade of 20,000 unionists was held in Chicago. The sympathy strike of the allied trades and financial donations from the Chicago Federation of Labor testified to general working-class support for the packinghouse workers.

As the strike dragged on into August, it was clear that the union had lost. Production at the packinghouses steadily climbed, and the packers, confident of their victory, refused to negotiate with the union. Only through the intervention of Chicago social reformers Jane Addams, Mary McDowell, and Dr. Cornelia DeBey did Armour finally agree to seek a settlement on September 3. The union agreed to send its workers back to the plants without a contract and without any protection against discrimination. Although the strikers rejected this offer in a referendum, Donnelly officially ended the strike on September 8. The union was completely routed.

Most skilled workers, except for union activists, returned to their jobs at the packinghouses. Many of the strikebreakers also remained. The Amalgamated was very nearly destroyed, and of the locals that did survive, all became strictly craft unions. The packinghouses soon offered welfare programs for the skilled workers, and the union's efforts at further organization stalled. Another wave of unionism engulfed the plants during World War I, but by 1923 it too suffered defeat. Only under the New Deal would packinghouse unionism finally succeed.

. Although defeated in 1904, the packinghouse workers showed that unions at the turn of the century could unite across skill, ethnic, race, and gender lines, if only temporarily. Critical in this effort was the willingness of skilled workers to strike over an issue—a minimum wage rate for the unskilled—that would directly benefit unskilled workers and largely new immigrant, black, and female workers. That these skilled workers acted out of what they perceived to be their own long-term interests cannot take away from the symbolic importance of their actions for the entire labor movement. [James D. Rose]

FURTHER READING

Barrett, James R. *Work and Community in the Jungle: Chicago's Packinghouse Workers, 1894–1922.* Urbana, IL: University of Illinois Press, 1987.

Brody, David. *The Butcher Workmen: A Study of Unionization.* Cambridge, MA: Harvard University Press, 1964.

Commons, John R. "Labor Conditions in Meat Packing and the Recent Strike." *The Quarterly Journal of Economics,* Vol. 14 (November, 1904), pp. 1–32.

Perlman, Selig, and Philip Taft. *History of Labour in the United States, 1896–1932,* Vol. 4. New York: Macmillan, 1935.

o   o   o

PAINT CREEK AND CABIN CREEK MINE STRIKES OF 1912. Attempts at unionization of the West Virginia mine fields failed regularly until 1902 when the United Mine Workers (UMW) managed to secure a contract for its members in the Kanawah coalfield in the southern part of the state. But the Kanawah miners were an isolated band of union workers in a sea of non-union coal production. On April 19, 1912, operators in the Paint Creek subdistrict of the Kanawah field refused to renew their contract and the Paint Creek miners went out on strike. Some of the operators sought court injunctions forbidding the UMW from organizing their mines, and all of them hired private guards from the Baldwin-Felts Company, a firm specializing in supplying security and strikebreakers and in other anti-union activities. When the Baldwin-Felts men set about evicting miners from company houses, the miners armed themselves and set up tent colonies near the mines.

The situation soon turned ugly. The miners complained to West Virginia's governor that the guards beat and mistreated them regularly and asked the governor to force them out of the state. When Governor

William E. Glassrock claimed that he had no such authority, the miners began to fight back on their own. As law enforcement officials looked on without interfering, the violence resulted in two deaths. The governor's desire to avoid alienating either party stemmed from his fear that to alienate the miners would lead to a strengthening of the Socialist Party which had garnered nearly a third of the votes in local elections in Kanawah County in 1912.

On August 3, 1912, the strike spread to neighboring Cabin Creek. At a UMW rally in Charleston the following day, Mother Jones, the legendary "miners' angel," inspired the strikers with a speech that likened their cause to "God's holy work," by "breaking the chains" that bound the miners. According to Mother Jones, "the whole damned lot" of Baldwin-Felts guards deserved bullets in the head.

While the governor tried to mediate, the violence spread. The local sheriff refused to arrest offenders and the National Guard could do nothing without a declaration of martial law. Glassrock took that step on September 2, 1912. By arresting miners who had committed criminal acts and by expelling the Baldwin-Felts guards from the strike zone, the National Guard ended the violence.

The operators were not pleased with the turn of events. They refused the governor's pleas that they meet with the UMW. The union, they claimed, had set about to destroy their property and kill or cripple their employees who were willing and anxious to work. The UMW, claimed the operators, would accept nothing but surrender, a path the companies flatly refused to consider. Instead, they called for law and order.

Thwarted in his various attempts at mediation, and with peace restored in the coalfields, Glassrock lifted martial law in mid-October. Almost immediately, the operators began to import strikebreakers. Advertisements offering a "good steady job all year round" to "family men of all nationalities" appeared in the metropolitan newspapers with the postscript that a strike was on.

The strikebreakers came on special trains. Violence erupted when the strikers tried to turn them back. The operators appealed to the governor for protection. Glassrock would not allow the Baldwin-Felts guards to return, but he did permit the companies to hire "watchmen" cleared by the National Guard. Most of the "watchmen" came from the ranks of the militia who had been on duty in the strike zone. They shifted their loyalties to the companies with little difficulty. Predictably, violence flared again and continued intermittently for the next four months in spite of the reimposition and lifting of martial law three times.

In March, Henry D. Hatfield, a surgeon and reformer, succeeded Glassrock as governor. Two weeks after his inauguration he inspected the strike zone. Under his administration the application of martial law by the National Guard became more evenhanded. Hatfield knew that only through the continuation of martial law could the operators be denied the use of Baldwin-Felts guards or private "watchmen." The introduction of these elements, he reasoned, had been responsible for the violence. Hatfield believed that workers did have a right "to meet and discuss conditions and organize into an association or union" for their welfare and protection.

When the operators rejected the governor's plea that they meet directly with the UMW, Hatfield was forced into the role of intermediary. The union had informed him that they would end the strike without union recognition if there would be no discrimination against UMW members and if a commission were selected to arbitrate disputes between the miners and the operators. The operators refused but did finally accept a compromise formulated by the governor that did include no discrimination against any miner (but without mention of the UMW), a nine-hour workday, the right of the miners to hire their own check weighman, and a twice-monthly payday. When the miners rejected this version, the governor threatened them with prosecution under martial law. In the face of this threat, and after a year of bitter strife and deprivation, the miners accepted Hatfield's compromise.

Hatfield lifted martial law on June 12, 1913, but when the operators refused to hire back 150 UMW members whom they claimed were leaders of the strike, the miners once again struck. This time Hatfield's intercession bore fruit. On August 1, 1913, he obtained a permanent settlement granting the miners the right to join the UMW without discrimination, guaranteeing union members the right to hold their meetings on company property, and providing for the appointment of a board of arbitration for future disputes. Two companies actually granted full recognition to the UMW. The victories in the Paint and Cabin Creek strikes, partial as they were, were the impetus for an organizing drive in West Virginia that by the summer of 1914 had brought 16,000 miners into the United Mine Workers. For their part, the operators regrouped to fight another day. They formed the Coal Operators Protective Association and pledged $1 million to protect their property against "the Socialists, otherwise known as the United Mine Workers of America." [Ronald L. Filippelli]

FURTHER READING

Lunt, Richard D. *Law and Order vs. the Miners: West Virginia, 1907–1933.* Hamden, CT: Archon Books, 1979.

o   o   o

PAPERWORKERS' LOCKOUT AND STRIKE OF 1987–1988. On March 27, 1987, twelve hundred fifty members of the United Paper Workers International Union (UPIU) were locked out of the International Paper (IP) Company Plant in Mobile, Alabama, after contract negotiations reached an impasse. Workers at Mobile, where the company demanded cuts in premium pay for overtime and holidays, were told that the plant would remain closed until the union accepted the company's final offer. Thus began a fifteen-month struggle that gained national attention. As much as any other labor dispute of the 1980s, the Paperworkers' lockout at Mobile and the strikes that followed at other IP locations embodied many of the tactics and attitudes that came to characterize industrial relations in that decade. Many in organized labor believed that the International Paper conflict was part of a general assault by corporate America on unions and on the standard of living of American workers.

Shortly after the lockout at Mobile, contracts at four other plants in the International Paper empire expired. The company had demanded concessions at each location. The first to vote to strike was the De Pere, Wisconsin, local. De Pere was followed in the next two weeks by strike votes at the IP plants in Jay, Maine, and Lock Haven, Pennsylvania.

Although the company had demanded some nineteen concessions and other contract changes from the union, including the right to contract out maintenance work, the key concession demands involved requiring workers to work ten holidays during the year and forfeit premium pay for work on Sundays and holidays. In exchange, IP offered improvements in the retirement allowance, medical insurance, and small wage increases over the length of a four-year contract. The union argued that the demands would amount to an annual loss of $3,200 for the average worker, or from 7 percent to 12 percent.

International Paper argued that it needed these concessions to stay competitive. The union, however, cited IP's balance sheet. In the previous ten years the company had been very successful. In 1988, sales and earnings reached record levels, with earnings rising 85 percent to $754 million. With its acquisition of the Hammermill Paper Company in 1986, IP became the largest primary paper producer in the United States.

IP's response to the shutdown of its four plants was the hiring of replacement workers. Recruitment was done with the assistance of a firm of management consultants, B.E.&K of Birmingham, Alabama. B.E.&K was representative of hundreds of management consulting and law firms that had emerged in the 1970s to advise businesses on how to keep their companies non-union and how to weaken unions where they already existed. In areas like Lock Haven, where unemployment was high, replacement workers could easily be recruited locally, badly dividing the communities in the process. The success of the tactic also served the company well by intimidating workers at other IP plants whose contracts were being negotiated at the same time. For example, when the company informed workers at its Pine Bluff, Arkansas, plant that they would be replaced if they struck, the workers voted to accept the concessionary contract. The plight of the workers at the struck plants, all of which were operating with permanent replacements, acted as an object lesson. In effect, IP had contained the spread of the conflict to its four closed plants. No other UPIU local rejected the company's demands after watching the decisive action taken by the company at Lock Haven, Mobile, De Pere, and Jay. The success of the company's strategy could be seen in the fact that in spite of the strike, IP's profits rose 33 percent in 1987.

With its traditional picketing tactics providing no progress, the UPIU turned to another strategy. On November 24, 1987, the union hired Ray Rogers, the head of Corporate Campaigns Inc., to devise a strategy to bring pressure on IP to settle and rehire the striking workers. Rogers had gained considerable fame for his innovative strategy to help the Amalgamated Clothing and Textile Workers Union successfully conduct the **J. P. Stevens Boycott** in the late 1970s. Rogers devised a campaign to bring the plight of the striking and locked-out paperworkers to the nation at large. He enlisted the aid of other unions and liberal groups to bring pressure on companies such as Avon Products, Coca-Cola, the Bank of Boston, Mellon Bank, Chase Manhattan Bank, and PNC Financial Corporation, whose officers also sat on the IP board of directors. The goal was to force them to resign from the IP board in order to shield their own companies from boycotts and bad publicity. Rogers also organized numerous caravans of IP workers to take the story of the strike on the road and raise money for the strikers. Attempts were also made to organize student support groups at colleges and universities and to force IP supporters and officials from boards of trustees.

While the corporate campaign seems to have had little success in resolving the dispute between the four striking locals and IP, it apparently did cause the company enough discomfort that IP began to offer non-concessionary contracts to locals that were still negotiating. It soon became clear to the UPIU's national leadership that no amount of public pressure was likely to bring IP to settle on any basis acceptable to the union. On October 7, 1988, leaders of the striking locals met at the UPIU's Nashville, Tennessee headquarters, where it was suggested that the strike be called off. Although representatives of the striking locals balked, believing that the corporate campaign was having an effect, Wayne Glenn, UPIU president, ordered the strike to end on October 10. The union had no funds to continue to support the strikers, particularly since the unemployment compensation benefits that workers in Jay, Maine and Lock Haven, Pennsylvania were receiving were coming to an end.

For the international union, the decision made some sense. To continue the strike might have meant the loss of the four local unions through decertification elections held among the replacement workers. With the settlement, although the workers did not receive their jobs back at once, the strikers did remain employees of the company with recall rights as openings occurred.

For the strikers, however, the settlement was a bitter pill to swallow. They had held firm for sixteen months under extreme hardship. Many had lost their homes or had seen their marriages dissolve. In spite of the difficulties, very few had crossed the picket lines to return to work. Many had spent countless hours manning food banks or traveling around the country speaking on the plight of the workers. For them, the defeat was total. The strikebreakers remained at work, represented by their union, while they were unemployed. While the settlement ended the strike, it left a residue of bitterness in the strike towns both against the company and the UPIU. [Ronald L. Filippelli]

FURTHER READING

Benjamin, Daniel. "Labor's Boardroom Guerrilla." *Time* (June 20, 1988), p. 50.

English, Carey W. "When Jobless Line Up for Strikers' Jobs." *U.S. News and World Report* (November 28, 1988), p. 89.

Marcial, Gene G. "What Weights International Paper Down?" *Business Week* (June 27, 1983), pp. 33–34.

Satchell, Michael. "The Strikers Strike Out." *U.S. News and World Report* (October 26, 1987), pp. 41–42.

o o o

PASSAIC, NEW JERSEY, TEXTILE STRIKE OF 1926. The strike in Passaic was precipitated by a 10 percent wage cut instituted in October 1925, and ongoing conditions considered unbearable by the workers' community. The strike extended from Passaic to Clifton, Lodi, and Garfield, New Jersey. The workers were largely of immigrant stock, mainly Polish and Italian. Low wages forced men to work extra shifts, women, often pregnant, to work nights, and children to leave school in order to supplement family incomes.

The strike was not only a struggle between labor and management. It drew hostile pressure from local society, drew police brutality, and caused an internecine battle between the leadership of the strike and the hierarchy of the American Federation of Labor (AFL). In addition, local church congregations were split in their allegiance.

Passaic is halved by a river. The countryside was dotted with Greek and Roman Catholic churches. People on the east side of the rail tracks were over 60 percent foreign born. Less than 10 percent of the millworkers lived on the west or better side of town. The east side was lined with dark tenements of a type long since outlawed in New York City. Rents for these flats were fifteen dollars per month for three dark rooms and up to thirty dollars for more cheerful quarters.

Textile factory wages lagged behind most industries, including its sister industry, the clothing trade. In addition, it continued to defy unionization. It was also one of the most protected industries in the country. Forty-seven percent of Passaic's textile workers earned less than $1,000 a year and 71 percent earned less than $1,200. Only the men who repaired the looms were paid a living wage of between thirty and forty dollars per week.

Many mothers on the east side of town were forced to work nights—a practice that was at that time outlawed in most American states. The New Jersey law was then in abeyance. These women earned around fifteen dollars per week. At the time of the strike, night work was almost universal for Passaic's working-class women. They worked as spinners, carders, and weavers. The work was heavy, required standing, lifting, and often constant walking. The number of workers had been reduced which increased the workload for those who remained. In addition, the noise level from machinery was high, oil soaked the floor, and the air was kept humid to prevent the threads on the looms from breaking.

Many women fell asleep at their machines, often damaging goods or injuring themselves. They worked well into their pregnancies, since a new birth would be a drain on the family budget. Giving birth on the mill floor was not uncommon.

Mill owners worked diligently against union organizing. They argued that they were experiencing hard times and could not afford to maintain wages, let alone raise them. Yet an independent study showed a 93 percent annual profit.

The 10 percent wage cut on October 5, 1925, literally meant starvation to many members of the millworkers' community—especially to young children and the elderly. A United Front committee began to be organized at the Botany Mill. By January of 1926, it had one thousand members. On January 26, Gustave Deak, president of Local 1603 of the United Textile Workers' (UTW), went to Colonel Johnson of Botany to present the workers' demand for an abrogation of the wage cut. Johnson responded by firing Deak and the committee. Then Botany's 1,000 union members led a walkout of its 6,000 employees. By the end of the week, two more mills and 3,000 more workers were on strike.

A parade of the strikers through the center of town included all ages and family members. The strikers demanded a restitution of the 10 percent wage cut and an additional 10 percent increase, the forty-four-hour workweek, decent working conditions, no discrimination against union workers, and union recognition.

The next goal of the strikers was to close the Forstman-Huffman plant. To this end, they marched across the Ackerman bridge to Clifton, from whence they were beaten back and chased by police, while the American press took pictures. By the end of the fourth week, the number of strikers reached 10,000, and Forstman-Huffman

closed the plant, claiming that it was for the protection of their workers.

By March, the strike spread to the Dundee Textile Company, a silk mill employing about 300 workers, and on March 11, it included about 4,000 workers from the National Silk Dyeing Company of Paterson, located in Lodi. In all, the strikers now numbered about 16,000.

They held firm against corrupt city officials' attempts to limit pickets and harass them. The American Civil Liberties Union charged that nearly 100 cases of uncalled for assaults against strikers by local police had occurred. On April 10, the strike leader, Albert Weisbord, was arrested without a warrant and held incommunicado for two days. He was charged with inciting to riot and released on a $50,000 bail bond.

Two days later, strikers and their supporters were arrested while dispersing in response to an order from the Bergen County sheriff. Bail for those arrested, including a representative of the American Civil Liberties Union and a member of the press, was set at $10,000 each. Meeting halls in Garfield were illegally closed, and Norman Thomas, Socialist Party chairman, was arrested there and released under another $10,000 bail bond.

Another major problem was the unwillingness of the American Federation of Labor to support the strike, largely because of antipathy toward the strike leader, Albert Weisbord. Weisbord was a native New Yorker, a graduate of City College and Harvard Law School. After passing his bar examinations he became a weaver in New England and worked at this trade there and in Paterson, New Jersey, where he was a member of the Associated Silk Workers of Paterson.

The objection of AFL president William Green to Weisbord was based on the charge that he was a Communist. The strikers in New Jersey either ignored the charge or considered it irrelevant. Weisbord appealed to Green to support the strike on the grounds that it represented legitimate labor demands against management.

The scene of the struggle, after six months of the strike, spread to Washington. Senators William Borah and Robert LaFollette and civic leader W. Jett Lauck attempted to intercede to end the strike. Colonel Johnson of Botany had indicated that he would negotiate with the strikers if Weisbord would leave. He indicated that he would be willing to negotiate with the United Textile Workers if they were affiliated with the AFL. Weisbord agreed to remove himself from the scene if it would mean AFL support for the union and the strike. This was accomplished when Weisbord stepped down from leadership of the strike the Thursday before Labor Day. It was a bittersweet moment for the 8,000 new members of the UTW/AFL. They had won half their battle—they were members of the mainstream of American labor, but the cost was the loss of a valued leader and a trusted friend.

Mainstream rank-and-file labor had supported Passaic all along. Among the unions who sent support to the strikers of Passaic were the Amalgamated Clothing Workers, the International Ladies' Garment Workers', United Mine Workers, branches of the Workmen's Circle, the Workers (Communist) Party, and various locals of the Bakers' Union. The last drew cheers when bringing truckloads of bread from New York. Three bakers were arrested by local police. Support was also forthcoming from such diverse figures as Elizabeth Gurley Flynn, Mrs. Gifford Pinchot, Dr. Stephen Wise, Mrs. Louise Wise, Justine Wise, Fanny Hurst, Rebecca West, and Jeanette Rankin.

Colonel Johnson then alienated the public by going back on his word and refusing to negotiate with the new AFL union or the Lauck committee or anyone else. He and his allies attempted to end the strike by simply declaring it over. This tactic did not work. Police harassment against strikers, their children, and any supporter of the strike continued. Unable to break the strike in the fall, mill owners charged twenty-one strikers with a bomb plot. This was never substantiated.

Civic and religious leaders now rallied to the cause of settlement. By November 1, the end was drawing near. On December 13, 333 days after the strike had begun, Botany capitulated to the union and settled. Workers were given the right to organize and bargain collectively; an impartial grievance arbitration system was put in place; there was to be no discrimination against union members who returned to their jobs.

The strike was notable for the unity of all ethnic groups and ages. Women were prominent among the pickets, arrestees, and organizers. One heroine of the strike was Lena Chernenco who symbolized the women who went out at four in the morning to picket duty, in winter or summer, in cold, snow, or rain.

By the new year, all the mills had settled. The strike was over, but the issue of labor solidarity contined to be unresolved. [Harriet Davis-Kram]

FURTHER READING

deLima, Agnes. *Night Workers in Textile Mills—Passaic, New Jersey.* New York: Consumers' League, 1920.

Siegel, Morton. *The Passaic Textile Strike of 1926.* Ph.D. dissertation, Columbia University, 1953.

Vorse, Mary Heaton. *The Passaic Textile Strike, 1926–1927.* Passaic, NJ: General Relief Committee of Textile Strikers, 1927.

Weisbord, Albert. *Passaic: The Story of a Struggle against Starvation Wages and for the Right to Organize.* Chicago, IL: The Daily Worker, 1926.

o   o   o

PATERSON, NEW JERSEY, STRIKE OF 1828. Although Paterson, New Jersey, has received far less attention from historians than many other northern factory towns, it was a key center of both industrial production and labor conflict in the early nineteenth century. Founded as the site of the nation's first planned manufacturing community in 1793, it experienced two major walkouts of cotton textile operatives in 1828 and 1835 [see **Paterson Strike of 1835**] and a strike by machine shop workers in 1836. A key element in accounting for the unusual level of tension between employers and wage earners was the nature of the local economy. Unlike their chief competitors in Lowell, Massachusetts, Paterson manufacturers did not draw upon the resources of major financial institutions to finance their cotton mills and machine shops. This resulted in the establishment of a host of chronically underfunded small and medium-sized factories. Ongoing efforts by mill and shop owners to increase output while keeping costs in check brought them into repeated conflict with their workers. The first of these confrontations arose during the summer of 1828. On July 16, 1828, the following notice appeared in the *Paterson Intelligencer*:

The subscribers hereby give notice to their workers and others, that after Saturday, the 19th July, 1828 they will stop their mills and factories, at half past seven o'clock in the morning, for breakfast, and at one o'clock P.M. for dinner. This arrangement we consider will divide the day in a more equal manner than heretofore, and prove of advantage to the workers.

Signed by twenty employers, including a weave shop owner, two millwrights, a dyer, a machinist, a turner, two blacksmiths and twelve cotton mill owners, the proposed changes affected nearly 50 percent of all Patersonians employed in manufacturing. On Saturday, July 19 at twelve o'clock noon, their usual lunch hour, factory operatives walked out of the mills without permission. The next day skilled carpenters, masons, and machine makers went on strike. By Monday, all but two of Paterson's textile mills were shut down as were two of its other shops.

Prior organization among local work-

ers contributed to the early success of the strike. It appears that trade societies of hatters, cordwainers, coopers, carpenters, and millwrights existed in Paterson as early as 1812. While both journeymen and master artisans originally joined these groups, they became bona fide workingmen's organizations by the third decade of the nineteenth century. Even mill employees had organized by the mid-1820s. Associations of cotton spinners and weavers, carrying beautifully decorated banners, marched in the annual July 4th parade in 1826. These groups doubtless took the lead in mobilizing the opposition to the actions of their employers.

The strikers and their local supporters held a public meeting on Tuesday, July 22 to draw up a set of demands to place before their employers. The first resolution passed at the meeting affirmed ". . . that from this day forward 12 o'clock shall be our dinner hour." While another one, put forward by skilled journeymen, stated that ten hours was to be ". . . considered a full day's work in the town of Paterson." The people attending the meeting decided to hold another one on the night of the 24th to ". . . establish a fund for the support of those who may be thrown out of employment in consequence of the above measures."

The accepted resolutions reflected two separate yet interrelated concerns. For the striking millhands, who were primarily adolescents and young women, the unilateral change in the lunch hour represented a direct attack by an organized group of employers against a time-honored condition of employment. Antebellum workers often viewed any alteration of customary work practices as a direct challenge to their basic rights as citizens. While switching the lunch hour also affected skilled craftsmen, their demand for a ten-hour workday mirrored the efforts of building tradesmen in Boston, Philadelphia, and New York to reduce their working time. They feared that consistently prolonged hours of labor jeopardized their ability to be with their families and prevented them from participating in the civic duties that were an integral part of citizenship in a republic. For both groups of wage earners, changes in the organization of work raised fundamental questions about their status in American society.

The regional press expressed great interest in the causes of the strike, its leadership, and the long-term implications of similar incidents. The *New York Evening Post* claimed that the turnout resulted from the efforts of weavers and spinners to gain a pay increase while the *Statesmen*, another New York newspaper, blamed agitators from England for the dispute. The *New York Commercial Advertiser* charged that the strikers were all supporters of Andrew Jackson's presidential drive and that they only shut down factories operated by their national Republican opponents. The *Evening Post*, a Democratic paper, turned this charge on its head by identifying the confrontation as an "Adams riot," since the mill owners provoked the incident in the first place by changing the lunch hour. Ultimately, the *Paterson Intelligencer* set its out-of-town rivals straight:

The misunderstanding was one purely of personal interest and convenience, and had no connection either with the supposed influence of the late tariff nor with the approaching presidential election. It originated from an attempt on the part of a number of proprietors to change the hours of dinner with a view to divide the time more equally; and an effort at the same time by the mechanics to reduce the number of working hours in a day from eleven to ten.

The strike continued for nearly three weeks. As in many other early industrial conflicts, there were a number of acts of sabotage. An arsonist unsuccessfully attempted to burn down one of the struck mills on the night of July 24, while unknown saboteurs cut out the warps on looms in the Phoenix Mill on the same evening. The latter case was unusual in that the Phoenix Mill was one of two Paterson textile factories to

remain in operation during the strike mainly because its owner had not attempted to change the lunch hour. Although rewards ranging from $50 to $500 were posted, the perpetrators were never found.

Although employers claimed that the walkout ended on their terms, a close reading of a letter to the *New York Commercial Advertiser* on August 8, 1828, indicates that at best the outcome was a draw:

I am happy to say that the children have yielded their position and most of the mechanics returned quietly to work, to take their dinner at 1 o'clock. Order being completely restored the employers re-established the hour of 12 for dinner. The children are perfectly docile and appear sorry for their conduct. The ringleaders of the mechanics, among whom were some Manchester Mobiles, have been discharged and things are going on quietly.

The very fact that the mill and shop owners restored the original lunch hour indicates that their triumph was far from complete. Unlike their northern New England counterparts, Paterson manufacturers lived and worked in town, often within sight of the factories and the homes of their employees. They never exercised the kind of control over local political or social institutions that mill owners in Lowell or Waltham did, their influence over their employees often extending only to the gates of their manufactories. The widespread coverage given the strike by newspapers in New York and surrounding communities did little to enhance Paterson's reputation as a place to invest in or settle. When combined with the unified opposition of a large segment of the town's work force, these factors eventually forced employers to alter their original plans.

The 1828 strike marked a decisive turning point in the relationship between employers and workers in Paterson. In the wake of the turnout, cotton mill owners accelerated their investment in power driven machinery in order to decrease their dependence on skilled workers. By 1832, they had all but eliminated the use of handlooms in both their mills and in the homes of outworkers. While some weavers found employment in the factories, many left Paterson to look for work elsewhere. Advances in the technology of cotton thread and yarn production also lessened the need for the services of highly skilled mule spinners. These changes, in turn, led to the collapse of local textile trade societies.

The election of Andrew Jackson to the presidency soon after the strike provided a political focus for the growing split between Paterson employers and workingmen. Although a number of mill and shop owners initially supported Jackson, they soon grew disenchanted with his economic policies and egalitarian rhetoric. By the mid-1830s, almost all of Paterson manufacturers had aligned themselves with the Whig Party, while the Democratic Party had emerged as the primary voice for the political concerns of both skilled and unskilled workers. The joining together of economic and political grievances proved to be a volatile combination that kept Paterson in turmoil for much of the decade. [Howard S. Harris]

FURTHER READING

DeVyver, Frank T. *Organization of Labor in New Jersey Before 1860.* Ph.D. dissertation, Princeton University, 1934.

Harris, Howard. *The Transformation of Ideology in the Early Industrial Revolution: Paterson, New Jersey, 1820–1840.* Ph.D. dissertation, City University of New York, 1985.

o   o   o

PATERSON, NEW JERSEY, STRIKE OF 1835. In response to a rapid rise in the cost of living in 1835, wage earners all across the United States walked off their jobs demanding pay increases and reductions in their hours of work. According to historian John R. Commons, at least sixty-five strikes occurred between January 31 and December 19 of that year. One of the bitterest con-

frontations took place in Paterson, New Jersey, when over 2,000 workers employed in the town's cotton and linen duck mills went on strike. The conflict deeply divided the community and became a *cause célèbre* for labor activists all across the country.

While the need for an increase in wages represented the immediate catalyst for the turnout, the young men and children who worked in the mills had other grievances as well. They were fined twenty-five cents if they failed to arrive at their machines before the actual start of the workday. The mill owners expected them to clean their machines at the end of their shift, thus adding at least an hour of unpaid labor to their daily schedules. In order to prevent their millhands from leaving their jobs without prior notice, employers often held back a week's wages as security. Workers claimed that they often had to work twelve or thirteen hours a day, especially during the summer months when conditions in the poorly ventilated mills often became unbearable. Attempts to protest fines or other examples of unfair treatment almost always resulted in automatic dismissal.

The strike began on July 3 and continued for six weeks, mainly because of the unwillingness of the manufacturers to consider any mediation of the dispute. Paterson mill owners repeatedly claimed that the women and children working in their manufactories had higher wages, more holidays, and better treatment than any other group of factory hands in the country. They pointed out that the young women performing more complex tasks received piece rates and that they actually requested more hours so as to increase their weekly take home pay. Employers perceived the strike as totally unnecessary, a rationalization which justified their unwillingness to meet with their employees or a committee of townspeople chosen to try and find some solution to the impasse.

In order to provide relief for the striking millhands, relatives and local supporters established the Paterson Association for the Protection of the Working Classes of Paterson. Members of the organization elected some of the town's most militant labor activists as their leaders. Peter Lydecker played a major role in the organization of journeymen carpenters and served as one of the Paterson delegates to the trades union in nearby Newark. Joseph Edwards who had five of his eight children working in the mills, served as the chairman of an initial meeting to establish a cordwainers union in town. Another shoeworker, Edward Earle, served as the Paterson correspondent for George Henry Evans' *Working Man's Advocate* of New York and played an important role in the founding of a local branch of the Anti-Union of Church and State Society. Under their leadership the Paterson Association became a key element in the strike and received much of the blame from the mill owners for the continuation of the dispute. They and their supporters singled out Edwards for particularly abusive treatment. In a letter to the *Paterson Intelligencer* on July 29, they charged that he lived off the wages of his children rather than making the effort to earn a decent living for his family. According to the letter, there was "none more conspicuous than a certain lazy shoemaker who instead of making shoes, makes speeches at the corners of the streets and in market places. Yes, instead of working for his children, his children work for him."

The tone of the letter reflected the anger and hostility generated by the strike. Textile manufacturers particularly resented the support given to the strike by organized workers in other towns. A delegation from the Newark Trades Union attended a meeting of the Paterson Association on July 27 to determine what kind of support they could provide for the workers. Mechanics in Belleville, New Jersey passed a resolution of support stating ". . . that we view with feelings of abhorrence the attempt of the employers to coerce by starvation, the women and

children by requiring of them 13.5 hours per day." The United Blacksmiths Society of New Haven, Connecticut, forwarded ten dollars "for those poor children in Paterson" while the *Daily Pittsburgh Gazette* lashed out at the mill owners:

To make a child of eight or twelve years of age labor thirteen hours a day is brutal tyranny. It is most unmanly and unnatural which not only makes a slave of the helpless creature for the time, which inflicts on it an injury for life, stinting the growth of its mind as well as body, and in many cases preventing it from attaining adult proportions.

A delegation of Boston trade unionists stopped over in Paterson on its way to a meeting with the Philadelphia Trades Union. After investigating conditions in the town, it moved on to Philadelphia accompanied by delegates from Paterson, Newark, and New York. This same group then travelled to New York where an unidentified Patersonian described the condition of the strikers for the delegates to the New York Trades Union. The union subsequently held a public meeting at Tammany Hall to build support for the Paterson workers. Each ward established a three-man committee to solicit funds for the factory operatives.

Workers in Newark provided the most consistent support for the walkout. After a meeting on July 26, each Newark trades union appointed a two-man committee to raise relief funds from their respective organizations. In three days they collected over $200. The trades union dispatched the money with a delegation to Paterson to decide ". . . the disposition thereof as will best carry into effect the intentions of the donors." The delegation also conducted an investigation of the progress of the strike, interviewing members of the Paterson Association, "respectable citizens," and individual strikers. They presented a lengthy report to a meeting of Newark workers on August

5. They observed that strikers remained away from their jobs because of the "arbitrary and uncompromising course by their employers."

The outside support given to the workers infuriated mill owners and their supporters:

The great length to which this "turnout" has extended is mainly to be attributed to the impertinent and unjustifiable interference of some persons connected with the trades union in Newark and New York, who have made it their business to visit this place with the express purpose of urging the children, by inflammatory speeches, to continue their present strike, and holding out to them promises that they should be sustained in it until the employers should accede to their terms.

Even with such support the mill operatives could not remain on strike indefinitely. By August 19, the *Intelligencer* reported that most, if not all, of the mills had reopened and that ". . . our town has again resumed its wanted cheerfulness and is now a scene of industry and contentment. . . ." Edward Earle confirmed the turn of events in a letter to the *Workingman's Advocate*. He claimed that employers refused to rehire some of the children because their parents had been active in supporting the strike and that notices had been posted at some of the mills identifying leaders of the Paterson Association. Some mill owners reportedly docked returning workers a week's pay in order to recoup some of their financial losses. Full-scale operations resumed in the mills by the first week of September. Factory owners officially blacklisted twenty-seven employees with the ban to remain in effect for a full year. Although the decision angered area trade unionists, there was little they could do to assist the Paterson workers.

The defeat of the strike and the advent of a nationwide economic depression two years later squelched any effort by the Paterson millworkers to improve their working conditions well into the 1850s. Although skilled craftsmen maintained an effective trades union organization for a period of time and conducted a successful strike against master machinists in 1836, they too fell victim to the collapse of the economy. The failure of workplace action convinced a number of labor leaders to invest more time and energy in electoral politics. Some of the men involved in the Paterson Association and the short-lived Paterson Trades Union, which was organized during the walkout, successfully ran for office on the Democratic Party ticket in the late 1830s and early 1840s. Although occasional, brief strikes took place in Paterson throughout the 1840s and 1850s, there was no further citywide mobilization of wage earners until 1863, when the hardships of the Civil War years sparked a new upsurge of labor activism across the United States. [Howard S. Harris]

FURTHER READING

DeVyver, Frank T. *Organization of Labor in New Jersey Before 1860.* Ph.D. dissertation, Princeton University, 1934.

Harris, Howard. *The Transformation of Ideology in the Early Industrial Revolution: Paterson, New Jersey, 1820–1840.* Ph.D. dissertation, City University of New York, 1985.

o   o   o

PATERSON, NEW JERSEY, TEXTILE STRIKE OF 1913. The strike by silk workers in the city of Paterson, New Jersey, which began in January 1913, and lasted until the end of July, allied laborers and intellectuals, reformers and revolutionaries, Socialists and syndicalists. Like the **Lawrence, Massachusetts, Textile Strike** a year earlier, the conflict in Paterson saw the Industrial Workers of the World (IWW), or Wobblies, assist a mass of theretofore unorganized workers effectively administer a protracted strike. Occurring only twenty-five miles west of Manhattan, the conflict in Paterson generated enormous publicity for the strikers and the IWW in the media and cultural capital of the American nation. During the course of the strike, such intellectuals and cultural rebels as John Reed, Walter Lippmann, Max Eastman, the painter John Sloan, and the famous Greenwich Village salon hostess, Mabel Dodge, experienced aspects of the class war in the United States through visits to Paterson or meetings with strikers and Wobblies. Before the strike ended, New York's bohemian intellectual community worked closely with the silk workers to stage one of the most famous events in American labor history, the "Paterson Strike Pageant," a full-scale dramatization of the industrial conflict that played before an overflow audience at Madison Square Garden.

In 1913, Paterson was one of the oldest industrial cities in the United States. Owing to its strategic location on a falls in the Passaic River, Paterson was chosen by Alexander Hamilton as early as the 1790s to be the site of the first major industrial development in the nation. Although Hamilton's plan never materialized, in the course of the nineteenth century Paterson developed a productive and profitable manufacturing economy built around the production of railroad locomotives and other metal products. As industry expanded, thousands of immigrants from the British Isles and Germany poured into the city's factories. By 1913, however, Paterson's economy had become less diverse while its laboring population had grown more polyglot. In 1913, the city led the nation in the production of silk, its more than 300 mills and dyehouses employing about 25,000 men, women, and children—a third of the city's work force. Some of the older British and German stock workers still found employment as the trade's most highly skilled employees in the weaving of silk ribbon. The dyehouses and the mills where cheaper grades of silk were produced, however, recruited the bulk of their workers from the Italian, Jewish, and other immigrant nationalities from the south and east of Europe.

If silk was the single most important product of Paterson in the year 1913, it was also an industry in economic peril. Newer, more modern, lower-cost silk mills in the southern part of the state, northeastern Pennsylvania, and elsewhere were capturing a larger share of the market. In order to compete, Paterson's manufacturers saw no alternative to reducing their cost of production than through lowering wages, intensifying labor, and introducing new machinery. As a consequence, the silk manufacturers threatened their employees' standards and traditions. And in Paterson, unlike Lawrence, Massachusetts, employers dealt with a work force that had a long history of unionism, strikes, and radicalism.

Ever since the 1870s, industrial conflict, unions, and socialism had been a part of Paterson's history. Shortly before the turn of the century, Italian immigrants had turned the city into a center for the propagation of anarchism. Moreover, since its founding in 1905, the Industrial Workers of the World (IWW) had maintained an organizational presence in Paterson. Even more important, the skilled ribbon weavers had a tradition of resistance to their employers that often expressed itself through strikes. Thus, as employers cut piece rates or demanded that workers tend four rather than two looms, Paterson's toilers resisted the changes spasmodically. Strikes and protests punctuated the year 1912, the result, according to one silk worker, ". . . of deep-seated grievances in the hearts and minds of the strikers." The skilled workers probably protested more to defend their traditional manner of work than their material standards which remained decent. Among the newer immigrant workers who labored as family units and who pooled their earnings to subsist, however, the intensification of labor and improved looms threatened to reduce employment opportunities. When, in January 1913, employees of Doherty and Company, the largest mill in Paterson, rebelled at the firm's decision to switch from the two-loom to the four-loom method, Local 152 of the IWW was ready to move into action. "There was a fruitful and fertile soil when the IWW dropped its seed . . . in Paterson," remembered one new recruit, "which rapidly took root and spread."

The IWW wasted little time capitalizing on the initial protest by the employees of Doherty. It spread its own message of rebellion and radicalism among all of the company's workers, and by February 1 it had succeeded in inducing a walkout among the firm's entire work force. From this firm, the Wobblies broadened their struggle to encompass all the silk workers in the city.

Because no single enterprise dominated the production of silk in Paterson, the strike leaders reasoned that only a general walkout could accomplish the workers' aims. Carrying their message from mill to mill, the agitators brought out growing numbers of workers; starting on February 25, 1,200 workers a day left their jobs until 25,000 silk workers had put down their tools and completely paralyzed the city's silk industry. At the time, the strikers had only two demands: the eight-hour workday and a minimum weekly wage of twelve dollars for dyehouse workers who performed the filthiest work in the industry.

When the strike began, Local 152 had at most 900 members. Two weeks later, it claimed 10,000, and its membership rolls continued to rise. As it had done in Lawrence, the IWW in Paterson formed the previously non-union strikers into a united and effective force. Each shop selected two delegates to represent it on a general strike committee that numbered 600 at full strength. The strike committee supervised all aspects of the conflict and had total responsibility for negotiating its resolution. When reporters asked members of the committee who their leaders were, the strike representatives responded: "We are all leaders." One of the national IWW leaders active in Paterson, Elizabeth Gurley Flynn, ex-plained more precisely how the strike was stimulated and administered. "The preparation and declaration as well as the stimulation of the strike was all done by the IWW, by the militant minority among the silk workers; the administering of the strike was done democratically by the silk workers themselves." That the IWW did a superb job in welding the disparate thousands of strikers firmly together was attested to by the social scientist and reformer, John Fitch, who wrote, "empty handed, with neither money nor credit nor with the prestige of a 2,000,000 membership, but willing to go to work and to go to jail. They [the Wobblies] have put into the 25,000 strikers a spirit that has made them stand together with a united determination for a period that must have tried the souls of the strongest."

As in Lawrence, the strikers in Paterson fought a largely peaceful struggle. To be sure, the silk workers used moral and communal suasion to intimidate potential strikebreakers in their ranks or neighborhoods, and harsh words, hostile looks, and fisticuffs were not uncommon. Overall, however, the strikers remained pacific in their behavior, heeding the advice of their leaders to engage in the most effective form of violence for workers, quitting the job. "Your power is your folded arms," said IWW speakers. "You have killed the mills; you have stopped production; you have broken off profits. Any other violence you may commit is less than this." The longer the strike lasted—and it went from February through March into April and on into the summer months—the harder the leaders struggled to maintain morale, to keep workers on the picket lines, and to preserve the peace.

Although the strikers waged a nonviolent battle, their enemies did not reciprocate. At one time or another, all the national and local IWW leaders involved in the conflict experienced some form of legal repression. William D. Haywood, Carlo Tresca, Elizabeth Gurley Flynn, Patrick Quinlan, and Adolph Lessig, among others were arrested, arraigned, jailed, indicted, and tried. Even the young journalist, poet, and rebel John Reed, who went to Paterson to write about the class war in America, ran afoul of the city's police, who arrested him during a melee with strikers. "There's war in Paterson," Reed wrote hyperbolically in the *Masses*. "But it's a curious kind of war. All the violence is the work of one side—the Mill Owners."

The manufacturers battled as hard as they did for good reason. Most of them saw their enterprises in peril if they conceded the strikers' demands for the eight-hour day, higher wages, and fewer looms to tend. Already, Paterson's employers could not compete equally with enterprises elsewhere that paid lower wages for higher production. Moreover, several of the larger Paterson firms operated lower-cost enterprises in other locations. They could shift production from Paterson to their other sites and ride out the strike with minimal loss in their market share. The will to survive economically, and in some cases the financial ability to do so, caused the silk manufacturers to endure a strike that began in February 1913, and persisted until July.

The length of the strike tried not only the workers' patience; it soon left them bereft of material resources. With income and credit vanished, the strikers depended for their sustenance on contributions from the IWW and other sympathizers. Neither the IWW nor the sympathizers, however, could provide as much as the strikers needed. As one alternative to surrender, the strike leaders transported the silk workers' children to foster families in other cities. John Reed and his friends in Greenwich Village suggested a better alternative: an elaborate public spectacle with script, music, and a cast composed of thousands of strikers to dramatize the cause of the strikers. Thus was born the "Paterson Strike Pageant." As scripted by Reed, designed by his strikers and their leaders, the "Pageant" was a grand success, packing Madison Square Garden

and winning fine reviews in New York's newspapers and magazines. Unfortunately, the performance itself produced no profits (precisely what its promoters expected of a single expensively mounted production) and generated much sympathy but far too little material support for the strikers. Dramatically the high point of the conflict in Paterson and also the apogee of cooperation between intellectuals and workers, strikers and bohemians, the "Pageant" ushered the strike into its final stage.

By early summer of 1913, few of the strikers had the will or the resources to continue their struggle. First, the skilled ribbon weavers and then the less skilled workers on the strike committee began to negotiate separate agreements with employers. On July 18, the English-speaking ribbon weavers separated themselves from the newer immigrants on the strike committee and came to their own agreement with employers. Cast adrift by their more skilled brothers, the remainder of the strikers rushed to settle on the best terms that they could command. By July 28, the strike was over and the workers were back in the mills having agreed to accept the wages and working conditions similar to those that had initially precipitated the conflict.

Not only did the great silk strike of 1913 end in defeat for the workers of Paterson, but it also ruptured the incipient alliance between intellectuals and labor radicals, workers and bohemians. IWW leaders blamed Greenwich Village cultural figures for misleading them about the potential rewards of the "Paterson Strike Pageant." The Village bohemians grew bored with revolutionaries who could not even win a strike and workers who surrendered meekly to their employers. Socialists castigated syndicalists for their loose talk of violence, and the latter ridiculed the former for preferring reform to revolution. And the silk workers of Paterson went back to their jobs, families, ethnic societies, and churches. Less than six months after the strike ended, Local

152's membership had declined from 10,000 to under 1,500 and was still falling.

The IWW, which had seemed a powerful radical presence after its victory in Lawrence in March 1912, was much diminished by its defeat in Paterson. As the labor economist Robert Hoxie reported after attending the convention of the IWW in 1913, the IWW "instead of being the grim, brooding power which it is pictured in popular imagination, is a body utterly incapable of strong, efficient, united action and the attainment of results of a permanent character; a body capable of local and spasmodic effort only . . . it has no present power . . . of constructive action." [Melvyn Dubofsky]

FURTHER READING

Dubofsky, Melvyn. *We Shall Be All: A History of the IWW*. Chicago, IL: Quadrangle Books, 1969.

Foner, Philip S. *History of the Labor Movement in the United States*, Volume 4: *The Industrial Workers of the World, 1905–1917*. New York: International Publishers, 1965.

Golin, Steve. *The Fragile Bridge; Paterson Silk Strike, 1913*. Philadelphia, PA: Temple University Press, 1988.

Tripp, Anne Huber. *The IWW and the Paterson Silk Strike of 1913*. Urbana, IL: University of Illinois Press, 1987.

o   o   o

PAWTUCKET, RHODE ISLAND, STRIKE OF 1824. The walkout of female operatives from the cotton mills of Pawtucket, Rhode Island, late in the spring of 1824 is considered to be the first bona fide strike of factory workers in the United States. Sparked by the efforts of the town's mill owners to cut wages and to increase the length of the workday, it represented more than just a protest against changes in working conditions. The strike reflected the growing concern of many people in the early nineteenth century over the economic, social, and political impact of centralized, factory-based production on their communities and the country at large. They viewed growing industrialization as a threat to the sense of themselves as free and independent citizens of a democratic nation.

Unlike many New England villages, Pawtucket had a viable manufacturing economy prior to the arrival of the cotton mills. Skilled artisans working in small shops produced a wide variety of iron goods, while a local shipyard built sailing vessels of all descriptions. Town craftsmen had close ties with area farmers, turning raw agricultural goods into finished commodities in grist, fulling, and linseed oil mills. Both groups envisioned themselves as independent producers free to choose when and how they would work. In their minds, economic freedom was directly linked with their heritage of political freedom derived from the American Revolution.

The building of Samuel Slater's cotton mill and others on the banks of the Blackstone River in the late 1700s and early 1800s represented a challenge to community values and customs. Mill dams interrupted the flow of water to non-cotton producers and interfered with the taking of fish from the river, an important part of the local agricultural economy. Area residents took both legal and direct action to force the mill owners to remove or modify their dams. This tradition of opposition was passed on to the offspring of local farmers and artisans who went to work in the mills.

The work experience in early cotton factories was very different from that which Pawtucket residents were used to. Fixed work hours and days regulated by the clock; direct supervision by overseers; stated policies, rules, and procedures; increased use of machinery; and the ever-present threat of arbitrary discharge ran counter to long-held traditions. Prior to the development of factories, people made little distinction between work and other aspects of their lives. If they felt like going fishing or berry picking they would pack up their tools and leave their shop or work bench. To celebrate the completion of a particular job, a master artisan would purchase a keg of beer for his journeymen and both he and his employees would get roaring drunk. Such behavior was unacceptable to cotton manufacturers who required a dependable, disciplined work force in order for their mills to turn a profit.

In addition to regulating the actions of their millhands on the shop floor, mill owners attempted to extend their control over their employees off the job as well. Employers whole-heartedly supported temperance crusades and moral reform societies and played a key role in the establishment of local churches. They believed that through the encouragement of such activities they could modify or eliminate patterns of behavior that interfered with the efficient operation of their mills. Pawtucket wage earners generally ignored these efforts where possible, continuing to act in accord with long-held habits and customs.

The gulf between manufacturers and their workers came into sharp focus late in the spring of 1824. On May 24, an organized group of mill owners announced that as of June 1 they planned to lengthen the workday by an hour while cutting the wages of their female handloom weavers by nearly 25 percent. Employers pointed out that a sharp drop in the value of finished cloth due to increased competition and an increase in the price of raw cotton threatened their ability to earn a sufficient level of profit. They also claimed that the hours worked in their mills were shorter than those of their competitors and that Pawtucket handloom weavers earned more than their counterparts in other sections of the country. The proposed changes would reduce their labor costs to an acceptable level.

As soon as the operatives learned of their employers decision they walked off their jobs. The striking millhands called a meeting where they decided that no one would return to work until the mill owners rescinded the wage cut. Two days after the turnout began, a large crowd gathered in the streets of Pawtucket to show their support for the operatives. Not only millworkers but also skilled craftsmen joined in the protest. They marched through the town, stopping at the homes of the mill owners to berate them for their mean-spirited and undemocratic behavior. One of the marchers threw a rock through the window of the "Yellow Mill," the only recorded incident of vandalism during the march. In response to the demonstration, employers shut down all of the town's cotton mills.

Five days later, someone attempted to set fire to that same Yellow Mill. Although the effort resulted in little damage, it represented an ominous threat to the interests of Pawtucket textile manufacturers. In the absence of formal trade union organization, sabotage of this kind represented a common form of worker protest during the first three decades of the nineteenth century. The wooden construction of most early mills made them extremely susceptible to fire. An identical incident occurred during a strike of cotton mill operatives in Paterson, New Jersey four years later. Although the arsonists remained anonymous in both fires, there is little doubt that they were directly related to the strikes.

The fire at the Yellow Mill apparently convinced Pawtucket manufacturers to end the conflict. During the first week of June, mill owners met on a number of occasions to come up with an acceptable solution of the strike. Although the exact terms of the settlement remain unknown, on June 5, the *Providence Patriot* reported that work had resumed at the mills under a planned compromise. In all likelihood employers either rescinded or modified their attempts to cut wages and extend the length of the workday.

The turnout provided a valuable lesson for Pawtucket's citizens. In the aftermath of the strike, both sides struggled to strengthen their positions in the community. Cotton manufacturers began to build fireproof mills, moved to gain control of the local political structure, and promoted

Sunday schools and temperance crusades as a means of exerting more influence over the behavior of a fiercely independent work force. Skilled male mule spinners took the first steps toward organizing a trade society in order to protect themselves from the arbitrary misuse of authority by their employers. In 1826, an alliance of local townspeople, including many wage earners, raised funds to install a clock in a new church to compete with the factory bells which rang every morning to summon the mill operatives to work. Even though mill owners dominated the local economy throughout the nineteenth century, they did not obtain real social or political control over the community and its people until well into the 1850s.

The 1824 Pawtucket turnout was significant for a number of reasons. In addition to being the first recorded strike of female factory operatives, it demonstrated the depth of the bonds that bound together wage earners in the New England town. Skilled male artisans and semiskilled female factory operatives shared a common concern over the changes that new forms of economic organization were bringing to their community. They interpreted those changes through a system of values and beliefs that predated the construction of the first cotton mill on the banks of the Blackstone River. As was the case in most early factory towns, people did not object to manufacturing per se, but rather to the violations of local customs and traditions that often accompanied the advent of mill-based manufacturing. The Pawtucket Strike of 1824 was the first in a series that erupted throughout the eastern United States in the 1820s and 1830s as the nation underwent its first period of sustained industrial growth. [Howard S. Harris]

FURTHER READING

Kulik, Gary. "Pawtucket Village and the Strike of 1824: The Origins of Class Conflict in Rhode Island." *Radical History Review*, Vol. 17 (Spring, 1978), pp. 5–37.

Werthheimer, Barbara. *We Were There: The Story of Working Women in America.* New York: Pantheon, 1977.

o o o

PENNSYLVANIA PUBLIC EMPLOYEES' STRIKE OF 1975. On July 1, 1975, following the failure to renegotiate a new contract, over 54,000 unionized workers withheld their services as employees of the Commonwealth of Pennsylvania. The strike was the first major statewide work stoppage since the passage of the Public Employee Relations Act on October 1, 1970, which extended collective bargaining rights to public employees in Pennsylvania. It was also the first general strike by state workers and the largest strike by public employees in the history of the United States. Participating in the strike were the American Federation of State, County and Municipal Employees (AFSCME), which represented 76,000 state employees; the Pennsylvania Social Service Union (PSSU), an affiliate of the Service Employees International Union, representing 10,000 state workers; the Retail Clerks Local 1357, which represented 3,000 state liquor store clerks; the Pennsylvania Nurses Association (PNA), which represented 3,300 nurses in state hospitals, and the Pennsylvania Employment Security Employees Associations (PESEA), which represented about 1,100 workers.

Bargaining strategies for both the commonwealth and the unions were affected by double-digit inflation during the 1973–1975 period. Negotiated pay increases since 1971 plus minimal service increments had kept average wages up to increases in the cost of living, and for lower job classifications, competitive with the private sector.

In addition, the budget for the commonwealth had been submitted to the legislature by Governor Milton J. Shapp in March, prior to any contract settlement with the unions. Pennsylvania's fiscal situation was tight, and the governor's budget had to reflect anticipated funding for negotiated increases that were not yet approved by the legislature. Shapp budgeted for a salary increase of 3.5 percent, well below what the unions were seeking. The commonwealth justified its position by arguing that in addition to any negotiated salary increase, a majority of state employees would receive a 5 percent non-negotiated annual increase in pay.

The general bargaining position of the unions was based on the inflation numbers, success in past contracts, and a recent 10 percent salary increase that had been gained by the state police and the Pennsylvania Turnpike employees. AFSCME, led by its executive director in Pennsylvania, Gerald McEntee, utilized a reopener clause in the contract to enter into bargaining with the commonwealth. The normal contract expiration date was July 1, 1976. AFSCME's initial demands included a $3,000-a-year salary increase, two cents per hour per employee for the health and welfare fund, a free dental insurance plan, full retirement at age sixty or with thirty years of service, a $3,600 minimum pension guarantee, and a cost-of-living escalator clause. In the final stage of bargaining, AFSCME reduced its wage demands and indicated a willingness to settle for a minimum 10 percent increase.

The Pennsylvania Social Services Union (PSSU) sought a one-year contract, a 15 percent salary increase, and a cost-of-living clause. The Retail Clerks Local 1357 wanted a three-year contract with terms similar to recently negotiated agreements with major supermarket chains in the area that included a 29 percent pay increase and a cost-of-living clause.

During the strike little time was spent in face-to-face bargaining. Brief meetings were held during which the parties did little more than exchange information on their respective positions. In anticipation of the strike, the commonwealth had prepared a two-prong plan: to continue to provide essential services by using supervisory personnel and to obtain court orders to force striking employees back to work. The law governing public-sector labor relations in Pennsylvania allowed the issuance of court injunctions if the commonwealth could show that the work stoppage threatened the health, safety, or welfare of the public. Injunctive relief proved to be one of the state's most effective weapons in diminishing the effect of the strike. On the first day of the strike, July 1, the commonwealth court issued back-to-work orders for prison guards and psychiatric security aides at eight correctional institutions and four state hospitals. The following day, the Pennsylvania Nurses Association (PNA) voluntarily entered a preliminary strike injunction in commonwealth court proceedings that resulted in sending 3,000 PNA employees back to work at general hospitals and state mental health and mental retardation institutions. According to one newspaper account, court orders resulted in forcing half of the striking employees back to work.

AFSCME's request to use binding arbitration to settle the dispute was rejected by the commonwealth on the basis of it not wanting a private third-party neutral to decide terms which could result in the citizens having to fund the settlement through increased taxes. The request for arbitration followed a failed attempt at mediation, a process mandated by law prior to any strike activity.

On July 4, the fourth day of the strike, following a nine-hour bargaining session, the 250-member AFSCME bargaining committee approved a two-year contract in a close vote. AFSCME's 650-member policy committee subsequently voted to accept the contract and workers from the largest state employees union began to return to work on July 6. The settlement was considered by many to be a victory for the governor since the wage increases did not exceed the 3.5 percent per year initially offered by the commonwealth. Also, while the total costs of the contract exceeded the budgeted $27.5

million by $6.8 million, the loss could be recovered from the $2 million to $3 million per day in labor costs saved by the state during the strike. In addition to the increase in wages, AFSCME obtained increases in the state's contribution to the health and welfare fund, and amnesty was granted to 5,000 first-level supervisors who struck illegally and to all state employees, including those charged with picketing violations.

The Pennsylvania Social Services Union and the Pennsylvania Employment Security Employees Association remained on strike until July 20. But in spite of two more weeks on the picket lines, the terms of their contracts differed little from the contract signed by AFSCME on July 5.

This first general strike against a state government demonstrated the effective use of back-to-work orders through court-imposed injunctions and indicated that public sector management in Pennsylvania was capable of holding their own in the collective bargaining arena. For the unions, the gain was in the demonstration of their ability to mobilize their members in support of a statewide strike. [Richard Z. Hindle]

FURTHER READING

The Philadelphia Inquirer (June 29–July 20, 1976).

Shapp, Milton J. "The Collective Bargaining Experience in Pennsylvania." *State Government: Public Sector Labor Relations*, (Autumn, 1976), pp. 263–267.

o   o   o

PHELPS-DODGE STRIKE OF 1983–1986. Phelps-Dodge Corporation is a mining operation that has come to symbolize the neo-robber baron or "copper king" mentality that dominated virtually all of the mining camps and smelters of the Far West in the first decades of this century. It was Phelps-Dodge that employed private militia to round up copper miners and others and run them out of town inn boxcars in 1916— the infamous "Bisbee deportation" in Arizona [see **Arizona Copper Strike of 1916**]. Phelps-Dodge dominated the politicians and local and state officials of Arizona. It advocated statehood for Arizona so that it could control political affairs far better than territorial government would allow, and it even employed religious bias in its corporate dominance.

Phelps-Dodge was the hard-liner of the eleven nonferrous companies that resisted a common expiration agreement in the industry, which led to the bitter eight-and-a-half-month strike in 1967–1968. Always known as the last of the industry holdouts in subsequent copper negotiations, Phelps-Dodge found that the political and economic climate in the first term of the administration of conservative Republican President Ronald Reagan provided an appropriate environment in which to eliminate its unions.

By June 1983, the copper industry was in a deep depression, and the country itself was experiencing the most severe recession since the 1930s. At one point in 1982, unemployment reached a rate of 10 percent of the national work force. More than 10 million workers were seeking jobs, and copper companies warned their reduced labor forces that the alternative to concessions could be a shutdown and reopening with an eager non-union pool.

It was going to be a difficult time for the primary unions and the 15,000 estimated workers in the industry under contract (down from more than 60,000 in 1968). The United Steel Workers of America (USWA) represented most of the copper workers, with the Machinists, Operating Engineers, Boilermakers, Teamsters, Electrical Workers, and a scattering of the building and metal trades bargaining for the others.

When Phelps-Dodge refused to go along with the other remaining copper employers (Kennecott, Asarco, Magma, and the one-time industry giant, Anaconda) who had reached "no-pay increase agreements" from the USWA-led coalition of unions, its workers went on strike on July 1, 1983. A dozen unions struck with the USWA.

"Impoverished and hungry workers, Phelps-Dodge believed, would not want to strike and would be willing to cross picket lines. Many were broke and in debt to the company for the housing it provided as well as for provisions from the company store— Phelps-Dodge Mercantile. Phelps-Dodge knew it could turn unemployment into a strikebreaking strategy. It did just that," according to one USWA account.

The union coalition sought only that the cost-of-living allowance (COLA) be retained. Five major producers agreed to the no-wage-increase contract but retained the COLA provision. "Phelps-Dodge rejected it and it even refused a last-minute union offer to drop the COLA. Phelps-Dodge wanted a strike it figured it could win," a union official recalled.

A month after the strike began, then-Arizona governor Bruce Babbitt, a Democrat in a state generally considered to be Republican and conservative in politics and attitudes, responded to the urgings of "law and order" advocates and called out the state's National Guard. It was the first time that the National Guard had been called to intervene in any significant labor dispute in almost half a century in the United States, and the action would in time affect not only the workers and their communities but also Babbitt's political fortunes.

The governor dispatched almost a thousand Guardsmen and members of the state police to concentrate in the towns of Clifton and Morenci, with instructions to defend the strikebreakers hired by the company. In a massive show of force, which some of the strikers who were Vietnam veterans said was "awesome," the state sent in armored personnel carriers, helicopters, SWAT teams with M-16 rifles, and snipers equipped with high-powered guns.

In the small Arizona mining town of Ajo, some 200 miles distant, 325 miners

were holding firm when on August 25 state police surrounded and invaded strikers' homes, and, without warrants, arrested forty people. On the first anniversary of the strike, a peaceful demonstration by strikers, families, and supporters in Clifton ended in a virtual riot when 200 officers of the Arizona Department of Public Safety in riot gear attacked the parade.

The dedication of the striking Phelps-Dodge workers and the loyalty of their families and of most members of the community was never at issue. What combined to wear them down during almost three years of job loss, dislocation, and harassment was a continued pattern of hostility from state law enforcement and federal judicial and labor relations agencies, reflecting the union-busting climate that had been established with President Reagan's mass firing of striking air traffic controllers in 1981 [see **Air Traffic Controllers' Strike of 1981**].

The deep depression in the copper industry had affected more than two-thirds of the jobs in the industry. Those laid off from the other companies found that the prospect of returning to their jobs was doubtful. The four Phelps-Dodge operations in Arizona and the one in El Paso, Texas, after being shut down by their own workers, now sought to employ scabs and targeted the jobless of the other companies.

The USWA assessment of the situation in 1986 captured what had gone from a strike to a desperate imbroglio: "When the company, in spite of its campaign of constant harassment and its vicious terrorizing of the strikers and their families, was unable to lure sufficient numbers of its own employees to come to work, it launched a recruiting program among the jobless of other companies," stated a USWA account.

"With the armed presence of the Arizona National Guard, the union picket lines were forced to give way and the strike by the valiant and determined workers was broken." Only scabs and non-strikers were eligible to vote in the National Labor Relations Board-sanctioned decertification election. The outcome was predictable, and protests about irregularities and company interference in the process were ruled out by the Reagan-dominated NLRB.

The Phelps-Dodge assault on the union became a *cause célèbre* among the emerging anti-Reagan coalition of the early 1980s, and the president of Morenci Local 616 of the USWA, along with others, journeyed to protest rallies in steel towns, union halls, and on college campuses to plead the cause. A "corporate campaign" sought to take the fight to the boardrooms of other companies which had Phelps-Dodge linkage, and it became an issue at the annual meeting of the company for a few years. The company's president declined an invitation to debate with the president of the USWA on the Dartmouth campus, his alma mater, where a student support group had formed.

A bitter legacy of dislocation, family disruption, community divisivenes, and political fallout were consequences of the Phelps-Dodge encounter. The company, which seventy years earlier had employed some of the last of the Western vigilantes to deport its workers, would, in the 1980s, seek protection in the courtrooms and from the administrative law judges of a President who had boasted of his strikebreaking. [Russell W. Gibbons]

FURTHER READING

Lens, Sidney. *Strikemakers and Strikebreakers*. New York: E. P. Dutton, 1985.

Steel Labor. Western Edition, March 1983–October 1986. United Steelworkers of America, Pittsburgh.

United Steelworkers of America. *Then and Now: The Road Between*, 2nd ed. Pittsburgh, PA: United Steelworkers of America, 1986.

o   o   o

PHILADELPHIA BOOKBINDERS' STRIKE OF 1836. While the demand for the ten-hour workday dominated labor conflict in 1835, unions returned to wage demands

the following year. The success of the shorter-hour movement had given hope to the new trade unions and citywide labor federations that had emerged since 1833. Sixty-nine strikes occurred during 1836, only one of which was for the ten-hour workday, while most of the rest centered on higher wages.

Much of this demand was fueled by the rapid inflation that had raised the price of food to double the 1833 level. In New York, the house carpenters, tin plate and sheet iron workers, handloom weavers, leather-dressers, cordwainers, shoebinders, and a dozen other trades declared their intention to strike to win a twenty-five-cents-a-day increase. In most cases the workers won.

Philadelphia experienced a similar surge of wage-driven strikes. Here, as in New York, the carpenters took the lead. Other trades followed. Unlike New York, however, two bitter disputes marred the Philadelphia movement. The most bitter involved the cordwainers who struck for at least three months for five and a quarter cents more on each pair of shoes, a sixty-cents-a-week increase. To counter a boycott of uncooperative employers by the union, the employers joined with shoe merchants, dry goods merchants, and leather dealers in a show of employer solidarity. Little is known about the outcome of the strike, except to note that in the face of the employer's united front, the shoemakers organized a cooperative in the second week of June 1835, to compete with their former masters

The strike that most galvanized the labor movement and the populace of Philadelphia, however, involved the bookbinders. The primary cause of the strike was to standardize the wages of bookbinders in the city and county of Philadelphia, where they varied from 25 to 50 percent. The workers drew up a bill of prices in October 1835, during the busy season of the trade, and got reluctant agreement from their employers. Soon after the beginning of 1836, however, when slow times returned, the employers cut the rates to the previous level. The journeymen refused to accept the lower wages and a strike began.

The employers were well prepared. They issued a list of the strikers for publication throughout the country in an attempt to blacklist unionists. Advertisements for skilled bookbinders were placed in other cities. Finally, the employers arranged that booksellers in the city would give no work to master binders who employed union members nor give work to any establishment that recognized a union. Given the wretched pay and working conditions of the bookbinders, even under the now-rejected price list, it seems clear that the real purpose of the employers was to break the union.

Unionists in other cities recognized the sophisticated employer response in Philadelphia as a threat to all unions, and they rallied around the bookbinders against their "self-styled masters." Fraternal support came from New York, Washington, Newark, and elsewhere and enabled the bookbinders to hold out. Indeed, so solid was the support for the bookbinders from other Philadelphia unions and unions elsewhere that the employers were forced, after six weeks, to offer to meet with the leaders of the strikers.

The effort resulted in nothing, and the strike lasted another six weeks before it was resolved with a victory for the workers. In thanking the other unions for the solidarity that made it possible for them to win, the bookbinders identified their struggle as "the sacred cause of every skilled labourer in the civilised world." While that was no doubt extreme, it is accurate to say that the Philadelphia bookbinders' strike did demonstrate the possibilities for coordination and support that the new city central federations offered to the fledgling labor movement of the antebellum period. [Ronald L. Filippelli]

FURTHER READING

Commons, John R., et al. *History of Labour in the United States*, Vol 1. New York: Macmillan, 1936.

Foner, Philip. *History of the Labor Movement in the United States: From Colonial Times to the Founding of the American Federation of Labor*, Vol. 1. New York: International Publishers, 1947.

o   o   o

PHILADELPHIA CARPENTERS' STRIKE OF 1791. The first known strike in the building trades occurred in Philadelphia in May of 1791 when the Journeymen Carpenters of the City and Liberties of Philadelphia struck against their employers, the master carpenters. Although the carpenters complained about low wages and the penchant of the masters to drive down wages, the strike was caused by a demand for a shorter day's work, with additional pay for overtime. The strikers agreed among themselves that they would not return to work until a day's work would begin at six in the morning and end at six in the evening.

The masters denied an interest in oppressing the carpenters and blamed the poor conditions in the trade on the difficulties of securing raw materials, supervising the workers, and providing tools—all of which left precious little profit for the employers. The masters were generally small contractors operating on a small margin. Most had been journeymen themselves. The cost of labor was essential to them in an industry characterized by competitive bidding for contracts offered by the merchant capitalists and landowners who financed the projects.

The carpenters lost the strike, but afterward they organized the Union Society of Carpenters, a cooperative, and advertised their willingness to "undertake buildings, or give designs, of any work in the line of our occupation . . . at 25 percent below the current rate established by the Master-Carpenters." The masters accused the strikers of reducing prices so as to force their submission and argued that the action would only work to the disadvantage of the carpenters and would not benefit anyone. [Ronald L. Filippelli]

FURTHER READING

Commons, John R., et al. *History of Labour in the United States*, Vol. 1. New York: Macmillan, 1936.

o   o   o

PHILADELPHIA CARPENTERS' STRIKE OF 1827. The modern American labor movement began in Philadelphia in 1827 as the result of the formation of a union of journeymen carpenters in order to secure the ten-hour workday. Failure in that struggle led to the formation of the first city central labor federation, the Mechanics Union of Trade Associations, and ultimately to a labor party that expanded its demands from the shorter workday to free public education, the end of imprisonment for debt, universal male suffrage, and other social and economic issues based on the principle of equality. In the course of this struggle, Philadelphia witnessed the creation of the first labor newspaper in America, *The Mechanics' Free Press*, and the first labor library, the Mechanics' Library Company of Philadelphia.

The genesis of the movement was the action by some 600 journeymen carpenters who went on strike in June for the ten-hour day. Carpenters, like most workers of the time, worked from sunrise to sunset. During the peak of the building season, from spring through early fall, this could mean a working day of twelve to fifteen hours. The master rejected the demand and regretted "the formation of any society that has a tendency to subvert good order, and coerce or mislead those who have been industriously pursuing their avocation and honestly maintaining their families." For support, the master carpenters, or contractors, turned to their employers, the merchant capitalists, for support.

The carpenters appointed a committee of twelve to manage the strike. It was charged with negotiating with the master carpenters, distributing funds to those carpenters in need of assistance, and receiving offers of employment for carpenters that they pledged to undertake "on reasonable terms, and execute in a workmanlike manner." The carpenters also publicly refuted the master carpenters' charge that a reduction in hours would mean loss to them of one-fifth of their usual time. In constructing their argument, the journeymen gave us an interesting glimpse into the work habits of the pre-industrial building trades. On the longest day of summer, they argued, when one subtracted two hours for meals, there remained only thirteen hours for work. On the shortest day, with but nine hours of sun, subtracting the one hour for a meal, eight hours were left for work. On a yearly basis, they contended, carpenters worked an average ten-and-a-half-hour day. They proposed to work ten hours without meals in the summer and as long as they could see in the winter, thus averaging nine and a half hours throughout the year. Thus, they argued, the loss in time would not be one-fifth, but rather one-twelfth. The journeymen further claimed that their system would end the practice, dear to the contractors, of employing the men during the long days of summer and either discharging them or reducing their wages in winter.

Following the example of the carpenters, the Journeymen House Painters and Glaziers of the City and County of Philadelphia called a meeting to demand the ten-hour day, and the bricklayers did the same. In the face of this rising tide of ten-hour sentiment among the city's tradesmen, the master carpenters advertised for journeymen to come to Philadelphia, but the journeymen countered with a circular that the invitation to carpenters to come to the city was "a most gross imposition upon the credulity of our working brethren." There were sufficient carpenters in Philadelphia to do all the work required.

After some ten days of agitation, the struggle of the carpenters receded from public view. The results are difficult to quantify. No doubt some of the carpenters achieved their goal, but most did not. Yet the greater impact of the strike lay in the impetus that it gave for the development of the labor movement in Philadelphia and ultimately in the nation as a whole. [Ronald L. Filippelli]

FURTHER READING:

Arky, Louis H. "The Mechanics Union of Trade Associations and the Formatin of the Philadelphia Workingmen's Movement." *Pennsylvania Magazine of History and Biography*, Vol. 76 (1952), pp. 142–176.

Commons, John R., et al. *History of Labour in the United States*, Vol. 1. New York: Macmillan, 1936.

Pessen, Edward. *Most Uncommon Jacksonians: The Radical Leaders of the Early Labor Movement*. Albany, NY: State University of New York Press, 1967.

o   o   o

PHILADELPHIA GENERAL STRIKE OF 1910. Late in the evening of March 2, 1910, the Philadelphia Central Labor Union (CLU) issued a proclamation to Mayor John Reyburn insisting that he force the city's transit company to arbitrate its labor dispute and that "he return the police to their regular duty and cease using them to man trolley cars." The proclamation demanded action by midnight on Friday, March 4, after which time "the working class will cease work . . . and remain on strike until further notice from duly accredited representatives." On March 5, between 50,000 and 100,000 workers either stopped or refused to report to work. Endorsed by the Building Trades Council, the CLU, and several independent unions, the number of strikers topped 125,000 the following week. The Philadelphia *Public Ledger* was hysterical. This "impossible strike," it reported, represented "an entirely new development in the history of combats between capital and labor in this country."

The Philadelphia General Strike originated in a long-running dispute between the Philadelphia Rapid Transit Company (PRT) and Division 477 of the Amalgamated Association of Street Car and Electric Railway Men of America. In May 1909, Division 477 struck the PRT when the company refused to recognize the union committee and its demands for an hourly wage of twenty-five cents, a shortening of the workday from the prevailing "swing run" (fourteen to eighteen hours) to ten hours, and freedom to buy uniforms in the open market rather than from the company. The PRT imported strikebreakers and violence ensued. Strikers and their sympathizers destroyed streetcars, track, and wiring, similar to the actions of crowds in earlier strikes against the unpopular and intrigue-riddled PRT. The use of scabs and the brutal treatment of strikers by the police evoked widespread support for Division 477. The CLU threatened a general strike of its 75,000 members before Mayor Reyburn urged the PRT to negotiate a compromise settlement that included recognition of the union.

Just seven months later, on January 1, 1910, the PRT triggered a renewal of the conflict. As Division 477 prepared to negotiate a new agreement, the company rejected a proposed wage increase and unilaterally implemented a welfare plan that included insurance and pensions. Two days later, the company fired seven employees who charged that the PRT intended to use the welfare plan to undermine the union and collective bargaining. Throughout January, Division 477 attempted to avoid a strike, seeking arbitration for the fired employees and appealing to Pennsylvania political boss James P. McNichol to intercede. Finally, a strike-authorization vote by frustrated Division 477 members on January 18 passed by a 5,121 to 233 margin, encouraging public interest groups to ask for intervention by the mayor. But arrogant PRT officials dismissed all requests for arbitration. On February 15, the company broke off all discussions with Division 477, and on February 19 it fired 173 more union members "for the good of the service."

The PRT's intransigence propelled a union counterattack. Within hours of the firings, Division 477 officers authorized a strike. Like workers on other big-city transit systems, PRT strikers were ideally positioned to build strike enthusiasm. Large numbers of transit workers routinely gathered at centrally located roundhouses, and streetcars provided an excellent means of informal communication through which workers could spread information and enlist support. Furthermore, the harsh conditions of streetcar employment were readily apparent to other workers. From the outset of the strike, crowds gathered to harass scabs and prevent the PRT's operation. Strike sympathizers battled police in Kensington and Germantown, threw stones at scab motormen, and demolished cars that attempted to leave the terminals. A crowd near the downtown Baldwin Locomotive Works seized and destroyed a car, knocking the motorman senseless. When police rushed the crowd, Baldwin's employees joined the strike sympathizers outside or threw nuts and bolts at the police from the upper-story factory windows.

Mayor Reyburn and the police added to public strike support by openly siding with the hated PRT. Reyburn sought to bolster the police by calling for 3,000 "citizen" volunteers and by enlisting the Pennsylvania Fencibles, a private military and social organization. The police arrested Division 477 president C. O. Pratt and CLU president John J. Murphy for inciting to riot and indiscriminately "clubbed, coerced and arrested innocent men." Five days after the strike began, at Reyburn's request, the despised State Constabulary arrived in the city, prompting union sympathizers to claim that Philadelphia was now "in the hands of Cossacks."

Mayor Reyburn's actions to quell the strike had the opposite result. Other workers throughout the city sporadically joined forces with the streetcar workers and disrupted production in several industries.

Union meetings expressed outrage at the PRT and City Hall which conspired to deny "the citizens of this city their God-given and constitutional rights." When Reyburn and the PRT continued to ignore ultimatums from labor organizations, workers attempted to halt all industry in the city. Well over 100,000 wage earners stopped work the week of March 5 to 12. These included not only union members but also formerly unorganized workers like the 12,000 employees at the Baldwin Locomotive Works. The general strike added to the ranks of every union in the city.

Police activity quickened with the spread of the strike. On March 5, 20,000 sympathy strikers ignored Mayor Reyburn's ban on public demonstrations and gathered at Independence Square. Mounted police with long night sticks charged the demonstrators, leaving hundreds injured. In response, Pennsylvania Federation of Labor (PFL) president Elmer E. Greenawalt threatened a statewide strike if the PRT had not settled by March 26. American Federation of Labor (AFL) president Samuel Gompers denounced Reyburn for treating American citizens the way that "Cossacks treat the Russian subjects."

Strike enthusiasm began to dissipate before the PFL could act, however. On March 22, large numbers of textile workers and metal workers returned to work. Two days later, United Mine Workers president J. L. Lewis declared that his union would not join a statewide general strike, dampening the prospects for a successful effort. Finally, on March 27, the day after the proposed statewide general strike was supposed to have begun, the CLU called off the Philadelphia General Strike. Only the streetcar employees remained off the job.

Division 477 continued to hold out and reject PRT offers that did not address all of the grievances. Political pressure and losses of $20,000 per day forced the PRT to moderate its position. A final compromise proposed by the company on April 15 included the reinstatement of all strikers, wage increases of one cent per hour every six months until the minimum reached twenty-five cents, the right of employees to join a union but without exclusive bargaining rights, and arbitration of the cases of the 173 men dismissed on February 19. While the rank and file narrowly rejected the offer, Division 477 officers accepted and called off the strike. Amid charges of a "sell out," union leader C. O. Pratt claimed he had promises from the company to honor the agreement. Within a year, however, the PRT took advantage of frustration and factionalism within Division 477 to implement a new welfare plan that effectively undercut union strength. For the next generation, Philadelphia Rapid Transit was a non-union bastion. [Ken Fones-Wolf]

FURTHER READING

Adams, Graham, Jr. *The Age of Industrial Violence, 1910–1915.* New York: Columbia University Press, 1966.

Foner, Philip S. *The AFL in the Progressive Era.* New York: International Publishers, 1980.

Fones-Wolf, Ken. "Mass Strikes, Corporate Strategies: The Baldwin Locomotive Works and the Philadelphia General Strike of 1910." *Pennsylvania Magazine of History and Biography,* Vol. 110 (July, 1986), pp. 447–457.

o   o   o

PHILADELPHIA PILOTS' STRIKE OF 1792. One of the earliest strikes for higher wages took place in Philadelphia in May of 1792. On the tenth of that month, the pilots of the port of Philadelphia refused to lead ships up and down the Delaware River unless their wages were raised. The job action lasted twelve days. The city's merchants petitioned the state government to stop the disruption that had virtually closed the nation's most important port to large-scale commerce. Eventually, after the Board of Wardens of the Port threatened to forbid the striking pilots to ever again practice their

trade in Philadelphia, the merchants and pilots compromised and successfully petitioned the state legislature for higher fees for the pilots. The legislation, however, also outlawed future work stoppages and authorized the use of substitute pilots in the event of a stoppage.

There is no evidence that Philadelphia's pilots had struck before 1792. In a city where merchant seamen and master cordwainers had pioneered in labor action and organization, the pilots were far from the most militant of Philadelphia's working class.

The strike began when the Board of Wardens, the agency charged with regulating the affairs of the port, decided to suspend port operations. The action was taken as the result of a dispute with the state legislature that had left the wardens without adequate funds to carry out their charge. When the legislature did not respond, the wardens resolved to close their office on April 10. The pilots, whose petitions to the legislature for increased pilotage fees had also been ignored, refused to conduct ships from the port until the legislature acted.

A few days later the governor of Pennsylvania ordered the state to provide the funds that the wardens needed but took no action on the pilots' grievances. When the Board of Wardens reopened the port, the pilots refused to return to work. The board then threatened to demand that the striking pilots turn in their licenses.

On May 10, the pilots met outside of the city at Marcus Hook, organized the Society of Delaware Pilots, and issued an ultimatum to the city's merchants demanding increased fees, assistance for aged pilots, and other things. The merchants, who were the employers of the pilots, ignored the ultimatum and enlisted the help of the Board of Wardens in forcing the pilots back to work. The merchants organized convoys of ships leaving port so that captains unfamiliar with the port could safely navigate to Delaware Bay. They also secured assistance from the Board of Wardens in escorting ships entering the river from the bay. In addition, the board advertised for scabs in the city's newspapers.

The mailed fist having been used, the merchants then turned to the velvet glove, offering to jointly petition the legislature for increased fees if the pilots would return to work. But the pilots, enraged by the convoys that were navigating the river, rejected the overture and attempted to block passage of the river. The action brought the displeasure of the city's press down on the striking pilots. Concerned primarily with the effect of the strike on the city's trade, the newspapers reported that ships had arrived and departed without incident. In general, the press condemned the strike as criminal at worst and to the detriment of the interests of commerce at best.

The strike ended on May 23 after a meeting of merchants and pilots at which it was agreed that higher fees were justified. While not all merchants agreed to the settlement, most apparently did, and the life of the port returned to normal. There is no indication that any of the striking pilots were prosecuted or lost their licenses.

After the strike, upon petition of the Society of Delaware Pilots, the legislature did revise the old port act to increase the fees of pilotage as the pilots had requested. However, the bill also prohibited any pilot from entering "into any combination with a view of preventing any other person from executing such duties." Pilots who combined with others to prevent work would lose their licenses, and the wardens were authorized to grant temporary licenses to replacement pilots. In short, the pilots got their money but the legislature took away their right to strike and to form organizations for concerted action. No other American seaport was regulated by such a statute. Nor did the legislature extend statutory restrictions upon concerted action to any other crafts. Undoubtedly, no other trade in the city had such a widespread effect on the prosperity of the population as did the pi-

lots. It was this public interest character of the pilots' trade that led the legislature to consider it suitable for regulation. The Society of Delaware Pilots appears to have vanished with the passage of the port act. [Ronald L. Filippelli]

FURTHER READING

Keller, Kenneth. "The Philadelphia Pilot's Strike of 1792." *Labor History*, Vol. 18 (1977), pp. 37–48.

o   o   o

PHILADELPHIA TEACHERS' STRIKE OF 1972–1973. The Philadelphia Federation of Teachers (PFT), an affiliate of the American Federation of Teachers (AFT), had represented teachers for purposes of collective bargaining since 1963. The Philadelphia Board of Education had resisted unionization vigorously, and the relationship between the board and the union had been problematic from the beginning. In 1970, the first teachers strike in the city's history closed the schools for four days. On the day it was settled, Pennsylvania's new law permitting strikes by public employees went into effect.

Against this background of strained labor relations, negotiations for the 1972 conflict began nearly a year in advance, in October of 1971. From the beginning, the board, pleading that it had no money to give, aggressively pushed for concessions in work rules and offered no salary increase. Thus, even though negotiations began early, no progress was made as the opening of the 1972 school year approached.

The board wanted to reorganize the assignment of teachers and change class size requirements so as to eliminate 478 teaching positions. The superintendent of schools, Matthew Costanzo, implemented the policy unilaterally in August, in the midst of negotiations. In addition, the board ordered retrenchments that saved $14 million in labor costs, thus reducing the base the union was attempting to increase. The proposals were an obvious challenge to the union—an invitation to strike.

On Tuesday, September 5, the first day teachers were expected to report to school, they formed picket lines instead. Part one of the first legal strike of teachers in Philadelphia began. One week later, the union offered to return to work under the old contract and continue to negotiate. But the board refused, having already imposed cost-cutting measures. The board acted with the knowledge that Philadelphia's mayor, Frank Rizzo, a law-and-order Democrat, was firmly behind the get-tough policy.

On September 26, D. Donald Jamieson, president judge of the Pennsylvania Court of Common Pleas, convinced the PFT and the board to agree to reopen the schools and negotiate under his supervision. For the union, the agreement was particularly important because it returned conditions in the schools, including class size, to what they had been before the board's unilateral action.

Nevertheless, even with the schools open, negotiations remained at an impasse. The union, as was its right under Pennsylvania law, called for impartial fact finding. Although the PFT's leaders were leery of fact finding, they reasoned that the fact finder would have to offer them something above the board's demands for concessions. They were wrong. Five days before Christmas, the fact finder made his report. It offered no pay raise for the first year and only 3 percent the following year. Preparation time for elementary teachers, a major issue, was placed in the recess and lunch periods of teachers. The only concession to the teachers came in the form of a 3 percent increase in the health and welfare fund. The union's membership overwhelmingly rejected the proposal.

The board now seized the high ground by accepting the fact finder's recommendations and announcing that since the school district had only $30 million to spend, the fact finder's recommendation would be the board's final offer. On January 1st, the agreement to work and negotiate expired. Seven days later, on a bitter January day, pickets appeared and phase two of the strike began. It would last fifty-two days.

Unlike during phase one, this time the board of education tried to keep the schools open. The students who attended found a small number of union teachers who had crossed the picket lines, administrators, volunteers, and new and often unqualified teachers who had been hired by the board. Nevertheless, probably less than a third of the students attended the hastily arranged classes.

On January 11, Judge Jamieson entered the strike again by issuing an injunction ordering the teachers back to work immediately. It had practically no effect. Judge Jamieson and the board had again miscalculated the determination of the teachers. Throughout the strike some 85 percent of the city's teachers, many of whom were not union members, honored the picket lines.

On January 15, Judge Jamieson held the PFT in contempt for violating the injunction to return to work. The contempt citation named twenty-eight union officials. A jury found the union's top negotiator, John Ryan, and its president, Frank Sullivan, and twenty-one other officials of the PFT guilty of contempt of court. Jamieson stunned the community when he sentenced Ryan and Sullivan to six months to four years in prison, imposed a $160,000 fine on the PFT, and an additional $10,000 fine for each day that the strike continued.

After the jailing of the PFT's officers, any hope of compromise vanished. Even the president of the board of education, William Ross, a hard-liner and, ironically, an official of the International Ladies Garment Workers Union (ILGWU), expressed concern that the judge had gone too far. Ross knew that the arrests would only make the teachers more militant. So too did hostile editorials in the city's newspapers and Mayor Rizzo who charged that the leaders of the PFT had "placed a gun to the heads" of the taxpayers.

With the jailing of their leaders, the attitude of the strikers toward strikebreakers became ugly. Those crossing the picket lines were subjected to villification and threats. When police tried to enforce the injunction by clearing picket lines, teachers responded with mass picketing. Wholesale arrests began. In all, 762 strikers were arrested between February 13 and February 19, 1973.

The jailing of the teachers also mobilized the Philadelphia labor movement. Edward Toohey, president of the Philadelphia Council of the AFL-CIO, created a United Labor Committee to support the teachers. The unions voted overwhelmingly to join the teachers' picket lines. At five o'clock in the morning of February 13, 5,000 trade unionists surrounded the Board of Education's headquarters. Philadelphia police took no action. The most important move made by Toohey's committee, however, was the decision to call a general strike. The twenty-four-hour walkout in sympathy with the teachers was set for February 28.

Pressure from the threat of a general strike put the elements of a solution in motion. At the same time as tensions in Philadelphia approached the crisis point, the AFL-CIO executive council was meeting in Miami. When President Richard Nixon met with the labor leaders to try to improve relations with organized labor, AFL-CIO president George Meany asked him to try to do something to settle the dispute in Philadelphia. Nixon agreed to send Under-Secretary of Labor William Usery to mediate the dispute. Meanwhile, in Philadelphia, school board president William Ross resigned under pressure from the Philadelphia labor movement and his own union, the ILGWU.

The mediation of Usery and the resignation of Ross created the context for the strike settlement. On the day before the proposed general strike, the PFT and the union reached a settlement. There were no union concessions in the package. Teachers won a pay increase totaling $99.9 million more than three times the board's final offer at the beginning of phase two of the strike. Fringe benefits were increased and teachers were guaranteed forty-five minutes each day for preparation. There were no layoffs of teachers.

Philadelphia's teachers union won more from this bitter strike than what appeared in the contract. The union came away having weathered an attack on its very existence. It had confronted a powerful employer, a popular mayor, a hostile press, and the judicial system. Any thoughts of turning labor relations in Philadelphia's school system back to the days before the union were dashed by the solidarity of the PFT. [Ronald L. Filippelli]

FURTHER READING

Sanzare, James. *A History of the Philadelphia Federation of Teachers*. Philadelphia, PA: Philadelphia Federation of Teachers, 1977.

o   o   o

PHILADELPHIA TRANSIT STRIKE OF 1944. As in many northern industrial cities, the need for labor in defense industries during World War II led to a dramatic change in the racial makeup of Philadelphia's population. The black population grew rapidly during the war and stood at 300,000 out of a general population of about 2 million by the end of hostilities. The increased contact between blacks and whites led to a heightening of racial tension in the city. So too did blacks' efforts to find better jobs. At first, whites were able to exclude blacks from all but the most menial jobs, but as the labor shortage intensified, and as the black community grew more aggressive in defense of its rights, tension sometimes escalated to conflict. Such was the case with the Philadelphia Transportation Company (PTC) in 1944.

The PTC employed some 11,000 workers, only some 500 of whom were blacks, and most of those were in the lowest paying, most menial jobs. The company seemed a perfect target for pressure from the black community. It played a vital role in defense production, carrying Philadelphia's workers to their jobs in defense-related industries. In addition, thousands of blacks rode the buses each day. Yet there were no black bus drivers. Appeals to the company for better jobs failed, however, as did similar calls to the Philadelphia Rapid Transit Employees Union (PRTEU). The workers then asked assistance from the local chapter of the National Association for the Advancement of Colored People (NAACP).

NAACP requests to the company were referred to the union, which in turn said that it had no jurisdiction over the hiring practices of the PTC. During these discussions, on January 11, 1943, the PTC asked the United States Employment Service (USES) for 100 white motormen. The War Manpower Commission (WMC), of which the USES was part, replied that the PTC should accept blacks for the positions. The company refused, claiming that, although nowhere were blacks mentioned, the contract with the PRTEU precluded any changes in past practice and customs during the life of the agreement. With this rebuff, the blacks turned for support to the federal Fair Employment Practices Committee (FEPC). FEPC officials extracted a statement from the company that stated that it would be willing to hire blacks if it were not a violation of the contract. When the union stalled, the FEPC ordered the PTC to end discrimination in hiring and employment against blacks.

The union then responded with a dual strategy. PRTEU president Frank Carney asked Virginia congressman Howard Smith, chairman of the House Committee to Investigate Executive Agencies and a bitter foe of the FEPC, to schedule a meeting of the FEPC. Carney also informed the PTC that it could not comply with the FEPC order

because it was in violation of the contract. The PTC then informed the FEPC that it could do nothing so long as the union contract was in effect.

Matters were complicated in early 1944 by a three-way struggle for the right to represent the PTC's employees. The CIO affiliate, the Transport Workers Union (TWU), had been trying to unseat PRTEU, an independent union, as had an AFL affiliate, the Amalgamated Association of Street and Electric Railway and Motor Coach Employees of America. The race issue became critical during the election, but in the end, the TWU, with a nondiscrimination policy, unseated the PRTEU. TWU's victory did not settle the race issue in the union. Many members remained intransigent. As negotiations with the PTC wore on, dissatisfaction with the TWU's negotiating ability played into the hands of the dissidents.

On the company side, a War Manpower Commission directive that all hiring had to be done through the USES, which adhered to a nondiscrimination policy, brought the PTC into line. The company hired three black applicants and promoted five black employees to be trained as streetcar operators. At 4:00 A.M. on August 1, the day that the black motormen took their first cars on the lines, a wildcat strike shut down most of Philadelphia's trolleys and buses. The strike committee, led by James McMenamin, and supported by Frank Carney, was largely made up of PRTEU adherents who probably saw the strike as a means to regain their lost power in the union. They argued that while the strike was clearly a protest against black motormen, it would also protect the seniority rights of white employees. That issue had long ago been disposed of in FEPC hearings. The seniority of all of the black motormen, even those who had already been employed by the PTC, started with their first day on the job.

The amount of sentiment for the strike was evident at the end of the first day when 3,500 workers rallied outside of one of the

PTC's carbarns. The rally gave the lie to the TWU's claim, in opposition to the strike, that it was the work of a small group of people out of touch with the wishes of the membership. Yet when 250 TWU members started a back-to-work movement, they were forced by their fellow workers to abandon it. Not only was the union unable to get the strikers back to work, but Major General Philip Hayes, head of the Army's Third Service Command, pleaded in vain with the strikers on the grounds of national defense. Mayor Bernard Samuel, mindful of the political minefield that the strike represented, made only a cursory appeal and contented himself with closing all of the city's taverns. Indeed, the organization most responsible for keeping violence from erupting was the NAACP which counseled blacks to use restraint in the volatile situation.

It became clear that only outside intervention could end the strike. William H. Davis, head of the War Labor Board, appealed to President Roosevelt for immediate action "in the interest of vital war production." The President responded on August 3, authorizing the secretary of war to take control of the Philadelphia Transit Company. Nevertheless, the strike committee voted to stay out until they received a written guarantee that blacks would not be employed as operators. When no such guarantee was forthcoming, the strike continued. So determined were the strikers that they risked the fines and imprisonment of the Smith-Connally Act, which forbade strikes against a facility in possession of the government.

Frustrated, General Hayes ordered troops to Philadelphia and gave strikers an ultimatum that Monday, August 7 was the deadline for returning to work. If they failed to respond, they would lose their jobs, be blacklisted by the War Manpower Commission during the war, and lose their draft deferments. In addition, McMenamin, Carney, and two other strike leaders were arrested for violation of the Smith-Connally

Act, a wartime labor law passed by Congress in angry reaction to the **Bituminous Coal Strike of 1943**. The sudden force of the government's action sobered the strikers. On Monday normal operations resumed. On August 9, seven of the eight black trainees resumed their training. The eighth had voluntarily withdrawn. The same day, an attractive contract between the TWU and the PTC went into effect. On August 11, the troops began to leave the city, and six days later General Hayes returned control of the PTC to its management. The volatile matter had been handled successfully and violence had been avoided.

The government's decisive action in upholding the rights of black workers had long-lasting effects. The intense resistance to black workers in skilled positions declined dramatically. By December, there were eighteen black operators. After the strike, a grand jury indicted thirty workers for violation of the Smith-Connally Act. The charges were dropped against three of the defendants, and the rest pled nolo contendere and paid $100 fines. [Ronald L. Filippelli]

FURTHER READING

Lipsitz, George. *Class and Culture in Cold War America: "A Rainbow at Midnight."* South Hadley, MA: J. F. Bergin Publishers, 1982.

Ross, Malcolm. *All Manner of Men.* New York: Reynal and Hitchcock, 1948.

Weaver, Robert C. *Negro Labor: A National Problem.* New York: Reynal and Hitchcock, 1946.

Winkler, Allan M. "The Philadelphia Transit Strike of 1944." *The Journal of American History*, Vol. 59 (1972), pp. 73–89.

o   o   o

PITTSBURGH POWER STRIKE OF 1946. During the strike-plagued year of 1946, one conflict dramatized not only worker resistance to attempts by management to turn back the gains that unions had made since the passage of the Wagner Act in 1935 but also the threat that militant trade union action posed to established labor leaders who had become responsible, in the eyes of government and industry, for stable labor relations.

Duquesne Power and Light Company supplied power to the city of Pittsburgh and the rest of Allegheny County. It had first become unionized in 1937 when employees formed an independent union, the Independent Association of Employees of Duquesne Light Company (IA). The union's refusal to join the American Federation of Labor or the Congress of Industrial Organizations made it an outsider in Pittsburgh's labor world. This fact of non-affiliation played a major role in the unfolding of the strike which began on September 10.

Duquesne Power and Light showed little interest in addressing the many demands of its varied work force. It counted on the natural divisions among construction workers, repairmen, clerks, and meter readers to keep the union weak. It also assumed that its status as a public utility would make it immune from a strike. Indeed, when the IA struck, the company was able to obtain a temporary restraining order barring any strike activity until a hearing could be held. George Mueller, IA president and the man who was to act as a lightning rod for criticism during the strike, argued that the court could not use the public interest argument to permit anti-labor actions by the company. When the court made the injunction permanent, Mueller derided the injunction publicly, calling it a "scrap of paper."

Probably in no major city in the country did organized labor have as good a working relationship with a mayor as it did with Pittsburgh's David Lawrence. But Lawrence, like many in the city, focused on what he considered to be Mueller's irresponsible leadership. He contrasted the IA's president with William Green, AFL president, and Philip Murray of the United Steel Workers of America, whom he praised for their "wise and competent counsel."

Yet Lawrence's attitudes did not reflect the sentiment of the membership of Mueller's union. They were angry and showed it by defying the injunction and striking on September 24. Mueller was immediately sentenced to one year in jail for fomenting the strike. In addition, the judge ordered the workers to return to their jobs or be jailed. The workers responded by rejecting the latest company offer overwhelmingly and vowing to stay on strike until the judge lifted the injunction and freed Mueller.

The court's harsh action had an effect opposite of what was intended. Sympathy strikes spread across Pittsburgh. Steelworkers shut down the vast Jones and Laughlin Steel southside works. Local bus and trolley transportation ground to a standstill. Five thousand workers rallied in front of the Allegheny County Jail demanding Mueller's release. In all, some 25,000 workers joined in the spontaneous uprising.

Demonstrations of this kind had not been seen in Pittsburgh since the great struggles to unionize the steel industry in 1892 and 1919. They sobered the judge who offered to free Mueller if he would recommend acceptance of the company offer to his membership. Mueller complied, but the rank and file rejected the offer out of hand and demanded that the injunction be lifted. Frustrated, Mayor Lawrence called upon AFL and CIO leaders to support him in his contest with Mueller in return for the lifting of the injunction. As their part of the bargain, AFL and CIO leaders ordered their members to return to work and to disregard IA picket lines. For their part, however, the utility workers held firm. Even with the injunction withdrawn, the company's offer included the contracting out of construction work and unsatisfactory compensation and vacation offers. The strike continued.

The action of AFL and CIO officials met opposition from some quarters. Members of various unions urged their leaders to support the strike, and some, like the Teamsters, defied the orders from their leaders and continued to honor the picket lines. The strike had now changed character. What had started out as a struggle for the right to strike, had now become a challenge to the authority of established labor leadership. To counter this threat, much of Pittsburgh's labor leadership joined with business and government to stop the strike. In so doing they used Mueller, who had been pilloried from every quarter for his intransigence, as the scapegoat.

The chamber of commerce offered to pay the costs of a mediated settlement. AFL and CIO officials intensified their campaign to deny the strikers any support from other unions. In addition, a dissident group within the IA was encouraged to challenge Mueller for leadership. The dissidents had the backing of District 50 of the United Mine Workers, a mixed district that included workers from a variety of occupations, including utility workers. Assailed on all sides, the strikers hit back. Several acts of sabotage caused power failures in sections of the city. Strikers also broke up meetings of the dissidents and intensified their aggressive picketing at sites throughout Pittsburgh. It was clear that the almost unanimous condemnation of the strike by the city's power structure had only served to intensify the solidarity and determination of the strikers. This became clear to all concerned when the IA overwhelmingly defeated three dissident groups in an NLRB-sponsored representation election.

Made more secure by their victory, the IA agreed to arbitration and ended the strike on October 20. They had held out for twenty-seven days, bolstered by rank-and-file support from other workers and attacked by the leadership of the labor movement. While the union made no great gains, it did survive and manage to turn back company attempts to weaken its contract at worst and to destroy the union at best. The strikers also demonstrated their willingness and ability to defy Pittsburgh's establishment—labor,

government, and industry, as well as much of public opinion—through tightly organized and mutually supportive collective action. [Ronald L. Filippelli]

FURTHER READING

Chamberlain, Neil. *Social Responsibility and Strikes.* New York: Harper, 1953.

Lipsitz, George. *Class and Culture in Cold War America: "A Rainbow at Midnight."* South Hadley, MA: J. F. Bergin Publishers, 1982.

o   o   o

POSTAL STRIKE OF 1970. The first nationwide strike by federal employees began on March 18, 1970, when 150,000 postal workers shut down the nation's mail system. After nearly a week of chaos, the walkout was ended by a combination of court injunctions, mediation, and congressional action.

The discontent of the postal workers had been building for some time. There was ample evidence of the rising militancy of the postal unions. Although, historically, postal unions had opposed strikes, both the United Federation of Postal Clerks and the National Postal Union had removed no-strike clauses from their constitutions during their 1968 conventions. In addition, union leaders hinted at the possibility of strikes during their lobbying efforts in Congress in 1969. The pressure on union leaders from their rank and file became difficult to contain. James Rademacher, president of the Letter Carriers, took the lead and announced that his union would strike on April 15 if promised pay increases to keep postal workers' pay comparable with the private sector were not forthcoming.

On March 12, the House of Representatives' Post Office and Civil Service Committee supported a postal reform-pay package that satisfied Rademacher but not his members. The biggest Letter Carriers local, New York City's No. 36, demanded that the members be polled on an immediate strike.

Rademacher told the New Yorkers that he was not prepared to call a nationwide strike. But the New York workers, angry over the size of the pay increases in the last two contracts, were adamant. They lived in one of the highest cost-of-living areas in the country, and many of their members could not support their families without second jobs or welfare payments. They also noted that the top pay of a letter carrier with twenty-one years of service was several thousand dollars below the government's estimated annual income necessary for a moderate standard of living in New York.

Not surprisingly, on March 17 the Local 36 members voted decisively for a strike. The leadership of the big Brooklyn local announced that his local would join in the strike, and the Postal Clerks agreed to honor the picket lines. By the morning of March 18 the wildcat strike was almost completely effective. The movement in New York spread quickly. By Thursday evening, March 19, letter carriers across the country had joined in the strike, including those in Akron, Boston, Buffalo, Pittsburgh, Houston, Detroit, and other cities.

Postmaster Winton M. Blount obtained an injunction ordering the workers back to work immediately. He also ordered strikers into a non-pay status, issued mail embargo orders, and suspended the postal monopoly for New York City. Nevertheless, the strikers stood firm. Blount knew that the tie-up could not be tolerated for long. In New York City alone the effects would be devastating. Most of the nation's financial paper moved through the city's postal system.

The dispute also proved to be a serious problem for the unions. At this point, only the Letter Carriers were out, and their action had not been sanctioned by the national union. But the longer the strike continued, the more difficult it became for the other unions to restrain their members from joining. To forestall this possibility, the leaders of the seven postal unions asked Secretary of Labor George Shultz to intervene. Shultz,

however, found Blount and other government officials reluctant to talk to the unions as long as an illegal strike was in effect. Under heavy pressure, Blount agreed to meet in secret with Shultz and the union leaders on March 20, the day the Letter Carriers' emergency conference was to decide on a formal national strike.

The meeting produced an agreement whereby the union leaders agreed to urge the strikers to return to work, and the postal service agreed to discuss all issues. Upon agreement, the service and the unions would present a united recommendation to Congress. Unfortunately, the rank and file did not accept the agreement. They had little faith in government promises. In fact, the situation had become worse, not better, as a result of the negotiations. The rejection of the compromise by the rank and file had put extra pressure on the union leaders to reassert their authority. One way to do this was to try to take control of the strike movement and lead it. In light of this failure, President Richard Nixon announced that if the strike had not ended by Monday, March 23, he would meet his constitutional obligation to assure that the mails would move. When the President's call went unheeded, he ordered troops into New York City. The troops were unarmed and were ordered to move the mails, nothing more. No one had any illusions about the government's ability to arrest 150,000 strikers. This was undoubtedly the reason that the government neglected to enforce the injunction until the very end of the walkout. Nixon added that no negotiations on the pay increase would begin without a back-to-work movement, and that if no such movement arose, then the government would enforce the court order.

Twenty-five hundred federal troops and 16,000 National Guardsmen replaced the striking 57,000 New York postal workers. The soldiers were put to work doing all of the operations of the post office. No home delivery was attempted. Indeed, few believed that the troops could bring the postal service back to normal. Their presence was symbolic—a reassertion of federal authority and a message to the strikers.

Nixon held to his promise to enforce the injunction. Local 36 president Gus Johnson was ordered to appear in federal court to show cause why he and his union should not be cited for contempt. Similar injunctions were obtained and enforced in other cities across the country. The combination of troops and injunctions stirred a back-to-work movement across the country. By Wednesday most of the strikers had returned to their stations. With the strike ended, negotiations could now begin. The union agreed on a package of proposals that would provide a 12 percent pay increase retroactive to October of 1969, fully paid health benefits, compression of top-pay length of service from twenty-one to eight years, area wages based on cost-of-living indexes, complete amnesty for workers involved in the strike, and collective bargaining and binding arbitration in the future. Postal authorities countered with an immediate 6 percent wage increase, retroactive to January 1970, and agreement for a joint sponsorship of postal reorganization that would include an additional 6 percent increase on the date of congressional enactment, compression of top-pay length of service to eight years, future collective bargaining on all issues with binding arbitration, and the withholding of disciplinary action until joint labor–management talks on amnesty could take place.

This was essentially the settlement agreed to on Thursday, April 2, with the exception of a slightly higher increase after postal reorganization was approved by Congress. Congress quickly approved the agreement, and President Nixon signed it on April 15. The next step was postal reorganization. The two sides agreed on a reorganization plan that traded the union's traditional lobbying role in Congress for more standard collective bargaining. The Postal Reorganization Act passed Congress on

August 6 and was signed by President Nixon on August 12, 1970.

Although postal reorganization had been in the works for some time, the wildcat strike of the letter carriers gave the movement considerable impetus because it dramatized the anomalies in the system for both sides. [Ronald L. Filippelli]

FURTHER READING

Loewenberg, J. Joseph. "The Post Office Strike of 1970." In *Collective Bargaining in Government: Readings and Cases.* J. Joseph Loewenberg and Michael H. Moskow, eds. Englewood Cliffs, NJ: Prentice Hall, 1972, pp. 192–202.

Shannon, Stephen C. "Work Stoppage in Government: The Postal Strike of 1970." *Monthly Labor Review,* Vol. 101, No. 7 (July 1978), pp. 14–22.

Woolf, Donald A. "Labor Problems in the Post Office." *Industrial Relations,* Vol. 9 (1969), pp. 29–34.

o   o   o

PULLMAN STRIKE AND BOYCOTT OF 1894. The Pullman Strike might more accurately be called the Chicago Railway Boycott and Strike of 1894. It derived its popular name from the small local strike of Pullman Palace Sleeping Car Company employees that began the affair. The greater strike went through three stages, beginning with the walkout of the sleeping car employees at the company town of Pullman, Illinois, just outside of Chicago, on May 11. To support those strikers, the American Railway Union (ARU) called a nationwide sympathy boycott, instructing its members on all railroads to refrain from handling any train which included Pullman cars after June 26. The boycott, in turn, quickly evolved into a general railway strike when railroad companies discharged employees for refusing to move trains as ordered, and the ARU responded by striking those roads.

Facing a tie-up of the nation's principal transportation network, railroad and government officials used armed force to reopen the lines and to suppress rioting by strikers and their sympathizers. Railroad guards, Pinkerton detectives, local police officers, state guards, swarms of deputy federal marshals, and units of the United States Army confronted and defeated mobs of ARU and other union members and their allies. Although the principal battles occurred in the Chicago area, other encounters took place at scores of communities all along the nation's railways.

The general railway strike ground to a halt between July 13, when rioting had been suppressed and trains were again running on schedule, and July 17, when federal marshals arrested Eugene V. Debs, president of the ARU, and other strike leaders. Meanwhile, the Pullman Company resumed operations on July 16. The affair culminated seventeen years of industrial warfare between militant railway workers and their employers that had begun with the **Railroad Strikes of 1877.** (*See also* **Union Pacific Strikes of 1884, Southwest Strikes of 1885–1886, Burlington Strike of 1888,** and **Great Northern Strike of 1894.**)

A failure of paternalism during the economic Panic of 1893 produced the initial strike. George M. Pullman, founder of the sleeping car firm and builder-owner of the company town which bore his name, designed the community as an example of how an enlightened employer should provide for his employees and their families. In fact, the project resulted in his dominating most aspects of their lives. He provided housing, parks, playgrounds, a school, a library, a shopping arcade, and most community services. He encouraged churches. He also managed the local government and excluded bars, brothels, and other corrupting influences from the town. Insistent on earning a 6 percent return on his investment, among other things, he gave preference to employees who lived in company housing, levied fees for using the library, and charged higher rents for arcade shops and company hous-

ing than landlords elsewhere.

To meet falling profits during the Panic of 1893, Pullman substantially reduced the labor force, cut wage rates, and spread work among his remaining employees by reducing the number of hours each worked. Rents on company housing, deducted directly from paychecks, went unchanged. The hard-pressed workers organized and affiliated their union with the American Railway Union (ARU), the industrial-type railway union that recently had won the Great Northern Railroad Strike. Pullman met with a committee of worker representatives but refused to restore wages or reduce rents and, shortly after, discharged members of the committee. The strike that followed attracted wide public sympathy but made little headway.

The strike was a month old when Pullman delegates to the annual convention of the ARU at Chicago presented their case against their employer. Debs, the president of the ARU, though sympathetic, cautioned against the proposed boycott of Pullman cars. He assumed railroad companies would resist and observed that armies of unemployed workers stood ready to take their jobs in the event of a strike. The convention, however, saw no alternative to assisting the members from Pullman. It therefore instructed Debs to negotiate with the sleeping car magnate, and if that failed, to launch the boycott.

The railroads and their allies took prompt measures to thwart the boycott even before it began. Among the first to act was Richard Olney, attorney general of the United States. A distinguished railroad lawyer from Boston, Olney, before, during, and after his tenure in office, was the legal counsel and a director of the Chicago, Burlington & Quincy Railroad, one of the lines soon to be struck. On June 23, when the ARU announced its intention to boycott if Pullman refused to negotiate, Olney ordered maps showing all railway postal routes in the United States. Three days later, when the boycott began and mail was delayed, he instructed U.S.

attorneys and marshals in potential trouble spots to protect trains carrying the mail in the usual way as directed by the postmaster general. He also authorized them to secure such warrants and court processes as might be needed and to swear in deputy marshals and posses as necessary.

Olney's purpose was to break the boycott by protecting mail trains. In the recent **Great Northern Railroad Strike**, the Justice Department had ruled that every car of every mail-carrying train, as made up by the company, was protected by federal law. Since passenger trains with Pullman cars carried mail, attempts by boycotters to cut off sleeping cars would violate federal law. Had the boycott not evolved into a major strike, Olney's strategy might have worked.

Meanwhile, the general managers of the twenty-four railroads centered in Chicago also moved against the boycott. Since 1892 they had worked closely together in a semi-secret organization, the Chicago General Managers' Association (GMA). Among other things, the GMA dealt with problems related to exchanging freight in the city and tried to establish common freight and passenger rates, wage scales, and labor policies. At a special meeting on June 25, 1894, the group agreed that their companies would act as one in resisting the pending boycott. Meeting daily to formulate policy during the difficulties, they designated a former member to direct the battle and serve as official spokesman for all. Not surprisingly, the general managers regarded disciplinary action as the way to suppress the boycott. All workers who refused to move sleeping cars would be discharged and replaced by persons recruited by a special GMA committee. It was this policy that converted the boycott into a strike on all of the railroads and brought rail traffic to a standstill.

Once the boycott-strike effectively tied up transportation, the GMA, on advice of its legal committee, sought closer ties with and more help from the Justice Department.

Attorney General Olney was receptive. Apparently at their request, he designated Edwin Walker as special attorney to direct the government's efforts against the strike at Chicago. Walker was the partner of a member of the GMA's legal committee.

The attorney general at once instructed Walker to petition the federal court in Chicago for an injunction against the boycott-strike. During such a strike, injunctions served two purposes: as grounds for sending federal troops directly into action against strikers, and for depriving strikes of leadership. Olney knew that ordinarily President Grover Cleveland would not send troops into a state unless requested to by the governor of that state. He agreed with most conservatives that Governor John Peter Altgeld of Illinois was pro-labor and probably would not ask for federal assistance. A few weeks before, however, the attorney general had devised a means for circumventing governors in securing federal intervention. In April, bands of unemployed men in the West were stealing trains to carry them to Washington to join Jacob S. Coxey's march for jobs. Federal judges issued injunctions against such acts and when mobs defied them, Cleveland, with or without a governor's request, sent in troops to uphold the judges. During the same incidents, when strikers and supporting mobs disregarded court orders, their leaders were arrested, brought before the judges, and punished summarily for contempt of court. Since juries were not involved, punishment in the form of jail terms, fines, or both was certain and swift. These precedents served Olney and the railroads well during the great boycott-strike.

In Chicago, the very judges who would later issue the injunctions, improperly assisted Walker in drafting his petition. Two laws originally designed to curb abuses by railroads and big businesses, the Interstate Commerce and Sherman Antitrust acts, served as the basis of the request. The sweeping injunction, handed down on July 2nd, prohibited any interference with interstate commerce or the mail; prohibited any activities that would injure or destroy tracks, switches, signals, or buildings; and prohibited any uncoupling of cars, engines, or parts of trains. Further, it prohibited Debs and "all other persons" from compelling or inducing railroad employees to refuse to perform their duties or to commit any act to further the strike. Neither were they to order, direct, aid, assist, or abet anyone engaged in such actions. United States attorneys in other jurisdictions soon sought and obtained similar injunctions.

On advice of counsel, Debs ignored the order and continued to direct the strike. On July 3, a mob at Blue Island, just outside Chicago, jeered and hooted a federal marshal who tried to read the injunction to them. They then dragged baggage cars across the tracks, obstructing passage of the mail. The marshal wired Olney for troops, declaring that he was unable to disperse the mob, clear the tracks, or arrest the troublemakers. A federal judge, the U.S. attorney, and special counsel Edwin Walker all countersigned the plea. President Cleveland at once authorized sending Army units to Chicago. Thereafter, federal troops were sent to various trouble spots around the country in response to similar requests.

Governor Altgeld, in two communications, protested the presence of the Army in Chicago as unnecessary and illegal. Illinois forces were adequate, he maintained, and would be used to preserve and maintain order. Cleveland, in terse responses allegedly drafted by Olney, denied that his act was unconstitutional since it was for the purpose of protecting the mail and enforcing U.S. court processes, both federal responsibilities.

As in the Railroad Strikes of 1877, federal troops generally commanded respect that local and state officers and troops and even federal marshals did not. Wherever they appeared, mobs generally tended to melt away. For example, at least thirteen were killed and fifty-three wounded in Chicago during the disorders, none by the U.S. Army which operated extensively in the area.

Debs recognized that when the army arrived to enforce the court order, the ARU's battle with the railroad companies had been transformed into a struggle with the federal government. It was a battle he could not win. The ARU leadership decided to end the matter by offering to call off the strike with the single condition that the men be rehired at their former jobs. Nothing else, not even recognition of the union, was sought.

Meanwhile, many workers and some unions such as the Knights of Labor joined the contest. Under pressure from leaders sympathetic to the ARU, Samuel Gompers, president of the American Federation of Labor, called a meeting of the general labor council of Chicago. Debs urged that body to convey his offer to end the strike to the GMA. If they rejected it, the council should order a general strike to force the GMA and Pullman to rehire the strikers. Conservative labor leaders including Gompers and the heads of the railway brotherhoods, long opposed to industrial unionism and Debs, declined to participate in what they saw as a doomed venture. Speaking for the majority, Gompers declared that a general strike would be "inexpedient, unwise and contrary to the best interests of the working people."

When the Army broke up the blocking of trains and federal marshals locked up Debs and the other strike leaders, the upheaval quickly came to an end. The impact on the workers varied. Although most returned to their old jobs, many were denied employment. The Pullman Company eventually rehired two-thirds of the men who had gone on strike, paying them the same wage that originally had led them to walk out. About a thousand either refused to return or were denied work and drifted to other jobs. Railroad strikers fared about the same. Most were rehired by the companies, but several thousand were blacklisted and denied jobs because they had been involved in violence or troublemaking during the strike. Many of that group never again worked for any railroad.

Both the ARU and the model company town of Pullman were also casualties of the great strike. Although Debs tried to keep the ARU alive, railroad detectives hounded his every move, and railway workers who joined his union were promptly discharged. In June 1897, the remnants of the union, still loyal to Debs, reorganized as the Social Democratic Party, a forerunner of the Socialist Party of America. As for the model community, shortly after the death of George M. Pullman in 1897, the Illinois Supreme Court ruled that the Pullman Company had exceeded its authority in building and managing the company town. As a result the company broke its ties to the town and over the next few years Pullman degenerated into one of the many dreary suburbs south of Chicago.

Debs and his principal aides received the brunt of the punishment for the strike. The federal court in Chicago found Debs guilty of contempt and sentenced him to six months in jail. On appeal to the United States Supreme Court, the justices, by unanimous vote, upheld the decision of the lower court. They ruled that the federal courts were correct to protect interstate commerce by issuing injunctions as was done at Chicago, and the President had been right to use the armed forces of the United States to uphold those injunctions. Moreover, accepting the grounds advanced by Olney in his argument before the court, those acts were justified, not by such "experimental" legislation as the Sherman Antitrust Act but by the constitutional grant to the federal government of control over interstate commerce. The decision was far reaching. Since any railroad strike of necessity threatened the movement of interstate commerce, it could be enjoined, and if continued, would

be suppressed. In effect, the decision outlawed strikes on the nation's railroads.

A parallel criminal case against Debs for conspiracy to obstruct the mail was postponed when a juror fell ill. Eventually, Attorney General Olney dropped the case, probably not wishing to risk an acquittal that would tarnish his earlier triumph before the Supreme Court. Debs served his term for contempt. His experiences led him into the Socialist movement where he soon emerged as its outstanding spokesman and frequent candidate for President of the United States.

The apparent total victory of the railroads proved to be short- lived. To the surprise of the railroad community, Olney seemed suddenly to shift sides. A few months after the strike, in a friend-of-the-court brief in another case, he argued that railway workers had the right to form unions. He continued to believe that the peculiar public service function of railway workers barred them from striking, but that being true, their rights somehow had to be protected. To that end, he proposed voluntary arbitration and helped draft what later became the Erdman Act, which set up a federal railway arbitration board.

Whatever Olney's motivation, he seems to have reacted to a change that took place in public opinion during or soon after the Pullman Strike. Generally it was agreed that the welfare of the nation demanded that the railroad network be kept open and operating at all times. When government intervened in railway strikes for that purpose, however, it should do so as a neutral, not as the champion of the companies against the workers. The objective should be to restore service by resolving the dispute, not to crush the workers. A lasting consequence of the Pullman Strike and Boycott was that few wished to repeat the experience. Railroad workers did not again engage in a massive strike until 1922. Gradually the companies extended tacit recognition to the railroad brotherhoods and informally negotiated labor problems with them. As for the federal government, whenever a railroad strike was threatened, Congress enacted special legislation or the executive intervened other than by force to ward off confrontations that no one wanted. [Gerald G. Eggert]

FURTHER READING

Buder, Stanley. *Pullman: An Experiment in Industrial Order and Community Planning.* New York: Oxford University Press, 1967.

Eggert, Gerald G. *Railroad Labor Disputes, The Beginnings of Federal Strike Policy.* Ann Arbor, MI: University of Michigan Press, 1967.

Ginger, Ray. *The Bending Cross, A Biography of Eugene Victor Debs.* New Brunswick, NJ: Rutgers University Press, 1949.

Lindsey, Almont. *The Pullman Strike.* Chicago, IL: University of Chicago Press, 1942.

Salvatore, Nick. *Eugene V. Debs, Citizen and Socialist.* Urbana, IL: University of Illinois Press, 1982.

o o o

R. J. REYNOLDS TOBACCO COM-
PANY STRIKE OF 1947. On May 1, 1947,
approximately 8,000 workers of the R. J.
Reynolds Tobacco Company in Winston-
Salem, North Carolina, walked off their
jobs. Representatives of their union, Local
22 of the Food, Tobacco, Agricultural and
Allied Workers (FTA), had been unable to
negotiate a new collective bargaining agreement with management, and union members refused to work without a contract.
Wages and benefits were important issues in
the dispute, but the company also claimed
the union's demand for a dues check-off (a
provision in previous contracts) violated
North Carolina's recently passed right-to-
work law. The thirty-eight-day strike gained
nationwide attention as singing workers
massed on the picket lines, and the company charged Communist domination of
the union.

The conflict between the largely black
work force and the R. J. Reynolds Tobacco
Company had a long history. The company
began doing business in 1875, one of a
number of small manufacturing firms that
stimulated the industrial expansion of the
postwar South. Its founder, R. J. Reynolds,
used aggressive merchandising to gain control of the market in chewing and smoking
tobacco in the late nineteenth century. With
the introduction of "Camels" in 1913, the
company also became a major producer of
cigarettes.

Black workers from the surrounding
countryside supplied the labor for the early
factories, much as their slave ancestors had
done in Virginia's antebellum factories.
Whites moved into the industry only after
the adoption of new technologies such as
the high-speed cigarette-making machine.
The labor-intensive jobs of stemming, cleaning, and conditioning the tobacco continued to be the province of blacks, and they
constituted a majority of the work force into
the 1960s. Labor relations were not far
removed from the plantation. White male
foremen exercised strict control on the shop
floor, while executives played the role of
distant paternalists. Conditions in the factories were hot and dirty, and wages were
among the lowest in the country.

The company and its executives
dominated the social, political, and economic life of Winston-Salem. In 1935, sociologist Charles S. Johnson described the city
this way: "Winston-Salem is built around a
single great industry, tobacco. So important
and powerful is the tobacco industry and the
R. J. Reynolds Tobacco Company, which is
the largest local plant, that the city in many
respects suggests a vast mill town. The influence of one company extends to practically
every phase of life of the town."

Reynolds employees had long complained about low wages, poor working
conditions, and racial discrimination; in the
summer of 1943, the rising cost of living and
a production speedup intensified those
chronic resentments. On June 17, women in
one of the factories sat down on their jobs,
sparking a plantwide strike. This action
provided the impetus for the rapid organization of workers into the United Cannery,
Agricultural, Packing and Allied Workers of
America (UCAPAWA). As one of the left-led
Congress of Industrial Organizations (CIO)

unions, UCAPAWA championed the black struggle for political as well as economic rights and employed a number of young radicals, including several black organizers. Local 22 of the renamed Food, Tobacco, Agricultural and Allied Workers won important concessions from Reynolds in 1944, 1945, and 1946. These included higher wages and benefits, seniority rights, and a grievance procedure establishing a system of industrial jurisprudence in the plants.

A variety of factors influenced the process of union building—the structure of labor law, the policies of the CIO, and the particular goals of the FTA. But Local 22 was not just an outpost of the industrial labor movement. It was a self-initiated working-class institution that drew on the organizational structure of the black church, the leadership skills of men and women, and a religious vision that sanctioned active opposition to oppression.

Armed with a union contract that provided a measure of employment security, black unionists used their new-found economic power to press for an expansion of their political and social rights. Voter registration topped the list of priorities. In the summer of 1944, the union established a political action committee to register black workers. By election time in November, the committee had added hundreds of new voters to the rolls. These efforts paid off in 1947, when the Reverend Kenneth Williams won a seat on the Board of Aldermen, becoming the first black in the South in the twentieth century to win an election against a white. Organization and political clout gave workers greater leverage at City Hall and at the county courthouse. Union officials participated effectively in debates on improved social services for the black community, minority representation on the police and fire departments, and low-cost public housing.

Marshaling its own enormous economic power, Reynolds fought back. Soon after the war ended, the company began installing new labor-saving machinery throughout its factories. Hardest hit were the stemmeries. Minimum wage laws and collective bargaining agreements had greatly increased the cost of production in these labor-intensive departments, and the black women employed there were the heart and soul of the union. When contract negotiations began in 1947, Reynolds indicated that it was unwilling to meet the union's request for further improvements. Unable to reach an agreement with the company, workers reluctantly voted to strike on May 1.

The black community provided crucial support for the strike, donating food to the soup kitchens, money for rent payments, and bodies for the picket lines. Barbers and beauticians pitched in by offering free services to workers. Union members traveled to New York, Philadelphia, and Detroit to raise money and win support for their boycott against Reynolds. The greatest show of solidarity came shortly after the strike when Paul Robeson sang for thousands of workers at an outdoor rally.

In the midst of the strike the *Winston-Salem Journal* charged that the Communist Party, which had recruited some members among the union's leaders, had "captured Local 22, the Reynolds union of the C.I.O. tobacco workers—lock, stock, and barrel." Statements identifying party members made by three former union officials—all white—accompanied articles written by the newspaper staff warning that the situation was leading from "peaceful picketing to open rioting." The House Committee on Un-American Activities ordered an immediate investigation and later called union leaders to Washington to testify.

The charges failed to bring Local 22 to the bargaining table on bended knees. But it did stir up a hornet's nest of reaction against the union in the white community. While the revelations of Communist Party activity dominated the headlines and hampered negotiations with the company, strikers continued to walk the picket line and support their elected leaders. The parties finally reached a settlement on June 7, a settlement that fell far short of the workers' demands. This also proved to be the last collective bargaining agreement signed by the Reynolds Tobacco Company.

Two factors contributed to the less than satisfactory results. First, Local 22 was never able to stop production as it had in 1943. Second, the union was operating in a radically transformed political environment. The passage of the Taft-Hartley bill put pressure on the union to sign a contract, and the anti-Communist hysteria that engulfed the nation in 1947 isolated the left-led unions from their old allies.

When the FTA's contract ran out in the spring of 1948, Reynolds refused further negotiations on the grounds that the union had not complied with the provisions of the recently-passed Taft-Hartley Act requiring all union officers to sign non-Communist affidavits. By the following fall, unionists began to feel the repercussions from the split between the center and the left-wing of the CIO. A rival CIO union, the United Transport Service Employees (UTSE), sent organizers to Winston-Salem to persuade black workers to reject Local 22. In the meantime, the FTA complied with the provisions of the Taft-Hartley Act and requested a new election. On March 8, 1950, the FTA won a plurality of the votes; a runoff two weeks later gave Local 22 a margin of fifty votes, but the NLRB accepted the challenged ballots of lower-level supervisors, and the union lost the election. [Robert Korstad]

FURTHER READING

Korstad, Robert R. "Those Who Were Not Afraid: Winston-Salem, 1943."In *Working Lives: The Southern Exposure History of Labor in the South.* Marc Miller, ed. New York: Pantheon, 1980, pp. 184–199.

——. *Daybreak of Freedom: Tobacco Workers and the CIO, Winston Salem, North Carolina,* *1943–1950.* Ph.D. dissertation, University of North Carolina, 1987.

Tilley, Nannie M. *The R. J. Reynolds Tobacco Company.* Chapel Hill, NC: University of North Carolina Press, 1985.

o   o   o

RADIO CORPORATION OF AMERICA (RCA) STRIKE OF 1936. This strike was the most dramatic event of a five-year struggle between what became Local 103 of the United Electrical, Radio, and Machine Workers of America (UE) and a company union sponsored by RCA.

RCA began manufacturing operations in 1930, when it purchased the former Victor Talking Machine plant in Camden, New Jersey. The company spent $5.5 million renovating and expanding the plant and employment rose from 7,000 to 20,000. By the end of 1931, as the Depression worsened, RCA slashed wages and salaries. By the summer of 1932, only about 5,000 workers retained jobs at the complex.

In March 1933, RCA announced new wage cuts and a speedup plan for incentive workers. A group of tool and die makers, some of whom were members of the Metal Workers Industrial Union, an affiliate of the Communist-led Trade Union Unity League (TUUL), threatened to strike and shut down the tool room for a day as a protest. They formed a new union, the RCA Victor Shop Association, and set out to organize the entire work force.

In response to this and to the nearly simultaneous passage of the National Industrial Recovery Act (NIRA), RCA decided to sponsor an employee representation plan. Each division elected representatives and the company appointed additional members to form a Joint Conference. The company union would discuss "all matters of mutual interest pertaining to working conditions," but all of its actions were subject to review by RCA.

The Shop Association initially tried to

take over the company union. Blocked in this effort, they withdrew, charging that it was company-dominated and contrary to Section 7(a) of the NIRA which gave workers the right to have unions of their own choosing. The Shop Association then changed its name to the Radio and Metal Workers Industrial Union (RMWIU). In response to these steps, the leaders of the Joint Conference modified its constitution, removing direct RCA sponsorship and changing its name to the Employees Committee Union (ECU).

From mid-1933 to early 1936 a stalemate existed. RCA management claimed impartiality and stated that it would discuss problems with any duly elected representatives of its employees and meet once a month with each group to discuss issues. The closest academic observer of RCA in this period wrote, "there is ample evidence that RCA strongly favored" the ECU. Improving profits and union pressure brought 10 percent wage hikes in July 1933, and April 1934, as well as time and a half for overtime and other gains. Management gave credit for the improvements to the ECU.

In March 1936, the RMWIU attended the founding convention of the UE and was chartered as Local 103. The union decided to attempt to break the deadlock with the ECU and RCA while business remained strong. Even though only about one-third of the workers were paying dues, the union believed that it had the allegiance of a majority. On May 20, 1936, the union asked for a signed contract, the abolition of the ECU, a 20 percent wage hike and a closed shop. RCA quickly rejected this proposal. It hired former NIRA chief Hugh Johnson as its "Special Labor Advisor" and continued inconclusive meetings with the UE.

A mass meeting of Local 103 on June 23 launched the strike. On the first day, as many as 80 percent of the production workers honored the strike call. RCA attempted to maintain production. The company hired over 1,000 strikebreakers, recruited private

guards through the Sherwood Detective Agency and employed two professional strikebreakers, Max Sherwood and George "Toupee" Williams to "organize community sentiment." The corporation spent over $244,000 on these efforts, plus another $586,000 on the subcontracting of partially completed orders. The ECU leadership, which urged its members to cross the picket lines, worked in close harmony with the company and local police and raised their own slogan of a closed shop for the ECU.

Throughout the strike, Local 103 maintained mass picket lines of 700 to 6,000 persons. Fist fights and stone-throwing incidents were daily events, and there were several stabbings on each side, none fatal. Large-scale arrests of strikers took place, reaching nearly 200 a day at times. Those arrested included almost all of the local's officers and UE national president James Carey. "Jersey Justice" became a byword for anti-labor judicial bias. Either Carey or UE secretary-treasurer Julius Emspak was on the scene for almost the entire strike, providing union direction. Strong support for the walkout came from the two UE locals at the nearby Philco plants in the form of pickets and over $50,000 in bail bond money.

Meanwhile, behind the scenes, Hugh Johnson and RCA president David Sarnoff were negotiating with the CIO's John L. Lewis, who had taken a strong interest in the strike from the beginning. Lewis had sent his assistant, Powers Hapgood, to assist in the strike and had helped mobilize support from the Camden shipyard workers.

An agreement was reached on July 21, 1936, to end the strike, as both sides were experiencing grave problems with its continuation. The liberal image of David Sarnoff had been badly damaged when his strike-breaking activities were widely publicized by the National Committee for the Defense of Political Prisoners. The union had filed an unfair labor practice charge against RCA with the National Labor Relations Board

(NLRB) for sponsoring a company union. Most importantly, the strike had been strong enough to nearly curtail production and to cause RCA to lose substantial business to its rival, Philco.

The UE was also feeling the pressure. Hundreds of its members had been jailed and over $2 million in bail bond money had been required. Worse, about half the pre-strike work force was now entering the plant daily, including 1,000 strikebreakers.

The contract called for all strikers to be rehired as business warranted. No outside employees were to be hired before March 31, 1937. RCA was, in a complex formula, to maintain wage and hour parity with Philco. Finally, RCA agreed to consent to an NLRB election and to recognize the union as the exclusive bargaining agent if it received a majority vote of the eligible employees.

The NLRB election was held on August 16, 1936. The ECU appeared on the ballot but a few days before the election, attempted to organize a boycott of the vote. The election results showed 3,016 votes for the UE and just 51 for the ECU out of an eligible pool of 9,752. On November 9, 1936, the NLRB certified UE Local 103 as the exclusive bargaining agent, because NLRB rules required only that the election winner receive a majority of the votes cast.

RCA, acting under Johnson's advice, continued to deny the UE exclusive bargaining recognition. Once again, there was a protracted stalemate between the union and the ECU. RCA failed to rehire almost 500 of the strikers and continued to meet and negotiate with both groups. There was "constant friction in the plants" and fights and short stoppages "became the order of the day."

In April 1937, an important turn in the situation occurred when the constitutionality of the National Labor Relations Act was upheld by the Supreme Court. Feeling certain that NLRB charges would now stick and that worker support for the ECU was waning, the company moved to settle the long

dispute. Johnson was removed from his position and replaced by Edward F. McGrady, one-time AFL official and a former assistant secretary of labor. Rapid progress was made. On October 8, 1937, an agreement was signed recognizing the UE as the exclusive bargaining agent and calling for a joint review of the cases of the 500 non-rehired strikers.

One week following the signing of the contract, the International Brotherhood of Electrical Workers (IBEW) granted the ECU a charter. In 1939, this IBEW local petitioned for a new NLRB representation election. UE Local 103 defeated it by a margin of 5,294 to 1,035. The ECU was finally dead. According to UE secretary-treasurer Julius Emspak, the 1936 RCA strike was decisive in establishing the UE as a strong, militant force in the industry and had a significant influence on the union's position at General Electric and Westinghouse. It was the first major strike test for the UE, a test the union survived. [Mark McColloch]

FURTHER READING

Derber, Milton. "Electrical Products." In *How Collective Bargaining Works*. Harry A., Millis, ed. New York: Twentieth Century Fund, 1942.

Galsenson, Walter. *The CIO Challenge to the AFL.* Cambridge, MA: Harvard University Press, 1960.

Matles, James J., and James Higgins. *Them and Us.* New York: Prentice-Hall, 1974.

o   o   o

RAILROAD SHOPMEN'S STRIKE OF 1922. The Railroad Shopmen's Strike of 1922 occurred against the backdrop of a postwar recession and an intensive campaign launched by railway management to roll back the significant wartime gains achieved by railroad shopcraft unions. Governmental control and operation of the nation's railroads during the war had been a boon to rail labor. Under the U.S. Railroad Administration's (USRA) auspices, the constituent unions of the American Federation of Labor's Railway Employees' Department (AFL-RED) increased their membership, gained the right to engage in collective bargaining, and won important concessions in wages and work rules embodied in the national agreements between the USRA and various railroad system federations. The railway unions hoped to sustain these gains by endorsing nationalization of the railroads in peacetime. Congress, however, rejected the proposed Plumb Plan and returned the railroads to private ownership under the Transportation Act of 1920. This act also established a nine-member Railroad Labor Board (RLB) (labor, management, and government represented by three members each) to handle grievances arising over wages, work rules, and working conditions.

From the outset, the railroad shopcraft unions viewed the new federal agency with skepticism. President Harding's appointments to the RLB reflected an anti-labor bias. Even its labor representatives were drawn from the more conservative locomotive brotherhoods and maintenance-of-way union. The Railway Employees' Department perceived the board as a preliminary step toward compulsory industrial arbitration which it opposed. Moreover, labor feared that the agency would serve as management's primary mechanism to depress wages and abrogate the national railroad agreements which had protected their interests.

Their fears were confirmed by the RLB decisions regarding wages and work rules between 1920 and 1922. Initially, the RLB granted railway employees a wage increase of thirteen cents per hour and continued to abide by the national agreements pending further review. The recession of 1921, however, legitimatized railway management's demand for wage deflation and work rule changes to cope with the economic crisis. The Association of Railroad Executives (ARE) persuasively argued before the board that wages had generally declined in non-transportation industries and that labor was available at much cheaper

rates than that prescribed by the board's ruling in 1920. As a result, the RLB ordered wage reductions ranging from five to eighteen cents an hour.

The railroad unions opposed the board-sanctioned wage reductions. Long denied a wage increase, they now felt that their organizations were the first to be subjected to management-induced wage deflation. The Federation Shop Crafts (composed of the railway mechanics) within the AFL-RED voted overwhelmingly to reject the wage slash. A threatened strike by the train service brotherhoods was only averted by the board's decision not to implement wage cuts until the thorny problem of work rule changes had been resolved.

In August 1921, the RLB began its overhaul of the national agreements, in effect, releasing railroads from the constraints of many labor-supported work rules. Management was no longer obligated to pay overtime rates for work on Sundays and legal holidays. The minimum guarantee of hours for employees to perform special work was reduced from five to four hours. Moreover, the board's abrogation of the national agreements necessitated the negotiation of new agreements between the carriers and various systems federations—a dismal prospect for the unions, given the poor state of the economy and the railroads' anti-union stance.

Officers of the AFL-RED cautioned its members against undertaking unauthorized strikes, but pledged not to incorporate any of the revisions in the new agreements. Member unions were instructed to strengthen their organizations and conserve finances in anticipation of a confrontation. In early 1922, however, the executive committees of each of the shopcraft unions accepted the work rule changes with the exception of the provision abolishing overtime pay for Sunday and holiday work.

Labor, meanwhile, chaffed under the carriers' anti-union policies and the recession's impact. Nearly 40 percent of the shopcraft and maintenance-of-way work force lay idle by the end of 1921. The AFL-RED charged that railway management contributed to unemployment by contracting out work to non-union shops. Several railroads, following the lead of the Pennsylvania and Erie railroads, established "contract shops" in an effort to circumvent union work rules and spread the piece rate system of remuneration. Railroad executives, on the whole, refused to engage in collective bargaining with their system federations. A few carriers even established company unions. The Pennsylvania Railroad flagrantly bypassed its system federation, conducted a separate election with its own slate of candidates, and concluded an agreement with an employee representation committee. Though the RLB ordered new elections and threatened to publicize the road's violation of the Transportation Act, the Pennsylvania Railroad obtained a federal court injunction enjoining the board from taking any action.

The board's inability to punish carriers violating its decisions brought the railway labor unions to the brink of a strike. A new round of wage cuts announced for July 1, 1922—reducing shopcraft wages by an average of 12 percent—constituted the final straw. The six shopcraft unions (including 120 system federations) and maintenance-of-way men voted to strike over three issues: the contracting out of work, the board's abolishment of overtime pay for Sunday and holiday work, and the latest installment of wage cuts. When the RLB rejected the AFL-RED's request for an early hearing to resolve its dispute with the carriers, the department authorized a strike.

On July 1, 400,000 railroad shopmen walked out in the nation's largest railway strike since the **Pullman Strike of 1894.** Though the maintenance-of-way men's union rescinded its strike call when the RLB acted swiftly on its appeal for a slight wage increment, the shopmen's walkout was 90 percent effective. Almost immediately, the nation's carriers were forced to curtail train service and shop operations. Violence erupted on some railroads, but the carriers suffered mainly from a paucity of skilled workers to repair and maintain locomotives. At Needles, California, Santa Fe train crews stranded 300 passengers as a protest against poorly repaired engines and the presence of armed guards on the trains.

From the strike's outset the Association of Railroad Executives sought to use the RLB as an instrument to break the strike and establish an open shop. On July 3, the board adopted a resolution condemning the strikers as "outlaws" and threatening them with a loss of seniority if they didn't return to work. Railway executives interpreted the resolution as a blank check to employ non-union replacement workers and strip striking shopmen of their seniority. The ARE refused to negotiate with the AFL-RED until the strikers returned to work. Seniority, rather than wages, now became the paramount issue in the strike. The railroad shopcraft union equated the attack on seniority as a threat against its existence.

As the strike wore on, it presented the nation and the administration of President Warren G. Harding with a grave crisis. Following on the heels of the national **Bituminous Coal Strike of 1922** launched by the United Mine Workers (UMW) in April, the rail strike and resulting transportation failure made the fuel shortage even more acute. The twin crisis divided Harding's cabinet. Commerce Secretary Herbert Hoover and Secretary of Labor James H. Davis attempted to bring together representatives of the AFL-RED and moderate railroad executives (such as Daniel Willard of the Baltimore & Ohio Railroad) in order to arrange a settlement which would keep the railway shopcraft unions intact. Attorney General Harry M. Daugherty urged vigorous federal intervention to end the strike. He dispatched federal marshals to protect railroad property and employed agents to gather evidence pursuant to an injunction to break the strike.

President Harding wavered between

the two positions. He first proposed a settlement whereby labor agreed to wage cuts, management restored full seniority rights, and the disputants pledged to abide by all future RLB decisions. Reeling from management's open-shop drive and financially drained, the striking shopmen were willing to settle on such unfavorable terms. However, the railway executives remained intransigent on the issue of seniority and refused to discharge replacement workers. The Association of Railroad Executives wanted nothing short of the railroad shopcraft unions' total capitulation.

In early August, Harding reversed his moderate position and embraced the virulent anti-union views of his attorney general. The month-long railroad shopmen's strike had paralyzed transportation and exacerbated the national coal shortage. Failing to win over railroad management, the President resolved to end the strike at labor's expense. He now proposed that striking workers resume work and submit the question of seniority rights to the RLB for a final decision—in effect resolving the dispute by compulsory arbitration. The unions rejected this solution as it had been the board's previous rulings that had initiated the strike. The stage was set for governmental intervention to break the strike.

On August 19, Harding addressed a joint session of Congress concerning the labor crisis. He accused the strikers of "cruelty and contempt" and engaging in a conspiracy to paralyze transportation against the public interest. His public statements, which glossed over management's violation of RLB decisions, were a prelude of things to come. Two weeks later, Attorney General Daugherty approached Federal District Judge James Wilkerson of Chicago and obtained a temporary restraining order to circumscribe the strikers' actions. The resulting blanket injunction, issued on September 23, was unprecedented. National in scope, it listed the officers of the AFL-RED, the shopcraft unions, and 120 system federations. More-

over, it banned virtually every action taken by the unions in support of the strike—including the dispensing of union funds. Symbolically, the injunction was a blow to organized labor and the principle of government impartiality in labor–management disputes. As a strikebreaking tactic it backfired. The injunction merely strengthened the strikers' resolve or had minimal impact as thousands of shopmen found other employment.

By September 1922, the two-month-old strike began to foment dissension within managerial ranks. Moderates, exasperated with the rapacious anti-labor policies of some carriers and fearful that the prolonged strike threatened their own financial stability, sought a solution outside the ARE. Led by Daniel Willard of the Baltimore & Ohio, they proposed to the Federated Shop Craft Policy Committee that separate settlements for each railroad be negotiated by joint commissions representing management and the respective system federation. Initially, the committee balked. Piecemeal settlements, they reasoned, undermined strikers' morale and unity against hard-line railroads such as the Pennsylvania Railroad. Moreover, intransigent carriers might exploit the arrangement by contracting out shop work to conciliatory railroads in order to break the strike. With the strike nearly lost and the railway shopcraft unions in dire financial straits, the committee reluctantly agreed to the "Baltimore Agreement" on September 13, 1922. Under this agreement, the committee authorized separate settlements that restored full seniority to striking workers and pledged the disputants to resolve their outstanding differences by establishing joint commissions.

In conjunction with the agreement, the B & O Railroad pioneered a labor–management cooperation plan which granted shopcraft unions recognition and greater responsibility at the shop floor level. The plan entailed the creation of joint shop committees composed of local managers and shopcraft employees who met regularly to devise ways to improve shop conditions and promote efficiency. The shop committees, however, did not function as forums to discuss wages and grievances. First installed in the B & O's Glenwood shops near Pittsburgh, the cooperation plan was extended to forty-five shops in the system. A joint system cooperation committee reviewed and advised upon the recommendations of the local shop committees and coordinated the cooperation plan for the B & O system. Though some unionists viewed the plan as a thinly veiled employee representation committee, others saw it as a mechanism that ensured the shopcraft unions' continued existence on the railroad.

Led by the B & O's example, 112 roads (including the New York Central and Erie Railroad) secured settlements with their system federations, though few adopted the ambitious labor–management cooperation plan. The agreements restored seniority status to over 225,000 shopmen. However, 130 carriers—led by the Pennsylvania Railroad—refused to settle under the terms of the "Baltimore Agreement." Their refusal prolonged the strike (the International Association of Machinists did not call off its strike until 1924) and resulted in 175,000 shopmen losing their seniority rights. Those who returned to work on the victorious railroads found themselves subjected to disadvantageous work rules and piece rates, and marshalled into company unions.

In retrospect, the settlement reached in the 1922 railroad shopmen's strike represented a salvaging operation for labor. Beyond the restoration of seniority rights for half of the striking shopmen and the shopcraft unions' continued existence, the strike achieved little. Defeat resulted in a precipitous decline in membership and the proliferation of company unionism in the locomotive shops. Moreover, the struggle indicated that a powerful anti-labor axis had been forged by government and railway management, creating a favorable environment for the "American Plan" to flourish. All pretenses of governmental impartiality had been stripped away by the RLB's actions and the Wilkerson injunction. As a result, labor engaged in independent political action to vent its frustration. The railway shopcraft unions proved instrumental in securing passage of the Railway Labor Act of 1926, which created the more impartial United States Board of Mediation to resolve railway labor disputes and endorsed railroad labor's right to organize and engage in collective bargaining. [James Quigel]

FURTHER READING

Perlman, Selig, and Philip Taft. *History of Labor in the United States 1896–1932*, Vol. IV, *Labor Movements*. New York: The Macmillan Company, 1935.

Troy, Leo. "Labor Representation on American Railways." *Labor History*, Vol. 2 (Fall, 1961), pp. 295–322.

Zieger, Robert. *Republicans and Labor 1919–1929*. Lexington, KY: University of Kentucky Press, 1969.

o   o   o

RAILROAD STRIKE OF 1946. The final major event of the great postwar strike wave of 1946 occurred on May 23 when railroad workers shut down the nation's entire railway system. Like workers in steel, auto, coal mining, electrical manufacturing, and a host of other industries, railroad workers had lost ground during the war as wages lagged significantly behind inflation. So long as overtime work was available, the effects of this loss were not so keenly felt. When the war ended, however, overtime disappeared, and unions throughout the economy struck to make up the differential. Nowhere had the decline in relative wages been greater than on the railroads. Indeed, the combination of the Great Depression and the wage controls of the war had reduced the wages of the railroad workers, in comparison with other industries, from first place in 1928 to twentieth in 1945.

In July of 1945, the five railroad brotherhoods formally submitted requests to the railroads for a 25 percent increase in wages, or approximately thirty cents an hour. In addition, they asked for standardization of basic rates of pay on a countrywide basis, revision of initial and final terminal delay rules, night differentials, time-and-a-half pay for Sunday and holiday work, limitations on the length of trains, and other adjustments involving a total of forty-four changes in work rules.

The two sides met through November and December, when the railroads declared that negotiations had reached an impasse and asked for the services of the National Mediation Board under the provisions of the Railway Labor Act. Early in 1946, two groups of railroad unions, one representing firemen, conductors, and switchmen, and the other representing the "nonoperating units," including shopcraft, maintenance-of-way, clerical, and other workers, agreed to submit their wage issues to arbitration. Two unions, however, the Brotherhood of Locomotive Engineers and the Brotherhood of Railroad Trainmen, refused the services of an arbitration board.

The fact that two arbitration boards were meeting concurrently, one for the three other brotherhoods, and one for the nonoperating unions, complicated the consideration of the case of the Engineers and Trainmen. Any settlement recommended for these unions would bring pressure on the Engineers and Trainmen as well. On April 3, the arbitration boards each awarded an increase of sixteen cents in the basic hourly rates. The Boards made few recommendations with regard to work rules changes, sending most back to the bargaining parties for resolution.

While the recommendations of the arbitration boards pleased none of the railroad unions, they did not directly involve the Engineers and Trainmen. The two brotherhoods had stayed aloof from the process from the beginning, and well before the boards' recommendations were announced,

they had taken a strike vote among their members that resulted in a 98 percent vote for a work stoppage on March 1, unless satisfactory terms were arranged. After the refusal of the Engineers and Trainmen to submit their dispute to arbitration, President Truman exercised his power under the Railway Labor Act to establish an emergency fact-finding board for these two unions. Truman's board recommended a settlement almost identical to that proposed by the arbitration boards. The two brotherhoods rejected it out of hand. In addition, although the other rail unions were more conciliatory, they still had not settled and were also preparing for a strike.

On May 14, President Harry Truman summoned railroad and union officials to separate conferences with government officials at the White House in an effort to avert the first nationwide railroad strike in a quarter of a century. Under pressure from the President, the unions did agree to postpone the strike for five days, from May 18 to May 23. Truman moved quickly to prepare for the worst. He invoked his powers under the wartime Smith-Connally Act on May 17 and seized the railroads. The Office of Defense Transportation was placed in control of operations. Truman's actions generated movement and on May 22, the railroads, the nonoperating unions, and the brotherhoods of the firemen, conductors, and switchmen accepted a compromise proposal from the President. It called for an eighteen-and-a-half cent hourly wage increase, and a withdrawal for one year of all requests for changes in work rules.

The next day, the strike deadline, the Engineers and Trainmen rejected the agreement, arguing that it was less favorable than the recommendations of the emergency fact-finding board that had considered their case. On the afternoon of May 23, all but a few of the 45,406 railroad trains of the United States came to a halt. All of the country suddenly felt the drastic, numbing effect of the rail shutdown. Trains scheduled to leave terminals after 4 P.M. on May 23 did not move, and those en route proceeded to specified terminals before being stopped. The action caused a mad scramble by commuters in the nation's major cities as the deadline neared. It was the first widespread strike by the railroad operating brotherhoods since the **Burlington Railroad Strike of 1888**. Although the two striking brotherhoods represented only 250,000 railroaders, the strike actually idled more than one million.

When the strike began, President Truman was entertaining wounded war veterans at a White House garden party. The next day he showed his anger at the defiance of the Engineers and Trainmen. In a nationwide radio broadcast he compared strike leaders A. F. Whitney of the Brotherhood of Railway Trainmen and Alvanley Johnston of the Brotherhood of Locomotive Engineers to the "foreign enemy" of Pearl Harbor. If the strikers did not return to work, said the President, railroad traffic would be ensured by federal troops. The intransigence of Whitney and Johnston had also aroused criticism from the nonstriking unions that had accepted the President's compromise. David B. Robertson, head of the Brotherhood of Locomotive Firemen, blasted the two strike leaders as "grasping for power" and "100 percent wrong."

Truman continued his offensive. On May 24, he went before Congress to ask for a law that would allow him to jail or draft any worker who would strike against the government. Significantly, Truman, who had always been considered friendly to the labor movement, also asked for the establishment of a joint congressional committee to study a revision of the nation's labor laws. Truman's strategy worked. Almost simultaneously with his appearance before Congress, Whitney and Johnston signed an agreement accepting the President's proposal of May 22 and ordered their members back to work. On May 26, the railroads were officially returned to private control.

Although the strike lasted only two days, its effects on labor relations were to prove much more enduring. Ever since the end of the war, through auto, steel, and electrical workers' strikes, the American public had remained more or less neutral. But when John L. Lewis, president of the United Mine Workers, called the **Bituminous Coal Strike of 1946** that browned out cities and endangered fuel supplies, anti-labor sentiment began to mount. The railroad strike brought that growing frustration to the surface even more as the public's patience with strikes began to wear thin.

The growing public perception that organized labor had become too powerful was also reflected in Congress. The House of Representatives had immediately passed the emergency bill that Truman had requested, and the Senate passed a modified version shortly after. Although these two bills were never reconciled, the Case Bill, which had been before Congress during the spring and was vigorously opposed by labor, was revised and approved by both houses. Ironically, only Truman's veto kept the strongly anti-labor bill from becoming law, but many of its provisions reappeared the following year in the Taft-Hartley Act, which significantly weakened the power of American unions. [Ronald L. Filippelli]

FURTHER READING

"The Great Train Strike." *Life* (June 3, 1946), pp. 27–33.

"Railroad Controversy Results in 2-Day Stoppage." *Monthly Labor Review*, Vol. 63 (July 1946), pp. 84–86.

o   o   o

RAILROAD STRIKES OF 1877. The Railroad Strikes of 1877 occurred between July 16 and August 5. Except for New England and the South, the wave of walkouts swept over most of the major railroad lines of the United States. The upheaval marked the onset of two decades of violent confrontation between railway workers and companies, culminating in the **Pullman Strike of 1894**. [*See also* **Union Pacific**, **Southwest**, **Burlington**, and **Great Northern** railroad strikes entries.] The suddenness, scale, and violence of the 1877 strikes took the nation by surprise. Such events were thought to be a European phenomenon, unlikely to happen in the United States. Although railway employees had suffered layoffs, pay reductions, and other consequences of the four years of depression that followed the Panic of 1873, they were generally better off than most workers. Moreover, there were no strong unions to call strikes or take over their direction once they began. The Brotherhood of Locomotive Engineers, following defeat in a strike against the Boston & Maine in February, had adopted a no-strike stance. Attempts in June to organize a Trainmen's Union embracing all railroaders may have galvanized some workers for what followed and provided a nucleus of strike leaders in a few communities, but the new union did not plan, organize, or direct the course of the strikes that summer. For the most part, they were spontaneous demonstrations against the railroads.

The troubles began with a series of wage cuts initiated by the eastern trunk lines (the Baltimore & Ohio, the Pennsylvania, the Erie, the New York Central, and the Grand Trunk). Following an agreement to end their ruinous rate wars, the companies decided to shore up their depression losses further by again reducing the wages of their employees. The Pennsylvania began the new round by lowering all wages in excess of one dollar a day by 10 percent on June 1. Other lines quickly followed. Until July 18 it seemed the workers would acquiesce. That day, however, Baltimore & Ohio workers at Martinsburg, West Virginia, threw down their tools and refused to move trains out of the yards.

Although there was no violence, railroad officials called upon Governor Henry M. Mathews of West Virginia for military assistance to put down a "riot" that local authorities were "powerless to suppress." Even with the state guard on hand, no one could be found to move the trains. At the urging of the B & O, Mathews called on President Rutherford B. Hayes for federal troops. The War Department replied that the President was averse to intervention unless there was an "insurrection" in progress that the state could not suppress. Mathews accordingly adopted the correct formula in his official request. Without independently checking into the nature of the so-called domestic insurrection, Hayes dispatched troops. With forces on hand less sympathetic to the workers than the state troopers had been, trains began moving and the yards were cleared.

The disorders, meanwhile, spread. Over the next few days, in railroad centers across the country—Baltimore, Pittsburgh, Buffalo, Columbus, Cleveland, Cincinnati, Indianapolis, Chicago, St. Louis, and San Francisco, to name but a few—throngs of the unemployed, the idle, the curious, and especially excitement-craving adolescents, joined the strikers. Railroaders themselves refused to move trains, and backed by angry crowds they prevented others from doing so. In Baltimore, state troops were called out to suppress strikers who were threatening railroad property. A mob of strike sympathizers stoned the troopers as they assembled at their armory, someone set the B & O depot on fire, and most windows in the riot area were smashed. Clashes between state guard units and rioters resulted in scores of casualties and the deaths of ten men and boys, none of them guardsmen or railroad employees.

The most serious rioting occurred at Pittsburgh where hostility focused on the Pennsylvania Railroad. Wage cuts by that company, its introduction of "double-headers" (longer trains pulled by two locomotives and manned by smaller crews), and the long history of its president, Thomas Scott, arrogantly manipulating the state legislature, made the Pennsylvania an obvious target of both railroaders and other disgruntled citizens. On July 19, railway workers in Pittsburgh refused to operate the new double-headers, thereby beginning a general tie-up of railroad traffic there. Trouble brewed as large numbers of people gathered. When neither local police nor state guard units from the Pittsburgh area could end the blockade, state troopers from Philadelphia were dispatched on July 21. The trains carrying them west encountered stone-throwing mobs at Harrisburg, Altoona, and Johnstown. At Pittsburgh, the Philadelphia units drew blood in a confrontation with those who were blocking trains. Angry mobs formed, set fire to the roundhouse where the Philadelphians spent the night, and subsequently drove them from the city. After two days of lawless rioting, looting, and destruction, the disorders burned themselves out about the time federal troops arrived on the scene.

Meanwhile, similar, though generally less spectacular affairs occurred across the railway network. Each community's experience had its unique feature. In Buffalo, local police, augmented by 300 special deputy sheriffs and a battalion of Civil War veterans, broke up the strike without state or federal assistance. The mayor of Indianapolis led a mob of jobless men to a large bakery and distributed free bread, then swore them in as special deputy police, and organized a citizen's committee to carry strikers' complaints to the railroads. About the same time, a federal judge in the same city organized a "committee of public safety" and swore in veterans and others as special deputy marshals to protect railroads in receivership from molestation by strikers.

A Marxist movement, the Workingmen's Party of the United States (WPUS), attempted to take over direction of the strike in several communities. It organized sympathetic mass meetings in New York, for example. In Chicago, the WPUS sought to convert the troubles into a general strike. Organized bands marched on the city's stockyards, planing mills, factories, and docks, calling out the workers. A combination of citizen's groups, veterans, local police, state guardsmen and federal troops, with some bloodshed, put down the disorders in the Windy City. Four sections of the WPUS in St. Louis met, declared their solidarity with the strikers, and marched en masse to a meeting of railroaders in the vast railyards across the river in East St. Louis, Illinois. For a week, strikers controlled the yards there. Meanwhile, back in St. Louis, the WPUS followed the example of their Chicago colleagues, calling upon all workers to walk out in support of the strike. Emboldened at their apparent success, the organizations' executive committee even offered to assist the mayor in preventing violence and tried to bargain with employers on behalf of the strikers. After a few days, the regular forces of law and order regained control of the situation and marched on the headquarters of the WPUS. The confrontation ended without a shot being fired. WPUS leaders who did not jump from the windows and flee were arrested. Not long after, federal forces retook possession of the yards in East St. Louis. The unique feature of the San Francisco disorders was a shift of the mob's target from the railroads to Chinese laborers who were widely perceived as the real cause of low wages and unemployment of white workers in the area.

Although the U.S. Army arrived in many of the trouble spots too late to deal with the most severe rioting, federal intervention was highly significant. There had been previous isolated instances when the Army suppressed strikes. However, until 1877, disputes between employees and employers were generally seen as well beyond the jurisdiction of the federal government. Matters of wages and working conditions were governed by market conditions, not statute law. Government, and especially the federal government, had no role. The intervention in 1877 for the first time fixed limits to this laissez faire attitude. Once a labor dispute erupted into violence and interfered with a federal function, it no longer was viewed as a labor dispute beyond the scope of government but as a disobedience of law that could not be tolerated. Beginning in 1877, the role of the federal government in strikes, and especially railroad strikes, became increasingly important.

It might seem that the strikes of 1877 crossed that new limit whenever they interfered with delivery of the mail or blocked interstate commerce. The Constitution itself specifically designated both as federal responsibilities. In fact, though each was offered as a justification for intervention, the Hayes administration did not cite either as grounds for sending in federal troops. In most instances, Hayes responded to requests of governors for assistance in suppressing domestic insurrection, to requests of federal judges for help against mobs who were defying injunctions that prohibited interference with bankrupt railroads in the hands of federal court receivers, or to protect federal property such as arsenals and treasury depositories from threatening mobs.

The possible use of troops to protect mail in 1877 was complicated by the willingness of strikers, and the unwillingness of railroad companies, to allow trains made up exclusively of mail cars to pass through blockades. Hayes did not wish to entangle himself in that dispute. Similarly, protecting interstate commerce by armed force, though no doubt constitutional, lacked strong historic precedent. By contrast, federal troops frequently had been employed during the recent Civil War and Reconstruction crises, and even before, to suppress domestic rebellion. This probably accounted for Hayes' willingness to use that justification, in spite of entries in his diary indicating that he saw the strikes not as rebellion against the government but as a response, however unjustified, of railroad workers to abuses by their employers.

The use of federal court injunctions as a major weapon against labor unions and strikes also emerged from the 1877 disorders. For several years the federal judges who handed down the injunctions in 1877 had played leading roles in developing railroad receiverships as a way of dealing with threatened railroad bankruptcies. The fact that railroads increasingly provided the primary means of transportation of persons and goods called for a means to protect those services when companies faced financial failure. The innovative judicial solution to this problem was for judges to take over the companies and operate them through court-appointed receivers. Judges traditionally protected the integrity of their courtrooms by summary contempt-of-court proceedings. Now, by extension, they protected railroad property in their care in the same manner. When strikers in 1877 threatened to prevent court appointed receivers from carrying out their duty to operate railroads in the custody of the courts, the judges issued injunctions warning against such actions. When those injunctions were ignored, the judges directed federal marshals to arrest the offenders and to bring them to court for summary punishment. The sheer number of offenders in 1877 prevented this means of enforcement, so courts called upon the President for troops and received them. In later strikes, federal judges would gradually broaden injunctions to protect not only railroads in receivership but also any line carrying interstate commerce or the mail.

Actually, Hayes had relatively few troops to use in suppressing the strikes. The Army consisted of only 25,000 men. Most were posted beyond the Mississippi River on the Mexican border or on the Indian frontier (the battle of the Little Big Horn had taken place only a year before). The skeleton forces scattered across the eastern portion of the nation were moved deftly. The Army Signal Corps, with men already stationed in all major cities as official weather observers, kept Washington reliably informed as to the strike's progress. Of necessity, only small detachments of soldiers could be sent to any one strike area. Although local police and state guard units suppressed most of the violence, wherever federal troops appeared, a quieting effect took place. The regular Army men were better disciplined than state guardsmen, looked and acted as if they meant business, and conducted themselves with restraint and calm under fire. Because they commanded respect, they were able to disperse crowds without the loss of a single soldier or the killing of a single civilian. By contrast, state troopers often were poorly trained and not used to military discipline. Themselves workers, many sympathized with the strikers. Crowds frequently taunted, assaulted, and even fired on them. Under pressure, the guards, sometimes with and sometimes without orders, opened fire on the crowds. Many rioters were reportedly killed. The number cannot be determined because most of the wounded and dying were carried from the scene and not reported.

The turning point of the strikes came near the end of July; on August 5, the Signal Corps reported quiet on all fronts. Trouble continued nonetheless in some communities. Coal miners in eastern Pennsylvania, whose employers for the most part were the so-called Anthracite Railroads, had struck in sympathy with the railroaders. When the latter returned to work at the end of July, the miners continued their walkout. A pitched battle took place on August 1 between miners and their sympathizers and the local police in Scranton. Again, many were wounded or killed. Four thousand state troops took up positions in the city for three months and over 1,400 federal soldiers and marines were on peace-keeping duty in the anthracite region until October 19.

At strikes' end, Hayes and his cabinet discussed the need for a federal policy for such emergencies. The President, in his diary, vaguely suggested education of the strikers, judicious control of the capitalists, and wise general policy to end or diminish the evil. When he called Congress into special session in October to consider a long-delayed Army appropriations bill, he praised the military for its prudent quelling of the disorders in July but made no suggestions for dealing with future railroad strikes or their causes. Congress, too, took little action. A bill to punish forcible obstruction of interstate commerce was introduced in each house, but never got out of committee, and nearly a year after the strikes, the House authorized a special congressional committee to investigate the causes of the depression, then in its fifth and last year.

The business community called for a larger Army and new and stronger laws to punish obstruction of trains. President Thomas Scott of the Pennsylvania Railroad argued that a railroad ought not have to be bankrupt to receive federal protection. He called upon federal judges to enjoin railroad strikes and recommended stationing Army units in major cities and at strategic points to enforce the injunctions. P. M. Arthur, head of the Brotherhood of Locomotive Engineers, on the other hand, called for a law requiring that all railway labor disputes be submitted to binding arbitration. Perhaps the most notable public attempts to prepare for future strikes were in states that enlarged their state guards, required better training, and built new fortress-like armories in some of the larger cities. Further actions for dealing with labor disputes would not come until violence again flared in later strikes and the railroads once more were shut down.

Workers, too, prepared for the future. Both concerned at the power of the forces arrayed against them and encouraged by their own strength, they stepped up their efforts to organize. The most immediate beneficiary was the Knights of Labor. It became a national union at its annual convention in 1878 and began an eight-year surge of growth that would sweep it briefly into the leadership of the American labor movement. [Gerald G. Eggert]

FURTHER READING

Bruce, Robert. *1877: Year of Violence.* Indianapolis, IN: Bobbs Merrill and Co., 1959.

Dacus, J. A. *Annals of the Great Strikes.* Chicago, IL: L. T. Palmer, 1877.

Eggert, Gerald G. *Railroad Labor Disputes, The Beginnings of Federal Strike Policy.* Ann Arbor, MI: University of Michigan Press, 1967.

Howe, George Frederick. "President Hayes's Notes of Four Cabinet Meetings." *American Historical Review,* Vol. 37 (January 1932), pp. 286–289.

o   o   o

RUBBER WORKERS' STRIKE OF 1913. By 1913, Akron, Ohio's rubber industry was solidly an open shop. A brief attempt at unionization of the industry by the American Federation of Labor (AFL) had been smashed in 1903. Thereafter, the Akron business community, with B.F. Goodrich, Goodyear, Firestone, and the other rubber companies in the lead, organized to make sure that unions could not gain a foothold in the city.

The lack of unionization was reflected in the conditions under which most of Akron's rubber workers toiled. The ten- to twelve-hour day and the six-day week were standard in the rubber industry. Most workers were on piece rates, while those on day wages earned seventeen and a half to twenty-five cents an hour. For piece-workers, rate reductions were common, and rubber workers were forced to work at a furious pace to earn a subsistence wage. Employers boasted that as a result of the speedup they could get 40 percent more production with the same number of men. In an industry that was increasingly consolidated and mechanized, the available pool of unskilled labor in Ohio, Pennsylvania, West Virginia, and Europe provided the companies with a reserve labor force whose presence further depressed wages and gave rubber workers second thoughts about any attempts at unionization.

In 1912, the Industrial Workers of the World (IWW) arrived in Akron, fresh from their great victory in the **Lawrence Textile Strike.** An IWW organizing drive began but made only halting progress until February 10, 1913, when the Firestone Tire Company announced a 35 percent cut in the piece-work rates paid in its auto tire department. The reduction caused a spontaneous strike which began with 150 tire builders and soon spread throughout the factory and beyond. The accumulated discontent that lay beneath the surface in Akron burst forth. By the next day, Goodyear and B.F. Goodrich workers had also turned out. Three days after the walkout began, some 4,000 rubber workers had left their posts. Overnight, the small band of IWW organizers had been presented with the opportunity to lead one of the great industrial uprisings in American history.

This show of militancy on the part of the heretofore docile Akron work force alarmed the authorities. Most of the workers were American born and because of this, company and political officials had assumed that they would have little interest in the appeal of the radical IWW. A plea from Mayor Frank Rockwell for state militia had been refused by the governor. Yet the strike continued to grow. By February 19, more than 15,000 rubber workers were on strike. The overwhelming majority were native Americans, with several thousand German and Hungarian immigrants in support.

The well-known talent of the IWW for dramatizing the plight of the strikers was fully in evidence in Akron. Parades swept through the city, strikers wore red ribbons to demonstrate their solidarity, and young women appeared on street corners to collect funds and support for the strikers. Rushing to capitalize on its unexpected good fortune, the IWW sent in veteran organizers such as George Speed, Arturo Giovannitti, W. E. Trautmann, and Bill Haywood.

At the beginning of the second week, the Committee of 100 that had been elected to direct the strike issued a nationwide call for support. Assistance came from Socialists

o

and AFL unions throughout Ohio and beyond. When the Akron Central Labor Union, an AFL affiliate, offered its support, however, AFL president Samuel Gompers warned them off, reminding them that the strike was being led by the IWW, Gompers' bitter enemy.

In the midst of the bickering with the AFL, which lasted throughout the strike, the strike committee presented its demands, calling for the reinstatement of all strikers without prejudice, the eight-hour workday, a uniform starting wage, and premium pay for overtime work. The wage demands across the many job classifications in the industry ranged from twenty to sixty cents per hour. The company refused to discuss the demands, blaming the strike on "outside agitators" with whom it would never negotiate. The Akron press fully supported the employers, concentrating on the radical tactics of the IWW and their implications for stability in the industry.

The employers' strategy involved the use of strikebreakers, a back-to-work movement, and the support of the local authorities. Labeling the strike "un-American," the companies formed the Citizen's Welfare League composed of business and professional men who pledged to protect the person and property of any workers wanting to return to work. Yet the solidarity of the strikers prevailed. Few chose to cross the picket lines. Addressing a strikers' rally on March 5, Bill Haywood urged them to stand firm and reject provocations to violence. This, however, was to prove difficult to do. On March 8, police charged an IWW "chain picket" and dispersed the strikers with clubs. A similar conflict occurred three days later. Scores of strikers were arrested in the riots that accompanied these assaults. Using the violence as justification, the sheriff issued an order which virtually placed the city under martial law. The mayor, for his part, called on the police to end the mass picketing, one of the IWW's most effective tactics. The strikers, he claimed, were being deceived by outsiders whose true goal was to cripple or ruin the industry.

Emboldened by the show of force by the police, anti-union citizens such as those in the Citizens' Welfare League entered the fray. Leaders of the strike were told to leave town or be removed forcibly. A Citizens Volunteer Police Association, whose members were deputized, organized "flying squadrons" that ranged throughout the city terrorizing the strikers and attacking IWW rallies. Union officials, such as Bill Haywood, were forced to leave Akron or risk injury or worse.

The Committee of 100 called off the strike at a mass rally on March 31. The combined force of the employers and the public officials had proved to be too much. The strike was an extraordinary example of spontaneous militancy against a powerful and entrenched industry. The leadership skills of the IWW had complemented the dedication of the local leaders of the strike for the first few weeks, but as in most other IWW efforts, skillful strike leadership did not translate into solid organization building. Six months after the great Akron strike, the IWW had practically disappeared from the city. [Ronald L. Filippelli]

FURTHER READING

Dubofsky, Melvyn. *We Shall Be All: A History of the Industrial Workers of the World.* Chicago, IL: Quadrangle, 1969.

Foner, Philip. *History of the Labor Movement in the United States: The Industrial Workers of the World, 1905–1917.* New York: International Publishers, 1965.

o   o   o

RUBBER WORKERS' STRIKE OF 1934. On June 19, 1934, eleven hundred rubber workers of the General Tire and Rubber Company in Akron, Ohio, led by the leaders of an American Federation of Labor (AFL) federal local union, began a seminal "sit-down" strike against their employer. This local union, which shortly afterward amalgamated into the Congress of Industrial Organizations' (CIO) United Rubber Workers (URW), pioneered the use of the sit-down strike tactic in the rubber industry and provided a living example of its potential as a method of employer confrontation. Other leaders of URW local unions in the Akron area would draw on this experience in much-publicized conflicts with their employers in 1935–1936, in the first of the CIO's founding strikes. In the wake of those engagements, the sit-down spread beyond the rubber industry and proved crucial in the founding of the industrial union movement in the United States.

Shortly after receiving a charter for their federal local union from the AFL in 1933, General Tire union activists made repeated but unsuccessful attempts to bargain collectively with their employer. General Tire management started an employee representation plan as an alternate, and less independent, form of collective representation. Continued employer refusal to bargain prompted local union president Rex Murray and his collaborators to begin planning for a possible recognition strike. At the behest of an anxious National Labor Board official and the supremely cautious AFL rubber industry organizer Coleman Claherty, both of whom counselled patience, the local's officers forsook any strike action through the spring of 1934. Finally, according to Murray, shop floor pressure mounted and forced the leaders' hands. "The people was becoming dissatisfied and discouraged with the progress that was being made," recalled Murray years later, "and they took the position of either get recognition or force the issue, one of the two."

The local union president wisely examined other strikes in the mass-production industries and concluded that the traditional strike methods were lacking. Employers could too easily get court injunctions to prevent or limit picketing, "and there was your labor organization, gone up the river," believed Murray. So he consulted with other area unionists: Wilmer Tate and Frank Petino, secretary and president, respectively, of the Akron central labor union; W. H. Wilson, another AFL organizer in the area; and of course Claherty. Murray proposed actually occupying the plant with the strikers. The others, especially the AFL's rubber industry organizer, thought it was a wild suggestion. But, Murray recalled, they had no other methods to offer that had not already been tried without success.

Murray's fellow local union leaders agreed that they had to assume the risks that such a tactic would entail. They thought that "it would be no different from insisting on our rights outside the plant and being arrested outside the plant. . . ." the local union officer later reminisced. In-plant supporters of the local were thereafter informed to stop work at a prearranged sign. This group then passed the information on to the less committed but still supportive rank-and-file workers. General Tire workers appeared to be ready for militant action.

When the company's management cut the piece-rate pay in the truck tire department, the local union's leaders finally had the critical issue they had been waiting for. They delivered an ultimatum to the company on June 18 to restore the rates. After several hedging responses from company officials, Murray began walking through the plant the evening of June 19, giving the prearranged signal to stop work. "That's when it started," he recalled, "and as fast as I could walk from one department to another, throughout the plant, that's when it went down." At shift change the workers smoothly exchanged places, "just like they was working."

The unified response and unexpected tactic confounded company executive Charles Jahant, vice-president of manufacturing. The local union's leaders allowed him to speak to the employees throughout the plant and then to a mass meeting outside the building. At that point, the local's officers decided to switch tactics and marched off of the company's property to a local high school, where action was taken to establish a traditional picket line. "The people thought they would have a lot more freedom," Murray said, "and it would eliminate considerable criticism that was developing because of the males and females both being in the plant, sitting down." The rubber workers' first sit-down lasted from 7:00 P.M. June 19 until the afternoon of June 20.

The rest of the strike continued for over a month. The company tried several times to defeat the unionists by trying to foster a back-to-work movement but failed. On July 18, 1934, General Tire company president William O'Neil agreed to a memo essentially granting the strikers' demands, which included an informal type of union recognition, pay rates comparable to the big three rubber companies, disestablishment of the employee representation plan, as well as restoration of the former piece rate. It was clearly a victory for the striking workers.

The 1934 General Tire sit-down strike's significance stemmed from more than simply being the "first" use of the sit-down tactic in the rubber industry. Previously, observers of the sit-downs concluded that the earliest sit-downs were unorganized protests. As the General Tire experience indicates, at least some local union officials consciously considered using the technique as a means of winning recognition before an outbreak of protest. Moreover, the sit-downers in the rubber industry in late 1935 and throughout 1936 were quite aware that their fellow unionists had used the tactic with success over a year previously. [Gilbert J. Gall]

FURTHER READING

Nelson, Daniel. "The Beginning of the Sit-Down Era: The Reminiscences of Rex Murray." *Labor History*, Vol. 15 (Winter, 1974), pp. 89–97.

Roberts, Harold. *The Rubber Workers*. New York: Harper, 1944.

o   o   o

RUBBER WORKERS' STRIKE OF 1936. Although the rubber workers briefly used the sit-down strike technique in a dispute with the General Tire and Rubber Company in Akron, Ohio, in 1934, it was not until 1936 that the sit-down came to be widely used as an effective labor weapon, drawing national attention and sparking the widespread use of that strike strategy beyond the rubber industry. Beginning in early 1936, five sit-down strikes against virtually every major Akron rubber company culminated in the great sit-down against industry leader Goodyear Tire and Rubber—the "first CIO strike"—as it came to be called. None of these sit-downs, however, were strikes that were "authorized" by the fledgling United Rubber Workers (URW) union which, in fact, opposed the use of the strategy. And, for the most part, they won only modest work-related gains. Nevertheless, the strikes proved vastly significant, and not only because they marked the emergence of the Committee of Industrial Organization (CIO) as an "effective" industrial union movement. In addition, they occurred just as the New Deal's labor relations innovations began to lose popularity, thus providing liberal politicians with the rationale for continued commitment to governmental intervention into industrial disturbances.

The Goodyear strike of February and March 1936 came on the heels of four similar contests. The Depression had hit the rubber industry hard in the early 1930s. Goodyear, which had a market share of 30 percent, had reduced its hours in 1931 in order to "share" the work, and Firestone, B. F. Goodrich, and others followed. In late 1935, Goodyear president Paul W. Litchfield began to reconsider because of a mild industry recovery. Rubber workers and the community feared the worse if the companies should increase the workday from six hours to eight: increasing unemployment, lowering of piece rates, and continued economic stagnation in the Akron area would likely result. The United Rubber Workers—created in September 1935 from the pre-existing American Federation of Labor (AFL) federal local unions—was in poor straits, with only 4,000 paying members and no funds to speak of. The companies had generally succeeded in forestalling independent unionization by fostering employee representation plans or "company" unions and had refused to recognize the URW locals for bargaining. In December 1935, CIO official Adolph Germer came to Akron to assist the unionists. More importantly, a fact-finding panel—convened by Secretary of Labor Frances Perkins under an agreement Goodyear had made to forestall a previous strike threat—issued a report that was quite critical of the company's plan to lengthen the workday and its refusal to negotiate with its workers. On January 19, 1936, a CIO-sponsored mass rally drew thousands of rubber workers to hear John L. Lewis attack the companies' instransigence.

Shortly afterward, on January 28, the tire builders at Firestone's Plant 1 sat down to protest the suspension of a URW Local 7 official for fighting with a non-union worker. This unplanned protest soon carried over into other departments, surprising the company and union officials. The local union, with the assistance of URW international union president Sherman H. Dalrymple, sought to negotiate an end to the stoppage. Finally, after a semi-concession by the company, Dalrymple settled the dispute on January 30. Workers quickly recognized that this was a "victory" and that it was due to their willingness to engage in militant confrontation.

Several other disputes followed quickly. On January 31, 1936, non-union tire builders at Goodyear Plant 1 sat down in anger over a cut in their piece rate. At first, URW Local 2 officers refused to involve themselves; soon, however, a surge of rubber workers wanting to join the union or pay their back dues stimulated local union interest, and the union moved to back the sit-

downers. On the heels of this dispute, Goodrich tire builders engaged in a similar protest for essentially the same reason on February 7. Again, the union acted as negotiating representatives but clearly the officers did not welcome this type of "unauthorized" production worker action. At a CIO rally, Dalrymple lectured workers that work stoppages of that type should be avoided. He said, "The proper way to handle grievances is through your union officers . . . . " Finally, on February 14, seventy largely non-union Goodyear tire builders received notice that they would be laid off as a result of the reinstallation of the eight-hour workday. The workers spontaneously elected a committee—C. D. Lesley, George Boyer, and James W. Jones—to press their grievance. After company refusals to do anything about the decision, the Lesley committee called a sit-down which lasted until 9 A.M. on February 15, ending only when the strikers received company assurances that a meeting with higher company officials would be arranged. URW Local 2 president John D. House offered the local's assistance even as the sit-down began again and spread to other shifts and departments. After a mass rally on February 17 at Local 2's union hall, Goodyear workers unpredictably marched to the plant and began to set up mass picket lines, a difficult proposition because the plant property ran for eleven miles and had forty-five separate entrances. Soon only 300 people remained in the plant; over 14,000 Goodyear workers had joined the strike. Before long, the strikers' spouses were serving pickets up to 5,000 meals per day.

To the company's consternation, the Akron community supported the rubber workers' demands. Though the company sought and received an injunction preventing mass picketing, the authorities hesitated at removing the strikers from the premises. Small business people donated $25,000 to strike relief, the newspapers maintained neutrality, and the Republican mayor of Akron, Lee D. Schroy, took great care in determining the role that the police force would play during the strike, after Akron's central labor council threatened a general strike if the pickets were forcibly removed. The CIO sent experienced leaders, such as Powers Hapgood, Rose Pesotta, and Leo Krzycki, among others, to aid the URW in organizing and maintaining the strike, guiding negotiations, and keeping emotions under control. The URW and its CIO advisers leased a local radio station which kept Goodyear workers apprised of strike news and played an important role in boosting morale.

Assistant Secretary of Labor Edward F. McGrady tried to mediate the dispute, and after two days recommended a return to work with the issues in disagreement to be submitted to arbitration. When this was presented to rubber workers on February 29, the more than 4,000 strikers in attendance shouted it down. Still, Goodyear president Paul Litchfield refused to countenance recognizing the union. "The Goodyear Tire and Rubber Company," he affirmed, "will not sign an agreement with the United Rubber Workers of America under any circumstances."

The strikers' solidarity changed his mind. On March 8, 1936, the company president began meeting covertly with URW officials to negotiate. The discussions continued, with John L. Lewis threatening a mass boycott of Goodyear rubber products if the company attempted to initiate any situation that might lead to violence. By March 22, the union's leaders had extracted concessions from the corporation. The company agreed to reinstate all workers with seniority rights and recognize that the URW spoke for those workers who joined the organization. Further, it promised advance notification for changes in piece rates and reduction of hours in some departments. That day, a crowd of 5,000 Goodyear rubber workers and URW members marched through Akron in victory.

The Goodyear settlement of March 22 was the CIO's first important victory and inaugurated a second wave of sit-down strikes through the rest of 1936. These conflicts, though, had important negative consequences. They undermined the previous public sympathy for the rubber workers plight, changed public officials' tolerant attitudes toward the unionists, and increased industrialists' willingness to relocate operations rather than face such militancy.

The sit-downs from spring to fall erupted unpredictably. There appeared to be no particular pattern to the repeated strike waves in various rubber plants and associated operations except for rank-and-file URW member protest against working with non-union employees. This grievance accounted for about one-third of these later sit-downs. Refusal of non-union workers to adhere to informal production limitations, wage adjustments, layoffs, and transfers were also common complaints, but often there were no substantive reasons. This exasperated URW officials who were trying to convince the company that they were responsible spokespersons for their members. "Sometimes it was laughable," observed URW Local 2 officer Charles L. Skinner subsequently. At other times, he asserted, he was "so damn mad I could have killed them all."

As the union struggled to quell this type of shop floor militancy, corporate officials began to announce their decision to "decentralize" operations to lessen the concentration of rubber work in Akron. In turn, this quickly turned local government officials and much of the Akron public against the sit-downers out of concern for the long range impact of decentralization on the community. Eventually, the URW's Dalrymple, believing that the union needed to get control of unauthorized strike actions, sponsored a convention resolution allowing expulsion of unionists who engaged in such actions without approval.

Thus, the sit-down strike technique that the rubber workers pioneered—and that other unionists were soon to adopt—had cut both ways. Through March 1936, it had helped build one of the first of the CIO's industrial unions through its success in challenging employer unfairness. The rubber industry's production workers at the rank-and-file level were responsible for lighting the fuse that resulted in the explosion of industrial union organizing in 1937. It remained for the URW's leaders to realize the necessity of harnessing and channeling that energy to build upon victories already won. [Gilbert J. Gall]

Further Reading

Bernstein, Irving. *Turbulent Years: A History of American Workers, 1933–1941.* Boston, MA: Houghton Mifflin, 1970.

Galenson, Walter. *The CIO Challenge to the AFL.* Cambridge, MA: Harvard University Press, 1960.

Nelson, Daniel. "Origins of the Sit-Down Era: Worker Militancy and Innovation in the Rubber Industry, 1934–1938." *Labor History*, Vol. 23 (Spring, 1982), pp. 198–225.

S

○ ○ ○ ○ ○ ○ ○ ○ ○ ○ ○

"SALT OF THE EARTH" STRIKE OF 1950–1952. The "Salt of the Earth" Strike was the longest, most controversial, and last great labor–management confrontation in New Mexico. It took place in the small mining town of Hanover, in the Pinos Altos mountains, and lasted for fifteen months, from October 1950 to January 1952. The conflict pitted the almost entirely Hispanic Local 890 of the International Union of Mine, Mill, and Smelter Workers against the Empire Zinc Corporation. The strike's importance far transcended the zinc mining fields of New Mexico because of the dramatization of the strike in the film, "Salt of the Earth," made by a group of directors, actors, and writers who, in the anti-Communist hysteria of the McCarthy era, had been blacklisted by the film industry because of their leftist politics.

The issue of anti-communism dominated the strike on the management side as well. The Mine, Mill, and Smelter Workers had been labeled a Communist-dominated union by the Congress of Industrial Organizations (CIO) and expelled from that body in 1950. Mine-Mill was directly descended from the Western Federation of Miners, a radical union of hardrock miners that was one of the founding organizations of the Industrial Workers of the World (IWW). Throughout this period, the federal government harassed Mine-Mill's leadership in the courts and in the National Labor Relations Board. Management used Mine-Mill's role in the strike to smear the action as part of a Communist (i.e., Soviet) plot to gain control of the American labor movement.

In fact, Empire Zinc was less interested in the politics of the union's leaders than it was in using the anti-Communist tactic to weaken the union in the metal mining industry. When negotiations for a new contract began between Local 890 and Empire Zinc on July 18, 1950, the company immediately began to charge that the Mexican-American miners were being misguided by Communist outsiders who wanted to use the strike as propaganda. For its part, the union charged that the company wanted to destroy the union in order to keep wages low for Mexican-American workers and thus divide them from the Anglo working class. This divide-and-conquer strategy was an old and familiar story in the Southwest.

The union's key demand centered on payment for all of the time that the miner was underground, rather than just for the time spent at the ore face. In the zinc fields, this was called "collar-to-collar" pay, while for coal miners the term used was "portal-to-portal" pay. This system was in effect in the other mines in the district owned by giants like Kennecott, and had been recommended by the War Labor Board. Other priority items for the union included six paid holidays and the removal of a "no strike" clause from the contract. Nevertheless, by the end of September, the company had resisted all the union's demands and had put forth no counterproposals of its own. Instead, Empire Zinc unilaterally announced a five-cents-an-hour wage increase and an eight-hour increase in the workweek. It was a take-it-or-leave-it offer.

Local 890 answered by striking. It was not a vain effort. The local covered a group of mines in the area, and the 128 employees of Empire Zinc made up only a small fraction of the membership. Thus, throughout the fifteen months of the conflict, contributions from the working members of the local, plus money from Mine-Mill and other locals, sustained the strikers.

From the beginning, the action in the strike was not at the bargaining table. Very little happened there as the company did little more than go through the motions of bargaining. Nor, for the first eight months of the strike, did the company attempt to open the mine with strikebreakers. The company's strategy was apparently to drain the union's financial resources and starve the strikers back to work. In the face of the stalemate, after eighteen weeks of the strike, the Mine-Mill Executive Board assumed control. The move reflected some dissension in the union between those who argued for compromise and those who were determined to stay out in support of the original demands.

Empire moved to exploit these cracks in the union's solidarity by writing to the strikers directly and inviting them to return to work. Few responded, but the company exaggerated the numbers and used the incident to publicize the existence of a "back-to-work" movement. Next, on June 7, 1951, Empire Zinc advertised that the company would reopen the mine. The company arranged with Sheriff Leslie Goforth and District Attorney Thomas Foy to provide funds for twenty-four special deputies to protect company property. Ernesto Velasquez, chairman of the strike committee, responded that the deputies real duty was to escort strikebreakers into the plant.

On June 11, the day of the mine's reopening, a large crowd of sympathizers joined the pickets to block any strikers from going back to work. Prominent in the crowd were many women and children who made their first entry into the strike on this date. The company immediately asked for and received an injunction to prohibit the union from blocking the road or coercing employ-

ees who wanted to work. Because the injunction named only union members, Local 890, after much debate, decided to turn the picket lines over to their wives, sisters, and mothers.

The ladies' auxiliary of Local 890 had assisted the strikers in many more traditional ways already, but their appearance on the picket line took the company and local police authorities by surprise. The women proved as tough as the men. After several days of hesitation, local authorities moved to regain control of the situation by escorting strikebreakers through the line. When the women refused to yield, mass arrests began and tear gas canisters were used, but other women stepped immediately in to take the place of their arrested sisters and held their ground. Passive resistance was replaced with struggle when police tried to take a convoy of strikebreakers through the line and the attempt failed.

The events on the picket line had given the small strike in New Mexico national prominence. The national media, including *Life* and the *New York Times* covered the story. The glare of the national spotlight brought an offer to arbitrate the strike from the Federal Mediation and Conciliation Service. The union agreed to take the risk, but the company refused. Events on the picket line had only made it more determined to reopen with non-union labor. Empire Zinc knew that any bad publicity that it received from the confrontation with the women was negated by Mine-Mill's association with communism in the public mind.

While they had won a moral victory of some significance, the strikers were no nearer to a settlement. In addition, as Mexican-Americans, they were isolated from any influence with the Anglo power structure of Grant County. From the beginning, the local press had moved from veiled opposition to open hostility for the strikers. The strikers' fierce loyalty to Mine-Mill had grown out of the fact that only the union had proved to be their champion over the years. As the prospects of economic victory waned, the strike became symbolically even more important as a demonstration of Mexican-American resistance to oppression.

Another critical blow against the union fell when women were included in the injunction and it was made permanent. Soon after, the National Labor Relations Board found the union guilty of trespassing on company property and coercing its employees. The union then agreed to accept a contract equal to any Mine-Mill contract then in effect in the district. Again the company refused.

Bitterness increased in proportion to the frustrations of the strikers as the strike wore on. By July, confrontations and conflicts on the picket lines became common. Officers beat pickets who forcefully impeded the entry of strikebreakers. Women threw chili powder into the eyes of "scabs," and police ran down several women with their cars as they rammed through the pickets.

On July 23, after a mass demonstration by strikers in his courtroom and in the streets surrounding the Grant County Courthouse in Silver City, District Judge Archibald W. Marshall found the union in contempt of court. He fined the local and international union $4,000 each, and three union officers and three members of the Local 890 negotiating team were sentenced to ninety days in jail.

Still, nothing broke the resolve of the strikers. Indeed, after the contempt-of-court charges were levied, the state police took over control of strike duty and managed it in an evenhanded manner. Governor Mecham of Arizona resisted pleas from the company and the local law enforcement authorities to send in the National Guard. In all, only about ten workers defied the union by returning to work, and the company was never able to resume operations. In addition, zinc prices were high and the other mines in the district provided jobs for a number of the strikers, thus reducing the

financial hardship on their families. Still, Empire Zinc remained determined to crush the union.

In August, the company began to use special deputies to provoke violence on the picket lines. This led to a series of incidents. On August 22, the sheriff agreed to lead a group of non-union Empire employees through the picket lines. The attempt failed, but it resulted in a riot, remembered as "The Bloody 23rd," that resulted in the running down of three women pickets and the injury of others, including strikebreakers. News of the events of August 22 triggered a general strike that shut down the entire district.

At this point, the Empire Zinc strike merged with a national walkout by Mine-Mill against Kennecott Copper and other mining companies in an attempt to achieve industrywide bargaining. The general strike and then the two-week walkout of Mine-Mill that closed most of the mines in the district brought the small businessmen of Grant County into the strike against the union. On the pretext that the strike was a Communist attempt to halt war production during the Korean conflict, they created a "law-and-order" movement to confront the "outside agitators" who had fomented the trouble. In addition to harassing strike leaders, the group tried in vain to have the governor send in the National Guard. Their most interesting tactic was to invite the United Steel Workers of America into the district to try to take over Local 890. The Steelworkers had been given Mine-Mill's jurisdiction by the CIO when the former was expelled. Since 1950, the two had been engaged in a struggle for dominance in the hardrock mining areas and in the smelting industry. The Steelworker attempt failed, largely because the union was insensitive to the ethnic issue.

Slowly, however, the enthusiasm for the strike began to dwindle. A second contempt motion had weakened the picket lines, and the number of strikebreakers entering the plant increased. Many of these workers had been recruited from other states. The anti-Communist attack on Mine-Mill grew daily, both in the local and the national press. Finally Governor Mecham, who had managed to stay out of the conflict, ordered the state police to assume complete control over the picket lines and to enforce the injunction. Also, the union was now subject to a possible $2,000 a day in fines for each day since the initial injunction had been issued.

Under these pressures, Mine-Mill asked for bargaining to resume. Surprisingly, Empire Zinc agreed. The union and the company both made concessions. The company made an attractive money offer, but it refused "collar-to-collar" pay. Benefit plans were also initiated or improved, but the company raised rents on company housing and refused to install hot water. The company also refused to drop court proceedings against the union, and strikebreakers retained their jobs. The no-strike clause remained in the contract.

The strikers ratified the contract. It was clearly not a victory in terms of the initial goals of the strike. But it was a great moral victory for the Mexican-American strikers. They had confronted the combined power of the company and the local government and had withstood a heavy barrage of criticism attacking them as pawns in a Communist conspiracy aimed at destroying the United States. Their dignity and solidarity would inspire future generations of Mexican-Americans in their struggle for justice. [Ronald L. Filippelli]

FURTHER READING

Biberman, Herbert. *Salt of the Earth: The Story of a Film.* Boston, MA: Beacon Press, 1965.

Cargill, Jack. "Empire and Opposition: 'The Salt of the Earth' Strike." In *Labor in New Mexico: Unions, Strikes, and Social History since 1881.* Robert Kern, ed. Albuquerque, NM: University of New Mexico Press, 1983, pp. 183–270.

Jensen, Vernon H. *Nonferrous Metals Industry Unionism, 1932–1954.* Ithaca, NY: Cornell University Press, 1954.

o o o

SAN FRANCISCO ANTI-CHINESE RIOTS OF 1877. The great **Railroad Strikes of 1877** swept across the country in July of that year leaving an untold number of dead and wounded and enormous property damage in its wake. It was the largest industrial uprising in American history. In San Francisco, the discontent among railroad workers combined with anti-Chinese feelings and led to mob attacks on the Chinese quarter of the city. Men were killed, and property was extensively damaged.

The roots of the savage anti-Chinese reaction in San Francisco lay in the defeat of the eight-hour-day movement by employers, and in effects of the depression of 1873. In fact, hard times came to California in advance of the rest of the country. Completion of the Central Pacific Railroad in 1869 left many thousands of construction workers, many of whom were Chinese, unemployed in San Francisco. In addition, many thousands of new immigrants poured into the city adding to the unemployment rolls which reached 20 percent by the mid-1870s. The Central Pacific also brought cheap goods from the East, thus destroying many California businesses. These circumstances were exacerbated with the collapse of the national economy in the Panic of 1873.

Under this combination of factors, the labor movement virtually collapsed. Anger among workers was directed at several causes: the railroad monopolies; the large-scale mechanized agriculture that used large gangs of seasonal laborers, who ended up in San Francisco in the off season, swelling the ranks of the unemployed; and the politicians whom they believed had betrayed them. But these were all powerful and distant targets. Most accessible as the brunt of the frustration and anger was San Francisco's large Chinese community.

The 1870 census showed just under 50,000 Chinese in California, with the largest concentration in San Francisco. White workers had long viewed the Chinese laborers as the main reason for low wages and high unemployment. The Chinese had long been victimized by state and local laws restricting their activity and by a variety of forms of intimidation from whites. When the news of the great railroad strikes reached San Francisco, it proved to be the match that set the tinder box of race relations in the city ablaze.

On the evening of July 23, a crowd assembled to hear speeches on the eight-hour workday and the nationalization of railroads. The meeting had been called by a group who identified with the Workingmen's Party of the United States. The small Socialist Party had been invigorated by the strikes in several eastern cities, especially St. Louis, where they were able to take control of the uprising for several days. The Socialists soon lost control, however, of the San Francisco meeting. Agitators from the city's "anticoolie" clubs disrupted the meeting and led many of the participants on a raid of the Chinese quarter. That night twenty or thirty Chinese wash houses were broken into and ransacked. The next day, the disturbances continued, resulting in killings, arson, and clashes with the police. On the third night, a battle between rioters and the police left several men dead and a large number injured.

One of the men who had been active in helping to put down the riots was Dennis Kearney, an Irish immigrant who had come to San Francisco in 1868 as chief mate on the clipper ship *Shooting Star*. By 1877, he was a small businessman in the moving and carting business. Kearney had shown little interest in politics prior to the riots, but after the events of July, he did an about face and positioned himself as the champion of the workingman. During September and October he spoke frequently on the streets, focusing his attacks on the Chinese, but aligning his anti-Oriental position with a Populist message that attacked the two-party system, capitalists, monopolists, the rich, and the corrupt. But Kearney also called for an end

to contract labor; an eight-hour law; equal pay for equal work for women; and free, compulsory education for children. His fame spread rapidly throughout the city, and his demand that "the Chinese must go" found a ready audience among the unemployed of the city. After he was rejected for membership in the Workingmen's Party of the United States by the Socialists, Kearney formed a new party, the Workingmen's Party of California, to serve as his vehicle to power. To Kearney, "the dignity of labor must be sustained, even if we have to kill every wretch that opposes it."

Kearney's demagogic speeches also attacked the San Francisco power structure, and that brought swift retribution. He was arrested on numerous occasions. The mayor proclaimed a state of emergency in San Francisco, and the California legislature passed a "gag law" making it a felony to "suggest or advise or encourage" any riotous action. All of this added to Kearney's fame. Upon release from jail he rode triumphantly at the head of the procession in the Workingmen's Thanksgiving Day parade. Among the units marching behind him were several of the city's trade unions.

Kearney's movement was intensely successful for several years, winning victories in both statewide and local elections, including the mayoralty of San Francisco. The intensity of the anti-Chinese sentiment stoked by Kearney and his partisans forced a number of employers to lay off Chinese workers and pledge to hire no more. Indeed, the California legislature, responding to pressure from Kearney's forces, passed a Chinese exclusion act. Yet by 1881, the force of the movement was spent. Kearney himself moved into the Greenback Labor Party, became a real estate agent, and then a stockbroker. By 1882, the Workingmen's Party of California, which had shaken San Francisco and California, and whose influence had reached Congress and the White House, had all but disappeared. [Ronald L. Filippelli]

FURTHER READING

Cross, Ira. *History of the California Labor Movement.* Berkeley, CA: University of California Press, 1935.

Sandmeyer, Elmer C. *The Anti-Chinese Movement in California.* Urbana, IL: The University of Illinois Press, 1939.

Saxton, Alexander. *The Indispensable Enemy: Labor and the Anti-Chinese Movement in California.* Berkeley, CA: University of California Press, 1971.

o   o   o

SAN FRANCISCO LONGSHORE-MEN'S STRIKE OF 1934. On May 9, 1934, longshoremen, represented by the International Longshoreman Association's (ILA) Local 38–79, went on strike in San Francisco, touching off a conflict that spread to numerous areas on the West Coast. In short order, the dispute escalated into a full-scale maritime strike and several days of violent rioting between workers and police in San Francisco, which ultimately experienced a citywide general strike as a result.

As with other disputes, the Great Depression's hard times helped create a climate ripe for labor militancy. After World War I, waterfront employers had beaten a previous ILA local union into nonexistence and replaced it with a pro-employer company union. Under the latter organization's regime, longshoremen saw little improvement in their pay and working conditions, the most hated of which was the "shape-up," the daily employment roll call. The "shape-up" had a long and dishonorable history in waterfront employment the world over, and in San Francisco it was no different. Crowds of desperate workers gathered on the docks early in the mornings to seek a day's work at the discretion of the foreman; it was a system that encouraged kickbacks, corruption, and debasement. The shape-up—combined with poor pay, the driving of the foremen, and terribly dangerous conditions, all of which intensified during the Depression—led to a festering sense of grievance.

No one felt this more than Harry Bridges, an Australian longshoreman resident in the United States since 1920. Bridges had fallen in love with the sea and had made a career of it for six years before becoming a longshoreman in San Francisco in 1922. He had flirted with unionism and radical ideas and by the early 1930s had become a Communist and a believer in the inevitability of the class struggle. In 1932, the Marine Workers Industrial Union (MWIU), which was led by Communists, began an organizing campaign in the maritime trades and recruited Bridges to its cause.

Early in 1933, a small group of longshoremen applied for and received a charter from the ILA, the dominant national union in the craft. San Francisco Local 38–79 quickly started attracting members in large numbers. Local union president Lee J. Holman well-represented the traditional business unionist approach that was dominant in the American Federation of Labor (AFL)–affiliated ILA. The much more radical Bridges-MWIU group joined the ILA, planning to eventually win leadership positions. Soon the new local began to condemn the longshore company union and led a brief strike at one company after four ILA members were fired. The San Francisco Labor Board, which had been set up to mediate labor disputes that were occurring under Section 7(a) of the National Recovery Act (NRA), ordered the company to reinstate the fired workers and to avoid future discrimination. With that victory workers rushed to sign up with the new independent union, and Local 38–79 became a force on the waterfront.

The Waterfront Employers' Association refused to recognize the ILA local. It raised wages unilaterally, forcing Local 38–79's leaders to demand even greater increases in order to prevent preemption. Holman proposed a basic hourly rate of one dollar an hour, the six-hour workday, and the thirty-hour workweek. The ILA also asked for a National Labor Board (NLB) election. None of the demands met with success. The Bridges group within the local then made its move by agitating for an even more ambitious set of requirements for an agreement and won the membership to their side. Now, in addition to the previous proposals, the basic demand of the union was the destruction of the shape-up and its replacement by a union-managed hiring hall. The local set a strike deadline for March 23, 1934.

Several weeks passed as government officials tried to mediate. At the request of President Roosevelt, the ILA suspended its intent to strike in favor of an investigation by a special labor board named by the President. This "Federal Mediation Board" held hearings and recommended representation elections, jointly-managed hiring halls, and arbitration of wage and hours questions. Within two days the longshoring employers stated that they would voluntarily deal with the ILA as majority representative, though at the same time still deal with the company union. Moreover, they implied that they would also agree to some type of jointly administered "dispatching hall." Wages and working conditions went unmentioned.

West Coast ILA leaders, including the current local union officers, wanted to accept. The Bridges group, with the support of the members, denounced the employers' statements and insisted on their previous demands. Shortly afterward, Local 38–79, with Bridges now firmly in control of rank-and-file sentiment, suspended Holman from the presidency. Strike votes up and down the West Coast backed a walkout, and on the evening of May 9, 1934, twelve major ports and many smaller ones stopped operating. The next day, over 1,000 ILA pickets marched in San Francisco. The employers tried to hire replacements and resume business, but by-and-large, the many strikebreakers did not have the experience to properly load cargo. Soon the local union also received the aid of Teamsters' Local 85, which voted not to pick up or deliver goods

to the docks. Furthermore, offshore maritime crafts—cooks, pilots, and sailors—followed the longshoremen's example and demanded recognition and resolution of their many grievances. By the third week in May, the strike had grown into a stoppage involving most, if not all, maritime workers.

The governors of California, Oregon, and Washington State appealed to the Roosevelt administration to mediate. Assistant Secretary of Labor Edward F. McGrady came to San Francisco hoping to resolve the dispute but failed. Into this increasingly confused situation stepped ILA president Joseph P. Ryan, who believed he could orchestrate a settlement. On May 28, Ryan signed an agreement between the employers and ILA officers in Seattle, San Francisco, Los Angeles, and Portland, essentially accepting what the companies had previously informally offered and the union had rejected. While Ryan, the employers, and the press ballyhooed the "settlement," pickets and police in San Francisco engaged in the first of their confrontations, with several pickets wounded by shotgun fire. When Ryan took his "agreement" to the ILA members, Bridges rejected it with the support of the membership.

Prominent San Francisco business elites—led by the Industrial Association, the city's most prominent anti-union business organization—now took over employer strike strategy. Increasingly, charges about the "radicalism" and "communism" of the elements within the ILA came to the fore. The tactic was in the time-honored tradition of using "red-baiting" to erode public support for labor and encourage public authorities to assist in breaking strikes. With general business backing, goods began to trickle from the docks through the city-owned belt line railroad, whose workers, as public employees, were prohibited from striking. Despite Teamster Local 85 president Mike Casey's opposition, truckers voted on June 7 not to haul this hot cargo, and all striking unions formed their own joint steering committee under Bridges leadership on June 18.

Before things worsened, San Francisco mayor Angelo J. Rossi attempted mediation. He coordinated an agreement attempting to address the hiring hall issue between the longshore employers and Ryan, along with a few other prominent union leaders present to give it credence. Bridges was excluded from the negotiations, and as might have been expected, longshoremen blasted Ryan because of the agreement's silence regarding the striking offshore trades. With the failure of this attempt, the Industrial Association became determined to reopen the port. The effort received the backing of Mayor Rossi and Chief of Police William J. Quinn. Meanwhile, President Roosevelt named a special National Longshoremen's Labor Board, chaired by San Francisco's Archbishop Edward J. Hanna, to try to resolve the dispute. On July 3 the employers restarted trucking shipments with their own shipping subsidiary. In mid-afternoon, 700 police, protecting the shipments, and thousands of pickets determined to prevent them from leaving, battled for four hours with billyclubs, baseball bats, bricks, and tear gas. The workers, retreating from the tear gas, could not prevent eighteen loads from leaving the piers. The next day, the Fourth of July, was quiet.

Then, on "Bloody Thursday," July 5, police and workers renewed their conflict. In a day-long industrial insurrection of great intensity, during which many bystanders and innocent citizens were seriously injured, running battles were fought throughout the warehouse district. Over the course of what was by now a major civil disturbance, the poorly armed pickets could not withstand the assaults of well-equipped police. The injured and dying lay in the streets. By evening two workers were dead and sixty-seven seriously injured. California governor Frank E. Merriam sent the National Guard into the city to restore order. With the public authorities in control, it now looked as though the employers might be able to break the strike.

The strikers petitioned for aid from the city's once-powerful labor movement. The San Francisco Central Labor Council debated Bridges request for assistance, and the Teamsters' rank and file, irate over the actions of the police, voted to stop work in sympathy on July 12. "In all my thirty years of leading these men I have never seen them so worked up," remarked Teamsters' local union president Mike Casey. The funeral for the two strikers who had been killed— Howard Sperry and Nick Bordoise—drew tens of thousands of silently respectful San Francisco workers. Their martyrdom— amplified by the moving spectacle of their funeral procession, during which the police wisely remained absent—fueled the sentiment for a general strike.

The National Longshoremen's Labor Board hoped to head off this development. In three days of hearings beginning on July 9, the board found Bridges and the employers still deadlocked. When the board asked the parties to submit the issues in the dispute to arbitration, the steamship companies—which employed the striking offshore crafts—spurned the suggestion.

Finally, labor sentiment for a general strike reached a peak. By Monday, July 16, sixty-three unions had voted to walk out in sympathy, despite pleas from Archbishop Hanna and Mayor Rossi. Conservative newspaper owners quickly used their publications to denounce the impending anarchy that the "communist"-inspired general strike would bring in the hope that government officials would be forced to use military power to break the strike and restore order. The chief of police, the mayor, and the governor all went along, to varying degrees; but the Roosevelt administration, ably represented by Secretary of Labor Frances Perkins, was not persuaded by the efforts of the publishers to create a climate of hysteria. Despite the entreaties of California senator Hiram Johnson, Perkins resisted using troops to assist California business interests in defeating the strikers. Instead, she worked harder to resolve the dispute, particularly the current sticking point of the refusal of ship owners to submit their interests to arbitration should bargaining break down with their protesting employees. She believed an equitable end would be brought about if those companies cast aside their obstinacy. Finally, Perkins convinced shipping executive Roger Lapham to present the Roosevelt position to the business group controlling strike strategy. The employers refused, even though 130,000 San Francisco workers were engaging in a general strike, closing much of the city down.

Luckily, there was no violence during the general strike, and within several days strikers began returning to work, urging their maritime brethren to arbitrate an end to the dispute. On July 19, the central labor council voted to end the general strike. As the workers returned, solidarity in the business groups began to erode. Moderate representatives in the Waterfront Employers, the Industrial Association, and among the newspaper publishers successfully pressured the steamship companies into accepting arbitration of the still-outstanding issues. When the longshore rank and file voted to accept arbitration of the hiring hall, the last obstruction to settlement was removed. On July 27, the seventy-nine-day strike ended. The National Longshoremen's Labor Board promulgated its decision on October 12, 1934. It granted jointly operated hiring halls, with the dispatcher to be chosen by the ILA. The board also awarded wage increases, the six-hour day, and the thirty-hour workweek. The board's decision was a triumph for Bridges and his longshoremen. Though the ILA and waterfront employers would again and again engage in economic battles, the 1934 struggle established the union and ended the hated shape-up.

Bridges went on to become one of the nation's best-known left-wing union leaders. Eventually, he broke with the ILA and

formed the International Longshoremen and Warehousemen's Union (ILWU), a CIO affiliate. The strike's long-term significance rests on its contribution to later labor militancy and its impact on policymakers at the federal level. Along with the **Toledo Auto-Lite Strike**, the **Minneapolis Teamsters' Strike**, and the **Textile Strike**, all in 1934, the San Francisco Longshoreman's strike played an important role in stimulating advances in federal labor legislation that would assist in peacefully resolving labor disputes and promote the process of collective bargaining. [Gilbert J. Gall]

FURTHER READING

Bernstein, Irving. *Turbulent Years: A History of the American Worker, 1933–1941.* Boston, MA: Houghton, Mifflin, 1970.

Brecher, Jeremy. *Strike!* San Francisco CA: Straight Arrow Books, 1972.

Larrowe, Charles P. *Harry Bridges: The Rise and Fall of Radical Labor in the United States.* New York: L. Hill, 1972.

———. "The Great Maritime Strike of '34." *Labor History,* Vol. 11 (1970), pp. 403–451; Vol. 12 (1971), pp. 3–37.

o   o   o

SAN FRANCISCO OPEN SHOP CAMPAIGN OF 1916. During the summer of 1916, a series of violent events racked San Francisco. The city had been a labor stronghold since well before the turn of the century, and the San Francisco business community, encouraged by the success of the **Los Angeles Open Shop Strikes of 1910**, set out to weaken the power of the labor movement.

On June 1, the longshoremen struck for higher wages. Employers claimed that the strikes were in violation of their contracts with the union and appealed for help to Secretary of Labor William B. Wilson who upheld the employers' claims and urged the men to return to work. As the longshoreman returned to their jobs, violence flared be-

461
o

tween the union men and strikebreakers, leaving several dead and injured on both sides. When the employers refused to withdraw the armed guards and the strikebreakers, the union struck again.

The chamber of commerce insisted that in the future it would insist on the right of employers to operate non-union if they so chose. A new "Law and Order Committee" was established to support the open shop. Before year's end, the committee had $2 million in its war chest.

The longshoremen ended their second strike on July 17, and the city returned to a short-lived calm. On July 22, twenty thousand people gathered downtown for a "preparedness parade," one of a number of such parades in major cities called by business leaders, chambers of commerce, and patriotic societies to arouse interest in national defense. Also on the agenda of the parade's sponsors was an attack on radicals and pacifists, as well as labor leaders, who opposed American involvement in the war in Europe. Indeed, so anti-union were the parade's sponsors that the labor movement had refused to participate in the ostensibly patriotic demonstration.

As the parade stepped off, at six minutes after two o'clock, a bomb exploded at the corner of Market and Stuart streets. Ten onlookers lay dead, with another forty wounded. In the midst of the hysteria and calls for revenge against the "radicals" that followed the incident, the Law and Order Committee called a mass protest meeting at which it managed to link the bombing to "labor violence" in the city.

Five days after the bombing, four men and one woman, all labor and radical activists, were arrested. Two, Tom Mooney and Warren Billings, were eventually tried and convicted of the crime. Billings, a member of the Boot and Shoe Workers Union, had been convicted three years earlier, at the age of nineteen, of carrying dynamite during a strike. But the man the authorities and the Law and Order Committee wanted most

was Tom Mooney. A molder by trade, Mooney was the leader of the left wing of the California Federation of Labor. He had been an unsuccessful candidate for superior court judge in 1910 and the following year ran unsuccessfully for sheriff on the Socialist ticket. By 1910, he had joined the radical Industrial Workers of the World (IWW). Authorities had failed to convict Mooney of carrying explosives during a strike of electrical workers against the Pacific Gas and Electric Company in 1913. Finally, just several days before the preparedness parade incident, Mooney had led an unsuccessful strike of streetcar workers against the United Railways.

Billing's was sentenced to life imprisonment and Mooney to death for the bombing. The evidence came from witnesses who were described as a prostitute, a drug addict, a psychopathic liar, and a woman suffering from spiritualistic hallucinations. The two key witnesses were later found to have perjured themselves. Nevertheless, the verdicts stood while radicals, liberals, and labor unions held protest rallies across the country. Indeed, the case became an international *cause célèbre* as well. Under unrelenting pressure from those who believed that Mooney and Billings had been convicted on false and perjured testimony, the governor of California commuted Mooney's sentence to life imprisonment. Not until 1939, after two decades of agitation and legal maneuvers on their behalf, did New Deal governor Culbert L. Olson pardon Mooney and Billings and release them from prison.

Against the background of the Preparedness Day bombing, the Law and Order Committee succeeded in having anti-picketing ordinances passed in San Francisco and several East Bay communities. The American entry into World War I interrupted the open shop campaign, but it returned in full force after the war ended.
[Ronald L. Filippelli]

FURTHER READING

Frost, Richard H. *The Mooney Case*. Stanford, CA: Stanford University Press, 1968.

Hunt, Henry Thomas. *The Case of Thomas J. Mooney and Warren K. Billings*. New York: Da Capo Press, 1971.

Gentry, Curt. *Frame-up: The Incredible Case of Tom Mooney and Warren Billings*. New York: Norton, 1967.

o   o   o

SAN FRANCISCO RESTAURANT WORKERS' STRIKE OF 1901. As it was in many trades, San Francisco was also a strong "union town" in the hotel and restaurant industry. As early as 1863, the city's cooks and waiters had organized and carried out a strike. By the turn of the century, organization had stabilized, with some 2,500 waiters, cooks, and bartenders affiliated with the Hotel and Restaurant Employees and Bartenders Union (HRE), an American Federation of Labor affiliate.

The union's strength lay in the small, moderately priced restaurants. In the spring of 1901, the restaurant workers set out to organize the large, expensive restaurants that made San Francisco famous among travelers as a city of fine and varied dining. By May, enough inroads had been made to call some 2,000 workers out on strike for the six-day workweek and pay raises. It was the largest strike in the union's brief history.

The restaurant owners, organized in one of the city's many employer associations, resisted. Wholesalers cut off supplies to restaurants that signed union shop agreements and displayed union house cards. In a counterdemonstration of solidarity, the bakery workers cut off supplies to non-union restaurants, and the butchers pressured their employers to supply only restaurants that had signed with the union.

Indeed, union solidarity throughout the city was a hallmark of the strike. In fact, the restaurant workers were the vanguard of an attempt by the city's central labor council to check a concerted anti-union, open-shop campaign by San Francisco employers. During 1901, bakery workers, longshoremen, brewers, and Teamsters, among others, also struck to hold onto previously won gains.

In spite of this support, however, the strike failed after three months. Ironically, strikes by other unions in the city, especially the Teamsters, made it impossible for them to contribute to a strike fund for the restaurant workers. Without this financial assistance, the international union's resources were not adequate to keep the strikers at even the level of bare subsistence. In fact, although HRE locals in other cities sent contributions, the financially strapped headquarters in Cincinnati could muster only $300 for the strike fund.

Although it lost the strike, the union regrouped and carried out successful organizing campaigns against individual restaurants in the following year. This tactic enabled non-striking workers to support those on strike for the time needed to bring employers to the bargaining table. Another important result of the restaurant workers' strike, along with the other conflicts that marked that year in San Francisco, was the election as mayor of Eugene E. Schmitz, a member of the Musicians Union, on the Union Labor Party ticket. During Schmitz's administration, the labor movement in San Francisco prospered. By 1902, the cooks achieved the six-day week and the union shop. Similar gains came for waiters during the rebuilding boom after the 1906 earthquake. [Ronald L. Filippelli]

FURTHER READING

Cross, Ira. *History of the Labor Movement in California.* Berkeley, CA: University of California Press, 1935.

Josephson, Matthew. *Union House, Union Bar: The History of the Hotel and Restaurant Employees and Bartenders International Union, AFL-CIO.* New York: Random House, 1956.

o o o

SANTA FE RAILROAD SHOPMEN'S STRIKES OF 1904–1905. A systemwide machinists strike began on the Santa Fe Railroad in late April of 1904. It resulted from the interplay of forces and pressures operating within and upon labor and management which led both parties to seek greater leverage over the workplace in order to advance their respective interests. It encapsulated a larger struggle played out across the industrial landscape—the clash between management's relentless drive for efficiency and greater productivity and labor's attempt to exert a measure of control over the workplace.

Having recently emerged from financial receivership, the Santa Fe launched an ambitious and expensive revitalization program to handle the growing freight and passenger traffic of its Southwest divisions. The railroad had expanded shop facilities, procured more powerful and complex motive power, and proposed work rule changes—including piece-rate payment to enhance operating efficiency. Its cost-conscious and anti-union stance had been intensified by rising locomotive maintenance and repair costs that the road attributed to labor's inefficiency and the shopcraft unions' growing influence—the machinists in particular. Though lacking a formal written agreement with the railroad (the exception being the railway carmen who agreed to work under a piece-rate system), Santa Fe shop mechanics enjoyed the status of quasi-recognition with a degree of bargaining leverage over wages, hours, and working conditions.

Between 1900 and 1904, returning prosperity replenished union ranks and invigorated its officers to take more forceful action. Santa Fe shopcraft unions staged sporadic strikes and work stoppages throughout the system and wrested concessions from management in the western and coast shops where their foothold was stronger. The machinists, whose constitution banned its members from working under piece rates and operating more than one machine simultaneously, spearheaded labor's insurgency.

Following a successful strike against the Union Pacific in 1903 to remove a piece-rate system, the International Association of Machinists (IAM) began an organizing drive on the Santa Fe system. Its principal goals included complete unionization of the Santa Fe shops, a uniform hourly wage rate of thirty-five cents for machinists (the prevailing union scale which the Santa Fe only accepted in its coast division shops due to the union's strength and a labor shortage), and a collective bargaining agreement governing work rules. IAM field organizers traveled the length of the Santa Fe system, recruiting new members, establishing new locals, and adjusting local grievances in the shops. Emboldened by the union's resurgent strength and the establishment of a district lodge at Topeka, IAM officers became more vociferous in their demands. Though elimination of the existing wage differential between western and eastern divisions had been a primary concern, resistance to the Santa Fe's hiring of non-union machinists and the union's insistence on the adoption of its own work rules became more important as the organizing drive intensified. Pressure by the machinists forced the railroad to temporarily recall its hiring agents from eastern locomotive centers (especially the Baldwin Locomotive Company of Philadelphia) where it recruited non-union machinists. Though the Santa Fe suspended its "labor survey," management still maintained its prerogative of employing non-union shop mechanics and operating on the "open shop" principle.

Shortly after establishment of a district lodge at Topeka, IAM district officers met with rank-and-file machinists to frame a collective bargaining agreement for the Santa Fe's consideration. The proposed agreement contained a list of twenty demands governing work rules for machinists, their helpers, and apprentices. Besides recognition and adoption of a uniform wage scale, provisions included: a journeyman-apprenticeship ratio of 5:1, ten hours' pay for a nine-hour workday on Saturdays, machinists' exemption from company imposed physical examinations as a condition of employment, and specified rules regarding overtime pay and grievance procedures. More importantly, the document broadly defined a machinist as a specialist competent in any single branch of machinist work. IAM leaders argued that these proposals had already been won by its organization on other roads. Actually, their demands represented a compendium of concessions gained piecemeal from the Santa Fe's coast division shops and other lines; nowhere had the IAM succeeded in getting their shop rules implemented in toto.

Santa Fe officials viewed the IAM's organizing drive and insurgency with disdain. They contrasted the machinists' truculence and Socialist proclivities with the conservative and amicable behavior of the locomotive brotherhoods and railway carmen whom the railroad placated with minor pay raises and concessions. Fearful of the IAM's deleterious influence on the other shopcraft unions, the railroad predicated its labor strategy on sequestering its eastern division shop mechanics (especially at its Topeka shop complex) from the machinists' agitation on the western lines. However, formation of the machinists district lodge at Topeka and the demands embodied in its proposed agreement represented a challenge the company could not ignore. Santa Fe president E. P. Ripley informed the railroad's executive committee that the struggle with the machinists was not over wages but for control over the shops. Acquiescence to their demands meant the wholesale spread of "soldiering," the deliberate slowing down of the pace of work, and inefficiency that pervaded its western and coast division shops. Management concluded that it would ultimately be cheaper to weather a strike than to operate on the basis of the machin-

ists' shop rules. After meeting with IAM district representatives in March 1904, the railroad formally rejected the proposed bargaining agreement. Both sides braced themselves for an impending strike.

For months, the Santa Fe had made elaborate strike preparations. It ordered additional engines, rolling stock, and equipment; stockpiled guns and ammunition; and retained Pinkerton agents to guard company property. Company spies infiltrated the IAM's district lodge, and informants provided management with daily reports of the union's activities. The labor survey conducted by the Santa Fe resulted in the hiring of a strikebreaking force of 600 men. To avoid detection, they were transported in small shipments over the Southern Pacific Railroad and housed in barracks on Catalina Island, California, until the strike began.

Management, confident of its resources and resolve to defeat the machinists, maneuvered to precipitate a strike. In April 1904, it announced the implementation of a new job and wage classification system for machinists. The prevailing union wage scale would only be paid to first-class machinists capable of operating all machinery and performing a variety of jobs. Other machinists with less skill were classified either as hands, handymen, or experienced helpers and paid on a declining basis. IAM officers denounced the system as a calculated move to reduce machinists to the status of "handymen" and demanded its immediate withdrawal from the shops. When the Santa Fe refused to discuss the matter, the district lodge officers wired the union's national headquarters in Washington and received the grand lodge's approval to strike.

Though the IAM's executive committee set May 2 as the strike date, over 300 machinists and their helpers walked out at various coast shops on April 28. At San Bernardino, California, and Albuquerque, New Mexico, boilermakers, blacksmiths, and other shopmen joined the machinists without their respective unions' sanctioning of a sympathy strike. Within a month, the conflagration had engulfed the entire Santa Fe system, involving over 1,000 shop mechanics.

The strike hampered locomotive maintenance and repair operations resulting in engine failures and costly delays to freight and passenger service. Even though minimal violence occurred during the strike, the Santa Fe had petitioned district courts along the entire system for injunctions to prevent the union's interference with company property and replacement workers. For the most part, machinists confined their efforts to picketing, inducing strikebreakers to quit the Santa Fe's employ, and waging a campaign to convince the public of the railroad's poorly repaired and unsafe locomotives.

The Santa Fe publicly minimized the disruption caused by the strike. Indeed, within two weeks after its outbreak, management declared the labor conflict over and decisively settled to its advantage. Replacement workers filled the vacancies left by striking shopmen, and the railroad announced it would no longer recognize nor deal with any shopcraft union. Despite evidence of poorly repaired engines and upheaval in its shops, Santa Fe officials maintained that the shops were operating more efficiently under a "betterment system" recently installed by efficiency expert Harrington Emerson. Though the IAM continued its struggle for four long years, its strike had been effectively crushed within the first few months. The union continued to picket outside the shops while inside important changes in work and remuneration were taking place beyond its control.

Prior to the strike, the Santa Fe had confined its betterment program to the physical reorganization of its shops. With the machinist union removed as an impediment, the railroad expanded its scope to include the adoption of scientific management and implementation of a bonus system for its shop employees. Seven months after

the strike began, Santa Fe machinists began receiving "Emerson bonus checks" based on their average monthly efficiency. The IAM denounced the bonus system as a glorified piece-rate and slave-wage system and demanded its removal from the shops as a condition for ending the strike. By early 1905, the machinists' control strike had merged with the system-wide upheaval accompanying extension of the Santa Fe's bonus system. Dissatisfaction with the new wage incentive scheme quickly spread among boilermakers, blacksmiths, and to a lesser extent, railway carmen. In April 1905, the International Brotherhood of Boilermakers (IBB) struck when the Santa Fe refused to rescind the bonus system. Though only a small proportion of its trade labored under bonus schedules at the time, boilermakers' fears had been heightened by machinists' charges of de-skilling, declining wage rates, and intensive supervision under the system.

The boilermakers' strike, however, was a repeat of the events of the previous year. The Santa Fe effectively undermined the strike by retaining strikebreakers and declaring its shops off limits to employees refusing to work under its bonus schedules. Scores of Santa Fe blacksmiths also joined the machinists and boilermakers rather than submit to the shop speedup. However, their depleted treasury precluded the financing of a systemwide strike on the Santa Fe. Despite machinists' efforts to coordinate a federated strike on the railroad, effective resistance to the bonus system collapsed by 1906. Within two years, the bonus system reigned supreme over the entire system, and the Santa Fe basked in the notoriety of being one of the first railroad systems in the country to widely use the principles of scientific management in a sweeping fashion.

The Santa Fe's victory over its shop mechanics had been costly. Nearly 5,000 employees had either struck or quit the railroad during the upheaval of 1904–1905. Before the machinists and boilermakers finally capitulated in 1908, the railroad had withstood a chronic labor shortage, poorly repaired motive power, and disruption to its freight and passenger traffic. Nevertheless, victory in the Santa Fe shopmen's strike enabled the railroad to operate virtually union-free and to pay its employees lower wage rates (notwithstanding premium payments) than unionized railroads operating in contiguous territories. Santa Fe officials credited the bonus system with keeping its shop force immune from the strikes which engulfed many of the nation's railroads between 1911 and 1915. Only the wartime emergency and direct government intervention revived the flagging fortunes of the Santa Fe shopcraft unions. In 1917, the United States Railway Administration forced the Santa Fe to abolish the bonus system, raise wage rates, and engage in collective bargaining with its shopmen. Government action had accomplished what the railway shopmen's strikes of 1904–1905 had failed to achieve. [James Quigel]

FURTHER READING

Bryant, Keith L., Jr. *History of the Atchison, Topeka and Santa Fe Railroad.* New York: Macmillan, 1974.

Graves, Carl. *Scientific Management and the Santa Fe Shopmen's Experience, 1900–1925.* Ph.D. dissertation, Harvard University, 1982.

o   o   o

SAVANNAH, GEORGIA, BLACK LABORERS' STRIKE OF 1891. The late nineteenth century was a period of rapid expansion for American industry but also a time of considerable conflict between labor and management. One of the less well known, but perhaps more significant conflicts between capital and labor in the late nineteenth century was the strike of the black laborers' in Savannah, Georgia, in 1891. Savannah was one of the leading ports in the southeastern United States, shipping both cotton and naval stores worth tens of millions of dollars annually. Essential to that commerce were black workers who loaded the cotton bales and barrels of naval stores from the freight cars of the Georgia Central, the Savannah, Florida, and Western railroads onto ships.

The strike of 1891 was not the first confrontation between the dock workers of Savannah and their employers. Four workers had been killed by police during a strike in 1881. Management was paying the laborers less in 1891 than had been the case in earlier years, and when a further cut from $1.25 a day to $1.10 was proposed, a small, short walkout ensued. Most of Savannah's dock workers were already members of the Labor Union and Protective Association (LUPA), which included nearly every black laborer in Savannah. Negotiations ensued, at which LUPA demanded a raise of five cents an hour, and management delayed. Meanwhile, municipal authorities in Savannah, led by Mayor John J. McDonough, called upon the local militia to "prevent any riotous disturbances."

The workers responded quietly but forcefully. They struck, but no riot ensued. Nonviolence was the order of the day, and the union countered management and municipal attempts at intimidation with union propaganda in the form of circulars warning blacks who might be potential strikebreakers to stay away from Savannah. LUPA sought the help of the black clergy in transmitting this message, and together with the use of "walking delegates," shut off almost completely the supply of labor to the docks. The union also attempted to reassure Savannah's white population, stressing their desire for "work," not "war."

With their economic well-being dependent on the port, much of the Savannah business community, including insurance and financial officials, began to agitate for a compromise settlement of the strike. The fact that nearly all black workers on the Savannah waterfront had joined the strike helped to encourage this movement on the part of significant parts of the Savannah white power structure. Under pressure from some of their colleagues, management offered a compromise, two and a half cents per hour, instead of the union's demand of five cents. The union's demand for weekly pay was also agreed to.

It was at this point that a fatal rift in LUPA began. While some black dock workers wanted to accept the offer, others held out for the full five cents, which would have represented up to a 40 percent pay increase for some dock workers. The employers' offer was rejected, but union unity was broken. Leaders of Savannah's business community, many of whom had sided with the dock workers, if only out of expediency, were outraged by LUPA's refusal to accept the compromise. White solidarity was restored, while at the same time the remarkable unity of the black community in support of the strikers was fractured. The strikers were also insistent on company recognition of their union. The break in the unity of the dock workers meant that an increasing number of outside strikebreakers, and many who had been strikers, drifted back to work, and a few short days later, the strike was lost. For several days, the black dock workers of Savannah had managed something that no other workers of their race managed in the South at that time, the use of a strike to force a compromise wage offer from a major employer. Perhaps the unique nature of that success prompted these brave and united workers to press their case too far. [Leslie S. Hough]

FURTHER READING

Wetherington, Mark V. "The Savannah Negro Laborers' Strike of 1891." *Southern Workers and their Unions, 1880–1975: Selected Papers, The Second Southern Labor History Conference, 1978.* Westport, CT: Greenwood Press, 1981.

Woodward, C. Vann. *Origins of the New South.* Baton Rouge, LA: Louisiana State University Press, 1971.

o   o   o

SEAMEN'S STRIKE OF 1921. The outbreak of World War I led to a substantial increase in the American merchant marine. The withdrawal of foreign flag ships from the shipping lanes had provided excellent opportunities for American companies. The labor shortages that accompanied the wartime boom also worked to the advantage of the seamen. Wages increased and working conditions improved. These improvements went hand in hand with unionization on both the Atlantic and Pacific coasts. By 1916, the International Seamen's Union of America (ISU) boasted 30,000 members, nearly double the number of 1914. Two years later, the union's membership had reached 50,000.

The outbreak of the war had demonstrated how dependent the United States was on foreign shipping. This knowledge resulted in a massive shipbuilding program under the direction of a special government agency, the Shipping Board. When the United States entered the war in April 1917, President Woodrow Wilson delegated to the board the authority to acquire, operate, and dispose of vessels. Under this mandate, the Shipping Board ran the American merchant marine. As the war progressed, this authority came to include labor relations in all of its aspects. The Shipping Board was given a general commission by both employers and the ISU to settle all marine labor questions arising during the war on the Atlantic and Gulf coasts. Only on the Pacific Coast did the parties continue with normal collective bargaining. Although the board never recognized the ISU or its affiliates as the official representative of the seamen, in general its stewardship of the merchant marine led to significant improvements in wages and working conditions.

After the war, the Shipping Board sold many of the ships built during the war to private owners and withdrew from direct operations. Relations between the operators and the union immediately began to deteriorate. The major issue was preferential hiring for union members. Members of the American Steamship Association termed it the "closed shop" and refused. The impasse on this and other issues resulted in a bitter strike in 1919 that paralyzed both coastal and trans-Atlantic shipping. The union won wage increases, the eight-hour workday, and other important gains. It did not, however, win the preferential union shop. Instead, under the prodding of the Shipping Board, the steamship owners agreed to allow union representatives on the docks and ships at certain times.

The coming of recession in the spring of 1920 reversed the balance of power in the industry, removing the leverage that the shortage of labor had provided for the ISU. As the level of freight rates dropped—descending more than two-thirds by the fall of 1921—the attitude of both private shipowners and the Shipping Board, which still operated a large number of ships, began to harden. This change of fortunes came at a time when the ISU's strength was at an all time high of 115,000 members. Some 90 percent of the seamen on both coasts were organized. Appearances were deceiving, however. The ISU had prospered largely because of factors beyond its control, including the growth of the merchant marine and the benevolence of the Shipping Board during the war and immediately after. Although the leaders of the union realized the danger of the new conditions, they were unable to adjust to the new reality.

The union faced other problems as well. Under the leadership of its founder, Andrew Furuseth, the ISU had always remained aloof from the unions of waterfront workers. This policy had developed because of jurisdictional problems and other grievances against the longshoremen. Internal revolts also distracted the ISU leaders. Militants wanted to merge all of the constituent craft unions in the ISU into one industrial union of seamen, but Furuseth rejected the plan. But the biggest problem faced by the union was the condition of the industry. By June 1921, over one-half of the Shipping Board's fleet tonnage was laid up because of lack of cargo. In addition, a deflationary spiral in the economy had actually reduced the cost of living by some 15 percent. Furuseth was pessimistic about the union's chances of weathering the storm without concessions.

The employers' offensive began on the Pacific Coast where owners wanted to end relations with the unions altogether. The Shipping Board hesitated to support such a drastic policy. Nevertheless, sentiment among the owners for an end to relations with the union was widespread on both coasts. In mid-April the owners proposed wage reductions of 20 to 40 percent, elimination of overtime pay, and the open shop.

Andrew Furuseth did everything possible to avoid a strike, but he was hemmed in on both sides. The owners had delivered an ultimatum, the Shipping Board refused to negotiate with the unions, and some of the ISU's own affiliates were eager to strike. In desperation, Furuseth, who knew that to surrender to the demands of the companies was to destroy the union, appealed to President Warren Harding to appoint a board of arbitration. Harding refused, relying instead on Admiral William S. Benson, his appointment as head of the Shipping Board. Benson, who had tried to maintain labor peace in the industry, had by now come to support the owners' position.

The Shipping Board and the private owners developed a coordinated strategy against the union. U.S. Navy personnel would man ships carrying the mail. All seamen who refused to sign on under the new work rules were ordered to leave the ships. Those who refused to sign were also effectively blacklisted. Benson threatened to withdraw government ships from any operators who dealt with the union. With 35,000 unemployed seamen on the Shipping Board's roster, it became rather simple to keep the ships crewed and sailing.

Efforts at mediation during the strike

by the secretary of labor and the secretary of commerce, Herbert Hoover, were opposed by the shipowners. With their members unemployed and facing the combined power of the government and the shipping industry, the only hope for the East Coast unions was the willingness of the skilled workers of the Marine Engineers Beneficial Association (MEBA) to stay on strike. That hope evaporated when the hard to replace engineers broke ranks with the other strikers and voted to accept the draconian contract offered by the owners. In the face of this critical defection, the ISU voted to return to work without an agreement several weeks later.

On the West Coast the situation was somewhat different. There there was much more solidarity between the seamen and the licensed trades, such as the masters, mates, pilots, and engineers. Men to replace the West Coast strikers had to be imported from the East Coast and this took time. The San Francisco local of MEBA refused to go along with the national union when it surrendered to the owners. Nevertheless, gradually the owners on the Pacific Coast were able to man their vessels with unemployed seamen, and on July 30, the strike ended in defeat on the West Coast as well. The debacle of 1921 resulted in the almost total destruction of the ISU. Until the revolution in American labor relations in the midst of the Great Depression of the 1930s, the shipowners enjoyed almost total control over labor relations on American vessels. [Ronald L. Filippelli]

FURTHER READING

Albrecht, Arthur E. *The International Seamen's Union*. Washington, DC: Government Printing Office, 1923.

Brown, Giles T. "The West Coast Phase of the Maritime Strike of 1921." *Pacific Historical Review*, Vol. 19 (1950), pp. 385–396.

Goldberg, Joseph P. *The Maritime Story: A Study in Labor-Management Relations*. Cambridge, MA: Harvard University Press, 1957.

o　　o　　o

SEAMEN'S STRIKE OF 1936. The National Industrial Recovery Act (NIRA), enacted in 1933 to regulate competition and increase aggregate demand, also breathed new life into the faltering labor movement. Section 7(a) of the act gave employees the right to organize and bargain collectively through representatives of their own choosing. The seamen were part of the widespread upsurge of unionization after the passage of the NIRA.

Militants among the seamen gained influence for several reasons. The lack of any adequate administrative machinery in the NIRA caused bitterness with the government's inability to enforce workers' rights to collective bargaining. The employers refused to abide by either the spirit or the letter of the law, choosing instead to fight unionization. The only seamen's union in existence, the venerable International Seamen's Union (ISU), was a small, conservative union that had virtually disappeared on the Pacific Coast and had assumed a docile posture toward the employers on the Atlantic and Gulf Coasts.

The impetus for the organizational drive came out of the West. During the great **San Francisco Longshoremen's Strike of 1934**, the seamen, organized in the ISU-affiliated Sailors' Union of the Pacific and the Communist-led Marine Workers International Union, joined with the men along the shore to form the Marine Federation of the Pacific. This organization lasted until political differences between the leaders of the seamen and longshoremen led to its demise in 1937.

The militancy of the West Coast seamen had paid off in better wages and working conditions, as well as union control of the hiring hall. These conditions did not exist on the East and Gulf coasts, where employers had been able to maintain complete control with the tacit compliance of the leaders of the ISU. Rank-and-file militants rose up to challenge the ISU leadership and to demand West Coast conditions as well as one national union for seamen.

Under pressure from this challenge from rank-and-file militants, the ISU leadership announced that they had decided to accept the East Coast companies' terms upon expiration of the contract in January, 1936. The terms, which also covered the Gulf Coast, provided for a wage scale five dollars below West Coast rates, as well as worse overtime and grievance provisions. In response to what they considered a sellout, 300 members of the crew of the Panama-Pacific Liner, *Pennsylvania*, who had shipped out in New York, walked off the ship in San Francisco on January 4, 1936. Soon after, the problems of the East Coast seamen were given a further airing on the West Coast. On March 2, 1936, crewmen of the intercoastal liner *California*, led by Joseph Curran, refused to cast off the lines until they received West Coast rates. It took the intervention of United States secretary of labor Frances Perkins to resolve the dispute and get the liner out of port by promising to use her influence to see that there were no charges brought against the strikers. Nevertheless, the ISU supported those who called the action mutiny, labeling the strike a breach of contract. When the ship returned to New York, sixty crewmen were discharged, some of whom were effectively blacklisted.

The ISU's repudiation of the *California* strikers worked to the advantage of the rank-and-file militants. In protest against the handling of the affair, they participated, along with Joseph Curran, in a wildcat strike on intercoastal ships. The ISU leadership denounced the strikers as "outlaws" and threatened them with expulsion. Curran was characterized as a "tool of the Communist Party." Nevertheless, the strikes spread to include 4,500 workers. West Coast seamen supported the tie-ups of East Coast ships in Pacific ports. The strike ended after nine weeks, when some 1,200 seamen voted to accept the terms of the ISU Executive Committee promising ISU assistance in preventing discrimination against the strikers, and implementation of the grievance procedure in the previous contract that had not been honored by the employers. The militants, including Curran, retreated to fight another day, waiting for the September 30 expiration of the West Coast agreements so that seamen on both coasts could confront employers together.

Negotiations on the West Coast began. The employers presented a united front to regain ground they had lost in the 1934 strike and the arbitration awards that had followed. Although the two sides differed on a variety of issues, the key stumbling block was the role of the union hiring hall. Although the stevedoring companies granted the demands of the International Longshoremen's Association on union control of the hiring hall, the issue proved insurmountable in the seamen's talks. The West Coast strike began at midnight October 30.

With the outbreak of the strike on the West Coast, the rank-and-file militants on the East Coast made plans to join in the West Coast strike. On October 30, the Seamen's Defense Committee, with Curran as chairman, ordered a sit-down strike on all ships to leave New York within twenty-four hours, in order to pressure the ISU leadership into participating in the strike. When the conservative leaders took only halfway measures, the Seamen's Defense Committee was reconstituted as a strike strategy committee with power to negotiate a new agreement meeting all West Coast provisions, including the union hiring hall. It called a strike on all East Coast ships on November 6. On November 23, the East Coast locals of the Masters, Mates, and Pilots' Association and the Marine Engineers Beneficial Association called their own strikes.

Citing their agreements with the ISU, the East Coast shippers called the strike an "outlaw" action led by a small group of militants who had forced the seamen out by threats of violence. The ISU leadership, in a fight for its life with the militants, lined up on the side of the shipping companies, tarring the strike as Communist inspired. Joseph Ryan, the conservative president of the International Longshoremen's Association, refused to permit his members to support the strikers on either coast. Both the Masters, Mates, and Pilots and the Marine Engineers called off their strikes, leaving the seamen alone. With these problems, the East Coast strike was called off after eighty-six days. Thirty thousand men had taken part at the beginning, but by January 24, Curran's committee could count no more than 3,000 still on strike.

The strike on the West Coast ended early in February after ninety-nine days. Unlike on the East Coast, the unions emerged victorious. Along with significant pay increases, job control through the longshoremen's and seamen's hiring halls was preserved and strengthened. The basic factor contributing to the success on the West Coast was the unity among the maritime unions.

On the East Coast, the debacle of the 1936–1937 strike signalled the end for the ISU. Even though the shipowners dealt with the ISU in negotiations that followed the strike's failure, the members no longer had any faith in the conservative, collaborationist, strategy of their leaders. During the strike a rival organization, the District Committee of the ISU, had been formed by the seamen. This group claimed a majority of the membership of the ISU. Soon, however, the interests of the rank-and-file group turned from taking over the ISU inside the American Federation of Labor to the creation of a new union as an affiliate of the newly formed Congress of Industrial Organizations. The first convention of the National Maritime Union (NMU) was held in July 1937. The new CIO union claimed a membership of 35,000. Joseph Curran was the new seamen's union's first president.

The appearance of the National Maritime Union also acted as a powerful stimu-

lant to reorganization on the West Coast. Whereas the West Coast had been the pacesetter in the past, the NMU now boasted a larger membership on the East Coast. When the NMU affiliated with the CIO, Harry Lundeberg, the head of the Sailor's Union of the Pacific, the old ISU affiliate, took his union back into the AFL. Lundeberg feared domination by Curran and his larger East Coast membership. Even though the aftermath of the strike left the seamen in two different unions, the settlements reached did bring long-term stability to the industry. Between January 1936 and June 1939, mandays lost to strikes declined by 90 percent. [Ronald L. Filippelli]

FURTHER READING

Bernstein, Irving. *The Turbulent Years: A History of the American Worker.* Boston, MA: Houghton Mifflin, 1970.

Galenson, Walter. *The CIO Challenge to the AFL: A History of the American Labor Movement, 1935–1941.* Cambridge, MA: Harvard University Press, 1960.

Goldberg, Joseph P. *The Maritime Story: A Study in Labor-Management Relations.* Cambridge, MA: Harvard University Press, 1957.

Lampman, Robert J. "The Rise and Fall of the Maritime Federation of the Pacific, 1935–1941." *Proceedings.* 25th Annual Conference. Pacific Coast Economic Association, 1950.

Stolberg, Benjamin. *The Story of the CIO.* New York: Viking Press, 1938.

o   o   o

SEATTLE GENERAL STRIKE OF 1919. The anti-radical hysteria that marked the great strike in Seattle had its roots in the intense bitterness between labor and capital that had long marked labor relations in that city. Much of this bitterness resulted from the strong presence in the city of the radical Industrial Workers of the World (IWW) and the fear and hatred that the "Wobblies" engendered among the respectable and conservative members of Seattle's middle and upper classes. The city was also home to small, but vocal, anarchist and Socialist communities. In addition, the anti-labor policies of the Seattle business community had resulted in the rise of a militant labor movement in the city, including one of the most radical central labor councils in the United States.

During World War I, the fear of the radicals' impact on labor relations merged with the citizenry's dislike for the anti-war stands of most of the city's radical groups, in particular the IWW. The first response to this was the creation of the Minute Men of Seattle in the summer of 1917. The group became the front line against radical influences in the city. Most of the Minute Men's anti-radical zeal was expended in the service of corporations, many of whom provided financial support for the organization. Many of the radicals tracked down by the Minute Men and later arrested were activists in the Seattle labor movement. Joining the Minute Men in the surveillance and suppression of radicals were the counterintelligence services of the Army and Navy. The latter, for example, policed the docks by searching and seizing members of the IWW without regard to constitutional due process.

The anxiety of Seattle's citizens and the pace of radical suppression quickened in the fall when the population was swelled by the annual migration of thousands of lumberjacks, harvest hands, and construction workers from the Pacific Northwest to the city. This migration, which in the past had had no serious political overtones, in the anti-radical climate of the war years became seen as a virtual IWW invasion to seize control of the city. This fear had been intensified by the IWW's recent organizing successes in the **Northwest Lumber Strike of 1917**, which had greatly increased the union's membership, insuring that a much larger percentage of the migrants would hold a Wobbly red card.

The combination of the anti-unionism, anti-IWW sentiment, anti-radicalism, and wartime hyper-patriotism prevalent in

Seattle reached as far as Washington where the administration of President Woodrow Wilson accepted sensationalist, xenophobic interpretations of what was going on in the city. Convinced that sedition in the Northwest threatened the war effort, the Wilson administration set in motion a widespread suppression of radicals and labor leaders. This federal initiative linked-up with the local efforts of the Seattle police and the Minute Men and, during 1917 and 1918, resulted in illegal arrests of IWW members on a large scale and the eventual deportation of seven IWW aliens for little more than the possession of IWW literature.

Against this background, the general labor unrest that marked America's transition from a wartime to a peacetime economy struck Seattle in 1919. One major cause was the marked increase in unemployment that accompanied the demobilization of the armed forces. In addition, war-induced inflation had left many workers eager to catch up. Unions, for their part, had grown during the war because of the federal government's interest in fostering labor peace in defense industries. The attempt by industry to roll back those gains after the war met with bitter resistance. When these trends came together in 1919, the result was the largest strike wave the country had ever seen. Over four million workers had gone on strike by the end of the year.

Complicating the massive industrial unrest was the deepening fear of many Americans, particularly those in the middle and upper classes, that the United States, as a result of the effects of the Bolshevik Revolution of 1917, was itself threatened by a Communist revolution. These fears seemed to be confirmed as the American left reorganized and grew rapidly after 1917, particularly among the immigrant industrial workers. In the minds of many then, the great strike wave of 1919, in which radicals of different persuasions played major roles, was the first battle in this revolution. The result was the anti-radical crusade, termed by historians the "Red Scare," which swept across the country during 1919 and 1920. Not surprisingly, given its tense social and labor climate, Seattle was one of the first cities to experience the effects of this confluence of events.

Thirty-five thousand Seattle shipyard workers struck on January 21, 1919, demanding more money and shorter hours. In essence, it was a strike against the government, because during the wartime emergency, shipping had been put under the control of the Emergency Fleet Corporation (EFC). When the EFC refused to discuss the issues during what it considered an illegal strike (the EFC's contracts with the seventeen shipyard unions still had two years to run), the Seattle Central Labor Council, temporarily in the hands of a radical minority, decided to call a general strike in the city in support of the shipyard workers. A measure of the radicalism of the Seattle labor movement was the fact that the city's American Federation of Labor (AFL) locals, contrary to the general conservatism of the craft-dominated federation, quickly supported the strike call.

The announcement of the strike call in the newspapers of February 3 sent a shock wave through the city. Panic buying began in grocery and drug stores. The Central Labor Council tried to calm this hysteria by assuring the citizens that the Committee of Fifteen, which had been appointed to direct the strike, would feed the people, keep medical facilities open, guarantee law and order, and run all industries necessary to the public health and welfare. These grandiose statements by labor leaders only served to heighten the fears that this was more than a strike, perhaps a revolution, particularly when the labor council boasted that the general strike would be the "most tremendous move ever made by labor in this country," and would lead down a road to "NO ONE KNOWS WHERE!" Indeed, the Seattle press fanned the fears by covering the story in sensationalist terms, emphasizing the role

of radicals and the revolutionary nature of the strike.

On February 16, some 60,000 workers in every line of work virtually paralyzed the city. Indeed, the Committee of Fifteen lived up to its pledges, and throughout the strike the city was well supplied with food, coal, water, heat, and light. In addition, there was no violence, and not one arrest occurred. In fact, for all of its revolutionary rhetoric, the aim of the strike was merely to force a settlement at the shipyard and to demonstrate labor's power to Seattle's bitterly anti-labor business establishment. News stories that described Seattle to the rest of the nation as in the grip of anarchy and revolution were without foundation. On the first day of the strike, newspaper headlines across the country greeted readers with the news that Seattle was in the hands of Communist revolutionaries.

Nevertheless, the city's political and business leadership used the strike as an opportunity to roll back the gains that labor had made during the war and to rid itself of the hated IWW. From the beginning, Mayor Ole Hanson described the strike as the first step in a Bolshevik attempt to overthrow the government of the United States. At his request federal troops entered the city on the first day of the strike, far too early for anyone to have determined that a state of emergency existed in the city. Hanson's appeals received a sympathetic hearing from many citizens who had been conditioned by Seattle's long war against radicals and labor. It was clear from the beginning that public opinion was running against the strike.

Pressure on the strikers also came from the labor movement. From the beginning, the AFL had been hostile to the strike, and had pressured its local affiliates to withdraw their support. This had an effect as the AFL locals brought pressure on the Central Labor Council, which they dominated, to call the general strike off on February 10.

Thus ended the general strike. It had lasted only five days and was, in reality, an almost wholly unremarkable labor dispute. Yet it engendered an orgy of hyperbole from politicians and newspapers across the country. Calls were heard in the United States Senate for the deportation of the strike leaders to Russia. Senator Knute Nelson of Minnesota declared that the events in Seattle posed a greater threat to Seattle than the war had. In this context, Seattle mayor Ole Hanson became a national hero for his defense of American values. Shortly after the strike, he resigned as mayor to capitalize on his new-found celebrity and tour the country giving lectures on the dangers of communism.

The importance of the Seattle general strike lay in the fact that it was the first incident in a series of great labor conflicts that marked 1919, and that the tactic of tarring labor disputes, and therefore the legitimacy of trade unions, with the brush of communism and revolution was used successfully for the first time. It would become a familiar story as the year wore on. [Ronald L. Filippelli]

FURTHER READING

Friedham, Robert L. *The Seattle General Strike.* Seattle, WA: University of Washington Press, 1964.

Murray, Robert K. *Red Scare: A Study of National Hysteria, 1919–1920.* Minneapolis, MN: University of Minnesota Press, 1955.

O'Connor, Harvey. *Revolution in Seattle: A Memoir.* New York: Monthly Review Press, 1964.

Preston, William, Jr. *Aliens and Dissenters: Federal Suppression of Radicals, 1903–1933.* Cambridge, MA: Harvard University Press, 1963.

o   o   o

SEATTLE POST-INTELLIGENCER STRIKE OF 1936. As in many other industries, the passage of the National Industrial Recovery Act led to an upsurge of union organizing among editorial employees on newspapers. This surge achieved national organization on December 15, 1933, when twenty-one local unions came together in Washington to form the American Newspaper Guild (ANG).

In its first year, the ANG achieved some success. It negotiated its first contract with the *Philadelphia Record*. But when the Guild began to act more like a trade union than a professional organization, publishers adopted a hard-line posture toward unionization of their editorial workers. A successful Guild boycott against the *Long Island Daily Press* and a bitter eighteen-week **Newark Star-Ledger Strike** did little to improve labor relations in the industry. Soon the small union was besieged on every side with disputes with publishers.

In 1936, the Guild affiliated with the American Federation of Labor and became involved in one of the most important strikes in its history. Thirty-six members struck William Randolph Hearst's *Seattle Post-Intelligencer* in protest against the discharge of two writers for union activity. The strike proved successful because of the solidarity shown by the rest of the Seattle labor movement. Teamsters, longshoremen, and woodworkers turned out to reinforce the Guild picket line.

Pressure for an end to the strike also came from the AFL. Charles P. Howard, the president of the International Typographical Union (ITU), whose members on the paper were idled by the strike, pushed the AFL Executive Council and AFL president William Green to intervene. The AFL proposed a return to work with the issues being submitted for resolution to a committee composed of Green and a representative of Hearst. Because the proposal did not return the two discharged men to work, the union refused. The Seattle Labor Council supported the Guild in its stand.

Faced with the united front of the Seattle labor movement, and with all hope of a mediated settlement gone, the *Post-Intelligencer*'s management gave in. The strike was settled on November 25, 1936. It was the first Guild victory against a major paper, although, in truth, it was a limited victory. The union received recognition for its dues-paying members through a management statement of policy, not a collective agreement. Nor were the two discharged writers returned to work. Nevertheless, the Guild did achieve improvements in wages and vacations and more importantly, it cracked the solid anti-union front of the Hearst chain, the most important in America. After the Seattle victory, a number of major newspapers signed with the Guild, including the *New York Daily News*, the largest paper in the country. [Ronald L. Filippelli]

FURTHER READING

Carlisle, Rodney, "William Randolph Hearst's Reaction to the American Newspaper Guild: A Challenge to New Deal Labor Legislation." *Labor History*, Vol. 10 (1969), pp. 74–99.

Leab, Daniel. *A Union of Individuals: the Formation of the American Newspaper Guild*. New York: Columbia University Press, 1970.

Galenson, Walter. *The CIO Challenge to the AFL*. Cambridge, MA: Harvard University Press, 1960.

o   o   o

SHARECROPPERS' AND FARM LABORERS' STRIKE OF 1935–1936. The formation of the Southern Tenant Farmers' Union in 1934 and its initiation of a sharecroppers and farm laborers' strike in 1935–1936 owed as much to the endemic inequality in the agricultural system as to the failure of the New Deal's agricultural policies. Even before the advent of the Great Depression and the collapse of "King Cotton," nearly 2 million Southern tenant farmers and sharecroppers lived a marginal existence. Disproportionately black and landless, they bargained their labor and mortgaged a share of their crops for the "privilege" of farming on land owned by wealthy white planters and corporations. The South's crop lien system had reduced them to virtual peonage. Plantation overseers and riding bosses exercised arbitrary authority and social control over black and white sharecroppers alike. Many became enmeshed in a vicious cycle of poverty, permanently indebted to unscrupulous merchants who charged exorbitant prices and rates of interest for the supplies and credit to sustain the system. This distinctive economic system reinforced the region's pattern of racial discrimination, in effect, creating a segregated rural lumpen proletariat.

The Great Depression heaped one more abuse upon the suffering of tenant farmers and sharecroppers—mass eviction from the land stemming from the Agricultural Adjustment Act's crop reduction program. Under the act, individual cotton farmers received rental and parity payments for reducing cultivation acreage and crop production. However, the act and its enforcement agency, the Agricultural Adjustment Administration (AAA), failed to address the peculiar problems of the plantation system and the vexing matter of landlord–tenant equity. Though Section 7 of the AAA's "Cotton Contract" vaguely pledged planters to share rental payments with "managing tenants" and to maintain the same number of sharecroppers, landlords circumvented the spirit of the contract. With less acreage to cultivate, planters began the wholesale eviction of sharecroppers from their lands. Landlords often withheld rental subsidies from tenants as a lien against accrued debts. More devious planters pocketed AAA subsidies by deliberately downgrading tenant farmers and "croppers" to the status of farm laborers, for whom they assumed no fiscal obligations. Planter domination of the AAA's county committees all but ensured their control over the distribution of subsidies and the perpetuation of abuses.

Sharecroppers residing in the fertile delta country of northeastern Arkansas bore the brunt of the AAA's misguided policies. There the high rate of farm tenancy (over 80 percent of the farming population in some counties) and absentee ownership of plantation lands compounded the problem of mass eviction. Early efforts by local Socialist activists to organize landless "croppers" into an "Unemployment Relief Army" resulted in the extension of some New Deal relief programs to the impoverished but failed to attack the fundamental causes of dislocation. Though some advocated building a strong state party organization to address the tenancy crisis, Socialist Party leader Norman Thomas proposed the formation of a bona fide sharecroppers' labor union to stem the tide of evictions and secure sharecropper and tenant rights under Section 7 of the cotton contract.

In July 1934, eighteen sharecroppers met in an abandoned school on the Norcross plantation near Tyronza, Arkansas, to establish the Southern Tenant Farmers Union (STFU) and plan an organization drive. There had been earlier sharecroppers' organizations. Most were short-lived however, casualties of planters' repression and the divisive issue of race. From the outset, STFU leaders decided to forge an interracial organization to enhance their collective bargaining power vis-à-vis the plantation owners. For the most part, they succeeded in convincing union members that their common problems took precedence over race. The STFU's executive committee included both black and white officers, and this racial balance filtered down to most union locals. Lingering prejudice in some areas of Arkansas' cotton counties, however, forced the union to adopt a "two local" strategy in organizing tenant farmers and sharecroppers.

Beside the problem of race, the STFU faced financial difficulties. Though dues payments were moderate, few sharecroppers could afford to pay. Without allowing membership to lapse, the union tolerated delinquent and non-payment of dues. Financially strapped, it depended upon the largesse of the Socialist Party and allied progressive organizations such as the League for Industrial Democracy, the American Civil Liberties Union, and the Washington Committee to Aid Agricultural Workers—the latter organization composed of sympathetic New Dealers. Several Communist-dominated organizations filtered money and support to the STFU, and party members from the radical Commonwealth Labor College in nearby Mena, Arkansas, provided invaluable aid during the union's organizing drive. Even the American Federation of Labor coordinated relief efforts on behalf of the STFU, though it sidestepped the union's proposal for direct affiliation.

Welcome as such aid was, STFU leaders feared that increasing dependence upon outside financial help might turn their union into a charity case. Direct action, they reasoned, had to be taken to secure better economic and living conditions for its members. The STFU embarked upon two fronts: initiating litigation to halt evictions, and waging strikes to obtain higher wages for cotton pickers and croppers. In December 1934, the union brought suit against Hiram Norcross, owner of the notorious Fairview (Norcross) Plantation. The plaintiffs, twenty-four tenant farmers, claimed that they had been unfairly evicted because of their membership in the STFU. In *West et al.* vs. *Norcross* the Arkansas Supreme Court dismissed the suit, ruling that sharecroppers were not parties to the AAA's cotton contract.

After this setback, the union and sympathetic liberals within the AAA's legal division began a campaign to achieve strict enforcement of tenant and sharecroppers' rights under Section 7. The STFU dispatched a small delegation to Washington, DC, to meet with Secretary of Agriculture Henry Wallace and chief AAA administrators. Though Wallace acknowledged that the AAA's cotton program had caused some dislocation and promised to undertake an impartial investigation of sharecroppers' complaints, he largely sided with the AAA's cotton division administrators. These officials dismissed the STFU's charges as exaggerated and attributed Arkansas' labor turbulence to Communist agitators from outside of the state. The cotton division white-washed and suppressed several independent reports on sharecroppers' conditions and convinced Wallace that Southern planters would not renew their cotton contracts if the legal division's interpretation of Section 7 was upheld. In a showdown between the AAA's legal and cotton divisions, Wallace sided with the latter. The subsequent purge of pro-STFU liberals from the AAA's legal division robbed the STFU of its most effective voice in addressing grievances at the federal level.

Emboldened by the cotton section's victory, Arkansas planters unleashed a three-month reign of terror in an attempt to bring the union to its knees. Local planters, sheriffs, and armed riding bosses disrupted union meetings, harassed and jailed STFU members, and enforced local ordinances banning union sponsored public rallies. At one outdoor rally at Birdsong, Arkansas, Socialist Party chairman Norman Thomas was forcibly removed from the stage by planters, while hired gangs indiscriminantly clubbed the union crowd. Night riders assaulted black union members and fired on the homes of STFU leaders. The spread of violence forced the union's executive committee to move its headquarters to Memphis, Tennessee. While the STFU cautioned against using violence and recommended passive resistance on the part of its members, it appealed to Wallace for direct federal intervention to advert the possibility of "class warfare" in Arkansas. Though the "reign of terror" engendered much national attention and was an embarrassment to Wallace and the AAA, the agency remained unmoved by the sharecroppers' pleas.

When the violence subsided, the STFU emerged weakened but still intact. By the summer of 1935, it had revived sufficiently to launch a new organizing drive and undertake a cotton pickers' strike. The union's action was taken to fend off a rival Communist sharecroppers' union in Alabama and to raise the wages of cotton pickers, which had

been reduced from sixty cents to forty cents per 100 pounds of cotton. At the union's first wage conference, representatives decided on a union scale of $1.00 and planned a strike at the peak of harvest season to achieve their goal. STFU wage committees were established in several counties to coordinate strike activity and distribute strike circulars among the cotton pickers.

By late September, Arkansas' delta cotton fields lay idle as thousands of pickers refused the call of the plantation bell. Fearing reprisals for their participation in the strike, many cited illness or the "misery," as the reason for not tending to the crop. To keep laborers out of the fields, STFU leaders spread rumors that "field scabs" had been killed for picking cotton. Violence did occur during the brief strike—mainly instigated by the planters. Despite planters' assertions that a sufficient labor supply existed to harvest the cotton crop, they capitulated and raised rates to an average of seventy-five cents. Fearing a revival of terrorism, the union called off the strike in October, though some locals held out longer and achieved the one-dollar rate.

The successful cotton pickers' strike swelled the ranks of the STFU. Within a few months membership rose to nearly 35,000 with new locals formed in Mississippi, Oklahoma, and Missouri. Geographical expansion and increased membership, however, brought with it attendant administrative problems—including the inability to collect dues and efforts by new Communist members to dominate internal union affairs. Moreover, the union confronted a new round of reprisals. Planters continued to evict tenants, blacklisted union croppers and farm laborers, and formed a rival sharecroppers' organization to entice white members from the STFU.

STFU leaders realized that continued outside financial support and national attention depended on the union's ability to wage another successful strike. In the spring of 1936, they initiated a strike to raise day rates for cotton croppers and to force plantation owners to sign contracts with the union. The STFU staged "picket marches" near targeted plantations to entice croppers to drop their hoes and abandon their fields. Unlike the previous strike, which caught planters off guard, the STFU's strike vote had been taken nearly three months before action commenced. Thus, plantation owners had plenty of time to prepare their own offensive. Roving bands of plantation deputies, armed with guns and baseball bats, patrolled highways and attacked peaceful marchers. At planters' insistence, the governor of Arkansas dispatched a contingent of National Guard troops to break the strike. Some planters even recruited "scab croppers" from the ranks of former Works Progress Administration employees who had been dropped from the relief rolls. Within six weeks, the union called off its strike. Cotton croppers' daily wages remained at $1.00 instead of the $1.50 demanded, and the union failed to obtain a written contract.

The defeat of the 1936 strike marked the beginning of the STFU's decline. For the remainder of its existence the union fell prey to an internecine struggle for control between its Communist and Socialist factions. Though its leaders hinged the union's future on direct affiliation with one of the labor federations, neither the AFL nor the Congress of Industrial Organizations (CIO) could afford to be the union's benefactor. The CIO offered indirect affiliation through the Communist-controlled United Cannery, Agricultural, Packing, and Allied Workers of America (UCAPAWA), which had taken the lead in organizing farm laborers and migrant workers.

In 1937, the STFU voted to affiliate with UCAPAWA under an ambiguous arrangement that nominally granted the union autonomy. Immediately, however, the two organizations argued over the collection and administration of dues. The STFU insisted that all dues payments be sent to its Memphis headquarters; UCAPAWA argued that the affiliation agreement granted them legal jurisdiction over the collection of sharecroppers' dues. Friction between the two unions intensified when the STFU expelled several Communists for fomenting dissension among its black members in an attempt to discredit the union's leadership. Angry at UCAPAWA's "rule or ruin" tactics, the STFU appealed to CIO president John L. Lewis. The CIO's decision to support UCAPAWA's position on the dues controversy all but sealed the STFU's fate. The sharecroppers' union severed connections with the international union and charted an independent course. Though it survived until 1941, the STFU ceased to become an effective force in the tenant farmers and sharecroppers' struggle to achieve better economic and living conditions.

Powerless to halt evictions under the AAA's cotton reduction program, the STFU tried to achieve limited economic objectives as opposed to fundamental reform of the plantation economy. The strikes of 1935–1936, however, focused national attention on the sharecroppers' plight and resulted in remedial legislation to ease their suffering. President Roosevelt appointed a special committee on farm tenancy to investigate and propose solutions to the tenancy crisis. STFU testimony at regional hearings conducted by the committee gave it an effective voice in helping to shape federal policy. Though Southern conservative congressmen succeeded in gutting the Bankhead-Jones Tenant Act in 1937, the bill's creation of the Farm Security Administration (FSA) revamped the Resettlement Administration and realized some of the STFU's aspirations. Under the FSA, the government initiated a home loan program for tenants and established "controversial" housing cooperatives in rural areas hardest hit by the cotton reduction program. The Resettlement Administration's experimental "Greenbelt Towns" were a far cry from the STFU's goal of establishing "cooperative plantations," owned and managed by tenants and sharecroppers themselves. The New Deal saw the tenancy crisis only in terms of home and land ownership, rather than in terms of an overhauling of the South's plantation and crop lien system. Ironically, it was not union or governmental action which achieved the demise of the plantation but the rise of agribusiness and mechanized cultivation of the land. These developments displaced more farm workers from the land, creating a pool of migratory farm laborers. Attempts to organize them into an effective union and gain concessions from powerful corporations posed a new challenge for activists and the labor movement. As the experience of the STFU indicated, that struggle would be long and difficult. [James Quigel]

FURTHER READING

Conrad, David Eugene. *The Forgotten Farmers: The Story of Sharecroppers in the New Deal*. Urbana, IL: University of Illinois Press, 1956.

Grubbs, Donald H. *Cry from the Cotton: The Southern Tenant Farmers' Union and the New Deal*. Chapel Hill, NC: University of North Carolina Press, 1971.

Mitchell, H. L. *Mean Things Happening in This Land*. Montclair, NJ: Allanheld, Osmun, and Co. Publishers, 1979.

o o o

SHOEMAKERS' STRIKE OF 1860. The Great Shoemakers' Strike of 1860 was the largest strike in the United States prior to the Civil War. Approximately 20,000 New England shoeworkers, men and women, ceased work in an effort to raise their wages and defend their standard of living. Their mass processions and parades through the streets of Lynn, Massachusetts, evoked considerable public sympathy in New England and widespread interest and curiosity elsewhere in the country. There was extensive coverage in the Boston press. Reporters and illustrators from national publications gave much attention to the strike, particularly the prominence of women workers.

The shoemakers' strike was a strike of mass participation and great excitement but of little violence and no bloodshed. There were few arrests and no prosecutions. There was anger but little hatred. In light of the extensive rioting that was common in nineteenth century American cities, the upheaval of 1860 was remarkably peaceful—impressive testimony to the discipline of the participants.

The strike took place in the towns and villages of New England where women's shoes were made, especially in Essex County north of Boston, in parts of Middlesex County farther west, and in southern New Hampshire. The making of shoes employed more people in the Bay State than any other branch of manufacturing, including textiles. But there was little strike activity among the makers of men's boots and shoes south of Boston.

The shoeworkers who struck were chiefly handworkers, not machine operators. They worked either at home or in small shops called "ten footers" near their homes, not in factories. The production of shoes took place within a putting-out system in which the employer, his assistants, and cutters in the central shop gave out cut materials to wage earners who worked with their own tools and returned the finished shoes to the employer.

The shoeworkers included both men and women. The women binders, or stitchers, sewed together the upper parts of the shoes. They were often the wives and daughters of the shoemakers, though a growing number were single women unattached to shoemaker families. The putting-out system enabled married women to combine wage work with their traditional domestic chores. The shoemakers, or cordwainers, were bottomers who fitted the uppers on lasts (wooden models of feet) and attached the uppers to the soles. In 1855, there were 45,000 male shoemakers and 33,000 binders in Massachusetts.

The strikers were mostly native born

but with a sprinkling of foreigners, mainly Irish. Immigrants were becoming an important part of the industry's work force, though less so than in textiles which employed machine operatives rather than handworkers. In Lynn, Massachusetts, approximately 10 percent of the shoemakers were Irish, but in Natick more than half were foreign-born, mostly German.

The main cause of the strike was the depressed condition of the shoe industry. Production increased more rapidly than demand as more and more "hands" entered the industry. Workers from the depressed countryside of Massachusetts, New Hampshire, and Maine poured into the manufacturing towns of Massachusetts, as did immigrants from Europe. Rural dwellers who stayed behind tried to eke out a living by combining farming and shoemaking. These thousands of outworkers living in the countryside made shoes for firms located in the large shoe towns like Lynn and Haverhill, Massachusetts. By 1855, more than half the shoes sold by Lynn employers were made by workers outside Lynn.

The shoe business was decentralized and highly competitive, with scores of firms that varied greatly in size. Some employed hundreds of workers, others scarcely a dozen. In the absence of expensive machinery, only small amounts of capital were needed to make a start. Competition was fierce. In Lynn alone there were over 100 shoe manufacturers in a city of 19,000. New firms appeared as well in New Hampshire and Maine to compete with Massachusetts employers. To make matters worse, New England emigrants to the west set up firms in New York, Ohio, and Wisconsin to compete with the communities they left behind. Competitive pressure also came from shoe merchants in Boston. They assembled large shipments for customers by purchasing shoes from small employers who competed vigorously for a share of the wholesale order.

The industry was unstable, beset by sharp cycles of boom and bust. Severe reductions hit in 1850, 1854, 1857, and 1859. Competition for work during slack periods drove wages down to three dollars per week for men and less for women who toiled for piece wages from dawn to dusk and even into the night when work was available.

Mechanization delivered another blow to the family wage. The sewing machine was the first important machine in the industry, enabling a skilled operator to stitch enough uppers to supply twenty bottomers or shoemakers. The demand for the machines was "immense and without a parallel," an observer reported in 1856. Women were hardest hit, but the whole family suffered. The number of binders dropped from 33,000 in 1855 to 19,000 in 1860. Some binders managed to purchase machines for home use. By 1860, hundreds had their own machines, competing with hand binders and the new "machine girls" who toiled either for manufacturers or their subcontractors, called "machine bosses," who owned dozens of sewing machines. Low wages, sharp fluctuations in the shoe trade, competition with rural outworkers, competition among scores of manufacturers, and mechanization all contributed to the worsening conditions that precipitated the upheaval of 1860.

The Great Shoemakers' Strike was not a spontaneous outburst among workers without structure or leadership. Organizing among shoemakers began two years before the outbreak of the strike. The first stirrings occurred in 1858. "Protective associations" or "benefit societies" appeared in eastern Massachusetts. In Lynn, shoemakers formed a mechanics association, levied dues of a penny a day, and established a newspaper, *The New England Mechanic*. In 1859, they drafted a "price list" of proposed wage rates and began to solicit the signatures of shoemakers who would abide by the new rates. By January 1860, the canvassers had obtained support from 1,100 cordwainers; only a few refused. Confident and determined, driven by a sense that it was their responsibility to bring order and justice to the industry, the shoemakers began to turn in their "wood" (lasts) and refused any more work until manufacturers signed the price list. The strike began in Natick, but the major turnout took place in Lynn on February 22, George Washington's Birthday. Nearly 3,000 shoemakers assembled in Lyceum Hall in what one witness called "the largest and most enthusiastic meeting of its kind ever held in New England."

Lynn, Massachusetts, became the focal point of the strike. The largest producer of women's shoes in the United States, Lynn was located a dozen miles from Boston on the north shore. A town of nearly 20,000, Lynn's population consisted largely of families employed in shoemaking and related trades.

The Lynn mechanics, or cordwainers, were a formidable group. Proud and disciplined, many were also self-educated and articulate. They were imbued with notions of the labor theory of value, equal rights, and the dignity of labor. Many were Methodists, veterans of such movements as temperance reform, free soilism, and the anti-Catholic American party. Lacking in deference, defenders of their craft, with a strong sense of self-esteem, they were the spearhead of the Great Shoemakers' Strike.

Their most important allies were the female stitchers who joined the shoemakers in early March. Their support was critical. A reduction in the supply of sewn uppers that were exported from Lynn to the outworkers in the country would make it more difficult for manufacturers to circumvent the Lynn shoemakers. The women adopted their own price list, held their own meetings, chose their own leaders, but they worked closely with the cordwainers, too closely some thought. The young, unmarried "machine girls," sewing machine operators, favored a more independent course and a higher price list. The home workers, mostly married women, supported closer ties with the male

shoemakers and were willing to adopt a lower price list if it promised an earlier victory for the men and preservation of the family wage.

The objective of the strike was to raise wages by forcing manufacturers to sign the price list. Shoeworkers pledged to abstain from work until all bosses had signed the list. But there were divisions among the strikers in Lynn over how to achieve that goal. All agreed that success depended chiefly on their ability to halt the making of shoes. The majority favored peaceful methods of moral suasion to enlist all shoemakers in a common effort. They dispatched representatives to the towns and villages of eastern Massachusetts and southern New Hampshire, vigorously promoting the strike among outworkers and exhorting them to join with Lynn cordwainers for the price list. But a strong and angry minority used other means. On the first day of the strike, they attempted to prevent shoe firms from sending raw materials to their many outworkers. Lynn bosses employed 6,000 shoemakers, but fewer than half lived in Lynn. The dissident minority obstructed the wagons carrying the materials and clashed with the express drivers and the marshals protecting them. The altercation and minor violence between strikers and expressmen became the official justification for the intervention in the strike by outside police.

Uniformed police from Boston arrived in Lynn on February 23 at the request of the mayor, Edward Davis. He also contacted Stephen C. Phillips, state attorney general, who activated the Lynn Light Infantry for possible use. Many Lynn citizens did not believe that minor incidents of fisticuffs warranted the intrusion of outside force into their city's internal affairs. The strikers themselves vowed to enforce their decision not to interfere with the express wagons. They saw the mayor's actions as a pretext for intervention on behalf of a minority—the manufacturers—who employed outworkers in place of Lynn citizens. "No rum and no outside police," was the cry of protest. Hundreds jeered the Boston police as they arrived in Lynn. So intimidated was Davis that he relented by withdrawing the police and ordering them back to Boston. He then pleaded ill health and took no further part in the strike. The strikers and their allies were not placated. Months later, they organized a workingmen's ticket and elected a shoemaker-Democrat as mayor of Lynn and other workers as aldermen and councilors. Leaders of the strike became the city marshal and deputy marshal, replacing those who had defended the expressmen. Cohesion from the strike persisted. In 1861, a group of shoeworkers formed Company C, the Lynn Mechanics' Phalanx, and enlisted in the Civil War, commanded by the leaders of their strike.

Strike activity revolved around the city of Lynn. Contingents of Lynn cordwainers tramped to the surrounding towns of Marblehead, South Reading, and Salem to bolster the resolve of shoemakers. In return, delegations of cordwainers from the smaller towns flocked to Lynn for the marches that displayed the numbers and might of the mechanics. In the evening, mass meetings assembled in Lyceum Hall to reaffirm collectively their determination to stand fast.

Highpoints of the strike were the large parades in Lynn. Altogether there were five during the six-week strike. The parade of March 7 attracted the attention of illustrators from New York magazines who featured the spectacle in their pages. Reporters were especially impressed by the determination and courage of the Lynn "ladies" who braved both the wet driving show and middle-class social convention to participate.

There was strong and widespread support for the shoeworkers. Unlike strikes in the twentieth century, which often involve only the workers, the 1860 shoemakers' strike witnessed the participation of many who themselves were not shoemakers. That support was evident in the largest parade on March 16, when 6,000 took part. Volunteer fire companies, marching bands, and militia companies from shoe towns in Essex and Middlesex counties joined the procession. Some ministers and priests preached support. Farmers in the countryside donated food and shopkeepers extended credit. Even a few manufacturers contributed to the strike fund.

Despite their fervor, strong organization, and considerable public support, the strikers were only partly successful. Some manufacturers agreed to pay the wages demanded by the shoemakers but refused to sign the price list. The strike began to peter out in early April as some cordwainers returned to work at the new rates, promising to contribute the increases they had won to a strike fund for their fellows.

The strike marked the end of the putting-out system and the dominance of the skilled handworker who labored with his fellows in the small shop. Within a few years, factories for the new Blake-McKay stitching machines would appear in shoe towns like Lynn. But individual conflict between manufacturers and shoeworkers so dramatically inaugurated in the 1860 strike, would remain a permanent feature of industrial relations in the industry for the next half century. [Paul Faler]

FURTHER READING

Blewett, Mary H. *Men, Women, and Work: Class, Gender, and Protest in the New England Shoe Industry, 1780–1910*. Urbana, IL: University of Illinois Press, 1988.

Dawley, Alan. *Class and Community: The Industrial Revolution in Lynn*. Cambridge, MA: Harvard University Press, 1976.

Faler, Paul G. *Mechanics and Manufacturers in the Early Industrial Revolution: Lynn, Massachusetts 1780–1860*. Albany, NY: State University of New York Press, 1981.

Foner, Philip S. *History of the Labor Movement in the United States*, Vol. 1, *From Colonial Times to the Founding of the American Federation of Labor*. New York: International Publishers, 1947.

Taylor, George Rogers. *The Transportation Revolution, 1815–1860*. New York: Holt, Rinehart and Winston, 1951.

o   o   o

SLAVE REBELLIONS. By the early part of the nineteenth century, life was changing for free and enslaved African-Americans in the southern states. As the main mass of workers in the region, they not only worked as common laborers in the fields, they also acquired various skilled trades. Despite the enactment of state laws to prevent them from receiving a formal education, many blacks learned how to read and acquired knowledge of the revolutionary age in which they lived. In the states of Virginia and South Carolina many of the slaves and free blacks lived in urban areas, and it was from their ranks that there emerged the leaders for the major slave revolts.

The three major revolts from 1800 to 1831 were led by men who were not "plantation laborers but persons who lived in or near an urban center." Gabriel Prosser, who led the revolt in Richmond, Virginia, in 1800 was a blacksmith who lived a few miles from this state capital. Denmark Vesey, who led the uprising in Charleston, South Carolina was a resident of that city. And Nat Turner, who led the insurrection in Southampton County, Virginia, in 1831, was a plantation slave, and a literate preacher. All three men then were skilled laborers who challenged an oppressive labor system that debased millions of African-Americans. While their efforts were not successful, they were among the many black leaders who dared to strike a blow for freedom and equality for all people in the United States.

Gabriel Prosser's Revolt

Gabriel Prosser and many of his co-conspirators were either free blacks or fugitive slaves who freely associated with slaves in Henrico County and adjoining counties in Virginia. These leaders either heard white men or read about efforts to free the thirteen colonies from British colonial rule. Influenced by this revolutionary fervor, they thought they were justified in seeking the freedom of their own people. What bothered them most was the fact that the new liberty for white people and the growth of abolitionism in the North did not seem to diminish the institution of slavery in the South. Thus the self-deterministic tendencies of these leaders persuaded them to revolt against the system of slavery in their region.

Gabriel Prosser emerged as the leader of the revolt in Henrico County because he had a grim sense of what had to be done to organize a revolt. He was not afraid to make decisions or delegate responsibilities to others and he was dedicated to his cause. Prosser's two brothers also joined him in planning the revolt and recruiting people for it. One of his brothers, Martin, was a preacher and the other, Solomon, was, like Gabriel, a blacksmith. When he told them of his plan to revolt they promised that they would work with him to the bitter end.

The Prosser brothers and their associates attended the religious services and social events of blacks in Henrico and the surrounding counties. They traveled as far away as Petersburg, Charlottesville, and Carterville. At the meetings they asked for volunteers who were willing to help them to recruit for the revolt. On August 10, 1800, Gabriel and his brothers attended a funeral for a little boy on William Young's plantation. After the service was over, Gabriel defied secrecy and asked the blacks present if they would join the revolt. Some of them hesitated, but he told them it was important to execute his plan because the summer was nearly over and the revolt had to occur before winter arrived. Martin also spoke to the crowd at the Young plantation and told them it was dangerous to delay the event any longer. The time was right to strike because the Revolutionary War was over, and the soldiers had been discharged. Hence, it was a good time to revolt. After they listened to the Prosser brothers and other leaders, many of those present agreed to join the revolt. With this show of support, Gabriel decided to hold another meeting on August 30 in front of Moore's schoolhouse, where a final decision would be made when to begin the revolt.

Knowing that he had limited resources and recruits, Gabriel decided that he would organize a small force of about 200 men who would enter Richmond at midnight and terrorize its inhabitants by burning the warehouse district. In the ensuing confusion, many white people would be killed, armaments would be taken, and the governor would be taken as a hostage. Once the initial revolt began, the Prosser brothers and their associates thought the French would join them in their battle against the pro-slavery forces in America, but events did not unfold as planned.

The leaders met again on August 30, six miles from Richmond, and 1,000 slaves met with them. They decided to march to the city, but a violent storm that day hampered their plans. Moreover, before Prosser could execute his plan, two or three slaves had told whites about the plot. This allowed Governor Monroe to mobilize more than 600 troops and alert all the militia units in Virginia. Numerous slaves were arrested and tried, but only thirty-five were executed. Gabriel Prosser was not captured until late September in Norfolk. He was returned to Richmond and tried, but he refused to talk to anyone about his revolt and he too was executed.

Gabriel Prosser's revolt was a bold movement by African-Americans in a slave society that had rising expectations. They did not want their people to remain indefinitely in a plantation economy. Prosser and his associates had had a taste of freedom. They had begun to be assimilated in urban communities in Virginia, and they had become versatile workers by acquiring different skills. If they could do this, they thought, why not try to change the old order and improve the lives of the masses of their people in bondage. Although the leaders were executed, white slave holders were not able to prevent further revolts in the South before the Civil War.

Denmark Vesey's Revolt

Twenty-two years after Prosser's revolt in Virginia, another major uprising occurred in Charleston, South Carolina. There were sporadic slave insurrections during the intervening years, but Vesey's revolt was on a grand scale and it caused a great deal of fear among Southerners. Denmark was a carpenter in Charleston who had purchased his freedom from slavery the same year of Prosser's rebellion. Like his predecessor, he too believed, that his people needed to live as free persons. This caused him to think about organizing a revolt against slave owners for more than twenty years. By 1822, he had chosen his compatriots carefully, and they accumulated 250 pike heads, bayonets, and 300 daggers.

Vesey and his associates were encouraged to revolt by rumors that reached Charleston at the time about the debates between the pro-slavery and anti-slavery forces in Congress on the Missouri Compromise. They thought that Congress had passed an emancipation act but that the slave owners refused to accept it. Thus they believed that their cause was justified. To help them achieve their goal, Vesey asked the nation of Haiti to assist them.

Like Prosser, Vesey and his cohorts traveled to rural areas beyond Charleston to ask slaves to join the revolt. At times they used appropriate passages from the Old Testament in the Bible to persuade people to unite with them. Vesey also appealed to their African heritage to inspire them to come with him. To stress this point, Vesey sent one of his associates, Gallah Jack, who had been born in Africa, to the Sea Islands near the coast to form African legions.

Vesey wanted the revolt to take place on the second Sunday in July 1822. When some white residents found out about it he changed the date to the second Sunday in August. However, because many of his co-leaders were miles away from Charleston recruiting, he did not reach them in time to let them know about the new date. During the one month lag, white men began to capture blacks suspected of being a part of the uprising. White people assumed that there were perhaps 9,000 African-Americans involved in the Vesey plot, but this was not verified. Nevertheless, 139 blacks were arrested and forty-seven were found guilty; and four white men were fined and put in prison for encouraging blacks to revolt. Vesey was executed on July 2, 1822.

The Vesey revolt had several negative effects on African-Americans in South Carolina and other southern states. After it was crushed, white people in the state decided to halt the work of the African Methodist Episcopal (AME) Church there because they felt that church members aided the revolters. This prompted their religious leader, the Reverend Morris Brown, to end the work in Charleston and move to the North to work with Bishop Richard Allen. Brown later became a bishop, and the AME Church did not reopen its work in South Carolina until the Civil War ended. A second result of the uprising was the enactment of a state law that made black seamen go to prison while their ships were berthed in state ports. Finally, as a result of the Vesey plot, and increased abolitionist activity in the northern states, southern intellectuals and religious leaders decided to solidify and strengthen their racial, religious, and cultural arguments to maintain the institution of slavery. Again, however, none of these measures stopped the revolts by some black workers on the plantations and in the cities.

Nat Turner's Revolt

Nat Turner was different from Gabriel Prosser and Denmark Vesey. They lived in urban centers, but Turner was a slave in rural Southampton County, Virginia. He was a deeply religious person, who was very unhappy with slavery. On one occasion he ran away but later returned to the planta-tion. By the time he came back, Turner had decided to organize a revolt against slave owners. He believed that celestial signs would let him know when to take action. Thus, after the solar eclipse in February 1831, he decided his revolt would occur on July 4. Because he was ill on the latter date, however, Turner waited for another heavenly sign. This came on August 13, when the sun became a "peculiar greenish blue."

The new date for the beginning of the revolt was August 21. By this time, scores of slaves had promised to join with Turner. On the designated day Turner killed his owner, Joseph Travis, and the rest of his family. Then he and his followers proceeded to kill sixty whites within twenty-four hours. Just as the uprising was gaining momentum, it was halted by state and federal troops. These forces killed more than 100 slaves and then hung thirteen others plus three free blacks immediately, but Turner was more difficult to apprehend. They finally caught him on October 30. His trial was a major event in Virginia that lasted for nearly two weeks and attracted a great deal of attention from white people throughout the South. Unlike Prosser and Vesey, who said little about their revolts, Turner's confession revealed much about his inner thoughts, religious beliefs, and how he planned the revolt. At the end of the trial Turner was found guilty, and he was hung on November 11, 1831.

As with the other two revolts, rumors and stories about Turner's revolt were greatly exaggerated. It was reported that hundreds of white persons were killed in southern Virginia. The event itself and the accounts of it caused many southern states to enact stronger black codes to greatly restrict the activities of the slaves, but they did not stop slave uprisings and conspiracies in the region. Between 1835 and the eve of the Civil War, revolts occurred in Georgia, Alabama, Louisiana, Mississippi, and North Carolina.

The three slave revolts discussed here indicate that the masses of African-American workers forced into being slaves throughout the South were not docile persons who accepted their fate. From colonial times to the Civil War, many of them tried to free their people from bondage. Their leaders, like Prosser, Vesey, and Turner, knew that their chances for success were grim, but they had to make the effort. Although they failed, they must be placed among those heroic figures who made their contributions to the struggle for freedom and equality in the United States. [Cyril Griffith]

FURTHER READING

Aptheker, Herbert. *American Negro Slave Revolts*. New York: International Publishers, 1969.

Carroll, Joseph C. *Slave Insurrections in the United States, 1800–1865*. New York: Negro Universities Press, 1968.

Frederickson, George M., and Christopher Lasch. "Resistance to Slavery." *Civil War History*. Vol. 13 (December 1967), pp. 315–329.

Genovese, Eugene D. *From Rebellion to Revolution, Afro-American Slave Revolts in The Making of the New World*. New York: Vintage Books, 1979.

Harding, Vincent. *There Is A River, The Black Struggle for Freedom in America*. New York: Vintage Books, 1983.

Kilson, Marion D. "Towards Freedom: An Analysis of Slave Revolts in the United States." *Phylon*, Vol. 25 (1954), pp. 175–189.

Killens, John Oliver. *The Trial Record of Denmark Vesey*. Boston, MA: Beacon Press, 1970.

Mullin, Gerald W. *Flight and Rebellion, Slave Resistance in Eighteenth-Century Virginia*. New York: Oxford University Press, 1972.

o   o   o

SOUTHERN LUMBER OPERATORS' LOCKOUT OF 1911–1913. This conflict was really a series of clashes between the Southern Lumber Operators Association (SLOA) and the Brotherhood of Timber Workers (BTW). The Association had been formed after a strike of workers in the southern timber industry occurred in 1907. It represented the owners of over 300 mills, most in Louisiana, Arkansas, Mississippi, North Carolina, Texas, and Virginia. Louisiana was the center of much of the discord in the timber mills during this period.

The Brotherhood of Timber Workers was founded in 1910, with its headquarters in Alexandria, Louisiana. The BTW seemed at first to owe more to the heritage of the Knights of Labor than to the Industrial Workers of the World (IWW), with which it was later associated. The Brotherhood initially expressed sympathy for the capitalist system and eschewed the use of violence, asking only that workers have the right to act through the union in their own interests.

One of the first challenges that the Brotherhood had to deal with was the issue of race. The BTW adopted the same approach as had the Populists, by organizing black locals. About half of the Brotherhood's membership was black, reflecting the large number of blacks employed in the lumber industry.

The lives most southern timber workers faced were difficult. Their wages, at $1.50 to $1.75 per day, were lower than those of lumber workers outside the South. Worse yet, pay came irregularly, sometimes only a few times a year. Wages were usually in scrip that was honored only at company stores, where prices were often half or more above other retailers. Hours of work were long, at least eleven per day. Timber workers usually labored in isolated locations, and they were therefore forced to live in shacks provided at high rents by the company. Medical care was poor, though workers were charged handsomely for this service. Company guards terrorized timber workers and their families, particularly union supporters.

The first convention of Louisiana BTW members, held in Alexandria in June 1911, addressed each of these areas of concern in the forests and mills. The demands of the lumber workers were for $2.00 per day, paid twice monthly in cash, not scrip. Company stores were to charge market prices, and the high rent charged for poor company housing was to be lowered as well. The inadequate and expensive medical insurance system was strongly criticized, as were the oppressive company police.

BTW members returned from the convention to press their demands, only to be confronted by slack demand for lumber and a militantly anti-union SLOA. John H. Kirby, owner of one of the largest lumber companies in the South, reacted to the claims of the BTW by accusing it of being a radical and Socialist organization, raising the specter of the IWW, and feigning friendship for the American Federation of Labor (AFL) as a legitimate labor organization. The Association's attacks were repeated widely in the press. The SLOA met frequently during the summer of 1911. At a meeting in New Orleans in July, the 125 members of the Association, running their mills at less than full capacity because of slack demand, agreed unanimously to lock out the timber workers in an attempt to break the BTW. Only the larger mills were closed, with those in Louisiana, where the Brotherhood was strongest, closing first.

The operators not only used the press to attack the BTW, but also formed local protective associations to fight the union. By the fall of 1911, mill owners felt that they could reopen the closed mills with non-union labor, and by the end of 1911, the lockout was officially ended, and the union forced out.

The Brotherhood reacted to the refusal of the SLOA to deal with them by embracing to a degree, the very ideology that the SLOA had attacked them for representing. The lockout of 1911 had weakened the BTW, and they were looking for help. The IWW was anxious to see the Brotherhood affiliate with it, and William "Big Bill" Haywood and Covington Hall, representing the IWW, attended the 1912 BTW Convention. The delegates voted at that meeting to affiliate with the IWW, and the BTW officially became the Southern Division of the National Industrial Union of Forest and Lumber Workers (IUFLW). Hall, a Mississippi born radical, played a key role from 1912 to 1914

in rallying timber workers, especially with his union newspaper, the *Lumberjack*.

At first, it would appear that the Brotherhood was playing into the hands of the SLOA by affiliating with the IWW. But initially the help of the IWW was useful in raising the hopes of southern lumber workers that they could fight the owners. After all, the IWW had beaten lumber operators in the Pacific Northwest. Therefore, the connection of the BTW and the IWW again enabled the Brotherhood to do battle with the Association.

By mid-1912, demand for lumber had increased significantly, and the saws in the woods and the mills were humming. The SLOA wanted to maintain full production. Similarly, the BTW, having been weakened by the lockout of 1911, was seeking to reorganize the timber industry, but it did not want an early confrontation with the owners.

Local union leaders in the area around Grabow, Louisiana, had a different idea. They struck the Galloway Lumber Company over the issue of pay twice a month. Unfortunately, the Brotherhood was not well prepared for this conflict. The company, given their desire to keep their mills running, decided to operate them with scab workers. This inevitably led to confrontations outside the mill, and on July 7, 1912, shooting outside the Galloway mill led to the death of two union members, a bystander, and a company guard. Nearly all BTW leaders were arrested as a result of this battle, and though they were eventually exonerated in a widely publicized trial, their absence while in jail still hurt the Brotherhood.

Merryville, Louisiana, was the site of the final confrontation between the Brotherhood and the Association. Despite the caution urged by the BTW leadership, workers at the American Lumber Company struck over the firing of fifteen of their fellow union members who had supported the BTW workers on trial at Grabow. At first, the

Merryville lumber workers showed remarkable solidarity, including the creation of a communal organization that Covington Hall called the "first American Soviet." A riot by company supporters in February 1914, literally drove most BTW members out of Merryville. Soon thereafter, the strike was lost, and so was the Brotherhood of Timber Workers.

Despite the disappearance of the BTW, the union had established that Southern workers were hardly a uniformly compliant lot, as often portrayed. The BTW brought together black and white workers in an industrial union. Workers were not intimidated by accusations of radicalism, as evidenced by their affiliation with the IWW. Premature confrontations at Grabow and Merryville with the SLOA certainly played a role in the demise of the Brotherhood, but lumber workers at the same time demonstrated that they could work together to resist the exploitation that has too often afflicted southern workers. [Leslie S. Hough]

FURTHER READING

Green, Jim. "The Brotherhood." *Working Lives: The Southern Exposure History of Labor in the South.* New York: Pantheon Books, 1980.

Reed, Merl E. "Lumberjacks and Longshoremen: The I.W.W. in Louisiana." *Labor History,* Vol. 13, No. 1 (Winter, 1972).

o   o   o

SOUTHERN TELEPHONE STRIKE OF 1955. In the years immediately following World War II, the Communications Workers of America (CWA) had only a tenuous foothold in the Bell System. The union had succeeded in making some gains after the disastrous nationwide **Telephone Strike of 1947**, but in the early fifties AT&T took the offensive. The union lost a bitter fifty-nine-day strike against the Indiana Bell Telephone Company and two battles with Western Electric that drained CWA's financial resources. It was clear that the company

was testing the union's strength. Nowhere did there seem to be greater prospects for success than in the Southern Bell bargaining unit.

Although unionism in the South had always been weak, CWA had managed to organize 32,000 workers in 126 locals throughout nine southern states. It amounted to one of American labor's biggest beachheads in the South. Nevertheless, the CIO postwar southern organizing drive and its counterpart in the AFL did not yield the desired results. After the passage of Taft-Hartley in 1947, most of the southern states adopted right-to-work laws and through a variety of anti-union measures, managed to limit union penetration. By 1955, only 15 percent of southern workers carried union cards. CWA learned the ferocity of anti-unionism in Dixie during a 1954 strike against the independent Alabama Telephone Company. Workers were discharged, several were jailed, and strikers were ostracized in the community.

Relations between Southern Bell and the union had been difficult from the beginning. Between 1947 and 1955, workers carried out some one hundred wildcat strikes over work related grievances that had been accumulating for years. Understandably, a no-strike guarantee was a high priority bargaining item for the company. But for the union, a no-strike clause meant the inability to respect a picket line of another CWA unit, such as, for example, telephone installers who worked for Western Electric. Also, because of the right-to-work laws in most southern states, the union could not bargain for the union-shop security clause as a quid pro quo for the blanket no-strike clause. In addition, Southern Bell refused to submit disputes arising during the administration of the contract to arbitration.

The strike began on March 14 when 50,000 telephone workers in nine states walked out. Almost immediately, the strike took a turn for the worse. Although picketing was generally peaceful, the company reported widespread sabotage of its cables. The union denied any complicity, but the events gained valuable publicity for the company's charges that the union was irresponsible, and sabotage marred the strike throughout. In addition, Southern Bell, like the rest of the Bell System, had an extremely high ratio of managers to workers. This enabled them to replace strikers with supervisory personnel who had been trained to handle the switchboard in anticipation of a strike. These supervisors were reinforced by thousands of college students from southern schools who signed on as strikebreakers even before the strike began.

Yet surprisingly, and with the exception of the college students, southerners were not generally hostile to the strikers. Indeed, in many communities, striking workers were afforded the use of public buildings and were given support from public officials. In part, this was probably the result of the fact that so many of the strikers were young white women, most of whom had graduated from high school, and who benefitted from the twin southern traditions of chivalry and paternalism. This also no doubt accounts in part for the reluctance of the police to interfere in strike activity in many communities. Also the strike took hold in hundreds of small communities where the telephone workers had frequent, often daily, contact with many of the citizens. Finally, the communities knew that whatever the outcome of the strike, Southern Bell was not able to leave their town, a threat that had been used effectively many times to blunt union drives in the South in industries such as textiles.

Nevertheless, the company was in no hurry to settle. After two months of the strike, it had proven its ability to operate with supervisory personnel and strikebreakers. Conversion to dial service and other technological improvements meant that local service—short of an equipment breakdown—was almost uninterruptible. Southern Bell could also count on the support of other companies in the Bell System, most of whom had already signed with the union, which assigned management people to go south and help to keep the company in operation. In these circumstances, the company had no incentive to bargain seriously, and it did not.

To counter these disadvantages, the union launched "operation zilch." This involved making constant person-to-person long distance calls, requiring operator assistance, to non-existent people. The union also set up a telephonic picket line whereby strikers made person-to-person calls which were answered by other strikers who then told the operator that the party could be reached at another number. At the second number, the referral was made to a third number, and so on. The goal was to tie up long distance service and cut down the company's profits.

The company responded to the tactic and to continued incidents of sabotage by seeking injunctions and threatening discharges. By April, the union was defending itself from hundreds of charges, including dozens of injunctions. Intimidation of strikers also increased, with frequent incidents of company employees and police harassing and threatening CWA supporters. Forty policemen and firemen used fire hoses to break up an "anti-scab" demonstration in Miami. In Tupelo, Mississippi, local police arrested fifty-two strikers in church for disturbing the peace. By the end of the strike, the company had discharged 249 strikers for offenses ranging from abusive language to sabotage. Southern Bell Company subsequently sued the union for $5 million in damages for what it claimed were 3,000 instances of destruction of company property.

The cost of the strike also drained the CWA. In seventy-two days the union spent almost $4.5 million. Other unions, particularly the Auto Workers, Steel Workers, and Amalgamated Clothing Workers, helped with solidarity contributions. With the financial drain a serious problem, and with the impasse in the talks, the Communications Workers began to search for external help to move the negotiations off dead center. Help was found in the person of Governor Bill Webb of Mississippi. Webb arranged for a conference of southern governors in Nashville that called for a return to work of the strikers and an agreement to negotiate on the disputed issues by the company. The initiative failed when the company ignored it, but it did put the union in a good light.

Above all, the company did not want third-party arbitration of the dispute. Its stand was not popular. The union had gained the high ground by publicly agreeing to impartial arbitration of outstanding issues. Several United States senators called for arbitration and several southern governors, stung by the company's rejection of their proposal, blasted the company for its refusal to submit the dispute for third-party resolution. When President Eisenhower moved cautiously toward an endorsement of arbitration, the pressure for the company to negotiate in good faith became much greater.

The strike ended on May 25, 1955, after seventy-two days. CWA emerged with wage increases of from one to four dollars a week. The union also made gains on impartial arbitration of disputes emerging under the contract, especially in the areas of suspension and discharge. There were also scheduling changes that amounted to a reduced workweek for many workers, including operators. The key union victory came on the no-strike issue. Southern Bell agreed that it would not discipline an employee solely for not crossing an authorized picket line during a lawful strike. In what became one of the largest arbitrations in American labor history, the company also agreed to submit the cases of workers discharged during the strike to arbitration. The majority were reinstated, though many came back with some loss of pay.

In retrospect, the Southern Bell strike was a remarkable achievement given the circumstances under which unions in the South had to operate. This was emphasized by the fact that it was maintained over seventy-two days over non-economic issues. Money was never the sticking point. The hard questions concerned the right to arbitration of grievances and especially the right to honor a union picket line without fear of discipline or dismissal. Joseph Beirne, president of CWA, later praised the southern workers for taking on one of the most powerful corporations in the world in an anti-union section of the country for the most basic of union principles: the right to strike or respect picket lines. [Ronald L. Filippelli]

FURTHER READING

Brooks, Thomas R. *Communications Workers of America: The Story of a Union.* New York: Mason/ Charter, 1977.

o   o   o

SOUTHWEST RAILROAD STRIKES OF 1885 AND 1886. The Southwest Strikes of 1885–1886 involved a series of strikes by railway workers belonging to the Knights of Labor (K of L). They were directed against companies controlled by Jay Gould, the notorious Wall Street financial manipulator. The series began between February 27 and March 9, 1885, as groups of workers on the Missouri Pacific, the Missouri, Kansas & Texas, and the Wabash went on strike because of wage reductions. When the companies rescinded those cuts on March 16, the first round of walkouts ended. Two months later, a second strike against the Wabash began in response to the firing of employees who belonged to the K of L. That strike ended when the company again yielded to the demands of the union on September 7. These important victories of the Knights were negated by the Southwest Strike of

1886. K of L workers, complaining that the Missouri Pacific was violating the terms of the 1885 settlement, again struck on March 6. As before, all Gould lines in the Southwest were involved. This strike ended when the companies, aided by state and federal judges, local police authorities, and state militias, crushed the disorders. At the request of a congressional committee of investigation, the national executive board of the Knights called off the lost strike on May 4, 1886.

The strikes of 1885 and 1886 were pivotal in the history of the Knights of Labor. The triumphs in 1885 brought tens of thousands of new members into the order, swelling its membership from 104,000 in July 1885, to a peak of 703,000 one year later. Although other factors were involved, the defeat in 1886 began the order's speedy slide to oblivion: 510,000 members by mid-1887, 260,000 a year later, 200,000 in mid-1889, and 100,000 by July 1890. The 1886 strike also witnessed a further perfecting of legal weapons for crushing railroad strikes that had begun with the **Railroad Strikes of 1877** and would culminate in the **Pullman Strike of 1894**. [*See also* **Union Pacific Strikes of 1884, Burlington Strike of 1888,** and **Great Northern Strike of 1894.**]

Neither the Grand Master Workman of the Knights, Terence Powderly, nor the order's national executive board actually controlled local units of the union during the Knights of Labor strikes in the 1880s. In some instances, workers struck, then organized into unions and affiliated with the Knights, as happened in the first of the 1884 Union Pacific Strikes. In other instances, local or district assemblies authorized strikes without the knowledge of, or contrary to the recommendations of, the national leadership. Only after strikes were underway did Powderly become involved. Often he bungled, sometimes he won credit for a victory, and on other occasions he tried to salvage what he could from defeat.

The initial difficulties in 1885 stemmed from wage cuts ordered over Gould's lines in response to an economic downturn. The Missouri Pacific reduced wages of shopmen and other employees by 10 percent in October 1884 and another 5 percent the following February 5. Unorganized, the workers submitted. Then, on February 26, the wages of Wabash workers were cut 10 percent. The next day, employees of that company at Moberly, Missouri, began a strike that quickly spread over the line. On March 7, Missouri Pacific employees at Sedalia joined in, laying down their tools, organizing a union, and forwarding demands to H. M. Hoxie, general manager of the company. They demanded restoration of their wages and steadier employment. Hoxie did not reply.

Meanwhile, Knights of Labor organizers helped the strikers form local assemblies all along the struck lines. The engineers, firemen, conductors, and brakemen, though members of the rival brotherhoods, gave the strike their full support. By March 9, traffic on all three of Gould's railroads ground to a halt. At the request of the companies, the governors of Kansas and Missouri sent in their militias to preserve peace. They did not, however, allow the troopers to act as strikebreakers. In fact, there was little turmoil. The strike leaders had complete control of their men, having set up a special force to protect railroad properties and to prevent violence. The prudent behavior, combined with the longstanding general distrust of Gould, and sympathy for the plight of the workers, won wide public support for the strikers. With the railroads paralyzed and business and political leaders demanding peace, the governors of Kansas and Missouri intervened on March 15. The Missouri Pacific and associated lines yielded, restoring wages to the level of September 1884, with time and a half for overtime, rehiring without prejudice those who had gone on strike, and promising not to alter wage rates without thirty days notice.

During April and May, however, the receiver of the Wabash began discharging shopmen who belonged to the Knights of Labor. The order's district assembly in Moberly, Missouri, interpreted this as a move to break K of L locals on the Wabash. Accordingly, it called a strike and appealed to the national executive board for help. Although eager to preserve its anti-strike policy, the board realized that the very existence of the order was at stake. When Wabash officials refused to end the layoffs and rehire those who had been locked out, the board threatened that all K of L members on the Wabash would be called out and Knights working on other railroads would boycott all traffic to and from that line. In fact, neither Powderly nor Gould wanted a strike. The Brotherhood of Locomotive Engineers had warned that it would not support the Knights in another strike, and Wall Street rivals were raiding Gould's properties on the stock exchange. The difficulty ended on September 7, when the receiver of the Wabash agreed that in filling vacancies the line would give preference to "old men" as opposed to "strangers or new men" and not enquire as to whether or not they were members of the Knights of Labor. Powderly, in turn, promised that no further strikes would be called against the Gould lines without first conferring with officials of the railroads.

As early as August 1885, the K of L District Assembly in Denison, Texas, charged the Missouri Pacific with not living up to the March agreement. The union's officers asked to discuss the matter with General Manager Hoxie. He in turn sent passes to enable the men to come to St. Louis. When they arrived, Hoxie was not available. After several days of waiting, the men returned home, leaving a statement of grievances behind. Later, in response to the strike in 1886, Hoxie denied ever having seen the report, which he called "ancient history," and complained that the Knights had called a strike without informing the company of grievances, much less giving it an opportunity to deal with them.

Meanwhile, local assemblies of the K of L on the various Gould lines joined together in a new district assembly made up entirely of railway employees. Martin Irons, who chaired the new executive board, put two questions to a mail vote of the local assemblies: should the district assembly demand recognition of the union as spokesmen of the employees (something that had not been done the previous March), and would the locals uphold the executive board if it demanded wages of no less than $1.50 per day for unskilled labor on all parts of the Gould Southwest System? By nearly a unanimous vote, both propositions carried. Although granted the power to strike, the board cautiously held it in reserve.

Following a meeting of the district assembly in February, the Texas and Pacific Railroad, a Gould property now in receivership, discharged C. A. Hall, Master Workman of the local in Marshall, Texas, for absenting himself from work. This happened in spite of Hall's having previously sought and received permission to attend the meeting. Irons again polled the locals. Would they support an action to have Hall reinstated? Again power to strike was granted. Irons asked the Texas and Pacific receivers to meet with his executive board. When the T&P sent three passes instead of the six needed to carry Hall and the five members of the executive board to Dallas, the board interpreted it as a denial of the union's right to speak for the men. They called a strike for March 6. To support the strike, the K of L called upon the Missouri Pacific to refuse to interchange traffic with the T&P. When the Missouri Pacific refused, the strike spread to that line, and in due course to the Wabash as well.

On March 9, the Missouri Pacific declared that all men who had walked out were no longer employees and must leave railroad property. Numerous state and federal judges in the various jurisdictions through which the railroad passed, at the company's request, issued injunctions forbidding strikers to use violence or enter railroad property.

Powderly and the national executive board learned of the new strike from the newspapers. Hurrying to the scene, the Grand Master Workman suggested to Hoxie that the matter be settled by extending the spirit and letter of the 1885 agreement to all parts of the Gould system and reinstating Hall. Hoxie denied that his company had violated the earlier settlement but charged that the union had because it had not first met with company officials as promised. He refused to deal with anyone other than employees of the line, and pointed out, correctly, that Hall had worked for the T&P, not the Missouri Central.

Ten days later, on March 28, Powderly met with Gould. The magnate pointed out that he was only one of several directors of the Missouri Pacific and that Hoxie, the general manager, alone could act. Given Gould's ability only a year before to act for all the lines, it is clear that his refusal was part of a careful strategy. In any event, Gould sent a telegram to Hoxie saying that when trains again were running, preference in hiring should be given to former employees, including strikers, so long as they were not guilty of violence or damaging railroad property. He also said he had no objection to arbitrating any past or future differences with employees.

Believing he had won, Powderly called off the strike and ordered the men back to work. To his chagrin, he learned that Hoxie and Gould were not willing to arbitrate. The angry and frustrated workers resumed their strike, and turning to violence, lost popular support. Their "killing" of trains and rioting led to intervention by the militia in several states. Pitched battles between strikers and the forces of law and order occurred in Fort Worth, Texas, and Parsons, Kansas, and lesser disorders hit other rail centers across the Southwest. Hoards of deputy United States marshals protected railroads in receivership, guarding scabs who were willing

to run trains and arresting strikers who defied injunctions. The climax came in East St. Louis on April 9 when a small party of deputies, threatened by strikers, opened fire, killing nine and wounding several others. The mob went wild, setting fire to both railroad property and private homes. The governor of Illinois placed the town under martial law. Elsewhere, the disorders continued sporadically until the end of April.

Meanwhile, following the troubles in East St. Louis, Powderly conferred in Washington with Congressman Andrew G. Curtin of Pennsylvania. Curtin, in turn, took him to meet President Grover Cleveland. Afterward, Cleveland told House leaders that he favored a congressional investigation of the strike, and a few days later, one was established with Curtin serving as chair. The committee travelled extensively over the lines involved in the strike. Its report, though admitting that the workers had grievances, blamed them on minor railroad officials, not Gould or Hoxie. The more proximate cause of the strike was the "cockiness" of the local K of L unions and the "dangerous if not pernicious" Martin Irons who led them. The report suggested no solution for avoiding future strikes. After noting that concentrations of wealth and power and various other oppressions were producing labor unrest, it concluded that the Interstate Commerce Commission, recently established by Congress, once appointed would probably make recommendations that would solve the whole matter.

Among its more important consequences, the strike of 1886 altered the status of unions on the railroads. The Knights of Labor rapidly lost power, leaving the skilled engineers, firemen, conductors, and brakemen as the only remaining groups. Led by brotherhoods notorious for their lack of militancy, railroad workers faced future strikes in which their opponents would be armed with even broader and more far reaching injunctions. [Gerald G. Eggert]

FURTHER READING

Allen, Ruth Alice. *The Great Southwest Strike*. Austin, TX: University of Texas Press, 1942.

Buchanan, Joseph Ray. *The Story of a Labor Agitator*. New York: The Outlook Company, 1903.

Eggert, Gerald G. *Railroad Labor Disputes, The Beginnings of Federal Strike Policy*. Ann Arbor, MI: University of Michigan Press, 1967.

Klein, Maury. *Life and Legend of Jay Gould*. Baltimore, MD: Johns Hopkins University Press, 1986.

Powderly, Terrence. *The Path I Trod*. New York: Columbia University Press, 1940.

o   o   o

STANDARD OIL STRIKES OF 1915 AND 1916. Bayonne, New Jersey, across New York harbor from Manhattan, was a company town as much as any Pennsylvania steel town or West Virginia coal patch. Tax revenues from the Standard Oil Company provided almost one-half of the city's budget. Local elected officials and law-enforcement officers worked as much for the corporation as for the citizens. This coalition of company and community power had kept Standard Oil union-free in Bayonne. Strikes in 1903 and 1913 were crushed with the use of strikebreakers protected by local police. In this environment, the possibility of unionization of Bayonne's largely immigrant workers was remote indeed.

The lack of success in unionization at Standard Oil did not reflect a shortage of grievances on the part of the workers. These grievances, based largely on poor pay and tyrannical foremen, burst forth again in the summer of 1915 when a group of stillcleaners, men who worked in temperatures up to 200° F, demanded a 15 percent wage hike, the fifty-hour workweek, and better treatment from the foremen. On July 15, the men, mostly Polish immigrants, walked off the job. By July 20, they had been joined by workers from almost all of the departments, bringing to almost 5,000 the number on strike. One day later, the strike spread to another Standard property, the Tidewater Oil Company, adding another several thousand to the strikers' ranks.

The company's response to the challenge was typical of the industrial warfare that marked the era. The company's attorney, Pierre Garvey, who was also mayor of Bayonne, advised Standard Oil to hire replacement workers through private agencies specializing in the recruitment of strikebreakers. The mayor also made the Bayonne police force available to break the strike. The combination led to violence at the Tidewater Oil plant on July 21, when armed strikebreakers, protected by police, fired into an angry crowd of strikers and sympathizers. When the smoke cleared, two strikers were dead and two fatally wounded.

The company blamed the killings on "professional agitators" who were stirring the workers up. Indeed, a number of unionists did come to Bayonne to heed the call of the unorganized strikers. Most significant were Frank Tannenbaum, a member of the radical Industrial Workers of the World (IWW), and Jeremiah Baly, a young Socialist. Both men had experience in organizing among immigrant workers, especially helpful in Bayonne where the strikers were made up of Polish, Hungarian, Italian, and American workers.

In addition to labeling the strike as the creation of radical outsiders, the company also publicized the fact that the shutdown would interrupt oil shipments to the allies, thus aiding the Germans. Strike leaders were alternately blasted for being "IWW revolutionists" and German agents.

The company combined adroit use of the press with the iron fist of repression. When the governor of New Jersey refused to send troops to escort strikebreakers into the plants, Standard Oil turned to the mayor of Bayonne and the county sheriff for help. Indeed, it was Sheriff Eugene Kincaid who effectively broke the strike. Kinkaid's men arrested and beat strike leaders Tannenbaum and Baly for being outside agitators and German agents. The company combined the velvet glove with the iron fist. Workers who heeded the sheriff's call to return to work would have their grievances considered by the company. The foreign workers refused, but the American workers, susceptible to being labeled disloyal to the United States and tools of foreign agitators, agreed to let the sheriff work out a settlement for them with Standard Oil. The return of 1,500 American workers broke the strike. Soon the foreign workers began to drift back. On July 28, the remaining strikers voted to return to work.

Standard Oil moved quickly to defuse any repeat of the events of the summer of 1915. Wage increases were immediately given, and the workweek was reduced from fifty-four to forty-eight hours. Special attention was paid to the needs of the more skilled, English-speaking workers. Union activists, on the other hand, were fired.

The tactics, however, did not work. On October 4, 1916, 600 paraffin workers at Standard Oil's Bayonne plant threatened to strike for higher wages. As in 1915, the strike soon spread to other workers. Once again the foreign workers were the backbone of the movement. And once again, the company used the same tactics to break the strike. English-speaking workers announced that they would not participate in the strike because the company had honored its promise to deal with their grievances after the last strike.

Sure of the support of its most skilled workers, Standard Oil locked out all of its workers. They then called on Mayor Garvey, an attorney for Standard Oil, to do his duty. On October 10, police began breaking up union meetings and arresting strikers. Police also marched into working-class neighborhoods, terrorizing inhabitants with their show of force. In the process eight strikers and one nonstriker were killed, and many others wounded.

Police violence and a back-to-work movement by the English-speaking workers, finally broke the strike. The Standard Oil company had employed all of the classic anti-union tactics of the period—strikebreakers, private guards, and police repression. But the crucial factor in breaking both strikes turned out to be the ability of the company, largely through its supporters in local government, to separate native-born, English-speaking workers from their immigrant brothers and sisters by appealing to their patriotism and status fears. [Ronald L. Filippelli]

FURTHER READING

Foner, Philip. *History of the Labor Movement in the United States*, Vol. 6. New York: International Publishers, 1982.

o   o   o

STEEL STRIKE OF 1901. The 1901 Steel Strike was an unequal match between the union of skilled employees in the steel industry—the Amalgamated Association of Iron, Steel, and Tin Workers (AA)—and the newly formed United States Steel Corporation (USS). The birth of USS climaxed a period of business consolidation in which companies in several branches of the steel industry had combined to dominate their particular markets. USS, the first billion-dollar corporation in the United States, in turn brought these merged steel companies under its financial control. J. P. Morgan, the New York banker, had raised the money to form USS and had assumed a stake in the holding company. The result of these business and financial maneuvers was to assemble a large number of formerly independent companies, each with its own history of labor relations, under one authority.

The Amalgamated Association had earlier lost most of its membership in the mills that produced raw (basic) steel and rod and wire products but retained a large membership in many of the mills that turned raw steel into other finished forms, particularly sheet steel, tin plate, and steel hoops.

These mills were run by companies that were now subsidiaries of USS. Some were under union contract, but others were not. Union officials were well aware of the anti-union policy that USS had inherited from its predecessors in the steel industry, and they resolved to bring more mills under contract before USS became impregnable to unions. The union's campaign was partly defensive as well, since the subsidiaries had begun to close their union mills and direct work toward non-union mills that could make the same products. Seeking to prevent this "whip-sawing" policy, the AA in 1901 adopted the goal of winning union contracts in all the mills of these subsidiaries.

The executive committee of USS, agreed to sign new contracts with the union but only for mills that were already unionized. But this policy was not followed by subsidiaries during negotiations in June 1901. There were marked differences between American Sheet Steel Company (ASSC) and American Tin Plate Company (ATPC), in their willingness to accommodate the union's demands. After denying certain union mills to the AA, the American Tin Plate Company offered to recognize the union in all of its mills if American Sheet Steel would do the same. But American Sheet Steel stuck fast to its refusal to offer contracts in any mill not previously organized by the union and even threatened to remove some that were under contract from the union column. With agreement nowhere in sight, T. J. Shaffer, president of the AA, called a strike of his members in the sheet and steel hoop mills on July 1, 1901.

During the strike, the AA negotiated with a divided employer group, which included both the subsidiary companies and the USS executives. The AA exploited the differences among the subsidiaries and between them and USS. The latter suffered from public mistrust of its vast assets and control of approximately 40 percent of the nation's steelmaking capacity and was constrained from acting too aggressively toward

the AA. The union hoped to bring pressure on the recalcitrant subsidiaries through their more vulnerable parent corporation. Thus it threatened to extend the strike to the tin plate mills unless the union won a settlement for the sheet and hoop mills.

At first, the union's strategy appeared to work. The executive committee of USS forced the firmly anti-union sheet mill managers to offer contracts in all but five plants. Confident of its ability to gain even better terms, and faithful to its original objective of recognition in all the subsidiaries' mills, the union rejected this compromise offer at a negotiating session two weeks after the walkout began. It also turned down a company offer to sign contracts wherever sheet steel workers had gone on strike. Steel hoop workers had shown enthusiasm in joining the strike, and the union saw the possibility of bringing many of them into the union if it continued the walkout. Carrying through on its threat, the AA sent out a strike call to the tin plate workers on July 15.

Ensuing discussions between the AA's top officers and J. P. Morgan, however, did not improve the union's options. T. J. Shaffer and John Williams, secretary of the AA, found Morgan congenial but unyielding in a meeting held in New York on July 27. They returned to Pittsburgh with an offer for contracts at all mills already unionized at the end of June 1901. This was less than AA's original proposal, and the AA's executive board rejected it. The entire board later traveled to New York to try to get Morgan's agreement covering both previously organized mills as well as the ones that were now being struck. Morgan turned this down and claimed that Shaffer and Williams had shown bad faith by not convincing their fellow executive board members to agree to his earlier offer.

Faced with a choice between accepting less than its goal of companywide unionization and raising its stake in the strike, the AA's executive committee opted for the latter course and authorized a strike in the basic steel mills. It realized that the sheet and tin plate operations had not been completely stopped and that USS was demonstrating its ability to withstand the strike. The executive board hoped that basic steel workers would respond to the union's call, despite the relatively low membership there. The union officers issued the strike call on August 10.

The AA's leaders had badly miscalculated their strength in basic steel. Membership among basic steel employees was too scattered to be decisive in the showdown, and the larger membership in the finishing mills was witnessing the resumption of work at their plants with strikebreakers. Contrary to the union's bedrock belief in its members' control of essential steelmaking skills, the subsidiary companies trained enough new recruits to run mill machinery and lift the union's siege.

The union by this point had committed itself too deeply to escape the strike without a sound beating, unless help came from other sources. When asked, however, the union's allies in the labor movement refused to become directly involved in the strike. USS finally drew the line at offering contracts only at mills where AA members were still out on strike in mid-August. Still resisting, President Shaffer of the AA hoped that miners and railroad workers would conduct sympathy strikes on behalf of his union, but this was mostly wishful thinking.

The agreement which ended the strike on September 14 not only reduced the number of mills under union contract but also bound the AA not to organize non-union mills.

The 1901 steel strike sharply reduced the presence of craft unionism in the steel industry's finishing mills. Despite its bitter experience in the 1890s in the basic steel mills, the AA persisted in its belief that skilled workers could indefinitely close plants simply by leaving their jobs. This illusion, in addition to errors in its negotiating tactics, led to a much worse outcome to the strike than might have occurred if the AA had been willing to capitalize on the short-run impact of the walkout. [Peter Gottlieb]

FURTHER READING

Brody, David. *Steelworkers in America. The Nonunion Era.* Cambridge, MA: Harvard University Press, 1960.

Couvares, Frank. *The Remaking of Pittsburgh. Class and Culture in an Industrial City, 1877–1919* Albany, NY: State University of New York Press, 1984.

Robinson, Jesse. *The Amalgamated Association of Iron, Steel, and Tin Workers* Baltimore, MD: Johns Hopkins University Press, 1920.

o o o

STEEL STRIKE OF 1919. World War I provided opportunities for organizing iron and steel workers that had not existed for many years. The federal government had brought about de facto recognition of unions in several key industries as a means of insuring cooperation between labor and management during the war. Though this by no means met all the demands of organized labor, it greatly encouraged workers in many open shop industries to seek the benefits of organization and collective bargaining. The rhetoric employed by federal government agencies to stimulate armed forces enlistments, donations to war bond drives, and greater productive efforts in American workshops also raised workers' expectations for a better way of life in the postwar era. As one Polish steelworker stated during the steel strike: "For why this war? For why we buy Liberty Bonds? For mills? No, for freedom and America—for everybody."

The American Federation of Labor (AFL) moved to tap these rising hopes before the war ended. Trade unionists in Chicago had succeeded in organizing employees in the meatpacking plants there by uniting all the labor organizations that claimed jurisdiction in the industry behind the unionization drive. John Fitzpatrick, president of the Chicago Federation of Labor, and William Z. Foster, an officer of the railway carmen's union, were the key figures in this campaign and the proponents of a similar drive in the iron and steel industry. During the summer of 1918, they convinced AFL leaders and officers of unions in the steel industry to discuss an organizing effort on the Chicago model. Out of these discussions came the National Committee for Organizing the Iron and Steel Workers (hereafter, the National Committee).

Both strengths and frailties lay in the composition of the National Committee. Being a council of representatives of twenty-four unions with claims on iron and steel industry employees, its very existence recognized the fact that modern industry, dominated by a small number of enormous companies, would quickly defeat the efforts of even the strongest single labor organization. Led by Fitzpatrick (chairman) and Foster (secretary-treasurer), the National Committee instituted financial procedures that equitably spread the expense of organizing among the member organizations. Though the Amalgamated Association of Iron, Steel, and Tin Workers (AA) covered the largest number of employees in the industry, all participating unions had a voice in making policy. Local chapters, called Iron and Steel Workers Councils, were set up in steelmaking centers, but the national unions reserved to themselves authority for the most important steps in the organizing campaign.

The problems of coordinating a national unionization campaign with two dozen independent unions undercut the advantages with which the war and the meatpacking industry success had endowed the National Committee. Participation in the drive was voluntary, and the National Committee had no real authority over its member unions. Jealous of their jurisdictions and prerogatives as independent organizations, the unions too often adhered to their own self-interests. For example, contributions of funds from the unions to the National Committee were not sufficient to cover expenses and provide the number of organizers required for success. Differences among the unions concerning the number of new members they could potentially gain from the organizing drive inevitably threw most of the burdens of sustaining the campaign on a few of them, and some of these succumbed to the shortsightedness that made their own small gains look more important than victory over the steel companies.

In spite of these structural problems within the National Committee, the organizing drive progressed rapidly. Beginning in the Chicago area in September 1918, organizers found rank-and-file steelworkers eager to enlist. "The campaign for organization in this district is in full blast," an organizer wrote excitedly from Gary, Indiana. The response was equally enthusiastic in other Midwest steel communities and in the Far West. The crucial Pittsburgh area was different. There the organizers had to wage a campaign for free speech and civil liberties during the late winter and early spring of 1919. Only then could they effectively work among steelworkers. Once local officials and company supervisors relaxed their grip on the mill communities in and around the city, the immigrant employees joined the drive. Pittsburgh-area native American workers—black as well as white—remained largely aloof from the campaign, refusing to participate in any movement with foreign-born workers.

Led by the largest producer, the United States Steel Corporation, the steel companies posed the basic issue as the closed shop versus American property rights. While the National Committee's chief objective clearly was union recognition, it officially adopted other demands ranging from higher wages and shorter hours to seniority and reinstatement of fired workers with back pay. Statements from steelworkers during the organizing drive stressed the shortening of the workday as the most important goal, especially the abolition of the twelve-hour day in continuous steelmaking processes.

Claiming to be ready to meet their own employees at any time to discuss grievances, the companies refused to meet with the National Committee to discuss its demands. The chairman of U.S. Steel, Judge Elbert Gary, refused to talk to the National Committee even after a strike vote taken between July 20 and August 20, 1919, demonstrated widespread support for action. United States President Woodrow Wilson intervened with Gary to seek a negotiating session but also failed.

The National Committee was caught between rising pressure from union members for a strike and resistance to any bargaining from the steel companies. AFL president Samuel Gompers, who had been leading delegations of the National Committee in visits to the White House, warned that striking before the steelworkers were thoroughly unionized would risk wrecking the union. Reports from organizers around the country, on the other hand, emphatically stated that refusal to call a strike would cause thousands of newly enlisted steelworkers to drop away from the organization and squander chances for success. With only about 20 percent of the industry work force organized in September 1919, the National Committee nonetheless authorized a strike for Monday, September 22, 1919. The majority of the participating unions voted on September 18 to stick to the strike deadline despite President Wilson's request to delay action until after the sessions of the Industrial Conference, which he had called to meet in Washington on October 6.

Approximately 250,000 steelworkers went on strike on September 22. This number was far more than the steel companies had thought were enrolled in the union; in some places, support for the strike also exceeded the National Committee's expectations. The walkout was most effective in closing mills in the West and Midwest. In the East and South, the strike's impact on production was mixed, from steep declines in output in Johnstown, Pennsylvania, and Wheeling, West Virginia, to virtually no drop in Duquesne, Pennsylvania. The vital Pittsburgh steel district was a microcosm of the uneven effect of the strike, but overall, production in this region was not seriously curtailed. Workers at Bethlehem Steel plants, hoping for some concessions from the company, did not join the strike until September 29, closing down the giant Lackawanna, New York, mill completely, but not impeding work significantly in Bethlehem, Pennsylvania.

As the strike approached, the steel companies threw all their resources into defeating the unions' campaign. Having tolerated civil liberties in Pennsylvania steel towns during most of the spring and summer, they called on county sheriff's deputies and the Pennsylvania constabulary to break up even the smallest union meetings, disperse union pickets, and arrest organizers on any pretext. Union members in the Sharon-Farrell steel district of Pennsylvania found all meeting places closed to them. They marched in a body to rallies held across the Ohio border where, according to one of the strikers," . . . we are back in America." The Indiana state militia mobilized to guard the streets of Gary, but a scuffle between strikers and strikebreakers seemed ominous enough to the city's mayor to justify requesting a U.S. Army unit. The troops placed Gary under martial law on October 6 to the great disadvantage of the strikers; the Indiana militia went to the steelmaking center of Indiana Harbor to hold the strikers there at bay.

The steel companies also formed an alliance with anti-union and zenophobic community groups to attack the strikers. In some Pittsburgh area mill towns, police and sheriffs deputized strikebreakers and assigned them to patrol mill gates and street corners where they inevitably clashed with union supporters. A group of businessmen and professionals led by a YMCA official met William Z. Foster at the Johnstown train station and forced him to leave town without contacting union members in the city. A union parade in Newcastle, Pennsylvania, was attacked by a crowd including members of the American Legion who claimed that immigrant strikers threatened both the companies and national institutions.

Public fear of subversion by foreign and radical groups accompanied the steel strike. Mounting to hysterical heights, this fear was fed by newspaper stories of secret meetings of revolutionary immigrant steelworkers, of William Z. Foster's beliefs in communism and syndicalism, and of disturbances to the public order in the strike zones. Investigations by state and national bodies—including U.S. Senate hearings on the strike—indicated that law enforcement agencies were responsible for most of the disturbances that the press headlined. But the intense public nervousness about the strikers' goals and actions effectively limited the unions' ability to maneuver against the steel companies. When striking became identified with disloyalty to the United States, native American steelworkers in particular felt pressure to cross picket lines.

The steel strike deepened divisions among the race and nationality groups in the industry. In mid-October, strikebreakers recruited by the companies began arriving in mill communities around the country. The use of blacks as strikebreakers was seen by some white unions as proof that blacks were more inclined to side with the employers than with their fellow steelworkers. The foreign-born workers' actions during the strike testified to their support for the union. Chased off the streets by police and company guards and vilified as foreign subversives in the national press, the immigrants in many mill towns still refused to go back to work. Though they had difficulty maintaining contact with the National Committee organizers and the local iron and steel workers councils, they sustained the strike by passing news through their fraternal organizations and informal community networks. They were increasingly hampered in demonstrating support for unionization as the strike continued but maintained a strong belief in the justice of the union cause. One reporter commented on the immigrant steelworkers' approach to the strike: " . . . this fight of the rank and file was not fed by oratory; it was not made by excitement. There was behind it a terrible patience."

President Wilson's Industrial Conference, held in Washington, DC, from October 6 to October 22, provided no respite for the National Committee. Representatives of unions, led by Samuel Gompers, failed to get the meeting to refer the steel strike to adjudication by a panel of six, to be chosen by the conference. The conference eventually foundered over disagreement between labor and employer representatives on a general statement of labor's rights. The failure of this meeting to draw up a blueprint for peaceful labor relations meant that the steel strike would be settled through the contest of strength between employers and unions.

The constituent unions in the National Committee did not help their own cause when steel companies began gaining the upper hand in mid-October. Although there had been tensions among the unions all along, they intensified during the strike crisis. Pessimism was added to mistrust when the walkout failed to produce quick results. The unions failed to fulfill even half their quotas for a $100,000 strike fund. The AA stood to gain the most from the organizing drive and the strike but flagrantly exploited the unionization drive to gain members without contributing its share of the necessary funds. Finally, the AA ordered its members who had been working under union contracts before the strike to return to their jobs. This caused an uproar on the National Committee, with charges of treason hurled against AA officials who responded with statements about the sanctity of their contracts.

Continuous pressure from steel companies, police, and local and national newspapers began to undermine the strike. Skilled, white, native Americans generally crossed picket lines first. This group had not strongly supported the strike in the Pittsburgh area to begin with, and the few who had struck were back at work by the end of October. Where the strike crumbled badly, stalwart unionists had no choice but to try to regain their jobs, too. Following the Pittsburgh workers' capitulation, steel men in Chicago began returning to the mills, and by November 21 between 75 and 85 percent were on the job. Youngstown, Johnstown, and Wheeling strikers gave up next, while those in Pueblo, Colorado, Lackawanna, New York, and Joliet, Illinois, stayed out the longest.

Reviewing the status of the strike on December 13, the National Committee acknowledged the seriousness of its position but voted with only two dissenting voices to continue the strike. By this time, it was clear that the companies refused to allow any third party to mediate a settlement and looked for a total victory over the unions. Such an outcome after eighteen months of campaigning was too bitter for the National Committee to accept. But the strike continued to disintegrate as winter approached. The National Committee faced the inevitable on January 8, 1920, and released all strikers who were still out to return to their former jobs.

The 1919 Steel Strike was a serious defeat for organized labor, both in the steel industry and in the modern, technologically advanced manufacturing sector of the economy in general. The unions' loss in this strike virtually halted the rapid growth in membership and economic power that had accompanied America's involvement in World War I. It also delayed the inception of collective bargaining in the steel industry for roughly twenty years. [Peter Gottlieb]

FURTHER READING

Brody, David. *Labor in Crisis. The Steel Strike of 1919.* Philadelphia, PA: Lippincott, 1965.

Foster, William Z. *The Great Steel Strike and Its Lessons.* New York: Huebsch, 1920.

Interchurch World Movement of North America. *Report on the Steel Strike of 1919.* New York: Inter-Church World Movement, 1923.

Murray, Robert K. "Communism and the Great Steel Strike of 1919." *Mississippi Valley Historical Review,* Vol. 38 (1951), pp. 445–466.

Warne, Colston E., ed. *The Steel Strike of 1919.* Boston, MA: Heath, 1963.

o   o   o

STEEL STRIKE OF 1937. The Little Steel Strike was among the most important of the Great Depression era. It forced a close examination of the new national labor relations system that had been codified in the mid-1930s. It also tested the power and morale of both the growing industrial unions and the staunchly open-shop firms in the vital steel industry.

This strike pitted one of the new industrial unions of the Committee for Industrial Organization (CIO)—the Steel Workers Organizing Committee—against several anti-union steel companies, collectively named "Little Steel" to distinguish them from the dominant company of the industry, the United States Steel Corporation. Formed in June 1936, the Steel Workers Organizing Committee (SWOC) surprised the country when it won recognition from U.S. Steel in March 1937. The giant steelmaker had bitterly fought unions since its creation in 1901 but suddenly switched policy and signed an agreement with the new steel union. This stunning victory was the greatest but by no means the only success for the fledgling union. It had won contracts with many smaller companies before U.S. Steel granted recognition; in May 1937, the Jones and Laughlin Steel Corporation—the fourth largest steel producer in the country—also signed a contract with SWOC, following a vote among company employees that gave the union a clear majority. In the days following SWOC's victory at Jones and Laughlin, several smaller steel companies also signed contracts with the union. As the summer of 1937 approached, SWOC seemed well on its way to unionizing all the important steel companies.

Philip Murray, the chairman of SWOC, and John L. Lewis, president of the CIO, developed a strategy for winning contracts with the Little Steel companies that depended on both the momentum gained from recent victories and the prospect of support from the federal government. Franklin D. Roosevelt had just begun his second term in office, following a landslide victory over the Republican Party in which organized labor had voted overwhelmingly for him and other New Deal Democrats. Interpreting the election results as an endorsement of the CIO's efforts to organize industrial workers, Murray and Lewis figured that assistance from federal agencies like the National Labor Relations Board and the Department of Labor, or from the White House itself, could be summoned if necessary.

The Little Steel companies—Republic Steel, Youngstown Sheet and Tube, Inland Steel, and Bethlehem Steel—had strong anti-union policies. Personified by executives such as Tom Girdler of Republic Steel and Eugene Grace of Bethlehem Steel, these companies adamantly refused to sign agreements with representatives of bona fide unions, referring to them consistently as "outside" agencies whose interests differed from those of the company and its employees. Girdler, whose reputation as a hard-boiled anti-union boss had been forged earlier when he had created a harsh open-shop environment at Jones and Laughlin's giant Aliquippa Works, reviled organized labor in general and the CIO unions in particular. "Before spending the rest of my life dealing with John Lewis," he asserted in 1934, "I am going to raise apples and potatoes."

Most of the Little Steel companies had established employee representation plans between 1933 and 1935 to meet the letter of federal laws that gave employees the right to organize unions and negotiate with employers. Bethlehem Steel's plan traced its origins further back to World War I. These company unions were closely controlled by the employers, even after the 1935 National Labor Relations Act made such control illegal. Though Little Steel firms converted their company unions into "independent" employees' associations to comply with the new law, these in-house organizations remained a strong buffer against real union organizing campaigns. They provided an arena for steel managers to propagate the values of teamwork between employees and supervisors, loyalty to the company, and distrust of outsiders who advocated real collective bargaining.

None of the Little Steel companies agreed to sign contracts with SWOC during an initial round of negotiations held in April 1937. Republic Steel told SWOC representatives that it was not obliged to sign an agreement under the terms of the federal labor relations law and would not do so even if a vast majority of its employees voted to have their interests represented by the CIO union. Inland Steel told SWOC negotiators that it was paying its employees as much as the companies that had signed contracts with SWOC and therefore saw no need to make a union agreement. Bethlehem Steel simply declined to meet with SWOC representatives.

In May 1937, SWOC turned its sights on Republic Steel, the third largest steel producer, distributing flyers to Republic workers, holding rallies, and signing up new members. Republic quickly countered by planting spies in SWOC local unions and intimidating organizers. The company also shut down its Canton, Ohio, mill on May 5 after SWOC had signed up 90 percent of the workers there. When SWOC expanded its campaign to the other Little Steel companies, they also resisted the organizing drive, though not as aggressively as had Republic Steel.

As the impasse between the union and the companies became clear, both sides began preparing for a strike. SWOC local bodies adopted resolutions to strike unless companies signed contracts. They formed committees to organize picketing squads. Republic Steel and Youngstown Sheet and Tube increased their existing stores of guns, ammunition, tear gas, and billy clubs, prepared their private forces of plant guards, and stockpiled the cots, kitchen equipment, and food that would be needed for strikebreakers to live inside the mills. Republic Steel's closure of its Massilon, Ohio, mill on May 20, as a way to avoid signing a union contract, brought the steelworkers' strike sentiment to a fever pitch. Following a vote in favor of striking by SWOC local union leaders at Republic, Youngstown Sheet and Tube, and Inland (Bethlehem Steel was not targeted by SWOC), the strike began on May 26.

In the steelmaking centers from Ohio to Illinois, where SWOC members walked out and set up their picket lines, the first days of the strike were deceptively peaceful. Most of the steel companies' employees supported SWOC at this point, the picket lines were large and orderly, and most of the Little Steel mills ceased operations. The most important theater of the strike was the Youngstown-Warren-Niles area of eastern Ohio, where Republic Steel and Youngstown Sheet and Tube had their chief operations. Since Republic Steel had been selected by SWOC as its foremost objective, all parties to the strike viewed the contest around this company's mills as decisive to the outcome of the entire strike.

The most dramatic episode of the Little Steel Strike took place in South Chicago, however, where a large Republic Steel mill remained in operation with about 1,000 nonstrikers after May 26. Chicago police and company guards skirmished with SWOC pickets regularly from the first day of the strike. The police stopped marches of union supporters during the first week of the strike and accused members of the Communist Party of agitating among the strikers and their sympathizers. Chicago SWOC leaders called a rally on Memorial Day (May 30) to protest the police actions against the Republic picketers. After listening to several speakers, the crowd of strikers and sympathizers formed a column to march to the plant gates. A combined force of more than 300 city police and company guards awaited them there.

When the marchers reached the line of police at the mill, there was a brief stand-off, followed by a sudden volley of gunfire from the police into the marchers. Though each side blamed the other for provoking the melee that followed, many eyewitnesses as well as movie film taken at the scene testified to the police's brutal actions once the marchers tried to escape. Many strikers and SWOC supporters were attacked and beaten by police as they were running away, some even after they had fallen down. Five of the marchers were killed in the first volley, and five more eventually died of gunshot wounds. Of the ten who died, seven were shot in the back, three in the side. None suffered wounds in the front of the body, though police witnesses consistently claimed that they had fired to protect themselves from the marchers' assault. Thirty other marchers were injured by gunshot, including two women and an eleven-year-old child, and twenty-eight received hospital treatment for beatings. Though the police claimed that the marchers brought guns to the rally, none of the sixteen police injured in the fight suffered wounds from gunshot.

Response to this "Memorial Day Massacre" was swift and emotional. Organized labor turned out in huge numbers to honor the dead at a mass funeral service in Chicago on June 3 and at protest meetings held at the Chicago Opera House and in the steelmaking center at Indiana Harbor. But the carnage at the Republic mill gates in Chicago did not give SWOC the moral advantage over the Little Steel companies that might have led to a strike victory. The steel companies stuck to their refusal to negotiate and to their open-shop principles, despite the pro-union sympathy which swelled around the country in the aftermath of the events on Memorial Day.

SWOC resorted to pressuring the Little Steel companies with effective picket lines, federal labor laws, and, when necessary, sympathy strikes by other unions. In most locations, the strikers' picket lines were well-managed and airtight. In Cleveland, for example, SWOC pickets peacefully closed Republic Steel's four mills and derailed the company's initial effort to orchestrate a return to work. But in places like Warren, Ohio, where mills continued partial operations with a force of nonstrikers, skirmishing between pickets, police, company guards, and strikebreakers went on continuously. When Republic officials failed during the first week of the strike to move supplies for its Warren mill past union pickets, it began an airlift to the besieged strikebreakers. Union supporters sniped at the planes. Republic later tried shipping supplies into the mill through the U.S. mail, but post office officials intervened to stop this ploy after SWOC leaders protested. The struggle between the union and the company over the use of the U.S. mail eventually led to U.S. Senate hearings and to additional national attention to the strike.

The Little Steel companies' resistance to SWOC did not weaken as the strike went on, nor did it provoke the federal government to step in and demand a settlement, as SWOC and CIO leaders had hoped. President Roosevelt demurred when SWOC implored him by telegram in early June to force the companies to come to terms. In its belief that Little Steel was violating the National Labor Relations Act by refusing to sign a contract, SWOC brought charges of unfair labor practices against the Inland

Steel Company (where the union felt it had the largest proportion of members of any of the Little Steel companies).

After the first week in June, Youngstown Sheet and Tube and Republic Steel began mounting a well-organized campaign against SWOC. They initiated petition drives through their employees' associations to demand a return to work, increased their efforts to move supplies across union picket lines, and orchestrated activities of local committees that purported to act in the public interest. These committees were often composed of anti-union businessmen and professionals with close ties to the steel companies. In Youngstown, the Citizens Committee publicly supported the local back-to-work drive. In Warren, the John Q. Public League recruited an extra-legal police force to exert pressure on SWOC. The Citizens Law and Order League in Canton demanded that local officials break up the picket lines and even led its own assault on union pickets on June 18.

The growing drumbeat of anti-strike sentiment in the Ohio mill towns began to sway the opinions of some local officials and strikers, though it also fostered unity among labor unions. The Youngstown City Council gave the mayor emergency powers, and the county sheriff recruited a large force of deputies from anti-union mill employees. The ultimate result of these rising tensions around the struck mills was foreshadowed in Monroe, Michigan, where the mayor obtained arms for a special police force from the Republic Steel mill in the town, spurned efforts by the governor of Michigan to negotiate, and then permitted the police on June 10 to attack SWOC pickets and lead nonstriking Republic employees through the mill gates.

The sudden spread of the strike to Bethlehem Steel's mills in Johnstown, Pennsylvania, revealed the way union, company, and public officials divided across the sharply drawn battle lines. SWOC members in Johnstown walked out of the mills on June

11 to support striking employees on a company-owned railroad and to pressure Bethlehem Steel to negotiate a contract with SWOC. A group of non-union employees kept the mills in operation, however, and a vociferous anti-strike campaign soon began, headed by Johnstown mayor Daniel Shields, who cooperated with the Johnstown Citizens Committee and purchased tear gas with funds from Bethlehem Steel to use against strikers.

Following an outbreak of violence between SWOC members and nonstrikers on the picket lines, Governor Earle of Pennsylvania ordered state police into Johnstown. Earle had been elected with strong support from Pennsylvania CIO forces, and he moved quickly to deploy the state's resources when Bethlehem executive Eugene Grace refused to close the mills. At this point, CIO president John L. Lewis also assumed a more direct role in the national strike as well as in the events in Johnstown. At a news conference on June 13, Lewis ordered coal miners at all mines operated by Little Steel companies to strike. He took the opportunity to voice his opinion of his arch-rival, Tom Girdler, calling him "a heavily armed monomaniac, with murderous tendencies, who has gone berserk." Meanwhile, miners in the Johnstown region prepared to march on the city to support the striking SWOC members. Anticipating a pitched battle between union and anti-union groups in Johnstown, Governor Earle on June 20 ordered state police to close Bethlehem Steel's giant mill complex and persuaded John L. Lewis to call off the miners' march.

But despite the strong support for SWOC from labor and state officials, events turned in Bethlehem Steel's favor. Reaction against Governor Earle's peace-keeping moves from business leaders around the country was intense. A nationwide public relations campaign supported by anti-labor businessmen created a great deal of negative opinion toward Lewis' apparent attempt to use his political allies to help unionize Beth-

lehem Steel employees. Governor Earle was forced to rescind his orders on June 25. Though state police remained in Johnstown, they only kept peace on the picket lines, and SWOC members watched their strike dwindle away in the next few days.

Efforts by other parties to mediate between the steel companies and SWOC also foundered. On the same day that SWOC members began their strike in Johnstown, Governor Davey of Ohio called a meeting of the representatives of SWOC, Republic Steel, and Youngstown Sheet and Tube in Columbus. Davey's proposed seven-point settlement was rebuffed by the companies, even though it would have granted much less than the union wanted. A second settlement offer was made at a subsequent meeting convened by Governor Davey on June 15. Under its terms an agreement between SWOC and the companies would not take effect until the question of whether or not signed contracts were legally mandatory had been decided by the courts. The steel companies rejected this proposal as well, and Governor Davey appealed to the federal government for help to settle the strike.

Before a federal mediation effort began, the tensions between strikers and nonstrikers in Youngstown broke out on June 19. Union pickets and their supporters (including the wives of some SWOC members) fought with company guards and Youngstown police, who had initiated the clash by using tear gas against a group of peaceful picketers. The "Stop 5 Gate Riot" killed two strikers and wounded twenty-three others on both sides.

Led by Youngstown Sheet and Tube, the Little Steel companies increased their pressure on the mayor and city council of Youngstown by showing a large number of petitions for returning to work signed by employees. Sheet and Tube chief executive Frank Purnell said that his company would reopen its mills as soon as local officials guaranteed protection for all who wanted to go back to their jobs. SWOC officials denounced the petitions as unreliable indicators of workers' sentiments, but with no progress in negotiations and the growing activity of anti-union groups in the steel towns, SWOC had little time or means to demonstrate its support among the employees.

Following the collapse of Governor Davey's mediation efforts, the Roosevelt administration tried its hand at settling the strike but with no greater success. Roosevelt set up a Federal Steel Mediation Board of three distinguished labor experts in mid-June 1937, to investigate the issues behind the strike, produce findings, and recommend ways to end the walkout, but he gave it no subpoena or enforcement powers. Seeing the board as a step toward its long-sought goal of federal government intervention, SWOC offered to cooperate at once. But the steel companies just as quickly denied the board's authority and criticized its members for being too pro-labor. As the board began its discussions with representatives of the steel companies, Youngstown Sheet and Tube announced the re-opening of its Youngstown mills, despite requests from Governor Davey and U.S. secretary of labor Frances Perkins to maintain the status quo until the Steel Mediation Board concluded its deliberations. On June 22, striking steelworkers massed at the mill gates in Youngstown, while city police, sheriff's deputies, and company guards prepared to assist the entrance of Sheet and Tube employees who wanted to return to work.

Fearing bloody clashes in Youngstown and other Ohio steel centers, Governor Davey called out the Ohio National Guard on June 22. Initially, the guardsmen evenhandedly patrolled the strike centers in the state. John Owens, the SWOC leader in Ohio, ordered pickets to keep away from the mill gates after the National Guard arrived. But the guardsmen under Ohio law had to follow orders from local law enforcement officials, not from the governor. Consequently, the soldiers in Youngstown soon were harassing

SWOC members and sympathizers, raiding SWOC offices, and strictly limiting the number of pickets by the mill entrances. In Warren, the guardsmen arrived just after an Ohio court had issued an injunction against SWOC's mass picketing there. Aroused by the emerging anti-strike combination of company and state government forces, the local labor movement called a citywide strike for June 23 of CIO members and employees on federal Works Progress Administration projects. The citywide strike began with a march of 2,000 angry SWOC members, their families, and supporters, during which two cars of strikebreakers were overturned as they attempted to enter mill gates.

The Steel Mediation Board's effort to settle the steel strike involved two different approaches. One was to win agreement from both SWOC and the steel companies to a proposal that made a negotiated settlement contingent on the union winning a majority of votes of employees in elections supervised by the National Labor Relations Board. SWOC agreed to study this idea, but the steel companies adhered to their position of not signing any contract with SWOC. The board's second approach was to bring President Franklin Roosevelt directly into the negotiations. Roosevelt declined, however, and the administrative order which had established the board lapsed on June 26. Five days later, the board members submitted their final report to President Roosevelt and ended their role in the strike.

The citizens committees and non-union steel workers in Ohio—both abetted by Youngstown Sheet and Tube and Republic Steel managers—increased their pressure on Governor Davey and on local officials to guarantee the safety of employees who wanted to begin working again. With no hope of bringing about a negotiated end to the strike, Governor Davey agreed to the reopening of these companies' mills and to the National Guard staying on duty to protect employees returning to work. Steel mills in Youngstown and Warren reopened on

June 25. A trickle of returning workers in Youngstown during the first days after the reopening soon swelled to a rush of employees back to work. In Warren, steelworkers returned more slowly, but mills there were completely manned by July 6.

The strike was not over, though. Despite the failure of its strategy, SWOC continued picketing peacefully and tried again to elicit support from President Roosevelt. At a press conference during the weekend of June 26–27, Roosevelt condemned both the union and the companies when asked about the conflict. Characterizing public opinion toward the antagonists in the strike with the phrase, "a plague on both your houses," Roosevelt conclusively removed himself from the struggle between labor and management in the steel industry. However, SWOC pursued its unfair labor practice charges against Inland Steel, having filed similar charges against Republic Steel.

While the strike was winding down in the first week of July 1937, in Johnstown, Pennsylvania, and in Canton, Warren, Niles, and Youngstown, Ohio, strikers resisted efforts to resume work at Republic Steel mills in Massilon and Cleveland. Police and company efforts to break their resistance led to more bloodshed. A special force of city police under the command of an anti-union World War I veteran attacked SWOC pickets in Massilon on July 11. After a gun battle that killed two union members and wounded several others, the police ransacked the local SWOC office. Republic's Massilon mill reopened soon after without further incident. In Cleveland, where the strike had kept Republic's four mills tightly shut, the attempts to resume operations also produced violence, despite the presence of the National Guard, a limitation on picketing by order of the sheriff, and the evidence of SWOC's retreat everywhere else. When a car driven by strikebreakers hit and killed a SWOC picket outside one of Republic's Cleveland mills on July 26, union members and non-union workers at the plant engaged

in a battle with rocks, clubs, and pick handles that ended in the flight of the picketers.

With the walkout crumbling by early July, SWOC badly needed even a small advance to avoid the impression of total defeat. It found solace with the help of the governor of Indiana, M. C. Townsend. Townsend and the Indiana commissioner of labor worked to forge settlements between SWOC and both Inland Steel and Youngstown Sheet and Tube mills in their state. These agreements allowed SWOC to claim victories for its members at the companies' mills at Indiana Harbor, though in reality they were face-saving devices that made it less painful for the union to halt picketing and send its members back to work. Youngstown Sheet and Tube contradicted Governor Townsend's announcement of an agreement to end the strike at the company's Indiana Harbor mill and vigorously denied having signed a contract with any organization regarding labor in that plant. Sheet and Tube managers in Indiana Harbor clearly stated their view of the terms worked out with the state government by unfurling a banner near the mill gates on which was printed: "We have not made any agreement or contract with any official person or organization. This plant is open for work on the conditions which existed when work was stopped on May 26th, 1937." With both SWOC and the steel companies sticking to their original bargaining positions, the strike faded away by the end of the summer of 1937.

The Little Steel Strike was one of the bloodiest labor conflicts of the 1930s. But its importance lay more in its impact on the alliance between the labor movement, the Democratic Party, and the federal government. The defeat of SWOC and its CIO parent in this strike produced tensions among these parties that were not soothed for many years. Never again was there as effective a partnership of unions, politicians, and elected officials for union organizing and collective bargaining as there had been before the strike. The steel companies' insistence that they could not be legally coerced to sign contracts with a union brought pressure on President Roosevelt to distance his administration from the CIO. This in turn caused a personal rift between Roosevelt and John L. Lewis that was never bridged.

Labor's setback in the Little Steel strike was only temporary. Neither SWOC nor the CIO collapsed after its defeat at the hands of Little Steel, as many had expected. Instead, the steel union persisted in its unfair labor practice charges before the National Labor Relations Board, eventually winning both the issue of mandatory signed contracts and reinstatement (with back pay) of union members fired during the organizing drive and strike. More importantly, SWOC resumed its effort to organize Bethlehem Steel in 1939 and finally won majorities in elections at the company's mills in 1941, leading to a signed agreement. Successful organizing followed at the other Little Steel companies. After bitterly fighting the union in 1937, Republic, Youngstown Sheet and Tube, and Inland also signed union contracts in 1942, even waiving the formality of elections in the face of overwhelming evidence that most of their employees wanted to be represented by SWOC. [Peter Gottlieb]

FURTHER READING

Bernstein, Irving. *The Turbulent Years: A History of the American Worker: 1933–1941*. Boston, MA: Houghton, Mifflin, 1970.

Galenson, Walter. *The CIO Challenge to the AFL*. Cambridge, MA: Harvard University Press, 1960.

Sofchalk, Donald. *The Little Steel Strike of 1937*. Ph.D. dissertation, Ohio State University, 1961.

Speer, Michael. "The 'Little Steel' Strike: Conflict for Control." *Ohio History*, Vol. 78 (1969), pp. 273–287.

o   o   o

STEEL STRIKE OF 1946. Almost five thousand strikes took place in the United States in 1946, the year after the end of World War II. Some 4.5 million workers participated in strikes that resulted in 116 million man-hours lost to American industry. Workers had made great sacrifices during the war when wages were carefully regulated and strikes were largely absent; and at war's end, when overtime work disappeared, they began to feel the pinch of the real earnings lost to inflation during the war. Although strikes occurred across the economy, perhaps the most important in setting the parameters for postwar labor relations took place in the steel industry.

The 1946 industrywide negotiations between big steel, led by the United States Steel Corporation, and the United Steel Workers of America (USWA) were the first in the steel industry's history to take place without the economic imperatives of depression or the political imperatives of war. Both the companies and the union made it clear that they would view the negotiations as an opportunity. For the union that meant continuing to build on the strength it had acquired under the benevolent eyes of the War Labor Board during the war, when it had become the country's largest union. For the companies it was the first opportunity since the unionization of the industry in the 1930s to stop the growing union penetration into management prerogatives and to reassert their control over labor relations.

The steel industry gave an indication of its strategy late in 1945 when it applied to the still-functioning wartime federal price control agency, the Office of Price Administration (OPA), for permission to raise prices by seven dollars a ton. The agency rejected the request, calling it inflationary. Quickly U.S. Steel's president Benjamin Fairless made it clear that there would be no wage increase granted in the 1946 negotiations with the USWA unless the company received permission to raise prices. By tying wage increases to price increases, the companies began a practice that was to continue through the 1950s and ultimately contribute to the decline of the competitiveness of the American steel industry.

With autoworkers already on strike and confrontations on the horizon in the coal and electrical manufacturing industries, as well as on the railroads, the thought of the economic impact of a strike in basic steel gravely worried President Harry S. Truman and his administration. Truman called Philip Murray, president of the USWA, and Fairless to the White House where the union agreed to reduce its demands to nineteen and a half cents an hour (down from twenty-five cents), and Truman reluctantly discarded his determination to hold the line on inflation and promised the company a four-dollar-a-ton price increase.

Unfortunately, Fairless could not convince the other steel companies to accept Truman's compromise. With the President's intervention in disarray, the strike began on January 20, 1946. America's largest and most basic industry was shut down. An embarrassed and angry Truman prophetically summed up the strike and its implications for the future of labor relations in the United States in a letter to his mother: "The steel people . . . would like to break the unions and the unions would like to break them so they probably will fight a while and then settle. . . ." But Truman concluded by writing that both would lose in the long run, and that "only the man in the street will pay the bill."

Although Truman personally found both sides in the struggle distasteful, he did realize that the devastation of a long steel strike at the beginning of the nation's reconversion period was more than the economy could take. Therefore, he moved once again to spark a settlement. This time the government's offer of a five-dollar-a-ton price increase, when coupled with an eighteen-and-a-half-cents-an-hour wage increase, met the approval of all twelve of the big inte-

grated steel companies engaged in industry-wide bargaining with the USWA. The strike ended on those terms on February 15.

The 1946 strike was important for a number of reasons. It forced Truman to discard his attempt to hold down postwar inflation. The inability to maintain wartime wage and price controls during postwar conversion became clear. It also opened the dikes for other inflationary wage and price settlements across American industry by setting the pattern for settlements in the auto and electrical manufacturing strikes in progress. Truman came out of the events of 1946 with a distrust of steel management, which had rejected his initial compromise settlement, thus thrusting him into a political quagmire. This hostility would contribute to his seizure of the steel mills during the **Steel Strike of 1952.** [Ronald L. Filippelli]

Further Reading

Bernstein, Barton. "The Truman Administration and the Steel Strike of 1946." *Journal of American History*, Vol. 52 (March 1966), pp. 791–803.

Nagle, Richard. *Collective Bargaining in Basic Steel and the Federal Government.* Ph.D. dissertation, Pennsylvania State University, 1978.

Tiffany, Paul A. *The Decline of American Steel: How Management, Labor and Government Went Wrong.* New York: Oxford University Press, 1988.

o   o   o

STEEL STRIKE OF 1952. Among labor disputes, the Steel Strike of 1952 was unique because it was the first time that the President of the United States seized a major portion of an American industry and provoked a historic confrontation over the constitutional question of the separation of powers.

The strike had its roots in the expansion of presidential power, the Korean War, and labor unrest following World War II. When North Korea invaded the Republic of Korea in 1950, the Truman administration hoped to support the South Koreans without a declaration of war or destabilizing the U.S. economy. To this end, Congress passed the Defense Production Act of 1950 (DPA) that provided the President with the authority to establish economic priorities and authorize material allocation, to induce the expansion of productive capacity, to control consumer spending and credit, and to requisition property if needed for the national defense. Further, Titles IV and V of the DPA provided the President with the power to develop wage and price control agencies and labor dispute settlement procedures that were not in conflict with the Labor Management Relations Act (LMRA).

As the Korean "police action" turned into a "limited national emergency," the expanded military spending, scare buying, and a rapidly advancing wage-price spiral resulting from the threat of controls, increased inflationary pressures and the cost of living. Using the DPA, the Truman administration organized the Office of Defense Mobilization (ODM) and its subsidiaries, the Economic Stabilization Agency (ESA), Office of Price Stabilization (OPS), and Wage Stabilization Board (WSB). In turn, these agencies revamped Truman's economic policy to include involuntary wage and price controls.

Organized labor was hostile to the imposition of mandatory wage and price controls. From their World War II experience, organized labor was convinced that under wage and price controls workers lost purchasing power while substandard wages and wage inequalities were inadequately addressed. To make matters worse, the United Labor Policy Committee, an advisory group headed by Phillip Murray, president of the United Steel Workers of America (USWA), and the CIO, believed that the ODM had been placed under the control of corporate executives who were unsympathetic to organized labor's concerns. Consequently, they were openly hostile to the appointment of Charles E. Wilson, president of General Electric, as director of ODM

and, in January 1951, organized labor's representatives withdrew from the WSB.

Truman appointed a National Advisory Committee on Mobilization Policy to study the issues raised by organized labor, and they recommended that the WSB be reconstituted, given more authority over wage policy, and if necessary, the power to arbitrate labor disputes. In effect, nonbinding compulsory arbitration had replaced collective bargaining as the preferred method of handling labor disputes. Soon thereafter, organized labor resumed its participation on the WSB, working to resolve wage policy issues. It was against this backdrop that the 1952 basic steel negotiations began.

In 1950, the major steel companies had prematurely renegotiated their wage agreements with USWA and simultaneously raised steel prices to avoid expected wage and price controls. This resulted in a new one-year contract granting a sixteen-cents-per-hour wage increase that expired on December 31, 1951.

The 1952 negotiations marked the first bargaining in five years over the total steel agreement. In addition to improvements in such economic issues as wages, shift and weekend premiums, holiday and vacation pay, and pension and insurance benefits, the USWA noneconomic demands included, among others: limitations on subcontracting; modifications of the grievance procedure, seniority, local work practices and job scheduling, and safety procedures; and, perhaps most important, a union shop agreement that included dues checkoff privileges.

When the negotiations began in November 1952, the steel industry was operating at full capacity and experiencing its most profitable period since World War I. The USWA wanted to share the immense profits, and at first, the companies seemed willing to accede to the union wage demands so long as they were assured of concurrent price increases. But given steel's profitability, the OPS was unwilling to revise its Industry

Earnings Standard and grant substantial price relief.

U.S. Steel–USWA negotiations were the pattern setter for the steel industry. Without guaranteed price increases, U.S. Steel took a hard-line position. The negotiations moved quickly to impasse, and the first of six strike deadlines was set. The steelworkers argued that the industry strategy was to force a strike, pressure the OPS for larger price increases, and blame any inflationary pressures on the union.

President Truman was not about to permit a strike in a crucial defense industry and immediately began "jawboning" the parties. To avert a strike, Truman convinced the union and the company to submit the dispute to the WSB. Truman reportedly offered the USWA the incentive of not invoking the national emergency procedures under the Taft-Hartley Act if the union agreed to the use of WSB.

Having little experience with labor disputes, the WSB appointed a panel of "experts" to hear the parties' presentations and to make recommendations. The WSB would use these recommendations to fashion a settlement. This procedure interjected further delays—time that the company used to organize a nationwide public relations campaign that discredited the union as "un-American" and emphasized the importance of price increases in maintaining industry growth. The vilification of the union antagonized an increasingly militant rank and file which had been frustrated by two strike deadline extensions necessitated by WSB delays.

On March 20, 1952, the WSB recommended an eighteen-month agreement that featured a twelve-and-a-half-cents-per-hour increase. Industry representatives on the WSB filed a dissenting opinion that suggested that the recommendations disregarded public interest and represented a capitulation to union interests. The recommendations were rejected by the steel companies but accepted by the union. On the

basis of the WSB recommendations, the USWA voted to resume negotiations but warned that if there was no agreement by April 4, 1952, it would give the steel companies a ninety-six-hour strike notice.

The ten days preceding the strike deadline were chaotic and filled with miscommunications and confusion. The most prominent involved Charles Wilson, director of the Office of Defense Mobilization, who misrepresented the Truman administration in public statements and offered the steel companies price relief in return for their acceptance of the WSB recommendation. Having compromised the stabilization program and the President, Wilson resigned.

As the strike deadline approached, a settlement seemed unlikely. In order to avoid a strike, Truman had three alternatives. He could use the national emergency procedures under Taft-Hartley with its eighty-day injunction requiring work and negotiations to continue, or he could seize the mills under Section 18 of the Selective Service Act—a provision that had been used to seize individual plants during World War II. A final alternative would be to seize the industry using the "inherent powers" of the Presidency contained in Article II of the Constitution. Truman chose the latter because it was thought that it offered a stronger legal basis for the seizure and because of the President's belief that the USWA was more likely to accept an industry seizure and call off the strike.

On April 8, 1952, President Truman announced the seizure in a nationwide radio and television broadcast that included a bitter condemnation of the recalcitrance of the steel companies. In turn, Secretary of Commerce Charles Sawyer wired eighty-six companies that he was taking possession of the mills and ordered them to perform their "usual functions and duties." The USWA acceded to Truman's requests and the seizure and called off the strike.

The steel companies were infuriated by the seizure and attempted to gain restraining orders and temporary injunctions. At first these efforts failed, but a consolidated hearing before Judge David A. Pine on April 25, 1952, resulted in a court finding five days later that the President had exceeded his constitutional and statutory authority. The USWA immediately authorized a strike. But once again the strike was postponed as the case moved quickly from the appellate level to the United States Supreme Court.

The Supreme Court case, *Youngstown Sheet and Tube* vs. *Sawyer*, was argued in mid-May and a decision was reached on June 2, 1952. The Supreme Court ruled that the seizure of the mills was unconstitutional. Two days later the workers began leaving the mills, and within twenty-four hours, 560,000 steelworkers and iron ore miners were on strike.

The United States Senate urged the President to initiate a Taft-Hartley injunction to stop the strike, but Truman refused, arguing that the steelworkers had postponed the strike for six months and that the steel companies were engaged in a "conspiracy against the public interest."

As negotiations continued during the strike, two things became clear to the USWA. First, the steelworkers realized that the industry's major concern was not only price but also the union shop agreement. Second, when the strike resulted in few shortages, the USWA also understood the extent to which the industry had stockpiled steel in preparation for the strike. This knowledge angered not only the USWA but also the entire labor community. So incensed by events was John L. Lewis, president of the United Mine Workers of America, that he made available $10 million to the USWA for the strike.

After fifty days of impasse, Truman brought Murray and U.S. Steel president Benjamin Fairless to the White House where he told them that if the strike was not settled in forty-eight hours, he would seize the mills under the provisions of the Selective Service Act. Within hours a two-year tentative agreement was reached. It contained a twenty-one-and-a-half-cents-per-hour increase in wages and benefits, a modified union shop agreement whereby new employees would become union members after thirty days unless they otherwise notified the employer in writing, and, for the companies, a $5.20 per ton increase in the price of steel.

After six strike deadlines, nearly seven months without a labor agreement, a constitutional crisis involving presidential authority—with the price stabilization program in shambles—the fifty-three-day steel strike ended on July 24, 1952. While it had been the longest strike to date in the steel industry, many remained perplexed and angered over how a strike in a so basic an industry could be tolerated in wartime. No doubt, this antagonism contributed to the outcome of the 1952 elections, to the negative perceptions of organized labor during the McCarthy era, and to labor unrest in the steel industry throughout the remainder of the decade. [John Russo]

FURTHER READING

Abel, I. W. *Collective Bargaining: Labor Relations in Steel, Then and Now*. New York: Columbia University Press, 1976.

Blackman, John L., Jr. *Presidential Seizures in Labor Disputes*. Cambridge, MA: Harvard University Press, 1967.

Marcus, Maeva. *Truman and the Steel Seizure Case: The Limits of Presidential Power*. New York: Columbia University Press, 1977.

Preis, Art. *Labor's Giant Step: Twenty Years of the CIO*. New York: Pioneer Publishers, 1964.

Shatz, Ronald W. "Battling Over Government's Role." In *Forging a Union of Steel: Phillip Murray, SWOC, and the Steelworkers*. Paul Clark, Donald Kennedy, and Peter Gottlieb, eds. Ithaca, NY: Cornell ILR Press, 1987.

"*Youngstown Sheet and Tube* vs. *Sawyer*, 343 US 579". In *Landmark Briefs and Arguments of the Supreme Court of the United States: Constitutional Law*. Philip B. Kirland and Gerhard Casper, eds. Arlington, VA: University Publications of America, 1975.

o   o   o

STEEL STRIKES OF 1956 AND 1959. A three-week strike in 1956 and the four-month strike in 1959 of over 500,000 steelworkers signalled the beginning of the dramatic decline of the American steel industry and the United Steel Workers of America (USWA), the union that represented its workers. In both strikes the negotiations took place in the context of a growing web of unfavorable conditions, some created by the past actions of the union and the companies, and others over which they had no control.

Both negotiations took place in the midst of inflationary pressures on the economy. Many observers blamed inflation on hefty wage and price hikes that had marked collective bargaining in steel since the end of World War II. In addition, the spiral of price and wage increases had put the American industry, overbuilt and with largely antiquated technology, in an increasingly unfavorable position with regard to foreign competitors in Europe, Japan, and the developing world.

Since the war, including the bitter nationwide **Steel Strike of 1952**, the company had conceded sizable wage gains to the union and then promptly raised prices and passed the additional costs and more on to the consumers. The pattern had been set in the **Steel Strike of 1946** when Philip Murray, president of the United Steel Workers of America had accepted a sizable wage settlement from the steel companies; and the federal government, relaxing price controls in effect during World War II, permitted the companies to raise prices to cover the costs of the new contract. In 1952, Murray, the founding president of the USWA, died suddenly. He was replaced by David J. McDonald, a veteran of the USWA leadership team who was perceived by steel management as more cooperative and understanding of the industry's position than Murray had been. But McDonald's hold on the leadership of the union was also a good

deal more tenuous than his predecessor's. He would experience two electoral challenges to his leadership between 1952 and 1960. Consequently, the companies appeared ready to assist McDonald to strengthen his hold on the union. The 1953 wage reopener negotiations ended amicably with the USWA receiving a generous wage increase. In late 1953 and 1954, McDonald and his industry counterpart, Benjamin Fairless of United States Steel, toured the company's mills together as a symbol of the new era of good labor relations in the steel industry. In 1954, negotiations again ended peacefully. Although a recession was underway, the union again achieved a good money settlement. As in 1953, the company quickly raised prices to allow for the increased labor costs.

In 1955, although the country was coming out a recession and U.S. Steel had record profits, bargaining became more difficult. Roger Blough, a tougher bargainer, had replaced Fairless at the top of U.S. Steel, the industry's pattern setter. Yet although negotiations went down to the wire in 1955, the results were more of the same: substantial wage increases for the union and higher prices for the companies. By 1956, however, the bargaining climate had changed considerably. Relations between Blough and McDonald were never good, and President Dwight Eisenhower's government, which had up to now stayed out of negotiations, began to consider intervention to stop the wage-price spiral in steel that it blamed for contributing massively to inflationary pressure.

McDonald came to the bargaining table in 1956 determined to win a big settlement in order to shore up his always shaky hold on the USWA. Key demands included wage increases, premium pay for weekend work, and supplemental unemployment benefits paid by the company. The industry, however, had determined to slow the union's steady march forward. Unlike the past when U.S. Steel had bargained with the union and the rest of the major steel companies had adopted the settlement, this time all twelve of the big steel companies bargained together. Although prepared to give substantial wage increases in a year of record earnings, the companies wanted a five-year contract without wage reopeners but with annual scheduled increases to provide labor stability. Despite attempts by the Eisenhower administration to forestall a strike, negotiations ended in impasse and the workers walked out on July 1. The settlement that finally emerged after considerable pressure from Eisenhower was a triumph for labor. Under pressure from a Republican president in an election year and at a time of increased fear of war because of the Suez crisis, the industry settled for a three-year contract, pay increases, a twice yearly cost-of-living escalator, and supplemental unemployment benefits. In all, the settlement added nearly 30 percent in pay raises over the life of the contract, putting steelworkers' pay 28 percent higher than the average hourly earnings in all manufacturing industries. Of American industrial workers, only coal miners earned more. Considering the size of the steel work force, the settlement was no doubt the richest on record in the history of collective bargaining in America.

Immediately after the end of the strike, the companies once again hiked prices. But although the companies had made a generous settlement, they had been willing to take a three-week strike in 1956. This signalled the beginning of a hardening industry stance toward the postwar pattern in steel. Some of this pressure came, no doubt, from the smaller companies who were part of the bargaining for the first time. Their ability to continue to pay the rich settlements agreed to by industry giant U.S. Steel was beginning to be in doubt. In addition, although steel imports still made up a tiny portion of the American market in 1956, they had increased 38 percent over 1955 levels. It was obviously becoming clear to steel management that, in the face of the challenge from cheaper foreign steel, its ability to pass increased labor costs on to the consumers was declining.

In August 1956, U.S. Steel announced that it would increase prices by 7.5 percent to offset the new contract with the union. The price increase, unlike those before it, received a hostile reaction from Congress which undertook a series of investigations of monopoly and pricing practices in the steel industry. The companies' and union's public images declined even more in 1957 and 1958 when the second and third year wage increases, plus the cost-of-living increases agreed upon in the 1956 settlement, went into effect. Nineteen fifty-seven was a recession year and at one time or another 400,000 steelworkers were laid off. The spectacle of wage and price increases under these conditions badly damaged the image of the steel companies and union in the eyes of Congress and the American people. Nevertheless, both prices and wages went up. McDonald, under political attack in the union, was in no mood to give the companies any relief. Nor, on the surface, did they appear to need it. Despite the economic slump, the companies made profits. The pattern of business as usual led to congressional cries for presidential intervention to stop the inflationary spiral. But although he referred to inflation as the greatest danger to the American people, Eisenhower refused.

These then were the circumstances under which the union and the companies entered bargaining in 1959. In that year, the volume of steel imported into America exceeded exports for the first time in the century. The ratio has not been reversed to this day. The vulnerability of the industry to foreign competition was finally becoming unmistakably clear. The industry was determined to hold the line on wages. McDonald was just as determined to protect the steelworkers from the effects of inflation. In the face of this clear standoff, President Eisenhower waffled, torn between his belief in letting market pressures force the participants to settle and the pragmatic need to hold wages and prices down and stop a strike.

The companies demanded a one-year contract with no raise and an end to the cost-of-living escalator clause, blaming the nation's inflation on high wages. In the midst of the recession, the companies seemed to have the upper hand. But unfortunately, company profits soared because nervous steel customers, expecting a strike, bought enormous amounts of steel in early 1959. The USWA seized on the profit figures to justify its demands for a wage hike. By the end of June, the talks were deadlocked. McDonald first appealed to Eisenhower to appoint a fact-finding board to help to resolve the dispute, and when Eisenhower rejected the idea, the USWA president gave ground and reduced the union's demands to no wage increases and a small increment in fringe benefits. But the industry, sensing its advantage, made a tactical error of considerable magnitude. It offered to accept the USWA's demands for a 3.4 percent increase in fringe benefits in exchange for union agreement to modify a number of work rules concerning local working conditions, incentives, employee scheduling, and seniority. The companies justified these demands for improved efficiency by pointing to the changed conditions in world trade. The demands were impossible for McDonald to meet and survive politically. His hold on the union was too shaky. The work rules issue was also the one he needed to rouse a rank and file that would probably have agreed reluctantly to the company demands on wages but who saw any attempt by the companies to make inroads on the shop floor as an attempt to break the union.

Some 500,000 steelworkers walked out on July 15, closing down the American steel industry. They stayed out for 116 days, making the 1959 steel walkout the longest industrial strike in American history up to that time. Only after two months of the strike did Eisenhower invoke the emer-gency strike provisions of the Taft-Hartley Act forcing the workers back to the mills for an eighty-day cooling off period. Just a few days before the end of the injunction, on January 4, 1960, the parties reached agreement. Once again the companies gave ground. The settlement included a small wage gain, fringe benefits improvements, and the continuation of the cost-of-living clauses. The volatile work rules issues were put aside to be studied by joint labor–management committees.

Although the 1959 strike was a victory for the union, it was a far cry from the enormous gains of 1956. Nor could the company, because of political pressures in an election year and the continuing recession, raise prices immediately after the settlement as it had done regularly in the past. In fact, for the first time since 1946, the negotiations had resulted in what could be considered a noninflationary settlement. But by 1960, the industry was already in decline and no labor settlement could have reversed it. Wages were 40 percent above the all-manufacturing average, and profits were high. But the mills were antiquated and lower-priced foreign steel, not to mention competing materials such as aluminum and pressed concrete, had gained an irreversible beachhead in the American market. [Ronald L. Filippelli]

FURTHER READING

Libertella, Anthony. *The Steel Strike of 1959: Labor, Management, and Government Relations*. Ph.D. dissertation, Ohio State University, 1972.

Nagle, Richard W. *Collective Bargaining in Basic Steel and the Federal Government*. Ph.D. dissertation, Pennsylvania State University, 1978.

Tiffany, Paul A. *The Decline of American Steel: How Management, Labor, and Government Went Wrong.* New York: Oxford University Press, 1988.

o   o   o

STUDEBAKER STRIKE OF 1913. The Industrial Workers of the World (IWW) were less important in the early auto industry than in industries such as textiles, mining, and lumber. However, the "Wobblies" did have a presence in Detroit soon after their founding in 1905. In 1910, in order to appeal to the city's growing number of metal workers, particularly auto workers, the IWW established a Metal and Machine Workers' Local No. 16. Progress was slow, however, but by 1913 the local had attracted over 400 members. Half of them worked in the auto industry.

The issues which troubled auto workers were similar to those which were arousing workers to protest across the country—the "drive system," the "foreman's empire," the speedup on the shop floor, the ten-hour workday, and low pay. Detroit employers, like their counterparts across the country, had formed their own association to control labor problems, the Employers' Association of Detroit, which kept its eye on the budding IWW movement and warned its members of the discontent simmering beneath the surface in the Motor City.

Before the strike broke out, the IWW's activities in Detroit in 1913 were not markedly different from those of earlier years. One method of proselytizing was to appear outside of the plant gates at lunchtime to speak on issues such as the eight-hour day and the speedup. An IWW attempt to speak to Ford workers of the Highland Park plant in the summer of 1913 came to nothing when the company refused to allow its employees to leave the factory. In addition, the Detroit police accommodated Ford by arresting IWW organizer Matilda Rabinowitz and several of her supporters after a brief scuffle. Thus frustrated, the IWW turned its attention to the Studebaker company where it had managed to attract some support. At the time there was discontent among Studebaker workers because of a unilateral change by the company from a weekly to biweekly pay system. In addition, when payday fell on Sunday or a holiday, the workers would be paid the day after, not the day before. To the auto workers, who lived from day to day, the

change created a major dislocation in their lives. The workers in the plant had organized to protest the change, and this fact gave the IWW militants an issue around which to organize auto workers.

The discontent built quickly when the company dismissed a workers' leader for circulating a petition on the pay issue. When the company delayed in responding to the protest against the firing, the workers at the Studebaker Plant No. 3, in Delray, walked off the job on June 17. Using IWW tactics of mass picketing, the strikers streamed to Studebaker Plants 1 and 5, where they called out their supporters. By the evening of the first day, some 6,000 men were on strike.

Most of the strikers were not skilled workers. They were operatives in the highly mechanized auto plants. The minority of skilled workers were organized into various American Federation of Labor (AFL) craft unions, and although some, like the metal polishers and iron molders, offered their moral support, others, such as the tool makers, refused to have anything to do with the IWW-led action. As in many other IWW strikes, the presence of conservative AFL craft unionists in struck plants proved to be a serious obstacle to the success of the strike. These skilled workers' unions were only a minor annoyance to the auto companies because with the transformation of work as a result of new technology, the skilled workers were becoming less and less of a factor in the industry.

Although the Detroit newspapers predictably branded the strike leaders as outside agitators and called on the auto workers to throw the IWW organizers out of the city, there was little trouble for the first two days. That changed on July 19, however, when the strikers marched to the Packard plant to try to persuade the workers to follow their example. Police broke up the meeting, injuring Jack Walsh, an IWW leader, and arresting several others.

On the fourth day of the strike, July 20, the strikers, under the leadership of

Matilda Rabinowitz, drew up a set of demands to present to the company. They included weekly paydays, the eight-hour day with no reduction in pay, and reinstatement of all strikers without prejudice. The formal demands came at the climax to the strike. Because the walkout had occurred during the summer slack season, there was a large pool of laid-off auto workers available to the employers. The strikers knew that to hold out much longer would mean their permanent replacement. The company also knew that time was in its favor, and refused to negotiate with the workers. On June 23, the men voted to return to work. The only concession that the company made was to modify the biweekly pay system to allow a worker to draw a portion of his wages in the first week.

The Studebaker Strike was the first major industrial conflict in the auto industry of Detroit. The spontaneous eruption at Studebaker gave the AFL hope that it could organize the auto workers, but the weak effort foundered on the rocks of exclusive craft jurisdiction. It was clear that the industry could only be organized on an industrial basis, and the willingness of the AFL craft unions to recognize that fact was years off in 1913. Although the IWW remained in Detroit after the Studebaker strike, it never again made serious inroads into the auto industry. [Ronald L. Filippelli]

FURTHER READING

Foner, Philip S. *History of the Labor Movement in the United States: The Industrial Workers of the World, 1905–1917*, Vol. 4. New York: International Publishers, 1965.

Peterson, Joyce Shaw. *American Automobile Workers, 1901–1933*. Albany, NY: State University of New York Press, 1987.

T

⚬ ⚬ ⚬ ⚬ ⚬ ⚬ ⚬ ⚬ ⚬ ⚬

⚬ ⚬ ⚬

TAMPA, FLORIDA, CIGAR WORK-
ERS' STRIKE OF 1931. This brief walkout
marked the last in a series of struggles that
pitted radical, immigrant cigar workers
against employers backed by the local elite,
which sought to prevent disruption of
Tampa's primary industry. Although another defeat for workers, the 1931 strike
showed the nature of their radicalism and
the forces arrayed against them.

Tampa's cigar industry dated from
1885, when Spanish and Cuban manufacturers relocated in the small port city of
Florida's Gulf Coast. Drawn by promises of
labor peace, cigar manufacturers brought
with them Cuban and Spanish-born cigar
makers who hand rolled clean Havana tobacco into luxury cigars. These highly skilled
workers carried with them a tradition of
militant trade unionism and radical politics.
As skilled workers, they had long exercised
enormous control over the production process, as evidenced by their practice of hiring
readers who read to them from texts they
selected.

The radicalism and collective strength
of Tampa cigar workers led to a series of
confrontations with employers over issues
of power, especially union recognition.
Despite widespread membership, first in
local, independent unions and later in the
Cigar Maker's International Union of the
American Federation of Labor, cigar workers failed to win union recognition in prolonged strikes in 1901, 1910, and 1920. In
each case, they confronted not only employers but also their allies in the local elite,
especially merchants and professionals, who

organized citizens' committees to repress
striking cigar workers. The illegal activities
of these vigilante groups included the forced
expulsion of strike leaders and the destruction of union offices and presses.

Cigar production peaked in 1929 and
then went into a deep decline. Reduced
demand led to unemployment and pay cuts
for workers. In an effort to fight back, half of
Tampa's 10,000 cigar workers joined the
Tobacco Workers Industrial Union (TWIU),
a union created by the Communist Party in
1931. Communists also organized protests
against evictions and campaigned for higher
unemployment relief in Tampa.

On November 7, 1931, Latin workers
staged a rally to celebrate the fourteenth
anniversary of the Russian Revolution. The
overflow crowd scuffled with police, and a
shot from an unknown source seriously
wounded a policeman. Arrests followed,
and seventeen people, including Communist organizers and several Latin women,
were charged with unlawful assembly, rioting, and assault to commit murder.

Cigar workers immediately began
collecting defense funds, and some staged
walkouts in protest against the arrests. On
November 26, cigar manufacturers decided
to ban the readers because, they claimed,
"All of the trouble is originating from the
readers' stand where fiery Communistic
translations from anarchistic publications
have constantly poured into the workers."

When cigar workers discover the readers' platforms dismantled the following
morning, they immediately walked out. They
then called a seventy-two-hour strike to
protest both the removal of the readers and

the continued imprisonment of the people arrested on November 7. The three-day demonstration became virtually a general strike in immigrant neighborhoods since most businesses closed in sympathy with the cigar workers. When the walkout ended, cigar workers found themselves locked out of the factories.

Manufacturers refused to indicate any conditions for a reopening of their factories, but they won support from Tampa's economic and political establishment. On the third day of the lockout, 300 leading Tampans organized a "secret committee of twenty-five outstanding citizens" to help cigar factory owners "wash the red out of their factories." According to a local newspaper, the new citizens' committee "was formed for the sole purposed of driving out the Communists." Assistance also came from Tampa police who, acting without a warrant, raided TWIU offices and seized union records. A federal judge issued a sweeping injunction that outlawed the Tobacco Workers Industrial Union and barred 140 individuals, including union leaders and publishers of two local Spanish-language newspapers, from interfering in any way with the peaceful conduct of Tampa's cigar industry.

During the second week of the lockout, "the secret committee of twenty-five" brought about the reopening of the cigar factories on terms that represented a complete victory for manufacturers. Employers agreed to reopen their plants, "provided the factories can be operated upon a basis of true Americanism." The owners spelled out "true Americanism" to include the open shop, nonrecognition of the TWIU or any group with "Communist affiliations," removal of the readers, and a ban on collections of any kind within the factories. Cigar workers agreed to accept these conditions if all workers were rehired to share existing work. With the full backing of the secret committee, cigar manufacturers reopened their factories on December 14, under the terms

previously announced. Workers showed their willingness to return, but only about 70 percent of those who had walked out in the seventy-two-hour sympathy strike were rehired. In the words of one industry spokesman, "Reds have been weeded out, and only the old faithful workers . . . were on the job." Gone too were the readers' platforms and any sign of the Tobacco Workers Industrial Union.

Leaders of the radical union remained locked up in jail after their arrest at the November 7 rally. In January 1932, the accused were tried under an 1866 Florida statute that made presence at an unlawful assembly sufficient to bring conviction for any assault that occurred. Charges against two of the defendants were dismissed, but the remaining fifteen were all found guilty and sentenced to prison terms ranging from one to ten years. In May 1933, after most of the convicted had completed their sentences, the Florida State Supreme Court reversed the convictions on a technicality.

A powerful alliance of forces killed the Tobacco Workers Industrial Union in Tampa. Supporters of cigar manufacturers depicted the struggle as more than a labor–management conflict. "It was not essentially a cigar strike, but a red revolution," a spokesman for the manufacturers claimed. Pictured in these terms, the fight to destroy the TWIU presumably justified any means.

The 1931 victory of manufacturers did not prevent the further decline of the luxury cigar industry. Production dropped, workers found themselves increasingly replaced by machines, and radios took the place of readers. [Robert P. Ingalls]

FURTHER READING

Ingalls, Robert P. *Urban Vigilantes in the New South: Tampa, 1882–1936.* Knoxville, TN: University of Tennessee Press, 1988.

Perez, Louis A. "Reminiscences of a Lector: Cuban Cigar Workers in Tampa." *Florida Historical Quarterly*, Vol. 53 (April 1974), pp. 443–449.

Yglesias, Jose. *The Truth About Them.* New York: Pantheon, 1971.

o   o   o

TELEPHONE STRIKE OF 1947. The 1947 national Telephone Strike by all accounts ended in defeat for telephone workers. Nevertheless, it signaled a new phase of labor–management relations in the telephone industry. Independent militant unionism among telephone workers had come of age by 1947, forcing the American Telephone and Telegraph Company (AT&T) to abandon its famed paternalism. The 1947 strike inaugurated a concerted systemwide effort by AT&T to destroy the telephone unions—organizations which, ironically, AT&T had given birth to and nurtured in their earliest form as company unions.

The militancy of the phone employees, 350,000 of whom walked out on the morning of April 7, 1947, had been slow in developing. In the 1920s and 1930s, company unionism flourished throughout the AT&T system—an empire that included the Bell Operating Companies (where AT&T retained control through stock ownership and administrative appointments) and other directly-owned subsidiaries such as the Long Lines Division, Western Electric, and Bell Laboratories. AT&T also offered its native-born, predominantly female work force "genteel respectability," white-collar status, and an elaborate benefit plan.

In 1937, prompted by the Supreme Court ruling upholding the Wagner Act and outlawing company unions, AT&T formally broke ties with the employee organizations it had spawned. But the legacy of employer domination lingered. Workers looked to AT&T for employment security, saw the company as all-knowing and all-powerful, and retained much of their customary deference and loyalty. A minority, however, threw off the "ingrained sense of inferiority" and went about building independent local unions. By 1939, they had created a systemwide confederation of autonomous locals, the National Federation of Telephone Workers (NFTW). Initial membership hovered near 100,000 and included 37 percent

of all Bell employees.

During World War II, telephone workers became increasingly restless and emboldened. Frustration over declining purchasing power and the unresponsiveness of the War Labor Board culminated in a 1944 strike in Dayton, Ohio. The walkout resulted in the establishment of a National Telephone panel which expedited the processing of War Labor Board cases and brought a measure of relief to phone employees. The NFTW enjoyed a new-found legitimacy and prestige arising from its handling of the strike and its pivotal position as the workers' representative on the panel. Membership leaped to 170,000 by 1945, and the number of NFTW affiliates doubled.

At the war's end, telephone workers joined with oil, auto, steel, and other workers in flexing their union muscles during the massive strike wave of 1945–1946. Some 200 stoppages occurred among Washington, DC, operators, for example, in the year following the war. Many of these were sympathy actions on behalf of outlying locals that lacked the strategic power of the Washington operators. Led by Mary Gannon, Washington's Traffic Local 2300 cut off telephone access to the White House and other government offices when necessary.

In this atmosphere of surging union temerity, the NFTW began preparations for its 1946 negotiations. Although hamstrung by the "autonomy clause" in the NFTW constitution, which granted affiliate unions control over their own bargaining, local presidents vowed nevertheless to stand united against the AT&T. Eventually, nearly half of the affiliates abandoned their pledge and accepted individual contracts, but Joseph Beirne, the newly elected president of NFTW, salvaged the negotiations on the national level through masterful maneuvering. Using the threat of a national strike and aided by pressure from the U.S. Conciliation Service and Secretary of Labor Lewis Schwellenbach, Beirne secured a national agreement from Cleo Craig, AT&T's vice-president for labor relations. The Beirne–Craig memorandum granted substantial wage increases, even in situations where the union had already settled with the local Bell company. The 1946 negotiations demonstrated in a concrete, highly-visible fashion the potential power of independent unionism among telephone workers, especially when that power was directed through a unified, disciplined national organization.

The scenario for 1947 unfolded in a dramatically different fashion. AT&T had learned its lesson. Determined to avoid the concessions of 1946, AT&T devised an aggressive strategy to weaken and hopefully destroy this new upstart unionism. There was to be no more industrywide bargaining—only local agreements—and wage and benefit advances were to be held to a minimum. In preparation for a national strike, AT&T hired additional supervisory personnel, replaced and repaired equipment, and trained its management for the ensuing test of wills.

On the other hand, "all pepped up and enthused" from its 1946 victory and unaware of AT&T's new hard-line stance, NFTW announced an ambitious list of demands, including systemwide bargaining, twelve-dollar-a-week wage increases, union shop, a minimum $100 monthly pension contribution, narrowing of geographical wage differentials, a compressed wage step chart, and improved vacation benefits. NFTW affiliates confidently renewed their unity pact and most anticipated major breakthroughs without a strike. A few foresaw a strike but assumed that service would grind to a halt forcing a quick conclusion through government intervention.

The early months of bargaining produced no wage offers from AT&T. Instead, they proposed local arbitration boards whose awards would be circumscribed by wage levels in the surrounding community. As the strike deadline approached, Joseph Beirne spoke against a national strike, arguing that the NFTW was unprepared financially and organizationally. "When the boss wants you to strike, don't," he reasoned. Only one other delegate shared his reticence. When the last-minute interventions of the U.S. Conciliation Service and the secretary of labor were ignored by AT&T and the union's final compromise had been rejected, the forty-nine-member National Bargaining Committee voted overwhelmingly to strike.

At 6 A.M. on April 7, the first nationwide strike in the history of the telephone industry began. With 350,000 employees out, 250,000 of them women, the strike was the largest walkout of women in U.S. history. It also reached into more communities than any previous strike, affecting every section of the country except New England. Carrying signs which proclaimed, "The Voice With a Smile Will be Gone for a While," around-the-clock pickets paraded throughout the South, the Midwest, and in rural towns across the United States. For many Americans, the 1947 Telephone Strike provided their first up-close view of unionism in action.

The strike was remarkably peaceful, although the union engaged in mass picketing while the employer countered with a flurry of injunctions and court orders. Twelve thousand women operators in New Jersey left their posts, defying a state law which called for jail sentences and steep fines for utility strikers. Major clashes occurred in Detroit, San Francisco, and Utah. In Chicago, police arrested over 1,000 workers, but, as one local union officer remembered, "the gals . . . were good strikers and hung on to the last."

Despite extensive support for the strike among employees, the company maintained its operations. Long distance service initially dropped 80 percent but soon recovered. Direct dial operations suffered even less. With no crises in service apparent, the government could hardly seize the industry. The NFTW was on its own against AT&T.

Even in the face of considerable public

sympathy for the strikers, AT&T refused to budge. Financial contributions from the garment unions, the mine workers, and others offset NFTW's nonexistent strike fund, but support services for the strikers remained primitive. As days lengthened into weeks, the strike began "crumbling around the edges."

On May 4, two NFTW affiliates in Illinois broke ranks and settled with Illinois Bell. Pressure mounted on the National Bargaining Committee as promising wage proposals flooded union offices. The "offers," all contingent on the negotiations occurring locally, excluded the National Bargaining Committee by prior agreement. Recognizing the inevitable, the national committee succumbed, disbanding on May 6. The local settlements began falling into place, and by May 31, even Washington, DC's operators, the last holdouts, were at their switchboards.

Although the NFTW failed to win any of its major demands, it did prevent AT&T from accomplishing its major goal: the destruction of national independent unionism in the phone company. On June 9, 1947, only weeks after the strike ended, thirty-two NFTW divisions representing 161,699 members met in Miami Beach and proceeded with their plans, formulated in 1946, to reconstitute themselves as the Communications Workers of America (CWA). In an unusual demonstration of farsightedness, local union officers voluntarily forfeited power and autonomy, setting up a national union with full authority over bargaining and strike action.

Some scholars have argued that the 1947 strike almost destroyed the impulse toward national unionism in the telephone industry. And certainly the strike took its toll on union membership and morale. But, for some unionists, the 1947 debacle hardened their resolve to build a "cohesive, unified, integrated union." Others, like John Moran, head of the Long Line Division, defected to the recently established CIO

organizing committee, but not because he rejected the idea of a militant national union: he simply desired stronger ties with the larger labor movement.

Even with the strike albatross around its neck, the new CWA represented 42 percent of AT&T employees, and the unaffiliated independents held 35 percent. The remainder belonged to the CIO's Telephone Workers Organizing Committee (TWOC) and the International Brotherhood of Electrical Workers. When the CWA affiliated with the CIO in 1949, absorbing TWOC's membership, telephone workers moved into the mainstream of the labor movement, breaking irrevocably with the provincialism and paternalism of the past.

Although AT&T continued to press its bargaining advantage in the late 1940s and 1950s, keeping wage rates in the phone industry substantially below those in other comparable settings, by the end of the 1950s it was clear that their decade-long campaign to eradicate independent unionism had failed. CWA had survived, in part, because it learned the lessons of 1947. Phone workers needed a national organization with sufficient power and financial resources to weather extended strikes. But realizing that strikes could be as much of a company as a union weapon, union leaders forged a central body that could also control the timing and extent of strike activity. They concentrated on building a structure that could match the company in discipline and unity without losing touch with the local rank-and-file militancy that had been so clearly revealed in the spring of 1947. [Dorothy Sue Cobble]

FURTHER READING

Barbash, Jack. *Unions and Telephones: The Story of the Communications Workers of America.* New York: Harper and Brothers, 1952.

Brooks, Thomas R. *Communications Workers of America: Story of a Union.* New York: Mason/Charter, 1977.

Schacht, John N. *The Making of Telephone Unionism, 1920–1947.* New Brunswick, NJ: Rutgers University Press, 1985.

o   o   o

TELLURIDE, COLORADO, MINERS' STRIKE OF 1903–1904. There were two fronts in the Colorado labor war of 1903–1904. While Colorado City mill workers and Cripple Creek miners battled in the center of the state, fellow members of the Western Federation of Miners (WFM) engaged in industrial warfare in the southwestern corner of Colorado. Like their counterparts in Cripple Creek, the Telluride miners faced the tightly interwoven opposition of corporate interests and state officials. Indeed, the line between public authority and private power virtually disappeared during this struggle.

By the summer of 1903, both labor and capital saw themselves on a collision course in San Miguel County. Mine operators had come to view WFM Local 63 as a haven for violent criminals. In particular, the murder in November 1902 of mine manager Arthur Collins, presumably by union miners, had forged an adamant anti-union attitude among operators. For hardrock labor, the events of 1903 had exacerbated discontent over the eight-hour issue. Although the Colorado electorate had amended the state constitution in 1902 to permit passage of an hours law, the subsequent legislative session had enacted no such protection. In July 1903, the Western Federation launched a statewide drive to win the eight-hour workday directly from employers.

Early in August, the San Juan District Union of the WFM called on employers to limit to eight hours the shifts worked by employees of ore-processing mills. The Telluride Mining Association (TMA) dismissed this proposal. The association argued that workers at a number of mills were bound for another year by a collective bargaining agreement that called for ten or more hours per day. Further, the operators attacked the demand that hours be reduced without a corresponding cut in daily pay. But when the union altered its demands to exclude employees under contract and to include a wage cut, the mine owners still made no concession.

On September 1, about 100 mill workers went on strike against six mills. This small work stoppage quickly grew in scope, encompassing most of the district. The mines supplying these ore-processing plants immediately laid off their 400 employees. In addition, a sympathy strike shut down two more local mining properties. That the operators intended to break the Telluride Miners' Union soon became clear when the Tomboy Gold Mining Company attempted to reopen its mill with non-union workers. The usual picket-line skirmishing between strikers and strikebreakers led local businessmen to organize a vigilante group, the Telluride Citizens' Alliance, early in October. This body was affiliated with the statewide citizens' alliance movement, whose primary aim was to eliminate the WFM from Colorado.

At the same time, the operators began to call on Governor James Peabody to send in the militia. Peabody lacked both a compelling substantive reason to commit state forces and the funds required for such an undertaking. Telluride gold mine owners, like their counterparts in Cripple Creek, surmounted these obstacles by offering to finance military intervention. Accordingly, on November 20 the governor sent more than 400 troops to San Miguel County under the command of Major Zeph Hill. Taking Peabody's advice to use vagrancy laws to purge the district of "the lawless, good-for-nothing, intimidating class," Hill arrested thirty-eight strikers on November 30, the first of many mass arrests of this sort.

With military protection, the systematic importation of strikebreakers began in earnest. A number of major firms resumed production in December, their mills working shifts of more than eight hours. Extremely eager to win the war, Major Hill could not confine himself to guarding company property. Hill urged the governor to send Pinkerton agents to infiltrate the miners' union to gather information. Peabody, however, thought that the TMA, not the state, should pay for the Pinkertons. When the major took his proposal to the operators' association, he was informed that it already had enough informants in Local 63.

Despite virtual tranquillity, Peabody declared "qualified martial law" on January 3, 1904, in order to give the National Guard and its patrons a free hand in annihilating the Telluride Miners' Union. Hill immediately broke up a strike meeting and arrested eighteen participants. These prisoners, together with thirteen others arrested elsewhere in town, were sent to Ridgeway, Colorado, forty-five miles away, and instructed not to come back. By the end of the month, Hill had expelled eighty-three unionists from the county. He had also ordered press censorship, limited the right of public assembly, imposed a 9:00 P.M. curfew, and collected many of the strikers' firearms. Especially fearful of the Italian immigrants in the union, he hired a Pinkerton to investigate their strike activities.

Meanwhile, the TMA and the citizens' alliance pressed the governor to establish a permanent military presence in Telluride. Peabody authorized the formation of a local cavalry troop of the Colorado National Guard. On January 11, this new unit, commanded by Captain Bulkeley Wells, manager of the Smuggler-Union mine, swore in forty-one recruits. On February 21, Major Hill and his men left the district in the safekeeping of this force. Not surprisingly, Captain Wells applied martial law in the same vigorous manner as his predecessor. Wells not only continued the censorship of news reports and the deportation of strikers but began to wiretap telephone calls to union members as well.

Despite strenuous military repression, the Telluride miners and mill workers persisted in their struggle for the eight-hour day. Hence, the operators decided to change strategy. On March 11, the governor deactivated the local militia troop and revoked "qualified martial law." Three days later, a contingent of fifty banned strikers returned to the district. Early the next morning, a large group of mine operators, bankers, gamblers, and other businessmen, equipped largely with Colorado National Guard weapons, rounded up more than seventy WFM members and supporters and put them on a train leaving town. Armed members of the citizens' alliance patrolled the streets. When the nearby Ouray Miners' Union assembled a sizable armed force to help its deported comrades return to their homes, Governor Peabody urged the WFM to pursue legal remedies. On March 22, the union obtained a court order that enjoined the citizens' alliance and the TMA from interfering with the return of expelled strikers.

Fearing an invasion, the operators prevailed upon the governor to reimpose martial law. Peabody called the local cavalry back to active duty on March 23, under the command of General Sherman Bell, assisted by Captain Wells. Military authorities permitted a few quiet union supporters to return to Telluride; "agitators" were redeported. On March 29, the National Guard arrested WFM international president Charles Moyer on grounds of "military necessity as well as military discretion." General Bell ignored numerous court orders to release Moyer and held him until June 15.

The Telluride Mining Association declared on April 5 that the strike was over and that they would have no further dealings with the WFM. Indeed, by this time the gold properties in the area were operating with a full complement of mine and mill employees. Within two weeks, General Bell had given command of the militia to Captain Wells and left town. Wells carried on the policy of expelling most strikers caught returning to their homes. On June 15, after Telluride's representative in Congress, H. M. Hogg, urged him to "call off this foolishness," Governor Peabody finally ended military rule.

The gold mine operators had crushed WFM Local 63. To prevent a resurgence of unionism, they instituted an elaborate blacklisting arrangement. Yet their victory was less than complete. Beginning in July, the Smuggler-Union and a number of other firms had to suspend operations due to a lack of competent workers. Moreover, in order to attract qualified employees, in December 1904, the operators began to employ all labor, including mill workers, on the eight-hour system, with a minimum wage of three dollars per day. These were precisely the terms for which the Telluride Miners' Union had struck. [Alan Derickson]

Further Reading

Jensen, Vernon H. *Heritage of Conflict: Labor Relations in the Nonferrous Metals Industry up to 1930.* Ithaca, NY: Cornell University Press, 1950.

Suggs, George G., Jr. *Colorado's War on Militant Unionism: James H. Peabody and the Western Federation of Miners.* Detroit, MI: Wayne State University Press, 1972.

o   o   o

TEN-HOUR MOVEMENT OF 1835. In the period from 1833 to 1837 a strike wave washed across the great cities of the Eastern Seaboard. These strikes came on the heels of the upsurge in unionization in a multitude of crafts. By 1835, approximately 100,000 skilled workers belonged to these new trade unions. As a consequence of the appearance of various organized trades in the cities of the Northeast, a movement toward the creation of citywide labor federations took hold. This resulted from a realization that each trade was far too weak to cope with employers alone. They also reflected the understanding that federation made the most sense in order for workers to participate in the political reform ferment that swept the country during the 1830s, ranging from the workingmen's parties, to Locofocoism, to Jacksonian Democracy.

The movement toward citywide fed-erations began in New York City in 1833 and quickly spread to Philadelphia, Boston, Baltimore, Washington, Pittsburgh, and a host of smaller cities. Although political action and education were primary goals of the federations, they devoted most of their time and resources to supporting affiliates in the strike wave which swept the country between 1833 and the depression of 1837. In the early years, most of these strikes were economic in nature, centering on wages and, in some cases, the closed shop. But by 1835, the struggle for the ten-hour workday had become the dominant preoccupation of the trades and the city labor federations.

The demand for ten hours had already been made in the 1820s, with little success. Only in New York City had the skilled trades succeeded, by 1829, in achieving ten hours on a reasonably widespread basis. In support of ten hours, workers advanced a bevy of arguments, some economic, some moral, and others civic. They argued that shorter hours would make them healthier, more productive workers and more active, in-formed participants in the democratic po-litical process. Leisure would also give them time for mental cultivation.

Employers took an entirely different viewpoint. More leisure time would result in intemperance and debauchery. By requiring long hours employers were not only con-tributing to the country's economic devel-opment but also to its moral soundness. Worker's countered that intemperance re-sulted from the exhaustion of long hours. When employers charged that shorter hours would lessen the amount of labor performed, workers argued that healthy, rested, and happy workers could perform more work from six to six than they did under the sunrise to sundown system.

The movement began in 1833, when workers in Baltimore and Washington demanded the ten-hour day. In Baltimore the campaign encompassed seventeen trades, a massive demonstration of cooperation and solidarity for that era. But 1835 proved to be the great year for the ten-hour movement. It started in Boston and spread to Baltimore, and a number of smaller cities, but Philadelphia proved to be the scene of its greatest success.

The Boston carpenters, who had tried unsuccessfully in 1825 and again in 1832, struck for ten-hours in 1835, in concert with the masons and stonecutters. Significantly, the strikers directed most of their ire toward the merchant capitalists—the owners of the buildings erected and the real estate brokers—not to the master craftsmen who were merely small contractors, middlemen, who, according to the strikers, "were slaves to the capitalists, as we are to them."

The strike gained great sympathy along the eastern seaboard as well as financial contributions from unions in a number of cities. Although the Boston building tradesmen lost their strike, their example set off a round of ten-hour actions in other cities. The Boston spark set off a blaze in Philadelphia. There the ten-hour movement included not only the building trades but mill workers, coal heavers, dock workers, and other common laborers also took part, as did hatters, tailors, bakers, printers, and most of the other trades of the city. Street parades and mass meetings were held. Most declared that they would not work without ten hours, and their solidarity was so impressive that the employers and city government caved in with practically no fight at all.

So swept up in the general excitement was most of the populace of the city that not only workers but also lawyers, physicians, merchants, and politicians supported the movement. At a huge rally in the State House yard on June 6, according to the *Pennsylvanian*, "the unanimity manifested throughout" was satisfactory proof that the feelings of the community were decidedly in favor of "the establishment on an immovable basis of the Ten-Hour system."

News of the great victory in Philadelphia inspired movements in smaller cities such as Paterson, New Jersey, Hartford,

Connecticut, and others. Even in cities in which no strikes took place, such as Newark, New Jersey, and Albany, New York, there is evidence that ten hours had been instituted as the normal workday in most trades. At the end of 1835, with the exception of Boston, ten hours had become the norm for most skilled workers in the eastern cities. [Ronald L. Filippelli]

FURTHER READING

Commons, John R., et al. *History of Labour in the United States*, Vol 1. New York: Macmillan, 1936.

Pressen, Edward. *Most Uncommon Jacksonians: The Radical Leaders of the Early Labor Movement*. Albany, NY: State University of New York Press, 1967.

o   o   o

TENNESSEE MINERS' STRIKE OF 1891. The common use of convict labor at low wages was long a feature of the South. The effect of this contract labor on free workers was not lost on the politically powerful Tennessee employers who benefited from the system. According to one Colonel Colyer, the leader of the Tennessee Democratic Party and the general counsel for the Tennessee Coal, Iron, and Railroad Company, free laborers were "loathe to enter upon strikes when they saw that the company was amply provided with convict labor." In the spring of 1891, at Briceville, in Anderson County, the country was given a demonstration of this principle.

The strike began when miners turned down a contract that ended grievance strikes, surrendered their hard-won right to their own checkweighman, and provided for payment in scrip redeemable only at the company store. On July 5, the first forty convicts arrived to replace the striking miners. Under orders from their guards, the convicts tore down the miners' houses and erected a stockade for their own use. Ten days later, fearing the arrival of even more convicts, the striking miners captured the stockade, marched the convicts and their guards to the depot at Coal Creek, and put them on the train to Knoxville.

Enraged by this challenge to civil authority, the governor personally led three companies of militia and a large contingent of convicts to Briceville. But the militia was largely made up of working men who fraternized freely with the strikers. The militiamen, like most of the citizens of Anderson County, were in sympathy with the strikers. A rash of requests for leave and the near desertion of an entire company testified to the unreliability of the citizen soldiers.

On July 20, 2,000 armed strikers and supporting miners from surrounding counties and as far afield as Kentucky marched on the struck mine. They sent a committee to demand the expulsion of the convicts. Faced with such a show of force, the militia and their wards moved once again to the depot and boarded the train to Knoxville. The same scenario was repeated at another nearby mine kept open by the use of convict labor.

The sparring between the governor and the strikers continued. Six hundred militiamen appeared in Anderson County. The miners agreed to a truce if the state legislature would repeal the convict lease law. When the employers' lobby proved too strong, the miners returned to the strike. By now, peaceful actions had yielded little success, and the leadership of the strike passed to more militant elements. On the evening of October 31, the miners once again took control of the stockade, but this time they released the 163 convicts held inside. In the following three days, two more stockades were emptied of prisoners and burned to the ground.

The actions seemed to have produced the desired results when coal operators hired the miners under the old terms. But the optimism was premature. In the middle of December, the governor announced that the convicts would return to the stockades at Briceville, Oliver Springs, and Coal Creek. A permanent military camp was established with 175 civil and military guards, and a Gatling gun overlooking the valley.

This emboldened the operators and angered the miners. When some operators began to introduce convicts into the mines, strikers once again captured a stockade and sent the convicts out of the county. But when they attempted to duplicate this success on August 15, the guards, instead of peacefully complying, opened fire and wounded several miners. In response, armed miners from the surrounding area commandeered trains and sped to Oliver Springs. There they marched to the stockade, disarmed the guards, burned the blockhouse, and returned guards and convicts to Knoxville.

In response, the militia arrested large numbers of strikers. Most of those arrested were later freed by local juries, but the overwhelming show of military force had succeeded in crushing the revolt of the Tennessee miners. Nevertheless, the episode made such an impression on state authorities that the convict lease system was soon abolished. [Ronald L. Filippelli]

FURTHER READING

Brecher, Jeremy. *Strike!* San Francisco, CA: Straight Arrow Books, 1972.

o o o

TEXTILE STRIKE OF 1934. In the United States, working-class unrest comes in waves. The years 1874, 1877, 1886, and 1919 all mark important watersheds in American labor history. The year 1934 belongs on this list as well. During that year, labor unrest exploded across the country as 1,470,000 men and women engaged in 1,856 work stoppages. Some of these convulsions engulfed entire cities and industries. Like other landmark years, the significance of 1934, however, lies not in statistics but in the tenor and aims of the conflicts. What distinguishes many of the strikes of 1934 were their lethal bitterness and commitment to shift the balance of state power in worker's favor.

The General Textile Strike was the largest upheaval of that tumultous year. Indeed, wrote one labor correspondent, "it was unquestionably the greatest single industrial conflict in the history of American organized labor." As much a political uprising as a trade union action, the strike swept like wildfire across the nation's textile belt which reached from Maine to Alabama. Launched on Labor Day, September 1, the strikers' ranks rapidly swelled to almost 500,000. Three weeks later, with supporters hungry from lack of funds, bruised by the combined might of the state and employers, and undermined by depression conditions, the General Textile Strike ended.

The origins of the strike lay in the 1920s. After World War I, as the textile industry fell into a steep depression, mill owners scurried to shore up dwindling profit margins. Stressing increased productivity, efficiency experts descended upon textile plants of all sizes. When they had finished, workers found themselves operating more machines for less pay. Across the nation, mill hands dubbed this assault the stretchout. "I used to run," one weaver recalled, "six frames and I now look after ten. It used to you git . . . [to] . . . rest now and then, so's you could bear the mill. but now you got to keep a-running all the time." Binding workers together in mutual suffering, the stretchout engendered factory-based solidarity, and textile operatives transformed their common anger into collective action. Between 1925 and 1933, local walkouts against the stretchout broke out in mill towns across the country.

The election of Franklin Roosevelt and the advent of the New Deal inspired textile workers to move from a local to national organizing plan. The first spark came from the National Industrial Recovery Act (NIRA) passed by Congress in June 1933. Section 7(a) of the act endorsed the workers' right to organize unions of their own choosing and to engage in collective bargaining. The NIRA also suspended antitrust laws and allowed trade associations to stabilize their industries through price fixing, if employers agreed to conform to codes of fair competition establishing minimum wages, maximum hours, and child labor prohibitions.

Racked by overproduction and cutthroat competition for more than a decade, representatives of the textile industry jumped at the opportunity to attach federal enforcement powers to their drive to regulate output and prices. Thus, the Cotton Textile Institute (CTI), formed in 1926 by a merger of northern and southern manufacturers' associations, pushed through the nation's first code of fair competition. Given the President's stamp of approval in July 1933, the code called for a minimum wage of twelve dollars in the South and thirteen dollars in the North, for a maximum workweek of forty hours. The stretchout, the foremost grievance of most mill workers, was not covered in the first draft of the code, but at the last moment, and then only at the insistence of South Carolina senator James Byrnes, did the planners address this issue. Written by CTI strategists, the stretchout plank predictably had no teeth.

Both employers and employees greeted the establishment of the textile code with applause. Mill owners broadcast their support in full-page advertisements set against the backdrop of the NIRA's symbol, the Blue Eagle, while mill hands marched in code parades carrying placards that read "Roosevelt is Our Leader" and danced through the night celebrating the promise of a New Deal. Beneath these initial endorsements, however, brewed a battle over the meaning of the code. Manufacturers backed the conservative sections, especially those that lifted antitrust statues and conceded mill owners large regulatory powers over the industry. Millhands highlighted those portions which backed unionization, stipulated minimum wage and maximum hour requirements, and pledged protection against the stretchout. Textile workers, moreover, heard in the rhetoric of the President what might be called a new nationalism. "The industrial recovery act is our industrial declaration of independence," proclaimed a southern weaver. Many millhands thus defined the defense of the New Deal against intractable employers as their patriotic duty and trade union membership as vigilant citizenship. "To refuse to join the union meant a worker was a slacker . . . [who] . . . violates the spirit of the law," avowed the education director of the AFL.

Workers' interpretation of the New Deal breathed life into the nearly moribund United Textile Workers of America (UTW). Founded in 1901, the union languished through the first three decades of the century. In 1932, the UTW's membership lists barely topped 20,000; this was out of 750,000 textile workers nationwide. Not even a handful of locals operated in the South, the regional leader in yarn and cloth production. After the adoption of the code, however, the union experienced meteoric growth; by May 1934, the UTW boasted a following of 300,000 for North and South. This phenomenal spurt took place without a coordinated unionization drive. Averring that the President wanted them to join the union, mill workers flocked into the UTW; they organized themselves for all practical purposes from the bottom up.

A brief recovery of textile industry profits abetted the UTW revival. The adoption of the code on August 1, 1933, combined with the impending imposition of a steep federal cotton processing tax, dragged the industry out of its depression lows. As an indicator, between the spring and summer of 1933, manufacturers hired 100,000 new employees.

The recovery proved short-lived. By fall, the scourge of overproduction again gripped the industry, triggering a familiar litany of events: cutthroat competition, vicious price cutting, the introduction of faster machines, and warehouses stuffed with unsold goods. In response, mill owners chiseled at the code. Workers in turn flooded

the Bruere Board—the textile code's titular arbitration authority—with letters. Scrawled often on course paper, these letters chronicle workers' grievances and reveal that they saw themselves as citizens whose voices ought to be heard and heeded. Millhands complained that employers violated the code by slashing skilled workers' wages, discriminating against unionists, and "stretching out of the stretch-out." "They doubled up on him so much that the work began to make him nervous and he began to loose weight," wrote Mrs. Tate of Raleigh, North Carolina, of her husband. When Jessie Beck of South Carolina became ill and could not keep up the increased workloads, she was fired. "We don't hardly have bread to eat," she informed a New Deal official. Beck closed her letter with a demand for government intervention so that she "could work and help make bread for my babies."

These letters had little impact. Between August 8, 1933, and August 8, 1934, the Bruere Board received almost 4,000 complaints, yet it conducted less than 100 investigations. The board's handling of even this miniscule number of inquiries was incredible. Usually it forwarded a grievance to the CTI, a representative of which contacted the complainant's employer. When the mill manager denied wrongdoing, the case was closed. In fact, the board resolved only a single dispute in a worker's favor.

As the Bruere Board's lackluster response to workers' complaints suggests employers had a larger voice in the administration of the code than employees. This trend continued through the summer of 1934. With the industry still plagued by overproduction, CTI representatives cajoled NRA officials into implementing a 25 percent reduction in production hours and a corresponding drop in pay. Frustrated by the board's pro-management stance and ready to flex its newly bulging organizational muscles, the UTW threatened a general strike if the order went into effect. But the union backed down and allowed the wage cut to go through, in exchange for a vague promise of union representation on the Bruere Board.

Many textile workers were furious at the UTW's surrender. On July 16, 1934, northern Alabama unionists took matters into their hands as forty UTW locals voted to strike, and within days, 23,000 workers had walked off the job. Many North Carolina workers wanted to join the strike but changed their minds after UTW leaders warned against such an action. On August 16, rejecting this cautious course, 2,000 mill operatives shut down a handful of Columbus, Georgia, plants.

Sprinting to catch up with the rank and file, UTW officials called a special convention in New York City on August 14. Southern militants swept the meeting. Fifty times they called for a general strike. An Alabama unionist, his head wrapped in bandages, endorsed one of these motions: "I have been wounded in the head and shot in the leg but I am ready to die for the union and I call upon you to do the same." With a mere ten dissenting votes, UTW representatives heeded his call, and the delegates vowed to support a general strike to begin on September 1, 1934. While the UTW copied Alabama strikers' list of demands for a twelve dollar minimum wage for a thirty-hour workweek, the abolition of the stretchout, and union recognition, most millhands saw the threatened showdown more starkly as a last ditch effort to make the owners and the government "live up to the code." Over the next two weeks, union officials sought a compromise, but the manufacturers rejected their overtures and President Roosevelt, who UTW vice-president Francis Gorman called the "only person in God's green world who can stop a general strike," remained aloof.

Textile workers answered the general strike call in numbers that startled owners, New Deal officials, and even UTW leaders. As strike director, Gorman coordinated millhands' activities across the country, and through his skillful use of the radio, bol-

stered workers' solidarity. Militant strikers, organized into "flying squadrons," fueled the strike's local fires. "Moving with the speed and force of a mechanized army, pickets in trucks and automobiles scurried about the countryside," wrote a reporter describing a Shelby, North Carolina, squadron, ". . . visiting mill towns and villages and compelling the closing of the plants." Flying squadrons forced plants to close "so rapidly that tabulators almost lost count." As a result, the strike spread rapidly throughout the nation. Newspapers estimated the strikers' ranks at 200,000 on September 4, 325,000 the next day, and 400,000 by the end of the first week.

The specter of the flying squadrons made northern and southern manufacturers who had long and violent histories of opposition to trade unionism, even more intransigent than usual. Mill owners petitioned public authorities to evict strikers, cut off public relief, issue injunctions against picketing, and above all, to have governors move troops into strike zones. Overnight, mills were transformed into armed fortresses patrolled by the state militiamen, National Guardsmen, and manufacturers' private armies of deputized loyal hands. These troops positioned machine gun nests above many mills and paraded around factories armed with rifles, picker sticks, and tear gas cannisters. One employer even rented an airplane to guard his factory. In Georgia, Governor Eugene Talmadge declared martial law and interned members of flying squadrons in a barbed-wire enclosed camp.

From the outset, confrontation and violence flared. Picket-line fistfights and shouting matches were commonplace. With the massing of force by the owners and the state, tensions escalated. On September 6, a striker and a special deputy were killed in Triton, Georgia, and in Augusta, a police officer shot three pickets, one fatally. The next day, at Honea Path, South Carolina, where the work force was divided about "half and half for and against the union," sheriff's deputies fired into a picket line set up by a flying squadron from a nearby mill town. Seven unionists were killed and a score wounded in the attack. On September 10, riots broke out across New England and nine days later, troops killed one striker and wounded several others in Saylesville, Rhode Island.

Despite the repression, the strikers' ranks did not crack easily. Indeed, throughout the second week, the strike held steady and even gained some support. A New England unionist captured the spirit of many millhands: "Don't think of yourself as a New Bedford worker—your fight is the fight of all textile workers." By the opening of the third week, however, the tide began to turn against the union, especially in the South. Employers there found replacement workers among the region's depression-beaten and impoverished rural citizens. Moreover, the UTW's inability to pay adequate strike relief took its toll on unionists and their families. By September 17, southern employers had surveyed the strike landscape and deemed themselves ready for a counteroffensive. Meeting in advance, they planned a "gigantic effort . . . to break through the strike lines and start the movement back to the mills." Two days later, an army of 25,000 militiamen and deputies assembled and pried open several southern mills. On September 21, Gorman declared that "force and hunger" were driving mill hands across picket lines.

On September 20, a mediation board chaired by former New Hampshire governor John G. Winant, appointed fifteen days earlier by the President, issued a report. The committee suggested that the Bruere Board be replaced by a new textile labor relations board staffed by "neutral" members, that the Federal Trades Commission study the capacity of the industry to raise wages, and that an ad hoc commission investigate the stretchout. The report offered no firm gains to either textile workers or their union. Nonetheless, the President asked the UTW to end the strike on the basis of the Winant Board's recommendations. On September 22, with the strike crumbling along both northern and southern fronts, Gorman bowed to Roosevelt's request and ordered UTW members back to work, telling them that they had scored an "overwhelming victory." Thus ended what may have been the largest single strike in American history.

Most millhands knew that they had won something less than a definite triumph. Despite the President's appeal to textile firms to rehire strikers without discrimination, on October 23, the UTW reported that 339 mills refused to do so, leaving thousands unemployed and with nothing to look forward to but "snow without clothes and Xmas without a penny." [Bryant Simon]

FURTHER READING

Allen, James E. "Eugene Talmadge and the Great Textile Strike in Georgia, September 1934." In *Essays in Southern Labor History: Selected Papers, Southern Labor History Conference, 1976.* Gary Fink and Merl E. Reed, eds. Westport, CT: Greenwood Press, 1977.

Bernstein, Irving. *Turbulent Years: A History of the American Worker, 1933–1941.* Boston, MA: Houghton Mifflin, 1970.

Hall, Jacquelyn Dowd, James Leloudis, Robert Korstad, Mary Murphy, Lu Ann Jones, and Christopher B. Day. *Like A Family: The Making of a Southern Cotton Mill Worker.* Chapel Hill, NC: The University of North Carolina Press, 1987.

Hodges, James A. *New Deal Labor Policy and the Southern Cotton Textile Industry, 1933–1941.* Knoxville, TN: University of Tennessee Press, 1986.

Irons, Janet C. *Testing the New Deal: The General Textile Strike of 1934.* Ph.D. dissertation, Duke University, 1988.

o   o   o

TOLEDO, OHIO, AUTO-LITE STRIKE OF 1934. Toledo, on the northwestern border of Ohio not far from Detroit, had become a major center of the automotive parts industry by the 1920s. In addition to its own vehicle manufacturer, Willys-Overland, the city boasted of Electric Auto-Lite, the largest independent supplier of auto parts, and its subsidiaries, Bingham

Stamping and Tool and Logan Gear, as well as the Spicer Manufacturing Company. When the Great Depression struck, Toledo suffered severe unemployment. As in many other industrial towns, the economic dislocation brought on political reform. In Toledo, as in the nation as a whole, this resulted in the election of Democrats in 1932.

For an independent producer such as Auto-Lite, survival depended on its ability to produce parts cheaper than the auto companies could make them. Thus, the downward pressure on wages that was felt everywhere during the Depression had an especially hard impact in Toledo. The company's determination to keep costs low extended to its determination to keep unions out. But the surge of union sentiment that followed the passage of the National Industrial Recovery Act in 1933 did not bypass Toledo. In August of 1933, the American Federation of Labor (AFL) issued a federal charter to workers at the four major Toledo auto parts plants. When the union presented demands for a 10 percent wage increase, a seniority system, and union recognition, the companies rejected them out of hand.

The strike began on February 23, 1934. With the help of a federal mediator, the workers accepted a 5 percent wage increase and a promise exacted from the company to set up machinery for negotiations on the other issues. But Auto-Lite went back on the agreement, refusing to negotiate with the local union. On April 12, the union called the workers out a second time. This time the response was not nearly so good, and the companies, sensing the union's weakness, kept the plants open and began to hire strikebreakers.

With its existence threatened, the union reached out for allies in the community. The American Workers Party (AWP) and the Lucas County Unemployed League offered assistance. The AWP was led by A. J. Muste, a Dutch-born minister who had become famous in labor circles by leading the Lawrence, Massachusetts, textile strike in 1919. Muste's AWP was a small Marxist party that was committed to working with unions. Another aspect of AWP's activities was the organization of the unemployed as a pressure group for government relief and as a means of keeping the jobless from taking the jobs of union men on strike.

The AWP could boast of talented and experienced leadership. This became apparent soon in Toledo when the party mobilized mass picketing of plant gates by the unemployed. When the companies secured an injunction limiting picketing, Louis Budenz, who was directing the strike for the AWP, ordered his followers to defy the order. The action resulted in the arrest of picketers on a number of occasions, but the tactic kept the unemployed league's members and the strikers mobilized and involved in the conflict.

In May, the companies hired and armed company guards to protect the strikebreakers. This escalation matched the increasing militancy of the strikers and their supporters as the daily crowds at the plant gates continued to grow. The tension alarmed the Lucas County sheriff who feared that sympathy for the strike was so widespread on the city police force that it would be unable to protect company property. He then took two related actions. He deputized special police and arranged for Auto-Lite to pay for them, and he jailed Budenz and four other pickets. The harsh actions of the special deputies and the arrests of their leaders agitated the crowd of 10,000 outside of Auto-Lite and set off what came to be called the "battle of Toledo."

The fighting on Wednesday, May 23, continued from afternoon until midnight. Fifteen hundred strikebreakers were effectively imprisoned inside the factory. Deputies fired tear gas canisters from the plant roof. The crowd replied with stones and bricks. On several occasions strikers broke into the building and were driven off in bitter fighting. While there were no deaths, the battle resulted in a number of serious injuries on both sides.

News of the events reached Columbus, the state capital, where the Ohio adjutant general ordered the National Guard to Toledo. The troops arrived on Thursday and dispersed the crowds. The trapped strikebreakers were freed and taken to their homes. The disorders of the previous day and the appearance of the heavily armed guard had sobered the combatants but only temporarily. That same afternoon, the anti-company crowds began to form again. This time the National Guardsmen became the focus of their anger. When the troops fired tear gas, the crowd surged forward, herding the soldiers toward the Auto-Lite factory gates. The guardsmen regrouped and carried out a bayonet charge. As the battle surged back and forth, the embattled guardsmen finally resorted to a volley into the crowd. Two were killed and fifteen wounded.

The killings only agitated the crowds more. In the evening of the May 24, they charged the factory once again. Once again, the guardsmen fired, wounding two. The adjutant general ordered the company to suspend work. The closing of the factory calmed the crowds, and subsequent outbreaks, while serious, did not reach the magnitude of the "battle of Toledo." The parties turned their attention to some kind of a mediated settlement assisted by Charles P. Taft, son of a former president, and a leading citizen of Ohio. Taft, who was sent by the Labor Department, pursued a strategy aimed at excluding the AWP from the negotiations. Only the AFL's federal local would be party to the talks. Taft's arrival coincided with a softening of the company's position. On Monday, June 4, with the help of Taft's assistant, Ralph A. Lind of the Cleveland Labor Board, Auto-Lite and the local union reached an agreement. The union won a five-cent general increase, a thirty-fivve-cent minimum wage, recognition of the union, voluntary arbitration of disputes arising during the life of the contract, and a priority system for reemployment that gave strikers priority second only to those company employees who had worked during the strike. Strikebreakers came last. In effect, this meant that all the strikers went back to work. The agreement excluded the American Workers Party. [Ronald L. Filippelli]

FURTHER READING

Bernstein, Irving. *A History of the American Worker, 1933–1941: The Turbulent Years.* Boston, MA: Houghton Mifflin, 1970.

Fine, Sidney. *The Automobile Under the Blue Eagle.* Ann Arbor, MI: University of Michigan Press, 1963.

o   o   o

TOMPKINS SQUARE RIOT OF 1874. The origins of the Tompkins Square Riot lie with the working-class movement for unemployed relief and public works which sprang up in New York City and other industrial towns in the United States during the early years of the 1873 depression. The riot itself was essentially the brutal dispersal of a public demonstration of 7,000 working-class New Yorkers by the New York City police. The preparations for the demonstration, the brutality of the police response, and the public sanction of it by most of the press and public authorities highlight the activities and the fear of working-class radicals during the depression of the mid-1870s.

The onset of the depression in mid-1873 hit New York's immigrant working class with high unemployment and crushing poverty. But the economic crisis also revitalized Socialist and Communist labor in the city, namely the badly split members of the First International. Concentrated in the city's Tenth Ward, members of the International and trade union activists organized numerous meetings of the unemployed beginning in November of 1873. Just like similar movements in cities such as Chicago, Cincinnati, and Philadelphia, the meetings usually passed resolutions asking for public relief, especially for employment of workers in public works projects for a minimum of eight hours a day at prevailing wages. In New York City, a regular network of ward organizations of the unemployed was also built, mostly by members of the International. Centered around the Tenth Ward but active in many working-class neighborhoods around the city, these groups numbered twenty-three by December of 1873 and claimed to have 10,000 followers organized on a neighborhood basis. The appeal of the organization seems to have been particularly strong among the German immigrant working class.

With response for the city authorities negative and evasive, the unemployed organizations called for a meeting on December 11, 1873, to air their grievances once more, pass a resolution, and send a delegation to City Hall. This meeting, the largest to date, was attended by more than 4,000 people and numerous resolutions were passed, among them some urging the unemployed to send their outstanding bills to the city treasurer. A Committee of Safety (whose name reminded New Yorkers of similarly named groups during the French Revolution, and more recently the Paris Commune) was formed, to further press for the demands of the unemployed. The Committee of Safety included workers from a variety of groups, freethinkers, trade unionists, communards, and members of the First International.

While the movement had been largely ignored up to then, by the middle-class press and the municipal authorities, the formation of the Committee of Safety and the December 11 meeting aroused a more aggressive negative response in many newspapers. Not only was there a general hostility to organized municipal relief among many politicians, the spectre of Socialist agitators with communard sympathies taking over in their city became increasingly threatening.

During the second half of December, the Committee of Safety and its ward-based affiliates, continued to hold numerous neighborhood meetings and announced a large-scale parade for January 13 to bring its demands directly to City Hall. At that point a rival organization sprang up, headed by a bricklayer named Patrick Dunn, who claimed to have thousands of followers behind a similar, though not Socialist-dominated movement. Dunn, whose uncertain allegiances and inflammatory rhetoric, incensed the members of the Committee of Safety, succeeded in leading a march to City Hall on January 5, 1874, without any concrete results however. Egged on by Dunn's effort to steal the show, the committee staged a mass rally on January 8, which saw thousands of workers march through the Lower East Side, demanding work and decent wages, with the carpenter P. J. McGuire, later a co-founder of the American Federation of Labor, giving speeches expressing the workers discontent and impatience.

Even though this parade was limited to the working-class districts of the Lower East Side, public authorities grew apprehensive over the prospect of an even larger demonstration on January 13 that was to lead thousands outside the confines of the Lower East Side to City Hall. Bowing to pressure from the Board of Police, which needed to issue a permit for the rally, the Committee of Safety changed the parade route, to end in a final rally at Union Square, at the edge of the Lower East Side. The committee also seemed anxious to appear a representative of honest and peaceful workingmen; it strove to keep unorganized outsiders out of the planned demonstration and invited New York's mayor to address the demonstrators at the end of the parade, which he initially agreed to do.

Tensions did not abate however, and at the last minute, on the night before the planned demonstration, the committee of Safety cancelled the entire parade and proceeded to prepare only for a rally on Tomkins Square. The committee did not succeed, however, in informing the participating organizations of this change, and they continued to anticipate a large-scale parade. At the same time, the Police Board and the Parks Commission met and cancelled the permit for the planned meeting entirely. They too failed to inform most of the participants of their actions.

Amidst this confusion, some 7,000 working-class men and women assembled on the frigid morning of January 13 on Tompkins Square in what looked to observers like a peaceful protest demonstration. After an hour, however, a police contingent of 1,600 men (almost two-thirds of the entire NYC police force) appeared on the scene, and its commander, Police Commissioner Abraham Duryea, ordered the demonstrators to disperse immediately. Without waiting for compliance, the police began an orgy of indiscriminate beating that lasted for a number of hours. Protesters and onlookers were pursued into the side streets of the Lower East Side. Even onlookers along the planned parade route were beaten by the police, some of whom were on horseback. A few of the demonstrators fought back with fists, sticks, or the tools of their trade. But whether they had weapons or were just marching with a red flag, like the well-known German-American Anarchist Justus Schwab, forty-six protesters, most of them German immigrants, were arrested and brought to the Fifth Precinct stationhouse where an angry crowd of workers gathered.

In the midst of this violence, the political issues that underlay the protest were almost completely lost. The mayor, with whom a delegation of workers met on January 14, joined a chorus of other public officials and the majority of the press which condemned the protesters for being radicals and Communists and approved of the police action as necessary. In fact, almost all newspapers and public spokesmen came forth to support the police actions. The only exceptions were the *Irish World*, the *New York Graphic,* and the *New York Sun* under its editor John Swinton. Swinton also gave the keynote address at a large protest meeting of workers which was held on January 20, and which demanded a public inquiry into the police actions. The inquiry was never held; instead, two of the arrested protesters were sentenced to up to six months in prison.

With public opinion in support of the police action, and the continuing hostility of public officials, the unemployed movement did not survive in the aftermath of the Tompkins Square Riot. Nevertheless, despite the increasing unemployment and poverty, and the scant resources of working-class organizations, the Socialist labor movement in New York City, reorganized toward the spring of 1874, this time eventually forming the New York City–based Social Democratic Workingmen's Party. [Dorothee Schneider]

FURTHER READING

Bernstein, Samuel. *The First International in America.* New York: Kelley, 1962.

Gutman, Herbert. "The Failure of the Movement by the Unemployed for Public Works." *Political Science Quarterly*, Vol. 80 (June 1965), pp. 254–276.

———. "The Tompkins Square 'Riot' of January 13, 1874: A Re-examination of Its Causes and Its Aftermath." *Labor History*, Vol. 6 (Winter, 1965), pp. 44–70.

o   o   o

TRANS WORLD AIRLINES FLIGHT ATTENDANTS' STRIKE OF 1986. The 1986 strike of the Independent Federation of Flight Attendants (IFFA) against Trans World Airlines (TWA) occurred for reasons specific to the mid-1980s airline industry. Even though the final bargaining impasse was, on the surface, a conventional disagreement about pay and work rules, that particular confrontation came about for a variety of reasons. They included the formation of an independent union by the flight attendants, the Airline Deregulation Act of 1978 and the resulting entry of new low-fare competitors, the takeover and merger movement in the airline industry, and an innovative attempt by TWA unions to influence the outcome of a takeover campaign.

Until the late 1960s, most airlines dismissed flight attendants when they married or reached an age ceiling of about thirty, so average seniority was under two years. As a result, flight attendants unions, too weak for independence, survived as subdivisions subordinated to the unions of other occupations, such as the pilots or transport workers. When marriage and age restrictions were finally dropped in the late 1960s, growing numbers of flight attendants with increasing seniority responded to women's movement themes. Several flight attendant groups broke away from parent unions to declare independent status, unaffiliated either with the AFL-CIO, other airline unions, or other flight attendant unions. Attendants at TWA formed the Independent Federation of Flight Attendants (IFFA) in March of 1977.

The deregulation of the airline industry in 1978 thrust TWA, IFFA, and the industry's other airlines and unions into an unfamiliar industrial relations environment. From 1938 to 1978, existing interstate airlines could raise or lower fares and add or drop routes only if they were given government approval. In exchange, they were protected from undue competition on profitable routes, from competition by new entrants to the industry, and they were, for all practical purposes, subsidized by the government. Airline managements that negotiated generous collective bargaining agreements were usually granted fare or rate adjustments by federal regulators. Although flight attendants remained the lowest paid occupation in the industry and negotiators from their parent unions, be they pilots or transport workers, seldom bargained for the issues that attendants themselves considered important, union representatives found the companies relatively amenable to negotiated improvements in a regulated environment.

Deregulation changed all that. It brought a virtual shakedown of the industry: new low-cost airlines entered and the fare wars, bankruptcies, mergers, and takeovers that regulation's advocates had envisioned became a reality. New entrants such as Texas Air and People Express challenged other managements to cut fares and labor costs. The 1982 declaration of bankruptcy and reemergence of Continental Airlines presented an additional alarming model of labor cost reduction. The unions, including the newly independent flight attendant groups like IFFA, were forced by the new fiercely competitive managements into an era of concession bargaining.

In May 1985, a rumor spread in the financial community that Carl Icahn, the "corporate raider," was preparing for a takeover of Trans World Airlines. Management, fearing that he would dismantle the airline, looked to Texas Air and its chairman Frank Lorenzo as an alternative buyer. Lorenzo had an antilabor reputation among airline unions. The three main unions, the Air Line Pilots Association (ALPA), the International Association of Machinists (IAM), and IFFA were alarmed. ALPA considered the possibility of an employee buyout, and the unions hired consultants to help them explore other options.

ALPA in particular decided that despite management's reluctance, Icahn was better for labor than Lorenzo, and it agreed to offer Icahn, but not Lorenzo, substantial pay cuts if he would proceed with his takeover bid. IAM and IFFA were less sure that Icahn was their saviour. Victoria Frankovich, IFFA president, told the press, "We don't want to run from a deal with Lorenzo if that means running from the frying pan into the fire . . . . these guys are all sharks and are trying to get a piece of our hides."

By late summer 1985, the pilots had agreed to pay cuts and work rule changes calculated to save about 30 percent in labor costs, the IAM to a 15 percent cut, and TWA management had decided to reject Lorenzo's bid and accede to Icahn's takeover. According to the *Wall Street Journal*, "Investment bankers say this may be the first takeover fight in which a major stock holder and a company's unions have banded together to defeat a merger favored by management." Another source speculated that this "may give rise to a new form of leverage for unions . . . . by forging an alliance early."

IFFA alone of the major unions had not come to agreement with Icahn. He insisted that IFFA take as great a percentage cut as the pilots, whose incomes were usually three or four times those of attendants. His insistence, attendants charged, was due to his arguably sexist belief that the attendants, who were overwhelmingly women, were not breadwinners. If TWA attendants' pay was higher than attendant pay on other airlines, as Icahn claimed, it was because a large proportion of TWA attendants had high seniority.

Personal animosity between Icahn and Frankovich, president of IFFA, did not make negotiations easier, and no agreement had been reached by March 1986. Their contract having been amendable since July of 1984 (airline negotiations can go on for, as in this case, years after the amendable date) and having waited out all the notification and cooling off periods required by the Railway Labor Act, IFFA struck TWA on March 7, 1986.

TWA's response was to quickly train reservation clerks and new hires as replacements for attendants, cut fares, and encourage strikers, especially those with little seniority, to take over the jobs that had previously gone only to attendants with considerable seniority. Pilots did not honor the IFFA's picket lines. IAM members at some locations did, but a court injunction ruled that their contract prohibited these actions.

By the end of March, the company claimed to be operating 100 percent of its normal schedule. After ten weeks, 1,500 union members had crossed the line to take jobs, and most other flight attendant jobs were filled by new trainees. The company had promised permanent jobs to new trainees and crossovers. Five thousand union members, many with substantial company seniority, had lost their jobs.

In mid-May, the IFFA offered an unconditional return to work. Icahn insisted that he could take back strikers only as jobs opened because of his commitment to new hires and crossovers. In fact, after the union's capitulation, the airline brought a last group of 463 trainees onto the job. All but about 500 of the strikers have now been called back to their jobs, by seniority, but they and the permanent replacements have been working under company-determined wages and work rules, since those matters were under discussion in the failed bargaining that led to the strike.

The strike may have ended with the union offer to return, but the hostilities have continued through numerous court battles, appeals, and three Supreme Court decisions. The Supreme Court confirmed a lower court's ruling that the 463 trainees TWA moved into jobs after the end of the strike did not have a right to their jobs and should be replaced by union members. In March 1988, the Court ruled that replacement workers must pay union dues, since the union security clause was not raised as a bargaining topic during the negotiations leading to the strike. Since Railway Labor Act contracts are amendable rather than fixed term, those parts of the contract not in dispute during negotiations, even if a contract is not agreed to, are considered still in effect. In February 1989, the Court overturned a lower court's ruling that the still-enforcable seniority provisions of the contract required the airline to replace junior union members who had taken jobs during the strike (crossovers) with more senior members who had continued to the strike's end. Several other matters are still in litigation at the time of this writing. The courts will have to decide if they should consider subjects one by one to determine which parts of the contract are still in effect. A private suit charges that by refusing to give striking attendants letters testifying to their employment experience so they could be given preference by other airlines under the deregulation act of 1978, TWA is liable to damages. The union is still charging TWA with bad-faith bargaining, asserting that Icahn has a sexist attitude about the occupation which has made him less open to good-faith bargaining with IFFA than with IAM or ALPA.

When Icahn took over TWA, he was perceived by many as labor's friend. Why did his first round of negotiations result in such a bitter strike, and why was IFFA the adversary? The pilots, of all the unions, were most anxious to avoid Lorenzo because of his harsh treatment of the pilots when he took over Continental. They were willing to support Icahn even if it meant pressuring the other unions. The IAM had enough bargaining power to resist that pressure. The IFFA did not, without a strike. The flight attendants were sensitive to slights to women and the occupation because of the union's experiences in the 1970s and 1980s, and they were now independent enough to make their own decisions. Because IFFA was no longer subordinate to a parent union, it could not be forced into an agreement it considered unfair. The IFFA's experience in this strike taught all the airline unions that in the new environment of deregulation, one union cannot strike without the active support of the others. [Frieda S. Rozen]

FURTHER READING

Cappelli, Peter. "Airlines." In *Collective Bargaining in American Industry*. David B. Lipsky and Clifford B. Donn, eds. Lexington, KY: Lexington Books, 1987, pp. 135–186.

Kaye, Tony, and Miriam Rozen. "Flight Attendants v. TWA: Icahn's Words Come Back to Haunt Him." *American Lawyer* (March, 1988), p. 21.

Loomis, Carol J. "The Comeuppance of Carl Icahn," *Fortune Magazine* (February 17, 1986), p. 19.

McKelvey, Jean T., ed. *Cleared for Takeoff: Airline Labor Relations Since Deregulation*. Ithaca, NY: Cornell ILR Press, 1988.

o   o   o

TRIANGLE FIRE OF 1911. On March 25, 1911, one of the worst occupational disasters in American history occurred. At 4:30 that Saturday afternoon, a fire started on the eighth floor of the Asch Building on the corner of Washington Place and Green Street in New York's Greenwich Village. In approximately fourteen minutes it claimed 146 lives.

The story of the Triangle Fire is much more than the story of one catastrophe. It also reflects the larger reality of the horrible working conditions then endemic in the clothing industry. The Triangle Fire became a national scandal because of the terrible toll it took in human lives. But workers were maimed or killed regularly in New York's garment industry.

Mass-produced clothing did not become a major industry until after the Civil War. The first clothes to be produced for a mass market were men's work clothes, followed by men's suits and coats. It was not until the last decade of the nineteenth century that women's ready-to-wear clothing acquired a mass market. By World War I it was the single largest industry in New York.

Around the turn of the century, Charles Dana Gibson designed a shirtwaist (blouse) that swept the fashion conscious world of America. Most women, whether shop girls or society matrons, donned the "Gibson Girl Look." This shirtwaist was generally made of a thin fabric such as lawn or batiste, it had a close fitted, ruffled bodice and leg-of-mutton sleeves. It was the ideal garment for the increasing numbers of women working in the offices and factories of America.

A shirtwaist factory was relatively easy to start. It required only the rental of a few sewing machines, some space—often crowded, dark, and dank—and the employment of several workers to assemble, press, and trim the garments. This was true of the entire clothing industry—men's and women's clothes, children's clothes, and white goods. The clothing industry had two kinds of shops—inside shops, where garments were designed and cut, and outside contractors' shops, where many manufacturers sent their cut goods to be assembled, pressed, and finished. It was in the latter that contractors most exploited and abused workers desperate for their jobs. Often, contractors produced their goods in tenement flats, where the workers included both the elderly and children as young as four or five. They worked from dawn to the early hours of the following morning. To such shops, inside shop workers sometimes brought home piecework after having already worked a ten- or twelve-hour day.

The shirtwaist trade grew so quickly that several successful entrepreneurs were able to establish large factories where garments were produced in their entirety in an inside shop. The most successful of these was the Triangle Shirtwaist Company, located on the eighth, ninth, and tenth floors of the Asch Building in lower Manhattan. The structure had been built in 1901, and was lauded as a state-of-the-art modern, healthy, and safe factory building.

The owners of Triangle, Isaac Harris and Max Blanck, were known among workers for their harsh treatment of employees. More than a year before the fire, an incident at Triangle was the precipitating event of the famous **"Uprising of the 20,000" of 1909**. But ironically, Triangle never accepted the shirtwaist makers union, Local 25 of the International Ladies' Garment Workers' Union (ILGWU), which grew out of that strike. However, because they were one of the only shops in the industry that generally had enough work to provide employment twelve months a year, in an industry where four to six months of unemployment was routine, they had no problem finding employees.

Most of the workers at Triangle were young women, between fifteen and twenty-five years old, mainly immigrants from southern or eastern Europe. One Italian family felt fortunate in having three members employed there, a mother and two teenage daughters. None survived the fire.

Blank and Harris ran an inside shop but managed to continue the worst abuses of the contracting system. They simply hired contractors to work inside the Triangle factory. The contractors were paid a lump sum and were in charge of hiring operators who were coerced into competing with each other through the speedup system, or they induced new immigrants to work as "trainees" for two to six weeks for no wages. The contractor was paid a single sum, and in turn had to pay his operatives. Obviously, the less he was able to pay his operators, the higher was his profit.

Discipline was strict; talking, singing, and gazing out of the window were not acceptable. Among the most abusive practice was the need for permission to go to the bathroom. The workroom was locked, and workers were checked before and after going to the bathroom and sometimes before leaving for the night to insure that no woman had hidden a piece of lace or a button in her hair.

The day of the fire was a Saturday. The office staff was short of personnel, including a competent telephone operator. At 4:30 in the afternoon, when union shops had been closed for three hours, someone on the eighth floor noticed smoke. The fire extinguisher on the wall was found to be unconnected to any water source, and workers on the eighth and ninth floors were locked in the workroom. Some found their way to a staircase and down to safety, others cleared the boxes away from the fire escape window and exited to safety that way. Meanwhile, a telephone call to the tenth floor alerted management to the fire. The telephone operator became hysterical and caused a panic among the rest of the staff. Amidst the ensuing chaos, the office employees and the owners were led to safety on the roof. No one alerted the ninth floor personnel.

The building next to the Asch Building

was owned in 1911, as it is today, by New York University (NYU). That afternoon a law class was in session. One of the students noticed the smoke from the factory and led a rescue party which proceeded to rescue anyone who made it to the roof of the Asch Building. This was not simple, because the NYU building was about twelve feet higher than the Asch Building.

The fire behaved in an unusual way. Instead of moving straight up to the ninth floor, it skipped a floor and went from eight to ten. By the time anyone on nine knew what was happening, they were sandwiched between two floors of flames. It was there that the greatest calamity struck.

Some workers became immobilized by fear—several froze at their machines. Fire inspectors later that afternoon described macabre scenes of burned bodies still at their machines. Others ran to exit doors where they died while clawing at the unyielding lock. Finally, someone remembered the fire escape and cleared a pathway to this exit. What they did not know was that by now the metal shutter on the eighth floor was so hot that it precluded further descent. Frantic women piled onto this last hope of survival, only to die when it collapsed into the courtyard below.

One scene that might have shocked the inhabitants of *Dante's Inferno* was the sight of women standing on the sills of windows, some throwing their pathetic pay envelopes to the wind before jumping nine stories to their death. Many jumped holding hands with one or two friends or co-workers—or perhaps even a sister. Efforts on the street to break the falls with blankets or firemen's nets proved futile.

The fire blazed only fifteen minutes— but that was long enough to cause 146 deaths. Frantic families and neighbors came running from the surrounding neighborhoods where most of the workers lived, hoping against hope to not find their loved ones among the wretched lines of corpses on the street.

The city morgue had neither the capacity nor the coffins to deal with the disaster. A makeshift morgue was set up on East 23rd Street, where grief stricken parents, husbands or children came to claim their own. Seven were never identified—they were too badly burned.

The fire galvanized the city, the nation, even distant corners of the world, particularly the victims' hometowns and provinces. A fund for survivors or orphaned children was rapidly organized and managed by the Red Cross and New York's organized labor community. Contributions came from diverse sources—in nickels and dimes from school children in Texas and in the form of a $5,000 check from Andrew Carnegie. Charity took the form of scholarships, or passage across the ocean to family, or the purchase of a small shop to keep a surviving remnant of a family together. Initially it was difficult to identify recipients who were too grief stricken to think of the future or too proud to accept handouts.

A mass funeral plan was rejected by the city, fearful of a riot, but a memorial march through a grey, rain-drenched city could not be stopped. A month later, a fundraising meeting at the Metropolitan Opera House was attended by every noted politician, labor leader, cleric, and civic leader in the city. After many speeches the audience was addressed by tiny Rose Schneiderman of the Women's Trade Union League:

I would be a traitor to those poor burned bodies if I were to talk good fellowship. We have tried you good people of the public and we have found you wanting.... The old inquisition had its rack and its thumb screw and its instruments of torture with iron teeth. We know what these things are today: the iron teeth are our necessities, the thumb screws are the high-powered and swift machinery to close to which we must work, and the rack is here in the firetrap structures that will destroy us the minute they catch fire.... We have tried you citizens! We are trying you now and you have a couple of dollars for the sorrowing mothers... by the way of a charity gift. But every time the workers come out in the only way they know how to protest against conditions which are unbearable, the strong hand of the law is allowed to press down heavily upon us . . . . I can't talk fellowship to you who are gathered here. Too much blood has been spilled. I know from experience it is up to the working people to save themselves and the only way is through a strong working class movement.

In the aftermath of the fire, New York State enacted the most stringent fire safety code in the nation—but its enforcement was done mostly by union members and the Joint Board of Sanitary Control—a creation of the negotiations which had ended the 1909 strike. Years after the Triangle tragedy, firetraps, and dark and unhealthy sweatshops continued to exist, due to the refusal of government to commit funds to police industrial safety hazards.

Blanck and Harris opened a new factory less than a week after the fire. Their trial ended when the judge, known for his hatred of labor all but directed the jury to bring in a verdict of not guilty. Blanck, for the rest of his life, took great pleasure in demonstrating a new lock which would not trap workers in the event of fire. The idea of ending the practice of locking workers into the shop apparently never occurred to him, or to many others in his position. Meanwhile, the owners of Triangle collected insurance payments for the material losses they incurred in the fire. Each year, on the fire's anniversary, a memorial ceremony at the sight of the Triangle Fire is hosted by one local of the ILGWU and the New York City fire department. [Harriet Davis-Kram]

FURTHER READING

Foner, Philip S. *Women and the American Labor Movement.* Vol. 1. New York: Free Press, 1979.

Schneiderman, Rose. *All For One.* New York: Paul S. Ericksson, 1967, pp. 97–103.

Stein, Leon. *The Triangle Fire.* New York: Carroll and Graff, 1962.

o   o   o

TROY, NEW YORK, COLLAR LAUNDRESSES' STRIKES OF 1869 AND 1886. These labor conflicts raise a question that has been central to analyses of women's labor activism: why did a smaller proportion of women than men form sustained organizations? Past answers focused on obstacles to women's organization related to links between women's work and family life. Highlighting stark contrasts between women and men drawn from conventional wisdom, this perspective viewed women as passive, unskilled, temporary workers who were more committed to family roles than unions. While this perspective sheds light on part of the picture, it is limited because it masks variations among women, overemphasizes the conservative influence of family roles on women's lives, and neglects ways in which family relationships may encourage women's activism, organization, and consciousness. Shifting the focus away from oppositional contrasts and examining differences among women in a variety of occupations, household economies, and communities reveals a new question: considering the barriers to permanent organization for women, under what conditions did some women form relatively successful unions, develop awareness of shared interests, and ally with male workers?

Troy is a good place to explore these questions because it had a major role in industrialization and the labor movements' efforts to organize nationally. Dominated by two major industries, one employing women and the other men, Troy's industrial structure provided employment for large numbers of the city's working-class population. The iron industry was a major producer of the region's iron products like stoves, bells, and nails. Troy earned its nickname, "Collar City," because the shirt, collar, and cuff industry produced 90 percent of the nation's detachable collars. The industry's nearly 3,000 largely Irish women workers included factory operatives who stitched men's detachable collars, laundresses who washed, starched, and ironed newly manufactured goods to be sold to retailers, and homeworkers. In comparison with other working women, collar women were relatively well organized. Although sewers, ironers, and starchers periodically went on strike, the ironers' union was the most continuous.

Troy's labor activity was characterized by cooperation between women and men workers. In this well-organized labor community, the Iron Molders' Union No. 2 was the collar laundresses' close ally and one of the strongest locals in a major national union, the Iron Molders' International Union. In 1864, molders helped laundresses to organize and in subsequent years continued to offer support. In 1866, during the **Iron Molders' Lockout**, laundresses showed their appreciation (and demonstrated financial solvency) by donating the immense sum of $500 to the molders' strike fund. Similarly, molders provided crucial support to the ironers' spring 1869 strike that followed several successful conflicts in previous years.

Analysis of the laundresses' success challenges conventional wisdom about working women. Laundresses maintained high wages and protected union members during illness and hard times in part because they were not unskilled, temporary workers who were uncommitted to their occupation. Although collar ironing, like other women's work, was defined as unskilled because it was related to household tasks, the ability to perform delicate operations with hot, heavy irons required a combination of physical strength, endurance, and dexterity that like other skills could only be acquired through experience. Laundry proprietors and manufacturers recognized that since skillful ironing required four to six weeks of training, they could not weaken the union simply by replacing union ironers. During the 1869 strike, employers had difficulty maintaining full production because inexperienced workers' skill was not equal to striking ironers' speed and dexterity. Employers admit-

ted that it took "some time to each newcomers the business."

Since Troy's collar industry offered relatively steady, well-paying employment to large numbers of women who needed employment at various stages of their lives, Troy's Irish working-class women were a permanent part of the city's labor force as a group. The significant proportion of Troy's Irish working-class women who were single worked most of their adult lives, and many who left work for marriage returned when they were widowed. Individuals who did not work were likely to know others in their family, neighborhood, or community who were currently employed or would be in the future. Since collar work had relatively high status in the community, those who returned to work probably entered the same occupation. Although collar laundresses' employment patterns differed from men's because their life cycle was different, their work can be more accurately described as interrupted or intermittent rather than temporary and transient.

The 1869 strike highlights the strengths and weaknesses of the laundresses' union and their bargaining position because collar manufacturers combined with laundry proprietors to prevent future wage increases by eliminating the union. In the past, collar workers bargained only with laundry owners who were relatively vulnerable to workers' demands because their small-scale businesses lacked extensive resources with which to weather reduced production during strikes. Collar manufacturers objected to laundresses' demands because the laundry proprietors' position in the business community enabled them to pass on increased costs to the manufacturers. Manufacturers absorbed increases for ironers the previous July and for starchers in March because they depended on laundries' services to prepare products for retailers. By the 1880s, manufacturers incorporated laundries into their factories, but in 1869 they combined with laundry owners.

The strike began at the end of May when laundry owners demanded that collar ironers equalize wages for work on different sized collars within each shop. The result of decreased rates for some work and increased rates for other work was an increase of about one and a half cents per dozen collars. Laundry owners not only declined to pay the increase but also refused to employ union ironers. The approximately 450 union ironers stayed away from their jobs, but collar sewers, washers, and starchers continued to work. Collar manufacturers met publicly on June 1 to plan strategies. They pressured laundry owners into holding out indefinitely by refusing to send new collars and cuffs to any laundry employing union ironers, and they assisted the owners obtain a new work force by helping to recruit and train new hands. They undermined union efforts to weather the strike by preventing the few collar manufacturers in other cities from patronizing the union's cooperative laundry which claimed to provide the same services for 25 percent less. Cooperating with manufacturers, the local press maintained that ironers received extraordinarily high wages, that women influenced by "outside busybodies" deserved to lose their jobs, and that Troy's collar factories were undersold by collar manufacturers in other cities. Troy's press also suppressed an essential fact revealed in New York City's newspapers: some employers offered to rehire striking ironers at slightly higher wages on the condition that they give up the union. Recognizing that the issue was the union's existence, Kate Mullaney, the ironers' president, told the New York City's Workingmen's Assembly on July 2 that their employers "do not care for the money." They were willing to increase wages but insisted that the ironers "must give up" their union.

Concerning an issue central to labor, workers' right to organize, the strike became a *cause célèbre* for New York State's labor movement. In the months of June and July, Troy's labor leaders organized fund-raising meetings, a mass rally in front of the courthouse, and a massive picnic attended by national labor leaders. Generous support from New York City's strong labor movement was a response to the centrality of the ironers' cause to trade union principles. Collar ironers were not only contributing to workers' right to organize but also to strategies that many trade unionists favored over strikes. In June they laid plans for a cooperative laundry, which if successful would transform them from wage earners to small entrepreneurs. In response to the ironers' request for strike contributions, William Jessup, the president of New York State's Workingmen's Assembly, argued that the collar ironers' strike and the New York City Bricklayers' strike for the eight-hour workday were the only two conflicts worthy of contributions that year. Jessup noted that "The Collar Laundry Union does not ask you to contribute to support them in idleness while they are on strike. They desire "to organize" manufactories of their own on the cooperative principle. The object is feasible . . . Let us all contribute with a willing heart and an open hand."

The laundresses' commitment to trade unionism included perceptions of themselves as women who were related to their identification with the working-class community. In early July, Esther Keegan, the ironers' vice-president, reported to the Workingmen's Assembly that they were holding firm. She said "You know what a union is, you know . . . the value of cooperation; we have been out of money six weeks and but two of our members have given in. I fancy but there are few men's organizations that can show such a record, and we are nothing but women." Mullaney and Keegan's remarks to the New York City's Workingwomen's Association, a middle-class organization formed by Susan B. Anthony, emphasized the ironers' perceptions of a division between themselves and middle-class women. Accompanied by Augusta Lewis of the typographers' union, Mullaney observed that she came to request contributions because she "understood that they were an association of working women." But as she looked around them she could tell that "they were not the working women whom she had been accustomed to see. She had to work all day in the shop, and this she did not think, judging from their appearance, that they did." Later Lewis reported that "Although the society comprises many wealthy ladies, they raised $30.00 for the laundresses of Troy. . . . Compared to the Workingwomen's Association, the laundresses' union was a "real workingwomen's association."

Trade union activity on the ironers' behalf continued until the end of July when those who were in financial need began to go back to work alongside newcomers at their former wages. But the union's demise did not mean the end of labor activity. Directed by Mullaney, Keegan, and another strike leader whom employers refused to rehire, the cooperative struggled on until at least 1872. The following winter, Susan B. Anthony, visiting Troy while waiting to change trains, found the three young women at work, dressed in the "simplest calico," in a shop on the upper floor of a large building. In the following decades, collar laundresses and later sewers, sometimes as union members and sometimes without the benefit of organization, continued to demand increases and react to changes in working conditions, including the introduction of machines.

Collar sewers and laundresses organized together in 1886 because of shifts in the relationship of laundresses, sewers, and iron workers to each other as well as to the nation's labor movement. Formed at the peak of the Knights of Labor's (K of L) influence, the Joan of Arc Assembly of ironers and starchers, reflected shifts in the industry and Knights' efforts to organize industrially. These shifts shaped labor activism. Ironers had less expertise and status in the 1880s because of changes in production, but they could depend on less-skilled starchers in labor struggles because they had more in common with workers. Laundresses who worked in departments of collar factories faced more powerful employers, but they shared more experiences with collar sewers, who by the 1880s were largely Irish. Collar sewers cooperated with laundresses in the 1886 lockout because they worked in the same factories, faced the same employers, and shared ethnic, family, and community ties.

The strike's issues was similar to the 1869 conflict: the workers' right to organize. In February 1886, shortly after an ironers' protest against machinery, the Knights' District Assembly 68 asked collar manufacturers to equalize wages in different factories and to pay an increase that restored previous year's wage cuts. Every employer complied, except George Ide. In mid-May, ironers and starchers in Ide's firm declared that they would not return to work unless Ide granted the increase. Ide responded by combining with other manufacturers in the association, which closed down the collar industry. The lockout involved thirty-three establishements and about 8,000 women, including homeworkers. Troy's Knights, and at first the national organization, supported the cause because the Joan of Arc Assembly demanded not only the restoration of wage cuts but also that employers recognize the Knights of Labor as their representative. Collar workers won part of the battle but not the war; they returned to work with a small increase and the promise of negotiations but rescinded demands for the Knights' representation.

Analyzed in relationship to other events, the strike reveals relationships between family ties, Troy's industrial structure, and labor activism. Locking out the entire industry over a demand for a small increase in one shop makes sense in light of the significance of the Knights' demands for recognition and some crucial events in the iron industry. The collar women's five-week conflict coincided with a four-month iron foundry strike, which ended at about the same time and involved a similar issue: the equalization of wages with molders in other cities and restoration of wage cuts. Although the molders' local was not officially affiliated with the Knights, some molders were Knights and their organizations were informally related.

Manufacturers' response to collar workers' demands was motivated in part by fears that the Joan of Arc Assembly would extend the Knights' influence even further. But labor leaders and others also suggested that manufacturers were in league with foundry owners. They argued that manufacturers locked out employees because they knew that throwing collar women out of work would be a hardship for molders' families who depended on the income of wives, daughters, and sisters who were collar workers. For labor leaders, the collar women's lockout was in part a strategy to pressure molders into a settlement favorable to foundry owners.

Whether or not this explanation is correct, it suggests that Troy's collar workers organized successfully partly because the city's industrial structure encouraged cooperation between workers of different sexes. Troy's workingmen wholeheartedly supported women's rights to earn wages and organize despite beliefs that women should not work, in part, because women employed in a different industry did not threaten men's livelihoods and contributed needed income. But more important, since striking men could depend on women family members' income, and vice versa, Troy's collar women also contributed to the labor movement's solidarity. This is not the only reason for Troy's high level of labor militancy; it suggests that relationships between industrial structure and family, neighborhood, and community patterns are an important part of the explanation.

What are the implications of these labor conflicts? Looking at conditions under which some women successfully organized suggests that nineteenth-century working women were not a homogeneous group on the lowest levels of the working class, but they included wage earners of diverse skills, earnings, commitment, work patterns, and relationships with male workers. This diversity emphasizes the inadequacy of conventional wisdom drawn from oppositional contrasts for understanding both women's and men's activism. A close look at the relationship between industrial structure and family, neighborhood, and community ties suggests that the family, formerly thought of as suited to understanding women, is also the key for analyzing a subject thought to be the domain of men, labor activism. Explanations that reserve family ties for understanding women and work experience for men lead to a narrow understanding of both sexes and neglect links between family, work, and industrial structure, all of which contribute to an understanding of a community's complex social life. [Carole Turbin]

FURTHER READING

Kessler-Harris, Alice. *Out of Work: A History of Wage-Earning Women in the United States.* New York: Oxford University Press, 1982.

Turbin, Carole. "'And We Are Nothing But Women': Irish Working Women in Troy, New York, 1864–1869." In *Women of America: A History.* Carol R. Berkin and Mary Beth Norton, eds. Boston, MA: Houghton Mifflin, 1978.

———. "Beyond Conventional Wisdom: Women's Wage Work, Household Economic Contribution, and Labor Activism in a Mid-Nineteenth Century Working Class Community." In *'To Toil the Livelong Day': America's Women at Work, 1780–1980.* Carol Gronman and Mary Beth Norton, eds. Ithaca, NY: Cornell University Press, 1987.

———. "Reconceptualizing Family, Work, and Labor Organizing: Working Women in Troy, New York, 1860–1890." *Review of Radical Political Economics.* Vol. 16 (Spring, 1984), pp 1–16.

Walkowitz, Daniel J. *Worker City, Company Town: Iron and Cotton Worker Protest in Troy and Cohoes, New York, 1855–1884.* Urbana, IL: University of Illinois Press, 1978.

U

● ● ● ● ● ● ● ● ● ●

● ● ●

UNION PACIFIC RAILROAD STRIKES OF 1884. Two closely related strikes occurred on the Union Pacific Railroad (UP) in 1884, the first running from May 4 to May 8, the second from August 13 to August 19. Both were easy victories over a large and powerful railroad company. Since the strikes involved the Knights of Labor, they gave that union an aura of success that contributed to its remarkable growth over the next two years. In fact, the role of the Knights was only incidental to the outcome of either strike.

On May 4, the Union Pacific announced 10 to 25 percent wage cuts for all employees except engineers and firemen. An angry machinist in one of the UP's shops in Denver tossed down his tools and refused to work. His fellow workers followed suit and within half an hour, as word spread, the entire work force joined in the wholly spontaneous walkout. Having no organization and needing advice on how to proceed, a small delegation called on Joseph R. Buchanan, editor of the *Labor Enquirer* and a charter member of a Knights of Labor (K of L) Assembly in Denver. At a mass meeting of the strikers, Buchanan helped draft a resolution calling upon all employees to refuse to work for the Union Pacific until the former wage rates were restored. All present signed it. Later in the day, workers from shops of another UP division in Denver joined in, also subscribing to the resolution. Forming themselves into the Union Pacific Employees' Protective Association, the strikers learned the next day that shopmen at all points on the Union Pacific had struck rather than accept the reductions. Although there were no unions in any of the shops when the company announced wage cuts, within thirty-six hours every shop on the Union Pacific and its branches from Omaha, Nebraska, to Ogden, Utah, had shut down. In all, some 12,000 workers were out. Orderly and well-disciplined, they mounted guard over company property to prevent damage by troublemakers. With the exception of two passenger trains, not a wheel turned during the entire strike. Meanwhile, impromptu leaders at the various strike centers, asked the Denver committee to act as spokesmen for all dealings with S. H. H. Clark, general manager of the railroad. Clark, after waiting in vain for instructions from his superiors in New York, acted on his own authority. On Saturday, May 6, he ordered reinstatement of the old wage rates effective May 8. The strikers went back to work, their four-day strike a total victory.

With some difficulty, Buchanan persuaded the shop and yardmen to maintain, rather than abandon, their new organization. Such an easy triumph led some workers to exaggerate their power. The company's surrender was complete, they argued; if not, the men could simply be called back on strike at any time and again bring the company to its knees. Buchanan more accurately predicted that the company would lower wages as soon as expedient, but piecemeal, in a manner less threatening to all workers at once. The Protective Association continued, affiliated with the Knights, and set up K of L assemblies in railroad towns all along the line.

On August 11, the Union Pacific announced wage cuts for fifteen first-class machinists in the shops at Ellis, Kansas, and discharged twenty men in the Denver shops. Included among the latter were several officers of the new union. After a day of hurried communications among union leaders, the workers began their second strike against the UP at noon, August 13. It was as complete as the earlier one had been. By evening of the first day, the officers of the company wired for the strikers' demands. Buchanan and two other representatives of the men went to Omaha to deal directly with company officials.

General Manager Clark listened to the complaints of the union that included, in addition to the wage cuts and firings, the arbitrary and petty behavior of foremen and other minor officials in the shops. Clark denied responsibility for these matters, told Buchanan he had not ordered the wage cuts in either May or August (the orders had come from the president's office, he said), and that he would be leaving his position on September 1 for reasons not related to the labor difficulties. He offered, however, to wire the union's demands to the UP's president, Charles Francis Adams, and assist in settling the matter.

The union called for full restoration of wages at Ellis, reinstatement of the twenty men at Denver, orders to superintendents not to discriminate against workers for union activities, and agreement that future retrenchments would not be in the form of hours or wage cuts. Further, the company was to recognize the union as the sole representative of the workers in matters relating to changes in wages or working conditions. When such negotiations broke down, disputed matters were to be submitted to arbitration. The Union Pacific haggled, agreeing at first only to restore wages at Ellis, then to rehire all those discharged at Denver except one, the secretary of the union committee. His "course" had been "very disagreeable and in bad taste on several occasions since the May strike . . ." The workers held their

ground, and on August 18, the company again yielded on all points. Until the whole K of L began to crumble later in the decade, the shop and yardmen in Union Pacific District 82 retained the respect of the company and had no further difficulties.

The success of the workers in the two UP strikes can be traced to several factors. First was the unexpected solidarity of the strikers, given their initial lack of organization and the way they were scattered out across several states. Without unity they would have lost. The cooperation of the operating trainmen, the Engineers and Firemen, also helped. But perhaps most important was the disarray of the company and its lack of determination to fight the matter through. The wage cut in May had been ordered on the assumption that, because pay on the UP was generally higher than for other lines, there would be no great outcry. None of the usual precautions of managers in that era were taken. The company had not arranged to bring eastern strikebreakers to the thinly settled West in the event of a walkout, nor did they have protection for scab workers had they been hired.

By August, new owners had taken control of the Union Pacific, putting its management in confusion. After long control by Jay Gould and a coterie of New Yorkers, the line was in financial difficulty. Congress threatened to investigate because of the UP's large indebtedness to the government. Only a month after the May strike, Boston interests acquired majority ownership and named Adams as president. Disliking Clark, whom he regarded as a Gould man, Adams secured his resignation but left him in power until a successor could be chosen. Given what happened in May, common sense should have dictated against further attempts to cut wages until the company was fully prepared. Instead, someone blundered. As Buchanan's account of negotiations indicate, Clark claimed not to be in charge or in sympathy with the company's course. But whether the second wage cut was Clark's, Adams's or someone else's idea, it again failed and handed the workers a second easy victory. [Gerald G. Eggert]

FURTHER READING

Buchanan, Joseph Ray. *The Story of a Labor Agitator.* New York: The Outlook Company, 1903.

Klein, Maury. *Life and Legend of Jay Gould.* Baltimore, MD: Johns Hopkins University Press, 1986.

New York Times (May 6–10, 1884).

o   o   o

"UPRISING OF THE 20,000" OF 1909. The "Uprising of the 20,000" was a turning point in the revolution that shook the labor movement in the first decade of the twentieth century. It was a workers' rebellion to regain control of the workplace, lost to employers in the current open-shop drive in manufacturing. It was infused with the energy of young immigrant women, who carried their traditions of resistance to political, religious, and social persecution from southern and eastern Europe to America. The powerful appeal of the new industrial unionism stunned the conservative craft unionists of the male-dominated American Federation of Labor (AFL) and transformed the struggling labor movement into a vital force with an effective strategy to combat the open-shop drive.

The uprising was part of a wave of unrest that brought semiskilled and unskilled immigrant workers to the forefront of the fight for industrial democracy in the Progressive era. Employers had cut piece rates and laid off workers in manufacturing industries nationwide after the depression of 1907–1908. The summer of 1909 was the climax of a year that included the **McKees Rocks Strike** at a United States Steel plant in response to the company's open-shop declaration, followed by strikes at the South Bethlehem and McKeesport, Pennsylvania, and Hammond, Indiana, plants, where skilled and unskilled, immigrant and "na-tive American" workers joined together to protest management speedups, increased production quotas, and union-breaking strategies. In each case, management's attempts to divide the workers united them in collective action.

New York City shirtwaist makers overcame deliberate stratification by age, sex, skill, and ethnicity to protest industry conditions in 1909. Shirtwaist makers worked fifty-six hours a week with extensive mandatory overtime. "Learners," who made up 25 percent of the work force, earned only three to four dollars a week, while "regular operators" made as much as twelve dollars. All workers paid for their own supplies and electrical power at inflated prices that profited employers. They were taxed for the use of their chairs and lockers and were fined for any imperfection in the product. Employers set time clocks to steal twenty precious minutes each day from their lunchtime. And "girl helpers" were subjected to arbitrary treatment by male inside contractors who distributed work, set piece rates, and assigned overtime.

A walkout over rates set by inside contractors in July 1909 at Rosen Brothers triggered strikes at the Triangle Shirtwaist Company and at Leiserson's. At Triangle, workers' frustration with a company union established in 1908 boiled over in September, and workers asked for support from the United Hebrew Trades and Local 25 of the International Ladies' Garment Workers' Union (ILGWU).

Local 25 had fewer than one hundred members and only four dollars in its treasury when it agreed to help the strikers. When Leiserson workers who met openly with the union were fired in September, the local struck. Leiserson recruited black scabs, hired professional strikebreakers, and called in favors from the city's police department and legal system. The Triangle Company paid prostitutes and pimps to taunt and tempt the strikers. Picket line beatings and arrests were daily events. Strikers who were sent to the workhouse waited while families and friends raised the enormous $2,500 bail.

In October, a committee of five met to consider a general strike. Clara Lemlich, a striker who was recovering from repeated picket line beatings, introduced the strike resolution at the impassioned meeting at Cooper Union in November, after Meyer London and Samuel Gompers, AFL president, among other speakers, had urged strikers to be cautious and patient. The young Leiserson worker challenged all present to take a revered Jewish oath: "If I turn traitor to the cause I now pledge, may this hand wither from the arm I now raise."

Within days, 15,000 shirtwaist and dressmakers from 500 shops walked out. More than 2,000 joined Local 25. Although they were harassed on the picket line and treated capriciously by the courts—one judge declared it "a strike against God"—their numbers swelled to almost 30,000 during the severe winter months.

The women organized and carried out every strike activity, with the exception of negotiating with the newly formed employers' association, a task reserved for the male leadership of Local 25. In 1909, nearly 32,000 workers were employed by 600 shops in New York City. Most shops employed twenty to fifty workers, but the seventy shops that dominated the industry employed from 100 to 300 workers each. Jewish and Italian women were a majority of the work force, and they were 90 percent of those who participated in the strike. Almost three-quarters were between sixteen and twenty-five years old. Although the patriarchy of the American Federation of Labor had limited their participation in union activities and organizing drives and had restricted them from holding leadership positions, many had worked for wages outside the home. While young Italian women were forbidden to attend union meetings at night, the leadership of their Jewish sisters in the 1902 Kosher Meat Riot and the 1907 rent strikes

in New York had met with cultural approval and community support.

Their principal demand was for the union shop. Local 25 also demanded a fifty-two-hour workweek with overtime limited to two hours per day; notice of no work in advance or upon arrival in the morning; a uniform price scale, negotiated in each shop; elimination of the ticket and subcontracting systems; and abolition of the charges for equipment and materials.

Clara Lemlich and the emerging rank-and-file leaders found critical support among women in the United Hebrew Trades, the Italian branch of the New York Socialist Party, and especially from the middle-class activists of the Women's Trade Union League (WTUL). The WTUL brought the strikers' case to the public by exposing working conditions and explaining strike demands, volunteering legal services, raising money for bail and operating expenses, and allowing themselves to be arrested on the picket line. The legitimacy that the "Mink Brigade" brought to the strike was instrumental in winning wide support across class lines.

The WTUL's most effective strategy linked the workers' fight for control at the workplace with the suffrage movement. In December, a march on City Hall and a follow-up meeting of 8,000 at the Hippodrome in support of "socialism, unionism, and suffrage" resulted in the first effort to settle the strike by arbitration. Marcus Marks, president of the Clothiers Association, and John Mitchell of the United Mine Workers set up a meeting between the manufacturers' representatives and Mitchell and Morris Hillquit for the workers, but the Clothiers Association refused to consider the union shop. On December 20 the strike spread to Philadelphia, where New York manufacturers were sending work to unorganized contractors. Just after Christmas, strikers angrily rejected a negotiated proposal that offered them a fifty-two-hour week, four paid holidays, and reinstatement without penalty but did not guarantee the union shop or prohibit working with unorganized contractors.

Negotiations broke down early in the new year. The strikers' refusal to settle for anything less than the union shop had alienated the American Federation of Labor. Support from women's organizations had declined after setbacks in the suffrage movement. Nineteen large manufacturers refused to recognize Local 25, and 356 of 450 shops signed weak, individual contracts. Small shops in financial distress subcontracted for larger manufacturers, and many strikers were forced to return to work under the same conditions that had inspired the first walkouts. On February 15, 1910, the leadership reluctantly called off the strike.

Although the strikers did not achieve all of their demands, the "Uprising of the 20,000" checked the momentum of the open-shop drive and opened the doors to women's participation in and leadership of the labor movement. Women who had never taken a public role emerged as political, social, and union spokespersons, and countless unnamed heroines were empowered and educated by their strike responsibilities.

The strike popularized the use of the general strike as a weapon in the open-shop drive and inspired the **Cloakmakers' Strike of 1910** where strikers who negotiated a preferential union shop and established a "Protocol of Peace" in the New York garment industry. The strike also established the reputation of the WTUL with workers and within the American Federation of Labor and forced the AFL to respond to concerns of progressive unionists who belonged to the Industrial Workers of the World or the Socialist Party. The strike created the first big local of the ILGWU and established the union's position as a force for social change in New York.

Veterans of the strike participated in the **Lawrence, Massachusetts, Textile Strike of 1912** and the **Paterson, New Jersey, Textile Strike of 1913**. Some became active in politics, like Rose Schneider-

man of the WTUL, the first woman to run for the United States Senate on the labor ticket in 1920. Others, including Theresa Malkiel, published fictionalized accounts and diaries of the strike. Most important, the "Uprising of the 20,000" proved that workers who had been considered "unorganizable"—women, immigrants, and the unskilled—could emerge from the sweatshop and inspire the labor movement to new standards of activism and solidarity. [Shelly G. Herochik]

FURTHER READING

Dye, Nancy Schrom. *As Equals and As Sisters: Feminism, the Labor Movement, and the Women's Trade Union League of New York.* Columbia, MO: University of Missouri Press, 1980.

Kessler-Harris, Alice. "Organizing the Unorganizable: Three Jewish Women and Their Union." In *The Labor History Reader.* Daniel J. Leab, ed. Urbana, IL: University of Illinois Press, 1985.

Lorwin, Louis. *The Women's Garment Workers: A History of the International Ladies' Garment Workers" Union.* New York: H. B. Huebsch, 1924.

Malkiel, Theresa S. *The Diary of a Shirtwaist Striker.* New York: Cooperative Press, 1910.

Schofield, Ann. "The Uprising of the 20,000: The Making of a Labor Legend." In *A Needle, A Bobbin, A Strike: Women Needleworkers in America.* Joan M. Jensen and Sue Davidson, eds. Philadelphia, PA: Temple University Press, 1984.

Schwartz, Maxine S. "The Uprising of the Twenty Thousand: Sex, Class and Ethnicity in the Shirtwaist Makers' Strike of 1909." In *Struggle a Hard Battle: Essays on Working Class Immigrants.* Dick Hoerder, ed. Normal, IL: Northern Illinois University Press, 1986.

Waldinger, Roger. "Another Look at the I.L.G.W.U.: Women, Industry Structure and Collective Action." In *Women, Work, and Protest: A Century of Women's Labor History.* Ruth Milkman, ed. New York: Routledge and Kegan Paul, 1985.

o   o   o

USX LOCKOUT AND BOYCOTT OF 1986. On July 31, 1986, USX Corporation, formerly United States Steel, locked out members of the United Steel Workers of America (USWA). This was the first nationwide labor dispute since the Depression that saw union picket lines go up in communities ravaged by plant closings and mass unemployment. The lockout passed without serious attempts by the company to operate its mills with strikebreakers. After six months, on January 31, 1987, the two sides reached a compromise concessionary agreement that fell far short of USX's expectations.

The combatants had been on a collision course for three years. As far back as July 1983, local union officers began complaining that management at what was then called U.S. Steel was violating contract provisions by contracting out bargaining unit work, ignoring seniority rules, and ordering employees to do work out of their job title. When workers complained, managers told them to file grievances; when the locals won their grievances, the company called for arbitration; when the union won in arbitration, the company paid back wages and continued violating the contract. These practices enabled U.S. Steel to increase productivity by 49 percent in the years 1983–1985, while reducing the company's unionized labor force by 11,500.

Before the 1986 bargaining round began, the six major steelmakers announced their decision to abandon industrywide bargaining, in part because U.S. Steel's confrontational tactics vis-à-vis the USWA presaged a strike that the other five steelmakers wanted no part of. The end of coordinated bargaining meant that the USWA would have to bargain individually with six different integrated steelmakers, each drained by the industry's prolonged decline, but each with different needs and problems.

The USWA's new president, Lynn Williams, brought to the 1986 bargaining round a complex strategy aimed at preserving as many steelmaking jobs as possible. To this end, Williams asked the largest steelmakers to join the union in lobbying Congress for protection from imports and other legislation to bolster the steel industry. U.S. Steel refused, but LTV, National, Bethlehem, Armco, and Inland joined with the

union in an extensive lobbying and public relations effort. The USWA placed at the center of its bargaining agenda the restriction of contracting out. The union also consciously bargained to give aid to those steelmakers deemed "needy and deserving"—LTV and Bethlehem—which were on the verge of bankruptcy, had shown a determination to modernize their mills, and were burdened with particularly high labor costs.

Pursuing this strategy, the USWA reached concessionary agreements with LTV, Bethlehem, Inland, and National. These contracts provided for wage and benefit cuts of $2.00 to $4.00 per hour, reducing each company's hourly labor costs to a narrow range around $22.80 per hour. In exchange, unionists received profit-sharing agreements. More importantly, the settlements barred contracting out.

When the U.S. Steel bargaining got underway on June 12, the company's chief negotiator, Bruce Johnston, made it clear that the company would not accept the pattern agreed to by its competitors. The company demanded far steeper wage and benefit reductions, offered no profit sharing, and refused to limit its practice of contracting out. Three weeks into the negotiations, on July 8, U.S. Steel chairman David Roderick announced that his firm was changing its name to USX, and restructuring so that steel would be just one of four separate corporate divisions. Although Roderick's announcement was widely interpreted as the prelude to a prolonged strike, the USW offered to continue working under the old contract. USX refused and the lockout was on.

The steelworkers won the first battle when state officials in Indiana, Utah, and Pennsylvania ruled that since USX had locked out its employees, they were eligible for unemployment compensation. A dramatic, winner-take-all showdown on the future of labor relations in steel was widely expected.

Outside events brought about a less than final solution, however. In the summer of 1986, takeover specialists began buying up the stock of USX, convinced that the company's energy assets were worth more than the price of its shares. On October 6, 1986, Carl Icahn, a leading takeover specialist, announced his intention to buy USX.

The Wall Street insider trading scandal that broke out in November 1986, blunted Icahn's campaign against USX management, but Icahn's intervention did precipitate a labor settlement. USWA president Lynn Williams considered and rejected an alliance with Icahn against Roderick, deeming a compromise settlement with USX preferable. David Roderick, for his part, recognized that an early settlement of its labor difficulties was essential if USX management were to survive. On October 29, the parties returned to the bargaining table.

Differences on give-backs and contracting-out blocked settlement until the parties agreed to mediation. But Sylvester Garrett, who had previously served as chairman of the U.S. Steel Board of Arbitration, successfully pressured both sides to accept a compromise.

The settlement gave USX wage and benefit savings of approximately $2.50 per hour, comparable to that received by its competitors. The final language on contracting out gave USX some minor exceptions that other companies had not gained. The press interpreted the pact as a victory for the union.

Some of the satisfaction unionists felt about their "victory" was dissipated just days after the contract's ratification, however. On February 4, 1987, USX announced that it would shut down an additional four mills. Workers at these mills, who had just voted in favor of concessions in the hope of saving their jobs, were furious. When the steel industry began to recover from its prolonged slump in 1988, labor relations at USX remained acrimonious. [David Bensman]

FURTHER READING

Hoerr, John. *And the Wolf Finally Came*. Pittsburgh, PA: University of Pittsburgh Press, 1988.

o   o   o

UTAH COAL STRIKE OF 1903–1904. The dream of unionization among Utah's miners had flared once before, in 1901, when a spontaneous strike by Carbon County miners had been defeated. Three years later, in the midst of a general upsurge in unionization across America, the desire for organization surfaced once again and resulted in Utah's greatest strike—a strike that lasted a full year and was spearheaded by Finnish, Slavic, and especially Italian immigrants.

In 1901, the strike had been without the direction of skilled union organizers, but by 1903, the United Mine Workers (UMW), fresh from successes in the East, were conducting an extensive organizing campaign in the coalfields of Colorado, Wyoming, and Utah. The Utah strike occurred at the same time as more well known strikes in the coalfields of Colorado—strikes that developed into industrial civil war. In Utah, as in Colorado, the main issue was the right of union recognition. The dispute centered on the Utah Fuel Company which had offered pay raises but refused to recognize the UMW. Believing that no gains could be held without union protection, the miner's struck.

The company blamed the trouble on the foreign miners and outside agitators. Indeed, outsiders did come to Carbon County but not until the miners, with the Italians in the lead, had taken their strike vote on November 12. The first attempt to bring in outside organizers failed when a delegation of miners on their way to meet a UMW official were turned back at gunpoint by company agents. Nevertheless, by November 17, Charles DeMolli, an Italian Socialist and a UMW organizer, with the help of an Italian fraternal lodge, "Miners'

Brotherhood," had succeeded in organizing a local with 468 members at Sunnyside. The miners voted overwhelmingly to stay out until the company recognized the UMW.

The company acted with dispatch in the face of the threat. All men not working were paid in full and discharged. A cash-only policy went into effect in the company store, and those strikers occupying company houses were ordered to vacate. An active campaign to hire strikebreakers succeeded in keeping the mines open at a significantly reduced level. In the meantime, the union extended its organizing drive to the other mining camps. The most significant success came with the closing of the company's Castle Gate mine, the only mine to be entirely closed during the strike.

With the spread of the strike, the Carbon County sheriff requested assistance from the governor who sent General John Q. Cannon of the Utah National Guard to assess the situation. Cannon noted that the coal camps were in a state of excitement. He also noted that the union drive was picking up momentum. Even though no violence had occurred, Cannon's report to the governor resulted in the sending in of the Utah National Guard. Their orders were to help local officials protect company property and prevent threats and acts of intimidation against miners who wanted to work.

One of the first assignments of the Guard was the arrest of organizer DeMolli in Scofield on November 25. The attempt to jail him failed when a sympathetic jury returned a verdict of not guilty on charges of disturbing the peace. With the failure of its attempt to remove DeMolli from the strike and thus weaken the strong Italian leadership of the conflict, the companies moved to counter his influence by bringing in the Italian consul in Denver, Giuseppe Cuneo. Cuneo had supported Pinkerton detectives in their hunt for Italians in the Colorado strike, but he quickly sensed the strong pro-strike sentiments of his countrymen in Utah and remained neutral.

DeMolli then tried to appeal to Governor Heber M. Wells to mediate the dispute. The appeal fell on deaf ears. Wells informed DeMolli that the strikers could not win and that if they did not soon end the strike "men from all over this state will shoulder their rifles and go down there and run the Italians out of the state."

In the face of this hostility, the strikers showed remarkable discipline. There was little or no violence as the strike ended its first month. This discipline held under a series of provocations. Anti-foreign sentiments were fanned by the companies. Italians took the brunt of the criticism and the major part of the harassment, both physical and legal. On December 8, the president and secretary of the Scofield union were arrested and jailed for twenty days for vagrancy. The secretary of the Sunnyside union served time for disturbing the peace. Similar sentences were imposed on a number of other union activists. Most important, however, was the arrest of A. B. Edler, a Socialist UMW attorney who had come to Scofield to defend the union men who had been arrested. Edler was arrested on charges of criminal libel for remarks about company guards that appeared in the newspapers.

One of the crucial factors in the strike was the involvement of the Mormon church. Most of the strikebreakers were Mormon farmers from the surrounding area. Church teachings against secret organizations (as the UMW was branded) and prejudice against foreigners made the Mormons willing strikebreakers. Wealthy Mormons also had substantial holdings in the coalfields. The UMW believed that the Mormon church acted in league with the Utah coal companies to prevent the success of the union in Utah. During the strike, anti-union statements were made in many Mormon meeting houses, as well as in the tabernacle in Salt Lake City. Indeed, in spite of official denials, Mormon church records later revealed that the church had instructed local Mormon authorities to support the company's strike-breaking activities.

In April, six months into the strike, the legendary Mary "Mother" Jones, the so-called miners' angel, arrived. Jones had been a militant supporter of labor causes for at least thirty years when she arrived in Helper, Utah, to support the strikers. During her stay, Jones was exposed to smallpox and quarantined. When she refused to remain out of circulation for the required fifteen days, the deputy sheriff moved to arrest her. He was prevented from making the arrest by at least 100 armed Italian miners. The sheriff requested the National Guard once again, but this time the governor refused. Instead, a posse was formed and 120 Italians taken into custody. The men were put into a "bullpen" patrolled by guards. They were subsequently taken in boxcars to Helper where they were tried on a multitude of charges, including rioting and disturbing the peace. By May 13, eleven had been found guilty and a like number discharged.

The constant harassment by local officials began to take its toll. The UMW had been defeated in the bloody strike in Colorado, and John Mitchell, president of the union, admitted that it was the most expensive effort in the union's history. Little was left in the union's treasury to carry on the fight in Utah. The union tried to arrange a meeting with the Utah Coal Company to agree to terms whereby the strikers could return to work. The company, knowing that victory was near, refused and set out to humiliate the strikers and the union. Company guards rounded up strikers and evicted them from Carbon County, threatening them with lynching if they returned.

Realizing that the strike was over, the UMW sent money to help strikers leave Carbon County. Many considered this a sellout by the union and refused the assistance. Most of the strikers never returned to the Utah mines. Some became farmers, others worked for the railroad, while still others went on to other mining camps where they would fight another day. [Ronald L. Filippelli]

FURTHER READING

Powell, Allan Kent. *The Next Time We Strike: Labor in Utah's Coal Fields, 1900–1933.* Logan, UT: Utah State University Press, 1985.

V

°°°°°°°°°°°

° ° °

VACAVILLE, CALIFORNIA, TREE
PRUNERS' STRIKE OF 1932. Two days
after the November 1932 elections, newly
elected California congressman Frank H.
Buck provoked a massive tree pruners' strike
when he announced a wage cut for pruners
on his ranch from $1.40 for an eight-hour
day to $1.25 for a nine-hour day. Buck, one
the largest growers in the Vacaville fruit
growing region, had raised wages to $1.40
during his congressional campaign, promising farmworkers even higher wages if he
won the election. Running under the campaign slogan "Give Government Back to the
People," Buck garnered nearly unanimous
support from farmworkers in the Vacaville
area. Within days of his victory, after securing the agreement of other orchardists in the
area, Buck announced that the 20 percent
wage cut would go into effect starting November 14.

On the day the pay cut was to go into
effect, 400 Mexican, Filipino, Japanese, and
white tree pruners walked off their jobs.
Unlike previous agricultural strikes in the
region, this was not a spontaneous walkout.
Unbeknownst to Buck, the Communist-led
Cannery and Agricultural Workers Industrial Union (CAWIU) had been actively
organizing workers in the area for several
months. By the time Buck made his announcement, more than 250 working tree
pruners had joined the union, and strike
plans were well developed. The tree pruners'
strike was to be the first deliberately organized strike since the CAWIU had started
organizing California agricultural workers
three years before.

The demands drawn up by the CAWIU
were similar in nature to those they had
made during earlier strikes: a $1.50 daily
minimum wage for a maximum eight-hour
workday; no evictions pending settlement
of the strike; no discrimination on the basis
of gender, race, or union activity; free transportation to and from the worksite; free
tools provided by the employer; and formal
recognition of the CAWIU.

Local ranchers responded by offering
$1.20 for an eight-hour day, with no recog-
nition of the union. The strikers rejected the
offer out of hand and the union moved to
solidify the strike by bringing in outside
legal and financial support. The communist
Worker's International Relief was mobilized
to bring in food and supplies, and the International Labor Defense provided its legal
services to strikers arrested during the frequent clashes with local authorities.

The first of these clashes occurred on
November 21 when strikers set up barricades to prevent trucks carrying scabs to the
orchards to pass through the center of town.
Police attempted to arrest six of the strike
leaders only to release them when a large
mob of pickets surrounded the outnumbered officers.

The growers moved quickly to mobi-
lize city, state, and county authorities as well
as the local citizenry to ensure that this
would not happen again. Local authorities
were especially predisposed to aid strikebreaking efforts because the mayor of Vacaville was himself one of the largest orchardists in the region. Newspapers, local ministers, and government officials attempted
to turn community sentiment against the

strikers by exploiting racial antagonism and through fervent anti-Communist appeals, charging the CAWIU with promoting and practicing violent sabotage. On December 2, ranchers, businessmen, American Legion members, and other community leaders staged a mass rally to "protest against Communism." Speakers such as the Rev. A. F. Fruehling declared that "a real menace confronts this community which must be met in the good old American way." A local judge then went on to explain that "the good old American way" meant nothing less than "the system that is used south of the Mason and Dixon line."

Just three days after the mass rally, lynch fever reached its peak when a mob of forty masked men, armed with the appropriate keys, dragged six strike leaders out of the Vacaville jail, drove them to a remote area twenty miles from town, and abandoned them after beating them with tug straps, shaving their heads with crude shears, and dousing them with red enamel. The local sheriff, who was absent when the kidnapping took place, claimed he had no idea who the vigilantes were or how they had gained possession of the keys to the jail.

During the first weeks of the strike, CAWIU picketers had been fairly successful in keeping scab labor out of the orchards. After repeated violent assaults from vigilantes, male pickets were replaced with women and children who courageously held the lines. But as time went on, the combined effects of continued vigilante attacks and dwindling relief supplies began to take their toll. A visiting delegation of American Federation of Labor (AFL) officials from the Sacramento Federated Trades Council helped turn the tide when they took the employers' side in the dispute. Many Filipino workers, after repeated violent attacks by local vigilantes, fled the region in fear for their lives. After two months of striking, with relief supplies severely depleted and attendance at strike meetings markedly declining, CAWIU members voted on January 20 to end the strike.

For the strikers, it was a bitter defeat. Not only had they lost all of their demands, but the growers had emerged from the strike better organized and more in control of their work force than ever before.

For the CAWIU the defeat was not as bitter. In Vacaville they learned important lessons in how to more effectively organize a multi-ethnic, migratory agricultural work force. Never again would they call a strike in pruning season, when the employers were under no pressure for immediate settlement. From that time on, CAWIU strikes would be targeted for harvest time, when growers would be most vulnerable to crop losses and most dependent on their work force. They had also learned that the more permanent family farmworkers, heretofore considered the most docile and least organizable workers, could become a solid and militant strike force, despite the fact that it took longer to mobilize them into action.

In January 1933, the CAWIU had yet to win a major strike. But under Sam Darcy's leadership they had developed a nucleus of dedicated and capable organizers who faced the turbulent months ahead with hard won recognition and respect from California farmworkers across the state. [Kate Bronfenbrenner]

FURTHER READING

Daniel, Cletus E. *Bitter Harvest: A History of California Farmworkers, 1870–1941.* Berkeley, CA: University of California Press, 1981.

Jamieson, Stuart. *Labor Unionism in American Agriculture.* U.S. Bureau of Labor Statistics Bulletin No. 836. Washington, DC: Government Printing Office, 1945.

McWilliams, Carey. *Factories in the Field: The Story of Migratory Labor in California.* Boston, MA: Little, Brown, 1939.

o   o   o

VIRGINIA INDENTURED SERVANTS' PLOT OF 1661. The first extensive indentured servants plot in Virginia occurred in 1661 and, as in the **Maryland Indentured Servants' Strike of 1663**, the key issue was a controversy over diet. It was customary to supply servants with meat three times a week. When the plantation owner, Major Goodwin, violated this custom by confining his servants to a diet of cornbread and water, the discontent surfaced. The leaders of the servants, Isaac Friend and William Cluton, proposed that they petition the king for redress.

According to one witness, the plot became more serious when Isaac Friend suggested "they would get a matter of Forty of them together and get Gunnes and hee would be the first and lead them and cry as they went along who would be for liberty and freed from bondage and that there would enough come to them and they would goe through the Countrey and Kill those that made any opposition and that they would either be free or dye for it."

Considering the inflammatory rhetoric and the general disturbances that it apparently caused, the York County court took suprisingly mild action in settling the case. William Cluton was bound over for inciting other servants to rebellion, but after several witnesses testified to his good character, the judge discharged him. Isaac Friend escaped punishment as well. The court did admonish the masters and magistrates to keep a close watch on the behavior of their servants. In 1662, a law was passed which restrained unlawful meetings of servants under heavy penalties. [Ronald L. Filippelli]

FURTHER READING

Morris, Richard B. *Government and Labor in Early America*. New York: Harper and Row, 1946.

Smith, Abbot E. *Colonists in Bondage: White Servitude and Convict Labor in America, 1607–1776*. Chapel Hill, NC: University of North Carolina Press, 1947.

W

∘∘∘∘∘∘∘∘∘∘

∘ ∘ ∘

WASHINGTON POST PRESSMEN'S STRIKE OF 1975 AND 1976. At midnight on September 30, one of the longest strikes in the history of the nation's capital began as the pressmen on the city's largest newspaper walked out. The intractability of the dispute was in evidence from the beginning. The pressmen left their workplace in a shambles. Huge sheets of paper hung in shreds from the presses and black printer's ink trickled from torn tubing. A foreman who tried to stop the destruction was badly beaten. Although the strike was the second in two years, nothing in the previous relations between the union and the newspaper gave any hint of the anger of the workers.

The printers' night of rage came after their contract had expired and negotiations seemed to be deadlocked. Behind the outburst were years of suspicion and insecurity as the *Post* moved to modernize its production facilities. The company, faced with shrinking profits, had long wanted to limit overtime and cut production costs through automation. Most importantly for the pressmen, this meant replacing the old "hot metal" printing systems with new photographic printing technology. The new technology, in addition to new training, would also require fewer workers.

The *Post* had been making plans for the confrontation. Rising labor costs had helped reduce the paper's share of the profits for its owner, the Washington Post Company, from 64 percent in 1970 to 38 percent in 1974. The company was also in a good position to take a strike because of its ownership of other profitable enterprises,

including *Newsweek* magazine, six broadcasting stations, and a paper mill. Nor did the *Post* hide its intentions from its unions. In 1974, a union representing 700 typographical workers softened their opposition to automation and allowed the company to begin regular use of photographic composition equipment. But the pressmen, who earned $15,000 a year plus significant amounts of overtime, resisted and walked out.

The vandalism of the newspaper's press room quickly led to a breach of union solidarity. The newspaper's chapter of the American Newspaper Guild, horrified by the destruction, and going against instructions from its national union, voted 270 to 251 not to support the strike. On the second day of the strike, some three-quarters of the paper's editorial and commercial employees crossed the picket lines and put out an edition of the paper. Throughout the long strike, the *Post* failed to publish the paper only once, on the first day of the conflict.

The *Post*'s ability to do this was also the result of careful forward planning. With their own presses out of order, the newspaper chartered helicopters at $108 an hour to fly copy from the roof of the building, out of the reach of angry pickets, to six other printing plants as far as 150 miles away. The *Post* had also hired Lawrence Wallace, a tough labor negotiator from the Knight newspaper chain. Despite the union's opposition to new labor-saving machinery, the company brought new photographic composition equipment into the building and began to train some 125 employees to use it. Much of the training occurred at the Newspaper Production and Research Center in Oklahoma City. The school was supported by the *Post* and some 200 other newspapers and directed by an ex-newspaper production manager who had broken printing unions at several newspapers. The pressmen considered the training center a "school for scabs."

After ten weeks of deadlocked negotiations, *Post* publisher Katharine Graham told the striking pressmen that unless they accepted the company's latest contract proposal, they would be replaced permanently by non-union pressmen. Meanwhile, temporary non-union replacements borrowed from out-of-town newspapers were helicoptered to the *Post* to begin manning the presses. The company provided bed and board, and issued workclothes to advertising and clerical employees who, along with management, did double duty as production workers.

To no one's surprise, the pressmen rejected the *Post*'s final offer. The offer had included a raise in base pay over three years of 25 percent, and $400,000 in bonuses to be distributed by the union in return for an end to featherbedding—the practice of overmanning—in the pressroom. The company coupled the offer with an invitation to "individual" union members to return to work.

By the end of the year, the presses were running again, although circulation was down slightly. The effects on the company had been minimal, a drop of some $800,000 in net income for the final quarter of 1975. The nine unions that had been supporting the strikers began to fall into line. The breakthrough came during the last week of February 1976, when the newspaper's mailers voted to accept a wage-and-benefits increase of 20 percent over three years. The photoengravers followed suit, and by the first of March members of some of the seven other unions honoring the picket line began drifting back to work. That left only the pressmen, all of whom had been replaced.

The strike left the members of the *Post*'s largest union, the Newspaper Guild, in disarray. A majority of its members stayed on the the job during the strike. After the Washington-Baltimore Guild charged them with strikebreaking, some of them banded together to form a new union. As a result, the *Post* refused to negotiate with the Guild on a contract due to expire in March, claiming that National Labor Relations Board rules forbade negotiations while certification of a new union was pending. Ultimately the company did agree to reestablish its relationship with the Guild, but the pressmen's union had been ousted for good. [Ronald L. Filippelli]

FURTHER READING

Elder, S. "Journalist versus the Unions at the *Washington Post*." *Columbia Journalism Review*, Vol. 15 (May, 1976), pp. 42–45.

Marshall, Elliot. "Striking Facts about the Post." *The New Republic* (October 25, 1975), pp. 9–12.

"The Post Settlement." *Newsweek* (March 1, 1976), p. 87.

"Showdown at the Post." *Newsweek* (December 22, 1975), p. 44.

"The Siege of Washington." *Time* (October 27, 1975), p. 76.

"Washington Luddites." *Time* (October 13, 1975), pp. 87–88.

o   o   o

WATERTOWN, CONNECTICUT, ARSENAL STRIKE OF 1909. Scientific management was one of the most important developments in the history of American industry. Near the end of the nineteenth century, Frederick Winslow Taylor proposed innovations in management that profoundly affected the relations between labor and capital. Workers and labor unions often vigorously resisted the changes brought about by the implementation of Taylor's techniques, and the dispute at the Watertown Arsenal clearly illustrates the nature of that conflict. Although the strike involved a small number of workers and lasted for only a week, it received substantial attention from the public and Congress. More than any other incident, it exemplified the fundamental issues of the managerial revolution then in progress.

Frederick Taylor began his career at the Midvale Steel Company near Philadelphia. Although he was born into a wealthy family, Taylor chose to become an apprentice at the Midvale works and to learn the trade of a machinist. He developed important new methods of cutting steel which established his early reputation as an engineer, but his real interest, and his enduring contribution, was in the area of managerial organization.

According to Taylor, the fundamental problem confronting managers at the time was that workers routinely engaged in the collective withholding of labor or "soldiering." He asserted that "by far the greatest evil from which both workmen and employers are suffering is the systematic soldiering which is almost universal under all of the ordinary schemes of management and which results from a careful study on the part of workmen of what they think will promote their best interests." Workers restricted their output, Taylor said, so as to prevent management from determining how fast a given amount of work could be done. If they produced more, workers believed that management would impose higher standards of production with no increase in pay and with resulting unemployment for some workers. Moreover, Taylor argued, workers relied on a "rule of thumb" method of accomplishing a job, in which skilled craftsmen retained individual control over the productive process. Such craft wisdom, in Taylor's view, was "the principal asset or possession of every tradesman."

Taylor's solution to the problem of "soldiering" involved several basic principles. First, Taylor said, management should acquire all knowledge of the productive processes and systematize that knowledge so it could be transmitted to other managers. Second, based on its more complete under-

standing of production, management should determine the standard of output that constituted a "fair day's work." Finally, management should retain detailed control over the planning and conception of all work; workers were responsible only for the execution of tasks assigned by the employer. Taylor added that labor unions were a hindrance to cooperation and prosperity in industry, because they encouraged soldiering. In his words, "The worst thing that a labor union can do for its members in the long run is to limit the amount of work which they allow each workman to do in a day."

The Watertown Arsenal is a federal armory located near Boston. In 1909, the arsenal was lagging in productivity compared to its private sector counterparts. The private competitors, primarily the Bethlehem and Midvale steel companies, had generally adopted scientific management techniques, and the commanding officer at Watertown concluded that he should undertake similar reforms at the arsenal. He contacted Taylor and one of Taylor's associates, Carl Barth; the two men visited the foundry and submitted proposals for reorganization of the facility. Among Barth's specific suggestions were the creation of a planning department and the development of a wage system based on premiums or bonuses for high productivity.

To implement the new compensation scheme, it was first necessary to standardize all pertinent jobs. Barth recommended that the arsenal employ Dwight Merrick, a specialist in time-and-motion study, to analyze tasks and to assign a standard rate to them. The purpose of the study was to ascertain the amount of time necessary to complete a job; if the task could be completed in less time, the system authorized a "bonus" payment to the faster workers. In June 1911, Merrick arrived at the arsenal to begin his work.

By August, Merrick had completed his time studies in the machine shop and moved into the foundry. On August 10, he timed a skilled worker making a mold for the metal frame of a packsaddle. After eliminating all "waste" or nonproductive time, Merrick concluded that a standard period for the task was twenty-four minutes, to which he added an additional two-thirds, arriving at a figure of forty minutes. If the job were completed in less time, the molder would be paid a premium.

While Merrick was timing the job with his stopwatch, another worker was conducting his own study using an ordinary clock. He found that the job required five minutes from beginning to end, without subtracting "waste" motion. The worker who made the mold objected to Merrick's conclusion that the job could be done in twenty-four minutes and pointed out, correctly, that Merrick's experience was in machine shops and that Merrick knew very little about foundry work. Merrick insisted that his analysis was "scientific" and objective and therefore beyond debate. The molders, however, concluded that the system was simply arbitrary.

That evening, the molders met to discuss the situation. They agreed that each would refuse to work under the stopwatch, and they drew up a formal petition protesting further application of the Taylor system. When they reported for work on August 11, Merrick was again present with his stopwatch. Merrick selected a job and directed the worker, Joseph Cooney, to proceed with the task. Cooney refused. The molders then presented their petition to the commanding officer, who summoned Cooney to discuss the matter. Cooney repeated that he would not work under the watch and was thereupon fired. Cooney's fellow molders learned of the discharge and walked out in a group. They neither notified their bargaining representative, the International Molders' Union, nor sought union approval for the work action.

The IMU promptly took up the molders' cause and met with management at the arsenal. Within a few days, the commanding officer agreed to investigate the grievances of the workers and invited them, including Cooney, to return to work. They did so on August 18.

The Watertown strike had important political repercussions. It intensified organized labor's opposition to the scientific management method, and particularly to the time studies and premium payment system. An official of the Machinists Union cogently summarized labor's position:

[W]e object to being reduced to a scientific formula, and we do not want to have the world run on that kind of basis at all. We would a good deal rather have the world run on the basis that everybody should enjoy some of the things in it, and if the people of the United States do not want to spend all their time working they have a right to say so, even though the scientific engineers claim that they can do five times as much as they are doing now.

Eventually, political pressure led to congressional investigation of the "efficiency experts" who followed Taylor's principles of work organization, and in 1915, Congress amended the Army appropriations bill to prohibit time studies in all establishments funded by the legislation. Watertown thus focused attention on the human costs of higher productivity and efficiency in the workplace. [Raymond L. Hogler]

FURTHER READING

Aitken, Hugh, G. J. *Taylorism at Watertown Arsenal: Scientific Management in Action, 1908–1915.* Cambridge, MA: Harvard University Press, 1960.

Hearing Before the Special Committee of the House of Representatives to Investigate the Taylor and Other Systems of Shop Management. 3 Vols., 62nd Congress, 2nd Session, Washington, DC: Government Printing Office, 1912.

o   o   o

WEST VIRGINIA COAL WARS OF 1920–1921. The speedup of the economy brought on by World War I provided a favorable environment for the growth of the American labor movement. Like many unions, the United Mine Workers (UMW) aggressively sought to expand their membership during this period. Some of the union's most intensive organizing efforts focused on the coal-rich state of West Virginia. By war's end, the UMW had succeeded in bringing West Virginia's stubborn central and northern coalfields into the union fold. In the years that followed, the UMW turned its attention to an even more ambitious organizing target—the southern West Virginia counties of Logan, Mingo, and McDowell. The violent confrontations between miners and operators that resulted came to be known as the "great West Virginia coal wars."

By 1919, most of the bituminous coalfields across the country had been organized by the UMW. Southern West Virginia was among the notable exceptions. The coalfields of this region were among the most productive and most profitable in the United States. Operated as a non-union haven by some of the largest coal companies in the country, they were of great strategic value to both the union and the companies. Without the higher wages and more restrictive work rules that accompanies unionization, the mines of southern West Virginia were able to undercut more expensive coal from union mines. The competition in the coal market that resulted placed limits on the gains the UMW could extract from unionized coal operators.

In an effort to extend its bargaining leverage across the coalfields, and to bring the benefits of unionism to a group of miners working under conditions well below those of union miners, the UMW mounted a determined effort to organize the southern West Virginia region during the postwar years. The coal operators of the region were equally determined to keep the union out. The conflict that ensued, as both sides resorted to physical force in an effort to achieve their goals, quickly escalated into violence on a level seldom seen in the annals of American labor history.

The historical record suggests that one of the primary factors responsible for the cycle of violence that gripped this region was the presence of hired gunmen, paid by the coal companies and deputized by sympathetic county officials. Ostensibly hired to guard company property and keep the peace, these private detectives spent much of their time harassing UMW officials and evicting thousands of union sympathizers from company-owned housing. Among the most celebrated of the inevitable confrontations between these parties occurred in the small Mingo County mining town of Matewan.

Following the outbreak of a strike against the Stone Mountain Coal Company in May 1920, thirteen deputized agents of the Baldwin-Felts Detective Agency were brought into Matewan to evict miners from their company homes. When Sid Hatfield, the local police chief and a miner sympathizer, attempted to intervene, a gun battle ensued. When the shootout was finished, nine people lay dead. Six of these were Baldwin-Felts men, including Albert and Lee Felts. Also killed were the mayor of Matewan, a miner, and a young boy. Sid Hatfield himself would later be gunned down by Baldwin-Felts men in a revenge shooting on the steps of the McDowell County Courthouse in Welch.

The violence continued over the next year, reaching its crest in the summer of 1921. By this time, strikes that had begun several months earlier in southern West Virginia had spread to other parts of the state and across the river into Kentucky. In the face of this turmoil, local officials had stepped up the use of private deputies and had even placed Mingo County under martial law.

In late August, union miners gathered in Marmet, a small mining camp ten miles up the Kanawha Valley from Charleston. There the decision was made to organize a march on Logan and Mingo counties in an effort to assist their beleaguered brothers. The approximately 6,000 miners and union sympathizers who assembled for the march were described as a motley "citizens army," complete with weapons and medical supplies. A few days after the march began, the mood of the marchers quickly turned ugly when word reached them that five union miners had been killed at one of the union camps organized for evicted strikers. Fighting quickly broke out in a number of places and an opposing force of 2,000 well-armed private gunmen and county deputies was hastily assembled. The two sides eventually clashed at Blair Mountain where thousands of rounds of gunfire were exchanged. Within days, the governor of West Virginia, declaring the miners' actions an insurrection against the state, asked President Warren Harding to intervene. Harding acted immediately, issuing a proclamation ordering the marchers to disperse and return to their homes on or before September 1.

To restore order, and enforce his directive, Harding sent a force of 2,150 regular Army troops of the 19th Infantry to West Virginia. The warlike atmosphere in Logan and Mingo counties was enhanced by the arrival of the military aircraft of the 88th Light Bombing Squadron. The troops, however, never saw action as some of the marchers surrendered and most, heeding the President's order, quietly dispersed. These events quickly ended the spiral of violence and the only casualties reported as a result of this episode were three Army officers and an enlisted man, killed when their Army plane crashed on the way back to their post.

As a result of their actions, 325 of the marchers were indicted for treason and another 200 were arrested for conspiracy and possession of weapons. The leader of the march, a UMW official named William Blizzard, stood trial for his part in the insurrection but was acquitted after five weeks. The charges against all the other marchers were eventually dropped. At least partly as a result of the military's intervention, the miners strike lost most of its momentum. It was called off in October 1922, more than

two years after it had begun. The termination of the strike effectively ended the UMW's effort to organize that part of the coalfields. It would not be until 1933, following the signing of the National Industrial Recovery Act (NIRA), that the miners' union would return to again try to organize southern West Virginia.

The struggle to unionize the coalfields of Logan, Mingo, and McDowell counties ranks among the bloodiest periods in labor's history. Its significance, however, goes beyond the level of violence that characterized the battle between union and management. The failure of the UMW underscores the long odds organized labor faced at a point in time when workers' rights to form and join unions had not yet been formally recognized. The episode also points out how integral government involvement was to the efforts of many employers to keep unions out of the workplace and the community prior to the passage of the National Labor Relations Act (NLRA) in 1935.

In reporting on the events of the period in 1922, Elliot Northcott, the United States attorney for West Virginia, accused coal operators and county officials of conspiring to deprive miners' of their basic constitutional rights. His investigation found that coal company officials had financed both the army of sheriff deputies and the corrupt political machine that kept sympathetic politicians in office. The politicians, in turn, put the authority and resources of local government at the disposal of the coal operators for use in their fight against the miners' union. This alliance between business and government was a phenomenon that would be seen often as employers resisted the growing intrusion of unionism in the late nineteenth and early twentieth centuries. [Paul F. Clark]

FURTHER READING

Coleman, McAlister. *Men and Coal*. New York: Arno, 1969.

Dubofsky, Melvyn, and Warren Van Tine. *John L. Lewis: A Biography*. New York: Quadrangle, 1977.

Lane, Winthrop. *Civil War in West Virginia: A Story of the Industrial Conflict in the Coal Mines.* New York: Oriole Chapbooks, 1969.

o   o   o

WHEATLAND, CALIFORNIA, HOP RIOT OF 1913. The first outburst of migratory farm labor in the twentieth century broke out in August 1913, on the hop ranch of E. B. Durst, California's largest single employer of agricultural migrants. Termed one of the most significant episodes in the long history of labor troubles in California, the Wheatland Hop Riot profoundly affected the future of the Industrial Workers of the World (IWW) on the West Coast and aroused some interest in the living and working conditions of agricultural workers in California.

The riot involved some 2,800 men, women, and children who had responded to Durst's newspaper advertisements for 2,700 hop pickers, twice as many as were needed, and the promise of ample work and high wages. On arrival to the ranch near Marysville, the migrants found intolerable living conditions: tents rented for $2.75 a week on a barren hillside, eight filthy outdoor toilets to be shared by all, irrigation ditches that were used for garbage disposal, and drinking wells a mile from the harvest site.

Durst altered piecework rates daily depending on the abundance or scarcity of pickers and never posted a flat piece rate for picking. In addition, he withheld 10 percent of the day's wages from every picker to be paid at the end of the season if the worker stayed through the harvest. He also required "extra clean" picking, which further reduced the workers' earnings.

Men, women, and children started work at 4 A.M. and often picked crops in 105° F heat during the day. No water was brought into the fields. Durst's cousin sold lunch wagon lemonade at five cents a glass. Because stores in surrounding towns were forbidden to send delivery trucks into the camp, the hop pickers were forced to buy food and supplies at a concession store on the ranch.

Only about 100 of the workers had been IWW members. About thirty immediately formed an IWW local on the ranch to protest living and working conditions. "It is suggestive," the official investigation report later stated, "that these thirty men through a spasmodic action, and with the aid of deplorable camp conditions, dominated a heterogeneous mass of 2,800 unskilled laborers in three days."

A mass meeting of the workers, held three days after their arrival at the ranch, chose a committee to demand drinking water in the fields twice a day, separate toilets for men and women, better sanitary conditions, and an increase in piece-rate wages. Two of the committee, Blackie Ford and Herman Suhr, had been in the **Free-Speech Fights of the Industrial Workers of the World.** Ranch owner Durst argued with committee members and slapped Ford across the face with his gloves.

The following day, August 3, the Wobblies called a mass meeting on a public spot they had rented for the occasion. Blackie Ford took a sick baby from its mother's arms and holding it before the crowd of some 2,000 workers, said, "It's for the kids that we are doing this." The meeting ended with the singing of IWW songwriter Joe Hill's parody, "Mr. Block." During the singing, two carloads of deputy sheriffs drove up with the district attorney from Marysville to arrest Ford. One of the deputies fired a shot over the head of the crowd to "sober the mob." Fighting broke out; the district attorney, a deputy sheriff, and two workers were killed; many were injured, and as the deputies left, another posse of armed citizens hurried to the ranch.

In the following panic and hysteria, the roads around the ranch were jammed with fleeing workers. California governor Hiram Johnson dispatched five companies of the National Guard to Wheatland "to overawe any labor demonstration and protect private property." Burns detectives rounded up hundreds of suspected IWW members throughout California and neighboring states. Some were severely beaten and tortured and kept incommunicado for weeks. One IWW prisoner committed suicide in prison, and another went insane from police brutality. A Burns detective was later convicted of assault on an IWW prisoner and jailed for a year.

At a trial eight months later, Ford and Suhr were charged with leading the strike meeting, which had preceded the shootings, and were convicted of second-degree murder. They were sentenced to life imprisonment and jailed for over ten years.

In his testimony before the Industrial Relations Commission in San Francisco in 1914, lawyer Austin Lewis, who defended Ford and Suhr at the Marysville trial, drew the parallel between conditions in agriculture and those in factory work. He called the Wheatland Riot "a purely spontaneous uprising . . . a psychological protest against factory conditions of hop picking . . . and the emotional result of the nervous impact of exceedingly irritating and intolerable conditions under which those people worked at the time."

IWW agitation about the Wheatland episode led to an investigation by the newly created Commission on Immigration and Housing in California, which made subsequent annual reports on the living and working conditions of migrants. In the year following Wheatland, forty new IWW locals started in California. Five national organizers and over 100 volunteer soapboxers agitated throughout the state, urging a boycott of the hop fields until living and working conditions improved and Ford and Suhr were released. In April 1915, an IWW meeting in Kansas City organized the Agricultural Workers' Organization, which continued as an IWW branch for many years and was the first union to organize and

successfully negotiate higher wage scales for harvest workers, one of the most dramatic union efforts ever to appear on the American scene.

Ranch owners like Durst financed their own private police forces of gunmen and detectives at an average of $10,000 a year for each farmer. A Farmers' Protective League, organized to quell potential strikes and riots, lobbied with the federal government for federal prosecution of the IWW. West Coast governors in 1915 urged President Wilson to immediately investigate the IWW to demonstrate its "lawlessness," since IWW activities it was claimed, "were a distinct menace to public welfare and particularly dangerous at a time when we require the unquestioned loyalty of all who live within our borders."

Two years later, with U.S. involvement in World War I, the U.S. Justice Department officially responded to Western fears of an IWW potential threat to agriculture, and thus to national security, by federally suppressing the Wobblies in 1917. [Joyce L. Kornbluh]

FURTHER READING

Brissenden, Paul F. *The I.W.W.; A Study of American Syndicalism*. New York: Columbia University Press, 1920.

McWilliams, Carey. *Factories in the Fields*. Boston, MA: Little, Brown, 1939.

Parker, Carleton H. *The Casual Laborer and Other Essays*. New York: Harcourt, Brace and Howe, 1920.

"Report on the Wheatland Riot," Official Report of the Commission on Immigration and Housing, Appendix i, 1914, State of California, Sacramento.

U.S. Commission on Industrial Relations. *Final Report and Testimony on Industrial Relations*, Vol. 5, 64th Congress, 1st Session. Washington, DC: Government Printing Office, 1916, pp. 4911–5027.

o　o　o

WILKES-BARRE, PENNSYLVANIA NEWSPAPER STRIKE OF 1978–1982. In October 1978, workers at the Wilkes-Barre *Times Leader*, a subsidiary of Capital Cities

Communications, struck the community's only daily newspaper. The conflict remains unresolved at the time of this writing. As part of their strategy to win new contracts, the four unions involved started a strike newspaper, the *Citizens Voice*. Ever since, the struggle in Wilkes-Barre and the Wyoming Valley has centered on the strike newspaper's competition with the *Times Leader*.

Wilkes-Barre, a city of approximately 50,000 residents, is located in northeastern Pennsylvania in the Wyoming Valley—the heart of the old anthracite coal region. This area is well known for many historic labor–management conflicts, particularly between coal operators and miners. These struggles forged traditions of community collective action, mutual self-help, and trade union solidarity, which were institutionalized in the area's strong families, ethnic neighborhoods, taverns, parishes, churches, fraternal, civic, and mutual benefit organizations. These traditions and institutions created the context in which the struggle between Capital Cities and the newspaper unions took place.

In May 1978, Capital Cities bought the Wilkes-Barre newspaper for $10.5 million, although similar papers elsewhere would have sold for between $20 million and $30 million. Capital Cities' purchase of the *Times Leader* meant that for the first time in the city's history, Wilkes-Barre's daily paper passed out of local hands. In 1978, Capital Cities was among the top fifteen newspaper chains and one of the top ten television conglomerates in the United States. After buying the *Times Leader*, Capital Cities continued to grow, moving into cable television and purchasing the American Broadcasting Company. The Wilkes-Barre newspaper unions were confronting one of the worlds largest media empires.

In addition to its reputation as a well-managed, profit-maximizing company, Capital Cities was known for aggressively pursuing changes in production that would enhance the profitability of its holdings. This aggressive reputation with its employees was vividly illustrated by well-publicized conflicts with the unions at several of its newspaper holdings prior to 1978. Therefore, it was not surprising that Capital Cities took a hard line when bargaining began with the *Times Leader*'s four unions—the guild employees, typographers, pressmen, and stereotypers. In fact, when the *Times Leader* was sold, the pressmen and the stereotypers were already working without a contract.

During bargaining sessions in the summer and fall of 1978, Capital Cities demanded fundamental changes in the union contracts. The company wanted to alter contract language on staffing that prevented reductions in personnel; it wanted to eliminate clauses that guaranteed job security for the life of the agreement; it wanted to change the contracts to allow the hiring of part-time workers; the company wanted to introduce a merit system that would be the sole judge of competence; it wanted to change the overtime provisions; it wanted to insert an ethics clause, and much more.

The members of the four unions involved in coordinated bargaining in Wilkes-Barre had enjoyed an excellent relationship with the locally owned newspaper and had negotiated strong contract language in the areas of job security, new technology, and control over the work process. Consequently, when Capital Cities called for dramatic changes in the organization and control of work, an impasse resulted, even though both sides were in agreement on a wage increase. This impasse occurred at a time when many unions in the United States were bargaining concessionary contracts and were being negatively affected by technological change. In fact, newspaper unions in several locations around the United States lost well-publicized strikes during the 1970s. The clash in Wilkes-Barre pitted a community with a strong tradition of collective action against a growing media conglomerate that had developed a labor relations strategy that raised the profitability of its holdings by gaining greater control of the work process.

As part of its overall strategy, Capital Cities built a twelve-foot-high chain link fence around the *Times Leader* facility, located in the heart of the Wilkes-Barre's downtown. The company also installed surveillance cameras throughout the newspaper building, and contracted with a security firm to send guards to Wilkes-Barre. The company placed guards at entrances and exits, in rest rooms, eating and break areas, and on the shop floor. Capital Cities also indicated that it would continue to publish in the event of a work stoppage by its employees, and after the strike began, the company sent a letter to its union members telling them that they would be replaced if they did not return to work by November 1, 1978.

On October 6, 1978, the unions struck the *Times Leader*. Over 200 union members supported the strike while twenty-five reported to work. Picket lines were established immediately and soon thereafter conflict broke out. Windows were broken, the company's building was defaced, some vehicles were destroyed, and confrontations occurred between guards and strikers. Four days later, at the urging of local officials, Capital Cities suspended publication of the *Times Leader* for four days. However, no progress was made in contract talks and when Capital Cities began publishing again, violence reoccurred. Open conflict gradually subsided until it ceased in the fall of 1982 when the pickets were withdrawn because the last of the four unions had been decertified.

A few days before the strike occurred, papers were filed in the county courthouse incorporating a strike newspaper called the *Citizens Voice* which was owned by the Wilkes-Barre Council of Newspaper Unions. The union council secured loans from some of the parent unions and received strike benefits to help them launch their paper. The council rented printing equipment, presses, and production facilities from a local paper. The unions agreed to a system of governance that gave each union an equal voice in the paper's management. The Unity Council, which was composed of members from each of the four unions, became the governing body. Its members were elected to one-year terms. The Unity Council formulates policy, manages finances, engages in long-range planning, assigns personnel, oversees the general operation of the paper, and conducts meetings. The *Citizens Voice* is not an employee-owned enterprise, but it is self-managed by workers who enjoy limited forms of workplace participation.

When the strike paper was first published, all workers, regardless of their job titles, received the same pay—$295 a week—which was less than they earned in their old positions. The Unity Council suspended the seniority principle and has been able to maintain solidarity among the unions throughout the strike. On the shop floor, traditional craft practices govern the organization and pace of work, and workers set up their own production teams, determine shift assignments, job duties, job content, days off, and vacation schedules.

Eventually, the newspaper unions bought a building, paid off their loans, and purchased a computerized printing system. The introduction of new technology did not result in any job losses because workers were reassigned to other duties when the new equipment was installed. In order to compete with the *Times Leader*, the editorial employees were forced to change as well. They pursued stories far more aggressively than they had before, provided independent accounts of local news events, added new sections on food and entertainment, added a photojournalist, daily columns, special features, and hired part-time workers.

In addition to creating an organization that could publish a viable newspaper, the unions involved also built coalitions with different groups in the community to insure that the *Citizens Voice* would survive. In this effort they relied heavily on three community groups—trade unions, politicians, and newspaper carriers. Unions in the area rallied to the cause of the *Citizens Voice* and made sure that local politicians supported the effort as well. According to the strike paper, approximately 800 of the 1,000 carriers in the area supported the strike and agreed to deliver the *Citizens Voice*. Newsstand operators refused to carry the *Times Leader*, while many merchants would not allow Capital Cities to put its paper in vending machines on their property.

A key to the survival of the *Citizens Voice* was the response to its efforts by the neighborhoods and towns in and about Wilkes-Barre. The unions rallied the citizenry by portraying Capital Cities as an outside force that threatened the community by publishing a "scab paper" that wanted to substitute prepackaged hard and soft features for local news. The *Citizens Voice* was able to portray Capital Cities as the moral equivalent of the coal operators, while the strikers were likened to the miners of an earlier era who battled to protect their human dignity against absentee owners. Consequently, most readers stopped buying the *Times Leader* and subscribed to the *Citizens Voice*.

Throughout the strike, local neighborhoods, many religious organizations, civic and voluntary associations, teachers unions, and elements of the middle class supported the *Citizens Voice*. Both newspapers struggled to capture advertising accounts of local businesses. In general, the *Citizens Voice* was successful in attracting the advertising of local businesses but far less successful in securing a reasonable share of national advertising. As a national chain the *Times Leader* attracted more national advertising accounts.

One of the key elements that led to this protracted struggle was the "deep pockets" of Capital Cities. By its own admission, the conglomerate lost $20 million in Wilkes-Barre the first year and has suffered continu-

ing losses of approximately $2 million a year since 1979. In addition, the struggle in Wilkes-Barre has dramatically reduced the market value of the *Times Leader*.

In fact, if it had not been for the unique cultural history of the Wilkes-Barre area, the strike, particularly in the political, economic, and social context of the late 1970s and 1980s, might well have been brief and successful from the corporation's point of view. Within a year the strikers could have been replaced, the unions decertified and the *Times Leader* been left free to grow and expand and compete with newspapers throughout northeastern Pennsylvania. Instead, at the time of this writing, the unions in Wilkes-Barre have been able to carry on one of the longest and most successful strike newspapers in the industry's history. [Donald Kennedy]

FURTHER READING

Keil, Thomas J. *On Strike! Capital Cities and the Wilkes-Barre Newspaper Unions*. Tuscaloosa, AL: University of Alabama Press, 1988.

o   o   o

WILLMAR, MINNESOTA, BANK STRIKE OF 1977–1979. Minnesota has a long tradition of farmer–labor activism and progressive politics, but those inherited Populist values rarely challenged the settled and hierarchical relations between the sexes. Yet on December 16, 1977, eight women bank employees, alleging sex discrimination and anti-union animus, struck the Citizens National Bank of Willmar, a religious, predominantly Democratic farmer–labor community of 16,000 in west central Minnesota. The first bank strike in Minnesota and the most infamous of the early assaults against women's secondary status in banking, the "Willmar 8 Strike" generated considerable debate and public attention and altered long-accepted practices among bank officials and union leaders in communities across the country.

Despite its "workingman" origins, the Citizens National Bank (CNB) of Willmar held to conservative yet typical approaches in its treatment of women. Historically, women bank employees have been relegated to the least prestigious, least powerful, and least lucrative positions. Even those few women designated as management have usually earned shockingly less than their male counterparts. At CNB, there were no male tellers or clericals, and except for one token female officer, all the upper-level jobs were occupied by men.

The breaking point for CNB's women employees came in 1976. Without considering its own veteran female employees for a newly-opened management trainee slot, CNB officials hired a young inexperienced man. They paid him $700 a month—more than every woman employee earned except for the one female officer, who with twelve years of banking experience made $750—and assigned their three top women to train him. When Irene Wallin, head teller, protested to Leo Pirsch, president of the bank, he responded, "We are not all equal, you know."

Irene Wallin was not the only outraged employee. In November, every woman in the bank signed a sex discrimination complaint with the Minnesota Department of Human Rights. The complaint, passed on to the U.S. Equal Employment Opportunity Commission (EEOC), languished for months. Undaunted, the women sought the aid of the local chapter of the National Organization of Women (NOW); NOW responded by picketing the bank and helping monitor the EEOC claim. The bank employees also turned to collective action: they formed the Willmar Bank Employees Association (WBEA), Local 1. In May, the WBEA won a secret ballot election, 9 to 2, becoming the first certified bank union in Minnesota. WBEA then affiliated with the Willmar Trades and Labor Association and initiated their first round of bargaining talks. Good news also emerged from the EEOC:

the initial investigation indicated that the women had "reasonable grounds" for a sex discrimination case.

The bank, however, was not to be so easily brought to justice. Backed by a powerful Minneapolis law firm and the unwavering arrogance of Pirsch—who stuck to his belief that not one of the female troublemakers was qualified for management—the bank denied every allegation of wrongful conduct and remained intransigent during the collective bargaining talks. According to union representatives, bank officials refused to include a nondiscrimination clause in the contract and at times turned their backs to the wall or read newspapers rather than engage the WBEA bargaining team in dialogue. Bank officials also shifted several women to the less desirable "drive-up window slots" and upped bank hours without warning. Emboldened by the EEOC finding and infuriated by the bank's treatment, the women walked out on December 16, 1977.

When they arrived that next morning to set up their first picket line in the freezing cold, little did they realize that their struggle would capture national attention and dominate their lives for years to come. Describing themselves as "small-town," church-going, and family-oriented, none of the eight had been politically active prior to the strike. Their actions sprang from a deep belief in American values rather than a rejection of those values. Their courage and optimism rested on a faith that the principles of "equal opportunity" and "workplace democracy" would triumph, that women as well as men could claim the heritage of equality, and that the American system of justice would catch the whale as well as the minnow. "If we don't win," one striker explained, "there's something wrong with the system."

Those beliefs were tested as the months lengthened into years. Letters of support flooded in from individual sympathizers—mainly women who, like the strikers, found themselves trapped in low-wage, dead-end jobs—but sustained support from established institutions was almost nonexistent. The local feminist community extended a helping hand, but nationally the women's movement appeared more interested in celebrating the breakthroughs of a few women super-achievers than backing the incremental collective advancement of a handful of women union sympathizers. Sectors of the labor movement were skeptical as well. Individuals stepped forward, such as the retired railway workers, who devoted almost full-time energy to the campaign, and local labor organizations— the Minnesota Education Association, the Willmar State Hospital Workers (AFSCME), the UAW, and the Teamster-affiliated Brinks drivers—donated thousands of dollars and organized a labor parade down Willmar's main street—a first for the town—but top-level commitment lagged. Sex discrimination issues were not yet central to labor's agenda and no national union had targeted bank employees for organization. Irene Wallin captured the frustration and confusion of the strikers: "It's a puzzle. Union leaders view the strike as a feminist issue while feminists see it as a union issue."

As the first year of the strike ended, the women realized that concessions were necessary. Despite daily picketing, the filing of unfair labor practice charges with the National Labor Relations Board (NLRB), and a moderately successful campaign urging townspeople to withdraw their funds from CNB, the bank had not budged. Faced with mounting financial pressures, the women agreed to an EEOC-negotiated conciliatory agreement in which they gained a modest back pay settlement of $11,750 (to be divided among eleven complainants), the promise from the bank to abide by the law, and an EEOC assurance to watchdog bank employment practices and prevent retaliation against whistleblowers. In return, the women gave up the right to sue and the possibility of immediate reinstatement and promotion. Several months later, in order to qualify for unemployment compensation,

the women announced an offer of "unconditional reinstatement." Pirsch declared the strike officially over, rehired one of the women, Doris Boshart—offering her a position several rungs below her former job as head bookkeeper—and told the others they had been permanently replaced.

Picketing continued as the women waited for justice through the NLRB. Appearances on the "Phil Donohue Show" on national television, the never-ending influx of encouraging letters, the news in February 1979 of Leo Pirsch's retirement, and a decision to sell the bank boosted their spirits, but after a disappointing NLRB decision in March, morale plummeted. Although the NLRB judge found the bank guilty of a multitude of unfair labor practices, it issued the mildest of reprimands to the bank, requiring it to post a notice of future intention to honor the law. He also denied the women their claim to immediate reinstatement; they were to be recalled as suitable positions opened.

The Willmar 8 picketed into the spring, but as the necessity for paid jobs became apparent, they eventually abandoned daily picketing. In May, after the union was safely decertified by the few initially loyal employees and the hand-picked strike replacements, the bank began offering employment to the strikers. But the openings were inferior to the former positions held by the women, and those who returned faced harassment and ostracism. The president of WBEA, Sylvia Erickson, was fired by the bank after she returned and never regained her job. By October of 1980 only one striker remained employed at CNB.

Although the strike ended in defeat, few of those who walked out expressed regret. The gains in personal dignity, self-awareness, and self-confidence had been enormous. Their assessment of the promises held out by American society had also changed. "Now . . . I know why our effort is so unique," WBEA treasurer Glennis Andresen told one reporter after hearing the NLRB ruling. "Everybody else knows it's useless to go looking for justice."

Ironically, the strike had its greatest impact after it was over. Film producer Mary Beth Yarrow, while visiting her hometown of Willmar over Christmas of 1978, decided to produce a film about the strike, and under the direction of actress Lee Grant and the co-production of Julie Thompson, "The Willmar 8," was released with suitable fanfare in the summer of 1980. In 1984, Yarrow secured Lee Grant once again to direct a National Broadcasting Company "docudrama" based on the strike entitled "A Matter of Sex." The plight of women bank employees as seen through the treatment of the Willmar 8 was impressed upon the conscience of millions of TV viewers.

The media attention in conjunction with the growing union willingness to organize bank employees stirred the labor movement into action. The UAW and the United Food and Commercial Workers Union reevaluated their stance toward organizing bank workers largely because of the Willmar 8 struggle. The UAW hired Andresen as an organizer and in 1983 won an election at the First American Bank and Trust in Willmar. Moreover, the banking community faced increasingly strident actions from women's groups such as the National Association of Working Women, and a blizzard of lawsuits from individual women alleging sex discrimination in pay and promotional practices. The Office of Federal Contract Compliance targeted the banking and insurance industry for special surveillance as well.

Banking officials responded in a variety of ways. In addition to sensitizing their personnel managers to the issue of sex discrimination through showings of "The Willmar 8," top advisors recommended certain concrete changes in banking practice. On the one hand, promotional opportunities were opened up to women and care exerted to abide by federal guidelines and procedures. On the other, union drives were met by fierce resistance, including the bending of the law and unfair labor practices.

Nevertheless, although the Willmar 8 strike sparked some changes among union and industry officials, the banking sector ultimately retained its highly segregated employment patterns and preserved its non-union status. The proportion of women bank "managers" doubled during the 1980s, but as bank management feminized, the pay, status, and power of these positions declined. As recent scholarly investigations have documented, bank management became internally segregated with women occupying the lowest rungs, and the pay gap persisted even as women secured management titles.

Just as important was the lack of collective advance through unionization. In the 1970s, only thirty out of 15,000 banks operated under collective bargaining agreements; that number dropped in the 1980s as banks resisted new union drives and refused to renew long-standing contracts. Thus, with little to fear from the law or government agencies, financial institutions found it easy to thwart workers such as the Willmar 8 who simply sought to realize age-old claims to industrial democracy and equality. [Dorothy Sue Cobble]

FURTHER READING

Amato, Joseph, David Nass, and T. C. Radzilowski. "The Women of Willmar," *The Progressive* (August 1978), pp. 125–127; and "A Year on the Line." *The Progressive* (February 1979), p. 41.

Perras, Richard A. "Effective Responses to Union Organizing Attempts in the Banking Industry." *Labor Law Journal*, Vol. 35 (February 1984), pp. 92–102.

"The Willmar 8." Documentary film by Lee Grant, Julie Thompson, and Mary Beth Yarrow, 1980.

The Willmar 8 Collection. Southwest Regional History Center. Marshall, MN: Southwest State University (includes newspaper clippings, legal briefs and rulings, interviews with the strikers and their attorney, and unpublished scholarly papers).

Y

° ° ° ° ° ° ° ° ° ° °

° ° °

YALE UNIVERSITY CLERICAL STRIKES OF 1984 AND 1985. In May of 1983, the National Labor Relations Board certified Local 34 of the Federation of University Employees as the representative of Yale University's clerical and technical employees. The bargaining unit was 80 percent female, and the victory in the organizing campaign was a landmark in the declining trade union movement's attempts to reverse its fortunes by organizing the growing service sector of the economy.

But as was so often the case in the 1980s, certification did not guarantee that negotiations would produce a collective bargaining agreement. When the negotiations began, it became clear that their significance would go beyond a contract between the university and its employees. The grievances of the women were clear. Many of the jobs they filled at Yale required special educational qualifications, such as foreign language skills and advanced degrees. Yet their average salary was approximately $13,000 a year, some $5,000 less than the university-paid truck drivers. Thus the negotiations centered on the issue of comparable worth—that wages in heavily female occupations were low because the workers were women, not because of the intrinsic worth of the job to the organization. Local 34 demanded equal pay for women's work that was "comparable" in terms of skills and experience to that done in jobs dominated by men.

After the victory of Local 34 in the NLRB election, Yale hired a law firm skilled in defeating unions as a consultant on the negotiations. It soon became clear that the university had no intention of agreeing to the comparable worth demand. The presidents of other ivy league universities urged President A. Bartlett Giamatti of Yale to hold the line. While the Yale negotiations were going on, both Harvard and Columbia were also involved in union organizing drives.

Following a year of desultory negotiations, Yale made a "final offer" of a 24 percent pay hike over three years. That fell far short of union demands for 38 percent and a recognition of the principle of comparable worth. Giamatti had refused binding arbitration, and had also refused to submit the outstanding issues in the strike to a committee of three faculty members chosen jointly by the Yale Corporation and the union. Although the proposed panel was to be made up of Yale faculty, Giamatti refused to allow "outside parties" to make decisions that would affect the "central mission" of the university.

The strike began on September 26 and promptly divided the university community. All but one of the student cafeterias shut down in a sympathy strike by dining hall workers. Some 400 classes were held off campus by supportive professors. Classes that could not be moved, those requiring special facilities such as laboratories and studios, were paralyzed. The strike also spawned a $14 million class-action suit by 102 students against the university. Two mass sit-ins resulted in over 630 arrests. Anti-union sentiment among some students led to confrontations with supporters of the pickets, and "Nuke Local 34" license plates became commonplace in New Haven. One low point in the strike came when someone broke into the law school library, dumped thirty-four card catalogue drawers out onto the floor, and spray-painted "Support Local 34" on the walls.

Because of Yale's prestige, the strike also became a point of debate across the country. When the strikers could not close the university, public relations became their main weapon. The university's reputation as a center of tolerance and liberal learning began to suffer as the union successfully publicized the plight of female employees of one of America's richest universities subsisting on fifty dollars per week in strike pay.

The agony of Yale ended in late January 1985. The nation's first comparable-worth strike had been a success. The resulting contract established a new salary structure that would enable workers to advance from previously dead-end jobs. Women who took time off to have children—or who shifted to new university jobs when grants expired—no longer had to begin again to accumulate seniority. The three-and-a-half-year contract also gave a financial boost to the lowest paid workers, a disproportionate number of whom were female and black or Hispanic. The average salary for current employees went from approximately $13,000 to $18,000 in three years. While not a complete victory for the union, the contract did recognize the principle of pay equity and made a down payment on its achievement. [Ronald L. Filippelli]

FURTHER READING

Bass, Carole and Paul. "Yale Teaches a Valuable Lesson." *The Progressive* (March 1985), p. 17.

Bell, D. A. "New Haven Diarist." *The New Republic* (December 3, 1984), p. 43.

"Bulldog, Bulldog, On Strike Now." *Newsweek* (October 8, 1984), p. 91.

"Women of Yale." *The Nation* (December 1, 1984), pp. 572–573.

o o o

YONKERS, NEW YORK, CARPET WEAVERS' STRIKE OF 1885. On February 20, 1885, 3,000 workers, mostly young women, struck the Alexander Smith Carpet Mills in Yonkers, New York. The strike was precipitated by the refusal of the company to reinstate a 10 percent pay cut instituted the previous December, to pay wages due, and to rehire at least twenty women fired for "obnoxious activity"—the latter being their active role in organizing a union.

During the 1870s, this branch of the textile industry underwent a transformation from small handcraft shops to large factories, and from a labor force of skilled male workers to one of unskilled women. In addition, the vagaries of the marketplace impelled management to continually lower wages. Growing economic crises in the industry led to long and militant strikes in 1878–1879 and 1884–1885.

The transformation of the carpet trade coincided with the rise in importance of the Knights of Labor. The Knights defined a working-class community and culture in opposition to emerging values of corporate America. Both wage-earning women and working-class housewives joined the Knights and demanded equal standing in the organization's priorities. They created a sphere of action and influence for working-class women that exceeded the bounds of nineteenth-century ideals of true womanhood, ideals that often negated the very existence of working-class women. These women, particularly those whose experiences were shaped by the labor and reform movements of the Gilded Age, used the language of domesticity to criticize the competitive capitalist system that they saw encroaching upon their rights, dignity, and comforts.

In a sense, the Knights legitimated a working-class feminine sphere distinct from the middle-class norm. During the 1885 strike, in which 90 percent of the workers were young women, the local Republican newspaper, the *Yonkers Statesman*, described union women as "Amazons" and questioned their right to the title of "lady." The editor cautioned the women "to go to Sunday School and be good girls" and "yet get good husbands and become honored members of society." The labor press, on the other hand, praised these women for their strength and dedication as trade unionists.

Late in 1883, New York City Knights secretly visited Yonkers and recruited seven of Alexander Smith's 3,000 workers. As prices fell in 1883, Smith workers secretly began building a strike fund. They kept themselves apprised of strikes and situations in other carpet centers, especially Philadelphia, and were ready to deal effectively with that city's attempt to recruit New York workers as strikebreakers. In December 1884, when Smith, the nation's largest carpet manufacturer, introduced a wage cut, workers knew that a strike was premature and would only benefit Smith. But in mid-February, when Smith identified and fired about twenty women for being union organizers, the workers were ready. On February 20, all the women in the tapestry rooms "paraded" into the street. At the end of the day, all 3,000 were locked out and the looms shut down.

A gradual deterioration in working conditions instituted by Smith gave the workers a clear-cut list of demands, most of which were related to ending punitive fines for behavioral infractions, a broken loom, or another worker's errors. The latter practice pitted one worker against another. In addition, they demanded an end to the use of spies and the blacklist which covered not only Yonkers but also New York and Philadelphia.

In April, Smith tried to break the strike and the union by opening the mill and offering to take back non-activist workers at a lower pay scale. He hoped that Philadelphia manufacturers' success in breaking their strike would work in Yonkers too. However, in Philadelphia the trade was spread through several small mills, the union was weak, and community support was absent. Smith was the largest employer in Yonkers, and the effect of the strike on the whole town made the workers' position much stronger. Attempts to break the strike with outsiders failed. Even the Yonkers police were sympathetic to the strikers.

Smith's workers were supported during the strike by an organized boycott of Smith's carpets by family and neighbors. Local shopkeepers offered extended credit and moral support to the strikers. The boycott, which was a favorite tactic of the Knights, was an outgrowth of its use by the Irish Land League. In 1885, the New York State Bureau of Labor gave boycotts considerable attention and noted that they often accompanied strikes.

After the arrest of three pickets at the Yonkers mills, the Central Labor Council of New York City sponsored a testimonial to the pickets. Delegates from every New York union were among the 2,000 guests. Seated beside the three honorees was New York labor journalist, John Swinton, who presented them with medals of honor. A local jury in Yonkers quickly acquitted them.

In June, Smith charged the strikers with attempted arson, but that was never substantiated. On July 16, Smith was forced to settle. The union called it a victory. The 10 percent wage cut was rescinded, all union members were rehired, the docking system was adjusted, and a union grievance committee was recognized. The union agreed to try to arbitrate grievances and to give notice of impending strikes.

After the strike, the carpet weavers became embroiled in the Knights' factionalism. Eventually this, plus the employers continued anti-union initiatives, weakened the weavers' national organization and led to the decline of the union in every mill. Months after the 1885 strike, Smith blacklisted some union members. In 1886, he declared an open shop and apparently was not opposed in any organized manner. By

1887, he began breaking the agreements reached in 1885.

With the national decline of the Knights after 1890, the support of working-class movements for women's issues diminished. While the Knights had attempted to include women's issues as integral to their movement, the trade union movement afterward assigned those concerns, and the women who held them, to as essentially auxiliary role. Domesticity became redefined along the lines of traditional nineteenth-century ideas, to the impoverishment of both home and union hall. [Harriet Davis-Kram]

FURTHER READING

Gordon, Michael. "The Labor Boycott in New York City, 1880–1886." *Labor History*, Vol. 16 (1975), pp. 184–229.

Levine, Susan. "Honor Each Noble Maid: Women Workers and the Yonkers Carpet Weavers' Strike of 1885." *New York History*, Vol. 62 (1981), pp. 153–176.

———. *Their Own Sphere: Women's Work, The Knights of Labor and the Transformation of the Carpet Trade, 1870–1890.* Ph.D. Dissertation, Graduate Center, City University of New York, 1980.

o   o   o

YOUNGSTOWN, OHIO, STEEL STRIKE OF 1915–1916. The steel strike in Youngstown and the violence and destruction that attended it grew out of the confluence of an immigrant labor force and the barbaric living and working conditions of an early-nineteenth-century American industrial city. Of greater Youngstown's approximately 100,000 inhabitants, a third were foreigners—mostly Lithuanians, Poles, and Serbs. Most of them depended on the steel industry for their livelihood. Carnegie Steel, Republic Iron and Steel, and the Youngstown Sheet and Tube Company together employed some 20,000 workers.

Youngstown's steelworkers, like their brothers in other cities, worked the standard twelve-hour day, although fourteen hours were not uncommon. For this effort they earned an average of $440 a year, hardly enough to fend off starvation. Workers' housing in Youngstown was among the worst of any city in the country. This poverty took a high toll. In 1913, 41 percent of all deaths in the city were of children under five.

Although the steel industry dominated the Mahoning River valley, its most imposing fortress rested in the borough of East Youngstown, the home of the Youngstown Sheet and Tube Company. The town had a population of 10,000 but only 450 registered voters. The almost totally immigrant population was kept in ignorance. In 1915, while East Youngstown had no churches and no English lessons for foreigners, it could boast of twenty-two saloons.

Total economic and political control of East Youngstown had led the company to miss the signs of change. The depression of 1913–1914 had ended. So too had the great flow of immigrants from Europe, which slowed to a trickle by World War I. Instead of cheap labor, Europe sent war orders, creating pressure on the existing labor force. Instead of fear of losing their jobs, the new tight labor market spurred workers to assert themselves and to demand changes in their working conditions.

The trouble in Youngstown began at the Republic works where a strike had closed the entire mill by the first week of January 1916. The strike fever spread to East Youngstown where, on January 5, 1916, workers closed the mill. The East Youngstown strikers demanded the same concessions as their brothers at Republic—a raise of six cents an hour, or approximately 30 percent, and double-time pay for Sunday work.

With 15,000 workers out and two of the city's largest mills shut down, the strikers planned a march to celebrate their success. They massed at the main entrance of Youngstown Sheet and Tube which was being guarded by company police. Hostility between the strikers and the guards soon resulted in bloodshed. Eight strikers were killed, and twelve wounded by a volley from the guards' guns. Enraged by the killings, the marchers turned a peaceful demonstration into an ugly riot. When the destruction stopped, the rioters had burned company property and four city blocks, including a bank and post office. Only the arrival of the National Guard calmed the city.

The extent of the workers' rage and the destruction that followed sobered all concerned. Both Republic Steel and Youngstown Sheet and Tube withdrew company guards and eschewed the use of strikebreakers in the volatile circumstances. For their part, the strikers returned to work on January 11 and 13, 1916. They had won a 10 percent wage increase, and at Republic, some concessions were given to the new unions organized by the AFL at the beginning of the strike.

The confrontation at Youngstown sent a warning signal to the rest of the steel industry. U.S. Steel, in its Carnegie Plant in Youngstown and throughout the country, raised wages 10 percent at the beginning of the strike. This is ironic since there is some evidence that it was U.S. Steel, under the direction of Elbert H. Gary, who dissuaded Republic Steel from offering a 10 percent increase to stop the strike from breaking out in the first place.

Following the settlement of the strike, a grand jury assigned responsibility for the killing of the eight strikers to the officers of United States Steel Corporation, which owned Carnegie Steel, and the Youngstown Sheet and Tube Company. In all, the grand jury indicted 113 corporations and corporate officers. It also censured the mayor and police force of East Youngstown. The Socialist newspaper, the *New York Call* predicted that there was not "the remotest possibility" that any of the indicted company officials would ever serve prison terms or pay fines for their illegal conduct. The *Call* was correct. On March 28, 1916, Judge W. S. Anderson dismissed the indictments. [Ronald L. Filippelli]

FURTHER READING

Foner, Philip S. *History of the Labor Movement in the United States*, Vol. 6, New York: International Publishers, 1982.

Index
○ ○ ○ ○ ○ ○ ○ ○ ○ ○